SOMETHING ABOUT THE AUTHOR®

Something about
the Author *was named
an "Outstanding
Reference Source,"*
*the highest honor given
by the American
Library Association
Reference and Adult
Services Division.*

ISSN 0276-816X

something ABOUT the AUThOR®

Facts and Pictures about Authors and Illustrators of Books for Young People

volume 205

GALE
CENGAGE Learning™

Detroit • New York • San Francisco • New Haven, Conn • Waterville, Maine • London

GALE
CENGAGE Learning™

Something about the Author, Volume 205

Project Editor: Lisa Kumar

Editorial: Laura Avery, Pamela Bow, Jim Craddock, Amy Fuller, Andrea Henderson, Margaret Mazurkiewicz, Tracie Moy, Jeff Muhr, Kathy Nemeh, Mary Ruby, Mike Tyrkus

Permissions: Jermaine Bobbitt, Sara Crane, Dean Dauphinais

Imaging and Multimedia: Dean Dauphinais, John Watkins

Composition and Electronic Capture: Amy Darga

Manufacturing: Drew Kalasky

Product Manager: Janet Witalec

For product information and technology assistance, contact us at
Gale Customer Support, 1-800-877-4253.
For permission to use material from this text or product,
submit all requests online at **www.cengage.com/permissions.**
Further permissions questions can be emailed to
permissionrequest@cengage.com

Gale
27500 Drake Rd.
Farmington Hills, MI, 48331-3535

LIBRARY OF CONGRESS CATALOG CARD NUMBER 62-52046

ISBN-13: 978-1-4144-4218-1
ISBN-10: 1-4144-4218-1

ISSN 0276-816X

This title is also available as an e-book.
ISBN-13: 978-1-4144-6437-4
ISBN-10: 1-4144-6437-1
Contact your Gale, Cengage Learning sales representative for ordering information.

Printed in the United States of America
1 2 3 4 5 6 7 14 13 12 11 10

Contents

Authors in Forthcoming Volumes vii

Introduction ix

SATA Product Advisory Board xi

Illustrations Index 189

Author Index 223

A

Abbott, Tony 1952- 1

Addasi, Maha 1968- 5

Aho, Julia Kay
    See Kay, Julia 94

Alda, Arlene 1933- 7

Allen, Raul 10

Amit, Ofra 1966- 11

B

Baldini, Michelle 12

Basye, Dale E. 13

Bok, Arthur
    See Bok, Chip 15

Bok, Chip 1952- 15

Bruel, Nick 17

Buller, Jon 1943- 19

Burgess, Starling
    See Tudor, Tasha 156

C

Calvert, Pam 1966- 23

Caparo, Antonio
    See Caparo, Antonio Javier 25

Caparo, Antonio Javier 25

Cheng, Andrea 1957- 26

Cousins, Lucy 1964- 31

Craig, David 36

Curtis, Stacy 38

D

D'Aluisio, Faith 1957- 40

de la Peña, Matt 49

Degen, Bruce 1945- 42

Dowell, Frances O'Roark 1964- 51

Dubin, Jill 55

Durney, Ryan 57

E

Ehrlich, Fred 58

Ehrlich, Fred, M.D.
    See Ehrlich, Fred 58

Ewart, Franzeska G. 1950- 59

F

Fabry, Glenn 1961- 60

Fearnley, Jan 1965- 62

Fernandes, Eugenie 1943- 65

Fowles, Shelley 1956- 70

Freitas, Donna 1972- 73

G

Gannon, Ned 1974- 75

Gibala-Broxholm, Scott 1959(?)- 75

Gibson, Barbara L.
    See Gibson, Barbara Leonard 76

Gibson, Barbara Leonard 76

Grey, Mini 78

H

Haley, Amanda 81

Hatton, Caroline 1957- 83

Hector, Julian 85

Hooper, Mary 1948- 86

J

Jackson Issa, Kai 90

Jennings, Patrick 1962- 90

K

Kay, Julia 94

Kim, Joung Un 1970- 95

Kuehnert, Stephanie 1979- 96

Kulikov, Boris 1966- 97

L

Laidlaw, Rob 102

Larson, Hope 1982- 102

Leick, Bonnie 103

Lewis, J. Patrick 1942- 104

M

Manushkin, Fran 1942- 112

Manushkin, Frances
    See Manushkin, Fran 112

Martin, Courtney Autumn 1984- 118

Mechner, Jordan 1964- 119

Mould, Chris 120

N

Nakata, Hiroe 123

Nugent, Cynthia 1954- 125

P

Page, Gail 1950- 128

Papp, Robert 1967- 129

Parker, Marjorie Blain 1960- 130

Puvilland, Alex 132

Puvilland, Alexandre
    See Puvilland, Alex 132

R

Ramos, Jorge 1958- 134

Robinson, Tim 1963- 136

Rosen, Elizabeth 1961- 137

S

Sanger, Amy Wilson 1967- 139

Shefelman, Janice 1930- 140

Shefelman, Janice Jordan
    See Shefelman, Janice 140

Somers, Kevin 142

Stone, Phoebe 143

Strachan, Bruce 1959- 146

T

Taylor, Brooke 148

Teague, Mark 1963- 149

Terry, Will 1966- 154

Thomson, Melissa 1979- 155

Tudor, Tasha 1915-2008
    Obituary Notice 156

W

Wales, Dirk 1931- 158

Walters, Eric 1957- 159

Walters, Eric Robert
    See Walters, Eric 159

Whiting, Sue 1960- 165

Whiting, Susan Allana
    See Whiting, Sue 165

Wilson, Martin 1973- 166

Wolf, Sallie 1950- 168

Wulf, Linda Press 170

Y

Yazzie, Johnson 1946- 172

Z

Ziefert, Harriet 1941- 172

Authors in Forthcoming Volumes

Below are some of the authors and illustrators that will be featured in upcoming volumes of *SATA*. These include new entries on the swiftly rising stars of the field, as well as completely revised and updated entries (indicated with *) on some of the most notable and best-loved creators of books for children.

David Acer ❚ Well known in his native Canada for his work as a comedian and magician, Acer is also one of the creative talents behind the long-running *Mystery Hunters,* an award-winning television program that explores life's mysteries. His books, which center on magic, include *Gotcha!: Eighteen Amazing Ways to Freak out Your Friends,* in which he shares nineteen magic tricks with young magicians.

*David Catrow ❚ Catrow, an award-winning political cartoonist whose work is syndicated to more than 900 newspapers in the United States and Canada, has also illustrated numerous children's books, working with authors ranging from Kathryn Lasky and William Kotzwinkle to Jerdine Nolan and Alan Katz. His work, which he also pairs with his original story in *Max Spaniel: Funny Lunch* and its sequel, is often cited for its dark, biting humor and for employing unusual, squiggly lines that recall the art of Dr. Seuss.

*Kate Feiffer ❚ Feiffer's humorous children's books are inspired by her home and family, particularly her daughter. *Double Pink* began her fictionalized family chronicle, and it has continued in *My Mom Is Trying to Ruin My Life, The Wild, Wild Inside: A View from Mommy's Tummy,* and *But I Wanted a Baby Brother!* On occasion, Feiffer has also collaborated with her father, noted cartoonist and writer Jules Feiffer, producing the dog-centered *Henry the Dog with No Tail* and *Which Puppy?,* the latter a story about the U.S. president's search for a "First Dog."

Liz Kessler ❚ A former teacher and journalist, Kessler is the author of the popular "Emily Windsnap" middle-grade novels. The series, which includes *The Tail of Emily Windsnap, Emily Windsnap and the Monster from the Deep,* and *Emily Windsnap and the Castle in the Mist,* features the adventures of a seventh grader who is half human and half mermaid and combine humor with fantasy and adventure.

Christina Meldrum ❚ Meldrum worked for several years as an attorney before turning to writing, and her debut young-adult novel, *Madapple,* quickly earned her critical recognition. Translated into several language, the story focuses on a young woman raised in isolation in Maine and her tragic experiences upon intersecting with modern culture.

*Laura Numeroff ❚ In her lighthearted picture books for children, Numeroff plays with language, pairing playful rhymes with her own bold artwork or illustrations by artists such as Felicia Bond, Lynn Munsinger, and David McPhail. Her children's story *If You Give a Mouse a Cookie* quickly became a childhood classic, and was followed by *If You Give a Moose a Muffin, If You Take a Mouse to School,* and *If You Give a Pig a Party.* Numeroff's other children's books, such as *When Sheep Sleep* and *Sometimes I Wonder if Poodles Like Noodles,* continue to engage nonsense lovers of all ages.

*Brian Pinkney ❚ Pinkney is an illustrator and author who works in a striking and unusual medium: oil painting over scratchboard, and his work is notable for revealing the diverse experiences of African Americans, their ancestors, and blacks in other parts of the world. The son of noted illustrator Jerry Pinkney, he is married to children's book author Andrea Davis Pinkney, with whom he has collaborated on picture books such as *Peggony-Po: A Whale of a Tale* and *Boycott Blues: How Rosa Parks Inspired a Nation,* in addition to creating several original self-illustrated stories.

Jim Rugg ❚ The work of cartoonist Rugg is familiar to teen fans of the "P.L.A.I.N. Janes" graphic-novel series, which features a story line by writer Cecil Castellucci. Rugg's renown extends beyond a young-adult audience, however. In addition to his collaboration with Castellucci, he has also worked with writer Brian Maruca on the "Street Angel" comics and the graphic novel *Afrodisiac.* In 2009 Rugg also teamed up with C. Allbritton Taylor to produce *One Model Nation,* a graphic-novel chronicle set in the 1970s that finds a West German industrial band caught up in the terrorist activities of the radical Baader Meinhoff Group.

Michael P. Waite ❚ In addition to working as a designer and executive in the computer-games industry, Waite has written more than twenty books for young readers, including works in the "Building Christian Character" and "Camp Windy Woods" series. Writing under the pseudonym Riford McKenzie, he has also released *The Witches of Dredmoore Hollow,* a fantasy-filled middle-grade novel that was honored as an Edgar Allen Poe Award finalist for best juvenile mystery in 2009.

*Helen Ward ❚ Ward is a British illustrator and author with more than forty children's books to her credit. Both her words and her detailed illustrations depict stories about animal life or retell classic fables through animal characters, and her artwork has also graced the pages of such famous works of English literature as Rudyard Kipling's *Just So Stories* and Kenneth Grahame's *The Wind in the Willows.*

Introduction

Something about the Author (*SATA*) is an ongoing reference series that examines the lives and works of authors and illustrators of books for children. *SATA* includes not only well-known writers and artists but also less prominent individuals whose works are just coming to be recognized. This series is often the only readily available information source on emerging authors and illustrators. You'll find *SATA* informative and entertaining, whether you are a student, a librarian, an English teacher, a parent, or simply an adult who enjoys children's literature.

What's Inside *SATA*

SATA provides detailed information about authors and illustrators who span the full time range of children's literature, from early figures like John Newbery and L. Frank Baum to contemporary figures like Judy Blume and Richard Peck. Authors in the series represent primarily English-speaking countries, particularly the United States, Canada, and the United Kingdom. Also included, however, are authors from around the world whose works are available in English translation. The writings represented in *SATA* include those created intentionally for children and young adults as well as those written for a general audience and known to interest younger readers. These writings cover the entire spectrum of children's literature, including picture books, humor, folk and fairy tales, animal stories, mystery and adventure, science fiction and fantasy, historical fiction, poetry and nonsense verse, drama, biography, and nonfiction. Obituaries are also included in *SATA* and are intended not only as death notices but also as concise overviews of people's lives and work. Additionally, each edition features newly revised and updated entries for a selection of *SATA* listees who remain of interest to today's readers and who have been active enough to require extensive revisions of their earlier biographies.

Autobiography Feature

Beginning with Volume 103, many volumes of *SATA* feature one or more specially commissioned autobiographical essays. These unique essays, averaging about ten thousand words in length and illustrated with an abundance of personal photos, present an entertaining and informative first-person perspective on the lives and careers of prominent authors and illustrators profiled in *SATA*.

Two Convenient Indexes

In response to suggestions from librarians, *SATA* indexes no longer appear in every volume but are included in alternate (odd-numbered) volumes of the series, beginning with Volume 57.

SATA continues to include two indexes that cumulate with each alternate volume: the Illustrations Index, arranged by the name of the illustrator, gives the number of the volume and page where the illustrator's work appears in the current volume as well as all preceding volumes in the series; the Author Index gives the number of the volume in which a person's biographical sketch, autobiographical essay, or obituary appears in the current volume as well as all preceding volumes in the series.

These indexes also include references to authors and illustrators who appear in *Gale's Yesterday's Authors of Books for Children, Children's Literature Review,* and *Something about the Author Autobiography Series.*

Easy-to-Use Entry Format

Whether you're already familiar with the *SATA* series or just getting acquainted, you will want to be aware of the kind of information that an entry provides. In every *SATA* entry the editors attempt to give as complete a picture of the person's life and work as possible. A typical entry in *SATA* includes the following clearly labeled information sections:

PERSONAL: date and place of birth and death, parents' names and occupations, name of spouse, date of marriage, names of children, educational institutions attended, degrees received, religious and political affiliations, hobbies and other interests.

ADDRESSES: complete home, office, electronic mail, and agent addresses, whenever available.

CAREER: name of employer, position, and dates for each career post; art exhibitions; military service; memberships and offices held in professional and civic organizations.

MEMBER: professional, civic, and other association memberships and any official posts held.

AWARDS, HONORS: literary and professional awards received.

WRITINGS: title-by-title chronological bibliography of books written and/or illustrated, listed by genre when known; lists of other notable publications, such as plays, screenplays, and periodical contributions.

ADAPTATIONS: a list of films, television programs, plays, CD-ROMs, recordings, and other media presentations that have been adapted from the author's work.

WORK IN PROGRESS: description of projects in progress.

SIDELIGHTS: a biographical portrait of the author or illustrator's development, either directly from the biographee—and often written specifically for the *SATA* entry—or gathered from diaries, letters, interviews, or other published sources.

BIOGRAPHICAL AND CRITICAL SOURCES: cites sources quoted in "Sidelights" along with references for further reading.

EXTENSIVE ILLUSTRATIONS: photographs, movie stills, book illustrations, and other interesting visual materials supplement the text.

How a *SATA* Entry Is Compiled

SATA editors examine a wide variety of published sources to gather information for an entry. Biographical and bibliographic sources are consulted, as are book reviews, feature articles, published interviews, and material sometimes obtained from the biographee's family, publishers, agent, or other associates. Whenever possible, the author or illustrator is sent a copy of the entry to check for accuracy and completeness.

Entries that have not been verified by the biographees or their representatives are marked with an asterisk (*).

Contact the Editor

We encourage our readers to examine the entire *SATA* series. Please write and tell us if we can make *SATA* even more helpful to you. Give your comments and suggestions to the editor:

Editor
Something about the Author
Gale, Cengage Learning
27500 Drake Rd.
Farmington Hills MI 48331-3535

Toll-free: 800-877-GALE
Fax: 248-699-8070

Something about the Author Product Advisory Board

The editors of *Something about the Author* are dedicated to maintaining a high standard of excellence by publishing comprehensive, accurate, and highly readable entries on a wide array of writers for children and young adults. In addition to the quality of the content, the editors take pride in the graphic design of the series, which is intended to be orderly yet inviting, allowing readers to utilize the pages of *SATA* easily and with efficiency. Despite the longevity of the *SATA* print series, and the success of its format, we are mindful that the vitality of a literary reference product is dependent on its ability to serve its users over time. As literature, and attitudes about literature, constantly evolve, so do the reference needs of students, teachers, scholars, journalists, researchers, and book club members. To be certain that we continue to keep pace with the expectations of our customers, the editors of *SATA* listen carefully to their comments regarding the value, utility, and quality of the series. Librarians, who have firsthand knowledge of the needs of library users, are a valuable resource for us. The *Something about the Author* Product Advisory Board, made up of school, public, and academic librarians, is a forum to promote focused feedback about *SATA* on a regular basis. The nine-member advisory board includes the following individuals, whom the editors wish to thank for sharing their expertise:

Eva M. Davis
Director,
Canton Public Library,
Canton, Michigan

Joan B. Eisenberg
Lower School Librarian,
Milton Academy,
Milton, Massachusetts

Francisca Goldsmith
Teen Services Librarian,
Berkeley Public Library,
Berkeley, California

Susan Dove Lempke
Children's Services Supervisor,
Niles Public Library District,
Niles, Illinois

Robyn Lupa
Head of Children's Services,
Jefferson County Public Library,
Lakewood, Colorado

Victor L. Schill
Assistant Branch Librarian/Children's Librarian,
Harris County Public Library/Fairbanks Branch,
Houston, Texas

Caryn Sipos
Community Librarian,
Three Creeks Community Library,
Vancouver, Washington

Steven Weiner
Director,
Maynard Public Library,
Maynard, Massachusetts

something about the author

ABBOTT, Tony 1952-

Personal

Born October 26, 1952, in Cleveland, OH; father a paratrooper, mother a teacher; married; children: two daughters. *Education:* University of Connecticut, B.A. *Hobbies and other interests:* Tennis, playing guitar, biking.

Addresses

Home—Trumbull, CT. *Agent*—George Nicholson, Sterling Lord Literistic, 65 Bleecker St., New York, NY 10012. *E-mail*—tonyabbott@sbcglobal.net.

Career

Writer. Formerly worked in bookstores, at a library, and for a publishing company.

Member

Society of Children's Book Writers and Illustrators, Connecticut Reading Association.

Awards, Honors

Golden Kite Award for fiction, Society of Children's Book Writers and Illustrators, 2007, for *Firegirl;* Edgar Allan Poe Award for best juvenile novel, Mystery Writers of America, 2009, for *The Postcard.*

Tony Abbott (Photograph by Neil Swanson. Reproduced by permission.)

Writings

Kringle, illustrated by Greg Call, Scholastic (New York, NY), 2005.
Firegirl, Little, Brown (New York, NY), 2006.
The Postcard, Little, Brown (New York, NY), 2008.
The Haunting of Derek Stone ("City of the Dead" series), Scholastic (New York, NY), 2009.

Author's books have been translated into Spanish, Italian, French, Russian, Polish, Turkish, Slovinian, Czech, Chinese, Korean, and Japanese.

"DANGER GUYS" SERIES

Danger Guys, illustrated by Joanne Scribner, HarperTrophy (New York, NY), 1994.
Danger Guys Blast Off, illustrated by Joanne Scribner, HarperTrophy (New York, NY), 1994.
Danger Guys: Hollywood Halloween, illustrated by Suwin Chan, HarperTrophy (New York, NY), 1994.
Danger Guys Hit the Beach, illustrated by Joanne Scribner, HarperTrophy (New York, NY), 1995.
Danger Guys on Ice, illustrated by Joanne Scribner, HarperTrophy (New York, NY), 1995.
Danger Guys and the Golden Lizard, illustrated by Joanne Scribner, HarperCollins (New York, NY), 1996.

"TIME SURFERS" SERIES

Space Bingo, illustrated by Kim Mulkey, Bantam (New York, NY), 1996.
Orbit Wipeout, Bantam (New York, NY), 1996.
Mondo Meltdown, Bantam (New York, NY), 1996.
Into the Zonk Zone, Bantam (New York, NY), 1996.
Splash Crash, Bantam (New York, NY), 1997.
Zero Hour, Bantam (New York, NY), 1997.
Shock Wave, Bantam (New York, NY), 1997.
Doom Star, Bantam (New York, NY), 1997.

"WEIRD ZONE" SERIES

Zombie Surf Commandos from Mars, illustrated by Broeck Steadman, Scholastic (New York, NY), 1996.
The Incredible Shrinking Kid, illustrated by Lori Savastano, Scholastic (New York, NY), 1996.
The Beast from beneath the Cafeteria, illustrated by Broeck Steadman and Peter Peebles, Scholastic (New York, NY), 1996.
Attack of the Alien Mole Invaders, illustrated by Lori Savastano, Scholastic (New York, NY), 1996.
The Brain That Wouldn't Obey, illustrated by Broeck Steadman and Lori Savastano, Scholastic (New York, NY), 1997.
Gigantopus from Planet X, illustrated by Broeck Steadman and Lori Savastano, Scholastic (New York, NY), 1997.
Cosmic Boy versus Mezmo Head, illustrated by Broeck Steadman and Lori Savastano, Scholastic (New York, NY), 1997.
Revenge of the Tiki Men, illustrated by Broeck Steadman and Lori Savastano, Scholastic (New York, NY), 1997.

"DON'T TOUCH THAT REMOTE!" SERIES

Sitcom School, Pocket Books (New York, NY), 1999.
The Fake Teacher, Pocket Books (New York, NY), 1999.

"SECRETS OF DROON" SERIES

The Hidden Stairs and the Magic Carpet, Scholastic (New York, NY), 1999.
Journey to the Volcano Palace, Scholastic (New York, NY), 1999.
The Mysterious Island, illustrated by David Merrell, Scholastic (New York, NY), 1999.
City in the Clouds, Scholastic (New York, NY), 1999.
The Great Ice Battle, illustrated by Tim Jessell, Scholastic (New York, NY), 1999.
The Sleeping Giant of Goll, illustrated by Tim Jessell, Scholastic (New York, NY), 2000.
Into the Land of the Lost, Scholastic (New York, NY), 2000.
The Golden Wasp, illustrated by Tim Jessell, Scholastic (New York, NY), 2000.
The Tower of the Elf King, illustrated by David Merrell, Scholastic (New York, NY), 2000.
Quest for the Queen, illustrated by David Merrell, Scholastic (New York, NY), 2000.
The Hawk Bandits of Tarkoom, illustrated by Tim Jessell, Scholastic (New York, NY), 2001.
Under the Serpent Sea, illustrated by Tim Jessell, Scholastic (New York, NY), 2001.
The Mask of Maliban, illustrated by Tim Jessell, Scholastic (New York, NY), 2001.
Voyage of the Jaffa Wind, illustrated by David Merrell, Scholastic (New York, NY), 2002.
The Moon Scroll, illustrated by Tim Jessell, Scholastic (New York, NY), 2002.
The Knights of Silversnow, illustrated by Tim Jessell, Scholastic (New York, NY), 2002.
Dream Thief, illustrated by David Merrell, Scholastic (New York, NY), 2003.
Search for the Dragon Ship, illustrated by Tim Jessell, Scholastic (New York, NY), 2003.
The Coiled Viper, illustrated by Tim Jessell, Scholastic (New York, NY), 2003.
In the Ice Caves of Krog, Scholastic (New York, NY), 2003.
Flight of the Genie, illustrated by David Merrell, Scholastic (New York, NY), 2004.
Isle of the Mists, Scholastic (New York, NY), 2004.
The Fortress of the Treasure Queen, Scholastic (New York, NY), 2004.
The Race to Doobesh, Scholastic (New York, NY), 2005.
The Riddle of Zorfendorf Castle, Scholastic (New York, NY), 2005.
The Moon Dragon, Scholastic (New York, NY), 2005.
The Chariot of Queen Zara, Scholastic (New York, NY), 2006.
In the Shadow of Goll, illustrated by David Merrell, Scholastic (New York, NY), 2006.
Pirates of the Purple Dawn, Scholastic (New York, NY), 2007.
Escape from Jabar-Loo, illustrated by David Merrell, Scholastic (New York, NY), 2007.

Queen of Shadowthorn, illustrated by David Merrell, Scholastic (New York, NY), 2007.

The Treasure of the Orkins, illustrated by Royce Fitzgerald, Scholastic (New York, NY), 2008.

Flight of the Blue Serpent, Scholastic (New York, NY), 2008.

In the City of Dreams, Scholastic (New York, NY), 2008.

The Lost Empire of Koomba, Scholastic (New York, NY), 2009.

"SECRETS OF DROON SPECIAL-EDITION" SERIES

The Magic Escapes, illustrated by Tim Jessell, Scholastic (New York, NY), 2002.

Wizard or Witch?, illustrated by David Merrell, Scholastic (New York, NY), 2004.

Voyagers of the Silver Sand, Scholastic (New York, NY), 2005.

Sorcerer, illustrated by David Merrell, Scholastic (New York, NY), 2006.

Moon Magic, illustrated by David Merrell, Scholastic (New York, NY), 2008.

Crown of Wizards, illustrated by David Merrell, Scholastic (New York, NY), 2009.

"CRACKED CLASSICS" SERIES

Dracula: Trapped in Transylvania, Volo (New York, NY), 2002.

Mississippi River Blues: The Adventures of Tom Sawyer, Volo (New York, NY), 2002.

What a Trip!: Around the World in Eighty Days, Volo (New York, NY), 2002.

Humbug Holiday: A Christmas Carol, Volo (New York, NY), 2002.

Treasure Island: X Marks the Spot, Volo (New York, NY), 2002.

Romeo and Juliet: Crushing on a Capulet, Volo (New York, NY), 2003.

Sidelights

Tony Abbott is the author of several popular series of books aimed at elementary-school students, particularly boys, among them the "Time Surfers," "Weird Zone," and "Secrets of Droon" stories. "From the practical to the spiritual, the series writer has a lot of balls to keep in the air," Abbott remarked in an online interview with Cynthia Leitich Smith for the *Cynsations* Web site. He continued, "You have to be the sort of person who doesn't recognize the concept of 'writer's block.' It doesn't exist; that's all. You have to be able to keep to a deadline. . . . You have to be constantly inventive. The question, 'where do you get your ideas?' has to be nonsensical to a series writer. You have to have a business side equal to your imaginative side, too, since series fiction tends to work in tandem with trends in the culture at large."

Abbott's first series, "Danger Guys," is a "good-natured parody of the likes of Indiana Jones films," explained a *Publishers Weekly* reviewer. The series features two school-aged sleuths, Noodle and Zeek, who constantly find themselves being sucked into fantastic, high-octane adventures. In the first book of the series, *Danger Guys,* Noodle and Zeek accidentally stow away with two kidnappers-cum-thieves and find the band's captives, a married couple of explorers. The boys free the couple and put a stop to the thieves' plan to steal artifacts from a prehistoric temple, all while escaping from a series of injurious obstacles that include trapdoors leading to unpleasant places, giant rolling boulders à la *Raiders of the Lost Ark,* and a nasty fate at the hands of the thieves themselves. "Readers will happily overlook the sheer implausibility of it all" and enjoy Abbott's "blithe caper," a *Publishers Weekly* reviewer concluded. In subsequent installments, Noodle and Zeek find themselves riding in a runaway rocket ship, slaying movie monsters come to life at Paragon Studio, and falling into the Pit of Death. "Struggling new readers will find the books exciting," concluded *Booklist* critic Mary Harris Veeder.

Abbott's longest-running series, "Secrets of Droon," takes place in a fantasy world that was described by the author on his Web site as "populated by wizards and sorcerers, helpful pillow-shaped folks called Purple

Abbott's imaginative middle-grade novel The Secrets of Droon: The Race to Doobesh *features artwork by David Merrell.* (Illustration copyright © 2005 by Scholastic Inc. Reprinted by permission of Scholastic, Inc.)

Cover of Abbott's novel The Coiled Viper, *a "Secrets of Droon" novel featuring artwork by Tim Jessell.* (Illustration copyright © 2003 by Tim Jessel. Reproduced by permission of Scholastic, Inc.)

Lumpies, [and] fleet six-legged beasts called pilkas." Three children—Eric, Julie, and Neal—discover a staircase in Eric's basement that leads to Droon, and they return again and again to help Droon's Princess Keeah defeat the wicked Lord Sparr. "I like to think of this fantasy series for second graders and up, as a single, multi-thousand-page saga," Abbott remarked to Smith. "When a young reader starts these books, and continues with them, he or she is reading a very complex and many-charactered drama. An epic in installments. I've been lucky enough to join a very small club in having so many books in a single series published."

In his "Cracked Classics" books, Abbott introduces young readers to the works of well-known writers such as Bram Stoker in *Dracula: Trapped in Transylvania*, Mark Twain in *Mississippi River Blues: The Adventures of Tom Sawyer*, Jules Vernes in *What a Trip!: Around the World in Eighty Days*, Charles Dickens in *Humbug Holiday: A Christmas Carol*, Robert Louis Stevenson in *Treasure Island: X Marks the Spot*, and William Shakespeare in *Romeo and Juliet: Crushing on a Capulet*. In the series, two reluctant students, Devin and Frankie (short for Francine), discover that the library's electronic security "zapper gates" also have the power to

zap the pair into a book. Their first trip into a story, *Dracula,* happens accidentally, but soon they realize that traveling into books is a good way to prepare for tests. "While it is clear that the message is 'reading is good, fun and important,'" Molly S. Kinney noted in *School Library Journal,* "the author delivers it through the characters and plot, rather than by lecturing." The "Cracked Classics" books are also extremely funny, critics generally agreed; a *Publishers Weekly* reviewer praised the "buoyant banter" in *Trapped in Transylvania,* while *School Library Journal* contributor Elaine E. Knight predicted that Abbott's "irreverent homage" to *The Adventures of Tom Sawyer* in *Mississippi River Blues* "would probably win a chuckle from Twain himself."

In addition to his series work, Abbott has written a number of highly regarded stand-alone titles. *Kringle,* a middle-grade novel that investigates the origins of Santa Claus, centers on a young man's epic struggle to rescue his mentor from villainous goblins. *Kringle,* Abbott remarked to Smith, "harks back to the classic English children's stories from *Peter Pan* to *The Hobbit,* and was written as something like a saint's biography, but with all the humor and adventure lacking from most of the classics in that genre." According to *Booklist* contributor Ilene Cooper, Abbott's "enticing premise, appealing young hero, and nonstop action will appeal to many fantasy lovers."

Firegirl, a Golden Kite Award winner, is based on an incident from Abbott's own life. The novel concerns Tom Bender, a sensitive, overweight seventh-grader, and his brief but life-altering relationship with Jessica Feeney, a girl who attends his school while receiving skin grafts at a local hospital for the horrible burns that cover her body. "Though fleeting and fragile, Tom's connection to Jessica changes his perspective on himself, his peers and friendship," a critic observed in *Publishers Weekly,* and Denise Moore, writing in *School Library Journal,* called the work "a touching story of friendship that is easy to read yet hard to forget."

Recipient of the Mystery Writers of America's Edgar Allan Poe Award for best juvenile novel, *The Postcard* was inspired in part by Abbott's collection of brightly colored linen postcards from the 1940s. As the author remarked in an online interview with Lesa Holstine, "There was a day when I was looking at my cards and wondered how interesting it would be if someone had included an almost invisible clue on an otherwise blank postcard that remained more or less undiscovered for seventy years. If someone found it now, what would they do?" *The Postcard* centers on Jason, a troubled thirteen year old who heads to St. Petersburg, Florida, to help his father settle the affairs of his deceased grandmother. A mysterious phone call, a story in a hardboiled pulp magazine, and the discovery of an old postcard lead Jason to investigate his grandmother's secret past. "Jason (paired nicely with a neighbor girl as sidekick) is a hero worth rooting for," Cooper noted, and

Nicki Clausen-Grace stated in *School Library Journal* that "the surprise ending to the mystery and the not-so-surprising ending to Jason's real-life drama are quite satisfying."

Abbott enjoys the rewards of writing for children and young adults. As he told an interviewer on the *Young Adult (& Kids) Books Central* Web site, "I suppose there is a part of me that likes the marvelous innocence and fun (and confusion, too?) of being young, and I like to portray those states using words. It all comes back to words, the desire to create worlds, situations, characters, emotions, using the unlimited resources of our wonderful language."

Biographical and Critical Sources

PERIODICALS

Booklist, August, 1994, Mary Harris Veeder, review of *Danger Guys* and *Danger Guys Blast Off,* p. 2040; October 15, 2005, Ilene Cooper, review of *Kringle,* p.

Abbott's picture book **In the City of Dreams** *is brought to life in artwork by Royce Fitzgerald.* (Illustration copyright © 2009 by Royce Fitzgerald. Reproduced by permission of Scholastic, Inc.)

48; July 1, 2006, Nancy Kim, review of *Firegirl,* p. 54; May 1, 2008, Ilene Cooper, review of *The Postcard,* p. 48; January 1, 2009, Ian Chipman, review of *City of the Dead,* p. 82.

Publishers Weekly, May 16, 1994, review of *Danger Guys,* p. 65; September 6, 1999, review of *Sitcom School,* p. 104; May 20, 2002, review of *Trapped in Transylvania,* p. 65; May 22, 2006, review of *Firegirl,* p. 52.

School Library Journal, July, 2002, Molly S. Kinney, review of *Trapped in Transylvania,* p. 113; January, 2003, reviews of *Mississippi River Blues* and *What a Trip!,* p. 133; July, 2006, Denise Moore, review of *Firegirl,* p. 97; April, 2008, Nicki Clausen-Grace, review of *The Postcard,* p. 139.

ONLINE

Cynsations Web log, http://cynthialeitichsmith.blogspot.com/ (September 10, 2008), Cynthia Leitich Smith, interview with Abbott.

Lesa's Book Critiques Web log, http://lesasbookcritiques.blogspot.com/ (May 22, 2009), Lesa Holstine, interview with Abbott.

Scholastic Web site, http://www2.scholastic.com/ (September 1, 2009), profile of Abbott.

Tony Abbott Home Page, http://www.tonyabbottbooks.com (September 1, 2009).

Young Adult (& Kids) Books Central Web site, http://www.yabookscentral.com/ (September 1, 2009), interview with Abbott.

*   *   *

ADDASI, Maha 1968-

Personal

Born 1968, in Kuwait; father a physician; married; husband's name Rami; children: Serena, Diana, Samer (son), Ramzy (son). *Education:* Butler University, B.A.; attended Vermont College of Fine Arts. *Hobbies and other interests:* Antique stores and yard sales, making bead bracelets, water-color painting.

Addresses

Home—Fairfax, VA. *E-mail*—Mahaaddasi@aol.com.

Career

Journalist and author. News correspondent and producer for Jordan and Dubai television and British Broadcasting Corporation (BBC); Noor Al Hussein Foundation, Jordan, worked in public relations.

Member

Authors Guild.

Awards, Honors

Smithsonian magazine Notable Book for Children designation, 2008, for *The White Nights of Ramadan.*

Writings

The White Nights of Ramadan (children's book), illustrated by Ned Gannon, Boyds Mills Press (Honesdale, PA), 2008.

Writer for *Heartbeat* (documentary television series). Author of weekly humor column for two years.

Sidelights

A native of Kuwait, Maha Addasi is the author of *The White Nights of Ramadan,* a picture book that examines Girgian, a Muslim celebration held during the month-long Muslim holiday of Ramadan in several countries located in the Persian Gulf region. "The idea of writing about Ramadan came from my own need to find a book about this month that was a fun read," Addasi stated in an online interview with Jama Rattigan. Noting that most books about Ramadan focus on fasting, a major part of the holiday, Addasi remarked that "what I wanted to show was that Ramadan is not a month of suffering, but a month that holds beautiful meanings of sharing and interacting with family and friends."

Maha Addasi shares the traditions of a major Muslim holiday in **The White Nights of Ramadan,** *a picture book illustrated by Ned Gannon.* (Boyds Mills Press, 2008. Illustration© 2008 by Ned Gannon. Reproduced by permission.)

Addasi developed a love of literature as a child, due in large part to her parents. As the author observed on her home page, "I remember a first-reader picture book I read some 600 times because my dad, a physician and a perfectionist, wanted it to sound impeccable and somehow the 599 other times did not make the cut." "The repeated reading gave me an appreciation for words even as early as age five," she added. Addasi's mother, who held a degree in literature, conducted early-morning study sessions centering on language and poetry. "I confess that, much as I writhed in agony about the early lessons then, I learned so much through them that I will forever be indebted to my mom for the time and energy she spent with me on language skills," Addasi recalled.

Attending Butler University in Indianapolis, Indiana, Addasi earned a bachelor's degree in journalism. She then returned to the Middle East and began a career as a news correspondent and producer for Jordan and Dubai television and for the British Broadcasting Corporation. After moving permanently to the United States in 1998 with her husband and children, Addasi decided to aim her writing at a younger audience. As she told Rattigan, "Turning to writing for children was much tougher than being a journalist. It took some seven years of work to re-craft my writing toward children's writing. . . . This writing field is so immense and there is always so much more to learn." Fortunately, she was able to draw on her journalistic background, noting that "it gave me several unique experiences and perspectives to draw on, and . . . it made me able to work fast."

In *The White Nights of Ramadan,* her debut work for young readers, Addasi introduces Noor, a young Kuwaiti girl who anxiously awaits the start of Girgian, the three-day festival that takes place in the middle of Ramadan, when the moon is full. With her younger brothers, Noor prepares candies made from honey, sugar, and nuts to share with the other children in her neighborhood. After a day of praying and fasting, the children carry lanterns and go door to door, collecting treats. Noor and her grandfather conclude the celebration by delivering a basket of food for the poor to their local mosque. *The White Nights of Ramadan* "underlines the gift of sharing during a month dedicated to self-improvement and community welfare," Fawzia Gilani-Williams remarked in her review of Addasi's story for *School Library Journal.*

Biographical and Critical Sources

PERIODICALS

Booklist, July 1, 2008, Hazel Rochman, review of *The White Nights of Ramadan,* p. 75.
Kirkus Reviews, July 1, 2008, review of *The White Nights of Ramadan.*
School Library Journal, September, 2008, Fawzia Gilani-Williams, review of *The White Nights of Ramadan,* p. 136.

ONLINE

Jama Rattigan's Alphabet Soup Web log, http://jama
   rattigan.livejournal.com/ (September 15, 2008), Jama
   Rattigan, interview with Addasi.
Maha Addasi Home Page, http://www.mahaaddasi.com
   (August 20, 2009).
Maha Addasi Web log, http://mahaaddasi.livejournal.com/
   (August 20, 2009).*

*   *   *

AHO, Julia Kay
See KAY, Julia

*   *   *

ALDA, Arlene 1933-

Personal

Born March 12, 1933, in New York, NY; daughter of
Simon (a lithographer) and Jeanette (a seamstress)
Weiss; married Alan Alda (an actor, writer, and director), March 15, 1957; children: Eve, Elizabeth, Beatrice. *Education:* Hunter College (now Hunter College
of the City University of New York), degree, 1954;
studied photography with Mort Shapiro and Lou Bernstein.

Addresses

Home—New York, NY; CA. *E-mail*—arlene@arlene
alda.com.

Career

Photographer, children's book author, and musician.
Houston Symphony, Houston, TX, assistant first clarinetist, 1956-57; photographer, 1967—; writer, beginning 1980. Performed with National Orchestral Association in New York, NY, and with suburban orchestras;
taught orchestral music in New York, NY; private clarinet instructor. Director of *Bravo Gloria* (documentary
film), Public Broadcasting Service (PBS), 1988. *Exhibitions:* Work included in exhibitions at Nikon House,
New York, NY; Soho Gallery, New York, NY; Fashion
Institute of Technology, New York, NY; Elaine Benson
Gallery, Bridgehampton, NY; and Mark Humphrey Gallery, Southampton, NY.

Member

Authors Guild, PEN, Phi Beta Kappa.

Awards, Honors

Fulbright scholarship for music study in Germany,
1954-55; New Jersey Institute of Technology award,
1983, for *Matthew and His Dad;* Silver Medal Award,
International Film and TV Festival of New York, and
John Muir Medical Film Festival award finalist, both
1988, both for *Bravo Gloria;* Notable Books for Children designation, American Library Association, 1999,
for *Arlene Alda's 1 2 3;* Chicago Graphics Award in the
communicating arts, for photo essay, "Allison's Tonsil-
lectomy"; Fulbright Association honor, 2000, for work
in the arts; honorary doctorate from Southampton College, 2003.

Writings

FOR CHILDREN

Hold the Bus: A Counting Book from 1 to 10, illustrated
   by Dan Regan, WhistleStop, 1996.
Hurry Granny Annie, illustrated by Eve Aldridge, Tricycle
   Press (Berkeley, CA), 1999.
Morning Glory Monday, illustrated by Maryann Kovalski,
   Tundra Books (Plattsburgh, NY), 2003.
Iris Has a Virus, illustrated by Lisa Desimini, Tundra
   Books (Plattsburgh, NY), 2008.

FOR CHILDREN; SELF-ILLUSTRATED WITH PHOTOGRAPHS

Arlene Alda's ABC Book, Celestial Arts, 1981, published
   as *ABC: What Do You See?,* Tricycle Press (Berkeley,
   CA), 1993.
Sonya's Mommy Works, Messner (New York, NY), 1982.
Matthew and His Dad, Little Simon (New York, NY),
   1983.
Sheep, Sheep, Sheep, Help Me Fall Asleep, Delacorte (New
   York, NY), 1992.
Pig, Horse, or Cow, Don't Wake Me Now, Doubleday (New
   York, NY), 1994.
Arlene Alda's 1 2 3: What Do You See?, Tricycle Press
   (Berkeley, CA), 1998.
The Book of ZZZs, Tundra Books (Plattsburgh, NY), 2005.
Did You Say Pears?, Tundra Books (Plattsburgh, NY),
   2006.
Here a Face, There a Face, Tundra Books (Plattsburgh,
   NY), 2008.
Hello, Good-bye, Tundra Books (Plattsburgh, NY), 2009.

OTHER

On Set: A Personal Story in Photographs and Words, Si-
   mon & Schuster (New York, NY), 1981.
(With husband, Alan Alda) *The Last Days of M*A*S*H*,*
   Unicorn Publishing, 1983.
(Illustrator) Linda Granfield, *97 Orchard Street, New York:
   Stories of Immigrant Life,* Tricycle (Berkeley, CA),
   1998.

Contributor to books, including *Women of Vision: Photographic Statements of Twenty Women Photographers,*
Unicorn Publishing, 1982. Contributor of photographs

to periodicals, including the *New York Times, Family Weekly, Life, Redbook, People, Vogue, Today's Health, Good Housekeeping,* and *Saturday Evening Post.*

Sidelights

Author and photographer Arlene Alda has earned critical praise for her self-illustrated children's books, which include *Arlene Alda's ABC Book, The Book of ZZZs,* and *Here a Face, There a Face.* Her works, while aimed at a young audience, hold a strong appeal for readers of all ages, as Alda stated in an *Open Book: Toronto* online interview. "I like to think that the readership spans from ages 4 to about 104," she remarked. "A lot of my humor and photos have a crossover 'audience.' But since I write for the picture book ages (3 to about 7 or 8), I actually keep that readership in mind."

Before marrying actor Alan Alda in 1957, Arlene was an accomplished clarinetist who began playing in high school, studied music in Europe on a Fulbright scholarship, and then joined the Houston Symphony. Although she gave up her professional music career to raise her children, she supported her struggling young husband in the early days of his acting career by giving private clarinet lessons and playing in obscure suburban orchestras.

In 1967, Arlene Alda took a course in photography, and the venture proved successful. Since her first efforts in the medium, she has gone on to exhibit her work in galleries, to contribute photographs to national magazines, and to write books that showcase her photos. For one project, the film *The Four Seasons,* the entire Alda family contributed their talents: Alan wrote, directed, and starred in the film, and the couple's two youngest daughters acted in it. With the assistance of her eldest daughter, Arlene supplied wacky vegetable photographs to appear as the work of an obsessive photographer. She remained on the set during the film's shooting and snapped pictures documenting its making. These behind-the-scenes observations were subsequently published as *On Set: A Personal Story in Photographs and Words.*

Alda's books for children showcase her photography, and some reviewers have particular praise for her images of animals. "Alda clearly possesses the skills to bring out every endearing quality of her animal subjects," claimed a reviewer in *Publishers Weekly.* In *Arlene Alda's ABC Book,* Alda discerns the shape of the letters of the alphabet in photographs of everyday objects; for example, the letter "A" can be detected in her photograph of a yellow sawhorse. The book "contributes a fresh look at commonplace, usually unnoticed things we find around us," according to reviewer Janice Del Negro in *Booklist.*

In similar fashion, the photographs in *Arlene Alda's 1 2 3: What Do You See?* depict the shapes of the numbers one through ten within the contours of objects and ani-

Arlene Alda's artful photographic images are a feature of concept books such as **Arlene Alda's 123.** (Copyright © 2004 by Arlene Alda. Used by permission of Tricycle Press, an imprint of the Crown Publishing Group, a division of Random House, Inc.)

mals. Examples include using the stem of a leaf to make the number "1," a banana peel to form the number "3," and a bagel cut in half to form an "8." Notes from Alda explain what each object is and how the numbers were formed.

In her *Horn Book* review of *Arlene Alda's 1 2 3,* Lolly Robinson remarked: "As she did in *Arlene Alda's ABC Book,* the photographer has kept the images and the format simple and accessible." Patricia Pearl Dole, a reviewer for *School Library Journal,* praised the "great imagination" exhibited in these photos, calling *Arlene Alda's 1 2 3* "a unique, challenging concept book." "This wonderful book," wrote David J. Whitin in *Teaching Children Mathematics,* "will help students recognize numerals and explore their own environments for other numerical shapes."

In other works for children, Alda incorporates a simple, rhyming text to accompany her photos of animals as seen from a child's viewpoint. In *Sheep, Sheep, Sheep, Help Me Fall Asleep,* for example, a child who cannot go to sleep closes her eyes and begins a search for some sheep to count to help her in her pursuit. Instead she finds a bevy of other animals. When she finally comes upon some sheep, more and more sheep appear, and the book becomes a counting exercise. "Alda's breezy rhyming text and arresting photographs make this a most engaging bedtime read-aloud," suggested a critic in *Publishers Weekly.* Likewise, in *Pig, Horse, or Cow, Don't Wake Me Now* Alda's rhyming text recounts

the early-morning chain reaction of waking on a farm. A peacock calling for his morning corn begins the process, awakening a variety of slumbering animals that culminates with a cat intruding on a little boy's sleep. "Early risers and sleepyheads will . . . have fun identifying the barnyard friends," claimed Mary Harris Veeder in a *Booklist* review of *Pig, Horse, or Cow, Don't Wake Me Now.*

Animals and humans at rest are the focus of *The Book of ZZZs,* a "perfect bedtime or sleepy storytime book," according to Denise Parrott in *Resource Links.* In the work, which features Alda's photographs accompanied by a brief caption, the author presents a host of creatures in repose, including a goat napping in the sun, a flamingo balancing on one leg, and a dog lounging in a chair. Other images capture a young boy catching a few winks while strapped in a car seat and a little girl fast asleep while sitting astride her father's shoulders. Parrott complimented Alda's "lovely, simple and poetic text," and a critic in *Publishers Weekly* noted that "anyone in the position of persuading a reluctant child to hit the hay may find this a useful tool."

In *Did You Say Pears?* Alda offers what *Booklist* reviewer GraceAnne A. DeCandido called a "marvelously imaginative pairing" of common homophones (words that are pronounced the same but differ in meaning and spelling) and homonyms (words having the same sound and often the same spelling but different meanings). "If a pitcher/could pour," for instance, is illustrated with a full-color photograph of a boy hurling a baseball opposite another photograph of a container made of blue china. DeCandido offered further praise for the work, commenting that the arrangements are "wrapped up in a rhyme of amazingly few words and terrific offbeat photographs."

In *Here a Face, There a Face,* a "perky photo-essay that blends poetry, art and elements of traditional seek-and-find books," according to a *Publishers Weekly* contributor, readers are challenged to find shapes resembling human features on a variety of natural and manmade objects. Alda presents photographs of such ordinary items as mailboxes, loaves of bread, clouds, water faucets, and trees, all of which seem to possess eyes, a nose, and a mouth, thanks to the human inclination to interpret patterns. "The short phrases that accompany the photos comment playfully on particular images," Carolyn Phelan remarked in *Booklist,* and a *Kirkus Reviews* contributor predicted that *Here a Face, There a Face* "will effectively spur young children to look more closely and imaginatively at their surroundings." Alda explores the concept of opposites in *Hello, Good-bye,* "Exceptionally fine color photographs bring clarity as well as beauty" to the work, Phelan stated.

In *97 Orchard Street, New York: Stories of Immigrant Life,* Alda provides photographs to illustrate a text written by Linda Granfield. The book tells the stories of four immigrant families that came to America from different countries and at different times but which all lived on New York City's Lower East Side. The Gumpertz family came from Prussia in the 1870s; the Rogarshevsky family came from Lithuania in 1901; the Jewish Confino family came from Greece in 1914; and the Baldizzi family came from Sicily in 1924. Despite their differences in background and language, the new immigrants faced many of the same challenges in their new homeland: finding work, learning a new language, and getting their children educated. "Their stories are not romanticized," Rhonda Cooper wrote in *Kliatt;* "Rather, the reader sees and feels the hardships and trials the succession of new immigrants endured." The book ends with information about the Lower East Side Tenement Museum, a place offering guided tours of the kinds of dwellings talked about in Granfield's story.

Alda also documents the lives of early immigrants in New York's Lower East Side in her book *Morning Glory Monday,* illustrated by Maryann Kovalski. The story is set during the 1930s and tells of a young Italian immigrant girl who is worried about her mother, who never smiles. In fact, the poverty of their home in New York's tenement district during the Great Depression makes the woman homesick for her native Italy. When the girl wins a packet of morning glory seeds at a fair, she decides to plant them in the window box to cheer up her mother. The pretty flowers do make her mother happy, and as time goes by, the flowers spread from the window box throughout the neighborhood, magically transforming the whole area into a lush garden and lifting the spirits of everyone. Alda's story is based on a real event during the Depression when a group of tenement residents decided to brighten up their neighborhood by planting flowers on all the fire escapes.

Gillian Engberg, reviewing *Morning Glory Monday* for *Booklist,* praised Alda's "spare, simple language," adding that the work "offers a glimpse of tenement living and an immigrant family's yearning." According to Rachel G. Payne in *School Library Journal,* "the cheerful tone and fanciful plot will enchant readers," while a critic for *Publishers Weekly* called *Morning Glory Monday* an "inspiring picture-book portrait of immigrant life."

In *Iris Has a Virus,* a picture book illustrated with cut-paper collages by Lisa Desimini, "Alda sensitively captures a kid's viewpoint on illness," observed Shelle Rosenfeld in *Booklist.* When young Iris comes down with a nasty stomach ailment, she heads to the doctor, who informs her that she has contracted a bug. Feverish dreams of fanciful bugs follow in the days ahead, as a bedridden Iris tries to recover in time to attend her grandfather's birthday party. "Alda's amusing text is a combination of rhyming couplets interspersed with prose," Kristine M. Casper wrote in *School Library Journal,* and a contributor for *Kirkus Reviews* described *Iris Has a Virus* as a "refreshing cup of literary chicken soup for illin' children."

Biographical and Critical Sources

BOOKS

Alda, Arlene, *Did You Say Pears?*, Tundra Books (Plattsburgh, NY), 2006.

PERIODICALS

Booklist, January 1, 1994, Janice Del Negro, review of *Arlene Alda's ABC Book,* p. 829; October 15, 1994, Mary Harris Veeder, review of *Pig, Horse, or Cow, Don't Wake Me Now,* p. 434; January 1, 2004, Gillian Engberg, review of *Morning Glory Monday,* p. 872; March 1, 2006, GraceAnne A. DeCandido, review of *Did You Say Pears?,* p. 94; February 15, 2008, Carolyn Phelan, review of *Here a Face, There a Face,* p. 83; October 15, 2008, Shelle Rosenfeld, review of *Iris Has a Virus,* p. 46; January 1, 2009, Carolyn Phelan, review of *Hello, Good-bye,* p. 90.
Dallas Morning News, September 11, 2002, Nancy Churnin, review of *Hurry Granny Annie.*
Horn Book, November, 1998, Lolly Robinson, review of *Arlene Alda's 1 2 3: What Do You See?,* pp. 708-710.
Kirkus Reviews, September 1, 2003, *Morning Glory Monday,* p. 1119; February 1, 2008, review of *Here a Face, There a Face;* August 1, 2008, review of *Iris Has a Virus;* February 15, 2009, review of *Hello, Good-bye.*
Kliatt, March, 2002, Rhonda Cooper, review of *97 Orchard Street, New York: Stories of Immigrant Life,* p. 34.
Plays, October, 2001, review of *97 Orchard Street, New York,* p. 70.
Publishers Weekly, November 16, 1992, review of *Sheep, Sheep, Sheep, Help Me Fall Asleep,* p. 60; October 10, 1994, review of *Pig, Horse, or Cow, Don't Wake Me Now,* p. 69; September 22, 2003, review of *Morning Glory Monday,* p. 104; February 21, 2005, review of *The Book of ZZZs,* p. 173; February 18, 2008, review of *Here a Face, There a Face,* p. 152.
Resource Links, October, 2003, Denise Parrot, review of *Morning Glory Monday,* p. 1; June, 2005, Denise Parrott, review of *The Book of ZZZs,* p. 1.
School Library Journal, December, 1998, Patricia Pearl Dole, review of *Arlene Alda's 1 2 3,* p. 98; November, 2003, Rachel G. Payne, review of *Morning Glory Monday,* p. 88; June, 2006, Jodi Kearns, review of *Did You Say Pears?,* p. 130; June, 2008, Carolyn Janssen, review of *Here a Face, There a Face,* p. 117; November, 2008, Kristine M. Casper, review of *Iris Has a Virus,* p. 84.
Teaching Children Mathematics, October, 1999, David J. Whitin, review of *Arlene Alda's 1 2 3,* p. 129.

ONLINE

Arlene Alda Home Page, http://www.arlenealda.com (September 1, 2009).
BookPage.com, http://www.bookpage.com/ (October, 1999), "Arlene Alda."
Open Book: Toronto Web site, http://www.openbook toronto.com/ (March 15, 2009), "Ten Questions with Arlene Alda."

*   *   *

ALLEN, Raul

Personal

Born in Valladolid, Spain. *Education:* Studied art in Salamanca, Spain, and Boston, MA.

Addresses

Home—Barcelona, Spain. *Agent*—Gerald and Cullen Rapp, 420 Lexington Ave., New York, NY 10170; inforappart.com. *E-mail*—raul@rrallen.com.

Career

Artist and illustrator. *Exhibitions:* Work exhibited in New York, NY, Boston, MA, and Madrid and Barcelona, Spain.

Awards, Honors

National Drawing Award, Foundation Gregorio Prieto; Artist Gallery Drawing Award.

Illustrator

Susan Lendroth, *Ocean Wide, Ocean Deep,* Tricycle Press (Berkeley, CA), 2007.
W.W. Jacobs, *The Monkey's Paw,* Benchmark Education (Pelham, NY), 2007.

Contributor to books, including *Bordes de la luz* by Luis Miguel Dos Santos Vicente, *Pizca y Mabú,* Diputación de Valladolid, 2005, *Cuentos y leyendas del amor,* Anaya, 2007, and *The Last Children's Book of American Birds,* Club Leteo, 2009. Contributor to periodicals, including *Business Week, Público, Rolling Stone, Madriz, Men's Health, Cinemanía, Gentleman's Quarterly, Foreign Policy,* and *El Duende.*

Biographical and Critical Sources

PERIODICALS

Kirkus Reviews, July 1, 2008, review of *Ocean Wide, Ocean Deep.*
Publishers Weekly, August 11, 2008, review of *Ocean Wide, Ocean Deep,* p. 45.
School Library Journal, October, 2008, Kathleen Whalin, review of *Ocean Wide, Ocean Deep,* p. 115.

ONLINE

Art Noveau Online, http://www.artnouveaumagazine.com/ (September 1, 2009), Kendrick Day, interview with Allen.

Digital Temple Web site, http://www.digital-temple.com/ (September 1, 2009), interview with Allen.

Raul Allen Home Page, http://www.rrallen.com (September 1, 2009).*

*   *   *

AMIT, Ofra 1966-

Personal

Born 1966, in Israel. *Education:* WIZO Haifa Academy of Design and Education, degree.

Addresses

Home and office—Tel Aviv, Israel. *E-mail*—studio@ofra-amit.com.

Career

Illustrator and graphic artist. *Exhibitions:* Work included in Society of Illustrators art exhibits, New York, NY, 2007, 2008.

Awards, Honors

Award of excellence, *Communication Arts Illustration Annual,* 2004, 2008; Award of Excellence, *Applied Arts Illustration Annual,* 2004; Ben Yitzhak Award for Children's Book Illustration silver medal, Israel Museum, 2006, 2008.

Illustrator

Kay Woodward, *Countdown!,* Gingham Dog Press (Grand Rapids, MI), 2006.

Laurie Friedman, *Angel Girl* (based on an unpublished memoir by Herman Rosenblat), Carolrhoda Books (Minneapolis, MN), 2008.

Illustrator of works published in Israel, including *The Princess Filly* by Mirik Snir, Kinneret Publishing House; *Grandpa Cooked a Soup* by Nira Harel, Hakibbutz Hameuchad Publishers; and *Balthazar* by Nurit Zarchi, Korim Publishers. Contributor to periodicals, including *Maariv* and *Einayim.*

Biographical and Critical Sources

PERIODICALS

Booklist, August 1, 2008, Hazel Rochman, review of *Angel Girl,* p. 65.

Kirkus Reviews, July 15, 2008, review of *Angel Girl.*

School Library Journal, August, 2008, Heidi Estrin, review of *Angel Girl,* p. 143.

ONLINE

Israeli Illustrators Directory Online, http://www.illustrators.co.il/ (October 10, 2009), "Omit Afra."

Ofra Amit Home Page, http://www.ofra-amit.com (October 10, 2009).

B

BALDINI, Michelle

Personal

Married; children: four. *Education:* Long Island University, M.L.S.

Addresses

Home—Silver Lake, OH. *Office*—Kent State University, School of Library and Information Science, 314 Library, Kent, OH 44242. *E-mail*—mbaldini@kent.edu.

Career

Author and administrator. Kent State University, Kent, OH, project coordinator at School of Library and Information Science.

Writings

(With Lynn Biederman) *Unraveling* (novel), Delacorte (New York, NY), 2008.

Sidelights

Unraveling, a young-adult novel coauthored by Michelle Baldini and Lynn Biederman, concerns a fifteen-year-old girl's difficult and often troubling search for love and acceptance. Published in 2008, the work was three years in the writing; the authors met while attending graduate school and decided to join forces after sharing their parenting experiences. "During class we had a lot to say," Baldini recalled to Dave O'Brien for the Ravenna *Record-Courier.* "I connected with her [Biederman], we had a lot in common."

Unraveling centers on Amanda Himmelfarb. A bright but insecure teen, Amanda suffers at the hands of her bitter, disapproving mother, whom Amanda has dubbed "The Captain." To bolster her self-esteem—as well as

Michelle Baldini (Reproduced by permission.)

her standing at school—Amanda begins pursuing a host of boys, allowing them to use her sexually. In exchange for a date to the homecoming dance, she agrees to surrender her virginity to Rick Hayes, a popular but less-than-trustworthy senior.

Unraveling "is a good story of family dynamics," wrote Myrna Marler in *Kliatt,* the critic adding that Baldini and Biederman's novel "demonstrat[es] . . . the self-absorption of a teenager that can lead to bad decision-making." A critic in *Publishers Weekly* also praised the work, stating that, "for great stretches, the verisimilitude is almost heartbreaking; luckily, Amanda speaks with wit and not self-pity." Michelle Roberts, reviewing the novel in *School Library Journal,* observed that *Unraveling* "moves at a quick pace . . . thanks to Amanda's honest and often humorous voice, as well as her thoughtful poetry interjected throughout."

Biographical and Critical Sources

PERIODICALS

Kirkus Reviews, June 15, 2008, review of *Unraveling.*

Kliatt, July, 2008, Myrna Marler, review of *Unraveling,* p. 7.

Publishers Weekly, June 30, 2008, review of *Unraveling,* p. 185.

Record-Courier (Ravenna, OH), June 20, 2008, Dave O'Brien, "Local Author's Book Explores Relationships."

School Library Journal, October, 2008, Michelle Roberts, review of *Unraveling,* p. 138.

ONLINE

e-Inside Online, http://einside.kent.edu/ (June 30, 2008), "Kent State Staff Member Publishes Debut Novel."

Michelle Baldini Home Page, http://www.michellebaldini.com (September 1, 2009).

Cover of Baldini and Lynn Biederman's collaborative young-adult novel Unraveling. (Jacket photographs © 2008 by Jack Hollingsworth. Used by permission of Delacorte Press an imprint of Random House's Children's Books, a division of Random House, Inc.)

BASYE, Dale E.

Personal

Born in Dallas, TX; children: Odgen. *Education:* Attended Academy of Art College, San Francisco State University, and San Francisco Art Institute. *Hobbies and other interests:* Writing music.

Addresses

Home—Portland, OR. *E-mail*—dale@interwonderland.com.

Career

Novelist, editor, and copywriter. *San Francisco Chronicle,* San Francisco, CA, editorial assistant, 1987-93; *Paperback Jukebox,* Portland, OR, editor and columnist, 1993-94; Tonic Publishing Inc., Portland, writer, editor, and publisher of *Tonic* (arts and entertainment newspaper), 1994-95; *Willamette Week,* Portland, writer, 1995-97, associated arts editor, 1997-98; Nike, Beaverton, OR, copywriter, 1997-99; freelance copywriter, 1999—; CyberSight, Portland, senior copywriter, 2000-01.

Awards, Honors

Coup d'CyberSight Award for Excellence; second-place award for best review, National Better Newspaper Association Awards, 1996; first-place award for arts and criticism, Society of Professional Journalists Awards, 1997; New Media Award Gold Medal, Summit Creative Awards, 2001; Web Site/Consumer Information Award Bronze Medal, Summit Creative Awards, 2001; Society of Professional Journalist awards for writing and design, both for *Tonic.*

Writings

"CIRCLES OF HECK" MIDDLE-GRADE NOVEL SERIES

Heck: Where the Bad Kids Go, illustrated by Bob Dob, Random House (New York, NY), 2008.

Rapacia: The Second Circle of Heck, illustrated by Bob Dob, Random House (New York, NY), 2009.

Blimpo: The Third Circle of Heck, illustrated by Bob Dob, Random House (New York, NY), 2010.

Also contributor of stories, essays, and reviews to periodicals.

Sidelights

Dale E. Basye, an award-winning journalist and copywriter, is the author of the "Circle of Heck" series of middle-grade novels, including *Heck: Where the Bad Kids Go,* an "uproarious send-up of all things purgato-

rial," observed a critic in *Publishers Weekly.* "I don't really write for kids," Basye remarked in an online interview for *Powells.com.* "I write for myself, and my psyche just so happens to have been frozen at about 12 years old or so, like Walt Disney's head, only just the inside, and much younger and without all the creepy talking animals and the absent father figures."

Born in Dallas, Texas, Basye grew up in California and studied at both San Francisco State University and the San Francisco Art Institute. After spending a number of years working as an editorial assistant at the *San Francisco Chronicle,* he ventured to Portland, Oregon, where he became writer, editor, and publisher of *Tonic,* a popular arts and entertainment newspaper. Basye later worked as a film critic for the *Willamette Week* before entering the world of advertising, working on campaigns for Nike, Quaker, Visa, and Wells Fargo, among other companies.

The idea for *Heck* came to Basye while he worked with a friend on a "mockumentary" film about the Devil. "While helping him to mine the topic for potential nuggets of humor, I unearthed the idea of an H-E-double-hockey-sticks Lite, just for children, which—of course—simply had to be called Heck," he stated in an essay on the Random House Web site. "I researched such classic works as Dante's Inferno and the phonebook (I wanted a pizza) and came up with a kid-ified underworld specifically designed to ignore the needs and enflame the misery of once-living children everywhere—in particular, the bad ones."

Heck focuses on Marlo and Milton Fauster, two siblings who are transported to Heck, a supernatural reform school, after perishing in a bizarre marshmallow explosion. There they meet Bea "Elsa" Bubb, the school's principal; Typhoid Mary, a biology teacher; and Virgil, a classmate who tries to help them escape through a maze of sewer pipes. "Puns and allusions abound, enough to sate the corniest appetite," Thom Barthelmess noted in *School Library Journal,* and a *Kirkus Reviews* contributor praised the "sly banter between characters and a richly imagined world" Basye creates.

Basye continues the adventures of Marlo and Milton in *Rapacia: The Second Circle of Heck* and *Blimpo: The Third Circle of Heck.* "I just seem to write for kids naturally," he stated in his *Powells.com* interview. "I also think you can get away with a lot more than you can writing for adults, not to mention have a profound effect on someone's life as kids haven't built up walls in their imaginations yet. They are eager to explore, open to just about anything, and if they are treated with respect, they will remember your story for years, maybe even incorporating some of what they've discovered into their personal, psychosocial Pee Chee folders. Or not. I just think it's a lot of fun."

Cover of Dale E. Basye's Heck: Where the Bad Kids Go, *which features artwork by Bob Dob.* (Illustration copyright © 2008 by Bob Dob. Reproduced by permission of Yearling, an imprint of Random House Children's Books, a division of Random House, Inc.)

Biographical and Critical Sources

PERIODICALS

Booklist, June 1, 2008, Thom Barthelmess, review of *Heck: Where the Bad Kids Go,* p. 76.
Kirkus Reviews, June 15, 2008, review of *Heck.*
Portland Tribune (Portland, OR), August 14, 2008, Eric Bartels, "Life with Children: *Heck* a Vivid Success."
Publishers Weekly, June 30, 2008, review of *Heck,* p. 184.
School Library Journal, September, 2008, Elaine E. Knight, review of *Heck,* p. 173.
Wall Street Journal, July 26, 2008, Meghan Cox Gurdon, review of *Heck,* p. W9.

ONLINE

Dale E. Basye Home Page, http://www.interwonderland. com (September 1, 2009).
Dale E. Basye Web log, http://wherethebadkidsgo. wordpress.com/ (September 1, 2009).
Powells.com, http://www.powells.com/ (August 20, 2009), "Kids' Q&A: Dale E. Basye."

Random House Web site, http://www.randomhouse.com/ (August 20, 2009), "Author Spotlight: Dale E. Basye." *Where the Bad Kids Go Web site,* http://www.wherethe badkidsgo.com/ (September 1, 2009).

*   *   *

BOK, Arthur
See BOK, Chip

*   *   *

BOK, Chip 1952-
(Arthur Bok)

Personal
Born Arthur Bok, July 25, 1952, in Dayton, OH; married; wife's name Deborah; children: four. *Education:* University of Dayton, B.A., 1974.

Addresses
Home—Akron, OH. *Agent*—(Literary) Nine Speakers, 2501 Calvert St. NW, Ste. 909, Washington, DC 20008-2620; (Editorial cartoons) Creators Syndicate, 5777 W. Century Blvd., Ste. 700, Los Angeles, CA 90045. *E-mail*—chip@bokbluster.com.

Career
Cartoonist. Worked for College Press Service, 1974-80; *Kettering-Oakwood Times,* Dayton, OH, freelance cartoonist, 1974-81; *Clearwater Sun,* Clearwater, FL, editorial cartoonist, 1981-82; *Miami Herald Sunday Magazine,* Miami, FL, illustrator of column for Dave Barry, 1982-84, creator of "Bok" (weekly cartoon), 1985-86; Viewtron, Miami, graphic designer, 1983-86; *Akron Beacon Journal,* Akron, OH, editorial cartoonist, 1987-2008; syndicated cartoonist, 2008—. University of Minnesota School of Journalism and Mass Communication, Silha lecturer, 2001. Also worked as a substitute teacher, wholesale drug salesman, and laborer.

Member
American Association of Editorial Cartoonists, Reporters Committee for Freedom of the Press (member of steering committee).

Awards, Honors
John Fischetti Award, Columbia College, 1988; named Best Editorial Cartoonist, Associated Press Society of Ohio, 1992, 1996, 1999, 2000; H.L. Mencken Award, Free Press Association, 1993; Berryman Editorial Cartooning Award, National Press Foundation, 1993; Best Editorial Cartoonist, National Cartoonist Society, 1995, 1999; Pulitzer Prize finalist, 1997; Cartoonist of the Year honor, *The Week* magazine, 2007; Top Ten Political Cartoons selection, 2008, *Time* magazine.

Chip Bok (Reproduced by permission.)

Writings
Bok!: The 9.11 Crisis in Political Cartoons, University of Akron Press (Akron, OH), 2002.
A Recent History of the United States in Political Cartoons: A Look Bok!, University of Akron Press (Akron, OH), 2005.

ILLUSTRATOR

Helen Thomas, *The Great White House Breakout,* Dial Books (New York, NY), 2008.

Regular contributing cartoonist for *Reason* magazine.

Sidelights
Chip Bok is a nationally renowned editorial cartoonist whose work has appeared in publications world wide, including in the pages of the London *Times, Chicago Tribune, New York Times, The Week, Time,* the *Washington Post,* and *Newsweek.* His cartoons are noted for their biting, satirical edge. "My job as a political cartoonist is to make fun of people and issues, and to provoke people to think," Bok told *Scholastic Update* contributors Tod Olson and Karen N. Peart. Bok is also the author of two cartoon-format history books and he served as the illustrator for *The Great White House Breakout,* a children's book written by longtime White House news correspondent Helen Thomas.

Born Arthur Bok in Dayton, Ohio, in 1952, the cartoonist took an early interest in the arts. "I was always the kid that could draw in my group of friends," he remarked to Olson and Peart. "I would draw hilarious caricatures of teachers and coaches." Bok entered the world of editorial cartooning almost as an afterthought. "My parents weren't too excited about it and I think my mother always wanted me to do something else to fall back on," he recalled. "But I think if you have something to fall back on, you usually do, and I wanted to put it all on the line."

Success did not come immediately for Bok. After working several years as a freelance cartoonist for Dayton's *Kettering-Oakwood Times,* he landed his first full-time position on the staff of Florida's *Clearwater Sun* in 1981. He lasted only six months on the job, however; Ray Jenkins, the editor who hired him, left the paper and the new editor said that Bok could stay on only if his cartoons focused on topics relating to Pinellas County. "It didn't take long before I had offended just about everybody in town [I wanted to impress] and probably most of the advertisers," Bok recalled to Sara Rimensnyder in *Reason.* He later created "Bok," a weekly cartoon on South Florida issues that ran in the *Miami Herald* Sunday magazine, *Tropic;* he also illustrated a column in the same publication for nationally syndicated humorist Dave Barry. After a stint as a graphic designer in Miami, he returned to Ohio and became the editorial cartoonist for the *Akron Beacon Journal,* where he worked for more than twenty years. Bok has received numerous honors during his career: he was

Self-caricature of author/illustrator Bok. (Illustration courtesy of Arthur (Chip) Bok.)

twice named best editorial cartoonist by the National Cartoonist Society, earned the H.L. Mencken Award, and was a finalist for the Pulitzer Prize.

In *The Great White House Breakout,* Thomas and Bok offer a fanciful and raucous tale about a youngster named Sam whose mother is president of the United States. Bored with his role as First Son and irritated by the constant presence of Secret Service agents, Sam conspires with his pet cat, Warren, and pet rat, Leonard, to escape the grounds of the White House and spend a day exploring the wonders of Washington, DC. When Sam finally grows homesick, Leonard concocts a wild plan to get back home that ends in chaos at the Washington Monument. "Bok's chipmunk-cheeked characters suit the irreverent mood of this high-energy story," Amy Rowland noted in *School Library Journal.* The cartoonist's "dynamic, detail-crammed illustrations will prove great fun for kids and a treat for adults alike," observed a *Kirkus Reviews* critic, also reviewing *The Great White House Breakout.*

Bok contributes his signature cartoon art to **The Great White House Breakout,** *a picture book by longtime journalist Helen Thomas.* (Illustration copyright © 2008 by Arthur (Chip) Bok. Reproduced by permission of Dial Books for Young Readers, a division of Penguin Putnam Books for Young Readers.)

Biographical and Critical Sources

PERIODICALS

Editor and Publisher, May 23, 2008, "Cartooning as a Life-saving Activity."
Kirkus Reviews, June 15, 2008, review of *The Great White House Breakout.*
Publishers Weekly, August 4, 2008, review of *The Great White House Breakout,* p. 61.
Reason, February, 2003, Sara Rimensnyder, "Drawing 9/11," p. 17.
Scholastic Update, October 7, 1994, Tod Olson and Karen N. Peart, "The Power of the Pen," p. 22.
School Library Journal, August, 2008, Amy Rowland, review of *The Great White House Breakout,* p. 103.

ONLINE

Cartoonist Group Web site, http://www.cartoonistgroup. com/ (September 1, 2009), "Chip Bok."
Chip Bok Home Page, http://www.bokbluster.com (September 1, 2009).
Creators Syndicate Web site, http://www.creators.com/ (September 1, 2009), "Chip Bok."

*   *   *

BRUEL, Nick

Personal

Son of Robert O. Bruel (a professor of psychology); married; wife's name Carina.

Addresses

Home—Tarrytown, NY. *E-mail*—nick@nickbruel.com.

Career

Cartoonist and children's book author. Presenter at schools and libraries.

Awards, Honors

Top-ten finalist, Dr. Seuss Picture-Book Contest, 1993; Gryphon Honor award, Center for Children's Books, 2009, for *Bad Kitty Gets a Bath.*

Writings

SELF-ILLUSTRATED

Boing, Roaring Brook Press (Brookfield, CT), 2004.
Bad Kitty, Roaring Brook Press (New Milford, CT), 2005, revised edition, 2007.

Who Is Melvin Bubble?, Roaring Brook Press (Brookfield, CT), 2006.
Poor Puppy, Roaring Brook Press (Brookfield, CT), 2007.
Bad Kitty Gets a Bath, Roaring Brook Press (New Milford, CT), 2008.
Little Red Bird, Roaring Brook Press (New York, NY), 2008.
Happy Birthday, Bad Kitty, Neal Porter Books (New York, NY), 2009.

Also author of *How to Be a Real Good Cartoonist,* 2003. Contributor to *Syncopated Comics.*

ILLUSTRATOR

Robert O. Bruel, *Bob and Otto,* Roaring Brook Press (New Milford, CT), 2007.
Dick King-Smith, *Hairy Hezekiah,* Roaring Brook Press (New York, NY), 2007.
Dick King-Smith, *Under the Mishmash Trees,* Roaring Brook Press (New York, NY), 2008.
Dick King-Smith, *Dinosaur Trouble,* Roaring Brook Press (New York, NY), 2008.
Dick King-Smith, *The Mouse Family Robinson,* Roaring Brook Press (New York, NY), 2008.
Dick King-Smith, *Clever Duck,* Roaring Brook Press (New York, NY), 2008.

Sidelights

Author and cartoonist Nick Bruel brings his quirky sense of humor to bear on children's literature in the picture books *Boing, Bad Kitty, Little Red Bird,* and

Cover of Robert O. Bruel's Bob and Otto, *a book featuring cartoon art by Nick Bruel.* (Illustration copyright © 2007 by Nick Bruel. Reprinted by arrangement with Henry Holt and Company, LLC.)

Who Is Melvin Bubble? Featuring cartoon-style water-color art, Bruel's books are particularly geared for beginning readers, combining engaging characters and an animated storyline. In *Little Red Bird,* an escape story featuring a tiny caged bird pairs what *Booklist* critic Krista Hutley described as an "appealingly bouncy" text with illustrations that "show an eye for comic-book-style story progression," according to *School Library Journal* critic Jayne Damron. A little boy and his family is profiled in the warmhearted art for *Who Is Melvin Bubble?,* a book that mixes "bright cartoon illustrations" and a "breezily positive" rhyming text, according to a *Kirkus Reviews* writer. *School Library Journal* critic Wendy Lukehart deemed *Who Is Melvin Bubble?* a "delightful choice" for storytimes that features "one cool kid," while a *Publishers Weekly* contributor noted that Bruel's "wry comments" make the book "a read-aloud treat—and fine inspiration for classroom biographies."

Dubbed a "bouncy solo debut" by a *Kirkus Reviews* contributor, *Boing* follows a young kangaroo as he learns how to jump from his mother. Despite being cheered on by animal friends Rabbit, Frog, Koala, and Grasshopper, the young kanga's hop turns into a flop every time, until it is discovered that he has stuffed his pouch too full of treasures to become sufficiently airborne. Praising the book for its "sunny watercolor and ink cartoons" and its toddler appeal, *Horn Book* contributor Christine Heppermann added that *Boing* "is an accomplishment designed to have preschoolers springing from their seats." A *Publishers Weekly* writer agreed, noting that because "Bruel's cartoons brim with energy and emotion," *Boing* is "not a book for bedtime."

A delightful romp disguised as an alphabet book, *Bad Kitty* finds the family cat perplexed when she realizes that her owners have run out of cat food. When she learns that the only edibles around are both healthy and nutritious, the cat's mood quickly goes from bad to worse. Kitty turns up her nose at the alphabetical array of foods that range from asparagus to zucchini, and retaliates with typical bad-cat abandon. Finally her repentant owners restock the kitchen with kitty favorites, including anchovies, shark sushi, and baked zebra ziti, and Bad Kitty is transformed into a very, very good kitty. "Even readers who've mastered their ABCs will laugh at Bruel's gleefully composed litanies and the can-you-top-this spirit that animates every page," commented a *Publishers Weekly* critic, while *School Library Journal* reviewer Maura Bresnahan concluded that *Bad Kitty* "will appeal to youngsters who like their stories more naughty than nice." In *Kirkus Reviews* a contributor predicted that "even the alphabet-experienced will love this bad, bad kitty!," while *Bookpage.com* reviewer Lynn Beckwith observed that "Bruel has created a joyfully silly portrait of a picky eater with attitude."

Bad Kitty returns in *Poor Puppy* as well as the chapter books *Bad Kitty Gets a Bath* and *Happy Birthday, Bad Kitty.* Described by *Booklist* critic Ilene Cooper as "a

funfest disguised as an alphabet book," *Poor Puppy* mixes alphabet and counting themes with a story about a frisky pup and its tour of twenty-six potentially favorite toys. Bad Kitty watches from the sidelines, sometimes becoming a potential plaything in a tale that is enhanced by "cartoon-style panels ablaze with color," according to *School Library Journal* critic Lynn K. Vanca.

Geared for more sophisticated, chapter-book readers, *Bad Kitty Gets a Bath* finds the kitty in question confronting a tub of water, something all kitties detest. Poor Puppy appears in the story as well, but when a bath is suggested his reaction is typically doglike: far less dramatic and fur-raising. *Happy Birthday, Bad Kitty* continues the feline saga, combining Bruel's stylized cartoon art with a humorous text in which the Bad One's birthday party includes a strange menagerie: Chatty Kitty, Strange Kitty, Stinky Kitty, and Mama Kitty. In what *Booklist* critic Shelle Rosenfeld described as a pairing of "witty asides and spastic, tongue-in-cheek commentaries" and "high-energy cartoon illustrations," *Bad Kitty Gets a Bath* salts an entertaining story with interesting cat facts—and dog facts too. In her *School Library Journal* review, Marilyn Ackerman called Bruel's tale "funny" and noted that the "zany" artwork features "numerous perspectives that heighten the humor." "Larded with science facts and plenty of laughs," according to a *Kirkus Reviews* writer, *Bad Kitty Gets a Bath* also contains a glossary of words that challenge

Bruel's illustrations are a highlight of Dick King-Smith's picture book **Dinosaur Trouble.** (Illustration copyright © 2008 by Nick Bruel. Reproduced by permission of Henry Holt and Company, LLC.)

developing readers. *Happy Birthday, Bad Kitty* continues the fun; "as usual, it's Bad Kitty's unapologetic, curmudgeon nature that delivers the laugh-out-loud fun," according to a *Publishers Weekly* critic.

In addition to creating original picture books, Bruel also illustrates texts by other writers, including Dick King-Smith and Bruel's father, Robert O. Bruel. The manuscript for Robert Bruel's *Bob and Otto,* a story about two best friends who learn to adapt to change, was discovered by son Nick after the elder Bruel's death. Nick Bruel tweaked the story, changed the title from "Two Worms," and created the artwork that appeared in the resulting picture book. Reviewing *Bob and Otto* in *School Library Journal,* Nancy Kunz wrote that Bruel's "bright, vibrant illustrations" bring to life a story that combines engaging characters and interesting science facts. In *Booklist* Julie Cummins cited the illustrator's "sturdy artwork, which mixes colors earthy and bright," while Danielle J. Ford commented in *Horn Book* that *Bob and Otto* combines an "engaging story" with "rich, not-to-be-missed visual details" that are also scientifically accurate.

Biographical and Critical Sources

PERIODICALS

Booklist, December 15, 2005, Ilene Cooper, review of *Bad Kitty,* p. 49; April 1, 2007, Julie Cummins, review of *Bob and Otto,* p. 55; July 9, 2007, review of *Poor Puppy,* p. 53; September 1, 2007, Ilene Cooper, review of *Poor Puppy,* p. 128; March 1, 2008, Suzanne Harold, review of *Dinosaur Trouble,* p. 67; April 15, 2008, Krista Hutley, review of *Little Red Bird,* p. 50; August 1, 2008, Shelle Rosenfeld, review of *The Mouse Family Robinson,* p. 72; October 15, 2008, Shelle Rosenfeld, review of *Bad Kitty Gets a Bath,* p. 39.
Horn Book, January-February, 2005, Christina M. Heppermann, review of *Boing,* p. 72; May-June, 2007, Danielle J. Ford, review of *Bob and Otto,* p. 262.
New York Times Book Review, January 15, 2006, Emily Jenkins, review of *Bad Kitty,* p. 18.
Kirkus Reviews, October 15, 2004, review of *Boing!,* p. 1002; September 15, 2005, review of *Bad Kitty,* p. 1022; July 1, 2006, review of *Who Is Melvin Bubble?,* p. 675; July 15, 2007, review of *Hairy Hezekiah;* April 15, 2008, review of *The Little Red Bird;* July 1, 2008, review of *Bad Kitty Gets a Bath;* July 15, 2008, review of *The Mouse Family Robinson;* September 1, 2008, review of *Clever Duck.*
Publishers Weekly, August 30, 2004, review of *Boing,* p. 53; October 17, 2005, review of *Bad Kitty,* p. 66; July 17, 2006, review of *Who Is Melvin Bubble?,* p. 156; August 6, 2007, review of *Hairy Hezekiah,* p. 189; September 7, 2009, review of *Happy Birthday, Bad Kitty,* p. 46.
School Library Journal, October, 2005, Maura Bresnahan, review of *Bad Kitty,* p. 109; August, 2006, Wendy Lukehart, review of *Who Is Melvin Bubble?,* p. 76; April, 2007, Nancy Kunz, review of *Bob and Otto,* p. 94; January, 2008, Lynn K. Vanca, review of *Poor Puppy,* p. 82; March, 2008, Kelly Roth, review of *Dinosaur Trouble,* p. 169; June, 2008, Jayne Damron, review of *Little Red Bird,* p. 96; August, 2008, Cheryl Ashton, review of *Under the Mishmash Trees,* p. 96; October, 2008, Marilyn Ackerman, review of *Bad Kitty Gets a Bath,* p. 102, and Donna Atmur, review of *The Mouse Family Robinson,* p. 114; December, 2008, Clare A. Dombrowski, review of *Clever Duck,* p. 94.

ONLINE

Macmillan Web site, http://us.macmillan.com/ (September 20, 2009), "Nick Bruel."
Nick Bruel Home Page, http://www.nickbruel.com (September 21, 2009).*

*   *   *

BULLER, Jon 1943-

Personal

Born 1943; married Susan Schade (an author and illustrator). *Education:* Columbia College, B.A., 1967.

Addresses

Home—Lyme, CT. *E-mail*—bullersooz@snet.net.

Career

Cartoonist and children's book illustrator. Has also worked for U.S. Postal Service; creator of "Bob Blob" and "Captain Connecticut" comic strips.

Writings

SELF-ILLUSTRATED; WITH WIFE, SUSAN SCHADE, EXCEPT WHERE NOTED

(Self-illustrated) *Fanny and May,* Crown (New York, NY), 1984.
I Love You, Good Night, Crown (New York, NY), 1984, board-book edition, illustrated by Bernadette Pons, Little Simon (New York, NY), 2006.
The Noisy Counting Book, Random House (New York, NY), 1987.
Space Rock, Random House (New York, NY), 1988.
No Tooth, No Quarter!, Random House (New York, NY), 1989.
20,000 Baseball Cards under the Sea, Random House (New York, NY), 1991.
Hello! Hello!, Simon & Schuster (New York, NY), 1991.
Mike and the Magic Cookies, Grosset & Dunlap (New York, NY), 1992.
Toad on the Road, Random House (New York, NY), 1992.

Jon Buller (Reproduced by permission.)

Yo! It's Captain Yo-Yo, Grosset & Dunlap (New York, NY), 1993.

Railroad Toad, Random House (New York, NY), 1993.

Snug House, Bug House!, Random House (New York, NY), 1994.

Toad Eats Out, Random House (New York, NY), 1995.

Felix and the 400 Frogs, Random House (New York, NY), 1996.

Ron Rooney and the Million Dollar Comic, Random House (New York, NY), 1996.

Snow Bugs, Random House (New York, NY), 1996.

Space Mall, Random House (New York, NY), 1997.

Toad Takes Off, Random House (New York, NY), 1997.

Pig at Work, Troll Books (New York, NY), 1997.

Pig at Play, Troll Books (New York, NY), 1998.

Baseball Camp on the Planet of the Eyeballs, Random House (New York, NY), 1998.

Cat on the Mat, Golden Books (New York, NY), 1999.

Cat at Bat, Golden Books (New York, NY), 2000.

Captain Zap and the Evil Baron von Fishhead, Random House (New York, NY), 2000.

Dinosaur Ed, Reader's Digest Children's Books (Pleasantville, NY), 2000.

Space Dog Jack, Scholastic (New York, NY), 2000.

Space Dog Jack and the Haunted Spaceship, Scholastic (New York, NY), 2001.

Cat on Ice, Golden Books (New York, NY), 2001.

Bungee Baboon Rescue, Scholastic (New York, NY), 2002.

Growling Grizzly, Scholastic (New York, NY), 2002.

Hawk Talk, Scholastic (New York, NY), 2002.

Back to the Bayou, Scholastic (New York, NY), 2003.

The Wright Brothers Take Off, Grosset & Dunlap (New York, NY), 2003.

(Wth others) *Smart about the Fifty States: A Class Report,* Grosset & Dunlap (New York, NY), 2003.

(With others) *Smart about the Presidents,* Grosset & Dunlap (New York, NY), 2004.

(With others) *Smart about the First Ladies,* Grosset & Dunlap (New York, NY), 2005.

The Travels of Thelonious (graphic novel; book one of "Fog Mound" trilogy), Simon & Schuster (New York, NY), 2006.

Faradawn (graphic novel; book two of "Fog Mound" trilogy), Simon & Schuster (New York, NY), 2007.

Simon's Dream (graphic novel; book three of "Fog Mound" trilogy), Simon & Schuster (New York, NY), 2008.

ILLUSTRATOR

Shari Lewis, *Shari Lewis Presents 101 Things for Kids to Do,* Random House (New York, NY), 1987.

Shari Lewis and Dick Zimmerman, *Shari Lewis Presents 101 Magic Tricks for Kids to Do,* Random House (New York, NY), 1990.

Faye Couch Reeves, *Howie Merton and the Magic Dust,* Random House (New York, NY), 1991.

Mark Saltzman, *Woodchuck Nation,* Random House (New York, NY), 1994.

Stuart J. Murphy, *Ready, Set, Hop!,* HarperCollins (New York, NY), 1996.

Sidelights

Jon Buller is a highly regarded author and illustrator of books for children, many of them done in collaboration with his wife, Susan Schade. Buller, who has earned notice for his humorous, energetic pictures, began drawing at the age of five, and by the age of eight he was writing and illustrating his own comic books. Buller later studied English in college and worked at a series of office jobs before creating his own comic strip, "Bob Blob," in 1974. After his strip came to the attention of a neighbor, author and illustrator Lucinda McQueen, she helped Buller create a portfolio of his work to show to children's book publishers in New York City. After seven years of effort, Buller completed his first title, *Fanny and May,* in 1984.

Buller notes that his artwork has been influenced by such celebrated figures as Ernest Shepard, who illustrated *Winnie-the-Pooh* and other works by A.A. Milne; Walt Kelly, creator of the *Pogo* comic strip; Ed Dodd, the originator of the "Mark Trail" comic strip; and and Bill Griffith, the creator of Zippy the Pinhead. Buller's literary inspirations include Margery Sharp, author of *The Rescuers;* Mary Norton, who wrote *The Borrowers;* and E.B. White, who penned such classics as *Stuart Little* and *Charlotte's Web.*

Buller's *The Noisy Counting Book* was the first work he both cowrote and co-illustrated with Schade. Describing their collaborative process in an interview on the *Miss Erin* blog, Buller stated that Schade "does most of the writing, and I do most of the illustrating, but we both do some of each." In their collaborative easy reader *Toad on the Road,* a bug-eyed toad climbs behind the wheel of a bright, red car and heads off for adventure

and fun. "Lively and colorful, the illustrations of Toad's madcap outing offer unexpected delights," a reviewer in *Publishers Weekly* commented. A pilot hands over the controls of his plane to Toad in *Toad Takes Off,* a book in which Buller's "brightly colored cartoonlike drawings" earned praised from *Booklist* contributor Carolyn Phelan.

In *Captain Zap and the Evil Baron von Fishhead,* Perry and Cosmo discover magic pencils that bring their drawings to life. After creating a superhero and his nemesis, however, the youngsters are transformed into their fictional characters. According to Phelan, the book's "snappy title and cartoonlike cover illustration will appeal to many primary-grade children." A feline with a passion for ice skating lands a role in a big ice show in *Cat on Ice.* Here Buller's "hilarious, exuberant pictures . . . will capture children," Gillian Enberg commented in *Booklist.*

Buller and Schade have also collaborated on *The Travels of Thelonious,* the first work in their "Fog Mound" graphic-novel trilogy for young readers. "Our first idea was to make [our tale] a conventional novel, with illustrations," Buller remarked in his *Miss Erin* online interview. "Susan wrote the text and then handed it to me to provide some illustrations. But at some point, while doing the illustrations, I got the idea that some chapters

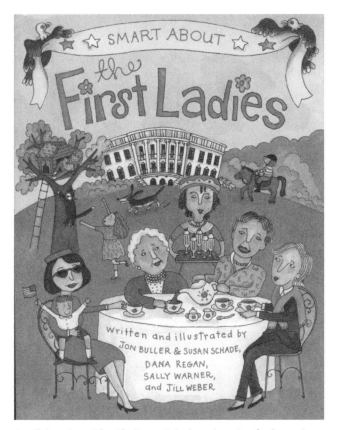

A collaboration with wife Susan Schade and a trio of other writers, Buller's **Smart about the First Ladies** *is illustrated by the authors.* (Reproduced by permission of Grosset & Dunlap, a division of Penguin Putnam Books for Young Readers.)

would work better if they were entirely done in cartoon format. It seemed a good way to draw people into the story."

Set in a future world where humans no longer exist, *The Travels of Thelonious* centers on Thelonious Chipmunk, an intelligent, curious creature who is swept from his home during a violent thunderstorm and lands in the Ruined City, which is ruled by a villainous Komodo dragon. Thelonious joins forces with Olive, a mechanically inclined bear; Fitzgerald, a porcupine librarian; and Brown, an enslaved lizard. The trio begins a dangerous journey to the Fog Mound, an idyllic land that holds the secrets to Earth's history. "Written in chapters that alternate between traditional prose and comic-book format, the story is a gentle introduction to graphic novels," wrote Heather M. Lisowski in *School Library Journal.*

Critics applauded Buller's contributions to *The Travels of Thelonious.* "The artwork's minimalist palette (black and blue) gives the story a quiet charm (even the prose sections contain an abundance of artwork)," observed a contributor in *Publishers Weekly.* Jesse Karp, writing in *Booklist,* commented that "the alternating chapters of illustrated prose and charming, highly detailed sequential art display a fascination with the power" of literature.

The "Fog Mound" series continues in *Faradawn,* as Thelonious and his friends return to the Ruined City to rescue an imprisoned group of birds and combat an invasion of crabs. Readers will enjoy "the tale's mix of narrow squeaks and set-piece celebrations," remarked a critic in *Kirkus Reviews,* and Karp noted that the story is "filled with the joy of exploration and discovery." *Simon's Dream,* the conclusion to the "Fog Mound" series, finds Thelonious and company engaged in a final battle with the evil forces that wish to destroy the utopian Fog Mound, among them the Dragon Lady and her band of vicious rat underlings. During their quest, the heroes also learn the sad fate of humanity that led to the rise of animal communities. Karp praised the "charming mixture of illustrated prose and purple-hued sequential art," and Larry Doyle, writing in the *New York Times Book Review,* observed that Schade and Buller "tell their story in alternating chapters of prose and graphics, and the combination works seamlessly, and delightfully." Comparing the trilogy to works such as *The Wizard of Oz* and *Planet of the Apes,* Doyle stated that "the 'Fog Mound' books read like breezy myth, with enough genuine invention and adventure to keep the story moving."

Biographical and Critical Sources

PERIODICALS

Booklist, September 15, 1996, Stephanie Zvirin, review of *Felix and the 400 Frogs,* p. 252; May 1, 1997, Carolyn Phelan, review of *Toad Takes Off,* p. 1505; Febru-

ary 15, 2001, Carolyn Phelan, review of *Captain Zap and the Evil Baron von Fishhead,* p. 1143; April 15, 2001, Gillian Engberg, review of *Cat on Ice,* p. 1569; September 1, 2004, Ilene Cooper, review of *Smart about the Presidents,* p. 116; April 15, 2006, Jesse Karp, review of *The Travels of Thelonious,* p. 48; September 15, 2007, Jesse Karp, review of *Faradawn,* p. 61; July 1, 2008, Jesse Karp, review of *Simon's Dream,* p. 62.

Kirkus Reviews, May 15, 2006, review of *The Travels of Thelonious,* p. 523; August 15, 2007, review of *Faradawn.*

New York Times Book Review, May 11, 2008, Larry Doyle, "Cracking the Comics Code," review of *Simon's Dream,* p. 19.

Publishers Weekly, June 22, 1992, review of *Toad on the Road,* p. 62; June 13, 1994, review of *Woodchuck Nation,* p. 63; August 21, 2006, review of *The Travels of Thelonious,* p. 68.

School Library Journal, November, 2003, Marlene Gawron, review of *Smart about the Fifty States: A Class Report,* p. 122; June, 2004, Christine E. Carr, review of *The Wright Brothers Take Off,* p. 124; April,

2005, Rebecca Luhman, review of *Smart about the First Ladies,* p. 118; July, 2006, Heather M. Lisowski and Philip S. Miller, review of *The Travels of Thelonious,* p. 129; September, 2008, Benjamin Russell, review of *Simon's Dream,* p. 216.

ONLINE

Childrensillustrators.com, http://www2.childrensillustrators.com/ (September 1, 2009), "Jon Buller."

Jon Buller and Susan Schade Home Page, http://www.bullersooz.com (September 1, 2009).

Miss Erin Blog, http://misserinmarie.blogspot.com/ (January 20, 2007), interview with Buller.

Newsarama.com, http://forum.newsarama.com/ (May 6, 2008), Zack Smith, "Jon Buller on the Fog Mound v3: *Simon's Dream.*"

*   *   *

BURGESS, Starling
See TUDOR, Tasha

C

CALVERT, Pam 1966-

Personal
Born 1966, in Rockledge, FL; married; children: four. *Hobbies and other interests:* Science, running, adventure racing, mountain biking, teaching, family, church life.

Addresses
Home—TX. *Agent*—Heacock Literary Agency, Inc., 507 Grand Blvd., P.O. Box 226, Cloudcroft, NM 88317-0226. *E-mail*—pam@pamcalvert.com.

Career
Writer. Taught high-school chemistry and physics, 1990-92; taught writing to grades 1-8 at a private school, 2003-06.

Member
Society of Children's Book Writers and Illustrators.

Awards, Honors
Received honors for newsletter; Cybils Award nomination, 2008, and Nevada Young Readers Award, 2010, both for *Princess Peepers.*

Writings

Flying Saucer, illustrated by Annie Cossette, StoryPlus, 2002.

Mystery of the Stolen Spider Stone ("Super Hero Hal" series), illustrated by Enrique Carballeira, StoryPlus, 2003.

Case of the Bunsen Burner Frame Up ("Super Hero Hal" series), illustrated by Enrique Carballeira, StoryPlus, 2004.

Pam Calvert (Photograph by Redfern Photography. Reproduced by permission.)

The Mat Maker, illustrated by Estella Hickman, Seedling Publications (Elizabethtown, PA), 2004.

Multiplying Menace: The Revenge of Rumpelstiltskin, illustrated by Wayne Geehan, Charlesbridge (Watertown, MA), 2006.

Clue School: Mystery at the Ballpark, illustrated by Richard Torrey, InnovativeKids (Norwalk, CT), 2007.

Princess Peepers, illustrated by Tuesday Mourning, Marshall Cavendish Children (New York, NY), 2008.

Multiplying Menace Divides!, illustrated by Wayne Geehan, Charlesbridge (Watertown, MA), 2010.

Contributor to periodicals, including *Odyssey: Adventures in Science, Nature's Friend, Highlights for Children,* and *Guideposts for Kids.* Former sports columnist.

Sidelights

A former high-school science teacher, Pam Calvert writes mysteries, adventure tales, picture books, and stories for young readers. "I didn't formally write for publication until I wrote a running club newsletter in 1993," she remarked to *California Readers* contributor Bonnie O'Brian. "It won awards and I got paid for a few articles in running magazines. Then I was offered a women's running column in a magazine, so I was hooked. I've been writing ever since." Calvert especially enjoys adding a whimsical touch to her works. "All of my picture books have an element of humor in them," she told interviewer Brian Humek. "Four of them have an educational slant and the rest are just humorous or whimsical books."

In *Multiplying Menace: The Revenge of Rumpelstiltskin* Calvert offers a unique take on the popular fairy tale. In the work, the menacing imp returns after a ten-year ab-

sence, threatening to wreak havoc upon the kingdom unless the queen's son joins him. In *Multiplying Menace Divides!* Rumplestiltskin is back with a sidekick witch, Matilda. Together they are on a quest to divide the kingdom, and yet again it is up to Prince Peter to save the day. *School Library Journal* reviewer Carol L. MacKay observed of *Multiplying Menace* that "Calvert has created an interesting vehicle for teaching children about the differences between multiplying with whole numbers and multiplying with fractions."

In the picture book *Princess Peepers* a youngster refuses to wear her eyeglasses—with predictably disastrous results—after her classmates at the Royal Academy for Perfect Princesses criticize her fashion tastes. Calvert was inspired to write the book by recalling her own bespectacled mishaps when she was a child. "I knew all too well what wearing glasses did to your self esteem," she explained in her Web log. "I was a little girl who wore glasses and remembered the teasing I suffered as a child. Maybe the comments weren't always there, but somewhere deep inside, I didn't like myself because I was different." "Calvert's tale of a bespectacled princess's rocky road to self-acceptance is rollicking good fun," a *Kirkus Reviews* critic noted of *Princess Peepers,* the critic adding that the entertaining story helps girls with their self esteem.

Discussing the joys of her literary career, Calvert stated to Humek: "I love the sheer pleasure of creating something that I know works. It might be a twist ending, a humorous scene that makes people laugh, or an interesting character. When I get the inspiration to write something unique that I think kids will want to read, the excitement is indescribable."

"I love to encourage children to achieve their dreams," Calvert told *SATA.* "I believe that if you put your mind to anything and work hard, you will attain success. It took me six years to see a book in print and eleven years of hard work to be able to stay home and write. One day, I hope to publish not only picture books but also novels and chapter books. I won't give up on my career dreams, and so I know it will happen one day.

"Don't let anyone tell you that you can't accomplish something," she added. "Just look them straight in the eye and say, 'I know I can.' And then go out and do it."

Calvert's elementary-grade novel Clue School: Mystery at the Ballpark *features artwork by Richard Torrey.* (Innovative Kids, 2007. Reproduced by permission.)

Biographical and Critical Sources

PERIODICALS

Kirkus Reviews, August 1, 2008, review of *Princess Peepers.*

Calvert teams up with illustrator Tuesday Mourning in the engaging picture book **Princess Peepers.** (Marshall Cavendish, 2008. Illustration copyright © 2008 by Tuesday Mourning. Reproduced by permission.)

School Library Journal, April, 2006, Carol L. MacKay, review of *Multiplying Menace: The Revenge of Rumpelstiltskin,* p. 97; October, 2008, Susan E. Murray, review of *Princess Peepers,* p. 102.

ONLINE

California Readers Web site, http://www.californiareaders. org/ (September 1, 2009), Bonnie O'Brian, "Meet Pam Calvert."

Pam Calvert Home Page, http://www.pamcalvert.com (September 1, 2009).

Pam Calvert Web log, http://www.pamcalvert.blogspot. com/ (September 1, 2009).

Persistent Picture Book Writer Web site, http://brianhumek. zachshouse.org/ (August 16, 2007), Brian Humek, interview with Calvert.

* * *

CAPARO, Antonio
See CAPARO, Antonio Javier

* * *

CAPARO, Antonio Javier
(Antonio Caparo)

Personal

Born in Cuba; immigrated to Canada.

Addresses

Home—Toronto, Ontario, Canada. *Agent*—Shannon Associates, 630 9th Ave., New York, NY 10036. *E-mail*—Ajcaparo@gmail.com.

Antonio Javier Caparo (Photograph by Adriana Garcia. Reproduced by permission.)

Career

Illustrator, comics artist, and graphic designer.

Illustrator

Yanitzia Canetti, *La culebra y el halcó,* Laredo (Beverly Hills, CA), 1995.

Sarah Prineas, *The Magic Thief,* HarperCollins (New York, NY), 2008.

Mary Anato, *Invisible Lines,* Egmont (New York, NY), 2009.

Sarah Prineas, *Lost,* HarperCollins (New York, NY), 2009.

Adam McKeown, reteller, *A Midsummer Night's Dream* (based on the play by William Shakespeare), Sterling (New York, NY), 2009.

Rick Riordan, *The Demigod Files,* Hyperion (New York, NY), 2009.

Katherine Marsh, *The Twilight Prisoner,* Hyperion (New York, NY), 2009.

Lauren St. John, *The Last Leopard,* Random House (New York, NY), 2009.

Victoria Laurie, *Oracles of Delphi Keep,* Random House (New York, NY), 2009.

Contributor to periodicals.

Sidelights

"I was born in Santa Clara, a small town in the center of Cuba," explained comics artist and designer Antonio Javier Caparo to *SATA.* "At the age of seventeen I moved to Havana to study graphic design and I soon discovered the marvelous world of illustration. In 1998 I moved to Colombia where I devoted myself completely to illustration. I also did some works in animation, another field I'm in love with. I've been living in Canada for the last few years where I discovered the

seasons, one of the most beautiful things in nature. The seasonal cycle also fertilizes the imagination; you only need a pen and a sketch pad in your backpack."

Biographical and Critical Sources

PERIODICALS

Booklist, May 15, 2008, Ilene Cooper, review of *The Magic Thief,* p. 59.

Horn Book, September-October, 2008, Anita L. Burkam, review of *The Magic Thief,* p. 594.

Kliatt, July, 2008, Paula Rohrlick, review of *The Magic Thief,* p. 20.

School Library Journal, June, 2008, Sue Giffard, review of *The Magic Thief,* p. 148.

ONLINE

Antonio Javier Caparo Web log, http://www.antoniocaparo. com (October 10, 2009).

*   *   *

CHENG, Andrea 1957-

Personal

Born September 19, 1957, in El Paso, TX; married Jim Cheng, 1982; children: Nicholas, Jane, Ann. *Education:* Cornell University, B.A. (English), 1979, M.S. (linguistics), 1982.

Addresses

Home—Cincinnati, OH.

Career

Educator and author. Cincinnati State Technical and Community College, Cincinnati, OH, instructor in English as a second language and director of department, 1996—.

Awards, Honors

Cooperative Children's Book Center (CCBC) Choice designation, 2000, and Society of School Librarians International Best Book Honor designation, 2001, both for *Grandfather Counts;* Young Reader selection, On the Same Page reading program (Cincinnati, OH), and Association of Jewish Librarians Notable Book of Jewish Content designation, both 2002, and Ohioana Book Award finalist in Juvenile Category, and New York Public Library Books for the Teen Age designation, both 2003, all for *Marika;* Parents' Choice Award, and Kansas National Education Association Recommended designation, both 2003, both for *Anna the Bookbinder;*

Andrea Cheng (Reproduced by permission.)

Parents' Choice recommendation, 2004, for *Honeysuckle House;* New York Public Library 100 Best Children's Books designation, 2005, and Bank Street College Children's Book of the Year, and Asian/Pacific American Honor Award, both 2006, all for *Shanghai Messenger; Smithsonian* magazine Notable Children's Book designation, and Bank Street College of Education Best Children's Books of the Year selection, both 2008, both for *The Bear Makers;* Ohioana Book Award finalist, and Bank Street College of Education Best Children's Books of the Year selection, both 2008, both for *Where the Steps Were.*

Writings

PICTURE BOOKS

Grandfather Counts, illustrated by Ange Zhang, Lee & Low (New York, NY), 2000.
When the Bees Fly Home, illustrated by Joline McFadden, Tilbury House (Gardiner, ME), 2002.
Anna the Bookbinder, illustrated by Ted Rand, Walker (New York, NY), 2003.
Goldfish and Chrysanthemums, illustrated by Michelle Chang, Lee & Low (New York, NY), 2003.
Shanghai Messenger, illustrated by Ed Young, Lee & Low (New York, NY), 2005.
The Lemon Sisters, illustrated by Tatjana Mai-Wyss, G.P. Putnam's (New York, NY), 2006.

Tire Mountain, illustrated by Ken Condon, Boyds Mills Press (Honesdale, PA), 2007.

MIDDLE-GRADE FICTION

Honeysuckle House, Front Street Books (Asheville, NC), 2004.
The Lace Dowry, Front Street Books (Asheville, NC), 2005.
Eclipse, Front Street Books (Asheville, NC), 2006.
The Bear Makers, Front Street Books (Asheville, NC), 2008.
(Self-illustrated) *Where the Steps Were,* Wordsong (Honesdale, PA), 2008.
Brushing Mom's Hair (verse novel), illustrated by Nicole Wong, Wordsong (Honesdale, PA), 2009.

OTHER

Marika (young-adult novel), Front Street Books (Asheville, NC), 2002.
The Key Collection (chapter book), illustrated by Yangsook Choi, Henry Holt (New York, NY), 2003.

Sidelights

Given her background, it seems only natural that Andrea Cheng would become a writer of children's books about the meeting of two cultures as well as a teacher of English as a second language. The daughter of Hungarian immigrants, Cheng grew up speaking Hungarian at home so that her grandmother—who spoke no English—would not be excluded from conversations. Her eventual marriage to the son of Chinese immigrants expanded her awareness of cultural boundaries still further. In addition to her background, her children have provided Cheng with further inspiration for many of her award-winning picture books and novels, which include *Goldfish and Chrysanthemums, The Key Collection, Shanghai Messenger,* and *The Bear Maker.* Her verse novel *Brushing Mom's Hair* had an even-more-personal inspiration: it was written for Cheng's daughter as a way to help the teen deal with Cheng's bout with cancer.

Although Cheng began submitting her work to publishers when her children were very young, it was not until 2000 that her first picture book, *Grandfather Counts,* was published. In the story, Helen, the eldest among her siblings, has to give up her bedroom when her grandfather comes from China to live with her family. At first she is upset and she also does not know how to connect with her grandfather, who only speaks Chinese. Soon Helen discovers that the two have something in common: her grandfather waves at the engineer of trains passing their house just like she does. Communication-building begins when they start counting the train cars together, once in Chinese and once in English. Dian S. Marton, writing in *School Library Journal,* described *Grandfather Counts* as "an affecting and tender addi-

tion to multicultural and intergenerational literature," while Ellen Mandel commented in *Booklist* that "Cheng's story hints honestly at the difficulties of resettling an aged, non-English speaking relative."

Cheng's picture books *When the Bees Fly Home* and *Anna the Bookbinder* explore the lives of two young people who realize their own strengths. In the former, Jonathan discovers he can use his artistic talent to help the family beekeeping business. Helen Rosenberg, writing in *Booklist,* considered the tale a "moving story of a boy whose search for acceptance leads him to discover his own abilities." In the latter, Anna saves the day by applying the skills her father has taught her about binding books. Here Cheng "establishes ambience and key relationships in just a few opening lines," noted a critic for *Publishers Weekly* in a review of *Anna the Bookbinder*, while Elizabeth A. McNichol wrote in *Childhood Education* that the tale is "loving and inspiring."

With *Goldfish and Chrysanthemums* Cheng returns to the theme of intergenerational and intercultural relationships. Nancy and Greg's grandmother, Ni Ni, discovers

Cover of Cheng's self-illustrated verse novel **Where the Steps Were.**
(Wordsong, 2008. Jacket photographs © 2008 by Andrea Cheng. Reproduced by permission.)

that her old house in China is going to be torn down. Nancy comes up with a plan to build the distressed Ni Ni a pond for goldfish in the backyard of their house, just like the one outside her home in China. "Cheng's story of intergenerational connection is a sweet one," noted a *Kirkus Reviews* contributor, and a *Publishers Weekly* critic cited the tale's "uplifting theme of the importance of familial ties and continuity." Ilene Cooper noted in her *Booklist* review of *Goldfish and Chrysanthemums* that "the telling is direct, and the message about bringing happiness to those one loves is clear."

Shanghai Messenger introduces eleven-year-old Xiao Mei, who is traveling to China for the first time to visit her extended family. Although she is nervous about going, her grandmother convinces her to be a "messenger": bring back all her memories to the United States. "Cheng does an admirable job of capturing this experience from the perspective of a child," wrote Grace Oliff in *School Library Journal*. According to a *Publishers Weekly* contributor, "readers of any ethnic background will enjoy learning about China through Xiao Mei's curious eyes," while a *Kirkus Reviews* contributor found Cheng's story to be "wonderfully evocative."

Focusing on intergenerational relationships in a different way, Cheng tells the story of three elderly sisters and a young trio of girls who celebrate an eightieth birthday in *The Lemon Sisters*. "Endearing, this will be a place for conversations to start between young and old," predicted Cooper, while Blair Christolon commented in *School Library Journal* that the tale "leaves readers with a warm glow inside."

In *Tire Mountain,* illustrated by Ken Condon, Cheng introduces a young boy named Aaron, who loves to play in the pile of automobile tires near his father's automotive shop. When Aaron's mother suggests that the family move to a more rural neighborhood, the young boy finds an imaginative way to let her know that his city neighborhood offers the same opportunities for energetic play that can be found in the country. *Tire Mountain* provides young children with "a kid's eye view of the world, where physical presences offer rock-solid comfort," according to a *Publishers Weekly* contributor, the critic dubbing Cheng's picture book "understated and affecting."

Although Cheng originally confined her writing to shorter works, she has increasingly turned to middle-grade fiction, and has also published chapter books and the young-adult novel *Marika*. "I didn't intend to write a novel but my writing group . . . helped me believe I could do it," Cheng explained to an interviewer for the Cincinnati *Enquirer*. *Marika* is drawn from Cheng's family history, and the title character is part of a well-off family living in Budapest during the 1930s. Although they are Jewish, Marika's family members attend a Roman Catholic church and consider themselves like all of their neighbors. When World War II breaks out, Marika is sent to live with Catholic friends who

The culture of China is the focus of Cheng's picture book Shanghai Messenger, *featuring paintings by Ed Young.* (Illustration copyright © 2005 by Ed Young. Reproduced by permission of Lee & Low Books, Inc.)

disguise her as a member of their own family. Tragically, the girl's mother is eventually sent to Auschwitz. Much of Marika's story comes from the recollections of Cheng's mother and grandmother, who lived through similar experiences. According to Lauren Adams in *Horn Book,* Cheng's "compelling" tale "is less a war story than it is the story of an interesting young life obscenely interrupted by Hitler's war." *Booklist* critic Hazel Rochman praised Cheng's "clear, quiet prose," while Amy Lilien-Harper noted in *School Library Journal* that the "deceptively simple . . . story, told in first person, captures a child's life as she grows into the realization of the horrors around her."

Cheng's first chapter book, *The Key Collection,* tells the story of Jimmy, whose grandmother is moving across the country to live with his aunt. Jimmy and his grandmother have always been very close; she tells him stories of each of the keys that belong to her key collection, and as she prepares to leave, both she and Jimmy realize that they can still be close, even if they live far away. *Booklist* critic Ed Sullivan considered the tale a "warm, reassuring story of intergenerational friendship," and a *Publishers Weekly* contributor dubbed *The Key Collection* a "gently delivered, tightly written novel." According to Joanna Rudge Long in *Horn Book,* "there's unusual warmth and depth in the details of the story," and in *School Library Journal,* Carol A. Ed-

wards deemed Cheng's novel "a quiet story with a strong heart and a clear picture of the way kids cope."

Like *Marika,* Cheng's middle-grade novel *The Lace Dowry* is set in Budapest in the 1930s, but it contains a very different story. Although Juli resists getting married, her mother insists on getting the young woman a lace tablecloth for her dowry. In Halas, where the best lace is made, Juli forges a relationship with a young lace maker and seeks to help her new friend when the girl's mother loses her sight. "Cheng captures Juli's voice, and that of her difficult mother, directly and simply," wrote a *Kirkus Reviews* contributor. Gillian Engberg noted in *Booklist* that the author "enrich[es] the theme with a vivid historical setting and Juli's strong narration." In her *Horn Book* review, Susan P. Bloom commented that, in *The Lace Dowry,* "Cheng presents each of the characters sympathetically and gives this tale, unusual in time and setting, poignant relevance and credibility."

Also based on Cheng's family history and set against the war-torn backdrop of Budapest, *The Bear Makers* takes place in 1948 as the Jewish Steiner family returns from their place of hiding. While they cannot reclaim their former lives, where Mr. Steiner owned a factory, the family also worries when the country's secret police, the AVO, force mass loyalty to the socialist workers' party. Eleven-year-old Kata is too young to under-

stand the looming political problems, but she does sense the worries of her older brother and of her father, who has been reduced to a part-time employee. Like her friend Eva, Kata joins a communist youth group, and also contributes to her family income by helping her mother sew stuffed bears and purses to sell on the street. A spark of hope comes for the family when Kata's brother escapes from Hungary, and the family prays that he leaves Europe for North America. "Kata's clear, first-person voice never loses the child's point of view," maintained *School Library Journal* contributor Kathleen Isaacs in her review of *The Bear Makers,* the critic calling Cheng's story "a thoroughly convincing recollection of a vanished world."

In *Eclipse* the year is now 1952 and eight-year-old Peti's Hungarian relatives have come to live with his family in America. Among them is his cousin Gabor, who is older and very belligerent. To escape Gabor's bullying, Peti hides in the local library, where he discovers a world of information and a friendship that illuminates his understanding of human resilience and the ways people deal with hardship. Peti's "naive, immediate viewpoint dramatizes issues—past and present," wrote *Booklist* contributor Hazel Rochman in a review of *Eclipse,* and in *School Library Journal* Lauralyn Persson praised Cheng for creating a "thoughtful novel" that "invites comparison with many situations in today's politically unstable world." "Short, episodic chapters and poetic prose" contribute to the appeal of Cheng's story for "those of a literary bent," according to a *Kirkus Reviews* writer.

Honeysuckle House focuses on two fourth graders who eventually become friends. At first, Sarah is upset because her teachers assume that, since she is Chinese American, she will happily befriend the new girl in class, Ting. Ting is shy and unsure of how to fit in and, although her interests are drastically different from Sarah's, the two girls soon begin to understand each other and provide each other with support. "Cheng proves herself a gifted and sympathetic observer of middle-graders' conflicts and concerns," wrote a critic for *Publishers Weekly,* while Persson commented in *School Library Journal* that, "with a strong social conscience behind it," Cheng's "absorbing novel has a lot going for it." In *Horn Book* Long maintained that "what distinguishes the story are the judiciously selected actions and details that give its characters vivid individuality."

A middle-grade novel featuring Cheng's original art, *Where the Steps Were* focuses on an encounter with racism and its impact on American history. In the novel free-verse narratives by five members of an inner-city third-grade class follow their experiences acting in the school play, studying the U.S. Civil War and the civil rights movement, and attending a professional theatrical performance, where they are asked to leave the theatre. In *Horn Book* Robin L. Smith praised the "remarkably emotional" wood-cut images Cheng creates to pair with her story, calling *Where the Steps Were* "a school story that gets the details right."

On her home page, Cheng discussed the inspiration behind her writing. "I don't really have a purpose in mind when I write," she explained."I usually start with an image rather than an idea or a purpose. For some reason, a certain image is stuck in my mind. I describe it, and the scene around it, and the characters involved, and that becomes a story. I don't have any purpose other than to evoke emotion in the reader." Cheng's poetic text "allows [her characters] . . . to speak their hopes, frustrations, and fears," asserted a *Kirkus Reviews* writer, while her original images "intensify . . . their emotional impact."

Biographical and Critical Sources

PERIODICALS

Booklist, December 15, 2000, Ellen Mandel, review of *Grandfather Counts,* p. 824; July, 2002, Helen Rosenberg, review of *When Bees Fly Home,* p. 1854; November 15, 2002, Hazel Rochman, review of *Marika,* p. 590; April 15, 2003, GraceAnne A. DeCandido, review of *Anna the Bookbinder,* p. 1476; April 15, 2003, Ed Sullivan, review of *The Key Collection,* p. 1471; July, 2003, Ilene Cooper, review of *Goldfish and Chrysanthemums,* p. 1896; April 1, 2005, Gillian Engberg, review of *The Lace Dowry,* p. 1360; August, 2005, Hazel Rochman, review of *Shanghai Messenger,* p. 1965; December 15, 2005, Ilene Cooper, review of *The Lemon Sisters,* p. 49; November 1, 2006, Hazel Rochman, review of *Eclipse,* p. 53; March 1, 2008, Hazel Rochman, review of *Where the Steps Were,* p. 70; December 1, 2008, Thom Barthelmess, review of *The Bear Makers,* p. 41.

Childhood Education, fall, 2003, Elizabeth A. McNichol, review of *Anna the Bookbinder,* p. 39.

Children's Bookwatch, October, 2005, review of *Shanghai Messenger.*

Enquirer (Cincinnati, OH), February 28, 2003, Sara Pearce, "Marika Describes Author's Real-Life Family."

Horn Book, November-December, 2002, Lauren Adams, review of *Marika,* p. 752; July-August, 2003, Joanna Rudge Long, review of *The Key Collection,* p. 452; July-August, 2004, Joanna Rudge Long, review of *Honeysuckle House,* p. 449; July-August, 2005, Susan P. Bloom, review of *The Lace Dowry,* p. 466; May-June, 2008, Robin L. Smith, review of *Where the Steps Were,* p. 309.

Journal of Adolescent and Adult Literacy, September, 2005, Vicki Balant, review of *The Lace Dowry,* p. 76.

Kirkus Reviews, August 1, 2002, review of *Marika,* p. 1124; February 15, 2003, review of *Anna the Bookbinder,* p. 302; March 1, 2003, review of *Goldfish and Chrysanthemums,* p. 380; June 1, 2003, review of *The Key Collection,* p. 801; March 15, 2004, review of *Honeysuckle House,* p. 267; April 1, 2005, review of *The Lace Dowry,* p. 414; August 1, 2005, review of *Shanghai Messenger,* p. 845; December 15, 2005, re-

view of *The Lemon Sisters,* p. 1319; September 1, 2006, review of *Eclipse,* p. 901; July 1, 2007, review of *Tire Mountain;* February 1, 2008, review of *Where the Steps Were;* October 1, 2008, review of *The Bear Makers.*

New York Times Book Review, July 13, 2003, review of *The Key Collection,* p. 20.

Publishers Weekly, September 16, 2002, review of *Marika,* p. 69; February 10, 2003, review of *Anna the Bookbinder,* p. 187; March 10, 2003, review of *Goldfish and Chrysanthemums,* p. 71; June 16, 2003, review of *The Key Collection,* p. 71; April 12, 2004, review of *Honeysuckle House,* p. 66; September 19, 2005, review of *Shanghai Messenger,* p. 66; December 18, 2006, review of *Eclipse,* p. 64; August 20, 2007, review of *Tire Mountain,* p. 67; March 3, 2008, review of *Where the Steps Were,* p. 47.

School Library Journal, November, 2000, Diane S. Marton, review of *Grandfather Counts,* p. 112; December, 2002, Amy Lilien-Harper, review of *Marika,* p. 132; April, 2003, Diane S. Marton, review of *Grandfather Counts,* p. 104; May, 2003, Louise L. Sherman, review of *Anna the Bookbinder,* p. 109; October, 2003, Carol A. Edwards, review of *The Key Collection,* p. 115; June, 2004, Lauralyn Persson, review of *Honeysuckle House,* p. 104; May, 2005, Barbara Auerbach, review of *The Lace Dowry,* p. 125; September, 2005, Grace Oliff, review of *Shanghai Messenger,* p. 167; January, 2006, Blair Christolon, review of *The Lemon Sisters,* p. 93; November, 2006, Lauralyn Persson, review of *Eclipse,* p. 130; May, 2008, Nina Lindsay, review of *Where the Steps Were,* p. 93; December, 2008, Kathleen Isaacs, review of *The Bear makers,* p. 120.

Voice of Youth Advocates, June, 2005, Mary Ann Harlan, review of *The Lace Dowry,* p. 126.

ONLINE

Andrea Cheng Home Page, http://www.andreacheng.com (June 21, 2006).

Front Street Books Web site, http://www.frontstreetbooks.com/ (June 21, 2006), profile of Cheng.

Lee & Low Web site, http://www.leeandlow.com/ (June 21, 2006), "Andrea Cheng."*

*   *   *

COUSINS, Lucy 1964-

Personal

Born February 10, 1964, in England; married; children: four. *Education:* Attended Canterbury Art College; Brighton Polytechnic, B.A. (graphic design; with honors); Royal College of Art, postgraduate degree.

Addresses

Home—Hampshire, England.

Career

Author and illustrator.

Awards, Honors

Ragazzi prize, 1997, for *Maisy's House;* National Art Illustration Award high commendation, 1997, for *Za Za's Baby Brother;* Nestlé Smarties Book Prize, 2002, for *Jazzy in the Jungle.*

Writings

SELF-ILLUSTRATED

Portly's Hat, Dutton (New York, NY), 1989.

(Adapter) *The Little Dog Laughed,* Macmillan (London, England), 1989, Dutton (New York, NY), 1990, published as *Lucy Cousins' Big Book of Nursery Rhymes,* Macmillan (London, England), 1998.

(Adapter) *Humpty Dumpty and Other Nursery Rhymes,* Dutton (New York, NY), 1989.

(Adapter) *Jack and Jill and Other Nursery Rhymes,* Dutton (New York, NY), 1989.

Country Animals, Walker Books (London, England), 1990, Tambourine Books (New York, NY), 1991.

Farm Animals, Walker (London, England), 1990, Tambourine Books (New York, NY), 1991.

Garden Animals, Walker (London, England), 1990, Tambourine Books (New York, NY), 1991.

Pet Animals, Walker (London, England), 1990, Tambourine Books (New York, NY), 1991.

What Can Rabbit Hear?, Walker (London, England), 1991, published as *What Can Pinky Hear?,* Candlewick Press (Cambridge, MA), 1997.

What Can Rabbit See?, Walker (London, England), 1991, published as *What Can Pinky See?,* Candlewick Press (Cambridge, MA), 1997.

(Reteller) *Noah's Ark,* Candlewick Press (Cambridge, MA), 1993, released with DVD, Walker (London, England), 2007.

My Toys, Candlewick Press (Cambridge, MA), 1995.

Za-Za's Baby Brother, Candlewick Press (Cambridge, MA), 1995.

Kathy Cat and Beaky Boo, Candlewick Press (Cambridge, MA), 1996.

Kathy Cat and Beaky Boo's Play Set, paper engineering by Lisa Boggiss and Rene Jablow, Candlewick Press (Cambridge, MA), 1997.

(Adapter) *Little Miss Muffett and Other Nursery Rhymes,* Dutton (New York, NY), 1997.

(Adapter) *Wee Willie Winkie and Other Nursery Rhymes,* Dutton (New York, NY), 1997.

Jazzy in the Jungle, Candlewick Press (Cambridge, MA), 2002.

Hooray for Fish!, Candlewick Press (Cambridge, MA), 2005.

Yummy: Eight Favorite Fairy Tales, Candlewick Press (Somerville, MA), 2009.

Also author of *Lucy Cousins' Nursery Rhyme Sticker Book.*

"MAISY" BOOKS; SELF ILLUSTRATED

Maisy Goes Swimming, Little, Brown (Boston, MA), 1990.

Maisy Goes to Bed, Little, Brown (Boston, MA), 1990, reprinted, Candlewick Press (Cambridge, MA), 2006.

Maisy Goes to School, Candlewick Press (Cambridge, MA), 1992.

Maisy Goes to the Playground, Candlewick Press (Cambridge, MA), 1992.

Maisy's ABC, Candlewick Press (Cambridge, MA), 1995.

Maisy's Pop-up Playhouse, paper engineering by Bruce Reifel, Candlewick Press (Cambridge, MA), 1995, published as *Maisy's House: A Pop-up and Play Book,* Walker Books (London, England), 1995.

Count with Maisy, Candlewick Press (Cambridge, MA), 1997.

Maisy's Colors, Candlewick Press (Cambridge, MA), 1997.

Happy Birthday, Maisy, paper engineering by Lisa Boggiss, Candlewick Press (Cambridge, MA), 1998.

Maisy at the Farm, paper engineering by Lisa Boggiss, Candlewick Press (Cambridge, MA), 1998.

Maisy's Bedtime, Candlewick Press (Cambridge, MA), 1999.

Maisy's Day (sticker book), Candlewick Press (Cambridge, MA), 1999.

Maisy's Mix-and-Match Mousewear, Candlewick Press (Cambridge, MA), 1999.

Maisy's Pool, Candlewick Press (Cambridge, MA), 1999.

Where Is Maisy?, Candlewick Press (Cambridge, MA), 1999.

Where Is Maisy's Panda?, Candlewick Press (Cambridge, MA), 1999.

Dress Maisy (sticker book), Candlewick Press (Cambridge, MA), 1999.

Maisy Dresses Up, Candlewick Press (Cambridge, MA), 1999.

Maisy Makes Gingerbread, Candlewick Press (Cambridge, MA), 1999.

Maisy Drives the Bus, Candlewick Press (Cambridge, MA), 2000.

Maisy Takes a Bath, Candlewick Press (Cambridge, MA), 2000.

Merry Christmas, Maisy, Candlewick Press (Cambridge, MA), 2000.

Maisy's Favorite Animals, Candlewick Press (Cambridge, MA), 2001.

Maisy's Favorite Clothes, Candlewick Press (Cambridge, MA), 2001.

Maisy's Favorite Things, Candlewick Press (Cambridge, MA), 2001.

Maisy's Favorite Toys, Candlewick Press (Cambridge, MA), 2001.

Maisy's Garden Sticker Book, Candlewick Press (Cambridge, MA), 2001.

Maisy's Morning on the Farm, Candlewick Press (Cambridge, MA), 2001.

Doctor Maisy, Candlewick Press (Cambridge, MA), 2001.

Maisy at the Beach (sticker book), Candlewick Press (Cambridge, MA), 2001.

Maisy at the Fair, Candlewick Press (Cambridge, MA), 2001.

Maisy Drives, Candlewick Press (Cambridge, MA), 2001.

Maisy Goes Shopping, Candlewick Press (Cambridge, MA), 2001.

Maisy Plays, Candlewick Press (Cambridge, MA), 2001.

Maisy's Big Flap Book, Candlewick Press (Cambridge, MA), 2001.

Maisy's Farm: A Pop-up and Play Set, paper engineering by Claire Jones, Candlewick Press (Cambridge, MA), 2001.

Maisy Cleans Up, Candlewick Press(Cambridge, MA), 2002.

Maisy Makes Lemonade, Candlewick Press (Cambridge, MA), 2002.

Maisy's Fire Engine, Candlewick Press (Cambridge, MA), 2002.

Maisy's First Clock, Candlewick Press (Cambridge, MA), 2002.

Maisy's Seasons, Candlewick Press (Cambridge, MA), 2002.

Maisy's Train, Candlewick Press (Cambridge, MA), 2002.

Maisy's Noisy Day, Candlewick Press (Cambridge, MA), 2002.

Go, Maisy, Go!, Candlewick Press (Cambridge, MA), 2003.

Maisy Likes Dancing, Candlewick Press (Cambridge, MA), 2003.

Maisy Loves You, Candlewick Press (Cambridge, MA), 2003.

Maisy's Best Friends, Candlewick Press (Cambridge, MA), 2003.

Maisy's Easter Egg Hunt (sticker book), Candlewick Press (Cambridge, MA), 2003.

Maisy's Rainbow Dress, Candlewick Press (Cambridge, MA), 2003.

Maisy's Snowy Christmas Eve, Candlewick Press (Cambridge, MA), 2003.

What Are You Doing, Maisy?, Candlewick Press (Cambridge, MA), 2003.

Where Are You Going, Maisy?, Candlewick Press (Cambridge, MA), 2003.

How Will You Get There, Maisy?, Candlewick Press (Cambridge, MA), 2004.

Is This Maisy's House?, Candlewick Press (Cambridge, MA), 2004.

Maisy Goes Camping, Candlewick Press (Cambridge, MA), 2004.

Maisy Likes Music, Candlewick Press (Cambridge, MA), 2004.

Maisy's Christmas Sticker Book, Candlewick Press (Cambridge, MA), 2004.

Maisy's Halloween, Candlewick Press (Cambridge, MA), 2004.

Maisy's Pirate Treasure Hunt, Candlewick Press (Cambridge, MA), 2004.

Maisy's Twinkly, Crinkly Counting Book, Candlewick Press (Cambridge, MA), 2004.

Smile, Maisy!, Candlewick Press (Cambridge, MA), 2004.

Squeak, Squeak, Maisy!: Squeak Me!, Candlewick Press (Cambridge, MA), 2004.

1, 2, 3, Maisy, Candlewick Press (Cambridge, MA), 2004.

Ha Ha, Maisy!, Candlewick Press (Cambridge, MA), 2005.

Maisy Goes to the Library, Candlewick Press (Cambridge, MA), 2005.

Maisy's Color Collection, Candlewick Press (Cambridge, MA), 2005.

Maisy's Traffic Jam, Candlewick Press (Cambridge, MA), 2005.

More Fun with Maisy!, Candlewick Press (Cambridge, MA), 2005.

Sweet Dreams, Maisy, Candlewick Press (Cambridge, MA), 2005.

With Love from Maisy, Candlewick (Cambridge, MA), 2005.

Maisy, Charley, and the Wobbly Tooth, Candlewick Press (Cambridge, MA), 2006.

Maisy's Valentine Sticker Book, Walker (London, England), 2006.

Maisy's First Game Book, Candlewick Press (Cambridge, MA), 2006.

Maisy's Wonderful Weather Book, Candlewick Press (Cambridge, MA), 2006.

Happy Easter, Maisy!, Candlewick Press (Cambridge, MA), 2007.

Maisy's Amazing Big Book of Words, Candlewick Press (Cambridge, MA), 2007.

Maisy Big, Maisy Small, Candlewick Press (Cambridge, MA), 2007.

Maisy Goes to the Hospital, Candlewick Press (Cambridge, MA), 2007.

Maisy Goes to the Museum, Candlewick Press (Cambridge, MA), 2008.

Maisy's Christmas Day, Candlewick Press (Cambridge, MA), 2008.

Maisy's House and Garden, Candlewick Press (Cambridge, MA), 2008.

Maisy's Nature Walk, Candlewick Press (Cambridge, MA), 2008.

Munch Munch, Maisy, Candlewick Press (Cambridge, MA), 2008.

Quack Quack, Maisy, Candlewick Press (Cambridge, MA), 2008.

Toot Toot, Maisy, Candlewick Press (Cambridge, MA), 2008.

Vroom Vroom, Maisy, Candlewick Press (Cambridge, MA), 2008.

Maisy Bakes a Cake, Candlewick Press (Somerville, MA), 2009.

Maisy Goes to Preschool (board book), Candlewick Press (Somerville, MA), 2009.

Maisy's Animals, Candlewick Press (Somerville, MA), 2009.

Maisy's Clothes, Candlewick Press (Somerville, MA), 2009.

Maisy's Food, Candlewick Press (Somerville, MA), 2009.

Maisy's Street, Candlewick Press (Somerville, MA), 2009.

Maisy's Toys, Candlewick Press (Somerville, MA), 2009.

Maisy's Book of Things That Go, Candlewick Press (Somerville, MA), 2010.

Where Are Maisy's Friends?, Candlewick Press (Somerville, MA), 2010.

Where Does Maisy Live?, Candlewick Press (Somerville, MA), 2010.

Where Is Maisy?, Candlewick Press (Somerville, MA), 2010.

Cousins' books have been translated into Afrikaans, French, and German.

Adaptations

The "Maisy" series was adapted as a television series, produced for Noggin network.

Sidelights

British author and illustrator Lucy Cousins is best known for creating the mouse character Maisy, which is featured in a multitude of books as well as in a television series. The bewhiskered character was born while Cousins was honing her illustrations skills in hopes of building a career in the children's-book field. She entered a competition for art students that was sponsored by Macmillan U.K. and when she placed second, *Portly's Hat,* her art school graduation project, was published. The win "gave me so much encouragement and it made it easier after college to approach publishers," Cousins later told Claudia Logan in an interview for *Publishers Weekly.* "I think it would have been much slower going without the competition."

Cousins followed *Portly's Hat* with several collections of nursery rhymes, each accompanied by her unique art style. *The Little Dog Laughed* is one of these; it has more recently been republished as *Lucy Cousins' Big Book of Nursery Rhymes.* The collection features forty of the illustrator's favorite poems accompanied by "amazing and vibrant art," according to Susan Fonseca in *Canadian Review of Materials.* "The art work is very bold," Fonseca continued, "using solid colors with definite black outlines." According to *Booklist* contributor Lauren Peterson, the collection contains "something familiar and something new in the same sitting."

In 1990, Cousins' most well-known character, Maisy, first appeared on the picture-book scene, taking center stage in *Maisy Goes Swimming* and *Maisy Goes to Bed.* A cheerful young mouse, Maisy has gone on to star in dozens of picture books, board books, pop-ups, and pull-the-flap books. According to Gillian Engberg, in a review of *Maisy's Rainbow Dream* for *Booklist,* Maisy has "legions of small fans." From the "beguiling twist on the alphabet-book genre" in *Maisy's ABC,* according to a *Publishers Weekly* contributor, to "a simple and effective counting book," as Lauren Adams described *Count with Maisy* in *Horn Book,* the little mouse educates as well as entertains. "Maisy makes preschool concepts fresh as a daisy," wrote a contributor to *Publishers Weekly* in a review of *Maisy's Colors,* and a *Kirkus Reviews* writer noted of *Maisy's Nature Walk* that Cousins' book "makes a welcome and invigorating addition to any toddler/preschooler science bookshelf."

Beyond concept books, the "Maisy" books often provide an entertaining story about friendship. *Maisy's Morning on the Farm* finds the "lovable pink-whiskered mouse," as she was called by a *Kirkus Reviews* contributor, doing morning chores and greeting each of the animals on a farm. *Where Are Maisy's Friends?* presents an interactive game of hide and seek in which young readers can lift flaps to discover where Maisy and her friends have gone, and *Maisy, Charley, and the Wobbly Tooth* finds the mouse comforting her toothy young friend Charley the crocodile during a frightening visit to the dentist. Olga R. Barnes deemed *Where Are Maisy's Friends?* "perfect for babies and toddlers" in her *School Library Journal* review, while *Booklist* critic

Lucy Cousins tells a humorous holiday story in her self-illustrated picture book **Maisy's Christmas Day.** (Illustration copyright © 2008 by Lucy Cousins. Reproduced by permission of the publisher Candlewick Press, Inc., Somerville, MA, on behalf of Walker Books, Ltd., London.)

Carolyn Phelan wrote of *Maisy, Charley, and the Wobbly Tooth* that "Cousins' distinctive artwork" enhances her story "with visual humor." In *Maisy Drives a Bus,* the character once again reveals "a charming personality with plenty of sparkle," according to Susan Marie Pitard in *School Library Journal.*

Along with her "Maisy" books, Cousins has published several standalone titles, among them *Jazzy in the Jungle,* which won the Nestlé Smarties Book Prize, and *Hooray for Fish!* In the latter, Little Fish explores the ocean and greets an array of friends. Bina Williams, reviewing *Hooray for Fish!* for *School Library Journal,* considered Cousins' "appealing oversize book . . . a swimming good time," while a *Publishers Weekly* contributor wrote that the author/illustrator's "exuberant illustrations bring new meaning to the old saying, 'plenty of fish in the sea.'"

Discussing her inspirations, Cousins explained to Logan that her own daughter began "reviewing" her mother's books at the age of seven months. Recalling the reception of some of her cloth books, Cousins told Logan: "She looked at it and chewed it and did all the right things." Cousins' own children have continued to inspire her career; as she wrote on the Candlewick Press Web site, she can "create better books and stories now that I have the insight into children's minds that all parents have. It's like having a market research team in my own home!"

Describing the process that results in each of her many books for children, Cousins noted on the Walker Books Web site: "I draw by heart. I think about what children would like by going back to my own childlike in-

stincts." Discussing her inspiration, the artist/illustrator added: "I get more pleasure and inspiration from walking around a primary school than from any art gallery."

Biographical and Critical Sources

PERIODICALS

Bookbird, summer, 1997, review of *Maisy's House: A Pop-up and Play Book,* p. 56.
Booklist, September 1, 1995, Hazel Rochman, review of *Za-Za's Baby Brother,* p. 84; February 1, 1996, review of *Maisy's Pop-up Playhouse,* p. 942; September 15, 1996, Carolyn Phelan, review of *Humpty Dumpty and Other Nursery Rhymes,* p. 246; April 1, 1999, Lauren Peterson, review of *Lucy Cousins' Book of Nursery Rhymes,* p. 1416; November 15, 1999, Carolyn Phelan, review of *Maisy Makes Gingerbread,* p. 633; October 1, 2001, Carolyn Phelan, review of *Doctor Maisy* and *Maisy's Morning on the Farm,* p. 324; December 1, 2003, Gillian Engberg, review of *Maisy's Rainbow Dream,* p. 684; April 1, 2005, Gillian Engberg, review of *Hooray for Fish!,* p. 1365; August, 2005, Carolyn Phelan, review of *Maisy Goes to the Library,* p. 2033; May 1, 2006, Carolyn Phelan, review of *Maisy, Charley, and the Wobbly Tooth,* p. 88; June 1, 2007, Gillian Engberg, review of *Maisy's Amazing Big Book of Words,* p. 81; October 15, 2008, Ilene Cooper, review of *Maisy Goes to the Museum,* p. 46.
Bulletin of the Center for Children's Books, October, 1996, review of *Humpty Dumpty and Other Nursery Rhymes,* p. 70.
Horn Book, November-December, 1993, Maeve Visser Knoth, review of *Noah's Ark,* p. 753; July-August,

1997, Lauren Adams, review of *Count with Maisy,* p. 442; July-August, 2004, Lauren Adams, review of *Maisy Goes Camping,* p. 434.

Kirkus Reviews, September 1, 2001, review of *Maisy's Morning on the Farm,* p. 1287; October 1, 2002, review of *Jazzy in the Jungle,* p. 1464; May 15, 2005, review of *Hooray for Fish!,* p. 586; August 1, 2005, review of *Maisy Goes to the Library,* p. 84; September 15, 2005, review of *Sweet Dreams, Maisy,* p. 1024; May 15, 2006, review of *Maisy, Charley, and the Wobbly Tooth,* p. 515; August 1, 2007, review of *Maisy Goes to the Hospital;* August 15, 2007, review of *Maisy Big, Maisy Small;* February 1, 2008, review of *Maisy's Nature Walk.*

Magpies, November, 1997, review of *Katy Cat and Beaky Boo Play Set,* p. 6; November, 1999, review of *Lucy Cousins' Nursery Rhyme Sticker Book,* p. 5; November, 2002, review of *Jazzy in the Jungle,* p. 26; March, 2005, Jo Goodman, "Before School," and review of *Hooray for Fish!,* p. 26.

New Statesman, December 4, 1998, review of *Lucy Cousins' Big Book of Nursery Rhymes,* p. 62.

Publishers Weekly, August 31, 1990, review of *Maisy Goes to Bed,* p. 62; March 1, 1991, Claudia Logan, "The Fresh Vision of Lucy Cousins," pp. 44-45; August 23, 1991, reviews of *What Can Rabbit Hear?* and *What Can Rabbit See?,* p. 61; February 20, 1995, review of *Maisy's ABC,* p. 204; July 17, 1995, review of *Za-Za's Baby Brother,* p. 229; August 5, 1996, review of *Jack and Jill and Other Nursery Rhymes,* p. 443; October 7, 1996, review of *Katy Cat and Beaky Boo,* p. 77; January 27, 1997, review of *Noah's Ark,* p. 108; May 14, 1997, reviews of *Maisy's Colors* and *Count with Maisy,* p. 74; October 19, 1998, review of *Maisy at the Farm,* p. 82; March 8, 1999, review of *Count with Maisy,* p. 70; April 5, 1999, review of *Maisy's Mix-and-Match Mousewear,* p. 243; April 12, 1999, review of *Country Animals,* p. 77; April 26, 1999, review of *Lucy Cousins' Book of Nursery Rhymes,* p. 84; August 2, 1999, review of *Maisy's Bedtime,* p. 86; May 1, 2000, "What a Character," p. 73; September

Cousins' adventurous mouse finds a way to reach her goal in the self-illustrated **Maisy Goes to the Museum.** (Illustration copyright © 2008 by Lucy Cousins. Reproduced by permission of the publisher Candlewick Press, Inc., Somerville, MA, on behalf of Walker Books, Ltd., London.)

25, 2000, review of *Merry Christmas, Maisy*, p. 75; October 21, 2002, review of *Jazzy in the Jungle*, p. 2002; September 22, 2003, review of *Maisy's Snowy Christmas Eve*, p. 73; May 30, 2005, review of *Hooray for Fish!*, p. 59.

School Librarian, autumn, 2000, review of *Maisie's Bathtime*, p. 130.

School Library Journal, July, 1995, Linda Wicher, review of *Maisy's ABC*, p. 55; January, 1997, Carolyn Jenks, review of *Katy Cat and Beaky Boo*, p. 76, and Vicki Emery, review of *Humpty Dumpty and Other Nursery Rhymes*, p. 83; August, 1998, review of *Maisy Goes Swimming*, p. 26; October, 1998, review of *Happy Birthday, Maisy*, p. 93; September, 1999, Gay Lynn Van Vleck, reviews of *Maisy's Pool* and *Maisy's Bedtime*, p. 179; June, 2000, Susan Marie Patard, review of *Maisy Drives the Bus*, p. 104; December, 2000, Olga R. Barnes, review of *Where Are Maisy's Friends?*, p. 106; December, 2001, Kathy M. Newby, review of *Doctor Maisy* and *Maisy's Morning on the Farm*, p. 97; April, 2002, Maria Otero-Boisvert, review of *Maisy Likes to Play*, p. S56; May, 2002, Wendy S. Carroll, review of *Maisy Cleans Up*, p. 105; December, 2002, Sheilah Kosco, review of *Jazzy in the Jungle*, p. 86; April, 2003, Melinda Piehler, review of *Go, Maisy, Go!*, p. 118; December, 2003, Melinda Piehler, review of *Maisy's Rainbow Dream*, p. 112; February, 2005, Andrea Tarr, review of *How Will You Get There, Maisy?*, p. 96; August, 2005, Bina Williams, review of *Hooray for Fish!*, p. 86, and Kristen M. Todd, review of *Maisy Goes to the Library*, p. 87; August, 2007, Andrea Tarr, review of *Maisy's Amazing Big Book of Words*, p. 78; November, 2007, G. Alyssa Parkinson, review of *Maisy Goes to the Hospital*, p. 88; September, 2008, Lynne Mattern, review of *Maisy Goes to the Museum*, p. 144.

Today's Parent, March, 1999, review of *Lucy Cousins' Big Book of Nursery Rhymes*, p. 14.

ONLINE

Canadian Review of Materials Online, http://www.umanitoba.ca/cm/ (April 28, 2000), Susan Fonseca, review of *Lucy Cousins' Big Book of Nursery Rhymes*.

Candlewick Press Web site, http://www.candlewick.com/ (June 25, 2006), profile of Cousins.

Maisy's Fun Club Web site, http://www.maisyfunclub.com/ (October 15, 2009).

Storyopolis, http://www.storyopolis.com/ (June 25, 2006), profile of Cousins.

Walker Books Web site, http://www.walker.co.uk/ (October 15, 2009), profile of Cousins.*

*   *   *

CRAIG, David

Personal

Born in Ottawa, Ontario, Canada.

Addresses

Home—Mississauga, Ontario, Canada. *E-mail*—david crg@rogers.com.

Career

Artist and illustrator. Storyboard and layout artist for periodicals, including *Chatelaine* and *Reader's Digest*, Montreal, Quebec, Canada, beginning 1967; worked for a design company in Toronto, Ontario, Canada; freelance illustrator based in Mississauga, Ontario, Canada. Designer of coins for Canadian Mint, including sesquicentennial silver dollar. *Exhibitions:* Work exhibited at O'Keefe Center, Toronto, Ontario, Canada.

Awards, Honors

Golden Cylinder Award, 2000; James Madison Book Award for Excellence (with Peter Busby), 2003, for *First to Fly*.

Illustrator

Shelley Tanaka, *Attack on Pearl Harbor: The True Story of the Day America Entered World War II* ("I Was There" series), Hyperion (New York, NY), 2001.

Peter Busby, *First to Fly: How Wilbur and Orville Wright Invented the Airplane*, Crown (New York, NY), 2002.

Maxine Trottier, *The Long White Scarf*, Fitzhenry & Whiteside (Markham, Ontario, Canada), 2005.

Shelley Tanaka, *Amelia Earhart: The Legend of the Lost Aviator*, Harry Abrams (New York, NY), 2008.

Mary Ann McCabe Riehle, *A Is for Airplane: An Aviation Alphabet*, Sleeping Bear Press (Chelsea, MI), 2009.

"A DAY THAT CHANGED AMERICA" SERIES; ILLUSTRATOR

Shelley Tanaka, *D-Day: They Fought to Free Europe from Hitler's Tyranny*, Hyperion (New York, NY), 2003.

Shelley Tanaka, *Gettysburg: The Legendary Battle and the Address That Inspired a Nation*, Hyperion (New York, NY), 2003.

Shelley Tanaka, *The Alamo: Surrounded and Outnumbered, They Chose to Make a Defiant Last Stand*, Hyperion (New York, NY), 2003.

Shelley Tanaka, *Earthquake!: On a Peaceful Spring Morning, Disaster Strikes San Francisco*, Hyperion (New York, NY), 2004.

"OUTWITTING THE ENEMY: STORIES FROM THE SECOND WORLD WAR" SERIES; ILLUSTRATOR

Stephen Shapiro and Tina Forrester, *Ultra Hush-Hush: Espionage and Special Missions*, Annick Press (Toronto, Ontario, Canada), 2003.

Stephen Shapiro and Tina Forrester, *Hoodwinked: Deception and Resistance*, Annick Press (Toronto, Ontario, Canada), 2004.

Sidelights

In addition to being a history buff, David Craig is also a highly regarded Canadian illustrator whose work has been featured in several nonfiction books, including Shelley Tanaka's *Attack on Pearl Harbor: The True Story of the Day America Entered World War II* and Peter Busby's *First to Fly: How Wilbur and Orville Wright*

David Craig's detailed paintings are a feature of Shelley Tanaka's **Amelia Earhart: The Legend of the Lost Aviator.** (Abrams Books for Young Readers, 2008. Illustration copyright © 2008 by David Craig. Reproduced by permission.)

Invented the Airplane. A professional artist since 1967, Craig has designed coins for the Canadian Mint and served such diverse clientele as Molson Brewery and the Canadian Football League.

In *Attack on Pearl Harbor* Tanaka views events as they played out in Hawai'i on the ill-fated day of December 7, 1941, through the eyes of four individuals: Peter Nottage, an eleven year old who witnessed the bombing raid; Mitsuo Fuchida, the commander of the Japanese fleet; George DeLong, a seaman aboard the USS *Oklahoma;* and Kazuo Sakamaki, a Japanese midget submariner who was taken prisoner. Eldon Younce, reviewing the title in *School Library Journal,* noted that Craig's "paintings are replete with action," and *Booklist* contributor Chris Sherman remarked that the illustrations "contribute much to the readers' understanding of the events."

Craig and Tanaka also collaborated on several books in the "A Day That Changed America" series. *D-Day: They Fought to Free Europe from Hitler's Tyranny,* an account of the invasion of Normandy, presents tales from four U.S. servicemen. Young praised the "colorful, action paintings" in the work. In *The Alamo: Surrounded and Outnumbered, They Chose to Make a Defiant Last Stand* Tanaka examines the final day of the siege that laid the groundwork for the Republic of Texas as well as the political and cultural forces that led to the conflict. "An array of maps, diagrams, and old photos enhances Craig's dramatic, detailed battle paintings," stated John Peters in *Booklist.* Tanaka explores a 1906 catastrophe through the eyes of four survivors in *Earthquake!: On a Peaceful Spring Morning, Disaster Strikes*

San Francisco. Craig's "colorful artwork" for this book drew notice from *School Library Journal* critic Patricia Manning.

Craig shared the James Madison Book Award for Excellence with Busby for *First to Fly,* a biography of Wilbur and Orville Wright. The book describes the fateful events of December 17, 1903, when Wilbur flew aloft for twelve seconds, and follows the Wright brothers' subsequent efforts to design airplanes. A contributor in *Publishers Weekly* cited Craig's "active, in-the-moment paintings imagining the Wrights' lives," while Harriett Fargnoli observed in *School Library Journal* that "the pages are filled with large, sumptuous paintings that add a flavor of realism and an almost nostalgic feel." Craig and Tanaka profile another celebrated pilot in *Amelia Earhart: The Legend of the Lost Aviator.* According to *School Library Journal* reviewer Donna Cardon, Craig's "realistic pictures are carefully researched and visually dramatic."

Craig has also contributed illustrations to the "Outwitting the Enemy: Stories from the Second World War" series written by Stephen Shapiro and Tina Forrester. In *Ultra Hush-Hush: Espionage and Special Missions* the coauthors describe clandestine war efforts, such as the work of the Navajo Code Talkers. Jennifer Baldwin, writing in *Kliatt,* noted that "Craig's dramatic illustrations . . . supplement the text." *Hoodwinked: Deception and Resistance* features stories about a variety of secret missions undertaken by Allied forces. The work offers "plenty of full-colour illustrations of acts of derring-do," as Greg Bak commented in *Resource Links.*

Biographical and Critical Sources

PERIODICALS

Booklist, August, 2001, Chris Sherman, review of *Attack on Pearl Harbor: The True Story of the Day America Entered World War II,* p. 2118; January 1, 2003, Carolyn Phelan, review of *First to Fly: How Wilbur and Orville Wright Invented the Airplane,* p. 874; August, 2003, Ed Sullivan, review of *Ultra Hush-Hush: Espionage and Special Missions,* p. 1975; October 15, 2003, John Peters, review of *The Alamo: Surrounded and Outnumbered, They Chose to Make a Defiant Last Stand,* p. 408; August, 2004, John Peters, review of *D-Day: They Fought to Free Europe from Hitler's Tyranny,* p. 1928; January 1, 2005, Roger Leslie, review of *Hoodwinked: Deception and Resistance,* p. 841; June 1, 2008, Ilene Cooper, review of *Amelia Earhart: The Legend of the Lost Aviator,* p. 94.

Kirkus Reviews, November 15, 2005, review of *The Long White Scarf,* p. 1236.

Kliatt, November, 2003, Jennifer Baldwin, review of *Ultra Hush-Hush,* p. 38.

Publishers Weekly, December 9, 2002, review of *First to Fly,* p. 84.

Resource Links, April, 2003, John Dryden, review of *Ultra Hush-Hush,* p. 28; February, 2005, Greg Bak, review of *Hoodwinked,* p. 49; February, 2006, Zoe Johnstone, review of *The Long White Scarf,* p. 14.

School Library Journal, November, 2001, Eldon Younce, review of *Attack on Pearl Harbor,* p. 187; March, 2003, Harriett Fargnoli, review of *First to Fly,* p. 248; February, 2004, John Sigwald, review of *The Alamo,* p. 170; May, 2004, Lynn Evarts, review of *Ultra Hush-Hush,* p. 174; August, 2004, Eldon Younce, review of *D-Day,* p. 145; October, 2004, Patricia Manning, review of *Earthquake!: On a Peaceful Spring Morning, Disaster Strikes San Francisco,* p. 195; April, 2006, Linda M. Kenton, review of *The Long White Scarf,* p. 119; November, 2008, Donna Cardon, review of *Amelia Earhart,* p. 148.

ONLINE

Annick Press Web site, http://www.annickpress.com/ (September 1, 2009), "David Craig."

David Craig Home Page, http://www.davidcraigart.com (September 1, 2009).*

* * *

CURTIS, Stacy

Personal

Married; wife's name Jann.

Addresses

Home—Oak Lawn, IL. *Agent*—Shannon Associates, 333 W. 57th St., Ste. 810, New York, NY 10019. *E-mail*—stacycurtis@hotmail.com.

Career

Cartoonist, illustrator, and printmaker. Editorial cartoonist for ten years, including work for *Times of Northwest Indiana,* Munster, IN; Mile 44 (printing company), cofounder, with Dave Windisch.

Member

National Cartoonists Society, Association of American Editorial Cartoonists, Society of Children's Book Writers and Illustrators.

Illustrator

Chaz Chapman, *You Know Your Dog Owns You If . . .,* Bowtie Press (Irvine, CA), 2004.

Lori Z. Scott, *Meghan Rose Has Ants in Her Pants,* Standard Publishing (Cincinnati, OH), 2007.

Lori Z. Scott, *Meghan Rose on Stage!,* Standard Publishing (Cincinnati, OH), 2007.

Lori Z. Scott, *Meghan Rose Has a Secret,* Standard Publishing (Cincinnati, OH), 2008.

Lori Z. Scott, *Meghan Rose All Dressed Up,* Standard Publishing (Cincinnati, OH), 2008.

Stephen Krensky, *Snack Attack,* Aladdin (New York, NY), 2008.

Mike Knudson and Steve Wilkinson, *Raymond and Graham Rule the School,* Viking (New York, NY), 2008.

Mike Knudson, *Raymond and Graham: Dancing Dudes,* Viking (New York, NY), 2008.

Sean Covey, *The Seven Habits of Happy Kids,* Simon & Schuster (New York, NY), 2008.

Mike Knudson, *Raymond and Graham: Bases Loaded,* Viking (New York, NY), 2010.

Contributor to periodicals, including *Highlights for Children, Cricket, Dog Fancy,* and *Chicago Tribune.*

Sidelights

Cartoonist, illustrator, and printmaker Stacy Curtis has provided the artwork for numerous children's books, including *Meghan Rose Has Ants in Her Pants* by Lori Z. Scott and *The Seven Habits of Happy Kids* by Sean Covey. "I love designing characters," Curtis remarked in an online interview with Wes Hargis for the *Three Men in a Tub Web log.* "Whether it's a picture book, a magazine cover, a spot illustration, etc., creating new characters is fun. Sometimes I can draw three versions

Stacy Curtis creates the artwork for the elementary-grade chapter book **Raymond and Graham Rule the School,** *by Mike Knudson and Steve Wilkinson.* (Illustration copyright © 2008 by Stacey Curtis. Reproduced by permission of Viking, a division of Penguin Putnam Books for Young Readers.)

of a moose and one of those three sketches hits the nail on the head. Other times, I may have to draw 60 versions of a moose until I get something that works. Either way, it's an enjoyable process."

Curtis illustrated the humorous chapter book *Raymond and Graham Rule the School,* coauthored by Mike Knudson and Steve Wilkinson. The work centers on a pair of lifelong friends who enter fourth grade expecting to be the kingpins of East Millcreek Elementary School. Instead, Raymond and Graham find themselves in the middle of a host of embarrassing situations: Graham accidentally shaves off one of his eyebrows, for instance, and Raymond suffers the aftereffects of devouring an entire jar of prunes. "Done in an exaggerated cartoon style, Curtis's occasional black-and-white illustrations perfectly suit the tone of the text," noted Andrea Tart in *School Library Journal.* In a sequel, *Raymond and Graham: Dancing Dudes,* written by Knudson, the pals learn that their class will perform a square dance for their fellow students on Valentine's Day. When Raymond volunteers for a special job that day, however, he is assigned a most surprising partner. Terrie Dorio, writing in *School Library Journal,* commented that the book is "illustrated with amusing cartoon drawings."

Biographical and Critical Sources

PERIODICALS

Kirkus Reviews, June 15, 2008, review of *Raymond and Graham Rule the School.*

School Library Journal, September, 2008, Andrea Tarr, review of *Raymond and Graham Rule the School,* p. 152; November, 2008, Terrie Dorio, review of *Raymond and Graham: Dancing Dudes,* p. 92

ONLINE

Shannon Associates Web site, http://www.shannon associates.com/ (September 1, 2009), "Stacy Curtis."

Stacy Curtis Home Page, http://www.stacycurtis.com (September 1, 2009).

Stacy Curtis Web log, http://stacycurtis.blogspot.com/ (September 1, 2009).

Three Men in a Tub Web log, http://threemeninatub. blogspot.com/ (October 6, 2008), Wes Hargis, interview with Curtis.*

D

D'ALUISIO, Faith 1957-

Personal
Born 1957; married Peter Menzel (a photojournalist); children: Josh, Jack, Adam, Evan.

Addresses
Office—Material World Books, 199 Kreuzer Ln., Napa, CA 94559. *E-mail*—fda@menzelphoto.com.

Career
Writer. Material World Books, Napa, CA, editor and lead writer. Former television news producer and documentary filmmaker.

Awards, Honors
Awards for documentaries and articles from Headlines Foundation, United Press International, Associated Press, and Radio-Television News Directors Association. (All with Peter Menzel) Books for the Teen Age selection, New York Public Library, 1996, for *Women in the Material World;* James Beard Foundation Award, 1999, for *Man Eating Bugs;* Best Science Portfolio Award, World Press Photo, and Independent Publisher Book Award, Science Category, both 2000, both for *Robo Sapiens;* Book of the Year selection, Harry Chapin World Hunger Media Foundation, 2005, and James Beard Foundation Award, 2006, both for *Hungry Planet.*

Writings

WITH HUSBAND, PETER MENZEL

Women in the Material World, illustrated with photographs, Sierra Club Books (San Francisco, CA), 1996.
Man Eating Bugs: The Art and Science of Eating Insects, illustrated with photographs by Menzel, Ten Speed Press (Berkeley, CA), 1998.

Robo Sapiens: Evolution of a New Species, illustrated with photographs by Menzel, MIT Press (Cambridge, MA), 2000.
Hungry Planet: What the World Eats, illustrated with photographs by Menzel, Ten Speed Press (Berkeley, CA), 2005, revised children's edition, Tricycle Press (Berkeley, CA), 2008.

Sidelights
Faith D'Aluisio, a former television news producer, and her husband, photojournalist Peter Menzel, have collaborated on a number of critically acclaimed nonfiction books, including *Hungry Planet: What the World Eats,* winner of the James Beard Foundation Award. The duo has traveled the globe in search of interesting stories; their works have introduced readers to a restaurant that serves live scorpions, the development of anthropomorphic robots, and the daily activities of a Mongolian family. "The parts of my television career that I enjoyed most were developing the narratives of the people that I was covering and that's what I do full time now, in every nook and cranny on the earth," D'Aluisio remarked in a *Photo.net* online interview with Philip Greenspun.

D'Aluisio and Menzel's first book, *Women in the Material World,* offers portraits of twenty women from such countries as China, Mali, Jordan, Italy, and Haiti. The work, which is illustrated with full-color photographs taken by a host of female photojournalists, includes interviews with these women, who discuss their day-to-day lives and reflect on social, cultural, and political issues in their native lands. In *Booklist* Leon Wagner described *Women in the Material World* as a "great book for a wide range of readers and thinkers."

In *Man Eating Bugs: The Art and Science of Eating Insects* D'Aluisio and Menzel present a global study of entomophagy, the practice of devouring bugs. While entomophagy is common in many parts of the world, including Asia and Africa, many Westerners frown upon it, D'Aluisio notes. As she told Jonathan Dyson in the

London *Independent,* "Here in the US we don't even know what our protein looks like other than that it's on a slab of Styrofoam in the grocer's freezer. We have developed our way out of knowing what we are eating and eating bugs is like one giant, atavistic, step backwards into our dark past." A reviewer in *Whole Earth* called *Man Eating Bugs* "by far the most informative, fun, and mind/stomach-bending book ever on insect eating." The critic added that D'Aluisio and Menzel's narrative "chronicles their journeys with lovely anecdotes of each day's new events."

D'Aluisio and Menzel profile the creation of synthetic beings in *Robo Sapiens: Evolution of a New Species.* The volume includes interviews with scientists who research and design robots, and it examines the different types of machines they construct, such as those with industrial and military applications and others that mimic human skills. Reviewing *Robo Sapiens* in *Publishers Weekly,* a critic deemed the work "an informative—and handsome—view of some current work in robotics, from out-there A[rtificial] I[ntelligence] research to practical (and profitable) surgical technology."

In *Hungry Planet* the husband-and-wife team describes the food consumption of families from more than twenty nations. Each entry opens with a photograph of family members standing with a week's worth of food purchases, along with a list of the items and their prices in both local and US currency. The work also includes narratives about the family members' lifestyles and the food traditions of their native lands. "Interestingly, the diets of the poorest families we have covered are often healthier than those of the richest," D'Aluisio told Jennifer Joe on the *Light Connection* Web site. "The poorer families themselves aren't the healthiest though, because with poverty comes limited access to health care and education. The best of both worlds may be good health care and a low calorie, grain based diet."

Hungry Planet, which was released in two versions—one for adults and another for younger readers—earned strong reviews. Gillian Engberg, writing in *Booklist,* called the book "a fascinating, sobering, and instructive look at daily life around the world," while a *Publishers Weekly* critic described it as a "beautiful, quietly pro-

In Hungry Planet: What the World Eats *Faith D'Aluisio and photographer Peter Menzel treat readers to a feast of knowledge.* (Tricycle Press, 2008. Photograph copyright © 2005 by Peter Menzel.)

vocative volume." In the words of *Geographical* critic Jo Sargent, by examining "how our spending patterns reflect cultural traditions and how globalisation is affecting our diet, *Hungry Planet* offers plenty of food for thought."

Discussing her literary partnership with Menzel, D'Aluisio remarked to Joe: "All of our books are meant to allow the reader the opportunity to compare and contrast cultures that he or she might never experience on his or her own."

Biographical and Critical Sources

PERIODICALS

Booklist, September 15, 1996, Leon Wagner, review of *Women in the Material World,* p. 186; March 15, 2000, review of *Man Eating Bugs: The Art and Science of Eating Insects,* p. 1360; July 1, 2008, Gillian Engberg, review of *Hungry Planet: What the World Eats,* p. 65.

Current Events, February 10, 2006, "Food for Thought: What the World Eats," p. S2.

Geographical, February, 2006, Jo Sargent, review of *Hungry Planet,* p. 90.

Independent (London, England), February 13, 1999, Jonathan Dyson, "Eating Insects," p. 28.

Publishers Weekly, July 3, 2000, review of *Robo Sapiens: Evolution of a New Species,* p. 55; August 22, 2005, review of *Hungry Planet,* p. 47.

School Library Journal, July, 2008, Joyce Adams Burner, review of *Hungry Planet,* p. 111.

Technology Review, September, 2000, Wade Roush, review of *Robo Sapiens,* p. 127.

USA Today, December 15, 2005, Shawn Sell, "Mom, What's for Dinner around the World?," interview with D'Aluisio and Menzel.

Whole Earth, spring, 1999, review of *Man Eating Bugs,* p. 73.

ONLINE

Light Connection Web site, http://www.lightconnection.us/ (November, 2008), Jennifer Joe, interview with D'Aluisio and Menzel.

Peter Menzel and Faith D'Aluisio Home Page, http://www.menzelphoto.com (September 1, 2009).

Photo.net, http://photo.net/ (April, 2007), Philip Greenspun, interview with D'Aluisio and Menzel.*

*   *   *

DEGEN, Bruce 1945-

Personal

Born June 14, 1945, in Brooklyn, NY; married Christine Bostard (a teacher and illustrator); children: Benjamin, Alexander. *Education:* Cooper Union, B.F.A., 1966; Pratt Institute, M.F.A., 1975.

Addresses

Home—CT.

Career

Author and illustrator. Director of artists' lithography studio in Ein Hod, Israel, beginning 1971. Instructor in illustration at School of Visual Arts, New York, NY; has also worked as an opera scenery painter, advertising designer, printmaker, and teacher of life drawing, printmaking, and calligraphy. *Exhibitions:* Works exhibited in New York, NY, at Master Eagle Gallery, Hempstead Municipal Gallery, and at Society of Illustrators' "Original Art" show.

Member

Society of Children's Book Writers and Illustrators.

Awards, Honors

Children's Choice selection, International Reading Association/Children's Book Council, 1982, for *Little Chick's Big Day,* and 1985, for *My Mother Didn't Kiss Me Good-Night;* Garden State Children's Book Award (Easy-to-Read category), New Jersey Library Association, 1983, for *Commander Toad in Space,* 1992, for *The Magic School Bus inside the Human Body,* 1993, for *The Magic School Bus Lost in the Solar System,* 1995, for *The Magic School Bus on the Ocean Floor,* 1998, for *The Magic School Bus inside a Hurricane,* and 1999, for *The Magic School Bus inside a Beehive;* Children's Books of the Year designation, Child Study Association of America, 1985, for *Jamberry,* and 1987, for *The Josefina Story Quilt;* Boston Globe/Horn Book nonfiction honor, 1987, for *The Magic School Bus at the Waterworks;* National Parenting Publications Award, 1994, for *The Magic School Bus in the Time of the Dinosaurs;* Best Books of the Year designation, *Parenting* magazine, 1999, for *The Magic School Bus Explores the Senses;* Oppenheim Toy Portfolio Gold Seal Award, 2000, for *Daddy Is a Doodlebug;* numerous other child-selected awards.

Writings

FOR CHILDREN; SELF-ILLUSTRATED

Aunt Possum and the Pumpkin Man, Harper (New York, NY), 1977.

The Little Witch and the Riddle, Harper (New York, NY), 1980.

Jamberry, Harper (New York, NY), 1983.

Teddy Bear Towers, Harper Collins (New York, NY), 1991.

Sailaway Home, Scholastic (New York, NY), 1996.

Daddy Is a Doodlebug, HarperCollins (New York, NY), 2000.

ILLUSTRATOR

Malcolm Hall, *Forecast,* Coward (New York, NY), 1977.

Stephen Krensky, *A Big Day for Scepters,* Atheneum (New York, NY), 1977.

Malcolm Hall, *Caricatures,* Coward (New York, NY), 1978.

Carol Chapman, *Ig Lives in a Cave,* Dutton (New York, NY), 1979.

Judy Delton, *Brimhall Turns to Magic,* Lothrop (New York, NY), 1979.

Marjorie Weinman Sharmat, *Mr. Jameson and Mr. Phillips,* Harper (New York, NY), 1979.

Claudia Louise Lewis, *Up and Down the River: Boat Poems,* Harper (New York, NY), 1979.

Charlotte Herman, *My Mother Didn't Kiss Me Good-Night,* Dutton (New York, NY), 1980.

Donald J. Sobol, *Encyclopedia Brown's Second Record Book of Weird and Wonderful Facts,* Delacorte (New York, NY), 1981.

Mary DeBall Kwitz, *Little Chick's Big Day,* Harper (New York, NY), 1981.

Clyde Robert Bulla, *Dandelion Hill,* Dutton (New York, NY), 1982.

Joel L. Schwartz, *Upchuck Summer,* Delacorte (New York, NY), 1982.

Malcolm Hall, *Deadlines,* Coward (New York, NY), 1982.

Mary DeBall Kwitz, *Little Chick's Breakfast,* Harper (New York, NY), 1983.

Lyn Littlefield Hoopes, *Daddy's Coming Home!,* Harper (New York, NY), 1984.

Joseph Slate, *Lonely Lula Cat,* Harper (New York, NY), 1985.

Bonnie Pryor, *Grandpa Bear,* Morrow (New York, NY), 1985.

Joel L. Schwartz, *Best Friends Don't Come in Threes,* Dell (New York, NY), 1985.

Eleanor Coerr, *The Josefina Story Quilt,* Harper (New York, NY), 1986.

Diane Stanley, *The Good-Luck Pencil,* Four Winds (New York, NY), 1986.

Bonnie Pryor, *Grandpa Bear's Christmas,* Morrow (New York, NY), 1986.

(With wife, Chris Degen) Aileen Lucia Fisher, *When It Comes to Bugs: Poems,* Harper (New York, NY), 1986.

Larry Weinberg, *The Forgetful Bears Meet Mr. Memory,* Scholastic (New York, NY), 1987.

Larry Weinberg, *The Forgetful Bears Help Santa,* Scholastic (New York, NY), 1988.

Joan Lowery Nixon, *If You Were a Writer,* Four Winds (New York, NY), 1988.

Mike Thaler, *In the Middle of the Puddle,* Harper (New York, NY), 1988.

Jan Wahl, *Tim Kitten and the Red Cupboard,* Simon and Schuster (New York, NY), 1988.

Barbara Brenner and William H. Hooks, *Lion and Lamb,* Bantam (New York, NY), 1989.

Joanna Cole, *Dinosaur Dances,* Putnam (New York, NY), 1990.

Barbara Brenner and William H. Hooks, *Lion and Lamb Step Out,* Bantam (New York, NY), 1990.

Barbara Brenner and William H. Hooks, *Ups and Downs with Lion and Lamb,* Bantam (New York, NY), 1991.

Tony Johnston, *Goblin Walk,* Putnam (New York, NY), 1991.

Mary DeBall Kwitz, *Little Chick's Friend, Duckling,* HarperCollins (New York, NY), 1992.

Jane Yolen, *Mouse's Birthday,* Putnam (New York, NY), 1993.

John Archambault, *A Beautiful Feast for a Big King Cat,* HarperCollins (New York, NY), 1994.

Joan Lowery Nixon, *Will You Give Me a Dream?,* Four Winds (New York, NY), 1994.

Gregory Valiska, *Shirley's Wonderful Baby,* HarperCollins (New York, NY), 2000.

Valiska Gregory, *Shirley's Wonderful Baby,* HarperCollins (New York, NY), 2002.

Stephanie Calmenson, *Jazzmatazz!,* HarperCollins (New York, NY), 2008.

"COMMANDER TOAD" SERIES; ILLUSTRATOR

Jane Yolen, *Commander Toad in Space,* Coward (New York, NY), 1980.

Jane Yolen, *Commander Toad and the Planet of the Grapes,* Coward (New York, NY), 1982.

Jane Yolen, *Commander Toad and the Big Black Hole,* Coward (New York, NY), 1983.

Jane Yolen, *Commander Toad and the Dis-Asteroid,* Coward (New York, NY), 1985.

Jane Yolen, *Commander Toad and the Intergalactic Spy,* Coward (New York, NY), 1986.

Jane Yolen, *Commander Toad and the Space Pirates,* Putnam (New York, NY), 1987.

Jane Yolen, *Commander Toad and the Voyage Home,* Putnam (New York, NY), 1997.

"JESSE BEAR" SERIES; ILLUSTRATOR

Nancy White Carlstrom, *Jesse Bear, What Will You Wear?,* Macmillan (New York, NY), 1986, Aladdin (New York, NY), 2005.

Nancy White Carlstrom, *Better Not Get Wet, Jesse Bear,* Macmillan (New York, NY), 1988.

Nancy White Carlstrom, *It's about Time, Jesse Bear,* Macmillan (New York, NY), 1990.

Nancy White Carlstrom, *How Do You Say It Today, Jesse Bear?,* Macmillan (New York, NY), 1992.

Nancy White Carlstrom, *Jesse Bear's Tra-La Tub,* Aladdin Books (New York, NY), 1994.

Nancy White Carlstrom, *Jesse Bear's Tum-Tum Tickle,* Aladdin Books (New York, NY), 1994.

Nancy White Carlstrom, *Jesse Bear's Yum-Yum Crumble,* Aladdin Books (New York, NY), 1994.

Nancy White Carlstrom, *Jesse Bear's Wiggle-Jiggle Jump-Up,* Aladdin Books (New York, NY), 1994.

Nancy White Carlstrom, *Happy Birthday, Jesse Bear,* Macmillan (New York, NY), 1994.

Nancy White Carlstrom, *Let's Count It Out, Jesse Bear,* Simon & Schuster (New York, NY), 1996.

Nancy White Carlstrom, *Guess Who's Coming, Jesse Bear?,* Simon & Schuster (New York, NY), 1997.

Nancy White Carlstrom, *Bizz Buzz Chug-A-Chug: Jesse Bear's Sounds,* Little Simon (New York, NY), 1997.

Nancy White Carlstrom, *Hooray for Me, Hooray for You, Hooray for Blue: Jesse Bear's Colors,* Little Simon (New York, NY), 1997.

Nancy White Carlstrom, *I Love You, Mama, Any Time of the Year,* Simon & Schuster (New York, NY), 1997.

Nancy White Carlstrom, *I Love You, Papa, in All Kinds of Weather,* Simon & Schuster (New York, NY), 1997.

Nancy White Carlstrom, *What a Scare, Jesse Bear!,* Simon & Schuster (New York, NY), 1999.

Nancy White Carlstrom, *Where Is Christmas, Jesse Bear?,* Simon & Schuster (New York, NY), 2000.

Nancy White Carlstrom, *Climb the Family Tree, Jesse Bear!,* Simon & Schuster (New York, NY), 2004.

"MAGIC SCHOOL BUS" SERIES; ILLUSTRATOR

Joanna Cole, *The Magic School Bus at the Waterworks,* Scholastic (New York, NY), 1986.

Joanna Cole, *The Magic School Bus inside the Earth,* Scholastic (New York, NY), 1987.

Joanna Cole, *The Magic School Bus inside the Human Body,* Scholastic (New York, NY), 1989.

Joanna Cole, *The Magic School Bus Lost in the Solar System,* Scholastic (New York, NY), 1990.

Joanna Cole, *The Magic School Bus on the Ocean Floor,* Scholastic (New York, NY), 1992.

Joanna Cole, *The Magic School Bus in the Time of the Dinosaurs,* Scholastic (New York, NY), 1994.

Joanna Cole, *The Magic School Bus inside a Hurricane,* Scholastic (New York, NY), 1995.

Joanna Cole, *The Magic School Bus inside a Beehive,* Scholastic (New York, NY), 1996.

Joanna Cole, *The Magic School Bus and the Electric Field Trip,* Scholastic (New York, NY), 1997.

Joanna Cole, *The Magic School Bus Explores the Senses,* Scholastic (New York, NY), 1999.

Joanna Cole, *The Magic School Bus and the Science Fair Expedition,* Scholastic (New York, NY), 2006.

"MS. FRIZZLE'S ADVENTURES" SERIES; ILLUSTRATOR

Joanna Cole, *Ms. Frizzle's Adventures: Ancient Egypt,* Scholastic (New York, NY), 2001.

Joanna Cole, *Ms. Frizzle's Adventures: Medieval Castle,* Scholastic (New York, NY), 2003.

Joanna Cole, *Ms. Frizzle's Adventures: Imperial China,* Scholastic (New York, NY), 2005.

Adaptations

Jamberry was adapted as a cassette by Live Oak Media (Pine Plains, NY), 1986. Degen's illustrations for Joanna Cole's "Magic School Bus" series served as the basis for the PBS-TV animated series of the same title.

Sidelights

Award-winning illustrator Bruce Degen is best known for his work for the "Commander Toad" series by Jane Yolen, Joanna Cole's "Magic School Bus" books, and Nancy White Carlstrom's "Jesse Bear" titles. In addition to such collaborative work, Degen has also illustrated several original stories, including *Jamberry, Sailaway Home,* and *Daddy Is a Doodlebug.* "The nice thing about books is that they go out into the world," he stated in an interview on the *Scholastic* Web site. "When a kid, parent, or teacher tells you how much he or she likes your book, you realize that you've given something that has become part of somone else's life."

Degen first discovered his talent as a young child, encouraged by his elementary school teacher to pursue his interest in drawing, which eventually led him to two degrees in the fine arts. After graduating from Cooper Union with a bachelor's degree, he worked as a director of an artists' lithography studio in Ein Hod, Israel. A number of other jobs followed, including work as a teacher. Two years after receiving his master's degree from the Pratt Institute, Degen published his first book for children.

Although not formally trained as an illustrator, Degen has had a fondness for books since he was a child growing up in New York City. "I have always loved books," he once told *SATA.* "As a child I would love to go to the library. If it was a nice day I wouldn't wait until I got home to read my books. I had to stop in the little park and begin my books under a tree." So, as he also once related, Degen was irresistibly drawn to children's book illustration. "After doing many different things in the field of art, I decided to go back to the root of what made drawing fun for me as a child—children's books."

Degen prefers to illustrate with line drawings and watercolors. His trademark spreads, filled with details and sight gags that supplement the text, showcase the artist's whimsical sense of humor and love of childhood stories. His style is considered especially well suited to Cole's "Magic School Bus" books, which aims to teach children about scientific facts with the help of humor and fantasy. "Collaborating with Joanna Cole on the 'Magic School Bus' series, Degen epitomized visual silliness," according to Suzy Schmidt in *Children's Books and Their Creators.* Schmidt added: "The crowded pages are absorbing as they display action, text, bubble-dialogue, and school reports. The result is an endlessly entertaining set of books with a wide and loyal readership." Degen's illustrations for the series have been roundly praised by reviewers. His drawings "fill the pages with plenty of action and intriguing details," said Carolyn Phelan in a *Booklist* review of *The Magic School Bus inside a Beehive.* Stephanie Zvirin, writing in another *Booklist* review, noted that Degen's illustrations help in "clarifying the concepts and adding comic relief" to Cole's text.

Each volume in the "Magic School Bus" series features a topic in science, from a study of the ocean floor to dinosaurs to electricity. Such topics are presented in a light and breezy manner, supposedly written by a grade-school class whose teacher, Ms. Frizzle, wears very bizarre and also thematically relevant clothing. For ex-

Cover of Joanna Cole's **The Magic School Bus: On the Ocean Floor,** *a book in the popular series that features Bruce Degen's cartoon art.* (Illustration copyright © 1992 by Bruce Degen. Reproduced by permission of Scholastic, Inc.)

ample, she might sport a dress with a frog print on it that indicates an upcoming topic in the series. Ms. Frizzle, or "The Friz" as her students lovingly refer to her, is also a fan of unorthodox teaching methods. Her hands-on approach involves continual field trips in the school bus to bore through the Earth's surface or perhaps travel through the circulatory system, depending upon the topic of the current book.

The Degen and Cole collaborative effort on the "Magic School Bus" books is thorough and time consuming, as the illustrator and author explained on the Scholastic Web site. First, Cole researches the topic at hand, reading books, visiting museums, and talking with experts in the field. She then works this information into a "dummy," or a rough outline of each page of the story, complete with sketch ideas for Degen and with speech bubbles containing possible jokes for the text. When this dummy is reviewed for accuracy, it is handed to Degen. "I take out the dummy Joanna has prepared, I

look at all the research books, I look at all the notes, and then I have a cup of coffee," Degen quipped on the Scholastic Web site. He then prepares sketch designs that will let the author know how every page will look, and then the two meet to hammer out the details. As reported on the Scholastic Web site, "Degen's favorite part of illustrating the 'Magic School Bus' is making bold fashion statements with Ms. Frizzle's weird outfits."

According to a contributor for the *Continuum Encyclopedia of Children's Literature,* Degen's "artistic interpretations bring alive often challenging scientific concepts" in the "Magic School Bus" series. The same writer also felt that scientific information presented in each book "is balanced through [Degen's] often humorous illustrations." This blend of text and humorous illustration presents "a remarkable achievement for a science series," according to Schmidt. With ten titles in the original series, scores of books in spin-off series,

and numerous episodes of the television adaptation aired, the series continues to garner critical acclaim. Reviewing *The Magic School Bus Explores the Senses,* Christine A. Moesch noted in *School Library Journal* that this volume serves as "another fun, fact-filled adventure in the series," and that Degen's artwork is "just as exciting and exacting as usual." Similarly, *Booklist* critic Lauren Peterson noted of this same title that the "innovative series continues to educate youngsters in fun and creative ways." In *The Magic School Bus and the Science Fair Expedition,* Ms. Frizzle travels through time with her students, who meet such luminaries as Galileo and Marie Curie. Here Degen's "instructive, funny, appealing illustrations" drew praise from *Booklist* reviewer Gillian Engberg.

In 2001, Degen and Cole decided to expand on their science series, and have the redoubtable Ms. Fizzle study world cultures and history. The result is the "Ms. Frizzle's Adventures" series, in which the school teacher

Degen teams up with writer Stephanie Calmenson for the high-energy picture book Jazzmatazz! (Illustration copyright © 2008 by Bruce Degen. Used by permission of HarperCollins Children's Books, a division of HarperCollins Publishers.)

discovers her own adventures while on vacation. Degen explained in an interview for *Reading Rockets Online* that it was decided also to change the size of the books as well as the style of painting. "All the original science books are in watercolor with a pen-and-ink line. Watercolor is a transparent, washy color. For the social studies series . . . I'm using something called gouache. Gouache is like poster paint that you had in elementary school. . . . It's opaque. It's thick. It's very bright, flat color, and so it has a whole different look."

In *Ms. Frizzle's Adventures: Ancient Egypt,* the teacher is off to Cairo, but, while parachuting from the plane she enters a time warp and arrives in ancient Egypt instead. Here, she and her companions make their way through pyramids and other ancient buildings, introducing readers to all manner of historical fact. Betsy Barnett, writing in *School Library Journal,* had high praise for the book, noting that Ms. Frizzle "has entered the realm of social studies with the same flair and excitement she took to science." Barnett further commented that "Degen's cartoon artwork gives readers even more helpful information," making the new series "a stunning success."

The timeline moves forward several centuries in *Ms. Frizzle's Adventures: Medieval Castle.* This time the teacher takes one of her students, Arnold, with her as she travels to the Middle Ages, where they enjoy life in a British castle until it comes under siege. Degen's illustrations "are brightly colored and the graphic design is reminiscent of comic books," observed Phelan in *Booklist,* and Anne Chapman Callaghan similarly noted in *School Library Journal* that the artist's "cartoon illustrations . . . are awash with action and scenery."

In *Ms. Frizzle's Adventures: Imperial China,* the intrepid educator leads a trio of students from a Chinatown celebration to an eleventh-century farming village. They decide to help a group of impoverished farmers on their journey to the Imperial Palace, where they hold a meeting with the emperor. According to Jennifer Mattson in *Booklist,* readers will "pore over Degen's delightfully cluttered compositions and lovely chinoiserie embellishments," and Margaret A. Chang, writing in *Horn Book,* remarked that the artist "opens himself to the influence of Chinese art, portraying ancient China with lighthearted but generally accurate illustrations." Comparing Degen's work in the "Ms. Frizzle's Adventures" books to his earlier efforts, *School Library Journal* critic Suzanne Myers Harold stated that the "cartoon illustrations . . . continue the frenetic, zany humor of the 'Magic School Bus' series."

Degen has also collaborated with other authors on series books with continuing characters, including the "Little Chick" stories by Mary DeBall Kwitz, the "Grandpa Bear" books by Bonnie Pryor, the "Lion and Lamb" books by Barbara Brenner and William H. Hooks, the "Forgetful Bears" by Larry Weinberg, the "Commander Toad" books by Jane Yolen, and the "Jesse Bear" series by Nancy White Carlstrom. Of these, the "Commander Toad" and "Jesse Bear" books have received the most attention. Yolen's books feature a very human-like toad who is commander of a space ship exploring the outer reaches of the galaxy. His crew drinks green tea and wolfs down "hop-corn" to keep healthy. Carlstrom's books, full of exuberant, creative rhymes, proved a perfect vehicle for some of Degen's best work. Schmidt has noted that Degen's strength is in his ability to collaborate well with authors: "[Degen's] work has contributed most to children's literature not by drawing attention to itself but by providing strong accompaniment to the texts."

In a review of *Jesse Bear, What Will You Wear?,* *School Library Journal* contributor Liza Bliss asserted that text and illustrations "interplay beautifully, each enhancing the other's brightness." Degen displays his usual sense of humor in the other "Jesse Bear" books as well. In *Better Not Get Wet, Jesse Bear,* for example, a portrait on the wall reacts in astonishment to Jesse Bear's watery mess. In *Guess Who's Coming, Jesse Bear?,* the bear is excited that someone is coming to dinner, until he finds out that the "someone" is his older and bossy cousin, Sara. Jesse changes his opinion during the visit, however, and does not want Sara to go home. Reviewing *Guess Who's Coming, Jesse Bear?,* Rachel Fox commented in *School Library Journal* that "Degen's bright . . . artwork [is] sure to entertain youngsters." A reunion featuring hayrides, boating, and a picnic is the focus of *Climb the Family Tree, Jesse Bear!* According to Wendy Woodfill in *School Library Journal,* here Degen's "watercolor-and-ink illustrations are bright, cheery, and uncluttered." Phelan also complimented the artwork, noting that the pictures, "brightened with colorful washes, reflect the genial tone of the words."

Halloween is featured in *What a Scare, Jesse Bear!,* in which Degen's artwork once again received praise. Anne Parker, writing in *School Library Journal,* remarked that his "brightly colored" illustrations are packed with "happy faces, showing that Halloween is a time for fun, not fright." In *Booklist* Lauren Peterson also commended Degen's "animated watercolor illustrations" for this "fun-filled episode in a delightful series." Another holiday is featured in *Where Is Christmas, Jesse Bear? New York Times Book Review* critic Margaret Moorman, writing about *Where Is Christmas, Jesse Bear?,* characterized the books in the series as "happy, gentle, well-rounded books" that are "perfect for their chosen audience." Moorman additionally described the series as presenting a "sunny world of daily rituals and seasonal celebrations enjoyed by a bear family of unwavering cub-centered love."

Degen tends to illustrate animal characters more frequently than humans, and some of his finest work, including his own book *Jamberry* as well as the "Jesse Bear" books, have bears as featured characters. *Jamberry* finds a boy and a bear happily lounging in a train-car full of berries and making up nonsense rhymes that

go along with the names of each different berry. Janie and Richard Jarvis, reviewing the title in the *Los Angeles Times Book Review,* called it a "joyous rhyming romp."

"People often ask me why I use animals," Degen once told *SATA.* "I think it is because they allow an easy fantasy identification, and the change of scale is cozy and attractive to children." Degen also does well creating pictures to accompany verse stories such as Yolen's *Mouse's Birthday.* As a *Publishers Weekly* reviewer wrote, "Degen's art is the ideal match for Yolen's jaunty rhyme." Other animals receive the Degen treatment, such as hippopotamuses in Valiska Gregory's *Shirley's Wonderful Baby.* When her mother brings home a new baby brother, big sister Shirley feels resentment toward the infant until a new baby-sitter helps change the young girl's perspective. Kristin de Lacoste, writing in *School Library Journal,* described the book as "beautifully illustrated in primary colors," and predicted that "the pictures of this hippopotamus family will delight readers." A critic for *Kirkus Reviews* dubbed the same artwork "eye-stopping." In Stephanie Calmenson's *Jazzmatazz!,* a piano-playing mouse inspires a houseful of animals to create their own music, and their infectious spirit soon spreads to the entire neighborhood. As Krista Hutley wrote in *Booklist,* Degen's illustrations "uniformly cheerful and effectively convey the concept of swelling, rhythmic sound in visual terms," and a critic in *Kirkus Reviews* remarked of *Jazzmatazz!* that each character has its "own onomatopoeic contribution to the jam that is mirrored in the illustrations."

Along with *Jamberry,* Degen has illustrated several other original stories. *Sailaway Home* is a simple rhyming story in which a young pig imagines going on a number of adventures while remaining safely near home. Calling the illustrations and rhymes "sweetly cheerful," *School Library Journal* commentator Lisa Dennis observed that in any other writer/illustrator's hands, the result would be "an unappealingly saccharine picture book, but in Degen's accomplished hands, these ingredients are melded into a delightful story." His self-illustrated title, *Daddy Is a Doodlebug,* is a "sweet, rhyming story," according to *Booklist* critic Marta Segal. Degen spotlights a little bug and its father spending a quiet day in each other's company. They enjoy drawing, which makes them "doodlebugs," but they also like sweets, which makes them "apple strudel bugs." Degen builds on this nonsense rhyme with a swing ride and car ride, playing on words to provide "plenty . . . to amuse older (adult) readers, too," as Segal further explained. Lisa Dennis, writing in *School Library Journal,* called the same work a "charming picture book full of clever wordplay and distinctive illustrations," adding that it serves as an "ode to the loving connection between parent and child." According to a contributor for *Publishers Weekly,* in *Daddy Is a Doodlebug* "Degen's noodle has come up with some fittingly quirky visuals for this splendoodle rhymoodle."

Even after illustrating scores of books for children, Degen continues to enjoy his career. "I believe that good children's book art will delight the child, and this is the work of lasting interest," he once remarked. "Being able to read to children, I can see by the children's candid reactions which elements truly communicate. Since I began, this work has involved me totally, and I hope I will be doing it as long as I can hold a pencil." In his *Reading Rockets Online* interview, Degen expanded on the benefits of his chosen career of book illustration: "You can do a painting, and it might end up being on somebody's wall, but if you do a book, it goes out to the world. It goes out in multiple copies; it's printed. It's in libraries. It's in homes. Somebody can have it here and there and everywhere. . . . There's nothing like that. There's nothing like the fact that you've actually become part of somebody's family life."

Biographical and Critical Sources

BOOKS

Continuum Encyclopedia of Children's Literature, Continuum Publishers (New York, NY), 2001.
Degen, Bruce, *Daddy Is a Doodlebug,* HarperCollins (New York, NY), 2000.
Children's Books and Their Creators, Houghton Mifflin (New York, NY), 1995.

PERIODICALS

Booklist, June 1-15, 1995, Stephanie Zvirin, review of *The Magic School Bus inside a Hurricane,* p. 776; September 1, 1996, Carolyn Phelan, review of *The Magic School Bus inside a Beehive,* p. 121; February 15, 1998, Lauren Peterson, review of *Guess Who's Coming, Jesse Bear?,* p. 1018; February 15, 1999, Lauren Peterson, review of *The Magic School Bus Explores the Senses,* p. 1061; September 1, 1999, Lauren Peterson, review of *What a Scare, Jesse Bear,* p. 147; June 1, 2000, Marta Segal, review of *Daddy Is a Doodlebug,* p. 1906; July, 2003, Carolyn Phelan, review of *Ms. Frizzle's Adventures: Medieval Castle,* p. 1881; August, 2004, Carolyn Phelan, review of *Climb the Family Tree, Jesse Bear!,* p. 1941; June 1, 2005, Jennifer Mattson, review of *Ms. Frizzle's Adventures: Imperial China,* p. 1815; September 15, 2006, Gillian Engberg, review of *The Magic School Bus and the Science Fair Expedition,* p. 63; January 1, 2008, Krista Hutley, review of *Jazzmatazz!,* p. 94.
Horn Book, January-February, 1998, Elizabeth S. Watson, review of *The Magic School Bus and the Electric Field Trip,* p. 90; July-August, 1999, Kathleen T. Horning, review of *The Magic School Bus Explores the Senses,* p. 480; November-December, 2001, Roger Sutton, review of *Ms. Frizzle's Adventures: Ancient Egypt,* pp. 769-770; September-October, 2005, Margaret A. Chang, review of *Ms. Frizzle's Adventures: Imperial China,* p. 600; November-December, 2006, Betty Carter, review of *The Magic School Bus and the Science Fair Expedition,* p. 732.

Kirkus Reviews, August 15, 2002, review of *Shirley's Wonderful Baby,* p. 1224; July 1, 2003, review of *Ms. Frizzle's Adventures: Medieval Castle,* p. 907; June 15, 2005, review of *Ms. Frizzle's Adventures: Imperial China,* p. 679; December 1, 2007, review of *Jazzmatazz!*

Los Angeles Times Book Review, April 11, 1999, Janie and Richard Jarvis, review of *Jamberry,* p. 6.

New York Times Book Review, December 17, 2000, Margaret Moorman, review of *Where Is Christmas, Jesse Bear?,* p. 30.

Publishers Weekly, March 8, 1993, review of *Mouse's Birthday,* p. 76; February 14, 2000, review of *Happy Birthday, Jesse Bear!,* p. 203; April 17, 2000, review of *Daddy Is a Doodlebug,* p. 78; November 5, 2001, review of *Ms. Frizzle's Adventures: Ancient Egypt,* p. 71; May 13, 2002, review of *Daddy Is a Doodlebug,* p. 72.

School Library Journal, April, 1986, Liza Bliss, review of *Jesse Bear, What Will You Wear?,* pp. 68-69; March, 1996, Lisa Dennis, review of *Sailaway Home,* p. 167; April, 1998, Rachel Fox, review of *Guess Who's Coming, Jesse Bear?,* p. 97; October, 1999, Anne Parker, review of *What a Scare, Jesse Bear,* p. 110; February, 1999, Christine A. Moesch, review of *The Magic School Bus Explores the Senses,* p. 96; April, 2000, Lisa Dennis, review of *Daddy Is a Doodlebug,* p. 97; September, 2001, Betsy Barnett, review of *Ms. Frizzle's Adventures: Ancient Egypt,* p. 212; November, 2002, Kristin de Lacoste, review of *Shirley's Wonderful Baby,* p. 124; July, 2003, Anne Chapman Callaghan, review of *Ms. Frizzle's Adventures: Medieval Castle,* p. 112; August, 2004, Wendy Woodfill, review of *Climb the Family Tree, Jesse Bear!,* p. 84; August, 2005, Suzanne Myers Harold, review of *Ms. Frizzle's Adventures: Imperial China,* p. 112; March, 2008, Kara Schaff Dean, review of *Jazzmatazz!,* p. 155.

ONLINE

Reading Rockets Online, http://www.readingrockets.org/ (September 1, 2009), video interview with Degen.

Scholastic Web Site, http://www.scholastic.com/ (September 1, 2009), "The Magic School Bus."*

*   *   *

de la PEÑA, Matt

Personal

Born in CA. *Education:* University of the Pacific, B.A.; San Diego State University, M.F.A. *Hobbies and other interests:* Basketball, reading, sad music, guitar.

Addresses

Home—Brooklyn, NY. *E-mail*—delapena_matt@yahoo.com.

Career

Writer. Also teaches at New York University and Gotham Writers' Workshop.

Matt de la Peña (Reproduced by permission.)

Awards, Honors

Best Books for Young Adults selection, American Library Association (ALA), and Quick Picks for Reluctant Young Adult Readers selection, ALA, both 2006, both for *Ball Don't Lie;* Top Ten Best Books for Young Adults selection, ALA, and Notable Books for a Global Society selection, International Reading Association, both 2009, both for *Mexican WhiteBoy.*

Writings

NOVELS

Ball Don't Lie (also see below), Delacorte Press (New York, NY), 2005.

Mexican WhiteBoy, Delacorte Press (New York, NY), 2008.

We Were Here, Delacorte Press (New York, NY), 2009.

OTHER

(With Brin Hill) *Ball Don't Lie* (screenplay; based on the author's novel), Slowhand Cinema 2008.

Contributor to *Does This Book Make Me Look Fat?,* edited by Marissa Walsh, Clarion (New York, NY),

2008. Also contributor to periodicals, including *Pacific Review, Vincent Brothers Review, Chiricú, Two Girl's Review, George Mason Review,* and *Allegheny Literary Review.*

Sidelights

Matt de la Peña, a former college basketball player, is the author of the award-winning *Ball Don't Lie,* a young-adult novel about a seventeen year old with a troubling background who finds solace on the basketball court. Discussing the significant role basketball has played in his writing career, de la Peña remarked on the Random House Web site: "No matter how far I move away from the game, into this new life as an author, no matter what strange direction my literary interests lead me in next, or where I go, or who I meet, I will always carry the game of basketball in my chest. This game was my best friend growing up. It was my confidante."

De la Peña was born and raised on the California coast. As a teen, the half-white, half-Mexican future author excelled at basketball, but he was also a reluctant reader who needed a push to boost his academic performance.

Cover of Matt de la Peña's young-adult novel Ball Don't Lie, *featuring cover art by Alex Williamson.* (Illustration copyright © 2005 by Alex Williamson. Used by permission of Dell Publishing, a division of Random House, Inc.)

"My mom told me to get a 3.2 GPA and she'd never bother me about homework," he told *Albuquerque Journal* contributor David Steinberg. "That's what I got and she allowed me to play high school basketball." De la Peña eventually earned an athletic scholarship to the University of the Pacific, where he played point guard for a squad that reached the NCAA tournament during his senior year.

Without his knowledge, several of de la Peña's professors submitted a graduate school application for him to San Diego State, and he eventually earned a master of fine arts degree in creative writing there. He published a number of short stories and poems before turning to novels; the idea for *Ball Don't Lie* came to him while driving in Los Angeles. In an online interview on the Gotham Writers' Workshop Web site, de la Peña recalled, "I pulled up to a light, . . . and there was this kid sitting at a bus stop with his hood up, headphones on. No one looked at him because his life wasn't interesting to them. But I wanted everyone to look at him for three hundred pages."

Ball Don't Lie concerns Travis "Sticky" Reichard, a teenager who has been shuttled from one foster home to another after his mother, a prostitute, committed suicide. Although he is skinny and demonstrates obsessive-compulsive behaviors, Sticky possesses incredible athletic gifts, and the white hoopster is adopted by his black peers at Lincoln Rec, a Los Angeles gym that is a proving ground for serious players. Sticky's dreams of obtaining a college scholarship and maintaining his relationship with a new girlfriend are threatened, however, by a past that continues to haunt him. "Jumping back and forth in time, this first novel has a unique narrative voice," Jack Forman commented in *School Library Journal,* and a *Kirkus Reviews* contributor observed that *Ball Don't Lie* has a "staccato effect that mimics a fast-paced hoops game." According to a critic in *Publishers Weekly,* readers "who don't mind mixing their sports stories with some true grit may find themselves hypnotized by Sticky's grim saga."

In *Mexican WhiteBoy,* de la Peña's second novel, a biracial teen struggles with issues of race and self-identity. The son of a Mexican father and a Caucasian mother, Danny Lopez feels uncomfortable around the primarily white classmates at his prestigious San Diego prep school. He decides to spend the summer with his estranged father's family in the border town of National City, and there Danny learns to take control of his life through his friendship with Uno, a tough-talking barrio kid who helps Danny hone his skill on the baseball diamond. In the words of *Horn Book* critic Jane Lopez-Santillana, *Mexican WhiteBoy,* "is unique in its gritty realism and honest portrayal of the complexities of life for inner-city teens." Lynn Rutan, writing in *Booklist,* remarked of the book that Danny's journey "to find his place will speak strongly to all teens but especially to those of mixed race."

"I honestly never thought I'd become a writer," de la Peña told SATA. "In third grade I went to school in the border town of National City in San Diego. My teacher wanted to hold me back a year claiming I couldn't read. I was an incredibly average student all the way through high school. It wasn't until college that I fell for books—it was Alice Walker's *The Color Purple* that first opened my eyes. By the end of college I decided to try and be a writer. I spent a good seven years with absolutely nothing. I moved to Los Angeles and made my way around the city by bus. I couldn't afford to take a girl on a date. But I wrote every single day. And fortunately a publisher bought my first book, *Ball Don't Lie,* and I moved to New York, where I now support myself as a novelist. But I still don't consider myself a 'smart' writer. I just work really hard. Like my dad and uncles, I show up everyday with my lunch pail ready to go. The only difference is, instead of concrete or sod I work with words.

"I'm incredibly humbled by the fact that some people read my books. And sometimes really like them. It makes my day when I get an e-mail or a letter from a reader. I read it in my rundown Brooklyn apartment with a giant smile on my face."

Biographical and Critical Sources

PERIODICALS

Albuquerque Journal, September 14, 2008, David Steinberg, "Basketball Fanatic Didn't Discover Passion for Books and Writing until College."

Booklist, November 15, 2005, Gillian Engberg, review of *Ball Don't Lie,* p. 55; August 1, 2008, Lynn Rutan, review of *Mexican WhiteBoy,* p. 60.

Horn Book, September-October, 2008, Jane Lopez-Santillana, review of *Mexican WhiteBoy,* p. 581.

Journal of Adolescent and Adult Literacy, March, 2009, Jessica Early, review of *Mexican WhiteBoy,* p. 540.

Kirkus Reviews, September 1, 2005, review of *Ball Don't Lie,* p. 971; July 15, 2008, review of *Mexican White-Boy.*

Kliatt, September, 2005, Claire Rosser, review of *Ball Don't Lie,* p. 7; July, 2008, Paula Rohrlick, review of *Mexican WhiteBoy,* p. 11.

Publishers Weekly, November 7, 2005, review of *Ball Don't Lie,* p. 76.

School Library Journal, November, 2005, Jack Forman, review of *Ball Don't Lie,* p. 132; September, 2008, Madeline Walton-Hadlock, review of *Mexican White-Boy,* p. 177.

ONLINE

Gotham Writers' Workshop Web site, http://www.writing classes.com/ (September 1, 2009), interview with de la Peña.

Matt de la Peña Home Page, http://www.mattdelapena. com (September 1, 2009).

Random House Web site, http://www.randomhouse.com/ (September 1, 2009), "Matt de la Peña.

* * *

DOWELL, Frances O'Roark 1964-

Personal

Born May 30, 1964, in Berlin, Germany; daughter of Del (a U.S. Army lawyer) and Jane (a homemaker) O'Roark; married Clifton Dowell (managing editor of a political newsletter); children: Jack, Will. *Education:* Wake Forest University, B.A.; University of Massachusetts, M.F.A.

Addresses

Home—Durham, NC. *E-mail*—fdowell@mindspring. com.

Career

Writer. Former editor and copublisher of *Dream/Girl* (arts magazine for girls). Worked variously as a paralegal, motel housekeeper, college English instructor, copywriter, and arts administrator.

Awards, Honors

Edgar Allan Poe Award for Best Juvenile Novel, Mystery Writers of America, 2001, and William Allen White Award, 2003, both for *Dovey Coe;* International Reading Association/Children's Book Council Children's Choice selection, for *Where I'd Like to Be;* Notable Children's Book selection, American Library Association, 2006, and Notable Book selection, National Council of Teachers of English, both 2005, both for *Chicken Boy; Boston Globe/Horn Book* Honor Book designation, 2008, and Christopher Award, 2009, both for *Shooting the Moon.*

Writings

YOUNG-ADULT FICTION

Dovey Coe, Atheneum (New York, NY), 2000.
Where I'd Like to Be, Atheneum (New York, NY), 2003.
The Secret Language of Girls, Atheneum (New York, NY), 2004.
Chicken Boy, Atheneum (New York, NY), 2005.
Shooting the Moon, Atheneum (New York, NY), 2008.
The Kind of Friends We Used to Be, Atheneum (New York, NY), 2009.
Falling In, Atheneum (New York, NY), 2010.

YOUNG-ADULT NOVELS; "FROM THE HIGHLY SCIENTIFIC NOTEBOOKS OF PHINEAS L. MacGUIRE" SERIES

Phineas L. MacGuire . . . Erupts!: The First Experiment, Atheneum (New York, NY), 2006.

Frances O'Roark Dowell (Reproduced by permission.)

Phineas L. MacGuire . . . Gets Slimed!, Atheneum (New York, NY), 2007.
Phineas L. MacGuire . . . Blasts Off!, Atheneum (New York, NY), 2007.

OTHER

Contributor of poetry to periodicals, including *Poetry East, Shenandoah,* and *New Delta Review.*

Sidelights

Frances O'Roark Dowell's books for young-adult readers explore issues of growing up, family and friend relationships, and overcoming adversity. Reviewing her novels, which include *Dovey Coe, The Secret Language of Girls,* and *Shooting the Moon,* critics have praised Dowell's well-developed and believable protagonists. In addition to her works for young adults, she has also written the popular "From the Highly Scientific Notebooks of Phineas L. MacGuire" series of stories aimed at middle-grade readers.

Although Dowell began writing poetry as a child, majored in English in college, and earned a master's degree in creative writing, she did not seriously pursue a career as an author until she was almost thirty years old. She wrote a draft of what would become her first novel, *Dovey Coe,* but put it aside, spending the next several years working at a variety of jobs, including motel housekeeper and legal secretary. After a friend put Dowell in touch with a children's-book editor, she began revising her manuscript for *Dovey Coe,* and the book was published in 2000.

Praised by critics, *Dovey Coe* features a spunky young heroine who is outspoken, assertive, and protective of her family. Dovey does not like Parnell, her older sister's suitor, particularly because he disrespects her family, and she is not afraid to say so. When Parnell takes Dovey's dog and threatens to kill it, the girl attempts to rescue her pet by attacking Parnell but is knocked unconscious. When she wakes up, both her dog and Parnell are dead, and Dovey must face a courtroom battle to prove her innocence. Betsy Fraser noted in *School Library Journal* that *Dovey Coe* "maintains a very fast pace" and features "an original character," adding that the story's "background and characters are carefully developed and appealing." In *Booklist* Frances Bradburn added that "Dowell has created a memorable character in Dovey, quick-witted and honest to a fault."

In an online interview for the *DreamGirl* Web site, Dowell discussed the inspiration behind *Dovey Coe.* "The reasons I wanted to set a book in the past is because I'm very interested in folklore and folkways—the ways people lived before we had so many time-saving devices and big grocery stores and all of our modern conveniences. I had been reading a lot of books about life in the Blue Ridge Mountains in earlier times, and I thought it would be fun to write a book using some of the knowledge I'd picked up."

Where I'd Like to Be is set in a home where orphaned children await foster homes. The protagonist, Maddie, makes the best of her bad situation and has a strong sense of herself. When a new girl, Murphy, arrives at the home, Maddie is captivated by the girl's story as well as by her imaginative personality. Dowell's cast of diverse young characters creates a family among themselves as they dream of becoming part of a permanent family. In *Booklist,* Linda Perkins wrote that in *Where I'd Like to Be* Maddie's "voice and views are consistently those of a perceptive eleven-year-old," and the novel provides "ample discussion possibilities." The story's characters were particularly impressive to Faith Brautigam, who commented in *School Library Journal* that "the foster children's backgrounds are believable, diverse, and engaging." In *Kirkus Reviews* a critic praised Dowell's characterizations, concluding that the novel's "talky pie-in-the-sky resolution mars the tightness of the narrative that precedes it, but taken as a whole, this is a lovely, quietly bittersweet tale of friendship and family." A *Publishers Weekly* reviewer deemed *Where I'd Like to Be* "a celebration of friendship and the powers of the imagination."

The way teenage girls grow apart from their friends is the subject of *The Secret Language of Girls.* Kate and Marylin have been friends since childhood, but as they

enter the sixth grade, their paths diverge. While Marylin gains access to the popular crowd, becomes a cheerleader, and is increasingly preoccupied by make-up and boys, Kate worries about her father's health and shies away from being noticed by her peers. In the end, the two girls find that their different lifestyles have not forced them as far apart as they thought. Martha P. Parravano, reviewing *The Secret Language of Girls* for *Horn Book,* observed that "Dowell's development of this familiar situation is refreshingly nonjudgmental" and the thoughtful tone of the novel is balanced by "supersonic pacing—a perspective that swings freely between Kate and Marylin, and vivid characterization." A *Publishers Weekly* reviewer described the book as a "perceptive slice-of-life novel" that will leave readers feeling "encouraged by the author's honest and sympathetic approach." B. Allison Gray maintained in *School Library Journal* that *The Secret Language of Girls* will ring true to young readers because of "excellent characterization, an accurate portrayal of the painful and often cruel machinations of preteens, and evocative dialogue."

Kate and Marylin return in *The Kind of Friends We Used to Be,* a sequel to *The Secret Language of Girls.* Now in seventh grade, the girls continue to pursue different interests—Marylin earns a spot on the cheerlead-

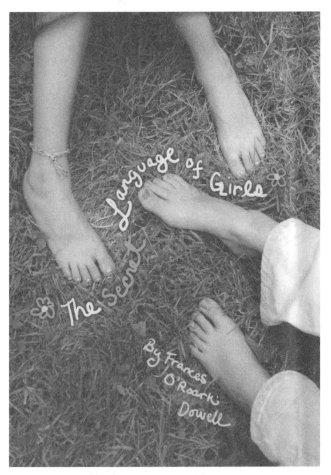

Cover of Dowell's young-adult novel The Secret Language of Girls, *featuring cover art by Michael Frost.* (Atheneum Books for Young Readers, 2004. Reproduced by permission.)

ing team and runs for student council while Kate is drawn to music and song writing—as they redefine their relationship. Told in the third-person from the perspective of both girls, *The Kind of Friends We Used to Be* earned solid reviews. Abby Nolan, writing in *Booklist,* praised Dowell's "light but observant style" in the novel and a *Publishers Weekly* critic noted that the story is "kept afloat by Dowell's smart insights into the way the middle school mind works." In the words of a *Kirkus Reviews* critic, "Dowell's characteristically sensitive exploration of the inner lives of these two girls will resonate long and loud."

Dowell features a male protagonist in *Chicken Boy,* "a story of friendship and family conflict that is both heart-wrenching and heartwarming," according to a reviewer in *Publishers Weekly.* The novel centers on Tobin "Toby" McCauley, a North Carolina seventh grader who is judged harshly by his peers, largely due to the antics of his disreputable family members. When classmate Henry Otis invites Tobin to help him raise chickens for a class project, the lonely and sensitive teen—who lost his mother years earlier—begins to gain confidence and develop a sense of purpose. "The beauty [of the tale] is that Tobin's growth emerges naturally through a gentle plot and amid a flock of well-defined characters," remarked Betty Carter in *Horn Book,* and in *School Library Journal* Cheryl Ashton called *Chicken Boy* "a refreshingly well-written encounter with richly developed and well-defined characters whom readers won't soon forget."

Shooting the Moon, a teen novel set during the Vietnam War, was based on an idea supplied by Dowell's husband. "The genesis . . . was this: I wrote a lousy book and was depressed about it," Dowell remarked in a *School Library Journal* interview with Elizabeth Bird. "My husband, trying to be helpful and supportive, suggested I write a book about an Army brat whose brother is a conscientious objector. I smiled and said, 'Yes, dear,' then filed his idea away under 'Things Other People Think I Should Write about and I Never Will' (a very thick file). But for some reason it stayed with me."

Shooting the Moon focuses on the Dexter family: twelve-year-old Jamie, Jamie's older brother T.J., and their father, a colonel in the U.S. Army. When T.J. enlists in the army's medical corps in 1969, his father disapproves and attempts to discourage his son from leaving. Once T.J. arrives in Vietnam, he begins sending home rolls of film for Jamie to develop; initially, he submits photographs of his favorite subject, the moon, but as time goes by, his images become grittier and more disturbing. "Dowell captures Jamie's growing self-awareness and maturity with the slightly detached, wistful tone of a memoir related well after the fact," commented Riva Pollard in *School Library Journal,* and a *Publishers Weekly* contributor observed that *Shooting the Moon* "succeeds in credibly depicting a girl's loss of innocence." Robin L. Smith, writing in

Cover of Dowell's middle-grade novel **Where I'd Like To Be,** *featuring cover art by Bruce Katz.* (Aladdin Paperbacks, 2003. Reproduced by permission.)

Horn Book, described the novel as "an important, timely story, sparely told, that stays true to its course."

Dowell created her "From the Highly Scientific Notebooks of Phineas L. MacGuire" series with her son, Jack, in mind. She noted on her home page that, "since he's pretty interested in scientific matters, I decided to write a book about a kid who's a serious scientist. It was fun for me and Jack to try out the experiments that Mac (a.k.a. Phineas L. MacGuire) does in the book." *Phineas L. MacGuire . . . Erupts!: The First Experiment* introduces the title character, a logically minded fourth-grader with a penchant for discovering new things. When Mac's best friend and science partner moves away suddenly, he is assigned to work with Ben, an obnoxious new student who alienates the rest of Mac's classmates. "Told in Mac's open, humorous, and self-effacing voice, the straightforward story is simple without being simplistic," Smith noted. In *Phineas L. MacGuire . . . Gets Slimed!* Mac takes on a new challenge: dedicating himself to the study of molds. According to a *Kirkus Reviews* critic, Mac's persona is "marked by both a disarming awareness of his own flaws and an unshakable faith in his friends' strengths." Mac attempts to raise money for Space Camp by caring

for a slobbery Labrador retriever in *Phineas L. MacGuire . . . Blasts Off!* This third entry in the series "is a refreshingly upbeat story, with a strong emphasis on cooperation," Elaine E. Knight commented in *School Library Journal.*

Asked if she had any advice for budding young authors, Dowell stated on her home page: "I don't know many writers, even famous writers, who just sit down and write brilliant books without breaking a sweat. Most writers I know, including myself, write lousy or only so-so first drafts, make improvements, get feedback, and revise, revise, revise. All this to say: don't expect to be perfect. Let yourself make mistakes. Do a lousy job—and then go back and do a better one."

Biographical and Critical Sources

PERIODICALS

Booklist, April 15, 2000, review of *Dovey Coe,* p. 1537; May 15, 2003, Linda Perkins, review of *Where I'd Like to Be,* pp. 1660-1661; August, 2007, Abby Nolan, review of *Phineas L. MacGuire . . . Gets Slimed!,* p. 77; March 1, 2009, Abby Nolan, review of *The Kind of Friends We Used to Be,* p. 46.

Horn Book, July-August, 2004, Martha P. Parravano, review of *The Secret Language of Girls,* p. 450; September-October, 2005, Betty Carter, review of *Chicken Boy,* p. 575; May-June, 2006, Robin Smith, review of *Phineas L. MacGuire . . . Erupts!: The First Experiment,* p. 313; September-October, 2007, Robin Smith, review of *Phineas L. MacGuire . . . Gets Slimed!,* p. 571; March-April, 2008, Robin L. Smith, review of *Shooting the Moon,* p. 216; July-August, 2008, Robin L. Smith, review of *Phineas L. MacGuire . . . Blasts Off!,* p. 443.

Kirkus Reviews, March 1, 2003, review of *Where I'd Like to Be,* p. 382; April 1, 2004, review of *The Secret Language of Girls,* p. 328; July 1, 2007, review of *Phineas L. MacGuire . . . Gets Slimed!;* May 1, 2008, review of *Phineas L. MacGuire . . . Blasts Off!;* December 1, 2008, review of *The Kind of Friends We Used to Be.*

Kliatt, January, 2008, Claire Rosser, review of *Shooting the Moon,* p. 5.

Publishers Weekly, February 24, 2003, review of *Where I'd Like to Be,* p. 73; May 31, 2004, review of *The Secret Language of Girls,* p. 74; October 24, 2005, review of *Chicken Boy,* p. 59; August 21, 2006, review of *Phineas L. MacGuire . . . Erupts!,* p. 68; December 17, 2007, review of *Shooting the Moon,* p. 51; December 8, 2008, review of *The Kind of Friends We Used to Be,* p. 58.

School Library Journal, May, 2000, review of *Dovey Coe,* p. 171; April, 2003, Faith Brautigam, review of *Where I'd Like to Be,* p. 158; May, 2004, B. Allison Gray, review of *The Secret Language of Girls,* p. 146; July, 2005, Cheryl Ashton, review of *Chicken Boy,* p. 101;

September, 2006, Terrie Dorio, review of *Phineas L. MacGuire . . . Erupts!*, p. 171; May, 2008, Riva Pollard, review of *Shooting the Moon*, p. 122; August, 2008, Elaine E. Knight, review of *Phineas L. MacGuire . . . Blasts Off!*, p. 86.

ONLINE

DreamGirl Web site, http://www.dgarts.com/ (February 2, 2005), interview with Dowell.
Frances O'Roark Dowell Home Page, http://www.frances dowell.com (September 1, 2009).
Frances O'Roark Dowell Web log, http://www.frances dowell.com/journal/ (September 1, 2009).
School Library Journal Web site, http://www.school libraryjournal.com/ (November 21, 2008), Elizabeth Bird, interview with Dowell."

*   *   *

DUBIN, Jill

Personal

Born in New York, NY; married; children: two. *Education:* Pratt Institute, B.F.A.

Addresses

Home and office—2070 Abby Ln., Atlanta, GA 30345. *Agent*—Lori Nowicki, Painted Words Licensing Group, Loripainted-words.com. *E-mail*—jill@jilldubin.com.

Career

Artist and book illustrator. Has created artwork for Texas Instruments, Great American Puzzle Factory, Fisher Price Toys, and Microsoft.

Member

Society of Children's Book Writers and Illustrators.

Awards, Honors

Mom's Choice Award Gold, 2009.

Writings

"LITTLE BITTIES" SERIES; SELF-ILLUSTRATED

Mother Goose Rhymes, Barron's (New York, NY), 1991.
The Farm, Barron's (New York, NY), 1991.
Puppies and Kittens, Barron's (New York, NY), 1991.
One Two Three, Barron's (New York, NY), 1991.
ABC, Barron's (New York, NY), 1991.
Things That Go, Barron's (New York, NY), 1991.

ILLUSTRATOR

Patricia Relf, *Sweet Sea, the Princess of Coral Kingdom*, Grosset & Dunlap (New York, NY), 1985.

Debby Slier, reteller, *The Gingerbread Boy*, Checkerboard Press (New York, NY), 1988.
Cindy West, reteller, *The Three Bears*, Checkerboard Press (New York, NY), 1988.
Don Estep, *Lucy's Early Day*, Checkerboard Press (New York, NY), 1990.
Don Estep, *Cat and Kittens*, Checkerboard Press (New York, NY), 1990.
Leslie McGuire, *Who Will Play with Me?*, Little & Woods Press (New York, NY), 1991.
Leslie McGuire, *Where Are My Toys?*, Little & Woods Press (New York, NY), 1991.
Leslie McGuire, *Big Bug, Little Bug*, Little & Woods Press (New York, NY), 1991.
Leslie McGuire, *Find the Kittens, One to Ten*, Little & Woods Press (New York, NY), 1991.
Nancy E. Krulik, *The Norfin Trolls: Ralph Troll's New Bicycle*, Scholastic (New York, NY), 1992.
Selena Richards, *Rebecca's Rainy Day*, Checkerboard Press (New York, NY), 1992.
Selena Richards, *Rebecca Goes to the Park*, Checkerboard Press (New York, NY), 1992.
Selena Richards, *Rebecca Goes to the Country*, Checkerboard Press (New York, NY), 1992.
Selena Richards, *Rebecca Goes Out*, Checkerboard Press (New York, NY), 1992.
Karen Berman Nagel, *The Norfin Trolls: Camp-out Adventure*, Scholastic (New York, NY), 1993.
Justine Korman, *The Krystal Princesses Shake up the Day*, Scholastic (New York, NY), 1993.
Ann D. Hardy, *ZooBC's!: An ABC Lift-the-Flap Book*, Ottenheimer Publishers (Owings Mills, MD), 1995.
Cindy Chang, *Where's the Mouse?*, Random House (New York, NY), 1995.
Cindy Chang, *Are You My Baby?*, Random House (New York, NY), 1996.
Cindy Chang, *What's for Lunch?*, Random House (New York, NY), 1996.
Cindy Chang, *Peekaboo!*, Random House (New York, NY), 1996.
Shirley Simon, *Benny's Baby Brother*, School Zone Publishing, 1996.
Kimberly Weinberger, *Winter Is Here!*, Scholastic (New York, NY), 1997.
Kimberly Weinberger, *We Love Fall!*, Scholastic (New York, NY), 1997.
Kimberly Weinberger, *Hello, Spring!*, Scholastic (New York, NY), 1998.
Steve Metzger, adaptor, *Little Red Caboose*, Scholastic (New York, NY), 1998.
Laura Wallace, *I Can Fly!: Fun with Our Animal Friends*, Ottenheimer Publishers (Owings Mills, MD), 1998.
Laura Wallace, *I Can Jump!: Fun with Our Animal Friends*, Ottenheimer Publishers (Owings Mills, MD), 1998.
Laura Wallace, *I Can Run!: Fun with Our Animal Friends*, Ottenheimer Publishers (Owings Mills, MD), 1998.
Laura Wallace, *I Can Splash!: Fun with Our Animal Friends*, Ottenheimer Publishers (Owings Mills, MD), 1998.
JoDee McConnaughhay, *Be Brave, Anna!*, Standard Publishing (Cincinnati, OH), 1999.

Jill Dubin's textured art brings to life Marianne Berkes' folk-song adaptation in Over in the Arctic. (Dawn Publications, 2008. Illustration copyright © 2008 by Jill Dubin. Reproduced by permission.)

Angela Shelf Medearis, *Seeds Grow!,* Scholastic (New York, NY), 1999.

Mimi, *Jake Is Up!,* Giggles Group (Highland Beach, FL), 2000.

Steve Metzger, adaptor, *You Are My Sunshine,* Scholastic (New York, NY), 2001.

My Music Maker: An Electronic Music Mixer and Songbook for Kids, Reader's Digest Children's Publishing (New York, NY), 2002.

Marcia Trimble, *Flower Green: A Flower for All Seasons,* Images Press (Los Altos Hills, CA), 2002.

Steve Metzger, *The Falling Leaves,* Scholastic (New York, NY), 2002.

Ivan Ulz, *Fire Truck!,* Scholastic (New York, NY), 2002.

Steve Metzger, *The Biggest Leaf Pile,* Scholastic (New York, NY), 2003.

David Parker, *I Can Cooperate!,* Scholastic (New York, NY), 2004.

David Parker, *I Can Make Good Choices!,* Scholastic (New York, NY), 2004.

Steve Metzger, *The Falling Leaves and the Scarecrow,* Scholastic (New York, NY), 2004.

David Parker, *I Can Share!,* Scholastic (New York, NY), 2005.

Marianne Berkes, *Over in the Arctic: Where the Cold Winds Blow,* Dawn Publications (Nevada City, CA), 2008.

Also illustrator of board books, activity books, sticker books, and coloring books. Contributor to periodicals, including *Reader's Digest* and *Ladybug.*

Sidelights

A graduate of the Pratt Institute, artist Jill Dubin has created artwork for such diverse clientele as Fisher Price Toys, Texas Instruments, the Great American Puzzle Factory, and Microsoft. In addition, she has contributed illustrations to more than fifty books for young readers. In *Flower Green: A Flower for All Seasons,* a work by Marcia Trimble, a sprout named Flower Green grows in a magical garden. After she draws a host of Flowerettes, Flower Green invites some neighboring flowers to a party in the hope of adding color and fragrance to her creations. Dubin's illustrations drew praise from *School Library Journal* critic Louise L. Sherman, who stated that "the flower-framed pages on which the blossoms open their invitations are striking."

Dubin also illustrated *Over in the Arctic: Where the Cold Winds Blow,* a picture book with a text by Marianne Berkes. Based on the traditional rhyme "Over in the Meadow," *Over in the Arctic* provides children with a glimpse of the many creatures that live in the tundra, including polar bears, snow geese, and arctic hares. "Graceful, stylish cut-paper collages in a mixture of

bright colors and patterns create icy backgrounds," remarked a contributor in *Kirkus Reviews*. Julie Roach, writing in *School Library Journal,* similarly noted that Dubin offers "chunky cut-paper collages in a cool palette."

Biographical and Critical Sources

PERIODICALS

Kirkus Reviews, August 1, 2008, review of *Over in the Arctic: Where the Cold Winds Blow.*

School Library Journal, April, 2002, Louise L. Sherman, review of *Flower Green: A Flower for All Seasons,* p. 126; September, 2008, Julie Roach, review of *Over in the Arctic,* p. 137.

ONLINE

Jill Dubin Home Page, http://jilldubin.com (September 1, 2009).

Painted Words Licensing Group Web site, http://painted-words.com/ (September 1, 2009), "Jill Dubin."*

*   *   *

DURNEY, Ryan

Personal

Married; wife's name Audrey (an illustrator). *Education:* Columbus College of Art and Design, B.F.A., 1999.

Addresses

Office—7920 San Felipe Blvd., Apt. 2704, Austin, TX 78729. *Agent*—Bernadette Szost, Portfolio Solutions, 136 Jameson Hill Rd., Clinton Corners, NY 12514. *E-mail*—ryandurney@hotmail.com; OnDrawnWings@excite.com.

Career

Artist and illustrator. Seedling Publications, Elizabethtown, PA, art director, illustrator, and head of graphic design department, 1999-2002; DSCI, artist and designer, 2005-06; also worked for Studio 612 (commercial photography studio). *Exhibitions:* Work exhibited by Society of Illustrators West, 2006.

Awards, Honors

Spot illustration contest winner, Young Isaac, Inc.; poster contest winner, Orton Cone Box Show; Best of Fantasy competition, ibooks, Inc./*3D World* magazine, 2004; blue ribbon, Highroad Gallery, 2005; Best 3D Christmas Image designation, Renderosity, 2008; Children's Choices selection, International Reading Association/Children's Book Council, 2008, for *Real-life Sea Monsters.*

Illustrator

Mike Sandven, *The Cold,* Trafford Publishing (Bloomington, IN), 2007.

Judith Jango-Cohen, *Real-life Sea Monsters,* Millbrook Press (Minneapolis, MN), 2008.

Also illustrator of books for Continental Press, including *The Little Rabbit Who Wanted Red Wings, Look, Bugs!, Puffins, Prairie Town, Weedy Sea Dragons, Scarlet Macaws,* and *The Contest.* Illustrator of magazine covers, including *Time for Kids, Clubhouse, Jr.,* and *Markets Media;* contributor of illustrations to magazines, including *Dark Realms* and *Odyssey.*

Biographical and Critical Sources

PERIODICALS

School Library Journal, September, 2007, Nancy Call, review of *Real-life Sea Monsters,* p. 183.

ONLINE

Ryan Durney Home Page, http://www.ryandurney.com (September 1, 2009).

Ryan Durney Web log, http://aliceinwonderland-book.blogspot.com/ (September 1, 2009).*

E-F

EHRLICH, Fred
(Fred Ehrlich, M.D.)

Personal
Male.

Addresses
Home—Lincoln, MA; Maplewood, NJ.

Career
Writer, pediatrician, and child psychiatrist.

Writings

A Valentine for Ms. Vanilla, illustrated by Martha Gradisher, Viking (New York, NY), 1991.

Lunch Boxes, illustrated by Martha Gradisher, Viking (New York, NY), 1991.

A Class Play with Ms. Vanilla, illustrated by Martha Gradisher, Viking (New York, NY), 1992.

(With Harriet Ziefert; as Fred Ehrlich, M.D.) *You Can't Take Your Body to a Repair Shop: A Book about What Makes You Sick,* illustrated by Amanda Haley, Blue Apple Books (Maplewood, NJ), 2004.

(As Fred Ehrlich, M.D.) *You Can't Use Your Brain If You're a Jellyfish: A Book about Animal Brains,* illustrated by Amanda Haley, Blue Apple Books (Maplewood, NJ), 2007.

(As Fred Ehrlich, M.D.) *You Can't Lay an Egg If You're an Elephant: A Book about How Animals Are Born,* illustrated by Amanda Haley, Blue Apple Books (Maplewood, NJ), 2007.

(As Fred Ehrlich, M.D.) *You Can't See a Dodo at the Zoo: A Book about Animals Endangered and Extinct,* illustrated by Amanda Haley, Blue Apple Books (Maplewood, NJ), 2007.

(With Harriet Ziefert) *A Bunny Is Funny: And So Is This Book!,* illustrated by Todd McKie, Blue Apple Books (Maplewood, NJ), 2008.

"EARLY EXPERIENCES" SERIES; AS FRED EHRLICH, M.D.

Does a Pig Flush?, illustrated by Emily Bolam, Blue Apple Books (Brooklyn, NY), 2002.

Does a Lion Brush?, illustrated by Emily Bolam, Blue Apple Books (Brooklyn, NY), 2002.

Does a Yak Get a Haircut?, illustrated by Emily Bolam, Blue Apple Books (Brooklyn, NY), 2003.

Does a Tiger Open Wide?, illustrated by Emily Bolam, Blue Apple Books (Brooklyn, NY), 2003.

Does a Panda Go to School?, illustrated by Emily Bolam, Blue Apple Books (Maplewood, NJ), 2003.

Does a Hippo Say Ahh?, illustrated by Emily Bolam, Blue Apple Books (Maplewood, NJ), 2003.

Does a Duck Have a Daddy?, illustrated by Emily Bolam, Blue Apple Books (Maplewood, NJ), 2004.

Does a Mouse Have a Mommy?, illustrated by Emily Bolam, Blue Apple Books (Maplewood, NJ), 2004.

Does a Chimp Wear Clothes?, illustrated by Emily Bolam, Blue Apple Books (Maplewood, NJ), 2005.

Does an Elephant Take a Bath?, illustrated by Emily Bolam, Blue Apple Books (Maplewood, NJ), 2005.

Does a Seal Smile?, illustrated by Emily Bolam, Blue Apple Books (Maplewood, NJ), 2006.

Does a Baboon Sleep in a Bed?, illustrated by Emily Bolam, Blue Apple Books (Maplewood, NJ), 2006.

Does a Giraffe Drive?, illustrated by Emily Bolam, Blue Apple Books (Maplewood, NJ), 2007.

Does a Camel Cook?, illustrated by Emily Bolam, Blue Apple Books (Maplewood, NJ), 2007.

Sidelights
A pediatrician and child psychiatrist, Fred Ehrlich has also written more than twenty books for young readers, including *Does a Lion Brush?* and other works in the "Early Experiences" series, illustrated by Emily Bolam. These books, which use a question-and-answer format, introduce facts about animals to help explain human behaviors, customs, and routines. In *Does a Seal Smile?* Ehrlich looks at the way creatures communicate with one another, and he explores personal hygiene in *Does an Elephant Take a Bath?* and *Does a Lion Brush?* Ha-

Dr. Fred Erlich creates the whimsical text for Does a Giraffe Drive?, *featuring artwork by Emily Bolam.* (Blue Apple Books, 2007. Illustration copyright © 2007 by Emily Bolam. Reproduced by permission.)

zel Rochman, reviewing *Does an Elephant Take a Bath?* in *Booklist,* noted that the combination of Ehrlich's narrative and Bolam's pictures "move easily from nonsense to fun facts and human connections." "By focusing on the creatures, the texts avoid being preachy and make the concepts fun," Julie Roach noted in *School Library Journal.*

Ehrlich has collaborated with Harriet Ziefert on a pair of titles, *You Can't Take Your Body to a Repair Shop: A Book about What Makes You Sick* and *A Bunny Is Funny: And So Is This Book!* In the former, the authors humorously explore a variety of maladies from the common cold to blisters. Gay Lynn Van Vleck, writing in *School Library Journal,* stated that the book offers "plenty of facts and lots of gross-out appeal." In *A Bunny Is Funny* Ehrlich and Ziefert present nineteen rhymes that celebrate the uniqueness of such creatures as an armadillo, flamingo, and crab. In *School Library Journal,* Wendy Woodfill called *A Bunny Is Funny* a "dynamic collection of short poems."

Biographical and Critical Sources

PERIODICALS

Booklist, August, 2004, Jennifer Mattson, review of *Does a Duck Have a Daddy?,* p. 1938; October 15, 2005, Hazel Rochman, review of *Does an Elephant Take a Bath?,* p. 57; December 1, 2005, Kay Weisman, review of *You Can't Use Your Brain If You're a Jellyfish: A Book about Animal Brains,* p. 66; May 15, 2006, Hazel Rochman, review of *Does a Baboon Sleep in a Bed?,* p. 48; August 1, 2006, Hazel Rochman, review of *Does a Seal Smile?,* p. 80.

Kirkus Reviews, November 15, 2004, review of *You Can't Take Your Body to a Repair Shop: A Book about What Makes You Sick,* p. 1095; March 15, 2005, review of *You Can't See a Dodo at the Zoo: A Book about Animals Endangered and Extinct,* p. 350; July 15, 2006, review of *Does a Seal Smile?,* p. 721; May 15, 2007, review of *You Can't Lay an Egg If You're an Elephant: A Book about How Animals Are Born.*

Publishers Weekly, December 9, 2002, reviews of *Does a Pig Flush?* and *Does a Lion Brush?,* p. 81.

School Library Journal, March, 2003, Olga R. Kuharets, reviews of *Does a Lion Brush?* and *Does a Pig Flush?,* p. 192; February, 2004, Julie Roach, reviews of *Does a Panda Go to School?* and *Does a Yak Get a Haircut?,* p. 112; August, 2004, Olga R. Kuharets, reviews of *Does a Duck Have a Daddy?* and *Does a Mouse Have a Mommy?,* p. 107; February, 2005, Gay Lynn Van Vleck, review of *You Can't Take Your Body to a Repair Shop,* p. 130; May, 2005, Rebecca Sheridan, review of *You Can't See a Dodo at the Zoo,* p. 106; September, 2005, Elaine Lesh Morgan, review of *A Class Play with Ms. Vanilla,* p. 167; November, 2005, Sandra Welzenbach, review of *You Can't Use Your Brain If You're a Jellyfish,* p. 114; July, 2007, Kathy Piehl, review of *You Can't Lay an Egg If You're an Elephant,* p. 90; July, 2008, Wendy Woodfill, review of *A Bunny Is Funny: And So Is This Book!,* p. 93.*

*   *   *

EHRLICH, Fred, M.D.
See EHRLICH, Fred

*   *   *

EWART, Franzeska G. 1950-

Personal

Born 1950, in Stranraer, Scotland; partner of Adam McLean (a writer). *Education:* Graduated from Glasgow University; Jordanhill College, primary teaching certificate. *Hobbies and other interests:* Music (flute and recorder), gardening, walking and cycling, painting, writing, frogs, cats.

Addresses

Home—Lochwinnoch, Scotland. *E-mail*—franzeska@franzeskaewart.com.

Career

Writer, educator, and puppeteer. Taught primary school in Glasgow, Scotland; also taught in Karachi, Pakistan, 1993. Conducts workshops on shadow puppetry. Also worked as a medical researcher.

Awards, Honors

Named Royal Literary Fund Writing fellow, 2009.

Franzeska G. Ewart (Reproduced by permission.)

Writings

JUVENILE FICTION

Columbine, Spindlewood (Barnstaple, England), 1995.

(Self-illustrated) *Putli's Puppet Magic,* Word Play (Glasgow, Scotland), 1996.

The Pen-Pal from Outer Space, illustrated by Simone Lia, Mammoth (London, England), 1998, published in *Alien Adventures: Three Stories in One,* Egmont (London, England), 2008.

Grandmother Georgia's Hats, illustrated by Anni Axworthy, Mammoth (London, England), 2000.

Shadowflight, illustrated by Derek Brazell, Mammoth (London, England), 2001.

Speak Up, Spike!, illustrated by Mark Oliver, Egmont (London, England), 2002, Crabtree Publishing (New York, NY), 2006.

Going Green!, illustrated by Georgie Birkett, Scholastic (London, England), 2003.

Bugging Miss Bannigan, illustrated by Georgie Birkett, Scholastic (London, England), 2003.

Bryony Bell Tops the Bill, illustrated by Kelly Waldek, A & C Black (London, England), 2004.

Bryony Bell's Star Turn, illustrated by Kelly Waldek, A & C Black (London, England), 2005.

Under the Spell of Bryony Bell, illustrated by Kelly Waldek, A & C Black (London, England), 2005.

Bima and the Water of Life, illustrated by Sandeep Kaushik, Barrington Stoke (Edinburgh, Scotland), 2007.

(Reteller) *William Shakespeare's The Tempest,* illustrated by David Wyatt, A & C Black (London, England), illustrated by David Watt, 2007.

Sita, Snake-Queen of Speed, illustrated by Helen Bate, Frances Lincoln (London, England), 2007, Frances Lincoln (New York, NY), 2008.

A Heart for Ruby, illustrated by Lauren Tobia, Walker (London, England), 2009.

Fire Mask, Barrington Stoke (Edinburgh, Scotland), 2010.

OTHER

Let the Shadows Speak: Developing Children's Language through Shadow Puppetry, Trentham (Stoke-on-Trent, England), 1998.

Biographical and Critical Sources

PERIODICALS

Guardian (London, England), June 1, 1999, October 1, 2001, Lindsey Fraser, review of *The Pen-Pal from Outer Space;* October 1, 2001, Lindsey Fraser, review of *Shadowflight;* October 8, 2002, Lindsey Fraser, review of *Speak Up, Spike!*

Herald (Glasgow, Scotland), June 23, 2001, Anne Johnstone, "Unlock the Imagination."

Kirkus Reviews, July 1, 2008, review of *Sita, Snake-Queen of Speed.*

Resource Links, April, 2006, Deb Nielsen, review of *Speak Up, Spike!,* p. 24.

Times Educational Supplement, March 11, 2005, Michael Thorn, review of *Under the Spell of Bryony Bell,* p. 12.

ONLINE

Franzeska G. Ewart Home Page, http://www.franzeskaewart.com (September 1, 2009).

Scottish Book Trust Web site, http://www.scottishbooktrust.com/ (September 1, 2009), "Franzeska G. Ewart."

*   *   *

FABRY, Glenn 1961-

Personal

Born March 24, 1961, in England; son of Ronald and Joan Anne Fabry; married, August 14, 1993; wife's name Nikki; children: Tom, Kitty. *Education:* Attended Twickenham Art College.

Addresses

Office—Glenn Fabry Studios, 116 Rodmell Ave., Brighton, East Sussex BN2 8PJ, England. *E-mail*—glenn fabrystudios@yahoo.co.uk.

Career

Artist and comic-book illustrator. Designer of computer game covers and game cards for *Magic the Gathering* and *World of Warcraft.* Has worked variously as a portrait artist, sign painter, tattoo artist, cartoonist, and cashier.

Awards, Honors

Eisner Award nominee for best cover artist, 1993, for *Hellblazer* and *The Spectre,* 1994, for *Hellblazer* and *Vertigo Jam,* 1998, for *Preacher,* 1999, for *Preacher, Hellblazer,* and *Aliens vs. Predator: Eternal,* and 2000, for *Preacher;* Eisner Award for best cover artist, 1995, for *Hellblazer;* Eisner Award for best anthology (with others), 2004, for *The Sandman: Endless Nights.*

Writings

SELF-ILLUSTRATED

(Author of foreword and commentary; with Garth Ennis) *Preacher: Dead or Alive* (collected covers), DC Comics (New York, NY), 2000.

(With Ben Cormack) *Anatomy for Fantasy Artists: An Illustrator's Guide to Creating Action Figures and Fantastical Forms,* Barron's (New York, NY), 2005.

Muscles in Motion: Figure Drawing for the Comic Book Artist, Watson-Guptill Publications (New York, NY), 2005.

Creator of "Jackinblack" (comic strip), published in *Strangled* (punk rock fanzine), 1981-86. Contributor of stories to comic books, including *A1,* Atomeka Press, 1989; *Bricktop A1 Special,* Atomeka Press, 2004; and *Bart Simpson's Treehouse of Horror,* Bongo Comics, 2008.

ILLUSTRATOR

Pat Mills, *Sláine the King* (first published in comic-book format), Titan (London, England), 1990.

Pat Mills, *The Collected Sláine* (first published in comic-book format), Titan (London, England), 1993.

Pat Mills, *Time Killer* (first published in comic-book format), Titan (London, England), 2003.

Neil Gaiman, *The Sandman: Endless Nights* (first published in comic-book format), DC Comics (New York, NY), 2003.

Garth Ennis, *The Authority: Kev* (first published in comic-book format), Wildstorm (La Jolla, CA), 2005.

Garth Ennis, *Midnighter: Killing Machine* (first published in comic-book format), Wildstorm (La Jolla, CA), 2007.

Mike Carey, *Neil Gaiman's Neverwhere,* Vertigo (New York, NY), 2007.

MAC, *Anna Smudge: Professional Shrink* ("Professionals" novel series), Toasted Coconut Media, (New York, NY), 2008.

Contributor to other comic-book series/graphic novels, including *2000 AD, 9-11, A1, All-New Official Handbook of the Marvel Universe A-Z, Atomika, The Authority: More Kev, Back Issue, Bart Simpson's Treehouse of Horror, The Batman/Judge Dredd Files, Batman/Judge Dredd: Die Laughing, Birds of Prey, Bricktop A1 Spe-*cial, *Crisis, Daredevil: The Target, Global Frequency, Greatest Hits, Hellblazer Special, Howard The Duck, JLA: Riddle of the Beast, Judge Dredd, Just a Pilgrim, MAD, Marvel Zombies: The Book of Angels, Demons and Various Monstrosities, Midnighter, Official Handbook of the Marvel Universe A to Z, The Quotable Sandman, The Sandman Companion, Slaine, Thor: Vikings, Time Twisters, Timeslip: The Collection, Transmetropolitan, Vertigo Secret Files: Hellblazer, The Worm,* and *X-Men: The Ultra Collection.*

Sidelights

Glenn Fabry, an Eisner Award-winning British illustrator, is best known for his work on the "Hellblazer" and "Preacher" series of comic books. In addition, Fabry has provided the artwork for *Anna Smudge: Professional Shrink,* the first work in the "Professionals" series of books geared for middle-grade readers. In an interview with Andy Serwin on the Wizard Universe Web site, Fabry admitted that the "Professionals" project, being a book, is "a little bit different from my bread and butter comic strip work." He added, however, that *Anna Smudge* afforded him the opportunity "to play around with my style and with the approach . . . a bit more, . . ., so I thought it'd be fun to be involved with that."

Written by MAC (an acronym for Melissa A. Calderone), *Anna Smudge* centers on the title character, an eleven-year-old therapist living in New York City. In the course of her work, Anna becomes embroiled in a mystery surrounded the diabolical Mr. Who, a criminal mastermind who has stolen top-secret materials from the Central Intelligence Agency. Fabry contributed more than a dozen black-and-white sketches to the work, bringing to life many of the story's grotesque characters. "I was going for more of a kind of a cartoony approach," the artist told Serwin. According to Nicki Clausen-Grace in *School Library Journal,* Fabry's illustrations "show each character in great detail and have a stylized nature that fits the genre to a tee." Bina Williams, writing in *Booklist,* noted that the pictures in *Anna Smudge* "add to the fun" of Calderone's text.

Biographical and Critical Sources

PERIODICALS

Arts and Activities, March, 2007, Jerome J. Hausman, review of *Anatomy for Fantasy Artists: An Illustrator's Guide to Creating Action Figures and Fantastical Forms,* p. 16.

Booklist, June 1, 2008, Bina Williams, review of *Anna Smudge: Professional Shrink,* p. 72.

School Library Journal, July, 2007, Heidi Dolamore, review of *Neil Gaiman's Neverwhere,* p. 127; June, 2008, Vicki Clausen-Grace, review of *Anna Smudge,* p. 146.

ONLINE

Comic Book Database, http://www.comicbookdb.com/ (September 1, 2009), "Glenn Fabry."

Glenn Fabry Home Page, http://www.glennfabry.co.uk (September 1, 2009).

Wizard Universe Web site, http://www.wizarduniverse. com/ (April 17, 2008), Andy Serwin, "The Wizard Q&A: Glenn Fabry."*

*   *   *

FEARNLEY, Jan 1965-

Personal

Born February 19, 1965, in South Shields, Tyne and Wear, England; married; husband's name Paul. *Education:* Degree (education); degree (graphic design). *Hobbies and other interests:* Walking in wilderness areas and on the beach, gardening, cycling.

Addresses

Home—England. *Agent*—David Higham Associates, 5-8 Lower John St., Golden Square, London W1F 9HA, England. *E-mail*—hello@janfearnley.com.

Career

Writer and illustrator. Has also worked as an early childhood educator in England.

Awards, Honors

Children's Book Award shortlist citations, 1999, for *Mr. Wolf's Pancakes,* 2001, for *A Perfect Day for It,* and 2003, for *Billy Tibbles Moves Out!;* Stockport Children's Book Award, 2001, for *Just like You;* Gold Award for Illustration, Association of Illustrators, 2002, for *Mr. Wolf and the Three Bears;* Oppenheim Portfolio Gold Award, 2002, for *A Perfect Day for It.*

Writings

SELF-ILLUSTRATED

Little Robin's Christmas, Little Tiger Press (Waukesha, WI), 1998, published as *Little Robin Red Vest,* Egmont Books (London, England), 1998, new edition, 2005.

Mabel and Max, Mammoth Books (London, England), 1998.

Mr. Wolf's Pancakes, Mammoth Books (London, England), 1999, Tiger Tales (Wilton, CT), 2001.

A Special Something, Hyperion Books for Children (New York, NY), 2000.

Just like You, Mammoth Books (London, England), 2000, Candlewick Press (Cambridge, MA), 2001.

Jan Fearnley (Photography by Egmont UK, Ltd. Reproduced by permission.)

Colin and the Curly Claw, Mammoth Books (London, England), 2001, Crabtree Publishing (New York, NY), 2002.

A Perfect Day for It, Egmont Children's Books (London, England), 2001, Harcourt (San Diego, CA), 2002.

Mr. Wolf and the Three Bears, Harcourt (San Diego, CA), 2002.

Billy Tibbles Moves Out!, Collins (London, England), 2003, HarperCollins (New York, NY), 2004.

Watch Out, Wilf!, Walker (London, England), 2004, published as *Watch Out!,* Candlewick Press (Cambridge, MA), 2004.

A Very Proper Fox, HarperCollins (London, England), 2006.

The Search for the Perfect Child, Candlewick Press (Cambridge, MA), 2006.

Are We There Yet?, HarperCollins (London, England), 2007.

Martha in the Middle, Candlewick Press (Cambridge, MA), 2008.

Mr Wolf and the Enormous Turnip, Egmont (London, England), 2008.

Milo Armadillo, Candlewick Press (Cambridge, MA), 2009.

The Baby Dragon Tamer, Egmont (London, England), 2009.

ILLUSTRATOR

Jeanne Willis, *Never Too Little to Love,* Walker (London, England), 2005.

Jeanne Willis, *Mummy, Do You Love Me?,* Walker (London, England), 2008, published as *Mommy Do You Love Me?,* Candlewick Press (Cambridge, MA), 2008.

Sidelights

Jan Fearnley worked as a preschool teacher before devoting herself to her first love: writing and illustrating books for children. With dual degrees in early childhood education and graphic art, Fearnley has learned how to entertain young listeners with brightly colored and engaging tales, many of which feature animals acting like children. Her popular self-illustrated books for young people have been published in both her native England and in North America and include *Mr. Wolf's Pancakes, Billy Tibbles Moves Out!, A Perfect Day for It,* and *Martha in the Middle.*

The youngest of six children, Fearnley grew up in England, where she sometimes found herself left behind while her older brothers played together. She entertained herself by drawing and making up stories, and by reading. In an interview for the *Year of Reading* Web site, the author-illustrator recalled: "A book can help you deal with emotions or problems, comfort you, make you laugh or move you to tears. They're powerful things. Have you got a favorite old book that you read over and over again, especially when you're feeling down? I rest my case!"

Fearnley broke into publishing with the Christmas story *Little Robin Red Vest*—released in the United States as *Little Robin's Christmas.* Little Robin has seven warm, red vests, one for each day of the week. As he sees

Fearnley pairs a gentle story with engaging watercolor art in her picture book **Just like You.** (Copyright © 2000. Used with permission of the publisher, Candlewick Press, Inc., Cambridge, MA.)

The lighthearted picture book **Mr. Wolf's Pancakes** *has inspired several more works by Fearnley.* (Tiger Tales, 2001. Illustration copyright © Jan Fearnley 1999. Reproduced by permission.)

other animals suffering from the cold, Robin gives his vests away one by one, until he is the one left shivering in the snow. Santa Claus rides to the rescue, endowing the little bird with a new vest made with a thread from his famous red coat. "Little Robin's unhesitating generosity will also kindle a response in young readers at any time of year," noted John Peters in a *Booklist* review of *Little Robin's Christmas*.

One of Fearnley's most popular characters is Mr. Wolf, an affable sort who knows how to get a job done. In *Mr. Wolf's Pancakes* he cannot seem to get any help from his neighbors—including a snobbish Chicken Little—in his efforts to cook up a batch of warm pancakes. Undaunted, Mr. Wolf sets to work in his kitchen, and when his neighbors smell the tantalizing results, they want to join him in the feast. He turns the tables on them with a comic twist. A *Publishers Weekly* reviewer predicted that youngsters would enjoy Fearnley's "sympathetic wolf and the savory surprise ending." A contributor to *Horn Book* praised Mr. Wolf as "likably drawn" and with a "gentle smile" that belies his quirky appetite.

Mr. Wolf makes return appearances in *Mr. Wolf and the Three Bears* and *Mr Wolf and the Enormous Turnip*. In *Mr. Wolf and the Three Bears* Wolf is hosting a birthday party for Baby Bear, and Grandma Wolf is providing the feast. The party is on the verge of ruin when Goldilocks crashes it and misbehaves, bringing Baby Bear to

tears and ignoring every plea to curb her nastiness. Grandma Wolf solves the problem by forbidding Goldilocks to go into the kitchen; a short time later she emerges from that very room, carrying a steaming hot pie. The wolf's effort to dig up a stubborn garden turnip for his turnip stew provides the drama in *Mr Wolf and the Enormous Turnip,* a story that provides "a sure antidote to the traditional fairy tale," according to a *Kirkus Reviews* writer. "Fearnley tells the story with enough of a wink and a nod so as not to alarm children," observed Rosalyn Pierini in a *School Library Journal* of *Mr. Wolf and the Three Bears,* while a *Publishers Weekly* reviewer deemed the book "archly hilarious" due to the wolf's "take-no-prisoners approach to etiquette."

Other Fearnley picture books include *Just like You, A Perfect Day for It, Billy Tibbles Moves Out!,* and *Mommy Do You Love Me?* In each story, likable animals provide chances for children to learn important messages about parental guidance, friendship, and sharing. The little mouse in *Just like You* wonders what his mother can do for him after seeing and hearing bigger, more powerful animals make promises to their children. Mother mouse assures him that her tiny size does not diminish the amount of love she holds for him. Martha Topol in *School Library Journal* observed that Fearnley's book "reminds readers of the daily expressions of unconditional love that make their relationship so unique." *Mommy Do You Love Me?* finds a young chick testing the limits of his own mother's affection, and here Fearnley's "soft watercolor-and-ink illustrations . . . perfectly enhance the [story's] sweetness," according to *Booklist* critic Randall Enos.

In *A Perfect Day for It* curious animals follow Bear to a mountaintop because he declares it is "a perfect day for it," while not specifying what "it" is. At the top, all the animals receive a great treat. Billy Tibbles, a cat with attitude, finds his comfortable world threatened in *Billy Tibbles Moves Out!* Told he must share his room with his brother, Billy rebels, until he discovers that having a roommate brings the chance for rowdy pillow fights and a chance to sleep with Dad. "Kids will immediately connect with Billy Tibbles," maintained Ilene Cooper in *Booklist,* while a *Publishers Weekly* contributor concluded that, "between giggles, youngsters should easily realize themselves" in Fearnley's "kid-pleasing" tale.

In *Martha in the Middle* a mouse child feels overlooked because she is overshadowed by her clear-thinking older sister and not as cute as little brother Ben. A meeting with a wise frog helps Martha realize that the center of things is possibly the most important part of all because it holds all the edges together. According to *School Library Journal* critic Ieva Bates, Fearnley's depiction of the story's animal characters is "expressive and entertaining," reflecting the "joyous nature" of the picture book. *Martha in the Middle* "combines a reassuring story with charming, rich watercolors," wrote Bina Williams in *Booklist,* and a *Publishers Weekly* critic predicted that Fearnley's inclusion of "witty details . . . [will] ramp up the fun on repeat readings."

Fido Farnsworth is a dog determined to find the perfect human child caretaker in *The Search for the Perfect Child.* But what is the perfect child like, exactly? Fearnley depicts a variety of children, and Fido's search reaches a happy end that "keep[s] little ones entertained," according to Cooper. Dubbing *The Search for the Perfect Child* a "celebration of childhood," a *Kirkus Reviews* writer concluded that Fearnley's "feel-good message . . . will not fail to draw a smile."

Biographical and Critical Sources

PERIODICALS

Booklist, September 15, 1998, John Peters, review of *Little Robin's Christmas,* p. 236; July, 2001, Cynthia Turnquest, review of *Just like You,* p. 2019; February 15, 2004, Ilene Cooper, review of *Billy Tibbles Moves Out!,* p. 1062; June 1, 2004, Julie Cummins, review of *Watch Out!,* p. 1741; February 1, 2005, Ilene Cooper, review of *Never Too Little to Love,* p. 966; December 1, 2006, Ilene Cooper, review of *The Search for the Perfect Child,* p. 51; March 15, 2008, Randall Enos, review of *Mommy Do You Love Me?,* p. 56; June 1, 2008, Bina Williams, review of *Martha in the Middle,* p. 90.

Horn Book, March, 2000, review of *Mr. Wolf's Pancakes,* p. 184.

Fearnley pairs two unusual friends in her self-illustrated picture book **Martha in the Middle.** (Illustration copyright © 2008 Jan Fearnley. Reproduced by permission of Candlewick Press, Inc., on behalf of Walker Books, London.)

Kirkus Reviews, January 1, 2006, review of *Mr Wolf and the Enormous Turnip,* p. 40; October 15, 2006, review of *The Search for the Perfect Child,* p. 1070.

Publishers Weekly, January 10, 2000, review of *Mr. Wolf's Pancakes,* p. 67; June 12, 2000, review of *A Special Something,* p. 71; March 25, 2002, review of *Mr. Wolf and the Three Bears,* p. 62; January 26, 2004, review of *Billy Tibbles Moves Out!,* p. 252; December 6, 2004, review of *Never Too Little to Love,* p. 59; February 25, 2008, review of *Mommy Do You Love Me?,* p. 78; June 9, 2008, review of *Martha in the Middle,* p. 49.

School Library Journal, August, 2000, Martha Topol, review of *A Special Something,* p. 154; April, 2001, Martha Topol, review of *Just like You,* p. 108; June, 2002, Rosalyn Pierini, review of *Mr. Wolf and the Three Bears,* p. 94; December, 2002, Olga R. Kuharets, review of *A Perfect Day for It,* p. 95; March, 2004, Bina Williams, review of *Billy Tibbles Moves Out!,* p. 157; April, 2004, Jane Barrer, review of *Watch Out!,* p. 110; November, 2006, Andrea Tarr, review of *The Search for the Perfect Child,* p. 92; April, 2008, Anne Parker, review of *Mommy Do You Love Me?,* p. 126; July, 2008, Ieva Bates, review of *Martha in the Middle,* p. 71.

ONLINE

David Higham Associates Web site, http://www.david higham.co.uk/ (February 3, 2004), "Jan Fearnley."

Jan Fearnley Home Page, http://www.janfearnley.com (October 15, 2009).

Year of Reading Web site, http://www.yearofreading.org. uk/ (October 1, 2004), "Jan Fearnley."*

*   *   *

FERNANDES, Eugenie 1943-

Personal

Born September 25, 1943, in Huntington, NY; daughter of Creig (an illustrator for DC Comics) and Marie Flessel (a homemaker); married Henry Fernandes (an illustrator), October 1, 1966; children: Kim, Matthew. *Education:* School of Visual Arts (New York, NY), degree, 1965. *Politics:* "Human." *Hobbies and other interests:* Painting, walking on the beach.

Addresses

Home—Peterborough, Ontario, Canada.

Career

Freelance illustrator and author, 1966—.

Awards, Honors

Independent Publisher Book Awards shortlist, Our Choice List inclusion, Cooperative Children's Book Center, and 3-Dimensional and Digital Illustrator Award,

all 2001, all for *Sleepy Little Mouse;* Our Choice listee, Canadian Children's Book Centre, Great Book selection, Canadian Toy Testing Council, and Children's Choices selection, International Reading Association (IRA) all 2003, all for *Busy Little Mouse;* Children's Choices selection, International Reading Association, and Debbie Zimmerman Early Years Literary Award shortlist, both 2005, both for *Big Week for Little Mouse;* Governor General's Award shortlist, 2006, and Golden Oak Award shortlist, and Amelia Frances Howard-Gibbon Illustrator's Award shortlist, both 2007, all for *Earth Magic; Skipping Stones* Honor Award, 2008, and Silver Birch Award shortlist, Best Bet for Children and Teens designation, Ontario Library Association, Children's Choices selection and Notable Book for a Global Society selection, both IRA, and Outstanding International Book designation, U.S. Board on Books for Young People, all 2009, all for *One Hen.*

Writings

SELF-ILLUSTRATED, EXCEPT WHERE NOTED

Wickedishrag, C.R. Gibson (Norwalk, CT), 1968.

Jenny's Surprise Summer, Western Publishing (Racine, WI), 1981.

The Little Boy Who Cried Himself to Sea, Kids Can Press (Toronto, Ontario, Canada), 1982.

A Difficult Day, black-and-white edition, Kids Can Press (Toronto, Ontario, Canada), 1983, color edition, 1987.

(Coauthor and co-illustrator with husband, Henry Fernandes) *Ordinary Amos and the Amazing Fish,* Western Publishing (Racine, WI), 1986.

The Very Best Picnic, Western Publishing (Racine, WI), 1988.

Jolly Book Box: Early Learning for Toddlers (contains "ABC and You," "Alone-Together," "Picnic Colors," "Dreaming Numbers," and "Busy Week"), Ladybird Books (Auburn, England), 1990.

(Co-illustrator with daughter, Kim Fernandes) *Just You and Me,* Annick Press (Toronto, Ontario, Canada), 1993.

Waves in the Bathtub, Scholastic Canada (Richmond Hill, Ontario, Canada), 1993.

The Tree That Grew to the Moon, North Winds (Richmond Hill, Ontario, Canada), 1994, Firefly Books (Buffalo, NY), 1998.

Little Toby and the Big Hair, illustrated by Kim Fernandes, Doubleday (Toronto, Ontario, Canada), 1997, Firefly Books (Buffalo, NY), 1998.

Baby Dreams, Stoddart Kids (New York, NY), 1999.

(Co-illustrator with Kim Fernandes) *Sleepy Little Mouse,* Kids Can Press (Niagara Falls, NY), 2000.

One More Pet, Scholastic (New York, NY), 2002.

Busy Little Mouse, illustrated by Kim Fernandes, Kids Can Press (Toronto, Ontario, Canada), 2002.

Big Week for Little Mouse, illustrated by Kim Fernandes, Kids Can Press (Toronto, Ontario, Canada), 2004.

Kitten's Spring, Kids Can Press (Toronto, Ontario, Canada), 2010.

Writer, designer, and producer of animated television-spots for *Sesame Street,* produced for Children's Television Workshop.

ILLUSTRATOR

Lucille Hammond, *Dog Goes to Nursery School,* Western Publishing (Racine, WI), 1982.

Stephanie Calmenson, *My Book of the Seasons,* Western Publishing (Racine, WI), 1982.

Ronne Peltzman, *Ned's Number Book,* Western Publishing (Racine, WI), 1982.

Lucille Hammond, *When Dog Was Little,* Western Publishing (Racine, WI), 1983.

Lucille Hammond, *The Adventures of Goat,* Western Publishing (Racine, WI), 1984.

Lucille Hammond, *The Good-by Day,* Western Publishing (Racine, WI), 1984.

Linda Hayward, *I Had a Bad Dream: A Book about Nightmares,* Western Publishing (Racine, WI), 1985.

Barbara Rennick, *Once upon a Time,* McGraw-Hill Ryerson (Toronto, Ontario, Canada), 1985.

Kathleen N. Daly, *Little Sister,* Western Publishing (Racine, WI), 1986.

Dorothy Marcic Hai, *Look at Me!: A Book of Occupations,* Western Publishing (Racine, WI), 1986.

Barbara Seuling, *Who's the Boss Here?: A Book about Parental Authority,* Western Publishing (Racine, WI), 1986.

Anne Baird, *Ride Away!,* Simon & Schuster (New York, NY), 1987.

Anne Baird, *Belly Buttons,* Simon & Schuster (New York, NY), 1987.

Lucille Hammond, *When Dog Grows Up,* Western Publishing (Racine, WI), 1987.

Richard Thompson, *Sky Full of Babies,* Annick Press (Toronto, Ontario, Canada), 1987.

Richard Thompson, *Foo,* Annick Press (Toronto, Ontario, Canada), 1988.

Richard Thompson, *I Have to See This!,* Annick Press (Toronto, Ontario, Canada), 1988.

Richard Thompson, *Gurgle, Bubble, Splash,* Annick Press (Toronto, Ontario, Canada), 1989.

Eve Merriam, *Daddies at Work,* Simon & Schuster (New York, NY), 1989.

Eve Merriam, *Mommies at Work,* Simon & Schuster (New York, NY), 1989.

Richard Thompson, *Effie's Bath,* Annick Press (Toronto, Ontario, Canada), 1990.

Richard Thompson, *Jesse on the Night Train,* Annick Press (Toronto, Ontario, Canada), 1990.

Marianne Borgardt, *Going to the Dentist* (case-bound pop-up), Simon & Schuster (New York, NY), 1991.

Stacie Strong, *Going to the Doctor* (case-bound pop-up), Simon & Schuster (New York, NY), 1991.

Jean Lewis, *Glow in the Dark—Under the Sea,* Western Publishing (Racine, WI), 1991.

Richard Thompson, *Maggee and the Lake Minder,* Annick Press (Toronto, Ontario, Canada), 1991.

Richard Thompson, *Tell Me One Good Thing: Bedtime Stories,* Annick Press (Toronto, Ontario, Canada), 1992.

Suzan Reid, *Grandpa Dan's Toboggan Ride,* Scholastic Canada (Richmond Hill, Ontario, Canada), 1992.

Lily Barnes, *Lace Them Up,* Somerville House (Toronto, Ontario, Canada), 1992.

Patricia Quinlan, *Brush Them Bright,* Somerville House (Toronto, Ontario, Canada), 1992.

Lucille Hammond, *Little Kitten Dress-Up,* Ladybird Books (Auburn, England), 1992.

Ginny Clapper, *My Mommy Comes Back* (book and tape), Western Publishing (Racine, WI), 1992.

Richard Thompson, *Don't Be Scared, Eleven,* Annick Press (Toronto, Ontario, Canada), 1993.

Judy Rothman, *Today I Took My Diapers Off* (book and tape), Western Publishing (Racine, WI), 1993.

David T. Suzuki, *Nature in the Home,* Stoddart (Toronto, Ontario, Canada), 1993.

Laurie Wark, *Katie's Hand-Me-Down Day,* Kids Can Press (Toronto, Ontario, Canada), 1994.

David T. Suzuki, *If We Could See Air,* Stoddart (Toronto, Ontario, Canada), 1994.

Larry Dane Brimner, *Elliot Fry's Good-Bye,* Boyds Mills Press (Honesdale, PA), 1994.

David T. Suzuki, *The Backyard Time Detectives,* Stoddart (Toronto, Ontario, Canada), 1995.

Marcia K. Vaughn, *Kapoc, the Killer Croc,* Silver Burdett Press (Morristown, NJ), 1995.

Lilly Barnes, *Make It Better,* Somerville House (Toronto, Ontario, Canada), 1996.

Patricia Quinlan, *On the Phone,* Somerville House (Toronto, Ontario, Canada), 1996.

Raffi, Bonnie Simpson, and Bert Simpson, *Rise and Shine,* Crown Publishers (New York, NY), 1996.

Troon Harrison, *Aaron's Awful Allergies,* Kids Can Press (Toronto, Ontario, Canada), 1996.

Susan Korman, *Wake Up, Groundhog!,* Golden Books (New York, NY), 1997.

Troon Harrison, *Lavender Moon,* Annick Press (Toronto, Ontario, Canada), 1997.

Budge Wilson, *The Long Wait,* Stoddart Kids (Toronto, Ontario, Canada), 1997.

Sylvia Fraser, *Tom and Francine: A Love Story,* Key Porter Kids (Toronto, Ontario, Canada), 1998.

Maria Coffey, *A Cat in a Kayak,* Annick Press (Willowdale, Ontario, Canada), 1998.

Troon Harrison, *The Memory Horse,* Tundra Books (Toronto, Ontario, Canada), 1999.

Robert Munsch, *Ribbon Rescue,* Scholastic (Toronto, Ontario, Canada), 1999, Scholastic (New York, NY), 2002.

Stephen Strauss, *How Big Is Big?,* Key Porter Kids (Toronto, Ontario, Canada), 1999.

Maria Coffey, *A Seal in the Family,* Annick Press (Toronto, Ontario, Canada), 1999.

Budge Wilson, *The Fear of Angelina Domino,* Stoddart Kids (Toronto, Ontario, Canada), 2000.

Ann Douglas, *Before You Were Born: The Inside Story!,* Owl Books (Toronto, Ontario, Canada), 2000.

Annie Sutton, *Oh, No!,* Pearson Educational (Toronto, Ontario, Canada), 2001.

Linda Ekblad, *The Number Eight,* Addison Wesley (Toronto, Ontario, Canada), 2002.

Kirsten Hall, *I'm So Scared!,* Scholastic (New York, NY), 2002.

Mary Ann Smith and Katie Smith Milway, *Cappuccina Goes to Town,* Kids Can Press (Toronto, Ontario, Canada), 2002.

Maria Coffey, *A Cat Adrift,* Firefly (New York, NY), 2002.

David L. Harrison, *The Mouse Was out at Recess,* Boyds Mills Press (Honesdale, PA), 2003.

Carl Nixon, *Three Blind Mice: A Play Based on a Nursery Rhyme,* Scholastic Canada (Markham, Ontario, Canada), 2003.

Judy Maus, *Jessie's Blessing,* AboutFace International (Toronto, Ontario, Canada), 2003.

Leta Potter, *The Pattern Farm,* Nelson (Toronto, Ontario, Canada), 2004.

Raffi, *Everything Grows,* Rounder Books (Cambridge, MA), 2004.

(With Michael Martchenko and Alan and Lea Daniel) Robert Munsch, *Munsch More!: A Robert Munsch Collection,* Scholastic Canada (Markham, Ontario, Canada), 2004.

Charles E. Hoce, *Beyond Old MacDonald: Funny Poems from Down on the Farm,* Boyds Mills Press (Honesdale, PA), 2005.

Dionne Brand, *Earth Magic,* Kids Can Press (Toronto, Ontario, Canada), 2006.

Laura Peetoom, *Mermaid in the Bathtub,* Fitzhenry & Whiteside (Markham, Ontario, Canada), 2006.

Eileen Spinelli, *Polar Bear, Arctic Hare: Poems of the Frozen North,* Boyds Mills Press (Honesdale, PA), 2007.

Katie Smith Milway, *One Hen: How One Small Loan Made a Big Difference,* A & C Black (London, England), 2008.

David T. Suzuki, *There's a Backyard in My Bedroom,* Greystone (Vancouver, British Columbia, Canada), 2008.

Contributor of illustrations to *Raffi Songs to Read,* Crown (New York, NY), 1988.

ILLUSTRATOR; BOARD BOOKS

My Bath Time Book, Ladybird Books (Auburn, England), 1987.

My Bedtime Book, (Auburn, England), 1987.

My Going Out Book, (Auburn, England), 1987.

My Playtime Book, (Auburn, England), 1987.

My Busy Day Book, (Auburn, England), 1988.

My Rainy Day Book, (Auburn, England), 1988.

My Sunny Day Book, (Auburn, England), 1988.

My Birthday Book, (Auburn, England), 1988.

Jan Colbert, *Good Morning,* HarperCollins (Toronto, Ontario, Canada), 1993.

Jan Colbert, *Good Night,* HarperCollins (Toronto, Ontario, Canada), 1993.

Sidelights

Eugenie Fernandes, a Canadian illustrator, has provided the artwork for more than one hundred children's books, including a host of self-illustrated titles. Among her

Eugenie Fernandes contributes her unique art to Eileen Spinelli's picture book **Polar Bear, Arctic Hare.** (Wordsong, 2007. Illustration copyright © 2007 by Eugenie Fernandes. Reproduced by permission.)

many efforts are Eileen Spinelli's *Polar Bear, Arctic Hare: Poems of the Frozen North* and Katie Smith Milway's *One Hen: How One Small Loan Made a Big Difference,* as well as *Just You and Me* and *Sleepy Little Mouse,* both written and illustrated with her daughter, artist Kim Fernandes.

Fernandes developed an early interest in the arts. "My father, a comic-book illustrator, had his studio overlooking Huntington Bay in Long Island," she recalled in an essay on her home page. "I had my own desk right next to his." As Fernandes once told *SATA:* "I spent much of my growing-up time in my father's studio. The rest of the time you could find me swimming with mermaids and romping with pirates, climbing trees, taking care of baby birds, and enjoying the picnic lunches that my mother often brought to the beach. *Tell Me One Good Thing: Bedtime Stories, Gurgle, Bubble, Splash,* and *Jenny's Surprise Summer* are filled with images of that childhood."

Fernandes later attended the School of Visual Arts in New York City, where, she stated in an interview on the Kids Can Press Web site, "my favorite class was illustrating children's books with Eric Blegvad (who illustrated *Hurry, Hurry, Mary Dear* by N.M. Bodecker)." Fernandes also recalled that her debut children's book had its beginnings there: "The first material I published was a story called *Wickedishrag,* that I wrote and illustrated for a class project when I was in art school in 1965." After graduation, she began designing greeting cards and tirelessly made the rounds of the publishing houses with her portfolio. She eventually drew the attention of editors and art directors after submitting stories with her art.

Among Fernandes's self-illustrated titles are *A Difficult Day* and *Waves in the Bathtub.* "The story for *A Difficult Day* was built around an angry moment that I shared with my son when he was five," she recalled to *SATA.* "He went to his room and slammed the door. 'You can't come in. Don't you try to come in,' he said. 'I don't like you any more. I don't like anybody!' Then there was a pause. By now I was listening very carefully and writing very quickly—because I knew that he

was giving me some important feelings. Then came his best line, 'Why don't you love me better!' I can feel the emotion in this story, both as the child and as the mother.

"*Waves in the Bathtub* is a story that has been with me since I was small enough to feel that the tub was huge. It brewed quietly over the years as I watched my own children play for hours in the tub with toy dolphins and boats and whales. And the song—I don't quite know where that came from. I just found myself singing it. The trick was putting it down on paper."

Told in verse, Fernandes's *Baby Dreams* was inspired by her granddaughter, who she often rocked to sleep. "Each illustration is a work of art," Susan Fonseca remarked in the *Canadian Review of Materials*. "Fernandes uses rich and vibrant colors that sweep across the page. She loves circles and swirls, shadows and light." In *One More Pet,* young Emily spends one summer collecting a houseful of stray animals, including a cat, a rabbit, a white rat, and a garden snake. When a farmer offers to give her a pony as a reward for helping him with some chores, Emily's mother finally objects to the growing menagerie, and the youngster instead receives a special present: a giant egg. Gwyneth Evans observed in *Quill & Quire* that "the cheerful, cozy mood of the tale is reflected in Fernandes's pictures, in their sunshine, open doors, rounded shapes and soft colours." Catherine Hoyt, writing in the *Canadian Review of Materials,* stated that "the quick rhyming text speeds the reader through the story. The storyline is cumulative," Hoyt added, "and children will be anxious to see what Emily's next new pet will be."

One of Fernandes's favorite works, *Just You and Me* tells of how young Heather and her mother wish to spend some time alone but must bring Heather's infant sibling with them on a walk after the baby refuses to fall asleep. No matter where they go—out to sea, up into the clouds, even to the moon—the baby remains awake. The baby finally falls asleep only after the other characters give up pursuing the task. *Quill & Quire* contributor Janet McNaughton dubbed the work a "winning effort," stating that "children five and under will appreciate the combination of the mundane and the wildly improbable in *Just You and Me.*"

Fernandes also collaborated with her daughter on *Busy Little Mouse,* a picture book designed to help children learn the various sounds that animals make. In the work, an energetic mouse spends a day cavorting with the creatures on a farm, including a wiggly pig and a noisy duck. The author's "rhyming text is bright and appealing," noted *Quill & Quire* reviewer Joanne Findon, who also observed that the "intricate three-dimensional Fimo illustrations are full of life and movement." In a sequel, *Sleepy Little Mouse,* the tiny protagonist has trouble falling asleep one night, and her tears flood the bedroom. Soon Little Mouse's bed floats from her home to the sea, where she plays with a group of friendly crea-

tures until her mother comes calling. *Sleepy Little Mouse* was also well received by critics. Jeffrey Canton, writing in *Quill & Quire,* described it as "a wonderfully gentle, whimsical bedtime story." In *Big Week for Little Mouse,* another work by Eugenie and Kim Fernandes, the title character prepares her house for a birthday party. The author's "rhythmic quatrains capture Little Mouse's energy as she excitedly gets ready for her big day," Jessica Kelley stated in *Quill & Quire.*

Fernandes has also contributed illustrations to a number of poetry collections, including David L. Harrison's *The Mouse Was out at Recess* and Charles E. Hoce's *Beyond Old MacDonald: Funny Poems from Down on the Farm.* In the former, Harrison describes the uproarious activities at an elementary school, which include a raucous bus ride, a chaotic field trip, and a disgusting cafeteria offering. According to a critic in *Kirkus Reviews,* Fernandes's pictures "are bright and lively and well suited to the material." Hoce offers some thirty selections about a variety of unusual animals, such as a cow that leaks milk, in *Beyond Old MacDonald.* Here "Fernandes's watercolor illustrations are clever and energetic and, in several instances, explain the verbal jokes," commented Shawn Brommer in *School Library Journal.*

Trinidad-born poet Dionne Brand collects twenty verses that describe her native land through the eyes of a young girl in *Earth Magic,* "an engaging picture of tropical life," noted Kathleen Whalin in *School Library Journal.* According to *Booklist* reviewer Gillian Engberg, Fernandes's "vibrantly colored scenes . . . amplify the sense of mysticism while reinforcing the poems' concrete images." In *Polar Bear, Arctic Hare,* a collection by Eileen Spinelli, young readers are introduced to the wonders of the far north. Michele Landsberg, writing in *Quill & Quire,* praised the "bright acrylic paintings, with their sweeps of movement and lush colour. Fernandes is at her best when she's evoking realistic animal behaviour: musk oxen huddling together against the wind, their young peeking out from behind the sheltering adults; an Arctic owl, swooping toward the reader with piercing yellow glare, the painting somehow conveying the silence of its swift approach."

Among Fernandes's other illustration projects is *Cappuccina Goes to Town,* a humorous picture book with a text by Mary Ann Smith and Katie Smith Milway. The work centers on an inquisitive cow named Cappuccina who takes advantage of a hole in a damaged fence to leave her pasture and venture into town. Once there, she decides to spruce up her image with a variety of hats, dresses, and wigs. When none of the wardrobe items fit her, Cappuccina turns to a clever hairdresser for help. In *Quill & Quire,* Bridget Donald observed that Fernandes "has added a few subtle interpretive touches, for instance where Cappuccina's tail overlaps the border, reinforcing the impression of a cow that cannot be contained."

Fernandes has also collaborated with Milway on *One Hen,* a picture book based on a true story. Set in an Ashanti village in Ghana, the story follows Kojo, an impoverished youngster who uses a microloan to buy a hen that produces eggs he can sell in the marketplace. Step by small step, Kojo builds the proceeds into a successful poultry farm that employs others from his region, and he eventually establishes a fund that provides microloans to members of the community. "Fernandes's large acrylic paintings capture the warmth of the climate and include numerous details, such as splashes of kente cloth, that authenticate the setting," Grace Oliff remarked in *School Library Journal,* and Linda Perkins, writing in *Booklist,* stated that the art in *One Hen* "reflects the optimistic tone of the story."

Fernandes once told *SATA:* "We moved to a lake in Ontario, Canada, in 1984. Before that my studio was always the corner of a bedroom, protected only by a strip of tape on the floor that said 'please knock.' Our two children were quite good about that invisible door. They often sat next to me creating pictures and stories of their own, just as I had done when I was a child sitting beside by my father, Creig Flessel. He was one of the early comic book artists in the 1930s with DC Comics.

"So . . . here I am in a nutshell, perhaps a coconut shell. I've always been grateful that my work could be done at home where I could be with the kids, snug as a bug on snowy days, splashing into the lake on hot summer afternoons, and doing something that I love: Writing and illustrating children's books."

Biographical and Critical Sources

BOOKS

Jones, Raymond E., and Jon C. Scott, *Canadian Children's Books: A Critical Guide to Authors and Illustrators,* Oxford University Press (Toronto, Ontario, Canada), 2000.

PERIODICALS

Booklist, May 15, 1999, Helen Rosenberg, review of *A Difficult Day,* p. 1702; April 15, 2002, Ellen Mandel, review of *Busy Little Mouse,* p. 1407; April 1, 2006, Gillian Engberg, review of *Earth Magic,* p. 38; April 15, 2007, Hazel Rochman, review of *Polar Bear, Arctic Hare: Poems of the Frozen North,* p. 48; June 1, 2008, Linda Perkins, review of *One Hen: How One Small Loan Made a Big Difference,* p. 82.
Canadian Children's Literature, summer, 1994, Hilary Turner, review of *Just You and Me,* p. 60.
Canadian Review of Materials, November, 1993, Jennifer Johnson, review of *Just You and Me,* p. 217; November 3, 2000, Susan Fonseca, review of *Baby Dreams;* September 6, 2002, Catherine Hoyt, review of *One More Pet.*
Childhood Education, fall, 2007, Connie Green, review of *Polar Bear, Arctic Hare,* p. 51.
Kirkus Reviews, August 15, 2003, review of *The Mouse Was out at Recess,* p. 1074.
Publishers Weekly, April 26, 1999, review of *A Difficult Day,* p. 81.
Quill & Quire, August, 1993, Janet McNaughton, review of *Just You and Me;* September, 2000, Jeffrey Canton, review of *Sleepy Little Mouse;* February, 2002, Joanne Findon, review of *Busy Little Mouse;* March, 2002, Bridget Donald, review of *Cappuccina Goes to Town;* April, 2002, Gwyneth Evans, review of *One More Pet;* February, 2004, Jessica Kelley, review of *Big Day for Little Mouse;* May, 2007, Michele Landsberg, review of *Polar Bear, Arctic Hare.*
Resource Links, April, 2002, Denise Parrott, review of *One More Pet,* p. 4; April, 2004, Adriane Pettit, review of *Big Week for Little Mouse,* p. 3; February, 2006, Suzanne Finkelstein, review of *Munsch More!: A Robert Munsch Collection,* p. 9; April, 2006, Linda Ludke, review of *Busy Little Mouse,* p. 4.
School Library Journal, August, 2002, Susan Marie Pitard, review of *Busy Little Mouse,* p. 155; July, 2003, Joyce Adams Burner, review of *Before You Were Born: The Inside Story!,* p. 77; September, 2003, John Peters, review of *The Mouse Was out at Recess,* p. 199; March, 2005, Shawn Brommer, review of *Beyond Old MacDonald: Funny Poems from Down on the Farm,* p. 194; July, 2006, Kathleen Whalin, review of *Earth Magic,* p. 118; May, 2007, Teresa Pfeifer, review of *Polar Bear, Arctic Hare,* p. 125; May, 2008, Grace Oliff, review of *One Hen,* p. 103.

ONLINE

Annick Press Web site, http://www.annickpress.com/ (September 1, 2009), "Eugenie Fernandes."
Kids Can Press Web site, http://www.kidscanpress.com/ (September 1, 2009), interview with Fernandes.*

*   *   *

FOWLES, Shelley 1956-

Personal

Born 1956, in South Africa. *Education:* Diploma (graphic art and design), M.A. (sequential design and illustration); pursuing practice-based Ph.D.

Addresses

Home—London, England. *E-mail*—shelley@leecom.demon.co.uk.

Career

Author, artist, and book illustrator. Designer of greeting cards and wrapping paper. *Exhibitions:* Work exhibited London and Brighton, England.

Awards, Honors

Marion Vannett Ridgway Honor Book Award, 2004, for *The Bachelor and the Bean.*

Shelley Fowles (Reproduced by permission.)

Writings

SELF-ILLUSTRATED

The Bachelor and the Bean: A Jewish Moroccan Folktale,
    Farrar, Straus & Giroux (New York, NY), 2003.
Climbing Rosa, Frances Lincoln (London, England), 2006.

ILLUSTRATOR

Ann Jungman, *The Most Magnificent Mosque,* Frances
    Lincoln (London, England), 2004.
James Riordan, *The Seven Voyages of Sinbad the Sailor,*
    Frances Lincoln (London, England), 2008.
Elizabeth Laird, reteller, *A Fistful of Pearls, and Other
    Tales from Iraq,* Frances Lincoln (London, England),
    2008.
Elizabeth Laird, reteller, *The Ogress and the Snake, and
    Other Stories from Somalia,* Frances Lincoln (London,
    England), 2009.

Sidelights

A native of South Africa, author and illustrator Shelley
Fowles lives and works in London, England. In addition to her work designing greeting cards, playing cards,

and wrapping paper, Fowles has also contributed artwork to a number of highly regarded children's books,
including her self-illustrated debut tale, *The Bachelor
and the Bean: A Jewish Moroccan Folktale,* which received the Marion Vannett Ridgway Honor Book Award.

The Bachelor and the Bean is set in a Moroccan village. Fowles' story concerns a grumpy old bachelor
who complains vociferously after dropping the last bean
from his plate down a well, which is inhabited by an
imp. Frustrated by the man's outburst, the imp gives
him a magic pot that produces food on command. When
the pot is stolen, the bachelor returns to the well and
secures a second pot, which provides him with beautiful glassware. That pot also goes missing, and the imp
finally offers a third pot, which is filled with water that
yields a reflection of the thief's identity: a jealous neighbor. When the bachelor confronts the woman, however,
he finds her surly behavior strangely appealing in what
Booklist critic Gillian Engberg described as a "lively,
funny, and perfectly paced" tale. A contributor in *Kirkus
Reviews* praised Fowles' illustrations, citing the "luminous watercolors that simply glow on the page like
stained glass," and Susan Perren, writing in the Toronto
Globe & Mail, observed that the author/illustrator "illuminates palm trees, brass cooking pots, mosques, mina-
rets and synagogues in a riot of colour, taste and sensa-
tion—a glorious excess."

Another self-illustrated work by Fowles, *Climbing Rosa,*
is based on an Hungarian folktale. When a king decides
that the time has come to marry off his son, a book
lover who does nothing but read all day, he announces
a contest: the woman who can fetch a handful of seeds
from an enormous tree will become the prince's bride.
A spunky villager with a penchant for climbing, Rosa
vies with her manipulative stepsister for the top prize.
"Ink-and-acrylic illustrations playfully illuminate the
humorous text," noted Kirsten Cutler in a review of
Climbing Rosa for *School Library Journal.* According
to a *Publishers Weekly* critic, "Fowles's talent for deliciously astringent prose . . . is matched by her gift for
creating scenes of dreamy, intensely hued romanticism."

Fowles has also illustrated books for other authors. *The
Most Magnificent Mosque,* a work by Ann Jungman,
centers on three rascally boys who create mischief at
the mosque in their Spanish town. After the trouble-
makers are caught red-handed, the local caliph orders
them to perform community service on the grounds of
the mosque. When the building is later threatened with
destruction by a Christian ruler, the trio—whose members have gained a greater appreciation for the structure—argues for its preservation. "Vibrant, colorful
paintings depict the action and setting of the story,"
Margaret R. Tassia commented in her review of *The
Most Magnificent Mosque* in *School Library Journal.*

In *The Seven Voyages of Sinbad the Sailor,* James Riordan retells the adventures of the legendary figure, including his excursions to the Isle of the Apes and the

Land of Sarandip. Farida S. Dowler, writing in *School Library Journal*, described Fowles' pictures for this work as "colorful and merry," and a contributor in *Kirkus Reviews* noted of *The Seven Voyages of Sinbad the Sailor* that the illustrator "adds comic notes with small, jewel-toned . . . illustrations done in an appealingly childlike style."

Biographical and Critical Sources

PERIODICALS

Booklist, March 15, 2003, Gillian Engberg, review of *The Bachelor and the Bean: A Jewish Moroccan Folktale,* p. 1328; April 1, 2006, Kathleen Odean, review of *Climbing Rosa,* p. 48.

Globe & Mail (Toronto, Ontario, Canada), February 24, 2004, Susan Perren, review of *The Bachelor and the Bean,* p. D10.

Kirkus Reviews, February 1, 2003, review of *The Bachelor and the Bean,* p. 228; May 1, 2008, review of *The Seven Voyages of Sinbad the Sailor.*

Publishers Weekly, February 3, 2003, review of *The Bachelor and the Bean,* p. 75; January 16, 2006, review of *Climbing Rosa,* p. 63.

School Library Journal, March, 2003, Kathy Piehl, review of *The Bachelor and the Bean,* p. 217; September, 2004, Margaret R. Tassia, review of *The Most Magnificent Mosque,* p. 170; May, 2006, Kirsten Cutler, review of *Climbing Rosa,* p. 110; August, 2008, Farida S. Dowler, review of *The Seven Voyages of Sinbad the Sailor,* p. 150.

ONLINE

Centre for Research and Development Web site, http://artsresearch.brighton.ac.uk/research/student/ (September 1, 2009), "Shelley Fowles."

Frances Lincoln Web site, http:www.franceslincoln.com/ (November 15, 2009), "Shelley Fowles."

James Riordan's adaptation of a traditional story is brought to life in Fowles' naïf-styled paintings for **The Seven Voyages of Sinbad the Sailor.**
(Frances Lincoln Children's Books, 2007. Illustration copyright © 2007 by Shelley Fowles. Reproduced by permission.)

World of Playing Cards Web site, http://www.wopc.co.uk/
   otc/ (September 1, 2009), "Shelley Fowles."

*   *   *

FREITAS, Donna 1972-

Personal

Surname pronounced FRAY-tis; born 1972, in RI. *Education:* Georgetown University, B.A., 1994; Catholic University of America, M.A., 1999, Ph.D., 2002.

Addresses

Home—New York, NY; and Boston, MA. *Office*—Boston University, Dept. of Religion, 147 Bay State Rd., Ste. 506, Boston, MA 02215. *Agent*—Miriam Altshuler Literary Agency, 53 Old Post Rd. North, Red Hook, NY 12571. *E-mail*—freitas@bu.edu.

Career

Author, theologian, and educator. Marymount University, Arlington, VA, lecturer, 2001; St. Johns University, Queens, NY, lecturer, 2002; Saint Michael's College, Colchester, VT, assistant professor, 2003-07; Education Sector, Washington, DC, senior fellow, 2005—; Boston University, Boston, MA, visiting research faculty, 2007, became assistant professor of religion. Georgetown University, Washington, DC, chaplain-in-residence, 2000-01; St. John's College High School, Washington, DC, dean of student life and director of peer ministry, 2000-01; New York University, New York, NY, community development educator, 2002-03. Commentator on National Public Radio's *All Things Considered.*

Member

American Academy of Religion, Religion Newswriters Association, Catholic Theological Society of America, Society for the Study of Christian Spirituality, National Association of Student Personnel Administrators.

Awards, Honors

St. Michael's College research grant, 2004; University of Manchester fellowship, 2004; Louisville Institute research grant, 2005-08.

Writings

FICTION

The Possibilities of Sainthood, Farrar, Straus & Giroux (New York, NY), 2008.

NONFICTION

(With Jason King) *Save the Date: A Spirituality of Dating, Love, Dinner, and the Divine,* Crossroad (New York, NY), 2003.

Becoming a Goddess of Inner Poise: Spirituality for the Bridget Jones in All of Us, Jossey-Bass (San Francisco, CA), 2005.
(With Jason King) *Killing the Imposter God: Philip Pullman's Spiritual Imagination in His Dark Materials,* Jossey-Bass (San Francisco, CA), 2007.
Sex and the Soul: Juggling Sexuality, Spirituality, Romance, and Religion on America's College Campuses, Oxford University Press (New York, NY), 2008.

Contributor to *Washington Post/Newsweek* online panel "On Faith," and *Beliefnet.com.* Contributor to periodicals, including *Publishers Weekly, Wall Street Journal, Washington Post, Christian Century,* and *School Library Journal.*

Sidelights

Donna Freitas, a noted theologian, writer, and educator, examines faith, relationships, and gender in books which include *Sex and the Soul: Juggling Sexuality, Spirituality, Romance, and Religion on America's College Campuses.* In 2008 Freitas released her first work of fiction, *The Possibilities of Sainthood,* a critically acclaimed young-adult novel. "It was the most fun thing I've ever written," Freitas told *Publishers Weekly* interviewer Sue Corbett. "I'm often writing about dark and serious topics in my work as a scholar, and it was so liberating to just go wherever my imagination wanted."

The idea for *The Possibilities of Sainthood,* a coming-of-age tale about a fifteen-year-old Catholic schoolgirl, emerged after Freitas read Louis Sachar's *Holes,* a Newbery Medal winner. "What I loved most were all the quirks—the characters' odd names and the interesting backstory," she remarked to Corbett. "When I finished it, I started to wonder, if I wrote a book, what would my main character's quirks be?" *The Possibilities of Sainthood* focuses on Antonia Lucia Labella, a boy-crazy teen who lives with her widowed mother in an Italian-American neighborhood in Providence, Rhode Island. When she is not swooning over heartthrob Andy Rottelini (who she hopes will deliver her first kiss), Antonia conducts extensive studies of the lives of the saints and frequently petitions the Vatican in the hope of achieving her life's goal: to become the first living saint in the history of the Catholic Church. "There are so many novels about teenagers who become famous but it's because they are royalty or celebrities," Freitas stated in her *Publishers Weekly* interview. "I thought this offbeat path to fame would be a strange but fun quest for a teenage girl."

The Possibilities of Sainthood garnered solid reviews. "While getting at serious issues," a *Publishers Weekly* contributor observed, "Freitas . . . wins readers over with a beautifully sustained light touch." In the words of *Booklist* critic Ilene Cooper, the author "hops into the romance genre and brightens and heightens it by providing characters who are anything but run-of-the-mill." Jennifer M. Brabander commented in her review

Cover of Donna Freitas's young-adult novel The Possibilities of Saint-hood, *featuring photography by Jeffrey Jenkins.* (Illustration copyright © 2008 by Jeffrey Jenkins. Reproduced by permission of Frances Foster Books, a division of Farrar, Straus & Giroux, LLC.)

for *Horn Book* that *The Possibilities of Sainthood* provides "a rare glimpse at how a passion for religion can happily co-exist alongside other, less-exalted kinds." "Like good homemade pasta," remarked a *Kirkus Reviews* contributor, "this satisfying novel balances lightness with substance and leaves teens wanting another serving."

Writing *The Possibilities of Sainthood* served as a catharsis for Freitas, who was then grieving over the recent deaths of her mother and grandmother. As she acknowledged to Corbett, "I was really sad about my mom, especially, so it was important that the book be lighthearted, because she was. I was trying to write my way out of my sadness." Once she began working on the book, Freitas added, the narrative "poured out. I wrote like a person possessed." The humorous aspects of Antonia's quest helped temper her sadness, the author told Jeannette Cooperman in the *National Catholic Reporter:* "In some ways, the saints are wonderfully kitschy, comedy-in-waiting. I don't mean that disre-

spectfully. People focus, and for good reason, on the darker side of Catholicism, but there's this wonderful lighthearted side that's filled with life."

Biographical and Critical Sources

PERIODICALS

Booklist, September 15, 2008, Ilene Cooper, review of *The Possibilities of Sainthood,* p. 59.

Christian Century, November 18, 2008, Amy Frykholm, review of *Sex and the Soul: Juggling Sexuality, Spirituality, Romance, and Religion on America's College Campuses,* p. 39.

Christianity Today, August, 2008, Katelyn Beatty, "Zipping It: Donna Freitas Says That When It Comes to Sexual Ethics, Nonreligious Schools Are Failing Their Students," p. 40.

Christian Science Monitor, May 28, 2008, Jane Lampman, review of *Sex and the Soul,* p. 25.

Commonweal, May 9, 2008, Jean Hughes Raber, review of *Sex and the Soul,* p. 32.

Herizons, spring, 2006, Heather Emberley, review of *Becoming a Goddess of Inner Poise: Spirituality for the Bridget Jones in All of Us,* p. 38.

Horn Book, November-December, 2008, Jennifer M. Brabander, review of *The Possibilities of Sainthood,* p. 703.

Kirkus Reviews, June 15, 2008, review of *The Possibilities of Sainthood.*

National Catholic Reporter, May 30, 2008, Kris Berggren, "Even on Catholic Campuses, Hookup Sex Prevails: Researcher Donna Freitas Finds College Students See No Connection between Religion and Sexual Behavior," p. 5; October 31, 2008, Jeannette Cooperman, "Donna Freitas," p. 20.

Publishers Weekly, September 13, 2004, review of *Becoming a Goddess of Inner Poise,* p. 75; June 11, 2007, review of *Killing the Imposter God: Philip Pullman's Spiritual Imagination in His Dark Materials,* p. 54; February 25, 2008, review of *Sex and the Soul,* p. 69; July 21, 2008, review of *The Possibilities of Sainthood,* p. 160; December 22, 2008, Sue Corbett, "Fall Flying Starts," p. 24.

School Library Journal, August, 2008, Cara von Wrangel Kinsey, review of *The Possibilities of Sainthood,* p. 120.

U.S. Catholic, November, 2008, "Sex, Lies, and Hook-up Culture," p. 12.

ONLINE

Boston University Web site, http://www.bu.edu/ (September 1, 2009), "Donna Freitas."

Donna Freitas Home Page, http://www.donnafreitas.com (September 1, 2009).

Macmillan Web site, http://us.macmillan.com/ (September 1, 2009), "Donna Freitas."*

G

GANNON, Ned 1974-

Personal

Born 1974; married; wife's name Sara; children: two. *Education:* Attended Kansas City Art Institute; School of Visual Arts, M.F.A.

Addresses

Home—WI. *E-mail*—nsgannon@charter.net.

Career

Illustrator, writer, educator, and fine-art painter. University of Wisconsin, Eau, Claire, teacher. *Exhibitions:* Work included in exhibits of Society of Illustrators (New York, NY) and *Communication Arts;* and in galleries in New York, NY.

Illustrator

Jane G. Meyer, *The Man and the Vine,* St. Vladimirs Seminary Press (Crestwood, NY), 2006.
Rebecca Hogue Wojahn, *Evan Early,* Woodbine House (Bethesda, MD), 2006.
Maha Addasi, *The White Nights of Ramadan,* Boyds Mills Press (Honesdale, PA), 2008.

Contributor to periodicals, including *Cobblestone.*

Biographical and Critical Sources

PERIODICALS

Booklist, July 1, 2008, Hazel Rochman, review of *The White Nights of Ramadan,* p. 75.
Kirkus Reviews, July 1, 2008, review of *The White Nights of Ramadan.*
School Library Journal, September, 2008, Fawzia Gilani-Williams, review of *The White Nights of Ramadan,* p. 136.

ONLINE

Ned Gannon Home Page, http://www.nedgannon.com (September 21, 2009).*

* * *

GIBALA-BROXHOLM, Scott 1959(?)-

Personal

Born c. 1959; married; wife's name Janice (an author); children: one son, one daughter.

Addresses

Home—Walworth, NY.

Career

Author and illustrator.

Writings

Scary Fright, Are You All Right?, Dial Books for Young Readers (New York, NY), 2002.

ILLUSTRATOR

Wendy Wax, *City Witch, Country Switch,* Marshall Cavendish Children (Tarrytown, NY), 2008.

Sidelights

Scott Gibala-Broxholm made his publishing debut with the self-illustrated chapter book *Scary Fright, Are You All Right?* Capturing the loving relationship between parent and child, the story focuses on a young monster who attracts the concern of her doting monster parents when her behavior suddenly undergoes a dramatic

change. Instead of icky slime, Scary Fright now prefers pizza for dinner, and she enjoys cute kittens as playmates rather than as a potential snack. Even more worrisome, cheerful singing has replaced the young monster's former snarling, growling, and howling at the moon. Hustled off to Dr. Ghastly by her worried monster mom and dad, Scary Fright is diagnosed with humanitis, a disease she contracted from her human playmates.

In *Booklist* Helen Rosenberg described *Scary Fright, Are You All Right?* as "hilarious," adding that Gibala-Broxholm's "nicely paced" text teams well with his "amusing, detailed" pencil-and-watercolor art. Storytime audiences will enjoy the story "of a girl who gets sent to her room for being good," quipped Maryann H. Owen in *School Library Journal,* and in *Kirkus Reviews* a critic described the book as a "year-round" favorite that is "packed with silly spooky humor."

In addition to his self-illustrated chapter book, Gibala-Broxholm has also created the artwork for Wendy Wax's picture book *City Witch, Country Switch.* A story based on the traditional folk tale "City Mouse and Country Mouse," *City Witch, Country Switch* is brought to life in artwork that is "full of humor," according to *School Library Journal* writer Maura Bresnahan, As a *Kirkus Reviews* writer concluded, the artist's detailed illustrations featuring two witch cousins "make the most of the absurd situations" in Wax's spell-laced story.

Scott Gibala-Broxholm creates the whimsical watercolor art that adds humor to City Witch, Country Witch *by Wendy Wax.* (Marshall Cavendish Children, 2008. Illustration copyright © 2008 by Scott Gibala-Broxholm. Reproduced by permission.)

Biographical and Critical Sources

PERIODICALS

Booklist, September 15, 2002, Helen Rosenberg, review of *Scary Fright, Are You All Right?,* p. 245.
Kirkus Reviews, June 15, 2002, review of *Scary Fright, Are You Alright?*; July 15, 2008, review of *City Witch, Country Switch.*
Publishers Weekly, August 12, 2002, review of *Scary Fright, Are You Alright?,* p. 300; October, 2008, Maura Bresnahan, review of *City Witch, Country Switch,* p. 128.
School Library Journal, August, 2002, Maryann H. Owen, review of *Scary Fright, Are You All Right?,* p. 155.*

*   *   *

GIBSON, Barbara L.
See GIBSON, Barbara Leonard

*   *   *

GIBSON, Barbara Leonard
(Barbara L. Gibson)

Personal
Married; husband's name Robert (a composer and director of University of Maryland School of Music). *Education:* Carnegie Mellon University, B.A. (fine art and design).

Addresses
Home—Olney, MD. *E-mail*—barbara@barbaragibson.com.

Career
Illustrator and fine arts painter.

Awards, Honors
Redbook Children's Picturebook Award, 1987, for *Creatures of the Desert World;* Art Director's Club award, 1991; Evelyn Thurman Young Readers Book Award, and Benjamin Franklin Award for Cover Design, Independent Book Publishers Association, both 2008, both for *The Dragonfly Door* by John Adams.

Illustrator
(Under name Barbara L. Gibson) Arnold B. Ajello and others, *How Things Are Made,* National Geographic Society (Washington, DC), 1981.
Susan McGrath, *Your World of Pets,* National Geographic Society (Washington, DC), 1985.
Toni Eugene, *Hide and Seek* (pop-up book), National Geographic Society (Washington, DC), 1985.

Barbara Leonard Gibson shares her knowledge of U.S. history in her artwork for Marie and Roland Smith's picture book **N Is for Our Nation's Capital.** (Sleeping Bear Press, 2005. Illustration copyright © 2005 Barbara Gibson. Reproduced by permission of Gale, a part of Cengage Learning.)

Jennifer C. Urquhart, *Creatures of the Desert World* (pop-up book), National Geographic Society (Washington, DC), 1987.

Peggy D. Winston, *Lets Explore a Tropical Forest* (pop-up book), National Geographic Society (Washington, DC), 1989.

Patricia F. Frakes, *My Own Little World,* National Geographic Society (Washington, DC), 1990.

ABC in the Woods, National Geographic Society (Washington, DC), 1990.

Pile of Puppies, National Geographic Society (Washington, DC), 1990.

Rainbow Books, National Geographic Society (Washington, DC), 1990.

Who's There?, National Geographic Society (Washington, DC), 1990.

Patricia F. Frakes, *My House,* National Geographic Society (Washington, DC), 1990.

Colonial Colors, Colonial Williamsburg Foundation (Williamsburg, VA), 1993.

Luise Woelflein, *Desert Animals,* Scholastic (New York, NY), 1993.

Luise Woelflein, *Forest Animals,* Scholastic (New York, NY), 1993.

Count with the Cooper, Colonial Williamsburg Foundation (Williamsburg, VA), 1993.

Animals at Colonial Williamsburg, Colonial Williamsburg Foundation (Williamsburg, VA), 1993.

Lisa A. Reinhard, *The Nutmeg Adventure,* Colonial Williamsburg Foundation (Williamsburg, VA), 1994.

Anne Miranda, *Cownting,* Time-Life for Children (Alexandria, VA), 1994.

Jonathan Grupper, *Spin's Really Wild Africa Tour,* National Geographic Society (Washington, DC), 1996.

Barbara Brownell, *Spin's Really Wild U.S.A. Tour,* National Geographic Society (Washington, DC), 1996.

C.L. Arbelbide, *The White House Easter Egg Roll,* White House Historical, 1997.

John Whitman, *Star Wars: The Death Star,* Little, Brown (Boston, MA), 1997.

Patricia Cornwell, *Life's Little Fable,* Putnam (New York, NY), 1999.

Audrey Penn, *The Whistling Tree,* Child & Family Press (Washington, DC), 2003.

Audrey Penn, *A Pocket Full of Kisses,* Child & Family Press (Washington, DC), 2004.

Marie Smith, *N Is for Our Nation's Capital: A Washington, DC, Alphabet,* Sleeping Bear Press (Chelsea, MI), 2005.

Audrey Penn, *A Kiss Goodbye,* Tanglewood Press (Terre Haute, IN), 2007.

John Adams, *The Dragonfly Door,* Feather Rock Books (Maple Plain, MN), 2007.

Audrey Penn, *Chester Raccoon and the Big Bad Bully,* Tanglewood Press (Terre Haute, IN), 2008.

Artie Knapp, *Stuttering Stan Takes a Stand,* Cincinnati Children's Hospital (Cincinnati, OH), 2008.

John Adams and Clea Adams, *The Dragonfly Secret,* Feather Rock Books (Maple Plain, MN), 2009.

Audrey Penn, *Chester Raccoon and the Acorn Full of Memories,* Tanglewood Press (Terre Haute, IN), 2009.

Lynn Friess, *A Western Lullaby,* Verve Communications, 2010.

Also illustrator of picture-book adaptations of *Dracula* by Bram Stoker, and *20,000 Leagues under the Sea* by Jules Verne. Contributor of artwork to periodicals, including *National Geographic, Washingtonian, Smithsonian, Ranger Rick, Your Big Backyard, Horticulturist, Scientific American, Equus,* and *Dressage Today.*

Sidelights

Working from her studio near Washington, DC, Barbara Leonard Gibson is a fine-arts painter whose interests include natural science, wildlife, seascapes, and landscapes. Her work spans portraits, advertising art, and book illustration, the last of which includes books published by the National Geographical Society, Time-Life Books, and the Colonial Williamsburg Foundation. Nature-based titles that feature Gibson's detailed paintings include *Hide and Seek, Creatures of the Desert World,* and *Explore a Tropical Rainforest,* while historical themes are the subject of her illustrations for *N Is for the Nation's Capital, Colonial Colors, Count with the Cooper,* and *The Nutmeg Adventure,* the last three produced for young visitors to Colonial Williamsburg in Williamsburg, Virginia.

Gibson's illustration projects also include creating art for picture-book stories by Audrey Penn that feature Chester the Raccoon and friends. In *A Pocket Full of Kisses,* Chester is having trouble with his mischievous little brother, and Gibson's detailed illustrations "depict an idyllic woodland populated with friendly beasts, birds, and bugs," according to *Booklist* contributor Carolyn Phelan. Reviewing the same book in *School Library Journal,* Gay Lynn Van Vleck observed that the artist's "crisp, realistic paintings are colorful," while a *Publishers Weekly* writer praised Gibson for "balanc-[ing] . . . the sentimental message" of Penn's "flowery, poignant prose" with "meticulously detailed" nature-based images. While Grace Oliff wrote in *School Library Journal* that *Chester Raccoon and the Big Bad Bully* "drips with . . . cloying sentimentality," Gibson's illustrations for the book "are bright and attractive, and the faces of the animals are . . . expressive."

Biographical and Critical Sources

PERIODICALS

Booklist, October 15, 2004, Carolyn Phelan, review of *A Pocket Full of Kisses,* p. 411.

Kirkus Reviews, July 1, 2008, review of *Chester Raccoon and the Big Bad Bully.*

Publishers Weekly, June 21, 2004, review of *A Pocket Full of Kisses,* p. 62.

School Library Journal, January, 2005, Gay Lynn Van Vleck, review of *A Pocket Full of Kisses,* p. 96; August, 2005, Pamela K. Bomboy, review of *N Is for Our Nation's Capital: A Washington, DC Alphabet,* p. 118; September, 2008, Grace Oliff, review of *Chester Raccoon and the Big Bad Bully,* p. 156.

ONLINE

Barbara Leonard Gibson Home Page, http://www.barbara gibson.com (September 20, 2009).

*   *   *

GREY, Mini

Personal

Born in Wales; partner's name Tony. *Education:* University College London, B.A. (English); studied theatre design; University of Brighton, M.A. (sequential design). *Hobbies and other interests:* Walking, cycling, "playing electric piano BADLY."

Addresses

Home—Oxford, England.

Career

Author and illustrator. Formerly worked as a puppet maker and theatre designer; teacher in South London, England, for six years; currently freelance illustrator.

Awards, Honors

Kate Greenaway Award shortlist, 2004, for *The Pea and the Princess;* Nestlé Smarties Gold Medal (Five Years and Under category), 2004, for *Biscuit Bear;* Boston Globe/Horn Book Award, 2006, for *Traction Man Is Here!;* Kate Greenaway Medal, 2007, for *The Adventures of the Dish and the Spoon.*

Writings

SELF-ILLUSTRATED

Egg Drop, Jonathan Cape (London, England), 2002, Knopf (New York, NY), 2009.

The Pea and the Princess, Jonathan Cape (London, England), 2003, published as *The Very Smart Pea and the Princess-to-Be,* Knopf (New York, NY), 2003.

Biscuit Bear, Jonathan Cape (London, England), 2004, published as *Ginger Bear,* Knopf (New York, NY), 2007.

Traction Man Is Here!, Knopf (New York, NY), 2005.

The Adventures of the Dish and the Spoon, Knopf (New York, NY), 2006.

Traction Man Meets Turbodog, Knopf (New York, NY), 2008.

ILLUSTRATOR

June Crebbin, *The Crocodile Is Coming!* (poems), Walker (London, England) 2005.

Lyn Gardner, *Into the Woods,* David Fickling (New York, NY), 2006.

Dick King-Smith, *The Twin Giants,* Walker (London, England), 2007, Candlewick Press (Cambridge, MA), 2008.

Sidelights

British-born author and illustrator Mini Grey has combined a degree in English, training in both theatre arts and fine arts, a job as a puppet-maker, and six years' experience working as a teacher in South London schools to fashion a career as an award-winning creator of children's picture books. In addition to her award-winning picture books *The Pea and the Princess*—published in the United States as *The Very Smart Pea and the Princess-to-Be*—and *Ginger Bear,* Grey is also the author and illustrator of *Egg Drop* and *Traction Man Is Here!* "Grey has a knack for reimagining nursery rhymes and other children's classics," wrote a *Publishers Weekly* critic in a review of *Ginger Bear,* a story that is based on the well-known tale of the Gingerbread Man.

Another well-known tale is turned topsy-turvy in *The Very Smart Pea and the Princess-to-Be,* as Grey recounts the classic test for princess-hood from the poor pea's point of view. Raised in a pod in the palace garden, this particular pea knows it has a higher purpose than the royal dining table, and sure enough, it is plucked by the queen and used as a way to test potential wives for her son, the prince. Realizing that the test is flawed after a number of highly qualified princesses sleep like babies atop the pile of mattresses under which the small pea has been placed, the pea decides to intervene; when the pretty young gardener who once tended it is tested for princess-hood, the little legume climbs the mattress mountain and whispers relentlessly about the lump in the girl's mattress. A *Kirkus Reviews* critic described the story as a "rib-tickling" tale, adding that Grey's illustrations contain "plenty of sight gags" that pair with her "chatty narrative." Susan Dove Lempke also praised the story in *Horn Book,* citing its "visual wit" and commenting on the "vegetable and fruit motifs" that appear in the painted illustrations.

In *Egg Drop,* Grey tells the story of an egg that knows its destiny is to fly, while *The Adventures of the Dish and the Spoon* follows the famed dish and spoon of "Hey Diddle Diddle" fame as the affectionate duo makes its way in the world, even resorting to robbery and the resulting jail time. Set during the Great Depression of the 1930s, *The Adventures of the Dish and the Spoon* draws on the popular culture of the era, from slapstick comedy to the mythos surrounding American bank robbers Bonnie and Clyde. In *Horn Book* Christine M. Heppermann cited Grey's "amusingly surreal mixed-media" illustrations as a feature of her "fanciful rags-to-riches tale." "Sprung from a familiar stanza," according to a *Publishers Weekly* critic, Grey's "inventive tale of true love will sustain many rereadings by readers of all ages." In the *New York Times Book Review* Jessica Bruder concluded that Grey's illustrations for *The Adventures of the Dish and the Spoon* "glow with humor and affection" and contain "plenty of comedic clues to reward careful readers."

Published in Grey's native England as *Biscuit Bear,* *Ginger Bear* finds Grey combining her multimedia art with an "edgy story" in which her "slightly arch tone . . . add[s] a lovely fairy-tale flavor," according to *School Library Journal* critic Susan Moorhead. In the tale, young Horace bakes a bear-shaped cookie that looks tempting to eat, but at his mother's urging he places the treat on his pillow to save it for another day. Then the fantasy begins: coming to life, the cookie-crisp Ginger Bear heads to the kitchen to bake some yummy new friends. Although many of the cookies wind up being eaten, Ginger Bear ultimately finds a safe home in the window of a local bakery. In *Kirkus Reviews* a critic dubbed *Ginger Bear* a "sweet little offering" that benefits from Grey's "graphic inventiveness," while in *Horn Book* Heppermann characterized the story as "a rambunctious, sometimes gleeful macabre foray into the world of baked goods." *Biscuit Bear* won the 2004 Smarties Prize, a significant achievement considering that it was Grey's third picture book.

Winner of the 2006 *Boston Globe/Horn Book* award, *Traction Man Is Here!* is the chronicle of a young boy's adventures while putting his brand new, camouflage-wearing action figure through its high-adventure paces. Told through the boy's eyes, the story follows Traction Man as he battles household horrors such as the Poisonous Dishcloth and rises above the indignity of wearing a green sweater knitted up by a loving grandma. In *School Library Journal* reviewer Marge Loch-Wouters dubbed *Traction Man Is Here!* an "imaginative and very funny romp."

Traction Man Meets Turbodog continues the story, as Traction Man find a messy adventure in the family compost heap, has fun cleaning up with new superfriend Scrubbing Brush, and ends the day with his human companion toasting marshmallows over a campfire. Grey's "inventive scenes celebrate the joy in . . . re-envisioning the everyday" and are full of "humor, deli-

cious language," and imaginative ideas, according to *School Library Journal* critic Wendy Lukehart. In *Publishers Weekly* a critic concluded that Grey's "real gift is in transforming an ordinary household into both thrilling stage and supporting cast," while Heppermann wrote that the author/illustrator's "irreverent wit" is a highlight of her "playful demonstration of why high-tech doesn't necessarily equal high-performance."

In creating her stories, Grey finds inspiration in both her home town and her own interests. "My stories often seem to take place in quite ordinary settings," she told Patricia Newman in *California Kids*. "For *Biscuit Bear* . . . ," Grey added, "I had to do detailed research into all types of biscuits and eat them!" "Picture books are a particular way of telling a story two ways at once," Grey added, ". . . and can be as simple or as complicated as anything else." An illustrator as well as an author, Grey has also contributed work to Lyn Gardner's middle-grade novel *Into the Woods*, where her "appealing" pen-and-ink images "add humor and detail to the story," according to *Booklist* critic Kay Weisman.

Biographical and Critical Sources

PERIODICALS

Booklist, March 1, 2005, Carolyn Phelan, review of *Traction Man Is Here!*, p. 1203; May 1, 2007, Kay Weisman, review of *Into the Woods*, p. 91; July 1, 2008, Carolyn Phelan, review of *The Twin Giants*, p. 75.

California Kids, September, 2005, Patricia Newman, "Who Wrote That?: Featuring Mini Grey."

Horn Book, November-December, 2003, Susan Dove Lempke, review of *The Very Smart Pea and the Princess-to-Be*, p. 730; March-April, 2005, Christine M. Heppermann, review of *Traction Man Is Here!*, p. 188; January-February, 2006, Mini Grey, transcript of *Boston Globe/Horn Book* Award acceptance speech, p. 17; May-June, 2006, Christine M. Heppermann, review of *The Adventures of the Dish and the Spoon*, p. 295; July-August, 2007, Christine M. Heppermann, review of *Ginger Bear*, p. 378, and Claire E. Gross, review of *Into the Woods*, p. 395; September-October, 2008, Christine M. Heppermann, review of *Traction Man Meets Turbodog*, p. 568.

Kirkus Reviews, August 15, 2003, review of *The Very Smart Pea and the Princess-to-Be*, p. 1073; March 15, 2005, review of *Traction Man Is Here!*, p. 352; May 15, 2007, reviews of *Ginger Bear* and *Into the Woods*.

New York Times Book Review, November 12, 2006, Jessica Bruder, review of *The Adventures of the Dish and the Spoon*, p. 21.

Publishers Weekly, March 7, 2005, review of *Traction Man Is Here!*, p. 67; March 13, 2006, review of *The Adventures of the Dish and the Spoon*, p. 65; May 21, 2007, review of *Ginger Bear*, p. 54; August 4, 2008, review of *Traction Man Meets Turbodog*, p. 60.

School Librarian, winter, 2002, review of *Egg Drop*, p. 186; autumn, 2003, review of *The Princess and the Pea*, p. 130; June, 2007, Margaret A. Chang, review of *Into the Woods*, p. 144.

School Library Journal, September, 2003, Wendy Woodfill, review of *The Very Smart Pea and the Princess-to-Be*, p. 179; June, 2005, Marge Loch-Wouters, review of *Traction Man Is Here!*, p. 115; April, 2006, Wanda Meyers-Hines, review of *The Adventures of the Dish and the Spoon*, p. 106; June, 2007, Susan Moorhead, review of *Ginger Bear*, p. 100; July, 2008, Mary-ann H. Owen, review of *The Twin Giants*, p. 76; August, 2008, Wendy Lukehart, review of *Traction Man Meets Turbodog*, p. 90.

ONLINE

Book Trust Web site, http://www.booktrusted.co.uk/ (December 1, 2005), Madelyn Travis, "Bear-faced Biscuit."

Random House Web site, http://www.randomhouse.com/ (September 20, 2009), "Mini Grey."

H

HALEY, Amanda

Personal

Married. *Education:* Art Institute of Chicago, B.F.A.

Addresses

Home—Chesapeake, VA. *Agent*—Shannon Associates, L.L.C., 630 9th Ave., Ste. 707, New York, NY 10036.

Career

Illustrator and graphic designer. Developer of advertising campaigns.

Awards, Honors

Teachers' Choice Award, International Reading Association, 2004, for *You Can't See Your Bones with Binoculars.*

Writings

SELF-ILLUSTRATED

Peek-a-boo Baby, Publications International (Lincolnwood, IL), 1998.
It's a Baby's World, Little, Brown (Boston, MA), 2001.
Doodle Studio, Pleasant Company (Middleton, WI), 2002.
Let Me Call You Sweetheart, HarperFestival (New York, NY), 2002.
Yankee Doodle, HarperFestival (New York, NY), 2002.
Easter Has Eggs, Sterling Publishing (New York, NY), 2008.
Kids Say the Cutest Things about God, West Side Publishing (Lincolnwood, IL), 2008.
If You're Happy and You Know It, Zonderkidz (Grand Rapids, MI), 2008.
3, 2, 1, School Is Fun, Children's Press (New York, NY), 2010.

ILLUSTRATOR

Shawn A. McMullen, *It's What's Inside That Counts,* Standard Publishing (Cincinnati, OH), 1991.
Shawn A. McMullen, *Justin Ordinary Squirrel,* Standard Publishing (Cincinnati, OH), 1991.
Andrea Posner, *Baby on Board,* Golden Books (New York, NY), 1999.
Robin Isabel Ahrens, *Dee and Bee,* Winslow Press (Delray Beach, FL), 2000.
Michelle Knudsen, *Love,* Little Simon (New York, NY), 2001.
Michelle Knudsen, *Cat Hat,* Golden Books (New York, NY), 2001.
Maxine A. Rock, *Me and My Dog,* Pleasant Company (Middleton, WI), 2001.
Deborah Mostow Zakarin, *Happening Hanukkah: Creative Ways to Celebrate,* Grosset & Dunlap (New York, NY), 2002.
Harriet Ziefert, *You Can't Taste a Pickle with Your Ear: A Book about Your Five Senses,* Blue Apple Books (Maplewood, NJ), 2002.
Harriet Ziefert, *You Can't Buy a Dinosaur with a Dime: Problem Solving in Dollars and Cents,* Blue Apple Books (Maplewood, NJ), 2003.
Joan Holub, *Fourth of July Sparkly Sky,* Little Simon (New York, NY), 2003.
Harriet Ziefert, *You Can't See Your Bones with Binoculars: A Guide to Your 206 Bones,* Blue Apple Books (Maplewood, NJ), 2003.
Margaret Frith, *Hooray for Ballet!,* Grosset & Dunlap (New York, NY), 2003.
Mary Packard, *The New Baby,* Children's Press (New York, NY), 2004.
Harriet Ziefert, *33 Uses for a Dad,* Blue Apple Books (Maplewood, NJ), 2004.
Harriet Ziefert and Fred Ehrlich, *You Can't Take Your Body to a Repair Shop: A Book about What Makes You Sick,* Blue Apple Books (Maplewood, NJ), 2004.
Harriet Ziefert, *Schools Have Learn,* Blue Apple Books (Maplewood, NJ), 2004.
Harriet Ziefert, *I Wish Santa Would Come by Helicopter,* Sterling Publishing (New York, NY), 2004.

Harriet Ziefert, *40 Uses for a Grandpa,* Blue Apple Books (Maplewood, NJ), 2005.

Harriet Ziefert, *41 Uses for a Grandma,* Blue Apple Books (Maplewood, NJ), 2005.

Harriet Ziefert, *Pizza and Other Stinky Poems,* Sterling Publishing (New York, NY), 2005.

Harriet Ziefert, *Ready, Alice?,* Sterling Publishing (New York, NY), 2005.

Fred Ehrlich, *You Can't See a Dodo at the Zoo,* Blue Apple Books (Maplewood, NJ), 2005.

Fred Ehrlich, *You Can't Use Your Brain If You're a Jellyfish,* Blue Apple Books (Maplewood, NJ), 2005.

Harriet Ziefert, *That's What Grandmas Are For,* Blue Apple Books (Maplewood, NJ), 2006.

Harriet Ziefert, *Dancing Class,* Sterling Publishing (New York, NY), 2006.

Harriet Ziefert, *Music Class,* Sterling Publishing (New York, NY), 2006.

Harriet Ziefert, *A Bath for a Princess,* Sterling Publishing (New York, NY), 2007.

Fred Ehrlich, *You Can't Lay an Egg If You're an Elephant,* Blue Apple Books (Maplewood, NJ), 2007.

Stephen Krensky, *Spark the Firefighter,* Dutton (New York, NY), 2008.

M.P. Hueston, *The All-American Jump and Jive Jig,* Sterling Publishing (New York, NY), 2010.

Contributor of illustrations to *Weekly Reader, American Girl, Girl's Life, Teen,* and *Better Homes & Gardens.*

Amanda Haley collaborates with prolific author Harriet Ziefert, creating the artwork for Ziefert's You Can't Taste a Pickle with Your Ear.
(Blue Apple Books, 2002. Illustration copyright © 2002 by Amanda Haley. Reproduced by permission.)

Sidelights

In addition to designing a variety of products, from gift wrap to stationery kits to children's lunch boxes, Amanda Haley has also contributed her artistic talents to children's literature. A graduate of the School of the Art Institute of Chicago, Haley creates pen-and-ink drawings that are tinted with bright water colors. In addition to producing self-illustrated stories of her own, Haley has worked extensively with noted writer Harriet Ziefert in addition to teaming up with authors such as Fred Ehrlich, M.D., and Stephen Krensky.

Haley began collaborating with Ziefert in 2002, publishing *You Can't Taste a Pickle with Your Ear: A Book about Your Five Senses,* the first of several titles about the human body that are geared toward younger readers. In *You Can't Taste a Pickle with Your Ear,* Ziefert offers children information about sensory organs, while her *You Can't See Your Bones with Binoculars: A Guide to Your 206 Bones* provides information about the shape and location of each bone in the human skeleton. Haley's illustrations for *You Can't Take Your Body to a Repair Shop: A Book about What Makes You Sick,* which is coauthored by Ziefert and Ehrlich, introduce common health problems and shows how they can be treated. Reviewing *You Can't Taste a Pickle with Your Ear,* a *Publishers Weekly* critic noted that Haley's "freewheeling watercolor-and-ink cartooning and frisky handwritten typography . . . add jolts of humor and energy" to the book's text.

In several of their collaborations, Haley and Ziefert focus on the complementary aspects of family members. Grandmothers earn special attention in *That's What Grandmas Are For,* while fathers receive top billing in *33 Uses for a Dad.* In the first-named book, children recount how grandmothers frequently indulge subsequent generations, and in the second, Ziefert highlights the many child-centered tasks that fathers undertake, from holding a child's hand to being a storyteller and campfire builder. In a review of *33 Uses for a Dad, School Library Journal* contributor Martha Topol wrote that Haley's pictures provide "a quiet, gentle charm that helps make this offering inviting," and a *Kirkus Reviews* critic concluded that the artist's "watercolor illustrations add warmth and humor."

Working as a duo, Haley and Ehrlich have also produced several books about the physical world, discussing extinct animals in *You Can't See a Dodo at the Zoo,* differences in cranial capacity in *You Can't Use Your Brain If You're a Jellyfish,* and reproductive qualities in *You Can't Lay an Egg If You're an Elephant.* "The bright cartoons add interest and appeal to the text," claimed Rebecca Sheridan in her *School Library Journal* review of *You Can't See a Dodo at the Zoo. Booklist* contributor Kay Weisman wrote that Haley's pictures "pick up key ideas from the text and add vivacity to" *You Can't Use Your Brain If You're a Jellyfish,* while a *Kirkus Reviews* critic concluded that the "cartoon-style illustra-

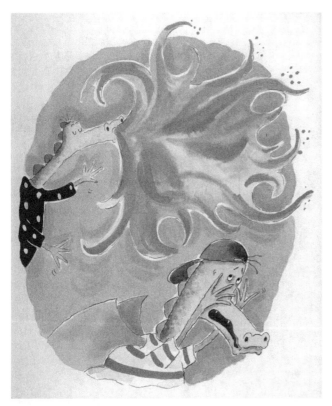

Haley's unique watercolor art brings to life Stephen Krensky's picture-book story in **Spark the Firefighter.** (Illustration copyright © 2008 by Amanda Haley. Reproduced by permission of Dutton Children's Books, a division of Penguin Putnam Books for Young Readers.)

tions" she contributes to *You Can't Lay an Egg If You're an Elephant* "nicely complement the text."

Fire safety is the focus of *Spark the Firefighter,* a story by Stephen Krensky that also features Haley's art. In the book, Spark, a young dragon, is afraid of fire, and he decides to overcome his fear by learning to be a volunteer firefighter. Hesitant at first, Spark succeeds in putting out several small fires before being called on to use his own fire-breathing ability to rescue farm animals trapped inside a burning barn. Haley's "amusing watercolors lighten up what could be a scary subject," concluded a *Kirkus Reviews* contributor in a review of *Spark the Firefighter,* while in *Booklist* Carolyn Phelan suggested that the artist's "deft line drawings, bright with colorful washes, offer plenty of drama as well as comic relief."

Biographical and Critical Sources

PERIODICALS

Booklist, April 15, 2000, GraceAnne A. DeCandido, review of *Dee and Bee,* p. 1550; March 15, 2001, Carolyn Phelan, review of *It's a Baby's World,* p. 1404; July, 2001, Gillian Engberg, review of *Cat Hat,* p. 2023; December 1, 2003, Gillian Engberg, review of

You Can't See Your Bones with Binoculars: A Guide to Your 206 Bones, p. 681; December 1, 2005, Kay Weisman, review of *You Can't Use Your Brain If You're a Jellyfish,* p. 66; November 1, 2008, Carolyn Phelan, review of *Spark the Firefighter,* p. 50.

Kirkus Reviews, November 15, 2002, review of *You Can't Taste a Pickle with Your Ear: A Book about Your Five Senses,* p. 1704; June 1, 2003, review of *You Can't Buy a Dinosaur with a Dime: Problem Solving in Dollars and Cents,* p. 813; December 15, 2003, review of *You Can't See Your Bones with Binoculars,* p. 1455; June 15, 2004, review of *33 Uses for a Dad,* p. 583; November 15, 2004, review of *You Can't Take Your Body to a Repair Shop: A Book about What Makes You Sick,* p. 1095; March 15, 2005, review of *You Can't See a Dodo at the Zoo,* p. 350; May 15, 2007, review of *You Can't Lay an Egg If You're an Elephant;* August 1, 2008, review of *Spark the Firefighter.*

Publishers Weekly, March 12, 2001, review of *It's a Baby's World,* p. 88; November 4, 2002, review of *You Can't Taste a Pickle with Your Ear,* p. 83.

School Library Journal, May, 2001, Sheryl L. Shipley, review of *It's a Baby's World,* p. 123; July, 2003, Leslie Barban, review of *You Can't Buy a Dinosaur with a Dime,* p. 120; September, 2003, Carol Schele, review of *Hooray for Ballet!,* p. 198; January, 2004, Dona Ratterree, review of *You Can't See Your Bones with Binoculars,* p. 123; October, 2004, Martha Topol, review of *33 Uses for a Dad,* p. 138; May, 2005, Maura Bresnahan, review of *Pizza and Other Stinky Poems,* p. 105, and Rebecca Sheridan, review of *You Can't See a Dodo at the Zoo,* p. 106; February, 2005, Roxanne Burg, review of *Schools Have Learn,* p. 114, and Gay Lynn Van Vleck, review of *You Can't Take Your Body to a Repair Shop,* p. 130; November, 2005, Sandra Welzenbach, review of *You Can't Use Your Brain If You're a Jellyfish,* p. 114; June, 2006, Kathleen Whalin, review of *That's What Grandmas Are For,* p. 130; July, 2007, Kathy Piehl, review of *You Can't Lay an Egg If You're an Elephant,* p. 90; September, 2008, Judith Constantinides, review of *Spark the Firefighter,* p. 152.*

*   *   *

HATTON, Caroline 1957-

Personal

Born 1957, in Normandy, France; married. *Education:* University of Paris, degree (pharmacy); University of California—Los Angeles, Ph.D. (chemistry). *Hobbies and other interests:* Crafts, horseback riding, backpacking.

Addresses

Home—Southern CA. *E-mail*—ch@carolinehatton.com.

Career

Writer, chemist, and French/English translator. University of California—Los Angeles, associate director of

Olympic Laboratory for more than ten years. Consultant to organizations that fight doping in sports. Presenter at schools and libraries.

Member

Society of Children's Book Writers and Illustrators, National Science Teachers Association, California Readers.

Writings

Véro and Philippe, illustrated by Preston McDaniels, Front Street Books (Chicago, IL), 2001.
The Night Olympic Team: Fighting to Keep Drugs out of the Games, Boyds Mills Press (Honesdale, PA), 2008.

Contributor to periodicals, including *Cricket, Highlights for Children, Schools Magazine, YES Mag,* and *Chao Ban Vietnam Adoption Newsletter.* Author of readers, including *Where Is My Puppy?, Surprise Moon,* and *A Pet for Grandma.*

Sidelights

Growing up in Paris, the daughter of Vietnamese immigrants, Caroline Hatton developed a love of writing. "When . . . I ran out of school library books to read, . . . I started writing (what must have been awful) novels," Hatton recalled during an online interview for the Tina Nichols Coury Web log. Although her love of writing was eventually superceded by a love of science and a career as a scientist specializing in detecting doping by athletes, Hatton returned to creative writing in her late thirties. "I chose to write for children because I had always known that good children's books are gems," she added. "As a teen, I'd walk to school through Paris even if it took an hour, to save my bus money to buy books, including picture books."

Hatton's children's stories and books are all written in English, even though she did not start learning English until age ten, and she did not move to the United States until age twenty-one. "I still love to learn new English words all the time and still speak French when yanked out of deep sleep," she admitted to *SATA.*

Hatton's first work of fiction, the upper elementary-grade novel *Véro and Philippe,* focuses on sibling rivalry and was inspired by Hatton's own memories of growing up between two cultures. Like their creator, the fictional Véronique and Philippe Vo move to Paris with their Vietnamese parents and must find a way to fit into their new culture, new city, and new school. Philippe, a bright and bookish twelve year old, is soon charged with caring for nine-year-old Véro after their nanny is fired, and his resentment of this responsibility stresses the sibling relationship until Véro and Philippe unite in their effort to regain their beloved nanny.

Hatton's work as a scientist is the focus of her nonfiction book *The Night Olympic Team: Fighting to Keep Drugs out of the Games.* Here she introduces readers to

Cover of Caroline Hatton's nonfiction book The Night Olympic Team, *which examines the science used in keeping sports fair.* (Boyds Mills Press, 2008. Jacket photograph © 2008 by Sam Kleinman/Corbis. Reproduced by permission.)

the work of the team of scientists entrusted with ensuring that the athletes competing at the Olympic Games do not benefit from performance-enhancing drugs. During the 2002 Winter Olympics in Salt Lake City, Utah, Hatton worked as part of the laboratory team that tested urine samples from athletes, double-checked results, and investigated any unusual results that might signal the presence of a new drug. In particular, they had to discover a way to test for NESP, a new blood booster that could increase athletes' endurance. In a review of *The Night Olympic Team* for *School Library Journal,* Marilyn Taniguchi praised Hatton's book as a "concise, readable account" of the chain of events that transpired after NESP was detected in three medal-winning cross-country skiers. Dubbing the book's subject "timely," Taniguchi went on to write that the author's "approach to the issues raised by the use of performance-enhancing drugs is fair-minded and kid-friendly." A *Kirkus Reviews* contributor called Hatton's work "readable" and a *Library Media Connection* critic dubbed it "outstanding."

When asked what she loves to do best, Hatton told *SATA:* "Exercising creativity! As a scientist, I wonder about different possibilities to solve mysteries. As a writer, I let my imagination run wild to get unstuck when I don't know what to write about. Getting a new

science or writing idea is a thrill." She also believes that, throughout life, each one of us should ask ourself, "What is your dream, and what are you doing about it?"

Biographical and Critical Sources

PERIODICALS

Kirkus Reviews, May 1, 2008, review of *The Night Olympic Team: Fighting to Keep Drugs out of the Games.*

Libraria Media Connection, October, 2008, review of *The Night Olympic Team.*

School Library Journal, December, 2001, review of *Véro and Philippe,* p. 103; June, 2008, interview with Hatton, p. 17, and Marilyn Taniguchi, review of *The Night Olympic Team,* p. 163.

ONLINE

Adopt Vietnam Web site, http://www.adoptvietnam.org/ (September 20, 2009), Allison Martin, interview with Hatton.

California Readers Web site, http://www.californiareaders. org/ (September 20, 2009), Bonnie O'Brian, interview with Hatton.

Caroline Hatton Home Page, http://www.carolinehatton. com (September 20, 2009).

Tina Nichols Coury Web log, http://www.tinanichols couryblog.com/ (May, 2008), interview with Hatton.

*   *   *

HECTOR, Julian

Personal

Born c. 1973, in Los Angeles, CA; son of biologists. *Education:* Parsons: The New School for Design, degree.

Addresses

Home—Brooklyn, NY. *Agent*—Conrad Rippy, Levine, Plotkin & Menin, 1740 Broadway, New York, NY 10019. *E-mail*—julian@julianhector.com.

Career

Author and illustrator. *Exhibitions:* Work included in group exhibition at Museum of American Illustration, 2008.

Writings

SELF-ILLUSTRATED

The Little Matador, Hyperion Books for Children (New York, NY), 2008.

The Gentleman Bug, Atheneum Books for Young Readers (New York, NY), 2010.

Author's work has been translated into Chinese.

ILLUSTRATOR

Laura Godwin, *This Is the Firefighter,* Disney/Hyperion (New York, NY), 2009.

Arthur A. Levine, *Monday Is One Day,* Scholastic Press (New York, NY), 2010.

Sidelights

Growing up in Texas, Julian Hector moved to New York City to attend Parsons' School of Design and has since made the city his home. His first book for children, the self-illustrated *The Little Matador,* was released in 2008 and quickly went into Chinese translation. A second picture book, *The Gentleman Bug,* further cemented Hector's budding career with its entertaining mix of whimsical story and subtly toned drawings.

In *The Little Matador* Hector focuses on a lad who is the youngest in a family full of bullfighters. Although the boy feels the weight of his parents' expectations that he, too, will become a matador, he would rather

Julian Hector introduces children to a Spanish tradition in his self-illustrated picture book **The Little Matador.** (Illustration © 2008 by Julian Hector. All rights reserved. Reprinted with permission of Disney Book Group.)

draw animals than fight them. In subtly hued images, Hector goes on to tell what Judith Constantinides described as a "succinct" story that depicts a "talent [that] is different but also special." In *Kirkus Reviews* a writer called Hector's inked illustrations for the story "wonderfully rendered," concluding of the mix between story and art: "It all works." Ilene Cooper wrote in her *Booklist* review of *The Little Matador* that the story's art, "with its unusual perspectives, both amuses and charms."

In addition to his original picture books, Hector has also worked as an illustrator, creating art to team with Laura Godwin's text for *This Is the Firefighter.* A rhyming story about a brave firefighter who rescues a girl's pet cat from a burning apartment building, *This Is the Firefighter* was acknowledged for its illustrations. In *Kirkus Reviews,* a contributor wrote that, through his use of primary colors, Hector creates a retro feel, "while at the same time incorporating modern art" into his reassuring images. With a similar reaction, Joanna Rudge Long concluded in *Horn Book* that Hector's "sturdy, simply modeled" characters are evocative of the illustrations of twentieth-century illustrator Lois Lenski.

Biographical and Critical Sources

PERIODICALS

Booklist, May 15, 2008, Ilene Cooper, review of *The Little Matador,* p. 49.
Horn Book, March-April, 2009, Joanna Rudge Long, review of *This Is the Firefighter,* p. 181.
Kirkus Reviews, June 15, 2008, review of *The Little Matador*; February 1, 2009, review of *This Is the Firefighter.*
School Library Journal, November, 2008, Judith Constantinides, review of *The Little Matador,* p. 90.

ONLINE

Julian Hector Home Page, http://www.julianhector.com (September 20, 2009).
Julian Hector Web log, http://julianhector.blogspot.com (September 20, 2009).*

* * *

HOOPER, Mary 1948-

Personal

Born July 23, 1948, in London, England; married; husband's name Richard; children: Gemma, Rowan. *Education:* Reading University, degree (English), 1990. *Hobbies and other interests:* Reading, painting furniture.

Addresses

Home—Henley on Thames, Oxfordshire, England. *Agent*—Rosemary Canter, PDF, Drury House, 34/43 Russell St., London WC2B 5HA, England. *E-mail*—contact@maryhooper.co.uk.

Career

Writer. Formerly worked as a secretary.

Member

Scattered Authors' Society.

Awards, Honors

North East Book Award, 2001, and Young Book Trust One Hundred Best Book listee, both for *Megan.*

Writings

JUVENILE AND MIDDLE-GRADE FICTION

Jodie, Nelson (Sunbury-on-Thames, England), 1978.
Only the Beginning, Nelson (Walton-on-Thames, England), 1981.
Love Emma XXX, Piccolo (London, England), 1982.
My Cousin Angie, Pan (London, England), 1984.
Follow That Dream, Pan (London, England), 1984.
Happy Ever After, Pan (London, England), 1984.
Janey's Diary, Methuen London (London, Englqnd), 1984.
A Love like Yours, Severn House (London, England), 1986.
Opposites Attract, Pan (London, England), 1986.
Lexie, Methuen Children's (London, England), 1987.
Janey's Summer, Magnet (London, England), 1987.
Making Waves, Methuen (London, England), 1988.
Short Cut to Love, Methuen (London, England), 1988.
Cassie, Teens Mandarin (London, England), 1990.
Katie: The Revolting Bridesmaid, Blackie (London, England), 1990, new edition, illustrated by Frederique Vaysierre, Bloomsbury (London, England), 2007.
Park Wood on Ice, Mammoth (London, England), 1991.
First Term, Mammoth (London, England), 1991.
Star, Mammoth (London, England), 1991.
The Boys Next Door, Mammoth (London, England), 1991.
Katie: The Revolting Wedding, Blackie (London, England), 1992, new edition, illustrated by Frederique Vaysierre, Bloomsbury (London, England), 2007.
Best Friends, Worst Luck, Walker (London, England), 1992.
Kate Goes to Chiddinghurst: The Four Katherines, Piccadilly (London, England), 1993.
There Goes Summer, Mammoth (London, England), 1993.
Spook Spotting, Walker (London, England), 1993.
Scandal Sheet, Mammoth (London, England), 1993.
Katie: The Revolting Baby, Blackie Children's Books (London, England), 1993.
The Pretend Princess, Heinemann (London, England), 1994.
The Boyfriend Trap, Walker (London, England), 1994.

Kae's Secret, Piccadilly Press (London, England), 1994.

Katie: The Revolting Holiday, Blackie Children's Books (London, England), 1995, new edition, illustrated by Frederique Vayssiere, Bloomsbury (London, England), 2008.

Carley's Story, Ginn (Aylesbury, England), 1995.

Two Naughty Angels: Down to Earth, illustrated by Lesley Harker, Bloomsbury Children's Books (London, England), 1995.

Ray's Story, Ginn (Aylesbury, England), 1995.

Jenny's Story, Ginn (Aylesbury, England), 1995.

Two Naughty Angels: The Ghoul at School, illustrated by Lesley Harker, Bloomsbury Children's Books (London, England), 1995.

Poppy's Big Push, Franklin Watts (London, England), 1996.

Poppy's Secret, Franklin Watts (London, England), 1996.

The Surprise Party, Heinemann (London, England), 1996.

Mad about the Boy, Walker (London, England), 1996.

The Lost Treasure, Franklin Watts (London, England), 1996.

Time Flies, Macdonald Young (Hemel Hempstead, England), 1996.

The Golden Key, Franklin Watts (London, England), 1996.

Freddie the Fibber, World International (Handforth, England), 1997.

Slow Down Sally, World International (Handforth, England), 1997.

Two Naughty Angels: Round the Rainbow, illustrated by Lesley Harker, Bloomsbury Children's Books (London, England), 1997.

House of Secrets, Ginn (Aylesbury, England), 1997.

Gita and Goldie, Bloomsbury (London, England), 1998.

The Peculiar Power of Tabitha Brown, Walker (London, England), 1998.

Paul and Percy, Bloomsbury (London, England), 1998.

Thirteen Candles, A. & C. Black (London, England), 1998.

Timmy and Tiger, Bloomsbury (London, England), 1998.

Two Sides of the Story, Bloomsbury (London, England), 1998.

Becky and Beauty, Bloomsbury Children's Books (London, England), 1998.

The Great Raj, Franklin Watts (London, England), 1998.

Spooks Ahoy!, Walker (London, England), 1998.

Bodies for Sale, Franklin Watts (London, England), 1999.

The Great Twin Trick, Walker (London, England), 1999.

The Never-ending Birthday, Macdonald Young (Hove, England), 1999.

The Genie, Barrington Stoke (Edinburgh, Scotland), 1999, illustrated by Jessica Fuchs, Stone Arch Books (Minneapolis, MN), 2007.

Lucy's Donkey Rescue, Macmillan Children's Books (London, England), 2000.

Lucy's Perfect Piglet, Macmillan Children's Books (London, England), 2000.

A Stormy Night for Lucy, Macmillan Children's Books (London, England), 2000.

Lucy's Badger Cub, Macmillan Children's Books (London, England), 2000.

Lucy's Wild Pony, Macmillan Children's Books (London, England), 2000.

A Lamb for Lucy, Macmillan Children's Books (London, England), 2000.

Nickie's Secrets, 4 Books (London, England), 2001.

Amber's Letter, Walker (London, England), 2002.

Spooks and Scares!, Young Hippo (London, England), 2002.

Letters to Liz: Nicki's Letter, Walker (London, England), 2002.

Letters to Liz: Jo's Letter, Walker (London, England), 2002.

Mischief and Mayhem, Scholastic (London, England), 2002.

The Genie, illustrated by Kirstin Holbrow, Barrington Stoke (Edinburgh, Scotland), 2003.

The New Girl, Barrington Stoke (Edinburgh, Scotland), 2003.

Haunted House, Scholastic (London, England), 2003.

Neighbourhood Witch, Walker (London, England), 2004.

Plague House, Scholastic (London, England), 2004.

Horror House, Scholastic (London, England), 2004.

Witch House, Scholastic (London, England), 2005.

The Haunting of Julia, illustrated by Maureen Gray, Stone Arch Books (Minneapolis, MN), 2008.

YOUNG-ADULT CONTEMPORARY FICTION

Chelsea and Astra: Two Sides of the Story, Bloomsbury (London, England), 1998.

Megan: The Biggest Decision of All, Bloomsbury (London, England), 1999.

Megan 2: And Then There Were Two, Bloomsbury (London, England), 1999.

Holly, Bloomsbury Children's Books (London, England), 2000.

Megan 3: Two's Company, Three's a Crowd, Bloomsbury Children's Books (London, England), 2001.

Amy, Bloomsbury (New York, NY), 2002.

Zara, Bloomsbury Children's (London, England), 2005.

YOUNG-ADULT HISTORICAL FICTION

At the Sign of the Sugared Plum, Bloomsbury Children's Books (New York, NY), 2003.

Petals in the Ashes (sequel to *At the Sign of the Sugared Plum*), Bloomsbury Children's Books (New York, NY), 2004.

The Remarkable Life and Times of Eliza Rose, Bloomsbury (New York, NY), 2006.

The Fever and the Flame (includes *At the Sign of the Sugared Plum* and *Petals in the Ashes*), Bloomsbury (London, England), 2006.

At the House of the Magician, Bloomsbury (London, England), 2007.

By Royal Command (sequel to *At the House of the Magician*), Bloomsbury (London, England), 2008.

Newes from the Dead, Roaring Brook Press (New York, NY), 2008.

The Betrayal (sequel to *By Royal Command*), Bloomsbury (London, England), 2009.

Contributor to books, including *The Not-so-Nice Victorians,* Franklin Watts (London, England), 2005.

Sidelights

Before becoming known for her young-adult historical fiction, British writer Mary Hooper worked as a secretary and raised her two children. She turned to writing after attending Reading University as an adult student and earning her college degree in English. Before tackling longer fiction, Hooper submitted hundreds of short stories to magazines catering to female readers. Her first novel, *Jodie,* was published in 1978, beginning a prolific career that includes beginning chapter books and middle-grade fiction as well as teen novels such as the popular "Megan" novels about a fifteen-year-old unwed mother. Most recently, Hooper has focused on historical fiction for older teens, producing the novels *At the Sign of the Sugared Plum, The Remarkable Life and Times of Eliza Rose,* and *Newes from the Dead,* as well as her "House of the Magician" series.

At the Sign of the Sugared Plum follows a young woman named Hannah, who travels to London in 1665, just as the bubonic plague is taking the city by storm. Hannah has come to the city to help her sister Sarah run Sarah's small sweets shop. Now, with horror and fear, the two

Cover of Mary Hooper's young-adult novel Amy, *which features a photograph by Yeti McCaldin.* (Bloomsbury, 2002. Jacket design © 2002 by Yeti McCaldin. Reproduced by permission.)

young women watch as the black death spreads, becoming a threat to all the city's inhabitants. "From the fetid smell of the streets to the ghastly sights of overwhelming cemeteries, the scope of the disaster is impressively wrought," commented Kristen Oravec in a review of *At the Sign of the Sugared Plum* for *School Library Journal.* A *Publishers Weekly* critic also enjoyed Hooper's novel, stating that, "So likeable is Hannah that readers will cheer when she and her sister accomplish the near-miracle of escaping from the quarantine city" in "a tale almost as tasty as the sisters' comfits."

Hannah's story continues in *Petals in the Ashes.* After narrowly escaping London, the she and Sarah visit their family home in Chertsey before returning to London. Once back in the city, Hannah finds herself trapped as the Great Fire breaks out, devouring all in its path. A strong heroine in her own right, Hannah bravely deals with the disaster and cares for those she loves. Renee Steinberg, reviewing the novel for *School Library Journal,* praised the book as "exemplary historical fiction, skillfully combining reality and imagination." Anne O'Malley, a reviewer for *Booklist,* also enjoyed the sequel, writing that "Hooper does a masterful job of portraying lively, realistic characters while also making history interesting and accurate." *At the Sign of the Sugared Plum* and *Petals in the Ashes,* were published in one volume as *The Fever and the Flame.*

A switch of two infants at birth provides the mystery at the core of *The Remarkable Life and Times of Eliza Rose,* a stand-alone historical novel by Hooper. In the story, fifteen-year-old Eliza Rose's search for her real parents leads her to seventeenth-century London, where her theft of a meat pie leads to Eliza's imprisonment. A pretty girl, Eliza is befriended by Ma Gwyn, who arranges the teen's release from the rat-infested prison and plans to turn her into a prostitute. Fortunately, Ma's daughter, the famous actress Nell Gwyn, takes Eliza as her companion, drawing the young woman into a world of intrigue, romance, and adventure that also holds the key to Eliza's past. In a *Kirkus Reviews* appraisal of *The Remarkable Life and Times of Eliza Rose,* a critic described Nell as a "vivid character" and noted the novel's "fairytale-like ending." "Hooper writes an earthy tale, rich in story and characters," according to *Booklist* critic Ilene Cooper, the critic predicting that the novel will appeal to readers due to "its mix of romance and raw detail." *The Remarkable Life and Times of Eliza Rose* was described by *School Library Journal* critic Connie Tyrrell Burns as an "engrossing, fast-paced" story featuring a "determined, well-drawn" heroine and a "winning combination of history and fairy-tale tropes."

Featuring the English setting that characterizes all Hooper's novels, the "House of the Magician" series includes *At the House of the Magician, By Royal Command,* and *The Betrayal.* In *At the House of the Magician* readers meet Lucy, a young woman whose dreams of working for a person connected to Queen Elizabeth I

Cover of Hooper's historical novel Petals in the Ashes, *the second in a series set in seventeenth-century London.* (Bloomsbury, 2004. Reproduced by permission.)

are answered when she becomes the servant of Dr. Dee, court magician and consultant to the queen. Due to her curiosity, Lucy learns of a threat to Elizabeth's life, and when her efforts thwart this impending evil, she becomes a spy to the queen. Continuing to live in the house of Dr. Dee in *The Royal Command* the young woman hears strange cries echoing through the house at night, cries that might signal that Dee and his colleague Mr. Kelly, are once again up to no good. In *The Betrayal,* the concluding volume in the "House of the Magician" series, Lucy enjoys a budding romance with the queen's fool until Elizabeth's lady-in-waiting becomes a rival for the young man's attention. Further problems arise for Lucy when her romantic rival shows signs that she may, in fact, be in league with Mary, Queen of Scots, and therefore another potential threat to the English monarch. Help is difficult to obtain, however, because Lucy's accusations are perceived by her friends as romantic jealousy.

Set half a century later, in 1650, *Newes from the Dead* features a haunting premise. Sentenced to death and hanged, twenty-two-year-old kitchen servant Anne Green awakes hours later, on a dissection table at Oxford University. Based on an actual story, *Newes from the Dead* is narrated by the young woman, who recounts how she was seduced by her master and then

unjustly accused of murdering her newborn child. A second narrator, the medical student Robert, who discovered that Green still lives, fills out the action, and an original account of Green's experience closes out Hooper's novel. While *Kliatt* contributor Claire Rosser found the book's structure "a bit awkward," the critic nonetheless described *Newes from the Dead* as "intriguing." Hooper creates a vivid sense of life in Cromwell's England, wrote *School Library Journal* contributor Rhona Campbell, and the story's "pervasive sense of injustice and indignity is vibrant enough" to balance Hooper's "unexpectedly positive ending."

Biographical and Critical Sources

PERIODICALS

Booklist, September 15, 2002, Gillian Engberg, review of *Amy,* p. 226; September 15, 2003, Kay Weisman, review of *At the Sign of the Sugared Plum,* p. 236; August, 2004, Anne O'Malley, review of *Petals in the Ashes,* p. 1934; September 15, 2006, Ilene Cooper, review of *The Remarkable Life and Times of Eliza Rose,* p. 69; May 1, 2008, Connie Fletcher, review of *Newes from the Dead,* p. 48.
Horn Book, May-June, 2008, Martha Walker, review of *Newes from the Dead,* p. 314.
Kirkus Reviews, August 1, 2002, review of *Amy,* p. 1132; July 1, 2003, review of *At the Sign of the Sugared Plum,* p. 911; June 1, 2004, review of *Petals in the Ashes,* p. 537; November 1, 2006, review of *The Remarkable Life and Times of Eliza Rose,* p. 1123; April 1, 2008, review of *Newes from the Dead.*
Kliatt, July, 2008, Claire Rosser, review of *Newes from the Dead,* p. 14.
New York Times Book Review, August 17, 2008, review of *Newes from the Dead,* p. 19.
Publishers Weekly, August 19, 2002, review of *Amy,* p. 90; August 25, 2003, review of *At the Sign of the Sugared Plum,* p. 65; May 12, 2008, review of *Newes from the Dead,* p. 55.
School Library Journal, September, 2002, Sharon Rawlins, review of *Amy,* p. 226; August, 2003, Kristen Oravec, review of *At the Sign of the Sugared Plum,* p. 160; August, 2004, Renee Steinberg, review of *Petals in the Ashes,* p. 123; December, 2006, Connie Tyrrell Burns, review of *The Remarkable Life and Times of Eliza Rose,* p. 146; January, 2008, Lisa Goldstein, review of *The Haunting of Julia,* p. 151; May, 2008, Rhona Campbell, review of *Newes from the Dead,* p. 126.

ONLINE

Bloomsbury Web site, http://www.bloomsbury.com/ (September 20, 2009), "Mary Hooper."
Mary Hooper Home Page, http://www.maryhooper.co.uk (September 20, 2009).*

J-K

JACKSON ISSA, Kai

Personal
Married; children: two. *Education:* Emory University, Ph.D.

Addresses
Home—Clarkston, GA. *E-mail*—kai@kaiwrites.com.

Career
Freelance writer and editor. Morehouse College, managing editor of Howard Thurman Papers Project.

Writings

Howard Thurman's Great Hope, illustrated by Arthur L. Dawson, Lee & Low (New York, NY), 2008.

Contributor to academic journals.

Sidelights
In addition to working as a freelance writer and editor, Kai Jackson Issa has also penned a children's picture book about the life of Howard Thurman. Thurman was an African-American minister who mentored leaders in the U.S. civil rights movement of the mid-twentieth century. Illustrated by Arthur L. Dawson, *Howard Thurman's Great Hope* shares with young readers the difficulties young Thurman encountered while earning an education. Growing up in rural, segregated Florida, African-American children like Thurman generally experienced limited educational opportunities, with few schools open to them and even fewer black families able to afford to send their sons and daughters to school instead of working at home to supplement the household income. Thurman, however, determined that college would be in his future, as his late father had hoped, and with the help of others in his town, he attended high school and graduated from both Morehouse College and Rochester Theological Seminary. This education set the young man on course to become an important advisor to civil rights leaders such as the Rev. Martin Luther King, Jr.

Writing in *School Library Journal,* Barbara Auerbach described *Howard Thurman's Great Hope* as an "accessible, engaging biography," while a *Kirkus Reviews* contributor wrote that Jackson Issa's book "introduces young readers to a Civil Rights Movement figure who should be better known." In *Booklist* Linda Perkins also commented on the limited attention paid to the contributions of Thurman, finding Jackson Issa's biography "a worthy title for social-studies units and Black History Month."

Biographical and Critical Sources

PERIODICALS

Booklist, November 15, 2008, Linda Perkins, review of *Howard Thurman's Great Hope,* p. 42.
Kirkus Reviews, August 1, 2008, review of *Howard Thurman's Great Hope.*
School Library Journal, September, 2008, Barbara Auerbach, review of *Howard Thurman's Great Hope,* p. 164.

ONLINE

Kai Jackson Issa Home Page, http://kaiwrites.com (September 25, 2009).*

* * *

JENNINGS, Patrick 1962-

Personal
Born February 25, 1962, in IN; son of Richard Jennings and Patricia Ann Utley; married Alison Kaplan (a book-

Patrick Jennings (Photograph by Alison Kaplan. Reproduced by permission.)

binder), August 2, 1997. *Education:* Arizona State University, B.F.A., 1985; attended San Francisco State University, 1987-91.

Addresses

Office—P.O. Box 1527, Port Townsend, WA 98368. *E-mail*—pjennings@patrickjennings.com.

Career

Author and librarian. Educator in San Francisco, CA, San Cristobal de las Casas, Chiapas, Mexico, and Bisbee, AZ, 1991-96; writer, 1991—; Copper Queen Library, AZ, library technician, beginning 1994.

Member

Society of Children's Book Writers and Illustrators.

Awards, Honors

Booklist Editors' Choice selection, 1996, for *Faith and the Electric Dogs;* PEN Center USA Literary Award finalist, 2002, and *Smithsonian* magazine Notable Book for Children designation, both for *The Beastly Arms;* Judy Lopez Memorial Award Honor Book, 2003, for *The Wolving Time;* Chicago Public Library Best of the Best selection, 2005, for *Out Standing in My Field.*

Writings

Faith and the Electric Dogs, Scholastic (New York, NY), 1996.
Faith and the Rocket Cat, Scholastic (New York, NY), 1998.
Putnam and Pennyroyal, illustrated by Jon J. Muth, Scholastic (New York, NY), 1999.
The Beastly Arms, Scholastic (New York, NY), 2001.
The Wolving Time, Scholastic (New York, NY), 2003.
Out Standing in My Field, Scholastic (New York, NY), 2005.
Wish Riders, Hyperion (New York, NY), 2006.
Barb and Dingbat's Crybaby Hotline, Hyperion (New York, NY), 2007.
We Can't All Be Rattlesnakes, Hyperion (New York, NY), 2009.

Contributor to periodicals, including *Horn Book.*

"IKE AND MEM" SERIES

The Bird Shadow, illustrated by Anna Alter, Holiday House (New York, NY), 2001.
The Tornado Watches, illustrated by Anna Alter, Holiday House (New York, NY), 2002.
The Weeping Willow, illustrated by Anna Alter, Holiday House (New York, NY), 2002.
The Lightning Bugs, illustrated by Anna Alter, Holiday House (New York, NY), 2003.
The Ears of Corn, illustrated by Anna Alter, Holiday House (New York, NY), 2003.
The Pup Tent, illustrated by Noel Tuazon, Holiday House (New York, NY), 2009.

Sidelights

Patrick Jennings, a librarian and educator, is the author of such award-winning works for young readers as *The Beastly Arms, The Wolving Time,* and *Out Standing in My Field.* His eclectic works have drawn praise for their entertaining plots, strong characters, and humorous dialog. "One of the most important themes in my work, and in my interactions with students," Jennings noted on the Scholastic Web site, "is the power language holds to excite the imagination, to express one's ideas and emotions, and to bring people closer through empathy and understanding."

In Jennings' *Faith and the Electric Dogs,* ten-year-old Faith is saved from bullies by a stray dog she names Edison (a stray dog in Mexico is called *un perro corriente,* or "electric dog"). Unhappy living in Mexico, Faith wants to return to San Francisco, and with Edison as her humorous, multilingual narrator and companion, she proceeds to build a rocket ship that takes the pair to a desert island. A *Kirkus Reviews* critic described Edison as "a witty ambassador of languages and cultures," and Susan Dove Lempke, writing in *Booklist,* attributed both "charm and substance" to Jennings' first novel.

Faith returns in *Faith and the Rocket Cat.* While her wish has been granted and she has moved back to San Francisco, Faith and Edison still find an excuse to take another rocket trip. By setting the story in the United States, Susan Dove Lempke noted in *Booklist,* Jennings has "an opportunity to skewer modern American educational techniques . . . and also to celebrate . . . multiple languages and ethnic groups."

Jennings is also the author of a series of short chapter books for early readers, collected as the "Ike and Mem Stories." These books feature simple tales about a brother and sister named Ike and Mem, their friends, and the small disputes and apologies that make up their lives. In the first book of the series, *The Bird Shadow,* Ike and Mem let their friend Dave bully them into trespassing on the property of a house they think is haunted. When Dave throws a rock through the window of a shed by the house, letting a flock of pigeons fly free, Ike and Mem wind up being confronted by the house's owner, Mr. Hawkins. The two guilty children eventually apologize and become friends with Mr. Hawkins, and all ends well. "This simple adventure will ring true with any children who have been goaded by a bully into participating in an activity they know is wrong," thought *School Library Journal* contributor Alice Casey Smith.

Cover of Jennings' middle-grade novel The Beastly Arms, *featuring detailed artwork by Brian Selznick.* (Illustration copyright © 2003 by Brian Selznick. Reproduced by permission of Scholastic, Inc.)

In addition, commented a *Publishers Weekly* reviewer, the book's "simple sentence structure and gentle repetition" will help to "instill a sense of confidence in readers just starting to tackle longer stories."

In *The Tornado Watches* Ike struggles to trust that his parents will take care of him when a tornado watch is declared, while he and his friend Buzzy have a falling out over how to build a tree house in *The Weeping Willow.* "The characters' dialogue and hurt feelings are adeptly expressed," JoAnn Jonas commented in her *School Library Journal* review of *The Weeping Willow,* and *Booklist* critic Shelle Rosenfeld described the same tale as "a well-written, perceptive story with likable characters." In *The Lightning Bugs,* Mem is appalled when Dave and Ike kill insects for fun. Linda B. Zeilstra, writing in *School Library Journal,* described the fourth work in the series as a "quiet, thoughtful story." Men and Ike pay a visit to their grandparents' farm and become angry when they are put to work in *The Ears of Corn.* According to *School Library Journal* critic Jean Lowery, "the story is resolved in a realistic fashion that will satisfy young readers."

Jennings's supernatural novel *The Wolving Time* is intended for slightly older readers. This story is set in the sixteenth century, in the Pyrenees mountains in the south of France. Laszlo Emberek is a thirteen-year-old shepherd from an unusual family: his parents are werewolves, and when he becomes a man he will turn into one too. Although there is a certain humorous potential in a story about werewolves keeping sheep, "this tale is no comedy," Joel Shoemaker noted in *School Library Journal,* "but rather a compelling, thoughtful story." In fact, the ability to turn into wolves comes in handy for these shepherds, as it allows them to negotiate, wolf-to-wolf, with the local packs in order to keep the wild wolves away from their flock. Even with this advantage, however, the Embereks barely make a living; they are shunned by their neighbors for being different and are persecuted by their village priest, a serious threat at a time when execution is accepted punishment for religious offenses. Yet despite the risk to themselves, the Embereks decide to take in Muno, an orphan whose parents were burned at the stake for being witches and who was subsequently turned into a near-slave by the priest.

The Wolving Time garnered solid reviews. "Readers are likely to identify with the werewolf metaphor, which evokes the physical and emotional changes that adolescents experience," noted Joel Shoemaker in *School Library Journal.* "This page-turner delivers a fascinating commentary on what constitutes true goodness," concluded a *Publishers Weekly* contributor in a review of *The Wolving Time,* and *Booklist* contributor Carolyn Phelan noted that, whether one considers the evil-versus-good role-reversal as "irony or revisionist history, Jennings makes his case with dramatic and ethical clarity."

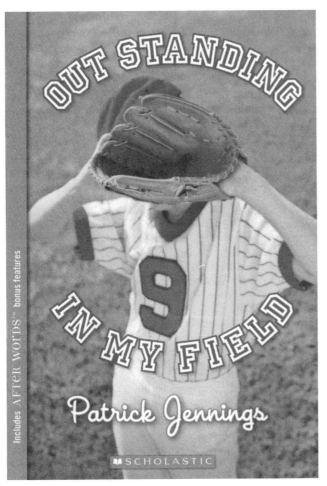

Cover of Jennings' elementary-grade novel **Out Standing in My Field**, *featuring a photograph by Kyo Morishima.* (Photograph copyright © by Kyo Morishima. Reproduced by permission of Scholastic, Inc. and the photographer.)

Taking place over the course of one Pee Wee League baseball game, *Out Standing in My Field* examines the life of eleven-year-old narrator Tyrus Cutter, the son of a frustrated former major leaguer. Lacking both athleticism and a love of the game, Ty proves a disappointment to his father, who serves as Ty's coach and has made the youngster the centerpiece of the team despite his obvious shortcomings. As the game progresses, Ty relates his tale in a stream-of-consciousness narrative that entertains via his "self-deprecating humor, [and] the way that he takes in his situation and fantasizes about a way out," as a *Publishers Weekly* critic noted. According to a contributor in *Kirkus Reviews, Out Standing in My Field* is "an unusual father-son story that goes far beyond the typical baseball novel."

Jennings blends elements of fantasy and historical fiction in *Wish Riders,* a "startlingly original tale set in a West Coast logging camp during the Depression," Vicky Smith remarked in *Horn Book.* The novel concerns a fifteen-year-old orphan known as Dusty who, along with several other young people, works long hours cooking and cleaning for the loggers. Dusty discovers that a seagull has mysteriously left some seeds in her hairbrush, and when she sows them, they grown into fine horses made of vegetation. Dusty and her coworkers use the creatures to escape into the woods, where they meet a strange and slightly threatening woman. "It's Edith's resourcefulness that sees the children through to places they can call home," Diana Tixier Herald commented in her *Booklist* review of *Wish Riders.*

Told through a series of phone conversations, *Barb and Dingbat's Crybaby Hotline* centers on the unlikely friendship between a pair of teenagers. Set in the mid-1970s, the work introduces Barb and Jeff, who become friends after Barb, as a favor to her friend, calls Jeff to inform him that he has been dropped as a boy friend. Barb and Jeff continue to stay in touch, and over time they gradually open up to one another. "The entire novel is made up of the phone conversations, . . . yet the characters are developed through their calls," observed Heather E. Miller in *School Library Journal,* while *Barb and Dingbat's Crybaby Hotline* was dubbed "compelling," by a critic in *Kirkus Reviews.*

A caged snake offers its views of human foibles in *We Can't All Be Rattlesnakes,* a "hilarious satire on modern American life," according to *Horn Book* contributor Susan Dove Lempke. When Gunnar, a lonely and insensitive youngster, captures a gopher snake, he names it Crusher and drops the creature into a terrarium. Unable to comprehend the strange world it has entered, Crusher communicates with Gunnar's other pets, a tortoise and a lizard, and develops a budding friendship with Breakfast, the live mouse that is supposed to serve as its meal. "The snake makes an entertaining (if understandably snarky) narrator," Carolyn Phelan stated in *Booklist,* and a *Publishers Weekly* reviewer commented that *We Can't All Be Rattlesnakes* "might encourage middle-graders to rethink their relationships to any pets that are incarcerated in cages."

Jennings once told *SATA:* "When I was ten, I wrote a play. I convinced my teacher to allow me to stage it (with me as director and star) and, with his consent, 'The Half-True Story of Jesse James' was presented to the student body of South Ward Elementary School, Crown Point, Indiana. It closed after only one performance. I kept writing after that. I wrote essays and stories and reviews and screenplays. (This was done in seats of higher learning, not in South Ward's.) I learned a lot about writing and a lot about what I do and don't like to do. I learned so much in fact, that I left film school and took a job as a preschool teacher. I chose preschool because I love kids. I mean that seriously. I have always loved to be around them. They know how to do what they like. Kids paint pictures then paint over them. They say memorable things, like 'I've hidden a whisper bomb in everybody's house.' They think screaming is exercise. They look at the bookshelf and never say, 'I really should read more.' You've got to like that.

"I read a lot of children's books at preschool. My exposure to children's literature up to then amounted to the

small collection of books I had as a child (Pooh, Dr. Seuss, Charlie Brown), the books I'd checked out of the Crown Point Public Library (Cleary, Dahl, E.B. White, Meindert DeJong, Michael Bond, Eleanor Cameron), and the books I'd studied in seats of higher learning (Huck Finn, Alice, *The Little Prince,* etc.). Consequently, I was unprepared for the great big happy bright world of books for children. *The Amazing Bone* stunned me, as did *The Night Kitchen,* not to mention *The Runaway Bunny, Madeline, The Tale of Peter Rabbit, A Hole Is to Dig,* and *Harold and the Purple Crayon.* Beyond their virtues of perfect pitch, rhythm, balance, and humor, these books *worked.* Children loved them, chanted them, used them in their play. (Alas, I discovered not all writers for children understand childhood so well. Some books read more like primers for adulthood than books for kids.)

"I began to read kid's books at home—just for my own pleasure! I reread Milne, White, Cleary, Seuss, Carroll, and Cameron. My books on deconstructionist filmmaking gathered dust. Then one day, as I read how James' parents were gobbled up by a rhinoceros, I decided to start a story of my own. The voice came first, just a whisper in my ear—a dog's voice. Then came the rocket ship and the rocket girl. Later, when I moved to Mexico, the story moved with me. The dog became electric, his narration, multilingual. Language became a key element of the story. Until I taught preschool, I labored under the typical adult delusion that children consider reading and writing to be chores tantamount to, say, yardwork. Nothing could be further from the truth. Language to children is like twittering is to birds, roaring to lions, grunting to pigs, barking to dogs. Kids chant and warble and make up very silly things to say. They bask in the sound of their voices. They smile when understood. And they adore stories—to tell, to hear, to look at, to read. Children love language, whether they are aware of it or not. This is why I write books for them."

Biographical and Critical Sources

PERIODICALS

Book, May-June, 2002, review of *The Beastly Arms,* p. 29.
Booklist, December 1, 1996, Susan Dove Lempke, review of *Faith and the Electric Dogs,* p. 653; September 15, 1998, review of *Faith and the Rocket Cat,* p. 230; November 15, 1999, Shelley Townsend-Hudson, review of *Putnam and Pennyroyal,* p. 626; May 1, 2001, Gillian Engberg, review of *The Beastly Arms,* p. 1678; August, 2002, GraceAnne A. DeCandido, review of *The Tornado Watches,* p. 1961; December 15, 2002, Shelle Rosenfeld, review of *The Weeping Willow,* p. 759; September 15, 2003, Carolyn Phelan, review of *The Wolving Time,* p. 231; March 15, 2005, Abby Nolan, review of *Out Standing in My Field,* p. 1294; January 1, 2007, Diana Tixier Herald, review of *Wish Riders,* p. 104; February 15, 2009, Carolyn Phelan, review of *We Can't All Be Rattlesnakes,* p. 84.

Childhood Education, 2003, Terre Sychterz, review of *The Weeping Willow,* p. 324.
Horn Book, January, 2000, review of *Putnam and Pennyroyal,* p. 77; July, 2001, review of *The Beastly Arms,* p. 454; January-February, 2003, Roger Sutton, review of *The Tornado Watches,* p. 75; September-October, 2006, Vicky Smith, review of *Wish Riders,* p. 587; March-April, 2009, Susan Dove Lempke, review of *We Can't All Be Rattlesnakes,* p. 197.
Kirkus Reviews, September 15, 1996, review of *Faith and the Electric Dogs,* pp. 1402-1403; January 1, 2002, review of *The Bird Shadow,* p. 47; June 15, 2002, review of *The Tornado Watches,* p. 882; October 15, 2002, review of *The Weeping Willow,* p. 1531; October 1, 2003, review of *The Wolving Time,* p. 1225; January 15, 2005, review of *Out Standing in My Field,* p. 122; August 15, 2006, review of *Wish Riders,* p. 844; December 1,2007, review of *Barb and Dingbat's Crybaby Hotline;* November 15, 2008, review of *We Can't All Be Rattlesnakes.*
New York Times Book Review, March 15, 2009, Julie Just, review of *We Can't All Be Rattlesnakes.* p. 13.
Publishers Weekly, October 28, 1996, review of *Faith and the Electric Dogs,* p. 82; April 30, 2001, review of *The Beastly Arms,* p. 79; December 10, 2001, review of *The Bird Shadow,* p. 70; December 1, 2003, review of *The Wolving Time,* p. 57, review of *The Beastly Arms,* p. 59; February 7, 2005, review of *Out Standing in My Field,* p. 60; January 19, 2009, review of *We Can't All Be Rattlesnakes,* p. 60.
School Library Journal, March, 2000, Arwen Marshall, review of *Putnam and Pennyroyal,* p. 239; April, 2001, John Peters, review of *The Beastly Arms,* p. 144; March, 2002, Alice Casey Smith, review of *The Bird Shadow,* p. 190; December, 2002, Shawn Brommer, review of *The Tornado Watches,* p. 98; February, 2003, JoAnn Jonas, review of *The Weeping Willow,* p. 114; August, 2003, Linda B. Zeilstra, review of *The Lightning Bugs,* p. 135; January, 2004, Joel Shoemaker, review of *The Wolving Time,* p. 130; February, 2004, Jean Lowery, review of *The Ears of Corn,* p. 114; April, 2005, Denise Moore, review of *Out Standing in My Field,* p. 134; February, 2008, Heather E. Miller, review of *Barb and Dingbat's Crybaby Hotline,* p. 116.

ONLINE

Kirby Larson Web log, http://kirbyslane.blogspot.com/ (April 13, 2009), "Patrick 'Tiger' Jennings."
Patrick Jennings Home Page, http://www.patrickjennings. com (September 1, 2009).
Scholastic Web site, http://www2.scholastic.com/ (September 1, 2009), "Patrick Jennings."*

*   *   *

KAY, Julia
(Julia Kay Aho)

Personal

Married; husband's name Zach. *Education:* Brigham Young University, B.A. (humanities, English emphasis

and studio art; magna cum laude, with honors), 2004; attended Santa Reparata International School of Art, 2003, and University of California, Los Angeles, 2007.

Addresses

Home—Rogers, AR. *E-mail*—julia@juliakay.com.

Career

Illustrator, writer, and graphic and Web designer. Worked variously as a corporate design director, product designer, and Web designer; *Insight* magazine, chief graphic designer, 2002-04; Pugster, product designer, 2005-06; Northwestern University, senior Web designer, 2007-09; *Eliza* magazine, fashion illustrator, 2007-09.

Member

Society of Illustrators, Phi Eta Sigma.

Writings

(Self-illustrated) *Gulliver Snip,* Henry Holt (New York, NY), 2008.

Sidelights

Artist and designer Julia Kay published her first book for children shortly after completing her college education. In *Gulliver Snip* she tells a rhyming tale about an imaginative young boy who transforms into a sea captain each evening when he climbs into the bathtub. Gulliver's bath-time adventures soon migrate from tub to the family living room, and the boy's rambunctious play serves as "a nice foray into the realm of imagination," according to a *Kirkus Reviews* writer. In her acrylic and oil pastel art for the story, Kay "makes some intriguing color choices," according to a *Publishers Weekly* contributor. Rather than blue, for example, the boy's imaginary ocean water is a vivid shade of green, clashed with dashes of purple and orange. According to Susannah Richards, reviewing *Gulliver Snip* for *School Library Journal,* Kay's story and art "creatively delineate both the real and imaginary worlds" of a small boy, making her debut picture book "a fun choice for bedtime sharing."

Biographical and Critical Sources

PERIODICALS

Kirkus Reviews, May 1, 2008, review of *Gulliver Snip.*
Publishers Weekly, June 9, 2008, review of *Gulliver Snip,* p. 49.
School Library Journal, August, 2008, Susannah Richards, review of *Gulliver Snip,* p. 94.

ONLINE

Gulliver Snip Home Page, http://www.gulliversnip.com (October 10, 2009).
Julia Kay Home Page, http://www.juliakay.com (October 10, 2009).

*   *   *

KIM, Joung Un 1970-

Personal

Born 1970. *Education:* Rhode Island School of Design, degree.

Addresses

Home—Anaheim, CA. *Agent*—Jane Feder, 305 E. 24th St., New York, NY 10010.

Career

Illustrator.

Illustrator

Sara Yamaka, *The Gift of Driscoll Lipscomb,* Simon & Schuster (New York, NY), 1995.
Bobbi Katz, *Could We Be Friends?: Poems for Pals,* Mondo (Greenvale, NY), 1997.
Ferida Wolff, *A Year for Kiko,* Houghton Mifflin (Boston, MA), 1997.
Kenneth Grahame, *Duck Song,* HarperFestival (New York, NY), 1998.
Betsy Franco, *Why the Frog Has Big Eyes,* Harcourt (San Francisco, CA), 2000.
Linda Hargrove, *Wings across the Moon,* HarperFestival (New York, NY), 2001.
Frances and Ginger Park, *The Have a Good Day Café,* Orchard Books (New York, NY), 2002.
Soyung Pak, *Sumi's First Day of School Ever,* Viking (New York, NY), 2003.
Elizabeth Cody Kimmel, *What Do You Dream?,* Candlewick Press (Cambridge, MA), 2003.
Candace Carter, *Sid's Surprise,* Harcourt (Orlando, FL), 2005.
Megan McDonald, *Hen Hears Gossip,* Greenwillow Books (New York, NY), 2008.

Sidelights

Educated at the Rhode Island School of Design, Joung Un Kim began illustrating children's books in the mid-1990s, starting her career by providing the artwork for Sara Yamaka's *The Gift of Driscoll Lipscomb* in 1995. Since then, the artist has continued her craft, teaming up with a variety of authors, including Betsy Franco, Linda Hargrove, Soyung Pak, and Megan McDonald, to create many well-received books for young readers.

Published in 2000 and 2001, respectively, Franco's *Why the Frog Has Big Eyes* and Hargrove's *Wings across the Moon* each share special stories about the natural

world with children. In the first book, Franco offers beginning readers a porquois lesson about how a boastful frog challenged a fish to a staring contest after defeating all of the other animals. The frog does not know, however, that fish cannot blink. Instead of besting the creature, Frog earns a pair of oversized eyeballs, strained from the unsuccessful effort. In *Wings across the Moon,* Hargrove presents a young mother and child as they watch the rising moon one evening. As the twilight approaches, nocturnal creatures begin to emerge in the darkness, providing youngsters with a new image of the nighttime world. Reviewing *Why the Frog Has Big Eyes* in *School Library Journal,* critic Laura Santoro thought Kim's "quirkily charming" illustrations "strongly support the easy text," while in the same periodical, contributor Olga R. Kuharets suggested that Kim's pictures for *Wings across the Moon* "set the tone for a calming story."

The first day of school, a fearful event for many children, becomes even more daunting in *Sumi's First Day of School Ever,* a story written by Pak about a young immigrant girl's experiences as she enters an American classroom. Featuring artwork by Kim, *Sumi's First Day of School Ever* shows readers both the good and bad experiences of Sumi, a new student from Korea who initially finds her school overwhelming, isolating, and confusing. Despite some teasing from other children, Sumi finds comfort in meeting a new friend and receiving a warm smile from her new teacher. "Kim's . . . soft-edged illustrations convey the poignant emotional content of each page," observed a critic in *Publishers Weekly.* A *Kirkus Reviews* contributor also commented favorably on Kim's pictures detailing this event experienced by children universally, claiming that "warm

Joung Un Kim contributes the graphic illustrations to Megan Mc-Donald's humorous picture book Hen Hears Gossip. (Illustration copyright © 2008 by Joung Un Kim. Used by permission of HarperCollins Publishers.)

smudges of color layer together to provide simple illustrations for this sweet tale."

In 2008, Kim joined with McDonald to produce *Hen Hears Gossip,* a lighthearted tale warning young readers about the consequences of spreading false information about other people. Listening in on a conversation between Cow and Pig, Hen attempts to share what she has heard to Duck, who then further distorts the story when retelling it to Goose. Eventually, the convoluted tale returns to Hen who decides to retrace the path of the now-hurtful gossip and uncover the actual facts from Cow. A *Kirkus Reviews* critic deemed Kim's "mixed-media illustrations" well-suited to McDonald's narrative, describing them as "bright, childlike and appropriately goofy." Comparing the artist's work to that of noted illustrator Leo Lionni, *Booklist* contributor Shelle Rosenfeld wrote that Kim's "collages . . . blend bold, blocky shapes with vivid, intricate patterns and texture."

Biographical and Critical Sources

PERIODICALS

Booklist, December 15, 1997, Ilene Cooper, review of *A Year for Kiko,* p. 714; October 1, 2000, Carolyn Phelan, review of *Why the Frog Has Big Eyes,* p. 352; April 15, 2001, Connie Fletcher, review of *Wings across the Moon,* p. 1564; August, 2003, Hazel Rochman, review of *Sumi's First Day of School Ever,* p. 1994; October 1, 2003, Lauren Peterson, review of *What Do You Dream?,* p. 328; July 1, 2008, Shelle Rosenfeld, review of *Hen Hears Gossip,* p. 72.

Horn Book, July-August, 2003, Johanna Rudge Long, review of *Sumi's First Day of School Ever,* p. 446.

Kirkus Reviews, June 15, 2003, review of *Sumi's First Day of School Ever,* p. 862; April 15, 2008, review of *Hen Hears Gossip.*

Publishers Weekly, May 15, 1995, review of *The Gift of Driscoll Lipscomb,* p. 72; July 28, 2003, review of *Sumi's First Day of School Ever,* p. 93.

School Library Journal, January, 2001, Laura Santoro, review of *Why the Frog Has Big Eyes,* p. 99; January, 2002, Olga R. Kuharets, review of *Wings across the Moon,* p. 100; August, 2003, Lisa Gangemi Kropp, review of *Sumi's First Day of School Ever,* p. 1994; February, 2004, Sandra Kitain, review of *What Do You Dream?,* p. 116; April, 2008, Jane Marino, review of *Hen Hears Gossip,* p. 116.*

* * *

KUEHNERT, Stephanie 1979-

Personal

Born 1979, in St. Louis, MO. *Education:* Attended Antioch College; Columbia College Chicago, B.A. (fiction writing), M.A., 2006. *Hobbies and other interests:* Music.

Addresses

Home—Forest Park, IL. *E-mail*—stephanie@stephanie kuehnert.com.

Career

Author. Worked variously in an office and as a bartender.

Writings

I Wanna Be Your Joey Ramone, Pocket Books/MTV Books (New York, NY), 2008.
Ballads of Suburbia, Pocket Books/MTV Books (New York, NY), 2009.

Columnist for *Forest Park (IL) Review.* Contributor to print and online periodicals.

Sidelights

Stephanie Kuehnert got her start by writing bad poetry about unrequited love and razor blades during junior-high school. In high school during the 1990s, she discovered punk rock and the riot grrrl movement and started producing D.I.Y. feminist 'zines. One of these zines, *Hospital Gown,* was featured in the book *Zine Scene* by Francesca Lia Block and Hillary Carlip. Since then Kuehnert has been writing about the kinds of characters she wanted to read about as a teen. "I want to give a voice to the kids who are searching for one: the misfits, the outcasts, the kids who are different and are facing seriously difficult situations and surviving them," the author told *SATA.*

Drawing from her own experiences coming of age amid the punk-rock culture of the 1980s and 1990s, with its focus on bands such as the the Clash, Social Distortion, Nirvana, and Patti Smith, Kuehnert created the character Emily Black, the heroine of her debut novel *I Wanna Be Your Joey Ramone.* (Because the book is a tribute to the female punk musicians the author admired while growing up, it is named for a Sleater-Kinney song.) In *I Wanna Be Your Joey Ramone,* "Kuehnert keeps the story raw and gritty," noted a *Publishers Weekly* contributor, and her references to the "drugs, sex, and rock-and-roll" aspects of punk culture have made her fiction popular among teen readers.

I Wanna Be Your Joey Ramone takes place in a small Wisconsin town, where Emily has been raised by her guitar-player father since her wild, punker mom abandoned the family. Missing her mother, Emily starts a punk band in order to be like her. In the novel, Kuehnert weaves together the stories of mother and daughter, showing their similarities as well as their contrasts. Although the *Publishers Weekly* contributor characterized the narrative style as sometimes overwrought, the critic concluded that "the intensity of the characters' emotions

and experiences will beguile" teens. "Kuehnert is acidly incisive and full-out entertaining" in her "classic tale of an artist coming into her own," wrote *Booklist* contributor Donna Seaman, and in *Kirkus Reviews* a critic dubbed the author's prose "slick." "The punk references bite with genuine angst and hunger," the *Kirkus Reviews* critic added, dubbing the character of Emily "tough" and "sardonic."

Kuehnert's second novel, *Ballads of Suburbia,* is set in the author's hometown of Oak Park, Illinois. Although it is not autobiographical, the book openly speaks about her own teenage struggles with self-injury, depression, and substance abuse. As Kuehnert told *SATA,* she wrote the book "in hopes to create a dialogue about the difficult issues that teens face that are too often kept secret." *Ballads of Suburbia* focuses on a conventional high-school freshman who deals with worries over her divorcing parents and the loss of a good friend by cutting herself. The punk culture soon touches Kara's life in the person of Maya, a new student who draws Kara into her misfit clique of punkers and drug users. *Ballads of Suburbia* "nails the raw vulnerability of teendom," wrote *Booklist* critic Annie McCormick, the critic adding of the novel that Kuehnert treats teen readers to "a hard-hitting and mesmerizing read."

Biographical and Critical Sources

PERIODICALS

Booklist, June 1, 2008, Donna Seaman, review of *I Wanna Be Your Joey Ramone,* p. 42; July 1, 2009, Annie McCormick, review of *Ballads of Suburbia,* p. 27.
Kirkus Reviews, June 15, 2008, review of *I Wanna Be Your Joey Ramone.*
Publishers Weekly, July 28, 2008, review of *I Wanna Be Your Joey Ramone,* p. 75.
Tribune Books (Chicago, IL), August 2, 2008, Kristin Kloberdanz, review of *I Wanna Be Your Joey Ramone,* p. 8.

ONLINE

Stephanie Kuehnert Home Page, http://www.stephanie kuehnert.com (October 10, 2009).

*   *   *

KULIKOV, Boris 1966-

Personal

Born 1966, in USSR (now Russia); immigrated to United States, 1997; married Yelena Romanova (a writer); children: Max, Andre. *Education:* Institute of Theatre, Music, and Cinema (St. Petersburg, Russia), graduated, 1992.

Boris Kulikov (Reproduced by permission.)

Addresses

Home and office—Brooklyn, NY. *E-mail*—boris.kulikov
@earthlink.net.

Career

Illustrator and painter. Formerly worked as a set and
costume designer in St. Petersburg, Russia. Also re-
stored murals and painted apartments; worked as an
electrician in the United States. *Exhibitions:* Work exhibited by Society of Illustrators, New York, NY, 2003,
2004, 2005, 2006, 2007, 2008. Work exhibited at Museum of Visual Arts, New York, NY, 2003; Society of
Illustrators Museum of American Illustration, New York,
NY, 1998, 2000, 2004, 2005; Katonah Museum of Art;
and Eric Carle Museum of Picture Book Art, Amherst,
MA, 2007.

Awards, Honors

Named among One Hundred Titles for Reading and
Sharing, New York Public Library, for *Fartiste* by Kathleen Krull and Paul Brewer, and *Sandy's Circus* by
Tanya Lee Stone; Sydney Taylor Book Award Honor
designation, 2008, for *The Castle on Hester Street* by
Linda Heller; numerous Best-Books designations from
periodicals.

Illustrator

Lore Segal, *Morris the Artist,* Farrar, Straus & Giroux
(New York, NY), 2003.
John Lithgow, *Carnival of the Animals,* Simon & Schuster
Books for Young Readers (New York, NY), 2004.

Nina Bernstein, *Magic by the Book,* Farrar, Straus & Gir-
oux (New York, NY), 2005.
Kathleen Krull, *Leonardo da Vinci* ("Giants of Science"
series), Viking (New York, NY), 2005.
Yelena Romanova, *The Perfect Friend,* Farrar, Straus &
Giroux (New York, NY), 2005.
B.G. Hennessy, reteller, *The Boy Who Cried Wolf,* Simon
& Schuster Books for Young Readers (New York,
NY), 2006.
Kathleen Krull, *Isaac Newton* ("Giants of Science" series),
Viking (New York, NY), 2006.
Kathleen Krull, *Sigmund Freud* ("Giants of Science" se-
ries), Viking (New York, NY), 2006.
Kate Banks, *Max's Words,* Farrar, Straus & Giroux (New
York, NY), 2006.
Nancy Crocker, *Betty Lou Blue,* Dial Books for Young
Readers (New York, NY), 2006.
Linda Heller, *The Castle on Hester Street* (twenty-fifth an-
niversary edition), Simon & Schuster (New York, NY),
2007.
Kathleen Krull, *Marie Curie* ("Giants of Science" series),
Viking (New York, NY), 2007.
John Lithgow, *Carnival of the Animals,* Aladdin (New
York, NY), 2007.
Kathleen Krull and Paul Brewer, *Fartiste,* Simon &
Schuster (New York, NY), 2008.
Kate Banks, *Max's Dragon,* Farrar, Straus & Giroux (New
York, NY), 2008.
Tanya Lee Stone, *Sandy's Circus: A Story about Alex-
ander Calder,* Viking (New York, NY), 2008.
Kate Banks, *The Eraserheads,* Farrar, Straus & Giroux
(New York, NY), 2010.
Kathleen Krull, *Albert Einstein* ("Giants of Science" se-
ries), Viking (New York, NY), 2010.

Contributor of illustrations to periodicals, including
Wall Street Journal, Los Angeles Times, and *New York
Times Book Review.*

Adaptations

Max's Words and *The Boy Who Cried Wolf* were adapted
for video, Weston Woods, 2007.

Sidelights

Born and educated in the former USSR, illustrator Boris
Kulikov has provided the artwork for a number of
highly regarded children's books, including *Magic by
the Book* by Nina Bernstein, *Max's Words* by Kate
Banks, and *The Perfect Friend,* the last by Kulikov's
wife, writer Yelena Romanova. His bold, textured artwork has drawn praise for its humor, energy, and theat-
ricality. The illustrator's "witty illustrations" for *The
Perfect Friend* "are sure to intrigue children and adults
alike," noted a *Publishers Weekly* contributor, while in
the same periodical another critic wrote that "Kulikov's
voluptuous pen-and-ink" drawings for *Magic by the
Book* add to the work's "elegant storybook feel." "I like
old times," the illustrator remarked to Julie Yates Walton in *Publishers Weekly.* "I do not like mass produc-
tion—contemporary architecture, chairs, tables, etc.

That is why often I use things from the past. I especially love the 1930s and '40s, and the Victorian and Renaissance styles."

Kulikov graduated from St. Petersburg's Institute of Theatre, Music, and Cinema before immigrating to the United States in 1997. He worked at a variety of odd jobs while working to establish his artistic career as an illustrator for the *New York Times Book Review.* Expanding his clients to include the *Wall Street Journal* and the *Los Angeles Times,* among others, Kulikov eventually found a way to make a much-hoped-for transition into children's-book illustration. His first illustration project, Lore Segal's *Morris the Artist,* drew critical praise and many other illustration opportunities.

Kulikov's illustrations for *Morris the Artist* stand out due to their contrast with Segal's modern story line about a creative boy who is unwilling to relinquish the gift of artist's paints he has brought to a friend's birthday party. Drawing from his training in theatrical cos-

tuming, Kulikov dresses the story's characters in clothing from a more-distant era, such as sailor suits, fedoras, and even knickers. The illustrator's "creative style . . . is enhanced by his brightly hued palette," commented a *Kirkus Reviews* critic, while a *Publishers Weekly* reviewer stated that "an off kilter, funhouse feeling pervades the full-spread compositions, and the children . . . sport big heads . . . and eyes with the unsettling fixed gaze of marionettes." Gillian Engberg, writing in *Booklist,* called Kulikov's artwork "noteworthy," writing that "an unusual, visually stimulating story about the dynamic of children's play and letting creativity loose."

Kulikov teamed up with B.G. Hennessy on *The Boy Who Cried Wolf,* a retelling of Aesop's fable about a mischievous youngster whose lies prove his undoing. The illustrations "show an outlandish village with skyscrapers" and "a funny, discordant mix of townspeople," Kirsten Cutler remarked in *School Library Journal,* and Joanna Rudge Long stated in *Horn Book* that Kulikov's

Kulikov's whimsical artwork matches well with Lore Segal's engaging story in **Morris the Artist.** (Illustration copyright © 2003 by Boris Kulikov. Used by permission of Farrar, Straus & Giroux, a division of Farrar, Straus & Giroux, LLC.)

depiction of the shepherd "fairly bursts from the page." A youngster who faces ridicule because of her huge feet comes to the rescue of her classmates in Nancy Crocker's *Betty Lou Blue.* A contributor in *Kirkus Reviews* praised the artist's "now recognizable style of large eyes and unexpected, ground-up perspectives," and *Booklist* critic Ilene Cooper similarly noted that "the imposing, deeply colored artwork, which makes use of unusual perspectives, commands attention."

Kulikov has served as the illustrator for the twenty-fifth-anniversary edition of Linda Heller's *The Castle on Hester Street,* an award-winning tale about Jewish immigrants. "Like the story," wrote a contributor in *Publishers Weekly,* "Kulikov's illustrations are beguiling, witty and filled with enough details for dozens of readings." A critic in *Kirkus Reviews* stated that the illustrator's "smiling, flexibly posed figures project an intimacy that will draw children in to this intergenerational interchange."

Kulikov has enjoyed a successful collaboration with Kathleen Krull on her "Giants of Science" series of picture-book biographies. In *Isaac Newton,* Krull examines the life of the English mathematician and scientist. According to Betty Carter in *Horn Book,* "half a dozen pen-and-ink illustrations emphasize Newton's characteristics: he was friendless, driven, vindictive, quirky, but always thinking." In *Sigmund Freud* Krull looks at the famed Austrian psychoanalyst. *Booklist* reviewer GraceAnne A. DeCandido remarked that "Kulikov provides knowing and witty illustrations" for this work, and Nancy Silverrod commented in *School Library Journal,* that his "sophisticated cartoon pen-and-ink drawings add to the text." A Nobel Prize-winning physicist is the focus on *Marie Curie.* Here Kulikov's pictures "further humanize the subject," wrote Kristen Oravec in *School Library Journal.*

Kulikov has also provided the artwork for *Fartiste,* a biography coauthored by Krull and Paul Brewer. The work describes the unusual talents of Joseph Pujol, a Frenchman who thrilled crowds in the late nineteenth century by passing gas at will, due to his remarkable ability to control the muscles of his intestines. "Kulikov draws each breaking of wind as a cross between a Botticelli-esque cloud and a comic-strip text balloon," a *Publishers Weekly* reviewer commented of the unusual picture book, and Catherine Threadgill, writing in *School Library Journal,* remarked that the illustrations "allude to the age of vaudevillian stage performance, painted playbills, [and] fire-hazard footlights that bronzed everything nearest them in golden warmth."

In Tanya Lee Stone's *Sandy's Circus: A Story about Alexander Calder,* the author profiles the preeminent American sculptor of the twentieth century, a man recognized as the inventor of the mobile. Kulikov's pictures for this book "are vibrant with energy and color," Long commented, "the fully formed humans standing out from the black-and-white linear objects whose simple lines pay tribute to Calder's wire medium."

Kulikov's art also graces the pages of *Max's Words* and *Max's Dragon,* a pair of picture books by Kate Banks. In the former, a youngster—intrigued by his older brothers' coin and stamp collections—decides to accumulate words from newspapers, magazines, and dictionaries. These words are then blended and rearranged to devise the imaginative tale "visualized in Kulikov's artwork," as Julie Cummins observed in *Booklist.* "Kulikov's clever illustrations feature Max's hundreds of words in different colors and fonts, sprinkled across the pages like confetti," a *Publishers Weekly* critic remarked. In Banks' rhyming text for *Max's Dragon* the word-loving boy creates his own mythical creature in the clouds from his collection of rhymes. "The unusual perspectives in the bright, textured artwork greatly enhance the story's drama," Engberg wrote, and in the *New York Times Book Review* Barbara Feinberg described Kulikov's illustrations for *Max's Dragon* as "warm and enveloping."

Biographical and Critical Sources

PERIODICALS

Booklist, August, 2003, Gillian Engberg, review of *Morris the Artist,* p. 1990; November 1, 2004, Diane Foote, review of *Carnival of the Animals,* p. 485; April 15,

Betty Lou Blue, **a picture book by Nancy Crocker, features playful gouache paintings by Kulikov.** (Illustration copyright © 2006 by Boris Kulikov. Reproduced by permission of Dial Books for Young Readers, a division of Penguin Putnam Books for Young Readers.)

2005, Jennifer Mattson, review of *Magic by the Book*, p. 1464; August 1, 2006, Ilene Cooper, review of *Betty Lou Blue*, p. 84; September 1, 2006, Julie Cummins, review of *Max's Words*, p. 132; December 1, 2006, GraceAnne A. DeCandido, review of *Sigmund Freud*, p. 36; December 15, 2007, John Peters, review of *Marie Curie*, p. 45, and Hazel Rochman, review of *The Castle on Hester Street*, p. 48; March 1, 2008, Gillian Engberg, review of *Max's Dragon*, p. 73; June 1, 2008, Gillian Engberg, review of *Sandy's Circus: A Story about Alexander Calder*, p. 106; August 1, 2008, Ilene Cooper, review of *Fartiste*, p. 75.

Horn Book, March-April, 2006, Joanne Rudge Long, review of *The Boy Who Cried Wolf*, p. 200; May-June, 2006, Betty Carter, review of *Isaac Newton*, p. 345; September-October, 2006, Betty Carter, review of *Sigmund Freud*, p. 607; November-December, 2007, Kitty Flynn, review of *Marie Curie*, p. 697; March-April, 2008, Robin L. Smith, review of *Max's Dragon*, p. 199; September-October, 2008, Christine M. Heppermann, review of *Fartiste*, p. 610, and Joanna Rudge Long, review of *Sandy's Circus*, p. 615.

Kirkus Reviews, May 1, 2003, review of *Morris the Artist*, p. 683; March 1, 2006, review of *Isaac Newton*, p. 233; September 15, 2006, review of *Betty Lou Blue*, p. 950; October 1, 2007, review of *The Castle on Hester Street*.

New York Times Book Review, October 14, 2007, "All Around the Town," review of *The Castle on Hester Street*, p. 18; November 9, 2008, Barbara Feinberg, review of *Max's Dragon*, p. 41.

Publishers Weekly, April 7, 2003, review of *Morris the Artist*, p. 66; June 30, 2003, Julie Yates Walton, "Flying Starts," p. 18; April 15, 2005, review of *Magic by the Book*, p. 57; July 17, 2006, review of *Max's Words*, p. 157; October 15, 2007, review of *The Castle on Hester Street*, p. 59; June 2, 2008, review of *Fartiste*, p. 46; September 15, 2008, review of *Sandy's Circus*, p. 67.

School Library Journal, March, 2005, Caitlin Augusta, review of *Magic by the Book*, p. 206; March, 2006, Kirsten Cutler, review of *The Boy Who Cried Wolf*, p. 208, and John Peters, review of *Isaac Newton*, p. 243; September, 2006, Maryann H. Owen, review of *Max's Words*, p. 158; December, 2006, Piper L. Nyman, review of *Betty Lou Blue*, p. 96, and Nancy Silverrod, review of *Sigmund Freud*, p. 164; December, 2007, Kristen Oravec, review of *Marie Curie*, p. 154; February, 2008, Marge Loch-Wouters, review of *Max's Dragon*, p. 82; July, 2008, Catherine Threadgill, review of *Fartiste*, p. 89; September, 2008, Barbara Elleman, review of *Sandy's Circus*, p. 169.

ONLINE

Boris Kulikov Home Page, http://www.boriskulikov.com (September 1, 2009).

L

LAIDLAW, Rob

Personal
Born in Canada.

Addresses
Home—Toronto, Ontario, Canada. *E-mail*—info@ animalconsultants.org.

Career
Animal advocate, biologist, and writer. Zoocheck Canada (wildlife protection charity), Toronto, Ontario, Canada, founder, 1984; cruelty inspector and chief inspector for Canadian human society, 1989-90; World Society for the Protection of Animals, project manager (Canada) and technical advisor, 2000-05.

Awards, Honors
School Library Journal Best Books inclusion, 2008, and Silver Birch Award nomination, Ontario Library Association, 2009, both for *Wild Animals in Captivity.*

Writings

Wild Animals in Captivity, Fitzhenry & Whiteside (Markham, Ontario, Canada), 2008.

Author, editor, and coauthor of professional reports, including *Zoos in Ontario: An Informal Look,* 1988; *Performing Prisoners: A Case against the Use of Animals in Circuses, Travelling Shows, and Novelty Acts,* 1997; *An Inquiry into Animal Welfare at Indonesian Zoos,* 2002; and *Scales and Tales: The Welfare and Trade of Reptiles Kept as Pets in Canada,* 2006. Contributor to periodicals, including *Satya.*

Biographical and Critical Sources

PERIODICALS

Kirkus Reviews, July 1, 2008, review of *Wild Animals in Captivity.*

School Library Journal, July, 2008, Ellen Heath, review of *Wild Animals in Captivity,* p. 114.

ONLINE

Animal Consultants Web site, http://www.animal consultants.org/ (October 15, 2009), "Rob Laidlaw."
Zoocheck Canada Web site, http://www.zoocheck.com/ (October 15, 2009).*

* * *

LARSON, Hope 1982-

Personal
Born 1982; married Bryan Lee O'Malley (a comics artist). *Education:* Art Institute of Chicago, degree.

Addresses
Home—Asheville, NC. *E-mail*—hope@hopelarson.com.

Career
Cartoonist, writer, and illustrator.

Awards, Honors
Ignatz Award for Promising New Talent, 2006; Special Recognition Eisner Award for New Cartooning Talent, 2007.

Writings

SELF-ILLUSTRATED

Salamander Dream, Adhouse Books, 2005.
Gray Horses/Chevaux gris, Oni Press (Portland, OR), 2006.

Chiggers, Ginee Seo/Simon & Schuster (New York, NY), 2008.

Contributor of illustrations to anthologies, including *Flight.*

Sidelights

A cartoonist, novelist, and author of children's books, Hope Larson established her creative career after graduating from the Art Institute of Chicago. Although her college studies had focused on print making, Larson was encouraged to explore comics by several people who worked in the field, and in comics she has ultimately found her niche, producing the graphic novels *Salamander Dream, Gray Horses,* and *Chiggers.* The recipient of a special Eisner award for new cartooning talent, Larson has also seen her artwork published in the *New York Times.*

Described by a *Publishers Weekly* contributor as "a whimsical, dreamlike flight of fancy" composed primarily of images, *Salamander Dream* recounts the stories exchanged by a fanciful young girl and her constant friend Salamander as the girl grows from a child into a young woman. Larson's second book, *Gray Horses,* also weaves fantasy with a coming-of-age theme as Noemie makes a new life for herself as an art student living in Paris. With a text in both English and French, the book is most remarkable for its art: with her "whimsical but sure touch," Larson uses black and yellow "to create the kind of swirling, beautiful spaces one imagines when exploring both a city and a dream," according to a *Publishers Weekly* contributor.

Larson's art reflects her interest in the work of manga artist Harold Sakuishi, and her Eisner Award-winning *Chiggers* was inspired by the author/illustrator's own experiences of growing up in North Carolina. It also shares her memories of what it was like to be a nerdy middle schooler. Using a comic-book format, the book's sequential images describe what transpires when shy teen Abby reunites with her summer-camp friend, Rose. As the sixth grader quickly discovers, Rose is three years older and her relative maturity now causes her to opt for the company of older teens. Abby is left to reach out to her fellow campers—such as Dungeons and Dragons fan Tiel and her new bunkmate Shasta—in order to find a new friend and thus avoid the ostracization that comes from being a loner. Although the novel covers "well-trod territory," according to *Booklist* contributor Stephanie Zvirin, *Chiggers* also features "a freshness, sureness, and understanding that speak[s] very well for Larson." Larson's "entertaining graphic novel" will attract younger teen readers who can "relate to Abby's friendship travails," predicted *Kliatt* reviewer George Galuschak, and in *School Library Journal* Sarah Krygier noted that the author "delicately handles both . . . middle-school angst and the . . . pressures that come with being somewhat different." Calling *Chiggers* a

"pitch-perfect graphic novel," a *Kirkus Reviews* writer added that Larson's self-illustrated story "effectively mixes magical realism with the timeless rituals of summer camp."

Biographical and Critical Sources

PERIODICALS

Booklist, April 15, 2008, Stephanie Zvirin, review of *Chiggers,* p. 39.
Kirkus Reviews, May 1, 2008, review of *Chiggers.*
Kliatt, September, 2008, George Galuschak, review of *Chiggers,* p. 33.
Publishers Weekly, July 18, 2005, review of *Salamander Dream,* p. 190; February 6, 2006, review of *Gray Horses,* p. 49; May 5, 2008, Heidi MacDonald, "Comics Class of '08," p. 34.
School Library Journal, July, 2008, Sarah Krygier, review of *Chiggers,* p. 120.

ONLINE

Hope Larson Home Page, http://www.hopelarson.com (October 15, 2009).

*   *   *

LEICK, Bonnie

Personal

Surname pronounced "like"; born in WI; married Douglas O'Leary; children: Ryan, Connor (stepsons). *Education:* California Institute of Art and Design, B.F.A (film/video-character animation).

Addresses

Home—Milwaukee, WI. *Agent*—Kid Shannon, 9001 W. Warnimont Ave., Milwaukee, WI 53228. *E-mail*—bonnieleick@hotmail.com.

Career

Illustrator. Animator for companies, including Disney, Creative Capers, and Warner Bros. *Exhibitions:* Work exhibited at Schlueter Art Gallery, Wisconsin Lutheran College, Milwaukee.

Member

Society of Children's Book Writers and Illustrators.

Illustrator

Lynn Huggins-Cooper, *Alien Invaders/Invasores Extraterrestres,* Raven Tree Press (Green Bay, WI), 2005.

Jane Leslie Conly, *Impetuous R., Secret Agent,* Hyperion (New York, NY), 2008.

Eye Find: A Picture Puzzle Book, Klutz Press (Palo Alto, CA), 2008.

Dawn Jeffers, *Beautiful Moon/Bella Luna,* Raven Tree Press (Green Bay, WI), 2009.

Katie McKy, *Wolf Camp,* Tanglewood (Terre Haute, IN), 2009.

Helen Ketteman, *Goodnight, Little Monster,* Marshall Cavendish (New York, NY), 2010.

Sidelights

Bonnie Leick grew up in rural Wisconsin, then left for the West coast where her life became a little bit more exciting: in addition to surviving a 6.7 earthquake in Northridge, California in 1964, she has also made it through three small tornados. Her luck with regard to weather also affected her career: Leick's art degree from the California Institute of Art and Design led to work in animation for firms such as Disney and Warner Brothers. More recently, Leick has turned to children's picture books, where her watercolor images have appeared alongside quirky tales in Lynn Huggins-Cooper's *Alien Invaders/Invasores Extraterrestres,* Katie McKy's *Wolf Camp,* and Jane Leslie Conly's *Impetuous R., Secret Agent.*

In the bilingual *Alien Invaders/Invasores Extraterrestres* a small boy sees garden bugs with an unusual perspective: to something smaller, they appear much as tall, large-eyed space aliens would appear to humans. Another insect—a cockroach—is the star of *Impetuous R., Secret Agent,* a picture book about a trio of young roaches that helps to save a struggling restaurant run by humans. Maddie, the star of *Wolf Camp,* comes home from an unusual summer camp transformed, and only a change of seasons can cure her of howling at the moon and baring her teeth. In reviewing *Impetuous R., Secret Agent* for *School Library Journal,* Elaine E. Knight cited Leick's pen-and-ink illustrations for revealing "an engaging bug's-eye view . . . and help[ing] to 'humanize' the [story's] insect characters." In the same periodical, Ann Welton praised Leick's inky colored images for *Alien Invader/Invasores Extraterrestres,* noting that the artist's ability to create "a luminous sheen adds to the menace" of a story with "plenty of child appeal." In *Kirkus Reviews* a critic also cited these same "shadowy" images, writing that Leick imbues her illustrations with "just enough humor to avoid real fright."

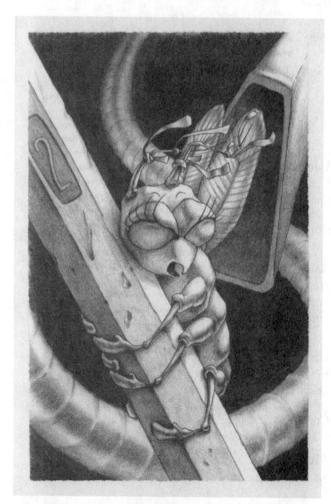

Jane Leslie Conly's Impetuous R., Secret Agent *features detailed watercolor illustrations by Bonnie Leick that depict events from a bug's perspective.* (Illustration copyright © 2008 by Bonnie Leick. All rights reserved. Reprinted with permission of Disney Book Group.)

Biographical and Critical Sources

PERIODICALS

Booklist, September 1, 2008, Francisca Goldsmith, review of *Impetuous R., Secret Agent,* p. 95.

Kirkus Reviews, June 1, 2005, review of *Alien Invaders/ Invasores Extraterrestres,* p. 638; June 15, 2008, review of *Impetuous R., Secret Agent.*

School Library Journal, October, 2005, Ann Welton, review of *Alien Invaders/Invasores Extraterrestres,* p. 149; November, 2008, Elaine E. Knight, review of *Impetuous R., Secret Agent,* p. 116.

ONLINE

Bonnie Leick Home Page, http://www.bonnieleick.com (October 15, 2009).

*   *   *

LEWIS, J. Patrick 1942-

Personal

Born May 5, 1942, in Gary, IN; son of Leo J. and Mary Lewis; married Judith Weaver, August 29, 1964 (divorced, 1983); married Susan G. Marceau, June 24, 1998; children: (first marriage) Beth, Matthew, Leigh Ann; (stepchildren) Kelly Marceau, Scott Marceau. *Edu-*

J. Patrick Lewis (Photograph by Susan Lewis. Reproduced with permission.)

cation: St. Joseph's College (Rensselaer, IN), B.A., 1964; Indiana University—Bloomington, M.A., 1965; Ohio State University, Ph.D., 1974.

Addresses

Home—Westerville, OH. *Agent*—Ginger Knowlton, Curtis Brown, Lt., 10 Astor Pl., New York, NY 10003. *E-mail*—jplewis42@aol.com.

Career

Author and educator. Otterbein College, Westerville, OH, professor of economics, 1974-98; poet and writer for children. Speaker at conferences; presenter at teachers' workshops.

Member

International Reading Association, Society of Children's Book Writers and Illustrators, National Council of Teachers of English.

Awards, Honors

Ohio Arts Council grant, 1989, 1991; Children's Book of the Year designation, Ohioana Library Association, 1989, for *The Tsar and the Amazing Cow;* Kentucky Bluegrass Award nomination, 1991, for *A Hippopotamusn't and Other Animal Verses;* Notable Book designation, American Library Association, 1992, for *The Moonbow of Mr. B. Bones,* 1995, for *Black Swan/White Crow,* 2002, for *Freedom like Sunlight; Parents* magazine honor book award, 1994, for *The Fat-Cats at Sea;* Kentucky Bluegrass Award, 1996, for *The Christmas of the Reddle Moon;* Hoosier Book Award nomination, 1998, for *Doodle Dandies;* Coretta Scott King Award nomination, 2000, for *Freedom like Sunlight; Storytell-*

ing World honor book designation, 2000, for *Isabella Abnormella;* Golden Kite Award, Society of Childrens Book Writers and Illustrators, 2001, for *The Shoe Tree of Chagrin;* Gold Book Award, National Association of Parent Publishers, and *New York Times* ten best illustrated books of the year listee, both 2002, and Ragazzi honor award, Bologna book festival, 2003, all for *The Last Resort;* Henry Bergh Children's Book Award for Poetry, American Society for the Prevention of Cruelty to Animals, 2003, and Golden Lamp Book of the Year Award, Association of Publishers, 2004, both for *Swan Song;* Alice Louise Wood Memorial Prize, Ohioana Awards, 2004, for lifetime achievement in children's literature; New York Public Library One Hundred Books for Reading and Sharing designation, 2005, for *Please Bury Me in the Library;* Family Choice Award for Educational Resources, 2005, and Books for the Teen Age listee, New York Public Library, Honor Book designation, Ragazzi Award, and Independent Publisher Book Award, all 2006, all for *VHERses;* IRA Teachers' Choices Award, and Independent Publisher Book Award, both 2006, both for *Galileo's Universe;* Silver Medal, Society of Illustrators, 2006, named among *Booklist* Ten Black History Books for Youth, 2007, Book of the Year Gold Award, *ForeWord* magazine, and Honor Book designation for Children's Poetry, Ragazzi Award, 2008; all for *Black Cat Bone;* IRA Teachers Choices Award, 2008, for *The Brothers' War;* Gold Medal for Nonfiction, *ForeWord* magazine, 2007, and Gold Medal, Independent Publisher Book Award, 2008, both for *Michelangelo's World;* (with Paul B. Janeczko) Parents' Choice Approved Award, 2008, and Best Children's Books of the Year designation, Bank Street College of Education, and Editor's Choice Award, Library Media Connection, both 2009, all for *Birds on a Wire;* Great Lakes Book Award finalist, 2009, for *The Underwear Salesman.*

Writings

FOR CHILDREN

The Tsar and the Amazing Cow, illustrated by Friso Henstra, Dial (New York, NY), 1988.

A Hippopotamusn't and Other Animal Verses, illustrated by Victoria Chess, Dial (New York, NY), 1990.

Two-legged, Four-legged, No-legged Rhymes, illustrated by Pamela Paparone, Knopf (New York, NY), 1991.

Earth Verses and Water Rhymes, illustrated by Robert Sabuda, Atheneum (New York, NY), 1991.

The Moonbow of Mr. B. Bones, illustrated by Dirk Zimmer, Knopf (New York, NY), 1992.

One Dog Day, illustrated by Marcy Dunn Ramsey, Atheneum (New York, NY), 1993.

(Reteller) *The Frog Princess: A Russian Folktale,* illustrated by Gennady Spirin, Dial (New York, NY), 1994.

July Is a Mad Mosquito, illustrated by Melanie W. Hall, Atheneum (New York, NY), 1994.

The Christmas of the Reddle Moon, pictures by Gary Kelley, Dial (New York, NY), 1994.

The Fat-Cats at Sea, illustrated by Victoria Chess, Knopf (New York, NY), 1994.

Black Swan/White Crow (haiku), woodcuts by Chris Manson, Atheneum (New York, NY), 1995.

Ridicholas Nicholas: More Animal Poems, pictures by Victoria Chess, Dial (New York, NY), 1995.

Riddle-icious, illustrated by Debbie Tilley, Knopf (New York, NY), 1996.

The Boat of Many Rooms, illustrated by Reg Cartwright, Atheneum (New York, NY), 1996.

The La-Di-Da Hare, illustrated by Diane Blumenthal, Dial (New York, NY), 1997.

Long Was the Winter Road They Traveled: A Tale of the Nativity, illustrated by Drew Bairley, Dial (New York, NY), 1997.

The Little Buggers: Insect and Spider Poems, illustrated by Victoria Chess, Dial (New York, NY), 1997.

Riddle-lightful, illustrated by Debbie Tilley, Knopf (New York, NY), 1998.

The House of Boo, illustrated by Katya Krenina, Atheneum (New York, NY), 1998.

Doodle Dandies: Poems That Take Shape, illustrated by Lisa Desimini, Atheneum (New York, NY), 1998.

BoshBlobberBosh: Runcible Poems for Edward Lear, illustrated by Gary Kelley, Harcourt (New York, NY), 1998.

At the Wish of the Fish: An Adaptation of a Russian Folktale, illustrated by Katya Krenina, Atheneum (New York, NY), 1999.

The Bookworm's Feast: A Potluck of Poems, Dial (New York, NY), 1999.

The Night of the Goat Children, illustrated by Alexi Natchev, Dial (New York, NY), 1999.

Isabella Abnormella and the Very, Very Finicky Queen of Trouble, illustrated by Kyrsten Brooker, DK Publishing (New York, NY), 2000.

Freedom like Sunlight: Praisesongs for Black Americans, Creative Editions (Mankato, MN), 2000.

Good Mousekeeping, and Other Animal Home Poems, illustrated by Lisa Desimini, Atheneum (New York, NY), 2001.

A Burst of Firsts: Doers, Shakers, and Record Breakers, illustrated by Brian Ajhar, Dial (New York, NY), 2001.

The Shoe Tree of Chagrin, illustrated by Chris Sheban, Creative Editions (Mankato, MN), 2001.

Arithme-Tickle: An Even Number of Odd Riddle-Rhymes, illustrated by Frank Remkiewicz, Harcourt (San Diego, CA), 2002.

A World of Wonders: Geographic Travels in Verse and Rhyme, ilustrated by Alison Jay, Dial (New York, NY), 2002.

The Last Resort, illustrated by Roberto Innocenti, Creative Editions (Mankato, MN), 2002.

The Snowflake Sisters, illustrated by Lisa Desimini, Atheneum (New York, NY), 2003.

Galileo's Universe, illustrated by Tim Curry, Creative Editions (Mankato, MN), 2003.

Swan Songs: Poems of Extinction, illustrated by Christopher Wormell, Creative Editions (Mankato, MN), 2003.

Scien-trickery: Riddles in Science, illustrated by Frank Remkiewicz, Silver Whistle (Orlando, FL), 2004.

Please Bury Me in the Library, illustrated by Kyle M. Stone, Harcourt (Orlando, FL), 2004.

The Stolen Smile, illustrated by Gary Kelley, Creative Editions (Mankato, MN), 2004.

Vherses: A Celebration of Outstanding Women, illustrated by Mark Summers, Creative Editions (Mankato, MN), 2005.

Monumental Verses, National Geographic (Washington, DC), 2005.

God Made the Skunk; and Other Animal Poems, Doggerel Daze, 2005.

Heroes and She-roes: Poems of Amazing and Everyday Heroes, illustrated by Jim Cooke, Dial (New York, NY), 2005.

Once upon a Tomb: Gravely Humorous Verses, illustrated by Simon Bartram, Candlewick Press (Cambridge, MA), 2006.

Blackbeard the Pirate King, National Geographic (Washington, DC), 2006.

Black Cat Bone: A Life of Blues Legend Robert Johnson in Verse, illustrated by Gary Kelley, Creative Editions (Mankato, MN), 2006.

Good Mornin', Ms. America: The U.S.A. in Verse, illustrated by Mark Clapsadle, Gingham Dog (Columbus, OH), 2006.

(With Paul B. Janczko) *Wing Nuts: Screwy Haiku,* illustrated by Tricia Tusa, Little, Brown (Boston, MA), 2006.

(With Rebecca Kai Dotlich) *Castles: Cold Stone Poems,* illustrated by Dan Burr, Boyds Mills Press (Honesdale, PA), 2007.

Tulip at the Bat, illustrated by Amiko Hirao, Little, Brown (Boston, MA), 2007.

Big Is Big (and Little Little): A Book of Contrasts, illustrated by Bob Barner, Holiday House (New York, NY), 2007.

The Brothers' War: Civil War Voices in Verse, National Geographic Society (Washington, DC), 2007.

Michelangelo's World, Creative Editions (Mankato, MN), 2007.

Under the Kissletoe: Christmastime Poems, illustrated by Rob Shepperson, Wordsong (Honesdale, PA), 2007.

(With Paul B. Janczko) *Birds on a Wire: A Renga 'Round Town,* illustrated by Gary Lippincott, Wordsong (Honesdale, PA), 2008.

The World's Greatest: Poems, illustrated by Keith Graves, Chronicle Books (San Francisco, CA), 2008.

Countdown to Summer: 180 Poems for Every Day of the School Year, illustrated by Ethan Long, Little, Brown (New York, NY), 2009.

The Underwear Salesman; and Other Jobs for Better or Verse, illustrated by Serge Bloch, Simon & Schuster (New York, NY), 2009.

(With Beth Zappitello) *First Dog,* illustrated by Tim Bowers, Sleeping Bear Press (Chelsea, MI), 2009.

The House, illustrated by Roberto Innocenti, Creative Editions (Mankato, MN), 2009.

The Kindergarten Cat, illustrated by Ailie Busby, Schwartz & Wade (New York, NY), 2009.

Skywriting: Poems to Fly, illustrated by Laszlo Kubinyi, Creative Editions (Mankato, MN), 2009.

Spot the Plot: A Riddle Book of Book Riddles, illustrated by Lynn Munsinger, Chronicle Books (San Francisco, CA), 2009.

Mr. Nickel and Mrs. Dime, illustrated by Valorie Fisher, Schwartz & Wade (New York, NY), 2010.

Contributor of children's poems to periodicals, including *Ahoy, Bookbird, Cricket, Journal of Children's Literature, Spider, Ladybug, Cicada, Odyssey, Ranger Rick, Reading Today, Highlights for Children, Ms., Your Big Backyard, Chickadee, Creative Classroom, Storytime,* and *Storyworks.* Contributor to anthologies.

"SHARING NATURE WITH CHILDREN" SERIES: NONFICTION

Earth and You, a Closer View: Nature's Features, Dawn Publications (Nevada City, CA), 2001.

Earth and Us, Continuous: Nature's Past and Future, Dawn Publications (Nevada City, CA), 2001.

Earth and Me, Our Family Tree, Dawn Publications (Nevada City, CA), 2002.

OTHER

Poems and short fiction included in anthologies. Contributor of book reviews to periodicals, including *New York Times, Nation, Progressive, Technology Review, Chicago Tribune,* and *San Francisco Chronicle;* contributor of articles and reviews to professional journals. Contributor of adult poems to periodicals, including *Gettysburgh Review, Dalhousie Review, New Letters, Seneca Review, Kansas Quarterly, Event, Spoon River Quarterly, Slate, American Literary Review, Yankee,* and *Southern Humanities Review.* Contributor of short fiction to *Wisconsin Review, Other Voices, Kansas Quarterly, Phoebe, Sun Dog, Madison Review,* and *New England Review.*

Sidelights

While working as a professor of economics at an Ohio university, J. Patrick Lewis led something of a double life. Beginning his career as a children's book author in the late 1980s, he wrote poems and stories for youngsters part time, and since his retirement he has devoted full time to children's literature. Influenced by such authors as Lewis Carroll, A.A. Milne, and Edward Lear, Lewis produces a wide range of entertaining prose and poetry for young and middle-grade readers, including *The Moonbow of Mr. B. Bones, The Shoe Tree of Chagrin, The Last Resort, Black Cat Bone: A Life of Blues Legend Robert Johnson in Verse,* and *The Brothers' War: Civil War Voices in Verse.* As Roger Sutton noted in his review of *The Brothers' War,* Lewis has gained a reputation "as a nimble, elegant and prolific" poet, and with this collection his talent for "apt rhyming" is further cemented.

In Lewis's first book for young readers, *The Tsar and the Amazing Cow,* he tells the story of an elderly couple who are finding it hard to get by until the milk of a

magic cow enables them to recapture the vigor of youth. When the greedy tsar hears of the wonderful cow, he orders the couple to St. Petersburg, but the cow manages to evade capture and ultimately all is well. Writing in *Booklist,* Ilene Cooper praised *The Tsar and the Amazing Cow* as a "well-told tale," and Margaret A. Bush described it in *Horn Book* as a "spare, well-paced narrative, adroitly embellished with an occasional richness of phrase." Another picture book by Lewis, *The Last Resort,* features illustrations by Roberto Innocenti; it won the Bologna Raggazi Honor Award and has been translated into fifteen languages.

The Moonbow of Mr. B. Bones, which continues in the folkloric tradition of *The Tsar and the Amazing Cow,* moves from Russia to the United States as Mr. B. Bones sells "magic jars with mysterious labels—Sundrops, Snowrays, Moonbows, Rainflakes, and Whistling Wind." He does a brisk business until someone claims that the jars are empty, but when Mr. B. opens a jar, a shining light convinces everyone that his "moonbows" are real. "A fine poet," Rochman wrote in *Booklist,* "Lewis tells the story with a lilting, colloquial rhythm." *School Library Journal* contributor Susan Scheps concluded that, "The folktale qualities of plot and narrative make this a good choice for reading aloud."

Also rooted in Russian folklore, *The Frog Princess* makes use of a story that some reviewers described as "complex." When a tsar commands each of his three sons to shoot an arrow into the forest and marry the woman who retrieves it, his youngest son winds up married to a frog, which has brought back his arrow. This frog is special; in fact it is a beautiful woman who has been placed under a curse by her father. "Lewis's retelling of this complex Russian tale," wrote *School Library Journal* contributor Linda Boyles, "is smooth and easy, lightened by touches of humor."

Other rhyming stories by Lewis include *The Fat-Cats at Sea* and *Tulip at the Bat,* the latter a comic send-up of the well-known poem "Casey at the Bat." *The Fat-Cats at Sea* finds a group of six nautical cats setting off to the Isle of Sticky-Goo to retrieve the island's famous sticky buns for the queen of Catmandoo. They go through the same adventures readers of sea tales have come to expect since Homer wrote his *Odyssey:* homesickness, hostile vessels, and washing up on the shores of a lotus-filled paradise. "The jaunty rhythms and smooth impeccable rhymes flow effortlessly, employing a highly appealing blend of downright silliness and a more sophisticated cleverness," stated a *Publishers Weekly* reviewer.

Described by *School Library Journal* contributor Carol Schene as a "unique take-off" of the classic baseball poem, *Tulip at the Bat* pits the New York Pets against the frightening lineup of the Boston Beasts during the World series. Lewis's description of the ballbark action is "witty and silly and lots of fun," added Schene.

In *The Snowflake Sisters* Lewis tells a more serene tale, narrowing readers' world view to that of two unique snowflakes falling on Christmas night, amid a sea of tiny ice crystals. Floating down through the night sky, sisters Crystal and Ivory catch a ride on Santa's sleigh, watch the ball drop in New York's Times Square, and drift to a quiet resting place on a friendly snowman. In *School Library Journal* Susan Patron praised the poet's "elegant and fluid rhymed text," while in *Booklist* Ilene Cooper called the text "clever" and had special praise for Lisa Desimini's illustrations, collages that "delightfully catch" Lewis's "wordplay." As a *Kirkus Reviews* writer noted, "never has the snowy season been celebrated with more joie de vivre."

While Lewis has authored several other prose texts, he is best known for his many verse collections, among them *A Hippopotamusn't and Other Animal Verses*, *Scien-Trickery: Riddles in Science*, *Once upon a Tomb: Gravely Humorous Verses*, and *Under the Kissletoe: Christmastime Poems*. *Scien-Trickery* contains eighteen science-inspired rhyming riddles that a *Kirkus Reviews* contributor predicted will "engage both the minds and the funny bones of young readers," while in *Horn Book* Claire E. Gross wrote that Lewis's "affable wit and infectious cadence bring fresh energy" to the holiday-themed verses in *Under the Kissletoe*.

Many of Lewis's verse collections for young readers focus on animal characters, and almost all feature word-

J. Patrick Lewis focuses his amusing verse on the traditions of the holiday season in **Under the Kissletoe,** *illustrated by Rob Shepperson.* (Wordsong Press, 2007. Illustration copyright © 2007 by Rob Shepperson. Reproduced by permission.)

play and engaging rhyme. *A Hippopotamusn't and Other Animal Verses* centers on birds and beasts; Hearne dubbed the book "playful, clever, and above all, freshly worded." In the book Lewis presents a variety of poetic forms, including quatrains, couplets, haiku, and limericks. In a review for *Horn Book*, Mary M. Burns pointed out Lewis's concise descriptions of animal characters as diverse as vultures and tomcats, concluding of *A Hippopotamusn't and Other Animal Verses:* "If there is anyone who doesn't chortle over this book, don't bother trying to please him or her—nothing ever will."

Other rhyming books include *Two-legged, Four-legged, No-legged Rhymes,* in which an assortment of creatures that includes cats, porcupines, and mosquitoes benefit from the Lewis treatment. Nesting habits are the focus of *Good Mousekeeping, and Other Animal Home Poems,* in which Lewis imagines the sort of homes wild animals—from flamingos to cats, to polar bears—might chose if they were human. In *Booklist* Kay Weisman praised *Good Mousekeeping* as an "imaginative, humorous collection" that is guaranteed to "delight even poetry curmudgeons," and Kathleen Whalin was prompted by the book to note in *School Library Journal* that "no one is better at clever wordplay than Lewis."

Lewis serves up more outlandish humor in *The Underwear Salesman: And Other Jobs for Better or Verse, Spot the Plot: A Riddle Book of Book Riddles,* and *Riddle-icious,* the last about which *Bulletin of the Center for Children's Books* reviewer Deborah Stevenson wrote: "Some books try to *make* language fun. This one knows it already is and invites readers to share in the revel." *Riddle-icious* consists of riddle-poems, while its follow up, *Riddle-lightful,* contains thirty-two additional simple-to-very-puzzling riddles. "Young wits will congratulate themselves when they figure out the answers to these clever brainteasers," maintained a *Publishers Weekly* critic in reviewing both works. "Puns are everywhere in this playful, rhyming survey of jobs," explained Hazel Rochman in her *Booklist* review of *The Underwear Salesman,* and a *Publishers Weekly* contributor cited the book's "sophisticated wordplay and his [Lewis's] willingness to push readers in terms of poetic conceits."

Lewis has sometimes stepped back to view the home all animals share. In *Earth Verses and Water Rhymes* his tone becomes "more sober," in the words of *Bulletin of the Center for Children's Books* contributor Betsy Hearne. Leone McDermott agreed in *Booklist,* writing that *Earth Verses and Water Rhymes* is a "pleasant book for curling up with at home or for reading aloud to a group." Praised by a *Publishers Weekly* reviewer as "a full-scale treat for the armchair traveler," *A World of Wonders: Geographic Travels in Verse and Rhyme* also scans the planet. Taking readers on trips alongside Christopher Columbus and others, Lewis also dispenses a wealth of geological and travel trivia. Other books that focus on the natural world are the three volumes in Lewis's "Sharing Nature with Children" series. *Earth*

and Us, Continuous serves as an introduction to the game board of life; the book describes the geology and ecology of planet Earth in verses that *Booklist* critic Gillian Engberg described as "written in sweeping language and poetic metaphors." Other volumes in the series include *Earth and Me, Our Family Tree* and *Earth and You, a Closer View.*

In *Doodle Dandies: Poems That Take Shape* Lewis again joins with artist Lisa Desimini, this time to present a series of concrete poems: verses where words are arranged in the shape of the thing they are describing. In a poem about a giraffe, for example, the word *tail* forms the tail of the giraffe and the word *stilts* is repeated four times to form the giraffe's four long legs. "These poems take both shape and flight as they soar through the imaginative landscape," enthused Lauren Adams in her *Horn Book* review of *Doodle Dandies.* Of this collaboration between author and artist, Adams called it "a true collaboration of text and art presenting poems that are pictures that are poems."

In addition to working with a variety of well-known illustrators in creating his verse collections, Lewis sometimes teams up with other poets, collaborating with Paul B. Janeczko on both *Wing Nuts: Screwy Haiku* and *Birds on a Wire: A Renga 'Round Town,* and with Rebecca Kai Dotlich on *Castles: Cold Stone Poems.* Describing Lewis and Janeczko as "two of the big kahunas of children's poetry," a *Kirkus Reviews* writer dubbed the twenty-six *senryu*-style haiku in *Wing Nuts* as "plenty of fun, with nary a screw up."

Some of Lewis's books feature Biblical themes. *The Boat of Many Rooms,* for instance, tells the story of Noah and his ark through a collection of rhythmic verses. A reviewer in *Publishers Weekly* applauded the narrative, commenting that "Lewis employs a wide variety of rhyme scheme and stanza length to convey the bustling energy." *Long Was the Winter Road They Traveled: A Tale of the Nativity,* another bible-based book, is, in the words of *Booklist* reviewer Susan Dove Lempke, "a reverent, tender look at the wonders of a night almost 2,000 years ago." *The House of Boo,* on the other hand, is a spooky poem in which Lewis celebrates a distinctly non-Christian holiday: Halloween.

Proving that truth proves as fascinating as fiction, Lewis delves into history in several illustrated books for slightly older readers. *Heroes and She-roes* contains twenty-one verses that bring to life individuals such as civil rights activist Rosa Parks, Indian pacifist Mahatma Gandhi, and Pakistani child activist Iqbal Mashih, as well as firefighters, teachers, and even an Alaskan rescue dog. The U.S. Civil War is the focus of *The Brothers' War,* a collection of eleven poems in which "Lewis [skillfully] honors fictionalized and historical heroes and does not shy away from the horrors of war," according to *School Library Journal* critic Donna Cardon.

Another work based on a true story, Lewis's *The Stolen Smile* focuses on suspected art thief Vincenzo Peruggia,

an employee of Paris's famous Louvre museum who was caught in 1913, two years after stealing the *Mona Lisa* and displaying it in his living quarters. Turning to the world of music, his *Black Cat Bone* contains nineteen verses that focus on the life of legendary Delta blues guitarist Robert Johnson and effectively "echo . . . Johnson's music," according to *School Library Journal* contributor Nina Lindsay.

In *The La-Di-Da Hare* Lewis pays tribute to nineteenth-century nonsense writers Lewis Carroll and Edward Lear, while also reflecting several other quirky influences in an upbeat story told, appropriately, in nonsense rhyme. Praising *The La-Di-Da Hare* as an "unpredictable and spirited romp," a *Publishers Weekly* critic wrote that Lewis has successfully mimicked the masters in a work that "blithely echoes classic nonsense poetry."

Focusing solely on Lear, Lewis's *BoshBlobberBosh* collects sixteen poems in various forms about the life of Lear, the unparalleled limericist and king of nonsense verse, or "bosh." Lewis explores Lear's childhood as the twentieth child in a family of twenty-one, his job as an art instructor to England's Queen Victoria, and even Lear's cat, Mr. Foss. Biographical notes explain the parts of Lear's life from whence the poems are drawn. "The verses are a bit more sweetly whimsical that Lear's angular nonsense," stated Deborah Stevenson in the *Bulletin of the Center for Children's Books,* "but they're enjoyable evocations of the poet's classic contributions, and Lewis has often caught his forerunner's tone." *School Library Journal* contributor Robin L. Gibson thought the collection to be a fitting pairing with Lear's original pen-and-ink drawings but added that "they are strong enough to stand on their own." A reviewer in *Publishers Weekly* approved of the tribute, writing that "literary chronicles seldom prove as amicable . . . and Lear himself would certainly be pleased that Lewis's limericks scan perfectly."

Lewis told *SATA:* "Long a college professor of economics, I didn't discover poetry until I was leaning into the sunset of forty. So I have had two great careers, though I now know that the present one is preeminently more satisfying.

"Briefly, I am trying to prove that there is no subject about which one cannot write a poem, which is why my books run helter-skelter through the Dewey Decimal system. Finding one's voice is the good advice coming out of creative writing workshops, but I would rather find a hundred voices so that no one will be able to pigeonhole my work. The poem is always more important than the poet. If a poem has any worth, one should be able to erase the poet's name from the bottom of the page. The poem has a chance of living on; the poet does not."

Biographical and Critical Sources

BOOKS

Copeland, Jeffrey S., and Vicky L. Copeland, editors, *Speaking of Poets 2: More Interviews with Poets,* National Council of Teachers of English, 1994.

Fletcher, Ralph, *Poetry Matters,* HarperCollins (New York, NY), 2002.

Lewis, J. Patrick, *The Moonbow of Mr. B. Bones,* Knopf (New York, NY), 1992.

PERIODICALS

Booklist, May 15, 1988, Ilene Cooper, review of *The Tsar and the Amazing Cow,* p. 1610; August, 1991, Hazel Rochman, review of *Two-legged, Four-legged, No-legged Rhymes,* p. 2150; October 1, 1991, Leone McDermott, review of *Earth Verses and Water Rhymes,* p. 320; January 15, 1992, Hazel Rochman, review of *The Moonbow of Mr. B. Bones,* p. 952; April 15, 1993, Christie Sylvester, review of *One Dog Day,* p. 1515; October 15, 1995, Carolyn Phelan, review of *Black Swan/White Crow,* p. 406; October 1, 1997, Susan Dove Lempke, review of *Long Was the Winter Road They Traveled: A Tale of the Nativity,* pp. 323-324; March 15, 2001, Stephanie Zvirin, review of *A Burst of Firsts: Doers, Shakers, and Record-breakers,* p. 1392, and Kay Weisman, review of *Good Mousekeeping,* p. 1394; September 1, 2001, Gillian Engberg, review of *Earth and Us, Continuous,* p. 111; December 15, 2001, Linda Perkins, review of *The Shoe Tree of Chagrin Falls,* p. 731; March 15, 2002, Carolyn Phelan, review of *A World of Wonders,* p. 1254; May 15, 2002, Diane Foote, review of *Arithme-Tickle: An Even Number of Odd Riddle-Rhymes,* p. 1595; November 15, 2003, Ilene Cooper, review of *The Snowflake Sisters,* p. 601; February 15, 2004, Carolyn Phelan, review of *Scien-Trickery: Riddles in Science,* p. 1055; January 1, 2005, Hazel Rochman, review of *Heroes and She-roes: Poems of Amazing and Everyday Heroes,* p. 849; December 15, 2005, Kay Weisman, review of *Vherses: A Celebration of Outstanding Women,* p. 44; August 1, 2006, John Peters, review of *Once upon a Tomb: Gravely Humorous Verses,* p. 81; October 1, 2006, Gillian Engberg, review of *Castles: Cold Stone Poems,* p. 51; January 1, 2007, Bill Ott, review of *Black Cat Bone: A Life of Blues Legend Robert Johnson in Verse,* p. 93; September 15, 2007, Carolyn Phelan, review of *Under the Kissletoe,* p. 69; March 1, 2009, Hazel Rochman, review of *The Underwear Salesman; and Other Jobs for Better of Verse,* p. 52.

Bulletin of the Center for Children's Books, July-August, 1988, Betsy Hearne, review of *The Tsar and the Amazing Cow,* pp. 232-233; July-August, 1990, Betsy Hearne, review of *A Hippopotamusn't and Other Animal Verses,* p. 271; January, 1992, Betsy Hearne, review of *Earth Verses and Water Rhymes,* p. 132; February, 1994, Roger Sutton, review of *July Is a Mad Mosquito,* p. 193; June, 1996, Deborah Stevenson, review of *Riddle-icious,* pp. 325-326; December, 1998, Deborah Stevenson, review of *BoshBlobberBosh: Runcible Poems for Edward Lear,* pp. 136-137.

Horn Book, May-June, 1988, Margaret A. Bush, review of *The Tsar and the Amazing Cow,* pp. 365-366; May-June, 1990, Mary M. Burns, review of *A Hippopotamusn't and Other Animal Verses,* p. 344; July-August, 1998, Lauren Adams, review of *Doodle Dandies,* pp. 505-506; March-April, 2002, Mary M. Burns, review of *A World of Wonders: Geographic Travels in Verse and Rhyme,* p. 224; February 1, 2002, Michael Cart, review of *The Last Resort,* p. 981; November-December, 2007, Claire E. Gross, review of *Under the Kissletoe: Christmastime Poems,* p. 632; January-February, 2008, Roger Sutton, review of *The Brothers' War: Civil War Voices in Verse,* p. 101; July-August, 2008, Elissa Gershowitz, review of *The World's Greatest: Poems,* p. 463.

Kirkus Reviews, July 1, 1991, review of *Two-legged, Four-legged, No-legged Rhymes,* pp. 858-859; September 1, 2001, review of *The Shoe Tree of Chagrin Falls,* p. 1295; January 1, 2002, review of *A World of Wonders,* p. 48; March 15, 2002, review of *Arithme-Tickle,* p. 417; September 15, 2003, review of *The Snowflake Sisters,* p. 1177; March 15, 2004, review of *Scien-Trickery,* p. 273; February 15, 2005, review of *Heroes and She-Roes,* p. 231; March 15, 2006, review of *Wing Nuts: Screwy Haiku,* p. 293; September 1, 2006, review of *Black Cat Bone,* p. 906; October 1, 2006, review of *Castles,* p. 1018; March 1, 2007, review of *Tulip at the Bat,* p. 226; May 1, 2007, review of *Big Is Big (and Little, Little);* August 15, 2008, review of *Birds on a Wire.*

New York Times Book Review, October 23, 2005, Jan Benzel, review of *Please Bury Me in the Library,* p. 21; July 9, 2006, Lawrence Downes, review of *Blackbeard: The Pirate King,* p. 16; April 13, 2008, review of *The World's Greatest,* p. 19.

Publishers Weekly, March, 1992, Susan Scheps, review of *The Moonbow of Mr. B. Bones,* p. 216; September 5, 1994, review of *The Fat-Cats at Sea,* p. 111; January 13, 1997, review of *The Boat of Many Rooms,* p. 71; March 24, 1997, review of *The La-Di-Da Hare,* p. 83; October 19, 1998, review of *BoshBlobberBosh,* p. 80; November 16, 1998, review of *Riddle-lightful,* p. 74; April 30, 2001, reviews of *Good Mousekeeping,* p. 77, and *A Burst of Firsts,* p. 78; January 7, 2002, review of *A World of Wonders,* p. 64; July 29, 2002, review of *The Last Resort,* p. 72; November 3, 2003, review of *Swan Song,* p. 75; August 28, 2006, reviews of *Once upon a Tomb* and *Black Cat Bone,* p. 53; January 22, 2007, review of *Tulip at the Bat,* p. 183; April 30, 2007, review of *Big Is Big (and Little, Little): A Book of Contrasts,* p. 159; December 3, 2007, review of *The Brothers' War,* p. 70; March 3, 2008, review of *The World's Greatest,* p. 46; January 19, 2009, review of *The Underwear Salesman,* p. 60.

School Library Journal, April, 1994, Judy Greenfield, review of *July Is a Mad Mosquito,* p. 120; September, 1994, Linda Boyles, review of *The Frog Princess,* p. 209; November, 1998, Robin L. Gibson, review of *BoshBlobberBosh,* p. 141; April, 2001, John Peters,

review of *Earth and You, a Closer View: Nature's Features,* p. 132; June, 2001, Kathleen Whalin, review of *Good Mousekeeping,* p. 138; February, 2002, Jane Marino, review of *The Shoe Tree of Chagrin Falls,* p. 108; April, 2002, Patricia Pearl Dole, review of *Earth and Me, Our Family Tree,* p. 114, Kathleen Whalin, review of *Arithme-Tickle,* p. 136, and Margaret Bush, review of *A World of Wonders,* p. 175; October, 2003, Susan Patron, review of *The Snowflake Sisters,* p. 65; December, 2003, Margaret Bush, review of *Swan Song,* p. 171; January, 2004, Joy Fleishhacker, review of *A World of Wonders,* p. 78; April, 2004, Corrina Austin, review of *Scien-Trickery,* p. 135; January, 2005, Wendy Lukehart, review of *The Stolen Smile,* p. 132; June, 2006, Nancy Palmer, review of *Please Bury Me in the Library,* p. 138; January, 2006, Marilyn Taniguchi, review of *Vherses,* p. 156; May, 2006, Teresa Pfeifer, review of *Wing Nuts,* p. 112; October, 2006, Jill Heritage Maza, review of *Castles,* p. 179; December, 2006, Rick Margolis, interview with Lewis, p. 34, Sally R. Dow, review of *Good Mornin', Ms. America: The USA in Verse,* p. 125, and Nina Lindsay, review of *Black Cat Bone,* and Daryl Grabarek, review of *Blackbeard: The Pirate King,* both p. 165; May, 2007, Marge Loch-Wouters, review of *Big Is Big (and Little Is Little),* p. 121; June, 2007, Carol Schene, review of *Tulip at the Bat,* p. 112; January, 2008, Donna Cardon, review of *The Brothers' War,* and Wendy Lukehart, review of *Michelangelo's World,* both p. 144; October, 2008, Donna Cardon, review of *Birds on a Wire,* p. 133.

ONLINE

J. Patrick Lewis Home Page, http://www.jpatricklewis.com (October 15, 2009).

M

MANUSHKIN, Fran 1942-
(Frances Manushkin)

Personal

Surname is pronounced "Ma-*nush*-kin"; born November 2, 1942, in Chicago, IL; daughter of Meyer (a furniture salesman) and Beatrice Manushkin. *Education:* Attended University of Illinois and Roosevelt University; Chicago Teachers College, North Campus (now Northeastern Illinois University), B.A., 1964. *Religion:* Jewish. *Hobbies and other interests:* Travel, swimming, bird watching, cat watching, reading, book collecting, snorkeling, theatergoing.

Addresses

Home—New York, NY. *E-mail*—franm@nyc.rr.com.

Career

Writer. Elementary teacher in Chicago, IL, 1964-65; Lincoln Center for Performing Arts, New York, NY, tour guide, 1966; Holt, Rinehart & Winston, Inc., New York, NY, secretary to college psychology editor, 1967-68; Harper & Row Publishers, Inc., New York, NY, secretary, 1968-72, associate editor of Harper Junior Books, 1973-78; Random House Inc, New York, NY, editor of Clubhouse K-2 (student paperback-book club), 1978-80. Mentor to adult writers in Eastern Europe through George Soros Foundation's Open Society program.

Member

PEN (co-chair of children's/young-adult book committee), Author's League of America, Author's Guild, Society of Children's Book Writers and Illustrators.

Awards, Honors

Pick of the Lists selection, American Booksellers Association, for *Latkes and Applesauce;* Notable Children's Book citation, Association of Jewish Libraries, 2000,

Fran Manushkin (Reproduced by permission.)

for *Come Let Us Be Joyful;* Notable Children's Book citation, American Library Association, for *The Matzah That Papa Brought Home;* One Hundred Books for Reading and Sharing inclusion, New York Public Library, 2006, for *The Shivers in the Fridge.*

Writings

FOR CHILDREN

Baby, illustrated by Ronald Himler, Harper (New York, NY), 1972, published as *Baby, Come Out!,* 1984, reprinted, Star Bright Books (New York, NY), 2002.

Bubblebath!, illustrated by Ronald Himler, Harper (New York, NY), 1974.

Shirleybird, illustrated by Carl Stuart, Harper (New York, NY), 1975.

Swinging and Swinging, illustrated by Thomas DiGrazia, Harper (New York, NY), 1976.

The Perfect Christmas Picture, illustrated by Karen A. Weinhaus, Harper (New York, NY), 1980.

Annie Finds Sandy, illustrated by George Wildman, Random House (New York, NY), 1981.

Annie Goes to the Jungle, illustrated by George Wildman, Random House (New York, NY), 1981.

Annie and the Desert Treasure, illustrated by George Wildman, Random House (New York, NY), 1982.

Annie and the Party Thieves, illustrated by George Wildman, Random House (New York, NY), 1982.

Moon Dragon, illustrated by Geoffrey Hayes, Macmillan (New York, NY), 1982.

The Tickle Tree, illustrated by Yuri Salzman, Houghton (Boston, MA), 1982.

The Roller Coaster Ghost, illustrated by Dave Ross, Scholastic (New York, NY), 1983.

Hocus and Pocus at the Circus, illustrated by Geoffrey Hayes, Harper (New York, NY), 1983.

The Adventures of Cap'n O.G. Readmore: To the Tune of "The Cat Came Back," illustrated by Manny Campana, Scholastic (New York, NY), 1984.

Buster Loves Buttons, illustrated by Dirk Zimmer, Harper (New York, NY), 1985.

Jumping Jacky, illustrated by Carolyn Bracken, Golden Books (New York, NY), 1986.

(With Lucy Bate) *Little Rabbit's Baby Brother,* illustrated by Diane de Groat, Crown (New York, NY), 1986.

Ketchup, Catch Up!, illustrated by Julie Durrell, Golden Books (New York, NY), 1987.

Beach Day, illustrated by Kathy Wilburn, Western Publishing (Racine, WI), 1988.

Puppies and Kittens, illustrated by Ruth Sanderson, Golden Books (New York, NY), 1989.

Latkes and Applesauce: A Hanukkah Story, illustrated by Robin Spowart, Scholastic (New York, NY), 1990.

(Compiler) *Glow in the Dark Mother Goose,* illustrated by Mary Grace Eubank, Western Publishing (Racine, WI), 1990.

(With Lucy Bate) *Be Brave, Baby Rabbit,* illustrated by Diane de Groat, Crown (New York, NY), 1990.

(Adaptor) *Walt Disney Pictures Presents: The Prince and the Pauper* (based on the film), illustrated by Russell Schroeder and Don Williams, Western Publishing (Racine, WI), 1990.

Hello World: Travel along with Mickey and His Friends, illustrated by Juan Ortiz and Phil Bliss, Disney Press (New York, NY), 1991.

Walt Disney's 101 Dalmatians: A Counting Book, illustrated by Russell Hicks, Disney Press (New York, NY), 1991.

The Best Toy of All, illustrated by Robin Ballard, Dutton (New York, NY), 1992.

My Christmas Safari, illustrated by R.W. Alley, Dial (New York, NY), 1993.

(Compiler) *Somebody Loves You: Poems of Friendship and Love,* illustrated by Jeff Shelly, Disney Press (New York, NY), 1993.

Let's Go Riding in Our Strollers, illustrated by Benrei Huang, Hyperion (New York, NY), 1993.

Peeping and Sleeping, illustrated by Jennifer Plecas, Clarion (New York, NY), 1994.

The Matzah That Papa Brought Home, illustrated by Ned Bittinger, Scholastic (New York, NY), 1995.

Starlight and Candles: The Joys of the Sabbath, illustrated by Jacqueline Chwast, Simon & Schuster (New York, NY), 1995.

Miriam's Cup: A Passover Story, illustrated by Bob Dacey, Scholastic (New York, NY), 1998.

Come, Let Us Be Joyful!: The Story of Hava Nagilah, illustrated by Rosalind Charney Kaye, UAHC Press (New York, NY), 2000.

Sophie and the Shofar: A New Year's Story, illustrated by Rosalind Charney Kaye, UAHC Press (New York, NY), 2001.

Daughters of Fire: Heroines of the Bible, illustrated by Uri Shulevitz, Harcourt Brace (San Diego, CA), 2001.

Hooray for Hanukkah!, illustrated by Carolyn Croll, Random House (New York, NY), 2001.

The Little Sleepyhead, illustrated by Leonid Gore, Dutton (New York, NY), 2004.

(With George Foreman) *Let George Do It!,* illustrated by Whitney Martin, Simon & Schuster (New York, NY), 2005.

The Shivers in the Fridge, illustrated by Paul O. Zelinsky, Dutton (New York, NY), 2006.

Ready, Set, Oops!, illustrated by Diane Palmisciano, Kane Press (New York, NY), 2007.

Elect Me!, illustrated by James Demski, Jr., Picture Windows Press (Minneapolis, MN), 2008.

How Mama Brought the Spring, illustrated by Holly Berry, Dutton (New York, NY), 2008.

The Tushy Book, illustrated by Tracy Dockray, Feiwel & Friends (New York, NY), 2009.

The Belly Book, illustrated by Tracy Dockray, Feiwel & Friends (New York, NY), 2010.

"ANGEL CORNERS" SERIES; FOR CHILDREN

Rachel, Meet Your Angel!!!, Puffin (New York, NY), 1995.
Toby Takes the Cake, Puffin (New York, NY), 1995.
Lulu's Mixed-up Movie, Puffin (New York, NY), 1995.
Val McCall, Ace Reporter?, Puffin (New York, NY), 1995.

"KATIE WOO" SERIES; FOR CHILDREN

The Big Lie, illustrated by Tammie Lyon, Picture Window Books (Minneapolis, MN), 2010.

Boss of the World, illustrated by Tammie Lyon, Picture Window Books (Minneapolis, MN), 2010.

Goodbye to Goldie, illustrated by Tammie Lyon, Picture Window Books (Minneapolis, MN), 2010.

A Happy Day, illustrated by Tammie Lyon, Picture Window Books (Minneapolis, MN), 2010.

No More Teasing, illustrated by Tammie Lyon, Picture Window Books (Minneapolis, MN), 2010.

Too Much Rain, illustrated by Tammie Lyon, Picture Window Books (Minneapolis, MN), 2010.

Sidelights

Fran Manushkin is the author of dozens of books for young readers, including such award-winning titles as *The Matzah That Papa Brought Home* and *The Shivers in the Fridge.* Noted for her whimsical imagination and her talent for creating lovingly drawn characters, Manushkin produces such entertaining picture books as *Baby, Moon Dragon,* and *The Tickle Tree,* as well as the novels *Lulu's Mixed-Up Movie* and *Val McCall, Ace Reporter?,* which are part of her "Angel Corners" series for girls. In addition, her stories portray youngsters and their parents celebrating both Jewish and Christian holidays. "I tell children that I don't get ideas—they get me!," Manuskin noted on her home page. "I get so excited about a line or a phrase or something I feel and see that I MUST write about it."

Born in Chicago, Illinois, in 1942, Manushkin never thought she would grow up to be an author. Instead,

Cover of Manushkin's elementary-grade novel Rachel, Meet Your Angel!, *featuring artwork by Sergio Giovine.* (Illustration copyright © 1995 by Sergio Giovine. Reproduced by permission of Puffin Books, a division of Penguin USA, Inc.)

upon graduating from high school, she went to college and earned a teaching certificate. After a four-month stint as a substitute teacher, however, Manushkin decided to abandon the idea of a career in teaching. What she really wanted was to live in New York City, and a job at the Illinois pavilion during the 1964 World's Fair got her there. After the fair ended, Manushkin remained in Manhattan and began a new career, this time in publishing. She worked for a series of book publishers, including Holt, Rinehart & Winston, Harper & Row, and Random House, where she met a host of people who inspired her to try her hand at writing books for children.

Manushkin's first book, *Baby,* was published in 1972; proving perennially popular with readers, it was reissued as *Baby, Come Out!* in 1984 and has been translated into several other languages. *Baby* is the light-hearted story of a not-quite-yet-born baby who decides that Mom's tummy suits her just fine—until Daddy comes home promising kisses that she cannot feel. *Horn Book* reviewer Sidney D. Long praised Manushkin's first effort as a "special book for mothers-to-be to share with their other children."

"My stories tend to grow from a single image," Manushkin once told *SATA.* "*Baby,* for example, blossomed from an image I had in my head of a mother communicating with her newborn baby. That image metamorphosed into a mother communicating with the child she is carrying in her womb. When the child said, 'I don't want to be born,' it just happened. I did not plan it. I didn't have a plot in mind." Before she became a writer herself, Manushkin believed that books "existed in a pure state in author's heads," with their endings perfectly well thought out. "That simply isn't true," she explained. "Books develop according to their own time. You cannot dictate that a book be born; neither can you dictate to a book. Listen," she added, "really listen, and your book will speak."

Baby was the first of many imaginative books that Manushkin has written for children, each one evolving out of an image or idea. In *Swinging and Swinging* a young girl on a swing soon finds that she has passengers; first a soft, puffy cloud, then the cheery sun, the moon, and a rain of stars join her. As she drifts into a drowsy half-sleep the moon and stars climb back up into the sky and night falls. In *The Tickle Tree* a young squirrel in the mood for a belly-grabbing tickle gets his friends to stack up and help him reach the top of a feather-leafed palm tree—which causes such a giggle that the animal tower soon topples like a laughing house of cards.

"Whether you know it or not, every book you write is about yourself," Manushkin explained. "*Hocus and Pocus at the Circus,* for example, is about my sister and myself—but I'm not telling who the nice sister is!" Geared for beginning readers, *Hocus and Pocus at the*

Manuskin shares her family's Jewish traditions in **The Matzah That Papa Brought Home,** *a picture book illustrated by Ned Bittinger.* (Illustration copyright © 1995 by Ned Bittinger. Reproduced by permission of Scholastic, Inc.)

Circus is about two witches—one mean, the other nice—who are busy laying plans for Halloween night. While Hocus plots to cause havoc at a circus, Pocus misspeaks her spells and ends up adding to the circusgoers' fun by turning rubber balls into puppies and herself into a squealing baby pig, and ends the evening by shooting her sister out of a cannon (harmlessly, of course!). A world where magic is possible also figures in *Moon Dragon,* a trickster tale wherein a tiny mouse devises a way to fool a huge, fire-breathing dragon that has eaten everything in sight and now wants the mouse for dessert. Noting that the author's "magic touch invests all her stories," a *Publishers Weekly* reviewer called *Moon Dragon* "one of [Manushkin's] best."

Manushkin has also written a number of well-received picture books for preschoolers, including *Let's Go Riding in Our Strollers* and *Peeping and Sleeping.* Featuring a lively, rhyming verse text, *Let's Go Riding in Our Strollers* presents all of the excitement of the urban outdoors as seen through the eyes of toddlers in strollers on their adventurous trip to the park. *Booklist* reviewer Ilene Cooper praised Manushkin's "exuberant text" in *Let's Go Riding in Our Strollers,* concluding that the book is "fun to look at and to read."

Peeping and Sleeping centers on a peeping noise that is keeping little Barry awake. Barry's father takes the young child out to the pond to investigate, and soon the boy's fears turn to curiosity and wonder at the busy activities of nocturnal creatures. *School Library Journal* contributor Lisa Wu Stowe praised "Manushkin's wonderfully realistic dialogue and evocative descriptions of a warm spring night's walk" in *Peeping and Sleeping.* A *Publishers Weekly* reviewer maintained: "Especially well captured is the trembling mixture of fear and giddiness that accompanies children's nighttime excursions." In another favorable estimation, *Booklist* reviewer Hazel Rochman asserted: "Although rooted in reality, the story with its gentle reversals creates a sense of hidden wonder, of magic and mischief in a hushed nighttime landscape."

Some of Manushkin's books for younger readers are designed as bedtime stories. *The Little Sleepyhead* features a young troublemaker who, after a day at play, wants to find a soft place to sleep. But grass tickles him, trees are too bumpy, and the bear snores. The child is eventually able to find a bed of feathers, and coaxes a lamb to snuggle with him as he drifts off to sleep. "The last sentence makes it perfect for the last story before bed," noted a critic for *Kirkus Reviews.* A *Publishers Weekly* contributor noted that Manushkin has created "an appealing toddler-size adventure, casting her spell from the opening words."

For older readers, Manushkin has created the "Angel Corners" series, which takes place in the town of Angel Corners and also has guardian angels as characters. In *Rachel, Meet Your Angel!*, the first book of the series, a lonely fifth grader who finds herself friendless after a move to a new town suddenly finds Merribel, a guardian-angel apprentice, looking over her shoulder. Things soon start to improve for Rachel; she meets three friends and together the girls find a way to raise the money needed to repair the town clock. "Middle-grade girls whose taste in novels runs to the fanciful will find the inaugural novel in the Angel Corners series a fun—if flighty—read," asserted a *Publishers Weekly* commentator. Other books in the series, each of which feature a different girl and her guardian angel, include *Toby Takes the Cake* and *Lulu's Mixed-Up Movie.*

In addition to her purely fictional tales, Manushkin has written several books that weave warm, joyous imagery into tradition-based religious holidays. Although Manushkin grew up in a Jewish home and is, herself, Jewish, her first holiday tales revolved around Christmas and include *My Christmas Safari,* a retelling of the "Twelve Days of Christmas" using African jungle motifs, and *The Perfect Christmas Picture.* The latter, which tells the story of perplexed photographer Mr. Green's attempts to get his whole family together for a holiday snapshot, "is about my family—the way I wish my family had been," the author explained to *SATA.* "I suppose the 'message' in that book has to do with acceptance in a rather odd, madcap family." The Green family is indeed madcap; the picture-taking process lasts a full nine months due to the fact that it is constantly thwarted by giggling, pinching, blinking eyes, and countless other minor disasters. *Horn Book* reviewer Mary M. Burns praised Manushkin for the "pleasant, unhackneyed lilt" she brings to the book's text.

Manushkin also creates books about traditional Jewish holidays, among them *The Matzah That Papa Brought Home, Miriam's Cup: A Passover Story,* and *Hooray for Hanukkah!* A cumulative Passover tale for preschoolers and beginning readers, *The Matzah That Papa Brought Home* was dubbed "a unique, lively offering" by *School Library Journal* contributor Marcia Posner. Stephanie Zvirin, writing in *Booklist,* maintained that "what the book actually does best is convey the feeling of closeness and community engendered by the celebration." *Miriam's Cup* compares a young girl named Miriam to her Biblical namesake in a retelling of the story of Passover. A *Publishers Weekly* reviewer felt that the book is "likely to become a favorite holiday read-aloud." *Hooray for Hanukkah!* explains the traditions of the winter holiday from the perspective of the family menorah. A *School Library Journal* reviewer called the book "a sweetly old-fashioned story."

Come Let Us Be Joyful: The Story of Hava Nagila explains the history of a popular Jewish song and centers on songwriter Moshe Nathanson, who became the cantor at the Society for the Advancement of Judaism in New York City. To research the work, Manushkin interviewed one of Nathanson's daughters, who lived just a few blocks from the author's home. *Sophie and the Shofar: A New Year's Story* is a tale of family, the High Holy Days, and the traditional blowing of the shofar. When young Sophie has a falling out with her cousin Sasha, newly arrival from Russia, she accuses her relative of stealing a precious family heirloom: the shofar that belongs to Sophie's father. On her home page, Manushkin stated that she enjoyed writing about a damaged relationship "that is healed on Rosh Hashana, a day for forgiveness."

In another Jewish-themed picture book, *How Mama Brought the Spring,* little Rosy is slow to leave her bed on a blustery winter's morning. To lighten the girl's spirits, Rosy's mother shows her how to make blintzes using a special recipe handed down by Rosy's grandmother, who grew up in snowy Minsk. Judith Constantinides, writing in *School Library Journal,* noted that "children will appreciate Manushkin's winning look at a different culture," and a *Kirkus Reviews* contributor stated that "this delicious picture book provides the perfect recipe for those who are sick of winter."

Manushkin confessed in an interview with Kathleen O'Grady on the Women's Studies Resources at the University of Iowa Web site that she was, at first, nervous

Holly Berry creates folk-style illustrations that reflect the traditional themes in Manushkin's picture book How Mama Brought the Spring.
(Illustration copyright © 2008 by Holly Berry. Reproduced by permission of Dutton Children's Books, a division of Penguin Putnam Books for Young Readers.)

about writing picture books about Judaism; her anxieties came to a head when she began working on *Daughters of Fire: Heroines of the Bible.* "I was terrified to do this book," she told O'Grady. "I thought only men with grey beards were allowed to write Jewish books." Unlike Manushkin's previous stories of Jewish tradition, *Daughters of Fire* collects the stories of ten women of the Hebrew Bible, revealing for young readers the history of Judaism as told from a feminine point of view. The tales of Eve, Miriam, Hannah, Queen Esther, and others are fleshed out by combining scripture with Jewish legends and folklore, giving them "the richness and complexity of the wider Jewish traditions," according to a reviewer for *Publishers Weekly.* "This is the longest book I've ever written," Manushkin told O'Grady. "It took me so long to realize that I had as much right to write these stories as so many other people." Amy Lilien-Harper noted in *School Library Journal* that "the author's lyrical, slightly old-fashioned writing fits her topic," while GraceAnne A. DeCandido, writing for *Booklist,* felt that in *Daughters of Fire* Manushkin "adds a spirited freshness to the tales."

Manushkin teamed up with former heavyweight champion and celebrity George Foreman on *Let George Do It!,* a book for young readers that depicts the chaotic preparations for a birthday party in the real-life Foreman household, where all the boys and their father are named George. "This family story packs a humorous punch," remarked a *Kirkus Reviews* contributor, and a *Publishers Weekly* critic noted that "youngsters will find plenty of laughs in the premise." In another collaboration, *Ready, Set, Oops!,* a clumsy youngster finds the inspiration for a class project after he literally bumps into a number of his schoolmates. Kelly Roth, writing in *School Library Journal,* described the work as "a fun mix of science and story."

A family of refrigerator magnets attempts to flee the confines of their chilly home in *The Shivers in the Fridge,* "a quirky perspective on a major appliance," in the words of a *Publishers Weekly* contributor. Although Sonny, Mama, Papa, Grandma, and Grandpa Shivers find themselves in a frigid, dark place, they harbor memories of a more-temperate environment. When an earthquake rattles their surrounding, accompanied by a bright light and a pair of monster hands, the Shivers decide to venture out in search of a safer home, but they must cross such formidable landmarks as Buttery Cliff and Mt. Ketchup. "Manushkin tells their story in colorful language and with a high humor," Ilene Cooper noted in *Booklist,* and *School Library Journal* reviewer Rebecca Sheridan called the work "a quirky and satisfying selection for those with a palate for adventure." In *The Tushy Book,* Manushkin depicts the many ways that toddlers can use their bottoms, such as sledding, spinning, and bouncing. The rhymes "are as much fun as the scenarios that celebrate the body and how it works," Rochman commented.

Manushkin once shared with *SATA* her advice for young writers-to-be: "In my years as a writer and editor I have learned a few things I would like to pass on: don't give up on a book even if lots of editors reject it, keep sending it around . . . and don't be nervous if you've started writing something but don't know where it is going—be willing to discover the book as it evolves."

Biographical and Critical Sources

PERIODICALS

Booklist, June 1, 1993, Ilene Cooper, review of *Let's Go Riding in Our Strollers,* p. 1858; June, 1994, Hazel Rochman, review of *Peeping and Sleeping,* p. 1841; January 15, 1995, Stephanie Zvirin, review of *The Matzah That Papa Brought Home,* p. 937; December 15, 2001, GraceAnne A. DeCandido, review of *Daughters of Fire: Heroines of the Bible,* p. 726; May 1, 2004, "Good Night, Sleep Tight," p. 1563; October 15, 2006, Ilene Cooper, review of *The Shivers in the Fridge,* p. 46; January 1, 2008, Julie Cummins, review of *How Mama Brought the Spring,* p. 94; March 15, 2009, Hazel Rochman, review of *The Tushy Book,* p. 68.

Bulletin of the Center for Children's Books, January, 2002, review of *Daughters of Fire,* p. 178.

Horn Book, June, 1972, Sidney D. Long, review of *Baby,* p. 261; December 1980, Mary M. Burns, review of *The Perfect Christmas Picture,* p. 626; November-December, 2006, Kitty Flynn, review of *The Shivers in the Fridge,* p. 700.

Kirkus Reviews, September 1, 2001, review of *Daughters of Fire,* p. 1296; May 1, 2004, review of *The Little Sleepyhead,* p. 445; May 1, 2005, review of *Let George Do It!,* p. 538; January 1, 2008, review of *How Mama Brought the Spring.*

Publishers Weekly, April 30, 1982, review of *Moon Dragon,* p. 59; April 25, 1994, review of *Peeping and Sleeping,* p. 77; February 6, 1995, review of *Rachel, Meet Your Angel!!,* p. 86; December 22, 1997, review of *Miriam's Cup: A Passover Story,* p. 54; August 27, 2001, review of *Daughters of Fire,* p. 81; September 24, 2001, review of *Hooray for Hanukkah!,* p. 48; May 31, 2004, review of *The Little Sleepyhead,* p. 73; May 23, 2005, review of *Let George Do It!,* p. 77; October 23, 2006, review of *The Shivers in the Fridge,* p. 49; December 10, 2007, review of *How Mama Brought the Spring,* p. 55.

Reading Teacher, April, 1999, review of *Miriam's Cup,* p. 762.

School Library Journal, June, 1994, Lisa Wu Stowe, review of *Peeping and Sleeping,* p. 110; February, 1995, Marcia Posner, review of *The Matzah That Papa Brought Home,* p. 76; February, 1998, Susan Pine, review of *Miriam's Cup,* p. 88; October, 2001, Amy Lilien-Harper, review of *Daughters of Fire,* p. 188; October, 2001, review of *Hooray for Hanukkah!,* p. 67; January, 2002, Linda R. Silver, review of *Sophie and the Shofar: A New Year's Story,* p. 106; September, 2004, Shelley B. Sutherland, review of *The Little Sleepyhead,* p. 173; January, 2006, Barbara Auerbach,

review of *Let George Do It!,* p. 96; October, 2006, Rebecca Sheridan, review of *The Shivers in the Fridge,* p. 118; September, 2007, Kelly Roth, review of *Ready, Set, Oops!,* p. 172; January, 2008, Judith Constantinides, review of *How Mama Brought the Spring,* p. 92; April, 2009, Maryann H. Owen, review of *The Tushy Book,* p. 112.

Social Education, May, 1999, review of *Miriam's Cup,* p. 14.

ONLINE

Fran Manushkin Home Page, http://www.franmanushkin. com (September 1, 2009).

Scholastic Web site, http://www2.scholastic.com/ (September 1, 2009), "Fran Manushkin."

Women's Studies Resources at the University of Iowa Web site, http://bailiwick.lib.uiowa.edu/wstudies/ (September 15, 2004), Kathleen O'Grady, interview with Manushkin.*

* * *

MANUSHKIN, Frances
See MANUSHKIN, Fran

* * *

MARTIN, Courtney Autumn 1984-

Personal

Born 1984; married Adam Hunter Peck (an artist), 2009. *Education:* Rhode Island School of Design, B.F.A. (illustration; with honors), 2006.

Addresses

Home—Somerville, MA. *E-mail*—camartin@c-a-martin. com.

Career

Illustrator and graphic artist. The Life Is Good Company, Boston, MA, Web designer, 2008—. *Exhibitions:* Muralist, with work exhibited at Mystic Seaport Museum, Mystic, CT. Paintings included in permanent collection at Noah Webster House, West Hartford, CT.

Member

Society of Children's Book Writers and Illustrators.

Illustrator

Sudipta Bardhan-Quallen, *Ballots for Belva,* Abrams Books for Young Readers (New York, NY), 2008.

Contributor to educational readers and to periodicals, including *Odyssey.*

Courtney Autumn Martin (Reproduced by permission.)

Sidelights

"Born and raised in Connecticut, I grew up as the middle of three creative siblings," Courtney Autumn Martin told *SATA.* "Me and my two sisters spent much of our childhood drawing, painting, and making home movies together. From early on, I loved art. By age nine I had written and illustrated my very first picture book, a biography about my best friend called *My Best Friend.*

"While attending the Rhode Island School of Design for illustration, I discovered my love of children's picture books and I have been collecting book after book ever since. Inspired by my favorite illustrators, I graduated and went on to pursue children's illustration as a career. Within two years of graduating from art school, I completed the work for my first published picture book, *Ballots for Belva.*

"I have many artistic interests including photography, book making, graphic design, and abstract painting. I also work as a Web designer and illustrate in my spare time. I and my husband, also an artist and designer, live happily near Boston with our black-and-white cat, Miette."

Biographical and Critical Sources

PERIODICALS

Booklist, November 15, 2008, Linda Perkins, review of *Ballots for Belva,* p. 47.

Kirkus Reviews, August 1, 2008, review of *Ballots for Belva.*

School Library Journal, September, 2008, Steven Engelfried, review of *Ballots for Belva,* p. 162.

ONLINE

Courtney Autumn Martin Home Page, http://c-a-martin. com (October 15, 2009).

Courtney Autumn Martin Web log, http://slumberlandbyday.blogspot.com (October 15, 2009).

* * *

MECHNER, Jordan 1964-

Personal

Born 1964. *Education:* Yale University, B.A.

Addresses

Home—CA.

Career

Author, screenwriter, producer, and videogame designer. Creator of videogames *Karateka, Prince of Persia, The Last Express, Prince of Persia: The Shadow and the Flame,* and *Prince of Persia: Sands of Time.* Smoking Car Productions (videogame development company), founder; Ubisoft Entertainment, videogame developer. Film work includes (executive producer) *Prince of Persia: The Sands of Time* and (director) *Chavez Ravine: A Los Angeles Story.*

Awards, Honors

Interactive Achievement Awards, Design Innovate Communicate Entertain (D.I.C.E.), for *Prince of Persia: The Sands of Time* (videogame); Best Short Documentary award, International Documentary Association, 2003, for *Chavez Ravine.*

Writings

(Author of screenplay) *Chavez Ravine: A Los Angeles Story,* Tiny Projects, 2003.

(Author of story) A.B. Sina, *Jordan Mechner's Prince of Persia* (graphic novel), illustrated by LeUyen Pham and Alex Puvilland, First Second Books (New York, NY), 2008.

(Author of screenplay) *Prince of Persia: The Sands of Time,* Walt Disney Productions (Burbank, CA), 2010.

(Author of story) *Solomon's Thieves* (graphic novel), illustrated by LeUyen Pham and Alex Puvilland, First Second Books (New York, NY), 2010.

Sidelights

After earning an undergraduate degree at Yale University, Jordan Mechner began developing the award-winning videogame *Prince of Persia,* setting in motion a story he would continue to develop for several decades. By combining a literary narrative with innovations in computer animation, Mechner earned widespread recognition for his adaptation of the traditional *Arabian Nights* folktale. The initial installment in the videogame series begins as an evil regent named Jaffar, ruling for an absent sultan, locks away a princess, hoping not only to win her hand in marriage but also her father's land. After working on the sequel, *Prince of Persia: The Sands of Time,* the designer partnered with Iranian poet A.B. Sina to pen a graphic-novel version of Mechner's fanciful tale, their text highlighted by the artwork of noted illustrators LeUyen Pham and Alex Puvilland.

In *Jordan Mechner's Prince of Persia* readers follow the threads of two different storylines set four hundred years apart. In one, a young prince named Guiv fights murderous family members bent upon destroying his ascension to the throne, while the other plotline features a beautiful young dancer who discovers a mysterious stranger living among the ruins of a once-great fortress. Based on Mechner's story, Sina's text "breathe[s] life, passion and legend into the original concept," according to a *Kirkus Reviews* critic who suggested teens would appreciate the "visually literate landscape of love, lore and violence." Writing in *Booklist,* Ian Chipman found *Jordan Mechner's Prince of Persia* "no mere videogame rip-off," but rather a "magnificent and complex graphic novel" featuring a multidimensional drama full of complexity and action. "Any readers looking for adventure should enjoy the chases, fights, and political intrigue," suggested *School Library Journal* contributor Andrea Lipinski, the critic adding that Mechner's afterword contributes further understanding to the development of the "Prince of Persia" fantasy world. While noting that some of the illustrated violence would not be appropriate for younger readers, *Kliatt* critic George Galuschak nonetheless found *Jordan Mechner's Prince of Persia* "a fascinating graphic novel that uses the trappings of Persian mythology to construct a rich, multifaceted world."

Furthering his reach into different mediums, Mechner has also adapted his "Prince of Persia" storyline into a motion picture, writing a screenplay for Walt Disney Productions. Produced by Jerry Bruckheimer and directed by Mike Newell, *Prince of Persia: The Sands of Time* stars Jake Gyllenhaal and Ben Kingsley. Following the videogame of the same name, the film features a

young orphan who becomes heir to the throne after winning the admiration of a Persian king. Mechner also planned two more sequels to the graphic-novel adaptation of the game, including *Solomon's Thieves.*

Biographical and Critical Sources

PERIODICALS

Booklist, September 1, 2008, Ian Chipman, review of *Jordan Mechner's Prince of Persia,* p. 58.

Hollywood Reporter, January 23, 2008, Paul Hyman, "A Games Guru Puts Persia on 2009 Big-Screen Map," p. 41.

Kirkus Reviews, July 15, 2008, review of *Jordan Mechner's Prince of Persia.*

Kliatt, September, 2008, George Galuschak, review of *Jordan Mechner's Prince of Persia,* p. 34.

Publishers Weekly, July 28, 2008, review of *Jordan Mechner's Prince of Persia,* p. 58.

School Library Journal, September, 2008, Andrea Lipinski, review of *Jordan Mechner's Prince of Persia,* p. 219.

ONLINE

Jordan Mechner Home Page, http://jordanmechner.com (September 25, 2009).*

*   *   *

MOULD, Chris

Personal

Born in England; married; children: two daughters. *Education:* Leeds Polytechnic, degree (illustration), 1991.

Addresses

Home—Bradford, West Yorkshire, England. *Agent*—Frances Mckay Illustration Agency, London, England, www.francesmckay.com. *E-mail*—chris@chrismouldink.com.

Career

Author and illustrator. Creator of illustrated images for television and film. *Exhibitions:* Work included in exhibitions in Abingdon, England, 1999; and Century Club, London, England, 2002.

Awards, Honors

Nottingham Children's Book Award; Sheffield Book Award commendation.

Writings

SELF-ILLUSTRATED

(With Michael Coleman) *Hank the Clank,* Oxford University Press (Oxford, England), 1994, Gareth Stevens (Milwaukee, WI), 1996.

(Adaptor) Charles Dickens, *A Christmas Carol,* Oxford University Press (Oxford, England), 1995.

(Adaptor) Charles Dickens, *Oliver Twist,* Oxford University Press (Oxford, England), 1996.

(Adaptor) Mary Shelley, *Frankenstein,* Oxford University Press (New York, NY), 1997.

(Adaptor) Robert Louis Stevenson, *Treasure Island,* Oxford University Press (Oxford, England), 1998.

(Adaptor) Arthur Conan Doyle, *The Hound of the Baskervilles,* Oxford University Press (Oxford, England), 1999.

(Adaptor) *Dr. Jekyll and Mr. Hyde,* Oxford University Press (Oxford, England), 2001.

(With Colin Thompson) *Gilbert* (picture book), Lothian Books (New York, NY), 2003.

Dust 'n' Bones: Ten Terrifying Classic and Original Ghost Stories, Hodder Children's (London, England), 2007.

76 Pumpkin Lane: Pop-up Spooky House, Hodder Children's (London, England), 2007.

Fangs 'n' Fire: Ten Dragon Tales, Hodder Children's (London, England), 2009.

Firefly Hollow, Hodder Children's (London, England), 2009.

SELF-ILLUSTRATED; "SOMETHING WICKEDLY WEIRD" SERIES

The Wooden Mile, Hodder Children's (London, England), 2007, Roaring Brook Press (New York, NY), 2008.

The Icy Hand, Hodder Children's (London, England), 2007, Roaring Brook Press (New York, NY), 2008.

The Silver Casket, Hodder Children's (London, England), 2007, Roaring Brook Press (New York, NY), 2009.

The Darkling Curse, Hodder Children's (London, England), 2008.

Smugglers' Mine, Hodder Children's (London, England), 2008.

The Treasure Keepers, Hodder Children's (London, England), 2009.

ILLUSTRATOR

Chris Ellis, *One Last Lie,* Educational Television Company (London, England), 1994.

Adam Bowett, *History's Big Mistakes,* Belitha (London, England), 1994.

Jeremy Strong, *The Desperate Adventures of Sir Rupert and Rosie Gusset,* A. & C. Black (London, England), 1995.

Michael Coleman, *Hank Clanks Again,* Oxford University Press (Oxford, England), 1995.

Adam Bowett, *History's Heros and Villains,* Belitha (London, England), 1995.

Philip Ardagh, *History's Travellers and Explorers,* Belitha (London, England), 1996.

Philip Ardagh, *History's Great Inventors,* Belitha (London, England), 1996.

Pauline Hall and Kevin Wooding, *Spooky Piano Time: Terrifying Pieces, Poems, and Puzzles,* Oxford University Press (New York, NY), 1997.

Nicholas Tulloch, *Alphabet Spook!: Spine-tingling Verse,* Oxford University Press (Oxford, England), 1997.

Judy Allen, *Aunties Billie's Greatest Inventions,* Walker (London, England), 1997.

Jeremy Strong, *Sir Rupert and Rosie Gusser in Deadly Danger,* A. & C. Black (London, England), 1999.

Philippa Gregory, *A Pirate Story,* Little Hippo (London, England), 1999.

Jan Dean, *Babysitting Jellyblob,* Macdonald Young (Hove, England), 1999.

Jan Dean, *Needlebelly and the Bully Boy,* Macdonald Young (Hove, England), 1999.

Jan Dean, *Kraxis and the Cow-Juice Soup,* Macdonald Young (Hove, England), 1999.

Jan Dean, *Frogsnot Ate My Goldfish,* Macdonald Young (Hove, England), 1999.

Clare Bevan, *Make 'em Laugh,* Macdonald Young (Hove, England), 1999.

Colin Thompson, *Fish Are So Stupid,* Hodder Wayland (London, England), 2000.

Phillip Steele, *Mummies,* Hodder Children's (London, England), 2000.

Pat Posner, *King Oftencross,* Scholastic Press (London, England), 2000.

Sue Pinkus, *Aliens,* Hodder Children's (London, England), 2000.

Keith Newstead, *Dinosaurs,* Arcturus (London, England), 2000.

Andrew Peters, *The Unidentified Frying Omelette,* Hodder Wayland (London, England), 2000.

Jan Dean, adaptor, *Much Ado about Nothing* (based on the play by William Shakespeare), Oxford University Press (New York, NY), 2000.

Andrew Peters, *Sadderday and Funday,* Hodder Wayland (London, England), 2001.

Margaret Mahy, *The Riddle of the Frozen Phantom,* Collins (London, England), 2001.

Jan Dean, *As You Like It* (based on the play by William Shakespeare), Hodder Wayland (London, England), 2001.

Jon Blake, *Space Rock and Five-a-Side,* Oxford University Press (Oxford, England), 2001.

Jan Dean, adaptor, *Twelfth Night* (based on the play by William Shakespeare), Oxford University Press (New York, NY), 2002.

Diana Wynne Jones, *Stopping for a Spell,* Collins Voyager (London, England), 2002.

Michael Lawrence, *Young Dracula,* Barrington Stoke (Edinburgh, England), 2002.

Martin Waddell, *Ronald the Tough Sheep,* Oxford University Press (Oxford, England), 2002, published as *Tough Ronald,* Picture Window Books (Minneapolis, MN), 2007.

Kaye Umansky, *Humble Tom's Big Trip: A Tudor Play,* Hodder Wayland (London, England), 2003.

Jan Dean, adaptor, *Geoffrey Chaucer's The Pardoner's Tale,* Hodder Wayland (London, England), 2002.

Jeanne Willis, *The Beast of Crowsfoot Cottage,* Macmillan Children's (London, England), 2003.

Kaye Umansky, *Meet the Weirds,* Barrington Stoke (Edinburgh, England), 2003.

Gervase Phinn, *Family Phantoms,* Puffin (London, England), 2003.

Kes Gray, *Duperball,* Oxford University Press (Oxford, England), 2003, Picture Window Press (Minneapolis, MN), 2007.

Michael Lawrence, *Young Monsters,* Barrington Stoke (Edinburgh, England), 2003.

Kaye Umansky, *Weird Happenings,* Barrington Stoke (Edinburgh, England), 2004.

Ian Ogilvy, *Measle and the Dragodon,* Oxford University Press (Oxford, England), 2004.

Ian Ogilvy, *Measle and the Wrathmonk,* Oxford University Press (Oxford, England), 2004.

Michaela Morgan, *The Beast,* Barrington Stoke (Edinburgh, England), 2004.

Kes Gray, *Vesuvius Poovius,* Hodder Children's (London, England), 2004.

Ian Ogilvy, *Measle and the Mallockee,* Oxford University Press (Oxford, England), 2005.

Kaye Umansky, *Wildly Weird,* Barrington Stoke (Edinburgh, England), 2006.

Gervase Phinn, *Don't Tell the Teacher,* Puffin (London, England), 2006.

Ian Ogilvy, *Measle and the Slitherghoul,* Oxford University Press (Oxford. England), 2006.

Alan MacDonald, *The Sand Witch,* Picture Window Press (Minneapolis, MN), 2007.

Ian Ogilvy, *Measle and the Doompit,* Oxford University Press (Oxford, England), 2007.

Rose Impey, *One Man Went to Mow,* Hodder Children's (London, England), 2007.

Tim Pigott-Smith, *The Dragon Tattoo,* Hodder Children's (London, England), 2008.

Michael Lawrence, *Young Wizards,* Barrington Stoke (Edinburgh, England), 2008.

Contributor to periodicals.

Sidelights

British artist and author Chris Mould began his career as a children's book illustrator after graduating from Leeds Polytechnic in 1991, with a determination to make art his life's work. At first Mould combined his art with jobs such as newspaper delivery and restaurant dishwasher and cook, but the success of his early illustrations work for authors such as Philip Ardagh, Philippa Green, Jeremy Strong, and Michael Coleman eventually allowed him to become a full-time artist. In addition to adapting several literary classics into heavily illustrated versions designed to lure reluctant readers, Mould has also turned author, collecting and retelling weird stories and penning novels that feature his quirky pen-and-ink art. Reviewing his version of Mary Shelley's *Frankenstein,* Hazel Rochman wrote in *Booklist* that Mould "manages to simplify the Victorian prose without losing . . . the terror and melancholy" of the original.

Mould's quirky pen-and-ink art is a feature of his "Something Wickedly Weird" middle-grade novel series. In the novels *The Wooden Mile, The Icy Hand, The*

Darkling Curse, Smugglers' Mine, The Treasure Keepers, and *The Silver Casket,* Mould recounts the story of Stanley Buggles, an eleven year old whose inheritance of a summer house in the coastal village of Crampton Rock yields him a series of amazing adventures. In *The Wooden Mile,* Stanley encounters a werewolf, converses with a dead trophy fish, and is stalked by a gang of scruffy and threatening pirates. These threats combine with a headless ghost in *The Icy Hand,* a skeleton army in *The Silver Casket,* and a pair of twins from a sinister family in *The Darkling Curse.* Emboldened by these adventures, Stanley risks his safety to follow a crumbling map to a possible treasure in *The Smugglers' Mine* and help capture a desperate criminal roaming the moors of Crampton Rock in *The Treasure Keepers.* In *School Library Journal,* Amanda Raklovits compared Mould's series with the books of Philip Ardagh, coauthors Paul Steward and Chris Riddell, and Lemony Snicket and wrote of *The Wooden Mile* that "the narrative moves quickly" and the illustrations "are well done." The book's "richly atmospheric ink drawings capture the rather macabre tone of the story," concluded *Booklist* critic Carolyn Phelan, and in *Horn Book* Tanya D. Auger dubbed Mould "a witty writer with a deft had for curious, wry details." The "Something Wickedly Weird" series is "deliciously, wickedly weird," Auger concluded.

Biographical and Critical Sources

PERIODICALS

Booklist, September 1, 1998, Hazel Rochman, review of *Frankenstein,* p. 120; October 14, 2008, Carolyn Phelan, review of *The Wooden Mile,* p. 42.

Horn Book, November-December, 2008, Tanya D. Auger, review of *The Wooden Mile,* p. 711.

Kirkus Reviews, June 1, 2004, review of *Vesuvius Poovius,* p. 537; July 15, 2008, review of *Something Wickedly Weird.*

Publishers Weekly, April 27, 1998, review of *Frankenstein,* p. 69.

School Librarian, February, 1995, review of *Hank the Clank,* p. 17; February, 1996, reviews of *A Christmas Carol,* p. 18, and *The Desperate Adventures of Sir Rupert and Rosie Gusset,* p. 22; August, 1995, review of *History's Big Mistakes,* p. 111; spring, 1998, reviews of *Frankenstein,* p. 35, and *Alphabet Spook!,* p. 46; summer, 1998, review of *Auntie Billie's Great Invention,* p. 76; winter, 2002, review of *The Day Our Teacher Went Batty,* p. 209; autumn, 2003, review of *The Beast of Crowsfoot Cottage,* p. 147; spring, 2007, Rosemary Woodman, review of *Dust 'n' Bones: Ten Terrifying Classic and Original Ghost Stories,* p. 34; spring, 2008, Martin Axford, review of *The Icy Hand,* p. 38; summer, 2008, Robin Barker, review of *Dust 'n' Bones,* p. 102.

School Library Journal, December, 2002, Nancy Menaldi-Scanlan, review of *Much Ado about Nothing,* p. 86; November, 2008, Amanda Raklovits, review of *The Icy Hand,* p. 132; April, 2009, Amanda Raklovitz, review of *The Wooden Mile,* p. 140; June, 2009, Elaine E. Knight, review of *The Silver Casket,* p. 132.

ONLINE

Chris Mould Home Page, http://www.chrismouldink.com (October 15, 2009).

Something Wickedly Weird Web site, http://www.something wickedlyweird.com/ (October 15, 2009).

N-P

NAKATA, Hiroe

Personal

Born in Hiroshima, Japan; immigrated to United States; children: Koharu (daughter). *Education:* Parsons School of Design, degree.

Addresses

Home—Brooklyn, NY. *Agent*—MB Artists, 10 E. 29th St., Ste. 40G, New York, NY 10016. *E-mail*—hinakata@earthlink.net.

Career

Illustrator of children's books.

Illustrator

Carol Shields Diggory, *Lucky Pennies and Hot Chocolate with Grandpa,* Dutton (New York, NY), 2000.

Joan Holub, *The Garden That We Grew,* Viking (New York, NY), 2001.

Miriam Chaikin, *Don't Step on the Sky: A Handful of Haiku,* Holt (New York, NY), 2002.

B.G. Hennessy, *My Book of Thanks,* Candlewick Press (Cambridge, MA), 2002.

Alyssa Satin Capucilli, *What Kind of Kiss?,* HarperFestival (New York, NY), 2002.

Jane Yolen, *Time for Naps,* Little Simon (New York, NY), 2002.

Caron Lee Cohen, *Everything Is Different at Nonna's House,* Clarion Books (New York, NY), 2003.

Jane Cutler, *The Birthday Doll,* Farrar, Straus (New York, NY), 2004.

Deborah Lee Rose, *Ocean Babies,* National Geographic Society (Washington, DC), 2004.

Deb Lund, *Tell Me My Story, Mama,* HarperCollins (New York, NY), 2004.

M.C. Helldorfer, *Got to Dance,* Doubleday (New York, NY), 2004.

Constance Levy, *The Story of the Red Rubber Ball,* Silver Whistle/Harcourt (Orlando, FL), 2004.

Dorothy Kunhardt, *Kitty's New Doll,* Golden Books (New York, NY), 2004.

Susan Myers, *This Is the Way a Baby Rides,* Abrams (New York, NY), 2005.

Mary Quattlebaum, *Winter Friends,* Doubleday (New York, NY), 2005.

Lynne Berry, *Duck Skates,* Holt (New York, NY), 2005.

Kristine O'Connell George, *Up!,* Clarion Books (New York, NY), 2005.

B.G. Hennessy, *Because of You,* Candlewick Press (Cambridge, MA), 2005.

Marsha Hayles, *Pajamas Anytime,* Putnam (New York, NY), 2005.

Wendy Cheyette Lewison, *Two Is for Twins,* Viking (New York, NY), 2006.

Dandi Daley Mackall, *God Made Me,* Little Simon Inspirations (New York, NY), 2006.

Dashka Slater, *Baby Shoes,* Bloomsbury (New York, NY), 2006.

Carol Hunt Senderak, *Mommy in My Pocket,* Hyperion (New York, NY), 2006.

Dennis R. Shealy, *Please and Thank You, God,* Golden Books (New York, NY), 2007.

Lynne Berry, *Duck Dunks,* Holt (New York, NY), 2008.

Marilyn Singer, *Shoe Bop!,* Dutton (New York, NY), 2008.

Lynne Berry, *Duck Tents,* Holt (New York, NY), 2009.

Victoria Adler, *Baby's Got Eyes,* Dial (New York, NY), 2009.

Sidelights

At the age of sixteen, Hiroe Nakata immigrated to New York City and eventually earned a degree at the Parsons School of Design. Since publishing her first illustrated work in 2000, Japanese-born artist Nakata has established a prolific career in children's books, adding the artwork to over twenty-five books in her first decade. Tracing the development of Nataka's work as an illustrator, *Bulletin of the Center for Children's Books* reviewer Hope Morrison suggested that since her picture-book debut—creating art for Carol Shields Diggory's *Lucky Pennies and Hot Chocolate with Grandpa*—the artist has "demonstrate[d] a knack for warm, domestic

Hiroe Nataka's gentle watercolor images pair with Deb Lund's rhyming text in Tell Me My Story, Mama. (Illustration copyright © 2004 by Hiroe Nakata. Used by permission of HarperCollins Publishers.)

details, highly expressive though stunningly simple faces, and a marked adeptness with cheerfully wet watercolors."

Other books featuring Nataka's art include Kristine O'Connell George's *Up!* and Mary Quattlebaum's *Winter Friends.* In her text for *Up!,* George follows the life of a toddler on the move as she rises in the morning, eats breakfast with her parents, and goes to the park to play with her father. *Winter Friends* collects a variety of poems by Quattlebaum, each illuminating the joys to be found during the colder months of the year, such as sledding, sipping hot chocolate, and making snow angels. Reviewing *Up!* in *Booklist,* Gillian Engberg wrote that "Nakata's airy, spirited watercolors beautifully expand on the words' carefree, physical elation." Engberg's sentiment was echoed by a *Kirkus Reviews* contributor who maintained that the artist's "watercolor illustrations burst off the pages in a riot of invigorating hues." According to Kara Schaff Dean in her *School Library Journal* review of *Winter Friends,* "Nakata's inspired illustrations perfectly complement the effortless verse" and a *Publishers Weekly* critic called the illustrator's "bright watercolors . . . stylish and elegantly concise."

Collaborating with writer Lynne Barry, Nataka helped bring to life the picture book *Duck Skates.* In the story, five ducks enjoy a day outdoors sledding, skating, and throwing snowballs, and through their adventures Barry introduces simple counting concepts to young readers.

The ducks return to enjoy a day at the beach in *Duck Dunks.* While following the young waterfowl as they play in the surf, fly a kite, and play tag in the sand, Barry's text also encourages children to count along with the story. Nataka's "watercolor-and-ink pictures convey the playfulness in warm, cozy tones," suggested *School Library Journal* critic Amelia Jenkins in a review of *Duck Skates,* while in the same periodical Jane Marino wrote of *Duck Dunks* that "the layout of pictures and lively, rhyming text complement the story perfectly." Barry and Nataka continue their picture-book collaboration about the small duck flock in *Duck Tents,* as the five feathered friends enjoy a night of camping. Reviewing *Duck Tents,* a *Publishers Weekly* contributor described the artist's depiction of the book's characters as "remarkably expressive."

Shoes take the main stage in two other books illustrated by Nakata: *Baby Shoes* by Dashka Slater and *Shoe Bop!* by Marilyn Singer. After picking out a new pair of shoes at the store, an active toddler does his best to make them his own in *Baby Shoes.* Going with his mother to the playground, the youngster manages to dirty his new shoes with grass stains, yellow road paint, and juice from fresh plums. In *Shoe Bop!* a second grader must trade in her worn purple shoes for a new pair. However, as she walks around the shoe store, she cannot make up her mind among all the variety of footwear, each possible pair of shoes described in Singer's verse. "The expressions on the characters' faces are particularly delightful," remarked *School Library Journal* critic Linda Zeilstra Sawyer in her review of *Baby Shoes.* Writing for the same periodical, Kathleen Kelly MacMillan voted "Nakata's vibrant, stylized watercolors . . . a perfect match for the bouncy text."

Nataka's engaging art is a feature of What Kind of Kiss?, *a picture book by Alyssa Satin Capucilli.* (Illustration copyright © 2002 by Alyssa Satin Capucilli. Used by permission of HarperCollins Publishers.)

Jane Cutler's picture book **The Birthday Doll** *features the gestured watercolor art Nataka is know for.* (Illustration copyright © 2004 by Hiroe Nakata. Used by permission of Farrar, Straus & Giroux, LLC.)

Biographical and Critical Sources

PERIODICALS

Booklist, February 1, 2005, Gillian Engberg, review of *Pajamas Anytime,* p. 965; March 1, 2005, Gillian Engberg, review of *Up!,* p. 1194; April 1, 2005, Carolyn Phelan, review of *Ocean Babies,* p. 1362; October 1, 2005, Hazel Rochman, review of *Duck Skates,* p. 61; November 1, 2005, Ilene Cooper, review of *Winter Friends,* p. 41; May 1, 2006, Carolyn Phelan, review of *Baby Shoes,* p. 84; May 15, 2006, Carolyn Phelan, review of *Two Is for Twins,* p. 50; September 1, 2008, Randall Enos, review of *Shoe Bop!,* p. 108; April 1, 2009, Carolyn Phelan, review of *Duck Tents,* p. 46.

Bulletin of the Center for Children's Books, July, 2004, Hope Morrison, "Hiroe Nakata."

Kirkus Reviews, November 15, 2001, review of *What Kind of Kiss?,* p. 1610; March 15, 2002, review of *Don't Step on the Sky: A Handful of Haiku,* p. 408; March 1, 2004, review of *Tell Me My Story, Mama,* p. 226; March 15, 2005, review of *Up!,* p. 351; September 15, 2005, review of *Winter Friends,* p. 1032; March 16, 2006, review of *Mommy in My Pocket,* p. 300; April 15, 2006, review of *Two Is for Twins,* p. 409.

Publishers Weekly, August 14, 2000, review of *Lucky Pennies and Hot Chocolate with Grandpa,* p. 354; March 11, 2002, review of *Don't Step on the Sky,* p. 70; April 18, 2003, review of *Everything Is Different at Nonna's House,* p. 68; February 2, 2004, review of *The Birthday Doll,* p. 76; March 1, 2004, review of *Tell Me My Story, Mama,* p. 67; May 3, 2004, review of *Got to Dance,* p. 190; March 28, 2005, review of *Ocean Babies,* p. 79; November 28, 2005, review of *Winter Friends,* p. 50; April 3, 2006, review of *Mommy in My Pocket,* p. 71; June 16, 2008, review of *Duck Dunks,* p. 47; April 20, 2009, review of *Duck Tents,* p. 48.

School Library Journal, September, 2000, Susan Hepler, review of *Lucky Pennies and Hot Chocolate with Grandpa,* p. 209; August, 2001, Carolyn Jenks, review of *The Garden That We Grew,* p. 153; December, 2001, Karen J. Tannenbaum, review of *What Kind of Kiss?,* p. 91; July, 2003, Jane Marino, review of *Everything Is Different at Nonna's House,* p. 88; March, 2004, Rosalyn Pierini, review of *The Birthday Doll,* p. 156; August, 2004, Liza Graybill, review of *Got to Dance,* p. 88; March, 2005, Rachel G. Payne, review of *Pajamas Anytime,* p. 172; October, 2005, Kara Schaff Dean, review of *Winter Friends,* p. 144; November, 2005, Amelia Jenkins, review of *Duck Skates,* p. 83; May, 2006, Linda Zeilstra Sawyer, review of *Baby Shoes,* p. 104; June, 2008, Jane Marino, review of *Duck Dunks,* p. 95; July, 2008, Kathleen Kelly MacMillan, review of *Shoe Bop!,* p. 92.

ONLINE

Time Out New York Kids Web site, http://newyorkkids. timeout.com (July, 2009), Eileen Clarke, interview with Nakata.*

*   *   *

NUGENT, Cynthia 1954-

Personal

Born 1954, in Canada. *Education:* B.A. (English literature; cum laude); graduate study (comparative literature). *Hobbies and other interests:* Playing guitar.

Addresses

Home—Vancouver, British Columbia, Canada.

Career

Author, illustrator, and educator. Langara College of Continuing Studies, Vancouver, British Columbia, Canada, instructor in writing. Judge for literary prizes; presenter at schools and libraries.

Member

Children's Writers and Illustrators of British Columbia.

Awards, Honors

Canadian Children's Book Centre (CCBC) Our Choice selection, Alberta Book Industry Book Illustration Award, Writers' Guild of Alberta Best Children's Book

Illustration honor, and Saskatchewan Children's Literature Award, all 1996, and Shining Willow Awards, 2003, all for *Mister Got to Go* by Lois Simmie; British Columbia Book Prize shortlist, 2005, and Manitoba Young Readers Choice shortlist, Chocolate Lily Award nomination, and CCBC Our Choice selection, both 2006, all for *Francesca and the Magic Bike;* Chocolate Lily Award nomination, and CCBC Our Choice selection, both 2006, both for *When Cats Go Wrong* by Norm Hacking; British Columbia Achievement Award for Early Literacy, 2008; Chocolate Lily Award for Best British Columbia Novel, 2008, for *Honey Cake.*

Writings

SELF-ILLUSTRATED

Francesca and the Magic Bike, Raincoast Books (Vancouver, British Columbia, Canada), 2004.
Fred and Pete at the Beach, Orca Book Publishers (Custer, WA), 2009.

ILLUSTRATOR

Lois Simmie, *Mister Got to Go: The Cat That Wouldn't Leave,* Red Dear College Press (Red Deer, Alberta, Canada), 1995.
Lois Simmie, *No Cats Allowed,* Chronicle Books (San Francisco, CA), 1996.
Terry Griggs, *Cat's Eye Corner,* Raincoast Books (Vancouver, British Columbia, Canada), 2000, Raincoast Books (Berkeley, CA), 2003.
Lois Simmie, *Mister Got to Go and Arnie,* Raincoast Books (Vancouver, British Columbia, Canada), 2001.
Lois Simmie, *Goodness Gracious, Gulliver Mulligan,* Raincoast Books (Berkeley, CA), 2002.
Terry Griggs, *Invisible Ink,* Raincoast Books (Vancouver, British Columbia, Canada), 2003.
Terry Griggs, *The Silver Door,* Raincoast Books (Vancouver, British Columbia, Canada), 2003.
Norm Hacking, *When Cats Go Wrong* (with CD), Raincoast Books (Vancouver, British Columbia, Canada), 2004, Raincoast Books (Berkeley, CA), 2006.
Jan Wells, *Memories,* Scholastic Canada (Markham, Ontario, Canada), 2005.
Simon Rose, *The Emerald Curse,* Tradewinds Books (Vancouver, British Columbia, Canada), 2006.
Joan Betty Stuchner, *Honey Cake,* Random House (New York, NY), 2008.
Bill Richardson, *The Aunts Come Marching,* Raincoast Books (Berkeley, CA), 2008.

Contributor of illustrations to periodicals.

Sidelights

Based in Vancouver, British Columbia, Canada, Cynthia Nugent is an award-winning author and illustrator. Her original self-illustrated stories include the highly praised

children's novel *Francesca and the Magic Bike* and the fanciful picture book *Fred and Pete at the Beach.* Nugent's computer-enhanced art, with its bright colors, can also be seen in picture books such as Norm Hacking's *When Cats Go Wrong* and Lois Simmie's award-winning *Mister Got to Go: The Cat That Wouldn't Leave,* as well as in Joan Betty Stuchner's middle-grade novel *Honey Cake* and Terry Griggs' "Cat's Eye Corner" fantasy series. Citing Nugent's "poster-art style" and use of "vibrant" colors, *School Library Journal* contributor Carol L. MacKay dubbed *When Cats Go Wrong* "an original and exhilarating blend of artwork, lyrics, and music," while a *Resource Links* writer described the book's illustrations as "vibrant" and "whimsical."

Nugent's original picture book *Francesca and the Magic Bike* was described by a *Resource Links* contributor as "an amazing and heartwarming tale about family relationships . . . and the power of forgiveness and believing in yourself." In the story, Francesca's mother dies and the ten year old is sent to live with a

Cynthia Nugent takes readers back to the tumultuous World War II era in her artwork for Joan Betty Stuchner's novel **Honey Cake.** (Illustration copyright © 2007 by Cynthis Nugent. Reproduced in the U.S. by permission of Stepping Stone Books, an imprint of Random House Children's Books, a division of Random House, Inc. In U.K. and Canada by permission of Tradewind Books.)

father she barely knows, whose life is too disruptive to give the girl a stable home. Although *School Library Journal* contributor Deanna Romriell found the book's ending somewhat unbelievable, her young heroine "is a sympathetic character" whose "journey provides some excitement and intrigue." Nugent's other self-illustrated story, *Fred and Pete at the Beach,* is based on her Vancouver neighbor Ron McDougall and his rescue dogs Fred and Pete, both of which were adopted from animal shelters and then trained in their important tasks.

To research the World-War-II setting for *Honey Cake,* Nugent traveled to Denmark, the setting for Stuchner's story about a Jewish family during the Nazi occupation of Copenhagen. Pen-and-ink illustrations bring to life the story of a ten-year-old boy and his experiences during a time of strife, uncertainty, and growing resistance to a looming threat of violence. The picture book *The Ants Come Marching,* in which writer Bill Richardson revises a well-known children's song, also benefits from Nugent's artwork, which "adds to the humour . . . and implies the mayhem created by the boisterous" characters, according to a *Resource Links* reviewer.

Nugent's watercolor art for *Mister Got to Go,* recounting the adventures of a stray city cat as it finds a permanent home in a Vancouver hotel, was credited by a *Resource Links* critic as "the book's strength"; her "bright . . . postcard-type scenes" are the sort "readers will want to examine more closely," the critic explained. Of the sequel, *Mister Got to Go and Arnie, School Library Journal* critic Linda Ludke wrote that "Nugent's colorful watercolors realistically capture cat demeanor" and contribute energy to Simmie's "humorous animal story."

Biographical and Critical Sources

PERIODICALS

Booklist, July 1, 2008, Hazel Rochman, review of *Honey Cake,* p. 66.

Canadian Review of Materials, May 24, 2002, review of *Mister Got to Go: The Cat That Wouldn't Leave*; May 9, 2003, review of *Goodness Gracious, Gulliver Mulligan.*

Canadian Book Review Annual, 1995, review of *Mister Got to Go,* p. 485; 2001, review of *Mister Got to Go and Arnie,* p. 468; 2002, review of *Goodness Gracious, Gulliver Mulligan,* p. 443; 2005, review of *Francesca and the Magic Bike,* p. 512; 2006, Deborah Dowson, review of *The Emerald Curse,* p. 510.

Kirkus Reviews, July 15, 2008, review of *Honey Cake.*

Quill & Quire, August, 1995, review of *Mister Got to Go,* p. 36; December, 2001, review of *Mister Got to Go and Arnie,* p. 26.

Resource Links, February, 2002, Denise Parrott, review of *Mister Got to Go and Arnie,* p. 8; August, 2002, Linda Ludke, review of *Mister Got to Go and Arnie,* p. 168;

Nugent's illustration projects include creating engaging watercolor art for Lois Simmie's **Mister Got to Go.** (Northern Lights Books for Children, 1995. Illustration copyright © 1995 by Cynthia Nugent. Reproduced by permission.)

June, 2003, Laura Reilly, review of *Good Gracious, Gulliver Mulligan,* p. 3; February, 2005, Elaine Rospad, review of *When Cats Go Wrong,* p. 4; June, 2007, Linda Berezowski, review of *The Aunts Come Marching,* p. 7; September, 2009, Deb Nielson, review of *Francesca and the Magic Bike,* p. 20.

School Librarian, November, 1996, review of *No Cats Allowed,* p. 147.

School Library Journal, April, 1997, Lisa Dennis, review of *No Cats Allowed,* p. 117; August, 2002, Linda Ludke, review of *Mister Got to Go and Arnie,* p. 168; August, 2003, Laura Reed, review of *Cat's Eye Corner,* p. 159; May, 2005, Carol L. MacKay, review of *When Cats Go Wrong,* p. 84; July, 2005, Deanna Romriell, review of *Francesca and the Magic Bike,* p. 107; September, 2006, Debbie Lewis O'Donnell, review of *Invisible Ink,* p. 207; January, 2007, Alana Abbott, review of *The Emerald Curse,* p. 107.

ONLINE

Children's Writers and Illustrators of British Columbia Web site, http://www.cwill.bc.ca/ (October 15, 2009), "Cynthia Nugent."

Cynthia Nugent Web log, http://www.cynthianugent.com (October 15, 2009).*

PAGE, Gail 1950-

Personal

Born 1950, in Sag Harbor, ME; children: Logan. *Education:* Fashion Institute of Technology, degree, 1970; studied privately.

Addresses

Home—Brooksville, ME. *E-mail*—gailpage@prexar. com.

Career

Painter, illustrator, and writer. Sue Brett Inc., New York, NY, dress designer, c. 1970s; Clover Embroidery Company, New York, NY, former graphic designer; clothing and textile designer, 1996; designer and manufacturer of floorcloths, beginning 1997; freelance designer and illustrator. *Exhibitions:* Work exhibited at numerous galleries in New England, New Jersey, New York, and Florida. Work included in permanent collection at Boston Children's Hospital; creator of mural installations at Bridgton Elementary School, Bridgton, ME, and at GoVap District Orphanage, Saigon, Vietnam.

Awards, Honors

Maine Arts Festival Poster Contest winner, 1999.

Gail Page mixes a humorous story with her topsy-turvy paintings in the picture book **How to Be a Good Dog.** (Bloomsbury Children's Books, 2006. Copyright © 2006 by Gail Page. Reproduced by permission.)

Writings

SELF-ILLUSTRATED

How to Be a Good Dog, Bloomsbury Children's Books (New York, NY), 2006.
Bobo and the New Neighbor, Bloomsbury U.S.A. Children's Books (New York, NY), 2008.

Contributor of illustrations to *Audio File* magazine.

Sidelights

Gail Page worked as a clothing and textile designer before moving to painting and illustration. In her paintings, done in acrylic on paper or board, as well as her unique floorcloths, Page uses bright, vibrant colors to render her stylized figures. In 2004 she turned her attention to an even larger canvas when she and her grown daughter met in Saigon, Vietnam, to help the children of the GoVap district orphanage paint the walls of their school's classrooms and hallways. "The experience confirmed our beliefs that art matters," Page recalled in her home page.

In her picture books *How to Be a Good Dog* and *Bobo and the New Neighbor* Page introduces Bobo, a loveable, floppy-eared white dog with a big black nose and a childlike good nature: Although Bobo has good intentions, he also has a knack for creating a bit of chaos in the life of his human owner, Mrs. Birdhead. In *How to Be a Good Dog* Bobo is banished to the dog house until fellow house pet Cat coaches him in the meaning behind "sit," "stay," and other doggy behaviors that are required to be readmitted into Mrs. Birdhead's home. In a sequel, *Bobo and the New Neighbor,* Bobo is again banished outside after creating havoc in the kitchen. A quick trip to the clothesline provides the dog with a clever disguise, and when he appears at his owner's door he is mistaken for a new neighbor, Mrs. Wrinklerump. The "quirky humor in the brief text is matched by the funny . . . illustrations," wrote a *Kirkus Reviews* writer of *How to Be a Good Dog.* Praising Page's colorful cartoon-style acrylic illustrations, *School Library Journal* contributor Linda M. Kenton dubbed *Bobo and the New Neighbor* "a fun read-aloud for a group," and Hazel Rochman predicted in *Booklist* that "kids will enjoy the [story's] farcical scenarios." In *School Library Journal,* DeAnn Okamura wrote that the "large acrylic paintings . . . and simple text" in Bobo's second book of adventures make them "a good choice to share with groups of young children," while a *Kirkus Reviews* writer dubbed *Bobo and the New Neighbor* an "offbeat tale" featuring "a wickedly ironic subtext" and "uncluttered illustrations."

Biographical and Critical Sources

PERIODICALS

Booklist, October 15, 2008, Hazel Rochman, review of *Bobo and the New Neighbor,* p. 45.

Do It Yourself, summer, 1998, profile of Page.

Kirkus Reviews, March 15, 2006, review of *How to Be a Good Dog,* p. 297; July 15, 2008, review of *Bobo and the New Neighbor.*

Publishers Weekly, March 6, 2006, review of *How to Be a Good Dog,* p. 72; June, 2006, Okamura DeAnn, review of *How to Be a Good Dog,* p. 124.

School Library Journal, December, 2008, Linda M. Kenton, review of *Bobo and the New Neighbor,* p. 98.

ONLINE

Gail Page Home Page, http://www.gailpage.com (October 15, 2009).*

*   *   *

PAPP, Robert 1967-

Personal

Born 1967; married; wife's name Lisa (an artist). *Hobbies and other interests:* Building furniture, spending time with family.

Addresses

Home—Bucks County, PA. *E-mail*—robert@robertpapp.com.

Career

Illustrator. *Exhibitions:* Work included in exhibitions at U.S. Capitol, Washington, DC.

Illustrator

Donald J. Sobol, *Encyclopedia Brown and the Case of the Jumping Frogs,* Delacorte Press (New York, NY), 2003.

Angela Shelf Medearis, *With Friends like These, Who Needs Enemies?,* Scholastic (New York, NY), 2003.

Angela Shelf Medearis, *Too Many Holidays?,* Scholastic (New York NY), 2003.

Gail Karwoski, *Quake!: Disaster in San Francisco, 1906,* Peachtree (Atlanta, GA), 2004.

Angela Shelf Medearis, *Best Friends Forever?,* Scholastic (New York, NY), 2004.

Angela Shelf Medearis, *The Case of the Missing Trophy,* Scholastic (New York, NY), 2004.

Trinka Hakes Noble, *The Scarlet Stockings Spy,* Sleeping Bear Press (Chelsea, MI), 2004.

Gertrude Chandler Warner, *The Clue in the Corn Maze,* Albert Whitman (Morton Grove, IL), 2004.

David Seidaman, *Kong: The Eighth Wonder of the World,* Meredith Books (Des Moines, IA), 2005.

Gertrude Chandler Warner, *The Ghost of the Chattering Bones,* Albert Whitman (Morton Grove, IL), 2005.

Gertrude Chandler Warner, *The Sword of the Silver Knight,* Albert Whitman (Morton Grove, IL), 2005.

Justine Simmons, *God, Can You Hear Me?,* Harper/Amistad (New York, NY), 2006.

Trinka Hakes Noble, *The Last Brother: A Civil War Tale,* Sleeping Bear Press (Chelsea, MI), 2006.

Gertrude Chandler Warner, *The Vanishing Passenger,* Albert Whitman (Morton Grove, IL), 2006.

Gertrude Chandler Warner, *The Rock 'n' Roll Mystery,* Albert Whitman (Morton Grove, IL), 2006.

Gertrude Chandler Warner, *The Giant Yo-Yo Mystery,* Albert Whitman (Morton Grove, IL), 2006.

Gertrude Chandler Warner, *The Creature in Ogopogo Lake,* Albert Whitman (Morton Grove, IL), 2006.

Steven L. Layne, *P Is for Princess: A Royal Alphabet,* Sleeping Bear Press (Chelsea, MI), 2007.

Gertrude Chandler Warner, *The Secret of the Mask,* Albert Whitman (Morton Grove, IL), 2007.

Gertrude Chandler Warner, *The Seattle Puzzle,* Albert Whitman (Morton Grove, IL), 2007.

Helen L. Wilbur, *M Is for Meow: A Cat Alphabet,* Sleeping Bear Press (Chelsea, MI), 2007.

Kathy-jo Wargin, *Mary's First Thanksgiving: An Inspirational Story of Greatfulness,* Zonderkidz (Grand Rapids, MI), 2008.

Laurence Yep, *Mia,* American Girl (Middleton, WI), 2008.

Laurence Yep, *Bravo, Mia!,* American Girl (Middleton, WI), 2008.

Marty Crisp, *Titanicat,* Sleeping Bear Press (Chelsea, MI), 2008.

Stephanie True Peters, *Rumble Tum,* Dutton Children's Books (New York, NY), 2009.

Gertrude Chandler Warner, *The Dog-Gone Mystery,* Albert Whitman (Morton Grove, IL), 2009.

Janice Shefelman, *Anna Maria's Gift,* Random House Children's Books (New York, NY), 2010.

Contributor of artwork to periodicals, including *Cooks Illustrated* and *Time.*

Sidelights

Robert Papp, an illustrator based in Bucks County, Pennsylvania, has created artwork for a number of children's picture books, among them stories by Marty Crisp, Trina Hakes Noble, Stephanie True Peters, Janice Shefelman, Angela Shelf Medearis, and Gertrude Chandler Warner. His illustrations for Noble's *The Last Brother: A Civil War Tale,* which focuses on two brothers who join the Union Army during the U.S. Civil War, were praised by *School Library Journal* contributor Christine Markley as "well-rendered" and "hauntingly detailed" paintings that "realistically convey the . . . intensity of battle, and the emotions of the characters." His work for another story by Noble, *The Scarlet Stockings Spy,* prompted Susan Scheps to dub Papp "a master of portraiture" in the same periodical, the critic adding that his "soft, realistic . . . oils are finely detailed." GraceAnne A. DeCandido compared the artist's "richly colored illustrations," with their "dramatic poses and fully realized figures," recall the work of turn-of-the-twentieth-century illustrator N.C. Wyeth.

Other books featuring Papp's detailed paintings include Crisp's *Titanicat,* a true story about a Irish cabin boy named Jim Mulholand who missed his assignment to sail on the fateful maiden voyage of the *Titanic* because he was assisting the ship's cat in moving its young litter of kittens ashore at the last minute. "Fresh-faced Jim and [Papp's] winsome kittens provide a sense of optimism" in Crisp's "amazing tale," according to *School Library Journal* critic Kara Schaff Dean. A *Kirkus Reviews* writer cited Papp's "photorealistic paintings," and in *Booklist* Ilene Cooper wrote that in his "lush, painterly artwork" Papp "plays with light and perspective."

Biographical and Critical Sources

PERIODICALS

Booklist, May 15, 2004, Carolyn Phelan, review of *Quake!: Disaster in San Francisco, 1906,* p. 1631; February 1, 2005, Ilene Cooper, review of *The Scarlet Stockings,* p. 959; September 1, 2006, GraceAnne A. DeCandido, review of *The Last Brother: A Civil War Tale,* p. 139; August 1, 2008, Ilene Cooper, review of *Titanicat,* p. 83.

Black Issues Book Review, March-April, 2007, review of *God, Can You Hear Me?,* p. 22.

Robert Papp collaborates with Marty Crisp, contributing detailed paintings to Crisp's true-to-life adventure in Titanicat. (Sleeping Bear Press, 2008. Illustration copyright © 2008 Robert Papp. Reproduced by permission of Gale, a part of Cengage Learning.)

Kirkus Reviews, May 1, 2008, review of *Titanicat.*

Publishers Weekly, November 27, 2006, review of *Can You Hear Me?,* p. 54.

School Library Journal, July, 2005, Susan Scheps, review of *The Scarlet Stockings Spy,* p. 79; December, 2006, Christine Markley, review of *The Last Brother,* p. 110; May, 2007, Kara Schaff Dean, review of *M Is for Meow: A Cat Alphabet,* p. 127; August, 2007, Linda L. Walkins, review of *God, Can You Hear Me?,* p. 92; July, 2008, Kara Shaff Dean, review of *Titanicat,* p. 68; October, 2008, Lisa Egly Lehmuller. review of *Mary's First Thanksgiving: An Inspirational Story of Greatfulness,* p. 128; November, 2008, Kelly Roth, reviews of *Mia* and *Bravo, Mia!,* both p. 104.

ONLINE

Robert Papp Home Page, http://www.robertpapp.com (October 15, 2009).

Robert Papp Web log, http://pappart.blogspot.com (October 15, 2009).*

*   *   *

PARKER, Marjorie Blain 1960-

Personal

Born March 2, 1960, in Edmonton, Alberta, Canada; daughter of William Ross (a lawyer), and Sandra Joan (a language arts teacher) Blain; married Jay Gordon Parker (a gas and electric distribution designer), September 27, 1986; children: Steven Maxwell, Casey Blain, Rachel Faye. *Ethnicity:* "Caucasian." *Education:* University of Calgary, bachelor of commerce (management information systems), 1982. *Religion:* Roman Catholic. *Hobbies and other interests:* Walking, cooking, reading, traveling, skiing.

Addresses

Home—Denver, CO. *E-mail*—marjorieblainparker@comcast.net.

Career

Author of children's books. Arthur Andersen, Calgary, Alberta, Canada, information systems consultant, 1982-86; Price Waterhouse, Denver, CO, information systems consultant, 1986-88; Software AG, Denver, technical software support, 1988-2002; freelance writer.

Member

Authors' Guild, Society of Children's Book Writers and Illustrators, Canadian Society of Children's Authors, Illustrators, and Performers, Colorado Council of the International Reading Association.

Awards, Honors

Henry Bergh Children's Book Award, American Society for the Prevention of Cruelty to Animals, and Silver

Marjorie Blain Parker (Photograph by Jay Parker. Reproduced by permission.)

Seal, Mr. Christie's Book Award, both 2002, and KIND Children's Book Award, National Association for Humane and Environmental Education, 2003, all for *Jasper's Day.*

Writings

FOR CHILDREN

Jasper's Day, illustrated by Janet Wilson, Kids Can Press (Toronto, Ontario, Canada), 2002.

Ice Cream Everywhere!, illustrated by Stephanie Roth, Scholastic (New York, NY), 2002.

Hello, School Bus!, illustrated by Bob Kolar, Cartwheel Books (New York, NY), 2004.

Hello, Fire Truck!, illustrated by Bob Kolar, Cartwheel Books (New York, NY), 2004.

Hello, Freight Train!, illustrated by Bob Kolar, Cartwheel Books (New York, NY), 2005.

Your Kind of Mommy, illustrated by Cyd Moore, Dutton Children's (New York, NY), 2007.

Mama's Little Duckling, illustrated by Mike Wohnoutka, Dutton Children's (New York, NY), 2008.

A Book about Dads, illustrated by R.W. Alley, Dutton Children's (New York, NY), 2009.

A Paddling of Ducks, illustrated by Joseph Kelly, Kids Can Press (Toronto, Ontario, Canada), 2010.

Contributor to children's magazines.

Sidelights

When Marjorie Blain Parker won her first ribbon for a poem published in the school bulletin during third grade, she was hooked on writing. Yet many years passed before this native Canadian returned to creative writing. After graduating from college with a business degree, Parker worked for an accounting firm, and in 1986 she moved to Denver, Colorado, with her American husband. Shortly thereafter, she took a correspondence course in writing for children. "I needed a hobby since I had to leave all my friends and family behind in Canada," Parker wrote on her home page. "I really enjoyed the writing and many of my pieces were published in children's magazines."

Parker's commitment to writing decelerated with the arrival of each of their three children, but once the kids were all of school age, she resumed her professional writing career. "In 1999, inspired by a writer friend, I decided to go for it," she continued. "My goal was to get a manuscript accepted before I turned forty." To this end she wrote stories, joined a critique group, and attended writers' conferences. Her first children's work *Jasper's Day,* an award-winning picture book about a boy's last day with his beloved dog, appeared in 2002, and her career as a children's author was begun.

In *Jasper's Day* the human family of Jasper, a golden retriever suffering from cancer, celebrates the day with meaningful activities before taking him to the veterinarian to be put to sleep and later interring him in the backyard. Several reviewers suggested that *Jasper's Day* would be useful for bibliotherapy, a *Kirkus Reviews* contributor remarking favorably upon Parker's "exquisite sensitivity" in telling the story. Finding "the difficult situation . . . described gently, but realistically," *School Library Journal* critic Lucinda Snyder Whitehurst added that the book might help children experiencing similar situations. Whitehurst also expressed concern that children with healthy pets might find *Jasper's Day* "upsetting," but *Booklist* critic Ilene Cooper concluded that the book offers "a celebration of life that will remind children to make the most of every moment with those they love."

Other works by Parker include *Your Kind of Mommy,* illustrated by Cyd Moore, and *Mama's Little Duckling,* a picture book with artwork by Mike Wohnoutka, as well as several beginning readers for Scholastic that feature cartoon art by Bob Kolar. "Original and sweet without being sappy," according to *School Library Journal* critic Martha Topol, *Your Kind of Mommy* describes the imaginative wanderings of a mother and child as they imagine how they would interact if they were a variety of animals rather than humans. Parker uses a repetitive text that is captured in Moore's "vibrant and expressive" paintings, wrote Topol, and her "gentle repetition of the verses is perfectly suited for . . . storytimes," according to a *Kirkus Reviews* contributor.

In *Mama's Little Ducking* Parker recounts the adventures of a curious little duckling after Mama Quack turns her tail feathers while hunting down a tasty meal. "This tender tale deals with a milestone every family faces," wrote a *Kirkus Reviews* writer, the critic adding that the story serves as a "delightful addition" to toddler libraries. In *School Library Journal,* Judith Constantinides noted that Parker's "text is lyrical, cleverly using repetitive phrases and rhyming words" and dubbed *Mama's Little Duckling* "a standout."

Discussing her work creating stories for young children, Parker once told *SATA* that she "loves the writing life" and "hopes to establish a body of work worthy of the respect of book lovers and the literary community."

Biographical and Critical Sources

PERIODICALS

Booklist, December 15, 2002, Ilene Cooper, review of *Jasper's Day,* p. 769; May 15, 2005, Gillian Engberg, review of *Hello, Freight Train!,* p. 1666.
Kirkus Reviews, September 15, 2002, review of *Jasper's Day,* pp. 1397-1398; February 1, 2007, review of *Your Kind of Mommy,* p. 128; January 15, 2008, review of *Mama's Little Duckling.*
Publishers Weekly, January 14, 2008, review of *Mama's Little Duckling,* p. 56.
Resource Links, October, 2002, Heather Hamilton, review of *Jasper's Day,* p. 8.
School Library Journal, January, 2003, Lucinda Snyder Whitehurst, review of *Jasper's Day,* p. 110; March, 2007, Martha Topol, review of *Your Kind of Mommy,* p. 184; February, 2008, Judith Constantinides, review of *Mama's Little Duckling,* p. 94.

ONLINE

Marjorie Blain Parker Home Page, http://www.marjorie blainparker.com (October 15, 2009).*

* * *

PUVILLAND, Alex (Alexandre Puvilland)

Personal
Born in France; married LeUyen Pham (an illustrator); children: Leo.

Addresses
Home—San Francisco, CA.

Career
Illustrator, animator, and creator of comics. Dreamworks Animation, Glendale, CA, layout artist, then illustrator and art director, beginning c. 1997.

Illustrator
(With wife, LeUyen Pham) A.B. Sina, *Jordan Mechner's Prince of Persia* (graphic novel), First Second (New York, NY), 2008.

Creator of online comics "The Fantastic Adventures of Pablo the Cuban Alligator" and "Soup-Opera."

Sidelights
In addition to his work in film animation, Alex Puvilland has also created online comics and collaborated with his wife, illustrator LeUyen Pham, on the graphic novel *Jordan Mechner's Prince of Persia.* Based on a 1990s video game designed by Mechner and featuring a text by poet A.B. Sina, the novel takes readers back in time, telling parallel stories set in the ninth and thirteenth centuries. In the city of Marv, the valiant Prince Guiv is denied the throne; he saves a beautiful princess and shoulders the battles of his people while he fights for his rightful inheritance. A second storyline takes place four centuries later, as a princess of Marv helps a young man break the hold of a deadly prophecy. As the story slips back and forth through time, Persian myth and prophecy sometimes mask and sometimes clarify reality, imbuing *Jordan Mechner's Prince of Persia* with a mystical quality suitable to its Middle Eastern setting.

Marjorie Blain Parker's gentle story in **Mama's Little Duckling** *is enhanced by Mike Wohnoutka's soft-edged illustrations.* (Illustration copyright © 2008 by Mike Wohnoutka. Reproduced by permission of Dutton Children's Books, a division of Penguin Putnam Books for Young Readers.)

In bringing to life the lyrical text of *Jordan Mechner's Prince of Persia,* Pham and Puvilland have recrafted the game's original characters, discarding some and revising others, such as Prince Guiv. Their efforts won the approval of several critics, Ian Chipman remarking in *Booklist* that the "magnificent and complex graphic novel" features "visual clues" that help readers follow Sima's intertwining story lines. According to a *Publishers Weekly* contributor, "the artwork by Pham and Puvilland is suitably vigorous and exotic," while Andrea Lipinski cited the illustrators' use of "vibrant colors and stirring images." In *School Library Journal* Lipinski explained that the multilevel story is enhanced by the couple's choice of a palette that transitions from "desert browns" to vibrant colors that "stand out . . . against the colors of sand and bone."

Biographical and Critical Sources

PERIODICALS

Booklist, September 1, 2008, Ian Chipman, review of *Jordan Mechner's Prince of Persia,* p. 98.

Kliatt, September, 2008, George Galuschak, review of *Jordan Mechner's Prince of Persia,* p. 34.

Publishers Weekly, July 28, 2008, review of *Jordan Mechner's Prince of Persia,* p. 58.

School Library Journal, September, 2008, Andrea Lipinski, review of *Jordan Mechner's Prince of Persia,* p. 219.

ONLINE

Alex Puvilland Home Page, http://alexpuvilland.com (October 15, 2009).

Alex Puvilland Web log, http://sickofpenguins.blogspot.com (October 15, 2009).*

*   *   *

PUVILLAND, Alexandre
See PUVILLAND, Alex

R

RAMOS, Jorge 1958-

Personal

Born March 16, 1958, in Mexico City, Mexico; married and divorced (twice); children: Paola, Nicolas. *Education:* Universidad Iberoamericana, degree (communications), 1981; attended University of California—Los Angeles.

Addresses

Home—Miami, FL.

Career

Journalist and author. Worked at radio and television stations in Mexico and Los Angeles, CA; *Noticiero Univision,* television news coanchor, 1986—, and host of *Al Punto,* beginning 2007.

Awards, Honors

(With others) eight Emmy awards, National Association of Television Arts and Sciences, 1986-2000; Suncoast Regional Emmy Award, 1991, 1992, 1995, 1996; Maria Moors Cabot Award, Columbia University, 2001; Ron Brown Award, National Child Labor Committee, 2002; David Brinkley Award for Excellence in Communication, Barry University, 2003; American Association of Publishers honor, 2004; Chairman's Humanitarian Award, Congressional Hispanic Caucus Institute, 2004; Emmy Award, 2005; Latino Book Award, Latino Literacy Now, 2006, for *Dying to Cross;* Hispanic Media Award, 2007; University of Richmond, honorary D.Lit., 2007; Distinguished Citizen Award, Commonwealth Club of San Francisco, 2008; Lifetime Achievement Award in Hispanic Television, *Multichannel News/ Broadcasting & Cable,* 2008.

Writings

Detrás de la máscara, Grijalbo (Mexico City, Mexico), 1998.

La otra cara de América: historias de los inmigrantes latinoamericanos que están cambiando a Estados Unitos, Grijalbo (Mexico City, Mexico), 2000, translated by Patricia J. Duncan as *The Other Face of America: Chronicles of the Immigrants Shaping Our Future,* Rayo (New York, NY), 2002.

A la caza de león, Grijalbo (Mexico City, Mexico), 2001.

No Borders: A Journalist's Search for Home (originally published in Spanish as *Atravesando fronteras*), translated by Patricia J. Duncan, Rayo (New York, NY), 2002.

The Latino Wave: How Hispanics Will Elect the Next American President (originally published in Spanish as *Ola Latina*), translated by Ezra E. Fitz, Rayo (New York, NY), 2004.

Morir en el intento: la peor tragedia de imigrantes en la historia de los Estados Unitos, HarperCollins (New York, NY), 2005, translated by Kristina Cordero as *Dying to Cross: The Worst Immigrant Tragedy in American History,* Rayo (New York, NY), 2005.

Lo que vi: experiencias de un periodista alrededor del mundo, Rayo (New York, NY), 2006.

El regalo del tiempo: cartas a mis hijos, HarperCollins (New York, NY), 2007, translated by Ezra E. Fitz as *The Gift of Time: Letters from a Father,* Morrow (New York, NY), 2008.

I'm Just like My Mom/me parezco tanto a mi mama, illustrated by Akemi Gutierrez, HarperCollins (New York, NY), 2008.

I'm Just like My Dad/me parezco tanto a mi papa, illustrated by Akemi Gutierrez, HarperCollins (New York, NY), 2008.

Tierra de todos: nuestro momento para crear una nacion de iguales, Vintage Español (New York, NY), 2009.

Columnist for weekly syndicated Spanish-language newspaper.

Sidelights

After studying at the Universidad Iberoamericana in his native Mexico, Jorge Ramos began a career in television, working on a news program for the country's

Grupo Televisa broadcasting company. Shortly into this job however, Ramos learned that his supervisors had edited his work, omitting material that might be interpreted as unfavorable to the president of Mexico. Unwilling to be censored as a journalist, Ramos decided to move to the United States, taking the first step toward becoming one of the most widely watched television news anchors in North America. In addition to his television duties as coanchor of Univision's popular Spanish-language news program *Noticiero Univision,* the Miami, Florida, resident has also shared through books and a syndicated newspaper column recounting his experiences as an immigrant. He also discusses events in the lives of other Hispanics living in the United States, those with and without legal-resident status.

After publishing a collection of interviews with famous world figures in *Detrás de la máscara,* Ramos chronicled the life of everyday Hispanics and their impact on their adopted country in *The Other Face of America: Chronicles of the Immigrants Shaping Our Future,* first published in Mexico as *La otra cara de América: Historias de los inmigrantes latinoamericanos que están cambiando a Estados Unitos. Atravesando fronteras*—published in English translation as *No Borders: A Journalist's Search for Home*—appeared in 2002 and outlines Ramos's early years in Mexico along with his decision to become a journalist in the United States. Information about his popularity as a television celebrity among a growing demographic can be found in *No Borders,* as well as glimpses from the news anchor's personal life as the divorced father of two children. According to a *Publishers Weekly* reviewer, "Readers from this large viewing audience will devour Ramos's inspiring immigrant story" in *No Borders,* while *Booklist* critic Vanessa Bush thought that "readers interested in the immigrant experience, particularly of Hispanics, will enjoy this insightful memoir."

Expanding his scope beyond adult readers, Ramos has also penned two books for younger children: *The Gift of Time: Letters from a Father* and the bilingual picture books *I'm Just like My Mom/me parezco tanto a mi mama* and *I'm Just like My Dad/me parezco tanto a mi papa.* Originally published as *El regalo del tiempo: cartas a mis hijos, The Gift of Time* appeared after the television anchor experienced a major automobile accident which caused him to refocus his priorities and put into words his love for his children. Featuring both Spanish and English texts, *I'm Just like My Mom/me parezco tanto a mi mama* and its companion title explain the many ways a child mirrors his or her same-sex parent in appearance and habit. Evaluating both books in *Kirkus Reviews,* a contributor applauded Ramos's overarching assertion that "love of the family means no child is alone," calling it "poignant and heartfelt." In *Booklist* Randall Enos predicted that "children will enjoy . . . discovering similarities and appreciating families," while *School Library Journal* reviewer Susan

Jorge Ramos focuses on the relationships within a close-knit family in **I'm Just like My Dad/me parezco tanto a mi papa,** *featuring artwork by Akemi Gutierrez.* (Illustration copyright © 2008 by Akemi Gutierrez. Used by permission of HarperCollins Publishers.)

E. Murray decided that the author's "gentle picture book[s] will open up conversations in many families."

Biographical and Critical Sources

PERIODICALS

Booklist, October 15, 2002, Vanessa Bush, review of *No Borders: A Journalist's Search for Home,* p. 364; October 15, 2008, Randall Enos, reviews of *I'm Just like My Mom/me parezco tanto a mi mama* and *I'm Just like My Dad/me parezco tanto a mi papa,* p. 46.

Broadcasting & Cable, October 20, 2008, Laura Mart, "Newsman of the Americas," p. A6.

Kirkus Reviews, December 1, 2001, review of *The Other Face of America: Chronicles of the Immigrants Shaping Our Future,* p. 1670; July 1, 2008, reviews of of *I'm Just like My Mom/me parezco tanto a mi mama* and *I'm Just like My Dad/me parezco tanto a mi papa.*

Latino Leaders, October-November, 2004, "Jorge Ramos," p. 20, and review of *The Latino Wave: How Hispanics Will Elect the Next American President,* p. 59.

Latin Trade, December, 2002, Andres Hernandez Alende, "An Immigrant's Tale," review of *No Borders,* p. 66.

Library Journal, January, 1999, Carmen J. Palmieri, review of *Detrás de la máscara,* p. 80; February 1, 2002, Boyd Childress, review of *The Other Face of America,* p. 119; April 15, 2005, Boyd Childress, review of *Dying to Cross: The Worst Immigrant Tragedy in American History,* p. 106.

Miami Herald, May 18, 2005, Andy Diaz, review of *Dying to Cross.*

New York Times Book Review, March 16, 2003, Shannon Brady Marin, review of *No Borders,* p. 24.

Publishers Weekly, January 21, 2002, review of *The Other Face of America,* p. 78; September 23, 2002, review of *No Borders,* p. 64; October 14, 2002, Adriana Lopez, "Man of La Media: Top-rated Spanish-language News Anchor Jorge Ramos Is Poised for Crossover Success," p. 20; May 31, 2004, review of *The Latino Wave,* p. 66.

School Library Journal, November, 2008, Susan E. Murray, reviews of of *I'm Just like My Mom/me parezco tanto a mi mama* and *I'm Just like My Dad/me parezco tanto a mi papa,* p. 98.

Television Week, May 30, 2005, Jennifer Pendleton, "Icon Anchor Staying Put at Flagship Newscast," p. 26.

Time, August 22, 2005, Tim Padgett, "The Man of the News Hour: Jorge Ramos," p. 53.

ONLINE

Jorge Ramos Home Page, http://www.jorgeramos.com (October 15, 2009).*

* * *

ROBINSON, Tim 1963-

Personal

Born 1963; married; wife's name Marguerite; children: Wyatt, Luke. *Education:* Syracuse University, B.F.A.

Addresses

Home—Croton-on-Hudson, NY. *E-mail*—TR@timrobinson.cc.

Career

Illustrator, author, songwriter, and performer. WBMG (publication design firm), New York, NY, designer; freelance illustrator beginning 1989. *Exhibitions:* Works exhibited at galleries in New York, NY, and Westchester County, NY, and in private collections.

Writings

SELF-ILLUSTRATED

Tobias, the Quig, and the Rumplenut Tree, Winslow Press (New York, NY), 2000.

ILLUSTRATOR

Margaret Kenda and Phyllis S. Williams, *Math Wizardry for Kids,* Barron's (Hauppague, NY), 1995.

Margaret Kenda, *Geography Wizardry for Kids,* Barron's (Hauppauge, NY), 1997.

Ruth Bell Alexander, *Fraction Jugglers: A Math Gamebook for Kids and Their Parents,* Workman (New York, NY), 2001.

Steve Sheinkin, *Two Miserable Presidents: Everything Your Schoolbooks Didn't Tell You about the Civil War,* Roaring Brook Press (New York, NY), 2008.

Steve Sheinkin, *King George: What Was His Problem?* (new edition of *Storyteller's History: The American Revolution*), Roaring Brook Press (New York, NY), 2008.

Contributor to periodicals, including *Boston Globe, Canadian Business, Harvard Business Review, Nation, New York Times,* and *Wall Street Journal.*

Sidelights

After spending a few years working for a New York City design firm, Tim Robinson became a freelance illustrator, producing his colorful, uniquely stylized art for corporations, high-profile periodicals, and Web sites. In 1995 he also moved into children's publishing, creating artwork for Margaret Kenda and Phyllis S. Williams' *Math Wizardry for Kids.* This title marked the first of many picture books Robinson has illustrated, both for educational and mainstream publishers; in 2000 he also created the original picture book *Tobias, the Quig, and the Rumplenut Tree.*

In *Tobias, the Quig, and the Rumplenut Tree* readers meet a boy whose father is a gardener and who understands the interdependence of plants and animals. Tobias knows that the nuts of the rumplenut tree can only be spread by a rare bird called the Quig. However, because the Quig lives in captivity, caged so that humans can enjoy its beautiful feathers, Tobias must find a way to free the bird and allow it to perform its destined task. In *School Library Journal* Robin L. Gibson cited the book's "playful rhymes" and noted that Robinson's use of "bright, saturated colors . . . have an appealing Seuss-like quality."

As an illustrator, Robinson has created artwork for several history-themed books by Steve Sheinkin, among them *King George: What Was His Problem?* and *Two Miserable Presidents: Everything Your Schoolbooks Didn't Tell You about the Civil War.* Sheinkin, a textbook writer by trade, created these two books to share the quirkier aspects of his historical research with middle-school students who many not find the study of history all that interesting. In *Booklist,* Carolyn Phelan noted that Robinson's "droll line drawings . . . suit the tone" of Sheinkin's humorous text.

Biographical and Critical Sources

PERIODICALS

Booklist, April 15, 2008, Hazel Rochman, review of *Two Miserable Presidents: Everything Your Schoolbooks*

Didn't Tell You about the Civil War, p. 44; August 1, 2008, Carolyn Phelan, review of *King George: What Was His Problem?,* p. 66.
Horn Book, July-August, 2008, Betty Carter, review of *King George,* p. 473.
School Library Journal, October, 2000, Robin L. Gibson, review of *Tobias, the Quig, and the Rumplenut Tree,* p. 134; October, 2008, Mary Mueller, review of *Two Miserable Presidents,* p. 175.

ONLINE

Tim Robinson Home Page, http://www.timrobinson.cc (October 15, 2009).
Mother Pie Web log, http://motherpie.typepad.com/ (January 13, 2009), "An Artist Captures Recession Stories."

* * *

ROSEN, Elizabeth 1961-

Personal
Born 1961. *Education:* Parsons School of Design, B.F.A. (communication design).

Addresses
Home—New York, NY; Woodstock, NY. *Agent*—Vicki Morgan and Gail Gaynin, Morgan Gaynin Inc., 194 3rd Ave., New York, NY 10003. *E-mail*—ERosenArt@aol.com.

Career
Illustrator, graphic designer, and fine-art painter. Formerly worked as art director of an advertising agency; founder of graphic design business. *Exhibitions:* Work included in exhibitions in galleries, including ZUNI, New York, NY.

Awards, Honors
Awards from Singapore Creative Circle, Australian Writers and Art Directors, *Print* magazine, Society of Publication Designers, and Art Directors Club.

Illustrator
Robyn Feller, *Qi Gong: The Energy of Harmony and Healing,* Monterey Books, 1997.
Julie Mars, *The Soul of Africa,* Andrews McMeel Publishing (Riverside, NJ), 2000.
Carole Lexa Schaefer, *Two Scarlet Songbirds: A Story of Anton Dvorak,* Alfred A. Knopf (New York, NY), 2001.
Malka Drucker, *Portraits of Jewish-American Heroes,* Dutton Children's Books (New York, NY), 2008.

Sidelights
Elizabeth Rosen spent many years working in New York City, first as an art director in the advertising industry and then as a freelance graphic artist. In addition to her commercial work and her fine-art painting, Rosen has also gained recognition as an illustrator of children's books and has created images to pair with texts by authors Carole Lexa Schaefer and Malka Drucker. Her colorful images, which often feature multi-cultural themes and radiate with an urban energy, are created using acrylics, mixed-media, and collage. In reviewing Rosen's work for Schaefer's *Two Scarlet Songbirds: A Story of Anton Dvorak, Booklist* contributor Carolyn Phelan concluded that the book's "painterly illustrations" are "defined by bold forms and colors," while Lucinda Snyder wrote in *School Library Journal* that Rosen's paintings, with their "thickly applied oils in vibrant swirls, . . . seem to have rhythm and movement of their own."

Rosen's use of mixed media is put to good use in her artwork for Drucker's *Portraits of Jewish-American Heroes.* In the portrait she creates to accompany a profile of Levi Strauss, the creator of the sturdy trousers now known as blue jeans, Rosen uses denim as a canvas, and her work for the book was praised as "creative and expressive" by *School Library Journal* contributor Heidi Estrin. Other portraits include images of Albert Einstein, Steven Spielberg, Ruth Bader Ginsburg, and Jonas Salk. Rosen's images were described by a *Kirkus Reviews* writer as an "eclectic mélange of various media of methods of collage . . . and paints, and in

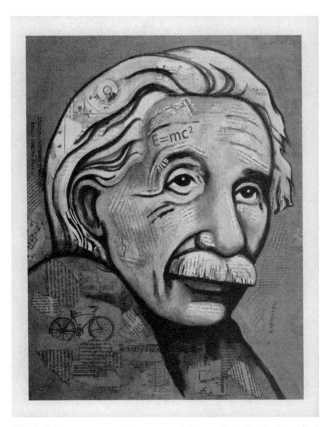

Elizabeth Rosen captures the essence of the notable individuals profiled in Malka Drucker's **Portraits of Jewish-American Heroes.** (Illustration copyright © 2008 by Elizabeth Rosen. Reproduced by permission of Dutton Children's Books, a division of Penguin Putnam Books for Young Readers.)

Booklist Hazel Rochman deemed *Portraits of Jewish-American Heroes* to be an "invitingly illustrated collective biography."

Biographical and Critical Sources

PERIODICALS

Booklist, December 14, 2001, Carolyn Phelan, review of *Two Scarlet Songbirds: A Story of Anton Dvorak,* p. 741; July 1, 2008, Hazel Rochman, review of *Portraits of Jewish-American Heroes,* p. 60.

Kirkus Reviews, July 1, 2008, review of *Portraits of Jewish-American Heroes.*

Publishers Weekly, June 30, 2008, review of *Portraits of Jewish-American Heroes,* p. 184.

School Library Journal, November, 2001, Lucinda Snyder Whitehurst, review of *Two Scarlet Songbirds,* p. 136; September, 2008, Heidi Estrin, review of *Portraits of Jewish-American Heroes,* p. 201.

ONLINE

Elizabeth Rosen Home Page, http://www.elizabethrosen. com (October 15, 2009).*

S

SANGER, Amy Wilson 1967-

Personal
Born 1967.

Addresses
Home—Woods Hole, MA.

Career
Author of children's books.

Writings

SELF-ILLUSTRATED; "WORLD SNACKS" SERIES

First Book of Sushi, Tricycle Press (San Francisco, CA), 2001.
Let's Nosh!, Tricycle Press (San Francisco, CA), 2002.
¡Hola! Jalapeño, Tricycle Press (San Francisco, CA), 2002.
Yum Yum Dim Sum, Tricycle Press (San Francisco, CA), 2003.
A Little Bit of Soul Food, Tricycle Press (San Francisco, CA), 2004.
Mangia! Mangia!, Tricycle Press (San Francisco, CA), 2005.
Chaat and Sweets, Tricycle Press (San Francisco, CA), 2007.

Sidelights
Though a series of self-illustrated board books, author Amy Wilson Sanger introduces young children to a variety of international cuisines, from Japanese delicacies in *First Book of Sushi,* to traditional Southern cooking in *A Little Bit of Soul Food.* Furthering her culinary journey around the world, the author/illustrator includes meals from China in *Yum Yum Dim Sum,* Italian dishes in *Mangia! Mangia!,* and food from India in *Chaat and Sweets.* In *Let's Nosh!,* Sanger extends her reach across religious and ethnic lines to focus on plates commonly prepared by American Jews with roots in Eastern Europe, including treats like rugelach, bagels, and noodle kugel.

With its "jaunty rhyming text," according to *School Library Journal* critic Ann Welton, Sanger's *¡Hola! Jalapeño* provides toddlers with "a good introduction to both the Spanish language and the cuisine of Mexico." Also writing in *School Library Journal,* Genevieve Gallagher suggested that "the rhymes in [*Yum Yum Dim Sum*] fit perfectly with the yummy illustrations." Other reviewers expressed favorable opinions of the artwork featured in each of Sanger's snack-inspired picture books, Mary N. Oluonye writing in *School Library Journal* that the author/illustrator's "three-dimensional collage images using wood, plastic, fabric, paper, and cross-stitching are wonderful" features of the books.

Biographical and Critical Sources

PERIODICALS

Kirkus Reviews, July 1, 2008, review of *Chaat and Sweets.*
Publishers Weekly, September 10, 2001, review of *First Book of Sushi,* p. 95; August 5, 2002, review of *Let's Nosh!,* p. 75; December 22, 2003, review of *Yum Yum Dim Sum,* p. 63.

Amy Wilson Sanger introduces young readers to a playful Chinese menu in **Yum Yum Dim Sum.** (Illustration copyright © 2004 by Amy Wilson Sanger. Used by permission of Tricycle Press, an imprint of the Crown Publishing Group, a division of Random House, Inc.)

School Library Journal, November, 2001, DeAnn Tabuchi, review of *First Book of Sushi,* p. 150; June, 2002, Ann Welton, review of *¡Hola! Jalapeño,* p. 129; January, 2004, Genevieve Gallagher, review of *Yum Yum Dim Sum,* p. 106; October, 2004, Mary N. Oluonye, review of *A Little Bit of Soul Food,* p. 129.*

*   *   *

SHEFELMAN, Janice 1930-
(Janice Jordan Shefelman)

Personal

Born April 12, 1930, in Baytown, TX; daughter of Gilbert John (a professor and writer) and Vera Jordan; married Thomas Whitehead Shefelman (an architect), September 18, 1954; children: Karl Jordan, Daniel

Whitehead. *Ethnicity:* "German/English." *Education:* Southern Methodist University, B.A., 1951, M.Ed., 1952; University of Texas—Austin, Library Certificate, 1980.

Addresses

Home—Austin, TX. *E-mail*—tjshef@aol.com.

Career

Author. Teacher at public schools in Dallas, TX, 1952-54, and Episcopal schools in Austin, TX, 1955-57; volunteer worker, 1957-80; Lake Travis Independent School District, Austin, librarian, 1980-84; full-time writer, 1980—. Storyteller and lecturer at public schools.

Member

Society of Children's Book Writers and Illustrators, Authors Guild, Austin Writers League of Texas.

Janice Shefelman (Reproduced by permission.)

Awards, Honors

Texas Bluebonnet Award Master List inclusion, Texas Library Association, 1985-86, for *A Paradise Called Texas;* Pick of the Lists designation, *American Bookseller;* Notable Children's Trade Book in the Field of Social Studies designation, and National Council for the Social Studies/Children's Book Council (CBC), both 1992, both for *A Peddler's Dream;* Best Books for the Teen Age designation, New York Public Library, Best Children's Book Award finalist, Texas Institute of Letters, and Children's Crown Award List inclusion, all for *Comanche Song;* Best Children's Book finalist, Texas Institute of Letters, for *Sophie's War;* Children's Choices selection, International Reading Association/ CBC, 2009, *Storytelling World* Award honor book designation, 2009, and Kids' Wings Award for Outstanding Literature, 2009-10, all for *I, Vivaldi.*

Writings

(As Janice Jordan Shefelman) *A Paradise Called Texas* ("Texas Trilogy"), illustrated by husband Tom Shefelman and sons Karl and Dan Shefelman, Eakin Press (Austin, TX), 1983.

(As Janice Jordan Shefelman) *Willow Creek Home* ("Texas Trilogy"), illustrated by Tom Shefelman and Karl and Dan Shefelman, Eakin Press (Austin, TX), 1985.

(As Janice Jordan Shefelman) *Spirit of Iron* ("Texas Trilogy"), illustrated by Tom Shefelman and Karl and Dan Shefelman, Eakin Press (Austin, TX), 1987.

Victoria House (picture book), illustrated by Tom Shefelman, Harcourt (San Diego, CA), 1988.

A Peddler's Dream (picture book), illustrated by Tom Shefelman, Houghton (Boston, MA), 1992.

A Mare for Young Wolf ("Young Wolf" series), illustrated by Tom Shefelman, Random House (New York, NY), 1993.

Young Wolf's First Hunt ("Young Wolf" series), illustrated by Tom Shefelman, Random House (New York, NY), 1995.

Young Wolf and Spirit Horse ("Young Wolf" series), illustrated by Tom Shefelman, Random House (New York, NY), 1997.

Comanche Song (middle-school historical novel), Eakin Press (Austin, TX), 2000.

Son of Spirit Horse (chapter book), illustrated by Tom Shefelman, Eakin Press (Austin, TX), 2004.

Sophie's War: The Journal of Anna Sophie Franziska, illustrated by Tom Shefelman, Eakin Press (Austin, TX), 2006.

I, Vivaldi (picture book), illustrated by Tom Shefelman, Eerdmans Books for Young Readers (Grand Rapids, MI), 2008.

Anna Maria's Gift, illustrated by Robert Papp, Random House (New York, NY), 2010.

Contributor to periodicals.

Sidelights

Writer and artist Janice Shefelman is the author of *I, Vivaldi,* an award-winning picture-book biography illustrated by her husband and frequent collaborator, Tom Shefelman. "For me writing is a visual art," she noted in an essay on her home page. "I make pictures in my head of the places, characters, and action, and then write what I see." Shefelman has also written several novels for young audiences, including *A Mare for Young Wolf* and other works in the "Young Wolf" series, as well as *Comanche Song.* Writing as Janice Jordan Shefelman, she has also completed the works in the "Texas Trilogy," which was inspired by events from her family's history.

I, Vivaldi, a *Storytelling World* Award honor book, was inspired by Janice and Tom Shefelman's love of classical music. "My childhood home was filled with music," Janice Shefelman noted in an interview on the *Eerdmans* Web site. "Mozart and Beethoven were my father's favorites. But as a teenager I became enamored of Frank Sinatra and popular music. Then I met Tom." She continued, "Together we listened to KMFA, our classical music radio station, and discovered *The Four Seasons* and a recording by Ofra Harnoy of Vivaldi's cello concertos. We began to wonder about the man who wrote such passionate, melodic music that touched our hearts across hundreds of years."

In *I, Vivaldi,* Shefelman offers a fictionalized account of the life of Antonio Vivaldi, an Italian violinist and composer who produced numerous instrumental and vo-

cal works during his lifetime. Born in Venice in 1648, Vivaldi was trained as a musician by his father; he later studied for the clergy and was ordained as a priest in 1703. He displayed little interest in religious matters, however, and was eventually relieved of his duties. Appointed as a violin teacher at the Ospitale della Pietà in Venice, Vivaldi organized and developed a group of orphaned girls into an internationally renowned chorus and orchestra.

Narrated by the young composer, *I, Vivaldi* earned solid reviews. "The few known facts about the composer's life are smoothly incorporated," remarked a critic in *Kirkus Reviews,* and a contributor in *Publishers Weekly* stated that "the first-person narration offers an accessible and personable view of Vivaldi's intense passion for music." Asked why she chose to profile the composer for young readers, Shefelman commented in her *Eerdmans* interview: "To enlarge their world both in time and space. To see the many possibilities in life. Everyone has a gift to give the world. Reading about those who have made the most of their gifts can inspire us all."

Shefelman once commented: "I have always thought of myself as a late bloomer, and I did not begin to write for children until I was forty-eight years old. Since my college days I have done freelance articles for magazines and newspapers, but it was not until I sat down at the proverbial dining room table and began to write *A Paradise Called Texas* that I found what it was I wanted to write: books for children.

"The idea for this first novel came from stories my father told me when I was a child, about how my great-grandfather left Germany in 1845 and brought his wife and young daughter with him to the Texas frontier. They had expected a paradise, but instead they found hardship, tragedy, and adventure. I wanted to make the daughter, Mina, come alive, and by writing her story, find out what she thought and felt. When I finished the book, the characters clamored for more adventures, so one book has grown into the 'Texas Trilogy.'

"Children's books have long been a favorite of mine ever since my father read *Winnie the Pooh* to me. As my two sons were growing up I read to them every night. At long last I decided that I too could write books like those I loved to read.

"A writer must read widely and live fully. One of my great pleasures is travel. When my husband and I married we sold all our possessions and traveled around the world for a year on freighters, living for several weeks in a Buddhist temple, all the while writing and illustrating our adventures for various newspapers. A dominant force in my life is the idea that one must dream and then go about making dreams come true. Perhaps this belief is the reason the story of my German ancestors' immigration to Texas was so appealing to me. The only

way to realize a dream is to begin—to write the outline of a book, then the first paragraph. Then, as Goethe said, 'the mind grows heated.'"

Biographical and Critical Sources

PERIODICALS

Booklist, February 15, 2001, Karen Hutt, review of *Comanche Song,* p. 1128.
Kirkus Reviews, December 15, 2007, review of *I, Vivaldi.*
Publishers Weekly, February 11, 2008, review of *I, Vivaldi,* p. 69.
School Library Journal, October, 2000, Coop Renner, review of *Comanche Song,* p. 171; March, 2008, Barbara Auerbach, review of *I, Vivaldi,* p. 189.

ONLINE

Eerdmans Web site, http://www.eerdmans.com/ (February, 2008), interview with Janice and Tom Shefelman.
Janice and Tom Shefelman Home Page, http://www.shefelmanbooks.com (September 1, 2009).

*   *   *

SHEFELMAN, Janice Jordan
See SHEFELMAN, Janice

*   *   *

SOMERS, Kevin

Personal

Male. *Education:* Antioch College, B.F.A.

Addresses

Home—Long Island City, NY. *E-mail*—kevin@somersaultstudio.com.

Career

Illustrator and writer. Marvel Comics Group, New York, NY, editor and artist; freelance illustrator and color artist.

Writings

Incredible Hulk, Project H.I.D.E., Marvel Comics (New York, NY), 1998.
Meaner than Meanest, illustrated by Diana Cain Bluthenthal, Hyperion Books for Children (New York, NY), 2001.

(Self-illustrated) *Sounds Funny! A Book about Comic Sounds,* Duo Press (New York, NY), 2008.

Sounds Tough! Big Noisy Machines, Duo Press (New York, NY), 2008.

Puck, *123 USA: A Cool Counting Book,* Duo Press (New York, NY), 2008.

Puck, *123 New York: A Cool Counting Book,* Duo Press (New York, NY), 2008.

Puck, *123 California: A Cool Counting Book,* Duo Press (New York, NY), 2008.

Puck, *123 Texas: A Cool Counting Book,* Duo Press (New York, NY), 2009.

Puck, *123 Chicago: A Cool Counting Book,* Duo Press (New York, NY), 2009.

Puck, *123 San Francisco: A Cool Counting Book,* Duo Press (New York, NY), 2009.

Sidelights

Kevin Somers worked for several years as a color artist and writer at Marvel Comics, and in the late 1990s he expanded his freelance career into children's-book publishing. His collaboration with illustrator Diana Cain Blumenthal resulted in the picture book *Meaner than Meanest,* and his original self-illustrated picture books include *Sounds Funny! A Book about Comic Sounds* and *Sounds Tough! Big Noisy Machines.* Other book illustration projects include a series of bilingual concept books for young children that have a regional focus; authored by Puck, the series includes *123 USA: A Cool Counting Book* and *123 San Francisco: A Cool Counting Book.*

Described by *School Library Journal* contributor Rosalyn Pierini as "an entertaining concoction" that is perfect for Halloween storytimes, *Meaner than Meanest* introduces a green-faced and ill-tempered witch who lives with Hisss the cat, a creature even meaner than she is. When the witch decides to brew up a creature that is the meanest in the world, her recipe of spiders, frog eyes, snails, and other nasties backfires. Out of the cauldron pops a sweet girl named Daisy, and the witch's evil mood now faces its strongest challenge yet. A *Publishers Weekly* critic called *Meaner than Meanest* a "haunted farce," and in *Kirkus Reviews* a critic had special praise for illustrator Diana Cain Blumenthal's "delightfully crabbed and scratchy artwork."

Somers creates a series of two-panel, sequential tales in his characteristic bold-colored, black-edged, comics-style art in both *Sounds Funny!* and *Sounds Tough!* In *Sounds Funny!* primary-colored illustrations depict the action that results in an object making its characteristic sound, whether it is an accelerating car, a startled dog, or a fragile soap bubble. The author/illustrator turns his attention to boy-friendly objects, such as a train, backhoe, tug boat, truck, and concrete mixer, in *Sounds Tough!,* which a *Kirkus Reviews* writer dubbed "a standout early board book" due to its "Roy Lichtenstein-inspired" art.

Biographical and Critical Sources

PERIODICALS

Kirkus Reviews, August 15, 2001, review of *Meaner than Meanest,* p. 1222; July 1, 2008, review of *Sounds Tough! Big Noisy Machines.*

Publishers Weekly, September 24, 2001, review of *Meaner than Meanest,* p. 42.

School Library Journal, November, 2001, Rosalyn Pierini, review of *Meaner than Meanest,* p. 136.

ONLINE

Kevin Somers Home Page, http://www.somersaultstudio.com (October 15, 2009).

*   *   *

STONE, Phoebe

Personal

Daughter of Walter (a professor and poet) and Ruth (a poet) Stone; married David Carlson (a photographer and designer); children: Ethan. *Education:* Attended Rhode Island School of Design.

Addresses

Home and office—Middlebury, VT. *E-mail*—phoebe@shoreham.net.

Career

Author, artist, and illustrator of children's books. Formerly worked as a fine arts painter; has taught painting at Castleton State College. *Exhibitions:* Work exhibited at Society of Illustrators' Original Art show, New York, NY, 1997, and at DeCordova Museum, Lincoln, MA, and various galleries in New England and New York City.

Awards, Honors

Two Vermont Council on the Fine Arts fellowships; Pick of the Lists selection, American Booksellers Association, 1999, for *Go Away, Shelly Boo!;* Marion Vannett Ridgeway Award finalist, for *In God's Name* by Sandy Eisenberg Sasso.

Writings

SELF-ILLUSTRATED

When the Wind Bears Go Dancing, Little, Brown (Boston, MA), 1997.

Phoebe Stone (Reproduced by permission.)

What Night Do the Angels Wander?, Little, Brown (Boston, MA), 1998.
Go Away, Shelley Boo!, Little, Brown (Boston, MA), 1999.

NOVELS

All the Blue Moons at the Wallace Hotel, Little, Brown (Boston, MA), 2000.
Sonata No. 1 for Riley Red, Little, Brown (Boston, MA), 2003.
Deep Down Popular, Little, Brown (Boston, MA), 2008.

OTHER

(Illustrator) Sandy Eisenberg Sasso, *In God's Name,* Jewish Lights (Woodstock, VT), 1994.

Sidelights

A highly regarded fine arts painter, Phoebe Stone is also the author and illustrator of a number of picture books for young readers, including *When the Wind Bears Go Dancing* and *What Night Do the Angels Wander?* Additionally, she has written the critically acclaimed young-adult novels *Sonata No. 1 for Riley Red* and *Deep Down Popular.* "Stone's books speak to the heart of youth—its frailty, wild ambitions, and promise," observed Liz Rosenberg in the *Boston Globe.* "Literature doesn't get much better than this."

Stone grew up in a creative, nurturing environment. Her father, a professor at Vassar College, wrote fiction and poetry, and her mother was a celebrated poet. "I was the artist in the family, and everything I did they loved," Stone recalled to *Boston Globe* interviewer Heather Stephenson. "My mother was always giving readings, or my father was giving poetry readings. I heard words nonstop, beautiful words, wonderful words from both

of them. I feel like I'm made out of their words somehow." Although her father committed suicide when Stone was eleven years old, her mother continued writing, inspiring young Phoebe to both paint and later, write books. Discussing the legacy of her father's death, Stone told Stephenson: "Of course I'll never be entirely the same person that I might have been. But you repair. The fabric may have a little lumpy, bumpy area where it's a little different as a result of the experience, but it's repaired. And when you look at the whole piece of fabric, it doesn't affect it; it's still beautiful."

Stone loved painting from a very young age, and she got her start in the world of children's books via her talent for drawing. After reviewing one of Stone's art exhibitions, an editor contacted her with a request to create the illustrations for Sandy Eisenberg Sasso's *In God's Name.* Since 1994, Stone has turned to children's books full time. "I was already working in sequences," she noted on her home page, "but at some point I began to realize that I could combine my love for images and words in picture books for children." She both wrote and illustrated *When the Wind Bears Go Dancing,* which was released in 1997. As she told Stephenson in Vermont's *Rutland Herald,* "You can be totally free and creative within the structure. You're still flying like a bird, but you're flying through a chute. You can't fly everywhere, but as long as you're flying, it's art. I want my work to be fine art and illustration at once."

When the Wind Bears Go Dancing tells the story of five, fuzzy bears who love to frolic, creating a wild wind as they go. Populated with other animals, including lions and tigers, the tale is narrated by a little girl who joins in the fun as the animals dance through the stormy sky. "The artwork is bold and colorful," Stephenson noted in the *Rutland Herald.* "The frisky bears romp across the blue and purple pages, dancing the heroine over the rooftops of her neighborhood as goldfish leap through the air and chipmunks read bedtime books down below." Praising the work as a "comforting" way to explain a "stormy night to an anxious child," Denise Furgione noted *School Library Journal* that the harmony between the illustrations and text creates a "delightful" presentation. Ilene Cooper, reviewing in *Booklist,* called *When the Wind Bears Go Dancing* a "warm, comforting" read for nights "when a mighty wind is blowing."

Stone's *What Night Do the Angels Wander?* is an exploratory tale about what angels might do to celebrate Christmas Eve. Once again, the author/illustrator uses simple rhymes and vibrant colors to create a world of celebration, weaving a "general spell" according to a *Kirkus Reviews* critic. Writing in *Booklist,* Cooper called Stone's "word imagery" "lovely," noting that the illustrations retain "the essence of a magical dream."

Go Away, Shelley Boo! is aimed at slightly older readers, and this time Stone delves into a little girl's anxiety as she anticipates the arrival of a new neighbor. Imagin-

ing that the new family's child will be a terror named Shelley Boo, little Emily Louise works herself into a whirl of dreaded expectations as she imagines "Shelley" stealing things, incessantly eating peanut butter, and engaging in various other childhood horrors. There is relief at the end of the book, however, when Emily finally meets her new neighbor, a harmless girl named Elizabeth. A *Kirkus Reviews* critic noted that young readers are sure to "identify" with Emily as she struggles to cope with the upcoming change. Judith Gloyer, writing in *School Library Journal,* was especially appreciative of Stone's artwork, lauding the "colorful pastel paintings" that accompany this "comforting story."

Deep Down Popular concerns the unlikely relationship between sixth-grade tomboy Jessie Lou Ferguson and her much-admired classmate Conrad Parker Smith. Although Jessie has pined for Conrad since the second grade, she finds him to be unapproachable until he injures his leg and is fitted for a brace, which greatly lessens his popularity. Jessie and Conrad, along with Quentin Duster, an unconventional fourth grader, find common ground in their outsider status, and they embark on a mission to help the local hardware store survive against a new, big-box company. Stone's "story explores the many varied and complicated aspects of status and fame," *Kliatt* reviewer Janis Flint-Ferguson remarked, and Cooper saw the work as "an ode to love in many forms."

In her first young-adult novel, *All the Blue Moons at the Wallace Hotel,* Stone writes about eleven-year-old Fiona's struggle to deal with the memory of her murdered father. Following his death, Fiona's artist mother

becomes very withdrawn and neglectful of Fiona, who leans heavily on her younger sister, Wallace, for comfort. Unfortunately, Wallace also runs away, leaving Fiona desolate and lonely. In order to cope with her losses and pain, Fiona turns to dance as a solace, hoping to become a ballerina. Although she cannot afford dance lessons, Fiona practices everyday and is given a chance to dance in a Christmas recital by a dance teacher who witnesses her talent. In prose that was dubbed "poetic" yet realistic by Emily-Greta Tabourin in the *New York Times Book Review,* Stone tells a powerful tale of what Tabourin decribed as "personal loss assuaged through the fulfillment of potential." *Booklist* critic Debbie Carton was also appreciative of Stone's "luminous writing," dubbing *All the Blue Moons at the Wallace Hotel* a "moving, tender story of familial love."

Set in the early 1960s, *Sonata No. 1 for Riley Red* focuses on Rachel Townsend, a Boston-area teen with an eccentric group of friends. When Desmona, a wealthy classmate who believes that everyone is destined to perform one extraordinary act, decides to free an elephant from a decrepit petting zoo, she recruits Rachel and friends Woolsey and Riley for the adventure. After the teens free the creature, they hide out in the woods for a week, during which their exploit creates headlines. "Stone's lively prose style makes this a good read," wrote *School Library Journal* critic Renee Steinberg, the critic adding that, "in spite of its bizarre plot, this story will find many fans." *Booklist* contributor Gillian Engberg noted the author's "ability to create a cast of passionate, artistic, likable characters," and Lynn Evarts wrote in *Voice of Youth Advocates* regarding "Stone's beautiful use of language and her ability to describe the surroundings in a dreamy, rose-colored-glasses tone."

Deep Down Popular concerns the unlikely relationship between sixth-grade tomboy Jessie Lou Ferguson and her much-admired classmate Conrad Parker Smith. Though Jessie has pined for Conrad since the second grade, she finds him to be unapproachable until he injures his leg and is fitted for a brace, which greatly lessens his popularity. Jessie and Conrad, along with Quentin Duster, an unconventional fourth grader, find common ground in their outsider status, and they embark on a mission to help the local hardware store survive against a new, big-box company. "The story explores the many varied and complicated aspects of status and fame," *Kliatt* reviewer Janis Flint-Ferguson remarked, and Cooper saw the work as "an ode to love in many forms." "Sweet and winning," wrote a *Kirkus Reviews* critic.

Biographical and Critical Sources

PERIODICALS

Booklist, January 1, 1998, Ilene Cooper, review of *When the Wind Bears Go Dancing,* p. 825; September 1, 1998, Ilene Cooper, review of *What Night Do the An-*

Stone creates ethnically inspired artwork to pair with Sandy Eisenberg Sasso's text in **In God's Name.** (Illustration copyright © 1994 by Jewish Lights Publishing, www.jewishlights.com. Reproduced by permission.)

gels Wander?, p. 134; December 1, 2000, Debbie Carton, review of *All the Blue Moons at the Wallace Hotel*, p. 713; January 1, 2004, Gillian Engberg, review of *Sonata No. 1 for Riley Red*, p. 862; March 15, 2008, Ilene Cooper, review of *Deep Down Popular*, p. 53.

Boston Globe, November 16, 1997, Heather Stephenson, interview with Stone; December 6, 1998, review of *What Night Do the Angels Wander?*; December 19, 1999, review of *Go Away, Shelley Boo!*; November 19, 2000, Liz Rosenberg, review of *All the Blue Moons at the Wallace Hotel*, p. E3; January 11, 2004, Liz Rosenberg, review of *Sonata No. 1 for Riley Red*.

Children's Book Review Service, November, 1998, review of *What Night Do the Angels Wander?*, p. 29.

Kirkus Reviews, August 15, 1997, review of *When the Wind Bears Go Dancing*, p. 1312; July 15, 1998, review of *What Night Do the Angels Wander?*, p. 1044; July 15, 1999, review of *Go Away, Shelley Boo!*, p. 1140; January, 2008, review of *Deep Down Popular*.

Kliatt, January, 2008, Janis Flint-Ferguson, review of *Deep Down Popular*, p. 12.

New York Times Book Review, February 11, 2001, Emily-Greta Tabourin, review of *All the Blue Moons at the Wallace Hotel*, p. 27.

Philadelphia Inquirer, October 15, 2000, Ann Waldron, review of *All the Blue Moons at the Wallace Hotel*.

Publishers Weekly, October 25, 1999, review of *What Is God's Name?*, p. 74; September 11, 2001, review of *All the Blue Moons at the Wallace Hotel*, p. 91; February 18, 2008, review of *Deep Down Popular*, p. 154.

Rutland (VT) Herald, September 21, 1997, Heather Stephenson, profile of Stone.

School Library Journal, January, 1998, Denise Furgione, review of *When the Wind Bears Go Dancing*, pp. 93-94; November, 1999, Judith Gloyer, review of *Go Away, Shelley Boo!*, p. 131; December, 2000, Carol A. Edwards, review of *All the Blue Moons at the Wallace Hotel*, p. 150; January, 2004, Renee Steinberg, review of *Sonata No. 1 for Riley Red*, p. 136; March, 2008, Lauralyn Persson, review of *Deep Down Popular*, p. 212.

Voice of Youth Advocates, February, 2001, Shari Fesko, review of *All the Blue Moons at the Wallace Hotel*, pp. 426-427; April, 2004, Lynn Evarts, review of *Sonata No. 1 for Riley Red*, p. 52.

ONLINE

Phoebe Stone Home Page, http://www.phoebestone.com (September 1, 2009).

Scholastic Web site, http://www2.scholastic.com/ (September 1, 2009), "Phoebe Stone."*

*   *   *

STRACHAN, Bruce 1959-

Personal

Born 1959.

Addresses

Home—Brooklyn, NY.

Career

Illustrator, painter, sculptor, and photographer.

The mysteries of a fascinating culture are revealed in Bruce Strachan's illustrations for his book **Ancient Egypt.** (Copyright © 2008 by Bruce Strachan. Reprinted by arrangement with Henry Holt & Company, LLC.)

Writings

(Illustrator) Robert Burleigh, *American Moments: Scenes from American History,* Holt (New York, NY), 2004.

(Self-illustrated) *Ancient Egypt: A First Look at People of the Nile,* Holt (New York, NY), 2008.

Sidelights

In addition to creating artwork for the *New York Times Book Review,* Bruce Strachan has also worked as a sculptor, photographer, and painter. In 2004, he added children's-book illustrator to his list of credits, providing the pictures for *American Moments: Scenes from American History,* a work for young readers written by Robert Burleigh. Featuring eighteen page-long accounts of important events in U.S. history, *American Moments* reflects not only on significant firsts, such as Charles Lindbergh's nonstop flight across the Atlantic, but also on notable cultural figures the nation has inspired, such as Georgia O'Keeffe capturing the arid beauty of the Southwest. "Startling 3-D tableaux steal the show in this historical parade," wrote a *Publishers Weekly* critic about Strachan's illustrations featuring characters crafted with clay and set in an intricate diorama. *School Library Journal* contributor Anne Chapman Callaghan similarly called Strachan's figures "real audience grabbers," claiming that "they clarify the text wonderfully."

In Strachan's original self-illustrated book, *Ancient Egypt: A First Look at People of the Nile,* young readers can learn about Egyptian culture during the time of the pharaohs, reading about mummies, pyramids, and royal tombs. To accompany his text, Strachan recreates ancient Egyptian scenes, using his oil-painted clay sculptures to depict a variety of subjects, from ancient statues like the Sphinx to historical figures like Queen Hatshepsut.

Biographical and Critical Sources

PERIODICALS

Booklist, July, 2004, Jennifer Mattson, review of *American Moments: Scenes from American History,* p. 1838.

Kirkus Reviews, May 15, 2004, review of *American Moments,* p. 488; July 15, 2008, review of *Ancient Egypt: A First Look at People of the Nile.*

Publishers Weekly, June 28, 2004, review of *American Moments,* p. 50.

School Library Journal, June, 2004, Anne Chapman Callaghan, review of *American Moments,* p. 124; August, 2008, John Peters, review of *Ancient Egypt,* p. 113.*

T

TAYLOR, Brooke

Personal
Female. *Hobbies and other interests:* Horseback riding, traveling.

Addresses
Home—OK.

Career
Author. Worked variously as a dude-ranch wrangler and for the travel industry.

Awards, Honors
Best Books for Young Adults nomination, and Quick Picks for Reluctant Readers nomination, both American Library Association, both 2009, both for *Undone.*

Writings

Undone, Walker (New York, NY), 2008.

Sidelights
Brooke Taylor wrote her first young-adult novel after working as a wrangler on a dude ranch and traveling internationally. "I started *Undone* intending to write a book about fate and what happens when you start living the life you've always envied," Taylor explained on her home page. "As the characters started opening up and coming to life, *Undone* became much more than just a careful-what-you-wish-for novel. It also became a novel about friendship, family, and the secrets we keep from the people we are closest to. And there's nothing more human (or fascinating!) than the need or desire to lead a secret life."

In *Undone* readers meet the beautiful but mysterious Kori Kitzler, a high-school sophomore who everyone recognizes as the class rebel but few students actually know. For quiet computer gamer Serena Moore, a chance meeting with the enigmatic Kori and an unusual team writing assignment inspires her to question whether it is better to avoid risk or pursue the things you really want out of life. As the two become friends, Serena slowly comes out of her shell and adopts Kori's rebel look. When Kori meets with tragedy, Serena finally discovers the secret that bound the two teens; now she must decide whether to reclaim her former life or fulfill Kori's dreams. In *School Library Journal* Jill Heritage Maza cited Taylor's talent for reproducing the "witty banter" characteristic of an "angst-ridden" teen narrator, and predicted that readers of *Undone* "will empathize with Serena's struggle to figure out who she is." Comparing the novel to works by Rachel Cohn, a *Kirkus Reviews* writer maintained that the inclusion of pop-culture references might date Taylor's story, while a *Publishers Weekly* critic observed that *Undone* "feels all the more familiar for every [plot] twist put in by [its] . . . debut author."

Biographical and Critical Sources

PERIODICALS

Kirkus Reviews, July 15, 2008, review of *Undone.*
Publishers Weekly, July 28, 2008, review of *Undone,* p. 75.
School Library Journal, August, 2008, Jill Maza, review of *Undone,* p. 135.

ONLINE

Brooke Taylor Home Page, http://www.brooketaylorbooks. com (October 15, 2009).
Class of 2K8 Web site, http://www.classof2k8.com/ (October 15, 2009), "Brooke Taylor."*

TEAGUE, Mark 1963-

Personal

Born February 10, 1963, in La Mesa, CA; son of John Wesley (an insurance agent) and Joan Teague; married Laura Quinlan (an insurance claims examiner), June 18, 1988; children: Lily, Ava. *Education:* University of California, Santa Cruz, B.A., 1985. *Politics:* Democrat. *Religion:* Christian. *Hobbies and other interests:* Soccer, running.

Addresses

Home—Coxsackie, NY.

Career

Freelance illustrator and writer, 1989—.

Member

Authors Guild, Authors League of America.

Awards, Honors

Christopher Award, 2003, for *Dear Mrs. LaRue.*

Writings

SELF-ILLUSTRATED

The Trouble with the Johnsons, Scholastic (New York, NY), 1989.
Moog-Moog, Space Barber, Scholastic (New York, NY), 1990.
Frog Medicine, Scholastic (New York, NY), 1991.
The Field beyond the Outfield, Scholastic (New York, NY), 1991.
Pigsty, Scholastic (New York, NY), 1994.
How I Spent My Summer Vacation, Crown (New York, NY), 1995.
The Secret Shortcut, Scholastic (New York, NY), 1996.
Baby Tamer, Scholastic (New York, NY), 1997.
The Lost and Found, Scholastic (New York, NY), 1998.
One Halloween Night, Scholastic (New York, NY), 1999.
Dear Mrs. LaRue: Letters from Obedience School, Scholastic (New York, NY), 2002.
Detective LaRue: Letters from the Investigation, Scholastic (New York, NY), 2004.
LaRue for Mayor: Letters from the Campaign Trail, Scholastic (New York, NY), 2008.
The Doom Machine (novel), Blue Sky Press (New York, NY), 2009.
Funny Farm, Orchard Books (New York, NY), 2009.
Firehouse!, Orchard Books (New York, NY), 2010.

ILLUSTRATOR

What Are Scientists, What Do They Do?, Scholastic (New York, NY), 1991.

Mark Teague (Photograph by Laura Teague. Reproduced by permission.)

Adventures in Lego Land, Scholastic (New York, NY), 1991.
Chris Babcock, *No Moon, No Milk!,* Crown (New York, NY), 1993.
Dick King-Smith, *Three Terrible Trins,* Crown (New York, NY), 1994.
Tony Johnston, *The Iguana Brothers, A Perfect Day,* Blue Sky Press (New York, NY), 1995.
Audrey Wood, *The Flying Dragon Room,* Blue Sky Press (New York, NY), 1996.
Dick King-Smith, *Mr. Potter's Pet,* Hyperion (New York, NY), 1996.
Cynthia Rylant, *Poppleton,* Blue Sky Press (New York, NY), 1997.
Cynthia Rylant, *Poppleton and Friends: Book Two,* Blue Sky Press (New York, NY), 1997.
Cynthia Rylant, *Poppleton Forever,* Blue Sky Press (New York, NY), 1998.
Audrey Wood, *Sweet Dream Pie,* Blue Sky Press (New York, NY), 1998.
Cynthia Rylant, *Poppleton Everyday,* Blue Sky Press (New York, NY), 1998.
Cynthia Rylant, *Poppleton in Fall,* Blue Sky Press (New York, NY), 1999.
Cynthia Rylant, *Poppleton in Spring,* Blue Sky Press (New York, NY), 1999.
Cynthia Rylant, *Poppleton Has Fun,* Blue Sky Press (New York, NY), 2000.
Cynthia Rylant, *Poppleton in Winter,* Blue Sky Press (New York, NY), 2001.
Cynthia Rylant, *The Great Gracie Chace,* Blue Sky Press (New York, NY), 2001.

Shana Corey, *First Graders from Mars: Episode One, Horus's Horrible Day,* Scholastic (New York, NY), 2001.

Shana Corey, *First Graders from Mars: Episode Two, The Problem with Pelly,* Scholastic (New York, NY), 2002.

Shana Corey, *First Graders from Mars: Episode Three, Nergal and the Great Space Race,* Scholastic (New York, NY), 2002.

Shana Corey, *First Graders from Mars: Episode Four, Tera, Star Student,* Scholastic (New York, NY), 2003.

Anne Isaacs, *Pancakes for Supper!,* Scholastic (New York, NY), 2006.

ILLUSTRATOR; "HOW DO DINOSAURS . . . ?" SERIES

Jane Yolen, *How Do Dinosaurs Say Goodnight?,* Blue Sky Press (New York, NY), 2000.

Jane Yolen, *How Do Dinosaurs Get Well Soon?,* Blue Sky Press (New York, NY), 2003.

Jane Yolen, *How Do Dinosaurs Clean Their Rooms?,* Blue Sky Press (New York, NY), 2004.

Jane Yolen, *How Do Dinosaurs Count to Ten?,* Blue Sky Press (New York, NY), 2004.

Jane Yolen, *How Do Dinosaurs Eat Their Food?,* Blue Sky Press (New York, NY), 2005.

Jane Yolen, *How Do Dinosaurs Learn Their Colors?,* Blue Sky Press (New York, NY), 2006.

Jane Yolen, *How Do Dinosaurs Play with Their Friends?,* Blue Sky Press (New York, NY), 2006.

Jane Yolen, *How Do Dinosaurs Go to School?,* Blue Sky Press (New York, NY), 2007.

Jane Yolen, *How Do Dinosaurs Say I Love You?,* Blue Sky Press (New York, NY), 2009.

Adaptations

The "How Do Dinosaurs . . . ?" series was adapted for audiobook and also released in boxed sets of board-book editions.

Sidelights

Author and illustrator Mark Teague has a quirky sense of humor, and the extent of his quirkiness can easily be discovered by reading any of his books for children. Peopled with characters with names like Elmo Freem, Wendell Fultz, Wallace Bleff, and Jack Creedle, Teague's books poke fun at things that kids dread—homework, cleaning one's room, ritual first-day-of-school haircuts, and the like—while his illustrations bring to life his quasi-realistic settings. Comparing the nostalgic quality of Teague's acrylic paintings to those of author/illustrator William Joyce, a *Publishers Weekly* contributor added that Teague's "combination of dead-pan text and unbridled art is a sure-fire recipe for a crowd-pleaser."

"I managed to graduate from college without having any idea what I was going to do with my life," Teague once admitted to *SATA*. "My degree was in U.S. history but I wasn't interested in teaching. I enjoyed art but had no formal training. I liked to write but was unsure how

to make it pay." The solution? Pack up the auto and head East to New York City. By the spring of 1986 Teague had arrived and was living with his brother, who helped the author-to-be get a job in the display department at the giant Barnes & Noble bookstore in Rockefeller Center. "The job provided a sort of crash course in design and graphic arts techniques," Teague explained, "and exposed me to a lot of new books. Looking at children's books in the store reminded me of how much I had enjoyed picture books as a child and how much fun it had been to write and illustrate my own stories at that age."

Remembering the fun of being an author sparked *The Trouble with the Johnsons,* Teague's first picture book for children. Published in 1989, the book tells the story of Elmo Freem, who longs to return to the country after his family moves to the big city. Together with his equally homesick cat, Elmo returns to the old house for a visit, where he meets the new owners, the Johnsons. While they seem nice enough, the Johnsons are a bit odd (for one thing, they are a family of dinosaurs). Ultimately, Elmo goes back to the city with the knowledge that home is really where your family is. "The book came out of my experience living in Brooklyn," Teague recalled to *SATA*. "The theme was somewhat melancholy, but I tried to offset this with humor and a plot which was energetic and bizarre." A *Publishers Weekly* commentator stated that "Teague's unique perspective is utilized magnificently both in words and pictures to produce a noteworthy first book." The same

Teague treats readers to a madcap story in his self-illustrated picture book **Pigsty!** (Copyright © 1994 by Mark Teague. Reproduced by permission of Scholastic, Inc.)

year as *The Trouble with the Johnsons* was accepted by its eventual publisher, Scholastic, Teague was able to escape the city, moving with his wife to upstate New York where he continues to make his home.

Elmo reemerges in Teague's next book, *Moog-Moog, Space Barber.* Taking as its premise "the apparently universal horror inspired by a bad haircut," according to Teague, *Moog-Moog, Space Barber* is much more a fantasy than *The Trouble with the Johnsons,* incorporating elements of science fiction as well. The amazingly calm Elmo awakes one morning to find several rotund space aliens—suitably green in color—hanging around the refrigerator in his kitchen. What has Elmo more concerned than close encounters of the alien kind is the razzing he expects to take from fellow schoolmates as a result of his perfectly horrid back-to-school haircut. Fortunately, the aliens are the ones to turn to when looking for a competent stylist; they fly Elmo off to Moog-Moog, barber to the extraterrestrials, and the boy's problems are solved. Stephanie Zvirin praised the book as "sure-footed silliness, sometimes amusingly sly, with just the right touch of irony," in her *Booklist* review.

Fans of Elmo get another glimpse of the boy's off-kilter world in *Frog Medicine,* which involves "that dreaded subject: homework," as well as giant frogs, and things of that sort," according to its author. Unfortunately for Elmo, fear of an impending book report causes him to sprout frog feet, and only a consultation with noted frog medicine practitioner Dr. Frank Galoof gives him hope of de-amphibianizing anytime soon. Once more, Teague reveals his "knack for dealing with the kinds of predicaments that loom large on children's horizons in a fresh and funny way," according to a *Publishers Weekly* contributor. *Frog Medicine* was also praised for containing acrylic illustrations with an attention to detail that reflects the hero's gradual transformation. "Every scene is bathed in curiously pure light," noted a *Kirkus Reviews* critic, "with plenty of clever, funny details to discover."

Equally bizarre is the world inhabited by one Wendell Fultz, who, in *Pigsty,* is not surprised to find a large hog dozing on his bed. In fact, the abominable condition of Wendell's room makes the pig the cleanest thing in it, but instead of cleaning up the mess like his mother requested, the sly Wendell just pushes a few things out of sight and settles in to play with his new porcine companion. Problems arise, however, after the rest of the curly tailed gang shows up, and their antics cause a commotion. Finally, Wendell himself is forced to lay down the law; the pigs grudgingly help clean up the room and then leave for messier parts. "Especially evident in [Teague's] artwork, there's enough fun to carry the story," maintained *Booklist* reviewer Ilene Cooper, while a *Publishers Weekly* critic lauded the author/illustrator's "gleefuly inventive imagination" and stated that "much of the tale's fun resides in [his] quirky acrylic art."

A dog decides to make a leap into local politics with humorous results in Teague's picture book **LaRue for Mayor.** (Illustration copyright © 2008 by Mark Teague. Reproduced by permission of Scholastic, Inc.)

More recent books by Teague continue to defy traditional classification. In *The Field beyond the Outfield,* a story about summer baseball camp becomes a full-scale fantasy involving a major-league playoff between teams of giant insects. Commenting on the story, *School Library Journal* critic Dorothy Houlihan wrote that "Teague's window to childhood is wide open, allowing him to address the realities of youthful fantasies without trivializing them." Readers opening the innocent-sounding *How I Spent My Summer Vacation* are drawn into the classroom of one Wallace Bleff and then immediately carried away to the Wild West, amid cowpokes, lariats, and stampeding cattle. Teague's story was described as "one rootin' tootin' tall tale" by a *Publishers Weekly* reviewer, the critic pointing out "some laugh-out-loud funny expressions on animal faces." *Baby Tamer,* Teague's 1997 contribution to the annals of quirky children's literature, depicts a face-off between incredibly competent, fully certified baby-sitter Amanda Smeedy and the Egmont children. When making a lot of noise does not cause even a raised eyebrow from the stoic Amanda, the twins grow desperate, finally resorting to producing a full-blown circus complete with fireworks before admitting defeat. Teague's "bright, sassy acrylics career across the pages at near-warp speed," according to a *Publishers Weekly* critic.

The mix of reality and fantasy that characterize the Halloween holiday provide the setting for *One Halloween Night*. Once again starring Wendell (from *Pigsty*) and his friends, *One Halloween Night* is the story of a perfectly awful Halloween: Wendell's "mad scientist" costume has turned pink in the wash, good candy is replaced by vegetable flavored candy, and school bully Leona Fleebish is determined to make the night even worse. Luckily for Wendell and company, their costumes give them special powers to deal with the night's problems. "Teague's illustrations are, as always, imaginative, quirky, and exuberant," wrote *Booklist* critic Susan Dove Lempke. Wendell and his friend Floyd also star in *The Lost and Found,* in which the two dive into the lost-and-found box at school only to get sucked into a realm of lost hats and missing items. "Teague's latest sly take on the wild flights of childhood fancy is as entertaining as always, and he doles out his deadpan artistic style with a wink," according to a reviewer for *Publishers Weekly*. As *Booklist* critic Stephanie Zvirin noted, "children will . . . love the crazy notion at the heart of the story."

Teague introduces his readers to Ike, a dog attending obedience school who is incredibly homesick for his owner, Mrs. LaRue, in *Dear Mrs. LaRue: Letters from Obedience School*. To hear Ike tell the tale, obedience training is worse than boot camp; Teague's clever illustrations show Ike's version of the tale in black and white, while in full color, the true story is revealed. The pup's reality is actually is not all that bad: Ike is actually being treated to a spa-style environment. The pup is not one to stay put, however, and he makes a break for freedom just in time to save Mrs. LaRue from danger. A *Publishers Weekly* critic dubbed *Dear Mrs. LaRue* "a tail-wagger of a book that will have readers howling with amusement." Roxanne Burg, writing in *School Library Journal,* considered Teague's "humorous acrylic illustrations" to be "a howl," while Cooper wrote that "the wonderfully arch text is matched with Teague's sly pictures." Sue Grossman, writing in *Childhood Education,* predicted that "children will have fun comparing Ike's story to what is really going on."

Ike's return in *Detective LaRue: Letters from the Investigation* finds him once again writing from prison—this time literally. Accused of kidnapping the neighbor's cats, Ike decides to clear his good name. As before, the dog's description of what is actually transpiring does not match actual events. Another outing, transcribed in *LaRue for Mayor: Letters from the Campaign Trail,* finds the clever pup chronicling his run for mayor in order to counter the anti-dog campaign of a local police chief. "Lively acrylics paired with comical correspondence result in a picture book that will have fans howling," wrote a reviewer in appraising *Detective LaRue* for *Publishers Weekly,* and a *Kirkus Reviews* contributor acknowledged that "Teague's innovative approach to storytelling is fun, but educational as well." Although Ike's colorful account of campaign hijinks and dirty tricks does not precisely coincide with Teague's black-and-white drawings of reality in *LaRue for Mayor,* "Kids will get a kick out of LaRue's unrepentant mischief," according to *Publishers Weekly* critic Krista Hutley.

In Teague's middle-grade novel *The Doom Machine* the illustrator treats readers to what a *Publishers Weekly* critic described as "a madcap . . . tale chockfull of malevolent aliens and superscience" and featuring a generous helping of "silliness." A member of a shiftless family, Jack Creedle lives with his Uncle Bud, a crazy inventor, and works as an auto mechanic. When a ship full of space aliens arrives in their quiet town, Jack, Bud, and a few other unsuspecting citizens are abducted and taken to the planet Skreepia. When it turns out that the Skreepian queen plans to use Bud's latest invention—the Dimensional Field Stabilizer—to conquer Earth, Jack and his captive neighbors must find a way to thwart her. Noting the novel's pulp-fiction feel and nostalgic 1950s setting, a *Kirkus Reviews* writer added that *The Doom Machine* showcases its author's "feeling for oddball characters and twists." Eric Norton also praised the novel in *School Library Journal,* writing of *The Doom Machine* that "Teague's signature artwork livens up an already gripping story" featuring "engaging characters and a good deal of humor."

Other original books by Teague include *Funny Farm* and *Firehouse!,* In *Funny Farm* a citified pup named Edward visits his rural relatives and learns several useful skills, such as tapping maple trees for syrup and tending sheep. In typical Teague fashion, "the narrative nature of the crisp oil illustrations reveals a much more entertaining version of the story than does the straightforward text," explained a *Publishers Weekly* contributor, while in *Booklist* Daniel Kraus called *Funny Farm* "weird, satirical, and surreal." "There is a confidence to Teague's artwork that will win over almost any reader," Kraus concluded.

In addition to creating original self-illustrated stories, Teague also creates artwork for text by other authors, such as Dick King-Smith, Audrey Wood, Anne Isaacs, and Cynthia Rylant. A *Publishers Weekly* contributor, appraising Wood's *The Flying Dragon Room,* asserted that the plot "gets a vital boost from Teague's buoyant whimsical art," while in *Booklist* Cooper noted of his work for Chris Babcock's *No Moon, No Milk!* that the illustrator's "ebullient artwork captures a very determined cow in . . . with humor and panache." Audrey Wood's "funny and clever" picture book *Sweet Dream* is "taken a notch further by Teague's illustrations," wrote Elizabeth Drennan in *Booklist,* and in *School Library Journal* Kathy Krasniewicz called his illustrations for Isaacs' *Pancakes for Supper* "brilliant" and featuring characters whose "faces . . . are overtly expressive and their stances just ooze attitude."

Working with author Shana Corey on the "First Graders from Mars" series, Teague has created a Martian vision of elementary school. The children are brilliantly col-

ored and have long tentacles; a *Publishers Weekly* critic called the setting a "Seussian landscape" in a review of the first title in the series, *First Graders from Mars: Episode One, Horus's Horrible Day.* Carol Schene, reviewing the same title, commented: "The nonhuman students are done in assorted colors from green to purple, and the teacher, Ms. Vortex, is really a standout with eyes . . . in the back of her head." Shelle Rosenfeld, writing about *First Graders from Mars: Episode Two, The Problem with Pelly* in *Booklist,* noted that Teague's "Martian setting clearly and humorously shows that normality is relative."

Teague has also teamed up with award-winning author Jane Yolen on the "How Do Dinosaurs . . . ?" picturebook series, which is intended to encourage good manners to readers through the humorous behaviors of dinosaur children. While the dinosaurs are depicted as having human parents, they are "specifically identified with cunningly placed labels within each double-paged spread," as well as at the end of the book, according to a critic for *Kirkus Reviews* in a review of *How Do Dinosaurs Get Well Soon?* Cooper observed of the same book that "Teague, always tops when it comes to mining humor in art, does a great job here." Reviewing *How Do Dinosaurs Go to School?, Horn Book* critic Martha V. Parravano wrote that the book's brightly colored acrylic paintings "play up . . . the dinos and the outrageousness of their behavior in exaggerated tableaux that put humor first."

As a father, Teague often gets inspiration from his two children. "My daughters keep it fresh for me. They provide all kinds of inspiration," he told an interviewer for the *Reading Is Fundamental Web site.* "They're very funny and we have a good time. I read to my daughters all the time," In the same interview, Teague gave his advice for young writers and illustrators: "Practice is everything. You should read a lot. I think that both writing and illustrating come from a love of books. That was the first thing for me. For as long as I remember, I just loved books."

Biographical and Critical Sources

PERIODICALS

Booklist, November 1, 1990, Stephanie Zvirin, review of *Moog-Moog, Space Barber,* p. 531; September 1, 1993, Ilene Cooper, review of *No Moon, No Milk!,* pp. 66-67; September 15, 1994, Ilene Cooper, review of *Pigsty,* p. 145; February 15, 1998, Elizabeth Drennan, review of *Sweet Dream,* p. 1021; July, 1998, Stephanie Zvirin, review of *The Lost and Found,* p. 1890; September 1, 1999, Susan Dove Lempke, review of *One Halloween Night,* p. 151; February 15, 2002, Shelle Rosenfeld, review of *First Graders from Mars: Episode Two, The Problem with Pelly,* p. 1019; November 1, 2002, Ilene Cooper, review of *Dear Mrs.*

LaRue: Letters from Obedience School, p. 494; January 1, 2003, Ilene Cooper, review of *How Do Dinosaurs Get Well Soon?,* p. 881; January 1, 2003, review of *Dear Mrs. LaRue,* p. 799; October 15, 2004, Jennifer Mattson, review of *Detective LaRue: Letters from the Investigation,* p. 411; July, 2005, Jennifer Mattson, review of *How Do Dinosaurs Eat Their Food?,* p. 1931; October 15, 2006, Gillian Engberg, review of *Pancakes for Supper!,* p. 46; April 1, 2007, Randall Enos, review of *How Do Dinosaurs Go to School?,* p. 61; December 15, 2007, Krista Hutley, review of *LaRue for Mayor: Letters from the Campaign Trail,* p. 50; November 15, 2008, Daniel Kraus, review of *Funny Farm,* p. 50.

Bulletin of the Center for Children's Books, April, 2008, Elizabeth Bush, review of *LaRue for Mayor,* p. 356.

Childhood Education, winter, 2001, Sue Grossman, review of *The Great Gracie Chase,* p. 112; spring, 2003, Sue Grossman, review of *Dear Mrs. LaRue,* p. 180.

Horn Book, March-April, 2003, Christine M. Hepperman, review of *How Do Dinosaurs Get Well Soon?,* p. 208; November-December, 2006, Barbara Bader, review of *Pancakes for Breakfast!,* p. 699; July-August, 2007, Martha V. Parravano, review of *How Do Dinosaurs Go to School?,* p. 388.

Instructor, August, 2001, Judy Freeman, review of *First Graders from Mars: Episode One, Horus's Horrible Day,* p. 22.

Kirkus Reviews, August 15, 1991, review of *Frog Medicine,* pp. 1094-1095; December 1, 2001, review of *First Graders from Mars: Episode Two,* p. 1683; August 1, 2002, review of *Dear Mrs. LaRue,* p. 1145; December 1, 2002, review of *How Do Dinosaurs Get Well Soon?,* p. 1776; August 15, 2004, review of *Detective LaRue: Letters from the Investigation,* p. 814; June 15, 2007, review of *How Do Dinosaurs Go to School?;* January 1, 2008, review of *LaRue for Mayor;* September 1, 2008, review of *The Doom Machine.*

Publishers Weekly, September 8, 1989, review of *The Trouble with the Johnsons,* p. 69; October 4, 1991, review of *Frog Medicine,* p. 88; July 11, 1994, review of *Pigsty,* p. 78; July 10, 1995, review of *How I Spent My Summer Vacation,* p. 56; January 22, 1996, review of *The Flying Dragon Room,* p. 73; August 26, 1996, review of *The Secret Shortcut,* p. 98; August 11, 1997, review of *Baby Tamer,* p. 401; July, 1998, Stephanie Zvirin, review of *The Lost and Found,* p. 1890; September 27, 1999, reviews of *One Halloween Night,* p. 47, and *The Secret Shortcut,* p. 107; July 16, 2001, review of *First Graders from Mars: Episode 1, Horus's Horrible Day,* p. 180; July 22, 2002, review of *Dear Mrs. LaRue,* p. 177; September 15, 2002, Jason Britton, "In the Studio with Mark Teague," pp. 23-24; July 19, 2004, review of *Detective LaRue,* p. 160; July 25, 2005, review of *How Do Dinosaurs Eat Their Food?,* p. 74; September 4, 2006, review of *Pancakes for Supper!,* p. 65; February 4, 2008, review of *LaRue for Mayor,* p. 56; March 2, 2009, review of *Funny Farm,* p. 61; October 5, 2009, review of *The Doom Machine,* p. 49.

School Library Journal, June, 1992, Dorothy Houlihan, review of *The Field beyond the Outfield,* pp. 103-104;

April, 2001, Beth Tegart, review of *The Great Gracie Chase,* p. 121; September, 2001, Carol Schene, review of *First Graders from Mars: Episode One,* p. 185; October, 2001, Patricia Manning, review of *Poppleton in Winter,* p. 130; April, 2002, Dona Ratterree, review of *First Graders from Mars: Episode Two,* p. 102; September, 2002, Roxanne Burg, review of *Dear Mrs. LaRue,* p. 207; February, 2003, Jody McCoy, review of *How Do Dinosaurs Get Well Soon?,* p. 126; October, 2004, Steven Engelfried, review of *Detective LaRue,* p. 135; August, 2005, Roxanne Burg, review of *How Do Dinosaurs Eat Their Food?,* p. 110; October, 2006, Kathy Krasniewicz, review of *Pancakes for Breakfast!,* p. 113; June, 2007, Neala Arnold, review of *How Do Dinosaurs Go to School?,* p. 128; March, 2008, Lee Bock, review of *LaRue for Mayor,* p. 178; April, 2009, Lee Bock, review of *Funny Farm,* p. 117; October, 2009, Eric Norton, review of *The Doom Machine,* p. 138.

Tribune Books (Chicago, IL), December 15, 2002, review of *Dear Mrs. LaRue,* p. 5.

ONLINE

Children's Book Council Magazine Online, http://cbcbooks.org/cbcmagazine/ (April 25, 2006), "Mark Teague."

Houghton Mifflin Education Place Web site, http://www.eduplace.com/kids/ (October 15, 2009), "Mark Teague."

Reading Is Fundamental Web site, http://www.rif.org/ (April 25, 2006), interview with Teague.

Scholastic Web site, http://www.scholastic.com/ (October 15, 2009), "Mark Teague."*

*   *   *

TERRY, Will 1966-

Personal

Born 1966; married; children. *Education:* Brigham Young University, degree (illustration). *Hobbies and other interests:* Snowboarding.

Addresses

Home—UT. *E-mail*—will@willterry.com.

Career

Illustrator, beginning 1992. Utah Valley State College, part-time instructor in illustration; speaker at schools.

Member

Society of Illustrators.

Awards, Honors

North Carolina Children's Book Award, for *Armadilly Chili* by Helen Ketteman; California Teacher's Association Illustrator, 2009-11.

Illustrator

Pat Bagley, *Mana, the No-Cow Wife,* Deseret Book (Salt Lake City, UT), 1993.

Rita Golden Gelman, *Pizza Pat,* Random House (New York, NY), 1999.

Marcia K. Vaughan, *The Treasure of Ghostwood Gully: A Southwest Mystery,* Rising Moon (Flagstaff, AZ), 2004.

Helen Ketteman, *Armadilly Chili,* Albert Whitman (Morton Grove, IL), 2004.

Eugene H. Peterson, *The Christmas Troll,* NavPress (Colorado Springs, CO), 2004.

Joan Holub, *More Snacks!: A Thanksgiving Play,* Aladdin Paperbacks (New York, NY), 2006.

Joan Holub, *Good Luck!: A St. Patrick's Day Story,* Aladdin Paperbacks (New York, NY), 2007.

Joan Holub, *Scaredy Pants!: A Halloween Story,* Aladdin Paperbacks (New York, NY), 2007.

Joan Holub, *Big Heart!: A Valentine's Day Story,* Aladdin (New York, NY), 2007.

Margaret Read MacDonald, *Little Rooster's Diamond Button,* Albert Whitman (Morton Grove, IL), 2007.

Teresa Bateman, *The Frog with the Big Mouth,* Albert Whitman (Morton Grove, IL), 2008.

Joan Holub, *Snow Day!: A Winter Tale,* Aladdin (New York, NY), 2008.

Joan Holub, *Picnic!: A Day in the Park,* Aladdin (New York, NY), 2008.

Joan Holub, *Spring Is Here!: A Story about Seeds,* Aladdin (New York, NY), 2008.

Shana Corey, *Monster Parade,* Random House (New York, NY), 2009.

Helen Ketteman, *The Three Little Gators,* Albert Whitman (Morton Grove, IL), 2009.

Contributor to periodicals, including *Time, Money, Wall Street Journal, Mac World, Seventeen, Arizona Highways,* and *Better Homes & Gardens.*

Sidelights

Will Terry considers himself fortunate in his career: he is able to create art and he gets to work with children. A freelance illustrator since graduating from college in the early 1990s, Terry earned his first picture-book contract almost immediately. In addition to creating artwork for a beginning-reader series by Joan Holub, his brightly colored, digital images can also be found in the pages of Helen Kettleman's *Armadilly Chili* and *The Three Little Gators,* Margaret Read MacDonald's *Little Rooster's Diamond Button,* and Teresa Bateman's *The Frog with the Big Mouth,* among other humorous picture books.

In *Armadilly Chili* Kettelman tells a Texas-styled version of "The Little Red Hen" that finds an armadillo asking several animal friends for some help in cooking up some of her special chili. Describing Terry's art for the book, a *Kirkus Reviews* critic praised the "swirls and curls of rich color" in the story's "big Southwestern scenes," and in *Booklist* Julie Cummins wrote that the artist "embellishes each [animal character] . . . with

Will Terry's stylized paintings bring to life Rita Golden Gelman's humorous story in **Pizza Pat.** (Illustration copyright © 1999 by Will Terry. Reproduced by permission of Random House Children's Books, a division of Random House, Inc.)

clever details." "Terry's vibrant cartoon artwork adds personality" to Kettelman's larger-than-life characters, according to Mary Elam in *School Library Journal.*

Terry's "eye-popping, comic illustrations" transform a "fresh version of an old folktale into a rollicking romp," wrote *Booklist* critic Connie Fletcher in her review of MacDonald's *Little Rooster's Diamond Button.* Based on a Hungarian folk tale, the book follows Little Rooster as he is robbed of a shiny diamond by a greedy king. The rooster avoids death by performing a series of amazing feats on the way to regaining his property, and his story is "given extra zest" in Terry's acrylic paintings, according to Fletcher. In *Kirkus Reviews* a contributor cited Terry's "energetic" artwork, while in *School Library Journal* Donna Cardon wrote that "rich, contrasting colors and exaggerated facial features . . . make the characters and scenes energetically funny." The artist's "googly-eyed characters look at home amid silly hysteria," wrote a *Publishers Weekly* critic, and "capture a world where anything is possible."

"I was one of those kids who didn't do very well in school," Terry noted on his home page. "It was hard for me to learn to read and stay focused during lessons. Staying on task was a struggle. I had a great attention span for day dreaming and most of my teachers thought I was lazy. My parents had me tested and found out that, indeed, I scored below average in reading compre-

hension. . . . Instead of labeling me and crushing my creativity, my parents got behind my aspirations and provided encouragement. I wouldn't be an illustrator without their love and support. I love to share this experience with children so that they realize they're not alone and that there's hope even if it seems bleak at the moment."

Biographical and Critical Sources

PERIODICALS

Booklist, June 1, 2004, Julie Cummins, review of *Armadilly Chili,* p. 1742; February 15, 2007, Connie Fletcher, review of *Little Rooster's Diamond Button,* p. 81.
Kirkus Reviews, February 15, 2004, review of *Armadilly Chili,* p. 180; January 15, 2007, review of *Little Rooster's Diamond Button,* p. 76; August 1, 2008, review of *The Frog with the Big Mouth,* p. 100.
Publishers Weekly, February 12, 2007, review of *Little Rooster's Diamond Button,* p. 85.
School Library Journal, May, 2004, Mary Elam, review of *Armadilly Chili,* p. 133; March, 2007, Donna Cardon, review of *Little Rooster's Diamond Button,* p. 198; September, 2008, Gay Lynn Van Vleck, review of *The Frog with the Big Mouth,* p. 137.

ONLINE

Will Terry Home Page, http://www.willterry.com (October 15, 2009).*

*   *   *

THOMSON, Melissa 1979-

Personal

Born 1979, in Charlotte, NC; daughter of Mark and Linda de Castrique; married Pete Thomson. *Education:* Davidson College, degree. *Hobbies and other interests:* Playing Scrabble.

Addresses

Home—New York, NY. *E-mail*—melissa@wjpthomson. com.

Career

Educator and author. Emery Elementary, Washington, DC, elementary teacher; teacher in New York NY.

Member

Society of Children's Book Writers and Illustrators.

Writings

Keena Ford and the Second-Grade Mix-up, illustrated by Frank Morrison, Dial Books (New York, NY), 2008.

Keena Ford and the Field Trip Mix-up, illustrated by Frank Morrison, Dial Books (New York, NY), 2009.

Sidelights

In addition to teaching elementary-grade students, Melissa Thomson established a second career as a children's author with her books *Keena Ford and the Second-Grade Mix-up* and *Keena Ford and the Field Trip Mix-up.* Based on her experiences teaching her second-graders in Washington, DC, Thomson's beginning chapter books introduce readers to a likeable seven year old whose class-time chronicles are brought to life in illustrations by Frank Morrison.

In *Keena Ford and the Second-Grade Mix-up* Keena is looking forward to starting second grade, but she worries when she learns that she will not be in the same class as her best friend, Eric. Despite the occasional mistake, misunderstanding, and misstep, the energetic Keena enjoys her new school experience. "Her escapades and the way she handles them ring with . . . emotional honesty," according to a *Kirkus Reviews*

Melissa Thomson attracts an elementary-grade readership with her series of books that includes **Keena Ford and the Second-Grade Mix-up,** *featuring artwork by Frank Morrison.* (Illustration © 2008 by Frank Morrison. Reproduced by permission of Dial Books for Young Readers, a division of Penguin Putnam Books for Young Readers.)

writer. A class trip to the U.S. Capitol is the backdrop for *Keena Ford and the Field Trip Mix-up,* in which the African-American girl describes an accident with scissors that resulted in the loss of one of her braids, as well as a scuffle with a U.S. congressman. In *School Library Journal* Debbie S. Hoskins praised *Keena Ford and the Field Trip Mix-up* as part of "a solid series" and cited the "distinctive illustrations" Morrison contributes to Keena's "entertaining" second chapter-book outing.

Biographical and Critical Sources

PERIODICALS

Kirkus Reviews, June 15, 2008, review of *Keena Ford and the Second-Grade Mix-up,* July 15, 2009, review of *Keena Ford and the Field Trip Mix-up.*
School Library Journal, October, 2008, Sharon R. Pearse, review of *Keena Ford and the Second-Grade Mix-Up,* p. 126; July, 2009, Debbie S. Hoskins, review of *Keena Ford and the Field Trip Mix-up,* p. 68.

ONLINE

Melissa Thomson Home Page, http://melissathomson.com (October 15, 2009).*

*　　*　　*

TUDOR, Tasha 1915-2008
(Starling Burgess)

OBITUARY NOTICE—

See index for *SATA* sketch: Born August 28, 1915, in Boston, MA; died June 18, 2008, in Marlboro, VT. Businesswoman, illustrator, and children's author. Tudor wrote and illustrated nearly fifty books between 1938 and 2003 and illustrated a similar number of works by other authors. Her delicate watercolor paintings and pencil drawings drew millions of children into enchanted lands where animals talked, dolls married, and modern-day living was not even on the horizon. It was a happy and secure world for children, a world of family, friendship, and small pleasures. Tudor was nominated for the prestigious Caldecott Medal for artists twice in her career: in 1945 for her illustrations in *Mother Goose* and in 1957 for her original counting book *1 Is One.* Nonetheless, she claimed that her books were part of a commercial, rather than an artistic, venture: she needed to earn a living. Her first self-illustrated book, *Pumpkin Moonshine,* languished for several years before it was published in 1938. Tudor spent the next few years primarily illustrating books for other authors, but she managed to publish an original title every year

or two. She created children's stories, holiday tales, and verse collections, all illustrated in her trademark Victorian style. In 1971 Tudor published *Corgiville Fair,* a book inspired by her love for the short-legged corgi dogs that she had welcomed into her life until there were more than a dozen of them on her New Hampshire farm. The book reportedly became her favorite, and Tudor published several sequels, including *Corgiville Christmas,* which appeared in 2003, when the author was nearly ninety years old. Tudor's books have remained in print for decades. Many were reprinted by the Jenny Wren Press, which she founded with a friend in 1989. Tudor's books have sometimes been described as akin to whimsical fantasies, but many of her stories were based on actual events from her life.

Tudor's life itself was in many ways a fantasy. A conventional childhood in Boston, where she was originally known as Starling Burgess, gave way to a more rustic adolescence in rural Connecticut, during which time she adopted her nickname "Tasha" and her mother's maiden name "Tudor" as her legal name. Tudor's love for nature and simplicity blossomed there, and she spent most of her adult years in idyllic, peaceful surroundings. If her drawings evoked nostalgia for the nineteenth century, her lifestyle personified it. Tudor wore period clothing, raised or grew her own food, spun cloth from flax, and sewed or knitted her own clothing for many years without benefit of electricity or running water. Her favorite time period began in 1830, when daily living was harder and simpler at the same time. She sometimes claimed to be the reincarnation of a sea captain's wife who had lived in the 1800s and she expressed the hope that she could return there when her life in the modern world was complete. Tudor left a substantial legacy to the future, in addition to nearly one hundred books full of her wistful illustrations. Her artwork and craft projects are part of a home-based family business begun by Tudor and perpetuated by her children and descendants. Tudor-decorated folk objects, from greeting cards to art prints, clothing, dolls, and home furnishings, seem likely to be available for many years to come.

OBITUARIES AND OTHER SOURCES:

BOOKS

Brown, Richard, *The Private World of Tasha Tudor,* Little, Brown (Boston, MA), 1992.

Davis, Harry, *The Art of Tasha Tudor,* Little, Brown (Boston, MA), 2000.

Hare, William John, and Priscilla T. Hare, *Tasha Tudor: The Direction of Her Dreams; The Bibliography and Collector's Guide,* Oak Knoll Press (New Castle, DE), 1999.

Tudor, Bethany, *Drawn from New England: Tasha Tudor,* Collins (New York, NY), 1979.

PERIODICALS

Chicago Tribune, June 20, 2008, sec. 2, p. 9.
Los Angeles Times, June 20, 2008, p. B6.
New York Times, June 20, 2008, p. C10.

W

WALES, Dirk 1931-

Personal
Born 1931.

Addresses
Home and office—Chicago, IL. *E-mail*—dirk@rainbow place.com.

Career
Writer, animator, and photographer. Collaborator, with Diane Kenna, on short animated films. *Exhibitions:* Work exhibited in galleries in Chicago, IL, and Santa Fe, NM; and in shows staged in Stockholm, Sweden, Austin, TX, Georgetown, DC, Taipei, Taiwan, El Paso, TX, Chicago, and Santa Fe. Photography included in private and corporate collections.

Awards, Honors
(With Diane Kenna) Numerous awards from film festivals for animated films based on *Ben's Dream* by Chris Van Allsburg and *New Friends* by James Stevenson.

Writings

FOR CHILDREN

A Lucky Dog: Owney, U.S. Rail Mail Mascot, illustrated by Diane Kenna, Great Plains Press (Chicago, IL), 2003.

Penny House, illustrated by Diane Kenna, Great Plains Press (Chicago, IL), 2005.

Twice a Hero: The Stories of Thaddeus Kosciuszko and Casimir Pulaski: Polish-American Heroes of the American Revolution (with DVD), illustrated by Lynn Ihsen Peterson, Great Plains Press (Chicago, IL), 2007.

Jack London's Dog, illustrated by Barry Moser, Great Plains Press (Chicago, IL), 2008.

The Further Adventures of a Lucky Dog: Owney, U.S. Rail Mail Mascot, illustrated by Catherine DeJong Artman and Tonwsend Artman, Great Plains Press (Chicago, IL), 2009.

OTHER

(And photographer) *Circle the Number You Love, Cross off the Number You Hate,* Great Plains Press (Chicago, IL), 1992.

(And photographer) *The Secret Heart of Numbers,* Sourcebooks (Naperville, IL), 1996.

Contributor of photography to periodicals, including *Avenue.*

Sidelights
Dirk Wales is a writer and photographer whose early work included short stories and poetry geared for adults. Turning from still photography to animation, Wales began a collaboration with artist Diane Kenna that resulted in several film-festival awards as well as their first picture-book collaboration: *A Lucky Dog: Owney, U.S. Rail Mail Mascot.* Wales has continued his work in children's picture books, producing a sequel to *A Lucky Dog* as well as a number of other books based on true stories, such as *Twice a Hero: The Stories of Thaddeus Kosciuszko and Casimir Pulaski: Polish-American Heroes of the American Revolution* and *Jack London's Dog.*

In both *A Lucky Dog* and *The Further Adventures of a Lucky Dog: Owney, U.S. Rail Mail Mascot* Wales tells the true tale of the homeless dog that was adopted as the mascot of the U.S. Postal Service in the late 1880s. Owney first appeared in the postal station in upstate New York, and when he began to ride the mail train around the country his story was taken up by the press and he became famous. In *Booklist* Diane Foote dubbed *A Lucky Dog* "a satisfying tale, all the more pleasing for being true."

Another well-known canine is the star of *Jack London's Dog,* Wales' story about the dog that inspired American writer Jack London to create the character of Buck in his famous novel *The Call of the Wild.* In what *School Library Journal* contributor Kathryn Kosiorek called "simple but eloquent language," Wales recounts the life of Jack the dog in Alaska's Yukon Territory after London returned to California and Jack left an abusive home for a life as an avalanche rescue dog. The dog's story is chronicled in "lovely engravings" by artist Barry Moser, according to a *Kirkus Reviews* writer, the critic adding that *Jack London's Dog* is a picture book with "visual interest."

Biographical and Critical Sources

PERIODICALS

Booklist, November 15, 2003, Diane Foote, review of *A Lucky Dog: Owney, U.S. Rail Mail Mascot,* p. 604; April 15, 2007, Carolyn Phelan, review of *Twice a Hero: The Stories of Thaddeus Kosciuszko and Casimir Pulaski: Polish-American Heroes of the American Revolution,* p. 40.
Kirkus Reviews, August 1, 2008, review of *Jack London's Dog.*
School Library Journal, January, 2006, Angela J. Reynolds, review of *Penny House,* p. 115; January, 2009, Kathryn Kosiorek, review of *Jack London's Dog,* p. 121.

ONLINE

Dirk Wales Home Page, http://www.rainbowplace.com/dirk/ (October 15, 2009).*

*   *   *

WALTERS, Eric 1957-
(Eric Robert Walters)

Personal

Born March 3, 1957, in Toronto, Ontario, Canada; son of Eric (a woodworker) and Christina (a homemaker) Walters; married December 28, 1984; wife's name Anita (a social worker); children: Christina, Nicholas, Julia. *Education:* York University, B.A. (with honors), 1979, B.S.W., 1983, M.S.W., 1985; University of Toronto, B.Ed., 1989. *Politics:* "Liberal." *Religion:* United Church of Canada. *Hobbies and other interests:* Playing and coaching basketball and soccer, music, travelling and spending time in Kenya.

Addresses

Home—Mississauga, Ontario, Canada. *E-mail*—ewalters@interlog.com.

Eric Walters (Reproduced by permission.)

Career

Writer and educator. Social worker affiliated with Children's Aid Society, Simcoe County, Ontario, Canada, 1979-81, Region of Peel, 1981-85; Strothers Treatment Centre, social worker, 1986-89; Emergency Department, Credit Valley Hospital, Mississauga, Ontario, crisis social worker, 1989-2008; Peel Region Board of Education, teacher, 1989-2005; writer, beginning 1992. Creation of Hope (charitable foundation), founder.

Member

Canadian Society of Children's Authors, Illustrators, and Performers, Writers' Union of Canada.

Awards, Honors

Silver Birch Award, Ontario Library Association, Blue Heron Book Award, and Children's Choice Award, Canadian Children's Book Centre (CCBC), all 1997, all for *STARS;* Silver Birch Award, CCBC Choice Award, and Ruth Schwartz Award nomination, all 1997, all for *Trapped in Ice;* Ruth Schwartz Award, CCBC Choice Award, New York Public Library Books for the Teen Age designation, and Canadian Library Book of the Year Honor selection, all 1998, all for *War of the Eagles;* CCBC Choice Award, and Red Cedar Award nomination, both 1998, both for *Diamonds in the Rough;* Canadian Library Association (CLA) Honour Book desig-

nation, 1998, for *The Hydrofoil Mystery;* CLA Book of the Year shortlist, 2000, and UNESCO Honor designation, 2003, both for *Caged Eagles;* Red Maple Award, and Snow Willow Award, both 2002, both for *Rebound;* CCBC Choice Award, and Red Maple Award finalist, both 2002, both for *The Bully Boys;* Silver Birch Award, and Arthur Ellis Award shortlist, both 2003, both for *Camp X;* Tiny Torgi Award, 2004, and Red Cedar Award nomination, 2005, both for *Run;* Red Cedar Award, 2004, for *Northern Exposures;* Red Maple Award nomination, 2004, for *Ricky;* White Pine Award, 2007, for *Shattered;* Red Maple Award, and Manitoba Young Readers Choice Award, both 2008, both for *We All Fall Down;* Red Maple Award, and Rocky Mountain Award, both 2008, both for *Safe as Houses;* Outdoor Education Award, 2008, for *The Pole.*

Writings

YOUNG-ADULT NOVELS

Stand Your Ground, Stoddart (Toronto, Ontario, Canada), 1994.
STARS, Stoddart (Toronto, Ontario, Canada), 1996.
Trapped in Ice, Viking Canada (Toronto, Ontario, Canada), 1997.
Diamonds in the Rough, Stoddart (Buffalo, NY), 1998.
War of the Eagles, Orca (Custer, WA), 1998.
Stranded, HarperCollins (Toronto, Ontario, Canada), 1998.
The Hydrofoil Mystery, Puffin (Toronto, Ontario, Canada), 1998.
Visions, HarperCollins (Toronto, Ontario, Canada), 1999.
Tiger by the Tail, HarperCollins (Toronto, Ontario, Canada), 1999.
The Money Pit Mystery, HarperCollins (Toronto, Ontario, Canada), 1999.
Caged Eagles (sequel to *War of the Eagles*), Orca (Custer, WA), 2000.
The Bully Boys, Viking Canada (Toronto, Ontario, Canada), 2000.
Rebound, Stoddart (Buffalo, NY), 2001.
Northern Exposures, HarperCollins (Toronto, Ontario, Canada), 2001.
Tiger in Trouble, Beach Holme (Vancouver, British Columbia, Canada), 2001.
Camp X, Penguin Canada (Toronto, Ontario, Canada), 2002.
Ricky, HarperCollins (Toronto, Ontario, Canada), 2002.
Tiger Town, Beach Holme (Vancouver, British Columbia, Canada), 2002.
Royal Ransom, Puffin Canada (Toronto, Ontario, Canada), 2003.
Run, Puffin (Toronto Ontario, Canada), 2003.
Overdrive, Orca (Custer, WA), 2004.
I've Got an Idea, HarperCollins (Toronto, Ontario, Canada), 2004.
Grind, Orca (Custer, WA), 2004.
Camp 30 (sequel to *Camp X*), Penguin Canada (Toronto, Ontario, Canada), 2004.

(With Kevin Spreekmeester) *Death by Exposure: An Interactive Mystery,* photography by Spreekmeester, Beach Holme (Vancouver, British Columbia, Canada), 2004, second edition, Sandcastle (Toronto, Ontario, Canada), 2007.
Elixir, foreword by Bob Banting, Viking Canada (Toronto, Ontario, Canada), 2005.
Juice, Orca (Victoria, British Columbia, Canada), 2005.
Stuffed, Orca (Victoria, British Columbia, Canada), 2006.
Laggan Lard Butts, Orca (Victoria, British Columbia, Canada), 2006.
We All Fall Down, CNIB (Toronto, Ontario, Canada), 2006.
Shattered, foreword by Roméo Dallaire, Viking Canada (Toronto, Ontario, Canada), 2006.
Camp X: Fools' Gold, Puffin Canada (Toronto, Ontario, Canada), 2006.
Sketches, Puffin Canada (Toronto, Ontario, Canada), 2007.
Safe as Houses, Doubleday Canada (Toronto, Ontario, Canada), 2007.
Tiger Trap, Dundurn (Toronto, Ontario, Canada), 2007.
(With Deborah Ellis) *Bifocal,* Fitzhenry & Whiteside (Markham, Ontario, Canada), 2007.
The Pole, Puffin (Toronto, Ontario, Canada), 2007.
House Party, Orca (Victoria, British Columbia, Canada), 2007.
In a Flash, Orca (Victoria, British Columbia, Canada), 2008.
Splat!, Orca (Victoria, British Columbia, Canada), 2008.
Alexandria of Africa, Doubleday Canada (Toronto, Ontario, Canada), 2008.
Voyageur, Puffin (Toronto, Ontario, Canada), 2008.
The Falls, Puffin (Toronto, Ontario, Canada), 2008.
Black and White, Puffin (Toronto, Ontario, Canada), 2009.
Special Edward, Orca (Victoria, British Columbia, Canada), 2009.
Wave, Random House (New York, NY), 2009.
Home Team, Orca (Victoria, British Columbia, Canada), 2010.
Branded, Orca (Victoria, British Columbia, Canada), 2010.
Trouble in Paradise, Penguin (Toronto, Ontario, Canada), 2010.
Nebala of North America, Random House (New York, NY), 2010.
The Matato Ride, Orca (Victoria, British Columbia, Canada), 2011.
Flyboy, Penguin (Toronto, Ontario, Canada), 2011.
End of Days, Doubleday (Toronto, Ontario, Canada), 2011.

Author's works have been translated into French, Dutch, Japanese, Korean, Italian, German, Swedish, Spanish, Norwegian, and Chinese.

"BASKETBALL" SERIES

Three on Three, Orca (Custer, WA), 1999.
Full Court Press, Orca (Custer, WA), 2000.
Hoop Crazy, Orca (Custer, WA), 2001.
Long Shot, Orca (Custer, WA), 2001.
Road Trip, Orca (Custer, WA), 2002.

Off Season, Orca (Victoria, British Columbia, Canada), 2003.

Underdog, Orca (Victoria, British Columbia, Canada), 2004.

(With Jerome "Junk Yard Dog" Williams) *Triple Threat,* Orca (Victoria, British Columbia, Canada), 2005.

(With Jerome "Junk Yard Dog" Williams and Johnnie Williams III) *Boot Camp,* Orca (Victoria, British Columbia, Canada), 2005.

OTHER

(With Norm Rippon) *Improve Your Child's Spelling 1,* Momentum Publishing, 1991.

(With Norm Rippon) *Improve Your Child's Spelling 2,* Momentum Publishing, 1993.

(With daughter, Christina Walters) *The True Story of Santa Claus,* illustrated by Andrew Gooderham, Chestnut Publishing (Toronto, Ontario, Canada), 2004.

(With Adrian Bradbury) *When Elephants Fight: The Lives of Children in Conflict in Afghanistan, Bosnia, Sri Lanka, Sudan, and Uganda,* Orca (Victoria, British Columbia, Canada), 2008.

(Editor) *Tell Me Why: How Young People Can Change the World,* Doubleday Canada (Toronto, Ontario, Canada), 2008.

Sidelights

The novels of Canadian author Eric Walters have been compared by critics to the work of well-known young-adult writers Gary Paulsen and Will Hobbs. As *Resource Links* contributor Gillian Richardson noted in a review of Walters' novel *Royal Ransom,* the author "excels at seizing the reader's attention with rapid-fire action scenes, often involving survival against nature." Walters' first novel, *Stand Your Ground,* sold out instantly, while *STARS* won both the Silver Birch Award and the Blue Heron Book Award. Books nominated for these awards are selected by juries of young adults, a testament to Walters' success at writing stories with which his audience can identify. His books have also proved popular because his teen protagonists invariably succeed despite the hurdles they face. This message—that obstacles can be overcome—is, in fact, what initially attracted Walters to writing for young adults. "I prefer writing children's novels because they are like morality plays," the prolific novelist once asserted. "There is much more right and wrong in them. In adult novels, it's almost as if you have to emphasize the bad or wrong, and I don't want the wrong people to win. I like happy endings."

Walters originally pursued a career as a social worker, but went on to become a teacher while continuing to work part-time as a crisis social worker in an emergency department. In 1991, inspired by the books he read aloud to his fifth-grade students, he decided to try his hand at writing his own books for children. His creative writing classes now became a sharing process for both Walters and his students; they took turns reading one another's writing, and he expected the students to give his work the same critical appraisal he gave theirs. In fact, it was his students' enthusiasm after hearing the first draft of *Stand Your Ground* that convinced Walters to send the completed draft to a publisher.

"The underlying theme of many of my books is about a sense of belonging," Walters once commented, "and about how you sometimes have to work to get to that place." His protagonists are frequently gifted teens to whom life has dealt a severe blow. Their stories revolve around the challenges they experience when they are suddenly offered an opportunity they had previously lacked. Will they recognize and accept it—or turn their backs? In both *Stand Your Ground* and *STARS,* seizing an opportunity involves rejecting the thrill of living outside the law and recognizing the value of the ordinary. In *Stand Your Ground,* for example, the protagonist comes to realize that he prefers living with his old-

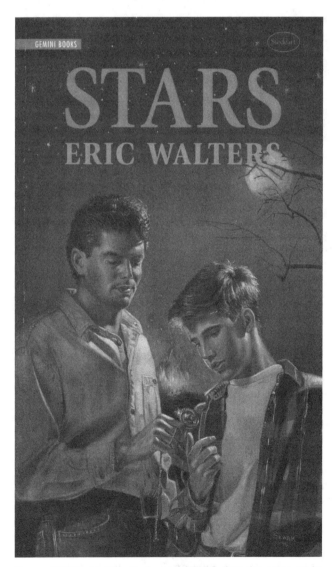

Cover of Walters' middle-grade novel STARS, *featuring cover art by Albert Slark.* (Stoddart, 1996. Copyright © 1996 by Eric Walters. Reproduced by permission.)

Ken Campbell created the dramatic cover art for Walters' middle-grade adventure novel Caged Eagles. (Book Publishers, 2000. Reproduced by permission.)

fashioned Dutch grandparents to wheeling deals with his con-artist father. In *STARS* a city boy spends his time planning his escape from a Northern Ontario camp for young offenders before he realizes how much he has come to love the wilderness.

Walters' street-smart but sensitive protagonists are based on children he remembers from growing up with in a troubled neighborhood in West-end Toronto. His mother died when he was four years old, and he and his older sister ended up raising themselves. For much of his youth, Walters ran wild, playing in neighboring stockyards, running through sewers, and fleeing the police. His world was populated by "smart people pushed in the wrong directions," as he once recalled, and these same people provide his stories with much of their drama. Like his protagonists, Walters managed to escape this world, a cultural move he once compared to immigrating to a new country: "You leave things behind and there's a sense of loss."

Walters' novel *Run* focuses on a true story: the 1980 effort of Canadian athlete Terry Fox to run across Canada following a leg amputation. The novel weaves Fox's story into the fictional story of Winston MacDonald, Jr., a student whose drinking and truancy have caused him

to be sent to live with his journalist father. When Winston's father is sent to cover Fox's Marathon of Hope, the teen has the chance to travel in Fox's support van and even runs alongside Fox, learning a lesson about perseverance and character. "It is a testament to Walters' talents that he manages to depict Terry as both a hero and a human," noted *Resource Links* reviewer Nadine d'Entremont, praising *Run* as an "excellent novel" that "skillfully explores a range of themes, including family, friendship, determination, and heroism." In writing *Run* Walters had the support of Fox's family, and he donated all royalties from the sale of the book to the Terry Fox Foundation to fund cancer research.

Taking place against a more contemporary backdrop, *Bifocal* is a collaborative novel by Walters and Deborah Ellis. Geared for younger teens, the story focuses on two boys whose lives are changed when their school is locked down during a hunt for a Muslim student suspected of terrorist activities. Jay, a football star, joins his team members as they brutishly vandalize property in the town's Muslim neighborhood in retaliation. Their activities extend to the home of Haroon, a bookish student, and the relationship between the two teens prompts both to stand up for what they believe is right. In *Kliatt* Clair Rosser praised *Bifocal* as a "suspenseful story" that "brings current issues to the forefront."

Another novel featuring contemporary teen issues, *Stuffed* focuses on a boy whose leadership role in boycotting a local fast-food restaurant results in legal threats. In *Northern Exposures* a teen ignored by his parents gets the chance to gain self-assurance and survival skills during a trip to northern Canada to photograph wildlife. The subject of performance-enhancing drugs in school athletics is the focus of *Juice,* as an easy-going football player nicknamed Moose begins to wonder what is in the energy drinks his new coach has been serving. In *School Library Journal* Michele Capozzella dubbed *Stuffed* "well written and thoughtful," and Philip Mills asserted in *Resource Links* that Walters' novel "contains a message to ponder over." "Walters knows about writing adventure stories for reluctant readers," according to Rosser, "and *Northern Exposures* . . . should attract many younger Yas" due to its suspense. Heather Empey wrote in the same periodical that *Juice* features a "likeable" protagonist and treats readers to an "engaging read," while *Booklist* contributor Ilene Cooper predicted that the novel's "simplicity will probably grab" the attention of reluctant readers. While noting that the story "could have been longer," Stephanie Squicciarini concluded in *Kliatt* that in *Juice* Walters serves up "a quick, well written and realistic read."

Several of Walters' novels are set during World War II. In *War of the Eagles* Jed, a Native American teen of the Tsimshian nation, learns about prejudice first hand as he watches the attitudes of his fellow townspeople change toward their Japanese neighbors as the war progresses and tensions mount in Jed's small Canadian fishing village. In the sequel to *War of the Eagles, Caged Eagles*

Walters focuses on the experiences of Jed's friend, fourteen-year-old Tadashi Fukushima, who, together with his Japanese-Canadian family and others from the village of similar heritage, is forced into an internment camp for the duration of the war. The boy does not understand his parents' fatalistic attitude in dealing with this humiliation; he grows angry as their possessions are taken from them and frustrated when he must live with the women in a makeshift hovel while his father lives elsewhere in the camp with the men. Together with a new friend, Tadashi finds a way to leave the camp undetected, and in an act of defiance he sinks the family's fishing boat—the source of their livelihood—to prevent it from being sold. Praising *Caged Eagles,* *Booklist* reviewer Chris Sherman noted that Walters "admirably succeeds" in helping readers understand the "humiliation, anger, and depression" of the Fukishima family while also weaving an element of adventure into Tadashi's story. In a *School Library Journal* review, Kathleen Isaacs called the book "a disturbing and convincing story that needs to be told," while in *Booklist* John Peters hailed *War of the Eagles* as "a multifaceted, well-knit" story that is enhanced by Walters' "fluent storytelling."

Cover of Walters' young-adult novel Sketches, *featuring artwork by* Anita Walters. (Orca Book Publishers, 2002. Reproduced by permission.)

In *Camp X* twelve-year-old George Braun and his older brother Jack are left alone when their father leaves to fight in World War II and their mother gets a job in a munitions factory. Exploring their new town of Whitby, Ontario, the boys stumble upon a secret military installation: a British-run camp to train Allied spies. As they learn more about the camp, they gain the confidence of the presiding director, and are ultimately asked to assist camp command in making deliveries to the munitions factory nearby. During their delivery run, George and Jack discover a plot to undermine the camp, and realize that not everyone they know can be trusted. Noting that *Camp X* is based on an actual military installation, *Resource Links* contributor Victoria Pennell praised the novel for containing "fast-moving action" that will appeal to upper-elementary-aged readers who enjoy military history.

Fans of *Camp X* will also appreciate *Camp 30* and *Camp X: Fools' Gold* In *Camp 30* George and Jack move from Whitby to nearby Bowmanville, where they discover a different type of camp: a prisoner of war camp that houses German soldiers. Like *Camp X, Camp 30* is also based on Canadian history; the camp in Bowmanville served as a temporary home for some of the highest-ranking German officers captured by Allied troops during the war. In *Camp X: Fools' Gold* the brothers find themselves in the center of a scheme by thieves to uncover the location of the fortune in gold that is supposedly hidden at Camp X. While noting that it recalls the popular "Hardy Boys" books of the early twentieth century, *Resource Links* critic David Ward added that *Camp 30* "promotes a part of Canadian history not often discussed or remembered," and Evette Berry noted in the same periodical that Walter's plot in *Camp X: Fools' Gold* "flows smoothly and . . . action sequences maintain the readers' interest throughout."

Turning to an even-earlier era, *Elixir* takes place in the early 1920s, as a Canadian preteen named Ruth Williams witnesses something amazing in the college research building where her mother works as a cleaning woman. At the University of Toronto's Institute of Biological Research two scientists are attempting to find a serum that will cure diabetes mellitus. Unfortunately, their experiments result in the death of many of the dogs used to test their serum, and animal rights activists now protest vehemently outside the doors of the institute. While Ruth becomes friends with the two scientists, she also makes a friend of one of the animal-rights activists. When she is asked to betray the scientists and help free the dogs, Ruth is confronted by a moral dilemma that has the potential to derail scientific advances. Noting that *Elixir* "will expose students to the incredible accomplishments" of two Canadian scientists, Teresa Hughes added in *Resource Links* that Walters' novel "brings [the men's] . . . personalities alive" for young readers.

In addition to problem novels featuring older teens, Walters is the author of a popular series of books for

young basketball fans. Beginning with *Three on Three,* the "Basketball" series includes the chapter books *Full Court Press, Long Shot, Hoop Crazy, Off Season, Road Trip, Laggan Lard Butts, House Party, In a Flash,* and *Splat!* among its titles. *Off Season* focuses on third-grade friends and basketball team members Nick and Kia, who travel to British Columbia to visit Nick's cousin Ned during summer vacation. Although the three spend some time shooting hoops on a rustic basketball court Ned's father has built, the city pair also learn to appreciate the ways of the wild when they become ringed in by flames during a forest fire. In *Road Trip* the boys hit the road, traveling to compete in a high-pressure tournament where the stakes are even higher for their coach. Praising the series' writing style as "easy and fast paced," *Resource Links* reviewer Stephanie Olson added in a review of *Road Trip* that "basketball fans will love the excitement" generated by the young team's competitive spirit.

The eighth book in the "Basketball" series, *Triple Threat,* was co-written by NBA star Jerome "Junk Yard Dog" Williams. Williams is also a character in the book and here he helps Nick and Kia overcome bullies. Walters and Williams team up again to write *Boot Camp,* this time joined by Williams' brother Johnnie Williams III. In this story, the friends tough it out at basketball camp during the summer of their sixth-grade year. Noting that "the authors' combined experience with the game is extraordinary," Ward added in a *Resource Links* review of *Boot Camp* that readers are treated to "an honest, realistic experience of an intensive . . . [sports] camp" experience.

Walters credits the popularity of his fiction to his realistic plots and vivid details. As he once explained to *SATA,* "I do a lot of personal research. I've hung out at a tough biker bar, white water rafted, rock climbed, played with people's pet lions and tigers and bears, spent days in a wheelchair, and stood outside in a blizzard in a T-shirt and shorts to find out what it was like to freeze to death."

Walters' own experiences as a youth, combined with things he has seen while working as a social worker, family therapist, and teacher, have convinced him that many good people caught in a dead end "don't get out alive." As a result, he has found writing about characters who *do* manage to escape to be a form of catharsis. He identifies so closely with his characters that he worries about them even after a book is finished. Recalling what people said of him when he was a youth, he once acknowledged: "A lot of my life has been dedicated to proving people wrong."

Biographical and Critical Sources

PERIODICALS

Booklist, December 15, 1998, John Peters, review of *War of the Eagles,* p. 752; June 1, 2000, Tim Arnold, re-

Walters turns to sports-minded young readers in his "Basketball" series novel Road Trip, *featuring cover art by John Mantha.* (Orca Book Publishers, 2002. Reproduced by permission.)

view of *Three on Three,* p. 1898; December 1, 2000, Chris Sherman, review of *Caged Eagles,* p. 702; April 1, 2001, Roger Leslie, review of *Full Court Press,* p. 1473; September 1, 2005, Ilene Cooper, review of *Juice,* p. 115; January 1, 2008, Frances Bradburn, review of *Sketches,* p. 63.

Bulletin of the Center for Children's Books, October, 2008, Deborah Stevenson, review of *In a Flash,* p. 98.

Kliatt, January, 2005, Claire Rosser, review of *Grind,* p. 18; July, 2005, Stephanie Squicciarini, review of *Juice,* p. 26; July, 2006, Stephanie Squicciarini, review of *Stuffed,* p. 22; November, 2007, Claire Rosser, review of *Bifocal,* p. 10; March, 2008, Ashleigh Larsen, review of *Splat!,* and Myrna Marler, review of *Sketches,* p. 21; November, 2008, Claire Rosser, review of *Northern Exposures,* p. 28.

Kirkus Reviews, January 1, 2008, review of *Sketches;* October 15, 2008, review of *Northern Exposures.*

Resource Links, February, 1998, review of *Trapped in Ice,* p. 113; October, 1998, review of *War of the Eagles,* p. 21; February, 2000, review of *Three on Three,* pp. 11-12, and review of *Stranded,* pp. 29-30; April, 2000, review of *The Bully Boys,* p. 12; October, 2000, review of *Caged Eagles,* p. 31; February, 2001, review of *Rebound,* p. 20; October, 2001, Shannon Danylko,

review of *Hoop Crazy!,* and Johal Jinder, review of *Tiger in Trouble,* p. 20; December, 2001, Shannon Danylko, review of *Long Shot,* p. 23; April, 2002, Victoria Pennell, review of *Camp X,* p. 42; October, 2002, Stephanie Olson, review of *Road Trip,* p. 18; February, 2003, Gillian Richardson, review of *Royal Ransom,* p. 19; April, 2003, review of *Tiger Town,* p. 54; June, 2003, Teresa Hughes, review of *Ricky,* p. 36, and Elaine Rosepad, review of *Off Season,* p. 47; October, 2003, Nadine d'Entremont, review of *Run,* p. 37; October, 2004, Antonia Gisler, review of *Underdog,* p. 21; December, 2004, David Ward, review of *Camp 30,* p. 24; February, 2005, Susan Miller, review of *Death by Exposure,* p. 61; April, 2005, Teresa Hughes, review of *Elixir,* p. 18; June, 2005, Deb Nielsen, review of *Triple Threat,* p. 23; June, 2006, Victoria Pennell, review of *We All Fall Down,* p. 28; October, 2006, Evette Berry, review of *Camp X: Fool's Gold,* p. 18, and Philip Mills, review of *Stuffed,* p. 55; April, 2007, David Ward, review of *Boot Camp,* p. 20; February, 2008, Margaret Mackey, review of *Bifocal,* p. 30.

School Library Journal, November, 2000, Kathleen Isaacs, review of *Caged Eagles,* p. 164; October, 2001, Janice C. Hayes, review of *Rebound,* p. 174; July, 2002, Kate Kohlbeck, review of *Long Shot,* p. 127; June, 2004, Margaret Mackey, review of *Overdrive,* p. 27; February, 2005, Heather Empey, review of *Grind,* p. 41; March, 2005, Kelly Czarnecki, review of *Triple Threat,* p. 220; August, 2005, Julie Webb, review of *Juice,* p. 138; October, 2005, Heather Empey, review of *Juice,* p. 38; February, 2006, Myra Junyk, review of *Shattered,* p. 53; October, 2006, Anne Hatcher, review of *Laggan Lard Butts,* p. 54, and Michele Capozzella, review of *Stuffed,* p. 163; June, 2007, Joanne de Groot, review of *Sketches,* p. 36; December, 2007, Gail Lennon, review of *House Party,* p. 44; March, 2008, Fawzia Gilani-Williams, review of *Bifocal,* p. 197; April, 2008, Diane P. Tuccillo, review of *Sketches,* p. 152.

Teacher Librarian, March-April, 1999, review of *War of the Eagles,* p. 22.

ONLINE

Canadian Review of Materials Online, http://www.umanitoba.ca/cm/ (September 26, 1998), Dave Jenkinson, interview with Walters.

Creation of Hope Web site, http://www.creationofhope.com (November 3, 2009).

Eric Walters Home Page, http://www.ericwalters.net (October 15, 2009).

*   *   *

WALTERS, Eric Robert
See WALTERS, Eric

WHITING, Sue 1960-
(Susan Allana Whiting)

Personal

Born 1960, in Sydney, New South Wales, Australia; married; children: two. *Education:* Attended teacher's college.

Addresses

Home—Australia.

Career

Author. Walker Books Australia, editor; previously worked as a primary school teacher.

Writings

Please Go to Sleep, illustrated by Michael Mucci, Banana Books (Otford, New South Wales, Australia), 2002.

Uncle Alien, illustrated by Michael Mucci, Banana Books (Otford, New South Wales, Australia), 2002.

Quacker, illustrated by Susie Boyer, Pearson Education (South Melbourne, Victoria, Australia), 2002.

Vamps Rule, illustrated by Conna Brecon, Pearson Education (South Melbourne, Victoria, Australia), 2002.

Eyes in the Paddock, illustrated by Tom Kurema, Macmillan Education Australia (South Yarra, New South Wales, Australia), 2003.

Living in the Outback, Rigby Harcourt Education (Port Melbourne, Victoria, Australia), 2003.

Pet Perspectives, Rigby Harcourt Education (Port Melbourne, Victoria, Australia), 2003.

My Yummy Treats, illustrated by Stuart Martin, Book Company (Sydney, New South Wales, Australia), 2004.

Battle of the Rats, Koala Books (Mascot, New South Wales, Australia), 2004.

Taming Butterflies, illustrated by Mini Goss, New Frontier Publishing (Epping, New South Wales, Australia), 2004.

All about Ants, National Geographic Society (Washington, DC), 2006.

Ancient Orbiters: A Guide to the Planets, National Geographic Society (Washington, DC), 2006.

The Hairy Legs Heist, New Frontier Publishing (Frenchs Forest, New South Wales, Australia), 2007.

Elephant Dance, illustrated by Nina Rycroft, Koala Books (Mascot, New South Wales, Australia), 2007.

The Firefighters, illustrated by Donna Rawlins, Candlewick Press (Cambridge, MA), 2008.

Dance of the Sugar Plum Fairy, illustrated by Sarah Davis, New Frontier Publishing (Frenchs Forest, New South Wales, Australia), 2008.

Looking for Animals, illustrated by David Stanley, Koala Books (Mascot, New South Wales, Australia), 2008.

Freaky, Walker Books (Newtown, New South Wales, Australia), 2009.

A Strange Little Monster, illustrated by Stephen Michael King, Penguin (Camberwell, New South Wales, Australia), 2010.
You Wish, Jellyfish, illustrated by Lee Krutop, Koala Books (Mascot, New South Wales, Australia), 2010.
To the Feral Tree, Walker Books (Newtown, New South Wales, Australia), 2010.

Also author of novelty books for Book Company. Author of books in Macmillan Australia's "Trekker" series, including *Great! Just Great!,* illustrated by Pete Beard, *The Baker and the Bush Beastie,* illustrated by Steven Hallam, *The Sea Storm Monster,* illustrated by Milo Kossowski, *A Fish out of Water,* illustrated by Hallam, and *Ants in His Pants,* illustrated by Craig Longmuir. Author of *Who Lives Here?, Make a Monster, The Shopping List,* and *Superdome,* all published by National Geographic, and *Mistie's Magic,* 2000.

Sidelights

Prior to becoming a children's author, Australian writer Sue Whiting worked as an elementary school teacher for a number of years, a job that developed her interest in youth literature. As she explained on her home page, when her children grew older Whiting began to have a few free moments in her day, allowing her to pursue a new career as a writer. "I wrote whenever I could and started sending manuscripts off to publishers, which of course were promptly returned with a 'thanks but no thanks' letter," the author noted. The author persevered, however and her first book was published in 2000.

Illustrated by Donna Rawlins, Whiting's *The Firefighters* reached American shores in 2008 and shares with young readers the experiences of a classroom of students learning about fire safety. Led by an enthusiastic teacher named Miss Iverson, the children pretend they live and work in a firehouse, exploring what it is like to be one of the men or women who fight fires. After playing in the school yard with fire trucks fashioned from cardboard boxes, the youngsters receive a surprise visit from a pair of firefighters who give them a tour of their fire truck and share their experiences as first responders to dangerous situations. Writing in *School Library Journal,* Linda Ludke deemed *The Firefighters* "a great choice for introducing not only fire safety, but also creative play." The same sentiment was expressed by a *Kirkus Reviews* critic who wrote that Whiting's book offers "a spark to imaginations, with a little fire safety on the side."

Whiting told *SATA:* "I am fiercely passionate about reading and literacy development, about the importance of story and storytelling. Stories explore the human experience. They help us to understand our place in the world. They pass down history, values, morals, and traditions. For me, writing books for children is both a joy and a privilege and there are few things I treasure more than having the opportunity to share my stories with keen young readers."

Biographical and Critical Sources

PERIODICALS

Booklist, September 1, 2008, Bina Williams, review of *The Firefighters,* p. 103.
Kirkus Reviews, July 15, 2008, review of *The Firefighters.*
School Library Journal, December, 2008, Linda Ludke, review of *The Firefighters,* p. 106.
Science and Children, November, 2007, Judy Kraus, review of *All about Ants,* p. 62.

ONLINE

Sue Whiting Home Page, http://www.suewhiting.com (September 20, 2009).

* * *

WHITING, Susan Allana
See WHITING, Sue

* * *

WILSON, Martin 1973-

Personal

Born 1973, in Tuscaloosa, AL. *Education:* Vanderbilt, B.A., 1995; University of Florida, M.F.A., 1998. *Hobbies and other interests:* Traveling, reading, exercising, spending time with friends and family.

Addresses

Home—New York, NY. *Agent*—George M. Nicholson, Sterling Lord Literistic, Inc., 65 Bleecker St., New York, NY 10012. *E-mail*—martin@martinwilsonwrites.com.

Career

Author and publicist. Worked previously as an editorial assistant, copyeditor, and managing editor at a publishing house in Austin, TX.

Awards, Honors

Henfield Foundation/*Transatlantic Review* Award for short story.

Writings

(With Adam McClellan) *Uniquely North Carolina,* Heinemann Library (Chicago, IL), 2004.
Uniquely Alabama, Heinemann Library (Chicago, IL), 2004.

Uniquely Mississippi, Heinemann Library (Chicago, IL), 2004.

What They Always Tell Us, Delacorte (New York, NY), 2008.

Contributor of short fiction to *Virgin Fiction 2, Pieces: A Collection of New Voices, Rebel Yell 2,* and *Rush Hour.*

Sidelights

Martin Wilson established himself as an author while working in the publishing industry on the editorial side. He began, like many writers, by publishing short stories in anthologies, all the while developing his prose style. Of note is a story he published in the literary journal *Rush Hour,* in which he creates a character named Alex who struggles not only with his emerging sexuality but also with his older brother, James. For the next several years, as Wilson recalled on his home page, he contemplated this relationship between brothers, and he eventually continued Alex's narrative in the manuscript that became his first published novel, *What They Always Tell Us.*

Growing up in Tuscaloosa, Alabama, Alex and James attend the same high school, where elder brother James has established a reputation as a star athlete and now has an attractive girlfriend. Alex, a solitary teen, finds himself even more outcast after he intentionally drinks a bottle of household cleaner during a party, leading to small-town gossip about his character. Embarrassed by his brother's suicide attempt, James feels relief when Alex regains the appearance of normalcy by joining the school's track team and developing a friendly relationship with Nathen. The brothers also begin to reconnect through their concern for their neighbor Henry, who at ten years old is often abandoned by his single mother. As the school year progresses, James and Alex turn to each other for support as James dreams of leaving the confining social strictures of his small Southern town and Alex slowly develops an intimate, romantic affair with Nathen.

"Wilson shows admirable control of a complicated story that in less-accomplished hands could have spun out of control," commented *Booklist* critic Ilene Cooper in a review of *What They Always Tell Us,* while a *Kirkus Reviews* contributor described the coming-of-age novel as "smoothly written and psychologically astute." Although offering a few reservations about the tale's narrative pace, *School Library Journal* critic Nora G. Murphy nonetheless recommended *What They Always Tell Us* to adolescents "grappling with decisions about the future, the frustrations of family, and the choices that relationships require of us." In *Publishers Weekly,* a critic described Wilson's story as "insightfully evoked," with characters who "will leave a lasting impression on readers."

***Cover of Martin Wilson's multilayered coming-of-age novel* What They Always Tell Us.**

Biographical and Critical Sources

PERIODICALS

Booklist, November 15, 2008, Ilene Cooper, review of *What They Always Tell Us,* p. 58.

Horn Book, September-October, 2008, Betty Carter, review of *What They Always Tell Us,* p. 599.

Kirkus Reviews, July 15, 2008, review of *What They Always Tell Us.*

Kliatt, July, 2008, Myrna Marler, review of *What They Always Tell Us,* p. 21.

Publishers Weekly, July 28, 2008, review of *What They Always Tell Us,* p. 75.

School Library Journal, September, 2008, Nora G. Murphy, review of *What They Always Tell Us,* p. 196.

ONLINE

Martin Wilson Home Page, http://martinwilsonwrites.com (September 25, 2009).

Martin Wilson Web Log, http://martinwilsonwrites.com/blog (September 25, 2009).*

WOLF, Sallie 1950-

Personal

Born Sarah Lloyd Wolf, February 28, 1950, in Charlottesville, VA; daughter of Barton Myers (a minister and career counselor) and Rosamond Lloyd; married Charles Beno Wolf (an attorney), September 1, 1973; children: Lou, Peter. *Education:* Brown University, B.A., 1972; Art Institute of Chicago, B.F.A., 1997. *Hobbies and other interests:* "Art, reading, listening to folk music, playing tennis, coaching, watching my boys play sports, and exploring the outdoors."

Addresses

Office—Calypso Moon Studio, 331 B Harrison St., Oak Park, IL 60304. *E-mail*—sallie@salliewolf.com.

Career

Artist and author. Northfield Mount Herman School, Northfield, MA, anthropology teacher, 1972-73; University of Chicago Press, Chicago, IL, typesetter and supervisor, 1974-79; artist and writer, 1979—. Conducts art and writing workshops for children and for adults through schools and art leagues. *Exhibitions:* Work included in solo shows at Oak Park Village Hall, Oak Park, IL, 1991; Harper College, Palatine, IL, 2001; Holderness School, Holderness, NH, 2003; Patricia Ladd Carega Gallery, Center Sandwich, NH, 2003, 2006; Adler Planetarium, Chicago, IL, 2005; Fermilab Art Gallery, Batavia, IL, 2006; Oak Park Hospital, Oak Park, 2007; and Oak Park Police Department Art Gallery, Oak Park, 2009; and Air Force Academy, Colorado Springs, CO, 2010. Group shows include Illinois Watercolor Society Annual Show, Schaumburg, 1999, 2000, 2002; Woman Made Gallery, Chicago, IL, 2003, 2005, 2008; Patricia Ladd Carega Gallery, 2004; Oak Park Public Library Art Gallery, 2006; Union Street Gallery, Chicago Heights, IL, 2006; Calypso Moon Studio, Oak Park, 2007; Maryland Federation of Art Circle Galleries, Annapolis, 2008; University of Chicago Gordon Center for Integrative Science, 2008; and Louisiana Art and Science Museum, 2009.

Member

Society of Children's Book Writers and Illustrators, Amnesty International, National Audubon Society, Sierra Club, Nature Conservancy, Appalachian Mountain Club, Chicago Children's Reading Round Table, Phi Beta Kappa.

Awards, Honors

First place, Oak Park Art League Abstract Show, 1999; Award of Excellence, Illinois Watercolor Society Annual Show, 1999; juror's award, Illinois Watercolor Society Annual Show, 2000, 2002; juror's award, Oak Park Art League Member's Show, 2002, 2005; Special assistance grant, Illinois Arts Council, 2005, 2006; Ragdale Foundation residency, 2003, 2004, 2007.

Writings

Peter's Trucks illustrated by Cat Bowman Smith, Albert Whitman (Morton Grove, IL), 1992.

Truck Stuck illustrated by Andy Roberts Davies, Charlesbridge (Watertown, MA), 2008.

(Self-illustrated) *The Robin Makes a Laughing Sound: A Birder's Journal,* Charlesbridge (Watertown, MA), 2010.

Sidelights

Sallie Wolf, a Chicago-area artist, is the author of the children's books *Peter's Trucks* and *Truck Stuck*. "I always loved children's books," Wolf told Katie Leimkuehler in a *Triblocal.com* interview. "I love that the message is everyday life is exciting." Wolf has also completed *The Robin Makes a Laughing Sound: A Birder's Journal,* a self-illustrated title that combines her poetry and journal excerpts with sketches and watercolor portraits of birds. "I like writing and art," she remarked to Leimkuehler. "I used to think they were at odds competing against each other. Now they are both tied together."

Wolf developed an early interest in the arts, she once recalled to *SATA*. "Reading and books were always important to me," she wrote. "As far back as I can remember, my parents read to my older brother and me. One of our favorite stories was 'The Bremen Town Musicians' because it had the word 'hobgoblins' in it, and we would burst into laughter whenever we would reach that line. I became a reader on my own when the school librarian finally let us out of the primary section. I was stunned and thrilled to learn that nonfiction books were organized by subject matter and that there were whole shelves of books on natural history, microscopes, American Indians, and history. It must have been about the eighth grade when I realized that books were written by people and that I could write stories myself.

"I had three career goals when I entered high school: to teach, to work for a publishing company, and to write and illustrate children's books. I think I chose children's literature because those were the books I had enjoyed most myself. Reading to my younger brother and sister gave me a new opportunity to explore picture books. I found their insights into the value and fun of everyday things and everyday life to be an important message that spoke to me."

Wolf later attended Brown University, where she earned a degree in anthropology and archaeology. "I went to art school to learn to draw people so I could illustrate children's books, and instead, I rediscovered my love of anthropology and natural history and found a way to use art as an entry back into these fields," she noted on her home page. After teaching anthropology at a boarding high school and working in the publishing industry as a typesetter, Wolf began keeping a journal while raising her two sons. "Writing in my journal became more

The busy characters in Sallie Wolf's board book **Truck Stuck** *come to life in Andy Robert Davies' art.* (Illustration copyright © 2008 by Andy Robert Davies. All

than just a habit," she stated on her home page. "It was the way I explored my world, thought about problems, filed away future story ideas. My journals filled up with the routines of my day, insights I gained, plans for what I wanted to do with my life, stories of Lou and Pete growing up."

Wolf's big break came after a chance meeting with an editor at a children's book conference. After learning that the editor was searching for a book about trucks, Wolf began writing what would eventually become *Peter's Trucks,* her picture book debut. The work centers on an eagle-eyed youngster who spots every truck that rolls through his neighborhood but cannot decide what each vehicle carries. A critic in *Kirkus Reviews* praised the "ingenious format" and "pleasantly cadenced, repetitive verse," and Susan Hepler, writing in *School Library Journal,* observed that Peter's observations "makes for some predictable hilarity" as he confuses one truck's cargo with that of another.

Following the success of *Peter's Trucks,* Wolf returned to school and earned a degree in painting and drawing from the School of the Art Institute of Chicago. Her work has been exhibited at numerous locations in Illinois, including the Adler Planetarium and the art gal-

lery of the Fermilab. Her next children's book, *Truck Stuck,* appeared sixteen years after her first. Told in verse, *Truck Stuck* examines the chaos that follows after an eighteen-wheeler becomes lodged beneath a viaduct. The resulting traffic jam proves a boon to a pair of budding entrepreneurs, who sell lemonade to a thirsty clown, a troop of Boy Scouts, and an Elvis impersonator, among others. "Kids who are crazy about vehicles will love this one: it's easy to read and a whole lot of fun," Robin L. Smith commented in *Horn Book,* and a *Kirkus Reviews* contributor deemed the story "a delirious age-appropriate romp."

"As a children's book author I get to write my own stories," Wolf stated on her home page. "I get to work with editors of publishing companies. I get to go to schools and teach writing workshops. So you can see that this is almost the perfect job for me. It meets all three of my career goals."

As Wolf explained to *SATA,* "All my art and writing begins in my journals. For a long time it felt as if the art was competing with the writing for my time and attention. With *The Robin Makes a Laughing Sound: A Birder's Journal,* the art already existed in my journals and suggested the book idea to me. That feels like a natural

way for me to work—the art leads me to what I want to write about, and that, in turn, inspires new art."

Biographical and Critical Sources

PERIODICALS

Booklist, February 17, 1992, review of *Peter's Trucks,* p. 61; March 1, 1992, Stephanie Zvirin, review of *Peter's Trucks,* p. 1287; March 1, 2008, Randall Enos, review of *Truck Stuck,* p. 74.

Bulletin of the Center for Children's Books, May, 1992, Stephanie Zvirin, review of *Peter's Trucks,* p. 251.

Chicago Tribune, June 26, 2005, Web Behrens, "The Aldler Explores Limits of Artistic Expression."

Horn Book, March-April, 2008, Robin L. Smith, review of *Truck Stuck,* p. 211.

Kirkus Reviews, February 1, 1992, review of *Peter's Trucks,* p. 191; December 15, 2007, review of *Truck Stuck.*

School Library Journal, June, 1992, Susan Hepler, review of *Peter's Trucks,* p. 105; February, 2008, Linda Staskus, review of *Truck Stuck,* p. 98.

ONLINE

Sallie Wolf Home Page, http://www.salliewolf.com (September 1, 2009).

Sallie Wolf Web log, http://truckstuck.blogspot.com/ (September 1, 2009).

Triblocal.com, http://www.triblocal.com/ (January 28, 2009), Katie Leimkuehler, "Oak Park Artist Creates Own Career Path."

*   *   *

WULF, Linda Press

Personal

Born in South Africa; married Stanley Wulf; children: Ami, Yoni (sons). *Education:* Obtained B.A. in South Africa; studied at University of California, Berkeley.

Addresses

Home—Berkeley, CA.

Career

Editor, journalist, and educator. Macmillan, Toronto, Ontario, Canada, editor for ten years.

Awards, Honors

Sydney Taylor Manuscript Award and Book Award Honor Book designation, California Writers Club First Prize for Children's Fiction, New York Public Library 100 Titles for Reading and Sharing inclusion, and *ForWord* magazine Best Children's Book designation, all 2006, all for *The Night of the Burning.*

Writings

The Night of the Burning: Devorah's Story (novel), Farrar, Straus & Giroux (New York, NY), 2006.

Sidelights

Linda Press Wulf is an editor, journalist, and educator. Wulf was born in South Africa but moved out of the country as soon as she finished her undergraduate studies, fearing that the apartheid situation in that country would become much worse, and even deadly. She pursued graduate studies at the University of California, Berkeley, and then lived and worked in Canada, Japan, and Israel before settling in the San Francisco Bay area.

In 2006 Wulf published her first book, *The Night of the Burning: Devorah's Story.* Twelve-year-old Devorah takes care of her younger sister, Nechama, after her parents die from typhus in war-torn Poland in the early 1920s. They are extracted from that country as part of a group of Jewish orphans and sent to South Africa for adoption. Upon arrival in Cape Town, she is adopted separately from her younger sister. Devorah, a character based closely on the life and experiences of Wulf's own mother-in-law, narrates the story and describes how she adapts to life in her new country as part of a less-financially secure family. She also reflects upon the life she knew in Poland, living with her biological parents and her sister. In the end, Devorah realizes that she must move forward and accept her present circumstances because it is impossible to return to the way life used to be.

Jill Murphy, writing for *Bookbag* online, noted that *The Night of the Burning* contains "some wonderful and homely descriptions of life in the Polish shtetls in the early part of the twentieth century." "Wulf draws some canny parallels between the treatment Devorah has received as a Jew and the colonial treatment of black people in South Africa," Murphy added. In a *MyShelf.com* review, Beverly J. Rowe related that the novel successfully recreates "the very real horrors of war, racism, and religious prejudice, and is also a wonderful story of triumph and joy that you will never forget." Also reviewing Wulf's tale, *Booklist* contributor Hazel Rochman commented that "the history of persecution and immigration will echo with many American families," and Janis Flint-Ferguson wrote in *Kliatt* that *The Night of the Burning* "sheds light on a little-known historical circumstance" that "enriches the story of Jewish struggle and survival." Sue Giffard, writing in *School Library Journal,* described the book as "an insightful exploration of the effects of traumatic" life events in which "the historical background in both countries is well por-

trayed." Giffard concluded that children in similar situations around the world "will take this story to their hearts," while a _Kirkus Reviews_ critic called Devorah "a sad, bittersweet, sometimes resentful, and starkly realistic" narrator.

Biographical and Critical Sources

PERIODICALS

Booklist, August 1, 2006, Hazel Rochman, review of _The Night of the Burning: Devorah's Story,_ p. 69.
Bulletin of the Center for Children's Books, December, 2006, Elizabeth Bush, review of _The Night of the Burning,_ p. 194.
Horn Book, November 1, 2006, Susan Dove Lempke, review of _The Night of the Burning,_ p. 728.
Kirkus Reviews, August 15, 2006, review of _The Night of the Burning,_ p. 854.

Kliatt, September, 2006, Janis Flint-Ferguson, review of _The Night of the Burning,_ p. 19.
Language Arts, May, 2007, Barbara Chatton, review of _The Night of the Burning,_ p. 497.
School Librarian, summer, 2007, Sarah Mears, review of _The Night of the Burning._
School Library Journal, January, 2007, Sue Giffard, review of _The Night of the Burning,_ p. 142.

ONLINE

Bookbag Web site, http://www.thebookbag.co.uk/ (February 5, 2008), Jill Murphy, review of _The Night of the Burning._
Linda Press Wulf Home Page, http://www.lindapresswulf. com (November 20, 2009).
MyShelf.com, http://www.myshelf.com/ (February 5, 2008), Beverly J. Rowe, review of _The Night of the Burning._*

Y-Z

YAZZIE, Johnson 1946-

Personal
Born 1946, in Pinon, AZ. *Education:* Attended University of Arts and Design (Helsinki, Finland), 2001; Northern Arizona University, B.F.A., 2002.

Addresses
Home—Heber, AZ.

Career
Illustrator, jewelry maker, and artist.

Writings

(Illustrator) Vee Browne, *The Stone Cutter and the Navajo Maiden,* translated by Lorraine Begay Manavi, Salina Bookshelf (Flagstaff, AZ), 2008.

Sidelights
Born on a Navajo reservation in the Four Corners region, artist Johnson Yazzie has built a career on capturing the natural beauty of the American Southwest on canvas. In 2008, Yazzie illustrated his first work for children, *The Stone Cutter and the Navajo Maiden,* a picture book written by Vee Browne. Interspersing Navajo vocabulary throughout, Browne tells the story of a young girl who accidentally breaks her deceased mother's *metate,* a kitchen implement used to grind corn. Looking to repair the object before her father's return, Cinnibah asks several artisans in her village for assistance, learning important traditions about her Navajo people along the way.

Writing in *School Library Journal,* Madeline J. Bryant maintained that Yazzie's "warm, impressionistic pastel and oil illustrations skillfully capture the desert landscape" in *The Stone Cutter and the Navajo Maiden,* while a *Kirkus Reviews* contributor commented favorably on the artist's use of color. The young protagonist's "red skirt and blue top provide vivid counterpoint to the ochres and browns of the desert landscape," the critic added.

Biographical and Critical Sources

PERIODICALS

Kirkus Reviews, June 15, 2008, review of *The Stone Cutter and the Navajo Maiden.*
School Library Journal, September, 2008, Madeline J. Bryant, review of *The Stone Cutter and the Navajo Maiden,* p. 140.

ONLINE

Johnson Yazzie Home Page, http://www.jjyazziearts.com (September 18, 2009).*

*   *   *

ZIEFERT, Harriet 1941-

Personal
Born July 7, 1941, in NJ. *Education:* Smith College, B.A.; New York University, M.A. (education).

Addresses
Office—Blue Apple Books, 515 Valley St., Ste. 108, Maplewood, NJ 07040.

Career
Writer and book packager, 1983—. Former elementary school teacher and school materials developer for Scholastic, New York, NY; publisher of Blue Apple Books and Begin Smart Books, Maplewood, NJ.

Awards, Honors

New Jersey Institute of Technology Award, 1987, for *Sarah's Questions* and *The Small Potatoes' Busy Beach Day*, 1988, for *Good Night, Jessie!, Hurry up, Jessie!, I Won't Go to Bed, Max and Diana and the Beach Day, Max and Diana and the Snowy Day, A New Coat for Anna, Pet Day, So Hungry!, Trip Day, Where's the Cat?, Where's the Dog?, Where's the Guinea Pig?,* and *Worm Day,* and 1990, for *Where Babies Come From: Stories to Help Parents Answer Preschoolers' Questions about Sex;* Outstanding Science Trade Book for Children designation, National Science Teachers Association/ Children's Book Council, 1990, for *Let's Get a Pet;* Teachers' Choice Award, International Reading Association, 2004, for *You Can't See Your Bones with Binoculars;* Best Children's Book of Year selection, Bank Street College of Education, for *Bigger than Daddy* and *Time Out, Buzzy.*

Writings

FOR CHILDREN

The Bath Book, Scholastic (New York, NY), 1981.

The Bed Book, Scholastic (New York, NY), 1981.

Clappity Clap!, photographs by Rudi Tesa, Viking (New York, NY), 1984.

Diggity Dig!, photographs by Rudi Tesa, Viking (New York, NY), 1984.

Zippety Zip!, photographs by Rudi Tesa, Viking (New York, NY), 1984.

Munchety Munch!, photographs by Rudi Tesa, Viking (New York, NY), 1984.

Baby Ben's Bow-Wow Book, illustrated by Norman Gorbaty, Random House (New York, NY), 1984.

Baby Ben's Busy Book, illustrated by Norman Gorbaty, Random House (New York, NY), 1984.

Baby Ben's Noisy Book, illustrated by Norman Gorbaty, Random House (New York, NY), 1984.

Flip the Switch!, illustrated by Norman Gorbaty, Grosset (New York, NY), 1984.

Push the Button, illustrated by Norman Gorbaty, Grosset (New York, NY), 1984.

Turn the Dial, illustrated by Norman Gorbaty, Grosset (New York, NY), 1984.

Turn the Key, illustrated by Norman Gorbaty, Grosset (New York, NY), 1984.

The Small Potatoes Club, illustrated by Richard Brown, Dell (New York, NY), 1984.

The Small Potatoes and the Magic Show, illustrated by Richard Brown, Dell (New York, NY), 1984.

Where Is My Dinner?, illustrated by Simms Taback, Grosset (New York, NY), 1984.

Where Is My Family?, illustrated by Simms Taback, Grosset (New York, NY), 1984.

Where Is My Friend?, illustrated by Simms Taback, Grosset (New York, NY), 1984.

Where Is My House?, illustrated by Simms Taback, Grosset (New York, NY), 1984.

On Our Way to the Barn, illustrated by Simms Taback, Harper (New York, NY), 1985.

On Our Way to the Forest, illustrated by Simms Taback, Harper (New York, NY), 1985.

On Our Way to the Water, illustrated by Simms Taback, Harper (New York, NY), 1985.

On Our Way to the Zoo, illustrated by Simms Taback, Harper (New York, NY), 1985.

Birthday Card, Where Are You?, illustrated by Richard Brown, Puffin (New York, NY), 1985.

The Small Potatoes and the Birthday Party, illustrated by Richard Brown, Dell (New York, NY), 1985.

The Small Potatoes and the Sleep-over, illustrated by Richard Brown, Dell (New York, NY), 1985.

Where's My Easter Egg?, illustrated by Richard Brown, Puffin (New York, NY), 1985.

Where's the Halloween Treat?, illustrated by Richard Brown, Puffin (New York, NY), 1985.

Baby Ben Gets Dressed, illustrated by Norman Gorbaty, Random House (New York, NY), 1985.

A Dozen Dogs, illustrated by Carol Nicklaus, Random House (New York, NY), 1985.

So Sick!, illustrated by Carol Nicklaus, Random House (New York, NY), 1985.

Lewis the Firefighter, illustrated by Carol Nicklaus, Random House (New York, NY), 1986.

Good Night, Lewis!, illustrated by Carol Nicklaus, Random House (New York, NY), 1986.

Keeping Daddy Awake on the Way Home from the Beach, illustrated by Seymour Chwast, Harper (New York, NY), 1986.

My Sister Says Nothing Ever Happens When We Go Sailing, illustrated by Seymour Chwast, Harper (New York, NY), 1986.

A New Coat for Anna, illustrated by Anita Lobel, Knopf (New York, NY), 1986.

All Clean!, illustrated by Henrik Drescher, Harper (New York, NY), 1986.

All Gone!, illustrated by Henrik Drescher, Harper (New York, NY), 1986.

Cock-a-Doodle-Doo!, illustrated by Henrik Drescher, Harper (New York, NY), 1986.

Run! Run!, illustrated by Henrik Drescher, Harper (New York, NY), 1986.

Bear All Year, illustrated by Arnold Lobel, Viking (New York, NY), 1986.

Bear Gets Dressed, illustrated by Arnold Lobel, Viking (New York, NY), 1986.

Bear Goes Shopping, illustrated by Arnold Lobel, Viking (New York, NY), 1986.

Bear's Busy Morning, illustrated by Arnold Lobel, Viking (New York, NY), 1986.

Sarah's Questions, illustrated by Susan Bonners, Lothrop (New York, NY), 1986.

The Small Potatoes and the Snowball Fight, illustrated by Richard Brown, Dell (New York, NY), 1986.

The Small Potatoes' Busy Beach Day, illustrated by Richard Brown, Dell (New York, NY), 1986.

Harry Takes a Bath, illustrated by Mavis Smith, Viking (New York, NY), 1986.

Dress Little Bunny, illustrated by Lisa Campbell Ernst, Viking (New York, NY), 1986.

Play with Little Bunny, illustrated by Lisa Campbell Ernst, Viking (New York, NY), 1986.

Let's Go! Piggety Pig, illustrated by David Prebenna, Little, Brown (New York, NY), 1986.

Listen! Piggety Pig, illustrated by David Prebenna, Little, Brown (New York, NY), 1986.

No More! Piggety Pig, illustrated by David Prebenna, Little, Brown (New York, NY), 1986.

Piggety Pig from Morning 'til Night, illustrated by David Prebenna, Little, Brown (New York, NY), 1986.

A New House for Mole and Mouse, illustrated by David Prebenna, Puffin (New York, NY), 1987.

Good Night, Jessie!, illustrated by Mavis Smith, Random House (New York, NY), 1987.

Harry Takes a Bath, illustrated by Mavis Smith, Viking (New York, NY), 1987.

So Big!, illustrated by Mavis Smith, Random House (New York, NY), 1987.

So Busy!, illustrated by Mavis Smith, Random House (New York, NY), 1987.

So Clean!, illustrated by Mavis Smith, Random House (New York, NY), 1987.

So Hungry!, illustrated by Mavis Smith, Random House (New York, NY), 1987.

So Little!, illustrated by Mavis Smith, Random House (New York, NY), 1987.

Mike and Tony: Best Friends, illustrated by Katherine Siracusa, Viking (New York, NY), 1987.

Say Good Night!, illustrated by Katherine Siracusa, Puffin (New York, NY), 1987.

Jason's Bus Ride, illustrated by Simms Taback, Viking (New York, NY), 1987.

Where's the Cat?, illustrated by Simms Taback, Harper (New York, NY), 1987.

Where's the Dog?, illustrated by Simms Taback, Harper (New York, NY), 1987.

Where's the Turtle?, illustrated by Simms Taback, Harper (New York, NY), 1987.

Where's the Guinea Pig?, illustrated by Simms Taback, Harper (New York, NY), 1987.

The Good-Day Bunnies, illustrated by Carol Nicklaus, Golden (New York, NY), 1987.

Lewis Said, Lewis Did, illustrated by Carol Nicklaus, Random House (New York, NY), 1987.

I Won't Go to Bed!, illustrated by Andrea Baruffi, Little, Brown (New York, NY), 1987.

Daddy, Can You Play with Me?, illustrated by Emilie Boon, Viking (New York, NY), 1988.

Mommy, Where Are You?, illustrated by Emilie Boon, Puffin (New York, NY), 1988.

Dark Night, Sleepy Night, illustrated by Andrea Baruffi, Viking (New York, NY), 1988.

Good Night, Everyone!, illustrated by Andrea Baruffi, Little, Brown (New York, NY), 1988.

Andy Toots His Horn, illustrated by Sanford Hoffman, Viking (New York, NY), 1988.

Chocolate Mud Cake, illustrated by Karen Gundersheimer, Harper (New York, NY), 1988.

Happy Birthday, Grandpa!, illustrated by Sidney Levitt, Harper (New York, NY), 1988.

Happy Easter, Grandma!, illustrated by Sidney Levitt, Harper (New York, NY), 1988.

Me, Too! Me, Too!, illustrated by Karen Gundersheimer, Harper (New York, NY), 1988.

Don't Cry, Baby Sam, illustrated by Richard Brown, Viking (New York, NY), 1988.

Egg-Drop Day, illustrated by Richard Brown, Little, Brown (New York, NY), 1988.

Here Comes a Bus, illustrated by Richard Brown, Puffin (New York, NY), 1988.

Mystery Day, illustrated by Richard Brown, Little, Brown (New York, NY), 1988.

Finding Robin Redbreast, illustrated by Mavis Smith, Puffin (New York, NY), 1988.

Strike Four!, illustrated by Mavis Smith, Viking (New York, NY), 1988.

What Do I Hear?, illustrated by Mavis Smith, Bantam (New York, NY), 1988.

What Do I See?, illustrated by Mavis Smith, Bantam (New York, NY), 1988.

What Do I Smell?, illustrated by Mavis Smith, Bantam (New York, NY), 1988.

What Do I Taste?, illustrated by Mavis Smith, Bantam (New York, NY), 1988.

What Do I Touch?, illustrated by Mavis Smith, Bantam (New York, NY), 1988.

A Clean House for Mole and Mouse, illustrated by David Prebenna, Viking (New York, NY), 1988.

Breakfast Time!, illustrated by Lisa Campbell Ernst, Simon & Schuster (New York, NY), 1988, reprinted, Blue Apple Books (Maplewood, NJ), 2006.

Bye-Bye, Daddy, illustrated by Lisa Campbell Ernst, Simon & Schuster (New York, NY), 1988.

Count with Little Bunny, illustrated by Lisa Campbell Ernst, Viking (New York, NY), 1988.

Feed Little Bunny, illustrated by Lisa Campbell Ernst, Viking (New York, NY), 1988.

Cat Games, illustrated by Claire Schumacher, Viking (New York, NY), 1988.

Snow Magic, illustrated by Claire Schumacher, Viking (New York, NY), 1988.

Good Morning, Sun!, illustrated by Lisa Campbell Ernst, Viking (New York, NY), 1988, Blue Apple Books (Maplewood, NJ), 2006.

Let's Get Dressed, illustrated by Lisa Campbell Ernst, Viking (New York, NY), 1988.

Going on a Lion Hunt, illustrated by Mavis Smith, Puffin (New York, NY), 1989.

In a Scary Old House, illustrated by Mavis Smith, Puffin (New York, NY), 1989.

My Getting-Ready-for-School Book, illustrated by Mavis Smith, Random House (New York, NY), 1989.

When the TV Broke, illustrated by Mavis Smith, Viking (New York, NY), 1989.

Animal Count, Puffin (New York, NY), 1989.

Bears 1, 2, 3, Random House (New York, NY), 1989.

Before I Was Born, illustrated by Rufus Coes, Knopf (New York, NY), 1989.

No More TV, Sleepy Dog, illustrated by Norman Gorbaty, Random House (New York, NY), 1989.

Boats, Puffin (New York, NY), 1989.

Can You Play?, Random House (New York, NY), 1989.

Dr. Cat, illustrated by Suzy Mandel, Viking (New York, NY), 1989.

Harry Goes to Fun Land, Puffin (New York, NY), 1989.

Let's Trade, illustrated by Mary Morgan, Puffin (New York, NY), 1989.

New Boots for Spring, illustrated by Deborah Kogan Ray, Viking (New York, NY), 1989.

No Ball Games Here, Puffin (New York, NY), 1989.

Please Let It Snow, illustrated by Amy Aitken, Viking (New York, NY), 1989.

The Prince Has a Boo-Boo!, illustrated by R.W. Alley, Random House (New York, NY), 1989.

Wait for Us!, illustrated by Amy Aitken, Random House (New York, NY), 1989.

Wish for a Fish, illustrated by Argus Childers, Random House (New York, NY), 1989.

With Love from Grandma, illustrated by Deborah Kogan Ray, Viking (New York, NY), 1989.

The Best Castle Ever, illustrated by Carol Nicklaus, Random House (New York, NY), 1989.

Henry's Wrong Turn, illustrated by Andrea Baruffi, Little, Brown (New York, NY), 1989, reprinted, Sterling Publishing (New York, NY), 2006.

How Big Is Big?, illustrated by Andrea Baruffi, Viking (New York, NY), 1989.

(With Martin Silverman) *Where Babies Come From: Stories to Help Parents Answer Preschoolers' Questions about Sex,* illustrated by Claire Schumacher, Random House (New York, NY), 1989.

The Big Birthday Box, illustrated by Laura Rader, Random House (New York, NY), 1989.

In My Kitchen, illustrated by Laura Rader, Random House (New York, NY), 1989.

Follow Me!, illustrated by Laura Rader, Puffin (New York, NY), 1990.

Getting Ready for the New Baby, illustrated by Laura Rader, Harper (New York, NY), 1990.

The Wheels on the Bus, illustrated by Andrea Baruffi, Random House (New York, NY), 1990.

Little Bunny's Melon Patch, illustrated by Lisa Campbell Ernst, Puffin (New York, NY), 1990.

I Want to Sleep in Your Bed!, illustrated by Mavis Smith, Harper (New York, NY), 1990.

Let's Get a Pet, illustrated by Mavis Smith, Houghton Mifflin (Boston, MA), 1990.

My Getting-Ready-for-Christmas Book, illustrated by Mavis Smith, Harper (New York, NY), 1990.

My Getting-Ready-for-Bed Book, illustrated by Mavis Smith, Harper (New York, NY), 1990.

Let's Swap, Puffin (New York, NY), 1990.

Parade, illustrated by Saul Mandel, Bantam (New York, NY), 1990.

The Prince's Tooth Is Loose, illustrated by R.W. Alley, Random House (New York, NY), 1990.

Stitches, illustrated by Amy Aitken, Puffin (New York, NY), 1990.

Tim and Jim Take Off, illustrated by Suzy Mandel, Viking (New York, NY), 1990.

Under the Water, illustrated by Suzy Mandel, Puffin (New York, NY), 1990.

Who Can Boo the Loudest?, Harper (New York, NY), 1990.

Noisy Barn!, illustrated by Simms Taback, Harper (New York, NY), 1990.

Zoo Parade!, illustrated by Simms Taback, Harper (New York, NY), 1990.

Penny Goes to the Movies, illustrated by Laura Rader, Viking (New York, NY), 1990.

A Car Trip for Mole and Mouse, illustrated by David Prebenna, Puffin (New York, NY), 1991.

Homes, Scholastic (New York, NY), 1991.

Sometimes I Share, illustrated by Carol Nicklaus, HarperCollins (New York, NY), 1991.

Later, Rover, illustrated by David Jacobson, Puffin (New York, NY), 1991.

Measure Me: A Counting Book, HarperCollins (New York, NY), 1991.

Take My Picture!, illustrated by Amy Aitken, HarperCollins (New York, NY), 1991.

When Daddy Had the Chicken Pox, illustrated by Lionel Kalish, HarperCollins (New York, NY), 1991.

Good Luck, Bad Luck, illustrated by Lillie James, Puffin (New York, NY), 1991.

Bob and Shirley: A Tale of Two Lobsters, illustrated by Mavis Smith, HarperCollins (New York, NY), 1991.

Harry Gets Ready for School, illustrated by Mavis Smith, Puffin (New York, NY), 1991.

Tommy the Winner, illustrated by Claire Schumacher, HarperCollins (New York, NY), 1991.

When Will Santa Come?, illustrated by Claire Schumacher, HarperCollins (New York, NY), 1991.

Bigger than a Baby, illustrated by Laura Rader, HarperCollins (New York, NY), 1991.

Dancing, illustrated by Laura Rader, HarperCollins (New York, NY), 1991.

Goody New Shoes, illustrated by Laura Rader, Puffin (New York, NY), 1991.

I Hate Boots!, illustrated by Laura Rader, HarperCollins (New York, NY), 1991.

Move Over, illustrated by Laura Rader, HarperCollins (New York, NY), 1991.

My Apple Tree, illustrated by Laura Rader, HarperCollins (New York, NY), 1991.

Big to Little, Little to Big, illustrated by Susan Baum, Simon & Schuster (New York, NY), 1991.

Empty to Full, Full to Empty, illustrated by Susan Baum, HarperCollins (New York, NY), 1992.

Clothes on, Clothes Off, illustrated by Susan Baum, HarperCollins (New York, NY), 1992.

Count up, Count Down, illustrated by Susan Baum, HarperCollins (New York, NY), 1992.

What Is Father's Day?, illustrated by Claire Schumacher, HarperCollins (New York, NY), 1992.

What Is Mother's Day?, illustrated by Claire Schumacher, HarperCollins (New York, NY), 1992.

What Is Halloween?, illustrated by Claire Schumacher, HarperCollins (New York, NY), 1992.

What Is Thanksgiving?, illustrated by Claire Schumacher, HarperCollins (New York, NY), 1992.

Come Visit My House!, illustrated by Mavis Smith, Viking (New York, NY), 1992.

Halloween Parade, illustrated by Lillie James, Puffin (New York, NY), 1992.

The Big, Red Blanket, illustrated by David Jacobson, HarperCollins (New York, NY), 1992.

Music Lessons, HarperCollins (New York, NY), 1992.

My Daddy, Viking (New York, NY), 1992.

My Mommy, Viking (New York, NY), 1992.

My Puppy, Viking (New York, NY), 1992.

The Princess Needs a Bath, HarperCollins (New York, NY), 1992.

Sam and Lucy, illustrated by Claire Schumacher, HarperCollins (New York, NY), 1992.

Who Spilled the Milk?, HarperCollins (New York, NY), 1992.

Here Comes a Truck, illustrated by Richard Brown, Puffin (New York, NY), 1992.

Where's Daddy's Car?, illustrated by Andrea Baruffi, HarperCollins (New York, NY), 1992.

Where's Mommy's Truck?, illustrated by Andrea Baruffi, HarperCollins (New York, NY), 1992.

What's a Birthday?, illustrated by Claire Schumacher, HarperFestival (New York, NY), 1993.

What's a Vacation?, illustrated by Claire Schumacher, HarperFestival (New York, NY), 1993.

What's a Wedding?, illustrated by Claire Schumacher, HarperFestival (New York, NY), 1993.

Scooter's Christmas, illustrated by Richard Brown, Harper (New York, NY), 1993.

Clown Games, illustrated by Larry Stevens, Puffin (New York, NY), 1993.

Three Wishes, illustrated by David Jacobson, Puffin (New York, NY), 1993.

Where's Bobo?, illustrated by Lillie James, Tambourine (New York, NY), 1993.

My Camera, illustrated by Laura Rader, illustrated by Laura Rader, Ziefert, Inc., 1993.

My Cassette Player, illustrated by Laura Rader, Ziefert, Inc., 1993.

My Telephone, illustrated by Laura Rader, Ziefert, Inc., 1993.

My Television, illustrated by Laura Rader, Ziefert, Inc., 1993.

My Valentines, illustrated by Laura Rader, Harper (New York, NY), 1993.

Bear's Colors, illustrated by Susan Baum, HarperCollins (New York, NY), 1993.

Bear's Numbers, illustrated by Susan Baum, HarperCollins (New York, NY), 1993.

Bear's Shapes, illustrated by Susan Baum, HarperCollins (New York, NY), 1993.

Bear's Weather, illustrated by Susan Baum, HarperCollins (New York, NY), 1993.

(Reteller) *Goldilocks and the Three Bears,* illustrated by Laura Rader, Tambourine (New York, NY), 1994.

Pete's Chicken, illustrated by Laura Rader, Tambourine (New York, NY), 1994.

(Reteller) *The Three Billy Goats Gruff,* illustrated by Laura Rader, Tambourine (New York, NY), 1994.

What Is Hanukkah?, illustrated by Rick Brown, HarperFestival (New York, NY), 1994.

What Is Passover?, illustrated by Lillie James, HarperFestival (New York, NY), 1994.

Where Is My Baby?, illustrated by Simms Taback, HarperFestival (New York, NY), 1994.

Animals of the Bible, illustrated by Letizia Galli, Doubleday (New York, NY), 1995.

The Best Smelling Alphabet Book, Little Simon (New York, NY), 1995.

Little Mouse Meets Santa, HarperFestival (New York, NY), 1995.

Little Mouse Meets the Easter Bunny, HarperFestival (New York, NY), 1995.

Scare the Moon, Candlewick Press (Cambridge, MA), 1995.

What Rhymes with Eel?, Viking (New York, NY), 1995.

What's Polite? Puffin (New York, NY), 1995.

What's Pretend?, Puffin (New York, NY), 1995.

(Reteller) *The Teeny-Tiny Woman,* illustrated by Laura Rader, Viking (New York, NY), 1995.

(Reteller) *The Three Little Pigs,* illustrated by Laura Rader, Viking (New York, NY), 1995.

Happy Birthday, Little Bear, illustrated by Susan Baum, Viking (New York, NY), 1995.

Take Care of Brown Bear, illustrated by Susan Baum, Viking (New York, NY), 1995.

(Reteller) *The Gingerbread Boy,* illustrated by Emily Bolam, Puffin (New York, NY), 1995.

(Reteller) *The Little Red Hen,* illustrated by Emily Bolam, Puffin (New York, NY), 1995.

Oh, What a Noisy Farm!, illustrated by Emily Bolam, Tambourine (New York, NY), 1995.

(Reteller) *The Princess and the Pea,* illustrated by Emily Bolam, Penguin (New York, NY), 1996.

The Turnip, illustrated by Laura Rader, Puffin (New York, NY), 1996.

Animal Play, DK (New York, NY), 1996.

My Clothes, DK (New York, NY), 1996.

My Food, DK (New York, NY), 1996.

Play Colors, DK (New York, NY), 1996.

Play Shapes, DK (New York, NY), 1996.

Rosie Rabbit's Easter, illustrated by Laura Rader, Candlewick Press (Cambridge, MA), 1996.

Rosie Rabbit's Valentine's Day, illustrated by Laura Rader, Candlewick Press (Cambridge, MA), 1996.

Rosie's Red String, DK (New York, NY), 1996.

Sam's Boo-Boo, DK (New York, NY), 1996.

Two Little Witches, illustrated by Simms Taback, Candlewick Press (Cambridge, MA), 1996.

Who Said Moo?, illustrated by Simms Taback, HarperFestival (New York, NY), 1996.

Benjy Bear's Christmas, illustrated by Emilie Boon, Candlewick Press (Cambridge, MA), 1996.

Benjy Bear's Halloween, illustrated by Emilie Boon, Candlewick Press (Cambridge, MA), 1996.

Little Hippo and the New Baby, illustrated by Emilie Boon, DK (New York, NY), 1997.

Eight Days of Hanukkah, illustrated by Melinda Levine, Viking (New York, NY), 1997.

Wee G., illustrated by Donald Saaf, Atheneum (New York, NY), 1997.

Baby Buggy, Buggy Baby, illustrated by Richard Brown, Houghton Mifflin (Boston, MA), 1997.

Night, Knight, illustrated by Richard Brown, Houghton Mifflin (Boston, MA), 1997.

Bears Odd, Bears Even, illustrated by Andrea Baruffi, Viking (New York, NY), 1997.

Math Riddles, illustrated by Andrea Baruffi, Viking (New York, NY), 1997.

Sleepy-O!, illustrated by Laura Rader, Houghton Mifflin (Boston, MA), 1997.

(Reteller) *Henny-Penny,* illustrated by Emily Bolam, Viking (New York, NY), 1997.

(Reteller) *The Magic Porridge Pot,* illustrated by Emily Bolam, Viking (New York, NY), 1997.

Mother Goose Math, illustrated by Emily Bolam, Viking (New York, NY), 1997.

The Cow in the House, illustrated by Emily Bolam, Puffin (New York, NY), 1997.

No Bath Tonight!, illustrated by Emily Bolam, DK (New York, NY), 1997.

(Reteller) *The Ugly Duckling,* illustrated by Emily Bolam, Puffin (New York, NY), 1997.

I Swapped My Dog, illustrated by Emily Bolam, Houghton Mifflin (Boston, MA), 1998.

A Polar Bear Can Swim, illustrated by Emily Bolam, Viking (New York, NY), 1998.

Rabbit and Hare Divide an Apple, illustrated by Emily Bolam, Viking (New York, NY), 1998.

Elomenopeo, illustrated by Donald Saaf, Houghton Mifflin (Boston, MA), 1998.

Max's Potty illustrated by Emily Bolam, DK (New York, NY), 1998.

Sarah's Potty, illustrated by Emily Bolam, DK (New York, NY), 1998.

Pushkin Meets the Bundle, illustrated by Donald Saaf, Atheneum (New York, NY), 1998.

Flip Flop Words, illustrated by Rick Brown, Dutton (New York, NY), 1998.

A Dozen Dozens, illustrated by Chris Demarest, Viking (New York, NY), 1998.

Bugs, Beetles, and Butterflies, illustrated by Lisa Flather, Viking (New York, NY), 1998.

(Reteller) *When I First Came to This Land,* illustrated by Simms Taback, Putnam (New York, NY), 1998.

Little Hippo's New Friend, illustrated by Emilie Boon, DK (New York, NY), 1998.

Little Hippo's New House, illustrated by Emilie Boon, DK (New York, NY), 1998.

Little Hippo's New School, illustrated by Emilie Boon, DK (New York, NY), 1998.

Mommies Are for Counting Stars, illustrated by Cynthia Jabar, Puffin (New York, NY), 1999.

Animal Music, illustrated by Donald Saaf, Houghton Mifflin (Boston, MA), 1999.

I Need a Valentine!, illustrated by Chris Demarest, Little Simon (New York, NY), 1999.

First Night, illustrated by S.D. Schindler, Putnam (New York, NY), 1999.

Daddies Are for Catching Fireflies, illustrated by Cynthia Jabar, Puffin (New York, NY), 1999.

I Need an Easter Egg!, illustrated by Laura Rader, Little Simon (New York, NY), 1999.

Talk, Baby!, illustrated by Emily Bolam, Henry Holt (New York, NY), 1999.

(Reteller) *Little Red Riding Hood,* illustrated by Emily Bolam, Viking (New York, NY), 2000.

Clara Ann Cookie Go to Bed! illustrated by Emily Bolam, Houghton Mifflin (Boston, MA), 2000.

Presents for Santa, illustrated by Laura Rader, Viking (New York, NY), 2000.

Pumpkin Pie, illustrated by Donald Dreifuss, Houghton Mifflin (Boston, MA), 2000.

Moonride, illustrated by Seymour Chwast, Houghton Mifflin (Boston, MA), 2000.

Hats off for the Fourth of July!, illustrated by Gustaf Miller, Viking (New York, NY), 2000.

Grandpas Are for Finding Worms, illustrated by Jennifer Plecas (New York, NY), 2000.

Grandmas Are for Giving Tickles, illustrated by Jennifer Plecas (New York, NY), 2000.

Train Song, illustrated by Donald Saaf, Orchard (New York, NY), 2000.

April Fool!, illustrated by Chris Demarest, Viking (New York, NY), 2000.

(Reteller) *The Snow Child,* illustrated by Julia Zanes, Viking (New York, NY), 2000.

First He Made the Sun, illustrated by Todd McKie, Putnam (New York, NY), 2000.

Ode to Humpty Dumpty, illustrated by Seymour Chwast, Houghton Mifflin (Boston, MA), 2001.

What Do Ducks Dream?, illustrated by Donald Saaf, Putnam (New York, NY), 2001.

Someday We'll Have Very Good Manners, illustrated by Chris Demarest, Putnam (New York, NY), 2001.

Ding-dong, Trick or Treat!, illustrated by Chris Demarest, Grosset (New York, NY), 2001.

Birdhouse for Rent, illustrated by Donald Dreifuss, Houghton Mifflin (Boston, MA), 2001.

Thirty-nine Uses for a Friend, illustrated by Rebecca Doughty, Putnam (New York, NY), 2001.

On Halloween Night, illustrated by Renee Andriani, Puffin (New York, NY), 2001.

Squarehead, illustrated by Todd McKie, Houghton Mifflin (Boston, MA), 2001.

No Kiss for Grandpa, illustrated by Emilie Boon, Orchard (New York, NY), 2001.

Murphy Meets the Treadmill, illustrated by Emily Bolam, Houghton Mifflin (Boston, MA), 2001.

Teachers Are for Reading Stories, illustrated by Emily Bolam, Puffin (New York, NY), 2002.

My Funny Valentine, illustrated by Emily Bolam, Puffin (New York, NY), 2002.

Cousins Are for Holiday Visits, illustrated by Emily Bolam, Puffin (New York, NY), 2002.

Egad Alligator!, illustrated by Todd McKie, Houghton Mifflin (Boston, MA), 2002.

You Can't Taste a Pickle with Your Ear: A Book about Your Five Senses, illustrated by Amanda Haley, Blue Apple (New York, NY), 2002.

Toes Have Wiggles, Kids Have Giggles, illustrated by Rebecca Doughty, Putnam (New York, NY), 2002.

Kitty Says Meow, illustrated by Santiago Cohen, Grosset (New York, NY), 2002.

From Kalamazoo to Timbuktu, illustrated by Gustaf Miller, Putnam (New York, NY), 2002.

Christmas Has Merry!, illustrated by Rebecca Doughty, Handprint (New York, NY), 2002.

A Dozen Dogs: A Math Reader, illustrated by Carol Nicklaus, Random House (New York, NY), 2003.

You Can't See Your Bones with Binoculars: A Guide to Your 206 Bones, illustrated by Amanda Haley, Blue Apple (Maplewood, NJ), 2003.

You Can't Buy a Dinosaur with a Dime: Problem Solving in Dollars and Cents, illustrated by Amanda Haley, Blue Apple (Maplewood, NJ), 2003.

Home for Navidad, illustrated by Santiago Cohen, Houghton Mifflin (Boston, MA), 2003.

Hey Irma!: This Is Halloween, illustrated by Barry Gott, Blue Apple (Brooklyn, NY), 2003.

A Dozen Ducklings Lost and Found, illustrated by Donald Dreifuss, Houghton Mifflin (Boston, MA), 2003.

Thirty-one Uses for a Mom, illustrated by Rebecca Doughty, Putnam (New York, NY), 2003.

Sleepy Dog, illustrated by Norman Gorbaty, Random House (New York, NY), 2003.

Lunchtime for a Purple Snake, illustrated by Todd McKie, Houghton Mifflin (Boston, MA), 2003.

This Little Egg Went to Market, illustrated by Emily Bolam, Puffin (New York, NY), 2003.

Buzzy's Big Bedtime Book, illustrated by Emily Bolam, Blue Apple Books (Maplewood, NJ), 2004.

Buzzy's Birthday, illustrated by Emily Bolam, Blue Apple Books (Maplewood, NJ), 2004.

Buzzy's Boo-boo, illustrated by Emily Bolam, Blue Apple Books (Maplewood, NJ), 2004.

Murphy Meets Paris, illustrated by Emily Bolam, Blue Apple Books (Maplewood, NJ), 2004.

Sometimes Buzzy Shares: A Lift-the-Flap Story, illustrated by Emily Bolam, Blue Apple Books (Maplewood, NJ), 2004.

Rockheads, illustrated by Todd McKie, Houghton Mifflin (Boston, MA), 2004.

Forty-four Uses for a Dog, illustrated by Todd McKie, Barnes & Noble Press (New York, NY), 2004.

Forty-one Uses for a Cat, illustrated by Todd McKie, Barnes & Noble Press (New York, NY), 2004.

Schools Have Learn, illustrated by Amanda Haley, Blue Apple (Maplewood, NJ), 2004.

One Smart Skunk, illustrated by Santiago Cohen, Blue Apple (Maplewood, NJ), 2004.

Thirty-three Uses for a Dad, illustrated by Amanda Haley, Blue Apple Books (Maplewood, NJ), 2004.

Bear's Busy Morning: A Guessing-game Story, illustrated by Arnold Lobel, Sterling Publishing (New York, NY), 2004.

Hey Irma!: It's Mother's Day, illustrated by Barry Gott, Blue Apple Books (Maplewood, NJ), 2004.

Hey, Irma!: It's a Contest, illustrated by Barry Gott, Blue Apple Books (Maplewood, NJ), 2004.

I Wish Santa Would Come by Helicopter, illustrated by Amanda Haley Sterling Publishing (New York, NY), 2004.

My Friend Grandpa, illustrated by Robert Wurzburg, Blue Apple Books (Maplewood, NJ), 2004.

Scare the Moon, illustrated by G. Brian Karas, Sterling Publishing (New York, NY), 2004.

This Is Thanksgiving, illustrated by Deborah Zemke, Blue Apple Books (Maplewood, NJ), 2004.

With Love from Grandma, illustrated by Deborah Kogan Ray, Sterling Publishing (New York, NY), 2004.

(With Fred Ehrlich, M.D.) *You Can't Take Your Body to a Repair Shop: A Book about What Makes You Sick,* illustrated by Amanda Haley, Blue Apple Books (Maplewood, NJ), 2004.

Noisy Forest!, illustrated by Simms Taback, Blue Apple Books (Maplewood, NJ), 2004.

Beach Party!, illustrated by Simms Taback, Blue Apple Books (Maplewood, NJ), 2005.

Thirty-five Uses for a Daughter, illustrated by Deborah Zemke, Blue Apple Books (Maplewood, NJ), 2005.

Thirty-eight Uses for a Husband, illustrated by Todd McKie, Sterling Publishing (New York, NY), 2005.

Thirty-nine Uses for a Wife, illustrated by Todd McKie, Sterling Publishing (New York, NY), 2005.

Forty Uses for a Grandpa, illustrated by Amanda Haley, Blue Apple Books (Maplewood, NJ), 2005.

Forty-one Uses for a Grandma, illustrated by Amanda Haley, Blue Apple Books (Maplewood, NJ), 2005.

All Dirty! All Clean!, illustrated by Rick Brown, Sterling Publishing (New York, NY), 2005.

Are We There Yet?, illustrated by Dale Gottlieb, Sterling Publishing (New York, NY), 2005.

Circus Parade, illustrated by Tanya Roitman, Blue Apple Books (Maplewood, NJ), 2005.

Families Have Together, illustrated by Deborah Zemke Blue Apple Books (Maplewood, NJ), 2005.

Go Away, Crows!, illustrated by Santiago Cohen, Sterling Publishing (New York, NY), 2005.

Good Dog, Rover, illustrated by Sanford Hoffman, Sterling Publishing (New York, NY), 2005.

Just like Mommy!, illustrated by Erik Brown, Sterling Publishing (New York, NY), 2005.

Night-night, Fuzzy!, illustrated by Elliot Kreloff, Blue Apple Books (Maplewood, NJ), 2005.

Pizza and Other Stinky Poems, illustrated by Amanda Haley, Sterling Publishing (New York, NY), 2005.

Ready, Alice?, illustrated by Amanda Haley, Sterling Publishing (New York, NY), 2005.

Take My Picture!, illustrated by Sanford Hoffman, Sterling Publishing (New York, NY), 2005.

The Big, Red Blanket, illustrated by David Jacobson, Sterling Publishing (New York, NY), 2005.

The Biggest Job of All, illustrated by Lauren Browne, Blue Apple Books (Maplewood, NJ), 2005.

The Pillow Fight, illustrated by Rich Rossi, Sterling Publishing (New York, NY), 2005.

The Prince's Tooth Is Loose, illustrated by R.W. Alley, Sterling Publishing (New York, NY), 2005.

Where Are the Dogsharks?, illustrated by Robert Wurzburg, Sterling Publishing (New York, NY), 2005.

Who Spilled the Milk?, illustrated by Martha Gradisher, Sterling Publishing (New York, NY), 2005.

If I Had a Robot Dog, illustrated by Andrea Baruffi, Sterling Publishing (New York, NY), 2005.

Silly Pig, illustrated by Laura Rader, Sterling Publishing (New York, NY), 2005.

Buzzy Had a Little Lamb, illustrated by Emily Bolam, Blue Apple Books (Maplewood, NJ), 2005.

Buzzy's Big Beach Book, illustrated by Emily Bolam, Blue Apple Books (Maplewood, NJ), 2006.

Fooba Wooba John, illustrated by Emily Bolam, Sterling Publishing (New York, NY), 2006.

Murphy Jumps a Hurdle, illustrated by Emily Bolam, Blue Apple Books (Maplewood, NJ), 2006.

Time Out, Buzzy, illustrated by Emily Bolam, Blue Apple Books (Maplewood, NJ), 2006.

A Bowlful of Rain, illustrated by R.W. Alley, Sterling Publishing (New York, NY), 2006.

Be Fair! Share!, illustrated by Pete Whitehead, Sterling Publishing (New York, NY), 2006.

Bigger than Daddy, illustrated by Elliot Kreloff, Blue Apple Books (Maplewood, NJ), 2006.

Dancing Class, illustrated by Amanda Haley, Sterling Publishing (New York, NY), 2006.

Fun Land Fun!, illustrated by Yukiko Kido, Sterling Publishing (New York, NY), 2006.

Grandma, It's for You!, illustrated by Lauren Browne, Blue Apple Books (Maplewood, NJ), 2006.

I'm Going to Boston to Visit the Ducks, illustrated by Tanya Roitman, Sterling Publishing (New York, NY), 2006.

I'm Going to Washington to Visit the President, illustrated by Tanya Roitman, Sterling Publishing (New York, NY), 2006.

In a Scary Old House, illustrated by Yukiko Kido, Sterling Publishing (New York, NY), 2006.

Just like Grandma!, illustrated by Erik Brown, Sterling Publishing (New York, NY), 2006.

Just like Grandpa!, illustrated by Erik Brown, Sterling Publishing (New York, NY), 2006.

Me! Me! ABC, illustrated by Ingri Von Bergen, Blue Apple Books (Maplewood, NJ), 2006.

No! Yes!, illustrated by Barry Gott, Sterling Publishing (New York, NY), 2006.

Ouch!, illustrated by Rich Rossi, Sterling Publishing (New York, NY), 2006.

Surprise!, illustrated by Richard Brown, Sterling Publishing (New York, NY), 2006.

That's What Grandmas Are For, illustrated by Amanda Haley, Blue Apple Books (Maplewood, NJ), 2006.

That's What Grandpas Are For, illustrated by Deborah Zemke, Blue Apple Books (Maplewood, NJ), 2006.

There Was a Little Girl, She Had a Little Curl, illustrated by Elliot Kreloff, Blue Apple Books (Maplewood, NJ), 2006.

Tic and Tac, illustrated by Elliot Kreloff, Sterling Publishing (New York, NY), 2006.

Too Much Tooting!, illustrated by Sanford Hoffman, Sterling Publishing (New York, NY), 2006.

A Bath for a Princess, illustrated by Amanda Haley, Sterling Publishing (New York, NY), 2007.

A Dozen Dozens, illustrated by Yukiko Kido, Sterling Publishing (New York, NY), 2007.

Christmas Is Coming!, illustrated by Chuck Nitzberg, Sterling Publishing (New York, NY), 2007.

Class Worms, illustrated by Barry Gott, Sterling Publishing (New York, NY), 2007.

Little Monster, illustrated by Pascale Constantin, Sterling Publishing (New York, NY), 2007.

Messy Bessie: Where's My Homework?, illustrated by Roger DeMuth, Blue Apple Books (Maplewood, NJ), 2007.

Buzzy's Balloon, illustrated by Emily Bolam, Blue Apple Books (Maplewood, NJ), 2007.

When Daddy Travels, illustrated by Emily Bolam, Sterling Publishing (New York, NY), 2007.

When Mommy Travels, illustrated by Emily Bolam, Sterling Publishing (New York, NY), 2007.

Lots and Lots, illustrated by Emily Bolam, Blue Apple Books (Maplewood, NJ), 2008.

ABC Dentist: Healthy Teeth from A to Z, illustrated by Liz Murphy, Blue Apple Books (Maplewood, NJ), 2008.

(With Fred Ehrlich) *A Bunny Is Funny: And So Is This Book!,* illustrated by Todd McKie, Blue Apple Books (Maplewood, NJ), 2008.

Baby Says, illustrated by Elliot Kreloff, Begin Smart Books (Maplewood, NJ), 2008.

Hanukkah Haiku, illustrated by Karla Gudeon, Blue Apple Books (Maplewood NJ), 2008.

Mighty Max!, illustrated by Elliot Kreloff, Blue Apple Books (Maplewood, NJ), 2008.

Mother Goose Manners, illustrated by Pascale Constantin, Blue Apple Books (Maplewood, NJ), 2008.

Peek-a-Boo What?, illustrated by Elliot Kreloff, Begin Smart Books (Maplewood, NJ), 2008.

Posey Paints a Princess, illustrated by Yukiko Kido, Blue Apple Books (Maplewood, NJ), 2008.

Posey Prefers Pink, illustrated by Yukiko Kido, Blue Apple Books (Maplewood, NJ), 2008.

Quack Shack, illustrated by Yukiko Kido, Blue Apple Books (Maplewood, NJ), 2008.

Snow Party, illustrated by Mark Jones, Blue Apple Books (Maplewood, NJ), 2008.

Wet Pet, illustrated by Yukiko Kido, Blue Apple Books (Maplewood, NJ), 2008.

By the Light of the Harvest Moon, illustrated by Mark Jones, Blue Apple Books (Maplewood, NJ), 2009.

Crab Cab, illustrated by Yukiko Kido, Blue Apple Books (Maplewood, NJ), 2009.

Live on Broadway: A Treasury of Theater from A to Z, introduction by Brian Stokes Mitchell, illustrated by Elliot Kreloff, Blue Apple Books (Maplewood, NJ), 2009.

My Forever Dress, illustrated by Liz Murphy, Blue Apple Books (Maplewood, NJ), 2009.

One Red Apple, illustrated by Karla Gudeon, Blue Apple Books (Maplewood, NJ), 2009.

Posey Plans a Party, illustrated by Yukiko Kido, Blue Apple Books (Maplewood, NJ), 2009.

Round Balls, Round Balls, illustrated with photographs by Will Winburn, Blue Apple Books (Maplewood, NJ), 2009.

You and Me: We're Opposites, illustrated by Ethan Long, Maplewood, NJ (Blue Apple Books), 2009.

Also author of school readers; author of *The Literature Experience,* 1991.

Ziefert's books have been translated into Spanish and French.

"NICKY" SERIES

Nicky's Christmas Surprise, illustrated by Richard Brown, Puffin (New York, NY), 1985.

Let's Watch Nicky, illustrated by Richard Brown, Viking (New York, NY), 1986.

Nicky's Friends, illustrated by Richard Brown, Viking (New York, NY), 1986.

Nicky's Noisy Night, illustrated by Richard Brown, Puffin (New York, NY), 1986.

Nicky's Picnic, illustrated by Richard Brown, Puffin (New York, NY), 1986.

No, No Nicky, illustrated by Richard Brown, Viking (New York, NY), 1986.

Nicky Upstairs and Down, illustrated by Richard Brown, Puffin (New York, NY), 1987.

Where Is Nicky's Valentine?, illustrated by Richard Brown, Puffin (New York, NY), 1987.

Thank You, Nicky, illustrated by Richard Brown, Puffin (New York, NY), 1988.

Oh No, Nicky!, illustrated by Richard Brown, Puffin (New York, NY), 1992.

Nicky, 1-2-3, illustrated by Emily Bolam, Puffin (New York, NY), 1995.

Nicky Visits the Airport, illustrated by Richard Brown, Puffin (New York, NY), 1997.

Nicky Visits the Fire Station, illustrated by Richard Brown, Puffin (New York, NY), 1997.

"MRS. ROSE'S CLASS" TRILOGY

Pet Day, illustrated by Richard Brown, Little, Brown (New York, NY), 1987.

Trip Day, illustrated by Richard Brown, Little, Brown (New York, NY), 1987.

Worm Day, illustrated by Richard Brown, Little, Brown (New York, NY), 1987.

"MAX AND DIANA" SERIES

Max and Diana and the Beach Day, illustrated by Lonni Sue Johnson, Harper (New York, NY), 1987.

Max and Diana and the Birthday Present, illustrated by Lonni Sue Johnson, Harper (New York, NY), 1987.

Max and Diana and the Shopping Day, illustrated by Lonni Sue Johnson, Harper (New York, NY), 1987.

Harriet Ziefert's many books for the youngest children include **Grandmas Are for Giving Tickles,** *a book featuring artwork by Jennifer Plecas.* (Illustration copyright © 2000 by Jennifer Plecas. Reproduced by permission of Puffin Books, a division of Penguin Putnam, Inc.)

Max and Diana and the Snowy Day, illustrated by Lonni Sue Johnson, Harper (New York, NY), 1987.

"JESSIE" SERIES

Hurry up, Jessie!, illustrated by Mavis Smith, Random House (New York, NY), 1987.

Come out, Jessie!, illustrated by Mavis Smith, Random House (New York, NY), 1988.

Dinner's Ready, Jessie!, illustrated by Mavis Smith, Random House (New York, NY), 1988.

FOR ADULTS

A Brides' Little Miseries, illustrated by Jennifer Rapp, Sterling Publishing (New York, NY), 2006.

Pregnancy's Little Miseries, illustrated by Jennifer Rapp, Sterling Publishing (New York, NY), 2006.

Adaptations

A New Coat for Anna was adapted for filmstrip, Random House (New York, NY), 1988.

Sidelights

Harriet Ziefert is the prolific author and packager of scores of easy-to-read picture books for very young readers. Among her popular titles are *A New Coat for Anna, Mommy, I Want to Sleep in Your Bed!*, and *ABC Dentist: Healthy Teeth from A to Z*, as well as series books such as the "Max and Diana" and "Jessie" sets. A former teacher, Ziefert saw a need for more simplified texts at the first-grade level. She has applied herself to filling that need, creating books that tell a story in a mere fifty to seventy-five words. Ziefert serves as the publisher of Blue Apple Books and Begin Smart Books, which focus on providing age-appropriate content for young audiences.

Born in 1941, Ziefert grew up in North Bergen, New Jersey, studied at Smith College, and earned a master's degree in education from New York University. Subsequently, she worked for many years in elementary schools, teaching at grade levels ranging from kindergarten to the fifth grade. When she had her own children, Ziefert quit teaching; as her children came of school age, she decided to return to work, but in the field of publishing. Working at Scholastic, Inc., she produced materials for kindergarten language-arts and social studies programs. While she hoped to become an editor, she was unsuccessful in finding a position; instead, she decided to write her own books.

Ziefert's resolve has spawned far more than a mere cottage industry. The list of the many titles she has released include concept books dealing with counting, the alphabet, rhyming, and questions as well as titles geared for pure enjoyment and featuring kittens, dogs, mice, chickens, and young boys and girls. Many of Ziefert's

Todd McKie's quirky cartoon art is a feature of Ziefert's humorous story **Rockheads.** (Illustration copyright © 2004 by Todd McKie. All right reserved. Reprinted by permission of Houghton Mifflin Harcourt Publishing Company.)

books are arranged in series, such as the "Mr. Rose's Class" trilogy: *Pet Day, Trip Day,* and *Worm Day.* These books feature, according to a *Publishers Weekly* reviewer, "a smart, bespectacled teacher who asks questions, interferes gently and nudges kids in his class to think about the world around them." Mr. Rose's students learn about pets, take an outing to a pond, and discover how worms mate in a series of books that "should appeal to beginning readers," according to *Booklist* contributor Denise M. Wilms.

Ziefert addresses basic pet recognition in *Where's the Dog?, Where's the Cat?, Where's the Guinea Pig?,* and *Where's the Turtle?* These board books "encourage the toddler to observe familiar pets in the house and yard as they run, eat, drink and rest," noted a *Kirkus Reviews* critic. Rhymed sentences introduce each animal, and a "lift-the-flap" picture allows young readers to discover the hidden animal. Heide Piehler, writing for *School Library Journal,* noted that children "will enjoy the recognizable creatures, the hiding game," and the series' illustrations by Simms Taback. Another of Ziefert's board-book series for toddlers features colorful animals enacting the same things most children do in their everyday lives. *So Big!, So Busy!, So Clean!, So Hungry!,* and *So Little!* demonstrate activities from getting dressed to playing with blocks and putting away toys. Sarah C. Vaughn, reviewing *So Hungry!* for *School Library Journal,* noted that an "added feature of this series is the note to parents that describes the various levels offered . . . and how best to use these books with children."

More animals make an appearance in a quartet of books illustrated by Henrik Drescher, each of which de-

scribes—in two-word sentences—how animals eat, drink, move, and make noise. *All Clean!, All Gone!, Cock-a-Doodle-Doo!,* and *Run! Run!* practice word skills while at the same time providing enjoyable reading via their "lively" texts, according to a reviewer in *Publishers Weekly.* "This foursome is fast-paced and fun," concluded the reviewer. Another of Ziefert's series for young readers includes *A New House for Mole and Mouse, Harry Takes a Bath, Jason's Bus Ride,* and *Mike and Tony: Best Friends.* The plotting for these stories is necessarily thin, "but illustrations are bold and bright," according to *Booklist* reviewer Ilene Cooper. As the series progresses, a pair of animal friends happily move into a new house; a hippo named Harry takes a messy bath; a dog blocks the street, halting a boy's bus ride for a time; and two young boys learn to be friends, sharing lunch and sleeping over at each other's houses. Cooper concluded that "the short sentences, repetitive words, and colorful, childlike artwork invite beginning readers." Ziefert's "On Our Way" series also employs animals and short, rhyming sentences designed to build reading skills. Of *On Our Way to the Forest,* a *Publishers Weekly* reviewer commented that it is virtually "guaranteed to entertain its audience" with its "zippy text and amiable art."

A humpback whale wanders into the busy mouth of New York's Hudson River instead of staying safely out to sea in *Henry's Wrong Turn,* which was inspired by actual events. Ziefert's whale tours Staten Island and buzzes by some ships before being guided back out to sea in a picture book "with simple prose that has a humorous edge," according to Denise M. Wilms in

Found an Apple, *with a toddler-friendly text by Ziefert, also features toddler-friendly art by Elliot Kreloff.* (Sterling Publishing Co., Inc, 2007. Illustration © 2007 by Elliot Kreloff. Reproduced by permission.)

Booklist. More humor is served up in *Oh, What a Noisy Farm!,* the story of a farmer's wife who yells at a bull chasing the farm's cow. The wife is joined by the husband and dog, all shouting and yapping at the bull, but when it and the cow become friends everybody settles down for a nap. Susan D. Lempke, writing for the *Bulletin of the Center for Children's Books,* noted that "children, who are fond of chasing each other and shouting, will particularly enjoy this simple, happy story (adults, on the other hand, may enjoy a grown-up giggle at the euphemistic 'friendship')."

Titles such as *Noisy Barn!, Zoo Parade!,* and *Beach Party!* feature more animal characters. In *Noisy Barn!* readers are encouraged to make the noises of the animals on the pages; at the end, all the animals—and their noises—are gathered together. *Zoo Parade* features animals "marching, jumping, and sauntering," explained Cooper in her *Booklist* review. Cooper concluded that the two books serve as "noisy, bouncy invitations" for young readers. In *Beach Party!* Ziefert describes the way various creatures, including a penguin, lobster, and octopus, traverse the pages as they head for a swim. Ziefert's "rhyming text ends abruptly

with a splash," Martha Topol commented in her *School Library Journal* review of *Beach Party!*

Poor Murphy is an overweight Labrador retriever who balks at exercise in *Murphy Meets the Treadmill.* It is only after his owner buys an exercise machine for the pudgy pooch that Murphy starts to get the hang of exercising, and all of the neighboring dogs soon notice the result. According to Louie Lahana, writing in *School Library Journal,* "the importance of exercise and a proper diet will be clear to children of all ages." Cooper pondered: "Maybe young couch potatoes will get Murphy's message: 'Exercise is worth it!'," while a critic for *Publishers Weekly* concluded that Ziefert and illustrator Emily Bolam have "mined a rich vein of wry, knowing humor." In a sequel titled *Murphy Meets Paris,* the adventurous canine heads to France with his owner, where he enjoys a luxurious stay at a posh hotel. Ziefert's "narration is light and direct," Catherine Threadgill remarked in *School Library Journal.*

Ziefert looks at a familiar childhood experience in *Buzzy Had a Little Lamb.* Buzzy, a little donkey preparing for his first day at school, learns that he must leave his beloved stuffed lamb at home. To ease his discomfort, Buzzy convinces his new schoolmates to join him in a host of imaginative games, including a rousing version of "Buzzy Had a Little Lamb." "While the text is episodic," as Rachel G. Payne noted in *School Library Journal,* "the situation is authentic and the donkey's reactions are age-appropriate." *A Bunny Is Funny: And So Is This Book!,* cowritten with Fred Ehrlich, offers concise, witty poems about a host of animals, including an armadillo, toucan, and butterfly. A critic in *Kirkus Reviews* recommended the collection as a read-aloud, stating that "young children will name all the creatures with enthusiasm."

In *Egad Alligator!* "Ziefert takes an alligator's eye-view" of the world, according to a reviewer for *Publishers Weekly.* Little Gator goes out exploring while his brother is taking a nap. However, every time he tries to befriend someone, from herons to kids playing baseball, they yell, "Egad Alligator!" Little Gator is confused about their reactions until he rests on a log and discovers it to be a snake; he himself cries out "Egad Python!" before running away. Kathy Broderick, writing in *Booklist,* pointed out "the story's valuable message about being able to understand the other fellow's point of view."

Like the message in *Egad Alligator!,* Ziefert's book *Squarehead* is about accepting and understanding differences. George is squareheaded, and his entire world is square. He hates anything that is round. One night, however, he has an encounter with the moon and realizes how beautiful it is. The earth, too, is big and round, and George realizes he has been missing a lot of beautiful things by limiting himself to squares. "This delightful read-aloud will teach . . . the value of appreciating differences," commented Kathy M. Newby in her

review of *Squarehead* for *School Library Journal.* A critic for *Publishers Weekly* commented that Ziefert and illustrator Todd McKie "adequately summarize and satirize prejudice through their geometric example."

Another of Ziefert's staples is the concept book. One such series employs a guessing game as its format and features a cheerful bear who appears in the titles *Bear All Year, Bear Gets Dressed, Bear Goes Shopping,* and *Bear's Busy Morning.* A *Kirkus Reviews* critic found Ziefert's "Bear" series to be composed of "delightful . . . concept books, with stiff, glossy card stock to make them durable with young children," and useful in helping with the development of such concepts as sequencing, time, days of the week, and seasons. Marge Loch-Wouters, writing in *School Library Journal,* noted that these "playful books are good choices for preschool story time and to put in the hands of young children who love the challenge of a guessing game." The "reason why" is at the heart of *Sarah's Questions,* the story of a young girl who asks her mother a variety of questions about the garden, the neighborhood animals, and other natural wonders. A contributor in *Publishers Weekly* felt that "the book's virtue is the quiet appreciation of everyday life," and a *Kirkus Reviews* critic dubbed Ziefert's award-winning title a "summer idyll."

The concepts of friendship and safety are explored by Ziefert in several "Nicky" books, including *Nicky's Friends, Let's Watch Nicky,* and *No, No Nicky.* The star of these books is a tiny, grey-striped kitten that makes friends with a boy and girl, mischievously goes after a goldfish, and stretches playfully. "These books are short, funny and very much to the point," noted a critic in *Publishers Weekly.* Reviewing *Nicky Upstairs and Down* for *Booklist,* Cooper maintained that this story of the kitten that runs all over the house is "just right for beginning readers."

Baby Buggy, Buggy Baby and *Night, Knight* introduce homonyms, while sibling relations are dealt with in *Chocolate Mud Cake, Me Too! Me Too!,* and *Bigger than a Baby.* Marge Loch-Wouters, writing in *School Library Journal,* called *Chocolate Mud Cake* and *Me Too! Me Too!* a "welcome change of pace from the many books on sibling rivalry." In the first book, sisters Molly and Jenny make mud pies and play dress-up on a rainy day. Molly, the older sister, generously includes her younger sibling in all these activities, inspiring *Booklist* reviewer Phillis Wilson to conclude that "Jenny and Molly are a delight to meet." *Bigger than a Baby* "help[s] youngsters understand and appreciate their new siblings," according to Dorothy Evans in *School Library Journal.* This book compares the development of a baby to the growth of its older sister, and thus might "be useful for children adjusting to new siblings or for other children having trouble feeling comfortable with new abilities and responsibilities," observed Kay Weisman in *Booklist.*

Bedtime is the focus of several of Ziefert's titles, including *I Won't Go to Bed!, Mommy, I Want to Sleep in Your Bed!,* and *Clara Ann Cookie, Go to Bed!* When Harry protests against bedtime in *I Won't Go to Bed!,*

Noisy Barn! *finds Ziefert teaming up with cartoon artist Simms Taback in a book that features bright colors and a simple text.* (Illustration copyright © 2003 by Simms Taback. Reproduced by permission of Blue Apple Books.)

his father allows him to stay up and promptly goes to bed himself, leaving Harry to roam about the house until he falls asleep on the floor. A *Publishers Weekly* reviewer commented that the book features a "traditional theme with a non-traditional treatment," while Cooper observed that in *I Won't Go to Bed!* Ziefert "catches the mood of children who fantasize about staying up all night." Clara Cookie also protests going to bed in *Clara Ann Cookie, Go to Bed!* When she is sent to her room to go to sleep by her parents, Clara orders all her stuffed animals to go to sleep. When her teddy bear, Popcorn, refuses, Clara tries all the techniques her parents use on her to get the bear to cooperate. Eventually, she lies down next to him and falls asleep herself. Piper L. Nyman, writing for *School Library Journal,* called *Clara Ann Cookie, Go to Bed!* "a book with persuasive potential in the never-ending going-to-bed battle." In *Mommy, I Want to Sleep in Your Bed!*, young Charlie has trouble staying in his room until he develops his own, special nighttime ritual. In *School Library Journal,* Maryann H. Owen described the work as a "gentle tale about a hard-learned lesson," and a *Kirkus Reviews* contributor deemed it "a perfect read before falling asleep."

Titles such as *Rockheads* and *A Dozen Ducklings Lost and Found* are designed to help students learn to develop their counting skills. In *Rockheads,* illustrator McKie used photographs of rocks with painted faces for the characters of the story. Ziefert and McKie begin with just one "Rockhead," then continue adding until there are a dozen. "Beware: may cause rock-crafting urges in older siblings," warned a critic for *Kirkus Reviews.* A mother duck takes her dozen ducklings for a walk in *A Dozen Ducklings Lost and Found.* Unknown to her, Farmer Donald has dug holes for a new fence, and before she realizes what is happening, several of her children are missing! She counts the children who are with her, then counts down from twelve to see if that will improve the situation. Farmer Donald realizes that the ducklings have only spilled down the holes and comes to the rescue. "The story works well as a concept book," praised Maryann H. Owen in *School Library Journal,* noting that Ziefert uses interesting techniques, such as counting numbers up to twelve instead of stopping at ten, as many counting books do. "Mother Duck's tendency to count both forwards and backwards is a nice touch," praised a critic for *Kirkus Reviews.*

Ziefert also covers holidays in many of her books, including *What Is Hanukkah?, Home for Navidad,* and *Hats off for the Fourth of July!* In *What Is Hanukkah?,* the author introduces the Festival of Lights with a repeated chant that "will have kids joining in" according to Rochman in *Booklist. Hanukkah Haiku* features eight verses, one for each night of the widely celebrated occasion. *Horn Book* reviewer Shoshana Flax described this volume by Ziefert as a "concisely poetic way to share the basics of the holiday."

Home for Navidad tells the story of a young Mexican girl whose mother has been working in the United States

Where's My Homework? joins an easy-reading Ziefert text with Roger de Muth's humorous illustrations. (Blue Apple Books, 2007. Illustration copyright © 2007 by Roger De Muth. Reproduced by permission.)

for three years to try to earn money for their family. The little girl is delighted when her mother sends a letter saying that she will be home for Christmas. A critic for *Kirkus Reviews* called this title "a beautiful new addition to the shelf of multicultural Chrismas stories." In her *School Library Journal* review, Susan Patron pointed out that the text is "sprinkled with many Spanish words," and that a glossary is provided at the end. Kitty Flynn, writing for *Horn Book,* complimented Ziefert's use of a "matter-of-fact, first-person narrative," while Rochman praised the "combination of simple words and bold, vibrant art."

The residents of Chatham, Massachusetts, celebrate in *Hats off for the Fourth of July!* Pictures focus on the parade and the celebration, ending with fireworks. "The text has the steady beat of a parade drummer," commented Susan Garland in *School Library Journal. Presents for Santa* tells of the mice who live at the North Pole. When the mother mouse asks her children what they should get Santa for Christmas, each mouse gives an idea that reflects what he actually wants for himself for Christmas. Carolyn Phelan, writing in *Booklist,* called *Presents for Santa* "an accessible holiday book," while a *School Library Journal* contributor described it as both "accessible and satisfying."

Counting and holidays are combined in *Two Little Witches,* in which little goblins learn to count to ten at Halloween, and *Eight Days of Hanukkah.* Counting is combined with ideas like friendship and relationships in books such as *Thirty-nine Uses for a Friend, Thirty-one Uses for a Mom* and *Forty-one Uses for a Cat.* In *Thirty-one Uses for a Mom,* a mother is depicted as many things: an alarm clock, a bank, a pitcher, catcher, and retriever (for baseball practice), and a friend. "Moms and kids alike should enjoy continuing the list," commented a *Kirkus Reviews* critic. Friends have such

uses as backrests, hairdressers, and accomplices in *Thirty-nine Uses for a Friend.* Cathy Broderick, in a review for *Booklist,* called the book "a fine manual of friendship," while Alison Kastner noted in *School Library Journal* that the book could be "useful as a springboard for discussion about friendship."

Ziefert's educational titles focus on mathematical and scientific topics for younger readers. *You Can't See Your Bones with Binoculars* introduces readers to the major and minor bones of the human skeleton. Both illustrations and text reveal the connections from the toes up to the skull. Gillian Engberg, writing in *Booklist,* considered this a "whimsical introduction to human anatomy." A critic for *Kirkus Reviews* was not as convinced, however, and found the text "too sophisticated for preschoolers . . . yet too simple for older kids." *You Can't Taste a Pickle with Your Ear* focuses on the five senses, and contains humor as well as questions for young readers to discuss with their parents. "Preschoolers . . . may develop a new awareness" of the senses, noted a reviewer for *Publishers Weekly. You Can't Buy a Dinosaur with a Dime* is a book about math skills using currency to teach its lessons. Though the book is more sophisticated than a typical counting book, Leslie Barban wrote in *School Library Journal* that the authors "know exactly how to make learning fun." A critic for *Kirkus Reviews* noted that "children who have learned the value of money and how to add coins will be able to put their skills to use." In *ABC Dentist,* Ziefert presents facts about teeth and gums as well as soothing advice about the goings-on in a dental office. *Booklist* reviewer Abby Nolan commented that this volume "seeks to offer plenty of knowledge as well as comfort."

Other popular titles by Ziefert include *A New Coat for Anna, Pete's Chicken,* and *Henry's Wrong Turn.* With *A New Coat for Anna,* Ziefert developed a larger storyline as well as a deeper thematic approach. In a book set just after World War II, Anna's mother trades a prized possession to create a new coat for her daughter. The coat is a year in the making: the wool is grown and spun, and the red dye extracted from berries. A *Kirkus Reviews* critic deemed the book a "warmly satisfying variation on a familiar story," while *Horn Book* contributor Ethel R. Twichell noted that the "simple text, based on a true story, carries the narrative along effectively." Susan Patron concluded in *School Library Journal* that "Ziefert's tale . . . will be understood and cherished by all ages."

Pete's Chicken is another longer and more ambitious picture book, the story of "an artistic rabbit" who "celebrates the true spirit of originality," according to a critic in *Publishers Weekly.* When his art teacher tells the class to draw a chicken, Pete lets loose with a purple-and-orange masterpiece that initially brings laughter from his schoolmates. The *Publishers Weekly* reviewer concluded that "Ziefert's uncluttered, boisterous text practically sings, filled with Pete's happy proc-

lamations of self-confidence," while in *Booklist* Cooper observed that "some of Pete's self-assurance might rub off on readers."

Ziefert has penned numerous retellings of popular folk and fairy tales, including *The Teeny-Tiny Woman, The Little Red Hen,* and *Goldilocks and the Three Bears.* Her *Ode to Humpty Dumpty* takes Mother Goose's rhyme and explores what happens after. Since no one could put Humpty back together, the king is mourning, and lead by a girl named Norma Jean Foote, all the townsfolk try to cheer him up by putting together a celebration in Humpty Dumpty's honor. In *First He Made the Sun* Ziefert bases her story on a traditional spiritual that retells the creation story from the Book of Genesis. God creates the sun and moon, then creates the animals to populate different places on earth. Ellen Mandel of *Booklist* and *School Library Journal* reviewer Kathy Piehl both noted that the illustrations might "encourage them to create their own artistic interpretations," in Mandel's words.

Ziefert stays close to the traditional versions of stories in her retellings of *The Snow Child* and *Little Red Riding Hood.* A Russian tale, *The Snow Child* describes a childless elderly couple who want more than anything to have a little one, so they create a child made of snow. When the old woman kisses the snow child, it comes to life, only to have to leave when the weather becomes warmer. The couple thinks that the child is gone forever, and is delighted when she returns the following winter. Anne Knickerbocker, reviewing *The Snow Child* for *School Library Journal,* called "the entire reading experience a pleasurable one," and Engberg commented in *Booklist* that Ziefert's "lovely offering" is enhanced by its "simple vocabulary." The well-known story of the girl with the red cape is told in its traditional form in Ziefert's *Little Red Riding Hood.* Here Little Red finally learns her lesson about not talking to strangers after the wolf eats her and she and her grandmother are rescued by a woodsman. "The story should provide a successful reading experience," noted Lisa Smith in *School Library Journal.*

Familial relationships are at the heart of many of Ziefert's books, among them *The Biggest Job of All, Bigger than Daddy,* and *It's for You!* A little girl contemplates the positives and negatives of a variety of occupations, including elephant washer, in *The Biggest Job of All.* According to a contributor in *Kirkus Reviews,* here "Ziefert's cozy tale encourages young dreamers to contemplate the possibilities of their own glorious futures." In *Bigger than Daddy,* young Edward spends a day exploring the world with his father, and the duo often reverse the roles of child and adult during their play. As Todd Morning remarked in *School Library Journal,* "Ziefert ably captures the teasing affection between a young preschool boy and his dad." Lulu fashions a unique gift from an old straw hat for her grandmother's birthday in *It's for You!* "This delightful story is perfect

for reading on Grandma's lap," Mary Hazelton commented in *School Library Journal*.

In all of her popular picture-book projects, Ziefert relies heavily on the work of illustrators to help carry her stories. The first challenge faced by the teacher-turned-author is to bring her story across with a limited number of words. To ensure that her new story comes across the way she wants it to, she works very closely with her illustrators—sometimes bringing in painters and artists who have never worked on children's books—to create the book as a whole, so that the art and the story flow together. "I'm very visual," Ziefert noted on the Penguin Books Web site. "I do a very loose text and try to develop it with an illustrator. I work with artists and turn them into illustrators. I like finding new artists and watching them grow."

Biographical and Critical Sources

PERIODICALS

Booklist, August, 1987, Ilene Cooper, review of "Hello Reading" series, p. 1754; September 1, 1987, Denise M. Wilms, review of *Pet Day,* pp. 75-76; November 15, 1987, Ilene Cooper, review of *I Won't Go to Bed!,* p. 574; December 1, 1987, Ilene Cooper, review of *Nicky Upstairs and Down,* p. 640; November 15, 1988, Phillis Wilson, reviews of *Chocolate Mud Cake* and *Me Too! Me Too!,* both p. 589; January 1, 1990, Denise M. Wilms, review of *Henry's Wrong Turn,* p. 922; December 15, 1991, Kay Weisman, review of *Bigger than a Baby,* p. 768; September 15, 1994, Ilene Cooper, review of *Pete's Chicken,* p. 146; October 15, 1999, Stephanie Zvirin, review of *Animal Music,* p. 457, and GraceAnne A. DeCandido, review of *First Night,* p. 458; February 15, 2000, Carolyn Phelan, review of *April Fool,* and Hazel Rochman, review of *Little Red Riding Hood,* both p. 1125; March 15, 2000, Marta Segal, review of *Moonride,* p. 1390; April 1, 2000, Carolyn Phelan, review of *Train Song,* p. 1472; April 15, 2000, Helen Rosenberg, review of *Hats off for the Fourth of July!* and Ellen Mandel, review of *First He Made the Sun,* both p. 1555; December 1, 2000, Todd Morning, review of *Pumpkin Pie,* p. 724, and Carolyn Phelan, review of *Presents for Santa,* and Gillian Engberg, review of *The Snow Child,* p. 727; February 15, 2001, Connie Fletcher, review of *Someday We'll Have Very Good Manners,* p. 1142; September 1, 2001, Ilene Cooper, review of *Murphy Meets the Treadmill,* p. 118; December 1, 2001, Cathy Broderick, review of *Thirty-nine Uses for a Friend,* p. 651; April 15, 2002, Kathy Broderick, review of *Egad Alligator!,* p. 1410; June 1, 2002, Ilene Cooper, review of *Toes Have Wiggles, Kids Have Giggles,* p. 1744; January 1, 2002, Ellen Mandel, review of *Thirty-one Uses for a Mom,* p. 911; March 15, 2003, Diane Foote, review of *A Dozen Ducklings Lost and Found,* p. 1335; September 1, 2003, Hazel Rochman, review of *Home for Navidad,* p. 136; November 1, 2003, Hazel Rochman, review of *What Is Hanukkah?,* p. 508; December 1, 2003, Gillian Engberg, review of *You Can't See Your Bones with Binoculars: A Guide to Your 206 Bones,* p. 681; March 1, 2004, Ilene Cooper, review of *Noisy Barn!,* p. 1199; July, 2005, Ilene Cooper, review of *Buzzy Had a Little Lamb,* p. 1931; May 1, 2006, Todd Morning, review of *Bigger than Daddy,* p. 94; November 15, 2008, Abby Nolan, review of *ABC Dentist: Healthy Teeth from A to Z,* p. 47; December 1, 2008, Hazel Rochman, review of *Mighty Max!,* p. 58.

Books for Keeps, September, 1994, Liz Waterland, review of *Let's Get a Pet,* p. 7.

Bulletin of the Center for Children's Books, May, 1995, Susan D. Lempke, review of *Oh, What a Noisy Farm!,* p. 328.

Horn Book, March, 1987, Ethel R. Twichell, review of *A New Coat for Anna,* p. 204; September-October, 2003, Kitty Flynn, review of *Home for Navidad,* p. 605; November-December, 2008, Shoshana Flax, review of *Hanukkah Haiku,* p. 655.

Junior Bookshelf, October, 1994, Marcus Crouch, review of *Let's Get a Pet,* p. 167.

Kirkus Reviews, August 15, 1986, review of *Bear All Year,* p. 1293; September 15, 1986, review of *Sarah's Questions,* p. 1447; October 15, 1986, review of *A New Coat for Anna,* p. 1582; June 1, 1987, review of *Where's the Dog?,* p. 864; August 15, 2001, review of *Birdhouse for Rent,* p. 1224; February 1, 2002, review of *Egad Alligator!,* p. 193; November 1, 2002, review of *Christmas Has Merry!,* p. 1628; November 15, 2002, review of *You Can't Taste a Pickle with Your Ear: A Book about Your Five Senses,* p. 1704; December 15, 2002, review of *Thirty-one Uses for a Mom,* p. 1860; February 1, 2003, review of *A Dozen Ducklings Lost and Found,* p. 244; June 1, 2003, review of *You Can't Buy a Dinosaur with a Dime: Problem Solving in Dollars and Cents,* p. 813; November 1, 2003, review of *Home for Navidad,* p. 1321; December 15, 2003, review of *You Can't See Your Bones with Binoculars,* p. 1455; April 1, 2004, review of *Rockheads,* p. 339; April 1, 2005, review of *Beach Party!,* p. 429; October 15, 2005, review of *Mommy, I Want to Sleep in Your Bed!,* p. 1149; November 1, 2005, review of *The Biggest Job of All,* p. 1189; May 1, 2006, review of *Bigger than Daddy,* p. 471; May 15, 2006, review of *Grandma, It's for You!,* p. 525; May 15, 2008, review of *A Bunny Is Funny;* November 15, 2008, review of *Mighty Max!*

Publishers Weekly, August 22, 1986, review of *Run! Run!,* and others, p. 92; October 31, 1986, review of *Sarah's Questions,* p. 64; November 28, 1986, review of *Nicky's Friends* and others, p. 72; June 26, 1987, review of *Pet Day,* p. 72; October 9, 1987, review of *I Won't Go to Bed!,* p. 167; June 21, 1993, review of *On Our Way to the Forest,* p. 103; June 27, 1994, review of *Pete's Chicken,* p. 78; June 5, 2000, review of *Hats off for the Fourth of July,* p. 93; March 26, 2001, review of *Ode to Humpty Dumpty,* p. 93; April 23, 2001, review of *Squarehead,* p. 77; June 4, 2001, review of *What Do Ducks Dream?,* p. 80; July 9, 2001, review of *Murphy Meets the Treadmill,* p. 67;

February 18, 2002, review *Egad Alligator!,* p. 95; November 4, 2002, review of *You Can't Taste a Pickle with Your Ear,* p. 83; February 3, 2003, reviews of *Lunchtime for a Purple Snake* and *A Dozen Ducklings Lost and Found,* both p. 75; September 22, 2003, review of *Home for Navidad,* p. 70; May 9, 2005, review of *Murphy Meets Paris,* p. 69; November 28, 2005, reviews of *The Biggest Job of All,* p. 50, and *Circus Parade,* p. 51.

School Library Journal, December, 1986, Susan Scheps, review of *A New Coat for Anna,* p. 97; January, 1987, Marge Loch-Wouters, review of *Bear All Year,* p. 69; November, 1987, Heide Piehler, review of *Where's the Dog?,* p. 98; March, 1988, Sarah C. Vaughn, review of *So Hungry!,* p. 180; December, 1988, Marge Loch-Wouters, reviews of *Chocolate Mud Cake* and *Me Too! Me Too!,* both p. 96; January, 1992, Dorothy Evans, review of *Bigger than a Baby,* p. 107; March, 2000, Diane Janoff, review of *April Fool!,* p. 220; April, 2000, Lisa Smith, review of *Little Red Riding Hood,* p. 128; May, 2000, Kathy Piehl, review of *First He Made the Sun,* p. 159; July, 2000, Susan Garland, review of *Hats off for the Fourth of July,* p. 90; October, 2000, review of *Presents for Santa,* p. 64, and Piper L. Nyman, review of *Pumpkin Pie* and *Clara Ann Cookie, Go to Bed!,* p. 144; December, 2000, Corinne Camarata, review of *Moonride,* p. 128; February, 2001, Carolyn Jenks, review of *Someday We'll Have Very Good Manners,* p. 108; March, 2001, Anne Knickerbocker, review of *The Snow Child,* p. 244; May, 2001, Kathy M. Newby, review of *Squarehead,* and Shara Alpern, review of *Ode to Humpty Dumpty,* p. 139; June, 2001, Joy Fleishhacker, review of *What Do Ducks Dream?,* p. 132; September, 2001, Wanda Meyers-Hines, review of *On Halloween Night,* and Lauralyn Persson, review of *Birdhouse for Rent,* both p. 210; October, 2001, Louie Lahana, review of *Murphy Meets the Treadmill,* December, 2001, Alison Kastner, review of *Thirty-nine Uses for a Friend,* p. 116; April, 2002, Maryann H. Owen, review of *Egad Alligator!,* p. 128; June, 2002, Rosalyn Pierini, review of *Toes Have Wiggles, Kids Have Giggles,* p.116; March, 2003, Maryann H. Owen, review of *A Dozen Ducklings Lost and Found,* and Rosalyn Pierini, review of *Thirty-one Uses for a Mom,* p. 211; April, 2003, Jody McCoy, review of *Lunchtime for a Purple Snake,* p. 144; July, 2003, Leslie Barban, review of *You Can't Buy a Dinosaur with a Dime,* p. 120; September, 2003, Grace Oliff, review of *A New Coat for Anna,* p. 86; October, 2003, Susan Patron, review of *Home for Navidad,* p. 69; January, 2004, Dona Ratterree, review of *You Can't See Your Bones with Binoculars,* p. 123; April, 2004, Donna Cardon, review of *Rockheads,* p. 144; May, 2005, Catherine Threadgill, review of *Murphy Meets Paris,* p. 106; August, 2005, Martha Topol, review of *Beach Party!,* and Rachel G. Payne, review of *Buzzy Had a Little Lamb,* both p. 110; October, 2005, Laura Scott, review of *Circus Parade,* p. 135; November, 2005, Maryann H. Owen, review of *Mommy, I Want to Sleep in Your Bed!,* p. 111; August, 2006, Mary Hazelton, reviews of *Bigger than Daddy* and *Grandma, It's for You!,* both p. 100; July, 2008, Wendy Woodfill, review of *A Bunny Is Funny: And So Is This Book!,* p. 93; October, 2008, Teri Markson, review of *Hanukkah Haiku,* p. 99; November, 2008, Nancy Baumann, review of *ABC Dentist,* p. 113.

ONLINE

Begin Smart Books Web site, http://www.beginsmartbooks.com/ (September 1, 2009), "Meet the Series Creator: Harriet Ziefert."

Penguin Books Web site, http://us.penguingroup.com/ (September 1, 2009), "Harriet Ziefert."*

Illustrations Index

(In the following index, the number of the *volume* in which an illustrator's work appears is given *before* the colon, and the *page number* on which it appears is given *after* the colon. For example, a drawing by Adams, Adrienne appears in Volume 2 on page 6, another drawing by her appears in Volume 3 on page 80, another drawing in Volume 8 on page 1, and so on and so on. . . .)

YABC

Index references to *YABC* refer to listings appearing in the two-volume *Yesterday's Authors of Books for Children,* also published by Gale, Cengage Learning. *YABC* covers prominent authors and illustrators who died prior to 1960.

A

Aas, Ulf *5:* 174
Abbe, S. van
    See van Abbe, S.
Abel, Raymond *6:* 122; *7:* 195; *12:* 3; *21:* 86; *25:* 119
Abelliera, Aldo *71:* 120
Abolafia, Yossi *60:* 2; *93:* 163; *152:* 202
Abrahams, Hilary *26:* 205; *29:* 24, 25; *53:* 61
Abrams, Kathie *36:* 170
Abrams, Lester *49:* 26
Abulafia, Yossi *154:* 67; *177:* 3
Accardo, Anthony *191:* 3, 8
Accornero, Franco *184:* 8
Accorsi, William *11:* 198
Acs, Laszlo *14:* 156; *42:* 22
Acuna, Ed *198:* 79
Adams, Adrienne *2:* 6; *3:* 80; *8:* 1; *15:* 107; *16:* 180; *20:* 65; *22:* 134, 135; *33:* 75; *36:* 103, 112; *39:* 74; *86:* 54; *90:* 2, 3
Adams, Connie J. *129:* 68
Adams, John Wolcott *17:* 162
Adams, Lynn *96:* 44
Adams, Norman *55:* 82
Adams, Pam *112:* 1, 2
Adams, Sarah *98:* 126; *164:* 180
Adamson, George *30:* 23, 24; *69:* 64
Addams, Charles *55:* 5
Addison, Kenneth *192:* 173
Addy, Sean *180:* 8
Ade, Rene *76:* 198; *195:* 162
Adinolfi, JoAnn *115:* 42; *176:* 2
Adkins, Alta *22:* 250
Adkins, Jan *8:* 3; *69:* 4; *144:* 2, 3, 4
Adler, Kelynn *195:* 47
Adler, Peggy *22:* 6; *29:* 31
Adler, Ruth *29:* 29
Adlerman, Daniel *163:* 2
Adragna, Robert *47:* 145
Agard, Nadema *18:* 1
Agee, Jon *116:* 8, 9, 10; *157:* 4; *196:* 3, 4, 5, 6, 7, 8
Agre, Patricia *47:* 195
Aguirre, Alfredo *152:* 218
Ahl, Anna Maria *32:* 24
Ahlberg, Allan *68:* 6, 7, 9; *165:* 5
Ahlberg, Janet *68:* 6, 7, 9
Aicher-Scholl, Inge *63:* 127
Aichinger, Helga *4:* 5, 45

Aitken, Amy *31:* 34
Akaba, Suekichi *46:* 23; *53:* 127
Akasaka, Miyoshi *YABC 2:* 261
Akib, Jamel *181:* 13; *182:* 99
Akino, Fuku *6:* 144
Alain *40:* 41
Alajalov *2:* 226
Albert, Chris *200:* 64
Alborough, Jez *86:* 1, 2, 3; *149:* 3
Albrecht, Jan *37:* 176
Albright, Donn *1:* 91
Alcala, Alfredo *91:* 128
Alcantará, Felipe Ugalde *171:* 186
Alcorn, John *3:* 159; *7:* 165; *31:* 22; *44:* 127; *46:* 23, 170
Alcorn, Stephen *110:* 4; *125:* 106; *128:* 172; *150:* 97; *160:* 188; *165:* 48; *201:* 113; *203:* 39
Alcott, May *100:* 3
Alda, Arlene *44:* 24; *158:* 2
Alden, Albert *11:* 103
Aldridge, Andy *27:* 131
Aldridge, George *105:* 125
Aldridge, Sheila *192:* 4
Alejandro, Cliff *176:* 75
Alex, Ben *45:* 25, 26
Alexander, Ellen *91:* 3
Alexander, Lloyd *49:* 34
Alexander, Martha *3:* 206; *11:* 103; *13:* 109; *25:* 100; *36:* 131; *70:* 6, 7; *136:* 3, 4, 5; *169:* 120
Alexander, Paul *85:* 57; *90:* 9
Alexeieff, Alexander *14:* 6; *26:* 199
Alfano, Wayne *80:* 69
Aliki
    See Brandenberg, Aliki
Allamand, Pascale *12:* 9
Allan, Judith *38:* 166
Alland, Alexandra *16:* 255
Allen, Gertrude *9:* 6
Allen, Graham *31:* 145
Allen, Jonathan *131:* 3, 4; *177:* 8, 9, 10
Allen, Joy *168:* 185
Allen, Pamela *50:* 25, 26, 27, 28; *81:* 9, 10; *123:* 4, 5
Allen, Rowena *47:* 75
Allen, Thomas B. *81:* 101; *82:* 248; *89:* 37; *104:* 9
Allen, Tom *85:* 176
Allender, David *73:* 223

Alley, R.W. *80:* 183; *95:* 187; *156:* 100, 153; *169:* 4, 5; *179:* 17
Allison, Linda *43:* 27
Allon, Jeffrey *119:* 174
Allport, Mike *71:* 55
Almquist, Don *11:* 8; *12:* 128; *17:* 46; *22:* 110
Aloise, Frank *5:* 38; *10:* 133; *30:* 92
Alsenas, Linas *186:* 2
Althea
    See Braithwaite, Althea
Altschuler, Franz *11:* 185; *23:* 141; *40:* 48; *45:* 29; *57:* 181
Alvin, John *117:* 5
Ambrus, Victor G. *1:* 6, 7, 194; *3:* 69; *5:* 15; *6:* 44; *7:* 36; *8:* 210; *12:* 227; *14:* 213; *15:* 213; *22:* 209; *24:* 36; *28:* 179; *30:* 178; *32:* 44, 46; *38:* 143; *41:* 25, 26, 27, 28, 29, 30, 31, 32; *42:* 87; *44:* 190; *55:* 172; *62:* 30, 144, 145, 148; *86:* 99, 100, 101; *87:* 66, 137; *89:* 162; *134:* 160
Ames, Lee J. *3:* 12; *9:* 130; *10:* 69; *17:* 214; *22:* 124; *151:* 13
Amon, Aline *9:* 9
Amoss, Berthe *5:* 5
Amstutz, Andre *152:* 102
Amundsen, Dick *7:* 77
Amundsen, Richard E. *5:* 10; *24:* 122
Ancona, George *12:* 11; *55:* 144; *145:* 7
Anderson, Alasdair *18:* 122
Andersen, Bethanne *116:* 167; *162:* 189; *175:* 17; *191:* 4, 5
Anderson, Bob *139:* 16
Anderson, Brad *33:* 28
Anderson, C.W. *11:* 10
Anderson, Carl *7:* 4
Anderson, Catherine Corley *72:* 2
Anderson, Cecil *127:* 152
Anderson, David Lee *118:* 176
Anderson, Derek *169:* 9; *174:* 180
Anderson, Doug *40:* 111
Anderson, Erica *23:* 65
Anderson, Laurie *12:* 153, 155
Anderson, Lena *99:* 26
Anderson, Peggy Perry *179:* 2
Anderson, Sara *173:* 3
Anderson, Scoular *138:* 13; *201:* 6
Anderson, Susan *90:* 12
Anderson, Tara *188:* 132
Anderson, Wayne *23:* 119; *41:* 239; *56:* 7; *62:* 26; *147:* 6; *202:* 4, 5

Andreasen, Daniel *86:* 157; *87:* 104; *103:* 201, 202; *159:* 75; *167:* 106, 107; *168:* 184; *180:* 247; *186:* 9
Andrew, Ian *111:* 37; *116:* 12; *166:* 2
Andrew, John *22:* 4
Andrews, Benny *14:* 251; *31:* 24; *57:* 6, 7; *183:* 8
Andrews, Vaughn *166:* 28
Anelay, Henry *57:* 173
Angel, Marie *47:* 22
Angelo, Valenti *14:* 8; *18:* 100; *20:* 232; *32:* 70
Anglund, Joan Walsh *2:* 7, 250, 251; *37:* 198, 199, 200
Anholt, Catherine *74:* 8; *131:* 7; *141:* 5
Anholt, Laurence *141:* 4
Anno, Mitsumasa *5:* 7; *38:* 25, 26, 27, 28, 29, 30, 31, 32; *77:* 3, 4; *157:* 10, 11
Antal, Andrew *1:* 124; *30:* 145
Antram, David *152:* 133
Apostolou, Christy Hale
  See Hale, Christy
Apple, Margot *33:* 25; *35:* 206; *46:* 81; *53:* 8; *61:* 109; *64:* 21, 22, 24, 25, 27; *71:* 176; *77:* 53; *82:* 245; *92:* 39; *94:* 180; *96:* 107; *152:* 4, 5; *162:* 192, 194; *173:* 44
Appleyard, Dev *2:* 192
Aragones, Sergio *48:* 23, 24, 25, 26, 27
Araneus *40:* 29
Arbo, Cris *103:* 4
Archambault, Matt *85:* 173; *138:* 19, 20; *143:* 33; *145:* 144; *179:* 103; *187:* 7
Archer, Janet *16:* 69; *178:* 156
Ardizzone, Edward *1:* 11, 12; *2:* 105; *3:* 258; *4:* 78; *7:* 79; *10:* 100; *15:* 232; *20:* 69,178; *23:* 223; *24:* 125; *28:* 25, 26, 27, 28, 29, 30, 31,33, 34, 35, 36, 37; *31:* 192, 193; *34:* 215, 217; *60:* 173; *64:* 145; *87:* 176; *YABC 2:* 25
Arena, Jill *176:* 49
Arenella, Roy *14:* 9
Argemi, David *197:* 2
Argent, Kerry *103:* 56; *138:* 17; *158:* 134
Arihara, Shino *201:* 98
Arisman, Marshall *162:* 50
Armer, Austin *13:* 3
Armer, Laura Adams *13:* 3
Armer, Sidney *13:* 3
Armitage, David *47:* 23; *99:* 5; *155:* 4
Armitage, Eileen *4:* 16
Armstrong, George *10:* 6; *21:* 72
Armstrong, Shelagh *102:* 114
Armstrong-Ellis, Carey *185:* 196
Arno, Enrico *1:* 217; *2:* 22, 210; *4:* 9; *5:* 43; *6:* 52; *29:* 217, 219; *33:* 152; *35:* 99; *43:* 31, 32, 33; *45:* 212, 213, 214; *72:* 72; *74:* 166; *100:* 169
Arnold, Alli *187:* 40, 41
Arnold, Caroline *174:* 5
Arnold, Emily *76:* 7, 9, 10
Arnold, Katya *115:* 11; *168:* 2, 3
Arnold, Tedd *116:* 14; *133:* 152; *160:* 5
Arnosky, Jim *22:* 20; *70:* 9, 10, 11; *118:* 3, 5; *160:* 8, 10; *189:* 5, 7, 8, 9, 10
Arnsteen, Katy Keck *105:* 97; *116:* 145
Arrowood, Clinton *12:* 193; *19:* 11; *65:* 210
Artell, Mike *89:* 8
Arting, Fred J. *41:* 63
Artzybasheff, Boris *13:* 143; *14:* 15; *40:* 152, 155
Aruego, Ariane *6:* 4
Aruego, José *4:* 140; *6:* 4; *7:* 64; *33:* 195; *35:* 208; *68:* 16, 17; *75:* 46; *93:* 91, 92; *94:* 197; *109:* 65, 67; *125:* 2, 3, 4, 5; *127:* 188; *143:* 25; *178:* 17, 19, 74; *188:* 166; *202:* 164
Arzoumanian, Alik *177:* 12; *194:* 115
Asare, Meshack *86:* 9; *139:* 19
Ascensios, Natalie *105:* 139
Asch, Frank *5:* 9; *66:* 2, 4, 6, 7, 9, 10; *102:* 18, 19,21; *154:* 12
Ashby, Gail *11:* 135
Ashby, Gil *146:* 4

Ashby, Gwynneth *44:* 26
Ashley, C.W. *19:* 197
Ashmead, Hal *8:* 70
Aska, Warabe *56:* 10
Assel, Steven *44:* 153; *77:* 22, 97
Astrop, John *32:* 56
Atene, Ann *12:* 18
Atherton, Lisa *38:* 198
Atkinson, Allen *60:* 5
Atkinson, J. Priestman *17:* 275
Atkinson, Janet *86:* 147; *103:* 138
Atkinson, Mike *127:* 74
Atkinson, Wayne *40:* 46
Attard, Karl *196:* 22, 23
Attebery, Charles *38:* 170
Atwell, Debby *150:* 6
Atwood, Ann *7:* 9
Aubrey, Meg Kelleher *77:* 159
Auch, Herm *173:* 7, 8
Auch, Mary Jane *173:* 7
Augarde, Steve *25:* 22; *159:* 7
Austerman, Miriam *23:* 107
Austin, Margot *11:* 16
Austin, Robert *3:* 44
Austin, Virginia *81:* 205; *127:* 221
Auth, Tony *51:* 5; *192:* 18
Avendano, Dolores *158:* 74
Avedon, Richard *57:* 140
Averill, Esther *1:* 17; *28:* 39, 40, 41
Axeman, Lois *2:* 32; *11:* 84; *13:* 165; *22:* 8; *23:* 49; *61:* 116; *101:* 124
Axtel, David *155:* 110
Ayer, Jacqueline *13:* 7
Ayer, Margaret *15:* 12; *50:* 120
Ayers, Alan *91:* 58; *107:* 169
Ayliffe, Alex *95:* 164
Ayto, Russell *111:* 5; *112:* 54
Azarian, Mary *112:* 9, 10; *114:* 129; *117:* 171; *137:* 163; *171:* 4, 5; *181:* 161; *188:* 128

B

B.T.B.
  See Blackwell, Basil T.
Babbitt, Bradford *33:* 158
Babbitt, Natalie *6:* 6; *8:* 220; *68:* 20; *70:* 242, 243; *194:* 8, 9
Baca, Maria *104:* 5
Bacchus, Andy *94:* 87
Bacha, Andy *109:* 169
Bachelet, Gilles *196:* 18
Bachem, Paul *48:* 180; *67:* 65; *144:* 206
Back, Adam *63:* 125
Back, George *31:* 161
Backes, Nick *190:* 72
Backhouse, Colin *78:* 142
Bacon, Bruce *4:* 74
Bacon, Paul *7:* 155; *8:* 121; *31:* 55; *50:* 42; *56:* 175; *62:* 82, 84
Bacon, Peggy *2:* 11, 228; *46:* 44
Baek, Matthew J. *169:* 95; *202:* 8
Baer, Julie *161:* 2
Baicker-McKee, Carol *177:* 15; *180:* 215
Bailey, Peter *58:* 174; *87:* 221; *194:* 12
Bailey, Sheila *155:* 11
Baker, Alan *22:* 22; *61:* 134; *93:* 11, 12; *146:* 6, 7, 10
Baker, Charlotte *2:* 12
Baker, Garin *89:* 65
Baker, Jeannie *23:* 4; *88:* 18, 19, 20
Baker, Jim *22:* 24
Baker, Joe *82:* 188; *111:* 55; *124:* 70; *197:* 73
Baker, Keith *179:* 6, 7
Baker, Leslie *112:* 214; *132:* 103, 246; *180:* 74, 246
Baldacci, Rudy *184:* 9
Baldridge, Cyrus LeRoy *19:* 69; *44:* 50
Baldus, Zachary *152:* 231; *187:* 60
Balet, Jan *11:* 22

Balian, Lorna *9:* 16; *91:* 16
Balit, Christina *102:* 24; *159:* 9; *162:* 118, 119
Ballantyne, R.M. *24:* 34
Ballis, George *14:* 199
Balouch, Kristen *176:* 11
Baltzer, Hans *40:* 30
Banbery, Fred *58:* 15
Banfill, A. Scott *98:* 7; *112:* 59
Bang, Molly Garrett *24:* 37, 38; *69:* 8, 9, 10; *111:* 7,9, 10, 11; *140:* 11; *158:* 37, 38, 39; *195:* 3
Banik, Yvette Santiago *21:* 136
Banner, Angela
  See Maddison, Angela Mary
Bannerman, Helen *19:* 13, 14
Banning, Greg *202:* 98
Bannon, Laura *6:* 10; *23:* 8
Bantock, Nick *74:* 229; *95:* 6
Banyai, Istvan *185:* 209; *193:* 14, 16
Baptist, Michael *37:* 208
Baracca, Sal *135:* 206
Baranaski, Marcin *182:* 113
Barasch, Lynne *126:* 16; *186:* 15
Barbarin, Lucien C., Jr. *89:* 88
Barbour, Karen *96:* 5; *74:* 209; *170:* 16
Bare, Arnold Edwin *16:* 31
Bare, Colleen Stanley *32:* 33
Barger, Jan *147:* 11
Bargeron, Geoffrey *14:* 258
Barkat, Jonathan *149:* 177; *164:* 254; *181:* 106; *184:* 186; *196:* 11; *198:* 148
Barker, Carol *31:* 27
Barker, Cicely Mary *49:* 50, 51
Barkley, James *4:* 13; *6:* 11; *13:* 112
Barks, Carl *37:* 27, 28, 29, 30, 31, 32, 33, 34
Barling, Joy *62:* 148
Barling, Tom *9:* 23
Barlow, Gillian *62:* 20
Barlow, Perry *35:* 28
Barlowe, Dot *30:* 223
Barlowe, Wayne *37:* 72; *84:* 43; *105:* 5
Barnard, Bryn *88:* 53; *13:* 55; *169:* 13; *193:* 194
Barner, Bob *29:* 37; *128:* 33; *136:* 19, 20; *177:* 27
Barnes, Hiram P. *20:* 28
Barnes, Tim *137:* 28
Barnes-Murphy, Rowan *88:* 22
Barnett, Charles II *175:* 150
Barnett, Ivan *70:* 14
Barnett, Moneta *16:* 89; *19:* 142; *31:* 102; *33:* 30, 31, 32; *41:* 153; *61:* 94, 97
Barney, Maginel Wright *39:* 32, 33, 34; *YABC 2:* 306
Barnum, Jay Hyde *11:* 224; *20:* 5; *37:* 189, 190
Baron, Alan *80:* 3; *89:* 123
Barr, George *60:* 74; *69:* 64
Barragan, Paula S. *134:* 116; *186:* 158
Barrall, Tim *115:* 152
Barraud, Martin *189:* 38
Barrauds *33:* 114
Barrer-Russell, Gertrude *9:* 65; *27:* 31
Barret, Robert *85:* 134
Barrett, Angela *40:* 136, 137; *62:* 74; *75:* 10; *76:* 142; *144:* 137; *145:* 14
Barrett, Jennifer *58:* 149
Barrett, John E. *43:* 119
Barrett, Moneta *74:* 5
Barrett, Peter *55:* 169; *86:* 111
Barrett, Robert *62:* 145; *77:* 146; *82:* 35
Barrett, Ron *14:* 24; *26:* 35
Barron, John N. *3:* 261; *5:* 101; *14:* 220
Barrow, Ann *136:* 27
Barrows, Walter *14:* 268
Barry, Ethelred B. *37:* 79; *YABC 1:* 229
Barry, James *14:* 25
Barry, Katharina *2:* 159; *4:* 22
Barry, Robert E. *6:* 12
Barry, Scott *32:* 35
Barshaw, Ruth McNally *203:* 9

Bartenbach, Jean *40:* 31
Barth, Ernest Kurt *2:* 172; *3:* 160; *8:* 26; *10:* 31
Bartholomew, Marie *200:* 66
Bartlett, Alison *101:* 88; *165:* 93
Barton, Byron *8:* 207; *9:* 18; *23:* 66; *80:* 181; *90:* 18, 19, 20, 21; *126:* 29, 30
Barton, Harriett *30:* 71
Barton, Jill *129:* 108; *135:* 120; *145:* 185, 189; *184:* 177
Bartram, Robert *10:* 42
Bartsch, Jochen *8:* 105; *39:* 38
Bascove, Barbara *45:* 73
Base, Graeme *101:* 15, 16, 17, 18; *162:* 8, 10, 12
Baseman, Gary *174:* 12
Bash, Barbara *132:* 9
Baskin, Leonard *30:* 42, 43, 46, 47; *49:* 125, 126, 128, 129,133; *173:* 120
Bass, Saul *49:* 192
Bassett, Jeni *40:* 99; *64:* 30
Basso, Bill *99:* 139; *189:* 134
Batchelor, Joy *29:* 41, 47, 48
Bate, Norman *5:* 16
Bates, Amy June *188:* 170; *189:* 27, 28
Bates, Leo *24:* 35
Batet, Carmen *39:* 134
Batherman, Muriel *31:* 79; *45:* 185
Battaglia, Aurelius *50:* 44
Batten, John D. *25:* 161, 162
Batten, Mary *162:* 14, 15
Battles, Asa *32:* 94, 95
Bauer, Carla *193:* 6
Bauer, Jutta *150:* 32
Bauernschmidt, Marjorie *15:* 15
Baum, Allyn *20:* 10
Baum, Willi *4:* 24, 25; *7:* 173
Bauman, Leslie *61:* 121
Baumann, Jill *34:* 170
Baumhauer, Hans *11:* 218; *15:* 163, 165, 167
Baxter, Glen *57:* 100
Baxter, Leon *59:* 102
Baxter, Robert *87:* 129
Bayer, Herbert *181:* 16
Bayley, Dorothy *37:* 195
Bayley, Nicola *40:* 104; *41:* 34, 35; *69:* 15; *129:* 33, 34, 35
Baylin, Mark *158:* 233
Baynes, Pauline *2:* 244; *3:* 149; *13:* 133, 135,137, 141; *19:* 18, 19, 20; *32:* 208, 213, 214; *36:* 105, 108; *59:* 12, 13, 14, 16, 17, 18, 20; *100:* 158, 159, 243; *133:* 3, 4
Beach, Lou *150:* 150
Beame, Rona *12:* 40
Bean, Jonathan *196:* 102
Bear's Heart *73:* 215
Beard, Dan *22:* 31, 32
Beard, J.H. *YABC 1:* 158
Bearden, Romare *9:* 7; *22:* 35
Beardshaw, Rosalind *169:* 22; *190:* 22
Beardsley, Aubrey *17:* 14; *23:* 181; *59:* 130, 131
Bearman, Jane *29:* 38
Beaton, Cecil *24:* 208
Beaton, Clare *125:* 28
Beauce, J.A. *18:* 103
Beaujard, Sophie *81:* 54
Beccia, Carlyn *189:* 29
Beck, Charles *11:* 169; *51:* 173
Beck, Ian *138:* 27; *182:* 150; *190:* 25
Beck, Melinda *203:* 112
Beck, Ruth *13:* 11
Becker, Harriet *12:* 211
Beckett, Sheilah *5:* 5; *33:* 37, 38
Beckhoff, Harry *1:* 78; *5:* 163
Beckhorn, Susan Williams *189:* 32
Beckman, Kaj *45:* 38, 39, 40, 41
Beckman, Per *45:* 42, 43
Beddows, Eric *72:* 70
Bedford, F.D. *20:* 118, 122; *33:* 170; *41:* 220, 221,230, 233

Bee, Joyce *19:* 62
Bee, William *188:* 6
Beeby, Betty *25:* 36
Beech, Carol *9:* 149
Beech, Mark *192:* 122
Beek *25:* 51, 55, 59
Beeke, Tiphanie *177:* 127; *204:* 140
Beekman, Doug *125:* 146, 148
Beerbohm, Max *24:* 208
Beeson, Bob *108:* 57
Begin, Maryjane *82:* 13
Beha, Philippe *172:* 85
Behr, Joyce *15:* 15; *21:* 132; *23:* 161
Behrens, Hans *5:* 97
Beier, Ellen *135:* 170; *139:* 47; *183:* 164
Beinicke, Steve *69:* 18
Beisner, Monika *46:* 128, 131; *112:* 127
Belden, Charles J. *12:* 182
Belina, Renate *39:* 132
Bell, Corydon *3:* 20
Bell, Graham *54:* 48
Bell, Julia *151:* 214
Bell, Julie *159:* 172; *165:* 18
Bell, Thomas P. *76:* 182
Bellamy, Glen *127:* 15
Bemelmans, Ludwig *15:* 19, 21; *100:* 27
Ben-Ami, Doron *75:* 96; *84:* 107; *108:* 132; *110:* 63; *159:* 157; *197:* 142
Bendall-Brunello, John *150:* 4; *157:* 163; *185:* 3, 4; *203:* 5
Benda, Wladyslaw T. *15:* 256; *30:* 76, 77; *44:* 182
Bender, Robert *77:* 162; *79:* 13; *160:* 23
Bendick, Jeanne *2:* 24; *68:* 27, 28
Benioff, Carol *121:* 42; *175:* 23
Benner, Cheryl *80:* 11
Bennett, Charles H. *64:* 6
Bennett, Erin Susanne *165:* 216
Bennett, F.I. *YABC 1:* 134
Bennett, James *146:* 240
Bennett, Jill *26:* 61; *41:* 38, 39; *45:* 54
Bennett, Rainey *15:* 26; *23:* 53
Bennett, Richard *15:* 45; *21:* 11, 12, 13; *25:* 175
Bennett, Susan *5:* 55
Benny, Mike *142:* 78; *203:* 13, 14
Benoit, Elise *77:* 74
Benson, Linda *60:* 130; *62:* 91; *75:* 101; *79:* 156; *134:* 129
Benson, Patrick *68:* 162; *147:* 17, 18, 19, 20
Bentley, Carolyn *46:* 153
Bentley, James *149:* 30
Bentley, Roy *30:* 162
Benton, Jim *172:* 22
Benton, Thomas Hart *2:* 99
Berelson, Howard *5:* 20; *16:* 58; *31:* 50
Berenstain, Jan *12:* 47; *64:* 33, 34, 36, 37, 38, 40, 42, 44; *135:* 25, 28, 31, 35
Berenstain, Stan *12:* 47; *64:* 33, 34, 36, 37, 38, 40, 42, 44; *135:* 25, 28, 31, 35
Berenzy, Alix *65:* 13; *73:* 6; *78:* 115
Berg, Joan *1:* 115; *3:* 156; *6:* 26, 58
Berg, Ron *36:* 48, 49; *48:* 37, 38; *67:* 72
Bergen, David *115:* 44
Berger, Barbara *77:* 14
Berger, Carin *185:* 6
Berger, William M. *14:* 143; *YABC 1:* 204
Bergherr, Mary *74:* 170; *151:* 123
Bergin, Mark *114:* 8, 9; *143:* 95; *160:* 26, 27
Bergstreser, Douglas *69:* 76
Bergum, Constance R. *121:* 14, 15
Bering, Claus *13:* 14
Berkeley, Jon *139:* 218
Berkowitz, Jeanette *3:* 249
Berman, Paul *66:* 14
Bernal, Richard *154:* 176
Bernadette
    See Watts, Bernadette
Bernardin, James *112:* 24; *167:* 94
Bernasconi, Pablo *183:* 10, 11

Bernath, Stefen *32:* 76
Bernhard, Durga *80:* 13
Bernstein, Michel J. *51:* 71
Bernstein, Ted *38:* 183; *50:* 131
Bernstein, Zena *23:* 46
Berridge, Celia *86:* 63
Berrill, Jacquelyn *12:* 50
Berry, Erick
    See Best, Allena
Berry, Holly *205:* 116
Berry, William D. *14:* 29; *19:* 48
Berry, William A. *6:* 219
Berson, Harold *2:* 17, 18; *4:* 28, 29, 220; *9:* 10; *12:* 19; *17:* 45; *18:* 193; *22:* 85; *34:* 172; *44:* 120; *46:* 42; *80:* 240
Bertholf, Bret *187:* 9; *189:* 32, 33
Berton, Patsy *99:* 16
Bertschmann, Harry *16:* 1
Besco, Don *70:* 99
Beskow, Elsa *20:* 13, 14, 15
Bess, Clayton *63:* 94
Best, Allena *2:* 26; *34:* 76
Betera, Carol *74:* 68
Bethell, Thomas N. *61:* 169
Bethers, Ray *6:* 22
Bettina
    See Ehrlich, Bettina
Betts, Ethel Franklin *17:* 161, 164, 165; *YABC 2:* 47
Betz, Rudolf *59:* 161
Bewick, Thomas *16:* 40, 41, 43, 44, 45, 47; *54:* 150; *YABC 1:* 107
Beyer, Paul J. III *74:* 24
Bezencon, Jacqueline *48:* 40
Biamonte, Daniel *40:* 90
Bianchi, John *91:* 19
Bianco, Pamela *15:* 31; *28:* 44, 45, 46
Bible, Charles *13:* 15
Bice, Clare *22:* 40
Biedrzycki, David *186:* 170
Bierman, Don *57:* 184
Biggers, John *2:* 123
Biggs, Brian *192:* 38; *196:* 15
Bikadoroff, Roxanna *201:* 74
Bileck, Marvin *3:* 102; *40:* 36, 37
Bilibin, Ivan *61:* 8, 9, 12, 13, 14, 15, 151, 152, 154, 162
Billington, Patrick *98:* 71
Billout, Guy *144:* 38, 39
Bimen, Levent *5:* 179
Binch, Caroline *81:* 18; *140:* 15, 16; *144:* 115
Binder, Hannes *169:* 163
Bing, Christopher *126:* 34
Binger, Bill *121:* 46
Binks, Robert *25:* 150
Binzen, Bill *24:* 47
Birch, Reginald *15:* 150; *19:* 33, 34, 35, 36; *37:* 196,197; *44:* 182; *46:* 176; *YABC 1:* 84; *2:* 34, 39
Birchall, Mark *123:* 188
Bird, Esther Brock *1:* 36; *25:* 66
Birdsong, Keith *167:* 85
Birkett, Georgie *204:* 121
Birkett, Rachel *78:* 206
Birling, Paul *109:* 30
Birmingham, Christian *132:* 243; *143:* 114
Birmingham, Lloyd P. *12:* 51; *83:* 13
Biro, Val *1:* 26; *41:* 42; *60:* 178; *67:* 23, 24; *84:* 242, 243
Bischoff, Ilse *44:* 51
Bishop, Don *199:* 133
Bishop, Gavin *97:* 17, 18; *144:* 42, 44
Bishop, Kathleen Wong *115:* 67
Bishop, Rich *56:* 43
Bite, I. *60:* 14
Bittinger, Ned *93:* 117; *205:* 115
Bjorklund, Lorence *3:* 188, 252; *7:* 100; *9:* 113; *10:* 66; *19:* 178; *33:* 122, 123; *35:* 36, 37, 38, 39,41, 42, 43; *36:* 185; *38:* 93; *47:* 106; *66:* 194; *YABC 1:* 242
Bjorkman, Steve *91:* 199; *160:* 110; *198:* 18

Black Sheep *164:* 100
Blackburn, Loren H. *63:* 10
Blackall, Sophie *194:* 140
Blackford, John *137:* 105; *180:* 36
Blackwell, Basil T. *YABC 1:* 68, 69
Blackwood, Freya *199:* 9
Blackwood, Gary L. *118:* 17
Blades, Ann *16:* 52; *37:* 213; *50:* 41; *69:* 21; *99:* 215
Blair, Jay *45:* 46; *46:* 155
Blaisdell, Elinore *1:* 121; *3:* 134; *35:* 63
Blake, Anne Catharine *189:* 71
Blake, Francis *198:* 4
Blake, Quentin *3:* 170; *10:* 48; *13:* 38; *21:* 180; *26:* 60; *28:* 228; *30:* 29, 31; *40:* 108; *45:* 219; *46:* 165, 168; *48:* 196; *52:* 10, 11, 12,13, 14, 15, 16, 17; *73:* 41, 43; *78:* 84, 86; *80:* 250, 251; *84:* 210, 211, 212; *87:* 177; *96:* 24, 26, 28; *124:* 79; *125:* 32, 34; *181:* 139
Blake, Robert J. *37:* 90; *53:* 67; *54:* 23; *160:* 28, 29
Blake, William *30:* 54, 56, 57, 58, 59, 60
Blanchard, N. Taylor *82:* 140
Blass, Jacqueline *8:* 215
Blazek, Scott R. *91:* 71
Bleck, Cathie *118:* 116
Bleck, Linda *204:* 124
Blegvad, Erik *2:* 59; *3:* 98; *5:* 117; *7:* 131; *11:* 149; *14:* 34, 35; *18:* 237; *32:* 219; *60:* 106; *66:* 16, 17, 18, 19; *70:* 233; *76:* 18; *82:* 106; *87:* 45; *100:* 188; *129:* 125; *132:* 17, 18, 19, 20; *176:* 14; *200:* 100; *YABC 1:* 201
Blessen, Karen *93:* 126
Bliss, Corinne Demas *37:* 38
Bliss, Harry *196:* 27, 28, 29
Blitt, Barry *179:* 199; *187:* 13
Bloch, Lucienne *10:* 12
Blondon, Herve *129:* 48; *183:* 22
Bloom, Lloyd *35:* 180; *36:* 149; *47:* 99; *62:* 117; *68:* 231; *72:* 136; *75:* 185; *83:* 99; *108:* 19
Bloom, Suzanne *172:* 23, 24
Blossom, Dave *34:* 29
Blumenschein, E.L. *YABC 1:* 113, 115
Blumer, Patt *29:* 214
Blundell, Kim *29:* 36
Bluthenthal, Diana Cain *93:* 32; *104:* 106; *177:* 26
Blythe, Benjamin *128:* 7
Blythe, Gary *112:* 52; *181:* 166; *182:* 64; *185:* 7; *186:* 116, 117
Boake, Kathy *176:* 185
Board, Perry *171:* 99
Boardman, Gwenn *12:* 60
Bober, Richard *125:* 145; *132:* 40
Bobri *30:* 138; *47:* 27
Bock, Vera *1:* 187; *21:* 41
Bock, William Sauts *8:* 7; *14:* 37; *16:* 120; *21:* 141; *36:* 177; *62:* 203
Bodecker, N(iels) M(ogens) *8:* 13; *14:* 2; *17:* 55, 56, 57; *73:* 22, 23, 24
Boehm, Linda *40:* 31
Bogacki, Tomek *138:* 31, 32; *144:* 123; *202:* 13
Bogan, Paulette *197:* 152; *201:* 17
Bogdan, Florentina *107:* 43
Bohdal, Susi *22:* 44; *101:* 20
Bohlen, Nina *58:* 13
Boies, Alex *96:* 53
Bok, Chip *205:* 16
Bolam, Emily *101:* 216; *159:* 12; *205:* 59
Bolian, Polly *3:* 270; *4:* 30; *13:* 77; *29:* 197
Bolle, Frank *87:* 100
Bollen, Roger *79:* 186; *83:* 16
Bolling, Vickey *114:* 44
Bollinger, Peter *101:* 7; *128:* 198; *172:* 26
Bolognese, Don *2:* 147, 231; *4:* 176; *7:* 146; *17:* 43; *23:* 192; *24:* 50; *34:* 108; *36:* 133; *71:* 24, 25; *103:* 131; *129:* 39, 40
Bolster, Rob *186:* 169

Bolton, A.T. *57:* 158
Bond, Arnold *18:* 116
Bond, Barbara Higgins *21:* 102
Bond, Bruce *52:* 97
Bond, Felicia *38:* 197; *49:* 55, 56; *89:* 170; *90:* 171; *126:* 37
Bond, Higgins *177:* 22, 23
Bonn, Pat *43:* 40
Bonner, Hannah *197:* 13, 14
Bonners, Susan *41:* 40; *85:* 36; *94:* 99, 100; *151:* 105, 106
Bono, Mary *184:* 73
Bonsall, Crosby *23:* 6
Boon, Debbie *103:* 6; *144:* 188
Boon, Emilie *86:* 23, 24
Boone, Debbie *165:* 77
Boore, Sara *60:* 73
Bootman, Colin *155:* 13; *159:* 35; *174:* 192
Booth, Franklin *YABC 2:* 76
Booth, George *191:* 13
Booth, Graham *32:* 193; *37:* 41, 42
Borda, Juliette *102:* 188
Bordier, Georgette *16:* 54
Boren, Tinka *27:* 128
Borges, Jose Francisco *119:* 62
Borja, Robert *22:* 48
Born, Adolf *49:* 63
Bornstein, Ruth *14:* 44; *88:* 45, 46; *107:* 30
Borten, Helen *3:* 54; *5:* 24
Bosin, Blackbear *69:* 104
Bossom, Naomi *35:* 48
Bostock, Mike *83:* 221; *114:* 14; *188:* 205
Boston, Peter *19:* 42
Bosustow, Stephen *34:* 202
Boszko, Ron *75:* 47
Bottner, Barbara *14:* 46
Boucher, Joelle *41:* 138
Boulat, Pierre *44:* 40
Boulet, Susan Seddon *50:* 47
Bouma, Paddy *118:* 25; *128:* 16
Bour, Daniele *66:* 145
Bourke-White, Margaret *15:* 286, 287; *57:* 102
Boutavant, Marc *200:* 136
Boutet de Monvel, M. *30:* 61, 62, 63, 65
Bowen, Betsy *105:* 222
Bowen, Richard *42:* 134
Bowen, Ruth *31:* 188
Bower, Ron *29:* 33
Bowers, David *95:* 38; *115:* 20; *127:* 169, 170; *165:* 57
Bowers, Tim *185:* 35; *201:* 41
Bowman, Claire *174:* 177
Bowman, Eric *151:* 23
Bowman, Leslie *85:* 203; *105:* 108; *116:* 76; *128:* 234; *182:* 24, 25
Bowman, Peter *146:* 214, 215; *150:* 115
Bowser, Carolyn Ewing *22:* 253
Boxall, Ed *178:* 28
Boyd, Aaron *158:* 242
Boyd, Patti *45:* 31
Boyle, Eleanor Vere *28:* 50, 51
Boynton, Sandra *57:* 13, 14, 15; *107:* 36, 37; *152:* 12, 13, 14
Bozzo, Frank *4:* 154
Brabbs, Derry *55:* 170
Brace, Eric *132:* 193, 194; *152:* 71; *184:* 195; *197:* 6; *201:* 54
Brackers de Hugo, Pierre *115:* 21
Bradford, June *158:* 138
Bradford, Ron *7:* 157
Bradley, David P. *69:* 105
Bradley, Richard D. *26:* 182
Bradley, William *5:* 164
Brady, Irene *4:* 31; *42:* 37; *68:* 191
Bragg, Michael *32:* 78; *46:* 31
Bragg, Ruth Gembicki *77:* 18
Brainerd, John W. *65:* 19
Braithwaite, Althea *23:* 12, 13; *119:* 16
Brak, Syd *146:* 187
Bralds, Braldt *90:* 28; *91:* 151
Bram, Elizabeth *30:* 67

Bramley, Peter *4:* 3
Brandenberg, Aliki *2:* 36, 37; *24:* 222; *35:* 49, 50, 51,52, 53, 54, 56, 57; *75:* 15, 17; *92:* 205; *113:* 18, 19, 20; *157:* 28; *156:* 111
Brandenburg, Alexa *75:* 19
Brandenburg, Jim *47:* 58; *150:* 212
Brandi, Lillian *31:* 158
Brandon, Brumsic, Jr. *9:* 25
Brannen, Sarah S. *202:* 15
Bransom, Paul *17:* 121; *43:* 44
Braren, Loretta Trezzo *87:* 193
Brassard, France *186:* 22
Braun, Wendy *80:* 17, 18
Brautigam, Don *115:* 175, 176
Brazell, Derek *75:* 105; *79:* 9
Breathed, Berkeley *86:* 27, 28, 29; *161:* 13, 14
Breckenreid, Julia *192:* 209
Breen, Steve *186:* 23
Brennan, Steve *83:* 230; *101:* 184
Brenner, Fred *22:* 85; *36:* 34; *42:* 34
Brett, Bernard *22:* 54
Brett, Harold M. *26:* 98, 99, 100
Brett, Jan *30:* 135; *42:* 39; *71:* 31, 32; *130:* 23, 24, 25, 26, 27; *171:* 15, 16
Brewer, Paul *106:* 115; *145:* 202
Brewer, Sally King *33:* 44
Brewster, Patience *40:* 68; *45:* 22, 183; *51:* 20; *66:* 144; *89:* 4; *97:* 30, 31
Brick, John *10:* 15
Brickman, Robin D. *131:* 88; *142:* 150; *155:* 18; *178:* 109; *184:* 32
Bridge, David R. *45:* 28
Bridgman, L.J. *37:* 77
Bridwell, Norman *4:* 37; *138:* 36, 37, 40
Brierley, Louise *91:* 22; *96:* 165; *183:* 51
Briggs, Harry *172:* 187
Briggs, Raymond *10:* 168; *23:* 20, 21; *66:* 29, 31, 32; *131:* 28, 29; *184:* 15, 16
Brigham, Grace A. *37:* 148
Bright, Robert *24:* 55
Brighton, Catherine *107:* 39
Brinckloe, Julie *13:* 18; *24:* 79, 115; *29:* 35; *63:* 140; *81:* 131
Brion *47:* 116
Brisley, Joyce L. *22:* 57
Brisson, James F. *110:* 60
Brittingham, Geoffrey *88:* 37
Brix-Henker, Silke *81:* 194
Brock, Charles E. *15:* 97; *19:* 247, 249; *23:* 224, 225; *36:* 88; *42:* 41, 42, 43, 44, 45; *100:* 189; *YABC 1:* 194, 196, 203
Brock, Emma *7:* 21
Brock, Henry Matthew *15:* 81; *16:* 141; *19:* 71; *34:* 115; *40:* 164; *42:* 47, 48, 49; *49:* 66
Brocksopp, Arthur *57:* 157
Broda, Ron *136:* 180; *174:* 123
Brodkin, Gwen *34:* 135
Brodovitch, Alexi *52:* 22
Bromhall, Winifred *5:* 11; *26:* 38
Bromley, Lizzy *159:* 179
Bronson, Linda *150:* 210; *174:* 133; *203:* 16, 17
Brooke, L. Leslie *16:* 181, 182, 183, 186; *17:* 15, 16, 17; *18:* 194
Brooker, Christopher *15:* 251
Brooker, Kyrsten *111:* 94; *140:* 28; *162:* 111; *175:* 108; *186:* 42, 225; *199:* 12; *201:* 30
Brooks, Erik *166:* 52; *182:* 30
Brooks, Karen Stormer *186:* 110
Brooks, Maya Itzna *92:* 153
Brooks, Ron *94:* 15; *197:* 188
Brooks, S.G. *178:* 127
Broomfield, Maurice *40:* 141
Brotman, Adolph E. *5:* 21
Brown, Buck *45:* 48
Brown, Calef *179:* 18
Brown, Christopher *62:* 124, 125, 127, 128
Brown, Craig McFarland *73:* 28; *84:* 65
Brown, Dan *61:* 167; *115:* 183, 184; *116:* 28, 29; *193:* 190; *200:* 21, 23
Brown, David *7:* 47; *48:* 52

Brown, Denise *11:* 213
Brown, Don *172:* 29
Brown, Elbrite *195:* 39; *198:* 5
Brown, Ford Madox *48:* 74
Brown, Hunter *191:* 111, 112
Brown, Judith Gwyn *1:* 45; *7:* 5; *8:* 167; *9:* 182, 190; *20:* 16, 17, 18; *23:* 142; *29:* 117; *33:* 97; *36:* 23, 26; *43:* 184; *48:* 201, 223; *49:* 69; *86:* 227; *110:* 188; *153:* 7
Brown, Kathryn *98:* 26
Brown, Lisa *187:* 175
Brown, Laurie Krasny *99:* 30
Brown, Marc (Tolon) *10:* 17, 197; *14:* 263; *51:* 18; *53:* 11, 12, 13, 15, 16, 17; *75:* 58; *80:* 24, 25, 26; *82:* 261; *99:* 29; *145:* 22, 23, 25, 27; *162:* 198
Brown, Marcia *7:* 30; *25:* 203; *47:* 31, 32, 33, 34, 35,36, 37, 38, 39, 40, 42, 43, 44; *YABC 1:* 27
Brown, Margery W. *5:* 32, 33; *10:* 3
Brown, Martin *101:* 43
Brown, Mary Barrett *97:* 74
Brown, Palmer *36:* 40
Brown, Paul *25:* 26; *26:* 107
Brown, Richard *61:* 18; *67:* 30
Brown, Rick *78:* 71; *150:* 154
Brown, Robert S. *85:* 33
Brown, Rod *157:* 142
Brown, Ruth *55:* 165; *86:* 112, 113; *105:* 16, 17, 18; *171:* 178
Brown, Trevor *99:* 160; *139:* 247; *189:* 206
Browne, Anthony *45:* 50, 51, 52; *61:* 21, 22, 23, 24, 25; *105:* 21, 22, 23, 25
Browne, Dik *8:* 212; *67:* 32, 33, 35, 37, 39
Browne, Gordon *16:* 97; *64:* 114, 116, 117, 119, 121
Browne, Hablot K. *15:* 65, 80; *21:* 14, 15, 16, 17, 18, 19,20; *24:* 25
Browne, Jane *165:* 222
Browning, Coleen *4:* 132
Browning, Mary Eleanor *24:* 84
Bruce, Robert *23:* 23
Brude, Dick *48:* 215
Bruel, Nick *166:* 41; *205:* 17, 18
Brule, Al *3:* 135
Brumbeau, Jeff *157:* 29
Bruna, Dick *43:* 48, 49, 50; *76:* 27, 28
Brundage, Frances *19:* 244
Brunhoff, Jean de *24:* 57, 58
Brunhoff, Laurent de *24:* 60; *71:* 35, 36, 37
Brunkus, Denise *84:* 50; *123:* 117; *178:* 209; *193:* 99; *204:* 10, 11, 12
Brunson, Bob *43:* 135
Bryan, Ashley *31:* 44; *72:* 27, 28, 29; *107:* 92; *116:* 192; *132:* 24; *178:* 33, 34, 35
Bryant, Laura J. *176:* 36; *183:* 168
Bryant, Michael *93:* 74
Brychta, Alex *21:* 21
Bryer, Diana *107:* 121
Bryson, Bernarda *3:* 88, 146; *39:* 26; *44:* 185; *131:* 40
Buba, Joy *12:* 83; *30:* 226; *44:* 56
Buchanan, George *166:* 198
Buchanan, Lilian *13:* 16
Buchanan, Rachel *171:* 71
Bucholtz-Ross, Linda *44:* 137
Buchs, Thomas *40:* 38
Buck, Margaret Waring *3:* 30
Buckhardt, Marc *172:* 59
Buckley, Mike *166:* 180
Budwine, Greg *175:* 172
Buehner, Mark *104:* 12, 15; *105:* 160; *119:* 98; *157:* 188; *159:* 39, 40, 43; *192:* 111
Buehr, Walter *3:* 31
Buff, Conrad *19:* 52, 53, 54
Buff, Mary *19:* 52, 53
Bull, Charles Livingston *18:* 207; *88:* 175, 176
Bullen, Anne *3:* 166, 167
Buller, Jon *205:* 21
Bullock, Kathleen *77:* 24
Bumgarner-Kirby, Claudia *77:* 194

Burbank, Addison *37:* 43
Burchard, Peter Duncan *3:* 197; *5:* 35; *6:* 158, 218; *143:* 17
Burckhardt, Marc *94:* 48; *110:* 89; *196:* 41; *199:* 116
Burger, Carl *3:* 33; *45:* 160, 162
Burgeson, Marjorie *19:* 31
Burgess, Anne *76:* 252
Burgess, Gelett *32:* 39, 42
Burgess, Mark *157:* 31
Burke, Lisa *187:* 19; *185:* 63
Burke, Phillip *95:* 117
Burkert, Nancy Ekholm *18:* 186; *22:* 140; *24:* 62, 63,64, 65; *26:* 53; *29:* 60, 61; *46:* 171; *YABC 1:* 46
Burkhardt, Bruce *142:* 86
Burkhardt, Melissa A. *142:* 86
Burleson, Joe *104:* 35; *172:* 139
Burn, Doris *6:* 172
Burn, Jeffrey *89:* 125; *152:* 132
Burn, Ted
  See Burn, Thomas E.
Burn, Thomas E. *151:* 41
Burnard, Damon *115:* 23
Burnett, Virgil *44:* 42
Burningham, John *9:* 68; *16:* 60, 61; *59:* 28, 29, 30,31, 32, 33, 35; *111:* 18, 19, 21; *160:* 37
Burns, Howard M. *12:* 173
Burns, Jim *47:* 70; *86:* 32; *91:* 197; *123:* 16
Burns, M.F. *26:* 69
Burns, Raymond *9:* 29
Burns, Robert *24:* 106
Burr, Dan *65:* 28; *108:* 134; *164:* 203; *182:* 68
Burr, Dane *12:* 2
Burra, Edward *YABC 2:* 68
Burrell, Galen *56:* 76
Burri, Rene *41:* 143; *54:* 166
Burridge, Marge Opitz *14:* 42
Burris, Burmah *4:* 81
Burroughs, John Coleman *41:* 64
Burroughs, Studley O. *41:* 65
Burton, Marilee Robin *46:* 33
Burton, Virginia Lee *2:* 43; *44:* 49, 51; *100:* 46, 47; *YABC 1:* 24; *147:* 56
Busoni, Rafaello *1:* 186; *3:* 224; *6:* 126; *14:* 5; *16:* 62, 63
Butchkes, Sidney *50:* 58
Butler, Geoff *94:* 20
Butler, Ralph *116:* 212
Butterfield, Ned *1:* 153; *27:* 128; *79:* 63
Butterworth, Ian *184:* 48, 49
Butterworth, Nick *106:* 43, 44; *149:* 34
Buxton, John *123:* 12
Buzelli, Christopher *105:* 149
Buzonas, Gail *29:* 88
Buzzell, Russ W. *12:* 177
Byard, Carole *39:* 44; *57:* 18, 19, 20; *60:* 60; *61:* 93, 96; *69:* 210; *78:* 246; *79:* 227
Byars, Betsy *46:* 35
Byfield, Barbara Ninde *8:* 18
Byfield, Graham *32:* 29
Bynum, Janie *176:* 50
Byrd, Robert *13:* 218; *33:* 46; *158:* 70
Byrd, Samuel *123:* 104

C

Cabat, Erni *74:* 38
Cabban, Vanessa *138:* 73; *176:* 39; *185:* 65
Cabrera, Jane *103:* 24; *152:* 27; *182:* 33, 34
Caceres, Ana Palmero *198:* 106
Caddy, Alice *6:* 41
Cady, Harrison *17:* 21, 23; *19:* 57, 58
Caffrey, Aileen *72:* 223; *141:* 154
Cairns, Julia *177:* 37
Caldecott, Randolph *16:* 98, 103; *17:* 32, 33, 36, 38, 39; *26:* 90; *100:* 49, 50; *YABC 2:* 172

Calder, Alexander *18:* 168
Calderón, Gloria *179:* 5
Calderon, W. Frank *25:* 160
Caldwell, Ben *105:* 75; *149:* 60; *195:* 61
Caldwell, Clyde *98:* 100; *116:* 39
Caldwell, Doreen *23:* 77; *71:* 41
Caldwell, John *46:* 225
Call, Greg *126:* 135; *165:* 49; *182:* 105, 163; *197:* 18, 19; *200:* 159
Callahan, Kevin *22:* 42
Callahan, Philip S. *25:* 77
Callan, Jamie *59:* 37
Calvin, James *61:* 92
Camburn-Bracalente, Carol A. *118:* 22
Cameron, Chad *190:* 144
Cameron, Julia Margaret *19:* 203
Cameron, Scott *99:* 18
Camm, Martin *140:* 208, 209, 210
Campbell, Ann *11:* 43; *123:* 182; *183:* 68
Campbell, Bill *89:* 39
Campbell, Ken *126:* 143; *205:* 162
Campbell, Robert *55:* 120
Campbell, Rod *51:* 27; *98:* 34
Campbell, Walter M. *YABC 2:* 158
Camps, Luis *28:* 120, 121; *66:* 35
Canga, C.B. *187:* 165
Caniglia, Jeremy *201:* 89
Cann, Helen *124:* 50; *141:* 78; *170:* 138; *179:* 22, 23
Cannell, Jon *196:* 43
Cannon, Janell *78:* 25; *128:* 40
Canright, David *36:* 162
Cantone, AnnaLaura *182:* 146; *196:* 80
Canty, Thomas *85:* 161; *92:* 47; *113:* 192; *134:* 60; *185:* 117
Canyon, Christopher *150:* 44; *151:* 112
Caparo, Antonio Javier *204:* 128
Caporale, Wende *70:* 42
Capp, Al *61:* 28, 30, 31, 40, 41, 43, 44
Cappon, Manuela *154:* 64
Caras, Peter *36:* 64
Caraway, Caren *57:* 22
Caraway, James *3:* 200, 201
Carbe, Nino *29:* 183
Cares, Linda *67:* 176
Carigiet, Alois *24:* 67
Carle, Eric *4:* 42; *11:* 121; *12:* 29; *65:* 32,33, 34, 36; *73:* 63, 65; *163:* 55, 56
Carling, Amelia Lau *164:* 46
Carlino, Angela *168:* 43; *188:* 20
Carlson, Nancy L. *41:* 116; *56:* 25; *90:* 45; *144:* 48, 50
Carlluccio, Maria *175:* 129
Carmi, Giora *79:* 35; *149:* 40
Carpenter, Nancy *76:* 128; *86:* 173; *89:* 171; *131:* 186; *134:* 8; *138:* 215; *153:* 204; *159:* 93; *165:* 232
Carr, Archie *37:* 225
Carrick, Donald *5:* 194; *39:* 97; *49:* 70; *53:* 156; *63:* 15, 16, 17, 18, 19, 21; *80:* 131; *86:* 151; *118:* 24
Carrick, Malcolm *28:* 59, 60
Carrick, Paul *118:* 26; *194:* 28
Carrick, Valery *21:* 47
Carrier, Lark *71:* 43
Carroll, Jim *88:* 211; *140:* 177; *153:* 99; *195:* 75
Carroll, Lewis
  See Dodgson, Charles L.
Carroll, Michael *72:* 5
Carroll, Pamela *84:* 68; *128:* 214; *199:* 130
Carroll, Ruth *7:* 41; *10:* 68
Carter, Abby *81:* 32; *97:* 121; *102:* 61; *163:* 139; *164:* 125; *184:* 22, 23; *191:* 85
Carter, Barbara *47:* 167, 169
Carter, David A. *114:* 24, 25; *170:* 42, 43
Carter, Don *124:* 54; *184:* 100; *192:* 43, 44, 45
Carter, Harry *22:* 179
Carter, Helene *15:* 38; *22:* 202, 203; *YABC 2:* 220, 221
Carter, Penny *173:* 91

Cartlidge, Michelle *49:* 65; *96:* 50, 51
Cartwright, Reg *63:* 61, 62; *78:* 26; *143:* 4
Cartwright, Shannon *176:* 81
Carty, Leo *4:* 196; *7:* 163; *58:* 131
Cary *4:* 133; *9:* 32; *20:* 2; *21:* 143
Cary, Page *12:* 41
Casale, Paul *71:* 63; *109:* 122; *136:* 28
Case, Sandra E. *16:* 2
Caseley, Judith *87:* 36; *159:* 47, 48, 49
Casilla, Robert *78:* 7; *167:* 124
Casino, Steve *85:* 193
Cassel, Lili
    See Wronker, Lili Cassel
Cassel-Wronker, Lili
    See Wronker, Lili Cassel
Cassels, Jean *8:* 50; *150:* 119; *173:* 37; *186:* 182
Cassen, Melody *140:* 51
Cassity, Don *104:* 24
Cassler, Carl *75:* 137, 138; *82:* 162
Casson, Hugh *65:* 38, 40, 42, 43
Castellon, Federico *48:* 45, 46, 47, 48
Castle, Jane *4:* 80
Castro, Antonio *84:* 71
Casu, Danny "casroc" *201:* 10
Catalano, Dominic *94:* 79; *163:* 60, 61; *162:* 54
Catalanotto, Peter *63:* 170; *70:* 23; *71:* 182; *72:* 96; *74:* 114; *76:* 194, 195; *77:* 7; *79:* 157; *80:* 28, 67; *83:* 157; *85:* 27; *108:* 11; *113:* 30, 31, 33, 34, 36; *114:* 27, 28, 29; *117:* 53; *124:* 168; *159:* 54, 55; *195:* 19, 20, 21, 22, 24, 174; *200:* 156
Catania, Tom *68:* 82
Cather, Carolyn *3:* 83; *15:* 203; *34:* 216
Catrow, David *117:* 179; *152:* 31, 33; *173:* 24
Cauley, Lorinda Bryan *44:* 135; *46:* 49
Cayard, Bruce *38:* 67
Cazet, Denys *52:* 27; *99:* 39, 40; *163:* 65, 66; *191:* 25, 27, 28
Ceccoli, Nicoletta *181:* 39; *188:* 99; *199:* 118
Cecil, Randy *127:* 132, 133; *187:* 16, 17; *191:* 168
Cellini, Joseph *2:* 73; *3:* 35; *16:* 116; *47:* 103
Cepeda, Joe *90:* 62; *109:* 91; *134:* 172; *159:* 57, 58, 164; *197:* 157; *203:* 69, 95
Chabrian, Debbi *45:* 55
Chabrian, Deborah *51:* 182; *53:* 124; *63:* 107; *75:* 84; *79:* 85; *82:* 247; *89:* 93; *101:* 197
Chagnon, Mary *37:* 158
Chalmers, Mary *3:* 145; *13:* 148; *33:* 125; *66:* 214
Chamberlain, Christopher *45:* 57
Chamberlain, Margaret *46:* 51; *106:* 89; *188:* 193
Chamberlain, Nigel *78:* 140
Chambers, C.E. *17:* 230
Chambers, Dave *12:* 151
Chambers, Jill *134:* 110
Chambers, Mary *4:* 188
Chambliss, Maxie *42:* 186; *56:* 159; *93:* 163, 164; *103:* 178; *186:* 33, 34; *196:* 39
Champlin, Dale *136:* 124
Chan, Harvey *96:* 236; *99:* 153; *143:* 218; *179:* 144
Chandler, David P. *28:* 62
Chaney, Howard *139:* 27
Chang, Warren *101:* 209
Chapel, Jody *68:* 20
Chapman, C.H. *13:* 83, 85, 87
Chapman, Frederick T. *6:* 27; *44:* 28
Chapman, Gaye *203:* 133
Chapman, Gaynor *32:* 52, 53
Chapman, Jane *145:* 186; *150:* 56; *166:* 220; *174:* 202; *176:* 43, 44; *179:* 131; *202:* 189
Chapman, Lynne *175:* 31; *197:* 25
Chappell, Warren *3:* 172; *21:* 56; *27:* 125
Charles, Donald *30:* 154, 155
Charlip, Remy *4:* 48; *34:* 138; *68:* 53, 54; *119:* 29, 30

Charlot, Jean *1:* 137, 138; *8:* 23; *14:* 31; *48:* 151; *56:* 21
Charlot, Martin *64:* 72
Charlton, Michael *34:* 50; *37:* 39
Charmatz, Bill *7:* 45
Chartier, Normand *9:* 36; *52:* 49; *66:* 40; *74:* 220; *145:* 169; *168:* 91; *177:* 108
Chase, Lynwood M. *14:* 4
Chast, Roz *97:* 39, 40
Chastain, Madye Lee *4:* 50
Chateron, Ann *152:* 19
Chatterton, Martin *68:* 102; *152:* 19
Chauncy, Francis *24:* 158
Chayka, Doug *145:* 97; *177:* 150; *196:* 46
Chee, Cheng-Khee *79:* 42; *81:* 224; *180:* 245
Chen, Chih-sien *90:* 226
Chen, Tony *6:* 45; *19:* 131; *29:* 126; *34:* 160
Chen, Yong *183:* 34
Cheney, T.A. *11:* 47
Cheng, Andrea *205:* 28
Cheng, Judith *36:* 45; *51:* 16
Chermayeff, Ivan *47:* 53
Cherry, David *93:* 40
Cherry, Lynne *34:* 52; *65:* 184; *87:* 111; *99:* 46, 47
Chesak, Lina *135:* 118
Chess, Victoria *12:* 6; *33:* 42, 48, 49; *40:* 194; *41:* 145; *69:* 80; *72:* 100; *92:* 33, 34; *104:* 167
Chessare, Michele *41:* 50; *56:* 48; *69:* 145
Chesterton, G.K. *27:* 43, 44, 45, 47
Chestnutt, David *47:* 217
Chesworth, Michael *75:* 24, 152; *88:* 136; *94:* 25; *98:* 155; *160:* 42
Chetham, Celia *134:* 34
Chetwin, Grace *86:* 40
Cheung, Irving *158:* 96
Chevalier, Christa *35:* 66
Chew, Ruth *7:* 46; *132:* 147
Chewning, Randy *92:* 206
Chichester Clark, Emma *72:* 121; *77:* 212; *78:* 209; *87:* 143; *117:* 37, 39, 40; *144:* 138; *156:* 24, 25
Chifflart *47:* 113, 127
Child, Lauren *119:* 32; *183:* 30, 31
Chin, Alex *28:* 54
Chitwood, Susan Tanner *163:* 16
Cho, Shinta *8:* 126
Chodos-Irvine, Margaret *52:* 102, 103, 107; *152:* 44
Choi, Yangsook *171:* 134; *173:* 135; *178:* 38, 39, 40
Chollat, Emilie *170:* 203
Chollick, Jay *25:* 175
Choma, Christina *99:* 169
Chomey, Steve *188:* 53
Chorao, Kay *7:* 200, 201; *8:* 25; *11:* 234; *33:* 187; *35:* 239; *69:* 35; *70:* 235; *123:* 174; *193:* 179
Chowdhury, Subrata *62:* 130; *162:* 22, 23
Christelow, Eileen *38:* 44; *83:* 198, 199; *90:* 57, 58; *184:* 26
Christensen, Bonnie *93:* 100; *153:* 67
Christensen, Gardell Dano *1:* 57
Christensen, James C. *140:* 226
Christiana, David *90:* 64; *135:* 13; *171:* 7; *195:* 26, 27
Christiansen, Per *40:* 24
Christie, R. Gregory *116:* 107; *127:* 20, 21; *162:* 179; *164:* 114; *165:* 137; *174:* 157; *179:* 172; *185:* 17, 18, 19; *200:* 2; *204:* 85
Christy, Howard Chandler *17:* 163, 164, 165, 168, 169; *19:* 186, 187; *21:* 22, 23, 24, 25
Christy, Jana *194:* 21
Chronister, Robert *23:* 138; *63:* 27; *69:* 167
Church, Caroline Jayne *179:* 27
Church, Frederick *YABC 1:* 155
Chute, Marchette *1:* 59
Chwast, Jacqueline *1:* 63; *2:* 275; *6:* 46, 47; *11:* 125; *12:* 202; *14:* 235

Chwast, Seymour *3:* 128, 129; *18:* 43; *27:* 152; *92:* 79; *96:* 56, 57, 58; *146:* 32, 33; *197:* 99
Cieslawksi, Steve *101:* 142; *127:* 116; *158:* 169, 171; *190:* 174
Cinelli, Lisa *146:* 253
Cirlin, Edgard *2:* 168
Clairin, Georges *53:* 109
Clapp, John *105:* 66; *109:* 58; *126:* 7; *129:* 148; *130:* 165; *195:* 48
Clark, Brenda *119:* 85; *153:* 55
Clark, David *77:* 164; *134:* 144, 145
Clark, Emma Chichester
    See Chichester Clark, Emma
Clark, Victoria *35:* 159
Clarke, Greg *169:* 134
Clarke, Gus *72:* 226; *134:* 31
Clarke, Harry *23:* 172, 173
Clarke, Peter *75:* 102
Claverie, Jean *38:* 46; *88:* 29
Clavis, Philippe Goossens *182:* 167
Clay, Wil *203:* 29
Clayton, Elaine *159:* 60
Clayton, Robert *9:* 181
Cleary, Brian P. *186:* 37
Cleaver, Elizabeth *8:* 204; *23:* 36
Cleland, T.M. *26:* 92
Clemens, Peter *61:* 125
Clement, Charles *20:* 38
Clement, Gary *186:* 79; *191:* 32
Clement, Janet *182:* 50
Clement, Nathan *200:* 30
Clement, Rod *97:* 42
Clement, Stephen *88:* 3
Clementson, John *84:* 213
Clemesha, David *192:* 49, 50
Clevin, Jorgen *7:* 50
Clifford, Judy *34:* 163; *45:* 198
Clokey, Art *59:* 44
Clouse, Dennis *187:* 158
Clouse, James *84:* 15
Clouse, Nancy L. *78:* 31; *114:* 90
Clover, Peter *152:* 45
Cneut, Carll *156:* 166; *165:* 67; *197:* 26
Coalson, Glo *9:* 72, 85; *25:* 155; *26:* 42; *35:* 212; *53:* 31; *56:* 154; *94:* 37, 38, 193
Cober, Alan E. *17:* 158; *32:* 77; *49:* 127
Cober-Gentry, Leslie *92:* 111
Cocca-Leffler, Maryann *80:* 46; *136:* 60; *139:* 193; *194:* 31, 33, 34
Cochran, Bobbye *11:* 52
CoConis, Ted *4:* 41; *46:* 41; *51:* 104
Cocozza, Chris *87:* 18; *110:* 173; *111:* 149
Cockroft, Jason *152:* 20
Coerr, Eleanor *1:* 64; *67:* 52
Coes, Peter *35:* 172
Cogancherry, Helen *52:* 143; *69:* 131; *77:* 93; *78:* 220; *109:* 204; *110:* 129; *203:* 92
Coggins, Jack *2:* 69
Cohen, Alix *7:* 53
Cohen, Miriam *155:* 23, 24
Cohen, Nancy R. *165:* 35
Cohen, Santiago *164:* 26
Cohen, Sheldon *105:* 33, 34; *166:* 46, 47
Cohen, Vincent O. *19:* 243
Cohen, Vivien *11:* 112
Coker, Paul *51:* 172
Colbert, Anthony *15:* 41; *20:* 193
Colby, C.B. *3:* 47
Cole, Babette *58:* 172; *96:* 63, 64; *155:* 29
Cole, Brock *68:* 223; *72:* 36, 37, 38, 192; *127:* 23; *136:* 64, 65; *197:*
Cole, Gwen *87:* 185
Cole, Henry *178:* 120; *181:* 42, 43; *189:* 60
Cole, Herbert *28:* 104
Cole, Michael *59:* 46
Cole, Olivia H.H. *1:* 134; *3:* 223; *9:* 111; *38:* 104
Colin, Paul *102:* 59; *123:* 118; *126:* 152; *192:* 129
Colley, Jacqui *202:* 20

Collicott, Sharleen *98:* 39; *143:* 29, 30
Collier, Bryan *126:* 54; *151:* 166; *174:* 16, 17, 18; *204:* 18, 19
Collier, David *13:* 127
Collier, John *27:* 179
Collier, Steven *50:* 52
Collier-Morales, Roberta *168:* 61
Collins, Heather *66:* 84; *67:* 68; *81:* 40; *98:* 192, 193; *129:* 95, 96, 98
Collins, Matt *167:* 90
Collins, Ross *140:* 23, 24; *200:* 36, 37
Colman, Audrey *146:* 161
Colón, Raul *108:* 112; *113:* 5; *117:* 167; *134:* 112; *146:* 23; *159:* 92; *166:* 73; *180:* 107; *186:* 156; *190:* 6; *193:* 24, 205; *202:* 21, 22, 23
Colonna, Bernard *21:* 50; *28:* 103; *34:* 140; *43:* 180; *78:* 150
Comport, Sally Wern *117:* 169; *169:* 104; *190:* 42
Conde, J.M. *100:* 120
Condon, Grattan *54:* 85 Condon, Ken *161:* 44; *195:* 28, 29
Cone, Ferne Geller *39:* 49
Cone, J. Morton *39:* 49
Conklin, Paul *43:* 62
Connelly, James *198:* 12
Connolly, Howard *67:* 88
Connolly, Jerome P. *4:* 128; *28:* 52
Connolly, Peter *47:* 60
Conoly, Walle *110:* 224
Conover, Chris *31:* 52; *40:* 184; *41:* 51; *44:* 79
Contreras, Gerry *72:* 9
Converse, James *38:* 70
Conway *62:* 62
Conway, Michael *69:* 12; *81:* 3; *92:* 108
Cook, Ande *188:* 135
Cook, G.R. *29:* 165
Cook, Joel *108:* 160
Cookburn, W.V. *29:* 204
Cooke, Donald E. *2:* 77
Cooke, Tom *52:* 118
Coomaraswamy, A.K. *50:* 100
Coombs, Charles *43:* 65
Coombs, Deborah *139:* 175
Coombs, Patricia *2:* 82; *3:* 52; *22:* 119; *51:* 32, 33, 34, 35, 36, 37, 38, 39, 40, 42, 43
Cooney, Barbara *6:* 16, 17, 50; *12:* 42; *13:* 92; *15:* 145; *16:* 74, 111; *18:* 189; *23:* 38, 89, 93; *32:* 138; *38:* 105; *59:* 48, 49, 51, 52, 53; *74:* 222; *81:* 100; *91:* 25; *96:* 71, 72, 74; *100:* 149; *YABC2:* 10
Cooper, Elisha *157:* 38, 39
Cooper, Floyd *79:* 95; *81:* 45; *84:* 82; *85:* 74; *91:* 118; *96:* 77, 78; *103:* 149; *144:* 54; *145:* 151; *159:* 198; *176:* 133, 134; *187:* 26, 27, 28, 29; *188:* 22; *199:* 175
Cooper, Heather *50:* 39
Cooper, Helen *102:* 42, 43, 44
Cooper, Mario *24:* 107
Cooper, Marjorie *7:* 112
Cope, Jane *61:* 201; *108* 52
Copeland, Mark *180:* 12
Copelman, Evelyn *8:* 61; *18:* 25
Copley, Heather *30:* 86; *45:* 57
Corbett, Grahame *30:* 114; *43:* 67
Corbino, John *19:* 248
Corcos, Lucille *2:* 223; *10:* 27; *34:* 66
Cordell, Matthew *197:* 93; *199:* 20, 21
Corey, Robert *9:* 34
Corlass, Heather *10:* 7
Cornell, James *27:* 60
Cornell, Jeff *11:* 58
Cornell, Laura *94:* 179; *95:* 25
Corr, Christopher *204:* 98
Corrigan, Barbara *8:* 37
Corrigan, Patrick *145:* 149
Corwin, Judith Hoffman *10:* 28
Corwin, Oliver *191:* 119
Cory, Fanny Y. *20:* 113; *48:* 29
Cosentino, Ralph *169:* 32

Cosgrove, Margaret *3:* 100; *47:* 63; *82:* 133
Costabel, Eva Deutsch *45:* 66, 67
Costanza, John *58:* 7, 8, 9
Costello, Chris *86:* 78
Costello, David F. *23:* 55
Côté, Geneviéve *184:* 37, 39
Cote, Nancy *126:* 139; *156:* 101; *174:* 101; *182:* 53, 54, 55
Cottenden, Jeff *190:* 45
Couch, Greg *94:* 124; *110:* 13; *162:* 31; *168:* 149; *199:* 22
Councell, Ruth Tietjen *79:* 29
Courtney, Cathy *58:* 69, 144; *59:* 15; *61:* 20, 87
Courtney, R. *35:* 110
Counihan, Claire *133:* 106
Cousineau, Normand *89:* 180; *112:* 76
Cousins, Lucy *172:* 53, 54; *205:* 34, 35
Couture, Christin *41:* 209
Covarrubias, Miguel *35:* 118, 119, 123, 124, 125
Coville, Katherine *32:* 57; *36:* 167; *92:* 38
Covington, Neverne *113:* 87
Cowdrey, Richard *169:* 170; *178:* 205; *204:* 22, 23
Cowell, Cressida *140:* 39
Cowell, Lucinda *77:* 54
Cowles, Rose *203:* 164, 167
Cox *43:* 93
Cox, Charles *8:* 20
Cox, David *56:* 37; *90:* 63; *119:* 38
Cox, Palmer *24:* 76, 77
Cox, Steve *140:* 96
Coxe, Molly *69:* 44
Coxon, Michele *158:* 80
Crabb, Gordon *70:* 39
Crabtree, Judith *98:* 42
Craft, Kinuko *22:* 182; *36:* 220; *53:* 122, 123, 148,149; *74:* 12; *81:* 129; *86:* 31; *89:* 139; *127:* 27, 28, 29; *132:* 142; *139:* 38
Craig, Daniel *177:* 67; *180:* 11; *185:* 203
Craig, David *136:* 198; *205:* 37
Craig, Helen *49:* 76; *62:* 70, 71, 72; *69:* 141; *94:* 42, 43, 44; *112:* 53; *135:* 101, 102
Crane, Alan H. *1:* 217
Crane, H.M. *13:* 111
Crane, Jack *43:* 183
Crane, Jordan *174:* 21
Crane, Walter *18:* 46, 47, 48, 49, 53, 54, 56, 57, 59, 60, 61; *22:* 128; *24:* 210, 217; *100:* 70, 71
Cravath, Lynne W. *98:* 45; *182:* 58, 59
Crawford, Denise *137:* 213
Crawford, Will *43:* 77
Credle, Ellis *1:* 69
Czernecki, Stefan *154:* 104; *178:* 68, 69
Crespi, Francesca *87:* 90
Cressy, Michael *124:* 55; *203:* 132
Crews, Donald *32:* 59, 60; *76:* 42, 43, 44
Crews, Nina *97:* 49
Crichlow, Ernest *74:* 88; *83:* 203
Croft, James *150:* 57
Crofut, Bob *80:* 87; *81:* 47
Crofut, Susan *23:* 61
Croll, Carolyn *80:* 137; *102:* 52
Cross, Peter *56:* 78; *63:* 60, 65
Crowe, Elizabeth *88:* 144
Crowell, Pers *3:* 125
Cruikshank, George *15:* 76, 83; *22:* 74, 75, 76, 77, 78, 79,80, 81, 82, 84, 137; *24:* 22, 23
Crump, Fred H. *11:* 62
Cruz, Ray *6:* 55; *70:* 234; *123:* 173; *172:* 192
Csatari, Joe *44:* 82; *55:* 152; *63:* 25, 28; *102:* 58
Cuetara, Mittie *158:* 85
Cuffari, Richard *4:* 75; *5:* 98; *6:* 56; *7:* 13,84, 153; *8:* 148, 155; *9:* 89; *11:* 19; *12:* 55, 96,114; *15:* 51, 202; *18:* 5; *20:* 139; *21:* 197; *22:* 14, 192; *23:* 15, 106; *25:* 97; *27:* 133; *28:* 196; *29:* 54; *30:* 85; *31:* 35; *36:* 101; *38:* 171; *42:* 97; *44:* 92, 192; *45:* 212, 213; *46:*

36, 198; *50:* 164; *54:* 80, 136, 137, 145; *56:* 17; *60:* 63; *66:* 49, 50; *70:* 41; *71:* 132; *77:* 157; *78:* 58, 149; *79:* 120; *85:* 2, 152
Cugat, Xavier *19:* 120
Cumings, Art *35:* 160
Cummings, Chris *29:* 167
Cummings, Michael *159:* 142
Cummings, Pat *42:* 61; *61:* 99; *69:* 205; *71:* 57,58; *78:* 24, 25; *93:* 75; *107:* 49, 50; *164:* 259; *203:* 45, 46
Cummings, Richard *24:* 119
Cunette, Lou *20:* 93; *22:* 125
Cunningham, Aline *25:* 180
Cunningham, David *11:* 13
Cunningham, Imogene *16:* 122, 127
Cunningham, Kelley *176:* 159
Cupples, Pat *107:* 12; *126:* 109; *182:* 13; *198:* 68
Curlee, Lynn *98:* 48; *141:* 39; *190:* 48
Currey, Anna *190:* 145; *202:* 130, 132
Curry, John Steuart *2:* 5; *19:* 84; *34:* 36; *144:* 126
Curry, Tom *127:* 131; *185:* 25, 26
Curtis, Bruce *23:* 96; *30:* 88; *36:* 22
Curtis, Neil *167:* 30
Curtis, Stacy *205:* 38
Cusack, Margaret *58:* 49, 50, 51
Cushman, Doug *65:* 57; *101:* 39, 40; *133:* 179; *157:* 45; *186:* 157
Cutting, Ann *196:* 194
Cyrus, Kurt *132:* 39; *179:* 36, 37
Czechowski, Alicia *95:* 21; *171:* 37
Czernecki, Stefan *117:* 173

D

Dabcovich, Lydia *25:* 105; *40:* 114; *99:* 75, 76
Dacey, Bob *82:* 175; *152:* 65
d'Achille, Gino *127:* 175, 176
Dailey, Don *78:* 197
Dain, Martin J. *35:* 75
Dale, Penny *127:* 224; *151:* 57; *160:* 89; *197:* 75
Dale, Rae *72:* 197
Daley, Joann *50:* 22
Dalton, Anne *40:* 62; *63:* 119
Daly, Deborah M. *74:* 213
Daly, Jim *103:* 60; *150:* 48
Daly, Jude *138:* 118, 119
Daly, Nicholas *37:* 53; *76:* 48, 49
Daly, Niki *107:* 15; *114:* 38, 39, 40; *164:* 86; *192:* 53; *198:* 26, 27
Daly, Paul *97:* 205
Dalziel, Brothers *33:* 113
D'Amato, Alex *9:* 48; *20:* 25
D'Amato, Janet *9:* 48; *20:* 25; *26:* 118
D'Amico, Steve *170:* 52
Danalis, Johnny *167:* 27
D'Andrea, Domenick *183:* 108
Daniel, Alan *23:* 59; *29:* 110; *76:* 50, 53, 55, 56; *153:* 76 *115:* 74; *134:* 70
Daniel, Lea *76:* 53, 55; *153:* 76
Daniel, Lewis C. *20:* 216
Daniels, Beau *73:* 4
Daniels, Steve *22:* 16
Daniels, Stewart *56:* 12
Dann, Bonnie *31:* 83
Dann, Penny *82:* 128
Danska, Herbert *24:* 219
Danyell, Alice *20:* 27
Darley, F.O.C. *16:* 145; *19:* 79, 86, 88, 185; *21:* 28,36; *35:* 76, 77, 78, 79, 80, 81; *YABC 2:* 175
Darling, Lois *3:* 59; *23:* 30, 31
Darling, Louis *1:* 40, 41; *2:* 63; *3:* 59; *23:* 30,31; *43:* 54, 57, 59; *121:* 53
Darrow, David R. *84:* 101
Darrow, Whitney, Jr. *13:* 25; *38:* 220, 221
Darwin, Beatrice *43:* 54

Darwin, Len *24:* 82
Dastolfo, Frank *33:* 179
Dauber, Liz *1:* 22; *3:* 266; *30:* 49
Daugherty, James *3:* 66; *8:* 178; *13:* 27, 28, 161; *18:* 101; *19:* 72; *29:* 108; *32:* 156; *42:* 84; *YABC 1:* 256; *2:* 174
d'Aulaire, Edgar Parin *5:* 51; *66:* 53
d'Aulaire, Ingri Parin *5:* 51; *66:* 53
Davalos, Felipe *99:* 197; *159:* 66; *174:* 163
Davenier, Christine *125:* 88; *127:* 32; *128:* 152; *179:* 39, 40
Davick, Linda *151:* 124
David, Jacques-Louis *193:* 22
David, Jonathan *19:* 37
Davidson, Kevin *28:* 154
Davidson, Raymond *32:* 61
Davie, Helen K. *77:* 48, 49
Davies, Andy Robert *205:* 169
Davis, Allen *20:* 11; *22:* 45; *27:* 222; *29:* 157; *41:* 99; *47:* 99; *50:* 84; *52:* 105
Davis, Bette J. *15:* 53; *23:* 95
Davis, Dimitris *45:* 95
Davis, Hendon *151:* 122
Davis, Jack E. *145:* 139; *175:* 84, 85
Davis, Jim *32:* 63, 64
Davis, Katie *152:* 52, 53, 54
Davis, Lambert *110:* 23, 24; *176:* 58
Davis, Marguerite *31:* 38; *34:* 69, 70; *100:* 34; *YABC 1:* 126, 230
Davis, Nelle *69:* 191
Davis, Paul *78:* 214
Davis, Yvonne LeBrun *94:* 144
Davisson, Virginia H. *44:* 178
DaVolls, Andy *85:* 53
Dawson, Diane *24:* 127; *42:* 126; *52:* 130; *68:* 104
Day, Alexandra *67:* 59; *97:* 54; *166:* 65; *169:* 40; *197:* 50, 51, 52, 54
Day, Larry *169:* 88; *185:* 59
Day, Rob *94:* 110; *127:* 24; *197:* 32
Dean, Bob *19:* 211
Dean, David *192:* 55
de Angeli, Marguerite *1:* 77; *27:* 62, 65, 66, 67, 69, 70, 72; *100:* 75, 76; *YABC 1:* 166
DeArmond, Dale *70:* 47
Deas, Michael *27:* 219, 221; *30:* 156; *67:* 134; *72:* 24; *75:* 155; *84:* 206; *88:* 124
Deas, Rich *191:* 87; *193:* 10
deBarros, Jim *196:* 60
Debon, Nicolas *151:* 60; *177:* 46
de Bosschere, Jean *19:* 252; *21:* 4; *186:* 44, 45
De Bruyn, M(onica) G. *13:* 30, 31
Decker, C.B. *172:* 120
De Cuir, John F. *1:* 28, 29
Deeter, Catherine *74:* 110; *103:* 150; *137:* 50
Degen, Bruce *40:* 227, 229; *57:* 28, 29; *56:* 156; *75:* 229; *76:* 19; *81:* 36, 37; *92:* 26; *93:* 199; *97:* 56, 58, 59; *124:* 40; *147:* 39, 40, 41; *168:* 23; *205:* 45, 46
De Grazia *14:* 59; *39:* 56, 57
DeGrazio, George *88:* 40
deGroat, Diane *9:* 39; *18:* 7; *23:* 123; *28:* 200, 201; *31:* 58, 59; *34:* 151; *41:* 152; *43:* 88; *46:* 40, 200; *49:* 163; *50:* 89; *52:* 30, 34; *54:* 43; *63:* 5; *70:* 136; *71:* 99; *73:* 117,156; *77:* 34; *85:* 48; *86:* 201; *87:* 142; *90:* 72, 73, 143; *95:* 182; *111:* 123; *118:* 160; *126:* 8; *130:* 130; *138:* 93, 94; *169:* 46, 47
de Groot, Lee *6:* 21
Deines, Brian *110:* 139
DeJohn, Marie *89:* 78
Dekhteryov, B. *61:* 158
de Kiefte, Kees *94:* 107
Delacre, Lulu *36:* 66; *156:* 35; *202:* 10, 53
Delaney, A. *21:* 78
Delaney, Michael *180:* 16
Delaney, Molly *80:* 43
Delaney, Ned *28:* 68; *56:* 80; *102:* 11
DeLange, Alex Pardo *179:* 128
DeLapine, Jim *79:* 21
De La Roche Saint Andre, Anne *75:* 37

de Larrea, Victoria *6:* 119, 204; *29:* 103; *72:* 203; *87:* 199
Delessert, Étienne *7:* 140; *46:* 61, 62, 63, 65, 67, 68; *130:* 38, 39, 40, 41, 42; *179:* 46, 47, 48, 49; *YABC 2:* 209
Delezenne, Christine *186:* 126
Del Negro, Janice *196:* 161
DeLorenzo, Christopher *154:* 149
Delulio, John *15:* 54
DeLuna, Tony *88:* 95
Demarest, Chris L. *45:* 68, 69, 70; *73:* 172, 173, 176; *78:* 106; *82:* 48, 49; *89:* 212; *92:* 86; *128:* 57, 58; *175:* 46, 48
De Mejo, Oscar *40:* 67
De Muth, Roger *205:* 184
Demi *11:* 135; *15:* 245; *66:* 129, 130; *89:* 216; *102:* 66, 67, 68
Denetsosie, Hoke *13:* 126; *82:* 34
Denise, Christopher *147:* 43, 44; *176:* 101; *193:* 35, 36, 37; *201:* 37
Dennis, Morgan *18:* 68, 69; *64:* 89
Dennis, Wesley *2:* 87; *3:* 111; *11:* 132; *18:* 71, 72, 73, 74; *22:* 9; *24:* 196, 200; *46:* 178; *69:* 94, 96; *129:* 62
Denos, Julia *202:* 26
Denslow, W.W. *16:* 84, 85, 86, 87; *18:* 19, 20, 24; *29:* 211; *100:* 21
Denton, Kady MacDonald *110:* 82; *130:* 70; *181:* 54, 55, 56; *192:* 75
Denton, Terry *72:* 163; *174:* 26; *186:* 52; *196:* 83, 84
DePalma, Mary Newell *132:* 114; *139:* 75; *185:* 30, 31; *186:* 121
dePaola, Tomie *8:* 95; *9:* 93; *11:* 69; *25*; *103*; *28:* 157; *29:* 80; *39:* 52, 53; *40:* 226; *46:* 187; *59:* 61, 62, 63, 64, 65, 66, 67, 68, 69, 71, 72, 74; *62:* 19; *108:* 63, 67, 68, 70; *155:* 62, 64, 66; *180:* 105; *200:* 47, 48, 49, 50
Deraney, Michael J. *77:* 35; *78:* 148
deRosa, Dee *70:* 48; *71:* 210; *91:* 78
Dervaux, Isabelle *111:* 117
DeSaix, Deborah Durland *180:* 15; *188:* 24
De Saulles, Tony *119:* 39
de Seve, Peter *146:* 261
Deshaprabhu, Meera Dayal *86:* 192
Desimini, Lisa *86:* 68; *94:* 47; *96:* 7; *104:* 107; *125:* 194; *131:* 180; *172:* 56
de St. Menin, Charles *70:* 17
Detmold, Edward J. *22:* 104, 105, 106, 107; *35:* 120; *64:* 5; *YABC 2:* 203
Detrich, Susan *20:* 133
Deutermann, Diana *77:* 175
DeVelasco, Joseph E. *21:* 51
de Veyrac, Robert *YABC 2:* 19
DeVille, Edward A. *4:* 235
de Visser, John *55:* 119
Devito, Bert *12:* 164
Devlin, Harry *11:* 74; *74:* 63, 65; *136:* 77, 78
Dewan, Ted *108:* 73; *157:* 55; *165:* 129
Dewar, Nick *133:* 122
Dewdney, Anna *184:* 43, 44
Dewey, Ariane *7:* 64; *33:* 195; *35:* 208; *68:* 16,17; *75:* 46; *93:* 91; *94:* 197; *109:* 65, 66, 67; *125:* 2, 3, 4, 5; *127:* 188; *143:* 25; *178:* 17, 19, 74; *188:* 166; *202:* 164
Dewey, Jennifer (Owings) *58:* 54; *64:* 214; *65:* 207; *88:* 169; *103:* 45
Dewey, Kenneth *39:* 52; *51:* 23; *56:* 163
de Zanger, Arie *30:* 40
Diakité, Baba Wagué *174:* 28
Diamond, Donna *21:* 200; *23:* 63; *26:* 142; *35:* 83, 84, 85, 86, 87, 88, 89; *38:* 78; *40:* 147; *44:* 152; *50:* 144; *53:* 126; *69:* 46, 47, 48, 201; *71:* 133; *123:* 19
Dias, Ron *71:* 67
Diaz, David *80:* 213; *96:* 83, 84; *108:* 228; *110:* 29; *149:* 106; *150:* 63; *179:* 160; *184:* 95, 97; *189:* 51, 52, 53
Dibley, Glin *138:* 83; *141:* 128
DiCesare, Joe *70:* 38; *71:* 63, 106; *79:* 214; *93:* 147; *116:* 217; *143:* 111; *166:* 57

Dick, John Henry *8:* 181
Dickens, Frank *34:* 131
Dickey, Robert L. *15:* 279
Dickson, Mora *84:* 21
Didier, Sam *166:* 114
Dietz, James *128:* 223; *193:* 136
di Fate, Vincent *37:* 70; *90:* 11; *93:* 60; *109:* 219, 220
Di Fiori, Lawrence *10:* 51; *12:* 190; *27:* 97; *40:* 219; *93:* 57; *130:* 45
Digby, Desmond *97:* 180
Dignan, James *196:* 143
Di Grazia, Thomas *32:* 66; *35:* 241
Dillard, Annie *10:* 32
Dillard, Sarah *136:* 186
Dillon, Corinne B. *1:* 139
Dillon, Diane *4:* 104, 167; *6:* 23; *13:* 29; *15:* 99; *26:* 148; *27:* 136, 201; *51:* 29, 48, 51, 52, 53, 54,55, 56, 57, 58, 59, 60, 61, 62; *54:* 155; *56:* 69; *58:* 127,128; *61:* 95; *62:* 27; *64:* 46; *68:* 3; *69:* 209; *74:* 89; *79:* 92; *86:* 89; *92:* 28, 177; *93:* 7, 210; *94:* 239, 240; *97:* 167; *106:* 58, 59,61, 64; *107:* 3; *139:* 246; *167:* 77; *189:* 202; *191:* 191; *194:* 45, 46, 48, 49
Dillon, Leo *4:* 104, 167; *6:* 23; *13:* 29; *15:* 99; *26:* 148; *27:* 136, 201; *51:* 29, 48, 51, 52, 53, 54,55, 56, 57, 58, 59, 60, 61, 62; *54:* 155; *56:* 69; *58:* 127,128; *61:* 95; *62:* 27; *64:* 46; *68:* 3; *69:* 209; *74:* 89; *79:* 92; *86:* 89; *92:* 28, 177; *93:* 7, 210; *94:* 239, 240; *97:* 167; *106:* 58, 59,61, 64; *107:* 3; *139:* 246; *167:* 77; *189:* 202; *191:* 191; *194:* 45, 46, 48, 49
Dillon, Sharon Saseen *59:* 179, 188
DiMaccio, Gerald *121:* 80
DiMaggio, Joe *36:* 22
DiMassi, Gina *169:* 17
Dinan, Carol *25:* 169; *59:* 75
Dines, Glen *7:* 66, 67
Dinesen, Thomas *44:* 37
Dinh, Pham Viet *167:* 184
Dinnerstein, Harvey *42:* 63, 64, 65, 66, 67, 68; *50:* 146
Dinsdale, Mary *10:* 65; *11:* 171
Dinyer, Eric *86:* 148; *109:* 163; *110:* 239; *124:* 11; *150:* 69; *170:* 4; *171:* 30
Dion, Nathalie *170:* 124
DiRocco, Carl *181:* 23
DiSalvo-Ryan, DyAnne *59:* 77; *62:* 185; *117:* 46; *144:* 64; *150:* 153; *186:* 162
Disney, Walt *28:* 71, 72, 73, 76, 77, 78, 79, 80, 81, 87, 88, 89,90, 91, 94
DiTerlizzi, Tony *105:* 7; *147:* 22; *154:* 31, 32, 33
Divito, Anna *83:* 159
Dixon, Don *74:* 17; *109:* 196
Dixon, Larry *127:* 125
Dixon, Maynard *20:* 165
Doares, Robert G. *20:* 39
Dob, Bob *205:* 14
Dobias, Frank *22:* 162
Dobrin, Arnold *4:* 68
Dobson, Steven Gaston *102:* 103
Dockray, Tracy *139:* 77
Docktor, Irv *43:* 70
Dodd, Ed *4:* 69
Dodd, Emma *203:* 57
Dodd, Julie *74:* 73
Dodd, Lynley *35:* 92; *86:* 71; *132:* 45, 46, 47
Dodge, Bill *96:* 36; *118:* 7, 8, 9; *133:* 135
Dodgson, Charles L. *20:* 148; *33:* 146; *YABC 2:* 98
Dodson, Bert *9:* 138; *14:* 195; *42:* 55; *54:* 8; *60:* 49; *101:* 125
Dodson, Liz Brenner *105:* 117; *111:* 15
Dohanos, Stevan *16:* 10
Dolce, J. Ellen *74:* 147; *75:* 41
Dolch, Marguerite P. *50:* 64
Dolesch, Susanne *34:* 49
Dollar, Diane *57:* 32

Dolobowsky, Mena *81:* 54
Dolson, Hildegarde *5:* 57
Domanska, Janina *6:* 66, 67; *YABC 1:* 166
Domi *134:* 113
Dominguez, El *53:* 94
Domjan, Joseph *25:* 93
Domm, Jeffrey C. *84:* 69; *135:* 70
Donahey, William *68:* 209
Donahue, Dorothy *76:* 170
Donahue, Vic *2:* 93; *3:* 190; *9:* 44
Donald, Elizabeth *4:* 18
Donalty, Alison *149:* 195, 196, 197
Donato *85:* 59; *149:* 204; *191:* 19
Donato, Michael A. *200:* 143
Doney, Todd L.W. *87:* 12; *93:* 112; *98:* 135;
   101: 57; *104:* 40; *118:* 163; *135:* 162, 163;
   151: 18
Donna, Natalie *9:* 52
Donohue, Dorothy *95:* 2; *132:* 30; *176:* 54, 55;
   178: 77, 78, 79
Dooling, Michael *82:* 19; *105:* 55; *106:* 224;
   125: 135; *171:* 46; *172:* 12; *176:* 120; *197:*
   89
Doran, Ben-Ami *128:* 189
Dore, Gustave *18:* 169, 172, 175; *19:* 93, 94,
   95, 96, 97, 98,99, 100, 101, 102, 103, 104,
   105; *23:* 188; *25:* 197, 199
Doremus, Robert *6:* 62; *13:* 90; *30:* 95, 96, 97;
   38: 97
Dorfman, Ronald *11:* 128
Doriau *86:* 59; *91:* 152
Dorman, Brandon *197:* 35; *204:* 6
Dormer, Frank W. *200:* 55
Dorros, Arthur *78:* 42, 43; *91:* 28
Doruyter, Karel *165:* 105
dos Santos, Joyce Audy *57:* 187, 189
Doty, Roy *28:* 98; *31:* 32; *32:* 224; *46:* 157;
   82: 71; *142:* 7
Doucet, Bob *132:* 238; *169:* 159
Dougherty, Charles *16:* 204; *18:* 74
Doughty, Rebecca *177:* 174
Doughty, Thomas *118:* 31; *140:* 60
Douglas, Aaron *31:* 103
Douglas, Carole Nelson *73:* 48
Douglas, Goray *13:* 151
Dow, Brian *150:* 92
Dowd, Jason *132:* 51, 52; *164:* 244
Dowd, Vic *3:* 244; *10:* 97
Dowden, Anne Ophelia *7:* 70, 71; *13:* 120
Dowdy, Mrs. Regera *29:* 100
Downard, Barry *202:* 32
Downes, Belinda *180:* 29
Downing, Julie *60:* 140; *81:* 50; *86:* 200; *99:*
   129
Doyle, Janet *56:* 31
Doyle, Richard *21:* 31, 32, 33; *23:* 231; *24:*
   177; *31:* 87
Draper, Angie *43:* 84
Drath, Bill *26:* 34
Drawson, Blair *17:* 53; *126:* 65
Dray, Matt *177:* 47
Drescher, Henrik *105:* 60, 62, 63; *172:* 72
Drescher, Joan *30:* 100, 101; *35:* 245; *52:* 168;
   137: 52
Dressell, Peggy *186:* 41
Drew, Janet *201:* 177
Drew, Patricia *15:* 100
Dronzek, Laura *199:* 28, 29
Drummond, V.H. *6:* 70
Drury, Christian Potter *105:* 97; *186:* 224
Dubanevich, Arlene *56:* 44
Dubin, Jill *205:* 56
Dubois, Claude K. *196:* 2
Dubois, Gerard *182:* 9
DuBurke, Randy *187:* 89
Ducak, Danilo *99:* 130; *108:* 214
Duchesne, Janet *6:* 162; *79:* 8
Duda, Jana *102:* 155
Dudash, Michael *32:* 122; *77:* 134; *82:* 149
Duer, Douglas *34:* 177
Duewell, Kristina *195:* 76

Duffy, Daniel Mark *76:* 37; *101:* 196; *108:*
   147, 148
Duffy, Joseph *38:* 203
Duffy, Pat *28:* 153
Dugan, Karen *181:* 26; *202:* 35
Dugin, Andrej *77:* 60
Dugina, Olga *77:* 60
Duke, Chris *8:* 195; *139:* 164
Duke, Kate *87:* 186; *90:* 78, 79, 80, 81; *192:*
   21, 59, 60, 61, 63
Duke, Marion *165:* 87
Dulac, Edmund *19:* 108, 109, 110, 111, 112,
   113, 114, 115, 117; *23:* 187; *25:* 152; *YABC
   1:* 37; *2:* 147
Dulac, Jean *13:* 64
Dumas, Philippe *52:* 36, 37, 38, 39, 40, 41, 42,
   43, 45; *119:* 40, 41, 42
Dunaway, Nancy *108:* 161
Dunbar, James *76:* 63
Dunbar, Polly *181:* 60, 61
Duncan, Beverly *72:* 92
Duncan, John *116:* 94
Dunn, H.T. *62:* 196
Dunn, Harvey *34:* 78, 79, 80, 81
Dunn, Iris *5:* 175
Dunn, Phoebe *5:* 175
Dunne, Jeanette *72:* 57, 173, 222
Dunnick, Regan *176:* 51; *178:* 83, 84
Dunnington, Tom *3:* 36; *18:* 281; *25:* 61; *31:*
   159; *35:* 168; *48:* 195; *79:* 144; *82:* 230
Dunn-Ramsey, Marcy *117:* 131
Dunrea, Olivier *59:* 81; *118:* 53, 54; *124:* 43
Duntze, Dorothee *88:* 28; *160:* 76
Dupasquier, Philippe *86:* 75; *104:* 76; *151:* 63
DuQuette, Keith *90:* 83; *155:* 73, 74
Durand, Delphine *200:* 56
Durham, Sarah *192:* 248
Duroussy, Nathalie *146:* 150
Durrell, Julie *82:* 62; *94:* 62
Dutz *6:* 59
Duvoisin, Roger *2:* 95; *6:* 76, 77; *7:* 197; *28:*
   125; *30:* 101, 102, 103, 104, 105, 107; *47:*
   205; *84:* 254
Dyer, Dale *141:* 71
Dyer, Jane *75:* 219; *129:* 28; *147:* 49, 50, 51;
   168: 121; *190:* 4; *191:* 57, 59, 60; *203:* 4
Dypold, Pat *15:* 37

E

E.V.B.
   See Boyle, Eleanor Vere (Gordon)
Eachus, Jennifer *29:* 74; *82:* 201; *164:* 153
Eadie, Bob *63:* 36
Eagle, Bruce *95:* 119
Eagle, Ellen *82:* 121; *89:* 3
Eagle, Jeremy *141:* 71
Eagle, Michael *11:* 86; *20:* 9; *23:* 18; *27:* 122;
   28: 57; *34:* 201; *44:* 189; *73:* 9; *78:* 235; *85:*
   43
Earl-Bridges, Michele *159:* 128
Earle, Edwin *56:* 27
Earle, Olive L. *7:* 75
Earle, Vana *27:* 99
Earley, Lori *132:* 2; *186:* 4; *195:* 8
Early, Margaret *72:* 59
East, Stella *131:* 223
Eastman, P.D. *33:* 57
Easton, Reginald *29:* 181
Eaton, Tom *4:* 62; *6:* 64; *22:* 99; *24:* 124
Ebbeler, Jeffrey *193:* 62
Ebel, Alex *11:* 89
Eberbach, Andrea *192:* 115
Ebert, Len *9:* 191; *44:* 47
Echevarria, Abe *37:* 69
Echo Hawk, Bunky *187:* 192
Eckersley, Maureen *48:* 62
Eckert, Horst *72:* 62
Ede, Janina *33:* 59

Edens, Cooper *49:* 81, 82, 83, 84, 85; *112:* 58
Edens, John *109:* 115
Edgar, Sarah E. *41:* 97
Edgerton, Perky *195:* 144
Edliq, Emily S. *131:* 107
Edrien *11:* 53
Edwards, Freya *45:* 102
Edwards, George Wharton *31:* 155
Edwards, Gunvor *2:* 71; *25:* 47; *32:* 71; *54:*
   106
Edwards, Jeanne *29:* 257
Edwards, Linda Strauss *21:* 134; *39:* 123; *49:*
   88, 89
Edwards, Michelle *152:* 62, 63
Edwards, Wallace *170:* 55
Egan, Tim *155:* 76, 77, 78
Egge, David *102:* 71
Eggenhofer, Nicholas *2:* 81
Eggleton, Bob *74:* 40; *81:* 190, 191; *105:* 6;
   121: 183; *149:* 203; *166:* 215
Egielski, Richard *11:* 90; *16:* 208; *33:* 236; *38:*
   35; *49:* 91, 92, 93, 95, 212, 213, 214, 216;
   79: 122; *106:* 67, 68, 69; *134:* 135; *144:*
   244; *163:* 82, 84
Ehlert, Lois *35:* 97; *69:* 51; *112:* 7; *113:* 208;
   128: 63, 64, 65; *172:* 77, 79, 80
Ehrlich, Bettina *1:* 83
Eitan, Ora *160:* 165
Eichenberg, Fritz *1:* 79; *9:* 54; *19:* 248; *23:*
   170; *24:* 200; *26:* 208; *50:* 67, 68, 69, 70,
   71, 72, 73,74, 75, 77, 79, 80, 81; *60:* 165;
   100: 137; *YABC 1:* 104, 105; *2:* 213
Einsel, Naiad *10:* 35; *29:* 136
Einsel, Walter *10:* 37
Einzig, Susan *3:* 77; *43:* 78; *67:* 155; *129:* 154
Eisner, Will *165:* 82, 83
Eitzen, Allan *9:* 56; *12:* 212; *14:* 226; *21:* 194;
   38: 162; *76:* 218
Eldridge, H. *54:* 109
Eldridge, Harold *43:* 83
Elgaard, Greta *19:* 241
Elgin, Kathleen *9:* 188; *39:* 69
Ellacott, S.E. *19:* 118
Elliot, David *192:* 26
Elliott, Mark *93:* 69; *105:* 108; *107:* 123; *140:*
   53; *165:* 189; *173:* 67; *195:* 95; *203:* 67
Elliott, Sarah M. *14:* 58
Ellis, Dianne *130:* 208
Ellis, Jan Davey *88:* 50; *115:* 80
Ellis, Richard *130:* 47, 48
Ellison, Chris *196:* 66; *199:* 131
Ellison, Pauline *55:* 21
Elmer, Richard *78:* 5
Elmore, Larry *90:* 8
Elschner, Géraldine *183:* 38
Elwell, Peter *195:* 150
Elwell, Tristan *110:* 39; *121:* 182; *127:* 46;
   137: 144; *141:* 173; *151:* 236; *158:* 264;
   167: 119, 120, 121; *169:* 20; *190:* 12; *202:*
   16
Elzbieta *88:* 80, 81
Emberley, Ed *8:* 53; *70:* 53, 54; *146:* 65, 69,
   70
Emberley, Michael *34:* 83; *80:* 72; *119:* 47,
   48; *147:* 100; *158:* 115; *189:* 62, 64; *203:*
   87, 89
Emerling, Dorothy *104:* 27
Emery, Leslie *49:* 187
Emmett, Bruce *49:* 147; *80:* 175; *101:* 206
Emry-Perrott, Jennifer *61:* 57
Emshwiller, Ed *174:* 45
Endle, Kate *191:* 167
Engel, Diana *70:* 57
Engle, Mort *38:* 64
Englebert, Victor *8:* 54
English, Mark *101:* 207
Enik, Ted *142:* 39
Enos, Randall *20:* 183
Enright, Maginel Wright *19:* 240, 243; *39:* 31,
   35, 36
Enrique, Romeo *34:* 135

Ensor, Barbara *180:* 30
Epstein, Stephen *50:* 142, 148
Erdogan, Buket *174:* 179
Erdrich, Louise *141:* 62
Erhard, Walter *1:* 152
Erickson, Jim *196:* 190
Erickson, Phoebe *11:* 83; *59:* 85
Erikson, Mel *31:* 69
Eriksson, Eva *63:* 88, 90, 92, 93; *203:* 99
Ering, Timothy Basil *131:* 100; *176:* 63, 64;
    202: 29; *204:* 8
Erlbruch, Wolf *181:* 66
Ernst, Lisa Campbell *47:* 147; *95:* 47; *154:* 46,
    47, 48; *164:* 88
Esco, Jo *61:* 103
Escourido, Joseph *4:* 81
Escrivá, Viví *119:* 51; *181:* 36
Essakalli, Julie Klear *200:* 58
Este, Kirk *33:* 111
Estep, David *73:* 57
Estes, Eleanor *91:* 66
Estoril, Jean *32:* 27
Estrada, Pau *74:* 76
Estrada, Ric *5:* 52, 146; *13:* 174
Etchemendy, Teje *38:* 68
Etheredges, the *73:* 12
Etienne, Kirk-Albert *145:* 184
Ets, Marie Hall *2:* 102
Ettlinger, Doris *171:* 98; *186:* 106; *197:* 126
Eulalie *YABC 2:* 315
Evans, Greg *73:* 54, 55, 56; *143:* 40, 41
Evans, Katherine *5:* 64
Evans, Leslie *144:* 227
Evans, Shane W. *159:* 142; *160:* 190; *168:* 39;
    188: 88; *189:* 66, 67, 68
Everitt, Betsy *151:* 110
Ewart, Claire *76:* 69; *145:* 59, 60
Ewing, Carolyn *66:* 143; *79:* 52
Ewing, Juliana Horatia *16:* 92
Eyolfson, Norman *98:* 154

F

Fabian, Limbert *136:* 114
Facklam, Paul *132:* 62
Falconer, Ian *125:* 66; *179:* 59
Falconer, Pearl *34:* 23
Falkenstern, Lisa *70:* 34; *76:* 133; *78:* 171;
    127: 16; *191:* 151
Falls, C.B. *1:* 19; *38:* 71, 72, 73, 74
Falter, John *40:* 169, 170
Falwell, Cathryn *118:* 77; *137:* 185; *196:* 71,
    72
Fancher, Lou *138:* 219; *141:* 64; *144:* 199;
    177: 51
Fanelli, Sara *89:* 63; *126:* 69
Faria, Rosana *150:* 143
Faricy, Patrick *185:* 182
Farmer, Andrew *49:* 102
Farmer, Peter *24:* 108; *38:* 75
Farnsworth, Bill *93:* 189; *116:* 147; *124:* 8;
    135: 52; *146:* 242, 243, 244; *182:* 176; *186:*
    31, 83, 84, 85; *191:* 197
Farquharson, Alexander *46:* 75
Farrell, David *40:* 135
Farrell, Russell *196:* 38
Farris, David *74:* 42
Fasolino, Teresa *118:* 145
Fatigati, Evelyn *24:* 112
Fatus, Sophie *182:* 74; *190:* 218
Faul-Jansen, Regina *22:* 117
Faulkner, Jack *6:* 169
Faulkner, Matt *161:* 174; *167:* 75
Fava, Rita *2:* 29
Fax, Elton C. *1:* 101; *4:* 2; *12:* 77; *25:* 107
Fay *43:* 93
Fearnley, Jan *153:* 82, 83; *205:* 63, 64, 65
Fearrington, Ann *146:* 80
Federspiel, Marian *33:* 51

Fedorov, Nickolai Ivanovich *110:* 102
Feelings, Tom *5:* 22; *8:* 56; *12:* 153; *16:* 105;
    30: 196; *49:* 37; *61:* 101; *69:* 56, 57; *93:* 74;
    105: 88
Fehr, Terrence *21:* 87
Feiffer, Jules *3:* 91; *8:* 58; *61:* 66, 67, 70, 74,
    76,77, 78; *111:* 47, 48, 49, 50; *132:* 122;
    157: 62; *201:* 48, 49, 50
Feigeles, Neil *41:* 242
Feldman, Elyse *86:* 7
Feller, Gene *33:* 130
Fellows, Muriel H. *10:* 42
Felstead, Cathie *116:* 85
Felts, Shirley *33:* 71; *48:* 59
Fennell, Tracy *171:* 69
Fennelli, Maureen *38:* 181
Fenton, Carroll Lane *5:* 66; *21:* 39
Fenton, Mildred Adams *5:* 66; *21:* 39
Ferguson, Peter *177:* 30, 31; *181:* 154; *197:* 4;
    199: 40
Ferguson, Walter W. *34:* 86
Fernandes, Eugenie *77:* 67; *205:* 68
Fernandes, Stanislaw *70:* 28
Fernandez, Fernando *77:* 57
Fernandez, Laura *77:* 153; *101:* 117; *131:* 222;
    170: 119; *175:* 182
Ferrari, Alex *188:* 121
Ferrington, Susan *172:* 22
Fetz, Ingrid *11:* 67; *12:* 52; *16:* 205; *17:* 59;
    29: 105; *30:* 108, 109; *32:* 149; *43:* 142; *56:*
    29; *60:* 34; *85:* 48; *87:* 146
Fiammenghi, Gioia *9:* 66; *11:* 44; *12:* 206; *13:*
    57, 59; *52:* 126, 129; *66:* 64; *85:* 83; *91:*
    161; *166:* 169
Fiedler, Joseph Daniel *96:* 42; *113:* 173; *129:*
    164; *146:* 17; *159:* 68; *162:* 104
Field, Rachel *15:* 113
Fielding, David *70:* 124
Fieser, Stephen *152:* 36
Fine, Howard *145:* 159; *159:* 64; *165:* 134;
    174: 129; *181:* 68
Fine, Peter K. *43:* 210
Finger, Helen *42:* 81
Fink, Sam *18:* 119
Finlay, Winifred *23:* 72
Finney, Pat *79:* 215
Fiore, Peter *99:* 196; *125:* 139; *144:* 225; *160:*
    169; *180:* 72
Fiorentino, Al *3:* 240
Firehammer, Karla *174:* 202
Firmin, Charlotte *29:* 75; *48:* 70
Firmin, Peter *58:* 63, 64, 65, 67, 68, 70, 71
Firth, Barbara *81:* 208; *127:* 218; *179:* 62
Fischel, Lillian *40:* 204
Fischer, Hans *25:* 202
Fischer-Nagel, Andreas *56:* 50
Fischer-Nagel, Heiderose *56:* 50
Fisher, Carolyn *154:* 50
Fisher, Chris *79:* 62; *158:* 248; *188:* 195
Fisher, Cynthia *117:* 45; *137:* 118; *195:* 40
Fisher, Jeffrey *142:* 80
Fisher, Leonard Everett *3:* 6; *4:* 72, 86; *6:*
    197; *9:* 59; *16:* 151, 153; *23:* 44; *27:* 134;
    29: 26; *34:* 87, 89, 90, 91, 93, 94, 95, 96;
    40: 206; *50:* 150; *60:* 158; *73:* 68, 70, 71,
    72, 73; *176:* 71, 72, 73; *YABC 2:* 169
Fisher, Lois *20:* 62; *21:* 7
Fisher, Valorie *177:* 55
Fisk, Nicholas *25:* 112
Fitschen, Marilyn *2:* 20, 21; *20:* 48
Fitz-Maurice, Jeff *175:* 2
Fitzgerald, F.A. *15:* 116; *25:* 86, 87
Fitzgerald, Joanne *157:* 153, 154; *198:* 34, 35
Fitzgerald, Royce *205:* 5
Fitzhugh, Louise *1:* 94; *9:* 163; *45:* 75, 78
Fitzhugh, Susie *11:* 117
Fitzpatrick, Jim *109:* 130
Fitzpatrick, Marie-Louise *125:* 69, 70; *189:* 72,
    73
Fitzsimmons, Arthur *14:* 128
Fix, Philippe *26:* 102

Flack, Marjorie *21:* 67; *100:* 93; *YABC 2:* 122
Flagg, James Montgomery *17:* 227
Flavin, Teresa *132:* 115; *186:* 119
Flax, Zeona *2:* 245
Fleetwood, Tony *171:* 51
Fleishman, Seymour *14:* 232; *24:* 87
Fleming, Denise *71:* 179; *81:* 58; *126:* 71, 72,
    73; *173:* 52, 53
Fleming, Guy *18:* 41
Flesher, Vivienne *85:* 55
Fletcher, Claire *80:* 106; *157:* 159
Flint, Russ *74:* 80
Floate, Helen *111:* 163
Floca, Brian *155:* 88, 89; *190:* 10, 66, 67
Floethe, Richard *3:* 131; *4:* 90
Floherty, John J., Jr. *5:* 68
Flook, Helen *81:* 68
Flora, James *1:* 96; *30:* 111, 112
Florczak, Robert *166:* 51
Florian, Douglas *19:* 122; *83:* 64, 65; *125:* 71,
    72, 74, 76; *128:* 130; *177:* 58, 60
Flory, Jane *22:* 111
Flower, Renee *125:* 109
Floyd, Gareth *1:* 74; *17:* 245; *48:* 63; *62:*
    35,36, 37, 39, 40, 41; *74:* 245; *79:* 56
Fluchere, Henri A. *40:* 79
Flynn, Alice *183:* 2
Flynn, Barbara *7:* 31; *9:* 70
Fogarty, Thomas *15:* 89
Foley, Greg *190:* 69
Folger, Joseph *9:* 100
Folkard, Charles *22:* 132; *29:* 128, 257, 258
Foott, Jeff *42:* 202
Forberg, Ati *12:* 71, 205; *14:* 1; *22:* 113; *26:*
    22; *48:* 64, 65
Ford, George *24:* 120; *31:* 70, 177; *58:* 126;
    81: 103; *107:* 91; *136:* 100; *194:* 47
Ford, Gilbert *199:* 10
Ford, H.J. *16:* 185, 186
Ford, Jason *174:* 119
Ford, Pamela Baldwin *27:* 104
Fordham, John *168:* 160, 161
Foreman, Michael *2:* 110, 111; *67:* 99; *73:* 78,
    79, 80,81, 82; *93:* 146; *135:* 55, 56, 57; *184:*
    58, 59
Forrester, Victoria *40:* 83
Forsey, Chris *140:* 210
Fortnum, Peggy *6:* 29; *20:* 179; *24:* 211; *26:*
    76, 77, 78; *39:* 78; *58:* 19, 21, 23, 27; *YABC*
    1: 148
Fortune, Eric *191:* 52
Foster, Brad W. *34:* 99
Foster, Genevieve *2:* 112
Foster, Gerald L. *7:* 78; *198:* 40
Foster, Jon *146:* 18; *198:* 7
Foster, Laura Louise *6:* 79
Foster, Marian Curtis *23:* 74; *40:* 42
Foster, Sally *58:* 73, 74
Foucher, Adele *47:* 118
Foust, Mitch *168:* 50
Fowler, Jim *184:* 190
Fowler, Mel *36:* 127
Fowler, Richard *87:* 219
Fowles, Shelley *165:* 127; *205:* 72
Fox, Charles Phillip *12:* 84
Fox, Christyan *188:* 36
Fox, Jim *6:* 187
Fox-Davies, Sarah *76:* 150; *182:* 63; *199:* 42,
    43
Frace, Charles *15:* 118
Frailey, Joy *72:* 108
Frame, Paul *2:* 45, 145; *9:* 153; *10:* 124; *21:*
    71; *23:* 62; *24:* 123; *27:* 106; *31:* 48; *32:*
    159; *34:* 195; *38:* 136; *42:* 55; *44:* 139; *60:*
    39, 40, 41, 42, 43, 44, 46; *73:* 183
Frampton, David *85:* 72; *102:* 33; *139:* 182;
    152: 37; *189:* 171
Francis, Guy *198:* 164
Francois, Andre *25:* 117
Francoise
    See Seignobosc, Francoise

Frank, Lola Edick 2: 199
Frank, Mary 4: 54; 34: 100
Franke, Phil 45: 91
Frankel, Alona 66: 70
Frankel, Julie 40: 84, 85, 202
Frankenberg, Robert 22: 116; 30: 50; 38: 92, 94, 95; 68: 111
Frankfeldt, Gwen 84: 223; 110: 92
Frankland, David 169: 137; 182: 164; 201: 159
Franklin, Ashton 165: 144
Franklin, John 24: 22
Franson, Leanne R. 111: 57, 58; 151: 7
Frascino, Edward 9: 133; 29: 229; 33: 190; 48: 80, 81, 82, 83, 84, 85, 86
Frasconi, Antonio 6: 80; 27: 208; 53: 41, 43, 45, 47,48; 68: 145; 73: 226; 131: 68
Fraser, Betty 2: 212; 6: 185; 8: 103; 31: 72,73; 43: 136; 111: 76
Fraser, Eric 38: 78; 41: 149, 151
Fraser, F.A. 22: 234
Fraser, James 171: 68
Fraser, Mary Ann 137: 63
Frasier, Debra 69: 60; 112: 67; 182: 81, 82, 83
Fraustino, Lisa Rowe 146: 87
Frazee, Marla 72: 98; 105: 79, 80; 151: 67, 68; 164: 165; 171: 190, 191; 187: 53, 54,55, 56, 143
Frazetta, Frank 41: 72; 58: 77, 78, 79, 80, 81, 82, 83
Frazier, Craig 177: 63
Freas, John 25: 207
Fredrickson, Mark 103: 33
Freeland, Michael J. 118: 115
Freeman, Don 2: 15; 13: 249; 17: 62, 63, 65, 67, 68; 18: 243; 20: 195; 23: 213, 217; 32: 155; 55: 129
Freeman, Irving 67: 150
Freeman, Laura 144: 111; 200: 62, 63
Freeman, Pietri 140: 223
Freeman, Tom 167: 118
Freeman, Tor 164: 93
Fregosi, Claudia 24: 117
Fremaux, Charlotte Murray 138: 29; 141: 95
French, Fiona 6: 82, 83; 75: 61; 109: 170; 132: 79, 80, 81, 82
French, Martin 163: 4
Frendak, Rodney 126: 97, 98
Freschet, Gina 175: 73
Freynet, Gilbert 72: 221
Fried, Janice 202: 121
Friedman, Judith 43: 197; 131: 221
Friedman, Marvin 19: 59; 42: 86
Frinta, Dagmar 36: 42
Frith, Michael K. 15: 138; 18: 120
Fritz, Ronald 46: 73; 82: 124
Fromm, Lilo 29: 85; 40: 197
Frost, A.B. 17: 6, 7; 19: 123, 124, 125, 126, 127, 128, 129,130; 100: 119; YABC 1: 156, 157, 160; 2: 107
Frost, Helen 183: 51
Frost, Kristi 118: 113
Frost, Michael 151: 209
Froud, Brian 150: 82, 83
Froud, Wendy 151: 237
Fry, Guy 2: 224
Fry, Rosalie 3: 72; YABC 2: 180, 181
Fry, Rosalind 21: 153, 168
Fryer, Elmer 34: 115
Fuchs, Bernie 110: 10; 162: 46
Fuchs, Erich 6: 84
Fuchshuber, Annegert 43: 96
Fufuka, Mahiri 32: 146
Fuge, Charles 144: 91, 93
Fujikawa, Gyo 39: 75, 76; 76: 72, 73, 74
Fulford, Deborah 23: 159
Fuller, Margaret 25: 189
Fulweiler, John 93: 99
Funai, Mamoru 38: 105
Funfhausen, Christian 196: 30
Funk, Tom 7: 17, 99

Furchgott, Terry 29: 86
Furness, William Henry, Jr. 94: 18
Furukawa, Mel 25: 42
Fusari, Erika 164: 227

G

Gaadt, David 78: 212; 121: 166; 201: 171
Gaadt, George 71: 9
Gaber, Susan 99: 33; 115: 57, 58; 164: 195; 169: 61, 62, 63; 185: 50, 51; 188: 124
Gaberell, J. 19: 236
Gable, Brian 195: 68, 69
Gabler, Mirko 99: 71; 195: 32
Gackenbach, Dick 19: 168; 41: 81; 48: 89, 90, 91, 92,93, 94; 54: 105; 79: 75, 76, 77
Gad, Victor 87: 161
Gaetano, Nicholas 23: 209
Gaffney-Kessell, Walter 94: 219; 174: 188
Gag, Flavia 17: 49, 52
Gag, Wanda 100: 101, 102; YABC 1: 135, 137, 138, 141, 143
Gagnon, Cecile 11: 77; 58: 87
Gaillard, Jason 200: 69; 204: 74
Gal, Laszlo 14: 127; 52: 54, 55, 56; 65: 142; 68: 150; 81: 185; 96: 104, 105
Galazinski, Tom 55: 13
Galbraith, Ben 200: 70
Galdone, Paul 1: 156, 181, 206; 2: 40, 241; 3: 42,144; 4: 141; 10: 109, 158; 11: 21; 12: 118, 210; 14: 12; 16: 36, 37; 17: 70, 71, 72, 73, 74; 18: 111, 230; 19: 183; 21: 154; 22: 150, 245; 33: 126; 39: 136, 137; 42: 57; 51: 169; 55: 110; 66: 80, 82, 139; 72: 73; 100: 84
Gale, Cathy 140: 22; 143: 52
Gall, Chris 176: 79, 80
Gallagher, Jack 187: 100
Gallagher, S. Saelig 105: 154; 198: 91
Gallagher, Sears 20: 112
Galloway, Ewing 51: 154
Galouchka, Annouchka Gravel 95: 55; 182: 40
Galster, Robert 1: 66
Galsworthy, Gay John 35: 232
Galvez, Daniel 125: 182
Gamble, Kim 112: 64, 65; 124: 77; 183: 40, 42, 43, 56, 57; 187: 170
Gammell, Stephen 7: 48; 13: 149; 29: 82; 33: 209; 41: 88; 50: 185, 186, 187; 53: 51, 52, 53, 54, 55, 56,57, 58; 54: 24, 25; 56: 147, 148, 150; 57: 27, 66; 81: 62, 63; 87: 88; 89: 10; 106: 223; 126: 2; 128: 71, 73, 74, 77; 154: 34
Gamper, Ruth 84: 198
Gampert, John 58: 94
Ganly, Helen 56: 56
Gannett, Ruth Chrisman 3: 74; 18: 254; 33: 77, 78
Gannon, Ned 205: 6
Gantschev, Ivan 45: 32
Garafano, Marie 73: 33
Garbot, Dave 131: 106
Garbutt, Bernard 23: 68
Garcia 37: 71
Garcia, Manuel 74: 145
Garcia-Franco, Rebecca 173: 46
Gardiner, Lindsey 178: 128; 186: 137
Gardner, Earle 45: 167
Gardner, Joan 40: 87
Gardner, Joel 40: 87, 92
Gardner, John 40: 87
Gardner, Lucy 40: 87
Gardner, Richard
    See Cummings, Richard
Gardner, Sally 171: 177; 177: 66, 68
Gargiulo, Frank 84: 158

Garland, Michael 36: 29; 38: 83; 44: 168; 48: 78, 221, 222; 49: 161; 60: 139; 71: 6, 11; 72: 229; 74: 142; 89: 187; 93: 183; 104: 110; 131: 55; 139: 209; 168: 56
Garland, Peggy 60: 139
Garland, Sarah 62: 45; 135: 67, 68; 171: 118
Garn, Aimee 75: 47
Garner, Joan 128: 170
Garneray, Ambroise Louis 59: 140
Garnett, Eve 3: 75
Garnett, Gary 39: 184
Garns, Allen 80: 125; 84: 39; 165: 231
Garófoli, Viviana 186: 123
Garraty, Gail 4: 142; 52: 106
Garrett, Agnes 46: 110; 47: 157
Garrett, Edmund H. 20: 29
Garrett, Tom 107: 194
Garrick, Jacqueline 67: 42, 43; 77: 94
Garrison, Barbara 19: 133; 104: 146; 109: 87
Garro, Mark 108: 131; 128: 210
Garvey, Robert 98: 222
Garza, Carmen Lomas 80: 211; 182: 86
Garza, Xavier 184: 64
Gates, Frieda 26: 80
Gaughan, Jack 26: 79; 43: 185
Gaver, Becky 20: 61
Gawing, Toby 72: 52
Gay, Marie-Louise 68: 76, 77, 78; 102: 136; 126: 76, 78, 81, 83; 127: 55, 56; 179: 70, 72, 73, 74
Gay, Zhenya 19: 135, 136
Gaydos, Tim 62: 201
Gazsi, Ed 80: 48
Gazso, Gabriel 73: 85
Geary, Clifford N. 1: 122; 9: 104; 51: 74
Geary, Rick 142: 44, 46
Gee, Frank 33: 26
Geehan, Wayne 157: 181
Geer, Charles 1: 91; 3: 179; 4: 201; 6: 168; 7: 96; 9: 58; 10: 72; 12: 127; 39: 156,157, 158, 159, 160; 42: 88, 89, 90, 91; 55: 111, 116
Geerinck, Manuel 173: 128
Gehm, Charlie 36: 65; 57: 117; 62: 60, 138
Geis, Alissa Imre 189: 77
Geisel, Theodor Seuss 1: 104, 105, 106; 28: 108, 109, 110,111, 112, 113; 75: 67, 68, 69, 70, 71; 89: 127, 128; 100: 106, 107, 108
Geisert, Arthur 92: 67, 68; 133: 72, 73, 74; 165: 97, 98; 171: 64, 65
Geldart, William 15: 121; 21: 202
Genia 4: 84
Gentry, Cyrille R. 12: 66
Genzo, John Paul 136: 74
George, Jean 2: 113
George, Lindsay Barrett 95: 57; 155: 97, 98
Geraghty, Paul 130: 60, 61
Gerard, Jean Ignace 45: 80
Gerard, Rolf 27: 147, 150
Gerber, Mark 61: 105
Gerber, Mary Jane 112: 124; 171: 56
Gerber, Stephanie 71: 195
Gerdstein, Mordecai 169: 105
Gergely, Tibor 54: 15, 16
Geritz, Franz 17: 135
Gerlach, Geff 42: 58
Gerrard, Roy 47: 78; 90: 96, 97, 98, 99
Gerritsen, Paula 177: 69
Gershinowitz, George 36: 27
Gerstein, Mordicai 31: 117; 47: 80, 81, 82, 83, 84, 85, 86; 51: 173; 69: 134; 107: 122; 142: 49, 52; 165: 209; 176: 119; 178: 95, 97, 99
Gervase 12: 27
Geter, Tyrone 146: 249; 150: 86
Getz, Arthur 32: 148
Gévry, Claudine 188: 47
Gewirtz, Bina 61: 81
Giancola, Donato 95: 146; 164: 226
Gibala-Broxholm, Scott 205: 76
Gibbons, Gail 23: 78; 72: 77, 78, 79; 82: 182; 104: 65; 160: 99, 100; 201: 59, 60, 62
Gibbs, Tony 40: 95

Gibran, Kahlil *32:* 116
Gibson, Barbara Leonard *205:* 77
Gider, Iskender *81:* 193
Giebfried, Rosemary *170:* 135
Giesen, Rosemary *34:* 192, 193
Giffard, Hannah *83:* 70
Giguere, George *20:* 111
Gilbert, John *19:* 184; *54:* 115; *YABC 2:* 287
Gilbert, W.S. *36:* 83, 85, 96
Gilbert, Yvonne *116:* 70; *128:* 84; *149:* 119; *185:* 69; *192:* 25; *195:* 81
Gilchrist, Jan Spivey *72:* 82, 83, 84, 85, 87; *77:* 90; *105:* 89, 91; *130:* 63, 64; *155:* 105, 107; *182:* 67
Giles, Will *41:* 218
Gili, Phillida *70:* 73
Gill, Margery *4:* 57; *7:* 7; *22:* 122; *25:* 166; *26:* 146, 147
Gillen, Denver *28:* 216
Gillette, Henry J. *23:* 237
Gilliam, Stan *39:* 64, 81
Gillies, Chuck *62:* 31
Gilliland, Jillian *87:* 58
Gillman, Alec *98:* 105
Gilman, Esther *15:* 124
Gilman, Phoebe *104:* 70, 71
Ginsberg, Sari *111:* 184
Ginsburg, Max *62:* 59; *68:* 194 *Girard, Roge 161:* 30
Girouard, Patrick *155:* 100
Giovanopoulos, Paul *7:* 104; *60:* 36
Giovine, Sergio *79:* 12; *93:* 118; *139:* 118; *205:* 114
Githens, Elizabeth M. *5:* 47
Gladden, Scott *99:* 108; *103:* 160; *193:* 46, 47
Gladstone, Gary *12:* 89; *13:* 190
Gladstone, Lise *15:* 273
Glanzman, Louis S. *2:* 177; *3:* 182; *36:* 97, 98; *38:* 120, 122; *52:* 141, 144; *71:* 191; *91:* 54, 56
Glaser, Byron *154:* 59, 60
Glaser, Milton *3:* 5; *5:* 156; *11:* 107; *30:* 26; *36:* 112; *54:* 141; *151:* 70
Glass, Andrew *36:* 38; *44:* 133; *48:* 205; *65:* 3; *68:* 43, 45; *90:* 104, 105; *150:* 89
Glass, Marvin *9:* 174
Glasser, Judy *41:* 156; *56:* 140; *69:* 79; *72:* 101
Glattauer, Ned *5:* 84; *13:* 224; *14:* 26
Glauber, Uta *17:* 76
Gleeson, J.M. *YABC 2:* 207
Glegg, Creina *36:* 100
Glienke, Amelie *63:* 150
Gliewe, Unada *3:* 78, 79; *21:* 73; *30:* 220
Gliori, Debi *72:* 91; *138:* 82; *162:* 37; *189:* 79, 81, 82
Glovach, Linda *7:* 105
Gobbato, Imero *3:* 180, 181; *6:* 213; *7:* 58; *9:* 150; *18:* 39; *21:* 167; *39:* 82, 83; *41:* 137, 251; *59:* 177
Goble, Paul *25:* 121; *26:* 86; *33:* 65; *69:* 68, 69; *131:* 79, 80
Goble, Warwick *46:* 78, 79; *194:* 143
Godal, Eric *36:* 93
Godkin, Celia *145:* 84, 86
Godfrey, Michael *17:* 279
Godon, Ingrid *166:* 163; *186:* 99
Goembel, Ponder *42:* 124
Goffe, Toni *61:* 83, 84, 85; *89:* 11; *90:* 124; *178:* 118
Goffstein, M.B. *8:* 71; *70:* 75, 76, 77
Golbin, Andre *15:* 125
Gold, Robert *166:* 151, 152
Goldfeder, Cheryl *11:* 191
Goldfinger, Jennifer P. *185:* 71
Goldsborough, June *5:* 154, 155; *8:* 92, *14:* 226; *19:* 139; *54:* 165
Goldsmith, Robert *110:* 77
Goldstein, Barry *198:* 147
Goldstein, Leslie *5:* 8; *6:* 60; *10:* 106

Goldstein, Nathan *1:* 175; *2:* 79; *11:* 41, 232; *16:* 55
Goldstrom, Robert *98:* 36; *145:* 51, 52
Golembe, Carla *79:* 80, 81; *136:* 91; *144:* 113; *193:* 53
Golin, Carlo *74:* 112
Gomez, Elena *188:* 122; *191:* 72
Gomez, Elizabeth *127:* 70; *133:* 76
Gomi, Taro *64:* 102; *103:* 74, 76
Gon, Adriano *101:* 112
Gonsalve, Ron *178:* 213
Gonzalez, Maya Christina *104:* 3; *136:* 92
Goodall, John S. *4:* 92, 93; *10:* 132; *66:* 92, 93; *YABC 1:* 198
Goode, Diane *15:* 126; *50:* 183; *52:* 114, 115; *76:* 195; *84:* 94; *99:* 141; *114:* 76, 77, 78; *170:* 99, 101
Goodelman, Aaron *40:* 203
Goodenow, Earle *40:* 97
Goodfellow, Peter *62:* 95; *94:* 202
Goodman, Joan Elizabeth *50:* 86
Goodman, Vivienne *82:* 251; *146:* 181, 182
Goodnow, Patti *117:* 33
Goodwin, Harold *13:* 74
Goodwin, Philip R. *18:* 206
Goor, Nancy *39:* 85, 86
Goor, Ron *39:* 85, 86
Goossens, Philippe *195:* 71
Gorbachev, Valeri *89:* 96; *112:* 97; *143:* 63, 64; *184:* 66, 67, 68, 101
Gordon, Gwen *12:* 151
Gordon, Margaret *4:* 147; *5:* 48, 49; *9:* 79
Gordon, Mike *101:* 62, 63, 64
Gordon, Russell *136:* 204; *137:* 214
Gordon, Walter *138:* 9
Gore, Leonid *89:* 51; *94:* 74; *136:* 8; *158:* 117; *166:* 136; *168:* 36; *170:* 107; *181:* 94; *185:* 73
Gorecka-Egan, Erica *18:* 35
Gorey, Edward *1:* 60, 61; *13:* 169; *18:* 192; *20:* 201; *29:* 90, 91, 92, 93, 94, 95, 96, 97, 98, 99, 100; *30:* 129; *32:* 90; *34:* 200, 65: 48; *68:* 24, 25; *69:* 79; *70:* 80, 82, 83, 84; *85:* 136; *127:* 62
Gorsline, Douglas *1:* 98; *6:* 13; *11:* 113; *13:* 104; *15:* 14; *28:* 117, 118; *YABC 1:* 15
Gorton, Julia *108:* 94; *178:* 81, 82
Gosfield, Josh *118:* 165, 166; *149:* 67
Gosner, Kenneth *5:* 135
Gosney, Joy *167:* 142
Gotlieb, Jules *6:* 127
Goto, Scott *115:* 86; *136:* 69; *203:* 77, 78
Gott, Barry *197:* 95
Gottlieb, Dale *67:* 162; *107:* 16; *149:* 6
Goudey, Ray *97:* 86
Gough, Alan *91:* 57
Gough, Philip *23:* 47; *45:* 90
Gould, Chester *49:* 112, 113, 114, 116, 117, 118
Gould, Jason *151:* 232
Gourbault, Martine *177:* 159
Govern, Elaine R. *26:* 94
Gower, Teri *102:* 184
Gowing, Toby *60:* 25; *63:* 33; *78:* 70, 252; *83:* 228; *86:* 187; *93:* 145; *108:* 133; *110:* 217; *184:* 125
Grabianski *20:* 144
Grabianski, Janusz *39:* 92, 93, 94, 95
Graboff, Abner *35:* 103, 104
Graef, Renée *61:* 188; *72:* 207; *204:* 45
Grafe, Max *156:* 173; *178:* 237; *192:* 240; *198:* 51
Graham, A.B. *11:* 61
Graham, Bob *101:* 66, 67, 68; *151:* 74, 75; *187:* 65, 67, 68, 70
Graham, Georgia *188:* 3; *190:* 75
Graham, L. *7:* 108
Graham, Margaret Bloy *11:* 120; *18:* 305, 307
Graham, Mark *88:* 208; *159:* 153; *182:* 3
Grahame-Johnstone, Janet *13:* 61
Grahame-Johnstone, Anne *13:* 61

Grainger, Sam *42:* 95
Gralley, Jean *166:* 86
Gramatky, Hardie *1:* 107; *30:* 116, 119, 120, 122, 123
Gran, Julie *168:* 118
Granahan, Julie *84:* 84
GrandPré, Mary *84:* 131; *109:* 199; *118:* 76; *180:* 65; *184:* 70, 71, 180; *192:* 87
Grandström, Brita *176:* 139
Grandville, J.J. *45:* 81, 82, 83, 84, 85, 86, 87, 88; *47:* 125; *64:* 10
Granger, Paul *39:* 153
Granström, Brita *162:* 35; *167:* 46
Grant, (Alice) Leigh *10:* 52; *15:* 131; *20:* 20; *26:* 119; *48:* 202
Grant, Gordon *17:* 230, 234; *25:* 123, 124, 125, 126; *52:* 69; *YABC 1:* 164
Grant, Melvyn *159:* 186, 187; *170:* 48, 49
Grant, Renee *77:* 40
Grant, Shirley *109:* 45
Graves, Elizabeth *45:* 101
Graves, Keith *167:* 89; *191:* 74
Gray, Harold *33:* 87, 88
Gray, Les *82:* 76; *83:* 232
Gray, Reginald *6:* 69
Greco, Tony *184:* 6
Greder, Armin *76:* 235
Green, Ann Canevari *62:* 48
Green, Eileen *6:* 97
Green, Elizabeth Shippen *139:* 109
Green, Jonathan *86:* 135; *105:* 109
Green, Ken *111:* 68
Green, Michael *32:* 216
Green, Robina *87:* 138
Green, Jonathan *157:* 105
Greene, Jeffrey *117:* 93
Greenaway, Kate *17:* 275; *24:* 180; *26:* 107; *41:* 222, 232; *100:* 115, 116; *YABC 1:* 88, 89; *2:* 131, 133, 136,138, 139, 141
Greenberg, Melanie Hope *72:* 93; *80:* 125; *101:* 174; *133:* 180; *186:* 189
Greenseid, Diane *178:* 106, 107
Greenstein, Elaine *150:* 100
Greenwald, Sheila *1:* 34; *3:* 99; *8:* 72
Greger, Carol *76:* 86
Gregorian, Joyce Ballou *30:* 125
Gregory, Emilian *177:* 146; *187:* 10
Gregory, Fran *130:* 4; *140:* 93
Gregory, Frank M. *29:* 107
Greiffenhagen, Maurice *16:* 137; *27:* 57; *YABC 2:* 288
Greiner, Robert *6:* 86
Gretter, J. Clemens *31:* 134
Gretz, Susanna *7:* 114
Gretzer, John *1:* 54; *3:* 26; *4:* 162; *7:* 125; *16:* 247; *18:* 117; *28:* 66; *30:* 85, 211; *33:* 235; *56:* 16
Grey, Mini *166:* 90; *192:* 71
Grey Owl *24:* 41
Gri *25:* 90
Grieder, Walter *9:* 84
Griesbach/Martucci *59:* 3
Grifalconi, Ann *2:* 126; *3:* 248; *11:* 18; *13:* 182; *46:* 38; *50:* 145; *66:* 99, 100, 101, 104, 106; *69:* 38; *70:* 64; *87:* 128; *90:* 53; *93:* 49; *128:* 48; *133:* 79, 81
Griffin, Gillett Good *26:* 96
Griffin, James *30:* 166
Griffin, John Howard *59:* 186
Griffin, Rachel *131:* 23
Griffith, Gershom *94:* 214
Griffiths, Dave *29:* 76
Griffiths, Dean *168:* 180; *169:* 182
Grimly, Gris *186:* 102; *192:* 112; *197:* 86
Grimsdell, Jeremy *83:* 75
Grimwood, Brian *82:* 89
Gringhuis, Dirk *6:* 98; *9:* 196
Gripe, Harald *2:* 127; *74:* 98
Grisha *3:* 71
Grobler, Piet *201:* 100
Grohmann, Susan *84:* 97

Gropper, William 27: 93; 37: 193
Gros 60: 199
Grose, Helen Mason YABC 1: 260; 2: 150
Grossman, Nancy 24: 130; 29: 101
Grossman, Robert 11: 124; 46: 39
Groth, John 15: 79; 21: 53, 54; 83: 230
Grover, Lorie Ann 168: 59
Grubb, Lisa 160: 116
Grue, Lisa 187: 193
Gruelle, Johnny 35: 107
Gschwind, William 11: 72
Guarnaccia, Steven 201: 170, 173
Guay-Mitchell, Rebecca 110: 95, 96; 135: 240; 180: 76; 181: 71, 73
Guback, Georgia 88: 102
Guerguerion, Claudine 105: 73
Guevara, Susan 97: 87; 167: 49; 194: 54
Guggenheim, Hans 2: 10; 3: 37; 8: 136
Guhathaakurta, Ajanta 183: 199
Guida, Lisa Chauncy 172: 188
Guilbeau, Honore 22: 69
Guillette, Joseph 137: 37
Guisewite, Cathy 57: 52, 53, 54, 56, 57
Gukova, Julia 95: 104; 154: 103; 168: 195
Gundersheimer, Karen 35: 240; 82: 100
Gunderson, Nick 57: 120
Gunnella 192: 144
Gurney, James 76: 97; 86: 32
Gurney, John Steven 75: 39, 82; 110: 175; 143: 67, 68; 169: 172
Gusman, Annie 38: 62
Gustafson, Scott 34: 111; 43: 40
Gustavson, Adam 104: 10; 171: 183; 176: 87; 197: 94; 204: 35
Guthridge, Bettina 108: 79; 186: 92
Guthrie, R. Dale 64: 143
Guthrie, Robin 20: 122
Gutierrez, Akemi 172: 87; 205: 135
Gutierrez, Alan 136: 31, 32
Gutierrez, Rudy 97: 162; 203: 79
Gutmann, Bessie Pease 73: 93, 94
Gwynne, Fred 41: 94, 95
Gyberg, Bo-Erik 38: 131

H

Haas, Irene 17: 77; 87: 46; 96: 117
Hack, Konrad 51: 127
Hader, Berta H. 16: 126
Hader, Elmer S. 16: 126
Haeffele, Deborah 76: 99
Haemer, Alan 62: 109
Hafner, Marylin 22: 196, 216; 24: 44; 30: 51; 35: 95; 51: 25, 160, 164; 86: 16; 105: 196; 121: 93, 94; 149: 208, 209; 179: 82, 83, 84, 115; 190: 200; 201: 29
Hagerty, Sean 62: 181
Hague, Michael 32: 128; 48: 98, 99, 100, 101, 103, 105,106, 107, 108, 109, 110; 49: 121; 51: 105; 64: 14, 15; 79: 134; 80: 91, 92; 83: 135; 100: 241; 102: 29; 129: 101, 103, 104; 185: 80, 81, 82
Hair, Jonathan 115: 135
Halas, John 29: 41, 47, 48
Haldane, Roger 13: 76; 14: 202
Hale, Bruce 203: 83
Hale, Christy 79: 124; 84: 200; 114: 201; 128: 2, 3; 146: 203; 158: 243; 167: 99; 179: 87
Hale, Irina 26: 97
Hale, James Graham 88: 207
Hale, Kathleen 17: 79; 66: 114, 116, 118
Haley, Amanda 205: 82, 83
Haley, Gail E. 43: 102, 103, 104, 105; 78: 65, 67; 136: 106, 107
Hall, Amanda 96: 110
Hall, Chuck 30: 189
Hall, Douglas 15: 184; 43: 106, 107; 86: 100; 87: 82; 129: 72
Hall, H. Tom 1: 227; 30: 210

Hall, Melanie 116: 48, 49; 169: 77, 78
Hall, Sydney P. 31: 89
Hall, Tim 164: 196; 202: 41
Hall, Vicki 20: 24
Hallinan, P.K. 39: 98
Hallman, Tom 98: 166
Hally, Greg 101: 200; 151: 224
Halperin, Wendy Anderson 96: 151; 125: 96, 97, 98, 99; 139: 22; 140: 84; 200: 77, 78
Halpern, Joan 10: 25
Halpern, Shari 174: 172
Halsey, Megan 96: 172; 114: 185; 180: 8; 185: 85
Halstead, Virginia 125: 105
Halverson, Janet 49: 38, 42, 44
Hallensleben, Georg 134: 5, 6; 172: 17
Hamanaka, Sheila 71: 100
Hamann, Brad 78: 151
Hamann, Sigune 104: 115
Hamberger, John 6: 8; 8: 32; 14: 79; 34: 136; 88: 78
Hamil, Tom 14: 80; 43: 163
Hamilton, Bill and Associates 26: 215
Hamilton, Helen S. 2: 238
Hamilton, J. 19: 83, 85, 87
Hamilton, Laurie 116: 210
Hamilton, Todd Cameron 84: 15
Hamlin, Janet 97: 136; 124: 90; 137: 157; 182: 117
Hamlin, Louise 71: 135
Hammond, Chris 21: 37
Hammond, Elizabeth 5: 36, 203
Hampshire, Michael 5: 187; 7: 110, 111; 48: 150; 51: 129
Hampson, Denman 10: 155; 15: 130
Hampton, Blake 41: 244
Handford, Martin 64: 105, 106, 107, 109
Handforth, Thomas 42: 100, 101, 102, 103, 104, 105, 107
Handville, Robert 1: 89; 38: 76; 45: 108, 109
Hane, Roger 17: 239; 44: 54
Haney, Elizabeth Mathieu 34: 84
Hanke, Ted 71: 10
Hankinson, Phil 181: 164
Hanley, Catherine 8: 161
Hann, Jacquie 19: 144
Hanna, Cheryl 91: 133
Hanna, Wayne A. 67: 145
Hannon, Mark 38: 37
Hanrahan, Kelly-Anne 203: 142
Hansen, Gaby 159: 11; 186: 25
Hansen, Mia 149: 76
Hanson, Joan 8: 76; 11: 139
Hanson, Peter E. 52: 47; 54: 99, 100; 73: 21; 84: 79; 116: 144
Hansson, Gunilla 64: 111, 112
Hardcastle, Nick 121: 82; 175: 185
Hardy, David A. 9: 96; 119: 74
Hardy, Paul YABC 2: 245 Haring, Keith 145: 65
Harlan, Jerry 3: 96
Harlin, Greg 89: 194; 103: 82; 118: 161; 121: 167; 182: 76; 201: 172
Harness, Cheryl 106: 80; 131: 87; 178: 111; 200: 39
Harnischfeger 18: 121
Harper, Arthur YABC 2: 121
Harper, Betty 126: 90
Harper, Jamie 174: 71
Harper, Piers 79: 27; 105: 102; 161: 67
Harrington, Glenn 82: 18; 94: 66, 68; 185: 118
Harrington, Jack 83: 162
Harrington, Richard 5: 81
Harris, Andrew N. 191: 78
Harris, Jim 127: 130; 183: 4
Harris, John 83: 25
Harris, Nick 86: 177
Harris, Susan Yard 42: 121
Harrison, Florence 20: 150, 152
Harrison, Harry 4: 103

Harrison, Jack 28: 149
Harrison, Mark 105: 157; 165: 190
Harrison, Ted 56: 73
Harsh, Fred 72: 107
Harston, Jerry 105: 143
Hart, Lewis 98: 115
Hart, Thomas 181: 165
Hart, William 13: 72
Hartland, Jessie 171: 80, 81; 186: 165
Hartung, Susan Kathleen 150: 107, 108; 173: 106; 175: 106; 192: 78
Hartelius, Margaret 10: 24
Hartshorn, Ruth 5: 115; 11: 129
Harvey, Amanda 145: 44
Harvey, Bob 48: 219
Harvey, Gerry 7: 180
Harvey, Lisa 97: 21
Harvey, Paul 88: 74
Harvey, Roland 71: 88; 123: 63; 179: 94
Haskamp, Steve 195: 36
Hassall, Joan 43: 108, 109
Hassell, Hilton YABC 1: 187
Hassett, John 162: 59
Hasselriis, Else 18: 87; YABC 1: 96
Hastings, Glenn 89: 183
Hastings, Ian 62: 67
Hauman, Doris 2: 184; 29: 58, 59; 32: 85, 86, 87
Hauman, George 2: 184; 29: 58, 59; 32: 85, 86, 87
Hausherr, Rosmarie 15: 29
Hawkes, Kevin 78: 72; 104: 198; 105: 197; 112: 109; 126: 87; 144: 88; 149: 210; 150: 110, 135; 156: 94; 164: 35; 186: 18; 190: 197; 198: 152; 201: 70, 71, 72
Hawkins, Jacqui 112: 86; 162: 64
Hawkinson, John 4: 109; 7: 83; 21: 64
Hawkinson, Lucy 21: 64
Hawthorne, Mike 140: 228
Haxton, Elaine 28: 131
Haydock, Robert 4: 95
Hayes, Geoffrey 26: 111; 44: 133; 91: 85
Haynes, Max 72: 107
Hays, Michael 73: 207; 83: 93; 139: 197; 146: 202, 250; 202: 47
Haywood, Carolyn 1: 112; 29: 104
Heale, Jonathan 104: 117
Healy, Daty 12: 143
Healy, Deborah 58: 181, 182; 101: 111
Heap, Sue 102: 207; 150: 113, 114; 187: 84, 85, 87
Hearn, Diane Dawson 79: 99; 113: 13
Hearon, Dorothy 34: 69
Hechtkopf, H. 11: 110
Heck, Ed 173: 81
Hector, Julian 205: 85
Hedderwick, Mairi 30: 127; 32: 47; 36: 104; 77: 86; 145: 91, 93, 95
Heffernan, Phil 146: 197; 195: 172
Hefter, Richard 28: 170; 31: 81, 82; 33: 183
Hehenberger, Shelly 126: 91
Heigh, James 22: 98
Heighway, Richard 25: 160; 64: 4
Heighway-Bury, Robin 159: 89
Heine, Helme 67: 86; 135: 91, 92
Heinly, John 45: 113
Hellard, Susan 81: 21; 204: 82
Heller, Linda 46: 86
Heller, Ruth M. 66: 125; 77: 30, 32
Hellmuth, Jim 38: 164
Helms, Georgeann 33: 62
Helquist, Brett 142: 203; 146: 133, 134; 156: 10; 173: 25; 180: 106; 187: 90, 91; 193: 12
Helweg, Hans 41: 118; 50: 93; 58: 22, 26
Hemphill, Helen 179: 95
Henba, Bobbie 90: 195
Henderson, Dave 73: 76; 75: 191, 192, 193, 194; 82: 4
Henderson, Douglas 103: 68

Henderson, Kathy *55:* 32; *155:* 118
Henderson, Keith *35:* 122
Henderson, Meryl *127:* 58, 60; *169:* 81
Hendrix, John *187:* 133
Hendry, Linda *80:* 104; *83:* 83; *164:* 216
Hengeveld, Dennis *142:* 86
Henkes, Kevin *43:* 111; *108:* 106, 107, 108
Henneberger, Robert *1:* 42; *2:* 237; *25:* 83
Henriksen, Harold *35:* 26; *48:* 68
Henriquez, Celeste *103:* 137
Henriquez, Elsa *82:* 260
Henriquez, Emile F. *89:* 88
Henry, Everett *29:* 191
Henry, Matthew *117:* 58
Henry, Paul *93:* 121; *194:* 125
Henry, Thomas *5:* 102
Hensel *27:* 119
Henshaw, Jacqui *141:* 127
Henstra, Friso *8:* 80; *36:* 70; *40:* 222; *41:* 250; *73:* 100, 101
Henterly, Jamichael *93:* 4
Heo, Yumi *89:* 85, 86; *94:* 89, 90; *146:* 40, 137, 138; *163:* 227; *201:* 192
Hepple, Norman *28:* 198
Herbert, Helen *57:* 70
Herbert, Jennifer *189:* 47
Herbert, Wally *23:* 101
Herbster, Mary Lee *9:* 33
Herder, Edwin *182:* 104
Herge
  See Remi, Georges
Hermansen, Pal *133:* 113
Hermanson, Dennis *10:* 55
Hermes, Gertrude *54:* 161
Herr, Margo *57:* 191
Herr, Susan *83:* 163
Herriman, George *140:* 74, 75, 76, 77, 78
Herriman, Lisa *87:* 190
Herring, Michael *121:* 76; *182:* 103
Herrington, Roger *3:* 161
Herscovici, C. *165:* 240
Hescox, Richard *85:* 86; *90:* 30; *139:* 35
Heslop, Mike *38:* 60; *40:* 130
Hess, Lydia J. *85:* 17
Hess, Mark *111:* 146; *113:* 207
Hess, Paul *134:* 47; *166:* 133; *193:* 13
Hess, Richard *42:* 31
Hester, Ronnie *37:* 85
Heuser, Olga J. *121:* 116
Heusser, Sibylle *168:* 195
Heustis, Louise L. *20:* 28
Hewgill, Jodi *201:* 90
Hewitson, Jennifer *74:* 119; *124:* 167
Hewitt, Kathryn *80:* 126; *149:* 105; *184:* 93; *196:* 36
Hewitt, Margaret *84:* 112
Heyduck-Huth, Hilde *8:* 82
Heyer, Carol *74:* 122; *130:* 72, 73; *192:* 35; *203:* 78
Heyer, Hermann *20:* 114, 115
Heyer, Marilee *102:* 108
Heyman, Ken *8:* 33; *34:* 113
Heyne, Ulrike *146:* 151
Heywood, Karen *48:* 114
Hickling, P.B. *40:* 165
Hickman, Stephen *85:* 58; *136:* 33; *171:* 128
Hierstein, Judy *56:* 40; *162:* 168
Higashi, Sandra *154:* 59, 60
Higginbottom, J. Winslow *8:* 170; *29:* 105, 106
Higgins, Chester *101:* 79
Higham, David *50:* 104
Hilb, Nora *176:* 8
Hildebrandt, Greg *8:* 191; *55:* 35, 36, 38, 39, 40, 42, 46; *172:* 110
Hildebrandt, Tim *8:* 191; *55:* 44, 45, 46
Hilder, Rowland *19:* 207
Hill, Eric *66:* 127, 128; *133:* 91
Hill, Gregory *35:* 190
Hill, Pat *49:* 120

Hillenbrand, Will *84:* 115; *92:* 76, 80; *93:* 131; *104:* 168; *128:* 137; *145:* 187; *146:* 184; *147:* 105, 106, 107; *152:* 59; *184:* 179; *195:* 34, 180; *196:* 125
Hilliard, Richard *183:* 74
Hillier, Matthew *45:* 205
Hillman, Priscilla *48:* 115
Hills, Tad *113:* 4; *137:* 147; *173:* 83
Himler, Ronald *6:* 114; *7:* 162; *8:* 17, 84, 125; *14:* 76; *19:* 145; *26:* 160; *31:* 43; *38:* 116; *41:* 44, 79; *43:* 52; *45:* 120; *46:* 43; *54:* 44, 83; *58:* 180; *59:* 38; *68:* 146; *69:* 231; *70:* 98; *71:* 177, 178; *77:* 219; *79:* 212; *83:* 62; *89:* 5; *91:* 160; *92:* 91, 92, 93; *94:* 93; *95:* 69, 174, 194; *99:* 99, 112; *113:* 92; *118:* 114; *137:* 73, 74, 77, 167; *163:* 99; *165:* 138; *178:* 9, 220; *183:* 77, 79, 80, 81; *184:* 80, 83
Himmelman, John *47:* 109; *65:* 87; *94:* 96, 97; *159:* 85
Hinds, Bill *37:* 127, 130
Hines, Anna Grossnickle *51:* 90; *74:* 124; *95:* 78, 79,80, 81
Hines, Bob *135:* 149, 150
Hirao, Amiko *203:* 98
Hiroko *99:* 61
Hiroshige *25:* 71
Hirsh, Marilyn *7:* 126
Hiscock, Bruce *137:* 80, 81; *204:* 51, 53
Hissey, Jane *103:* 90; *130:* 81
Hitch, Jeff *99:* 206; *128:* 86
Hitz, Demi *11:* 135; *15:* 245; *66:* 129, 130; *152:* 94, 95
Hnizdovsky, Jacques *32:* 96; *76:* 187
Ho, Kwoncjan *15:* 132
Hoban, Lillian *1:* 114; *22:* 157; *26:* 72; *29:* 53; *40:* 105, 107, 195; *41:* 80; *69:* 107, 108; *71:* 98; *77:* 168; *106:* 50; *113:* 86; *136:* 118
Hoban, Tana *22:* 159; *104:* 82, 83, 85
Hobbie, Jocelyn *190:* 78; *196:* 92
Hobbie, Nathaniel *196:* 92
Hobbs, Leigh *166:* 95
Hoberman, Norman *5:* 82
Hobson, Sally *77:* 185
Hockerman, Dennis *39:* 22; *56:* 23
Hodgell, P.C. *42:* 114
Hodges, C. Walter *2:* 139; *11:* 15; *12:* 25; *23:* 34; *25:* 96; *38:* 165; *44:* 197; *45:* 95; *100:* 57; *YABC 2:* 62, 63
Hodges, David *9:* 98
Hodgetts, Victoria *43:* 132
Hofbauer, Imre *2:* 162
Hoff, Syd *9:* 107; *10:* 128; *33:* 94; *72:* 115,116, 117, 118; *138:* 114, 115
Hoffman, Rosekrans *15:* 133; *50:* 219; *63:* 97
Hoffman, Sanford *38:* 208; *76:* 174; *88:* 160, 161; *151:* 156
Hoffmann, Felix *9:* 109
Hoffnung, Gerard *66:* 76, 77
Hofsinde, Robert *21:* 70
Hogan, Inez *2:* 141
Hogan, Jamie *192:* 94; *198:* 177
Hogarth, Burne *41:* 58; *63:* 46, 48, 49, 50, 52, 53, 54, 55,56
Hogarth, Paul *41:* 102, 103, 104; *YABC 1:* 16
Hogarth, William *42:* 33
Hogenbyl, Jan *1:* 35
Hogner, Nils *4:* 122; *25:* 144
Hogrogian, Nonny *3:* 221; *4:* 106, 107; *5:* 166; *7:* 129; *15:* 2; *16:* 176; *20:* 154; *22:* 146; *25:* 217; *27:* 206; *74:* 127, 128, 129, 149, 152; *127:* 99; *YABC 2:* 84, 94
Hokanson, Lars *93:* 111; *172:* 137
Hokusai *25:* 71
Hol, Colby *126:* 96
Holberg, Richard *2:* 51
Holbrook, Kathy *107:* 114
Holdcroft, Tina *38:* 109
Holden, Caroline *55:* 159
Holder, Heidi *36:* 99; *64:* 9
Holder, Jim *204:* 163
Holder, Jimmy *151:* 224

Hole, Stian *204:* 55
Holiday, Henry *YABC 2:* 107
Holl, F. *36:* 91
Holland, Brad *45:* 59, 159
Holland, Gay W. *128:* 105
Holland, Janice *18:* 118
Holland, Marion *6:* 116
Holldobler, Turid *26:* 120
Holliday, Keaf *144:* 236
Holling, Holling C. *15:* 136, 137
Hollinger, Deanne *12:* 116
Holm, Sharon Lane *114:* 84; *115:* 52
Holmes, B. *3:* 82
Holmes, Bea *7:* 74; *24:* 156; *31:* 93
Holmes, Dave *54:* 22
Holmes, Lesley *135:* 96
Holmgren, George Ellen *45:* 112
Holmlund, Heather D. *150:* 140
Holt, Norma *44:* 106
Holt, Pater *151:* 188
Holtan, Gene *32:* 192
Holub, Joan *149:* 72
Holyfield, John *149:* 231
Holz, Loretta *17:* 81
Hom, Nancy *79:* 195
Homar, Lorenzo *6:* 2
Homer, Winslow *128:* 8; *YABC 2:* 87
Honey, Elizabeth *112:* 95, 96; *137:* 93, 94
Honeywood, Varnette P. *110:* 68, 70
Hong, Lily Toy *76:* 104
Honigman, Marian *3:* 2
Honore, Paul *42:* 77, 79, 81, 82
Hood, Alun *69:* 145, 218; *72:* 41; *80:* 226; *87:* 4; *95:* 139
Hood, Susan *12:* 43
Hook, Christian *104:* 103
Hook, Frances *26:* 188; *27:* 127
Hook, Jeff *14:* 137; *103:* 105
Hook, Richard *26:* 188
Hooks *63:* 30
Hooper, Hadley *177:* 145
Hoover, Carol A. *21:* 77
Hoover, Russell *12:* 95; *17:* 2; *34:* 156
Hope, James *141:* 116
Hopkins, Chris *99:* 127
Hopkinson, Leigh *202:* 70
Hopman, Philip *178:* 184
Hoppin, Augustus *34:* 66
Horacek, Petr *163:* 117
Horder, Margaret *2:* 108; *73:* 75
Horen, Michael *45:* 121
Horne, Daniel *73:* 106; *91:* 153; *109:* 127; *110:* 232; *164:* 176
Horne, Richard *111:* 80
Horowitz, Dave *204:* 58
Horse, Harry *128:* 195; *169:* 86
Horvat, Laurel *12:* 201
Horvath, David *192:* 95
Horvath, Ferdinand Kusati *24:* 176
Horvath, Maria *57:* 171
Horwitz, Richard *57:* 174
Hotchkiss, De Wolfe *20:* 49
Hough, Charlotte *9:* 112; *13:* 98; *17:* 83; *24:* 195
Houlihan, Ray *11:* 214
House, Caroline *183:* 121
Housman, Laurence *25:* 146, 147
Houston, James *13:* 107; *74:* 132, 134, 135
Hovland, Gary *88:* 172; *171:* 148
Hoyt, Eleanor *158:* 231
How, W.E. *20:* 47
Howard, Alan *16:* 80; *34:* 58; *45:* 114
Howard, Arthur *165:* 111, 112; *190:* 5
Howard, J.N. *15:* 234
Howard, John *33:* 179
Howard, Kim *116:* 71
Howard, Paul *142:* 126, 129; *144:* 187
Howard, Rob *40:* 161
Howarth, Daniel *170:* 34
Howe, John *115:* 47; *176:* 106
Howe, John F. *79:* 101; *80:* 150

Howe, Phillip *79:* 117; *175:* 115
Howe, Stephen *1:* 232
Howell, Karen *119:* 123
Howell, Pat *15:* 139
Howell, Troy *23:* 24; *31:* 61; *36:* 158; *37:* 184; *41:* 76, 235; *48:* 112; *56:* 13; *57:* 3; *59:* 174; *63:* 5; *74:* 46; *89:* 188; *90:* 231; *95:* 97; *98:* 130; *99:* 189; *153:* 156, 157, 158; *176:* 104; *199:* 96, 98
Howes, Charles *22:* 17
Hoyt, Ard *145:* 141; *190:* 82
Hranilovich, Barbara *127:* 51
Hu, Ying-Hwa *116:* 107; *152:* 236; *173:* 171
Huang, Benrei *137:* 55
Huang, Zhong-Yang *117:* 30, 32
Hubbard, Woodleigh Marx *98:* 67; *115:* 79; *160:* 138
Hubley, Faith *48:* 120, 121, 125, 130, 131, 132, 134
Hubley, John *48:* 125, 130, 131, 132, 134
Hudak, Michal *143:* 74
Hudnut, Robin *14:* 62
Huerta, Catherine *76:* 178; *77:* 44, 45; *90:* 182
Huffaker, Sandy *10:* 56
Huffman, Joan *13:* 33
Huffman, Tom *13:* 180; *17:* 212; *21:* 116; *24:* 132; *33:* 154; *38:* 59; *42:* 147
Hughes, Arthur *20:* 148, 149, 150; *33:* 114, 148, 149
Hughes, Darren *95:* 44
Hughes, David *36:* 197
Hughes, Shirley *1:* 20, 21; *7:* 3; *12:* 217; *16:* 163; *29:* 154; *63:* 118; *70:* 102, 103, 104; *73:* 169; *88:* 70; *110:* 118, 119; *159:* 103
Hugo, Victor *47:* 112
Huliska-Beith, Laura *204:* 108
Hull, Cathy *78:* 29
Hull, Richard *95:* 120; *123:* 175; *172:* 195
Hulsmann, Eva *16:* 166
Hume, Lachie *189:* 93
Hummel, Berta *43:* 137, 138, 139
Hummel, Lisl *29:* 109; *YABC 2:* 333, 334
Humphrey, Henry *16:* 167
Humphreys, Graham *25:* 168
Humphries, Tudor *76:* 66; *80:* 4; *124:* 4, 5
Huneck, Stephen *183:* 88, 89
Hunt, James *2:* 143
Hunt, Jonathan *84:* 120
Hunt, Paul *119:* 104; *129:* 135; *139:* 160; *173:* 112
Hunt, Robert *110:* 206, 235; *147:* 136, 137; *170:* 3
Hunt, Scott *190:* 143
Hunter, Anne *133:* 190; *178:* 150
Huntington, Amy *180:* 99
Hurd, Clement *2:* 148, 149; *64:* 127, 128, 129, 131, 133, 134,135, 136; *100:* 37, 38
Hurd, Peter *24:* 30, 31,; *YABC 2:* 56
Hurd, Thacher *46:* 88, 89; *94:* 114, 115, 116; *123:* 81, 82, 84
Hurlimann, Ruth *32:* 99
Hurst, Carol Otis *185:* 92
Hurst, Philip *196:* 79
Hurst, Tracey *192:* 238
Hussar, Michael *114:* 113; *117:* 159
Hustler, Tom *6:* 105
Hutchins, Laurence *55:* 22
Hutchins, Pat *15:* 142; *70:* 106, 107, 108; *178:* 131, 132
Hutchinson, Sascha *95:* 211
Hutchinson, William M. *6:* 3, 138; *46:* 70
Hutchison, Paula *23:* 10
Hutton, Clarke *YABC 2:* 335
Hutton, Kathryn *35:* 155; *89:* 91
Hutton, Warwick *20:* 91
Huyette, Marcia *29:* 188
Hyatt, John *54:* 7
Hyatt, Mitch *178:* 162
Hyde, Maureen *82:* 17; *121:* 145, 146
Hyman, David *117:* 64

Hyman, Trina Schart *1:* 204; *2:* 194; *5:* 153; *6:* 106; *7:* 138, 145; *8:* 22; *10:* 196; *13:* 96; *14:* 114; *15:* 204; *16:* 234; *20:* 82; *22:* 133; *24:* 151; *25:* 79, 82; *26:* 82; *29:* 83; *31:* 37, 39; *34:* 104; *38:* 84, 100, 128; *41:* 49; *43:* 146; *46:* 91, 92, 93, 95, 96, 97, 98, 99, 100, 101, 102, 103, 104, 105,108, 109, 111, 197; *48:* 60, 61; *52:* 32; *60:* 168; *66:* 38; *67:* 214; *72:* 74; *75:* 92; *79:* 57; *82:* 95, 238; *89:* 46; *95:* 91, 92, 93; *100:* 33, 199; *132:* 12; *147:* 33, 35, 36; *167:* 58, 60; *177:* 189, 190

I

Ibarra, Rosa *147:* 91
Ibatoulline, Bagram *156:* 48; *174:* 33, 82; *202:* 30
Ichikawa, Satomi *29:* 152; *41:* 52; *47:* 133, 134,135, 136; *78:* 93, 94; *80:* 81; *146:* 143, 145, 146
Ide, Jacqueline *YABC 1:* 39
Ilsley, Velma *3:* 1; *7:* 55; *12:* 109; *37:* 62; *38:* 184
Imai, Ayano *190:* 85, 86
in den Bosch, Nicole *150:* 204
Inga *1:* 142
Ingman, Bruce *134:* 50; *182:* 91, 92
Ingpen, Robert *109:* 103, 104; *132:* 138; *137:* 177; *166:* 103; *181:* 140
Ingraham, Erick *21:* 177; *84:* 256; *103:* 66
Inkpen, Mick *99:* 104, 105; *106:* 44
Innerst, Stacy *149:* 104
Innocenti, Roberto *21:* 123; *96:* 122; *159:* 111, 197; *199:* 176
Inoue, Yosuke *24:* 118
Iofin, Michael *97:* 157
Iosa, Ann *63:* 189
Ipcar, Dahlov *1:* 124, 125; *49:* 137, 138, 139, 140, 141, 142,143, 144, 145; *147:* 122, 124, 126
Irvin, Fred *13:* 166; *15:* 143, 144; *27:* 175
Irving, Jay *45:* 72
Irving, Laurence *27:* 50
Isaac, Joanne *21:* 76
Isaacs, Gary *170:* 188
Isadora, Rachel *43:* 159, 160; *54:* 31; *79:* 106, 107,108; *121:* 100, 102; *165:* 116, 117; *204:* 61, 63, 64
Ishmael, Woodi *24:* 111; *31:* 99
Ives, Ruth *15:* 257
Iwai, Melissa *149:* 233; *183:* 92; *199:* 115

J

Jabar, Cynthia *101:* 201
Jackness, Andrew *94:* 237
Jackson, Julian *91:* 104, 106
Jackson, Michael *43:* 42
Jackson, Shelley *79:* 71; *99:* 109; *187:* 82
Jacob, Murv *89:* 30
Jacobi, Kathy *62:* 118
Jacobs, Barbara *9:* 136
Jacobs, Lou, Jr. *9:* 136; *15:* 128
Jacobsen, Laura *176:* 98; *177:* 85, 86
Jacobson, Rick *131:* 222; *170:* 119
Jacobus, Tim *79:* 140; *109:* 126; *129:* 180
Jacques, Robin *1:* 70; *2:* 1; *8:* 46; *9:* 20; *15:* 187; *19:* 253; *32:* 102, 103, 104; *43:* 184; *73:* 135; *YABC 1:* 42
Jaeggi, Yoshiko *186:* 184
Jaffee, Al *66:* 131, 132
Jagr, Miloslav *13:* 197
Jahn-Clough, Lisa *88:* 114; *152:* 104; *193:* 70, 71
Jahnke, Robert *84:* 24

Jainschigg, Nicholas *80:* 64; *91:* 138; *95:* 63; *99:* 25; *108:* 50; *171:* 41
Jakesavic, Nenad *85:* 102
Jakobsen, Kathy *116:* 83
Jakubowski, Charles *14:* 192
Jambor, Louis *YABC 1:* 11
James, Ann *73:* 50; *82:* 113; *158:* 61; *183:* 44
James, Brian *140:* 91
James, Curtis E. *182:* 93
James, Derek *35:* 187; *44:* 91; *61:* 133; *74:* 2; *80:* 57; *86:* 88; *130:* 30; *179:* 29
James, Gilbert *YABC 1:* 43
James, Gordon C. *195:* 89
James, Harold *2:* 151; *3:* 62; *8:* 79; *29:* 113; *51:* 195; *74:* 90
James, Kennon *126:* 211
James, Robin *50:* 106; *53:* 32, 34, 35
James, Simon *202:* 73, 74
James, Will *19:* 150, 152, 153, 155, 163
Janosch
  See Eckert, Horst
Janovitch, Marilyn *68:* 168
Janovitz, Marilyn *87:* 187; *130:* 198; *194:* 91
Jansons, Inese *48:* 117
Jansson, Tove *3:* 90; *41:* 106, 108, 109, 110, 111, 113, 114
Jaques, Faith *7:* 11, 132, 133; *21:* 83, 84; *69:* 114,116; *73:* 170
Jaques, Frances Lee *29:* 224
Jarrett, Clare *201:* 77
Jauss, Anne Marie *1:* 139; *3:* 34; *10:* 57, 119; *11:* 205; *23:* 194
Jay, Alison *158:* 97, 98; *183:* 126, 127; *196:* 95, 96, 97, 98; *200:* 72, 73, 74
Jeffers, Oliver *175:* 111
Jeffers, Susan *17:* 86, 87; *25:* 164, 165; *26:* 112; *50:* 132, 134, 135; *70:* 111, 112, 113; *137:* 107, 108, 109, 110, 111; *202:* 77, 78
Jefferson, Louise E. *4:* 160
Jenkin-Pearce, Susie *78:* 16
Jenkins, Debra Reid *85:* 202; *114:* 89; *173:* 134
Jenkins, Jean *98:* 79, 102
Jenkins, Leonard *157:* 169; *167:* 128; *189:* 96, 97; *190:* 89
Jenkins, Patrick *72:* 126
Jenkins, Steve *124:* 177; *154:* 90, 91, 92, 93; *185:* 194; *188:* 81, 82, 83, 84, 85, 86
Jenks, Aleta *73:* 117; *124:* 225
Jenkyns, Chris *51:* 97
Jensen, Bruce *95:* 39
Jensinius, Kirsten *56:* 58
Jeram, Anita *89:* 135; *102:* 122, 123; *129:* 112; *154:* 96, 97, 98; *164:* 154; *203:* 123, 124
Jernigan, E. Wesley *85:* 92
Jerome, Karen A. *72:* 194
Jeruchim, Simon *6:* 173; *15:* 250
Jeschke, Susan *20:* 89; *39:* 161; *41:* 84; *42:* 120
Jessel, Camilla *29:* 115
Jessell, Tim *159:* 3; *177:* 87; *181:* 95; *205:* 4
Jeyaveeran, Ruth *182:* 100
Jiang, Cheng An *109:* 108
Jiang, Wei *109:* 108
Jimenez, Maria *77:* 158; *93:* 127
Jobling, Curtis *138:* 74
Jocelyn, Marthe *118:* 83; *137:* 219; *163:* 119, 120; *198:* 62
Joerns, Consuelo *38:* 36; *44:* 94
John, Diana *12:* 209
John, Helen *1:* 215; *28:* 204
Johns, Elizabeth *127:* 33
Johns, Jasper *61:* 172
Johns, Jeanne *24:* 114
Johnson, Adrian *143:* 50
Johnson, Bruce *9:* 47
Johnson, Cathy *92:* 136
Johnson, Crockett
  See Leisk, David
Johnson, D. William *23:* 104

Johnson, D.B. *183:* 98, 139
Johnson, David *175:* 18; *191:* 91
Johnson, Gillian *119:* 175; *164:* 217
Johnson, Harper *1:* 27; *2:* 33; *18:* 302; *19:* 61;
  31: 181; *44:* 46, 50, 95
Johnson, Ingrid *37:* 118
Johnson, James Ralph *1:* 23, 127
Johnson, James David *12:* 195
Johnson, Jane *48:* 136
Johnson, Joel Peter *98:* 18; *128:* 111; *201:* 13
Johnson, John E. *34:* 133
Johnson, Kevin *72:* 44
Johnson, Kevin Eugene *109:* 215
Johnson, Larry *47:* 56; *123:* 107; *159:* 203
Johnson, Layne *187:* 94
Johnson, Margaret S. *35:* 131
Johnson, Meredith Merrell *71:* 181; *83:* 158;
  89: 103; *104:* 88
Johnson, Milton *1:* 67; *2:* 71; *26:* 45; *31:* 107;
  60: 112; *68:* 96
Johnson, Pamela *16:* 174; *52:* 145; *62:* 140;
  73: 116; *85:* 64
Johnson, Paul Brett *83:* 95; *132:* 119
Johnson, Stephen T. *80:* 15; *131:* 35; *141:* 96;
  145: 40; *164:* 187; *175:* 32; *189:* 99, 100
Johnson, Steve *138:* 219; *141:* 64; *144:* 199;
  177: 51
Johnson, William R. *38:* 91
Johnson-Petrov, Arden *115:* 206
Johnston, David McCall *50:* 131, 133
Johnston, Lynne *118:* 85, 87, 89
Johnstone, Anne *8:* 120; *36:* 89
Johnstone, Janet Grahame *8:* 120; *36:* 89
Jonas, Ann *50:* 107, 108, 109; *135:* 113
Jones, Bob *71:* 5; *77:* 199
Jones, Carol *5:* 131; *72:* 185, 186; *153:* 111,
  112
Jones, Chuck *53:* 70, 71
Jones, Davy *89:* 176
Jones, Douglas B. *185:* 192; *202:* 82
Jones, Elizabeth Orton *18:* 124, 126, 128, 129
Jones, Harold *14:* 88; *52:* 50
Jones, Holly *127:* 3
Jones, Jeff *41:* 64
Jones, Laurian *25:* 24, 27
Jones, Margaret *74:* 57
Jones, Noah Z. *182:* 37; *203:* 159
Jones, Randy *131:* 104
Jones, Richard *127:* 222
Jones, Robert *25:* 67
Jones, Wilfred *35:* 115; *YABC 1:* 163
Jordan, Charles *89:* 58
Jordan, Jess *158:* 136; *203:* 111
Jordan, Martin George *84:* 127
Jordan, Richard *84:* 36
Jorgenson, Andrea *91:* 111
Jorisch, Stéphane *153:* 56, 193; *177:* 29; *178:*
  138, 139; *187:* 23
Joseph, James *53:* 88
Joudrey, Ken *64:* 145; *78:* 6
Joyce, William *72:* 131, 132, 133, 134; *73:*
  227; *145:* 37
Joyner, Jerry *34:* 138
Juan, Ana *175:* 38; *179:* 111, 112
Jucker, Sita *5:* 93
Judge, Lita *192:* 99
Judkis, Jim *37:* 38
Juhasz, Victor *31:* 67
Jullian, Philippe *24:* 206; *25:* 203
Jung, Tom *91:* 217
Junge, Alexandra *183:* 37
Junge, Walter *67:* 150
Jupo, Frank *7:* 148, 149
Jurisch, Stephane *154:* 105
Justice, Martin *34:* 72

K

Kabatova-Taborska, Zdenka *107:* 153
Kachik, John *165:* 230
Kaczman, James *156:* 98
Kadair, Deborah Ousley *184:* 45, 89
Kahl, David *74:* 95; *97:* 35; *109:* 174; *110:*
  213; *198:* 15
Kahl, M.P. *37:* 83
Kahl, Virginia *48:* 138
Kahn, Katherine Janus *90:* 135
Kakimoo, Kozo *11:* 148
Kalett, Jim *48:* 159, 160, 161
Kalin, Victor *39:* 186
Kalman, Maira *96:* 131, 132; *137:* 115
Kalmenoff, Matthew *22:* 191
Kalow, Gisela *32:* 105
Kamen, Gloria *1:* 41; *9:* 119; *10:* 178; *35:*
  157; *78:* 236; *98:* 82
Kaminsky, Jef *102:* 153
Kandell, Alice *35:* 133
Kane, Henry B. *14:* 90; *18:* 219, 220
Kane, Robert *18:* 131
Kanfer, Larry *66:* 141
Kangas, Juli *200:* 88
Kappes, Alfred *28:* 104
Karalus, Bob *41:* 157
Karas, G. Brian *80:* 60; *99:* 179; *115:* 41; *118:*
  50; *136:* 168; *145:* 166; *149:* 245; *159:* 65;
  171: 192; *178:* 142, 143; *202:* 38
Karasz, Ilonka *128:* 163
Karlin, Eugene *10:* 63; *20:* 131
Karlin, Nurit *63:* 78; *103:* 110
Karpinski, Tony *134:* 160
Kasamatsu, Shiro *139:* 155
Kasparavicius, Kestutis *139:* 210
Kassian, Olena *64:* 94
Kastner, Jill *79:* 135; *117:* 84, 85
Kasuya, Masahiro *41:* 206, 207; *51:* 100
Kasza, Keiko *191:* 99, 100, 101, 102, 103
Katona, Robert *21:* 85; *24:* 126
Katz, Avi *199:* 55
Katz, Karen *158:* 123
Kauffer, E. McKnight *33:* 103; *35:* 127; *63:* 67
Kaufman, Angelika *15:* 156
Kaufman, Joe *33:* 119
Kaufman, John *13:* 158
Kaufman, Stuart *62:* 64; *68:* 226; *137:* 44
Kaufmann, John *1:* 174; *4:* 159; *8:* 43, 1; *10:*
  102; *18:* 133, 134; *22:* 251
Kaye, Graham *1:* 9; *67:* 7, 8
Kaye, M.M. *62:* 95
Kazalovski, Nata *40:* 205
Keane, Bil *4:* 135
Kearney, David *72:* 47; *121:* 83
Keating, Pamel T. *77:* 37
Keats, Ezra Jack *3:* 18, 105, 257; *14:* 101,
  102; *33:* 129; *57:* 79, 80, 82, 83, 84, 87
Keegan, Charles *166:* 211
Keegan, Marcia *9:* 122; *32:* 93
Keeler, Patricia A. *81:* 56; *183:* 102, 103
Keely, Jack *119:* 95
Keely, John *26:* 104; *48:* 214
Keen, Eliot *25:* 213
Keep, Richard C. *170:* 122
Keeping, Charles *9:* 124, 185; *15:* 28, 134; *18:*
  115; *44:* 194, 196; *47:* 25; *52:* 3; *54:* 156;
  69: 123, 124; *74:* 56; *155:* 9
Keeter, Susan *168:* 46; *183:* 192
Keith, Eros *4:* 98; *5:* 138; *31:* 29; *43:* 220; *52:*
  91, 92, 93, 94; *56:* 64, 66; *60:* 37; *79:* 93
Keleinikov, Andrei *65:* 101, 102
Kelen, Emery *13:* 115
Keller, A.J. *62:* 198
Keller, Arthur I. *26:* 106
Keller, Dick *36:* 123, 125
Keller, Holly *45:* 79; *76:* 118, 119, 120, 121;
  108: 137, 138, 140; *157:* 117, 118, 119
Keller, Katie *79:* 222; *93:* 108
Keller, Laurie *196:* 105, 106

Keller, Ronald *45:* 208
Kelley, Gary *183:* 105
Kelley, True *41:* 114, 115; *42:* 137; *75:* 35;
  92: 104, 105; *124:* 62; *130:* 100, 101; *179:*
  120, 121, 122; *192:* 251
Kellogg, Steven *8:* 96; *11:* 207; *14:* 130; *20:* ;
  201: 38 58; *29:* 140, 141; *30:* 35; *41:* 141;
  57: 89, 90, 92,93, 94, 96; *59:* 182; *73:* 141;
  77: 129; *130:* 105, 106; *177:* 94, 95, 96, 97;
  199: 57; *YABC 1:* 65, 73
Kelly, Billy *158:* 143
Kelly, Geoff *97:* 196; *112:* 25
Kelly, Irene *147:* 134
Kelly, John *194:* 186
Kelly, Joseph *174:* 94
Kelly, Kathleen M. *71:* 109
Kelly, Laura *89:* 217
Kelly, True *163:* 87
Kelly, Walt *18:* 136, 137, 138, 139, 140, 141,
  144, 145, 146, 148, 149
Kemble, E.W. *34:* 75; *44:* 178; *YABC 2:* 54,
  59
Kemp-Welsh, Lucy *24:* 197; *100:* 214
Kendall, Jane *150:* 105; *186:* 109
Kendall, Peter *152:* 85
Kendrick, Dennis *79:* 213
Kennaway, Adrienne *60:* 55, 56; *171:* 88, 89
Kennedy, Doug *189:* 104
Kennedy, Paul Edward *6:* 190; *8:* 132; *33:* 120
Kennedy, Richard *3:* 93; *12:* 179; *44:* 193;
  100: 15; *YABC 1:* 57
Kent, Jack *24:* 136; *37:* 37; *40:* 81; *84:* 89;
  86: 150; *88:* 77
Kent, Rockwell *5:* 166; *6:* 129; *20:* 225, 226,
  227,229; *59:* 144
Kenyon, Tony *81:* 201; *127:* 74
Kepes, Juliet *13:* 119
Kerins, Anthony *76:* 84
Kerr, Judith *24:* 137
Kerr, Phyllis Forbes *72:* 141
Kessler, Leonard *1:* 108; *7:* 139; *14:* 107, 227;
  22: 101; *44:* 96; *67:* 79; *82:* 123
Kest, Kristin *168:* 99; *173:* 23
Kesteven, Peter *35:* 189
Ketcham, Hank *28:* 140, 141, 142
Kettelkamp, Larry *2:* 164
Key, Alexander *8:* 99
Khalsa, Dayal Kaur *62:* 99
Kiakshuk *8:* 59
Kidd, Chip *94:* 23
Kidd, Richard *152:* 110
Kidd, Tom *64:* 199; *81:* 189; *185:* 173
Kiddell-Monroe, Joan *19:* 201; *55:* 59, 60; *87:*
  174; *121:* 112
Kidder, Harvey *9:* 105; *80:* 41
Kidwell, Carl *43:* 145
Kieffer, Christa *41:* 89
Kiesler, Kate *110:* 105; *136:* 142
Kiff, Ken *40:* 45
Kilbride, Robert *37:* 100
Kilby, Don *141:* 144
Kim, David *201:* 79; *202:* 97
Kim, Glenn *99:* 82
Kimball, Anton *78:* 114; *119:* 105
Kimball, Yeffe *23:* 116; *37:* 88
Kimber, Murray *171:* 91
Kimmel, Warren *176:* 112
Kincade, Orin *34:* 116
Kindersley, Barnabas *96:* 110
Kindred, Wendy *7:* 151
King, Colin *53:* 3
King, Robin *10:* 164, 165
King, Stephen Michael *141:* 31; *197:* 191
King, Tara Calahan *139:* 172
King, Tony *39:* 121
Kingman, Dong *16:* 287; *44:* 100, 102, 104
Kingsley, Charles *YABC 2:* 182
Kingston, Julie *147:* 14
Kingston, Maxine Hong *53:* 92
Kinney, Jeff *187:* 97
Kipling, John Lockwood *YABC 2:* 198

Illustrations Index

Kipling, Rudyard *YABC 2:* 196
Kipniss, Robert *29:* 59
Kirchherr, Astrid *55:* 23
Kirchhoff, Art *28:* 136
Kirk, Daniel *153:* 115, 116, 117; *173:* 101; *196:* 113, 114, 115, 116
Kirk, David *117:* 88, 89; *161:* 97, 98
Kirk, Ruth *5:* 96
Kirk, Steve *170:* 37
Kirk, Tim *32:* 209, 211; *72:* 89; *83:* 49
Kirmse, Marguerite *15:* 283; *18:* 153
Kirsch, Vincent X. *124:* 207
Kirschner, Ruth *22:* 154
Kirwan, Wednesday *198:* 73
Kish, Ely *73:* 119; *79:* 2
Kitamura, Satoshi *62:* 102; *98:* 91; *101:* 147; *138:* 2; *143:* 83, 85, 86; *201:* 83
Kiss, Andrew *168:* 115
Kitchel, JoAnn E. *133:* 32
Kitchen, Bert *70:* 126; *193:* 49
Kittelsen, Theodor *62:* 14
Kiuchi, Tatsuro *114:* 71
Kiwak, Barbara *172:* 135
Klahr, Susan *176:* 196
Klapholz, Mel *13:* 35
Klein, Bill *89:* 105
Klein, Robert *55:* 77
Klein, Suzanna *63:* 104
Kleinman, Zalman *28:* 143
Kleven, Elisa *173:* 96, 97
Kliban, B. *35:* 137, 138
Kline, Michael *127:* 66
Klise, M. Sarah *180:* 117, 118; *181:* 97
Knabel, Lonnie *73:* 103; *75:* 187, 228; *194:* 216
Kneen, Maggie *140:* 139
Knight, Ann *34:* 143
Knight, Christopher *13:* 125
Knight, Hilary *1:* 233; *3:* 21; *15:* 92, 158, 159; *16:* 258, 259, 260; *18:* 235; *19:* 169; *35:* 242; *46:* 167; *52:* 116; *69:* 126, 127; *132:* 129; *YABC 1:* 168, 169, 172
Knorr, Laura *200:* 91
Knorr, Peter *126:* 92, 93
Knotts, Howard *20:* 4; *25:* 170; *36:* 163
Knutson, Barbara *112:* 134; *202:* 108
Knutson, Kimberley *115:* 90
Kobayashi, Ann *39:* 58
Kochalka, James *196:* 120, 121, 122
Kocsis, J.C.
  See Paul, James
Kodman, Stanislawa *201:* 85
Koehler, Hanne Lore *176:* 203
Koehn, Ilse *34:* 198; *79:* 123
Koelsch, Michael *99:* 182; *107:* 164; *109:* 239; *138:* 142; *150:* 94; *176:* 105; *187:* 63; *198:* 63
Koering, Ursula *3:* 28; *4:* 14; *44:* 5; *64:* 140,141; *85:* 46
Koerner, Henry
  See Koerner, W.H.D.
Koerner, W.H.D. *14:* 216; *21:* 88, 89, 90, 91; *23:* 211
Koetsch, Mike *166:* 68
Koffler, Camilla *36:* 113
Kogan, Deborah Ray *161:* 101, 102
Koide, Yasuko *50:* 114
Kolado, Karen *102:* 228
Komoda, Kiyo *9:* 128; *13:* 214
Kompaneyets, Marc *169:* 92
Konashevich, Vladimir *61:* 160
Konashevicha, V. *YABC 1:* 26
Konigsburg, E.L. *4:* 138; *48:* 141, 142, 144, 145; *94:* 129, 130, 131; *126:* 129, 130, 131; *194:* 95, 98
Kono, Erin Eitter *177:* 99
Kooiker, Leonie *48:* 148
Koonook, Simon *65:* 157
Koontz, Robin Michal *136:* 155
Koopmans, Loek *101:* 121
Kopelke, Lisa *154:* 107

Kopper, Lisa *72:* 152, 153; *105:* 135, 136
Korach, Mimi *1:* 128, 129; *2:* 52; *4:* 39; *5:* 159; *9:* 129; *10:* 21; *24:* 69
Koren, Edward *5:* 100; *65:* 65, 67
Kosaka, Fumi *164:* 130
Koscielniak, Bruce *99:* 122; *153:* 120, 121, 122
Koshkin, Alexander *92:* 180
Kossin, Sandy *10:* 71; *23:* 105
Kostin, Andrej *26:* 204
Kosturko, Bob *164:* 56
Kotzky, Brian *68:* 184
Kovacevic, Zivojin *13:* 247
Kovalski, Maryann *58:* 120; *84:* 88; *97:* 124, 125, 126; *158:* 3; *186:* 80
Krahn, Fernando *2:* 257; *34:* 206; *49:* 152
Kramer, Anthony *33:* 81
Kramer, David *96:* 162; *109:* 132; *150:* 220
Kramer, Frank *6:* 121
Krantz, Kathy *35:* 83
Kratter, Paul *139:* 65
Kraus, Robert *13:* 217; *65:* 113; *93:* 93, 94
Krause, Jon *176:* 62
Krauss, Trisha *174:* 10
Kredel, Fritz *6:* 35; *17:* 93, 94, 95, 96; *22:* 147; *24:* 175; *29:* 130; *35:* 77; *YABC 2:* 166, 300
Kreloff, Eliot *189:* 107, 108; *205:* 182
Krementz, Jill *17:* 98; *49:* 41
Krenina, Katya *117:* 106; *125:* 133; *176:* 117
Kresin, Robert *23:* 19
Krieger, Salem *54:* 164
Kriegler, Lyn *73:* 29
Krinitz, Esther Nisenthal *193:* 196
Krommes, Beth *128:* 141; *149:* 136; *181:* 100, 101; *184:* 105; *188:* 125
Krone, Mike *101:* 71
Kronheimer, Ann *135:* 119
Krosoczka, Jarrett J. *155:* 142; *200:* 93, 94
Kruck, Gerald *88:* 181
Krudop, Walter Lyon *199:* 19
Krupinski, Loretta *67:* 104; *102:* 131; *161:* 105, 106
Krupp, Robin Rector *53:* 96, 98
Krush, Beth *1:* 51, 85; *2:* 233; *4:* 115; *9:* 61; *10:* 191; *11:* 196; *18:* 164, 165; *32:* 72; *37:* 203; *43:* 57; *60:* 102, 103, 107, 108, 109
Krush, Joe *2:* 233; *4:* 115; *9:* 61; *10:* 191; *11:* 196; *18:* 164, 165; *32:* 72, 91; *37:* 203; *43:* 57; *60:* 102, 103, 107, 108, 109
Krych, Duane *91:* 43
Krykorka, Vladyana *96:* 147; *143:* 90, 91; *168:* 14
Kubick, Dana *165:* 91
Kubinyi, Laszlo *4:* 116; *6:* 113; *16:* 118; *17:* 100; *28:* 227; *30:* 172; *49:* 24, 28; *54:* 23; *167:* 149
Kubricht, Mary *73:* 118
Kucharik, Elena *139:* 31
Kuchera, Kathleen *84:* 5
Kuhn, Bob *17:* 91; *35:* 235
Kulikov, Boris *163:* 185; *185:* 23; *205:* 99, 100
Kulka, Joe *188:* 110
Kukalis, Romas *90:* 27; *139:* 37
Kuklin, Susan *63:* 82, 83, 84
Kunhardt, Dorothy *53:* 101
Kunhardt, Edith *67:* 105, 106
Kunstler, Mort *10:* 73; *32:* 143
Kurchevsky, V. *34:* 61
Kurczok, Belinda *121:* 118
Kurelek, William *8:* 107
Kuriloff, Ron *13:* 19
Kurisu, Jane *160:* 120
Kuskin, Karla *2:* 170; *68:* 115, 116; *111:* 116
Kutzer, Ernst *19:* 249
Kuzma, Steve *57:* 8; *62:* 93
Kuznetsova, Berta *74:* 45
Kvasnosky, Laura McGee *93:* 103; *142:* 83; *182:* 108
Kwas, Susan Estelle *179:* 116

Kyong, Yunmee *165:* 139

L

LaBlanc, Andre *24:* 146
Laboccetta, Mario *27:* 120
LaBrose, Darcie *157:* 134
Labrosse, Darcia *58:* 88; *108:* 77; *178:* 89
LaCava, Vince *95:* 118
Laceky, Adam *32:* 121
Lacis, Astra *85:* 117
Lacome, Julie *174:* 96, 97
La Croix *YABC 2:* 4
Ladwig, Tim *98:* 212; *117:* 76
La Farge, Margaret *47:* 141
LaFave, Kim *64:* 177; *72:* 39; *97:* 146; *99:* 172; *106:* 123; *149:* 126; *196:* 128, 129
Lafontaine, Roger *167:* 158
Lafrance, Marie *197:* 109
Lagarrigue, Jerome *136:* 102; *187:* 81
Laimgruber, Monika *11:* 153
Laite, Gordon *1:* 130, 131; *8:* 209; *31:* 113; *40:* 63; *46:* 117
Laliberté, Louise-Andrée *169:* 98
LaMarche, Jim *46:* 204; *61:* 56; *94:* 69; *114:* 22; *129:* 163; *162:* 78, 80
Lamb, Jim *10:* 117
Lambase, Barbara *101:* 185; *150:* 221; *166:* 234
Lambert, J.K. *38:* 129; *39:* 24
Lambert, Sally Anne *133:* 29
Lambert, Saul *23:* 112; *33:* 107; *54:* 136
Lambert, Stephen *109:* 33; *174:* 99
Lambo, Don *6:* 156; *35:* 115; *36:* 146
Lamontagne, Jacques *166:* 227
Lamut, Sonja *57:* 193
Lamut, Sonya *85:* 102
Landa, Peter *11:* 95; *13:* 177; *53:* 119
Landau, Jacob *38:* 111
Landis, Joan *104:* 23; *203:* 32
Landon, Lucinda *79:* 31
Landshoff, Ursula *13:* 124
Landström, Lena *146:* 165, 166
Landström, Olof *146:* 166, 168; *170:* 22
Lane, Daniel *112:* 60
Lane, John R. *8:* 145
Lane, John *15:* 176, 177; *30:* 146
Lane, Nancy *166:* 74
Lang, G.D. *48:* 56
Lang, Gary *73:* 75
Lang, Jerry *18:* 295
Langdon, Bryan *186:* 187; *191:* 113, 114, 115
Lange, Dorothea *50:* 141
Langley, Jonathan *162:* 128
Langner, Nola *8:* 110; *42:* 36
Lanino, Deborah *105:* 148
Lantz, Paul *1:* 82, 102; *27:* 88; *34:* 102; *45:* 123
Larkin, Bob *84:* 225
Laroche, Giles *126:* 140; *146:* 81
LaRochelle, David *171:* 97
Larrecq, John *44:* 108; *68:* 56
Larsen, Suzanne *1:* 13
Larson, Gary *57:* 121, 122, 123, 124, 125, 126, 127
Larsson, Carl *35:* 144, 145, 146, 147, 148, 149, 150, 152, 153, 154
Larsson, Karl *19:* 177
Lartitegui, Ana G. *105:* 167
LaRue, Jenna *167:* 20
La Rue, Michael D. *13:* 215
Lasker, Joe *7:* 186, 187; *14:* 55; *38:* 115; *39:* 47; *83:* 113, 114, 115
Latham, Barbara *16:* 188, 189; *43:* 71
Lathrop, Dorothy *14:* 117, 118, 119; *15:* 109; *16:* 78, 79, 81; *32:* 201, 203; *33:* 112; *YABC 2:* 301
Lattimore, Eleanor Frances *7:* 156
Lauden, Claire *16:* 173

Lauden, George, Jr. *16:* 173
Laune, Paul *2:* 235; *34:* 31
Laure, Jason *49:* 53; *50:* 122
Lauter, Richard *63:* 29; *67:* 111; *77:* 198
Lavallee, Barbara *74:* 157; *92:* 154; *96:* 126; *145:* 193; *166:* 125, 126; *186:* 155; *192:* 172
Lave, Fitz Hugh *59:* 139
Lavis, Stephen *43:* 143; *87:* 137, 164, 165
Layton, Neal *152:* 120, 121; *182:* 65; *187:* 103, 105, 106
Law, Jenny *201:* 31
Lawrason, June *168:* 30
Lawrence, John *25:* 131; *30:* 141; *44:* 198, 200
Lawrence, Stephen *20:* 195
Lawson, Carol *6:* 38; *42:* 93, 131; *174:* 56; *189:* 89
Lawson, George *17:* 280
Lawson, Robert *5:* 26; *6:* 94; *13:* 39; *16:* 11; *20:* 100, 102, 103; *54:* 3; *66:* 12; *100:* 144, 145; *YABC 2:* 222, 224, 225, 227, 228, 229, 230, 231, 232, 233, 234, 235, 237, 238, 239, 240, 241
Layfield, Kathie *60:* 194
Lazare, Jerry *44:* 109; *74:* 28
Lazarevich, Mila *17:* 118
Lazarus, Claire *103:* 30
Lazarus, Keo Felker *21:* 94
Lazzaro, Victor *11:* 126
Lea, Bob *166:* 208; *203:* 108
Lea, Tom *43:* 72, 74
Leacroft, Richard *6:* 140
Leaf, Munro *20:* 99
Leake, Donald *70:* 41
Leander, Patricia *23:* 27
Lear, Edward *18:* 183, 184, 185
Lear, Rebecca *149:* 46
Lebenson, Richard *6:* 209; *7:* 76; *23:* 145; *44:* 191; *87:* 153
Le Cain, Errol *6:* 141; *9:* 3; *22:* 142; *25:* 198; *28:* 173; *68:* 128, 129; *86:* 49
Lechon, Daniel *113:* 211
Leder, Dora *129:* 172
Ledger, Bill *181:* 58
Leduc, Bernard *102:* 36
Lee, Alan *62:* 25, 28
Lee, Bryce *99:* 60; *101:* 195; *196:* 53
Lee, Chinlun *181:* 138; *182:* 112
Lee, Declan *191:* 20
Lee, Dom *83:* 118, 120; *93:* 123; *121:* 121, 126; *146:* 174, 175, 206, 207; *174:* 204
Lee, Doris *13:* 246; *32:* 183; *44:* 111
Lee, Hector Viveros *115:* 96
Lee, Ho Baek *200:* 160
Lee, Jeanne M. *158:* 56
Lee, Jared *93:* 200; *157:* 229
Lee, Jody *81:* 121; *82:* 225; *91:* 155; *100:* 182
Lee, Jody A. *127:* 124, 126, 127
  See also Lee, Jody
Lee, Manning de V. *2:* 200; *17:* 12; *27:* 87; *37:* 102, 103, 104; *YABC 2:* 304
Lee, Marie G. *138:* 157
Lee, Paul *97:* 100; *105:* 72, 209; *109:* 177; *128:* 113; *202:* 45
Lee, Robert J. *3:* 97; *67:* 124
Lee, Victor *96:* 228; *105:* 182; *140:* 196
Leech, Dorothy *98:* 76
Leech, John *15:* 59
Leedy, Loreen *84:* 142; *128:* 144, 145, 146; *175:* 125, 126, 127
Leeman, Michael *44:* 157
Leeming, Catherine *87:* 39
Lees, Harry *6:* 112
LeFever, Bill *88:* 220, 221
Legenisel *47:* 111
Legrand, Edy *18:* 89, 93
Lehman, Barbara *73:* 123; *170:* 130
Lehrman, Rosalie *2:* 180
Leichman, Seymour *5:* 107
Leick, Bonnie *205:* 104

Leighton, Clare *25:* 130; *33:* 168; *37:* 105, 106, 108,109
Leisk, David *1:* 140, 141; *11:* 54; *30:* 137, 142, 143,144
Leister, Brian *89:* 45; *106:* 37; *114:* 67; *149:* 236
Leloir, Maurice *18:* 77, 80, 83, 99
Lemaître, Pascal *144:* 175; *176:* 130; *189:* 135
Lemieux, Michele *100:* 148; *139:* 153
Lemke, Horst *14:* 98; *38:* 117, 118, 119
Lemke, R.W. *42:* 162
Lemon, David Gwynne *9:* 1
LeMoult, Adolph *82:* 116
Lenn, Michael *136:* 89
Lennon, John *114:* 100
Lennox, Elsie *95:* 163; *143:* 160
Lenski, Lois *1:* 144; *26:* 135, 137, 139, 141; *100:* 153, 154
Lent, Blair *1:* 116, 117; *2:* 174; *3:* 206, 207; *7:* 168, 169; *34:* 62; *68:* 217; *133:* 101; *183:* 60
Leonard, Richard *91:* 128
Leone, Leonard *49:* 190
Lerner, Carol *86:* 140, 141, 142
Lerner, Judith *116:* 138
Lerner, Sharon *11:* 157; *22:* 56
Leroux-Hugon, Helene *132:* 139
Leslie, Cecil *19:* 244
Lessac, Frané *80:* 182, 207; *96:* 182; *202:* 58
Lessing, Erich *167:* 52; *173:* 60
Lester, Alison *50:* 124; *90:* 147, 148; *129:* 130
Lethcoe, Jason *191:* 116, 117
Le Tord, Bijou *49:* 156; *95:* 112
Leutz, Emanuel *165:* 27
Levai, Blaise *39:* 130
Levin, Ted *12:* 148
Levine, David *43:* 147, 149, 150, 151, 152; *64:* 11
Levine, Joe *71:* 88
Levine, Marge *81:* 127
Levinson, David *178:* 232
Levit, Herschel *24:* 223
Levstek, Ljuba *131:* 192; *134:* 216; *149:* 65; *168:* 180
Levy, Jessica Ann *19:* 225; *39:* 191
Levy, Lina *117:* 126
Lewin, Betsy *32:* 114; *48:* 177; *90:* 151; *91:* 125; *92:* 85; *115:* 105; *169:* 110, 111; *178:* 47; *186:* 188; *194:* 201
Lewin, Ted *4:* 77; *8:* 168; *20:* 110; *21:* 99,100; *27:* 110; *28:* 96, 97; *31:* 49; *45:* 55; *48:* 223; *60:* 20, 119, 120; *62:* 139; *66:* 108; *71:* 12; *72:* 21; *74:* 226; *76:* 139, 140; *77:* 82; *79:* 87; *85:* 49, 177; *86:* 55; *88:* 182; *93:* 28, 29; *94:* 34, 182, 194; *99:* 156; *104:* 8; *115:* 123; *118:* 74; *119:* 114, 116; *131:* 54; *145:* 99; *165:* 151; *177:* 75; *178:* 42; *190:* 30; *192:* 86; *195:* 101, 102; *203:* 52
Lewis, Allen *15:* 112
Lewis, E.B. *88:* 143; *93:* 109; *119:* 79; *124:* 113; *128:* 49; *151:* 167; *168:* 110; *173:* 121; *174:* 66; *176:* 7; *184:* 150; *185:* 191
Lewis, H.B. *170:* 124
Lewis, J. Patrick *162:* 83
Lewis, Jan *81:* 22
Lewis, Kim *136:* 165
Lewis, Richard W. *52:* 25
Lewis, Robin Baird *98:* 193
Leydon, Rita Floden *21:* 101
Li, Xiojun *187:* 172
Liao, Jimmy *202:* 100
Lichtenheld, Tom *152:* 125, 126
Lieblich, Irene *22:* 173; *27:* 209, 214
Lieder, Rick *108:* 197; *199:* 58, 59, 60
Lies, Brian *92:* 40; *141:* 101; *150:* 138; *190:* 97, 98, 99,
Liese, Charles *4:* 222
Life, Kay *79:* 49
Lifton, Robert Jay *66:* 154
Lightburn, Ron *86:* 153; *91:* 122
Lightfoot, Norman R. *45:* 47

Lignell, Lois *37:* 114
Lill, Debra *121:* 70
Lilly, Charles *8:* 73; *20:* 127; *48:* 53; *72:* 9,16; *77:* 98; *102:* 94
Lilly, Ken *37:* 224
Lim, John *43:* 153
Limona, Mercedes *51:* 183
Lin, Grace *143:* 217; *162:* 86, 87; *174:* 185
Lincoln, Patricia Henderson *27:* 27; *78:* 127
Lindahn, Ron *84:* 17
Lindahn, Val *84:* 17
Lindberg, Howard *10:* 123; *16:* 190
Lindberg, Jeffrey *64:* 77; *77:* 71; *79:* 54; *80:* 149; *174:* 109; *179:* 52
Linden, Seymour *18:* 200, 201; *43:* 140
Lindenbaum, Pija *144:* 143; *183:* 113
Linder, Richard *27:* 119
Lindman, Maj *43:* 154
Lindsay, Norman *67:* 114
Lindsay, Vachel *40:* 118
Lindstrom, Jack *145:* 118
Line, Les *27:* 143
Linell
  See Smith, Linell
Lionni, Leo *8:* 115; *72:* 159, 160, 161
Lipinsky, Lino *2:* 156; *22:* 175
Lippincott, Gary A. *70:* 35; *119:* 118
Lippman, Peter *8:* 31; *31:* 119, 120, 160
Lisi, Victoria *89:* 145
Lisker, Emily *169:* 114
Lisker, Sonia O. *16:* 274; *31:* 31; *44:* 113, 114
Lisowski, Gabriel *47:* 144; *49:* 157
Lissim, Simon *17:* 138
Little, Ed *89:* 145; *151:* 53
Little, Harold *16:* 72
Little, Mary E. *28:* 146
Littlewood, Karen *165:* 126
Litty, Julie *111:* 63
Litzinger, Rosanne *151:* 101; *176:* 118; *196:* 133, 134, 135
Liu, Lesley *143:* 72
Livesly, Lorna *19:* 216
Livingston, Susan *95:* 22
Liwska, Renata *164:* 113; *199:* 25, 69
Ljungkvist, Laura *180:* 120
Llerena, Carlos Antonio *19:* 181
Lloyd, Errol *11:* 39; *22:* 178
Lloyd, Megan *77:* 118; *80:* 113; *97:* 75; *117:* 94, 95; *189:* 121, 122
Lloyd, Sam *183:* 116, 117
Lo, Beth *165:* 154
Lo, Koon-chiu *7:* 134
Loates, Glen *63:* 76
Lobel, Anita *6:* 87; *9:* 141; *18:* 248; *55:* 85,86, 87, 88, 93, 104; *60:* 67; *78:* 263; *82:* 110; *96:* 157, 159; *101:* 84; *132:* 35; *162:* 93, 94
Lobel, Arnold *1:* 188, 189; *5:* 12; *6:* 147; *7:* 167, 209; *18:* 190, 191; *25:* 39, 43; *27:* 40; *29:* 174; *52:* 127; *55:* 89, 91, 94, 95, 97, 98, 99, 100, 101, 102,103, 105, 106; *60:* 18, 31; *66:* 181, 183; *75:* 57; *82:* 246; *136:* 146
Lobel, Gillian *190:* 21
Locker, Thomas *109:* 134
Lodge, Bernard *107:* 125, 126; *153:* 93
Loeb, Jeph *153:* 177
Lodge, Jo *112:* 119
Loefgren, Ulf *3:* 108
Loescher, Ann *20:* 108
Loescher, Gil *20:* 108
Loew, David *93:* 184; *171:* 120
Lofting, Hugh *15:* 182, 183; *100:* 161, 162
Lofts, Pamela *60:* 188
Loh, George *38:* 88
Lomberg, Jon *58:* 160
Lonette, Reisie *11:* 211; *12:* 168; *13:* 56; *36:* 122; *43:* 155
Long, Ethan *168:* 146; *178:* 12; *182:* 120, 121; *196:* 124
Long, Laurel *162:* 135; *190:* 11; *203:* 113, 114
Long, Loren *99:* 176; *172:* 65; *182:* 78; *188:* 114, 115

Long, Melinda *152:* 128
Long, Miles *115:* 174
Long, Sally *42:* 184
Long, Sylvia *74:* 168; *132:* 63; *179:* 134
Longoni, Eduardo *73:* 85
Longtemps, Ken *17:* 123; *29:* 221; *69:* 82
Looser, Heinz *YABC 2:* 208
Lopez, Loretta *190:* 100
López, Rafael *197:* 160; *198:* 85
Lopshire, Robert *6:* 149; *21:* 117; *34:* 166; *73:* 13
Lord, John Vernon *21:* 104; *23:* 25; *51:* 22
Lorenz, Albert *40:* 146; *115:* 127
Loretta, Sister Mary *33:* 73
Lorraine, Walter H. *3:* 110; *4:* 123; *16:* 192; *103:* 119
Los, Marek *146:* 22; *193:* 23
Loss, Joan *11:* 163
Louderback, Walt *YABC 1:* 164
Lousada, Sandra *40:* 138
Louth, Jack *149:* 252; *151:* 191, 192
Love, Judy *173:* 43; *196:* 40
Low, Joseph *14:* 124, 125; *18:* 68; *19:* 194; *31:* 166; *80:* 239
Low, William *62:* 175; *80:* 147; *112:* 194; *150:* 202; *169:* 175; *177:* 110; *192:* 27
Lowe, Vicky *177:* 130
Lowenheim, Alfred *13:* 65, 66
Lowenstein, Sallie *116:* 90, 91
Lowitz, Anson *17:* 124; *18:* 215
Lowrey, Jo *8:* 133
Lubach, Vanessa *142:* 152
Lubell, Winifred *1:* 207; *3:* 15; *6:* 151
Lubin, Leonard B. *19:* 224; *36:* 79, 80; *45:* 128, 129,131, 132, 133, 134, 135, 136, 137, 139, 140, 141; *70:* 95; *YABC2:* 96
Lucht, Irmgard *82:* 145
Ludwig, Helen *33:* 144, 145
Lufkin, Raymond *38:* 138; *44:* 48
Luhrs, Henry *7:* 123; *11:* 120
Lujan, Tonita *82:* 33
Lupo, Dom *4:* 204
Lustig, Loretta *30:* 186; *46:* 134, 135, 136, 137
Luthardt, Kevin *172:* 125, 126
Luxbacher, Irene *153:* 145
Luzak, Dennis *52:* 121; *99:* 142
Lydbury, Jane *82:* 98
Lydecker, Laura *21:* 113; *42:* 53
Lynch, Charles *16:* 33
Lynch, Marietta *29:* 137; *30:* 171
Lynch, P.J. *126:* 228; *129:* 110; *132:* 247; *183:* 64
Lyne, Alison Davis *188:* 118, 198
Lyon, Carol *102:* 26
Lyon, Elinor *6:* 154
Lyon, Fred *14:* 16
Lyon, Tammie *175:* 170
Lyons, Oren *8:* 193
Lyster, Michael *26:* 41

M

Maas, Dorothy *6:* 175
Maas, Julie *47:* 61
Macaulay, David *46:* 139, 140, 141, 142, 143, 144, 145, 147, 149, 150; *72:* 167, 168, 169; *137:* 129, 130, 131, 132
MacCarthy, Patricia *69:* 141
Macdonald, Alister *21:* 55
Macdonald, Roberta *19:* 237; *52:* 164
MacDonald, Norman *13:* 99
MacDonald, Ross *201:* 103
MacDonald, Suse *54:* 41; *109* 138; *130:* 156; *193:* 106, 107, 109, 110
Mace, Varian *49:* 159
Macguire, Robert Reid *18:* 67
Machetanz, Fredrick *34:* 147, 148
MacInnes, Ian *35:* 59

MacIntyre, Elisabeth *17:* 127, 128
Mack, Jeff *161:* 128; *194:* 119, 120
Mack, Stan *17:* 129; *96:* 33
Mackay, Donald *17:* 60
MacKaye, Arvia *32:* 119
Mackenzie, Robert *204:* 78
Mackenzie, Stuart *73:* 213
MacKenzie, Garry *33:* 159
Mackie, Clare *87:* 134
Mackinlay, Miguel *27:* 22
MacKinstry, Elizabeth *15:* 110; *42:* 139, 140, 141, 142, 143,144, 145
MacLeod, Lee *91:* 167
Maclise, Daniel *YABC 2:* 257
Macnaughton, Tina *182:* 145
MacRae, Tom *181:* 112
Madden, Don *3:* 112, 113; *4:* 33, 108, 155; *7:* 193; *78:* 12; *YABC 2:* 211
Maddison, Angela Mary *10:* 83
Madsen, Jim *146:* 259; *152:* 237; *184:* 106; *197:* 21; *202:* 103, 104
Maestro, Giulio *8:* 124; *12:* 17; *13:* 108; *25:* 182; *54:* 147; *59:* 114, 115, 116, 117, 118, 121, 123, 124, 125,126, 127; *68:* 37, 38; *106:* 129, 130, 131, 136, 137, 138
Maffia, Daniel *60:* 200
Maggio, Viqui *58:* 136, 181; *74:* 150; *75:* 90; *85:* 159; *90:* 158; *109:* 184; *193:* 113
Magnus, Erica *77:* 123
Magnuson, Diana *28:* 102; *34:* 190; *41:* 175
Magoon, Scott *181:* 104
Magovern, Peg *103:* 123
Maguire, Sheila *41:* 100
Magurn, Susan *91:* 30
Mahony, Will *37:* 120
Mahony, Will *85:* 116
Mahood, Kenneth *24:* 141
Mahurin, Matt *164:* 225; *175:* 95; *189:* 37; *196:* 14
Maik, Henri *9:* 102
Maione, Heather *106:* 5; *178:* 8; *189:* 126, 127; *193:* 58
Maisto, Carol *29:* 87
Maitland, Antony *1:* 100, 176; *8:* 41; *17:* 246; *24:* 46; *25:* 177, 178; *32:* 74; *60:* 65, 195; *67:* 156; *87:* 131; *101:* 110
Majewski, Dawn W. *169:* 95
Mak, Kam *72:* 25; *75:* 43; *87:* 186; *97:* 24; *102:* 154; *149:* 195; *186:* 28
Makie, Pam *37:* 117
Maktima, Joe *116:* 191
Maland, Nick *99:* 77
Male, Alan *132:* 64
Malone, James Hiram *84:* 161
Malone, Nola Langner *82:* 239
Malone, Peter *191:* 121, 122, 123
Malsberg, Edward *51:* 175
Malvern, Corinne *2:* 13; *34:* 148, 149
Manchess, Gregory *165:* 241; *203:* 119
Mancusi, Stephen *63:* 198, 199
Mandelbaum, Ira *31:* 115
Manders, John *138:* 152, 155; *188:* 171; *190:* 92; *199:* 5
Manet, Edouard *23:* 170
Mangiat, Jeff *173:* 127
Mangurian, David *14:* 133
Manham, Allan *42:* 109; *77:* 180; *80:* 227
Manley, Matt *103:* 167; *117:* 98; *172:* 49
Manna, Giovanni *178:* 44
Manniche, Lise *31:* 121
Manning, Jane *96:* 203
Manning, Jo *63:* 154
Manning, Lawrence *191:* 153
Manning, Mick *176:* 139
Manning, Samuel F. *5:* 75
Mantel, Richard *57:* 73; *63:* 106; *82:* 255
Mantha, John *205:* 164
Maraja *15:* 86; *YABC 1:* 28; *2:* 115

Marcellino, Fred *20:* 125; *34:* 222; *53:* 125; *58:* 205; *61:* 64, 121, 122; *68:* 154, 156, 157, 158, 159; *72:* 25; *86:* 184; *98:* 181; *118:* 129, 130, 131; *149:* 218; *194:* 7
Marchesi, Stephen *34:* 140; *46:* 72; *50:* 147; *66:* 239; *70:* 33; *73:* 18, 114, 163; *77:* 47, 76,147; *78:* 79; *80:* 30; *81:* 6; *89:* 66; *93:* 21,130; *94:* 94; *97:* 66; *98:* 96; *114:* 115, 116
Marchiori, Carlos *14:* 60
Marciano, John Bemelmans *118:* 133; *167:* 110, 111, 112
Marcus, Barry David *139:* 248; *145:* 18
Maren, Julie *199:* 73
Margules, Gabriele *21:* 120
Mariana
　See Foster, Marian Curtis
Mariano, Michael *52:* 108
Marino, Dorothy *6:* 37; *14:* 135
Mario, Heide Stetson *101:* 202
Maris, Ron *71:* 123
Maritz, Nicolaas *85:* 123
Mark, Mona *65:* 105; *68:* 205; *116:* 213
Markham, R.L. *17:* 240
Marks, Alan *104:* 104; *109:* 182; *164:* 92; *185:* 134; *187:* 120, 121, 122
Marks, Cara *54:* 9
Marks, Colin *203:* 129
Marokvia, Artur *31:* 122
Marquez, Susan *108:* 121
Marrella, Maria Pia *62:* 116
Marriott, Pat *30:* 30; *34:* 39; *35:* 164, 165, 166; *44:* 170; *48:* 186, 187, 188, 189, 191, 192, 193; *91:* 92
Mars, W.T. *1:* 161; *3:* 115; *4:* 208, 225; *5:* 92, 105, 186; *8:* 214; *9:* 12; *13:* 121; *27:* 151; *31:* 180; *38:* 102; *48:* 66; *62:* 164, 165; *64:* 62; *68:* 229; *79:* 55
Marschall, Ken *85:* 29
Marsh, Christine *3:* 164
Marsh, James *73:* 137
Marsh, Reginald *17:* 5; *19:* 89; *22:* 90, 96
Marshall, Anthony D. *18:* 216
Marshall, Felicia *170:* 190
Marshall, James *6:* 160; *40:* 221; *42:* 24, 25, 29; *51:* 111, 112, 113, 114, 115, 116, 117, 118, 119, 120, 121; *64:* 13; *75:* 126, 127, 128, 129; *102:* 10, 12
Marshall, Janet *97:* 154
Marstall, Bob *55:* 145; *84:* 153, 170; *104:* 145; *154:* 166, 167, 168
Martchenko, Michael *50:* 129, 153, 155, 156, 157; *83:* 144,145; *154:* 137, 138, 139
Marten, Ruth *129:* 52
Martin, Brad *199:* 186
Martin, Charles E. *70:* 144
Martin, David Stone *24:* 232; *62:* 4
Martin, Fletcher *18:* 213; *23:* 151
Martin, Rene *7:* 144; *42:* 148, 149, 150
Martin, Richard E. *51:* 157; *131:* 203
Martin, Ron *32:* 81
Martin, Stefan *8:* 68; *32:* 124, 126; *56:* 33
Martin, Whitney *166:* 137
Martinez, Ed *58:* 192; *72:* 231; *77:* 33; *80:* 214; *167:* 123
Martinez, John *6:* 113; *118:* 13; *139:* 143
Martinez, Sergio *158:* 190
Martini, Angela *183:* 161
Martiniere, Stephan *171:* 130
Marton, Jirina *95:* 127, 128; *144:* 145
Martorell, Antonio *84:* 6; *97:* 161
Martucci, Griesbach *52:* 106
Marvin, Frederic *83:* 86
Marx, Robert F. *24:* 143
Marzollo, Jean *190:* 127
Masefield, Judith *19:* 208, 209
Masheris, Robert *78:* 51
Masiello, Ralph *186:* 171
Mason, George F. *14:* 139
Mason, Robert *84:* 96
Massey, Barbara *68:* 142

Massie, Diane Redfield 16: 194
Massie, Kim 31: 43
Mataya, David 121: 66
Mathers, Petra 119: 135; 163: 104; 176: 143,
144; 187: 142; 196: 101
Mathewuse, James 51: 143
Mathieu, Joseph 14: 33; 39: 206; 43: 167; 56:
180; 79: 126; 94: 147; 185: 140
Matje, Martin 169: 177, 178; 172: 180
Matsubara, Naoko 12: 121
Matsuda, Shizu 13: 167
Matsuoka, Mei 192: 135
Matte, L'Enc 22: 183
Mattelson, Marvin 36: 50, 51
Matteson, Jenny 180: 132
Matthews, Elizabeth 194: 128
Matthews, F. Leslie 4: 216
Matthews, Tina 190: 130
Mattingly, David 71: 76, 77; 82: 64; 91: 216,
217; 109: 25
Matulay, Laszlo 5: 18; 43: 168
Matus, Greta 12: 142
Maughan, William 181: 31
Mauldin, Bill 27: 23
Mauterer, Erin Marie 119: 5
Mawicke, Tran 9: 137; 15: 191; 47: 100
Mawson, Matt 74: 115
Max, Peter 45: 146, 147, 148, 149, 150
Maxie, Betty 40: 135
Maxwell, John Alan 1: 148
May, Steve 204: 30
Mayan, Earl 7: 193
Mayer, Bill 200: 138
Mayer, Danuta 117: 103
Mayer, Marianna 32: 132
Mayer, Mercer 11: 192; 16: 195, 196; 20: 55,
57; 32: 129, 130, 132, 133, 134; 41: 144,
248, 252; 58: 186; 73: 140, 142, 143; 137:
137, 138
Mayforth, Hal 166: 77
Mayhew, James 85: 121; 138: 187; 149: 140;
204: 81
Mayhew, Richard 3: 106
Mayo, Gretchen Will 38: 81; 84: 166
Mays, Victor 5: 127; 8: 45, 153; 14: 245; 23:
50; 34: 155; 40: 79; 45: 158; 54: 91; 66:
240
Mazal, Chanan 49: 104
Maze, Deborah 71: 83
Mazellan, Ron 75: 97, 98
Mazetti, Alan 112: 72
Mazille, Capucine 96: 168
Mazza, Adriana Saviozzi 19: 215
Mazzella, Mary Jo 82: 165
Mazzetti, Alan 45: 210
McAfee, Steve 135: 146; 167: 176; 191: 84
McAlinden, Paul 112: 128
McBride, Angus 28: 49; 103: 40
McBride, Will 30: 110
McCaffery, Janet 38: 145
McCallum, Graham 78: 78
McCallum, Stephen 141: 143; 156: 5; 166:
228
McCann, Gerald 3: 50; 4: 94; 7: 54; 41: 121
McCarthy, Dan 174: 74
McCarthy, Linda 177: 128
McCarthy, Meghan 168: 134; 199: 74
McCauley, Adam 157: 36; 184: 199; 193: 100
McCay, Winsor 41: 124, 126, 128, 129, 130,
131; 134: 77, 79
McClary, Nelson 1: 111
McClements, George 196: 146
McClintock, Barbara 57: 135; 95: 130; 146:
190
McClintock, Theodore 14: 141
McCloskey, Robert 1: 184, 185; 2: 186, 187;
17: 209; 39: 139, 140, 141, 142, 143, 146,
147, 148; 85: 150, 151; 100: 172, 173, 174
McClung, Robert 2: 189; 68: 166, 167
McClure, Gillian 31: 132; 150: 53
McConnel, Jerry 31: 75, 187

McConnell, Mary 102: 49
McCord, Kathleen Garry 78: 236
McCormack, John 66: 193
McCormick, A.D. 35: 119
McCormick, Dell J. 19: 216
McCrady, Lady 16: 198; 39: 127
McCrea, James 3: 122; 33: 216
McCrea, Ruth 3: 122; 27: 102; 33: 216
McCue, Lisa 65: 148, 149; 77: 54; 80: 132;
175: 33; 177: 133, 135
McCully, Emily Arnold 2: 89; 4: 120, 121,
146, 197; 5: 2, 129; 7: 191; 11: 122; 15:
210; 33: 23; 35: 244; 37: 122; 39: 88; 40:
103; 50: 30,31, 32, 33, 34, 35, 36, 37; 52:
89, 90; 57: 6; 62: 3; 70: 195; 86: 82; 96:
192; 97: 93; 110: 143,144; 117: 47; 167: 96
McCurdy, Michael 13: 153; 24: 85; 81: 160;
82: 157, 158; 86: 125; 97: 92; 117: 178;
132: 6; 147: 159, 160
McCusker, Paul 99: 19
McDaniel, Jerry 132: 135
McDaniel, Preston 160: 206; 170: 139
McDermott, Beverly Brodsky 11: 180
McDermott, Gerald 16: 201; 74: 174, 175;
163: 150, 151
McDermott, Mike 96: 187
McDonald, Jill 13: 155; 26: 128
McDonald, Mercedes 169: 118
McDonald, Ralph J. 5: 123, 195
McDonnell, Flora 146: 199, 200
McDonnell, Patrick 179: 153, 154
McDonough, Don 10: 163
McElligott, Matt 196: 147
McElmurry, Jill 137: 148; 163: 141; 202: 186
McElrath-Eslick, Lori 129: 145; 142: 21; 173:
123; 202: 194; 204: 88, 89
McEntee, Dorothy 37: 124
McEwan, Keith 88: 116; 165: 122, 123
McEwen, Katharine 169: 34
McFall, Christie 12: 144
McFeely, Daniel 160: 213
McGaw, Laurie 109: 243; 143: 216
McGee, Barbara 6: 165
McGee, Marni 163: 153
McGillvray, Kim 158: 171; 165: 213; 186:
183; 190: 175
McGinley-Nally, Sharon 131: 19
McGinnis, Robert 110: 113; 177: 80
McGovern, Tara 98: 171
McGraw, Sheila 83: 146
McGregor, Barbara 200: 155
McGregor, Malcolm 23: 27
McGrory, Anik 193: 120
McGuire, Robert 204: 57
McGuirk, Leslie 152: 159
McHale, John 138: 190
McHenry, E.B. 193: 122
McHugh, Tom 23: 64
McIntosh, Jon 42: 56
McKay, Donald 2: 118; 32: 157; 45: 151, 152
McKean, Dave 150: 71; 174: 156; 197: 83,
118
McKeating, Eileen 44: 58
McKee, David 10: 48; 21: 9; 70: 154, 155;
107: 139, 140, 141; 134: 218; 158: 148, 149,
150, 151
McKee, Diana 109: 185
McKelvey, Patrick 164: 141
McKendry, Joe 170: 136
McKeveny, Tom 164: 60; 173: 79
McKie, Roy 7: 44
McKie, Todd 205: 181
McKillip, Kathy 30: 153
McKinney, Ena 26: 39
McKinnon, James 136: 75
McKowen, Scott 172: 63; 202: 49
McLachlan, Edward 5: 89
McLaren, Chesley 133: 53
McLaren, Kirsty 123: 99; 124: 226
Mclean, Andrew 113: 117, 118, 120, 121; 172:
130, 131

McLean, Janet 172: 130
McLean, Meg 94: 196
McLean, Sammis 32: 197
McLean, Wilson 90: 29; 113: 195
McLoughlin, John C. 47: 149
McLoughlin, Wayne 102: 230; 134: 178
McMahon, Robert 36: 155; 69: 169
McManus, Shawn 85: 71
McMenemy, Sarah 156: 139
McMillan, Bruce 22: 184
McMullan, James 40: 33; 67: 172; 87: 142;
99: 63, 64; 189: 133; 196: 51
McMullen, Nigel 146: 177
McNeely, Tom 162: 55
McNaught, Harry 12: 80; 32: 136
McNaughton, Colin 39: 149; 40: 108; 92: 144,
145, 146; 134: 104, 106
McNicholas, Maureen 38: 148
McNicholas, Shelagh 173: 61; 191: 125, 126
McPhail, David 14: 105; 23: 135; 37: 217,
218, 220,221; 47: 151, 152, 153, 154, 155,
156, 158, 159, 160, 162, 163, 164; 71: 211;
81: 139, 140, 142; 86: 123; 132: 150; 140:
129, 131, 132; 183: 134, 135, 137; 189: 132
McPhee, Richard B. 41: 133
McPheeters, Neal 78: 132; 86: 90; 99: 162;
111: 141; 142: 162
McQuade, Jacqueline 124: 223
McQueen, Lucinda 28: 149; 41: 249; 46: 206;
53: 103
McQuillan, Mary 153: 97; 200: 140
McVay, Tracy 11: 68
McVicker, Charles 39: 150
Mead, Ben Carlton 43: 75
Meade, Holly 90: 102; 94: 101; 149: 8; 151:
107
Mecray, John 33: 62
Meddaugh, Susan 20: 42; 29: 143; 41: 241;
77: 50; 84: 173, 174, 175, 176, 177, 178;
125: 160, 161, 162; 176: 148, 149, 150, 151
Meehan, Dennis B. 56: 144
Meents, Len W. 73: 147, 150
Meers, Tony 99: 113
Meisel, Paul 98: 137; 124: 18; 162: 180; 179:
16; 181: 62; 194: 154
Melanson, Luc 149: 229; 198: 97, 98
Melendez, Francisco 72: 180
Melling, David 202: 199
Melnychuk, Monika 153: 65
Melo, Esperança 196: 90
Melo, John 16: 285; 58: 203
Meloni, Maria Teresa 98: 62
Meltzer, Ericka
See O'Rourke, Ericka
Menasco, Milton 43: 85
Menchin, Scott 188: 129
Mendelson, Steven T. 86: 154
Mendelssohn, Felix 19: 170
Mendola, Christopher 88: 223
Meng, Heinz 13: 158
Merian, Maria Sibylla 140: 88
Mero, Lee 34: 68
Merrell, David 205: 3
Merrill, Frank T. 16: 147; 19: 71; YABC 1:
226, 229,273
Merriman, Rachel 98: 108; 114: 122; 149: 142
Merveille, David 200: 142
Meryman, Hope 27: 41
Meryweather, Jack 10: 179
Meseldzija, Petar 168: 97
Meserve, Jess 184: 137
Messick, Dale 64: 150, 151, 152
Meth, Harold 24: 203
Meyer, Herbert 19: 189
Meyer, Renate 6: 170
Meyers, Bob 11: 136
Meyers, Nancy 172: 124
Meynell, Louis 37: 76
Micale, Albert 2: 65; 22: 185
Miccuci, Charles 82: 163; 144: 150
Micich, Paul 164: 163

Middleton, Jeffrey *177:* 173
Middleton-Sandford, Betty *2:* 125
Mieke, Anne *45:* 74
Mighell, Patricia *43:* 134
Miglio, Paige *101:* 203; *151:* 223; *201:* 118, 119; *204:* 162
Mikec, Larry *204:* 125
Mikolaycak, Charles *9:* 144; *12:* 101; *13:* 212; *21:* 121; *22:* 168; *30:* 187; *34:* 103, 150; *37:* 183; *43:* 179; *44:* 90; *46:* 115, 118, 119; *49:* 25; *78:* 121, 122, 205, 207; *81:* 4
Milelli, Pascal *129:* 66; *135:* 153; *187:* 45
Miles, Elizabeth *117:* 77
Miles, Jennifer *17:* 278
Milgrim, David *158:* 157; *187:* 125, 126, 128
Milhous, Katherine *15:* 193; *17:* 51
Millais, John E. *22:* 230, 231
Millar, H.R. *YABC 1:* 194, 195, 203
Millard, C.E. *28:* 186
Millard, Kerry *105:* 124; *204:* 93, 94
Miller, Don *15:* 195; *16:* 71; *20:* 106; *31:* 178
Miller, Edna *29:* 148
Miller, Edward *115:* 64; *183:* 140, 141
Miller, Frank J. *25:* 94
Miller, Grambs *18:* 38; *23:* 16
Miller, Ian *99:* 128
Miller, Jane *15:* 196
Miller, Marcia *13:* 233
Miller, Marilyn *1:* 87; *31:* 69; *33:* 157
Miller, Mitchell *28:* 183; *34:* 207
Miller, Phil *175:* 150
Miller, Shane *5:* 140
Miller, Virginia *81:* 206
Millman, Isaac *172:* 18
Mills, Elaine *72:* 181
Mills, Judith Christine *130:* 168, 169
Mills, Lauren *92:* 170
Mills, Yaroslava Surmach *35:* 169, 170; *46:* 114
Millsap, Darrel *51:* 102
Milone, Karen *89:* 169
Milord, Susan *147:* 163, 164; *200:* 144
Milton, Debbie *162:* 161
Mims, Ashley *170:* 51
Miner, Julia *98:* 69
Minor, Wendell *39:* 188; *52:* 87; *56:* 171; *58:* 116; *62:* 56; *66:* 109; *74:* 93; *78:* 129; *94:* 67; *117:* 12, 13; *124:* 84, 86; *136:* 121; *164:* 168, 169; *170:* 71; *199:* 79, 80, 81, 82
Minter, Daniel *176:* 154; *179:* 177
Mirocha, Paul *81:* 133; *192:* 148; *194:* 36
Misako Rocks! *192:* 149, 150
Mitchell, Judith *109:* 117
Mitchell, Mark *91:* 208
Mitchell, Tracy *190:* 15
Mitgutsch, Ali *76:* 161
Mitsuhashi, Yoko *45:* 153
Miyake, Yoshi *38:* 141
Mizumura, Kazue *10:* 143; *18:* 223; *36:* 159
Mochi, Ugo *8:* 122; *38:* 150
Mock, Paul *55:* 83; *123:* 32
Modarressi, Mitra *90:* 236; *126:* 168; *173:* 165, 166; *200:* 147, 148
Modell, Frank *39:* 152
Mogenson, Jan *74:* 183
Mohn, Susan *89:* 224
Mohr, Mark *133:* 201
Mohr, Nicholasa *8:* 139; *113:* 127
Molan, Christine *60:* 177; *84:* 183
Moldon, Peter L. *49:* 168
Molk, Laurel *92:* 150
Mollica, Gene *197:* 11
Momaday, N. Scott *48:* 159
Mombourquette, Paul *112:* 91; *126:* 142
Monk, Julie *165:* 231; *191:* 96
Monks, Lydia *189:* 136, 137
Monroy, Manuel *199:* 192
Montgomery, Lucy *150:* 126
Montgomery-Higham, Amanda *169:* 131
Monteiel, David *201:* 95
Montiel, David *69:* 106; *84:* 145

Montijo, Rhode *193:* 164
Montresor, Beni *2:* 91; *3:* 138; *38:* 152, 153, 154,155, 156, 157, 158, 159, 160; *68:* 63
Montserrat, Pep *128:* 135; *181:* 119; *184:* 53
Moon, Carl *25:* 183, 184, 185
Moon, Eliza *14:* 40
Moon, Ivan *22:* 39; *38:* 140
Moore, Adrienne *67:* 147
Moore, Agnes Kay Randall *43:* 187
Moore, Cyd *117:* 107, 108; *159:* 137, 138; *186:* 148, 149, 151; *203:* 15
Moore, Gustav *127:* 181, 182; *170:* 162, 163
Moore, Jackie *128:* 79
Moore, Janet *63:* 153
Moore, Margie *176:* 156
Moore, Mary *29:* 160
Moore, Patrick *184:* 121
Moore, Yvette *101:* 11, 12; *154:* 141
Mora, Giovanni *179:* 127; *184:* 11
Mora, Raul Mina *20:* 41
Moraes, Odilon *102:* 144
Morales, Yuyi *154:* 144
Moran, Rosslyn *111:* 26
Moran, Tom *60:* 100
Mordan, C.B. *193:* 115
Mordvinoff, Nicolas *15:* 179
Moreno, René Rey *59:* 59; *190:* 133, 209
Morgan, Barbara *169:* 116
Morgan, Jacqui *58:* 57
Morgan, Mary *114:* 133, 134, 135; *123:* 11
Morgan, Tom *42:* 157
Morgan, Pierr *173:* 148
Morgenstern, Michael *158:* 7, 57; *171:* 103; *174:* 60
Morice, Dave *93:* 142
Morin, Paul *73:* 132; *79:* 130; *88:* 140; *137:* 143
Moriuchi, Mique *177:* 203
Morning, Tuesday *205:* 25
Morozumi, Atsuko *110:* 155
Morrill, Leslie *18:* 218; *29:* 177; *33:* 84; *38:* 147; *42:* 127; *44:* 93; *48:* 164, 165, 167, 168, 169, 170,171; *49:* 162; *63:* 136, 180; *70:* 72; *71:* 70, 91,92; *72:* 228; *80:* 163, 164, 165; *90:* 121; *121:* 88; *178:* 117
Morrill, Rowena A. *84:* 16; *98:* 163
Morris *47:* 91
Morris, Frank *55:* 133; *60:* 28; *76:* 2
Morris, Harry O. *119:* 138
Morris, Jackie *128:* 194; *144:* 119; *151:* 146; *202:* 126, 127; *204:* 83
Morris, Jennifer E. *179:* 157
Morris, Oradel Nolen *128:* 180
Morris, Tony *62:* 146; *70:* 97
Morrison, Bill *42:* 116; *66:* 170; *69:* 40
Morrison, Gordon *87:* 150; *113:* 93; *128:* 181, 182; *183:* 144, 145, 146
Morrison, Frank *169:* 162; *205:* 156
Morrison, Taylor *159:* 144, 145; *187:* 131
Morrow, Gray *2:* 64; *5:* 200; *10:* 103, 114; *14:* 175
Morse, Scott *200:* 149, 150
Morton, Lee Jack *32:* 140
Morton, Marian *3:* 185
Mosberg, Hilary *117:* 195; *118:* 164; *149:* 55
Moser, Barry *56:* 68, 117, 118, 119, 120, 121, 122, 123, 124; *59:* 141; *60:* 160; *79:* 91, 147, 149, 151, 152; *82:* 81; *90:* 118; *91:* 35; *95:* 210; *97:* 91, 93; *102:* 152; *126:* 4; *128:* 175; *133:* 141; *138:* 167, 171, 174; *153:* 205; *174:* 130; *185:* 152, 154; *195:* 163; *204:* 115
Moser, Cara *90:* 118; *138:* 167
Moses, Grandma *18:* 228
Moses, Will *178:* 170, 171
Moskof, Martin Stephen *27:* 152
Mosley, Francis *57:* 144
Moss, Donald *11:* 184
Moss, Geoffrey *32:* 198
Moss, Marissa *71:* 130; *104:* 127; *163:* 156
Most, Bernard *48:* 173; *91:* 142, 143; *134:* 120

Mowll, Joshua *188:* 133
Mowry, Carmen *50:* 62
Moxley, Sheila *96:* 174; *169:* 26
Moyers, William *21:* 65
Moyler, Alan *36:* 142
Mozley, Charles *9:* 87; *20:* 176, 192, 193; *22:* 228; *25:* 205; *33:* 150; *43:* 170, 171, 172, 173, 174; *YABC2:* 89
Mueller, Hans Alexander *26:* 64; *27:* 52, 53
Mugnaini, Joseph *11:* 35; *27:* 52, 53; *35:* 62
Mujica, Rick *72:* 67; *88:* 95; *111:* 53; *180:* 185; *197:* 70
Mullen, Douglas *180:* 178
Muller, Robin *86:* 161
Muller, Steven *32:* 167
Muller, Jorg *35:* 215; *67:* 138, 139
Mulock, Julie *163:* 112
Mullins, Edward S. *10:* 101
Mullins, Patricia *51:* 68
Multer, Scott *80:* 108
Munari, Bruno *15:* 200
Munch, Edvard *140:* 143
Munowitz, Ken *14:* 148; *72:* 178, 179
Munro, Roxie *58:* 134; *136:* 177; *137:* 218; *184:* 133, 134
Munsinger, Lynn *33:* 161; *46:* 126; *71:* 92; *82:* 80; *89:* 218; *92:* 125; *94:* 157, 158, 159, 160; *98:* 196; *103:* 198; *142:* 143; *145:* 133, 134, 136; *153:* 203; *176:* 162; *177:* 140, 141, 142; *189:* 113, 114, 116, 117; *201:* 42
Munson, Russell *13:* 9
Munster, Sebastian *166:* 107
Munoz, William *42:* 160
Munzar, Barbara *149:* 75
Murdocca, Salvatore *73:* 212; *98:* 132; *111:* 168; *157:* 228; *164:* 257
Murphy, Bill *5:* 138; *130:* 170
Murphy, Jill *37:* 142; *70:* 166; *142:* 132, 134
Murphy, Kelly *130:* 212; *143:* 119; *176:* 158; *190:* 135
Murphy, Mary *196:* 158
Murphy, Tom *192:* 40
Murr, Karl *20:* 62
Murray, Joe *175:* 37
Murray, Ossie *43:* 176
Mussino, Attilio *29:* 131; *100:* 164
Mutchler, Dwight *1:* 25
Myers, Bernice *9:* 147; *36:* 75; *81:* 146, 147, 148
Muth, Jon J. *165:* 169; *167:* 109; *190:* 227; *193:* 59
Myers, Christopher *183:* 150; *193:* 139
Myers, Duane O. *99:* 145
Myers, Tim *147:* 168
Myers, V.G. *142:* 41
Myers, Lou *11:* 2

N

Nachreiner, Tom *29:* 182
Nacht, Merle *65:* 49
Nadler, Ellis *88:* 91
Nagle, Shane *180:* 223
Nagy, Ian *195:* 64
Najaka, Marlies *62:* 101
Nakai, Michael *30:* 217; *54:* 29
Nakata, Hiroe *157:* 156; *162:* 30; *205:* 124, 125
Nakatani, Chiyoko *12:* 124
Narahashi, Keiko *77:* 188; *82:* 213; *115:* 142, 143, 144
Nascimbene, Yan *133:* 128; *173:* 132, 133
Nash, Lesa *87:* 135
Nash, Linell *46:* 175
Nash, Scott *130:* 36; *188:* 196
Naso, John *33:* 183
Nason, Thomas W. *14:* 68
Nasser, Muriel *48:* 74

Nast, Thomas *21:* 29; *28:* 23; *51:* 132, 133, 134, 135,136, 137, 138, 139, 141
Nasta, Vincent *78:* 185
Natale, Vincent *76:* 3; *78:* 125; *112:* 47; *166:* 81; *174:* 189; *185:* 212; *197:* 59
Natchev, Alexi *96:* 177
Nathan, Charlott *125:* 151
Nathan, Cheryl *150:* 104; *186:* 112
Natti, Susanna *20:* 146; *32:* 141, 142; *35:* 178; *37:* 143; *71:* 49; *93:* 98; *125:* 166, 168; *126:* 228; *151:* 6; *178:* 8; *188:* 106
Navarra, Celeste Scala *8:* 142
Naylor, Penelope *10:* 104
Nazz, James *72:* 8
Nebel, M. *45:* 154
Neebe, William *7:* 93
Needham, Dave *196:* 85
Needler, Jerry *12:* 93
Neel, Alice *31:* 23
Neely, Beth *119:* 184
Neely, Keith R. *46:* 124
Neff, Leland *78:* 74
Negri, Rocco *3:* 213; *5:* 67; *6:* 91, 108; *12:* 159
Negrin, Fabian *174:* 125; *175:* 15
Neidigh, Sherry *128:* 53; *204:* 101, 102, 103
Neilan, Eujin Kim *180:* 241; *200:* 151, 152
Neill, John R. *18:* 8, 10, 11, 21, 30; *100:* 22
Neilsen, Cliff *158:* 131; *177:* 112, 121
Neilsen, Terese *116:* 74
Nelson, Craig *62:* 151; 153; *183:* 86
Nelson, Gail White *68:* 140
Nelson, Jennifer *129:* 152; *199:* 132
Nelson, Kadir *151:* 185; *154:* 146, 147; *157:* 189, 222; *181:* 122, 124; *197:* 155
Nelson, S.D. *131:* 34; *181:* 126, 127
Ness, Evaline *1:* 164, 165; *2:* 39; *3:* 8; *10:* 147; *12:* 53; *26:* 150, 151, 152, 153; *49:* 30, 31, 32; *56:* 30; *60:* 113
Neubecker, Robert *170:* 143
Neville, Vera *2:* 182
Nevins, Daniel *191:* 173
Nevwirth, Allan *79:* 168
Newberry, Clare Turlay *1:* 170
Newbold, Greg *108:* 125; *145:* 199; *151:* 23; *193:* 178; *197:* 10; *199:* 92, 93
Newfeld, Frank *14:* 121; *26:* 154
Newman, Andy *149:* 61; *195:* 63
Newman, Ann *43:* 90
Newman, Barbara Johansen *191:* 137, 138
Newsham, Ian *143:* 162
Newsom, Carol *40:* 159; *44:* 60; *47:* 189; *65:* 29; *70:* 192; *80:* 36; *85:* 137, 138; *92:* 167; *191:* 82
Newsom, Tom *49:* 149; *71:* 13, 62; *75:* 156; *91:* 113
Newton, Jill *83:* 105; *200:* 154
Ng, Michael *29:* 171
Ng, Simon *167:* 7
Nguyen, Vincent *189:* 49
Nicholson, William *15:* 33, 34; *16:* 48
Nickens, Bessie *104:* 153
Nicklaus, Carol *45:* 194; *62:* 132, 133
Nickle, John *181:* 128
Nickless, Will *16:* 139
Nicholas, Corasue *154:* 20
Nicolas *17:* 130, 132, 133; *YABC 2:* 215
Niebrugge, Jane *6:* 118
Nielsen, Cliff *95:* 207, 208; *105:* 58; *114:* 112; *124:* 12; *125:* 91, 92; *132:* 224; *135:* 187; *136:* 40; *137:* 168; *145:* 54; *149:* 28; *158:* 129; *165:* 64, 158; *168:* 169; *170:* 6; *175:* 114, 116; *187:* 75, 76; *194:* 107; *197:* 172; *201:* 14
Nielsen, Jon *6:* 100; *24:* 202
Nielsen, Kay *15:* 7; *16:* 211, 212, 213, 215, 217; *22:* 143; *YABC 1:* 32, 33
Niemann, Christoph *191:* 141
Nikola-Lisa, W. *180:* 180
Niland, Deborah *25:* 191; *27:* 156; *135:* 50; *172:* 143

Niland, Kilmeny *25:* 191; *75:* 143
Nino, Alex *59:* 145
Ninon *1:* 5; *38:* 101, 103, 108
Nissen, Rie *44:* 35
Nithael, Mark *158:* 237
Nivola, Claire A. *78:* 126; *140:* 147
Nixon, K. *14:* 152
Nobati, Eugenia *194:* 118
Noble, Louise *61:* 170
Noble, Marty *97:* 168; *125:* 171
Noble, Trinka Hakes *39:* 162; *84:* 157
Noda, Takayo *168:* 143
Noguchi, Yoshie *30:* 99
Nolan, Dennis *42:* 163; *67:* 163; *78:* 189; *82:* 225; *83:* 26; *92:* 169, 170; *103:* 166; *111:* 35; *112:* 213; *127:* 171; *166:* 161; *194:* 218
Noll, Sally *82:* 171
Nolte, Larry *121:* 63, 65
Nones, Eric Jon *61:* 111; *76:* 38; *77:* 177
Noonan, Daniel *100:* 224
Noonan, Julia *4:* 163; *7:* 207; *25:* 151; *91:* 29; *95:* 149
Norcia, Ernie *108:* 155; *140:* 47
Nordenskjold, Birgitta *2:* 208
Noreika, Robert *173:* 20
Norling, Beth *149:* 153, 154
Norman, Elaine *77:* 72, 176; *94:* 35; *136:* 63; *178:* 42
Norman, Mary *36:* 138, 147
Norman, Michael *12:* 117; *27:* 168
Northway, Jennifer *85:* 96
Nostlinger, Christiana *162:* 131
Novak, Linda *166:* 205
Novak, Matt *104:* 132, 133; *165:* 173, 174; *204:* 104, 106
Novelli, Luca *61:* 137
Nugent, Cynthia *106:* 189; *205:* 126, 127
Numeroff, Laura Joffe *28:* 161; *30:* 177
Nurse, Chris *164:* 91
Nussbaumer, Paul *16:* 219; *39:* 117
Nutt, Ken *72:* 69; *97:* 170
Nyce, Helene *19:* 219
Nygren, Tord *30:* 148; *127:* 164

O

Oakley, Graham *8:* 112; *30:* 164, 165; *84:* 188,189, 190, 191, 192
Oakley, Thornton *YABC 2:* 189
Oberheide, Heide *118:* 37
Obligado, Lilian *2:* 28, 66, 67; *6:* 30; *14:* 179; *15:* 103; *25:* 84; *61:* 138, 139, 140, 141, 143
Oblinski, Rafael *190:* 139
Obrant, Susan *11:* 186
O'Brien, Anne Sibley *53:* 116, 117; *155:* 115
O'Brien, John *41:* 253; *72:* 12; *89:* 59, 60; *98:* 16; *161:* 185; *169:* 16; *180:* 196
O'Brien, Patrick *193:* 142, 143, 144
O'Brien, Teresa *87:* 89
O'Brien, Tim *93:* 25; *136:* 94; *164:* 57; *169:* 57; *173:* 55; *175:* 86; *184:* 192; *191:* 134; *193:* 137
O'Clair, Dennis *127:* 25
O'Connor, George *183:* 153
Odell, Carole *35:* 47
Odem, Mel *99:* 164; *167:* 84, 87
O'Donohue, Thomas *40:* 89
Oechsli, Kelly *5:* 144, 145; *7:* 115; *8:* 83, 183; *13:* 117; *20:* 94; *81:* 199
Offen, Hilda *42:* 207
Ogden, Bill *42:* 59; *47:* 55
Ogg, Oscar *33:* 34
Ogle, Nancy Gray *163:* 144
Ohi, Ruth *90:* 175, 177; *131:* 63; *135:* 106; *175:* 107; *179:* 55
Ohlsson, Ib *4:* 152; *7:* 57; *10:* 20; *11:* 90; *19:* 217; *41:* 246; *82:* 106; *92:* 213
Ohtomo, Yasuo *37:* 146; *39:* 212, 213
O'Keefe, Jennifer *136:* 184

O'Kelley, Mattie Lou *36:* 150
Olbinski, Rafal *149:* 27; *158:* 77; *203:* 36
Oleynikov, Igor *202:* 134
Oliver, Isaac *171:* 182
Oliver, Jenni *23:* 121; *35:* 112
Oliver, Narelle *152:* 192; *197:* 129, 130
Oller, Erika *128:* 186; *134:* 126
Olschewski, Alfred *7:* 172
Olsen, Ib Spang *6:* 178, 179; *81:* 164
Olson, Alan *77:* 229
Olson-Brown, Ellen *183:* 154
Olugebefola, Ademola *15:* 205
O'Malley, Kevin *94:* 180; *106:* 8; *113:* 108; *136:* 70; *157:* 193; *191:* 146; *203:* 78
O'Neil, Dan IV *7:* 176
O'Neill, Catharine *72:* 113; *84:* 78; *134:* 153
O'Neill, Jean *22:* 146
O'Neill, Martin *187:* 39; *203:* 118
O'Neill, Michael J. *54:* 172
O'Neill, Rose *48:* 30, 31
O'Neill, Steve *21:* 118
Ono, Chiyo *7:* 97
Orbaan, Albert *2:* 31; *5:* 65, 171; *9:* 8; *14:* 241; *20:* 109
Orbach, Ruth *21:* 112
Orback, Craig *197:* 132
Orfe, Joan *20:* 81
Org, Ed *119:* 93
Ormai, Stella *72:* 129
Ormerod, Jan *55:* 124; *70:* 170, 171; *90:* 39; *132:* 172, 173, 174; *147:* 98
Ormsby, Virginia H. *11:* 187
O'Rourke, Ericka *108:* 216; *117:* 194; *111:* 142; *119:* 194; *137:* 152; *150:* 134; *167:* 64; *172:* 164; *188:* 163; *191:* 172; *201:* 15; *203:* 75
O'Rourke, Ericka Meltzer
  See O'Rourke, Ericka
Orozco, Jose Clemente *9:* 177
Orr, Forrest W. *23:* 9
Orr, N. *19:* 70
Ortiz, Vilma *88:* 158
Osborn, Kathy *152:* 232; *199:* 101, 102
Osborn, Robert *65:* 49
Osborne, Billie Jean *35:* 209
Osmond, Edward *10:* 111
O'Sullivan, Tom *3:* 176; *4:* 55; *78:* 195
Otani, June *124:* 42; *156:* 53
Otis, Rebecca *185:* 92
Ottley, Matt *147:* 221; *171:* 133
Otto, Svend *22:* 130, 141; *67:* 188, 189
Oudry, J.B. *18:* 167
Oughton, Taylor *5:* 23; *104:* 136
Overeng, Johannes *44:* 36
Overlie, George *11:* 156
Owens, Carl *2:* 35; *23:* 521
Owens, Gail *10:* 170; *12:* 157; *19:* 16; *22:* 70; *25:* 81; *28:* 203, 205; *32:* 221, 222; *36:* 132; *46:* 40; *47:* 57; *54:* 66, 67, 68, 69, 70, 71, 72, 73; *71:* 100; *73:* 64; *77:* 157; *80:* 32; *82:* 3; *99:* 226
Owens, Mary Beth *113:* 202, 203; *191:* 148, 149
Owens, Nubia *84:* 74
Oxenbury, Helen *3:* 150, 151; *24:* 81; *68:* 174, 175,176; *81:* 209; *84:* 213, 245; *129:* 56; *149:* 159; *184:* 181
Oz, Robin *88:* 167; *185:* 181

P

Padgett, Jim *12:* 165
Page, Gail *205:* 128
Page, Homer *14:* 145
Page, Mark *162:* 70
Paget, Sidney *24:* 90, 91, 93, 95, 97
Paget, Walter *64:* 122
Paillot, Jim *173:* 89
Pajouhesh, Noushin *160:* 121

Pak *12:* 76
Pak, Yu Cha *86:* 174
Paladino, Lance *134:* 30
Palazzo, Tony *3:* 152, 153
Palecek, Josef *56:* 136; *89:* 158
Palen, Debbie *135:* 88; *195:* 148, 149
Palencar, John Jude *84:* 12, 45; *85:* 87; *92:* 187; *99:* 128; *110:* 204; *150:* 122; *171:* 86
Palin, Nicki *81:* 201; *89:* 161
Palladini, David *4:* 113; *40:* 176, 177, 178, 179, 181,224, 225; *50:* 138; *78:* 186
Pallarito, Don *43:* 36
Palmer, Carol *158:* 230; *195:* 187
Palmer, Heidi *15:* 207; *29:* 102
Palmer, Jan *42:* 153; *82:* 161
Palmer, Judd *153:* 160, 161
Palmer, Juliette *6:* 89; *15:* 208
Palmer, Kate Salley *104:* 143; *154:* 169
Palmer, Lemuel *17:* 25, 29
Palmisciano, Diane *110:* 62; *162:* 26; *202:* 138, 139
Palmquist, Eric *38:* 133
Panesis, Nicholas *3:* 127
Panter, Gary *182:* 191
Panton, Doug *52:* 99
Paparone, Pamela *129:* 174
Papas, William *11:* 223; *50:* 160
Papin, Joseph *26:* 113
Papish, Robin Lloyd *10:* 80
Papp, Robert *198:* 41; *205:* 130
Paradis, Susan *40:* 216
Paraquin, Charles H. *18:* 166
Paris, Peter *31:* 127
Parisi, Elizabeth B. *141:* 82; *164:* 57
Park, Nick *113:* 143
Park, Seho *39:* 110
Park, W.B. *22:* 189
Parker, Ant *82:* 87, 88; *104:* 121
Parker, Lewis *2:* 179
Parker, Nancy Winslow *10:* 113; *22:* 164; *28:* 47, 144; *52:* 7; *69:* 153; *91:* 171, 174; *132:* 175
Parker, Robert *4:* 161; *5:* 74; *9:* 136; *29:* 39
Parker, Robert Andrew *11:* 81; *29:* 186; *39:* 165; *40:* 25; *41:* 78; *42:* 123; *43:* 144; *48:* 182; *54:* 140; *74:* 141; *91:* 24; *111:* 115; *151:* 201; *154:* 156; *200:* 163, 164
Parker-Rees, Guy *149:* 145; *193:* 149, 150
Parkin, Trevor *140:* 151
Parkins, David *114:* 123; *146:* 176; *176:* 168; *192:* 107
Parkinson, Kathy *71:* 143; *144:* 234
Parkinson, Keith *70:* 66
Parks, Gordon, Jr. *33:* 228
Parnall, Peter *5:* 137; *16:* 221; *24:* 70; *40:* 78; *51:* 130; *69:* 17, 155; *136:* 22, 23, 24
Parnall, Virginia *40:* 78
Parow, Lorraine *158:* 127
Parr, Todd *134:* 139, 140; *179:* 163, 164, 165
Parrish, Anne *27:* 159, 160
Parrish, Dillwyn *27:* 159
Parrish, Maxfield *14:* 160, 161, 164, 165; *16:* 109; *18:* 12, 13; *YABC 1:* 149, 152, 267; *2:* 146, 149
Parry, David *26:* 156
Parry, Marian *13:* 176; *19:* 179
Parsons, Garry *197:* 135
Partch, Virgil *45:* 163, 165
Pascal, David *14:* 174
Paschkis, Julie *177:* 153, 154
Pasquier, J.A. *16:* 91
Pastel, Elyse *201:* 123
Pasternak, Robert *119:* 53
Paterson, Diane *13:* 116; *39:* 163; *59:* 164, 165, 166,167; *72:* 51, 53; *129:* 175; *177:* 156, 157
Paterson, Helen *16:* 93
Patkau, Karen *112:* 123
Paton, Jane *15:* 271; *35:* 176
Patrick, John *139:* 190
Patrick, Pamela *90:* 160; *93:* 211; *105:* 12

Patrick, Tom *190:* 103
Patterson, Geoffrey *54:* 75
Patterson, Robert *25:* 118
Patti, Joyce *187:* 145, 146
Patz, Nancy *111:* 40; *154:* 161
Paul, James *4:* 130; *23:* 161
Paul, Korky *102:* 85
Paull, Grace *24:* 157; *87:* 127
Paulsen, Ruth Wright *79:* 160, 164; *189:* 146
Pavlov, Elena *80:* 49
Payne, Adam S. *135:* 166
Payne, C.F. *145:* 138, 140; *179:* 168
Payne, Joan Balfour *1:* 118
Payne, Tom *170:* 27
Payson, Dale *7:* 34; *9:* 151; *20:* 140; *37:* 22
Payzant, Charles *21:* 147
Peacock, Ralph *64:* 118
Peake, Mervyn *22:* 136, 149; *23:* 162, 163, 164; *YABC2:* 307
Pearson, Larry *38:* 225
Pearson, Tracey Campbell *64:* 163, 164, 167, 168, 169; *118:* 51; *156:* 169, 171, 172; *163:* 140
Peat, Fern B. *16:* 115
Peck, Anne Merriman *18:* 241; *24:* 155
Peck, Beth *66:* 242; *79:* 166; *80:* 136; *91:* 34; *95:* 9; *101:* 77; *164:* 197; *190:* 170
Peddicord, Jane Ann *199:* 106
Pedersen, Janet *193:* 152
Pedersen, Judy *66:* 217; *121:* 36; *172:* 67
Pedersen, Vilhelm *YABC 1:* 40
Pederson, Sharleen *12:* 92
Pedlar, Elaine *161:* 45
Peek, Merle *39:* 168
Peet, Bill *2:* 203; *41:* 159, 160, 161, 162, 163; *78:* 158, 159, 160, 161
Peguero, Adrian *116:* 133
Peguero, Gerard *116:* 133
Pels, Winslow Pinney *55:* 126
Peltier, Leslie C. *13:* 178
Peltzer, Marc *202:* 92
Penberthy, Mark *171:* 78
Pendle, Alexy *7:* 159; *13:* 34; *29:* 161; *33:* 215; *86:* 62
Pendola, Joanne *76:* 203; *81:* 125; *105:* 181; *178:* 152, 153
Pene du Bois, William *4:* 70; *10:* 122; *26:* 61; *27:* 145, 211; *35:* 243; *41:* 216; *68:* 180, 181; *73:* 45
Penfound, David *102:* 185
Pennington, Eunice *27:* 162
Peppe, Mark *28:* 142
Peppe, Rodney *4:* 164, 165; *74:* 187, 188, 189
Pepper, Hubert *64:* 143
Percy, Graham *63:* 2
Pericoli, Matteo *178:* 177
Perini, Ben *173:* 77
Perkins, David *60:* 68
Perkins, Lucy Fitch *72:* 199
Perkins, Lynne Rae *172:* 146
Perl, Susan *2:* 98; *4:* 231; *5:* 44, 45, 118; *6:* 199; *8:* 137; *12:* 88; *22:* 193; *34:* 54, 55; *52:* 128; *YABC 1:* 176
Perrone, Donna *78:* 166
Perry, Marie Fritz *165:* 180
Perry, Patricia *29:* 137; *30:* 171
Perry, Roger *27:* 163
Perske, Martha *46:* 83; *51:* 108, 147
Persson, Stina *175:* 166
Pesek, Ludek *15:* 237
Petach, Heidi *149:* 166; *200:* 207
Peters, David *72:* 205; *182:* 116
Petersen, Jeff *181:* 95
Petersham, Maud *17:* 108, 147, 148, 149, 150, 151, 152, 153
Petersham, Miska *17:* 108, 147, 148, 149, 150, 151, 152, 153
Peterson, Eric *109:* 125
Peterson, Nisse *99:* 27
Peterson, R.F. *7:* 101
Peterson, Russell *7:* 130

Petie, Haris *2:* 3; *10:* 41, 118; *11:* 227; *12:* 70
Petricic, Dusan *153:* 75, 76, 77; *170:* 12; *172:* 13; *176:* 170; *179:* 56
Petrides, Heidrun *19:* 223
Petrone, Valeria *159:* 160; *171:* 92; *186:* 173; *204:* 49
Petrosino, Tamara *177:* 40; *193:* 154, 155
Petruccio, Steven James *67:* 159; *127:* 5
Pettingill, Ondre *64:* 181; *70:* 64
Peyo *40:* 56, 57
Peyton, K.M. *15:* 212
Pfeifer, Herman *15:* 262
Pfister, Marcus *83:* 165, 166, 167; *146:* 152; *150:* 160
Pfloog, Jan *124:* 60
Pham, LeUyen *160:* 48; *175:* 154, 156; *179:* 149; *201:* 124, 125, 126, 127; *204:* 28
Phelan, Matt *182:* 160; *184:* 222
Phillips, Craig *70:* 151
Phillips, Douglas *1:* 19
Phillips, F.D. *6:* 202
Phillips, Louise *133:* 67
Phillips, Matt *184:* 173
Phillips, Thomas *30:* 55
Philpot, Glyn *54:* 46
Phiz
 See Browne, Hablot K.
Piatti, Celestino *16:* 223
Pica, Steve *115:* 181
Picarella, Joseph *13:* 147
Picart, Gabriel *121:* 165; *201:* 169
Pichon, Liz *174:* 139
Pickard, Charles *12:* 38; *18:* 203; *36:* 152
Picken, George A. *23:* 150
Pickens, David *22:* 156
Pickering, Jimmy *195:* 152; *197:* 163
Pienkowski, Jan *6:* 183; *30:* 32; *58:* 140, 141, 142,143, 146, 147; *73:* 3; *87:* 156, 157; *131:* 189
Pieper, Christiane *200:* 168
Pignataro, Anna *163:* 220 *Pileggi, Steve 145:* 122
Pilkey, Dav *68:* 186; *115:* 164, 166; *166:* 173, 174, 175
Pimlott, John *10:* 205
Pincus, Harriet *4:* 186; *8:* 179; *22:* 148; *27:* 164, 166; *66:* 202
Pini, Wendy *89:* 166
Pinkett, Neil *60:* 8
Pinkney, Brian *81:* 184, 185; *94:* 107; *113:* 146, 147; *117:* 121, 166; *132:* 145; *158:* 108, 191; *189:* 200: 8
Pinkney, Jerry *8:* 218; *10:* 40; *15:* 276; *20:* 66; *24:* 121; *33:* 109; *36:* 222; *38:* 200; *41:* 165, 166, 167, 168, 169, 170, 171, 173, 174; *44:* 198; *48:* 51; *53:* 20; *56:* 61, 68; *58:* 184; *60:* 59; *61:* 91; *71:* 146, 148, 149; *72:* 17; *73:* 149; *74:* 159,192; *75:* 45; *80:* 206; *81:* 44; *85:* 144; *95:* 50; *107:* 158, 159, 160; *108:* 164; *112:* 114, 115; *133:* 58; *195:* 140
Pinkwater, Daniel Manus *46:* 180, 181, 182, 185, 188, 189, 190; *151:* 161 76: 178, 179, 180
Pinkwater, Manus *8:* 156; *46:* 180
 See also Pinkwater, Daniel Manus
Pinkwater, Jill *114:* 160, 161; *158:* 179; *188:* 143, 145, 146
Pinto, Ralph *10:* 131; *45:* 93
Pinto, Sara *200:* 165
Pinon, Mark *74:* 22
Piven, Hanoch *173:* 142
Pistolesi *73:* 211
Pitcairn, Ansel *188:* 10
Pittman, Helena Clare *71:* 151
Pitz, Henry C. *4:* 168; *19:* 165; *35:* 128; *42:* 80; *YABC 2:* 95, 176
Pitzenberger, Lawrence J. *26:* 94
Pitzer, Susanna *181:* 131
Player, Stephen *82:* 190
Plecas, Jennifer *84:* 201; *106:* 124; *149:* 168; *205:* 180

Ploog, Mike *180:* 19
Plowden, David *52:* 135, 136
Plume, Ilse *170:* 149
Plummer, William *32:* 31
Podevin, Jean François *184:* 185
Podwal, Mark *56:* 170, 173; *101:* 154, 155, 157; *149:* 176; *160:* 194
Pogany, Willy *15:* 46, 49; *19:* 222, 256; *25:* 214; *44:* 142, 143, 144, 145, 146, 147, 148
Pohrt, Tom *67:* 116; *104:* 80; *152:* 199; *195:* 154; *199:* 85
Poirson, V.A. *26:* 89
Polacco, Patricia *74:* 195, 196, 197, 198; *123:* 121, 122, 123; *180:* 189, 190, 191, 193, 194
Polgreen, John *21:* 44
Politi, Leo *1:* 178; *4:* 53; *21:* 48; *47:* 173,174, 176, 178, 179, 180, 181
Pollema-Cahill, Phyllis *123:* 126
Pollen, Samson *64:* 80
Polonsky, Arthur *34:* 168
Polseno, Jo *1:* 53; *3:* 117; *5:* 114; *17:* 154; *20:* 87; *32:* 49; *41:* 245
Pomaska, Anna *117:* 148
Pons, Bernadette *184:* 100
Ponter, James *5:* 204
Poole, Colin *111:* 27
Poortvliet, Rien *6:* 212; *65:* 165, 166, 167
Pope, Kevin *183:* 158
Popp, Wendy *72:* 122; *158:* 68
Poppel, Hans *71:* 154, 155
Porfirio, Guy *76:* 134
Portal, Colette *6:* 186; *11:* 203
Porter, George *7:* 181
Porter, Janice Lee *136:* 175; *164:* 37
Porter, John *113:* 47
Porter, Pat Grant *84:* 112; *125:* 101
Porter, Sue *146:* 246, 247
Porter, Walter *124:* 175
Posada, Mia *187:* 151
Posen, Michael *175:* 82
Posthuma, Sieb *150:* 163
Postier, Jim *202:* 140; *204:* 25
Postma, Lidia *79:* 17
Potter, Beatrix *100:* 194, 195; *132:* 179, 180, 181, 182; *YABC 1:* 208, 209, 210, 212, 213
Potter, Giselle *117:* 123; *143:* 44; *144:* 170, 197; *149:* 7; *150:* 165; *187:* 152, 153; *190:* 198; *196:* 152; *200:* 12
Potter, Katherine *104:* 147; *171:* 135; *173:* 136
Potter, Miriam Clark *3:* 162
Poulin, Stephane *98:* 140, 141
Poullis, Nick *146:* 210
Powell, Constance Buffington *174:* 141
Powell, Gary *151:* 208
Powell, Ivan *67:* 219
Power, Margaret *105:* 122
Powers, Daniel *161:* 173
Powers, Richard M. *1:* 230; *3:* 218; *7:* 194; *26:* 186
Powledge, Fred *37:* 154
Powzyk, Joyce *74:* 214
Poydar, Nancy *96:* 149; *190:* 180, 181, 182
Pracher, Richard *91:* 166
Prachaticka, Marketa *126:* 126
Prange, Beckie *181:* 169
Prap, Lila *177:* 165
Prater, John *103:* 142, 143, 144; *149:* 172
Pratt, Charles *23:* 29
Pratt, George *116:* 208
Pratt, Pierre *150:* 73; *166:* 183; *168:* 172; *201:* 27
Prebenna, David *73:* 174
Preiss-Glasser, Robin *123:* 176; *152* 40; *172:* 194
Press, Jenny *116:* 95
Preston, Mark *152:* 162
Pretro, Korinna *91:* 126
Price, Christine *2:* 247; *3:* 163, 253; *8:* 166
Price, Cynthia *118:* 156
Price, Edward *33:* 34
Price, Garrett *1:* 76; *2:* 42

Price, Hattie Longstreet *17:* 13
Price, Norman *YABC 1:* 129
Price, Willard *48:* 184
Priceman, Marjorie *81:* 171; *136:* 169; *156:* 200; *168:* 153, 154; *188:* 45
Priestley, Alice *168:* 33
Priestley, Chris *198:* 144
Primavera, Elise *26:* 95; *58:* 151; *73:* 37; *80:* 79; *86:* 156; *105:* 161
Primrose, Jean *36:* 109
Prince, Alison *86:* 188, 189
Prince, Leonora E. *7:* 170
Pritchett, Shelley *116:* 148
Prittie, Edwin J. *YABC 1:* 120
Proimos, James *176:* 4
Proimos, John *173:* 144
Prosmitsky, Jenya *132:* 33
Provensen, Alice *37:* 204, 215, 222; *70:* 176, 177, 178, 180; *71:* 213; *147:* 184; *191:* 190
Provensen, Martin *37:* 204, 215, 222; *70:* 176, 177, 178, 180; *71:* 213; *191:* 190
Pucci, Albert John *44:* 154
Pudlo *8:* 59
Puggaard, Ulla *196:* 25
Pulver, Harry, Jr. *129:* 159
Pulver, Robin *160:* 4
Punchatz, Don *99:* 57
Purdy, Susan *8:* 162
Pursell, Weimer *55:* 18
Purtscher, Alfons *97:* 6
Puskas, James *5:* 141
Pyk, Jan *7:* 26; *38:* 123
Pyle, Chuck *99:* 149; *191:* 83
Pyle, Howard *16:* 225, 226, 227, 228, 230, 231, 232, 235; *24:* 27; *34:* 124, 125, 127, 128; *59:* 132; *100:* 198

Q

Quackenbush, Robert *4:* 190; *6:* 166; *7:* 175, 178; *9:* 86; *11:* 65, 221; *41:* 154; *43:* 157; *70:* 185, 186; *71:* 137; *85:* 47; *92:* 148; *133:* 154, 164, 169
Qualls, Sean *177:* 167, 168; *193:* 43
Quennell, Marjorie (Courtney) *29:* 163, 164
Quidor, John *19:* 82
Quirk, John *62:* 170
Quirk, Thomas *12:* 81

R

Rackham, Arthur *15:* 32, 78, 214-227; *17:* 105, 115; *18:* 233; *19:* 254; *20:* 151; *22:* 129, 131, 132, 133; *23:* 175; *24:* 161, 181; *26:* 91; *32:* 118; *64:* 18; *100:* 9, 16, 203, 204; *YABC 1:* 25, 45, 55, 147; *2:* 103, 142, 173, 210
Racz, Michael *56:* 134
Raczka, Bob *191:* 155, 156
Radcliffe, Andrew *82:* 215
Rader, Laura *101:* 219; *197:* 147; *203:* 53
Radunsky, Vladimir *177:* 170; *192:* 30
Rafilson, Sidney *11:* 172
Raglin, Tim *125:* 24
Raible, Alton *1:* 202, 203; *28:* 193; *35:* 181; *110:* 207
Raine, Patricia *82:* 74; *88:* 154
Ramá, Sue *173:* 45; *185:* 186; *190:* 184
Ramhorst, John *117:* 11
Ramirez, Gladys *177:* 19
Ramsey, James *16:* 41
Ramsey, Marcy Dunn *82:* 11; *180:* 186
Ramus, Michael *51:* 171
Rand, Paul *6:* 188

Rand, Ted *67:* 9, 10, 121, 123; *74:* 190; *84:* 170; *103:* 170; *112:* 6; *114:* 73; *139:* 168; *143:* 194; *156:* 154; *161:* 9, 10; *200:* 38; *204:* 7
Randazzo, Tony *81:* 98
Randell, William *55:* 54
Rane, Walter *93:* 144; *143:* 109; *184:* 126
Rankin, Joan *163:* 40
Rankin, Laura *176:* 173, 174; *179:* 150
Ransome, Arthur *22:* 201
Ransome, James E. *74:* 137; *75:* 80; *84:* 181; *94:* 108; *117:* 115; *123:* 128, 129, 130; *158:* 101, 102; *159:* 205; *178:* 188, 189, 190
Rantz, Don *119:* 184
Rao, Anthony *28:* 126
Raphael, Elaine *23:* 192; *71:* 24, 25
Rappaport, Eva *6:* 190
Raschka, Chris *80:* 187, 189, 190; *97:* 211; *115:* 210; *117:* 151, 152, 153, 154; *143:* 195; *145:* 153; *166:* 190, 191; *170:* 114
Rash, Andy *158:* 178; *162:* 172
Raskin, Ellen *2:* 208, 209; *4:* 142; *13:* 183; *22:* 68; *29:* 139; *36:* 134; *38:* 173, 174, 175, 176, 177, 178,179, 180, 181; *60:* 163; *86:* 81
Rathmann, Peggy *93:* 32; *94:* 168; *157:* 212, 214
Ratkus, Tony *77:* 133
Ratzkin, Lawrence *40:* 143
Rau, Margaret *9:* 157
Raverat, Gwen *YABC 1:* 152
Ravid, Joyce *61:* 73
Ravielli, Anthony *1:* 198; *3:* 168; *11:* 143
Ravilious, Robin *77:* 169
Rawlins, Donna *72:* 198; *73:* 15, 129
Rawlins, Janet *76:* 79
Rawlings, Steve *143:* 139; *151:* 54
Rawlinson, Debbie *75:* 132
Ray, Deborah Kogan *8:* 164; *29:* 238; *50:* 112, 113; *62:* 119; *78:* 191; *203:* 149, 150, 151
Ray, Jane *96:* 166; *97:* 104; *152:* 208; *190:* 221; *196:* 165
Ray, Ralph *2:* 239; *5:* 73
Rayann, Omar *162:* 205; *186:* 29, 30
Rayevsky, Robert *64:* 17; *70:* 173; *80:* 204; *117:* 79; *190:* 187, 188
Raymond, Larry *31:* 108; *97:* 109
Rayner, Hugh *151:* 170
Rayner, Mary *22:* 207; *47:* 140; *72:* 191; *87:* 171, 172; *192:* 104
Rayner, Shoo
    See Rayner, Hugh
Raynes, John *71:* 19
Raynor, Dorka *28:* 168
Raynor, Paul *24:* 73
Rayyan, Omar *110:* 222; *112:* 17; *125:* 131
Razzi, James *10:* 127
Read, Alexander D. *20:* 45
Reader, Dennis *71:* 157
Reasoner, Charles *53:* 33, 36, 37
Rebenschied, Shane *203:* 76
Reczuch, Karen *115:* 132; *145:* 131
Redlich, Ben *163:* 221; *198:* 193
Reddy, Mike *203:* 67
Reed, Joseph *116:* 139
Reed, Lynn Rowe *115:* 173; *171:* 146
Reed, Tom *34:* 171
Reeder, Colin *74:* 202; *77:* 113
Rees, Mary *134:* 219
Reese, Bob *60:* 135
Reeve, Philip *171:* 50
Reeves, Eira B. *130:* 173, 174; *141:* 151
Reeves, Rick *181:* 179
Reeves, Rosie *202:* 200
Regan, Dana *117:* 116
Regan, Laura *103:* 198; *153:* 206
Reichert, Renée *169:* 127
Reid, Barbara *82:* 178; *92:* 17; *93:* 169, 170
Reid, Stephen *19:* 213; *22:* 89
Reim, Melanie *104:* 151; *150:* 98
Reinert, Kirk *89:* 138; *195:* 129
Reinertson, Barbara *44:* 150; *62:* 103

Reiniger, Lotte *40:* 185
Reisberg, Mira *119:* 2
Reisch, Jesse *158:* 130
Reiser, Lynn *81:* 175; *138:* 184; *180:* 200
Reiss, John J. *23:* 193
Relf, Douglas *3:* 63
Relyea, C.M. *16:* 29; *31:* 153
Remi, Georges *13:* 184
Remington, Frederic *19:* 188; *41:* 178, 179, 180, 181, 183,184, 185, 186, 187, 188; *62:* 197
Remkiewicz, Frank *67:* 102; *77:* 171; *80:* 130; *113:* 107; *152:* 116; *152:* 211, 212; *157:* 148
Rendon, Maria *116:* 141; *192:* 134; *134:* 152
Renfro, Ed *79:* 176
Renier, Aaron *202:* 141
Renlie, Frank *11:* 200
Reschofsky, Jean *7:* 118
Rethi *60:* 181
Rethi, Lili *2:* 153; *36:* 156
Reusswig, William *3:* 267
Revell, Cindy *195:* 93
Rex, Adam *156:* 172; *169:* 91; *186:* 178, 179
Rex, Michael *157:* 147; *191:* 159, 160
Rey, H.A. *1:* 182; *26:* 163, 164, 166, 167, 169; *69:* 172, 173, 174, 175; *86:* 195, 196, 197; *100:* 211; *YABC 2:* 17
Rey, Luis V. *201:* 162
Reynolds, Adrian *192:* 159, 160
Reynolds, Doris *5:* 71; *31:* 77
Reynolds, Peter H. *142:* 12; *179:* 175, 176; *202:* 113, 114
Rhead, Louis *31:* 91; *100:* 228
Rhodes, Andrew *38:* 204; *50:* 163; *54:* 76; *61:* 123, 124; *87:* 200
Ribbons, Ian *3:* 10; *37:* 161; *40:* 76
Ricci, Regolo *93:* 22; *164:* 148
Rice, Elizabeth *2:* 53, 214
Rice, Eve *34:* 174, 175; *91:* 172
Rice, James *22:* 210; *93:* 173
Rich, Martha *195:* 16
Richards, Chuck *170:* 154
Richards, George *40:* 116, 119, 121; *44:* 179
Richards, Henry *YABC 1:* 228, 231
Richardson, Ernest *2:* 144
Richardson, Frederick *18:* 27, 31
Richardson, John *110:* 88
Richman, Hilda *26:* 132
Richmond, George *24:* 179
Riddell, Chris *114:* 170, 195; *166:* 179; *199:* 164, 166, 167
Riddle, Tohby *74:* 204; *151:* 179
Riding, Peter *63:* 195
Rieniets, Judy King *14:* 28
Riger, Bob *2:* 166
Riggio, Anita *73:* 191; *85:* 63; *137:* 184; *172:* 165
Riley, Jon *74:* 70
Riley, Kenneth *22:* 230
Riley, Terry *203:* 100
Riley-Webb, Charlotte *153:* 143
Rinaldi, Angelo *165:* 60, 69
Ringgold, Faith *71:* 162; *114:* 173, 174, 176; *187:* 160, 161, 163
Ringi, Kjell *12:* 171
Rios, Tere
   See Versace, Marie
Ripper, Charles L. *3:* 175
Ripplinger, Henry *117:* 31
Ritchie, William *74:* 183
Ritter, John *175:* 14
Ritz, Karen *41:* 117; *72:* 239; *87:* 125; *102:* 7; *106:* 6
Rivers, Ruth *178:* 193
Rivkin, Jay *15:* 230
Rivoche, Paul *45:* 125
Roach, Marilynne *9:* 158
Robbin, Jodi *44:* 156, 159
Robbins, Frank *42:* 167
Robbins, Ken *147:* 191, 192
Robbins, Ruth *52:* 102

Roberts, Cliff *4:* 126
Roberts, David *154:* 4, 6; *191:* 162; *196:* 184; *197:* 105
Roberts, Doreen *4:* 230; *28:* 105
Roberts, Jim *22:* 166; *23:* 69; *31:* 110
Roberts, Tony *109:* 195, 214
Roberts, W. *22:* 2, 3
Robertson, M.P. *197:* 153
Robins, Arthur *137:* 172; *151:* 225; *204:* 161
Robinson, Aminah Brenda Lynn *86:* 205; *103:* 55; *159:* 175
Robinson, Charles [1870-1937] *17:* 157, 171, 172, 173, 175, 176; *24:* 207; *25:* 204; *YABC 2:* 308, 309, 310, 331
Robinson, Charles *3:* 53; *5:* 14; *6:* 193; *7:* 150; *7:* 183; *8:* 38; *9:* 81; *13:* 188; *14:* 248, 249; *23:* 149; *26:* 115; *27:* 48; *28:* 191; *32:* 28; *35:* 210; *36:* 37; *48:* 96; *52:* 33; *53:* 157; *56:* 15; *62:* 142; *77:* 41; *111:* 148
Robinson, Jerry *3:* 262
Robinson, Joan G. *7:* 184
Robinson, Lolly *90:* 227
Robinson, T.H. *17:* 179, 181, 182, 183; *29:* 254
Robinson, W. Heath *17:* 185, 187, 189, 191, 193, 195, 197, 199, 202; *23:* 167; *25:* 194; *29:* 150; *YABC 1:* 44; *2:* 183
Rocco, John *187:* 4; *188:* 151
Roche, Christine *41:* 98
Roche, Denis *99:* 184; *180:* 32; *196:* 168
Roche, P.K. *57:* 151, 152
Rocker, Fermin *7:* 34; *13:* 21; *31:* 40; *40:* 190,191
Rocklen, Margot *101:* 181
Rockwell, Anne *5:* 147; *33:* 171, 173; *71:* 166, 167,168; *114:* 183, 184; *194:* 152, 155
Rockwell, Gail *7:* 186
Rockwell, Harlow *33:* 171, 173, 175
Rockwell, Lizzy *114:* 182; *162:* 182; *185:* 189
Rockwell, Norman *23:* 39, 196, 197, 199, 200, 203, 204, 207; *41:* 140, 143; *123:* 47; *YABC 2:* 60
Rockwood, Richard *119:* 75
Rodanas, Kristina *156:* 183, 184
Rodegast, Roland *43:* 100
Rodgers, Frank *69:* 177
Rodriguez, Albert G. *182:* 50
Rodriguez, Christina *184:* 12
Rodriguez, Edel *204:* 86
Rodriguez, Joel *16:* 65
Rodriguez, Robert *145:* 145
Rodriguez-Howard, Pauline *177:* 18
Roeckelein, Katrina *134:* 223
Roennfeldt, Robert *66:* 243
Roever, J.M. *4:* 119; *26:* 170
Roffey, Maureen *33:* 142, 176, 177
Rogasky, Barbara *46:* 90
Rogé *173:* 160
Rogers, Carol *2:* 262; *6:* 164; *26:* 129
Rogers, Chris M. *150:* 59; *196:* 61
Rogers, Forest *87:* 160; *101:* 76
Rogers, Frances *10:* 130
Rogers, Gregory *104:* 76; *126:* 57; *171:* 26
Rogers, Jacqueline *78:* 249; *80:* 34; *86:* 54 *103:* 70; *115:* 72; *129:* 173; *131:* 57, 225; *143:* 211; *153:* 100; *193:* 186; *203:* 51
Rogers, Sherry *191:* 66
Rogers, Walter S. *31:* 135, 138; *67:* 65, 168; *100:* 81
Rogers, William A. *15:* 151, 153, 154; *33:* 35
Rogoff, Barbara *95:* 20
Rohmann, Eric *103:* 152; *198:* 151
Rojankovsky, Feodor *6:* 134, 136; *10:* 183; *21:* 128,129, 130; *25:* 110; *28:* 42; *68:* 120
Rolfsen, Alf *62:* 15
Romain, Trevor *134:* 157
Roman, Barbara J. *103:* 171
Romas *114:* 111; *165:* 63
Romano, Robert *64:* 68
Romero, Alejandro *187:* 185
Roos, Maryn *168:* 198

Root, Barry *80:* 212; *90:* 196; *146:* 78; *156:* 165; *159:* 161; *182:* 18, 172
Root, Kimberly Bulcken *86:* 72; *98:* 21; *108:* 111; *127:* 114; *159:* 162; *176:* 134; *192:* 163
Roper, Bob *65:* 153
Roraback, Robin *111:* 156
Rorer, Abigail *43:* 222; *85:* 155
Rosales, Melodye *80:* 35
Rosamilia, Patricia *36:* 120
Rose, Carl *5:* 62
Rose, David S. *29:* 109; *70:* 120
Rose, Gerald *68:* 200, 201; *86:* 48
Rose, Ted *93:* 178
Rosen, Elizabeth *205:* 137
Rosenbaum, Jonathan *50:* 46
Rosenberg, Amye *74:* 207, 208
Rosenberry, Vera *87:* 22, 26; *144:* 212, 213; *158:* 120
Rosenblum, Richard *11:* 202; *18:* 18
Rosenstiehl, Agnès *203:* 153
Rosier, Lydia *16:* 236; *20:* 104; *21:* 109; *22:* 125; *30:* 151, 158; *42:* 128; *45:* 214; *77:* 227, 228
Rosing, Jens *85:* 142
Ross
   See Thomson, Ross
Ross, Christine *83:* 172, 173
Ross, Clare Romano *3:* 123; *21:* 45; *48:* 199
Ross, Dave *32:* 152; *57:* 108
Ross, Graham *199:* 4
Ross, Herbert *37:* 78
Ross, John *3:* 123; *21:* 45
Ross, Johnny *32:* 190
Ross, Larry *47:* 168; *60:* 62
Ross, Ruth *109:* 233
Ross, Tony *17:* 204; *56:* 132; *65:* 176, 177, 179; *90:* 123; *123:* 186, 187, 190; *130:* 188, 190, 191, 192; *132:* 242; *174:* 159; *176:* 181, 182, 183; *202:* 198
Rossetti, Dante Gabriel *20:* 151, 153
Rostant, Larry *180:* 221; *194:* 108; *195:* 96; *197:* 12
Roth, Arnold *4:* 238; *21:* 133
Roth, Julie Jersild *180:* 206
Roth, Marci *135:* 223
Roth, R.G. *184:* 50
Roth, Rob *105:* 98; *146:* 41
Roth, Robert *176:* 159
Roth, Roger *61:* 128; *190:* 192
Roth, Stephanie *136:* 171, 172
Roth, Susan L. *80:* 38; *93:* 78; *134:* 165, 166; *181:* 145, 146
Rothenberg, Joani Keller *162:* 190, 191
Rothman, Michael *139:* 62; *184:* 34 Rotman, Jeffrey L. *145:* 30
Rotondo, Pat *32:* 158
Roughsey, Dick *35:* 186
Rouille, M. *11:* 96
Rounds, Glen *8:* 173; *9:* 171; *12:* 56; *32:* 194; *40:* 230; *51:* 161, 162, 166; *56:* 149; *70:* 198, 199; *YABC 1:* 1, 2, 3; *112:* 163
Roundtree, Katherine *114:* 88; *168:* 102
Rovetch, Lissa *201:* 164
Rowan, Evadne *52:* 51
Rowe, Eric *111:* 161
Rowe, Gavin *27:* 144; *72:* 47; *88:* 201
Rowe, John *132:* 70, 71; *180:* 126
Rowell, Kenneth *40:* 72
Rowen, Amy *52:* 143
Rowena *116:* 101
Rowland, Andrew *164:* 136
Rowland, Jada *83:* 73
Rowles, Daphne *58:* 24
Roy, Jeroo *27:* 229; *36:* 110
Royo *118:* 32; *144:* 105, 106, 108; *165:* 19; *166:* 166
Rubel, Nicole *18:* 255; *20:* 59; *81:* 66, 67; *95:* 169, 170; *119:* 60; *135:* 177, 179, 180; *169:* 68; *181:* 150
Rubel, Reina *33:* 217
Rud, Borghild *6:* 15

Ruddell, Gary *110:* 238; *116:* 207
Rudolph, Norman Guthrie *17:* 13
Rue, Leonard Lee III *37:* 164
Rueda, Claudia *183:* 170, 171
Ruelle, Karen Gray *126:* 193
Ruff, Donna *50:* 173; *72:* 203; *78:* 49; *80:* 120,121; *93:* 162; *164:* 121
Ruffins, Reynold *10:* 134, 135; *41:* 191, 192, 193, 194, 195, 196; *125:* 187, 188, 189; *162:* 197
Ruhlin, Roger *34:* 44
Ruiz, Art *95:* 154; *110:* 91
Rumford, James *193:* 167
Runnerstroem, Bengt Arne *75:* 161
Ruse, Margaret *24:* 155
Rush, Ken *98:* 74
Rush, Peter *42:* 75
Russell, Charles M. *167:* 171
Russell, E.B. *18:* 177, 182
Russell, Jim *53:* 134
Russell, P. Craig *80:* 196; *146:* 102; *162:* 186
Russo, Marisabina *84:* 51; *106:* 164; *151:* 183; *188:* 153, 154, 155, 156
Russo, Susan *30:* 182; *36:* 144
Russon, Mary *87:* 145
Ruth, Greg *183:* 125
Ruth, Rod *9:* 161
Rutherford, Alexa *110:* 108
Rutherford, Jenny *78:* 5
Rutherford, Meg *25:* 174; *34:* 178, 179; *69:* 73; *72:* 31
Rutland, Jonathan *31:* 126
Ruurs, Margriet *147:* 195
Ruzzier, Sergio *159:* 176, 177; *163:* 184
Ryan, Amy *188:* 50
Ryan, Will *86:* 134
Ryden, Hope *8:* 176
Rylant, Cynthia *112:* 170, 172
Rymer, Alta M. *34:* 181
Ryniak, Christopher *178:* 11
Rystedt, Rex *49:* 80

S

Saaf, Chuck *49:* 179
Saaf, Donald *101:* 220; *124:* 180
Sabaka, Donna R. *21:* 172
Sabin, Robert *45:* 35; *60:* 30; *99:* 161
Sabuda, Robert *170:* 166, 167, 168
Sacker, Amy *16:* 100
Saelig, S.M. *129:* 73; *173:* 59
Saffioti, Lino *36:* 176; *48:* 60
Saflund, Birgitta *94:* 2
Sagsoorian, Paul *12:* 183; *22:* 154; *33:* 106; *87:* 152
Sahara, Tony *168:* 106; *177:* 181; *178:* 228; *186:* 132
Sahlberg, Myron *57:* 165
Saidens, Amy *145:* 162; *191:* 131
Saint Exupery, Antoine de *20:* 157
Saint James, Synthia *152:* 220; *188:* 90; *200:* 7
Saldutti, Denise *39:* 186; *57:* 178
Sale, Morton *YABC 2:* 31
Sale, Tim *153:* 177
Salerno, Steven *150:* 79; *176:* 188; *202:* 39
Salter, George *72:* 128, 130
Saltzberg, Barney *135:* 184, 185; *194:* 160
Saltzman, David *86:* 209
Salwowski, Mark *71:* 54
Salzman, Yuri *86:* 12
Sambourne, Linley *YABC 2:* 181
Sampson, Katherine *9:* 197
Samson, Anne S. *2:* 216
San Souci, Daniel *40:* 200; *96:* 199, 200; *113:* 171; *157:* 149; *170:* 69; *192:* 167, 168
Sancha, Sheila *38:* 185
Sanchez, Enrique O. *155:* 84
Sand, George X. *45:* 182
Sandberg, Lasse *15:* 239, 241
Sanders, Beryl *39:* 173
Sanderson, Ruth *21:* 126; *24:* 53; *28:* 63; *33:* 67; *41:* 48, 198, 199, 200, 201, 202, 203; *43:* 79; *46:* 36,44; *47:* 102; *49:* 58; *62:* 121, 122; *85:* 3; *109:* 207, 208, 209, 210; *172:* 157, 158
Sandia *119:* 74
Sandin, Joan *4:* 36; *6:* 194; *7:* 177; *12:* 145,185; *20:* 43; *21:* 74; *26:* 144; *27:* 142; *28:* 224, 225; *38:* 86; *41:* 46; *42:* 35; *59:* 6; *80:* 136; *94:* 188; *140:* 116; *153:* 179, 180; *197:* 168
Sandland, Reg *39:* 215
Sandoz, Edouard *26:* 45, 47
Sanford, John *66:* 96, 97
Sanger, Amy Wilson *205:* 140
Sankey, Tom *72:* 103
Sano, Kazuhiko *153:* 208; *195:* 171; *203:* 21
Santat, Dan *188:* 160
Santore, Charles *54:* 139; *200:* 171, 172
Santoro, Christopher *74:* 215
Santos, Jesse J. *99:* 24
Sapieha, Christine *1:* 180
Saport, Linda *123:* 137, 138
Sara
    See De La Roche Saint Andre, Anne
Sardinha, Rick *175:* 151
Sarg, Tony *YABC 2:* 236
Sargent, Claudia *64:* 181
Sargent, Robert *2:* 217
Saris *1:* 33
Sarony *YABC 2:* 170
Saroff, Phyllis V. *202:* 160
Sasaki, Goro *170:* 46
Sasek, Miroslav *16:* 239, 240, 241, 242
Sassman, David *9:* 79
Satty *29:* 203, 205
Sauber, Robert *40:* 183; *76:* 256; *78:* 154; *87:* 92
Saunders, Dave *85:* 163, 164, 165
Savadier, Elivia *84:* 50; *145:* 45; *164:* 206
Savage, Naomi *56:* 172
Savage, Steele *10:* 203; *20:* 77; *35:* 28
Savage, Stephen *174:* 182
Savio *76:* 4
Savitt, Sam *8:* 66, 182; *15:* 278; *20:* 96; *24:* 192; *28:* 98
Sawyer, Kem Knapp *84:* 228, 229
Say, Allen *28:* 178; *69:* 182, 183, 232; *110:* 194, 195,196; *161:* 154, 155
Sayles, Elizabeth *82:* 93; *105:* 155; *109:* 116; *180:* 64
Scabrini, Janet *13:* 191; *44:* 128
Scanlan, Peter *83:* 27; *153:* 165; *187:* 149
Scanlon, Paul *83:* 87
Scannell, Reece *105:* 105
Scarry, Huck *35:* 204, 205
Scarry, Richard *2:* 220, 221; *18:* 20; *35:* 193, 194, 195,196, 197, 198, 199, 200, 201, 202; *75:* 165, 167, 168
Schachner, Judith Byron *88:* 180; *92:* 163; *93:* 102; *142:* 82; *178:* 199, 200; *190:* 140
Schade, Susan *205:* 21
Schaeffer, Mead *18:* 81, 94; *21:* 137, 138, 139; *47:* 128
Schaffer, Amanda *90:* 206
Schanzer, Rosalyn *138:* 192, 193
Scharl, Josef *20:* 132; *22:* 128
Scheel, Lita *11:* 230
Scheffler, Axel *180:* 23, 24
Scheib, Ida *29:* 28
Schermer, Judith *30:* 184
Schick, Eleanor *82:* 210, 211; *144:* 222
Schick, Joel *16:* 160; *17:* 167; *22:* 12; *27:* 176; *31:* 147, 148; *36:* 23; *38:* 64; *45:* 116, 117; *52:* 5, 85; *104:* 159
Schields, Gretchen *75:* 171, 203
Schindelman, Joseph *1:* 74; *4:* 101; *12:* 49; *26:* 51; *40:* 146; *56:* 158; *73:* 40
Schindler, Edith *7:* 22
Schindler, S.D. *38:* 107; *46:* 196; *74:* 162; *75:* 172, 173; *99:* 133; *112:* 177; *118:* 185, 186; *121:* 71; *136:* 159; *143:* 45; *149:* 120; *156:* 30; *169:* 135; *171:* 161, 162, 163; *172:* 9; *186:* 163; *194:* 109; *195:* 35; *198:* 170, 171, 172
Schlesinger, Bret *7:* 77
Schmid, Eleanore *12:* 188; *126:* 196, 197
Schmiderer, Dorothy *19:* 224
Schmidt, Bill *73:* 34; *76:* 220, 222, 224
Schmidt, Elizabeth *15:* 242
Schmidt, George Paul *132:* 122
Schmidt, Karen Lee *54:* 12; *71:* 174; *92:* 56; *94:* 190, 191; *127:* 103
Schmidt, Lynette *76:* 205
Schneider, Christine M. *171:* 165
Schneider, Howie *181:* 159
Schneider, Rex *29:* 64; *44:* 171
Schnurr, Edward *170:* 62
Schoberle, Cecile *80:* 200; *92:* 134
Schoenherr, Ian *32:* 83; *173:* 41
Schoenherr, John *1:* 146, 147, 173; *3:* 39, 139; *17:* 75; *29:* 72; *32:* 83; *37:* 168, 169, 170; *43:* 164, 165; *45:* 160, 162; *51:* 127; *66:* 196, 197, 198; *68:* 83; *72:* 240; *75:* 225; *88:* 176
Scholder, Fritz *69:* 103
Schomburg, Alex *13:* 23
Schongut, Emanuel *4:* 102; *15:* 186; *47:* 218, 219; *52:* 147, 148, 149, 150; *185:* 27
Schoonover, Frank *17:* 107; *19:* 81, 190, 233; *22:* 88,129; *24:* 189; *31:* 88; *41:* 69; *YABC 2:* 282, 316
Schories, Pat *164:* 210
Schottland, Miriam *22:* 172
Schramm, Ulrik *2:* 16; *14:* 112
Schreiber, Elizabeth Anne *13:* 193
Schreiber, Ralph W. *13:* 193
Schreiter, Rick *14:* 97; *23:* 171; *41:* 247; *49:* 131
Schroeder, Binette *56:* 128, 129
Schroeder, E. Peter *12:* 112
Schroeder, Ted *11:* 160; *15:* 189; *30:* 91; *34:* 43
Schrotter, Gustav *22:* 212; *30:* 225
Schubert, Dieter *101:* 167, 168
Schubert-Gabrys, Ingrid *101:* 167, 168
Schucker, James *31:* 163
Schuett, Stacey *72:* 137
Schulder, Lili *146:* 29
Schulke, Debra *57:* 167
Schulke, Flip *57:* 167
Schulz, Barbara *167:* 24
Schulz, Charles M. *10:* 137, 138, 139, 140, 141, 142; *118:* 192, 193, 194, 196, 199
Schutzer, Dena *109:* 32
Schwark, Mary Beth *51:* 155; *72:* 175
Schwartz, Amy *47:* 191; *82:* 100; *83:* 178, 179, 180,181; *129:* 107; *131:* 197, 198; *189:* 166, 168
Schwartz, Carol *124:* 41; *130:* 199
Schwartz, Charles *8:* 184
Schwartz, Daniel *46:* 37
Schwartz, Joanie *124:* 170
Schwartzberg, Joan *3:* 208
Schwarz, Viviane *204:* 132
Schweitzer, Iris *2:* 137; *6:* 207
Schweninger, Ann *29:* 172; *82:* 246; *159:* 202; *168:* 166
Schwinger, Laurence *84:* 44; *91:* 61
Scofield, Penrod *61:* 107; *62:* 160
Scott, Anita Walker *7:* 38
Scott, Art *39:* 41
Scott, Frances Gruse *38:* 43
Scott, Julian *34:* 126
Scott, Roszel *33:* 238
Scott, Sally *87:* 27
Scott, Steve *166:* 230, 231; *171:* 93
Scott, Trudy *27:* 172
Scrace, Carolyn *143:* 95, 96
Scrambly, Crab *198:* 196

Scribner, Joanne *14:* 236; *29:* 78; *33:* 185; *34:* 208; *78:* 75; *164:* 237; *203:* 73
Scrofani, Joseph *31:* 65; *74:* 225
Scroggs, Kirk *187:* 169
Seaman, Mary Lott *34:* 64
Searle, Ronald *24:* 98; *42:* 172, 173, 174, 176, 177, 179; *66:* 73, 74; *70:* 205, 206, 207
Searle, Townley *36:* 85
Sebree, Charles *18:* 65
Sedacca, Joseph M. *11:* 25; *22:* 36
Seder, Jason *108:* 102
Seeger, Laura Vaccaro *172:* 162
Seegmiller, Don *174:* 57
Seely, David *164:* 173
Seeley, Laura L. *97:* 105
Segal, John *178:* 202
Segar, E.C. *61:* 179, 181
Segur, Adrienne *27:* 121
Seibold, J. Otto *83:* 188, 190, 191; *149:* 212, 214, 215, 216; *196:* 177, 179
Seignobosc, Francoise *21:* 145, 146
Sejima, Yoshimasa *8:* 187
Selig, Sylvie *13:* 199
Seltzer, Isadore *6:* 18; *133:* 59
Seltzer, Meyer *17:* 214
Selven, Maniam *144:* 133
Selway, Martina *169:* 157
Selznick, Brian *79:* 192; *104:* 25; *117:* 175; *126:* 156; *134:* 171; *158:* 76, 78; *169:* 70; *171:* 172, 173; *191:* 106; *192:* 130; *197:* 158; *203:* 35; *205:* 92
Sempe, Jean-Jacques *47:* 92; *YABC 2:* 109
Sendak, Maurice *1:* 135, 190; *3:* 204; *7:* 142; *15:* 199; *17:* 210; *27:* 181, 182, 183, 185, 186, 187, 189,190, 191, 192, 193, 194, 195, 197, 198, 199, 203; *28:* 181, 182; *32:* 108; *33:* 148, 149; *35:* 238; *44:* 180, 181; *45:* 97, 99; *46:* 174; *73:* 225; *91:* 10, 11 *YABC1:* 167; *113:* 163, 165, 167, 168; *118:* 153; *127:* 161
Senders, Marci *180:* 79
Sengler, Johanna *18:* 256
Senn, Steve *60:* 145
Seredy, Kate *1:* 192; *14:* 20, 21; *17:* 210
Sergeant, John *6:* 74
Servello, Joe *10:* 144; *24:* 139; *40:* 91; *70:* 130, 131; *146:* 159
Seton, Ernest Thompson *18:* 260-269, 271
Seuss, Dr.
    See Geisel, Theodor
Severin, John Powers *7:* 62
Sewall, Marcia *15:* 8; *22:* 170; *37:* 171, 172, 173; *39:* 73; *45:* 209; *62:* 117; *69:* 185, 186; *71:* 212; *90:* 232; *96:* 127; *102:* 101; *107:* 129; *119:* 176, 177, 178, 180
Seward, James *70:* 35
Seward, Prudence *16:* 243
Sewell, Helen *3:* 186; *15:* 308; *33:* 102; *38:* 189, 190, 191, 192
Seymour, Stephen *54:* 21
Sfar, Joann *182:* 183
Shachat, Andrew *82:* 179
Shadbolt, Robert *203:* 68
Shahn, Ben *39:* 178; *46:* 193
Shalansky, Len *38:* 167
Shanks, Anne Zane *10:* 149
Shannon, David *57:* 137; *107:* 184; *112:* 216; *135:* 12; *152:* 223, 224, 225; *158:* 192
Sharp, Paul *52:* 60
Sharp, William *6:* 131; *19:* 241; *20:* 112; *25:* 141
Sharratt, Nick *102:* 207, 208; *104:* 163; *153:* 198; *175:* 176; *192:* 208; *199:* 141, 142, 143, 184, 187, 188
Shaw, Barclay *74:* 14, 16; *118:* 138
Shaw, Charles *21:* 135; *38:* 187; *47:* 124; *126:* 219
Shaw, Charles G. *13:* 200
Shaw-Smith, Emma *144:* 117
Shea, Edmund *56:* 19
Shearer, Ted *43:* 193, 194, 195, 196

Sheban, Chris *182:* 185; *190:* 102, 104; *202:* 28; *204:* 112, 114
Shecter, Ben *16:* 244; *25:* 109; *33:* 188, 191; *41:* 77
Shed, Greg *74:* 94; *84:* 204; *129:* 149, 167; *91:* 179: 192
Sheeban, Chris *144:* 190; *158:* 163
Shefcik, James *48:* 221, 222; *60:* 141
Shefelman, Karl *58:* 168
Shefelman, Tom *204:* 137
Shefts, Joelle *48:* 210
Shein, Bob *139:* 189
Sheinkin, Stephen *204:* 139
Shekerjian, Haig *16:* 245
Shekerjian, Regina *16:* 245; *25:* 73
Sheldon, David *184:* 174; *185:* 204
Shelley, John *186:* 223
Shemie, Bonnie *96:* 207
Shenton, Edward *45:* 187, 188, 189; *YABC 1:* 218, 219, 221
Shepard, Ernest H. *3:* 193; *4:* 74; *16:* 101; *17:* 109; *25:* 148; *33:* 152, 199, 200, 201, 202, 203, 204, 205, 206,207; *46:* 194; *98:* 114; *100:* 111, 178, 179, 217, 219, 220,221; *YABC 1:* 148, 153, 174, 176, 180, 181
Shepard, Mary *4:* 210; *22:* 205; *30:* 132, 133; *54:* 150, 152, 153, 157, 158; *59:* 108, 109, 111; *100:* 246
Shepherd, Amanda *198:* 14
Shepherd, Irana *171:* 112
Sheppard, Kate *195:* 176
Shepperson, Rob *96:* 153; *177:* 163; *178:* 204; *197:* 34; *205:* 108
Sheridan, Brian *196:* 193
Sherman, Theresa *27:* 167
Sherwan, Earl *3:* 196
Shields, Charles *10:* 150; *36:* 63
Shields, Leonard *13:* 83, 85, 87
Shiffman, Lena *139:* 167; *168:* 136
Shigley, Neil K. *66:* 219
Shillabeer, Mary *35:* 74
Shilston, Arthur *49:* 61; *62:* 58
Shimin, Symeon *1:* 93; *2:* 128, 129; *3:* 202; *7:* 85; *11:* 177; *12:* 139; *13:* 202, 203; *27:* 138; *28:* 65; *35:* 129; *36:* 130; *48:* 151; *49:* 59; *56:* 63, 65, 153
Shine, Andrea *104:* 165; *128:* 34
Shinn, Everett *16:* 148; *18:* 229; *21:* 149, 150, 151; *24:* 218
Shinn, Florence Scovel *63:* 133, 135
Shore, Robert *27:* 54; *39:* 192, 193; *YABC 2:* 200
Shortall, Leonard *4:* 144; *8:* 196; *10:* 166; *19:* 227, 228, 229, 230; *25:* 78; *28:* 66, 167; *33:* 127; *52:* 125; *73:* 12, 212
Shortt, T.M. *27:* 36
Shpitalnik, Vladimir *83:* 194
Shropshire, Sandy *170:* 191
Shtainments, Leon *32:* 161
Shulevitz, Uri *3:* 198, 199; *17:* 85; *22:* 204; *27:* 212; *28:* 184; *50:* 190, 191, 192, 193, 194, 195, 196,197, 198, 199, 201; *106:* 181, 182, 183; *165:* 203, 205; *166:* 138
Shulman, Dee *180:* 140
Shupe, Bobbi *139:* 80, 81
Shute, A.B. *67:* 196
Shute, Linda *46:* 59; *74:* 118
Siberell, Anne *29:* 193
Sibley, Don *1:* 39; *12:* 196; *31:* 47
Sibthorp, Fletcher *94:* 111, 112
Sidjakov, Nicolas *18:* 274
Siebel, Fritz *3:* 120; *17:* 145
Siebold, J. Otto *158:* 227
Siegel, Hal *74:* 246
Sieger, Ted *189:* 172
Siegl, Helen *12:* 166; *23:* 216; *34:* 185, 186
Silin-Palmer, Pamela *184:* 102
Sill, John *140:* 194; *141:* 157
Sills, Joyce *5:* 199
Silva, Simon *108:* 122
Silver, Maggie *85:* 210

Silveria, Gordon *96:* 44
Silverstein, Alvin *8:* 189
Silverstein, Shel *33:* 211; *92:* 209, 210
Silverstein, Virginia *8:* 189
Silvey, Joe *135:* 203
Simard, Remy *95:* 156
Simmons, Elly *110:* 2; *127:* 69; *134:* 181
Simon, Eric M. *7:* 82
Simon, Hilda *28:* 189
Simon, Howard *2:* 175; *5:* 132; *19:* 199; *32:* 163, 164, 165
Simont, Marc *2:* 119; *4:* 213; *9:* 168; *13:* 238,240; *14:* 262; *16:* 179; *18:* 221; *26:* 210; *33:* 189, 194; *44:* 132; *58:* 122; *68:* 117; *73:* 204, 205, 206; *74:* 221; *126:* 199, 200; *133:* 195; *164:* 128
Sims, Agnes *54:* 152
Sims, Blanche *44:* 116; *57:* 129; *75:* 179, 180; *77:* 92; *104:* 192; *152:* 117; *156:* 160; *160:* 70; *168:* 174, 175; *198:* 17
Singer, Edith G. *2:* 30
Singer, Gloria *34:* 56; *36:* 43
Singer, Julia *28:* 190
Singh, Jen *178:* 146
Siomades, Lorianne *134:* 45; *204:* 48
Simont, Marc *163:* 40
Siracusa, Catherine *68:* 135; *82:* 218
Sís, Peter *67:* 179, 181, 183, 184, 185; *96:* 96, 98; *106:* 193, 194, 195; *149:* 224, 226; *180:* 177; *192:* 180, 182
Sivard, Robert *26:* 124
Sivertson, Liz *116:* 84
Skardinski, Stanley *23:* 144; *32:* 84; *66:* 122; *84:* 108
Slack, Michael *185:* 108; *189:* 173, 174
Slackman, Charles B. *12:* 201
Slade, Christian *193:* 187; *204:* 134
Slade, Paul *61:* 170
Slark, Albert *99:* 212; *205:* 161
Slater, Rod *25:* 167
Slavin, Bill *182:* 14, 15; *196:* 90; *199:* 148, 149, 150
Sloan, Joseph *16:* 68
Sloane, Eric *21:* 3; *52:* 153, 154, 155, 156, 157, 158, 160
Sloat, Teri *164:* 231
Slobodkin, Louis *1:* 200; *3:* 232; *5:* 168; *13:* 251; *15:* 13, 88; *26:* 173, 174, 175, 176, 178, 179; *60:* 180
Slobodkina, Esphyr *1:* 201
Slonim, David *166:* 167, 168
Small, David *50:* 204, 205; *79:* 44; *95:* 189, 190, 191; *126:* 203, 204; *136:* 119; *143:* 201, 202, 203; *144:* 246; *150:* 5; *161:* 176; *183:* 181, 182, 183, 184; *200:* 211
Small, W. *33:* 113
Smalley, Janet *1:* 154
Smath, Jerry *198:* 179, 180
Smedley, William T. *34:* 129
Smee, David *14:* 78; *62:* 30
Smee, Nicola *167:* 156
Smith, A.G., Jr. *35:* 182
Smith, Ali *204:* 68
Smith, Alvin *1:* 31, 229; *13:* 187; *27:* 216; *28:* 226; *48:* 149; *49:* 60
Smith, Andy *188:* 20
Smith, Anne *194:* 147
Smith, Anne Warren *41:* 212
Smith, Barry *75:* 183
Smith, Brian *200:* 183
Smith, Carl *36:* 41
Smith, Cat Bowman *146:* 39; *164:* 219; *201:* 55, 184
Smith, Craig *97:* 197; *172:* 175
Smith, Donald A. *178:* 7
Smith, Doris Susan *41:* 139
Smith, Douglas *189:* 159
Smith, Duane *171:* 152
Smith, E. Boyd *19:* 70; *22:* 89; *26:* 63; *YABC 1:* 4, 5, 240, 248, 249
Smith, Edward J. *4:* 224

Smith, Elwood H. *157:* 231; *181:* 79; *203:* 160, 161, 162
Smith, Eunice Young *5:* 170
Smith, Gary *113:* 216
Smith, George *102:* 169
Smith, Howard *19:* 196
Smith, J. Gerard *95:* 42
Smith, Jacqueline Bardner *27:* 108; *39:* 197
Smith, Jay J. *61:* 119
Smith, Jeff *93:* 191
Smith, Jessie Willcox *15:* 91; *16:* 95; *18:* 231; *19:* 57, 242; *21:* 29, 156, 157, 158, 159, 160, 161; *34:* 65; *100:* 223; *YABC 1:* 6; *2:* 180, 185, 191, 311, 325
Smith, Jos. A. *52:* 131; *72:* 120; *74:* 151; *84:* 147, 148; *85:* 146; *87:* 96; *94:* 219; *96:* 97; *104:* 33; *108:* 126, 127, 128; *111:* 140; *136:* 145; *181:* 173; *200:* 213; *201:* 94
Smith, Kenneth R. *47:* 182
Smith, Kevin Warren *89:* 112
Smith, L.H. *35:* 174
Smith, Lane *76:* 211, 213; *88:* 115; *105:* 202, 203,204, 205; *131:* 207; *160:* 217, 221; *179:* 183, 184, 185, 186; *199:* 122, 123, 124, 126
Smith, Lee *29:* 32
Smith, Linell Nash *2:* 195
Smith, Maggie Kaufman *13:* 205; *35:* 191; *110:* 158; *178:* 226; *190:* 204
Smith, Mavis *101:* 219
Smith, Moishe *33:* 155
Smith, Philip *44:* 134; *46:* 203
Smith, Ralph Crosby *2:* 267; *49:* 203
Smith, Robert D. *5:* 63
Smith, Sally J. *84:* 55
Smith, Susan Carlton *12:* 208
Smith, Terry *12:* 106; *33:* 158
Smith, Virginia *3:* 157; *33:* 72
Smith, William A. *1:* 36; *10:* 154; *25:* 65
Smith-Moore, J.J. *98:* 147
Smolinski, Dick *84:* 217
Smoljan, Joe *112:* 201
Smollin, Mike *39:* 203
Smyth, Iain *105:* 207
Smyth, M. Jane *12:* 15
Smythe, Fiona *151:* 213
Smythe, Theresa *141:* 37
Snair, Andy *176:* 4
Sneed, Brad *125:* 25; *191:* 175, 176
Snyder, Andrew A. *30:* 212
Snyder, Jerome *13:* 207; *30:* 173
Snyder, Joel *28:* 163
So, Meilo *162:* 201
Soentpiet, Chris K. *97:* 208; *110:* 33; *159:* 184; *161:* 10; *163:* 130
Sofia *1:* 62; *5:* 90; *32:* 166; *86:* 43
Sofilas, Mark *93:* 157
Sohn, Jiho *182:* 78
Sokol, Bill *37:* 178; *49:* 23
Sokolov, Kirill *34:* 188
Solbert, Ronni *1:* 159; *2:* 232; *5:* 121; *6:* 34; *17:* 249
Solomon, Michael *174:* 115
Solonevich, George *15:* 246; *17:* 47
Soma, Liana *81:* 118
Soman, David *90:* 122; *102:* 126; *140:* 120; 93; *188:* 43, 89; *200:* 180, 181
Sommer, Robert *12:* 211
Song, Jae *203:* 27
Soo, Kean *201:* 185
Sorel, Edward *4:* 61; *36:* 82; *65:* 191, 193; *126:* 214
Sorensen, Henri *196:* 58
Sorensen, Henrik *62:* 16
Sorensen, Svend Otto *22:* 130, 141; *67:* 188, 189
Sorra, Kristin *155:* 80
Sosa, Hernan *198:* 66
Sostre, Maria *187:* 36
Sotomayor, Antonio *11:* 215
Souhami, Jessica *112:* 128; *176:* 193
Souza, Diana *71:* 139

Sovak, Jan *115:* 190
Soyer, Moses *20:* 177
Spaenkuch, August *16:* 28
Spafford, Suzy *160:* 228
Spain, Valerie *105:* 76
Spain, Sunday Sahara *133:* 204
Spalenka, Greg *149:* 69; *151:* 228; *184:* 195; *191:* 21; *196:* 12; *198:* 181, 182, 201
Spanfeller, James *1:* 72, 149; *2:* 183; *19:* 230, 231,232; *22:* 66; *36:* 160, 161; *40:* 75; *52:* 166; *76:* 37
Sparks, Mary Walker *15:* 247
Spears, Rick *182:* 187
Speidel, Sandra *78:* 233; *94:* 178; *134:* 180
Speirs, John *67:* 178
Spence, Geraldine *21:* 163; *47:* 196
Spence, Jim *38:* 89; *50:* 102
Spencer, Laurie *113:* 12
Spencer, Mark *57:* 170
Spengler, Kenneth J. *146:* 256
Sperling, Andrea *133:* 182
Spiegel, Beth *184:* 203
Spiegel, Doris *29:* 111
Spiegelman, Art *109:* 227
Spier, Jo *10:* 30
Spier, Peter *3:* 155; *4:* 200; *7:* 61; *11:* 78; *38:* 106; *54:* 120, 121, 122, 123, 124, 125, 126, 127, 128, 129, 130,131, 132, 133, 134
Spilka, Arnold *5:* 120; *6:* 204; *8:* 131
Spirin, Gennady *95:* 196, 197; *113:* 172; *128:* 9; *129:* 49; *134:* 210; *153:* 9; *204:* 143, 144, 145
Spivak, I. Howard *8:* 10; *13:* 172
Spohn, David *72:* 233
Spohn, Kate *87:* 195; *147:* 201, 202
Spollen, Christopher J. *12:* 214
Spooner, Malcolm *40:* 142
Spowart, Robin *82:* 228; *92:* 149; *133:* 131; *176:* 163; *177:* 183, 184
Sprague, Kevin *150:* 60; *196:* 62
Spranger, Nina *201:* 199
Sprattler, Rob *12:* 176
Spring, Bob *5:* 60
Spring, Ira *5:* 60
Springer, Harriet *31:* 92
Spudvilas, Anne *110:* 74; *197:* 192; *199:* 154
Spurll, Barbara *78:* 199; *88:* 141, 142; *99:* 215
Spurrier, Steven *28:* 198
Spuvilas, Anne *85:* 114
Spy
  See Ward, Leslie
Squires, Stuart *127:* 74
St. Aubin, Bruno *179:* 54
St. John, J. Allen *41:* 62
Stabin, Victor *101:* 131; *164:* 158
Stadler, John *62:* 33; *204:* 149
Staffan, Alvin E. *11:* 56; *12:* 187
Stahl, Ben *5:* 181; *12:* 91; *49:* 122; *71:* 128; *87:* 206; *112:* 107
Stair, Gobin *35:* 214
Stallwood, Karen *73:* 126
Stamaty, Mark Alan *12:* 215
Stammen, JoEllen McAllister *113:* 14
Stampnick, Ken *51:* 142
Stanbridge, Joanne *150:* 91
Stanley, Diane *3:* 45; *37:* 180; *80:* 217, 219
Stanley, Sanna *145:* 228
Starcke, Helmut *86:* 217
Stark, Ken *197:* 102
Starr, Branka *73:* 25
Stasiak, Krystyna *49:* 181; *64:* 194
Staub, Leslie *103:* 54
Staunton, Ted *112:* 192
Stawicki, Matt *164:* 250
Stead, L. *55:* 51, 56
Steadman, Broeck *97:* 185, 186; *99:* 56; *121:* 48
Steadman, Ralph *32:* 180; *123:* 143, 145
Stearn, Nick *183:* 26
Steckler, June *90:* 178
Steele, Robert Gantt *169:* 174

Steichen, Edward *30:* 79
Steig, William *18:* 275, 276; *70:* 215, 216, 217, 218; *111:* 173, 174, 175, 176, 177
Stein, Harve *1:* 109
Steinberg, Saul *47:* 193
Steinel, William *23:* 146
Steiner, Charlotte *45:* 196
Steiner, Joan *110:* 219; *199:* 160, 161
Steirnagel, Michael *80:* 56
Stemp, Eric *60:* 184
Stephens, Alice Barber *66:* 208, 209
Stephens, Charles H. *YABC 2:* 279
Stephens, Pam *198:* 69
Stephens, Pat *126:* 110; *128:* 101
Stephens, William M. *21:* 165
Steptoe, Javaka *151:* 203, 204; *190:* 169
Steptoe, John *8:* 197; *57:* 9; *63:* 158, 159, 160, 161,163, 164, 165, 166, 167; *96:* 4; *105:* 87
Stern, Simon *15:* 249, 250; *17:* 58; *34:* 192, 193
Sterret, Jane *53:* 27
Stetsios, Debbie *165:* 108, 109
Steven, Kat *158:* 237
Stevens, David *62:* 44
Stevens, Helen *189:* 31
Stevens, Janet *40:* 126; *57:* 10, 11; *80:* 112; *90:* 221, 222; *109:* 156; *130:* 34; *166:* 202; *176:* 53, 116; *193:* 199, 200, 202
Stevens, Mary *11:* 193; *13:* 129; *43:* 95
Stevenson, Harvey *66:* 143; *80:* 201, 221; *153:* 60; *191:* 166
Stevenson, James *42:* 182, 183; *51:* 163; *66:* 184; *71:* 185, 187, 188; *78:* 262; *87:* 97; *113:* 182, 183,184, 185; *161:* 182, 183
Stevenson, Sucie *92:* 27; *104:* 194, 195; *112:* 168; *160:* 202; *194:* 172, 173; *195:* 166
Stewart, April Blair *75:* 210
Stewart, Arvis *33:* 98; *36:* 69; *60:* 118; *75:* 91; *127:* 4
Stewart, Charles *2:* 205
Stewart, Joel *151:* 205
Stieg, William *172:* 58
Stiles, Fran *26:* 85; *78:* 56; *82:* 150
Stillman, Susan *44:* 130; *76:* 83
Stimpson, Tom *49:* 171
Stinemetz, Morgan *40:* 151
Stinson, Paul *110:* 86
Stirnweis, Shannon *10:* 164
Stites, Joe *86:* 96
Stobbs, William *1:* 48, 49; *3:* 68; *6:* 20; *17:* 117, 217; *24:* 150; *29:* 250; *60:* 179; *87:* 204, 205,206
Stock, Catherine *37:* 55; *65:* 198; *72:* 7; *99:* 225; *114:* 197, 198, 199; *126:* 3; *145:* 161; *161:* 82; *173:* 149
Stockman, Jack *113:* 24
Stoeke, Janet Morgan *90:* 225; *136:* 196; *202:* 182, 183
Stoerrle, Tom *55:* 147
Stolp, Jaap *49:* 98
Stolp, Todd *89:* 195
Stone, David L. *87:* 154
Stone, David *9:* 173
Stone, David K. *4:* 38; *6:* 124; *9:* 180; *43:* 182; *60:* 70
Stone, Helen V. *6:* 209
Stone, Helen *44:* 121, 122, 126
Stone, Kazuko G. *134:* 43
Stone, Kyle M. *202:* 185
Stone, Phoebe *86:* 212; *134:* 213; *162:* 188; *205:* 145
Stone, Steve *166:* 213
Stone, Tony *150:* 34, 35
Storrings, Michael *191:* 108
Stoud, Virginia A. *89:* 31
Stover, Jill *82:* 234
Strachan, Bruce *205:* 146
Stratton, Helen *33:* 151
Stratton-Porter, Gene *15:* 254, 259, 263, 264, 268, 269
Straub, Matt *192:* 176

Straub, Phillip *197:* 22
Streano, Vince *20:* 173
Street, Janet Travell *84:* 235
Streeter, Clive *121:* 2
Stringer, Lauren *129:* 187; *154:* 172, 173; *161:* 127; *183:* 187, 188
Strodl, Daniel *47:* 95
Strogart, Alexander *63:* 139
Stromoski, Rick *111:* 179; *124:* 161, 190
Strong, Joseph D., Jr. *YABC 2:* 330
Stroyer, Poul *13:* 221
Strugnell, Ann *27:* 38
Struzan, Drew *117:* 6
Stubbs, William *73:* 196
Stubis, Talivaldis *5:* 182, 183; *10:* 45; *11:* 9; *18:* 304; *20:* 127
Stubley, Trevor *14:* 43; *22:* 219; *23:* 37; *28:* 61; *87:* 26
Stuck, Marion *104:* 44
Stuecklen, Karl W. *8:* 34, 65; *23:* 103
Stull, Betty *11:* 46
Stutzman, Mark *119:* 99
Stutzmann, Laura *73:* 185
Suarez, Maribel *162:* 208; *200:* 202
Suba, Susanne *4:* 202, 203; *14:* 261; *23:* 134; *29:* 222; *32:* 30
Sueling, Barbara *98:* 185
Sueling, Gwenn *98:* 186
Sugarman, Tracy *3:* 76; *8:* 199; *37:* 181, 182
Sugimoto, Yugo *170:* 144
Sugita, Yutaka *36:* 180, 181
Suh, John *80:* 157
Sullivan, Dorothy *89:* 113
Sullivan, Edmund J. *31:* 86
Sullivan, James F. *19:* 280; *20:* 192
Sully, Tom *104:* 199, 200; *182:* 77
Sumichrast, Jozef *14:* 253; *29:* 168, 213
Sumiko *46:* 57
Summers, Leo *1:* 177; *2:* 273; *13:* 22
Summers, Mark *118:* 144
Summers, Mike *190:* 176
Sutton, Judith *94:* 164
Svarez, Juan *56:* 113
Svendsen, Mark *181:* 176
Svolinsky, Karel *17:* 104
Swain, Carol *172:* 182
Swain, Su Zan Noguchi *21:* 170
Swan, Susan *22:* 220, 221; *37:* 66; *60:* 146; *145:* 205; *181:* 168
Swann, Susan *86:* 55
Swanson, Karl *79:* 65; *89:* 186
Swarner, Kristina *203:* 62
Swayne, Sam *53:* 143, 145
Swayne, Zoa *53:* 143, 145
Swearingen, Greg *152:* 56; *165:* 135; *173:* 2
Sweat, Lynn *25:* 206; *57:* 176; *73:* 184; *168:* 178
Sweet, Darrell K. *60:* 9; *69:* 86; *74:* 15; *75:* 215; *76:* 130, 131; *81:* 96, 122; *82:* 253; *83:* 11; *84:* 14; *85:* 37; *89:* 140; *90:* 6; *91:* 137,139; *95:* 160, 161; *126:* 25; *185:* 175; *195:* 132
Sweet, Darrell K. *1:* 163; *4:* 136; *164:* 175
Sweet, Melissa *71:* 94; *72:* 172; *111:* 82; *139:* 53, 58; *141:* 88; *142:* 231; *155:* 121; *159:* 121, 122; *172:* 185; *188:* 127
Sweet, Ozzie *31:* 149, 151, 152
Sweetland, Robert *12:* 194
Swiatkowska, Gabi *132:* 43; *175:* 139; *180:* 218; *183:* 176
Swope, Martha *43:* 160; *56:* 86, 87, 89
Sylvada, Peter *154:* 174
Sylvester, Natalie G. *22:* 222
Szafran, Gene *24:* 144
Szasz, Susanne *13:* 55, 226; *14:* 48
Szekeres, Cyndy *2:* 218; *5:* 185; *8:* 85; *11:* 166; *14:* 19; *16:* 57, 159; *26:* 49, 214; *34:* 205; *60:* 150, 151, 152, 153, 154; *73:* 224; *74:* 218; *131:* 213, 215
Szpura, Beata *81:* 68; *119:* 65; *168:* 201

T

Taback, Simms *40:* 207; *52:* 120; *57:* 34; *80:* 241; *104:* 202, 203; *170:* 176, 177; *205:* 183
Taber, Patricia *75:* 124
Tabor, Nancy Maria Grande *89:* 210; *161:* 188
Taddei, Richard *112:* 13, 14
Tadgell, Nicole *150:* 77; *161:* 20; *177:* 186
Tadiello, Ed *133:* 200
Tafuri, Nancy *39:* 210; *75:* 199, 200; *92:* 75; *130:* 215, 216, 217
Tailfeathers, Gerald *86:* 85
Tait, Douglas *12:* 220; *74:* 105, 106
Takabayashi, Mari *113:* 112; *130:* 22; *156:* 169
Takahashi, Hideko *136:* 160; *187:* 6
Takakjian, Portia *15:* 274
Takashima, Shizuye *13:* 228
Talarczyk, June *4:* 173
Talbott, Hudson *84:* 240; *163:* 100
Tallarico, Tony *116:* 197
Tallon, Robert *2:* 228; *43:* 200, 201, 202, 203, 204, 205,206, 207, 209
Tamaki, Jillian *201:* 188
Tamas, Szecsko *29:* 135
Tamburine, Jean *12:* 222
Tandy, H.R. *13:* 69
Tandy, Russell H. *65:* 9; *100:* 30, 131
Tang, Charles *81:* 202; *90:* 192
Tang, Susan *80:* 174; *108:* 158
Tang, You-shan *63:* 100
Tankersley, Paul *69:* 206; *133:* 219
Tannenbaum, Robert *48:* 181
Tanner, Jane *87:* 13; *97:* 37
Tanner, Tim *72:* 192; *84:* 35
Tanobe, Miyuki *23:* 221
Tarabay, Sharif *110:* 149; *113:* 123; *169:* 83
Tarkington, Booth *17:* 224, 225
Tarlow, Phyllis *61:* 198
Tate, Don *159:* 141, 191; *183:* 69; *186:* 120
Tauss, Herbert *95:* 179
Tauss, Marc *117:* 160; *126:* 155; *178:* 221; *197:* 7
Tavares, Matt *159:* 192, 193; *198:* 188, 189, 190; *199:* 86
Taylor, Ann *41:* 226
Taylor, Dahl *129:* 157
Taylor, Geoff *93:* 156; *197:* 173, 175; *204:* 151, 152
Taylor, Isaac *41:* 228
Taylor, Mike *143:* 99, 100
Teague, Mark *83:* 6; *139:* 241; *170:* 180, 181; *205:* 150, 151
Teale, Edwin Way *7:* 196
Teason, James *1:* 14
Teckentrup, Britta *200:* 191, 192
Teeple, Lyn *33:* 147
Tee-Van, Helen Damrosch *10:* 176; *11:* 182
Teicher, Dick *50:* 211
Teichman, Mary *77:* 220; *124:* 208; *127:* 22; *197:* 33
Temertey, Ludmilla *96:* 232; *104:* 43, 45; *109:* 244
Tempest, Margaret *3:* 237, 238; *88:* 200
Temple, Frances *85:* 185, 186, 187
Temple, Herbert *45:* 201
Templeton, Owen *11:* 77
ten Cate, Marijke *183:* 193
Tenggren, Gustaf *18:* 277, 278, 279; *19:* 15; *28:* 86; *YABC2:* 145
Tennent, Julie *81:* 105
Tenneson, Joyce *153:* 166
Tenney, Gordon *24:* 204
Tenniel, John *74:* 234, 235; *100:* 89; *YABC 2:* 99; *153:* 63
Tepper, Matt *116:* 80
Terkel, Ari *103:* 162
Terry, Michael *180:* 209
Terry, Will *131:* 73; *205:* 155
Teskey, Donald *71:* 51
Tessler, Manya *200:* 193

Thacher, Mary M. *30:* 72
Thackeray, William Makepeace *23:* 224, 228
Thamer, Katie *42:* 187
Tharlet, Eve *146:* 149
Thelwell, Norman *14:* 201
Theobalds, Prue *40:* 23
Theurer, Marilyn Churchill *39:* 195
Thiesing, Lisa *89:* 134; *95:* 202; *156:* 190; *159:* 195
Thiewes, Sam *133:* 114
Thistlethwaite, Miles *12:* 224
Thollander, Earl *11:* 47; *18:* 112; *22:* 224
Thomas, Allan *22:* 13
Thomas, Art *48:* 217
Thomas, Eric *28:* 49
Thomas, Harold *20:* 98
Thomas, Jacqui *125:* 95
Thomas, Jan *197:* 180
Thomas, Mark *42:* 136
Thomas, Martin *14:* 255
Thomas, Middy *177:* 114
Thompson, Arthur *34:* 107
Thompson, Carol *85:* 189; *95:* 75; *102:* 86; *147:* 166; *189:* 179, 180, 181; *190:* 84
Thompson, Colin *95:* 204
Thompson, Ellen *51:* 88, 151; *60:* 33; *67:* 42; *77:* 148; *78:* 75, 219; *79:* 122, 170; *84:* 219; *85:* 97; *87:* 37; *88:* 192, 194; *89:* 80; *93:* 37; *98:* 59; *132:* 14
Thompson, George W. *22:* 18; *28:* 150; *33:* 135
Thompson, John *58:* 201; *102:* 226; *124:* 154; *128:* 228; *129:* 157; *150:* 49; *185:* 160; *191:* 192
Thompson, Julie *44:* 158
Thompson, Katherine *132:* 146
Thompson, K. Dyble *84:* 6
Thompson, Miles *152:* 77
Thompson, Sharon *74:* 113; *158:* 60; *165:* 87
Thomson, Arline K. *3:* 264
Thomson, Bill *186:* 160
Thomson, Hugh *26:* 88
Thomson, Ross *36:* 179
Thorkelson, Gregg *95:* 183, 184; *98:* 58; *165:* 30, 31
Thorn, Lori *189:* 119
Thornberg, Dan *104:* 125
Thornburgh, Rebecca McKillip *143:* 37
Thorne, Diana *25:* 212
Thornhill, Jan *77:* 213
Thorpe, Peter *58:* 109
Thorvall, Kerstin *13:* 235
Threadgall, Colin *77:* 215
Thurber, James *13:* 239, 242, 243, 245, 248, 249
Thurman, Mark *63:* 173; *168:* 116
Thurman, Mark *63:* 173; *168:* 116
Tibbles, Jean-Paul *115:* 200
Tibbles, Paul *45:* 23
Tibo, Gilles *67:* 207; *107:* 199, 201
Tichenor, Tom *14:* 207
Tichnor, Richard *90:* 218
Tiegreen, Alan *36:* 143; *43:* 55, 56, 58; *77:* 200; *94:* 216, 217; *121:* 54, 59
Tierney, Tom *113:* 198, 200, 201
Tilley, Debbie *102:* 134; *133:* 226; *137:* 101; *159:* 96; *190:* 211, 212
Tilney, F.C. *22:* 231
Timbs, Gloria *36:* 90
Timmins, Harry *2:* 171
Timmons, Bonnie *194:* 189
Tinkelman, Murray *12:* 225; *35:* 44
Titherington, Jeanne *39:* 90; *58:* 138; *75:* 79; *135:* 161
Tobin, Nancy *145:* 197
Toddy, Irving *172:* 144
Tokunbo, Dimitrea *181:* 183; *187:* 182, 183
Tolbert, Jeff *128:* 69
Toledo, Francisco *197:* 182; *198:* 199
Toledo, Natalia *197:* 182
Tolford, Joshua *1:* 221
Tolkien, J.R.R. *2:* 243; *32:* 215

Tolman, Marije *195:* 43
Tolmie, Ken *15:* 292
Tomei, Lorna *47:* 168, 171
Tomes, Jacqueline *2:* 117; *12:* 139
Tomes, Margot *1:* 224; *2:* 120, 121; *16:* 207;
  18: 250; *20:* 7; *25:* 62; *27:* 78, 79; *29:* 81,
  199; *33:* 82; *36:* 186, 187, 188, 189, 190;
  46: 129; *56:* 71; *58:* 183; *70:* 228; *75:* 73,
  75; *80:* 80; *83:* 97; *90:* 205
Tommaso, Rich *200:* 198
Toner, Raymond John *10:* 179
Tong, Gary *66:* 215
Tongier, Stephen *82:* 32
Tooke, Susan *173:* 162
Toothill, Harry *6:* 54; *7:* 49; *25:* 219; *42:* 192
Toothill, Ilse *6:* 54
Topolski, Feliks *44:* 48
Torbert, Floyd James *22:* 226
Torgersen, Don *55:* 157
Torline, Kevin *169:* 171
Tormey, Bertram M. *75:* 3, 4
Torrecilla, Pablo *176:* 207
Torres, Leyla *156:* 199, 201
Torrey, Helen *87:* 41
Torrey, Marjorie *34:* 105
Torrey, Richard *189:* 182; *205:* 24
Toschik, Larry *6:* 102
Totten, Bob *13:* 93
Toy, Julie *128:* 112
Trachok, Cathy *131:* 16
Tracy, Libba *82:* 24
Trago, Keith *158:* 253
Trail, Lee *55:* 157
Trang, To Ngoc *167:* 180
Trang, Winson *89:* 151
Trapani, Iza *116:* 202
Travers, Bob *49:* 100; *63:* 145
Treatner, Meryl *95:* 180
Tremain, Ruthven *17:* 238
Tresilian, Stuart *25:* 53; *40:* 212
Trez, Alain *17:* 236
Trezzo, Loretta *86:* 45
Trier, Walter *14:* 96
Trimby, Elisa *47:* 199
Trinkle, Sally *53:* 27
Triplett, Gina *182:* 193; *188:* 100; *198:* 38
Tripp, F.J. *24:* 167
Tripp, Wallace *2:* 48; *7:* 28; *8:* 94; *10:* 54,76;
  11: 92; *31:* 170, 171; *34:* 203; *42:* 57; *60:*
  157; *73:* 182
Trivas, Irene *53:* 4; *54:* 168; *82:* 46, 101
Trnka, Jiri *22:* 151; *43:* 212, 213, 214, 215;
  YABC 1: 30, 31
Trondheim, Lewis *182:* 183
Troughton, Joanna *37:* 186; *48:* 72
Troyer, Johannes *3:* 16; *7:* 18
Trudeau, G.B. *35:* 220, 221, 222; *48:* 119,
  123, 126, 127,128, 129, 133; *168:* 189
Trueman, Matthew *165:* 208; *183:* 191
Truesdell, Sue *55:* 142; *108:* 219, 220
Tryon, Leslie *84:* 7; *139:* 214; *143:* 10; *181:*
  10
Tseng, Jean *72:* 195; *94:* 102; *119:* 126; *151:*
  106; *173:* 138, 139; *200:* 158
Tseng, Mou-sien *72:* 195; *94:* 102; *119:* 126;
  151: 106; *173:* 138, 139; *200:* 158
Tsinajinie, Andy *2:* 62
Tsinganos, Jim *180:* 142
Tsugami, Kyuzo *18:* 198, 199
Tucker, Ezra *156:* 31
Tuckwell, Jennifer *17:* 205
Tudor, Bethany *7:* 103
Tudor, Tasha *18:* 227; *20:* 185, 186, 187; *36:*
  111; *69:* 196, 198; *100:* 44;
  YABC 2: 46, 314; *160:* 234
Tuerk, Hanne *71:* 201
Tugeau, Jeremy *199:* 170; *203:* 96
Tulloch, Maurice *24:* 79
Tunis, Edwin *1:* 218, 219; *28:* 209, 210, 211,
  212
Tunnicliffe, C.F. *62:* 176; 177; 178, 179; 181

Turkle, Brinton *1:* 211, 213; *2:* 249; *3:* 226;
  11: 3; *16:* 209; *20:* 22; *50:* 23; *67:* 50; *68:*
  65; *79:* 205, 206, 207; *128:* 47; *YABC 1:* 79
Turnbull, Christopher J. *143:* 99, 100
Turner, Gwenda *59:* 195
Turner, Helen *203:* 154
Turska, Krystyna *12:* 103; *31:* 173, 174, 175;
  56: 32,34; *100:* 66
Tusa, Tricia *72:* 242; *111:* 180, 181; *157:* 165;
  164: 186; *189:* 40; *201:* 9
Tusan, Stan *6:* 58; *22:* 236, 237
Tworkov, Jack *47:* 207
Tyers, Jenny *89:* 220
Tylden-Wright, Jenny *114:* 119
Tyrol, Adelaide Murphy *103:* 27
Tyrrell, Frances *107:* 204
Tzimoulis, Paul *12:* 104

U

Uchida, Yoshiko *1:* 220
Uderzo *47:* 88
Udovic, David *189:* 185; *195:* 201
Ueno, Noriko *59:* 155
Ugliano, Natascia *196:* 186
Ulm, Robert *17:* 238
Ulrich, George *73:* 15; *75:* 136, 139; *99:* 150
Ulriksen, Mark *101:* 58; *182:* 43
Unada *84:* 67
  See Gliewe, Unada
Underhill, Liz *53:* 159
Underwood, Beck *192:* 36
Underwood, Clarence *40:* 166
Unger, Jim *67:* 208
Ungerer, Tomi *5:* 188; *9:* 40; *18:* 188; *29:*
  175; *33:* 221, 222, 223, 225; *71:* 48; *106:*
  209, 210, 211, 212
Unwin, Nora S. *3:* 65, 234, 235; *4:* 237; *44:*
  173, 174; *YABC 1:* 59; *2:* 301
Upitis, Alvis *145:* 179
Urban, Helle *149:* 243
Urbanovic, Jackie *86:* 86; *189:* 186, 187
Uris, Jill *49:* 188, 197
Ursell, Martin *50:* 51
Utpatel, Frank *18:* 114
Utz, Lois *5:* 190

V

Vagin, Vladimir *66:* 10; *142:* 215
Vaillancourt, Francois *107:* 199
Vainio, Pirkko *123:* 157, 158
Valério, Geraldo *180:* 225; *194:* 116
Vallejo, Boris *62:* 130; *72:* 212; *91:* 38; *93:* 61
Van Abbe, S. *16:* 142; *18:* 282; *31:* 90; *YABC
  2:* 157, 161
Van Allsburg, Chris *37:* 205, 206; *53:* 161,
  162, 163, 165,166, 167, 168, 169, 170, 171;
  105: 215, 216, 217, 218; *156:* 176, 177, 178
Vance, James *65:* 28
Van Der Linde, Henry *99:* 17
van der Meer, Ron *98:* 204, 205
van der Meer, Atie *98:* 204, 205
Vandivert, William *21:* 175
Van Dongen, H.R. *81:* 97
Van Dusen, Chris W. *173:* 169
Van Everen, Jay *13:* 160; *YABC 1:* 121
Van Fleet, John *165:* 12, 13
Van Frankenhuyzen, Gijsbert *145:* 230; *149:*
  164; *184:* 151
van Genechten, Guido *165:* 226
van Haeringen, Annemarie *193:* 206
Van Horn, William *43:* 218
van Hout, Mies *195:* 191
van Kampen, Vlasta *194:* 217
van Lawick, Hugo *62:* 76, 79

Van Lieshout, Maria *201:* 196
Van Loon, Hendrik Willem *18:* 285, 289, 291
van Ommen, Sylvia *186:* 192
Van Patter, Bruce *183:* 195
Van Rynbach, Iris *102:* 192
Van Sciver, Ruth *37:* 162
VanSeveren, Joe *63:* 182
Van Stockum, Hilda *5:* 193
Van Wassenhove, Sue *202:* 193
Van Wely, Babs *16:* 50; *79:* 16
Van Wright, Cornelius *72:* 18; *102:* 208; *116:*
  107; *152:* 236; *173:* 170, 171; *199:* 185
Van Zyle, Jon *103:* 125; *160:* 181, 182; *176:*
  199, 200
Vardzigulyants, Ruben *90:* 54
Varga, Judy *29:* 196
Vargo, Kurt *79:* 224
Varley, Susan *61:* 199; *63:* 176, 177; *101:* 148;
  134: 220
Varon, Sara *195:* 208
Vasconcellos, Daniel *80:* 42
Vasiliu, Mircea *2:* 166, 253; *9:* 166; *13:* 58;
  68: 42
Vaughn, Frank *34:* 157
Vavra, Robert *8:* 206
Vawter, Will *17:* 163
Vayas, Diana *71:* 61
Vazquez, Carlos *125:* 184
Veeder, Larry *18:* 4
Velasquez, Eric *45:* 217; *61:* 45; *63:* 110, 111;
  88: 162; *90:* 34, 144; *94:* 213; *107:* 147;
  132: 192; *138:* 213; *159:* 126; *181:* 184;
  184: 96; *191:* 16; *192:* 234
Velasquez, Jose A. *63:* 73
Velez, Walter *71:* 75; *91:* 154; *121:* 181; *168:*
  49
Velthuijs, Max *110:* 228, 229
Vendrell, Carme Sole *42:* 205
Venezia, Mike *54:* 17
Venti, Anthony Bacon *124:* 103; *126:* 26
Venturo, Piero *61:* 194, 195
Ver Beck, Frank *18:* 16, 17
Verkaaik, Ben *110:* 209
Verling, John *71:* 27
Verney, John *14:* 225; *75:* 8
Vernon, Ursula *204:* 157
Verrier, Suzanne *5:* 20; *23:* 212
Versace, Marie *2:* 255
Verstraete, Randy *108:* 193
Vestal, H.B. *9:* 134; *11:* 101; *27:* 25; *34:* 158
Vestergaard, Hope *190:* 203
Vicatan *59:* 146
Vickrey, Robert *45:* 59, 64
Victor, Joan Berg *30:* 193
Viereck, Ellen *3:* 242; *14:* 229
Vigna, Judith *15:* 293; *102:* 194, 195, 196, 197
Vilato, Gaspar E. *5:* 41
Villiard, Paul *51:* 178
Vimnera, A. *23:* 154
Vincent, Eric *34:* 98
Vincent, Felix *41:* 237
Vincent, Gabrielle *121:* 175
Vip *45:* 164
Viskupic, Gary *83:* 48
Vitale, Stefano *109:* 71, 107; *114:* 219, 220;
  123: 106; *138:* 232; *180:* 228, 229
Vivas, Julie *51:* 67, 69; *96:* 225; *197:* 190;
  199: 71
Voake, Charlotte *114:* 221, 222; *180:* 232
Vo-Dinh, Mai *16:* 272; *60:* 191
Vogel, Ilse-Margret *14:* 230
Voigt, Erna *35:* 228
Vojnar, Kamil *95:* 31; *114:* 4; *115:* 62; *121:*
  90; *124:* 72; *130:* 31; *141:* 81; *146:* 196;
  150: 123; *158:* 5, 6; *158:* 154; *171:* 119,
  188; *179:* 15; *180:* 112; *203:* 74
Vojtech, Anna *42:* 190; *108:* 222, 223; *150:*
  203; *174:* 173
von Buhler, Cynthia *149:* 237; *162:* 177; *177:*
  205; *180:* 77; *185:* 214, 215, 216

von Roehl, Angela *126:* 191
von Schmidt, Eric *8:* 62; *50:* 209, 210
von Schmidt, Harold *30:* 80
Vosburgh, Leonard *1:* 161; *7:* 32; *15:* 295, 296; *23:* 110; *30:* 214; *43:* 181
Voss, Tom *127:* 104
Voter, Thomas W. *19:* 3, 9
Vroman, Tom *10:* 29
Vulliamy, Clara *72:* 65

W

Waber, Bernard *47:* 209, 210, 211, 212, 213, 214; *95:* 215, 216, 217; *156:* 203, 205, 206, 207
Wachenje, Benjamin *194:* 170
Wack, Jeff *95:* 140; *110:* 90
Wagner, John *8:* 200; *52:* 104
Wagner, Ken *2:* 59
Waide, Jan *29:* 225; *36:* 139
Wainwright, Jerry *14:* 85
Waites, Joan C. *171:* 2
Wakeen, Sandra *47:* 97
Wakiyama, Hanako *171:* 96; *192:* 236; *200:* 16
Waldherr, Kris *81:* 186
Waldman, Bruce *15:* 297; *43:* 178
Waldman, Neil *35:* 141; *50:* 163; *51:* 180; *54:* 78; *77:* 112; *79:* 162; *82:* 174; *84:* 5, 56, 106; *94:* 232, 233, 234; *96:* 41; *111:* 139; *113:* 9; *118:* 30; *142:* 220, 223; *203:* 173, 174
Waldrep, Richard *111:* 147; *198:* 202
Walker, Brian *144:* 128
Walker, Charles *1:* 46; *4:* 59; *5:* 177; *11:* 115; *19:* 45; *34:* 74; *62:* 168; *72:* 218
Walker, Dugald Stewart *15:* 47; *32:* 202; *33:* 112
Walker, Gil *8:* 49; *23:* 132; *34:* 42
Walker, Jeff *55:* 154; *123:* 116
Walker, Jim *10:* 94
Walker, Mort *8:* 213
Walker, Norman *41:* 37; *45:* 58
Walker, Stephen *12:* 229; *21:* 174
Wallace, Beverly Dobrin *19:* 259
Wallace, Cly *87:* 93
Wallace, Ian *53:* 176, 177; *56:* 165, 166; *58:* 4; *98:* 4; *101:* 191; *112:* 124; *141:* 197, 198, 199, 200; *151:* 212
Wallace, John *105:* 228
Wallace, Nancy Elizabeth *141:* 204; *186:* 195, 197, 199
Wallenta, Adam *123:* 180
Waller, S.E. *24:* 36
Wallner, Alexandra *15:* 120; *156:* 183
Wallner, John C. *9:* 77; *10:* 188; *11:* 28; *14:* 209; *31:* 56, 118; *37:* 64; *51:* 186, 187, 188, 189, 190, 191,192, 193, 194, 195; *52:* 96; *53:* 23, 26; *71:* 99; *73:* 158; *89:* 215; *141:* 9
Wallner, John *162:* 17
Wallower, Lucille *11:* 226
Walotsky, Ron *93:* 87
Walsh, Ellen Stoll *99:* 209; *147:* 219; *194:* 194, 195, 196
Walsh, Rebecca *158:* 193
Walsh, Vivian *149:* 215; *158:* 227
Walters, Anita *205:* 163
Walters, Audrey *18:* 294
Walther, Tom *31:* 179
Walton, Garry *69:* 149
Walton, Tony *11:* 164; *24:* 209; *153:* 8; *177:* 73
Waltrip, Lela *9:* 195
Waltrip, Mildred *3:* 209; *37:* 211
Waltrip, Rufus *9:* 195
Wan *12:* 76
Wang, Suling *191:* 183
Warburton, Sarah *154:* 187
Wappers, G. *121:* 40
Ward, Fred *52:* 19

Ward, Helen *72:* 244; *144:* 240, 242
Ward, John *42:* 191; *96:* 54; *97:* 110; *123:* 105; *124:* 71; *173:* 66
Ward, Keith *2:* 107; *132:* 69
Ward, Leslie *34:* 126; *36:* 87
Ward, Lynd *1:* 99, 132, 133, 150; *2:* 108, 158, 196, 259; *18:* 86; *27:* 56; *29:* 79, 187, 253, 255; *36:* 199,200, 201, 202, 203, 204, 205, 206, 207, 209; *43:* 34; *56:* 28; *60:* 116; *100:* 65
Ward, Peter *37:* 116
Waring, Geoff *172:* 84
Warhola, James *92:* 5; *115:* 85, 87; *118:* 174, 175, 177; *176:* 84; *187:* 189, 190
Warner, Ben *159:* 171
Warner, Peter *14:* 87
Warnes, Tim *175:* 159; *202:* 188
Warnick, Elsa *113:* 223
Warren, Betsy *2:* 101
Warren, Jim *85:* 81
Warren, Marion Cray *14:* 215
Warshaw, Jerry *30:* 197, 198; *42:* 165
Wasden, Kevin *102:* 162
Washington, Nevin *20:* 123
Washington, Phyllis *20:* 123
Wasserman, Amy L. *92:* 110
Waterman, Stan *11:* 76
Watkins-Pitchford, D.J. *6:* 215, 217
Watling, James *67:* 210; *78:* 112; *101:* 81; *117:* 189, 190; *127:* 119, 120
Watson, Aldren A. *2:* 267; *5:* 94; *13:* 71; *19:* 253; *32:* 220; *42:* 193, 194, 195, 196, 197, 198, 199, 200, 201; *YABC 2:* 202
Watson, G. *83:* 162
Watson, Gary *19:* 147; *36:* 68; *41:* 122; *47:* 139
Watson, J.D. *22:* 86
Watson, Jesse Joshua *197:* 124; *199:* 181; *202:* 136
Watson, Karen *11:* 26
Watson, Mary *117:* 193
Watson, Richard Jesse *62:* 188, 189
Watson, Wendy *5:* 197; *13:* 101; *33:* 116; *46:* 163; *64:* 12; *74:* 242, 243; *91:* 21; *142:* 228
Watt, Mélanie *136:* 206; *193:* 211
Wattenberg, Jane *174:* 200; *185:* 46; *187:* 108
Watterson, Bill *66:* 223, 225, 226
Watts, Bernadette *4:* 227; *103:* 182, 183
Watts, James *59:* 197; *74:* 145; *86:* 124
Watts, John *37:* 149
Watts, Leslie Elizabeth *150:* 207; *165:* 106
Watts, Stan *116:* 205
Weatherby, Mark Alan *77:* 141
Webb, Jennifer *110:* 79
Webb, Lanny *142:* 175
Webb, Sophie *135:* 214
Webber, Helen *3:* 141
Webber, Irma E. *14:* 238
Weber, Erik *56:* 19, 20
Weber, Florence *40:* 153
Weber, Jill *127:* 227, 228; *189:* 163
Weber, Roland *61:* 204
Weber, Sam *190:* 227
Weber, William J. *14:* 239
Webster, Jean *17:* 241
Weeks, Sarah *162:* 39
Wegman, William *78:* 243
Wegner, Fritz *14:* 250; *20:* 189; *44:* 165; *86:* 62
Weidenear, Reynold H. *21:* 122
Weigel, Jeff *170:* 193
Weihs, Erika *4:* 21; *15:* 299; *72:* 201; *107:* 207, 208
Weil, Lisl *7:* 203; *10:* 58; *21:* 95; *22:* 188,217; *33:* 193
Weiman, Jon *50:* 162, 165; *52:* 103; *54:* 78, 79, 81; *78:* 80; *82:* 107; *93:* 82; *97:* 69; *105:* 179; *193:* 65
Weiner, Sandra *14:* 240
Weiner, Scott *55:* 27
Weinhaus, Karen Ann *53:* 90; *71:* 50; *86:* 124

Weinman, Brad *197:* 20
Weinstock, Robert *204:* 165, 166
Weisgard, Leonard *1:* 65; *2:* 191, 197, 204, 264, 265; *5:* 108; *21:* 42; *30:* 200, 201, 203, 204; *41:* 47; *44:* 125; *53:* 25; *85:* 196, 198, 200, 201; *100:* 139,207; *YABC 2:* 13
Weisman, David *173:* 47
Weiss, Ellen *44:* 202
Weiss, Emil *1:* 168; *7:* 60
Weiss, Harvey *1:* 145, 223; *27:* 224, 227; *68:* 214; *76:* 245, 246, 247
Weiss, Nicki *33:* 229
Weissman, Bari *49:* 72; *90:* 125; *139:* 142
Weitzman, David L. *172:* 199
Welch, Sheila Kelly *130:* 221
Welkes, Allen *68:* 218
Wellington, Monica *99:* 223; *157:* 259, 260, 261
Welliver, Norma *76:* 94
Wellner, Fred *127:* 53
Wells, Frances *1:* 183
Wells, H.G. *20:* 194, 200
Wells, Haru *53:* 120, 121
Wells, Robert E. *184:* 208
Wells, Rosemary *6:* 49; *18:* 297; *60:* 32; *66:* 203; *69:* 215, 216; *114:* 227; *118:* 149, 150; *156:* 188, 189, 190, 191
Wells, Rufus III *56:* 111, 113
Wells, Susan *22:* 43
Wendelin, Rudolph *23:* 234
Wengenroth, Stow *37:* 47
Weninger, Brigitte *189:* 192, 194
Werenskiold, Erik *15:* 6; *62:* 17
Werner, Honi *24:* 110; *33:* 41; *88:* 122
Werth, Kurt *7:* 122; *14:* 157; *20:* 214; *39:* 128
Wesson,
West, Harry A. *124:* 38
Westcott, Nadine Bernard *68:* 46; *84:* 49; *86:* 133; *106:* 199; *111:* 78; *113:* 111; *130:* 224; *139:* 54; *158:* 256; *194:* 199
Westerberg, Christine *29:* 226
Westerduin, Anne *105:* 229
Westerman, Johanna *162:* 206
Weston, Martha *29:* 116; *30:* 213; *33:* 85, 100; *53:* 181, 182, 183, 184; *77:* 95; *80:* 152; *119:* 196,197, 198, 199; *127:* 189; *133:* 196
Wetherbee, Margaret *5:* 3
Wexler, Jerome *49:* 73; *150:* 129
Whalley, Peter *50:* 49
Whatley, Bruce *186:* 93, 95
Wheatley, Arabelle *11:* 231; *16:* 276
Wheeler, Cindy *49:* 205
Wheeler, Dora *44:* 179
Wheelright, Rowland *15:* 81; *YABC 2:* 286
Whelan, Michael *56:* 108; *70:* 27, 29, 67, 68, 148; *74:* 18; *84:* 14; *91:* 195, 196; *95:* 147; *98:* 150, 151; *106:* 157; *113:* 218, 220; *116:* 99, 100
Whelan, Patrick *135:* 145
Whistler, Rex *16:* 75; *30:* 207, 208
White, Craig *110:* 130; *119:* 193; *130:* 33; *179:* 31
White, David Omar *5:* 56; *18:* 6
White, Joan *83:* 225
White, Martin *51:* 197; *85:* 127
Whitear *32:* 26
Whitehead, Beck *86:* 171
Whitehead, S.B. *154:* 132
Whithorne, H.S. *7:* 49
Whitney, George Gillett *3:* 24
Whitney, Jean *99:* 53
Whitson, Paul *102:* 161
Whittam, Geoffrey *30:* 191
Whyte, Mary *96:* 127
Wiberg, Harald *38:* 127; *93:* 215
Wick, Walter *77:* 128
Wickstrom, Sylvie *106:* 87; *169:* 180
Wickstrom, Thor *200:* 205
Widener, Terry *105:* 230; *106:* 7; *163:* 23; *200:* 17

Wiese, Kurt *3:* 255; *4:* 206; *14:* 17; *17:* 18, 19; *19:* 47; *24:* 152; *25:* 212; *32:* 184; *36:* 211,213, 214, 215, 216, 217, 218; *45:* 161; *100:* 92

Wiesner, David *33:* 47; *51:* 106; *57:* 67; *58:* 55; *64:* 78, 79, 81; *69:* 233; *72:* 247, 248, 249, 251,252, 253, 254; *83:* 134; *104:* 31; *117:* 197, 199, 200, 202; *139:* 223, 224; *151:* 51; *181:* 189, 190

Wiesner, William *4:* 100; *5:* 200, 201; *14:* 262

Wiggins, George *6:* 133

Wijngaard, Juan *111:* 36; *114:* 124

Wikkelsoe, Otto *45:* 25, 26

Wikland, Ilon *5:* 113; *8:* 150; *38:* 124, 125, 130; *127:* 162

Wikler, Madeline *114:* 233

Wilbur, C. Keith, M.D. *27:* 228

Wilburn, Kathy *53:* 102; *68:* 234

Wilcox, Cathy *105:* 123

Wilcox, J.A.J. *34:* 122

Wilcox, R. Turner *36:* 219

Wild, Jocelyn *46:* 220, 221, 222; *80:* 117

Wilde, George *7:* 139

Wildsmith, Brian *16:* 281, 282; *18:* 170, 171; *66:* 25; *69:* 224, 225, 227; *77:* 103; *83:* 218; *124:* 214,217, 219

Wildsmith, Mike *140:* 229

Wilhelm, Hans *58:* 189, 191; *73:* 157; *77:* 127; *135:* 229, 230, 233, 234; *196:* 209

Wilkin, Eloise *36:* 173; *49:* 208, 209, 210

Wilkinson, Barry *50:* 213

Wilkinson, Gerald *3:* 40

Wilkon, Jozef *31:* 183, 184; *71:* 206, 207, 209; *133:* 222

Wilks, Mike *34:* 24; *44:* 203

Willems, Mo *154:* 245, 246, 247; *180:* 236, 237, 239

Willey, Bee *103:* 129; *139:* 159; *173:* 115

Willhoite, Michael A. *71:* 214

William, Maria *168:* 51

Williams, Berkeley, Jr. *64:* 75

Williams, Ferelith Eccles *22:* 238

Williams, Garth *1:* 197; *2:* 49, 270; *4:* 205; *15:* 198, 302, 304, 307; *16:* 34; *18:* 283, 298, 299, 300, 301; *29:* 177, 178, 179, 232, 233, 241, 242, 243, 244, 245, 248; *40:* 106; *66:* 229, 230, 231, 233, 234; *71:* 192; *73:* 218, 219, 220; *78:* 261; *100:* 251, 252, 255; *136:* 117; *YABC 2:* 15, 16, 19

Williams, J. Scott *48:* 28

Williams, Jennifer *102:* 201

Williams, Jenny *60:* 202; *81:* 21; *88:* 71

Williams, Kent *180:* 18

Williams, Kit *44:* 206, 207, 208, 209, 211, 212

Williams, Marcia *97:* 214; *159:* 208, 209

Williams, Maureen *12:* 238

Williams, Patrick *14:* 218

Williams, Richard *44:* 93; *72:* 229; *74:* 133; *78:* 155, 237; *91:* 178; *110:* 212; *136:* 201, 202, 203; *152:* 115

Williams, Sam *124:* 222; *153:* 11; *177:* 201, 202; *180:* 34

Williams, Sophy *135:* 236

Williams, Vera B. *53:* 186, 187, 188, 189; *102:* 201, 202, 203

Williamson, Alex *177:* 180; *205:* 50

Williamson, Mel *60:* 9

Willingham, Fred *104:* 206; *154:* 157

Willis, Adam *181:* 75

Willmore, J.T. *54:* 113, 114

Wilsdorf, Anne *180:* 122; *189:* 124; *191:* 195

Wilson, Anne *160:* 114

Wilson, Charles Banks *17:* 92; *43:* 73

Wilson, Connie *113:* 179

Wilson, Dagmar *10:* 47

Wilson, Dawn *67:* 161; *81:* 120; *113:* 158

Wilson, Edward A. *6:* 24; *16:* 149; *20:* 220, 221; *22:* 87; *26:* 67; *38:* 212, 214, 215, 216, 217

Wilson, Forrest *27:* 231

Wilson, Gahan *35:* 234; *41:* 136

Wilson, George *76:* 87

Wilson, Helen Miranda *140:* 61

Wilson, Jack *17:* 139

Wilson, Janet *77:* 154; *96:* 114; *99:* 219, 220; *153:* 64 *106:* 122; *130:* 210; *145:* 178; *173:* 64

Wilson, John *22:* 240

Wilson, Maurice *46:* 224

Wilson, Patten *35:* 61

Wilson, Peggy *15:* 4; *84:* 20

Wilson, Phil *181:* 29

Wilson, Rowland B. *30:* 170

Wilson, Sarah *50:* 215

Wilson, Tom *33:* 232

Wilson, W.N. *22:* 26

Wilson-Max, Ken *170:* 196; *180:* 181

Wilton, Nicholas *103:* 52; *183:* 111

Wilwerding, Walter J. *9:* 202

Wimmer, Mike *63:* 6; *70:* 121; *75:* 186; *76:* 21,22, 23; *91:* 114; *97:* 45, 68; *98:* 28; *107:* 130; *146:* 21; *149:* 47; *173:* 126; *193:* 21, 25; *194:* 204, 205

Winborn, Marsha *78:* 34; *99:* 70; *192:* 20

Winch, John *165:* 233

Winchester, Linda *13:* 231

Wind, Betty *28:* 158

Windham, Kathryn Tucker *14:* 260

Windham, Sophie *184:* 212

Winfield, Alison *115:* 78

Winfield, Wayne *72:* 23

Wing, Gary *64:* 147

Wing, Ron *50:* 85

Wingerter, Linda S. *132:* 199; *174:* 181; *200:* 196

Winick, Judd *124:* 227, 228, 229

Winn-Lederer, Ilene *202:* 91

Winslow, Will *21:* 124

Winstead, Rosie *180:* 243

Winsten, Melanie Willa *41:* 41

Winter, Jeanette *151:* 240, 241, 242; *184:* 215, 217, 218, 219

Winter, Milo *15:* 97; *19:* 221; *21:* 181, 203, 204, 206; *64:* 19; *YABC 2:* 144

Winter, Paula *48:* 227

Winter, Susan *163:* 177; *182:* 201

Winters, Greg *70:* 117

Winters, Nina *62:* 194

Wise, Louis *13:* 68

Wiseman, Ann *31:* 187

Wiseman, B. *4:* 233

Wishnefsky, Phillip *3:* 14

Wiskur, Darrell *5:* 72; *10:* 50; *18:* 246

Wisniewski, David *95:* 220, 221

Wisniewski, Robert *95:* 10; *119:* 192

Witschonke, Alan *153:* 149, 150

Witt, Dick *80:* 244

Wittmann, Patrick *162:* 204

Wittman, Sally *30:* 219

Wittner, Dale *99:* 43

Wittwer, Hala *158:* 267; *195:* 80

Woehr, Lois *12:* 5

Wohlberg, Meg *12:* 100; *14:* 197; *41:* 255

Wohnoutka, Mike *137:* 68; *190:* 199; *195:* 218; *205:* 132

Wojtowycz, David *167:* 168

Woldin, Beth Weiner *34:* 211

Wolf, Elizabeth *133:* 151

Wolf, J. *16:* 91

Wolf, Janet *78:* 254

Wolf, Linda *33:* 163

Wolfe, Corey *72:* 213

Wolfe, Gillian *199:* 193

Wolff, Ashley *50:* 217; *81:* 216; *156:* 216, 217; *170:* 57; *174:* 174; *184:* 72; *203:* 181, 182, 183, 184

Wolff, Glenn *178:* 230

Wolfsgruber, Linda *166:* 61

Wondriska, William *6:* 220

Wong, Janet S. *98:* 225; *152:* 43

Wong, Nicole *174:* 13

Wonsetler, John C. *5:* 168

Wood, Audrey *50:* 221, 222, 223; *81:* 219, 221; *198:* 206

Wood, Don *50:* 220, 225, 226, 228, 229; *81:* 218, 220; *139:* 239, 240

Wood, Grant *19:* 198

Wood, Heather *133:* 108

Wood, Ivor *58:* 17

Wood, Muriel *36:* 119; *77:* 167; *171:* 55; *187:* 46

Wood, Myron *6:* 220

Wood, Owen *18:* 187; *64:* 202, 204, 205, 206, 208, 210

Wood, Rob *193:* 48

Wood, Ruth *8:* 11

Woodbridge, Curtis *133:* 138; *204:* 113

Wooding, Sharon L. *66:* 237

Woodruff, Liza *132:* 239; *182:* 46, 204

Woodruff, Thomas *171:* 73

Woods, John, Jr. *109:* 142

Woodson, Jack *10:* 201

Woodson, Jacqueline *94:* 242

Woodward, Alice *26:* 89; *36:* 81

Wool, David *26:* 27

Woolley, Janet *112:* 75

Woolman, Steven *106:* 47; *163:* 73

Wooten, Vernon *23:* 70; *51:* 170

Worboys, Evelyn *1:* 166, 167

Word, Reagan *103:* 204

Wormell, Christopher *154:* 251; *202:* 206

Worth, Jo *34:* 143

Worth, Wendy *4:* 133

Wosmek, Frances *29:* 251

Wrenn, Charles L. *38:* 96; *YABC 1:* 20, 21

Wright, Barbara Mullarney *98:* 161

Wright, Cliff *168:* 203

Wright, Dare *21:* 206

Wright-Frierson, Virginia *58:* 194; *110:* 246

Wright, George *YABC 1:* 268

Wright, Joseph *30:* 160

Wronker, Lili Cassel *3:* 247; *10:* 204; *21:* 10

Wu, Donald *200:* 18

Wummer, Amy *154:* 181; *168:* 150; *176:* 85; *201:* 202, 203

Wyant, Alexander Helwig *110:* 19

Wyatt, David *97:* 9; *101:* 44; *114:* 194; *140:* 20; *167:* 13; *188:* 48

Wyatt, Stanley *46:* 210

Wyeth, Andrew *13:* 40; *YABC 1:* 133, 134

Wyeth, Jamie *41:* 257

Wyeth, N.C. *13:* 41; *17:* 252, 253, 254, 255, 256, 257, 258, 259, 264, 265, 266, 267, 268; *18:* 181; *19:* 80, 191, 200; *21:* 57, 183; *22:* 91; *23:* 152; *24:* 28, 99; *35:* 61; *41:* 65; *100:* 206; *YABC1:* 133, 223; *2:* 53, 75, 171, 187, 317

Wyman, Cherie R. *91:* 42

X

Xuan, YongSheng *119:* 202, 207, 208; *140:* 36; *187:* 21

Y

Yaccarino, Dan *141:* 208, 209; *147:* 171; *192:* 244, 245

Yakovetic, Joe *59:* 202; *75:* 85

Yalowitz, Paul *93:* 33

Yamaguchi, Marianne *85:* 118

Yamasaki, James *167:* 93

Yang, Belle *170:* 198

Yang, Jay *1:* 8; *12:* 239

Yap, Weda *6:* 176

Yaroslava
  See Mills, Yaroslava Surmach

Yashima, Taro *14:* 84

Yates, John *74:* 249, 250
Yayo *178:* 88
Yee, Cora *166:* 233
Yee, Wong Herbert *115:* 216, 217; *172:* 204, 205; *194:* 59
Yelchin, Eugene *204:* 4
Yeo, Brad *135:* 121; *192:* 106
Yerxa, Leo *181:* 195
Yezerski, Thomas F. *162:* 29
Ylla
    See Koffler, Camilla
Yohn, F.C. *23:* 128; *YABC 1:* 269
Yoo, Taeeun *191:* 198
Yorinks, Adrienne *144:* 248; *200:* 214
Yorke, David *80:* 178
Yoshida, Toshi *77:* 231
Yoshikawa, Sachiko *168:* 104; *177:* 28; *181:* 196, 197
Youll, Paul *91:* 218
Youll, Stephen *92:* 227; *118:* 136, 137; *164:* 248; *202:* 92
Young, Amy L. *185:* 218; *190:* 46
Young, Cybéle *167:* 9
Young, Ed *7:* 205; *10:* 206; *40:* 124; *63:* 142; *74:* 250, 251, 252, 253; *75:* 227; *81:* 159; *83:* 98; *94:* 154; *115:* 160; *137:* 162; *YABC 2:* 242; *173:* 174, 175, 176; *205:* 29
Young, Mary O'Keefe *77:* 95; *80:* 247; *134:* 214; *140:* 213
Young, Noela *8:* 221; *89:* 231; *97:* 195
Young, Paul *190:* 222
Young, Selina *153:* 12; *201:* 204, 205
Yun, Cheng Mung *60:* 143

Z

Zacharow, Christopher *88:* 98
Zacks, Lewis *10:* 161
Zadig *50:* 58
Zaffo, George *42:* 208
Zagwyn, Deborah Turney *138:* 227
Zahares, Wade *193:* 219
Zaid, Barry *50:* 127; *51:* 201
Zaidenberg, Arthur *34:* 218, 219, 220
Zalben, Jane Breskin *7:* 211; *79:* 230, 231, 233; *170:* 202
Zallinger, Jean *4:* 192; *8:* 8, 129; *14:* 273; *68:* 36; *80:* 254; *115:* 219, 220, 222
Zallinger, Rudolph F. *3:* 245
Zakrajsek, Molly *177:* 146
Zappa, Ahmet *180:* 250
Zebot, George *83:* 214
Zeck, Gerry *40:* 232
Zeff, Joe *181:* 98
Zeifert, Harriet *154:* 265, 267
Zeiring, Bob *42:* 130
Zeldich, Arieh *49:* 124; *62:* 120
Zeldis, Malcah *86:* 239; *94:* 198; *146:* 265, 266
Zelinsky, Paul O. *14:* 269; *43:* 56; *49:* 218-223; *53:* 111; *68:* 195; *102:* 219, 222, 221, 222; *154:* 255, 256, 257; *171:* 141; *185:* 96
Zelvin, Diana *72:* 190; *76:* 101; *93:* 207
Zemach, Kaethe *149:* 250
Zemach, Margot *3:* 270; *8:* 201; *21:* 210, 211; *27:* 204, 205, 210; *28:* 185; *49:* 22, 183, 224; *53:* 151; *56:* 146; *70:* 245, 246; *92:* 74

Zeman, Ludmila *153* 212
Zemsky, Jessica *10:* 62
Zepelinsky, Paul *35:* 93
Zerbetz, Evon *127:* 34; *158:* 109
Zezejl, Daniel *197:* 74
Zhang, Ange *101:* 190; *172:* 41
Zhang, Son Nang *163:* 113; *170:* 206
Ziegler, Jack *84:* 134
Zimdars, Berta *129:* 155
Zimet, Jay *147:* 94; *152:* 74; *196:* 75
Zimic, Tricia *72:* 95
Zimmer, Dirk *38:* 195; *49:* 71; *56:* 151; *65:* 214; *84:* 159; *89:* 26; *147:* 224
Zimmer, Tracie Vaughn *169:* 183
Zimmerman, Andrea *192:* 49, 50
Zimmermann, H. Werner *101:* 223; *112:* 197
Zimnik, Reiner *36:* 224
Zingone, Robin *180:* 134
Zinkeisen, Anna *13:* 106
Zinn, David *97:* 97
Zoellick, Scott *33:* 231
Zollars, Jaime *190:* 190
Zonia, Dhimitri *20:* 234, 235
Zorn, Peter A., Jr. *142:* 157
Zudeck, Darryl *58:* 129; *63:* 98; *80:* 52
Zug, Mark *88:* 131; *204:* 169
Zulewski, Tim *164:* 95
Zuma *99:* 36
Zvorykin, Boris *61:* 155
Zweifel, Francis *14:* 274; *28:* 187
Zwerger, Lisbeth *54:* 176, 178; *66:* 246, 247, 248; *130:* 230, 231, 232, 233; *181:* 92; *194:* 224, 225, 226
Zwinger, Herman H. *46:* 227
Zwolak, Paul *67:* 69, 71, 73, 74

Author Index

The following index gives the number of the volume in which an author's biographical sketch, Autobiography Feature, Brief Entry, or Obituary appears.

This index includes references to all entries in the following series, which are also published by The Gale Group.

YABC—*Yesterday's Authors of Books for Children: Facts and Pictures about Authors and Illustrators of Books for Young People from Early Times to 1960*
CLR—*Children's Literature Review: Excerpts from Reviews, Criticism, and Commentary on Books for Children*
SAAS—*Something about the Author Autobiography Series*

A

Aardema, Verna 1911-2000 .... *107*
  Obituary *119*
  Earlier sketches in SATA *:4, 68*
  See also CLR *17*
  See also SAAS *8*
Aaron, Chester 1923- *74*
  Earlier sketch in SATA *9*
  See also SAAS *12*
Aaseng, Nate
  See Aaseng, Nathan
Aaseng, Nathan 1953- *172*
  Brief entry *38*
  Earlier sketches in SATA *51, 88*
  See also CLR *54*
  See also SAAS *12*
Abadzis, Nick 1965- *193*
abalos, Rafael 1956- *197*
Abbas, Jailan 1952- *91*
Abbey, Lynn
  See Abbey, Marilyn Lorraine
Abbey, Marilyn Lorraine 1948- *156*
Abbott, Alice
  See Borland, Kathryn Kilby
  and Speicher, Helen Ross S(mith)
Abbott, Jacob 1803-1879 .... *22*
Abbott, Manager Henry
  See Stratemeyer, Edward L.
Abbott, R(obert) Tucker 1919-1995 .... *61*
  Obituary *87*
Abbott, Sarah
  See Zolotow, Charlotte
Abbott, Tony 1952- *205*
  Earlier sketch in SATA *159*
Abdelsayed, Cindy 1962- *123*
Abdul, Raoul 1929- *12*
Abeele, Veronique van den *196*
Abel, Raymond 1911- *12*
Abell, Kathleen 1938- *9*
Abelove, Joan *110*
Abels, Harriette S(heffer) 1926- *50*
Abercrombie, Barbara 1939- *182*
  Earlier sketch in SATA *16*
Abercrombie, Barbara Mattes
  See Abercrombie, Barbara
Abercrombie, Lynn
  See Sorrells, Walter
Abernethy, Robert G(ordon) 1927- *5*

Abisch, Roslyn Kroop 1927- *9*
Abisch, Roz
  See Abisch, Roslyn Kroop
Ablow, Gail 1962- *198*
Abodaher, David J. (Naiph) 1919- *17*
Abolafia, Yossi 1944-
  See Abulafia, Yossi
Abouzeid, Chris *175*
Abrahall, Clare Hoskyns
  See Hoskyns-Abrahall, Clare (Constance Drury)
Abrahams, Hilary (Ruth) 1938- *29*
Abrahams, Peter 1947- *194*
Abrahams, Robert David 1905-1998 .... *4*
Abramovitz, Anita (Zeltner Brooks) 1914- *5*
Abrams, Joy 1941- *16*
Abrams, Lawrence F. *58*
  Brief entry *47*
Abrashkin, Raymond 1911-1960 .... *50*
Abulafia, Yossi 1944- *177*
  Brief entry *46*
  Earlier sketch in SATA *60*
Acampora, Paul *175*
Accardo, Anthony *191*
Acer, David *206*
Achebe, Albert Chinualumogu
  See Achebe, Chinua
Achebe, Chinua 1930- *40*
  Brief entry *38*
  Earlier sketch in SATA *38*
  See also CLR *20*
Ackerman, Diane 1948- *102*
Ackerman, Eugene (Francis) 1888-1974 ...... *10*
Ackerman, Karen 1951- *126*
Ackerman, Susan Yoder 1945- *92*
Ackison, Wendy Wassink 1956- *103*
Ackley, Peggy Jo 1955- *58*
Ackroyd, Peter 1949- *153*
Acorn, John (Harrison) 1958- *79*
Acredolo, Linda (Potter) 1947- *159*
Acs, Laszlo (Bela) 1931- *42*
  Brief entry *32*
Acuff, Selma Boyd 1924- *45*
Ada, Alma Flor 1938- *181*
  Earlier sketches in SATA *43, 84, 143*
  See also CLR *62*
Adair, Gilbert 1944- *98*
Adair, Ian 1942- *53*
Adair, Margaret Weeks (?)-1971 .... *10*

Adam, Cornel
  See Lengyel, Cornel Adam
Adam, Mark
  See Alexander, Marc
Adam, Robert 1948- *93*
Adams, Adrienne 1906- *90*
  Earlier sketch in SATA *8*
  See also CLR *73*
Adams, Andy 1859-1935
  See YABC *1*
Adams, Barbara Johnston 1943- *60*
Adams, Bruin
  See Ellis, Edward S.
Adams, Captain Bruin
  See Ellis, Edward S.
Adams, Captain J. F. C.
  See Ellis, Edward S.
Adams, Dale
  See Quinn, Elisabeth
Adams, Daniel
  See Nicole, Christopher (Robin)
Adams, Debra
  See Speregen, Devra Newberger
Adams, Douglas 1952-2001 .... *116*
  Obituary *128*
Adams, Douglas Noel
  See Adams, Douglas
Adams, Edith
  See Shine, Deborah
Adams, Florence 1932- *61*
Adams, Harriet S(tratemeyer) 1892(?)-1982 .. *1*
  Obituary *29*
Adams, Harrison
  See Rathborne, St. George (Henry)
  and Stratemeyer, Edward L.
Adams, Hazard 1926- *6*
Adams, Hazard Simeon
  See Adams, Hazard
Adams, John Anthony 1944- *67*
Adams, Laurie 1941- *33*
Adams, Lowell
  See Joseph, James (Herz)
Adams, Nicholas
  See Pine, Nicholas
Adams, Nicholas
  See Smith, Sherwood
Adams, Nicholas
  See Doyle, Debra
  and Macdonald, James D.

Adams, Pam 1919- *112*
Adams, Pamela
    See Adams, Pam
Adams, Richard (George) 1920- *69*
    Earlier sketch in SATA 7
    See also CLR *121*
Adams, Ruth Joyce *14*
Adams, Tricia
    See Kite, Pat
Adams, William Taylor 1822-1897 .... *28*
Adam Smith, Janet (Buchanan) 1905-1999 .. *63*
Adamson, Gareth 1925-1982(?) *46*
    Obituary *30*
Adamson, George 1906-1989
    Obituary *63*
Adamson, George (Worsley) 1913-2005 ...... *30*
Adamson, Graham
    See Groom, Arthur William
Adamson, Joy(-Friederike Victoria)
    1910-1980 .... *11*
    Obituary *22*
Adamson, Wendy Writson 1942- *22*
Addasi, Maha 1968- *205*
Addison, Kenneth 1949(?)-2005 .... *187*
Addison, Kenneth L.
    See Addison, Kenneth
Addona, Angelo F. 1925- *14*
Addy, Sharon Hart 1943- *192*
    Earlier sketch in SATA *108*
Addy, Ted
    See Winterbotham, R(ussell) R(obert)
Adelberg, Doris
    See Orgel, Doris
Adelson, Leone 1908- *11*
Adinolfi, JoAnn *176*
Adkins, Jan 1944- *144*
    Earlier sketches in SATA 8, 69
    See also CLR 77
    See also SAAS 19
Adler, C(arole) S(chwerdtfeger) 1932- *126*
    Earlier sketches in SATA 26, 63, 102
    See also CLR 78
    See also SAAS 15
Adler, David A. 1947- *178*
    Earlier sketches in SATA 14, 70, 106, 151
    See also CLR 108
Adler, Irene
    See Penzler, Otto
    and Storr, Catherine (Cole)
Adler, Irving 1913- *29*
    Autobiography Feature *164*
    Earlier sketch in SATA *1*
    See also CLR 27
    See also SAAS 15
Adler, Larry 1939- *36*
Adler, Peggy *22*
Adler, Ruth 1915-1968 .... *1*
Adlerman, Daniel (Ezra) 1963- *163*
    Earlier sketch in SATA 96
Adlerman, Kim
    See Adlerman, Kimberly M(arie)
Adlerman, Kimberly M(arie) 1964- *163*
    Earlier sketch in SATA 96
Adoff, Arnold 1935- *96*
    Earlier sketches in SATA 5, 57
    See also CLR 7
    See also SAAS 15
Adoff, Jaime *163*
Adoff, Jaime Levi
    See Adoff, Jaime
Adorjan, Carol (Madden) 1934- *71*
    Earlier sketch in SATA *10*
Adrian, Frances
    See Polland, Madeleine A(ngela Cahill)
Adrian, Mary
    See Jorgensen, Mary Venn
Adshead, Gladys L(ucy) 1896-1985 .... *3*
Aesop 620(?)B.C.-560(?)B.C. *64*
    See also CLR *14*
Aesop, Abraham
    See Newbery, John

Affabee, Eric
    See Stine, R.L.
Agapida, Fray Antonio
    See Irving, Washington
Agard, John 1949- *138*
Agard, Nadema 1948- *18*
Agarwal, Deepa 1947- *141*
Agee, Jon 1960- *196*
    Earlier sketches in SATA *116, 157*
Agell, Charlotte 1959- *150*
    Earlier sketch in SATA *99*
Agent Orange
    See Moseley, James W(illett)
Aghill, Gordon
    See Garrett, Randall
    and Silverberg, Robert
Agle, Nan Hayden 1905- *3*
    See also SAAS *10*
Agnew, Edith J(osephine) 1897-1988 .... *11*
Agonito, Joseph *177*
Agonito, Rosemary 1937- *177*
Ahern, Margaret McCrohan 1921- *10*
Ahl, Anna Maria 1926- *32*
Ahlberg, Allan 1938- *165*
    Brief entry *35*
    Earlier sketches in SATA 68, 120
    See also CLR 18
Ahlberg, Janet 1944-1994 .... *120*
    Brief entry *32*
    Obituary *83*
    Earlier sketch in SATA 68
    See also CLR 18
Aho, Julia Kay
    See Kay, Julia
Aichinger, Helga 1937- *4*
Aiken, Clarissa (M.) Lorenz 1899-1992 .... *12*
    Obituary *109*
Aiken, Conrad 1889-1973 .... *30*
    Earlier sketch in SATA *3*
Aiken, Conrad Potter
    See Aiken, Conrad
Aiken, Joan (Delano) 1924-2004 .... *73*
    Autobiography Feature *109*
    Obituary *152*
    Earlier sketches in SATA 2, 30
    See also CLR 90
    See also SAAS *1*
Aillaud, Cindy Lou 1955- *184*
Ainsley, Alix
    See Steiner, Barbara A(nnette)
Ainsworth, Catherine Harris 1910- *56*
Ainsworth, Norma 1911-1987 .... *9*
Ainsworth, Ruth (Gallard) 1908- *73*
    Earlier sketch in SATA 7
Ainsworth, William Harrison 1805-1882 ...... *24*
Aistrop, Jack 1916- *14*
Aitken, Amy 1952- *54*
    Brief entry *40*
Aitken, Dorothy 1916- *10*
Aitmatov, Chingiz 1928-2008 .... *56*
Aitmatov, Chingiz Torekulovich
    See Aitmatov, Chingiz
Akaba, Suekichi 1910- *46*
Akers, Floyd
    See Baum, L. Frank
Akib, Jamel *181*
Aks, Patricia 1926-1994 .... *68*
Alagoa, Ebiegberi Joe 1933- *108*
Alain
    See Brustlein, Daniel
Alajalov, Constantin 1900-1987
    Obituary *53*
Alalou, Ali *203*
Alalou, Elizabeth *203*
Alan, David
    See Horsfield, Alan
Alan, Robert
    See Silverstein, Robert Alan
Alarcon, Francisco X. 1954- *104*
Alarcon, Francisco Xavier
    See Alarcon, Francisco X.

Alarcon, Karen Beaumont
    See Beaumont, Karen
Albert, Burton 1936- *22*
Albert, Louise 1928- *157*
Albert, Michael 1966- *202*
Albert, Richard E. 1909-1999 .... *82*
Albert, Susan Wittig 1940- *107*
Alberts, Frances Jacobs 1907-1989 .... *14*
Albertson, Susan
    See Wojciechowski, Susan
Albion, Lee Smith *29*
Alborough, Jez 1959- *149*
    Earlier sketch in SATA *86*
Albrecht, Lillie (Vanderveer H.)
    1894-1985 .... *12*
Albyn, Carole Lisa 1955- *83*
Alchemy, Jack
    See Gershator, David
Alcock, Gudrun 1908- *56*
    Brief entry *33*
Alcock, Vivien (Dolores) 1924-2003 .... *76*
    Brief entry *38*
    Obituary *148*
    Earlier sketch in SATA *45*
    See also CLR 26
Alcorn, John 1935- *31*
    Brief entry *30*
Alcorn, Stephen 1958- *110*
Alcott, Louisa May 1832-1888 .... *100*
    See also YABC *1*
    See also CLR *109*
Alda, Arlene 1933- *205*
    Brief entry *36*
    Earlier sketches in SATA 44, 106, 158
    See also CLR 93
Alden, Isabella (Macdonald) 1841-1930 ..... *115*
    See also YABC 2
Alden, Sue
    See Francis, Dorothy
Alderman, Clifford Lindsey 1902-1988 .... *3*
Alderson, Sue Ann 1940- *59*
    Brief entry *48*
Alding, Peter
    See Jeffries, Roderic
Aldis, Dorothy (Keeley) 1896-1966 .... *2*
Aldiss, Brian W. 1925- *34*
Aldiss, Brian Wilson
    See Aldiss, Brian W.
Aldon, Adair
    See Meigs, Cornelia Lynde
Aldous, Allan (Charles) 1911- *27*
Aldrich, Ann
    See Meaker, Marijane
Aldrich, Bess Streeter 1881-1954
    See CLR 70
Aldrich, Thomas (Bailey) 1836-1907 .... *114*
    Earlier sketch in SATA *17*
Aldridge, (Harold Edward) James 1918- *87*
Aldridge, Josephine Haskell *14*
Aldridge, Sheila 1974- *192*
Aleas, Richard
    See Appelt, Kathi
Alegria, Malin 1974(?)- *190*
Alegria, Ricardo E(nrique) 1921- *6*
Aleksin, Anatolii Georgievich 1924- *36*
Alenov, Lydia 1948- *61*
Alex, Ben (a pseudonym) 1946- *45*
Alex, Marlee (a pseudonym) 1948- *45*
Alexander, Anna B(arbara Cooke) 1913- *1*
Alexander, Anne
    See Alexander, Anna B(arbara Cooke)
Alexander, Ellen 1938- *91*
Alexander, Frances (Laura) 1888-1979 .... *4*
Alexander, Janet 1907-1994 .... *97*
    Earlier sketch in SATA *1*
Alexander, Jocelyn Anne Arundel 1930- *22*
Alexander, Linda 1935- *2*

Alexander, Lloyd 1924-2007 .... *135*
    Obituary *182*
    Earlier sketches in SATA *3, 49, 81, 129*
    See also CLR *48*
    See also SAAS *19*
Alexander, Lloyd Chudley
    See Alexander, Lloyd
Alexander, Marc 1929- *117*
Alexander, Martha 1920- *136*
    Earlier sketches in SATA *11, 70*
Alexander, Rae Pace
    See Alexander, Raymond Pace
Alexander, Raymond Pace 1898-1974 .... *22*
Alexander, Robert *200*
Alexander, Rod
    See Pellowski, Michael (Joseph)
Alexander, Sally Hobart 1943- *84*
Alexander, Sue 1933-2008 .... *136*
    Obituary *195*
    Earlier sketches in SATA *12, 89*
    See also SAAS *15*
Alexander, Vincent Arthur 1925-1980
    Obituary *23*
Alexeieff, Alexandre A. 1901-1979 .... *14*
Alger, Horatio, Jr.
    See Stratemeyer, Edward L.
Alger, Horatio, Jr. 1832-1899 .... *16*
    See also CLR *87*
Alger, Leclaire (Gowans) 1898-1969 .... *15*
Aliki
    See Brandenberg, Aliki
Alkema, Chester Jay 1932- *12*
Al-Khalili, Jim 1962- *124*
Alkiviades, Alkis 1953- *105*
Alkouatli, Claire *186*
Allaby, John Michael
    See Allaby, Michael
Allaby, Michael 1933- *167*
Allamand, Pascale 1942- *12*
Allan, Mabel Esther 1915-1998 .... *75*
    Earlier sketches in SATA *5, 32*
    See also CLR *43*
    See also SAAS *11*
Allan, Nicholas 1956- *123*
    Earlier sketch in SATA *79*
Allan-Meyer, Kathleen 1918- *51*
    Brief entry *46*
Allard, Harry
    See Allard, Harry G(rover), Jr.
Allard, Harry G(rover), Jr. 1928- *102*
    Earlier sketch in SATA *42*
    See also CLR *85*
Allee, Marjorie Hill 1890-1945 .... *17*
Allen, Adam
    See Epstein, Beryl
    and Epstein, Samuel
Allen, Alex B.
    See Heide, Florence Parry
Allen, Allyn
    See Eberle, Irmengarde
Allen, Betsy
    See Harrison, Elizabeth (Allen) Cavanna
Allen, Bob 1961- *76*
Allen, Gertrude E(lizabeth) 1888-1984 .... *9*
Allen, Grace
    See Hogarth, Grace (Weston Allen)
Allen, Jeffrey (Yale) 1948- *42*
Allen, John
    See Perry, Ritchie (John Allen)
Allen, Jonathan 1957- *177*
    Earlier sketch in SATA *131*
Allen, Jonathan Dean
    See Allen, Jonathan
Allen, Judy (Christina) 1941- *124*
    Earlier sketch in SATA *80*
Allen, Kenneth S. 1913-1981 .... *56*
Allen, Leroy 1912- *11*
Allen, Linda 1925- *33*
Allen, Marjorie 1931- *22*
Allen, Maury 1932- *26*
Allen, Merritt Parmelee 1892-1954 .... *22*

Allen, Nancy Kelly 1949- *171*
    Earlier sketch in SATA *127*
Allen, Nina (Stroemgren) 1935- *22*
Allen, Pamela (Kay) 1934- *123*
    Earlier sketches in SATA *50, 81*
    See also CLR *44*
Allen, Raul *205*
Allen, Rodney F. 1938-1999 .... *27*
Allen, Roger MacBride 1957- *105*
Allen, Ruth
    See Peterson, Esther (Allen)
Allen, Samuel W(ashington) 1917- *9*
Allen, T. D.
    See Allen, Terril Diener
Allen, Terril Diener 1908- *35*
Allen, Terry D.
    See Allen, Terril Diener
Allen, Thomas B. 1929- *193*
    Earlier sketches in SATA *45, 140*
Allen, Thomas B. 1929- *193*
Allen, Thomas Benton
    See Allen, Thomas B.
Allen, Tom
    See Allen, Thomas B.
Allende, Isabel 1942- *163*
    See also CLR *99*
Allerton, Mary
    See Govan, (Mary) Christine Noble
Alley, Robert W.
    See Alley, R.W.
Alley, R.W. *169*
Alleyn, Ellen
    See Rossetti, Christina
Allington, Richard L(loyd) 1947- *39*
    Brief entry *35*
Allison, Amy 1956- *138*
Allison, Bob *14*
Allison, Diane Worfolk *78*
Allison, Jennifer *173*
Allison, Linda 1948- *43*
Allison, Margaret
    See Klam, Cheryl
Allman, Barbara 1950- *137*
Allmendinger, David F(rederick), Jr. 1938- . *35*
Allred, Alexandra Powe 1965- *144*
Allred, Gordon T(hatcher) 1930- *10*
Allsop, Kenneth 1920-1973 .... *17*
Allsopp, Sophie *188*
Alma, Ann 1946- *201*
Almedingen, E. M.
    See Almedingen, Martha Edith von
Almedingen, Martha Edith von 1898-1971 .... *3*
Almon, Russell
    See Clevenger, William R.
    and Downing, David A(lmon)
Almond, David 1951- *158*
    Earlier sketch in SATA *114*
    See also CLR *85*
Almond, Linda Stevens 1881(?)-1987
    Obituary *50*
Almquist, Don 1929- *11*
Alonzo, Sandra *199*
Alphin, Elaine Marie 1955- *139*
    Autobiography Feature *139*
    Earlier sketches in SATA *80, 130*
Alsenas, Linas 1979- *186*
Alsop, Mary O'Hara 1885-1980 .... *34*
    Obituary *24*
    Earlier sketch in SATA *2*
Alter, Anna 1974- *206*
    Earlier sketch in SATA *135*
Alter, Judith (MacBain) 1938- *101*
    Earlier sketch in SATA *52*
Alter, Judy
    See Alter, Judith (MacBain)
Alter, Robert Edmond 1925-1965 .... *9*
Alter, Stephen 1956- *187*
Althea
    See Braithwaite, Althea
Altman, Linda Jacobs 1943- *21*

Altman, Suzanne
    See Orgel, Doris
    and Schecter, Ellen
Alton, Steve *169*
Altschuler, Franz 1923- *45*
Altsheler, Joseph A(lexander) 1862-1919
    See YABC *1*
Alvarez, John
    See del Rey, Lester
Alvarez, Joseph A. 1930- *18*
Alvarez, Julia 1950- *129*
al-Windawi, Thura
    See Windawi, Thura al-
Alyer, Philip A.
    See Stratemeyer, Edward L.
Amado, Elisa *193*
Amann, Janet 1951- *79*
Amato, Carol A. 1942- *92*
Amato, Mary 1961- *178*
    Earlier sketch in SATA *140*
Ambrose, Stephen E. 1936-2002 .... *138*
    Earlier sketch in SATA *40*
Ambrose, Stephen Edward
    See Ambrose, Stephen E.
Ambrus, Gyozo Laszlo 1935- *1*
    See also SAAS *4*
Ambrus, Victor G.
    See Ambrus, Gyozo Laszlo
Amend, Bill 1962- *147*
Amerman, Lockhart 1911-1969 .... *3*
Ames, Evelyn 1908-1990 .... *13*
    Obituary *64*
Ames, Gerald 1906-1993 .... *11*
    Obituary *74*
Ames, Lee J(udah) 1921- *151*
    Earlier sketch in SATA *3*
Ames, Mildred 1919-1994 .... *85*
    Earlier sketches in SATA *22, 81*
Amico, Tom 1960(?)- *176*
Amit, Ofra 1966- *205*
Ammon, Richard 1942- *124*
Amon, Aline 1928- *9*
Amoss, Berthe 1925- *112*
    Earlier sketch in SATA *5*
Anastasio, Dina 1941- *94*
    Brief entry *30*
    Earlier sketch in SATA *37*
Anaya, Rudolfo 1937-
    See CLR *129*
Anaya, Rudolfo A.
    See Anaya, Rudolfo
Anaya, Rudolpho Alfonso
    See Anaya, Rudolfo
Anckarsvard, Karin Inez Maria 1915-1969 .... *6*
Ancona, George 1929- *192*
    Earlier sketches in SATA *12, 85, 145*
    See also SAAS *18*
Anders, C. J.
    See Bennett, Cherie
Anders, Isabel 1946- *101*
Anders, Lou *176*
Andersdatter, Karla M(argaret) 1938- *34*
Andersen, Bethanne 1954- *191*
Andersen, Hans Christian 1805-1875 .... *100*
    See also YABC *1*
    See also CLR *113*
Andersen, Ted
    See Boyd, Waldo T.
Andersen, Yvonne 1932- *27*
Anderson, Bernice G(oudy) 1894-1997 .... *33*
Anderson, Bob 1944- *139*
    Earlier sketch in SATA *136*
Anderson, Brad(ley Jay) 1924- *33*
    Brief entry *31*
Anderson, C. C.
    See Anderson, Catherine Corley
Anderson, C(larence) W(illiam) 1891-1971 . *11*
Anderson, Catherine C.
    See Anderson, Catherine Corley
Anderson, Catherine Corley 1909-2001 .... *72*

Anderson, Clifford
    See Gardner, Richard (M.)
Anderson, Daryl Shon 1963- 93
Anderson, Dave
    See Anderson, David
Anderson, David 1929- 60
Anderson, Derek 1969- 169
Anderson, Eloise Adell 1927- 9
Anderson, George
    See Groom, Arthur William
Anderson, Grace Fox 1932- 43
Anderson, J(ohn) R(ichard) L(ane)
    1911-1981 15
    Obituary 27
Anderson, Jodi Lynn 182
Anderson, John David 1975- 197
Anderson, John L. 1905- 2
Anderson, Joy 1928- 1
Anderson, Kevin J. 1962- 117
    Earlier sketch in SATA 74
Anderson, Kevin James
    See Anderson, Kevin J.
Anderson, Kirsty 1978- 108
Anderson, K.J.
    See Moesta, Rebecca
Anderson, Laurie Halse 1961- 186
    Earlier sketches in SATA 95, 132
    See also CLR 138
Anderson, LaVere Francis Shoenfelt
    1907-1998 27
Anderson, Leone Castell 1923- 53
    Brief entry 49
Anderson, Lisa G. 1963- 108
Anderson, Lonzo
    See Anderson, John L.
Anderson, Lucia (Lewis) 1922- 10
Anderson, Madelyn Klein 1926-2005 28
Anderson, Margaret J(ean) 1931- 27
    See also SAAS 8
Anderson, Marilyn D. 1943- 144
Anderson, Mary 1939- 82
    Earlier sketch in SATA 7
    See also SAAS 23
Anderson, Matthew Tobin
    See Anderson, M.T.
Anderson, Mona 1910-2004 40
Anderson, Mrs. Melvin
    See Anderson, Catherine Corley
Anderson, M.T. 1968- 182
    Earlier sketches in SATA 97, 146
Anderson, Norman Dean 1928- 22
Anderson, Peggy Perry 1953- 179
    Earlier sketch in SATA 84
Anderson, Poul 1926-2001 90
    Autobiography Feature 106
    Brief entry 39
    See also CLR 58
Anderson, Poul William
    See Anderson, Poul
Anderson, Rachel 1943- 86
    Earlier sketch in SATA 34
    See also SAAS 18
Anderson, Rebecca M.
    See Moesta, Rebecca
Anderson, Rebecca Moesta
    See Moesta, Rebecca
Anderson, Richard
    See Anderson, J(ohn) R(ichard) L(ane)
Anderson, Sara 173
Anderson, Scoular 201
Anderson, (Tom) Scoular 138
Anderson, Susan 1952- 90
Anderson, Thomas Scoular
    See Anderson, Scoular
Anderson, W. B.
    See Schultz, James Willard
Anderson, Wayne 1946- 202
    Earlier sketches in SATA 56, 147
Andersson, Kenneth 1970- 200
Andre, Evelyn M(arie) 1924- 27
Andreasen, Dan 186

Andreassen, Karl
    See Boyd, Waldo T.
Andreassi, K. Robert
    See DeCandido, Keith R.A.
Andree, Louise
    See Coury, Louise Andree
Andrew, Ian 1962- 166
    Earlier sketch in SATA 116
Andrew, Ian Peter
    See Andrew, Ian
Andrew, Prudence (Hastings) 1924- 87
Andrews, Benny 1930-2006 31
    Obituary 178
Andrews, Eleanor Lattimore
    See Lattimore, Eleanor Frances
Andrews, Elton V.
    See Pohl, Frederik
Andrews, F(rank) Emerson 1902-1978 22
Andrews, J(ames) S(ydney) 1934- 4
Andrews, Jan 1942- 167
    Brief entry 49
    Earlier sketches in SATA 58, 98
Andrews, Julie 1935- 153
    Earlier sketch in SATA 7
    See also CLR 85
Andrews, Laura
    See Coury, Louise Andree
Andrews, Roy Chapman 1884-1960 19
Andrews, Tamra 1959- 129
Andrews, V(irginia) C(leo) 1924(?)-1986
    Obituary 50
Andrews, Wendy
    See Sharmat, Marjorie Weinman
Andrews, William G(eorge) 1930- 74
Andrezel, Pierre
    See Blixen, Karen
Andriani, Renee
    See Williams-Andriani, Renee
Andriola, Alfred J. 1912-1983
    Obituary 34
Andrist, Ralph K. 1914-2004 45
Andronik, Catherine M. 189
Andryszewski, Tricia 1956- 148
    Earlier sketch in SATA 88
Angel, Ann 1952- 192
Angel, Carl 178
Angel, Marie 1923- 47
Angeles, Peter A. 1931- 40
Angeletti, Roberta 1964- 124
Angeli, Marguerite (Lofft) de
    See de Angeli, Marguerite (Lofft)
Angell, Judie 1937- 78
    Earlier sketch in SATA 22
    See also CLR 33
Angell, Madeline 1919- 18
Angelo, Valenti 1897- 14
Angelou, Maya 1928- 136
    Earlier sketch in SATA 49
    See also CLR 53
Angier, Bradford -1997 12
Angle, Kimberly Greene 203
Angle, Paul M(cClelland) 1900-1975
    Obituary 20
Anglund, Joan Walsh 1926- 2
    See also CLR 94
Ango, Fan D.
    See Longyear, Barry B(rookes)
Angrist, Stanley W(olff) 1933- 4
Anholt, Catherine 1958- 131
    Earlier sketch in SATA 74
Anholt, Laurence 1959- 141
    Earlier sketch in SATA 74
Anita
    See Daniel, Anita
Anmar, Frank
    See Nolan, William F(rancis)
Annett, Cora
    See Scott, Cora Annett (Pipitone)
Annie-Jo
    See Blanchard, Patricia
    and Suhr, Joanne

Annixter, Jane
    See Sturtzel, Jane Levington
Annixter, Paul
    See Sturtzel, Howard A(llison)
Anno, Mitsumasa 1926- 157
    Earlier sketches in SATA 5, 38, 77
    See also CLR 122
Anrooy, Francine Van
    See Van Anrooy, Francine
Ansary, Mir Tamim 1948- 140
Anstey, Caroline 1958- 81
Antell, Will D. 1935- 31
Anthony, Barbara
    See Barber, Antonia
Anthony, C. L.
    See Smith, Dorothy Gladys
Anthony, Edward 1895-1971 21
Anthony, John
    See Beckett, Ronald Brymer
    and Ciardi, John (Anthony)
    and Sabini, John Anthony
Anthony, Joseph Patrick 1964- 103
Anthony, Patricia 1947- 109
Anthony, Piers 1934- 129
    Autobiography Feature 129
    Earlier sketch in SATA 84
    See also CLR 118
    See also SAAS 22
Anthony, Susan C(arol) 1953- 87
Anticaglia, Elizabeth 1939- 12
Antilles, Kem
    See Moesta, Rebecca
Antle, Nancy 1955- 102
Antolini, Margaret Fishback 1904-1985
    Obituary 45
Anton, Michael J(ames) 1940- 12
Antonacci, Robert J(oseph) 1916- 45
    Brief entry 37
Anvil, Christopher
    See Crosby, Harry C., Jr.
Anzaldua, Gloria (Evanjelina) 1942-2004
    Obituary 154
Aoki, Hisako 1942- 45
Apfel, Necia H(alpern) 1930- 51
    Brief entry 41
Aphrodite, J.
    See Livingston, Carole
Apikuni
    See Schultz, James Willard
Apostolina, M. 184
Apostolina, Michael
    See Apostolina, M.
Apostolou, Christine Hale 1955- 179
    Earlier sketches in SATA 82, 128
Appel, Allen (R.) 1945- 115
Appel, Benjamin 1907-1977 39
    Obituary 21
Appel, Martin 1948- 45
Appel, Martin Eliot
    See Appel, Martin
Appel, Marty
    See Appel, Martin
Appelbaum, Diana Muir Karter 1953- 132
Appelt, Kathi 1954- 190
    Earlier sketches in SATA 83, 129
Apperley, Dawn 1969- 135
Appiah, Peggy 1921-2006 84
    Earlier sketch in SATA 15
    See also SAAS 19
Apple, Margot 152
    Brief entry 42
    Earlier sketch in SATA 64
Applebaum, Stan 1922- 45
Applegate, K.A.
    See Applegate, Katherine
Applegate, Katherine 1956- 196
    Earlier sketches in SATA 109, 162
    See also CLR 90
Applegate, Katherine Alice
    See Applegate, Katherine

Appleton, Victor
  See Barrett, Neal, Jr.
  and Doyle, Debra
  and Macdonald, James D.
  and Stratemeyer, Edward L.
  and Vardeman, Robert E(dward)
Appleton, Victor II
  See Goulart, Ron
Apsler, Alfred 1907-1982 .... *10*
Aragones, Sergio 1937- *48*
  Brief entry *39*
Araujo, Frank P. 1937- *86*
Arbo, Cris 1950- *103*
Arbuckle, Dorothy Fry 1910-1982
  Obituary *33*
Arbuthnot, May Hill 1884-1969 .... *2*
Archambault, John *163*
  Earlier sketches in SATA *67, 112*
Archbold, Rick 1950- *97*
Archer, Colleen Rutherford 1949- *164*
Archer, Frank
  See O'Connor, Richard
Archer, Jules 1915- *85*
  Earlier sketch in SATA *4*
  See also SAAS *5*
Archer, Lily 1981- *193*
Archer, Marion Fuller 1917- *11*
Archer, Nathan
  See Watt-Evans, Lawrence
Archer, Peggy 1947- *199*
Archibald, Joe
  See Archibald, Joseph S(topford)
Archibald, Joseph S(topford) 1898-1986 .... *3*
  Obituary *47*
Ard, William
  See Jakes, John
Ardagh, Philip 1961- *154*
Ardai, Charles 1969- *85*
Arden, Barbi
  See Stoutenburg, Adrien (Pearl)
Arden, William
  See Lynds, Dennis
Ardizzone, Edward (Jeffrey Irving)
  1900-1979 .... *28*
  Obituary *21*
  Earlier sketch in SATA *1*
  See also CLR *3*
Ardley, Neil (Richard) 1937- *121*
  Earlier sketch in SATA *43*
Arehart-Treichel, Joan 1942- *22*
Arena, Felice 1968- *151*
Arenella, Roy 1939- *14*
Argent, Kerry 1960- *138*
Argueta, Jorge *179*
Arihara, Shino 1973- *201*
Arkin, Alan 1934- *59*
  Brief entry *32*
Arkin, Alan Wolf
  See Arkin, Alan
Arksey, Neil *158*
Arlen, Leslie
  See Nicole, Christopher (Robin)
Arley, Robert
  See Jackson, Mike
Armer, Alberta (Roller) 1904-1986 .... *9*
Armer, Laura Adams 1874-1963 .... *13*
Armistead, John 1941- *130*
Armitage, David 1943- *155*
  Brief entry *38*
  Earlier sketch in SATA *99*
Armitage, Frank
  See Carpenter, John
Armitage, Ronda (Jacqueline) 1943- *155*
  Brief entry *38*
  Earlier sketches in SATA *47, 99*
Armour, Richard (Willard) 1906-1989 .... *14*
  Obituary *61*
Armstrong, Alan 1939- *172*
Armstrong, Alan W.
  See Armstrong, Alan
Armstrong, George D. 1927- *10*

Armstrong, Gerry (Breen) 1929- *10*
Armstrong, Jeannette (C.) 1948- *102*
Armstrong, Jennifer 1961- *165*
  Autobiography Feature *120*
  Earlier sketches in SATA *77, 111*
  See also CLR *66*
  See also SAAS *24*
Armstrong, Louise *43*
  Brief entry *33*
Armstrong, Martin Donisthorpe
  1882-1974 .... *115*
Armstrong, Matthew 1975- *188*
Armstrong, Matthew S.
  See Armstrong, Matthew
Armstrong, Ralph Richard
  See Armstrong, Richard
Armstrong, Richard 1903-1986 .... *11*
Armstrong, William H(oward) 1914-1999 ..... *4*
  Obituary *111*
  See also CLR *117*
  See also SAAS *7*
Armstrong-Ellis, Carey (Fraser) 1956- *145*
Arndt, Ursula (Martha H.) *56*
  Brief entry *39*
Arneson, D(on) J(on) 1935- *37*
Arnett, Caroline
  See Cole, Lois Dwight
Arnett, Jack
  See Goulart, Ron
Arnette, Robert
  See Silverberg, Robert
Arno, Enrico 1913-1981 .... *43*
  Obituary *28*
Arnold, Caroline 1944- *174*
  Brief entry *34*
  Earlier sketches in SATA *36, 85, 131*
  See also CLR *61*
  See also SAAS *23*
Arnold, Elizabeth 1944- *164*
Arnold, Elliott 1912-1980 .... *5*
  Obituary *22*
Arnold, Emily 1939- *134*
  Autobiography Feature *134*
  Earlier sketches in SATA *5, 50, 76, 110*
  See also CLR *46*
  See also SAAS *7*
Arnold, Gillian Clare
  See Cross, Gillian
Arnold, Katya 1947- *168*
  Earlier sketches in SATA *82, 115*
Arnold, Louise *175*
Arnold, Marsha Diane 1948- *147*
  Earlier sketch in SATA *93*
Arnold, Nick 1961- *113*
Arnold, Oren 1900-1980 .... *4*
Arnold, Susan (Riser) 1951- *58*
Arnold, Tedd 1949- *160*
  Earlier sketches in SATA *69, 116*
Arnoldy, Julie
  See Bischoff, Julia Bristol
Arnosky, James Edward 1946- *189*
  Earlier sketches in SATA *70, 118*
  See also CLR *93*
Arnosky, Jim
  See Arnosky, James Edward
Arnott, Kathleen 1914- *20*
Arnov, Boris, Jr. 1926- *12*
Arnow, Harriette (Louisa) Simpson
  1908-1986 .... *42*
  Obituary *47*
Arnsteen, Katy Keck 1934- *68*
Arnstein, Helene S(olomon) 1915- *12*
Arntson, Herbert E(dward) 1911-1982 .... *12*
Aroner, Miriam *82*
Aronin, Ben 1904-1980
  Obituary *25*
Aronson, Marc 1950- *189*
  Autobiography Feature *189*
  Earlier sketches in SATA *126, 175*
Aronson, Marc Henry
  See Aronson, Marc

Aronson, Sarah *196*
Aronson, Virginia 1954- *122*
Arora, Shirley (Lease) 1930- *2*
Arrasmith, Patrick *176*
Arrick, Fran
  See Angell, Judie
Arrigan, Mary 1943- *142*
Arrington, Aileen *183*
Arrington, Stephen L. 1948- *97*
Arrington, Stephen Lee
  See Arrington, Stephen L.
Arrley, Richmond
  See Delany, Samuel R., Jr.
Arrowood, (McKendrick Lee) Clinton
  1939- *19*
Arrowsmith, Pat 1930- *59*
Artell, Mike 1948- *183*
  Earlier sketches in SATA *89, 134*
Arthur, Robert (Andrew) 1909-1969
  See Arthur, Robert, (Jr.)
Arthur, Robert, (Jr.) 1909-1969 .... *118*
Arthur, Ruth M(abel) 1905-1979 .... *26*
  Earlier sketch in SATA *7*
Artis, Vicki Kimmel 1945- *12*
Artzybasheff, Boris (Miklailovich)
  1899-1965 .... *14*
Aruego, Ariane
  See Dewey, Ariane
Aruego, Jose 1932- *178*
  Earlier sketches in SATA *6, 68, 125*
  See also CLR *5*
Aruego, Jose Espiritu
  See Aruego, Jose
Arundel, Honor (Morfydd) 1919-1973 .... *4*
  Obituary *24*
  See also CLR *35*
Arundel, Jocelyn
  See Alexander, Jocelyn Anne Arundel
Arvey, Michael 1948- *79*
Arzoumanian, Alik *177*
Asare, Meshack (Yaw) 1945- *139*
  Earlier sketch in SATA *86*
Asaro, Catherine 1955- *165*
  Earlier sketch in SATA *101*
Asaro, Catherine Ann 1955-
  See Asaro, Catherine
Asay, Donna Day 1945- *127*
Asbjornsen, Peter Christen 1812-1885 .... *15*
  See also CLR *104*
Asch, Frank 1946- *154*
  Earlier sketches in SATA *5, 66, 102*
Ash, Jutta 1942- *38*
Ashabranner, Brent 1921- *166*
  Earlier sketches in SATA *1, 67, 130*
  See also CLR *28*
  See also SAAS *14*
Ashabranner, Brent Kenneth
  See Ashabranner, Brent
Ashbless, William
  See Blaylock, James P.
  and Powers, Tim
Ashby, Gil 1958- *146*
Ashby, Gwynneth 1922- *44*
Ashby, Ruth *170*
Ashby, Yvonne 1955- *121*
Ashe, Arthur (Robert, Jr.) 1943-1993 .... *65*
  Obituary *87*
Ashe, Geoffrey (Thomas) 1923- *17*
  Autobiography Feature *125*
Ashe, Mary Ann
  See Lewis, Mary
Asher, Bridget
  See Baggott, Julianna
Asher, Sandra Fenichel
  See Asher, Sandy
Asher, Sandy 1942- *71*
  Autobiography Feature *158*
  Brief entry *34*
  Earlier sketch in SATA *36*
  See also SAAS *13*

Asheron, Sara
See Moore, Lilian
Ashey, Bella
See Breinburg, Petronella
Ashford, Daisy
See Ashford, Margaret Mary
Ashford, Jeffrey
See Jeffries, Roderic
Ashford, Margaret Mary 1881-1972 10
Ashley, Bernard (John) 1935- 155
Brief entry 39
Earlier sketches in SATA 47, 79
See also CLR 4
Ashley, Elizabeth
See Salmon, Annie Elizabeth
Ashley, Ray
See Abrashkin, Raymond
Ashman, Linda 1960- 203
Earlier sketch in SATA 150
Ashton, Lorayne
See Gottfried, Theodore Mark
Ashton, Warren T.
See Adams, William Taylor
Asimov, Isaac 1920-1992 74
Earlier sketches in SATA 1, 26
See also CLR 79
Asinof, Eliot 1919-2008 6
Asinof, Eliot Tager
See Asinof, Eliot
Aska, Warabe
See Masuda, Takeshi
Asprin, Robert L. 1946-2008 92
Asprin, Robert Lynn
See Asprin, Robert L.
Asquith, Cynthia Mary Evelyn (Charteris)
1887-1960 107
Asquith, Ros 153
Astley, Juliet
See Lofts, Norah (Robinson)
Aston, Dianna Hutts 1964- 176
Aston, James
See White, T(erence) H(anbury)
Ata, Te 1895-1995 119
Atene, Ann
See Atene, (Rita) Anna
Atene, (Rita) Anna 1922- 12
Atheling, William, Jr.
See Blish, James
Atkins, Catherine 160
Atkins, Jeannine 1953- 172
Earlier sketch in SATA 113
Atkinson, Allen G. 1953(?)-1987 60
Brief entry 46
Obituary 55
Atkinson, M. E.
See Frankau, Mary Evelyn Atkinson
Atkinson, Margaret Fleming 14
Atteberry, Kevan J. 186
Attema, Martha 1949- 156
Earlier sketch in SATA 94
Atticus
See Davies, Hunter
and Fleming, Ian
and Pawle, Gerald Strachan
and Wilson, (Thomas) Woodrow
Atwater, Florence (Hasseltine Carroll)
1896-1979 66
Earlier sketch in SATA 16
See also CLR 19
Atwater, Montgomery Meigs 1904-1976 15
Atwater, Richard (Tupper) 1892-1948 66
Brief entry 27
Earlier sketch in SATA 54
See also CLR 19
Atwater-Rhodes, Amelia 1984- 170
Earlier sketch in SATA 124
Atwell, Debby 1953- 150
Earlier sketch in SATA 87
Atwood, Ann (Margaret) 1913-1992 7
Atwood, Margaret 1939- 170
Earlier sketch in SATA 50

Atwood, Margaret Eleanor
See Atwood, Margaret
Aubrey, Meg Kelleher 1963- 83
Aubry, Claude B. 1914-1984 29
Obituary 40
Auch, Herm 173
Auch, Mary Jane 173
Earlier sketch in SATA 138
Auch, M.J.
See Auch, Mary Jane
Auclair, Joan 1960- 68
Auel, Jean 1936- 91
Auel, Jean M.
See Auel, Jean
Auel, Jean Marie
See Auel, Jean
Auer, Martin 1951- 77
Augarde, Steve 1950- 159
Earlier sketch in SATA 25
Augelli, John P(at) 1921- 46
Augustine, Mildred
See Benson, Mildred
Ault, Phil
See Ault, Phillip H(alliday)
Ault, Phillip H(alliday) 1914- 23
Ault, Rosalie Sain 1942- 38
Ault, Roz
See Ault, Rosalie Sain
Aung, (Maung) Htin 1909- 21
Auntie Deb
See Coury, Louise Andree
Auntie Louise
See Coury, Louise Andree
Aunt Weedy
See Alcott, Louisa May
Auseon, Andrew 1976- 166
Austen, Carrie
See Bennett, Cherie
Austin, Carrie
See Seuling, Barbara
Austin, Elizabeth S. 1907-1977 5
Austin, Harry
See McInerny, Ralph
Austin, Margot 1909(?)-1990 11
Obituary 66
Austin, Michael 178
Austin, Oliver L(uther), Jr. 1903-1988 7
Obituary 59
Austin, Patricia 1950- 137
Austin, R. G.
See Gelman, Rita Golden
and Lamb, Nancy
Austin, Virginia 1951- 152
Earlier sketch in SATA 80
Auteur, Hillary
See Gottfried, Theodore Mark
Auth, Tony
See Auth, William Anthony, Jr.
Auth, William Anthony, Jr. 1942- 192
Autry, Gloria Diener
See Allen, Terril Diener
Auvil, Peggy A 1954- 122
Auvil, Peggy Appleby
See Auvil, Peggy A
Aveni, Anthony F. 1938- 181
Aveni, Anthony Francis
See Aveni, Anthony F.
Averbeck, Jim 1963- 201
Averill, Esther (Holden) 1902-1992 28
Obituary 72
Earlier sketch in SATA 1
Avery, A. A.
See Montgomery, Rutherford George
Avery, Al
See Montgomery, Rutherford George
Avery, Gillian (Elise) 1926- 137
Autobiography Feature 137
Earlier sketches in SATA 7, 75
See also SAAS 6
Avery, Kay 1908- 5

Avery, Lorraine
See Older, Effin
and Older, Jules
Avery, Lynn
See Cole, Lois Dwight
Avi 1937- 190
Earlier sketches in SATA 14, 71, 108, 156
See also CLR 68
Avishai, Susan 1949- 82
Avril, Francois 1961- 191
Avril, Lynne
See Cravath, Lynne W.
Awdry, Christopher Vere 1940- 67
Awdry, Wilbert Vere 1911-1997 94
See also CLR 23
Axelrod, Amy 131
Axelsen, Stephen 1953- 165
Axton, David
See Koontz, Dean R.
Ayars, James S(terling) 1898-1986 4
Aye, A. K.
See Edwards, Hazel (Eileen)
Ayer, Eleanor H. 1947-1998 121
Earlier sketch in SATA 78
Ayer, Jacqueline 1930- 13
Ayer, Margaret (?)-1981 15
Aylesworth, Jim 1943- 139
Earlier sketches in SATA 38, 89
See also CLR 89
Aylesworth, Thomas G(ibbons) 1927-1995 .. 88
Earlier sketch in SATA 4
See also CLR 6
See also SAAS 17
Ayliffe, Alex 190
Aylward, Marcus
See Alexander, Marc
Aymar, Brandt 1911- 22
Ayme, Marcel (Andre) 1902-1967 91
See also CLR 25
Ayres, Becky
See Hickox, Rebecca (Ayres)
Ayres, Katherine 1947- 187
Ayres, Pam 1947- 90
Ayres, Patricia Miller 1923-1985
Obituary 46
Aytmatov, Chingiz
See Aitmatov, Chingiz
Ayto, Russell 1960- 206
Earlier sketches in SATA 111, 166
Azaid
See Zaidenberg, Arthur
Azar, Penny 1952- 121
Azarian, Mary 1940- 171
Earlier sketch in SATA 112
Azore, Barbara 1934- 188

B

Baastad, Babbis Friis
See Friis-Baastad, Babbis Ellinor
Bab
See Gilbert, W(illiam) S(chwenck)
Babbis, Eleanor
See Friis-Baastad, Babbis Ellinor
Babbitt, Lucy Cullyford 1960- 85
Babbitt, Natalie 1932- 194
Earlier sketches in SATA 6, 68, 106
See also CLR 141
See also SAAS 5
Babbitt, Natalie Zane Moore
See Babbitt, Natalie
Babcock, Chris 1963- 83
Babcock, Dennis 1948- 22
Babcock, Dennis Arthur
See Babcock, Dennis
Baber, Carolyn Stonnell 1936- 96
Baboni, Elena 198
Baca, Ana 1967- 191
Baca, Maria 1951- 104

Bach, Alice (Hendricks) 1942- 93
  Brief entry 27
  Earlier sketch in SATA 30
Bach, Bellamy
  See Windling, Terri
Bach, Mary 1960- 125
Bach, Richard 1936- 13
Bach, Richard David
  See Bach, Richard
Bache, Ellyn 1942- 124
Bachel, Beverly K. 1957- 142
Bachelet, Gilles 1952- 196
Bachman, Fred 1949- 12
Bachman, Richard
  See King, Stephen
Bachrach, Deborah 80
Backus, James Gilmore 1913-1989
  Obituary 63
Backus, Jim
  See Backus, James Gilmore
Bacmeister, Rhoda W(arner) 1893-1991 11
Bacon, Betty
  See Bacon, Elizabeth
Bacon, Elizabeth 1914-2001 3
  Obituary 131
Bacon, Joan Chase
  See Bowden, Joan Chase
Bacon, Josephine Dodge (Daskam)
  1876-1961 48
Bacon, Margaret Frances
  See Bacon, Peggy
Bacon, Margaret Hope 1921- 6
Bacon, Martha Sherman 1917-1981 18
  Obituary 27
  See also CLR 3
Bacon, Melvin 1950- 93
Bacon, Melvin L.
  See Bacon, Melvin
Bacon, Peggy 1895-1987 50
Bacon, R(onald) L(eonard) 1924- 84
  Earlier sketch in SATA 26
Baden, Robert 1936- 70
Baden-Powell, Robert (Stephenson Smyth)
  1857-1941 16
Badt, Karin L(uisa) 1963- 91
Bae, Hyun-Joo 186
Baehr, Kingsley M. 1937- 89
Baehr, Patricia 1952- 65
Baehr, Patricia Goehner
  See Baehr, Patricia
Baek, Matthew J. 1971- 202
Baer, Jill
  See Gilbert, (Agnes) Joan (Sewell)
Baer, Judy 1951- 71
Baer, Julie 1960- 161
Baer-Block, Roxanna 172
Baerg, Harry J(ohn) 1909-1996 12
Baeten, Lieve 1954- 83
Bagert, Brod 1947- 191
  Earlier sketch in SATA 80
Baggette, Susan K. 1942- 126
Baggott, Julianna 1969- 197
Bagnold, Enid 1889-1981 25
  Earlier sketch in SATA 1
Baguley, Elizabeth 1959- 199
Bahlke, Valerie Worth -1994
  See Worth, Valerie
Bahous, Sally 1939- 86
Bahr, Mary (Madelyn) 1946- 95
Bahr, Robert 1940- 38
Bahti, Tom 1926-1972 57
  Brief entry 31
Baicker-McKee, Carol 1958- 177
Bailey, Alice Cooper 1890-1978 12
Bailey, Anne 1958- 71
Bailey, Bernadine (Freeman) 1901-1995 14
Bailey, Carolyn Sherwin 1875-1961 14
Bailey, Debbie 1954- 123
Bailey, Donna (Veronica Anne) 1938- 68
Bailey, Jane H(orton) 1916- 12
Bailey, John (Robert) 1940- 52

Bailey, Len 193
Bailey, Linda 1948- 182
  Earlier sketch in SATA 107
Bailey, Maralyn Collins (Harrison) 1941- 12
Bailey, Matilda
  See Radford, Ruby L(orraine)
Bailey, Maurice Charles 1932- 12
Bailey, Pearl (Mae) 1918-1990 81
Bailey, Peter 1946- 194
Bailey, Ralph Edgar 1893-1982 11
Bailey, Sheila (Lucas) 1960- 155
Baillie, Allan 1943- 151
  Earlier sketch in SATA 87
  See also CLR 49
  See also SAAS 21
Baillie, Allan Stuart
  See Baillie, Allan
Baines, John (David) 1943- 71
Bains, Larry
  See Sabin, Louis
Baird, Alison 1963- 138
Baird, Bil 1904-1987 30
  Obituary 52
Baird, Thomas (P.) 1923-1990 45
  Brief entry 39
  Obituary 64
Baird, William Britton
  See Baird, Bil
Baity, Elizabeth Chesley 1907-1989 1
Baiul, Oksana 1977- 108
Bajoria, Paul 1964- 187
Bakeless, John (Edwin) 1894-1978 9
Bakeless, Katherine Little 1895-1992 9
Baker, Alan 1951- 146
  Earlier sketches in SATA 22, 93
Baker, Augusta 1911-1998 3
Baker, Barbara 1947- 192
Baker, Betty Lou 1928-1987 73
  Obituary 54
  Earlier sketch in SATA 5
Baker, Carin Greenberg 1959- 79
Baker, Charlotte 1910- 2
Baker, Christina
  See Kline, Christina Baker
Baker, Christopher W. 1952- 144
Baker, Deirdre 1955- 195
Baker, E.D. 190
Baker, (Mary) Elizabeth (Gillette) 1923- 7
Baker, Gayle Cunningham 1950- 39
Baker, James W. 1924- 65
  Earlier sketch in SATA 22
Baker, James W. 1926- 122
Baker, Janice E(dla) 1941- 22
Baker, Jeanette 178
Baker, Jeannie 1950- 156
  Earlier sketches in SATA 23, 88
  See also CLR 28
Baker, Jeffrey J(ohn) W(heeler) 1931- 5
Baker, Jim
  See Baker, James W.
Baker, Keith 1953- 179
Baker, Ken 1962- 133
Baker, Laura Nelson 1911- 3
Baker, Margaret 1890-1965 4
Baker, Margaret J(oyce) 1918- 12
  See also SAAS 8
Baker, Mary Gladys Steel 1892-1974 12
Baker, (Robert) Michael (Graham) 1938- 4
Baker, Nina (Brown) 1888-1957 15
Baker, Pamela J. 1947- 66
Baker, Rachel 1904-1978 2
  Obituary 26
Baker, Roberta 206
Baker, Rosalie F. 1945- 166
Baker, Samm Sinclair 1909-1997 12
  Obituary 96
Baker, Susan (Catherine) 1942-1991 29
Balaam
  See Lamb, G(eoffrey) F(rederick)
Balan, Bruce 1959- 113
Balcavage, Dynise 1965- 137

Balch, Glenn 1902-1989 3
  Obituary 83
  See also SAAS 11
Baldacci, David 1960- 184
Baldacci, David G.
  See Baldacci, David
  and Baldacci, David
Balderose, Nancy Ward 1952- 93
Balderson, Margaret 1935- 151
Baldini, Michelle 205
Baldry, Cherith 1947- 167
  Earlier sketch in SATA 72
Balducci, Carolyn 1946- 5
Balducci, Carolyn Feleppa
  See Balducci, Carolyn
Baldwin, Alex
  See Griffin, W.E.B.
Baldwin, Anne Norris 1938- 5
Baldwin, Clara 11
Baldwin, Gordo
  See Baldwin, Gordon C(ortis)
Baldwin, Gordon C(ortis) 1908-1983 12
Baldwin, James 1841-1925 24
Baldwin, James 1924-1987 9
  Obituary 54
Baldwin, Louis 1919- 110
Baldwin, Margaret
  See Weis, Margaret
Baldwin, Stan(ley C.) 1929- 62
  Brief entry 28
Bales, Carol Ann 1940- 57
  Brief entry 29
Balet, Jan (Bernard) 1913- 11
Balgassi, Haemi 1971- 131
Balian, Lorna 1929- 91
  Earlier sketch in SATA 9
Balit, Christina 1961- 159
  Earlier sketch in SATA 102
Ball, Duncan 1941- 73
Ball, Zachary
  See Janas, Frankie-Lee
  and Masters, Kelly R(ay)
Ballantine, Lesley Frost
  See Frost, Lesley
Ballantyne, R(obert) M(ichael) 1825-1894 ... 24
  See also CLR 137
Ballard, James G.
  See Ballard, J.G.
Ballard, James Graham
  See Ballard, J.G.
Ballard, Jane
  See Gorman, Carol
Ballard, J.G. 1930-2009 93
  Obituary 203
Ballard, Jim G.
  See Ballard, J.G.
Ballard, John 1945- 110
Ballard, Lowell C(lyne) 1904-1986 12
  Obituary 49
Ballard, (Charles) Martin 1929- 1
Ballard, Mignon F. 1934- 64
  Brief entry 49
Ballard, Mignon Franklin
  See Ballard, Mignon F.
Ballard, Robert D(uane) 1942- 85
  See also CLR 60
Ballard, Robin 1965- 126
Balliett, Blue 1955- 156
Ballinger, Bryan 1968- 161
Ballouhey, Pierre 1944- 90
Balogh, Penelope 1916-1975 1
  Obituary 34
Balouch, Kristen 176
Balow, Tom 1931- 12
Baltazzi, Evan S(erge) 1921- 90
Balterman, Marcia Ridlon 1942- 22
Baltimore, J.
  See Catherall, Arthur
Baltzer, Hans (Adolf) 1900- 40
Balzano, Jeanne (Koppel) 1912- 7
Bambara, Toni Cade 1939-1995 112

Bamfylde, Walter
  See Bevan, Tom
Bamman, Henry A. 1918- 12
Banat, D. R.
  See Bradbury, Ray
Bancroft, Griffing 1907-1999 6
Bancroft, Laura
  See Baum, L. Frank
Bandel, Betty 1912- 47
Baner, Skulda Vanadis 1897-1964 10
Banerjee, Anjali 174
Banfill, A. Scott 1956- 98
Bang, Betsy 1912- 48
  Brief entry 37
Bang, Garrett
  See Bang, Molly
Bang, Molly 1943- 158
  Earlier sketches in SATA *24, 69, 111*
  See also CLR *8*
Bang, Molly Garrett
  See Bang, Molly
Bang-Campbell, Monika 1975(?)- 195
  Earlier sketch in SATA *140*
Banjo, The
  See Paterson, A(ndrew) B(arton)
Banke, Cecile de
  See de Banke, Cecile
Banks, Kate 1960- 200
  Earlier sketches in SATA *134, 172*
Banks, Laura Stockton Voorhees 1908(?)-1980
  Obituary 23
Banks, Lynne Reid
  See Reid Banks, Lynne
Banks, Merry 197
Banks, Michael A. 1951- 101
Banks, Paul 1952- 174
Banks, Sara (Jeanne Gordon Harrell) 26
  See Harrell, Sara (Jeanne) Gordon
Bannatyne-Cugnet, Elizabeth Jo-Anne
  See Bannatyne-Cugnet, Jo
Bannatyne-Cugnet, Jo 1951- 101
Banner, Angela
  See Maddison, Angela Mary
Bannerman, Helen (Brodie Cowan Watson)
  1862(?)-1946 19
  See also CLR *144*
Banning, Evelyn I. 1903-1993 36
Bannon, Laura (?)-1963 6
Bannor, Brett 1959- 143
Banta, Susan 181
Bantock, Nick 1950(?)- 95
Banyai, Istvan 193
Barakat, Ibtisam 1963- 186
Barasch, Lynne 1939- 186
  Earlier sketches in SATA *74, 126*
Barbalet, Margaret 1949- 77
Barbary, James
  See Baumann, Amy Beeching
  and Beeching, Jack
Barbash, Shepard 1957- 84
Barbe, Walter Burke 1926- 45
Barber, Antonia 1932- 163
  Earlier sketch in SATA *29*
Barber, Atiim Kiambu
  See Barber, Tiki
Barber, Lynda
  See Graham-Barber, Lynda
Barber, Lynda Graham
  See Graham-Barber, Lynda
Barber, Richard (William) 1941- 35
Barber, Ronde 1975- 182
Barber, Tiki 1975- 182
Barbera, Joe 1911-2006 51
  Obituary 179
Barbera, Joseph
  See Barbera, Joe
Barbera, Joseph Roland
  See Barbera, Joe
Barberis, Juan C(arlos) 1920- 61
Barbour, Karen 1956- 170
  Earlier sketches in SATA *63, 121*

Barbour, Ralph Henry 1870-1944 16
Barclay, Bill
  See Moorcock, Michael
Barclay, Isabel
  See Dobell, I(sabel) M(arian) B(arclay)
Barclay, William Ewert
  See Moorcock, Michael
Bardhan-Quallen, Sudipta 168
Bardoe, Cheryl 181
Bare, Arnold Edwin 1920- 16
Bare, Colleen Stanley 32
Bar-el, Dan 199
Barenholtz, Bernard 1914-1989
  Obituary 64
Bargar, Gary W. 1947-1985 63
Barger, Jan 1948- 147
Barish, Matthew 1907-2000 12
Barkan, Joanne 127
  Earlier sketch in SATA *77*
Barker, Albert W. 1900- 8
Barker, Carol (Minturn) 1938- 31
Barker, Cicely Mary 1895-1973 49
  Brief entry 39
  See also CLR *88*
Barker, Melvern 1907-1989 11
Barker, S. Omar 1894-1985 10
Barker, Squire Omar
  See Barker, S. Omar
Barker, Will 1913-1983 8
Barkin, Carol 1944- 52
  Earlier sketch in SATA *42*
Barklem, Jill 1951- 96
  See also CLR *31*
Barkley, Brad 178
Barkley, James Edward 1941- 6
Barks, Carl 1901-2000 37
Barley, Janet Crane 1934- 95
Barnaby, Ralph S(tanton) 1893-1986 9
Barnard, A. M.
  See Alcott, Louisa May
Barnard, Bryn 1956- 169
  Earlier sketch in SATA *115*
Barne, Kitty
  See Barne, Marion Catherine
Barne, Marion Catherine 1883-1957 97
Barneda, David 206
Barner, Bob 1947- 136
  Earlier sketch in SATA *29*
Barnes, Dawn 1957- 175
Barnes, Derrick 191
Barnes, Derrick D.
  See Barnes, Derrick
Barnes, (Frank) Eric Wollencott 1907-1962 . 22
Barnes, Joyce Annette 1958- 85
Barnes, Laura T. 1958- 119
Barnes, Loutricia
  See Barnes-Svarney, Patricia L(ou)
Barnes, Malcolm 1909(?)-1984
  Obituary 41
Barnes, Michael 1934- 55
Barnes-Murphy, Frances 1951- 88
Barnes-Murphy, Rowan 1952- 88
Barnes-Svarney, Patricia L(ou) 1953- 67
Barnet, Nancy 1954- 84
Barnett, Ivan 1947- 70
Barnett, Lincoln (Kinnear) 1909-1979 36
Barnett, Moneta 1922-1976 33
Barnett, Naomi 1927- 40
Barney, Maginel Wright 1881(?)-1966 39
  Brief entry 32
Barnhart, Clarence L(ewis) 1900-1993 48
  Obituary 78
Barnouw, Adriaan Jacob 1877-1968
  Obituary 27
Barnouw, Victor 1915-1989 43
  Brief entry 28
Barnstone, Willis 1927- 20
Barnum, Jay Hyde 1888(?)-1962 20
Barnum, P. T., Jr.
  See Stratemeyer, Edward L.

Barnum, Richard 67
  Earlier sketch in SATA *1*
Barnum, Theodore
  See Stratemeyer, Edward L.
Barnwell, Ysaye M. 1946- 200
Baron, Kathy 1954- 90
Baron, Virginia Olsen 1931- 46
  Brief entry 28
Barr, Donald 1921-2004 20
  Obituary 152
Barr, George 1907-1992 2
Barr, Jene 1922-1985 16
  Obituary 42
Barr, Nevada 1952- 126
  Earlier sketch in SATA *115*
Barrer, Gertrude
  See Barrer-Russell, Gertrude
Barrer-Russell, Gertrude 1921- 27
Barrett, Angela (Jane) 1955- 145
  Earlier sketch in SATA *75*
Barrett, Ethel 87
  Brief entry 44
Barrett, Joyce Durham 1943- 138
Barrett, Judi 204
  See Barrett, Judith
Barrett, Judith 1941- 26
  See also CLR *98*
  See Barrett, Judi
Barrett, Robert T(heodore) 1949- 92
Barrett, Ron 1937- 14
Barrett, Susan (Mary) 1938- 113
Barrett, Tracy 1955- 156
  Earlier sketches in SATA *84, 115*
Barrett, William E(dmund) 1900-1986
  Obituary 49
Barretta, Gene 176
Barretton, Grandall
  See Garrett, Randall
Barrie, Baronet
  See Barrie, J(ames) M(atthew)
Barrie, J(ames) M(atthew) 1860-1937 100
  See also YABC *1*
  See also CLR *124*
Barringer, William 1940-1996 153
Barrington, Michael
  See Moorcock, Michael
Barris, George 1925- 47
Barrol, Grady
  See Bograd, Larry
Barron, Rex 1951- 84
Barron, T.A. 1952- 192
  Earlier sketches in SATA *83, 126*
  See also CLR *86*
Barron, Thomas Archibald
  See Barron, T.A.
Barron, Tom
  See Barron, T.A.
Barrow, Lloyd H. 1942- 73
Barrows, Annie 1962- 180
Barry, Dan 1958- 177
Barry, Dana (Marie Malloy) 1949- 139
Barry, James P(otvin) 1918- 14
Barry, Katharina Watjen 1936- 4
Barry, Robert (Everett) 1931- 6
Barry, Scott 1952- 32
Barry, Sheila Anne -2003 91
Barshaw, Ruth McNally 203
Bartell, Susan S. 175
Bartenbach, Jean 1918- 40
Barth, Edna 1914-1980 7
  Obituary 24
Barth, Kelly L. 1964- 152
Barthelme, Donald 1931-1989 7
  Obituary 62
Barth-Grozinger, Inge 1950- 185
Bartholomew, Barbara 1941- 86
  Brief entry 42
Bartholomew, Jean
  See Beatty, Patricia (Robbins)
Bartlett, Alison 153
Bartlett, Philip A. 1

Bartlett, Robert Merrill 1899-1995 .... *12*
Bartoletti, Susan Campbell 1958- *173*
  Earlier sketches in SATA *88, 129, 135*
Barton, Byron 1930- *126*
  Earlier sketches in SATA *9, 90*
Barton, Jill(ian) 1940- *75*
Barton, May Hollis *67*
  Earlier sketch in SATA *1*
Barton, Pat
  See Arrowsmith, Pat
Bartos-Hoeppner, Barbara 1923- *5*
Bartram, Simon *156*
Bartsch, Jochen 1906- *39*
Baruch, Dorothy W(alter) 1899-1962 .... *21*
Barunga, Albert 1912(?)-1977 .... *120*
Baryshnikov, Mikhail 1948- *192*
Bas, Rutger
  See Rutgers van der Loeff-Basenau, An(na)
  Maria Margaretha
Base, Graeme 1958- *162*
  Earlier sketches in SATA *67, 101*
  See also CLR *22*
Base, Graeme Rowland
  See Base, Graeme
Baseman, Gary 1960- *174*
Bash, Barbara 1948- *132*
Bashevis, Isaac
  See Singer, Isaac Bashevis
Bashevis, Yitskhok
  See Singer, Isaac Bashevis
Bashista, Adrienne Ehlert *203*
Basile, Gloria Vitanza 1929- *180*
Baskin, Leonard 1922-2000 .... *120*
  Brief entry *27*
  Earlier sketch in SATA *30*
Baskin, Nora Raleigh 1961- *189*
  Earlier sketch in SATA *129*
Bason, Lillian 1913- *20*
Bass, L. G.
  See Geringer, Laura
Bassett, Jeni 1959- *64*
  Brief entry *43*
Bassett, John Keith
  See Keating, Lawrence A.
Bassett, Lisa 1958- *61*
Bassil, Andrea
  See Nilsen, Anna
Bastyra, Judy *108*
Basye, Dale E. *205*
Bat-Ami, Miriam 1950- *150*
  Autobiography Feature *150*
  Earlier sketches in SATA *82, 122*
Bate, Lucy 1939-1993 .... *18*
Bate, Norman (Arthur) 1916- *5*
Bateman, Colin 1962- *172*
Bateman, Donna M. *190*
Bateman, Teresa 1957- *168*
  Earlier sketch in SATA *112*
Bates, Amy June *189*
Bates, Barbara S(nedeker) 1919- *12*
Bates, Betty
  See Bates, Elizabeth
Bates, Dianne 1948- *147*
Bates, Elizabeth 1921- *19*
Bates, Ivan *175*
Bates, Katharine Lee 1859-1929 .... *113*
Bates, Martine
  See Leavitt, Martine
Bateson, Catherine 1960- *197*
  Earlier sketch in SATA *157*
Batey, Tom 1946- *52*
  Brief entry *41*
Bath, Kevin P.
  See Bath, K.P.
Bath, K.P. 1959- *171*
Batherman, Muriel
  See Sheldon, Muriel
Batson, Larry 1930- *35*
Batt, Tanya Robyn 1970- *131*
Battaglia, Aurelius 1910- *50*
  Brief entry *33*

Batten, H(arry) Mortimer 1888-1958 .... *25*
Batten, Mary 1937- *162*
  Earlier sketches in SATA *5, 102*
Batterberry, Ariane Ruskin 1935- *13*
Batterberry, Michael Carver 1932- *32*
Battle-Lavert, Gwendolyn 1951- *155*
  Earlier sketches in SATA *85, 131*
Battles, (Roxy) Edith 1921- *7*
Baudouy, Michel-Aime 1909- *7*
Bauer, A.C.E. *201*
Bauer, Caroline Feller 1935- *98*
  Brief entry *46*
  Earlier sketch in SATA *52*
  See also SAAS *24*
Bauer, Fred 1934- *36*
Bauer, Helen 1900-1988 .... *2*
Bauer, Joan 1951- *160*
  Earlier sketch in SATA *117*
Bauer, Jutta 1955- *150*
Bauer, Marion Dane 1938- *192*
  Autobiography Feature *144*
  Earlier sketches in SATA *20, 69, 113, 144*
  See also SAAS *9*
Bauer, Michael Gerard 1955(?)- *167*
Bauer, Steven 1948- *125*
Bauerschmidt, Marjorie 1926- *15*
Baughman, Dorothy 1940- *61*
Baum, Allyn Z(elton) 1924-1997 .... *98*
  Earlier sketch in SATA *20*
Baum, L. Frank
  See Thompson, Ruth Plumly
Baum, L. Frank 1856-1919 .... *100*
  Earlier sketch in SATA *18*
  See also CLR *107*
Baum, Louis 1948- *182*
  Brief entry *52*
  Earlier sketch in SATA *64*
Baum, Louis F.
  See Baum, L. Frank
Baum, Lyman Frank
  See Baum, L. Frank
Baum, Maxie *188*
Baum, Willi 1931- *4*
Baumann, Amy Beeching 1922- *10*
Baumann, Amy Brown Beeching
  See Baumann, Amy Beeching
Baumann, Hans 1914- *2*
  See also CLR *35*
Baumann, Kurt 1935- *21*
Baumgartner, Barbara 1939- *86*
Baurys, Flo(rence) 1938- *122*
Bausum, Ann *173*
Bawden, Nina 1925- *132*
  Earlier sketches in SATA *4, 72*
  See also CLR *51*
  See also SAAS *16*
Bawden, Nina Mary Mabey
  See Bawden, Nina
Baxter, Valerie
  See Meynell, Laurence Walter
Bay, Jeanette Graham 1928- *88*
Bayer, Harold
  See Gregg, Andrew K.
Bayer, Jane E. (?)-1985
  Obituary *44*
Bayley, Nicola 1949- *129*
  Earlier sketches in SATA *41, 69*
Baylor, Byrd 1924- *136*
  Earlier sketches in SATA *16, 69*
  See also CLR *3*
Baynes, Pauline 1922-2008 .... *133*
  Obituary *196*
  Earlier sketches in SATA *19, 59*
Baynes, Pauline Diana
  See Baynes, Pauline
Bayoc, Cbabi *186*
BB
  See Watkins-Pitchford, Denys James
Beach, Charles
  See Reid, (Thomas) Mayne
Beach, Charles Amory *1*

Beach, Edward L. 1918-2002 .... *12*
  Obituary *140*
Beach, Edward Latimer
  See Beach, Edward L.
Beach, Lisa 1957- *111*
Beach, Lynn
  See Lance, Kathryn
Beach, Stewart T(aft) 1899-1979 .... *23*
Beachcroft, Nina 1931- *18*
Beagle, Peter S. 1939- *130*
  Earlier sketch in SATA *60*
Beagle, Peter Soyer
  See Beagle, Peter S.
Beaglehole, Helen 1946- *117*
Beale, Fleur *107*
Bealer, Alex W(inkler III) 1921-1980 .... *8*
  Obituary *22*
Beales, Valerie 1915- *74*
Beals, Carleton 1893-1979 .... *12*
Beals, Frank Lee 1881-1972
  Obituary *26*
Beam, Matt 1970- *187*
Beame, Rona 1934- *12*
Beamer, (George) Charles (Jr.) 1942- *43*
Bean, Jonathan 1979- *194*
Bean, Normal
  See Burroughs, Edgar Rice
Beaney, Jan
  See Udall, Jan Beaney
Beaney, Jane
  See Udall, Jan Beaney
Bear, Carolyn
  See Rayban, Chloe
Bear, Greg(ory Dale) 1951- *105*
  Earlier sketch in SATA *65*
Bearanger, Marie
  See Messier, Claire
Beard, Charles A(ustin) 1874-1948 .... *18*
Beard, Dan(iel Carter) 1850-1941 .... *22*
Beard, Darleen Bailey 1961- *96*
Bearden, Romare (Howard) 1914(?)-1988 ... *22*
  Obituary *56*
Beardmore, Cedric
  See Beardmore, George
Beardmore, George 1908-1979 .... *20*
Beardshaw, Rosalind 1969- *190*
Beardsley, Martyn R. 1957- *150*
Bearman, Jane (Ruth) 1917- *29*
Beaton, Clare 1947- *125*
Beatty, Elizabeth
  See Holloway, Teresa (Bragunier)
Beatty, Hetty Burlingame 1907-1971 .... *5*
Beatty, Jerome, Jr. 1918- *5*
Beatty, John (Louis) 1922-1975 .... *6*
  Obituary *25*
Beatty, Patricia (Robbins) 1922-1991 .... *73*
  Obituary *68*
  Earlier sketches in SATA *1, 30*
  See also SAAS *4*
Beaty, Andrea *186*
Beaty, Mary (T.) 1947- *146*
Beaumont, Karen 1954- *204*
Beccia, Carlyn *189*
Bechard, Margaret 1953- *164*
  Earlier sketch in SATA *85*
Bechtel, Louise Seaman 1894-1985 .... *4*
  Obituary *43*
Beck, Barbara L. 1927- *12*
Beck, Ian 1947- *190*
  Earlier sketch in SATA *138*
  See Beck, Ian Archibald
Beck, Peggy 1949- *171*
Beck, Scott *197*
Becker, Beril 1901-1999 .... *11*
Becker, Bonny *184*
Becker, Deborah Zimmett 1955- *138*
Becker, Helaine 1961- *142*
Becker, John (Leonard) 1901- *12*
Becker, John E(mil) 1942- *148*
Becker, Joyce 1936- *39*
Becker, May Lamberton 1873-1958 .... *33*

Becker, Neesa 1951- 123
Becker, Shari 174
Beckerman, Chad W. 198
Beckett, Sheilah 1913- 33
Beckhorn, Susan Williams 1953- 189
Beckles Willson, Robina 1930- 27
Beckman, Delores 1914-1994 51
Beckman, Gunnel 1910- 6
  See also CLR 25
  See also SAAS 9
Beckman, Kaj
  See Beckman, Karin
Beckman, Karin 1913- 45
Beckman, Per (Frithiof) 1913- 45
Bedard, Michael 1949- 154
  Earlier sketch in SATA 93
  See also CLR 35
Beddor, Frank 194
Beddows, Eric
  See Nutt, Ken
Bedford, A. N.
  See Watson, Jane Werner
Bedford, Annie North
  See Watson, Jane Werner
Bedford, David 159
Bedoukian, Kerop 1907-1981 53
Bee, Jay
  See Brainerd, John W(hiting)
Bee, William 188
Beebe, B. F.
  See Johnson, B. F.
Beebe, (Charles) William 1877-1962 19
Beeby, Betty 1923- 25
Beech, Mark 1971- 191
Beech, Webb
  See Griffin, W.E.B.
Beecham, Jahnna 161
Beechcroft, William
  See Hallstead, William F(inn III)
Beeching, Jack 1922- 14
Beeke, Tiphanie 163
Beeler, Janet
  See Shaw, Janet
Beeler, Nelson F(rederick) 1910-1978 13
Beere, Peter 1951- 97
Beers, Dorothy Sands 1917- 9
Beers, Lorna 1897-1989 14
Beers, V(ictor) Gilbert 1928- 130
  Earlier sketch in SATA 9
Beeton, Max
  See Redding, Robert Hull
Begay, Shonto 1954- 137
Begaye, Lisa Shook
  See Beach, Lisa
Begin, Mary Jane 1963- 82
Begin-Callanan, Mary Jane
  See Begin, Mary Jane
Begley, Kathleen A. 1948- 21
Begley, Kathleen Anne
  See Begley, Kathleen A.
Behan, Leslie
  See Gottfried, Theodore Mark
Behler, Deborah A. 1947- 145
Behler, John L. 1943-2006 145
  Obituary 173
Behler, John Luther
  See Behler, John L.
Behn, Harry 1898-1973 2
  Obituary 34
Behnke, Frances L. 8
Behr, Joyce 1929- 15
Behrens, June York 1925- 19
Behrman, Carol H(elen) 1925- 144
  Earlier sketch in SATA 14
Beifuss, John, (Jr.) 1959- 92
Beil, Karen Magnuson 1950- 124
Beiler, Edna 1923- 61
Beinicke, Steve 1956- 69
Beirne, Barbara 1933- 71
Beiser, Arthur 1931- 22
Beiser, Germaine 1931- 11

Belair, Richard L. 1934- 45
Belaney, Archibald Stansfeld 1888-1938 24
  See also CLR 32
Belbin, David 1958- 164
  Earlier sketch in SATA 106
Belden, Wilanne Schneider 1925- 56
Belfrage, Sally 1936-1994 65
  Obituary 79
Belknap, B. H.
  See Ellis, Edward S.
Belknap, Boynton
  See Ellis, Edward S.
Belknap, Boynton M.D.
  See Ellis, Edward S.
Bell, Anthea 1936- 148
  Earlier sketch in SATA 88
Bell, Cathleen Davitt 1971- 203
Bell, Cece 202
Bell, Clare (Louise) 1952- 99
Bell, Corydon Whitten 1894-1980 3
Bell, David Owen 1949- 99
Bell, Emerson
  See Stratemeyer, Edward L.
Bell, Emily Mary
  See Cason, Mabel Earp
Bell, Frank
  See Benson, Mildred
Bell, Gertrude (Wood) 1911-1987 12
Bell, Gina
  See Balzano, Jeanne (Koppel)
Bell, Hilari 1958- 197
  Earlier sketch in SATA 151
Bell, Jadrien
  See Golden, Christie
Bell, Janet
  See Clymer, Eleanor
Bell, Janet Cheatham 1937- 127
Bell, Krista 1950- 126
Bell, Krista Anne Blakeney
  See Bell, Krista
Bell, Margaret E(lizabeth) 1898-1990 2
Bell, Mary Reeves 1946- 88
Bell, Norman (Edward) 1899- 11
Bell, Raymond Martin 1907-1999 13
Bell, Siobhan 177
Bell, Thelma Harrington 1896-1985 3
Bell, William 1945- 90
  See also CLR 91
Bellairs, John (Anthony) 1938-1991 160
  Obituary 66
  Earlier sketches in SATA 2, 68
  See also CLR 37
Beller, Susan Provost 1949- 128
  Earlier sketch in SATA 84
  See also CLR 106
Bellingham, Brenda 1931- 99
  Brief entry 51
Bello, Rosario de
  See De Bello, Rosario
Belloc, (Joseph) Hilaire (Pierre Sebastien Rene
  Swanton) 1870-1953 112
  See also YABC 1
  See also CLR 102
Belloc, Joseph Peter Rene Hilaire
  See Belloc, (Joseph) Hilaire (Pierre Sebastien
  Rene Swanton)
Belloc, Joseph Pierre Hilaire
  See Belloc, (Joseph) Hilaire (Pierre Sebastien
  Rene Swanton)
Belloli, Andrea P. A. 1947- 86
Bell-Rehwoldt, Sheri 1962- 199
Bellville, Cheryl Walsh 1944- 54
  Brief entry 49
Bell-Zano, Gina
  See Balzano, Jeanne (Koppel)
Belpre, Pura 1899-1982 16
  Obituary 30
Belting, Natalia Maree 1915-1997 6
Belton, John Raynor 1931- 22
Belton, Sandra 1939- 186
  Earlier sketches in SATA 85, 134

Belton, Sandra Yvonne
  See Belton, Sandra
Belton, Sandra Yvonne
  See Belton, Sandra
Beltran, Alberto 1923- 43
Beltran-Hernandez, Irene 1945- 74
Belvedere, Lee
  See Grayland, Valerie (Merle Spanner)
Bemelmans, Ludwig 1898-1962 100
  Earlier sketch in SATA 15
  See also CLR 93
Benander, Carl D. 1941- 74
Benary, Margot
  See Benary-Isbert, Margot
Benary-Isbert, Margot 1889-1979 2
  Obituary 21
  See also CLR 12
Benasutti, Marion 1908-1992 6
Benatar, Raquel 1955- 167
Benchley, Nathaniel (Goddard) 1915-1981 .. 25
  Obituary 28
  Earlier sketch in SATA 3
Benchley, Peter 1940-2006 164
  Earlier sketches in SATA 3, 89
Benchley, Peter Bradford
  See Benchley, Peter
Bendall-Brunello, John 185
Bender, Edna 1941- 92
Bender, Esther 1942- 88
Bender, Lucy Ellen 1942- 22
Bender, Robert 1962- 160
  Earlier sketch in SATA 79
Bendick, Jeanne 1919- 135
  Earlier sketches in SATA 2, 68
  See also CLR 5
  See also SAAS 4
Bendick, Robert L(ouis) 1917- 11
Benedetto, William R. 1928- 180
Benedetto, William Ralph
  See Benedetto, William R.
Benedict, Andrew
  See Arthur, Robert, (Jr.)
Benedict, Dorothy Potter 1889-1979 11
  Obituary 23
Benedict, Lois Trimble 1902-1967 12
Benedict, Rex 1920-1995 8
Benedict, Stewart H(urd) 1924- 26
Beneduce, Ann Keay 128
Benet, Laura 1884-1979 3
  Obituary 23
Benet, Stephen Vincent 1898-1943
  See YABC 1
Benet, Sula 1906-1982 21
  Obituary 33
Ben-Ezer, Ehud 1936- 122
Benezra, Barbara (Beardsley) 1921- 10
Benham, Leslie 1922- 48
Benham, Lois (Dakin) 1924- 48
Benham, Mary Lile 1914-1991 55
Benjamin, E. M. J.
  See Bache, Ellyn
Benjamin, Floella 1949- 206
Benjamin, Nora
  See Kubie, Nora Gottheil Benjamin
Benjamin, Saragail Katzman 1953- 86
Benner, Cheryl 1962- 80
Benner, Judith Ann 1942- 94
Bennett, Alice
  See Ziner, Florence
Bennett, Cherie 1960- 158
  Earlier sketch in SATA 97
Bennett, Dorothea
  See Young, Dorothea Bennett
Bennett, Holly 1957- 181
Bennett, Holly 1957- 181
Bennett, James (W.) 1942- 153
  Autobiography Feature 153
  Earlier sketches in SATA 93, 148

Bennett, Jay 1912- 87
   Brief entry 27
   Earlier sketch in SATA *41*
   See also SAAS *4*
Bennett, Jill (Crawford) 1934- 41
Bennett, John 1865-1956
   See YABC *1*
Bennett, Penelope (Agnes) 1938- 94
Bennett, Rachel
   See Hill, Margaret (Ohler)
Bennett, Rainey 1907-1998 15
   Obituary 111
Bennett, Richard 1899- 21
Bennett, Russell H(oradley) 1896- 25
Bennett, Veronica 1953- 178
Bennett, William (John) 1943- 102
Benning, Elizabeth
   See Rice, Bebe Faas
Benny, Mike 1964- 203
Benson, Elizabeth P(olk) 1924- 65
Benson, Kathleen 1947- 183
   Earlier sketches in SATA *62, 111*
Benson, Linda M(aria) 1959- 84
Benson, Mildred 1905-2002 100
   Obituary 135
   Earlier sketches in SATA *1, 65, 67*
Benson, Mildred Augustine Wirt
   See Benson, Mildred
Benson, Mildred Wirt
   See Benson, Mildred
Benson, Millie
   See Benson, Mildred
Benson, Patrick 1956- 147
Benson, Sally 1900-1972 35
   Obituary 27
   Earlier sketch in SATA *1*
Bentley, Judith (McBride) 1945- 89
   Earlier sketch in SATA *40*
Bentley, Karen
   See Taschek, Karen
Bentley, Nancy (L.) 1946- 78
Bentley, Nicolas Clerihew 1907-1978
   Obituary 24
Bentley, Phyllis Eleanor 1894-1977 6
   Obituary 25
Bentley, Roy 1947- 46
Bentley, William (George) 1916- 84
Benton, Jim 1963- 172
ben Uzair, Salem
   See Horne, Richard Henry Hengist
Bercaw, Edna Coe 1961- 124
Berck, Judith 1960- 75
Berelson, Howard 1940- 5
Berends, Polly Berrien 1939- 50
   Brief entry 38
Berenstain, Jan 1923- 135
   Earlier sketches in SATA *12, 64, 129*
   See also CLR *19*
   See also SAAS *20*
Berenstain, Janice
   See Berenstain, Jan
Berenstain, Michael 1951- 45
Berenstain, Mike
   See Berenstain, Michael
Berenstain, Stan 1923-2005 135
   Obituary 169
   Earlier sketches in SATA *12, 64, 129*
   See also CLR *19*
   See also SAAS *20*
Berenstain, Stanley
   See Berenstain, Stan
Berenzy, Alix 1957- 168
   Earlier sketch in SATA *65*
Beresford, Elisabeth 1928- 141
   Earlier sketches in SATA *25, 86*
   See also SAAS *20*
Berg, Adriane G(ilda) 1948- 152
Berg, Dave
   See Berg, David
Berg, David 1920-2002 27
   Obituary 137

Berg, Elizabeth 1948- 104
Berg, Jean Horton 1913-1995 6
Berg, Joan
   See Victor, Joan Berg
Berg, Ron 1952- 48
Bergaust, Erik 1925-1978 20
Bergel, Colin J. 1963- 137
Bergen, Joyce 1949- 95
Berger, Barbara (Helen) 1945- 77
Berger, Carin 185
Berger, Gilda 1935- 88
   Brief entry 42
Berger, Josef 1903-1971 36
Berger, Melvin H. 1927- 158
   Autobiography Feature 124
   Earlier sketches in SATA *5, 88*
   See also CLR *32*
   See also SAAS *2*
Berger, Phil 1942-2001 62
Berger, Samantha (Allison) 1969- 140
Berger, Terry 1933- 8
Bergey, Alyce (Mae) 1934- 45
Bergin, Mark 1961- 160
   Earlier sketch in SATA *114*
Berglin, Ruth Marie 1970- 181
Bergman, Donna 1934- 73
Bergman, Mara 1956- 196
Bergman, Tamar 1939- 95
Bergren, Lisa T.
   See Bergren, Lisa Tawn
Bergren, Lisa Tawn 200
Bergsma, Jody Lynn 163
Bergum, Constance R. 1952- 121
Berkebile, Fred D(onovan) 1900-1978
   Obituary 26
Berkeley, Jon 1962- 204
Berkes, Marianne 173
Berkey, Barry Robert 1935- 24
Berkowitz, Freda Pastor 1908-1994 12
Berkus, Clara Widess 1909- 78
Berlan, Kathryn Hook 1946- 78
Berlfein, Judy Reiss 1958- 79
Berlin, Eric 195
Berliner, Don 1930- 33
Berliner, Franz 1930- 13
Berlitz, Charles (L. Frambach) 1914-2003 ... 32
   Obituary 151
Berman, Linda 1948- 38
Berman, Paul (Lawrence) 1949- 66
Berna, Paul 1910-1994 15
   Obituary 78
   See also CLR *19*
Bernadette
   See Watts, (Anna) Bernadette
Bernard, Bruce 1928-2000 78
   Obituary 124
Bernard, George I. 1949- 39
Bernard, Jacqueline (de Sieyes) 1921-1983 ... 8
   Obituary 45
Bernard, Patricia 1942- 181
   Earlier sketch in SATA *106*
Bernard, Trish
   See Bernard, Patricia
Bernardin, James (B.) 1966- 112
Bernardo, Anilu 184
Bernards, Neal 1963- 71
Bernasconi, Pablo 1973- 183
Bernays, Anne 1930- 32
Bernhard, Durga T. 1961- 80
Bernhard, Emery 1950- 80
Bernheimer, Kate 201
Bernier-Grand, Carmen T. 1947- 202
Bernstein, Daryl (Evan) 1976- 81
Bernstein, Joanne E(ckstein) 1943- 15
Bernstein, Margery 1933- 114
Bernstein, Nina 1949- 180
Bernstein, Theodore M(enline) 1904-1979 ... 12
   Obituary 27
Berrien, Edith Heal
   See Heal, Edith
Berrill, Jacquelyn (Batsel) 1905- 12

Berrington, John
   See Brownjohn, Alan
Berry, B. J.
   See Berry, Barbara J.
Berry, Barbara J. 1937- 7
Berry, Erick
   See Best, (Evangel) Allena Champlin
Berry, James 1924- 110
   Earlier sketch in SATA *67*
   See also CLR *143*
Berry, Jane Cobb 1915(?)-1979
   Obituary 22
Berry, Joy
   See Berry, Joy Wilt
Berry, Joy Wilt 1944- 58
   Brief entry 46
Berry, Lynne 190
Berry, William D(avid) 1926- 14
Bersani, Shennen 1961- 164
Berson, Harold 1926- 4
Bertagna, Julie 1962- 151
Bertholf, Bret 189
Bertin, Charles-Francois
   See Berlitz, Charles (L. Frambach)
Bertolet, Paul
   See McLaughlin, Frank
Berton, Pierre (Francis de Marigny)
   1920-2004 99
   Obituary 158
Bertrand, Cecile 1953- 76
Bertrand, Diane Gonzales 1956- 177
   Earlier sketch in SATA *106*
Bertrand, Lynne 1963- 164
   Earlier sketch in SATA *81*
Beskow, Elsa (Maartman) 1874-1953 20
   See also CLR *17*
Bess, Clayton
   See Locke, Robert
Besson, Luc 1959- 199
Best, (Evangel) Allena Champlin 1892-1974 . 2
   Obituary 25
Best, Cari 1951- 200
   Earlier sketches in SATA *107, 149*
Best, (Oswald) Herbert 1894-1980 2
Bestall, A(lfred) E(dmeades) 1892-1986 97
   Obituary 48
Betancourt, Jeanne 1941- 148
   Brief entry 43
   Earlier sketches in SATA *55, 96*
Beth, Mary
   See Miller, Mary Beth
Bethancourt, T. Ernesto
   See Paisley, Tom
Bethel, Dell 1929- 52
Bethell, Jean (Frankenberry) 1922- 8
Bethers, Ray 1902-1973 6
Bethke, Bruce Raymond 1955- 114
Bethlen, T.D.
   See Silverberg, Robert
Bethune, J. G.
   See Ellis, Edward S.
Bethune, J. H.
   See Ellis, Edward S.
Betteridge, Anne
   See Potter, Margaret
Bettina
   See Ehrlich, Bettina Bauer
Bettmann, Otto Ludwig 1903-1998 46
Bettoli, Delana 187
Betts, James
   See Haynes, Betsy
Betz, Eva Kelly 1897-1968 10
Bevan, Tom 1868-1930(?)
   See YABC *2*
Bevis, Mary 1939- 202
Bewick, Thomas 1753-1828 16
Beyer, Audrey White 1916- 9
Beyer, Paul J. III 1950- 74
Beynon, John
   See Harris, John (Wyndham Parkes Lucas)
   Beynon

Bezencon, Jacqueline (Buxcel) 1924- *48*
Bhatia, Jamunadevi 1919- *48*
Bhatia, June
    See Bhatia, Jamunadevi
Bial, Morrison David 1917- *62*
Bial, Raymond 1948- *165*
    Earlier sketches in SATA *76, 116*
Biala
    See Brustlein, Janice Tworkov
Biale, Rachel 1952- *99*
Bialk, Elisa
    See Krautter, Elisa (Bialk)
Bianchi, John 1947- *91*
Bianchi, Robert S(teven) 1943- *92*
Bianco, Margery
    See Bianco, Margery Williams
Bianco, Margery Williams 1881-1944 .... *15*
    See also CLR *146*
Bianco, Pamela 1906- *28*
Bibby, Violet 1908-1996 .... *24*
Bible, Charles 1937- *13*
Bibo, Bobette
    See Gugliotta, Bobette
Bice, Clare 1909-1976 .... *22*
Bickerstaff, Isaac
    See Swift, Jonathan
Bidner, Jenni 1963- *193*
Biegel, Paul 1925- *79*
    Earlier sketch in SATA *16*
    See also CLR *27*
    See also SAAS *18*
Biemiller, Carl L(udwig), Jr.) 1912-1979 ..... *40*
    Obituary *21*
Bienenfeld, Florence L(ucille) 1929- *39*
Bierhorst, John (William) 1936- *149*
    Autobiography Feature *149*
    Earlier sketches in SATA *6, 91*
    See also SAAS *10*
Biggar, Joan R(awlins) 1936- *120*
Biggle, Lloyd, Jr. 1923-2002 .... *65*
Biggs, Brian 1968- *192*
Bilal, Abdel W(ahab) 1970- *92*
Bilbrough, Norman 1941- *111*
Bildner, Phil *173*
Bileck, Marvin 1920- *40*
Bilibin, Ivan (Iakolevich) 1876-1942 .... *61*
Bill, Alfred Hoyt 1879-1964 .... *44*
Billam, Rosemary 1952- *61*
Billings, Charlene W(interer) 1941- *41*
Billingsley, Franny 1954- *132*
Billington, Elizabeth T(hain) *50*
    Brief entry *43*
Billout, Guy (Rene) 1941- *144*
    Earlier sketch in SATA *10*
    See also CLR *33*
Bilson, Geoffrey 1938-1987 .... *99*
Binch, Caroline (Lesley) 1947- *140*
    Earlier sketch in SATA *81*
Bing, Christopher (H.) *126*
Bingham, Caroline 1962- *158*
Bingham, Jane M. 1941- *163*
Bingham, Jane Marie
    See Bingham, Jane M.
Bingham, Janet 1959- *200*
Bingham, Sam(uel A.) 1944- *96*
Bingley, Margaret (Jane Kirby) 1947- *72*
Binkley, Anne
    See Rand, Ann (Binkley)
Binzen, Bill
    See Binzen, William
Binzen, William *24*
Birch, David (W.) 1913-1996 .... *89*
Birch, Reginald B(athurst) 1856-1943 .... *19*
Birchman, David 1949- *72*
Birchmore, Daniel A. 1951- *92*
Bird, Carmel 1940- *124*
Bird, E(lzy) J(ay) 1911- *58*
Birdsall, Jeanne 1952(?)- *170*
Birdseye, Tom 1951- *148*
    Earlier sketches in SATA *66, 98*
Birenbaum, Barbara 1941- *65*

Birmingham, Lloyd P(aul) 1924- *83*
    Earlier sketch in SATA *12*
Birmingham, Ruth
    See Sorrells, Walter
Birney, Betty G. 1947- *169*
    Earlier sketch in SATA *98*
Biro, B.
    See Biro, B. S.
Biro, B. S. 1921- *1*
    See also CLR *28*
    See also SAAS *13*
Biro, Val
    See Biro, B. S.
Bischoff, Julia Bristol 1899-1970 .... *12*
Bishop, Bonnie 1943- *37*
Bishop, Claire Huchet 1899(?)-1993 .... *14*
    Obituary *74*
    See also CLR *80*
Bishop, Courtney
    See Ruemmler, John D(avid)
Bishop, Curtis (Kent) 1912-1967 .... *6*
Bishop, Elizabeth 1911-1979
    Obituary *24*
Bishop, Gavin 1946- *144*
    Earlier sketch in SATA *97*
Bishop, Kathleen Wong 1954- *120*
Bishop, Kathy
    See Bishop, Kathleen Wong
Bishop, Nic 1955- *161*
    Earlier sketch in SATA *107*
Bisset, Donald 1910-1995 .... *86*
    Earlier sketch in SATA *7*
Bisson, Terry 1942- *99*
Bisson, Terry Ballantine
    See Bisson, Terry
Bitter, Gary G(len) 1940- *22*
Bixby, William (Courtney) 1920-1986 .... *6*
    Obituary *47*
Bjoerk, Christina 1938- *99*
    Earlier sketch in SATA *67*
    See also CLR *22*
Bjork, Christina
    See Bjoerk, Christina
Bjorklund, Lorence F. 1913-1978 .... *35*
    Brief entry *32*
Bjorkman, Steve *163*
Black, Algernon David 1900-1993 .... *12*
    Obituary *76*
Black, Holly 1971- *147*
Black, Irma Simonton 1906-1972 .... *2*
    Obituary *25*
Black, Mansell
    See Trevor, Elleston
Black, MaryAnn
    See Easley, MaryAnn
Black, Susan Adams 1953- *40*
Blackall, Bernie 1956- *126*
Blackall, Sophie *182*
Blackburn, Claire
    See Altman, Linda Jacobs
Blackburn, John(ny) Brewton 1952- *15*
Blackburn, Joyce Knight 1920- *29*
Blacker, Terence 1948- *194*
Blacker, Tina
    See Louise, Tina
Blackett, Veronica Heath 1927- *12*
Blackie, Jean Cutler 1943- *79*
Blacklin, Malcolm
    See Chambers, Aidan
Blacklock, Dyan 1951- *112*
Blackman, Malorie 1962- *196*
    Earlier sketches in SATA *83, 128*
Blackton, Peter
    See Wilson, Lionel
Blackwood, Alan 1932- *70*
Blackwood, Freya *199*
Blackwood, Gary L. 1945- *169*
    Earlier sketches in SATA *72, 118*

Blade, Alexander
    See Garrett, Randall
    and Hamilton, Edmond
    and Silverberg, Robert
Blades, Ann (Sager) 1947- *69*
    Earlier sketch in SATA *16*
    See also CLR *15*
Bladow, Suzanne Wilson 1937- *14*
Blaine, Chris
    See Gardner, Craig Shaw
Blaine, John
    See Goodwin, Harold L(eland)
Blaine, Marge
    See Blaine, Margery Kay
Blaine, Margery Kay 1937- *11*
Blair, Alison
    See Lerangis, Peter
Blair, Anne Denton 1914-1993 .... *46*
Blair, David Nelson 1954- *80*
Blair, Eric 1903-1950 .... *29*
    See also CLR *68*
Blair, Jay 1953- *45*
Blair, Lucile
    See Yeakley, Marjory Hall
Blair, Margaret Whitman 1951- *124*
Blair, Mary 1911-1978 .... *195*
Blair, Pauline Hunter
    See Clarke, Pauline
Blair, Ruth Van Ness 1912-1999 .... *12*
Blair, Shannon
    See Kaye, Marilyn
Blair, Walter 1900-1992 .... *12*
    Obituary *72*
Blaisdell, Bob
    See Blaisdell, Robert
Blaisdell, Robert 1959- *105*
Blake, Bronwyn 1940- *149*
Blake, Francis *198*
Blake, Jon 1954- *171*
    Earlier sketch in SATA *78*
Blake, Olive
    See Supraner, Robyn
Blake, Quentin (Saxby) 1932- *125*
    Earlier sketches in SATA *9, 52, 96*
    See also CLR *31*
Blake, Robert 1949- *42*
Blake, Robert J. *160*
Blake, Walker E.
    See Griffin, W.E.B.
Blake, William 1757-1827 .... *30*
    See also CLR *52*
Blakely, Gloria 1950- *139*
Blakely, Roger K. 1922- *82*
Blakeney, Jay D.
    See Chester, Deborah
Blakey, Nancy 1955- *94*
Blanc, Esther S. 1913-1997 .... *66*
Blanc, Mel 1908-1989
    Obituary *64*
Blanchard, Patricia *125*
Blanchet, M(uriel) Wylie 1891-1961 .... *106*
Blanco, Richard L(idio) 1926- *63*
Bland, E.
    See Nesbit, E.
Bland, Edith Nesbit
    See Nesbit, E.
Bland, Fabian
    See Nesbit, E.
Blane, Gertrude
    See Blumenthal, Gertrude
Blank, Clarissa Mabel 1915-1965 .... *62*
Blankenship, LeeAnn 1944- *181*
Blassingame, Wyatt Rainey 1909-1985 .... *34*
    Obituary *41*
    Earlier sketch in SATA *1*
Blatchford, Claire H. 1944- *94*
Blauer, Ettagale 1940- *49*
Bledsoe, Glen L. 1951- *108*
Bledsoe, Glen Leonard
    See Bledsoe, Glen L.

Bledsoe, Karen E. 1962- 167
    Earlier sketch in SATA 108
Bledsoe, Karen Elizabeth
    See Bledsoe, Karen E.
Bledsoe, Lucy Jane 1957- 162
    Earlier sketch in SATA 97
Bleeker, Sonia
    See Zim, Sonia Bleeker
Blegen, Daniel M. 1950- 92
Blegvad, Erik 1923- 132
    Earlier sketches in SATA 14, 66
Blegvad, Lenore 1926- 176
    Earlier sketches in SATA 14, 66
Bley, Anette 1967- 188
Blish, James 1921-1975 66
Blish, James Benjamin
    See Blish, James
Blishen, Edward (William) 1920-1996 66
    Obituary 93
    Earlier sketch in SATA 8
Bliss, Corinne Demas 1947- 131
    Earlier sketch in SATA 37
    See Demas, Corinne
Bliss, Frederick
    See Card, Orson Scott
Bliss, Gillian
    See Paton Walsh, Jill
Bliss, Harry 1964- 196
    Earlier sketch in SATA 156
Bliss, Reginald
    See Wells, H(erbert) G(eorge)
Bliss, Ronald G(ene) 1942- 12
Blitt, Barry 187
Bliven, Bruce, Jr. 1916-2002 2
Blixen, Karen 1885-1962 44
Blizzard, Gladys S. (?)-1992 79
Blobaum, Cindy 1966- 123
Bloch, Lucienne 1909-1999 10
Bloch, Marie Halun 1910-1998 6
    See also SAAS 9
Bloch, Robert (Albert) 1917-1994 12
    Obituary 82
Blochman, Lawrence G(oldtree)
    1900-1975 22
Block, Francesca Lia 1962- 158
    Earlier sketches in SATA 80, 116
    See also CLR 116
    See also SAAS 21
Block, Irvin 1917- 12
Blomgren, Jennifer (Alice) 1954- 136
Blood, Charles Lewis 1929- 28
Bloom, Barbara Lee 1943- 146
Bloom, Freddy 1914-2000 37
    Obituary 121
Bloom, Lloyd 1947- 108
    Brief entry 43
Bloom, Suzanne 1950- 172
Bloomfield, Michaela 1966- 70
Bloor, Edward 1950- 201
    Earlier sketches in SATA 98, 155
Bloor, Edward William
    See Bloor, Edward
Blos, Joan W. 1928- 153
    Autobiography Feature 153
    Brief entry 27
    Earlier sketches in SATA 33, 69, 109
    See also CLR 18
    See also SAAS 11
Blos, Joan Winsor
    See Blos, Joan W.
Blough, Glenn O(rlando) 1907-1995 1
Blue, Rose 1931- 166
    Autobiography Feature 117
    Earlier sketches in SATA 5, 91, 93
    See also SAAS 24
Blue, Zachary
    See Stine, R.L.
Bluggage, Oranthy
    See Alcott, Louisa May
Blumberg, Leda 1956- 59

Blumberg, Rhoda 1917- 123
    Earlier sketches in SATA 35, 70
    See also CLR 21
Blume, Judy 1938- 195
    Earlier sketches in SATA 2, 31, 79, 142
    See also CLR 69
Blume, Judy Sussman
    See Blume, Judy
Blume, Lesley M.M. 1975- 180
Blumenthal, Deborah 204
    Earlier sketch in SATA 161
Blumenthal, Gertrude 1907-1971
    Obituary 27
Blumenthal, Shirley 1943- 46
Blutig, Eduard
    See Gorey, Edward (St. John)
Bly, Janet (Chester) 1945- 43
Bly, Stephen A(rthur) 1944- 116
    Earlier sketch in SATA 43
Blyler, Allison Lee 1966- 74
Blythe, Gary 1959- 185
Blyton, Carey 1932-2002 9
    Obituary 138
Blyton, Enid 1897-1968 25
    See also CLR 31
Blyton, Enid Mary
    See Blyton, Enid
Bo, Ben
    See Richardson, V.A.
Boardman, Fon Wyman, Jr. 1911-2000 6
Boardman, Gwenn R.
    See Petersen, Gwenn Boardman
Boase, Wendy 1944-1999 28
    Obituary 110
Boatner, Mark Mayo III 1921- 29
Bobbe, Dorothie de Bear 1905-1975 1
    Obituary 25
Bober, Natalie S. 1930- 134
    Earlier sketch in SATA 87
    See also SAAS 23
Bobette, Bibo
    See Gugliotta, Bobette
Bobri, Vladimir V. 1898-1986 47
    Brief entry 32
Bobritsky, Vladimir
    See Bobri, Vladimir V.
Bochak, Grayce 1956- 76
Bock, Hal
    See Bock, Harold I.
Bock, Harold I. 1939- 10
Bock, William Sauts Netamux'we 1939- 14
Bodanis, David 179
Bode, Janet 1943-1999 96
    Obituary 118
    Earlier sketch in SATA 60
Bode, N.E.
    See Baggott, Julianna
Bodecker, N(iels) M(ogens) 1922-1988 73
    Obituary 54
    Earlier sketch in SATA 8
Boden, Hilda
    See Bodenham, Hilda Morris
Bodenham, Hilda Morris 1901- 13
Bodett, Thomas Edward 1955- 70
Bodett, Tom
    See Bodett, Thomas Edward
Bodie, Idella F(allaw) 1925- 89
    Earlier sketch in SATA 12
Bodker, Cecil
    See Bodker, Cecil
Bodker, Cecil 1927- 133
    Earlier sketch in SATA 14
    See also CLR 23
Bodsworth, (Charles) Fred(erick) 1918- 27
Boeckman, Charles 1920- 12
Boegehold, Betty (Doyle) 1913-1985
    Obituary 42
Boelts, Maribeth 1964- 200
    Earlier sketches in SATA 78, 163
Boerst, William J. 1939- 170
    Earlier sketch in SATA 121

Boesch, Mark J(oseph) 1917- 12
Boesen, Victor 1908- 16
Bogacki, Tomek 1950- 138
Bogaerts, Gert 1965- 80
Bogan, Paulette 1960- 201
    Earlier sketch in SATA 129
Bogart, Jo Ellen 1945- 92
    See also CLR 59
Boggs, Ralph Steele 1901-1994 7
Bograd, Larry 1953- 89
    Earlier sketch in SATA 33
    See also SAAS 21
Bogue, Gary 1938- 195
Bogue, Gary L.
    See Bogue, Gary
Bohdal, Susi 1951- 101
    Earlier sketch in SATA 22
Bohlen, Nina 1931- 58
Bohlmeijer, Arno 1956- 94
Bohner, Charles (Henry) 1927- 62
Bohnhoff, Maya Kaathryn 1954- 88
Boiger, Alexandra 178
Boissard, Janine 1932- 59
Bojunga, Lygia
    See Nunes, Lygia Bojunga
Bojunga-Nunes, Lygia
    See Nunes, Lygia Bojunga
Bok, Arthur
    See Bok, Chip
Bok, Chip 1952- 205
Bolam, Emily 1969- 206
Boland, Janice 98
Bolden, Tonya 1959- 188
    Earlier sketches in SATA 79, 138
Bolden, Tonya Wilyce
    See Bolden, Tonya
Boles, Paul Darcy 1916-1984 9
    Obituary 38
Bolian, Polly 1925- 4
Bollen, Roger 1941(?)- 83
    Brief entry 29
Bolliger, Max 1929- 7
Bollinger, Max 1929- 167
Bollinger, Peter 172
Bolognese, Don(ald Alan) 1934- 129
    Earlier sketches in SATA 24, 71
Bolognese, Elaine 1933- 23
Bolotin, Norman (Phillip) 1951- 93
Bolton, Carole 1926- 6
Bolton, Elizabeth
    See St. John, Nicole
Bolton, Evelyn
    See Bunting, Eve
Bonar, Veronica
    See Bailey, Donna (Veronica Anne)
Bond, B. J.
    See Heneghan, James
Bond, Bruce 1939- 61
Bond, Felicia 1954- 126
    Earlier sketch in SATA 49
Bond, Gladys Baker 1912- 14
Bond, Higgins 1951- 177
    Earlier sketch in SATA 83
Bond, J. Harvey
    See Winterbotham, R(ussell) R(obert)
Bond, (Thomas) Michael 1926- 157
    Earlier sketches in SATA 6, 58
    See also CLR 95
    See also SAAS 3
Bond, Nancy 1945- 159
    Autobiography Feature 159
    Earlier sketches in SATA 22, 82
    See also CLR 11
    See also SAAS 13
Bond, Nancy Barbara
    See Bond, Nancy
Bond, Rebecca 1972- 130
Bond, Ruskin 1934- 87
    Earlier sketch in SATA 14
Bondie, J. D.
    See Cunningham, Chet

Bondoux, Anne-Laure 1971- *175*
Bone, Ian 1956- *158*
  Earlier sketch in SATA *117*
Bonehill, Captain Ralph
  See Stratemeyer, Edward L.
Bonestell, Chesley 1888-1986
  Obituary *48*
Bonham, Barbara Thomas 1926- *7*
Bonham, Frank 1914-1989 .... *49*
  Obituary *62*
  Earlier sketch in SATA *1*
  See also SAAS *3*
Boniface, William 1963- *182*
  Earlier sketch in SATA *102*
Bonino, Louise
  See Williams, Louise Bonino
Bonk, John J. *189*
Bonn, Pat
  See Bonn, Patricia Carolyn
Bonn, Patricia Carolyn 1948- *43*
Bonner, Hannah *197*
Bonner, Mary Graham 1890-1974 .... *19*
Bonner, Mike 1951- *121*
Bonners, Susan 1947- *85*
  Brief entry *48*
Bonnett-Rampersaud, Louise *173*
Bonning, Tony 1948- *169*
Bonsall, Crosby Barbara (Newell)
  1921-1995 .... *23*
  Obituary *84*
Bonsall, Joseph S. 1948- *119*
Bonsignore, Joan 1959- *140*
Bontemps, Arna 1902-1973 .... *44*
  Obituary *24*
  Earlier sketch in SATA *2*
  See also CLR *6*
Bontemps, Arnaud Wendell
  See Bontemps, Arna
Bonzon, Paul-Jacques 1908-1978 .... *22*
Boock, Paula 1964- *134*
Booher, Dianna Daniels 1948- *33*
Book, Rick 1949- *119*
Book, Rita
  See Holub, Joan
Bookman, Charlotte
  See Zolotow, Charlotte
Boon, Debbie 1960- *103*
Boon, Emilie (Laetitia) 1958- *86*
Boone, Charles Eugene
  See Boone, Pat
Boone, Pat 1934- *7*
Boorman, Linda (Kay) 1940- *46*
Boorstin, Daniel J(oseph) 1914-2004 .... *52*
Boos, Ben 1971- *206*
Booth, Coe *187*
Booth, Ernest Sheldon 1915-1984 .... *43*
Booth, George 1926- *191*
Booth, Graham (Charles) 1935- *37*
Bootman, Colin *159*
Borden, Louise 1949- *190*
  Autobiography Feature *141*
  Earlier sketches in SATA *68, 104, 141*
Bordier, Georgette 1924- *16*
Borgman, James
  See Borgman, Jim
Borgman, James Mark
  See Borgman, Jim
Borgman, Jim 1954- *122*
Borgo, Lacy Finn 1972- *194*
Boring, Mel 1939- *168*
  Earlier sketch in SATA *35*
Borja, Corinne 1929- *22*
Borja, Robert 1923- *22*
Borland, Hal
  See Borland, Harold Glen
Borland, Harold Glen 1900-1978 .... *5*
  Obituary *24*
Borland, Kathryn Kilby 1916- *16*
Borlenghi, Patricia 1951- *79*
Born, Adolf 1930- *49*

Bornstein, Ruth Lercher
  See Bornstein-Lercher, Ruth
Bornstein-Lercher, Ruth 1927- *88*
  Autobiography Feature *107*
  Earlier sketch in SATA *14*
Borski, Lucia Merecka *18*
Borten, Helen Jacobson 1930- *5*
Bortolotti, Dan 1969- *157*
Borton, Elizabeth
  See Trevino, Elizabeth B(orton) de
Borton, Lady 1942- *98*
Borton de Trevino, Elizabeth
  See Trevino, Elizabeth B(orton) de
Bortstein, Larry 1942- *16*
Bortz, Alfred B(enjamin) 1944- *139*
  Earlier sketch in SATA *74*
Bortz, Fred
  See Bortz, Alfred B(enjamin)
Bosch, Pseudonymous *199*
Bosco, Jack
  See Holliday, Joseph
Boshell, Gordon 1908-1991 .... *15*
Boshinski, Blanche 1922- *10*
Bosman, Paul 1929- *107*
Bosse, Malcolm (Joseph, Jr.) 1926-2002 .... *136*
  Earlier sketch in SATA *35*
Bosserman, (Charles) Phillip 1931- *84*
Bossom, Naomi 1933- *35*
Bostock, Mike 1962- *114*
Boston, L(ucy) M(aria Wood) 1892-1990 .... *19*
  Obituary *64*
  See also CLR *3*
Bostrom, Kathleen (Susan) Long 1954- *139*
Bostrom, Kathy
  See Bostrom, Kathleen (Susan) Long
Bosworth, J. Allan 1925- *19*
Bothwell, Jean (?)-1977 .... *2*
Botkin, B(enjamin) A(lbert) 1901-1975 .... *40*
Botsford, Ward 1927-2004 .... *66*
Botting, Douglas (Scott) 1934- *43*
Bottner, Barbara 1943- *170*
  Autobiography Feature *121*
  Earlier sketches in SATA *14, 93*
  See also SAAS *26*
Bottone, Frank G., Jr. 1969- *141*
Bouchard, David 1952- *117*
Boucher, (Clarence) Carter 1954- *129*
Boudelang, Bob
  See Pell, Ed(ward)
Boughton, Richard 1954- *75*
Boulet, Susan Seddon 1941- *50*
Boulle, Pierre (Francois Marie-Louis)
  1912-1994 .... *22*
  Obituary *78*
Boulton, Jane 1921- *91*
Bouma, Paddy 1947- *128*
Bour, Daniele 1939- *62*
Bourbonniere, Sylvie 1966- *182*
Bourdon, David 1934-1998 .... *46*
Bourgeois, Paulette 1951- *153*
Bourne, Lesley
  See Marshall, Evelyn
Bourne, Miriam Anne 1931-1989 .... *16*
  Obituary *63*
Boutavant, Marc 1970- *200*
Boutet de Monvel, (Louis) M(aurice)
  1850(?)-1913 .... *30*
  See also CLR *32*
Bova, Ben 1932- *133*
  Earlier sketches in SATA *6, 68*
  See also CLR *96*
Bova, Benjamin William
  See Bova, Ben
Bovaird, Anne E(lizabeth) 1960- *90*
Bow, Patricia 1946- *168*
Bowden, Joan Chase 1925- *51*
  Brief entry *38*
Bowe, Julie 1962- *194*
Bowen, Alexandria Russell *97*
Bowen, Andy Russell
  See Bowen, Alexandria Russell

Bowen, Anne 1952- *202*
  Earlier sketch in SATA *170*
Bowen, Betty Morgan
  See West, Betty
Bowen, Catherine (Shober) Drinker
  1897-1973 .... *7*
Bowen, David
  See Bowen, Joshua David
Bowen, Fred 1953- *136*
Bowen, Joshua David 1930- *22*
Bowen, Rhys
  See Quin-Harkin, Janet
Bowen, Robert Sydney 1900-1977 .... *52*
  Obituary *21*
Bowermaster, Jon 1954- *135*
  Earlier sketch in SATA *77*
Bowers, Terrell L. 1945- *101*
Bowers, Terry
  See Bowers, Terrell L.
Bowers, Tim *185*
Bowie, C. W.
  See Old, Wendie C(orbin)
  and Wirths, Claudine (Turner) G(ibson)
Bowie, Jim
  See Norwood, Victor G(eorge) C(harles)
  and Stratemeyer, Edward L.
Bowkett, Stephen 1953- *67*
Bowler, Jan Brett
  See Brett, Jan
Bowler, Tim 1953- *149*
Bowman, Catherine
  See Smith, Cat Bowman
Bowman, Crystal 1951- *105*
Bowman, James Cloyd 1880-1961 .... *23*
Bowman, John S(tewart) 1931- *16*
Bowman, Kathleen (Gill) 1942- *52*
  Brief entry *40*
Bowman, Leslie
  See Bowman, Leslie W.
Bowman, Leslie W. *182*
Bowsher, Melodie *195*
Boxall, Ed *178*
Boyce, Frank Cottrell *182*
Boyce, George A(rthur) 1898- *19*
Boyd, Candy Dawson 1946- *72*
  See also CLR *50*
Boyd, Pauline
  See Schock, Pauline
Boyd, Selma
  See Acuff, Selma Boyd
Boyd, Waldo T. 1918- *18*
Boyden, Linda 1948- *143*
Boyer, Allen B. 1963- *153*
Boyer, Robert E(rnst) 1929- *22*
Boyes, Vivien 1952- *106*
Boyes, Vivien Elizabeth
  See Boyes, Vivien
Boyle, Ann (Peters) 1916- *10*
Boyle, Eleanor Vere (Gordon) 1825-1916 .... *28*
Boyle, Robert H. 1928- *65*
Boylston, Helen Dore 1895-1984 .... *23*
  Obituary *39*
Boyne, John 1971- *181*
Boynton, Sandra (Keith) 1953- *152*
  Brief entry *38*
  Earlier sketches in SATA *57, 107*
  See also CLR *105*
Boz
  See Dickens, Charles (John Huffam)
Braasch, Gary *201*
Bracken, Charles
  See Pellowski, Michael (Joseph)
Brackers de Hugo, Pierre 1960- *115*
Brackett, Dolli Tingle 1911-1993 .... *137*
Brackett, Virginia 1950- *166*
  Earlier sketch in SATA *121*
Brackett, Virginia Roberts Meredith
  See Brackett, Virginia
Bradbury, Bianca (Ryley) 1908-1982 .... *56*
  Earlier sketch in SATA *3*

Bradbury, Edward P.
  See Moorcock, Michael
Bradbury, Ray 1920- 123
  Earlier sketches in SATA *11, 64*
Bradbury, Ray Douglas
  See Bradbury, Ray
Bradby, Marie 161
Bradfield, Carl 1942- 91
Bradford, Ann (Liddell) 1917- 56
  Brief entry 38
Bradford, Barbara Taylor 1933- 66
Bradford, Karleen 1936- 96
  Earlier sketch in SATA *48*
Bradford, Lois J(ean) 1936- 36
Bradford, Richard (Roark) 1932-2002 59
  Obituary 135
Bradley, Duane
  See Sanborn, Duane
Bradley, Kimberly Brubaker 1967- 179
Bradley, Marion Zimmer 1930-1999 139
  Obituary 116
  Earlier sketch in SATA *90*
Bradley, Timothy J. 193
Bradley, Virginia 1912- 23
Bradley, Will
  See Strickland, Brad
Bradman, Tony 1954- 152
  Earlier sketch in SATA *81*
Bradshaw, Gillian (Joan) 1949- 118
Bradshaw, Gillian 1956- 127
Bradshaw, Gillian Marucha
  See Bradshaw, Gillian
Bradstreet, T. J.
  See Thesman, Jean
Brady, Esther Wood 1905-1987 31
  Obituary 53
Brady, Irene 1943- 4
Brady, Kimberley S. 1953- 101
Brady, Kimberley Smith
  See Brady, Kimberley S.
Brady, Lillian 1902- 28
Bragdon, Elspeth MacDuffie 1897-1980 6
Bragdon, Lillian Jacot 24
Brager, Bruce L. 1949- 146
Bragg, Mabel Caroline 1870-1945 24
Bragg, Michael 1948- 46
Bragg, Ruth Gembicki 1943- 77
Brahm, Sumishta 1954- 58
Brailsford, Frances
  See Wosmek, Frances
Brainerd, John W(hiting) 1918- 65
Braithwaite, Althea 1940- 23
  Autobiography Feature 119
  See also SAAS *24*
Bram, Elizabeth 1948- 30
Brancato, Robin F(idler) 1936- 97
  See also CLR *32*
  See also SAAS *9*
Branch, Muriel Miller 1943- 152
  Earlier sketch in SATA *94*
Brand, Christianna
  See Lewis, Mary
Brand, Rebecca
  See Charnas, Suzy McKee
Brande, Robin 194
Brandel, Marc 1919- 71
Brandenberg, Alexa (Demetria) 1966- 97
Brandenberg, Aliki 1929- 157
  Earlier sketches in SATA *2, 35, 75, 113*
  See also CLR *71*
Brandenberg, Franz 1932- 75
  Earlier sketches in SATA *8, 35*
Brandenburg, Jim 1945- 87
Brandhorst, Carl T(heodore) 1898-1988 23
Brandis, Marianne 1938- 149
  Earlier sketches in SATA *59, 96*
Brandon, Brumsic, Jr. 1927- 9
Brandon, Curt
  See Bishop, Curtis (Kent)
Brandreth, Gyles 1948- 28

Brandreth, Gyles Daubeney
  See Brandreth, Gyles
Brandt, Catharine 1905-1997 40
Brandt, Keith
  See Sabin, Louis
Brandt, Sue R(eading) 1916- 59
Branfield, John (Charles) 1931- 11
Branford, Henrietta 1946-1999 106
Branley, Franklyn M(ansfield) 1915-2002 .. 136
  Earlier sketches in SATA *4, 68*
  See also CLR *13*
  See also SAAS *16*
Brannen, Sarah S. 202
Branscum, Robbie (Tilley) 1937-1997 72
  Obituary 96
  Earlier sketch in SATA *23*
  See also SAAS *17*
Bransom, (John) Paul 1885-1979 43
Brashares, Ann 1967- 188
  Earlier sketch in SATA *145*
  See also CLR *113*
Brassard, France 1963- 186
Braswell, E.J.
  See Lynn, Tracy
Braswell, Elizabeth J.
  See Lynn, Tracy
Braswell, Liz
  See Lynn, Tracy
Bratton, Helen 1899-1986 4
Bratun, Katy 1950- 160
  Earlier sketch in SATA *83*
Braude, Michael 1936- 23
Braun, Lilian Jackson 1916(?)- 109
Brautigan, Richard 1935-1984 56
Brautigan, Richard Gary
  See Brautigan, Richard
Bray, Libba 203
  Earlier sketch in SATA *159*
Bray, Martha E.
  See Bray, Libba
Braymer, Marjorie Elizabeth 1911-1988 6
Breathed, Berke 1957- 161
  Earlier sketch in SATA *86*
Breathed, Guy Berkeley
  See Breathed, Berke
Brecht, Edith 1895-1975 6
  Obituary 25
Breck, Vivian
  See Breckenfeld, Vivian Gurney
Breckenfeld, Vivian Gurney 1895-1992 1
Breda, Tjalmar
  See DeJong, David C(ornel)
Bredeson, Carmen 1944- 163
  Earlier sketch in SATA *98*
Breen, Steve 1970- 186
Breinburg, Petronella 1927- 11
  See also CLR *31*
Breisky, William J(ohn) 1928- 22
Brenaman, Miriam 172
Brennan, Caitlin
  See Tarr, Judith
Brennan, Gale (Patrick) 1927- 64
  Brief entry 53
Brennan, Herbie 1940- 183
  Earlier sketch in SATA *140*
Brennan, James Herbert
  See Brennan, Herbie
Brennan, Jan
  See Brennan, Herbie
Brennan, J.H.
  See Brennan, Herbie
Brennan, Joseph Lomas 1903-2000 6
Brennan, Linda Crotta 1952- 130
Brennan, Tim
  See Conroy, John Wesley
Brennan-Nelson, Denise 203
Brenner, Anita 1905-1974 56
Brenner, Barbara (Johnes) 1925- 124
  Earlier sketches in SATA *4, 42, 76*
  See also SAAS *14*

Brenner, Fred 1920- 36
  Brief entry 34
Brent, Hope 1935(?)-1984
  Obituary 39
Brent, Stuart 14
Breskin, Jane
  See Zalben, Jane Breskin
Breslin, Theresa 128
  Autobiography Feature 128
  Earlier sketch in SATA *70*
Breslow, Maurice 1935- 72
Breslow, Maurice A
  See Breslow, Maurice
Breslow, Susan 1951- 69
Brett, Bernard 1925- 22
Brett, Grace N(eff) 1900-1975 23
Brett, Jan 1949- 171
  Earlier sketches in SATA *42, 71, 130*
  See also CLR *27*
Brett, Jan Churchill
  See Brett, Jan
Brett Bowler, Jan
  See Brett, Jan
Brewer, Heather 1973- 196
Brewer, James D. 1951- 108
Brewer, Sally King 1947- 33
Brewster, Benjamin
  See Folsom, Franklin (Brewster)
Brewster, Hugh 1950- 191
  Earlier sketch in SATA *95*
Brewster, Patience 1952- 97
Brewton, John E(dmund) 1898-1982 5
Brian, Janeen (Paulette) 1948- 141
Briant, Ed 180
Brick, John 1922-1973 10
Brickman, Robin D. 1954- 155
Bride, Nadja
  See Nobisso, Josephine
Bridgers, Sue Ellen 1942- 90
  Autobiography Feature 109
  Earlier sketch in SATA *22*
  See also CLR *18*
  See also SAAS *1*
Bridges, Laurie
  See Bruck, Lorraine
Bridges, Ruby (Nell) 1954- 131
Bridges, William (Andrew) 1901-1984 5
Bridwell, Norman (Ray) 1928- 138
  Earlier sketches in SATA *4, 68*
  See also CLR *96*
Brier, Howard M(axwell) 1903-1969 8
Brierley, (Louise) 1958- 59
Briggs, Katharine Mary 1898-1980 101
  Obituary 25
Briggs, Peter 1921-1975 39
  Obituary 31
Briggs, Raymond 1934- 184
  Earlier sketches in SATA *23, 66, 131*
  See also CLR *10*
Briggs, Raymond Redvers
  See Briggs, Raymond
Bright, Paul 1949- 182
Bright, Robert Sr.) 1902-1988 63
  Obituary 60
  Earlier sketch in SATA *24*
Bright, Robert Douglas
  See Bright, Robert Sr.)
Bright, Sarah
  See Shine, Deborah
Brightfield, Richard 1927- 65
  Brief entry 53
Brightfield, Rick
  See Brightfield, Richard
Brighton, Catherine 1943- 206
  Earlier sketches in SATA *65, 107*
Brill, Marlene Targ 1945- 124
  Earlier sketch in SATA *77*
Brimberg, Stanlee 1947- 9
Brimner, Larry Dane 1949- 170
  Autobiography Feature 112
  Earlier sketch in SATA *79*

Brin, David 1950- 65
Brin, Ruth Firestone 1921- 22
Brinckloe, Julie 1950- 13
Brinckloe, Julie Lorraine
    See Brinckloe, Julie
Brindel, June (Rachuy) 1919- 7
Brindle, Max
    See Fleischman, Sid
Brindze, Ruth 1903-1984 23
Brink, Carol Ryrie 1895-1981 100
    Obituary 27
    Earlier sketches in SATA *1, 31*
    See also CLR *30*
Brinsmead, H. F(ay)
    See Brinsmead, H(esba) F(ay)
Brinsmead, H. F.
    See Brinsmead, H(esba) F(ay)
Brinsmead, H(esba) F(ay) 1922- 78
    Earlier sketch in SATA *18*
    See also CLR *47*
    See also SAAS *5*
Briquebec, John
    See Rowland-Entwistle, (Arthur) Theodore
    (Henry)
Brisbane, Henry R.
    See Ellis, Edward S.
Brisco, P. A.
    See Matthews, Patricia
Brisco, Patty
    See Matthews, Patricia
    and Matthews, Clayton (Hartley)
Briscoe, Jill (Pauline) 1935- 56
    Brief entry 47
Brisley, Joyce Lankester 1896-1978 22
    Obituary 84
Brissenden, Connie
    See Brissenden, Constance
Brissenden, Constance 1947- 150
Brisson, Pat 1951- 177
    Autobiography Feature 133
    Earlier sketches in SATA *67, 128, 133*
Britt, Albert 1874-1969
    Obituary 28
Britt, Dell 1934- 1
Brittain, Bill
    See Brittain, William
Brittain, C. Dale 1948- 82
Brittain, William 1930- 76
    Earlier sketch in SATA *36*
    See also SAAS *7*
Brittingham, Geoffrey (Hugh) 1959- 76
Britton, Kate
    See Stegeman, Janet Allais
Britton, Louisa
    See McGuire, Leslie (Sarah)
Britton, Rick 1952- 82
Bro, Margueritte (Harmon) 1894-1977 19
    Obituary 27
Broach, Elise 1963- 173
Broadhead, Helen Cross 1913- 25
Brochmann, Elizabeth 1938- 41
Brock, Betty (Carter) 1923-2003 4
    Obituary 150
Brock, C(harles) E(dmund) 1870-1938 42
    Brief entry 32
Brock, Delia
    See Ephron, Delia
Brock, Emma L(illian) 1886-1974 8
Brock, H(enry) M(atthew) 1875-1960 42
Brockett, Eleanor Hall 1913-1967 10
Brockman, C(hristian) Frank 1902-1985 26
Brockmeier, Kevin 1972- 176
Broderick, Dorothy M. 1929- 5
Brodeur, Ruth Wallace
    See Wallace-Brodeur, Ruth
Brodie, Sally
    See Cavin, Ruth (Brodie)
Brodsky, Beverly
    See McDermott, Beverly Brodsky
Brody, Wendy
    See Staub, Wendy Corsi

Broeger, Achim 1944- 31
Broekel, Rainer Lothar 1923- 38
Broekel, Ray
    See Broekel, Rainer Lothar
Broekstra, Lorette 1964- 189
    Earlier sketch in SATA *124*
Brogden, Sherryl
    See Jordan, Sherryl
Broger, Achim
    See Broeger, Achim
Broida, Marian 154
Brokamp, Marilyn 1920- 10
Broman, Fred
    See Moseley, James W(illett)
Bromhall, Winifred 26
Brommer, Gerald F(rederick) 1927- 28
Brondfield, Jerome 1913-1998 22
Brondfield, Jerry
    See Brondfield, Jerome
Bronner, Stephen Eric 1949- 101
Bronowski, Jacob 1908-1974 55
Bronson, Alice
    See Watkins, Dawn L.
Bronson, Linda 203
Bronson, Lynn
    See Lampman, Evelyn Sibley
Bronson, Wilfrid Swancourt 1894-1985
    Obituary 43
Brook, Judith (Penelope) 1926- 59
    Brief entry 51
Brook, Judy
    See Brook, Judith (Penelope)
Brooke, L(eonard) Leslie 1862-1940 17
    See also CLR *20*
Brooke, William J. 1946- 139
Brooke-Haven, P.
    See Wodehouse, P(elham) G(renville)
Brooker, Kyrsten 199
Brookins, Dana 1931- 28
Brooks, Anita
    See Abramovitz, Anita (Zeltner Brooks)
Brooks, Bill 1939- 59
Brooks, Bruce 1950- 112
    Brief entry 53
    Earlier sketch in SATA *72*
    See also CLR *25*
Brooks, Caryl 1924- 84
Brooks, Charlotte K(endrick) 1918-1998 24
    Obituary 112
Brooks, Erik 1972- 182
    Earlier sketch in SATA *152*
Brooks, George
    See Baum, L. Frank
Brooks, Gwendolyn 1917-2000 6
    Obituary 123
    See also CLR *27*
Brooks, Gwendolyn Elizabeth
    See Brooks, Gwendolyn
Brooks, Jerome 1931- 23
Brooks, Kevin 1959- 197
    Earlier sketch in SATA *150*
Brooks, Kevin M.
    See Brooks, Kevin
Brooks, Lester 1924- 7
Brooks, Martha 1944- 134
    Autobiography Feature 134
    Earlier sketches in SATA *68, 121*
Brooks, Maurice (Graham) 1900- 45
Brooks, Polly Schoyer 1912- 12
Brooks, Ron 1948- 94
    Brief entry 33
Brooks, Ronald George
    See Brooks, Ron
Brooks, Terry 1944- 60
Brooks, Walter R(ollin) 1886-1958 17
Brooks-Hill, Helen (Mason) 1908-1994 59
Broome, Errol 1937- 158
    Earlier sketch in SATA *105*
Brophy, Nannette 1963- 73
Brosnan, James Patrick 1929- 14

Brosnan, Jim
    See Brosnan, James Patrick
Brostoff, Anita 1931- 132
Brothers Grimm
    See Grimm, Jacob Ludwig Karl
    and Grimm, Wilhelm Karl
Brothers Hildebrandt, The
    See Hildebrandt, Greg
    and Hildebrandt, Tim
Broun, Emily
    See Sterne, Emma Gelders
Brouwer, S. W.
    See Brouwer, Sigmund (W.)
Brouwer, Sigmund (W.) 1959- 109
Brow, Thea 1934- 60
Brower, Millicent 8
Brower, Pauline 1929- 22
Browin, Frances Williams 1898-1986 5
Brown, Alexis
    See Baumann, Amy Beeching
Brown, Anne Ensign 1937- 61
Brown, Beverly Swerdlow 97
Brown, Bill
    See Brown, William L(ouis)
Brown, Billye Walker
    See Cutchen, Billye Walker
Brown, Bob
    See Brown, Robert Joseph
Brown, Buck 1936- 45
Brown, Calef 179
Brown, Cassie 1919-1986 55
Brown, Charlotte Lewis 181
Brown, Conrad 1922- 31
Brown, Craig McFarland 1947- 73
Brown, David
    See Brown, David A(lan)
    and Myller, Rolf
Brown, Dee 1908-2002 110
    Obituary 141
    Earlier sketch in SATA *5*
Brown, Dee Alexander
    See Brown, Dee
Brown, Don 1949- 200
    Earlier sketch in SATA *172*
Brown, Drew T. III 1955- 83
Brown, Drollene P. 1939- 53
Brown, Elbrite 198
Brown, Eleanor Frances 1908-1987 3
Brown, Elizabeth Ferguson 1937- 153
Brown, Elizabeth M(yers) 1915- 43
Brown, Fern G. 1918- 34
Brown, (Robert) Fletch 1923- 42
Brown, Fornan 1901-1996 71
    Obituary 88
Brown, George Earl 1883-1964 11
Brown, George Mackay 1921-1996 35
Brown, Irene Bennett 1932- 3
Brown, Irving
    See Adams, William Taylor
Brown, Ivor (John Carnegie) 1891-1974 5
    Obituary 26
Brown, Jane Clark 1930- 81
Brown, Janet Mitsui 87
Brown, Jo 1964- 170
Brown, Joanne 1933- 147
Brown, Joe David 1915-1976 44
Brown, Joseph E(dward) 1929- 59
    Brief entry 51
Brown, Judith Gwyn 1933- 20
Brown, Kathryn 1955- 168
    Earlier sketch in SATA *98*
Brown, Kathy
    See Brown, Kathryn
Brown, Ken (James) 129
Brown, Kevin 1960- 101
Brown, Laurene Krasny 1945- 99
    Earlier sketch in SATA *54*
Brown, Laurie Krasny
    See Brown, Laurene Krasny
Brown, Lloyd Arnold 1907-1966 36

Brown, Mahlon A.
See Ellis, Edward S.
Brown, Marc (Tolon) 1946- 145
Earlier sketches in SATA 10, 53, 80
See also CLR 29
Brown, Marcia (Joan) 1918- 47
Earlier sketch in SATA 7
See also CLR 12
Brown, Margaret Wise 1910-1952 100
See also YABC 2
See also CLR 107
Brown, Margery (Wheeler) 78
Earlier sketch in SATA 5
Brown, Marion Marsh 1908-2001 6
Brown, Myra Berry 1918- 6
Brown, Palmer 1919- 36
Brown, Pamela (Beatrice) 1924-1989 5
Obituary 61
Brown, Peter 1979- 178
Brown, Rachel W.N. 1947- 203
Brown, Reeve Lindbergh
See Lindbergh, Reeve
Brown, Richard E. 1946- 61
Brown, Robert Joseph 1907-1989 14
Brown, Roderick (Langmere) Haig-
See Haig-Brown, Roderick (Langmere)
Brown, Rosalie
See Moore, Rosalie (Gertrude)
Brown, Roswell
See Webb, Jean Francis (III)
Brown, Roy (Frederick) 1921-1982 51
Obituary 39
Brown, Ruth 1941- 170
Earlier sketch in SATA 105
Brown, Scott 1971- 134
Brown, Sue Ellen 1954- 81
Brown, Tricia 1954- 114
Brown, Vinson 1912-1991 19
Brown, Walter R(eed) 1929- 19
Brown, Will
See Ainsworth, William Harrison
Brown, William L(ouis) 1910-1964 5
Browne, Anthony 1946- 163
Brief entry 44
Earlier sketches in SATA 45, 61, 105
See also CLR 19
Browne, Anthony Edward Tudor
See Browne, Anthony
Browne, Dik
See Browne, Richard Arthur Allen
Browne, Hablot Knight 1815-1882 21
Browne, Matthew
See Rands, William Brighty
Browne, Nicki M.
See Browne, N.M.
Browne, Nicky Matthews
See Browne, N.M.
Browne, N.M. 1960- 167
Browne, Richard Arthur Allen 1917-1989 ... 67
Brief entry 38
Browne, Vee F(rances) 1956- 90
Browning, Robert 1812-1889
See YABC 1
See also CLR 97
Brownjohn, Alan 1931- 6
Brownlee, Walter 1930- 62
Brownlie, Betty 1946- 159
Brownlow, Kevin 1938- 65
Brownlow, Mike 183
Brownridge, William R(oy) 1932- 94
Broyles, Anne 1953- 201
Bruce, Dorita Fairlie 1885-1970
Obituary 27
Bruce, (William) Harry 1934- 77
Bruce, Mary 1927- 1
Bruchac, Joseph III
See Bruchac, Joseph
Bruchac, Joseph 1942- 176
Autobiography Feature 176
Earlier sketches in SATA 42, 89, 131
See also CLR 46

Bruchac, Margaret M.
See Bruchac, Marge
Bruchac, Marge 181
Bruck, Lorraine 1921- 55
Brief entry 46
Bruel, Nick 205
Earlier sketch in SATA 166
Bruel, Robert O. 1929-2002 189
Bruemmer, Fred 1929- 47
Brugman, Alyssa (F.) 1974- 152
Brumbeau, Jeff 1955- 157
Bruna, Dick 1927- 76
Brief entry 30
Earlier sketch in SATA 43
See also CLR 7
Brunhoff, Jean de 1899-1937 24
See also CLR 116
Brunhoff, Laurent de 1925- 150
Earlier sketches in SATA 24, 71
See also CLR 116
Brunkus, Denise 204
Brunskill, Elizabeth Ann Flatt
See Flatt, Lizann
Brush, Karen A(lexandra) 1960- 85
Brussel-Smith, Bernard 1914- 58
Brust, Steven 1955- 121
Earlier sketch in SATA 86
Brust, Steven K. Zoltan
See Brust, Steven
Brustlein, Daniel 1904- 40
Brustlein, Janice Tworkov -2000 40
Obituary 126
Brutschy, Jennifer 1960- 84
Bryan, Ashley 1923- 178
Earlier sketches in SATA 31, 72, 132
See also CLR 66
Bryan, Ashley F.
See Bryan, Ashley
Bryan, Dorothy M. 1896(?)-1984
Obituary 39
Bryan, Jennifer 190
Bryan, Sean 192
Bryant, Bernice (Morgan) 1908-1976 11
Bryant, Jen 1960- 175
Earlier sketch in SATA 94
Bryant, Jennifer
See Bryant, Jen
Bryant, Jennifer Fisher
See Bryant, Jen
Bryant, Laura J. 176
Brychta, Alex 1956- 21
Brynie, Faith H. 1946- 113
Brynie, Faith Hickman
See Brynie, Faith H.
Bryson, Bernarda 1903-2004 9
Buba, Joy Flinsch 1904- 44
Buchan, Bryan 1945- 36
Buchan, John 1875-1940
See YABC 2
Buchan, Stuart 1942-1987
Obituary 54
Buchanan, Debby 1952- 82
Buchanan, Deborah Leevonne
See Buchanan, Debby
Buchanan, Jane 1956- 160
Buchanan, Paul 1959- 116
Buchanan, Sue 1939- 139
Buchheimer, Naomi Barnett
See Barnett, Naomi
Buchignani, Walter 1965- 84
Buchmann, Stephen L. 194
Buchwald, Art 1925-2007 10
Buchwald, Arthur
See Buchwald, Art
Buchwald, Emilie 1935- 7
Buck, Gisela 1941- 101
Buck, Lewis 1925- 18
Buck, Margaret Waring 1905-1997 3
Buck, Nola
See Godwin, Laura

Buck, Pearl S. 1892-1973 25
Earlier sketch in SATA 1
Buck, Pearl Sydenstricker
See Buck, Pearl S.
Buck, Siegfried 1941- 101
Buckalew, Clare B.
See Dunkle, Clare B.
Buckeridge, Anthony (Malcolm)
1912-2004 85
Earlier sketch in SATA 6
Buckholtz, Eileen (Garber) 1949- 54
Brief entry 47
Buckler, Ernest 1908-1984 47
Buckless, Andrea K. 1968- 117
Buckley, Helen E(lizabeth) 1918- 90
Earlier sketch in SATA 2
Buckley, James, Jr. 1963- 166
Earlier sketch in SATA 114
Buckley, Michael 177
Buckley, Susan 184
Buckley, Susan Washburn
See Buckley, Susan
Buckley-Archer, Linda 185
Buckmaster, Henrietta
See Stephens, Henrietta Henkle
Bucks, Brad
See Holub, Joan
Budd, E. S.
See Sirimarco, Elizabeth
Budd, Lillian (Peterson) 1897-1989 7
Budhos, Marina 173
Buehler, Stephanie Jona 1956- 83
Buehner, Caralyn (M.) 1963- 159
Earlier sketch in SATA 104
Buehner, Mark 1959- 159
Earlier sketch in SATA 104
Buehr, Walter Franklin 1897-1971 3
Buell, Ellen Lewis
See Cash, Ellen Lewis Buell
Buell, Janet 1952- 185
Earlier sketch in SATA 106
Buergel, Paul-Hermann H. 1949- 83
Buettner, Dan 1960- 95
Buff, Conrad 1886-1975 19
Buff, Mary (E. Marsh) 1890-1970 19
Buffett, Jimmy 1946- 110
Earlier sketch in SATA 76
Buffie, Margaret 1945- 161
Earlier sketches in SATA 71, 107
See also CLR 39
Bugbee, Emma 1888(?)-1981
Obituary 29
Bugni, Alice 1951- 122
Buhhos, Marina Tamar
See Budhos, Marina
Bujold, Lois McMaster 1949- 136
Bulfinch, Thomas 1796-1867 35
Bulion, Leslie 1958- 161
Bull, Angela (Mary) 1936- 45
Bull, Emma 1954- 190
Autobiography Feature 103
Earlier sketch in SATA 99
Bull, Norman John 1916- 41
Bull, Peter (Cecil) 1912-1984
Obituary 39
Bull, Schuyler M. 1974- 138
Bulla, Clyde R. 1914-2007 139
Obituary 182
Earlier sketches in SATA 2, 41, 91
See also SAAS 6
Bullard, Lisa 1961- 142
Buller, Jon 205
Bullock, Kathleen (Mary) 1946- 77
Bullock, Robert (D.) 1947- 92
Bulpin, (Barbara) Vicki 92
Bumstead, Kathleen Mary 1918-1987 53
Bundles, A'Lelia Perry 1952- 76
Bunin, Catherine 1967- 30
Bunin, Sherry 1925- 30
Bunkers, Suzanne L. 1950- 136

Bunting, A.E.
See Bunting, Eve
Bunting, Anne Evelyn
See Bunting, Eve
Bunting, Eve 1928- *196*
Earlier sketches in SATA *18, 64, 110, 158*
See also CLR *82*
Bunting, Glenn (Davison) 1957- *22*
Bunyan, John 1628-1688
See CLR *124*
Bupp, Walter
See Garrett, Randall
Burack, Sylvia K. 1916-2003 .... *35*
Obituary *143*
Burbank, Addison (Buswell) 1895-1961 ...... *37*
Burch, Joann J(ohansen) *75*
Burch, Robert J(oseph) 1925- *74*
Earlier sketch in SATA *1*
See also CLR *63*
Burchard, Peter Duncan 1921- *143*
Earlier sketches in SATA *5, 74*
See also SAAS *13*
Burchard, S. H.
See Burchard, Sue
Burchard, Sue 1937- *22*
Burchardt, Nellie 1921- *7*
Burckhardt, Marc 1962- *196*
Burdett, Lois *117*
Burdick, Eugene (Leonard) 1918-1965 .... *22*
Burford, Eleanor
See Hibbert, Eleanor Alice Burford
Burg, Shana 1968- *204*
Burgan, Michael 1960- *167*
Earlier sketch in SATA *118*
Burger, Carl 1888-1967 .... *9*
Burgess, Ann Marie
See Gerson, Noel Bertram
Burgess, Barbara Hood 1926- *69*
Burgess, Em
See Burgess, Mary Wyche
Burgess, (Frank) Gelett 1866-1951 .... *32*
Brief entry *30*
Burgess, Mark *157*
Burgess, Mary Wyche 1916- *18*
Burgess, Melvin 1954- *198*
Earlier sketches in SATA *96, 146*
Burgess, Michael
See Gerson, Noel Bertram
Burgess, Robert F(orrest) 1927- *4*
Burgess, Starling
See Tudor, Tasha
Burgess, Thornton Waldo 1874-1965 .... *17*
Burgess, Trevor
See Trevor, Elleston
Burgwyn, Mebane Holoman 1914-1992 .... *7*
Burke, David 1927- *46*
Burke, Diana G.
See Gallagher, Diana G.
Burke, Diana Gallagher
See Gallagher, Diana G.
Burke, Dianne O'Quinn 1940- *89*
Burke, Janine 1952- *139*
Burke, Jim 1973- *179*
Burke, John
See O'Connor, Richard
Burke, Katie 1953- *168*
Burke, Patrick 1958- *114*
Burke, Ralph
See Garrett, Randall
and Silverberg, Robert
Burkert, Nancy Ekholm 1933- *24*
See also SAAS *14*
Burkett, D. Brent *194*
Burke-Weiner, Kimberly 1962- *95*
Burks, Brian 1955- *95*
Burland, Brian (Berkeley) 1931- *34*
Burland, C. A.
See Burland, Cottie (Arthur)
Burland, Cottie (Arthur) 1905-1983 .... *5*
Burleigh, Robert 1936- *193*
Earlier sketches in SATA *55, 98, 146*

Burlingame, (William) Roger 1889-1967 .... *2*
Burman, Alice Caddy 1896(?)-1977
Obituary *24*
Burman, Ben Lucien 1896-1984 .... *6*
Obituary *40*
Burn, Doris 1923- *1*
Burn, Ted
See Burn, Thomas E.
Burn, Thomas E. 1940- *150*
Burnard, Damon 1963- *115*
Burnett, Constance Buel 1893-1975 .... *36*
Burnett, Frances (Eliza) Hodgson
1849-1924 .... *100*
See also YABC *2*
See also CLR *122*
Burnett Bossi, Lisa *193*
Burney, Anton
See Hopkins, (Hector) Kenneth
Burnford, Sheila (Philip Cochrane Every)
1918-1984 .... *3*
Obituary *38*
See also CLR *2*
Burnham, Gretchen
See Sprague, Gretchen
Burnham, Nicole 1970- *161*
Burnham, Niki
See Burnham, Nicole
Burnham, Sophy 1936- *65*
Burningham, John 1936- *160*
Earlier sketches in SATA *16, 59, 111*
See also CLR *9*
Burns, Diane L. 1950- *81*
See also SAAS *24*
Burns, Eloise Wilkin
See Wilkin, Eloise
Burns, Florence M. 1905-1988 .... *61*
Burns, Khephra 1950- *92*
Burns, Loree Griffin *193*
Burns, Marilyn 1941- *96*
Brief entry *33*
Burns, Olive Ann 1924-1990 .... *65*
Burns, Paul C. *5*
Burns, Ray
See Burns, Raymond (Howard)
Burns, Raymond (Howard) 1924- *9*
Burns, Theresa 1961- *84*
Burns, William A. 1909-1999 .... *5*
Burr, Dan 1951- *65*
Burr, Lonnie 1943- *47*
Burrell, Roy E(ric) C(harles) 1923- *72*
Burroughs, Edgar Rice 1875-1950 .... *41*
Burroughs, Jean Mitchell 1908- *28*
Burroughs, Polly 1925- *2*
Burroway, Janet (Gay) 1936- *23*
Burstein, Chaya M(alamud) 1923- *64*
Burstein, Fred 1950- *83*
Burstein, John 1949- *54*
Brief entry *40*
Burstein, Stanley M.
See Burstein, Stanley Mayer
Burstein, Stanley Mayer 1941- *175*
Bursztynski, Sue 1953- *114*
Burt, Jesse Clifton 1921-1976 .... *46*
Obituary *20*
Burt, Olive Woolley 1894-1981 .... *4*
Burtinshaw, Julie *185*
Burton, Gennett 1945- *95*
Burton, Hester (Wood-Hill) 1913-2000 .... *74*
Earlier sketch in SATA *7*
See also CLR *1*
See also SAAS *8*
Burton, Leslie
See McGuire, Leslie (Sarah)
Burton, Marilee Robin 1950- *82*
Earlier sketch in SATA *46*
Burton, Maurice 1898-1992 .... *23*
Burton, Rebecca 1970- *183*
Burton, Robert (Wellesley) 1941- *22*
Burton, Virginia Lee 1909-1968 .... *100*
Earlier sketch in SATA *2*
See also CLR *11*

Burton, William H(enry) 1890-1964 .... *11*
Busby, Ailie *192*
Busby, Cylin 1970- *118*
Busby, Edith (A. Lake) (?)-1964
Obituary *29*
Buscaglia, (Felice) Leo(nardo) 1924-1998 ... *65*
Buscaglia, Leo F.
See Buscaglia, (Felice) Leo(nardo)
Busch, Phyllis S. 1909- *30*
Bush, Anne Kelleher
See Kelleher, Anne
Bush, Catherine 1961- *128*
Bushmiller, Ernest Paul 1905-1982 .... *31*
Bushmiller, Ernie
See Bushmiller, Ernest Paul
Bushnell, Jack 1952- *86*
Busoni, Rafaello 1900-1962 .... *16*
Buss, Helen M.
See Clarke, Margaret
Busse, Sarah Martin *194*
Busselle, Rebecca 1941- *80*
Bustard, Anne 1951- *173*
Butcher, Kristin 1951- *140*
Butenko, Bohdan 1931- *90*
Butler, Beverly Kathleen 1932- *7*
Butler, Bill
See Butler, William Vivian
and Butler, Ernest Alton
and Butler, William Huxford
Butler, Charles 1963- *175*
Earlier sketch in SATA *121*
Butler, Charles Cadman
See Butler, Charles
Butler, Dori Hillestad 1965- *164*
Butler, Dorothy 1925- *73*
Butler, Geoff 1945- *94*
Butler, M. Christina 1934- *170*
Earlier sketch in SATA *72*
Butler, Octavia 1947-2006 .... *84*
See also CLR *65*
Butler, Octavia E.
See Butler, Octavia
Butler, Octavia Estelle
See Butler, Octavia
Butler, Vivian
See Butler, William Vivian
Butler, William
See Butler, William Vivian
Butler, William Vivian 1927-1987 .... *79*
Butters, Dorothy Gilman
See Gilman, Dorothy
Butterworth, Emma Macalik 1928- *43*
Butterworth, Nick 1946- *149*
Earlier sketch in SATA *106*
Butterworth, Oliver 1915-1990 .... *1*
Obituary *66*
Butterworth, W.E.
See Griffin, W.E.B.
Butterworth, William E.
See Griffin, W.E.B.
Butterworth, William Edmund III
See Griffin, W.E.B.
Butts, Ed 1951- *177*
Butts, Edward P.
See Butts, Ed
Butts, Ellen R(ubinstein) 1942- *93*
Buxton, Ralph
See Silverstein, Alvin
and Silverstein, Virginia B.
Buzzeo, Toni 1951- *135*
Byalick, Marcia 1947- *141*
Earlier sketch in SATA *97*
Byard, Carole (Marie) 1941- *57*
Byars, Betsy 1928- *163*
Autobiography Feature *108*
Earlier sketches in SATA *4, 46, 80*
See also CLR *72*
See also SAAS *1*
Byars, Betsy Cromer
See Byars, Betsy
Byfield, Barbara Ninde 1930- *8*

Byman, Jeremy 1944- *129*
Bynum, Janie *133*
Byrd, Elizabeth 1912-1989 .... *34*
Byrd, Nicole
  See Zach, Cheryl (Byrd)
Byrd, Robert (John) 1942- *158*
  Earlier sketches in SATA *33, 112*
Byrne, Mary Gregg 1951- *162*

C

C. 3. 3.
  See Wilde, Oscar
C. E. M.
  See Mastrangelo, Charles E(lmer)
Cabaniss, J(ames) Allen 1911-1997 .... *5*
Cabat, Erni 1914- *74*
Cabban, Vanessa 1971- *176*
Cable, Mary 1920- *9*
Cabot, Meg 1967- *175*
  Earlier sketch in SATA *127*
  See also CLR *85*
Cabot, Meggin
  See Cabot, Meg
Cabot, Meggin Patricia
  See Cabot, Meg
Cabot, Patricia
  See Cabot, Meg
Cabral, O. M.
  See Cabral, Olga
Cabral, Olga 1909- *46*
Cabrera, Cozbi A. 1963- *177*
Cabrera, Jane 1968- *182*
  Earlier sketches in SATA *103, 152*
Cabrera, Marcela 1966- *90*
Caddy, Alice
  See Burman, Alice Caddy
Cade, Toni
  See Bambara, Toni Cade
Cadmus and Harmonia
  See Buchan, John
Cadnum, Michael 1949- *165*
  Earlier sketches in SATA *87, 121*
  See also CLR *78*
Caduto, Michael J. 1955- *103*
Cadwallader, Sharon 1936- *7*
Cady, (Walter) Harrison 1877(?)-1970 .... *19*
Caffey, Donna (J.) 1954- *110*
Cagle, Malcolm W(infield) 1918- *32*
Cahn, Rhoda 1922- *37*
Cahn, William 1912-1976 .... *37*
Cain, Arthur H(omer) 1913-1981 .... *3*
Cain, Christopher
  See Fleming, Thomas
Cain, Sheridan 1952- *186*
Caine, Geoffrey
  See Walker, Robert W.
Caines, Jeannette (Franklin) 1938- *78*
  Brief entry *43*
  See also CLR *24*
Cairns, Trevor 1922- *14*
Calabro, Marian 1954- *79*
Caldecott, Moyra 1927- *22*
Caldecott, Randolph (J.) 1846-1886 .... *100*
  Earlier sketch in SATA *17*
  See also CLR *110*
Calder, Charlotte 1952- *125*
Calder, David 1932-1997 .... *105*
Calder, Lyn
  See Calmenson, Stephanie
Calder, Marie D(onais) 1948- *96*
Calderone-Stewart, Lisa
  See Calderone-Stewart, Lisa-Marie
Calderone-Stewart, Lisa-Marie 1958- *123*
Caldwell, Doreen (Mary) 1942- *71*
Caldwell, John C(ope) 1913-1984 .... *7*
Caletti, Deb 1963- *171*
Calhoun, B. B. 1961- *98*

Calhoun, Chad
  See Barrett, Neal, Jr.
  and Cunningham, Chet
  and Goulart, Ron
Calhoun, Dia 1959- *183*
  Earlier sketch in SATA *129*
Calhoun, Mary
  See Wilkins, Mary Huiskamp
Calhoun, T.B.
  See Bisson, Terry
Cali, Davide 1972- *190*
Calif, Ruth 1922- *67*
Calkins, Franklin
  See Stratemeyer, Edward L.
Call, Greg *197*
Call, Hughie Florence 1890-1969 .... *1*
Callahan, Dorothy M(onahan) 1934- *39*
  Brief entry *35*
Callahan, Philip Serna 1923- *25*
Callan, Jamie 1954- *59*
Callan, Jim 1951- *181*
Callaway, Bernice (Anne) 1923- *48*
Callaway, Kathy 1943- *36*
Callen, Larry
  See Callen, Lawrence Willard, Jr.
Callen, Lawrence Willard, Jr. 1927- *19*
Calley, Karin 1965- *92*
Calmenson, Stephanie 1952- *139*
  Brief entry *37*
  Earlier sketches in SATA *51, 84*
Calvert, Elinor H.
  See Lasell, Elinor H.
Calvert, John
  See Leaf, (Wilbur) Munro
Calvert, Pam 1966- *205*
Calvert, Patricia 1931- *132*
  Earlier sketches in SATA *45, 69*
  See also SAAS *17*
Camburn, Carol A.
  See Camburn-Bracalente, Carol A.
Camburn-Bracalente, Carol A. 1962- *118*
Cameron, Ann 1943- *129*
  Earlier sketches in SATA *27, 89*
  See also SAAS *20*
Cameron, Edna M. 1905-1999 .... *3*
Cameron, Eleanor (Frances) 1912-1996 .... *25*
  Obituary *93*
  Earlier sketch in SATA *1*
  See also CLR *72*
  See also SAAS *10*
Cameron, Elizabeth
  See Nowell, Elizabeth Cameron
Cameron, Elizabeth Jane 1910-1976 .... *32*
  Obituary *30*
Cameron, Ian
  See Payne, Donald Gordon
Cameron, M(alcolm) G(ordon) Graham
  See Graham-Cameron, M(alcolm) G(ordon)
Cameron, M. Graham
  See Graham-Cameron, M(alcolm) G(ordon)
Cameron, Mike Graham
  See Graham-Cameron, M(alcolm) G(ordon)
Cameron, Polly 1928- *2*
Cameron, Scott 1962- *84*
Camp, Charles L. 1893-1975
  Obituary *31*
Camp, Lindsay 1957- *133*
Camp, Madeleine L'Engle
  See L'Engle, Madeleine
Camp, Walter (Chauncey) 1859-1925
  See YABC *1*
Campbell, (Elizabeth) Andrea 1963- *50*
Campbell, Ann R. 1925- *11*
Campbell, Bill 1960- *89*
Campbell, Bruce
  See Epstein, Samuel
Campbell, Camilla 1905-1992 .... *26*
Campbell, Carole R. 1939- *125*
Campbell, Hope 1925- *20*
Campbell, Hugh 1930- *90*

Campbell, Jane
  See Edwards, Jane Campbell
Campbell, Julie
  See Tatham, Julie Campbell
Campbell, Patricia J(ean) 1930- *45*
Campbell, Patty
  See Campbell, Patricia J(ean)
Campbell, Peter A. 1948- *99*
Campbell, R. W.
  See Campbell, Rosemae Wells
Campbell, Robin
  See Strachan, Ian
Campbell, Rod 1945- *98*
  Brief entry *44*
  Earlier sketch in SATA *51*
Campbell, Rosemae Wells 1909- *1*
Camper, Cathy 1956- *170*
Campion, Nardi Reeder 1917-2007 .... *22*
Campling, Elizabeth 1948- *53*
Campoy, F. Isabel 1946- *181*
  Earlier sketch in SATA *143*
Camps, Luis 1928- *66*
Canales, Viola 1957- *141*
Candell, Victor 1903-1977
  Obituary *24*
Canfield, Dorothea F.
  See Fisher, Dorothy (Frances) Canfield
Canfield, Dorothea Frances
  See Fisher, Dorothy (Frances) Canfield
Canfield, Dorothy
  See Fisher, Dorothy (Frances) Canfield
Canfield, Jack 1944- *164*
Canfield, Jane White 1897-1984 .... *32*
  Obituary *38*
Canfield, Muriel 1935- *94*
Caniff, Milton 1907-1988
  Obituary *58*
Caniff, Milton Arthur Paul
  See Caniff, Milton
Cann, Helen 1969- *179*
  Earlier sketch in SATA *124*
Cann, Kate 1954- *152*
  Earlier sketch in SATA *103*
Cannan, Joanna
  See Pullein-Thompson, Joanna Maxwell
Cannell, Jon *196*
Cannell, Jonathan C.
  See Cannell, Jon
Cannon, A.E. *202*
  Earlier sketches in SATA *93, 163*
Cannon, Ann Edwards
  See Cannon, A.E.
Cannon, Bettie (Waddell) 1922- *59*
Cannon, Curt
  See Hunter, Evan
Cannon, Eileen E(mily) 1948- *119*
Cannon, Frank
  See Mayhar, Ardath
Cannon, Janell 1957- *128*
  Earlier sketch in SATA *78*
  See also CLR *120*
Cannon, Marian G. 1923- *85*
Cannon, Taffy
  See Cannon, Eileen E(mily)
Cantone, AnnaLaura *182*
Canusi, Jose
  See Barker, S. Omar
Canyon, Christopher 1966- *150*
  Earlier sketch in SATA *104*
Caparo, Antonio
  See Caparo, Antonio Javier
Caparo, Antonio Javier *205*
Capek, Michael 1947- *142*
  Earlier sketch in SATA *96*
Capes, Bernard (Edward Joseph)
  1854-1918 .... *116*
Caple, Kathy *193*
Caple, Laurie 1958- *201*
Caplin, Alfred Gerald 1909-1979 .... *61*
  Obituary *21*
Caponigro, John Paul 1965- *84*

Capote, Truman 1924-1984 91
Capp, Al
    See Caplin, Alfred Gerald
Cappel, Constance 1936- 22
Cappetta, Cynthia 1949- 125
Cappo, Nan Willard 1955- 143
Capps, Benjamin (Franklin) 1922- 9
Cappy Dick
    See Cleveland, George
Captain Kangaroo
    See Keeshan, Robert J.
Captain Wheeler
    See Ellis, Edward S.
Captain Young of Yale
    See Stratemeyer, Edward L.
Capucilli, Alyssa Satin 1957- 203
    Earlier sketches in SATA *115, 163*
Capucine
    See Mazille, Capucine
Caraher, Kim(berley Elizabeth) 1961- 105
Caraker, Mary 1929- 74
Caras, Roger A(ndrew) 1928-2001 12
    Obituary 127
Caravantes, Peggy 1935- 140
Caraway, Caren 1939- 57
Carbone, Elisa 1954- 173
    Earlier sketches in SATA *81, 137*
Carbone, Elisa Lynn
    See Carbone, Elisa
Carbonnier, Jeanne 1894-1974 3
    Obituary 34
Card, Orson Scott 1951- 127
    Earlier sketch in SATA *83*
    See also CLR *116*
Care, Felicity
    See Coury, Louise Andree
Carew, Jan 1925- 51
    Brief entry 40
Carew, Jan Rynveld
    See Carew, Jan
Carey, Bonnie
    See Marshall, Bonnie C.
Carey, Charles W., Jr. 1951- 170
Carey, Ernestine Gilbreth 1908-2006 2
    Obituary 177
Carey, Janet Lee 1954(?)- 185
Carey, Lisa 110
Carey, M. V.
    See Carey, Mary V(irginia)
Carey, Mary V(irginia) 1925-1994 44
    Brief entry 39
Carey, Peter 1943- 94
Carey, Peter Philip
    See Carey, Peter
Carey, Valerie Scho 1949- 60
Carheden, Goorel Kristina
    See Naaslund, Goorel Kristina
Carigiet, Alois 1902-1985 24
    Obituary 47
    See also CLR *38*
Carini, Edward 1923- 9
Carkeet, David 1946- 75
Carle, Eric 1929- 163
    Earlier sketches in SATA *4, 65, 120*
    See also CLR *72*
    See also SAAS *6*
Carleton, Captain L. C.
    See Ellis, Edward S.
Carleton, Captain Latham C.
    See Ellis, Edward S.
Carleton, Latham C.
    See Ellis, Edward S.
Carley, V(an Ness) Royal 1906-1976
    Obituary 20
Carling, Amelia Lau 1949- 164
    Earlier sketch in SATA *119*
Carlisle, Carolyn
    See Hawes, Louise
Carlisle, Clark
    See Holding, James (Clark Carlisle, Jr.)
Carlisle, Olga Andreyev 1930- 35

Carlock, Miriam
    See Eyerly, Jeannette
Carls, Claudia 1978- 198
Carlsen, G(eorge) Robert 1917- 30
Carlsen, Ruth C(hristoffer) 1918- 2
Carlson, Bernice Wells 1910- 8
Carlson, Christopher C. 202
Carlson, Dale (Bick) 1935- 1
Carlson, Daniel (Bick) 1960- 27
Carlson, Kirsten 1968- 192
Carlson, Kirsten M.
    See Carlson, Kirsten
Carlson, Laurie 1952- 173
    Earlier sketch in SATA *101*
Carlson, Laurie Winn
    See Carlson, Laurie
Carlson, Melody 1956- 171
    Earlier sketch in SATA *113*
Carlson, Nancy L.
    See Carlson, Nancy L(ee)
Carlson, Nancy L(ee) 1953- 144
    Brief entry 45
    Earlier sketches in SATA *56, 90*
Carlson, Natalie Savage 1906-1997 68
    Earlier sketch in SATA *2*
    See also SAAS *4*
Carlson, Susan Johnston 1953- 88
Carlson, Vada F. 1897- 16
Carlstrom, Nancy White 1948- 156
    Brief entry 48
    Earlier sketches in SATA *53, 92*
Carlton, Keith
    See Robertson, Keith (Carlton)
Carlton, Susan 1960- 195
Carlyon, Richard 55
Carman, Patrick 1966- 197
    Earlier sketch in SATA *161*
Carmer, Carl (Lamson) 1893-1976 37
    Obituary 30
Carmer, Elizabeth Black 1904- 24
Carmi, Giora 1944- 149
    Earlier sketch in SATA *79*
Carmichael, Carrie
    See Carmichael, Harriet
Carmichael, Harriet 40
Carmody, Isobelle 1958- 191
    Earlier sketch in SATA *161*
Carmody, Isobelle Jane
    See Carmody, Isobelle
Carney, Elizabeth 1981- 199
Carney, Jeff 1962- 196
Carney, Mary Lou 1949- 170
Carol, Bill J.
    See Knott, William C(ecil, Jr.)
Caron, Romi
    See Caron-Kyselkova', Romana
Caron-Kyselkova', Romana 1967- 94
Caroselli, Remus F(rancis) 1916- 36
Carpelan, Bo 1926- 8
Carpelan, Bo Gustaf Bertelsson
    See Carpelan, Bo
Carpenter, (John) Allan 1917- 81
    Earlier sketch in SATA *3*
Carpenter, Angelica Shirley 1945- 153
    Earlier sketch in SATA *71*
Carpenter, Frances 1890-1972 3
    Obituary 27
Carpenter, John 1948- 58
Carpenter, John Howard
    See Carpenter, John
Carpenter, Johnny
    See Carpenter, John
Carpenter, Patricia (Healy Evans) 1920- 11
Carr, Glyn
    See Styles, (Frank) Showell
Carr, Harriett H(elen) 1899-1977 3
Carr, Jan 1953- 132
    Earlier sketch in SATA *89*
Carr, M. J.
    See Carr, Jan

Carr, Mary Jane 1899-1988 2
    Obituary 55
Carr, Philippa
    See Hibbert, Eleanor Alice Burford
Carr, Roger Vaughan 1937- 95
Carrel, Annette Felder 1929- 90
Carrick, Carol (Hatfield) 1935- 118
    Earlier sketches in SATA *7, 63*
    See also SAAS *18*
Carrick, Donald (F.) 1929-1989 63
    Earlier sketch in SATA *7*
Carrick, Malcolm 1945- 28
Carrick, Paul 1972- 194
Carrier, Lark 1947- 71
    Brief entry 50
Carrier, Roch 1937- 166
    Earlier sketch in SATA *105*
Carrighar, Sally 1898-1985 24
Carrington, G. A.
    See Cunningham, Chet
Carrington, Marsha Gray 1954- 168
    Earlier sketch in SATA *111*
Carris, Joan 1938- 182
    Brief entry 42
    Earlier sketch in SATA *44*
Carris, Joan Davenport
    See Carris, Joan
Carroll, Curt
    See Bishop, Curtis (Kent)
Carroll, Elizabeth
    See Barkin, Carol
    and James, Elizabeth
Carroll, Jaye
    See Carroll, Michael
Carroll, Jenny
    See Cabot, Meg
Carroll, (Archer) Latrobe 1894-1996 7
Carroll, Laura
    See Parr, Lucy
Carroll, Lewis 1832-1898 100
    See also YABC *2*
    See also CLR *108*
Carroll, Michael 1966- 203
Carroll, Raymond 1924- 86
    Brief entry 47
Carruth, Hayden 1921-2008 47
    Obituary 197
Carryl, Charles E. 1841-1920 114
Carryl, Charles Edward
    See Carryl, Charles E.
Carse, Robert 1902-1971 5
Carson, J(ohn) Franklin 1920-1981 1
    Obituary 107
Carson, Mary Kay 1964- 200
    Earlier sketch in SATA *150*
Carson, Rachel 1907-1964 23
Carson, Rachel Louise
    See Carson, Rachel
Carson, Rosalind
    See Chittenden, Margaret
Carson, S. M.
    See Gorsline, (Sally) Marie
Carson, William C. 1928- 154
Carter, Abby 184
Carter, Alden R 1947- 137
    Earlier sketch in SATA *67*
    See also CLR *22*
    See also SAAS *18*
Carter, Alden Richardson
    See Carter, Alden R
Carter, Andy 1948- 134
Carter, Angela 1940-1992 66
    Obituary 70
Carter, Angela Olive
    See Carter, Angela
Carter, Anne Laurel 1953- 135
Carter, Asa Earl
    See Carter, Forrest
Carter, Avis Murton
    See Allen, Kenneth S.

Carter, Bruce
   See Hough, Richard (Alexander)
Carter, Carol S(hadis) 1948- 124
Carter, David A. 1957- 170
   Earlier sketch in SATA *114*
Carter, Don 1958- 192
   Earlier sketch in SATA *124*
Carter, Dorothy Sharp 1921- 8
Carter, Forrest 1927(?)-1979 32
Carter, Helene 1887-1960 15
Carter, (William) Hodding, Jr. 1907-1972 2
   Obituary 27
Carter, James Earl, Jr.
   See Carter, Jimmy
Carter, Jimmy 1924- 79
Carter, Katharine J(ones) 1905-1984 2
Carter, Lin(wood Vrooman) 1930-1988 91
Carter, Mike 1936- 138
Carter, Nick
   See Avallone, Michael (Angelo, Jr.)
   and Ballard, (Willis) Todhunter
   and Crider, Bill
   and Cassiday, Bruce (Bingham)
   and Chastain, Thomas
   and Dey, Frederic (Merrill) Van Rensselaer
   and Garside, Jack
   and Hayes, Ralph E(ugene)
   and Henderson, M(arilyn) R(uth)
   and Lynds, Dennis
   and Lynds, Gayle (Hallenbeck)
   and Randisi, Robert J.
   and Rasof, Henry
   and Stratemeyer, Edward L.
   and Smith, Martin Cruz
   and Swain, Dwight V(reeland)
   and Vardeman, Robert E(dward)
   and Wallmann, Jeffrey M(iner)
   and White, Lionel
Carter, Peter 1929- 57
Carter, Phyllis Ann
   See Eberle, Irmengarde
Carter, Samuel (Thomson) III 1904-1988 37
   Obituary 60
Carter, William E. 1926-1983 1
   Obituary 35
Cartlidge, Michelle 1950- 96
   Brief entry 37
   Earlier sketch in SATA *49*
Cartner, William Carruthers 1910- 11
Cartwright, Ann 1940- 78
Cartwright, Reg(inald Ainsley) 1938- 64
Cartwright, Sally 1923- 9
Carusone, Al 1949- 89
Carvell, Marlene 172
Carver, John
   See Gardner, Richard (M.)
Carwell, L'Ann
   See McKissack, Patricia C.
Cary
   See Cary, Louis F(avreau)
Cary, Barbara Knapp 1912(?)-1975
   Obituary 31
Cary, Kate 1967(?)- 174
Cary, Louis F(avreau) 1915- 9
Caryl, Jean
   See Kaplan, Jean Caryl Korn
Casanova, Mary 1957- 186
   Earlier sketches in SATA *94, 136*
Cascone, A.G.
   See Cascone, Annette
   and Cascone, Gina
Cascone, Annette 1960- 103
Cascone, Gina 1955- 103
Case, Marshal T(aylor) 1941- 9
Case, Michael
   See Howard, Robert West
Caseley, Judith 1951- 159
   Brief entry 53
   Earlier sketch in SATA *87*
Casewit, Curtis W(erner) 1922-2002 4

Casey, Barbara (Louise) 1944- 147
   Earlier sketch in SATA *79*
Casey, Brigid 1950- 9
Casey, Tina 1959- 141
Cash, Ellen Lewis Buell 1905-1989
   Obituary 64
Cash, Megan Montague 160
Cashore, Kristin 1976(?)- 206
Casilla, Robert 1959- 146
   Earlier sketch in SATA *75*
Cason, Mabel Earp 1892-1965 10
Cass, Joan E(velyn) 1
Cass-Beggs, Barbara 1904- 62
Cassedy, Patrice (Rinaldo) 1953- 149
Cassedy, Sylvia 1930-1989 77
   Obituary 61
   Earlier sketch in SATA *27*
   See also CLR *26*
Cassel, Lili
   See Wronker, Lili Cassel
Cassels, Jean 173
Cassidy, Anne 1952- 166
Cassidy, Cathy 1962- 183
Casson, Hugh Maxwell 1910-1999 65
   Obituary 115
Cassutt, Michael 1954- 78
Cassutt, Michael Joseph
   See Cassutt, Michael
Castaldi, Elicia 194
Castaldo, Nancy Fusco 1962- 151
   Earlier sketch in SATA *93*
Castaneda, Omar S. 1954- 71
Castell, Megan
   See Williams, Jeanne
Castellanos, Jane Mollie Robinson
   1913-2001 9
Castellon, Federico 1914-1971 48
Castellucci, Cecil 1969- 176
Castillo, Edmund L. 1924-2005 1
   Obituary 167
Castillo, Lauren 195
Castle, Lee
   See Ogan, George F.
   and Ogan, Margaret E. (Nettles)
Castle, Paul
   See Howard, Vernon (Linwood)
Castle, Robert
   See Hamilton, Edmond
Castrovilla, Selene 1966- 186
Caswell, Brian 1954- 171
   Earlier sketch in SATA *97*
Caswell, Helen (Rayburn) 1923- 12
Catalano, Dominic 1956- 163
   Earlier sketch in SATA *76*
Catalano, Grace (A.) 1961- 99
Catalanotto, Peter 1959- 195
   Autobiography Feature 113
   Earlier sketches in SATA *70, 114, 159*
   See also CLR *68*
   See also SAAS *25*
Catanese, P.W. 1961- 179
Cate, Annette LeBlanc 196
Cate, Dick
   See Cate, Richard Edward Nelson
Cate, Richard Edward Nelson 1932- 28
Cather, Willa 1873-1947 30
   See also CLR *98*
Catherall, Arthur 1906-1980 74
   Earlier sketch in SATA *3, 4*
Cathon, Laura E(lizabeth) 1908-1991 27
Catlett, Elizabeth 1919(?)- 82
Catlin, Wynelle 1930- 13
Catlow, Nikalas
   See Catlow, Niki
Catlow, Niki 1975- 193
Cato, Heather 105
Cato, Sheila 114
Catran, Ken 1944- 190
Catrow, David 206
   See Catrow, David J. III

Catrow, David J. III 152
   See Catrow, David
Catt, Louis
   See French, Vivian
Cattell, James 1954- 123
Catton, (Charles) Bruce 1899-1978 2
   Obituary 24
Catz, Max
   See Glaser, Milton
Caudell, Marian 1930- 52
Caudill, Rebecca 1899-1985 1
   Obituary 44
Cauley, Lorinda Bryan 1951- 46
   Brief entry 43
Caulfield, Peggy F. 1926-1987
   Obituary 53
Cauman, Samuel 1910-1971 48
Causley, Charles (Stanley) 1917-2003 66
   Obituary 149
   Earlier sketch in SATA *3*
   See also CLR *30*
Cavallaro, Ann (Abelson) 1918- 62
Cavallo, Diana 1931- 7
Cavanagh, Helen (Carol) 1939- 98
   Brief entry 37
   Earlier sketch in SATA *48*
Cavanah, Frances 1899-1982 31
   Earlier sketch in SATA *1*
Cavanna, Betty
   See Harrison, Elizabeth (Allen) Cavanna
Cavanna, Elizabeth
   See Harrison, Elizabeth (Allen) Cavanna
Cave, Kathryn 1948- 123
   Earlier sketch in SATA *76*
Cavendish, Peter
   See Horler, Sydney
Cavin, Ruth (Brodie) 1918- 38
Cavoukian, Raffi 1948- 68
Cawley, Winifred 1915- 13
Caxton, Pisistratus
   See Lytton, Edward G(eorge) E(arle) L(ytton)
   Bulwer-Lytton Baron
Cazeau, Charles J(ay) 1931- 65
Cazet, Denys 1938- 191
   Brief entry 41
   Earlier sketches in SATA *52, 99, 163*
Cazzola, Gus 1934- 73
Cebulash, Mel 1937- 91
   Earlier sketch in SATA *10*
Ceccoli, Nicoletta 181
Cecil, Randy 1968- 187
Cecka, Melanie 199
Ceder, Georgiana Dorcas -1985 10
Celenza, Anna Harwell 133
Celestino, Martha Laing
   See Laing, Martha
Cepeda, Joe 159
Cerf, Bennett (Alfred) 1898-1971 7
Cerf, Christopher (Bennett) 1941- 2
Cermak, Martin
   See Duchacek, Ivo D(uka)
Cerullo, Mary M. 1949- 145
   Earlier sketch in SATA *86*
Cervon, Jacqueline
   See Moussard, Jacqueline
Cetin, Frank Stanley 1921- 2
Chabon, Michael 1963- 145
Chaconas, D.J.
   See Chaconas, Dori
Chaconas, Dori 1938- 175
   Earlier sketch in SATA *145*
Chaconas, Doris J.
   See Chaconas, Dori
Chadwick, Lester 67
   Earlier sketch in SATA *1*
Chaffee, Allen 3
Chaffin, Lillie D(orton) 1925- 4
Chaikin, Miriam 1924- 152
   Earlier sketches in SATA *24, 102*
Chall, Marsha Wilson 150
Challand, Helen J(ean) 1921- 64

Challans, Mary 1905-1983 23
    Obituary 36
Chalmers, Mary (Eileen) 1927- 6
    See also SAAS 14
Chamberlain, Barbara A.
    See Azore, Barbara
Chamberlain, Margaret 1954- 46
Chamberlin, Kate 1945- 105
Chamberlin, Mary 1960- 177
Chamberlin, Rich 177
Chamberlin, Richard
    See Chamberlin, Rich
Chambers, Aidan 1934- 171
    Earlier sketches in SATA *1, 69, 108*
    See also SAAS 12
Chambers, Bradford 1922-1984
    Obituary 39
Chambers, Catherine E.
    See St. John, Nicole
Chambers, John W. 1933- 57
    Brief entry 46
Chambers, Kate
    See St. John, Nicole
Chambers, Margaret Ada Eastwood 1911- 2
Chambers, Peggy
    See Chambers, Margaret Ada Eastwood
Chambers, Robert W(illiam) 1865-1933 107
Chambliss, Maxie 186
Chan, Gillian 1954- 147
    Earlier sketch in SATA *102*
Chance, James T.
    See Carpenter, John
Chance, John T.
    See Carpenter, John
Chance, Stephen
    See Turner, Philip (William)
Chandler, Caroline A(ugusta) 1906-1979 22
    Obituary 24
Chandler, David P(orter) 1933- 28
Chandler, Edna Walker 1908-1982 11
    Obituary 31
Chandler, Jennifer
    See Westwood, Jennifer
Chandler, Karen 1959- 122
Chandler, Linda S(mith) 1929- 39
Chandler, Pauline 175
Chandler, Robert 1953- 40
Chandler, Ruth Forbes 1894-1978 2
    Obituary 26
Chandonnet, Ann F. 1943- 92
Chaney, Jill 1932- 87
Chang, Chih-Wei 1966- 111
Chang, Cindy 1968- 90
Chang, Margaret 1941- 71
Chang, Margaret Scrogin
    See Chang, Margaret
Chang, Raymond 1939- 142
    Earlier sketches in SATA *71, 142 PEN*
Chanin, Michael 1952- 84
Channel, A. R.
    See Catherall, Arthur
Chapian, Marie 1938- 29
Chapin, Alene Olsen Dalton 1915(?)-1986
    Obituary 47
Chapin, Tom 1945- 83
Chapman, Allen 67
    Earlier sketch in SATA *1*
Chapman, Cheryl O(rth) 1948- 80
Chapman, (Constance) Elizabeth (Mann)
    1919- 10
Chapman, Gaye 1970- 200
Chapman, Gaye Coralie
    See Chapman, Gaye
Chapman, Gaynor 1935- 32
Chapman, Gillian 1955- 120
Chapman, Jane 1970- 176
    Earlier sketch in SATA *122*
Chapman, Jean 104
    Earlier sketch in SATA *34*
    See also CLR 65

Chapman, John Stanton Higham 1891-1972
    Obituary 27
Chapman, Lee
    See Bradley, Marion Zimmer
Chapman, Lynne 1960- 197
Chapman, Lynne F(erguson) 1963- 150
    Earlier sketch in SATA *94*
Chapman, Maristan
    See Chapman, John Stanton Higham
Chapman, Vera (Ivy May) 1898-1996 33
Chapman, Walker
    See Silverberg, Robert
Chappell, Audrey 1954- 72
Chappell, Crissa-Jean 198
Chappell, Warren 1904-1991 68
    Obituary 67
    Earlier sketch in SATA *6*
    See also SAAS 10
Chapra, Mimi 182
Charbonneau, Eileen 1951- 118
    Earlier sketch in SATA *84*
Charbonnet, Gabrielle 1961- 81
Chardiet, Bernice (Kroll) 1927(?)- 27
Charest, Emily MacLachlan 198
Charles, Donald
    See Meighan, Donald Charles
Charles, Louis
    See Stratemeyer, Edward L.
Charles, Nicholas
    See Kuskin, Karla
Charles, Nicholas J.
    See Kuskin, Karla
Charles, Norma 153
Charles, Veronika Martenova 182
Charlip, Remy 1929- 119
    Earlier sketches in SATA *4, 68*
    See also CLR 8
Charlot, Jean 1898-1979 8
    Obituary 31
Charlot, Martin (Day) 1944- 64
Charlton, Michael (Alan) 1923- 34
Charlton-Trujillo, e.E. 189
Charmatz, Bill 1925-2005 7
Charnas, Suzy McKee 1939- 110
    Earlier sketch in SATA *61*
Charosh, Mannis 1906- 5
Chartier, Normand L. 1945- 66
Chase, Alice
    See McHargue, Georgess
Chase, Alyssa 1965- 92
Chase, Andra 1942- 91
Chase, Emily
    See Aks, Patricia
    and Garwood, Julie
    and Sachs, Judith
    and White, Carol
Chase, Mary (Coyle) 1907-1981 17
    Obituary 29
Chase, Mary Ellen 1887-1973 10
Chase, Richard 1904-1988 64
    Obituary 56
Chase, Samantha
    See Glick, Ruth (Burtnick)
Chast, Roz 1954- 97
Chastain, Madye Lee 1908-1989 4
Chataway, Carol 1955- 140
Chatterjee, Debjani 1952- 83
Chauncy, Nan(cen Beryl Masterman)
    1900-1970 6
    See also CLR 6
Chaundler, Christine 1887-1972 1
    Obituary 25
Chayka, Doug 196
Chbosky, Stephen 1972- 164
Cheaney, Janie B.
    See Cheaney, J.B.
Cheaney, J.B. 1950- 188
Chee, Cheng-Khee 1934- 79
Cheese, Chloe 1952- 118
Chekhonte, Antosha
    See Chekhov, Anton (Pavlovich)

Chekhov, Anton (Pavlovich) 1860-1904 90
Chelushkin, Kirill 1968- 186
Chen, Anthony 1929- 6
Chen, Chih-Yuan 1975- 155
Chen, Ju-Hong 1941- 78
Chen, Pauline 1966- 202
Chen, Sara
    See Odgers, Sally Farrell
Chen, Tony
    See Chen, Anthony
Chen, Yong 1963- 183
Chen, Yuan-tsung 1932- 65
Chenault, Nell
    See Smith, Linell Nash
Chenery, Janet (Dai) 1923- 25
Cheney, Cora 1916-1999 3
    Obituary 110
Cheney, Glenn (Alan) 1951- 99
Cheney, Lynne V. 1941- 152
Cheney, Lynne Vincent
    See Cheney, Lynne V.
Cheney, Ted
    See Cheney, Theodore Albert
Cheney, Theodore A. Rees
    See Cheney, Theodore Albert
Cheney, Theodore Albert 1928- 11
Cheng, Andrea 1957- 205
    Earlier sketches in SATA *128, 172*
Cheng, Christopher 1959- 173
    Earlier sketch in SATA *106*
Cheng, Judith 1955- 36
Cheng, Shan
    See Jiang, Cheng An
Cheripko, Jan 1951- 155
    Earlier sketch in SATA *83*
Chermayeff, Ivan 1932- 47
Chernenko, Dan
    See Chernenko, Dan
Chernoff, Dorothy A.
    See Ernst, (Lyman) John
Chernoff, Goldie Taub 1909- 10
Cherry, Carolyn Janice
    See Cherryh, C.J.
Cherry, Lynne 1952- 99
    Earlier sketch in SATA *34*
Cherryh, C.J. 1942- 172
    Earlier sketch in SATA *93*
Cherryholmes, Anne
    See Price, Olive
Cheshire, Simon 172
Chesler, Bernice 1932-2002 59
Chess, Victoria (Dickerson) 1939- 92
    Earlier sketch in SATA *33*
Chessa, Francesca 191
Chester, Deborah 1957- 85
Chester, Kate
    See Guccione, Leslie Davis
Chesterton, G(ilbert) K(eith) 1874-1936 27
Chesworth, Michael 160
Chetin, Helen 1922- 6
Chetwin, Grace 86
    Brief entry 50
Chevalier, Christa 1937- 35
Chevalier, Tracy 1962- 128
Chew, Ruth 1920- 7
Chichester Clark, Emma 1955- 69
    Earlier sketches in SATA *117, 156*
Chidsey, Donald Barr 1902-1981 3
    Obituary 27
Chiefari, Janet D. 1942- 58
Chien, Catia 193
Chien-min, Lin
    See Rumford, James
Child, L. Maria
    See Child, Lydia Maria
Child, Lauren 1965- 183
    Earlier sketches in SATA *119, 160*
Child, Lincoln 1957- 113
Child, Lincoln B.
    See Child, Lincoln
Child, Lydia Maria 1802-1880 67

Child, Mrs.
See Child, Lydia Maria
Child, Philip 1898-1978 47
Children's Shepherd, The
See Westphal, Arnold Carl
Childress, Alice 1920-1994 81
Earlier sketches in SATA 7, 48
See also CLR 14
Childs, H(alla) Fay (Cochrane) 1890-1971 1
Obituary 25
Chilton, Charles (Frederick William)
1917- 102
Chima, Cinda Williams 192
Chimaera
See Farjeon, Eleanor
Chin, Richard (M.) 1946- 52
Chinery, Michael 1938- 26
Chin-Lee, Cynthia 1958- 102
Chin-Lee D., Cynthia
See Chin-Lee, Cynthia
Chippendale, Lisa A. 158
Chipperfield, Joseph Eugene 1912-1980(?) .. 87
Earlier sketch in SATA 2
Chisholm, P. F.
See Finney, Patricia
Chislett, Gail (Elaine) 1948- 58
Chittenden, Elizabeth F. 1903-1999 9
Chittenden, Margaret 1935- 28
Chittum, Ida 1918- 7
Chitwood, Suzanne Tanner 1958- 160
Chmielarz, Sharon Lee 1940- 72
Choate, Judith (Newkirk) 1940- 30
Chocolate, Debbi 1954- 96
Chocolate, Deborah M. Newton
See Chocolate, Debbi
Chodos-Irvine, Margaret 152
Choi, Sook Nyul 1937- 73
Autobiography Feature 126
See also CLR 53
Choi, Yangsook 178
Choldenko, Gennifer 1957- 182
Earlier sketch in SATA 135
Chorao, (Ann Mc)Kay (Sproat) 1936- 162
Earlier sketches in SATA 8, 69
Choron, Sandra (Zena Samelson) 1950- 146
Choung, Eun-hee 199
Chown, Marcus 1959- 137
Choyce, Lesley 1951- 165
Earlier sketch in SATA 94
Chrisman, Arthur Bowie 1889-1953 124
See also YABC 1
Christelow, Eileen 1943- 184
Autobiography Feature 120
Brief entry 35
Earlier sketches in SATA 38, 90
Christensen, Bonnie 1951- 157
Earlier sketch in SATA 110
Christensen, Gardell Dano 1907-1991 1
Christensen, Laurie
See Steding, Laurie
Christesen, Barbara 1940- 40
Christgau, Alice Erickson 1902-1977 13
Christian, Mary Blount 1933- 9
Christiana, David 195
Christie, Agatha (Mary Clarissa)
1890-1976 36
Christie, Ann Philippa
See Pearce, Philippa
Christie, Gregory
See Christie, R. Gregory
Christie, Philippa
See Pearce, Philippa
Christie, R. Gregory 1971- 185
Earlier sketch in SATA 127
Christopher, John
See Youd, Samuel
Christopher, Louise
See Hale, Arlene

Christopher, Matt(hew Frederick)
1917-1997 80
Obituary 99
Earlier sketches in SATA 2, 47
See also CLR 119
See also SAAS 9
Christopher, Milbourne 1914(?)-1984 46
Christy, Howard Chandler 1873-1952 21
Chrustowski, Rick 176
Chrystie, Frances N(icholson) 1904-1986 60
Chu, Daniel 1933- 11
Chukovsky, Kornei (Ivanovich) 1882-1969 . 34
Earlier sketch in SATA 5
Church, Caroline Jayne 179
Church, Richard 1893-1972 3
Churchill, E(lmer) Richard 1937- 11
Churchill, Elizabeth
See Hough, Richard (Alexander)
Chute, B(eatrice) J(oy) 1913-1987 2
Obituary 53
Chute, Marchette (Gaylord) 1909-1994 1
Chwast, Jacqueline 1932- 6
Chwast, Seymour 1931- 146
Earlier sketches in SATA 18, 96
Ciardi, John (Anthony) 1916-1986 65
Obituary 46
Earlier sketch in SATA 1
See also CLR 19
See also SAAS 26
Ciccone, Madonna Louise Veronica
See Madonna
Ciment, James D. 1958- 140
Cirrone, Dorian 182
Cisneros, Sandra 1954-
See CLR 123
Citra, Becky 1954- 137
Citrin, Michael 1965(?)- 183
Clair, Andree 19
Clampett, Bob 1914(?)-1985 44
Obituary 38
Clampett, Robert
See Clampett, Bob
Clapp, John 1968- 109
Clapp, Patricia 1912- 74
Earlier sketch in SATA 4
See also SAAS 4
Clare, Ellen
See Sinclair, Olga
Clare, Helen
See Clarke, Pauline
Claremont, Chris 1950- 87
Claremont, Christopher Simon
See Claremont, Chris
Clark, Ann Nolan 1896-1995 82
Obituary 87
Earlier sketch in SATA 4
See also CLR 16
See also SAAS 16
Clark, Champ 1923-2002 47
Clark, Christopher (Anthony) Stuart
See Stuart-Clark, Christopher (Anthony)
Clark, Clara Gillow 1951- 154
Earlier sketch in SATA 84
Clark, David
See Hardcastle, Michael
Clark, David Allen
See Ernst, (Lyman) John
Clark, Emma Chichester
See Chichester Clark, Emma
Clark, Frank J(ames) 1922- 18
Clark, Garel
See Garelick, May
Clark, Halsey
See Deming, Richard
Clark, Joan
See Benson, Mildred
Clark, Joan 1934- 182
Earlier sketches in SATA 59, 96
Clark, Leonard 1905-1981 30
Obituary 29

Clark, M. R.
See Clark, Mavis Thorpe
Clark, Margaret (D.) 1943- 126
Clark, Margaret Goff 1913- 82
Earlier sketch in SATA 8
Clark, Mary Higgins 1929- 46
Clark, Mavis Thorpe 1909-1999 74
Earlier sketch in SATA 8
See also CLR 30
See also SAAS 5
Clark, Merle
See Gessner, Lynne
Clark, Patricia Denise 1921- 117
Clark, Patricia Finrow 1929- 11
Clark, Ronald Harry 1904-1999 193
Clark, Ronald William 1916-1987 2
Obituary 52
Clark, Sherryl 1956- 149
Clark, Van D(eusen) 1909-1974 2
Clark, Virginia
See Gray, Patricia (Clark)
Clark, Walter Van Tilburg 1909-1971 8
Clarke, Arthur
See Clarke, Arthur C.
Clarke, Arthur C. 1917-2008 115
Obituary 191
Earlier sketches in SATA 13, 70
See also CLR 119
Clarke, Arthur Charles
See Clarke, Arthur C.
Clarke, Clorinda 1917- 7
Clarke, Gus 1948- 134
Clarke, J.
See Clarke, Judith
Clarke, James Hall
See Rowland-Entwistle, (Arthur) Theodore
(Henry)
Clarke, Joan B. 1921- 42
Brief entry 27
Clarke, John
See Laklan, Carli
and Sontup, Dan(iel)
Clarke, Judith 1943- 164
Earlier sketches in SATA 75, 110
See also CLR 61
Clarke, Julia 1950- 138
Clarke, Kenneth 1957- 107
Clarke, Lea
See Rowland-Entwistle, (Arthur) Theodore
(Henry)
Clarke, Margaret 1941-
See CLR 99
Clarke, Mary Stetson 1911-1994 5
Clarke, Michael
See Newlon, (Frank) Clarke
Clarke, Pauline 1921- 131
Earlier sketch in SATA 3
See also CLR 28
Clarke-Rich, Elizabeth L. 1934- 103
Clarkson, E(dith) Margaret 1915- 37
Clarkson, Ewan 1929- 9
Claudia, Susan
See Goulart, Ron
and Johnston, William
Claverie, Jean 1946- 38
Clay, Patrice 1947- 47
Clay, Wil 203
Clayman, Deborah Paula
See Da Costa, Deborah
Claypool, Jane
See Miner, Jane Claypool
Clayton, Elaine 1961- 159
Earlier sketch in SATA 94
Clayton, Lawrence (Otto, Jr.) 1945- 75
Clayton, Sandra 1951- 110
Cle, Troy 202
Clea, Super
See Hantman, Clea

Cleary, Beverly 1916- *121*
  Earlier sketches in SATA *2, 43, 79*
  See also CLR *72*
  See also SAAS *20*
Cleary, Beverly Atlee Bunn
  See Cleary, Beverly
Cleary, Brian P. 1959- *186*
  Earlier sketches in SATA *93, 132*
Cleaver, Bill
  See Cleaver, William J.
Cleaver, Carole 1934- *6*
Cleaver, Elizabeth (Ann Mrazik)
  1939-1985 .... *23*
  Obituary *43*
  See also CLR *13*
Cleaver, Hylton Reginald 1891-1961 .... *49*
Cleaver, Vera 1919-1993 .... *76*
  Earlier sketch in SATA *22*
  See also CLR *6*
Cleaver, Vera Allen
  See Cleaver, Vera
Cleaver, William J. 1920-1981 .... *22*
  Obituary *27*
  See also CLR *6*
Cleishbotham, Jebediah
  See Scott, Sir Walter
Cleland, Mabel
  See Widdemer, Mabel Cleland
Clem, Margaret H(ollingsworth) 1923- *90*
Clemens, Samuel
  See Twain, Mark
Clemens, Samuel Langhorne
  See Twain, Mark
Clemens, Virginia Phelps 1941- *35*
Clement, Gary *191*
Clement, Janet *182*
Clement, Nathan 1966- *200*
Clement, Priscilla Ferguson 1942- *171*
Clement, Rod *97*
Clement-Moore, Rosemary *188*
Clements, Andrew 1949- *203*
  Earlier sketches in SATA *104, 158*
Clements, Bruce 1931- *178*
  Earlier sketches in SATA *27, 94*
Clemesha, David *192*
Clemons, Elizabeth
  See Nowell, Elizabeth Cameron
Clerk, N. W.
  See Lewis, C.S.
Cleveland, Bob
  See Cleveland, George
Cleveland, George 1903(?)-1985
  Obituary *43*
Cleveland-Peck, Patricia *80*
Cleven, Cathrine
  See Cleven, Kathryn Seward
Cleven, Kathryn Seward *2*
Clevenger, William R. 1954- *84*
Clevenger, William Russell
  See Clevenger, William R.
Clevin, Joergen 1920- *7*
Clevin, Jorgen
  See Clevin, Joergen
Clewes, Dorothy (Mary) 1907-2003 .... *86*
  Obituary *138*
  Earlier sketch in SATA *1*
Clifford, David
  See Rosenberg, Eth Clifford
Clifford, Eth
  See Rosenberg, Eth Clifford
Clifford, Harold B(urton) 1893-1988 .... *10*
Clifford, Margaret Cort 1929- *1*
Clifford, Martin
  See Hamilton, Charles (Harold St. John)
Clifford, Mary Louise Beneway 1926- *23*
Clifford, Peggy
  See Clifford, Margaret Cort
Clifford, Rachel Mark
  See Lewis, Brenda Ralph

Clifton, Lucille 1936- *128*
  Earlier sketches in SATA *20, 69*
  See also CLR *5*
Clifton, Thelma Lucille
  See Clifton, Lucille
Climo, Shirley 1928- *166*
  Autobiography Feature *110*
  Brief entry *35*
  Earlier sketches in SATA *39, 77*
  See also CLR *69*
Cline-Ransome, Lesa *201*
Clinton, Catherine 1952- *203*
Clinton, Cathryn 1957- *136*
Clinton, Dirk
  See Silverberg, Robert
Clinton, Jon
  See Prince, J(ack) H(arvey)
Clippinger, Carol *193*
Clish, (Lee) Marian 1946- *43*
Clive, Clifford
  See Hamilton, Charles (Harold St. John)
Clokey, Art 1921- *59*
Cloudsley-Thompson, J(ohn) L(eonard)
  1921- *19*
Clouse, Nancy L. 1938- *78*
Clover, Peter 1952- *152*
Clutha, Janet Paterson Frame
  See Frame, Janet
Clymer, Eleanor 1906-2001 .... *85*
  Obituary *126*
  Earlier sketch in SATA *9*
  See also SAAS *17*
Clyne, Patricia (Edwards) *31*
Cneut, Carll 1969- *197*
Coalson, Glo 1946- *94*
  Earlier sketch in SATA *26*
Coates, Anna 1958- *73*
Coates, Belle 1896-1986 .... *2*
Coates, Ruth Allison 1915- *11*
Coats, Alice M(argaret) 1905-1976 .... *11*
Coatsworth, Elizabeth (Jane) 1893-1986 .... *100*
  Obituary *49*
  Earlier sketches in SATA *2, 56*
  See also CLR *2*
Cobalt, Martin
  See Mayne, William (James Carter)
Cobb, Jane
  See Berry, Jane Cobb
Cobb, Mary 1931- *88*
Cobb, Vicki 1938- *136*
  Autobiography Feature *136*
  Earlier sketches in SATA *8, 69, 131*
  See also CLR *2*
  See also SAAS *6*
Cobbett, Richard
  See Pluckrose, Henry (Arthur)
Cober, Alan E(dwin) 1935-1998 .... *7*
  Obituary *101*
Cobham, Sir Alan
  See Hamilton, Charles (Harold St. John)
Coburn, Jake 1978- *155*
Cocagnac, Augustin Maurice(-Jean) 1924- *7*
Cocca-Leffler, Maryann 1958- *194*
  Earlier sketches in SATA *80, 136*
Cochran, Bill *187*
Cochran, Bobbye A. 1949- *11*
Cochran, Thomas 1955- *198*
Cockett, Mary *3*
Cocks, Peter *204*
Cocovini, Abby *202*
Coddell, Esme Raji
  See Codell, Esme Raji
Codell, Esme Raji 1968- *160*
Cody, C. S.
  See Waller, Leslie
Cody, Jess
  See Cunningham, Chet
Coe, Anne (E.) 1949- *95*
Coe, Douglas
  See Epstein, Beryl
  and Epstein, Samuel

Coe, Lloyd 1899(?)-1976
  Obituary *30*
Coen, Rena Neumann 1925- *20*
Coerr, Eleanor (Beatrice) 1922- *67*
  Earlier sketch in SATA *1*
Cofer, Judith Ortiz 1952- *164*
  Earlier sketch in SATA *110*
Coffelt, Nancy 1961- *189*
Coffey, Brian
  See Koontz, Dean R.
Coffin, Geoffrey
  See Mason, F(rancis) van Wyck
Coffin, M. T.
  See Stanley, George Edward
Coffman, Ramon Peyton 1896-1989 .... *4*
Cogan, Karen 1954- *125*
Coggins, Jack (Banham) 1911-2006 .... *2*
Cohen, Barbara 1932-1992 .... *77*
  Obituary *74*
  Earlier sketch in SATA *10*
  See also SAAS *7*
Cohen, Daniel (E.) 1936- *70*
  Earlier sketch in SATA *8*
  See also CLR *43*
  See also SAAS *4*
Cohen, Deborah Bodin 1968- *180*
Cohen, Jan Barger
  See Barger, Jan
Cohen, Jene Barr
  See Barr, Jene
Cohen, Joan Lebold 1932- *4*
Cohen, Judith Love 1933- *78*
Cohen, Miriam 1926-1955 .... *155*
  Earlier sketches in SATA *29, 106*
  See also SAAS *11*
Cohen, Nora *75*
Cohen, Paul S. 1945- *58*
Cohen, Peter Zachary 1931- *150*
  Earlier sketch in SATA *4*
Cohen, Robert Carl 1930- *8*
Cohen, Sholom 1951- *94*
Cohn, Angelo 1914-1997 .... *19*
Cohn, Diana *194*
Cohn, Rachel 1968- *161*
Coit, Margaret Louise 1922-2003 .... *2*
  Obituary *142*
Colato Lainez, Rene 1970- *176*
Colbert, Anthony 1934-2007 .... *15*
Colbert, Nancy A. 1936- *139*
Colby, C(arroll) B(urleigh) 1904-1977 .... *35*
  Earlier sketch in SATA *3*
Colby, Jean Poindexter 1909-1993 .... *23*
Cole, Annette
  See Steiner, Barbara A(nnette)
Cole, Babette 1949- *155*
  Earlier sketches in SATA *61, 96*
Cole, Betsy 1940- *83*
Cole, Brock 1938- *200*
  Earlier sketches in SATA *72, 136*
  See also CLR *18*
Cole, Davis
  See Elting, Mary
Cole, Hannah 1954- *74*
Cole, Henry 1955- *181*
Cole, Jack -1974
  See Stewart, John
Cole, Jackson
  See Curry, Thomas Albert
  and Germano, Peter B.
  and Heckelmann, Charles N(ewman)
  and Newton, D(wight) B(ennett)
  and Schisgall, Oscar
Cole, Jennifer
  See Zach, Cheryl (Byrd)
Cole, Joanna 1944- *168*
  Brief entry *37*
  Earlier sketches in SATA *49, 81, 120*
  See also CLR *40*
Cole, Lois Dwight 1903-1979 .... *10*
  Obituary *26*
Cole, Michael 1947- *59*

Cole, Samantha
  See Cole, Stephen
Cole, Sheila 1939- 171
  Earlier sketches in SATA 24, 95
Cole, Sheila R.
  See Cole, Sheila
Cole, Sheila Rotenberg
  See Cole, Sheila
Cole, Stephen 1971- 161
Cole, William (Rossa) 1919-2000 71
  Earlier sketch in SATA 9
  See also SAAS 9
Coleman, Andrew
  See Pine, Nicholas
Coleman, Clare
  See Bell, Clare (Louise)
  and Easton, M(alcolm) Coleman
Coleman, Janet Wyman 184
Coleman, Loren 1947- 164
Coleman, Loren Elwood, Jr.
  See Coleman, Loren
Coleman, Mary Ann 1928- 83
Coleman, Michael
  See Jones, Allan Frewin
Coleman, Michael 1946- 199
  Autobiography Feature 133
  Earlier sketches in SATA 108, 133
Coleman, Rowan 187
Coleman, William L(eRoy) 1938- 49
  Brief entry 34
Coles, Robert (Martin) 1929- 23
Colfer, Eoin 1965- 197
  Earlier sketch in SATA 148
  See also CLR 112
Colin, Ann
  See Ure, Jean
Collard, Sneed B. III 1959- 184
  Earlier sketches in SATA 84, 139
Colledge, Anne 1939- 142
Colley, Jacqui 1965- 202
Collicott, Sharleen 1937- 143
  Earlier sketch in SATA 98
Collier, Bryan 204
  Earlier sketches in SATA 126, 174
Collier, Christopher 1930- 70
  Earlier sketch in SATA 16
  See also CLR 126
Collier, Ethel 1903-1999 22
Collier, James Lincoln 1928- 166
  Earlier sketches in SATA 8, 70
  See also CLR 126
  See also SAAS 21
Collier, Jane
  See Collier, Zena
Collier, Kristi 182
Collier, Steven 1942- 61
Collier, Zena 1926- 23
Collings, Gillian 1939- 102
Collington, Peter 1948- 99
  Earlier sketch in SATA 59
Collins, Ace 1953- 82
Collins, Andrew J.
  See Collins, Ace
Collins, David R(aymond) 1940-2001 121
  Earlier sketch in SATA 7
Collins, Heather 1946- 81
Collins, Hunt
  See Hunter, Evan
Collins, Michael
  See Lynds, Dennis
Collins, Michael 1930- 58
Collins, Pat(ricia) Lowery 1932- 151
  Earlier sketch in SATA 31
Collins, Paul 1954- 126
Collins, Ross 1972- 200
Collins, Ruth Philpott 1890-1975
  Obituary 30
Collins, Suzanne 180
Collins, Yvonne 194
Collinson, A. S.
  See Collinson, Alan S.

Collinson, Alan S. 1934- 80
Collinson, Roger (Alfred) 1936- 133
Collison, Linda 1953- 185
Collodi, Carlo
  See Lorenzini, Carlo
Colloms, Brenda 1919- 40
Colman, Hila 53
  Earlier sketch in SATA 1
  See also SAAS 14
Colman, Morris 1899(?)-1981
  Obituary 25
Colman, Penny (Morgan) 1944- 160
  Autobiography Feature 160
  Earlier sketches in SATA 77, 114
Colman, Warren (David) 1944- 67
Colombo, John Robert 1936- 50
Colon, Raul 156
Colon, Raul 1952- 202
Colonius, Lillian 1911-1992 3
Colorado, Antonio J.
  See Colorado (Capella), Antonio J(ulio)
Colorado (Capella), Antonio J(ulio)
  1903-1994 23
  Obituary 79
Colquhoun, Glenn 1964- 165
Colston, Fifi E. 1960- 150
Colt, Martin
  See Epstein, Beryl
  and Epstein, Samuel
Colum, Padraic 1881-1972 15
  See also CLR 36
Columbus, Chris 1959- 97
Columbus, Christopher
  See Columbus, Chris
Columella
  See Moore, Clement Clarke
Colver, Anne 1908- 7
Colvin, James
  See Moorcock, Michael
Colwell, Eileen (Hilda) 1904-2002 2
Colwyn, Stewart
  See Pepper, Frank S.
Coman, Carolyn 1951- 197
  Earlier sketch in SATA 127
Combs, Lisa M.
  See McCourt, Lisa
Combs, Robert
  See Murray, John
Comfort, Jane Levington
  See Sturtzel, Jane Levington
Comfort, Mildred Houghton 1886-1976 3
Comins, Ethel M(ae) 11
Comins, Jeremy 1933- 28
Commager, Henry Steele 1902-1998 23
  Obituary 102
Comora, Madeleine 190
Compere, Mickie
  See Davidson, Margaret
Compestine, Ying Chang 1963- 187
  Earlier sketch in SATA 140
Comport, Sally Wern 190
Compton, Patricia A. 1936- 75
Comte, The Great
  See Hawkesworth, Eric
Comus
  See Ballantyne, R(obert) M(ichael)
Comyns, Nance
  See Comyns-Toohey, Nantz
Comyns-Toohey, Nantz 1956- 86
Conan Doyle, Arthur
  See Doyle, Sir Arthur Conan
Condie, Ally 204
Condie, Allyson B.
  See Condie, Ally
Condit, Martha Olson 1913- 28
Condon, Bill 1949- 142
Condon, Judith 83
Condon, Ken 195
Condy, Roy 1942- 96
Cone, Ferne Geller 1921- 39

Cone, Molly (Lamken) 1918- 151
  Autobiography Feature 151
  Earlier sketches in SATA 1, 28, 115
  See also SAAS 11
Cone, Patrick 1954- 89
Coney, Michael G. 1932-2005 61
  Obituary 170
Coney, Michael Greatrex
  See Coney, Michael G.
Coney, Mike
  See Coney, Michael G.
Conford, Ellen 1942- 162
  Earlier sketches in SATA 6, 68, 110
  See also CLR 71
Conger, Lesley
  See Suttles, Shirley (Smith)
Conklin, Gladys Plemon 1903- 2
Conklin, Paul S. 1929(?)-2003 43
  Brief entry 33
  Obituary 147
Conkling, Hilda 1910-1986 23
Conlan, Kathleen Elizabeth 1950- 145
Conlan, Kathy
  See Conlan, Kathleen Elizabeth
Conley, Robyn 1963- 125
Conley-Weaver, Robyn
  See Conley, Robyn
Conlon-McKenna, Marita 1956- 71
Conly, Jane Leslie 1948- 164
  Earlier sketches in SATA 80, 112
Conly, Robert Leslie 1918(?)-1973 23
  See also CLR 2
Connell, Kirk
  See Chapman, John Stanton Higham
Connell, Tom 206
Connelly, Marc(us Cook) 1890-1980
  Obituary 25
Connolly, Jerome P(atrick) 1931- 8
Connolly, Pat 1943- 74
Connolly, Peter 1935- 105
  Earlier sketch in SATA 47
Conover, Chris 1950- 31
Conquest, Owen
  See Hamilton, Charles (Harold St. John)
Conrad, Joseph 1857-1924 27
Conrad, Pam 1947-1996 133
  Brief entry 49
  Obituary 90
  Earlier sketches in SATA 52, 80
  See also CLR 18
  See also SAAS 19
Conroy, Jack
  See Conroy, John Wesley
Conroy, John Wesley 1899-1990 19
  Obituary 65
Conroy, Robert
  See Goldston, Robert (Conroy)
Constable, Kate 1966- 172
Constant, Alberta Wilson 1908-1981 22
  Obituary 28
Constantin, Pascale 185
Conway, Diana C(ohen) 1943- 91
Conway, Gordon
  See Hamilton, Charles (Harold St. John)
Cook, Ande 192
Cook, Bernadine 1924- 11
Cook, Fred J(ames) 1911-2003 2
  Obituary 145
Cook, Glen 1944- 171
  Earlier sketch in SATA 108
Cook, Glen Charles
  See Cook, Glen
Cook, Hugh 1956- 85
Cook, Hugh, Walter Gilbert
  See Cook, Hugh
Cook, Jean Thor 1930- 94
Cook, Joel 1934- 79
Cook, Joseph Jay 1924- 8
Cook, Lisa Broadie 157
Cook, Lyn
  See Waddell, Evelyn Margaret

Cook, Roy
    See Silverberg, Robert
Cook, Trish 175
Cooke, Ann
    See Cole, Joanna
Cooke, Arthur
    See Lowndes, Robert A(ugustine) W(ard)
Cooke, Barbara
    See Alexander, Anna B(arbara Cooke)
Cooke, David Coxe 1917- 2
Cooke, Donald Ewin 1916-1985 2
    Obituary 45
Cooke, Frank E. 1920- 87
Cooke, Jean (Isobel Esther) 1929- 74
Cooke, John Estes
    See Baum, L. Frank
Cooke, Trish 1962- 129
Cookson, Catherine (McMullen) 1906-1998 .. 9
    Obituary 116
Cooley, Regina Francoise 1940- 177
Coolidge, Olivia E(nsor) 1908- 26
    Earlier sketch in SATA *1*
Cooling, Wendy 169
    Earlier sketch in SATA *111*
Coombs, Charles I(ra) 1914-1994 43
    Earlier sketch in SATA *3*
    See also SAAS *15*
Coombs, Chick
    See Coombs, Charles I(ra)
Coombs, Jonathan 204
Coombs, Kate 190
Coombs, Patricia 1926- 51
    Earlier sketch in SATA *3*
    See also SAAS *22*
Cooney, Barbara 1917-2000 96
    Obituary 123
    Earlier sketches in SATA *6, 59*
    See also CLR *23*
Cooney, Caroline B. 1947- 179
    Brief entry 41
    Earlier sketches in SATA *48, 80, 113, 130*
Cooney, Doug 181
Cooney, Nancy Evans 1932- 42
Coontz, Otto 1946- 33
Cooper, Ann (Catharine) 1939- 104
Cooper, Dutch
    See Kuyper, Sjoerd
Cooper, Elisha 1971- 157
    Earlier sketch in SATA *99*
Cooper, Elizabeth Keyser -1992 47
Cooper, Floyd 187
    Earlier sketches in SATA *96, 144*
    See also CLR *60*
Cooper, Gordon 1932- 23
Cooper, Helen 1963- 169
    Earlier sketch in SATA *102*
Cooper, Henry S(potswood) F(enimore), Jr.
    1933- 65
Cooper, Ilene 1948- 145
    Earlier sketches in SATA *66, 97*
Cooper, James Fenimore 1789-1851 19
    See also CLR *105*
Cooper, John R. 1
Cooper, Kay 1941- 11
Cooper, Lee Pelham 1926- 5
Cooper, Lester (Irving) 1919-1985 32
    Obituary 43
Cooper, Lettice (Ulpha) 1897-1994 35
    Obituary 82
Cooper, Louise 1952-2009 152
Cooper, M.E.
    See Lerangis, Peter
Cooper, M.E.
    See Davis, Maggie S.
Cooper, Melrose
    See Kroll, Virginia L.
Cooper, Michael L. 1950- 181
    Earlier sketches in SATA *79, 117*
Cooper, Patrick 1949- 134

Cooper, Susan 1935- 151
    Earlier sketches in SATA *4, 64, 104*
    See also CLR *67*
    See also SAAS *6*
Cooper, Susan Mary
    See Cooper, Susan
Cope, Jane U(rsula) 1949- 108
Copeland, Helen 1920- 4
Copeland, Mark 1956- 180
Copeland, Paul W. 23
Coplans, Peta 1951- 84
Copley (Diana) Heather Pickering 1918- 45
Coppard, A(lfred) E(dgar) 1878-1957
    See YABC *1*
Copper, Melinda 1952- 172
Copper, Melinda McConnaughey
    See Copper, Melinda
Coralie
    See Anderson, Catherine Corley
Corbett, Grahame 43
    Brief entry 36
Corbett, Scott 1913- 42
    Earlier sketch in SATA *2*
    See also CLR *1*
    See also SAAS *2*
Corbett, Sue 174
Corbett, W(illiam) J(esse) 1938- 102
    Brief entry 44
    Earlier sketch in SATA *50*
    See also CLR *19*
Corbin, Sabra Lee
    See Malvern, Gladys
Corbin, William
    See McGraw, William Corbin
Corbman, Marjorie 1987- 179
Corby, Dan
    See Catherall, Arthur
Corcoran, Barbara (Asenath) 1911- 77
    Autobiography Feature 125
    Earlier sketch in SATA *3*
    See also CLR *50*
    See also SAAS *20*
Corcos, Lucille 1908-1973 10
Cordell, Alexander
    See Graber, Alexander
Cordell, Alexander
    See Graber, (George) Alexander
Cordell, Matthew 1975- 199
Corder, Zizou
    See Young, Louisa
Corella, Joseph
    See Odgers, Sally Farrell
Coren, Alan 1938-2007 32
    Obituary 187
Corey, Dorothy 23
Corey, Shana 1974- 133
Corfe, Thomas Howell 1928- 27
Corfe, Tom
    See Corfe, Thomas Howell
Corfield, Robin Bell 1952- 74
Corlett, William 1938-2005 46
    Brief entry 39
Cormack, M(argaret) Grant 1913- 11
Cormack, Maribelle B. 1902-1984 39
Cormier, Robert 1925-2000 83
    Obituary 122
    Earlier sketches in SATA *10, 45*
    See also CLR *55*
Cormier, Robert Edmund
    See Cormier, Robert
Cornelius, Carol 1942- 40
Cornelius, Kay 1933- 157
Cornell, J.
    See Cornell, Jeffrey
Cornell, James (Clayton, Jr.) 1938- 27
Cornell, Jean Gay 1920- 23
Cornell, Jeffrey 1945- 11
Cornell, Laura 189
Cornish, D.M. 1972- 185
Cornish, Sam(uel James) 1935- 23

Cornwall, Nellie
    See Sloggett, Nellie
Cornwell, Autumn 195
Corr, Christopher 1955- 189
Correy, Lee
    See Stine, G(eorge) Harry
Corrick, James A. 1945- 76
Corrigan, (Helen) Adeline 1909- 23
Corrigan, Barbara 1922- 8
Corrigan, Eireann 1977- 163
Corrin, Sara 1918- 86
    Brief entry 48
Corrin, Stephen 86
    Brief entry 48
Corsi, Wendy
    See Staub, Wendy Corsi
Cort, M. C.
    See Clifford, Margaret Cort
Cort, Margaret
    See Clifford, Margaret Cort
Corwin, Judith H(offman) 1946- 10
Corwin, Oliver
    See Corwin, Oliver J.
Corwin, Oliver J. 206
Cory, Rowena
    See Lindquist, Rowena Cory
Cosby, Bill 1937- 110
    Earlier sketch in SATA *66*
Cosby, William Henry, Jr.
    See Cosby, Bill
    and Cosby, Bill
Cosentino, Ralph 169
Cosgrave, John O'Hara II 1908-1968
    Obituary 21
Cosgrove, Margaret (Leota) 1926- 47
Cosgrove, Stephen E(dward) 1945- 53
    Brief entry 40
Coskey, Evelyn 1932- 7
Cosner, Shaaron 1940- 43
Cossi, Olga 1921- 102
    Earlier sketch in SATA *67*
Costabel, Eva Deutsch 1924- 45
Costabel-Deutsch, Eva
    See Costabel, Eva Deutsch
Coste, Marion 1938- 183
Costello, David 174
Costello, David F(rancis) 1904-1990 23
Cte, Genevieve 1964- 184
Cote, Nancy 1952- 182
Cott, Jonathan 1942- 23
Cottam, Clarence 1899-1974 25
Cotten, Cynthia 188
Cottle, Joan 1960- 135
Cottler, Joseph 1899-1996 22
Cottonwood, Joe 1947- 92
Cottrell, Leonard 1913-1974 24
Cottringer, Anne 1952- 150
    Earlier sketch in SATA *97*
Couch, Greg 199
Coulman, Valerie 1969- 161
Couloumbis, Audrey 173
Counsel, June 1926- 70
Countryman, The
    See Whitlock, Ralph
Courlander, Harold 1908-1996 6
    Obituary 88
Coursen, Valerie 1965(?)- 102
Courtis, Stuart Appleton 1874-1969
    Obituary 29
Courtland, Tyler
    See Stevens, Serita
Courtney, Dayle
    See Goldsmith, Howard
Coury, Louise Andree 1895(?)-1983
    Obituary 34
Cousins, Linda 1946- 90
Cousins, Lucy 1964- 205
    Earlier sketch in SATA *172*
Cousins, Margaret 1905-1996 2
    Obituary 92

Cousteau, Jacques-Yves 1910-1997 98
    Earlier sketch in SATA 38
Couture, Christin 1951- 73
Couvillon, Jacques 195
Covert, Ralph 1968- 197
Coville, Bruce 1950- 155
    Autobiography Feature 155
    Earlier sketches in SATA 32, 77, 118
Covington, Dennis 109
Covington, Linda
    See Windsor, Linda
Cowan, Catherine 121
Cowan, Rebecca M.
    See Moesta, Rebecca
Cowan, Rebecca Moesta
    See Moesta, Rebecca
Coward, Fiona 1963- 178
Cowdrey, Richard 1959- 204
Cowell, Cressida 1966- 140
Cowen, Eve
    See Werner, Herma
Cowen, Ida 1898-1993 64
Cowie, Leonard W(allace) 1919- 4
Cowles, Kathleen
    See Krull, Kathleen
Cowley, Cassia Joy
    See Cowley, Joy
Cowley, Joy 1936- 164
Cowley, (Cassia) Joy 1936- 90
    Autobiography Feature 118
    Earlier sketch in SATA 4
    See also CLR 55
    See also SAAS 26
Cowley, Marjorie 1925- 111
Cox, (Christopher) Barry 1931- 62
Cox, Clinton 1934- 108
    Earlier sketch in SATA 74
Cox, David (Dundas) 1933- 56
Cox, Donald William 1921- 23
Cox, Jack
    See Cox, John Roberts
Cox, John Roberts 1915-1981 9
Cox, Judy 1954- 198
    Earlier sketches in SATA 117, 160
Cox, Marion Monroe 1898-1983
    Obituary 34
Cox, Palmer 1840-1924 24
    See also CLR 24
Cox, Vic 1942- 88
Cox, Vicki 1945- 158
Cox, Victoria
    See Garretson, Victoria Diane
Cox, Wallace 1924-1973 25
Cox, Wally
    See Cox, Wallace
Cox, William R(obert) 1901-1988 46
    Brief entry 31
    Obituary 57
Coxe, Molly 1959- 101
    Earlier sketch in SATA 69
Coxon, Michele 1950- 158
    Earlier sketch in SATA 76
Coy, Harold 1902-1986 3
Coy, John 1958- 171
    Earlier sketch in SATA 120
Craats, Rennay 1973- 131
Crabtree, Judith 1928- 98
    Earlier sketch in SATA 63
Cracker, Edward E.B.
    See Odgers, Sally Farrell
Craft, Elizabeth 1971(?)- 204
Craft, K. Y.
    See Craft, Kinuko Y(amabe)
Craft, Kinuko
    See Craft, Kinuko Y(amabe)
Craft, Kinuko Y(amabe) 1940- 127
    Earlier sketch in SATA 65
Craft, Ruth 1935- 87
    Brief entry 31
Craig, A. A.
    See Anderson, Poul

Craig, Alisa
    See MacLeod, Charlotte (Matilda)
Craig, David 205
    See James, Bill
Craig, Helen 1934- 94
    Earlier sketches in SATA 46, 49
Craig, Joe 1979- 198
Craig, Joe Alexander
    See Craig, Joe
Craig, John Eland
    See Chipperfield, Joseph Eugene
Craig, John Ernest 1921- 23
Craig, Kit
    See Reed, Kit
Craig, M. F.
    See Craig, Mary (Francis) Shura
Craig, M. Jean 17
Craig, M. S.
    See Craig, Mary (Francis) Shura
Craig, Margaret (Maze) 1911-1964 9
Craig, Mary
    See Craig, Mary (Francis) Shura
Craig, Mary Shura
    See Craig, Mary (Francis) Shura
Craig, Mary (Francis) Shura 1923-1991 86
    Obituary 65
    Earlier sketch in SATA 6
    See also SAAS 7
Craig, Ruth 1922- 95
Craik, Mrs.
    See Craik, Dinah Maria (Mulock)
Craik, Dinah Maria (Mulock) 1826-1887 34
Crandall, Court 1965- 175
Crandell, Rachel 1943- 152
Crane, Barbara (Joyce) 1934- 31
Crane, Caroline 1930- 11
Crane, Jordan 1973- 174
Crane, M. A.
    See Wartski, Maureen (Ann Crane)
Crane, Royston Campbell 1901-1977
    Obituary 22
Crane, Stephen 1871-1900
    See YABC 2
    See also CLR 132
Crane, Stephen Townley
    See Crane, Stephen
Crane, Walter 1845-1915 100
    Earlier sketch in SATA 18
    See also CLR 56
Crane, William D(wight) 1892-1976 1
Cranfield, Ingrid 1945- 74
Cranshaw, Stanley
    See Fisher, Dorothy (Frances) Canfield
Crary, Elizabeth (Ann) 1942- 99
    Brief entry 43
Crary, Margaret (Coleman) 1906-1986 9
Craste, Marc 201
Cravath, Lynne Avril
    See Cravath, Lynne W.
Cravath, Lynne W. 1951- 182
    Earlier sketches in SATA 98, 148
Craven, Thomas 1889-1969 22
Crawford, Charles P. 1945- 28
Crawford, Deborah 1922- 6
Crawford, John E(dmund) 1904-1971 3
Crawford, K(aren) Michael 1959- 155
Crawford, Mel 1925- 44
    Brief entry 33
Crawford, Phyllis 1899- 3
Crawley, Dave 177
Cray, Roberta
    See Emerson, Ru
Crayder, Dorothy 7
Crayder, Teresa
    See Colman, Hila
Crayon, Geoffrey
    See Irving, Washington
Craz, Albert G. 1926- 24
Crebbin, June 1938- 169
    Earlier sketch in SATA 80

Crecy, Jeanne
    See Williams, Jeanne
Credle, Ellis 1902-1998 1
Creech, Sharon 1945- 172
    Earlier sketches in SATA 94, 139
    See also CLR 89
Creeden, Sharon 1938- 91
Creel, Ann Howard 1953- 187
Creighton, (Mary) Helen 1899-1989
    Obituary 64
Creighton, Jill 1949- 96
Crenson, Victoria 1952- 159
    Earlier sketch in SATA 88
Cresp, Gael 1954- 119
Crespo, George 1962- 82
Cresswell, Helen 1934-2005 79
    Obituary 168
    Earlier sketches in SATA 1, 48
    See also CLR 18
    See also SAAS 20
Cressy, Michael 1955- 124
Cressy, Mike
    See Cressy, Michael
Cretan, Gladys (Yessayan) 1921- 2
Cretzmeyer, Stacy (Megan) 1959- 124
Crew, Gary 1947- 163
    Earlier sketches in SATA 75, 110
    See also CLR 42
Crew, Helen (Cecilia) Coale 1866-1941
    See YABC 2
Crew, Linda (Jean) 1951- 137
    Earlier sketch in SATA 71
Crews, Donald 1938- 76
    Brief entry 30
    Earlier sketch in SATA 32
    See also CLR 7
Crews, Nina 1963- 158
    Earlier sketch in SATA 97
Crichton, John Michael
    See Crichton, Michael
Crichton, Michael 1942-2008 88
    Obituary 199
    Earlier sketch in SATA 9
Crider, Allen Billy
    See Crider, Bill
Crider, Bill 1941- 99
Crilley, Mark 1966- 148
    Autobiography Feature 148
    Earlier sketch in SATA 120
Crimi, Carolyn 1959- 176
Cripps, Enid Margaret
    See Appiah, Peggy
Crisler, Curtis L. 188
Crisman, Ruth 1914- 73
Crisp, Marta Marie 1947- 128
Crisp, Marty
    See Crisp, Marta Marie
Crispin, A(nn) C(arol) 1950- 86
Crist, James J. 1961- 168
Cristall, Barbara 79
Crist-Evans, Craig 1954- 153
Crocker, Carter 193
Crocker, Nancy 1956- 185
Crofford, Emily (Ardell) 1927- 61
Crofut, William E. III 1934- 23
Croggon, Alison 1962- 194
Croll, Carolyn 1945- 102
    Brief entry 52
    Earlier sketch in SATA 56
Croman, Dorothy Young
    See Rosenberg, Dorothy
Cromie, Alice Hamilton 1914-2000 24
Cromie, William J(oseph) 1930- 4
Crompton, Anne Eliot 1930- 73
    Earlier sketch in SATA 23
Crompton, Richmal
    See Lamburn, Richmal Crompton
Cronbach, Abraham 1882-1965 11
Crone, Ruth 1919-2003 4
Cronin, A(rchibald) J(oseph) 1896-1981 47
    Obituary 25

Cronin, Doreen (A.) 125
Cronin, Doreen 1966(?)- 178
   See also CLR 136
Cronin, Doreen A.
   See Cronin, Doreen
Crook, Beverly Courtney 38
   Brief entry 35
Crook, Connie Brummel 1930- 168
   Earlier sketch in SATA 98
Crook, Constance
   See Crook, Connie Brummel
Crosby, Alexander L. 1906-1980 2
   Obituary 23
Crosby, Harry C., Jr. 102
Crosby, Margaret
   See Rathmann, Peggy
Crosher, G. R. 14
Cross, Gilbert B. 1939- 60
   Brief entry 51
Cross, Gillian 1945- 178
   Autobiography Feature 178
   Earlier sketches in SATA 38, 71, 110, 165
   See also CLR 28
Cross, Gillian Clare
   See Cross, Gillian
Cross, Helen Reeder
   See Broadhead, Helen Cross
Cross, Peter 1951- 95
Cross, Shauna 1976(?)- 196
Cross, Tom 1954- 146
Cross, Verda 1914- 75
Cross, Wilbur Lucius III 1918- 2
Crossland, Caroline 1964- 83
Crossley-Holland, Kevin 1941- 165
   Earlier sketches in SATA 5, 74, 120
   See also CLR 84
   See also SAAS 20
Crossley-Holland, Kevin John William
   See Crossley-Holland, Kevin
Crouch, Marcus 1913-1996 4
Crout, George C(lement) 1917- 11
Crow, Donna Fletcher 1941- 40
Crow, Francis Luther
   See Luther, Frank
Crowe, Andrew 111
Crowe, Carole 1943- 204
Crowe, Chris 206
Crowe, Ellie 203
Crowe, John
   See Lynds, Dennis
Crowe, (Bettina) Peter Lum 1911- 6
Crowell, Grace Noll 1877-1969 34
Crowell, Pers 1910-1990 2
Crowell, Robert Leland 1909-2001 63
Crowfield, Christopher
   See Stowe, Harriet (Elizabeth) Beecher
Crowley, Arthur McBlair 1945- 38
Crowley, John 1942- 140
   Earlier sketch in SATA 65
Crowley, Suzanne 1963- 196
Crowley, Suzanne Carlisle
   See Crowley, Suzanne
Crownfield, Gertrude 1867-1945
   See YABC 1
Crowther, James Gerald 1899-1983 14
Crowther, Robert 1948- 163
Cruikshank, George 1792-1878 22
   See also CLR 63
Cruise, Robin 1951- 179
Crum, Shutta 192
   Earlier sketch in SATA 134
Crummel, Susan Stevens 1949- 176
   Earlier sketch in SATA 130
Crump, Fred H., Jr. 1931- 76
   Earlier sketch in SATA 11
Crump, J(ames) Irving 1887-1979 57
   Obituary 21
Crump, William D(rake) 1949- 138
Crunden, Reginald
   See Cleaver, Hylton Reginald

Crunk, T.
   See Crunk, Tony
Crunk, Tony 1956- 130
Crutcher, Chris 1946- 196
   Earlier sketches in SATA 52, 99, 153
   See also CLR 28
Crutcher, Christopher C.
   See Crutcher, Chris
Cruz, Ray(mond) 1933- 6
Cruz Martinez, Alejandro (?)-1987 74
Crystal, Billy 1947- 154
Ctvrtek, Vaclav 1911-1976
   Obituary 27
Cuetara, Mittie 1957- 158
   Earlier sketch in SATA 106
Cuffari, Richard 1925-1978 66
   Obituary 25
   Earlier sketch in SATA 6
Cuffe-Perez, Mary 1946- 199
Cullen, Countee 1903-1946 18
Cullen, Lynn 190
Culliford, Pierre 1928-1992 40
   Obituary 74
Cullinan, Bernice E(llinger) 1926- 135
Culp, Louanna McNary 1901-1965 2
Culper, Felix
   See McCaughrean, Geraldine
Cumbaa, Stephen 1947- 72
Cumming, Peter 1951- 168
Cumming, Primrose Amy 1915- 24
Cumming, Robert 1945- 65
Cummings, Betty Sue 1918- 15
   See also SAAS 9
Cummings, Mary 1951- 185
Cummings, Parke 1902-1987 2
   Obituary 53
Cummings, Pat 1950- 203
   Earlier sketches in SATA 42, 71, 107
   See also CLR 48
   See also SAAS 13
Cummings, Phil 1957- 123
   Earlier sketch in SATA 74
Cummings, Priscilla 1951- 170
   Earlier sketch in SATA 129
Cummings, Richard
   See Gardner, Richard (M.)
Cummins, Julie 200
Cummins, Maria Susanna 1827-1866
   See YABC 1
Cuneo, Mary Louise -2001 85
Cunliffe, John Arthur 1933- 86
   Earlier sketch in SATA 11
Cunliffe, Marcus (Falkner) 1922-1990 37
   Obituary 66
Cunnane, Kelly 175
Cunningham, Bob
   See May, Julian
Cunningham, Captain Frank
   See Glick, Carl (Cannon)
Cunningham, Cathy
   See Cunningham, Chet
Cunningham, Chet 1928- 23
Cunningham, Dale S(peers) 1932- 11
Cunningham, Dru 91
Cunningham, E. V.
   See Fast, Howard
Cunningham, Julia (Woolfolk) 1916- 132
   Earlier sketches in SATA 1, 26
   See also SAAS 2
Cunningham, Lawrence J. 1943- 125
Cunningham, Virginia
   See Holmgren, Virginia C(unningham)
Curiae, Amicus
   See Fuller, Edmund (Maybank)
Curie, Eve 1904-2007 1
   Obituary 188
Curlee, Lynn 1947- 190
   Earlier sketches in SATA 98, 141
Curley, Daniel 1918-1988 23
   Obituary 61

Curley, Marianne 1959- 175
   Earlier sketch in SATA 131
Currey, Anna 194
Currie, Robin 1948- 120
Currie, Stephen 1960- 132
   Earlier sketch in SATA 82
Curry, Ann (Gabrielle) 1934- 72
Curry, Jane L(ouise) 1932- 138
   Autobiography Feature 138
   Earlier sketches in SATA 1, 52, 90
   See also CLR 31
   See also SAAS 6
Curry, Peggy Simson 1911-1987 8
   Obituary 50
Curry, Tom 185
Curtis, Bruce (Richard) 1944- 30
Curtis, Chara M(ahar) 1950- 78
Curtis, Christopher Paul 1954(?)- 187
   Earlier sketches in SATA 93, 140
   See also CLR 68
Curtis, Gavin 1965- 107
Curtis, Jamie Lee 1958- 144
   Earlier sketch in SATA 95
   See also CLR 88
Curtis, Jennifer Keats 185
Curtis, Marci 160
Curtis, Munzee
   See Caseley, Judith
Curtis, Neil 1950-2006 202
Curtis, Patricia 1921- 101
   Earlier sketch in SATA 23
Curtis, Peter
   See Lofts, Norah (Robinson)
Curtis, Philip (Delacourt) 1920- 62
Curtis, Richard 1937- 29
Curtis, Richard Alan
   See Curtis, Richard
Curtis, Richard Hale
   See Deming, Richard
   and Levinson, Leonard
   and Rothweiler, Paul Roger
Curtis, Stacy 205
Curtis, Wade
   See Pournelle, Jerry (Eugene)
Curtiss, A(rlene) B. 1934- 90
Cusack, Margaret 1945- 58
Cushman, Doug 1953- 157
   Earlier sketches in SATA 65, 101
Cushman, Jerome 2
Cushman, Karen 1941- 147
   Earlier sketch in SATA 89
   See also CLR 55
Cusick, Richie Tankersley 1952- 140
   Earlier sketch in SATA 67
Cutbill, Andy 1972- 201
Cutchen, Billye Walker 1930- 15
Cutchins, Judy 1947- 59
Cutler, Daniel S(olomon) 1951- 78
Cutler, Ebbitt 1923- 9
Cutler, Ivor 1923-2006 24
   Obituary 174
Cutler, Jane 1936- 162
   Earlier sketches in SATA 75, 118
Cutler, May Ebbitt
   See Cutler, Ebbitt
Cutler, Samuel
   See Folsom, Franklin (Brewster)
Cutlip, Kimbra L(eigh-Ann) 1964- 128
Cutrate, Joe
   See Spiegelman, Art
Cutt, W(illiam) Towrie 1898-1981 16
   Obituary 85
Cuyler, Margery 1948- 195
   Earlier sketches in SATA 39, 99, 156
Cuyler, Margery Stuyvesant
   See Cuyler, Margery
Cuyler, Stephen
   See Bates, Barbara S(nedeker)
Cyrus, Kurt 1954- 179
   Earlier sketch in SATA 132
Czernecki, Stefan 1946- 178

D

Dabba Smith, Frank 174
Dabcovich, Lydia 99
  Brief entry 47
  Earlier sketch in SATA 58
Dace, Dolores B(oelens) 1929- 89
Da Costa, Deborah 193
Daddo, Andrew 1967- 198
Dadey, Debbie 1959- 136
  Earlier sketch in SATA 73
Dahl, Borghild (Margarethe) 1890-1984 7
  Obituary 37
Dahl, Roald 1916-1990 73
  Obituary 65
  Earlier sketches in SATA 1, 26
  See also CLR 111
Dahlberg, Maurine F. 1951- 171
Dahlstedt, Marden (Stewart) 1921-1983 8
  Obituary 110
Dahme, Joanne 206
Dain, Martin J. 1924-2000 35
Dakos, Kalli 1950- 115
  Earlier sketch in SATA 80
Dale, Anna 1971- 170
Dale, Gary
  See Reece, Colleen L.
Dale, George E.
  See Asimov, Isaac
Dale, Jack
  See Holliday, Joseph
Dale, Kim 1957- 123
Dale, Margaret J(essy) Miller 1911- 39
Dale, Mitzi
  See Hemstock, Gillian
Dale, Norman
  See Denny, Norman (George)
Dale, Penny 1954- 151
  Earlier sketch in SATA 70
Daley, Michael J. 170
Dalgliesh, Alice 1893-1979 17
  Obituary 21
  See also CLR 62
Dalkey, Kara 1953- 132
Dalkey, Kara Mia
  See Dalkey, Kara
Dallas, Ruth 1919- 86
Dalmas, John
  See Jones, John R(obert)
Dalton, Alene
  See Chapin, Alene Olsen Dalton
Dalton, Annie 1948- 140
  Earlier sketch in SATA 40
Dalton, Kit
  See Cunningham, Chet
Dalton, Pamela
  See Johnson, Pamela
Dalton, Sean
  See Chester, Deborah
Dalton, Sheila 1949- 108
D'Aluisio, Faith 1957- 205
Daly, Jim
  See Stratemeyer, Edward L.
Daly, Jude 1951- 177
Daly, Kathleen N(orah) 124
  Brief entry 37
Daly, Maureen 1921-2006 129
  Obituary 176
  Earlier sketch in SATA 2
  See also CLR 96
  See also SAAS 1
Daly, Nicholas 1946- 164
  Earlier sketches in SATA 37, 76, 114
  See also CLR 41
  See also SAAS 21
  See Daly, Niki
Daly, Niki 198
  See Daly, Nicholas
D'Amato, Alex 1919- 20
D'Amato, Janet (Potter) 1925- 9
Damerow, Gail 1944- 83

Damerow, Gail Jane
  See Damerow, Gail
D'Amico, Carmela 170
D'Amico, Steve 170
Damrell, Liz 1956- 77
Damrosch, Helen
  See Tee-Van, Helen Damrosch
Dana, Barbara 1940- 22
Dana, Richard Henry, Jr. 1815-1882 26
Danachair, Caoimhin O
  See Danaher, Kevin
Danaher, Kevin 1913-2002 22
Danakas, John 1963- 94
Dandi
  See Mackall, Dandi Daley
D'Andrea, Kate
  See Steiner, Barbara A(nnette)
Dangerfield, Balfour
  See McCloskey, (John) Robert
Daniel, Alan 1939- 76
  Brief entry 53
Daniel, Anita 1893(?)-1978 23
  Obituary 24
Daniel, Anne
  See Steiner, Barbara A(nnette)
Daniel, Becky 1947- 56
Daniel, Claire 1949- 164
Daniel, Colin
  See Windsor, Patricia
Daniel, Hawthorne 1890- 8
Daniel, (Donna) Lee 1944- 76
Daniel, Rebecca
  See Daniel, Becky
Daniels, Guy 1919-1989 11
  Obituary 62
Daniels, Lucy
  See Oldfield, Jenny
Daniels, Max
  See Gellis, Roberta
Daniels, Olga
  See Sinclair, Olga
Daniels, Patricia 1955- 93
Daniels, Zoe
  See Laux, Constance
Dank, Gloria Rand 1955- 56
  Brief entry 46
Dank, Leonard D(ewey) 1929- 44
Dank, Milton 1920- 31
Dann, Max 1955- 62
Danneberg, Julie 1958- 173
Dantz, William R.
  See Philbrick, Rodman
Danziger, Paula 1944-2004 149
  Brief entry 30
  Obituary 155
  Earlier sketches in SATA 36, 63, 102
  See also CLR 20
Darby, Gene Kegley
  See Darby, Jean (Kegley)
Darby, J. N.
  See Govan, (Mary) Christine Noble
Darby, Jean (Kegley) 1921- 68
Darby, Patricia (Paulsen) 14
Darby, Ray(mond) 1912-1982 7
d'Arcy, Willard
  See Cox, William R(obert)
Dare, Geena
  See McNicoll, Sylvia (Marilyn)
Darian, Shea 1959- 97
Daringer, Helen Fern 1892-1986 1
Darke, Marjorie 1929- 87
  Earlier sketch in SATA 16
Darley, F(elix) O(ctavius) C(arr)
  1822-1888 35
Darling, David J. 1953- 60
  Brief entry 44
Darling, Kathy
  See Darling, Mary Kathleen
Darling, Lois (MacIntyre) 1917-1989 3
  Obituary 64

Darling, Louis, (Jr.) 1916-1970 3
  Obituary 23
Darling, Mary Kathleen 1943- 124
  Earlier sketches in SATA 9, 79
Darling, Sandra Louise Woodward
  See Day, Alexandra
Darnell, K(athryn) L(ynne) 1955- 150
Darroll, Sally
  See Odgers, Sally Farrell
Darrow, Sharon 181
Darrow, Whitney, (Jr.) 1909-1999 13
  Obituary 115
Darwin, Len
  See Darwin, Leonard
Darwin, Leonard 1916- 24
Dasent, Sir George Webbe 1817-1896 62
  Brief entry 29
Dash, Joan 1925- 142
Daskam, Josephine Dodge
  See Bacon, Josephine Dodge (Daskam)
D'ath, Justin 1953- 174
  Earlier sketch in SATA 106
Dauer, Rosamond 1934- 23
Daugherty, Charles Michael 1914- 16
Daugherty, James (Henry) 1889-1974 13
  See also CLR 78
Daugherty, Richard D(eo) 1922- 35
Daugherty, Sonia Medwedeff (?)-1971
  Obituary 27
d'Aulaire, Edgar Parin 1898-1986 66
  Obituary 47
  Earlier sketch in SATA 5
  See also CLR 21
d'Aulaire, Ingri 1904-1980 66
  Obituary 24
  Earlier sketch in SATA 5
  See also CLR 21
d'Aulaire, Ingri Mortenson Parin
  See d'Aulaire, Ingri
Dave, Dave
  See Berg, David
Daveluy, Paule Cloutier 1919- 11
Davenier, Christine 1961- 179
  Earlier sketch in SATA 127
Davenport, John 1960- 156
Daves, Michael 1938- 40
David, A. R.
  See David, A(nn) Rosalie
David, A(nn) Rosalie 1946- 103
David, Jonathan
  See Ames, Lee J(udah)
David, Lawrence 1963- 165
  Earlier sketch in SATA 111
David, Peter 1956- 72
David, Peter Allen
  See David, Peter
David, Rosalie
  See David, A(nn) Rosalie
Davidson, Alice Joyce 1932- 54
  Brief entry 45
Davidson, Basil 1914- 13
Davidson, (Marie) Diane 1924- 91
Davidson, Hugh
  See Hamilton, Edmond
Davidson, Jessica 1915-1986 5
Davidson, Judith 1953- 40
Davidson, Lionel 1922-2009 87
Davidson, Margaret 1936- 5
Davidson, Marion
  See Garis, Howard R.
Davidson, Mary R. 1885-1973 9
Davidson, Mary S. 1940- 61
Davidson, Mickie
  See Davidson, Margaret
Davidson, Nicole
  See Jensen, Kathryn
Davidson, R.
  See Davidson, Raymond
Davidson, Raymond 1926- 32
Davidson, Rosalie 1921- 23

Davie, Helen K(ay) 1952- *148*
  Earlier sketch in SATA 77
Davies, Andrew (Wynford) 1936- *27*
Davies, Andy Robert *200*
Davies, Bettilu D(onna) 1942- *33*
Davies, Hunter 1936- *55*
  Brief entry *45*
Davies, Jacqueline 1962- *186*
  Earlier sketch in SATA 155
Davies, Joan 1934- *50*
  Brief entry *47*
Davies, Nicola 1958- *182*
  Earlier sketches in SATA 99, 150
Davies, Peter J(oseph) 1937- *52*
Davies, Sumiko 1942- *46*
Davis, (A.) Aubrey 1949- *153*
Davis, Barbara Steincrohn
  See Davis, Maggie S.
Davis, Bette J. 1923- *15*
Davis, Burke 1913- *4*
Davis, Christopher 1928- *6*
Davis, D(elbert) Dwight 1908-1965 .... *33*
Davis, Daniel S(heldon) 1936- *12*
Davis, David R. 1948- *106*
Davis, Donald 1944- *169*
  Earlier sketch in SATA 93
Davis, Donald D.
  See Davis, Donald
Davis, Emma
  See Davis, Maggie S.
Davis, Gibbs 1953- *102*
  Brief entry *41*
  Earlier sketch in SATA 46
Davis, Grania 1943- *88*
  Brief entry *50*
Davis, H(arold) L(enoir) 1896-1960 .... *114*
Davis, Hubert J(ackson) 1904-1997 .... *31*
Davis, Jacky *204*
Davis, James Robert 1945- *32*
Davis, Jenny 1953- *74*
Davis, Jim
  See Davis, James Robert
Davis, Julia 1900(?)-1993 .... *6*
  Obituary *75*
Davis, Karen (Elizabeth) 1944- *109*
Davis, Katie 1959(?)- *152*
Davis, Lambert *176*
Davis, Leslie
  See Guccione, Leslie Davis
Davis, Louise Littleton 1921- *25*
Davis, Maggie S. 1943- *57*
Davis, Marguerite 1889- *34*
Davis, Mary L(ee) 1935- *9*
Davis, Mary Octavia 1901-1976 .... *6*
Davis, Nelle 1958- *73*
Davis, Ossie 1917-2005 .... *81*
  See also CLR 56
Davis, Paxton 1925-1994 .... *16*
Davis, Rich 1958- *206*
Davis, Robert 1881-1949
  See YABC 1
Davis, Robin W(orks) 1962- *87*
Davis, Russell Gerard 1922- *3*
Davis, Tim(othy N.) 1957- *94*
Davis, Verne Theodore 1889-1973 .... *6*
Davis, Yvonne 1927- *115*
Davol, Marguerite W. 1928- *146*
  Earlier sketch in SATA 82
DaVolls, Andy (P.) 1967- *85*
DaVolls, Linda 1966- *85*
Davys, Sarah
  See Manning, Rosemary
Dawes, Claiborne 1935- *111*
Dawson, Elmer A. *67*
  Earlier sketch in SATA 1
Dawson, Imogen (Zoe) 1948- *126*
  Earlier sketch in SATA 90
Dawson, Janine 1957- *196*
Dawson, Mary 1919- *11*
Day, A(rthur) Grove 1904-1994 .... *59*

Day, Alexandra 1941- *197*
  Autobiography Feature *197*
  Earlier sketches in SATA 67, 97, 169
  See also CLR 22
  See also SAAS 19
Day, Beth (Feagles) 1924- *33*
Day, Donna
  See Asay, Donna Day
Day, Edward C. 1932- *72*
Day, Jon 1936(?)- *79*
Day, Karen *187*
Day, Larry 1956- *181*
Day, Nancy 1953- *140*
Day, Nancy Raines 1951- *148*
  Earlier sketch in SATA 93
Day, Shirley 1962- *94*
Day, Thomas 1748-1789
  See YABC 1
Day, Trevor 1955- *124*
Dazey, Agnes J(ohnston) *2*
Dazey, Frank M. *2*
Deacon, Alexis 1978- *139*
Deacon, Eileen
  See Geipel, Eileen
Deacon, Richard
  See McCormick, (George) Donald (King)
Deadman, Ronald 1919-1988(?)
  Obituary *56*
Deak, Erzsi 1959- *152*
Dean, Anabel 1915- *12*
Dean, Carolee 1962- *148*
Dean, David 1976- *192*
Dean, Karen Strickler 1923- *49*
Dean, Ruth (Brigham) 1947- *145*
Dean, Zoey
  See Bennett, Cherie
de Angeli, Marguerite (Lofft) 1889-1987 ... *100*
  Obituary *51*
  Earlier sketches in SATA 1, 27
  See also CLR 1
Deans, Karen *195*
Deans, Sis Boulos 1955- *136*
  Earlier sketch in SATA 78
DeArmand, Frances Ullmann 1904(?)-1984 . *10*
  Obituary *38*
DeArmond, Dale 1914- *70*
DeArmond, Dale Burlison
  See DeArmond, Dale
Deary, Terry 1946- *171*
  Brief entry *41*
  Earlier sketches in SATA 51, 101
Deaver, Julie Reece 1953- *68*
de Banke, Cecile 1889-1965 .... *11*
De Bello, Rosario 1923- *89*
Debon, Nicolas *186*
  Earlier sketch in SATA 151
de Bono, Edward 1933- *66*
de Brissac, Malcolm
  See Dickinson, Peter
de Brunhoff, Jean
  See Brunhoff, Jean de
De Brunhoff, Laurent
  See Brunhoff, Laurent de
De Bruyn, Monica G. 1952- *13*
De Bruyn, Monica Jean Grembowicz
  See De Bruyn, Monica G.
DeBry, Roger K. 1942- *91*
de Camp, Catherine Crook 1907-2000 .... *83*
  Earlier sketch in SATA 12
de Camp, L. Sprague 1907-2000 .... *83*
  Earlier sketch in SATA 9
de Camp, Lyon Sprague
  See de Camp, L. Sprague
DeCandido, Keith R.A. *112*
Dechausay, Sonia E. *94*
Decker, C.B. *172*
Decker, Cynthia B.
  See Decker, C.B.
Decker, Duane 1910-1964 .... *5*
Decker, Timothy 1974- *197*

DeClements, Barthe (Faith) 1920- *131*
  Earlier sketches in SATA 35, 71
  See also CLR 23
de Clercq Zubli, Rita la Fontaine 1929- *199*
de Conte, Sieur Louis
  See Twain, Mark
Dedman, Stephen *108*
Dee, Catherine 1964- *138*
Dee, Ruby
  See Wallace, Ruby Ann
Deedy, Carmen Agra 1960- *196*
Deedy, John 1923- *24*
Deegan, Paul Joseph 1937- *48*
  Brief entry *38*
Deem, James M. 1950- *191*
  Autobiography Feature *191*
  Earlier sketches in SATA 75, 134
Deem, James Morgan
  See Deem, James M.
Deeter, Catherine 1947- *137*
DeFelice, Cynthia 1951- *165*
  Earlier sketches in SATA 79, 121
DeFelice, Cynthia C.
  See DeFelice, Cynthia
Defoe, Daniel 1660(?)-1731 .... *22*
  See also CLR 61
DeFord, Deborah H. *123*
deFrance, Anthony
  See DiFranco, Anthony (Mario)
Degen, Bruce 1945- *205*
  Brief entry *47*
  Earlier sketches in SATA 57, 97, 147
DeGering, Etta (Belle) Fowler 1898-1996 ..... *7*
De Goldi, Kate
  See De Goldi, Kathleen Domenica
De Goldi, Kathleen Domenica 1959- *123*
de Goursac, Olivier 1959- *184*
De Grazia, Ettore 1909-1982 .... *39*
De Grazia, Ted
  See De Grazia, Ettore
deGroat, Diane 1947- *169*
  Earlier sketches in SATA 31, 90
deGros, J. H.
  See Villiard, Paul
de Grummond, Lena Young *62*
  Earlier sketch in SATA 6
de Hamel, Joan Littledale 1924- *86*
De Haven, Tom 1949- *72*
de Hugo, Pierre
  See Brackers de Hugo, Pierre
Deiss, Joseph Jay 1915- *12*
de Jenkins, Lyll Becerra 1925-1997 .... *102*
DeJong, David C(ornel) 1905-1967 .... *10*
de Jong, Dola 1911-2003
  See de Jong, Dorothea Rosalie
de Jong, Dorothea Rosalie 1911-2003 .... *7*
  Obituary *149*
DeJong, Meindert 1906-1991 .... *2*
  Obituary *68*
  See also CLR 73
DeJonge, Joanne E. 1943- *56*
Deka, Connie
  See Laux, Constance
de Kay, Ormonde (Jr.) 1923-1998 .... *7*
  Obituary *106*
de Kiriline, Louise
  See Lawrence, Louise de Kiriline
Dekker, Carl
  See Laffin, John (Alfred Charles)
  and Lynds, Dennis
deKruif, Paul (Henry) 1890-1971 .... *50*
  Earlier sketch in SATA 5
Delacre, Lulu 1957- *156*
  Earlier sketch in SATA 36
DeLaCroix, Alice 1940- *195*
  Earlier sketch in SATA 75
de la Cruz, Melissa 1971- *179*
De la Garza, Phyllis 1942- *169*
De Lage, Ida 1918- *11*
de la Mare, Walter (John) 1873-1956 .... *16*
  See also CLR 23

Delaney, Harry 1932- 3
Delaney, Joseph 1945- 172
Delaney, M.C.
    See Delaney, Michael
Delaney, Michael 1955- 180
    Earlier sketch in SATA 96
Delaney, Michael Clark
    See Delaney, Michael
Delaney, Ned
    See Delaney, Thomas Nicholas III
Delaney, Thomas Nicholas III 1951- 28
Delano, Hugh 1933- 20
Delany, Samuel R., Jr. 1942- 92
Delany, Samuel Ray
    See Delany, Samuel R., Jr.
de la Pena, Matt 205
De La Ramee, Marie Louise 1839-1908 20
de la Roche, Mazo 1879-1961 64
De La Roche Saint Andre, Anne 1950- 75
Delaune, (Jewel) Lynn (de Grummond) 7
DeLaurentis, Louise Budde 1920- 12
del Barco, Lucy Salamanca 1900(?)-1989
    Obituary 64
Delderfield, Eric R(aymond) 1909-1995 14
Delderfield, Ronald Frederick 1912-1972 20
DeLeeuw, Adele (Louise) 1899-1988 30
    Obituary 56
    Earlier sketch in SATA 1
De Leon, Nephtali 1945- 97
Delessert, Etienne 1941- 179
    Brief entry 27
    Earlier sketches in SATA 46, 130
    See also CLR 81
Delgado, James P. 1958- 122
de Lint, Charles 1951- 157
    Earlier sketch in SATA 115
de Lint, Charles Henri Diederick Hofsmit
    See de Lint, Charles
Delmar, Roy
    See Wexler, Jerome (LeRoy)
Del Negro, Janice M. 197
Deloria, Vine, Jr. 1933-2005 21
    Obituary 171
Deloria, Vine Victor, Jr.
    See Deloria, Vine, Jr.
del Rey, Lester 1915-1993 22
    Obituary 76
Delrio, Martin
    See Doyle, Debra
    and Macdonald, James D.
Delton, Judy 1931-2001 77
    Obituary 130
    Earlier sketch in SATA 14
    See also SAAS 9
Delulio, John 1938- 15
Delving, Michael
    See Williams, Jay
de Marcken, Gail 186
Demarest, Chris L. 1951- 175
    Brief entry 44
    Earlier sketches in SATA 45, 82, 128
Demarest, Christopher Lynn
    See Demarest, Chris L.
Demarest, Doug
    See Barker, Will
De Mari, Silvana 1953- 193
Demas, Corinne 203
    See Bliss, Corinne Demas
Demas, Vida 1927- 9
Dematons, Charlotte 1957- 203
DeMatteis, J.M. 1953- 180
DeMatteis, John Marc
    See DeMatteis, J.M.
De Mejo, Oscar 1911-1992 40
Demers, Dominique 1956- 177
de Messieres, Nicole 1930- 39
Demi
    See Hitz, Demi
Demijohn, Thom
    See Disch, Thomas M.
    and Sladek, John

Deming, Richard 1915-1983 24
Deming, Sarah 191
de Monfreid, Dorothee 1973- 189
Demuth, Patricia Brennan 1948- 84
    Brief entry 51
Dendinger, Roger E. 1952- 158
Denenberg, Barry 1940- 175
Dengler, Marianna (Herron) 1935- 103
Dengler, Sandy 1939- 54
    Brief entry 40
Denim, Sue
    See Pilkey, Dav
Denise, Christopher 1968- 193
    Earlier sketch in SATA 147
Denman, K.L. 1957- 186
Denmark, Harrison
    See Zelazny, Roger
Dennard, Deborah 1953- 136
    Earlier sketch in SATA 78
Denney, Diana 1910-2000 25
    Obituary 120
Dennis, Morgan 1891(?)-1960 18
Dennis, Wesley 1903-1966 18
Denniston, Elinore 1900-1978
    Obituary 24
Denny, Norman (George) 1901-1982 43
Denos, Julia 202
Denslow, Sharon Phillips 1947- 142
    Earlier sketch in SATA 68
Denslow, W(illiam) W(allace) 1856-1915 16
    See also CLR 15
Dent, Grace 1973- 187
Denton, Kady MacDonald 181
    Earlier sketches in SATA 66, 110
    See also CLR 71
Denton, Terry 1950- 186
Denver, Walt
    See Redding, Robert Hull
    and Sherman, Jory (Tecumseh)
Denzel, Justin F(rancis) 1917-1999 46
    Brief entry 38
Denzer, Ann Wiseman
    See Wiseman, Ann (Sayre)
DePalma, Mary Newell 1961- 185
    Earlier sketch in SATA 139
De Palma, Toni 199
dePaola, Thomas Anthony 1934- 155
    Earlier sketches in SATA 11, 59, 108
    See also CLR 81
    See also SAAS 15
    See dePaola, Tomie
dePaola, Tomie 200
    See dePaola, Thomas Anthony
deParrie, Paul 1949- 74
DePauw, Linda Grant 1940- 24
DeRan, David 1946- 76
Derby, Ken 1956- 181
Derby, Kenneth R.
    See Derby, Ken
Derby, Pat 1942- 172
Derby, Sally 1934- 189
    Earlier sketches in SATA 89, 132
de Regniers, Beatrice Schenk (Freedman)
    1914-2000 68
    Obituary 123
    Earlier sketch in SATA 2
    See also SAAS 6
Dereske, Jo 1947- 72
Derleth, August (William) 1909-1971 5
Derman, Martha (Winn) 74
Derman, Sarah Audrey 1915- 11
DeRoberts, Lyndon
    See Silverstein, Robert Alan
de Roo, Anne Louise 1931-1997 84
    Earlier sketch in SATA 25
    See also CLR 63
deRosa, Dee 70
Derrick, Lionel
    See Cunningham, Chet
Derrickson, Jim 1959- 141

Derry Down Derry
    See Lear, Edward
Dervaux, Isabelle 1961- 106
Derwent, Lavinia 14
Desai, Anita 1937- 126
    Earlier sketch in SATA 63
DeSaix, Deborah Durland 188
De Saulles, Tony 1958- 119
Desbarats, Peter 1933- 39
de Selincourt, Aubrey 1894-1962 14
de Seve, Randall 198
Deshpande, Chris 1950- 69
Desimini, Lisa 1964- 148
    Earlier sketch in SATA 86
Desjarlais, John 1953- 71
Desjarlais, John J.
    See Desjarlais, John
Desmoinaux, Christel 1967- 149
    Earlier sketch in SATA 103
Desmond, Adrian J(ohn) 1947- 51
Desmond, Alice Curtis 1897-1990 8
Desnoettes, Caroline 183
DeSpain, Pleasant 1943- 87
Desputeaux, Helene 1959- 95
Dessen, Sarah 1970- 172
    Earlier sketch in SATA 120
Detine, Padre
    See Olsen, Ib Spang
de Trevino, Elizabeth B.
    See Trevino, Elizabeth B(orton) de
de Trevino, Elizabeth Borton
    See Trevino, Elizabeth B(orton) de
Detwiler, Susan Dill 1956- 58
Deuker, Carl 1950- 196
    Earlier sketches in SATA 82, 150
Deutsch, Babette 1895-1982 1
    Obituary 33
Deutsch, Eva Costabel
    See Costabel, Eva Deutsch
Deutsch, Helen 1906-1992 76
Deutsch, Kurt
    See Singer, Kurt D.
De Valera, Sinead 1879(?)-1975
    Obituary 30
Devaney, John 1926-1994 12
de Varennes, Monique 1947- 168
de Varona, Frank J. 1943- 83
Devereux, Frederick L(eonard), Jr.
    1914-1993 9
Devi, Nila
    See Woody, Regina Jones
deVinck, Christopher 1951- 85
DeVita, James 195
DeVito, Cara 1956- 80
Devlin, Dorothy Wende
    See Devlin, Wende
Devlin, Harry 1918-2001 136
    Earlier sketches in SATA 11, 74
Devlin, Wende 1918-2002 74
    Earlier sketch in SATA 11
Devon, Paddie 1953- 92
Devons, Sonia 1974- 72
Devorah-Leah 111
de Vos, Gail 1949- 122
DeVries, Douglas 1933- 122
De Waard, E(lliott) John 1935- 7
Dewan, Ted 1961- 157
    Earlier sketch in SATA 108
Dewdney, Anna 184
Dewdney, Selwyn (Hanington) 1909-1979 ... 64
DeWeese, Gene
    See DeWeese, Thomas Eugene
DeWeese, Jean
    See DeWeese, Thomas Eugene
DeWeese, Thomas Eugene 1934- 46
    Brief entry 45
Dewey, Ariane 1937- 178
    Earlier sketches in SATA 7, 109
Dewey, Jennifer (Owings) 1941- 103
    Brief entry 48
    Earlier sketch in SATA 58

Dewey, Kenneth Francis 1940- *39*
De Wire, Elinor 1953- *180*
deWit, Dorothy (May Knowles) 1916-1980 . *39*
  Obituary *28*
Dexter, Alison 1966- *125*
Dexter, John
  See Bradley, Marion Zimmer
Deyneka, Anita 1943- *24*
Deyrup, Astrith Johnson 1923- *24*
Dezern, Chad *201*
Dhami, Narinder 1958- *152*
Dhondy, Farrukh 1944- *152*
  Earlier sketch in SATA *65*
  See also CLR *41*
Diakite, Baba Wague 1961- *174*
Diakite, Penda 1993(?)- *174*
Diamond, Arthur 1957- *76*
Diamond, Donna 1950- *69*
  Brief entry *30*
  Earlier sketch in SATA *35*
Diamond, Petra
  See Sachs, Judith
Diamond, Rebecca
  See Sachs, Judith
Dias, Earl Joseph 1916- *41*
Dias, Ron 1937- *71*
Diaz, David 1959(?)- *189*
  Earlier sketches in SATA *96, 150*
  See also CLR *65*
Dibley, Glin *188*
DiCamillo, Kate 1964- *202*
  Earlier sketches in SATA *121, 163*
  See also CLR *117*
Di Certo, J(oseph) J(ohn) 1933- *60*
DiCianni, Ron 1952- *107*
Dick, Trella Lamson 1889-1974 .... *9*
Dickens, Charles (John Huffam)
  1812-1870 .... *15*
  See also CLR *95*
Dickens, Frank
  See Huline-Dickens, Frank William
Dickens, Monica (Enid) 1915-1992 .... *4*
  Obituary *74*
Dickerson, Roy Ernest 1886-1965
  Obituary *26*
Dickinson, Emily 1830-1886 .... *29*
Dickinson, Emily Elizabeth
  See Dickinson, Emily
Dickinson, Mary 1949- *48*
  Brief entry *41*
Dickinson, Mary-Anne
  See Rodda, Emily
Dickinson, Peter 1927- *150*
  Earlier sketches in SATA *5, 62, 95*
  See also CLR *125*
Dickinson, Peter Malcolm de Brissac
  See Dickinson, Peter
Dickinson, Susan 1931- *8*
Dickinson, Terence 1943- *102*
Dickinson, W(illiam) Croft 1897-1963 .... *13*
Dickson, Gordon R. 1923-2001 .... *77*
Dickson, Gordon Rupert
  See Dickson, Gordon R.
Dickson, Helen
  See Reynolds, Helen Mary Greenwood Campbell
Dickson, Naida 1916- *8*
Diehn, Gwen 1943- *80*
Dierssen, Andreas 1962- *190*
Diesen, Deborah 1967- *200*
Dieterich, Michele M. 1962- *78*
Dietz, David H(enry) 1897-1984 .... *10*
  Obituary *41*
Dietz, Lew 1907-1997 .... *11*
  Obituary *95*
Diffily, Deborah *159*
Di Fiori, Larry
  See Di Fiori, Lawrence
Di Fiori, Lawrence 1934- *130*
DiFranco, Anthony (Mario) 1945- *42*
Digby, Anne 1935- *72*

Digges, Jeremiah
  See Berger, Josef
Digman, Kristina 1959- *176*
D'Ignazio, Fred(erick) 1949- *39*
  Brief entry *35*
Di Grazia, Thomas (?)-1983 .... *32*
Dijkstra, Lida 1961- *195*
Dikty, Julian May
  See May, Julian
Dillard, Annie 1945- *140*
  Earlier sketch in SATA *10*
Dillard, Kristine 1964- *113*
Dillard, Polly Hargis 1916- *24*
Diller, Harriett 1953- *78*
Dillon, Barbara 1927- *44*
  Brief entry *39*
Dillon, Diane 1933- *194*
  Earlier sketches in SATA *15, 51, 106*
  See also CLR *44*
Dillon, Diane Claire
  See Dillon, Diane
Dillon, Eilis 1920-1994 .... *74*
  Autobiography Feature *105*
  Obituary *83*
  Earlier sketch in SATA *2*
  See also CLR *26*
Dillon, Jana (a pseudonym) 1952- *117*
Dillon, Leo 1933- *194*
  Earlier sketches in SATA *15, 51, 106*
  See also CLR *44*
Dillon, Sharon Saseen
  See Saseen, Sharon (Dillon)
Dils, Tracey E. 1958- *83*
Dilson, Jesse 1914-1988 .... *24*
Dinan, Carolyn *59*
  Brief entry *47*
Dines, Carol 1956- *175*
Dines, (Harry) Glen 1925-1996 .... *7*
Dinesen, Isak
  See Blixen, Karen
Dinessi, Alex
  See Schembri, Jim
Dinneen, Betty 1929- *61*
Dinnerstein, Harvey 1928- *42*
Dinsdale, Tim(othy Kay) 1924-1987 .... *11*
Diop, Birago (Ismael) 1906-1989
  Obituary *64*
Diouf, Sylviane A. *168*
Diouf, Sylviane Anna
  See Diouf, Sylviane A.
DiPucchio, Kelly *204*
  Earlier sketch in SATA *159*
Dirk
  See Gringhuis, Richard H.
Dirks, Wilhelmina 1916- *59*
Dirks, Willy
  See Dirks, Wilhelmina
Dirtmeister
  See Tomecek, Steve
DiSalvo, DyAnne 1960- *144*
  Earlier sketch in SATA *59*
DiSalvo-Ryan, DyAnne
  See DiSalvo, DyAnne
Disch, Thomas M. 1940-2008 .... *92*
  Obituary *195*
  See also CLR *18*
  See also SAAS *15*
Disch, Thomas Michael
  See Disch, Thomas M.
Disch, Tom
  See Disch, Thomas M.
Disher, Garry 1949- *125*
  Earlier sketch in SATA *81*
Disney, Walt(er Elias) 1901-1966 .... *28*
  Brief entry *27*
Ditchfield, Christin 1973- *189*
DiTerlizzi, Tony 1969- *154*
Divakaruni, Chitra Banerjee 1956- *160*
Di Valentin, Maria (Amelia) Messuri
  1911-1985 .... *7*

Divine, Arthur Durham 1904-1987
  Obituary *52*
Divine, David
  See Divine, Arthur Durham
Dixon, Ann R. 1954- *127*
  Earlier sketch in SATA *77*
Dixon, Ann Renee
  See Dixon, Ann R.
Dixon, Dougal 1947- *190*
  Earlier sketches in SATA *45, 127*
Dixon, Franklin W.
  See Barrett, Neal, Jr.
  and Goulart, Ron
  and Lantz, Francess L(in)
  and Lerangis, Peter
  and McFarlane, Leslie
  and Stanley, George Edward
  and Stratemeyer, Edward L.
Dixon, Jeanne 1936- *31*
Dixon, Paige
  See Corcoran, Barbara (Asenath)
Dixon, Peter L(ee) 1931- *6*
Dixon, Rachel 1952- *74*
Djoleto, (Solomon Alexander) Amu 1929- ... *80*
d'lacey, Chris 1949- *165*
Doak, Annie
  See Dillard, Annie
Doane, Pelagie 1906-1966 .... *7*
Dobell, I(sabel) M(arian) B(arclay)
  1909-1998 .... *11*
Dobie, J(ames) Frank 1888-1964 .... *43*
Dobkin, Alexander 1908-1975
  Obituary *30*
Dobler, Lavinia G. 1910- *6*
Dobrin, Arnold 1928- *4*
Dobson, Jill 1969- *140*
Dobson, Julia 1941- *48*
Dobson, Mary 1954- *117*
Docherty, James
  See Docherty, Jimmy
Docherty, Jimmy 1976- *204*
Dockery, Wallene T. 1941- *27*
Dockray, Tracy 1962- *139*
Dockrey, Karen 1955- *103*
Doctor, Bernard
  See Doctor, Bernard Aquina
Doctor, Bernard Aquina 1950- *81*
Doctor X
  See Nourse, Alan E(dward)
Dodd, Ed(ward Benton) 1902-1991 .... *4*
  Obituary *68*
Dodd, Emma 1969- *203*
Dodd, Lynley (Stuart) 1941- *132*
  Earlier sketches in SATA *35, 86*
  See also CLR *62*
Dodd, Marty 1921- *142*
Dodd, Quentin 1972- *137*
Dodds, Bill 1952- *78*
Dodds, Dayle Ann 1952- *201*
  Earlier sketches in SATA *75, 150*
Doder, Josh 1968- *187*
Dodge, Bertha S(anford) 1902-1995 .... *8*
Dodge, Fremont
  See Grimes, Lee
Dodge, Gil
  See Hano, Arnold
Dodge, Mary (Elizabeth) Mapes
  1831(?)-1905 .... *100*
  Earlier sketch in SATA *21*
  See also CLR *62*
Dodgson, Charles Lutwidge
  See Carroll, Lewis
Dodson, Kenneth MacKenzie 1907-1999 ..... *11*
Dodson, Susan 1941- *50*
  Brief entry *40*
Dogyear, Drew
  See Gorey, Edward (St. John)
Doherty, Berlie 1943- *111*
  Earlier sketch in SATA *72*
  See also CLR *21*
  See also SAAS *16*

Doherty, Charles Hugh 1913- 6
Doherty, Craig A. 1951- *169*
  Earlier sketch in SATA *83*
Doherty, Katherine M(ann) 1951- 83
Doherty, Kieran 1945- *164*
Dokey, Cameron 1956- 97
Dolan, Edward F(rancis), Jr. 1924- 94
  Brief entry *31*
  Earlier sketch in SATA *45*
Dolan, Ellen M(eara) 1929-1998 88
Dolan, Sean J. 1958- 74
Dolce, J. Ellen 1948- 75
Dolch, Edward William 1889-1961 50
Dolch, Marguerite Pierce 1891-1978 50
Dollar, Diane (Hills) 1933- 57
Dolson, Hildegarde
  See Lockridge, Hildegarde (Dolson)
Domanska, Janina 1913(?)-1995 68
  Obituary 84
  Earlier sketch in SATA *6*
  See also CLR *40*
  See also SAAS *18*
Dominguez, Angel 1953- 76
Domino, John
  See Averill, Esther (Holden)
Domjan, Joseph (Spiri) 1907-1992 25
Domm, Jeffrey C. 1958- 84
Donahue, Dorothy *178*
Donald, Rhonda Lucas 1962- *147*
Donalds, Gordon
  See Shirreffs, Gordon D(onald)
Donaldson, Bryna
  See Stevens, Bryna
Donaldson, Gordon 1913-1993 64
  Obituary 76
Donaldson, Joan 1953- 78
Donaldson, Julia 1948- *180*
  Earlier sketches in SATA *82, 132*
Donaldson, Stephen R. 1947- *121*
Donaldson, Stephen Reeder
  See Donaldson, Stephen R.
Doner, Kim 1955- 91
Doney, Todd L. W. 1959- *104*
Dong-Sung, Kim 1970- *195*
Dong-Sung Kim
  See Dong-Sung, Kim
Donkin, Nance (Clare) 1915- 95
Donna, Natalie 1934-1979 9
Donnelly, Elfie 1950-
  See CLR *104*
Donnelly, Jennifer 1963- *154*
Donnelly, Matt 1972- *148*
Donnio, Sylviane *188*
Donoghue, Emma 1969- *101*
Donohue, Moira Rose 1954- *201*
Donoughue, Carol 1935- *139*
Donovan, Frank (Robert) 1906-1975
  Obituary 30
Donovan, John 1928-1992 72
  Brief entry 29
  See also CLR *3*
Donovan, Mary Lee 1961- 86
Donovan, William
  See Berkebile, Fred D(onovan)
Donze, Mary Terese 1911- 89
Doob, Leonard W(illiam) 1909-2000 8
Dooley, Norah 1953- 74
Dooling, Michael 1958- *105*
Dor, Ana
  See Ceder, Georgiana Dorcas
Dore, (Louis Christophe Paul) Gustave
  1832-1883 19
Doremus, Robert 1913- 30
Doren, Marion (Walker) 1928- 57
Dorenkamp, Michelle 1957- 89
Dorflinger, Carolyn 1953- 91
Dorfman, Joaquin 1979- *180*
Dorfman, Joaquin Emiliano
  See Dorfman, Joaquin
Dorian, Edith M(cEwen) 1900-1983 5

Dorian, Harry
  See Hamilton, Charles (Harold St. John)
Dorian, Marguerite 7
Dorin, Patrick C(arberry) 1939- 59
  Brief entry 52
Dorman, Brandon *194*
Dorman, Michael 1932- 7
Dorman, N. B. 1927- 39
Dormer, Frank W. *200*
Dorris, Michael 1945-1997 75
  Obituary 94
  See also CLR *58*
Dorris, Michael A.
  See Dorris, Michael
Dorris, Michael Anthony
  See Dorris, Michael
Dorritt, Susan
  See Schlein, Miriam
Dorros, Alex 1991- *194*
Dorros, Arthur 1950- *168*
  Earlier sketches in SATA *78, 122*
  See also CLR *42*
  See also SAAS *20*
Dorros, Arthur M.
  See Dorros, Arthur
Dorson, Richard M(ercer) 1916-1981 30
Doss, Helen (Grigsby) 1918- 20
Doss, Margot Patterson 6
dos Santos, Joyce Audy 1949- 57
  Brief entry 42
Dothers, Anne
  See Chess, Victoria (Dickerson)
Dotlich, Rebecca Kai 1951- *182*
Dottig
  See Grider, Dorothy
Dotts, Maryann J. 1933- 35
Doty, Jean Slaughter 1929- 28
Doty, Roy 1922- 28
Doubtfire, Dianne (Abrams) 1918- 29
Doucet, Sharon Arms 1951- *144*
  Autobiography Feature *144*
  Earlier sketch in SATA *125*
Dougherty, Charles 1922- 18
Dougherty, Terri (L.) 1964- *146*
Doughty, Rebecca 1955- *174*
Douglas, Blaise 1960- *101*
Douglas, Carole Nelson 1944- 73
Douglas, Garry
  See Kilworth, Garry
Douglas, James McM.
  See Griffin, W.E.B.
Douglas, Kathryn
  See Ewing, Kathryn
Douglas, Leonard
  See Bradbury, Ray
Douglas, Lola
  See Zeises, Lara M.
Douglas, Marjory Stoneman 1890-1998 10
Douglas, Michael
  See Bright, Robert Sr.)
Douglas, Michael
  See Crichton, Michael
Douglas, Shirley Stewart
  See Tepper, Sheri S.
Douglass, Barbara 1930- 40
Douglass, Frederick 1817(?)-1895 29
Douglass, Keith
  See Cunningham, Chet
Douty, Esther M(orris) 1909-1978 8
  Obituary 23
Dow, Emily R. 1904-1987 10
Dow, Vicki
  See McVey, Vicki
Dowd, John David 1945- 78
Dowd, Siobhan 1960-2007 .... *204*
Dowdell, Dorothy (Florence) Karns 1910- ... 12
Dowden, Anne Ophelia Todd 1907-2007 7
  Obituary *180*
  See also SAAS *10*
Dowdey, Landon Gerald 1923- 11

Dowdy, Mrs. Regera
  See Gorey, Edward (St. John)
Dowell, Frances O'Roark *205*
  Earlier sketch in SATA *157*
Dower, Laura *185*
Dowling, Terry 1947- *101*
Downard, Barry 1956- *202*
Downer, Ann 1960- *155*
Downer, Marion 1892(?)-1971 25
Downes, Belinda 1962- *180*
Downey, Fairfax D(avis) 1893-1990 3
  Obituary 66
Downey, Lynn 1961- *185*
Downham, Jenny 1964- *192*
Downie, John 1931- 87
Downie, Mary Alice 1934- *171*
  Earlier sketches in SATA *13, 87*
Downie, Mary Alice Dawe
  See Downie, Mary Alice
Downing, David A(lmon) 1958- 84
Downing, Johnette *184*
Downing, Julie 1956- *148*
  Earlier sketch in SATA *81*
Downing, Paula E. 1951- 80
Downing, Warwick 1931- *138*
Downing, Wick
  See Downing, Warwick
Dowswell, Paul 1957- *184*
Doyle, A. Conan
  See Doyle, Sir Arthur Conan
Doyle, Sir Arthur Conan 1859-1930 24
  See also CLR *106*
Doyle, Brian 1935- *156*
  Earlier sketches in SATA *67, 104*
  See also CLR *22*
  See also SAAS *16*
Doyle, Charlotte 1937- *178*
  Earlier sketch in SATA *94*
Doyle, Charlotte Lackner
  See Doyle, Charlotte
Doyle, Conan
  See Doyle, Sir Arthur Conan
Doyle, Debra 1952- *165*
  Earlier sketch in SATA *105*
Doyle, Donovan
  See Boegehold, Betty (Doyle)
Doyle, John
  See Graves, Robert
Doyle, Malachy 1954- *165*
  Earlier sketch in SATA *120*
  See also CLR *83*
Doyle, Richard 1824-1883 21
Doyle, Sir A. Conan
  See Doyle, Sir Arthur Conan
Dr. A
  See Asimov, Isaac
  and Silverstein, Alvin
  and Silverstein, Virginia B.
Dr. Alphabet
  See Morice, Dave
Dr. Fred
  See Bortz, Alfred B(enjamin)
Dr. Laura
  See Schlessinger, Laura (Catherine)
Seuss, Dr.
  See Dr. Seuss
Dr. Seuss 1904-1991 .... *100*
  Obituary 67
  Earlier sketches in SATA *1, 28, 75*
  See also CLR *100*
Dr. Zed
  See Penrose, Gordon
Drabble, Margaret 1939- 48
Drackett, Phil(ip Arthur) 1922- 53
Draco, F.
  See Davis, Julia
Dracup, Angela 1943- 74
Dragisic, Patricia *116*

Dragonwagon, Crescent 1952- *186*
    Autobiography Feature *186*
    Earlier sketches in SATA *11, 41, 75, 133*
    See also SAAS *14*
Drake, David 1945- *85*
Drake, David Allen
    See Drake, David
Drake, Frank
    See Hamilton, Charles (Harold St. John)
Drake, Jane 1954- *82*
Drakeford, Dale B 1952- *113*
Drakeford, Dale Benjamin
    See Drakeford, Dale B
Draper, Hastings
    See Jeffries, Roderic
Draper, Sharon
    See Draper, Sharon M.
Draper, Sharon M. 1948- *195*
    Autobiography Feature *146*
    Earlier sketches in SATA *98, 146*
    See also CLR *57*
Draper, Sharon Mills
    See Draper, Sharon M.
Drapier, M. B.
    See Swift, Jonathan
Drawson, Blair 1943- *126*
    Earlier sketch in SATA *17*
Dray, Matt 1967- *177*
Dray, Matthew Frederick
    See Dray, Matt
Dresang, Eliza (Carolyn Timberlake) 1941- . *19*
Drescher, Henrik 1955- *172*
    Earlier sketches in SATA *67, 105*
    See also CLR *20*
Drescher, Joan E(lizabeth) 1939- *137*
    Earlier sketch in SATA *30*
Dressen-McQueen, Stacey *191*
Dreves, Veronica R. 1927-1986
    Obituary *50*
Drew, Patricia (Mary) 1938- *15*
Drewery, Mary 1918- *6*
Drewery, Melanie 1970- *165*
Drewry, Henry N(athaniel) 1924- *138*
Dreyer, Ellen *177*
Drial, J. E.
    See Laird, Jean E(louise)
Drimmer, Frederick 1916-2000 .... *60*
    Obituary *124*
Driskill, J. Lawrence 1920- *90*
Driskill, Larry
    See Driskill, J. Lawrence
Driving Hawk, Virginia
    See Sneve, Virginia Driving Hawk
Dron, Laura
    See Matthews, L.S.
Dronzek, Laura *199*
Drucker, Malka 1945- *111*
    Brief entry *29*
    Earlier sketch in SATA *39*
Drucker, Olga Levy 1927- *79*
Druitt, Tobias
    See Purkiss, Diane
Drummond, V(iolet) H(ilda) 1911-2000 .... *6*
Drummond, Walter
    See Silverberg, Robert
Drury, Clare Marie
    See Hoskyns-Abrahall, Clare (Constance Drury)
Drury, Roger W(olcott) 1914-1996 .... *15*
Druse, Eleanor
    See King, Stephen
Dryden, Pamela
    See St. John, Nicole
D.T., Hughes
    See Hughes, Dean
Duane, Diane (Elizabeth) 1952- *145*
    Brief entry *46*
    Earlier sketches in SATA *58, 95*
Dubanevich, Arlene 1950- *56*
Dubelaar, Thea 1947- *60*
Dubin, Jill *205*

du Blane, Daphne
    See Groom, Arthur William
Duble, Kathleen Benner 1958- *164*
Dubois, Claude K. 1960- *196*
DuBois, Rochelle Holt 1946- *41*
Du Bois, Shirley Graham 1907(?)-1977 .... *24*
    See Graham, Shirley
Du Bois, W. E. B. 1868-1963 .... *42*
Du Bois, William Edward Burghardt
    See Du Bois, W. E. B.
du Bois, William Pene
    See Pene du Bois, William (Sherman)
Duboise, Novella 1911-1999 .... *88*
Dubosarsky, Ursula 1961- *193*
    Earlier sketches in SATA *107, 147*
DuBose, LaRocque (Russ) 1926- *2*
Dubrovin, Vivian 1931- *139*
    Earlier sketch in SATA *65*
DuBurke, Randy *172*
Ducey, Jean Sparks 1915- *93*
Duchacek, Ivo D(uka) 1913-1988
    Obituary *55*
Du Chaillu, Paul (Belloni) 1835(?)-1903 ..... *26*
Ducharme, Dede Fox
    See Ducharme, Lilian Fox
Ducharme, Lilian Fox 1950- *122*
Ducornet, Erica 1943- *7*
Ducornet, Rikki
    See Ducornet, Erica
Duden, Jane 1947- *136*
Duder, Tessa 1940- *117*
    Earlier sketch in SATA *80*
    See also CLR *43*
    See also SAAS *23*
Dudley, Helen
    See Hope Simpson, Jacynth
Dudley, Martha Ward 1909(?)-1985
    Obituary *45*
Dudley, Nancy
    See Cole, Lois Dwight
Dudley, Robert
    See Baldwin, James
Dudley, Ruth H(ubbell) 1905-2001 .... *11*
Dudley-Smith, T.
    See Trevor, Elleston
Due, Linnea A. 1948- *64*
Dueck, Adele 1955- *97*
Dueland, Joy V(ivian) *27*
Duerr, Gisela 1968- *89*
Duey, Kathleen 1950- *199*
    Earlier sketch in SATA *132*
Dufault, Joseph Ernest Nephtali
    See James, Will(iam Roderick)
Duff, Annis (James) 1904(?)-1986
    Obituary *49*
Duff, Maggie
    See Duff, Margaret K(app)
Duff, Margaret K(app) 1916-2003 .... *37*
    Obituary *144*
Duffey, Betsy (Byars) 1953- *131*
    Earlier sketch in SATA *80*
Duffie, Charles 1960- *144*
Duffield, Katy S. 1961- *147*
Duffy, Carol Ann 1955- *165*
    Earlier sketch in SATA *95*
Dugan, Jack
    See Griffin, W.E.B.
Dugan, John Kevin
    See Griffin, W.E.B.
Dugan, Karen *202*
Dugan, Karen M.
    See Dugan, Karen
Dugan, Michael (Gray) 1947- *15*
Duggan, Alfred Leo 1903-1964 .... *25*
Duggan, Maurice (Noel) 1922-1974 .... *40*
    Obituary *30*
Duggleby, John 1952- *94*
Dugin, Andrej 1955- *77*
Dugina, Olga 1964- *77*
du Jardin, Rosamond Neal 1902-1963 .... *2*

Duka, Ivo
    See Duchacek, Ivo D(uka)
Duke, Kate 1956- *192*
    Earlier sketches in SATA *90, 148*
    See also CLR *51*
Duke, Will
    See Gault, William Campbell
Dulac, Edmund 1882-1953 .... *19*
Dumas, Alexandre (pere) 1802-1870 .... *18*
    See also CLR *134*
Dumas, Jacqueline 1946- *55*
Dumas, Philippe 1940- *119*
    Earlier sketch in SATA *52*
du Maurier, Daphne 1907-1989 .... *27*
    Obituary *60*
Dumbleton, Mike 1948- *206*
    Earlier sketches in SATA *73, 124*
Dunbar, Fiona 1961- *167*
Dunbar, Joyce 1944- *162*
    Earlier sketches in SATA *76, 112*
Dunbar, Paul Laurence 1872-1906 .... *34*
Dunbar, Polly 1980(?)- *181*
Dunbar, Robert E(verett) 1926- *32*
Duncan, Alexandra
    See Moore, Ishbel (Lindsay)
Duncan, Alice Faye 1967- *168*
    Earlier sketch in SATA *95*
Duncan, Gregory
    See McClintock, Marshall
Duncan, Jane
    See Cameron, Elizabeth Jane
Duncan, Julia K.
    See Benson, Mildred
Duncan, Lois 1934- *141*
    Autobiography Feature *141*
    Earlier sketches in SATA *1, 36, 75, 133*
    See also CLR *129*
    See also SAAS *2*
Duncan, Norman 1871-1916
    See YABC *1*
Duncan, Terence
    See Nolan, William F(rancis)
Duncombe, Frances (Riker) 1900-1994 .... *25*
    Obituary *82*
Dungy, Anthony
    See Dungy, Tony
Dungy, Tony 1955- *206*
Dunham, Montrew 1919- *162*
Dunham, Montrew Goetz
    See Dunham, Montrew
Dunkle, Clare B. 1964- *155*
Dunlap, Julie 1958- *84*
Dunleavy, Deborah 1951- *133*
Dunlop, Agnes M. R. (?)-1982 .... *87*
Dunlop, Eileen (Rhona) 1938- *76*
    Earlier sketch in SATA *24*
    See also SAAS *12*
Dunmore, Helen 1952- *201*
Dunn, Anne M. 1940- *107*
Dunn, Harvey T(homas) 1884-1952 .... *34*
Dunn, Herb
    See Gutman, Dan
Dunn, John M. (III) 1949- *93*
Dunn, Judy
    See Spangenberg, Judith Dunn
Dunn, Mary Lois 1930- *6*
Dunnahoo, Terry Janson 1927- *7*
Dunne, Jeanette 1952- *72*
Dunne, Kathleen 1933- *126*
Dunne, Marie
    See Clark, Ann Nolan
Dunne, Mary Collins 1914- *11*
Dunne, Mary Jo
    See Dunne, Mary Collins
Dunnett, Kaitlyn
    See Emerson, Kathy Lynn
Dunnett, Margaret (Rosalind) 1909-1977 ..... *42*
Dunnick, Regan *178*
Dunrea, Olivier 1953- *160*
    Brief entry *46*
    Earlier sketches in SATA *59, 118*

Dunrea, Olivier Jean-Paul Dominique
See Dunrea, Olivier
Dunton, Dorothy 1912- 92
Dupasquier, Philippe 1955- 151
Earlier sketch in SATA 86
DuPrau, Jeanne 1944- 144
Dupuy, T(revor) N(evitt) 1916-1995 4
Obituary 86
DuQuette, Keith 1960- 155
Earlier sketch in SATA 90
Duran, Gloria 1924- 171
Duran, Gloria Bradley
See Duran, Gloria
Duranceau, Suzanne 1952- 162
Durand, Delphine 1971- 200
Durango, Julia 1967- 173
Durant, Alan 1958- 165
Earlier sketch in SATA 121
Durant, John 1902- 27
Durbin, William 1951- 174
Earlier sketch in SATA 143
Durell, Ann 1930- 66
Durkee, Sarah 173
Durney, Ryan 205
Durrant, Lynda 1954- 148
Earlier sketch in SATA 96
Durrell, Gerald (Malcolm) 1925-1995 8
Obituary 84
Durrell, Julie 1955- 94
Durrett, Deanne 1940- 144
Earlier sketch in SATA 92
Durst, Sarah Beth 1974- 203
Du Soe, Robert C. 1892-1958
See YABC 2
Dussling, Jennifer 1970- 143
Earlier sketch in SATA 96
DuTemple, Lesley A. 1952- 113
Dutton, Sandra 191
Dutz
See Davis, Mary Octavia
Duval, Katherine
See James, Elizabeth
Duval, Kathy 1946- 181
Duvall, Aimee
See Thurlo, Aimee
and Thurlo, David
Duvall, Evelyn Millis 1906- 9
Duvall, Jill D(onovan) 1932- 102
Duvoisin, Roger (Antoine) 1904-1980 30
Obituary 23
Earlier sketch in SATA 2
See also CLR 23
Dwiggins, Don(ald J.) 1913-1988 4
Obituary 60
Dwight, Allan
See Cole, Lois Dwight
Dwyer, Deanna
See Koontz, Dean R.
Dwyer, K.R.
See Koontz, Dean R.
Dyck, Peter J. 1914- 75
Dyer, James (Frederick) 1934- 37
Dyer, Jane 191
Earlier sketch in SATA 147
Dyess, John (Foster) 1939- 76
Dygard, Thomas J. 1931-1996 97
Obituary 92
Earlier sketch in SATA 24
See also SAAS 15
Dyke, John 1935- 35

E

E. V. L.
See Lucas, E(dward) V(errall)
Eagar, Frances (Elisabeth Stuart)
1940-1978 11
Obituary 55

Eager, Edward (McMaken) 1911-1964 17
See also CLR 43
Eager, George 1921- 56
Eager, George B.
See Eager, George
Eagle, Ellen 1953- 61
Eagle, Kin
See Adlerman, Daniel (Ezra)
and Adlerman, Kimberly M(arie)
Eagle, Mike 1942- 11
Earle, Olive L(ydia) 1888-1982 7
Earle, William
See Johns, W(illiam) E(arle)
Earls, Nick 1963- 156
Earlier sketch in SATA 95
Early, Jack
See Scoppettone, Sandra
Early, Jon
See Johns, W(illiam) E(arle)
Early, Margaret 1951- 72
Earnshaw, Brian 1929- 17
Earnshaw, Micky
See Earnshaw, Spencer Wright
Earnshaw, Spencer Wright 1939- 88
Easley, MaryAnn 94
Eason, Alethea 1957- 197
Eastman, Charles A(lexander) 1858-1939
See YABC 1
Eastman, P(hilip) D(ey) 1909-1986 33
Obituary 46
Easton, Kelly 1960- 192
Earlier sketch in SATA 141
Eastwick, Ivy (Ethel) O(live) 3
Eaton, Anne T(haxter) 1881-1971 32
Eaton, Anthony 1971- 167
Eaton, George L.
See Verral, Charles Spain
Eaton, Janet
See Givens, Janet E(aton)
Eaton, Jeanette 1886-1968 24
Eaton, Maxwell III 1981- 199
Eaton, Tom 1940- 22
Ebbeler, Jeff
See Ebbeler, Jeffrey
Ebbeler, Jeffrey 1974- 206
Ebel, Alex 1927- 11
Eber, Dorothy (Margaret) Harley 1930- 27
Eberhart, Sheri S.
See Tepper, Sheri S.
Eberle, Irmengarde 1898-1979 2
Obituary 23
Eble, Diane 1956- 74
Eboch, Chris 113
Eccles Williams, Ferelith 1920- 22
Echlin, Kim 1955- 166
Eckblad, Edith Berven 1923- 23
Ecke, Wolfgang 1927-1983
Obituary 37
Eckert, Allan W. 1931- 91
Brief entry 27
Earlier sketch in SATA 29
See also SAAS 21
Eckert, Horst 1931- 72
Earlier sketch in SATA 8
See also CLR 26
Ecklar, Julia (Marie) 1964- 112
Eddings, David 1931-2009 91
Eddings, David Carroll
See Eddings, David
Ede, Janina 1937- 33
Edell, Celeste 12
Edelman, Lily (Judith) 1915-1981 22
Edelson, Edward 1932- 51
Edens, Cooper 1945- 166
Earlier sketches in SATA 49, 112
Edens, (Bishop) David 1926- 39
Edey, Maitland A(rmstrong) 1910-1992 25
Obituary 71
Edgerton, Perky 196
Edgeworth, Maria 1768-1849 21

Edgy, Wardore
See Gorey, Edward (St. John)
Edison, Theodore
See Stratemeyer, Edward L.
Edler, Tim(othy) 1948- 56
Edmiston, Jim 1948- 80
Edmonds, I(vy) G(ordon) 1917- 8
Edmonds, Walter D(umaux) 1903-1998 27
Obituary 99
Earlier sketch in SATA 1
See also SAAS 4
Edmund, Sean
See Pringle, Laurence
Edsall, Marian (Stickney) 1920- 8
Edwards, Al
See Nourse, Alan E(dward)
Edwards, Anne 1927- 35
Edwards, Audrey 1947- 52
Brief entry 31
Edwards, Becky (Jane) 1966- 125
Edwards, Bertram
See Edwards, Herbert Charles
Edwards, Bronwen Elizabeth
See Rose, Wendy
Edwards, Cecile Pepin 1916- 25
Edwards, David 1962- 198
Edwards, Dorothy 1914-1982 88
Obituary 31
Earlier sketch in SATA 4
Edwards, F. E.
See Nolan, William F(rancis)
Edwards, Frank B. 1952- 93
Edwards, Gunvor 32
Edwards, Harvey 1929- 5
Edwards, Hazel (Eileen) 1945- 135
Edwards, Herbert Charles 1912- 12
Edwards, Jane Campbell 1932- 10
Edwards, Julia
See Stratemeyer, Edward L.
Edwards, Julie
See Andrews, Julie
Edwards, Julie Andrews
See Andrews, Julie
Edwards, June
See Bhatia, Jamunadevi
Edwards, Linda Strauss 1948- 49
Brief entry 42
Edwards, Margaret (Alexander) 1902-1988
Obituary 56
Edwards, Michelle 1955- 152
Earlier sketch in SATA 70
Edwards, Monica le Doux Newton
1912-1998 12
Edwards, Olwen
See Gater, Dilys
Edwards, Page (Lawrence, Jr.) 1941-1999 ... 59
Edwards, Pamela Duncan 189
Edwards, R. T.
See Goulart, Ron
Edwards, Sally (Cary) 1929- 7
Edwards, Samuel
See Gerson, Noel Bertram
Edwards, Wallace 1957(?)- 170
Egan, E(dward) W(elstead) 1922- 35
Egan, Kerry 175
Egan, Lorraine Hopping 1960- 134
Earlier sketch in SATA 91
Egan, Tim 1957- 191
Earlier sketches in SATA 89, 155
Egermeier, Elsie E(milie) 1890-1986 65
Eggenberger, David 1918- 6
Eggleston, Edward 1837-1902 27
Egielski, Richard 1952- 163
Earlier sketches in SATA 11, 49, 106
Egypt, Ophelia Settle 1903-1984 16
Obituary 38
Ehlert, Lois 1934- 172
Earlier sketches in SATA 35, 69, 128
See also CLR 28
Ehlert, Lois Jane
See Ehlert, Lois

Ehling, Katalin Olah 1941- *93*
Ehrenfreund, Norbert 1921- *86*
Ehrenhaft, Daniel 1970- *185*
Ehrhardt, Karen 1963- *184*
Ehrlich, Amy 1942- *132*
    Earlier sketches in SATA 25, 65, 96
Ehrlich, Bettina Bauer 1903-1985 .... *1*
Ehrlich, Fred *205*
Ehrlich, Fred M.D.
    See Ehrlich, Fred
Ehrlich, H. M.
    See Ziefert, Harriet
Eichenberg, Fritz 1901-1990 .... *50*
    Earlier sketch in SATA 9
Eichler, Margrit 1942- *35*
Eichner, James A. 1927- *4*
Eidson, Thomas 1944- *112*
Eifert, Virginia (Louise) S(nider) 1911-1966 . *2*
Eige, (Elizabeth) Lillian 1915- *65*
Eiken, J. Melia 1967- *125*
Einhorn, Edward 1970- *204*
Einsel, Naiad *10*
Einsel, Walter 1926- *10*
Einzig, Susan 1922- *43*
Eiseman, Alberta 1925- *15*
Eisenberg, Azriel (Louis) 1903-1985 .... *12*
Eisenberg, Lisa 1949- *155*
    Brief entry *50*
    Earlier sketch in SATA 57
Eisenberg, Phyllis Rose 1924- *41*
Eisner, Vivienne
    See Margolis, Vivienne
Eisner, Will 1917-2005 .... *165*
    Earlier sketch in SATA 31
Eisner, William Erwin
    See Eisner, Will
Eitzen, Allan 1928- *9*
Eitzen, Ruth (Carper) 1924- *9*
Ekwensi, C. O. D.
    See Ekwensi, Cyprian
Ekwensi, Cyprian 1921-2007 .... *66*
Ekwensi, Cyprian Odiatu Duaka
    See Ekwensi, Cyprian
Elam, Richard M(ace, Jr.) 1920- *9*
Elborn, Andrew
    See Clements, Andrew
    and Clements, Andrew
Elboz, Stephen 1956- *152*
Eldin, Peter 1939- *154*
Eldon, Kathy 1946- *107*
Eldridge, Marion *199*
Elfman, Blossom 1925- *8*
Elgin, Kathleen 1923- *39*
Elia
    See Lamb, Charles
Eliot, A. D.
    See Jewett, (Theodora) Sarah Orne
Eliot, Alice
    See Jewett, (Theodora) Sarah Orne
Eliot, Anne
    See Cole, Lois Dwight
Eliot, Dan
    See Silverberg, Robert
Elish, Dan 1960- *204*
    Earlier sketches in SATA 68, 129
Elisha, Ron 1951- *104*
Elisofon, Eliot 1911-1973
    Obituary *21*
Elkeles, Simone 1970- *187*
Elkin, Benjamin 1911-1995 .... *3*
Elkins, Dov Peretz 1937- *5*
Ellacott, S(amuel) E(rnest) 1911- *19*
Elleman, Barbara 1934- *147*
Ellen, Jaye
    See Nixon, Joan Lowery
Eller, Scott
    See Holinger, William (Jacques)
    and Shepard, Jim
Ellestad, Myrvin
    See Ellestad, Myrvin H.
Ellestad, Myrvin H. 1921- *120*

Elliot, David 1952- *122*
Elliott, Bruce
    See Field, Edward
Elliott, David 1947- *201*
    Earlier sketch in SATA 163
Elliott, Don
    See Silverberg, Robert
Elliott, Elizabeth Shippen Green
    See Green, Elizabeth Shippen
Elliott, Janice 1931-1995 .... *119*
Elliott, Joey
    See Houk, Randy
Elliott, Laura Malone 1957- *197*
Elliott, Louise *111*
Elliott, Odette 1939- *75*
Elliott, Patricia 1946- *176*
Elliott, Sarah M(cCarn) 1930- *14*
Elliott, (Robert) Scott 1970- *153*
Elliott, William
    See Bradbury, Ray
Elliott, Zetta *206*
Ellis, (Mary) Amabel (Nassau Strachey)
    Williams
    See Williams-Ellis, (Mary) Amabel (Nassau
    Strachey)
Ellis, Anyon
    See Rowland-Entwistle, (Arthur) Theodore
    (Henry)
Ellis, Carson 1975- *190*
Ellis, Carson Friedman
    See Ellis, Carson
Ellis, Deborah 1960- *187*
    Earlier sketch in SATA 129
Ellis, E. S.
    See Ellis, Edward S.
Ellis, Edward S. 1840-1916
    See YABC 1
Ellis, Edward Sylvester
    See Ellis, Edward S.
Ellis, Ella Thorp 1928- *127*
    Earlier sketch in SATA 7
    See also SAAS 9
Ellis, Harry Bearse 1921-2004 .... *9*
Ellis, Herbert
    See Wilson, Lionel
Ellis, Mel(vin Richard) 1912-1984 .... *7*
    Obituary *39*
Ellis, Richard 1938- *130*
Ellis, Sarah 1952- *179*
    Earlier sketches in SATA 68, 131
    See also CLR 42
Ellison, Chris *196*
Ellison, Emily *114*
Ellison, Lucile Watkins 1907(?)-1979 .... *50*
    Obituary *22*
Ellison, Virginia H(owell) 1910- *4*
Ellsberg, Edward 1891-1983 .... *7*
Ellsworth, Loretta 1954- *199*
Ellsworth, Mary Ellen (Tressel) 1940- *146*
Elmer, Robert 1958- *154*
    Earlier sketch in SATA 99
Elmore, (Carolyn) Patricia 1933- *38*
    Brief entry *35*
El-Moslimany, Ann P(axton) 1937- *90*
Elschner, Geraldine 1954- *183*
Elspeth
    See Bragdon, Elspeth MacDuffie
Elster, Jean Alicia 1953- *150*
Elting, Mary 1906- *88*
    Earlier sketch in SATA 2
    See also SAAS 20
Elvgren, Jennifer Riesmeyer *179*
Elwart, Joan Potter 1927- *2*
Elwood, Ann 1931- *55*
    Brief entry *52*
Elwood, Roger 1943-2007 .... *58*
Elya, Susan Middleton 1955- *202*
    Earlier sketches in SATA 106, 159
Elzbieta *88*
Ember, Kathi *190*

Emberley, Barbara A. 1932- *146*
    Earlier sketches in SATA 8, 70
    See also CLR 5
Emberley, Barbara Anne
    See Emberley, Barbara A.
Emberley, Ed 1931- *146*
    Earlier sketches in SATA 8, 70
    See also CLR 81
Emberley, Edward Randolph
    See Emberley, Ed
Emberley, Michael 1960- *189*
    Earlier sketches in SATA 34, 80, 119
Embry, Margaret Jacob 1919-1975 .... *5*
Emecheta, Buchi 1944- *66*
Emecheta, Florence Onye Buchi
    See Emecheta, Buchi
Emerson, Alice B.
    See Benson, Mildred
Emerson, Kathy Lynn 1947- *63*
Emerson, Ru 1944- *107*
    Earlier sketch in SATA 70
Emerson, Sally 1952- *111*
Emerson, William K(eith) 1925- *25*
Emert, Phyllis R(aybin) 1947- *93*
Emery, Anne (McGuigan) 1907- *33*
    Earlier sketch in SATA 1
Emmens, Carol Ann 1944- *39*
Emmett, Jonathan 1965- *188*
    Earlier sketch in SATA 138
Emmons, Della (Florence) Gould 1890-1983
    Obituary *39*
Emory, Jerry 1957- *96*
Emrich, Duncan (Black Macdonald)
    1908-1970(?) *11*
Emshwiller, Carol 1921- *174*
    Autobiography Feature *174*
Emshwiller, Carol Fries
    See Emshwiller, Carol
Emslie, M. L.
    See Simpson, Myrtle L(illias)
Ende, Michael (Andreas Helmuth)
    1929-1995 .... *130*
    Brief entry *42*
    Obituary *86*
    Earlier sketch in SATA 61
    See also CLR 138
Enderle, Dotti 1954- *203*
    Earlier sketch in SATA 145
Enderle, Judith (Ann) Ross 1941- *89*
    Autobiography Feature *114*
    Earlier sketch in SATA 38
    See also SAAS 26
Enell, Trinka (Gochenour) 1951- *79*
Enfield, Carrie
    See Smith, Susan Vernon
Engdahl, Sylvia Louise 1933- *4*
    Autobiography Feature *122*
    See also CLR 2
    See also SAAS 5
Engel, Diana 1947- *70*
Engelbreit, Mary 1952- *169*
Engelhart, Margaret S. 1924- *59*
Engelmann, Kim (V.) 1959- *87*
England, George Allan 1877-1936 .... *102*
Englart, Mindi Rose 1965- *146*
Engle, Eloise
    See Paananen, Eloise (Katherine)
Engle, Margarita 1951- *193*
Englebert, Victor 1933- *8*
English, James W(ilson) 1915- *37*
English, Karen *202*
Engstrom, Elizabeth 1951- *110*
Enright, D(ennis) J(oseph) 1920-2002 .... *25*
    Obituary *140*
Enright, Dominique *194*
Enright, Elizabeth (Wright) 1909-1968 .... *9*
    See also CLR 4
Ensor, Barbara *180*
Ensor, Robert (T.) 1922- *93*
Enthoven, Sam 1974- *187*

Entwistle, (Arthur) Theodore (Henry) Rowland
  See Rowland-Entwistle, (Arthur) Theodore
  (Henry)
Enys, Sarah L.
  See Sloggett, Nellie
Epanya, Christian A(rthur Kingue) 1956- *91*
Ephraim, Shelly S(chonebaum) 1952- *97*
Ephron, Delia 1944- *197*
  Brief entry *50*
  Earlier sketch in SATA *65*
Epler, Doris M. 1928- *73*
Epp, Margaret A(gnes) 1913- *20*
Eppenstein, Louise (Kohn) 1892-1987
  Obituary *54*
Epple, Anne Orth 1927- *20*
Epstein, Anne Merrick 1931- *20*
Epstein, Beryl 1910- *31*
  Earlier sketch in SATA *1*
  See also CLR *26*
  See also SAAS *17*
Epstein, Beryl M. Williams
  See Epstein, Beryl
Epstein, Perle S(herry) 1938- *27*
Epstein, Rachel S. 1941- *102*
Epstein, Samuel 1909-2000 .... *31*
  Earlier sketch in SATA *1*
  See also CLR *26*
  See also SAAS *17*
Erdman, Loula Grace 1905(?)-1976 .... *1*
Erdoes, Richard 1912- *33*
  Brief entry *28*
Erdogan, Buket *187*
Erdrich, Karen Louise
  See Erdrich, Louise
Erdrich, Louise 1954- *141*
  Earlier sketch in SATA *94*
Erickson, Betty J. 1923- *97*
Erickson, Betty Jean
  See Erickson, Betty J.
Erickson, John R. 1943- *136*
  Earlier sketch in SATA *70*
Erickson, Jon 1948- *141*
Erickson, Phoebe *59*
Erickson, Russell E(verett) 1932- *27*
Erickson, Sabra Rollins 1912-1995 .... *35*
Erickson, Walter
  See Fast, Howard
Ericson, Walter
  See Fast, Howard
Ericsson, Jennifer A. *170*
Erikson, Mel 1937- *31*
Ering, Timothy Basil *176*
Erlanger, Baba
  See Trahey, Jane
Erlbach, Arlene 1948- *160*
  Earlier sketches in SATA *78, 115*
Erlbruch, Wolf 1948- *181*
Erlich, Lillian (Feldman) 1910-1983 .... *10*
Erlings, Fridrik 1962- *196*
Erlingsson, Frierik
  See Erlings, Fridrik
Ermatinger, James W. 1959- *170*
Ernest, William
  See Berkebile, Fred D(onovan)
Ernst, (Lyman) John 1940- *39*
Ernst, Kathleen
  See Ernst, Kathleen A.
Ernst, Kathleen A. 1959- *162*
Ernst, Kathryn (Fitzgerald) 1942- *25*
Ernst, Lisa Campbell 1957- *154*
  Brief entry *44*
  Earlier sketches in SATA *55, 95*
Erskine, Kathryn *193*
Ervin, Janet Halliday 1923- *4*
Erwin, Will
  See Eisner, Will
Esbaum, Jill *174*
Esbensen, Barbara J(uster) 1925-1996 .... *97*
  Brief entry *53*
  Earlier sketch in SATA *62*
Eschbacher, Roger *160*

Eschmeyer, R. E. 1898-1989 .... *29*
Escriva, Vivi *182*
Eseki, Bruno
  See Mphahlele, Es'kia
Esekie, Bruno
  See Mphahlele, Es'kia
Eshmeyer, Reinhart Ernst
  See Eschmeyer, R. E.
Eskridge, Ann E. 1949- *84*
Espeland, Pamela (Lee) 1951- *128*
  Brief entry *38*
  Earlier sketch in SATA *52*
Espinosa, Laura *203*
Espinosa, Leo *203*
Espriella, Don Manuel Alvarez
  See Southey, Robert
Espy, Willard R(ichardson) 1910-1999 .... *38*
  Obituary *113*
Essakalli, Julie Klear *200*
Essrig, Harry 1912- *66*
Estep, Irene Compton *5*
Esterl, Arnica 1933- *77*
Estes, Eleanor (Ruth) 1906-1988 .... *91*
  Obituary *56*
  Earlier sketch in SATA *7*
  See also CLR *70*
Estoril, Jean
  See Allan, Mabel Esther
Estrada, Pau 1961- *200*
  Earlier sketch in SATA *74*
Etchemendy, Nancy 1952- *166*
  Earlier sketch in SATA *38*
Etchemendy, Nancy Elise Howell
  See Etchemendy, Nancy
Etchison, Birdie L(ee) 1937- *38*
Etchison, Craig 1945- *133*
Etherington, Frank 1945- *58*
Eton, Robert
  See Meynell, Laurence Walter
Ets, Marie Hall 1893-1984 .... *2*
  See also CLR *33*
Ettlinger, Doris 1950- *173*
Eunson, (John) Dale 1904-2002 .... *5*
  Obituary *132*
Evan, Frances Y. 1951- *167*
Evanoff, Vlad 1916- *59*
Evans, Cambria 1981- *178*
Evans, Douglas 1953- *144*
  Earlier sketch in SATA *93*
Evans, Eva (Knox) 1905-1998 .... *27*
Evans, Freddi Williams 1957- *134*
Evans, Greg 1947- *143*
  Earlier sketch in SATA *73*
Evans, Hubert Reginald 1892-1986 .... *118*
  Obituary *48*
Evans, Katherine (Floyd) 1901-1964 .... *5*
Evans, Larry
  See Evans, Laurence Chubb
Evans, Laurence Chubb 1939- *88*
Evans, Lawrence Watt
  See Watt-Evans, Lawrence
Evans, Lezlie *180*
Evans, Mari 1923- *10*
Evans, Mark *19*
Evans, Nancy 1950- *65*
Evans, Nate *201*
Evans, Patricia Healy
  See Carpenter, Patricia (Healy Evans)
Evans, (Alice) Pearl 1927- *83*
Evans, Shane W. *189*
Evans, Shirlee 1931- *58*
Evans, Tabor
  See Cameron, Lou
  and Knott, William C(ecil, Jr.)
  and Wallmann, Jeffrey M(iner)
  and Whittington, Harry (Benjamin)
Evarts, Esther
  See Benson, Sally
Evarts, Hal G., (Jr.) 1915-1989 .... *6*
Everett, Gail
  See Hale, Arlene

Evernden, Margery 1916- *5*
Eversole, Robyn 1971- *74*
Eversole, Robyn H.
  See Eversole, Robyn
Eversole, Robyn Harbert
  See Eversole, Robyn
Evslin, Bernard 1922-1993 .... *83*
  Brief entry *28*
  Obituary *77*
  Earlier sketch in SATA *45*
Ewart, Claire 1958- *145*
  Earlier sketch in SATA *76*
Ewart, Franzeska G. 1950- *205*
Ewen, David 1907-1985 .... *4*
  Obituary *47*
Ewing, Juliana (Horatia Gatty) 1841-1885 ... *16*
  See also CLR *78*
Ewing, Kathryn 1921- *20*
Eyerly, Jeannette 1908-2008 .... *86*
  Obituary *196*
  Earlier sketch in SATA *4*
  See also SAAS *10*
Eyerly, Jeannette Hyde
  See Eyerly, Jeannette
Eyre, Dorothy
  See McGuire, Leslie (Sarah)
Eyre, Frank 1910-1988
  Obituary *62*
Eyre, Katherine Wigmore 1901-1970 .... *26*
Ezzell, Marilyn 1937- *42*
  Brief entry *38*

F

Fabe, Maxene 1943- *15*
Faber, Doris (Greenberg) 1924- *78*
  Earlier sketch in SATA *3*
Faber, Harold 1919- *5*
Fabre, Jean Henri (Casimir) 1823-1915 .... *22*
Fabry, Glenn 1961- *205*
Facklam, Margaret
  See Thomas, Peggy
Facklam, Margery (Metz) 1927- *132*
  Earlier sketches in SATA *20, 85*
Fadden, David Kanietakeron *196*
Fadiman, Clifton (Paul) 1904-1999 .... *11*
  Obituary *115*
Fagan, Cary 1957- *186*
Fahs, Sophia Blanche Lyon 1876-1978 ...... *102*
Failing, Barbara Larmon *182*
Fain, Sarah 1971- *204*
Fair, David 1952- *96*
Fair, Sylvia 1933- *13*
Fairfax-Lucy, Brian (Fulke Cameron-Ramsay)
  1898-1974 .... *6*
  Obituary *26*
Fairfield, Flora
  See Alcott, Louisa May
Fairlie, Gerard 1899-1983
  Obituary *34*
Fairman, Joan A(lexandra) 1935- *10*
Faithfull, Gail 1936- *8*
Falcone, L(ucy) M. 1951- *155*
Falconer, Ian 1959- *179*
  Earlier sketch in SATA *125*
  See also CLR *146*
Falconer, James
  See Kirkup, James
Falconer, Lee N.
  See May, Julian
Falkner, Brian 1962- *206*
Falkner, Leonard 1900-1977 .... *12*
Fall, Andrew
  See Arthur, Robert, (Jr.)
Fall, Thomas
  See Snow, Donald Clifford
Faller, Regis 1968- *187*
Falls, C(harles) B(uckles) 1874-1960 .... *38*
  Brief entry *27*

Falstein, Louis 1909-1995 .... *37*
Falwell, Cathryn 1952- *196*
Fancher, Lou 1960- *177*
Fanelli, Sara 1969- *126*
  Earlier sketch in SATA *89*
Fanning, Leonard M(ulliken) 1888-1967 .... *5*
Faralla, Dana 1909- *9*
Faralla, Dorothy W.
  See Faralla, Dana
Farb, Peter 1929-1980 .... *12*
  Obituary *22*
Farber, Norma 1909-1984 .... *75*
  Obituary *38*
  Earlier sketch in SATA *25*
Fardell, John 1967- *195*
Farish, Terry 1947- *146*
  Earlier sketch in SATA *82*
Farjeon, (Eve) Annabel 1919-2004 .... *11*
  Obituary *153*
Farjeon, Eleanor 1881-1965 .... *2*
  See also CLR *34*
Farley, Carol (J.) 1936- *137*
  Earlier sketch in SATA *4*
Farley, Terri *165*
Farley, Walter (Lorimer) 1915-1989 .... *132*
  Earlier sketches in SATA *2, 43*
Farlow, James O(rville, Jr.) 1951- *75*
Farmer, Nancy 1941- *161*
  Earlier sketches in SATA *79, 117*
Farmer, Patti 1948- *79*
Farmer, Penelope (Jane) 1939- *105*
  Brief entry *39*
  Earlier sketch in SATA *40*
  See also CLR *8*
  See also SAAS *22*
Farmer, Peter 1950- *38*
Farmer, Philip Jose
  See Farmer, Philip Jose
Farmer, Philip Jose 1918-2009 .... *93*
  Obituary *201*
Farmer, Philipe Jos
  See Farmer, Philip Jose
Farnham, Burt
  See Clifford, Harold B(urton)
Farnsworth, Bill 1958- *186*
  Earlier sketches in SATA *84, 135*
Farquhar, Margaret C(utting) 1905-1988 ...... *13*
Farquharson, Alexander 1944- *46*
Farquharson, Martha
  See Finley, Martha
Farr, Diana *82*
  Earlier sketch in SATA *3*
Farr, Finis (King) 1904-1982 .... *10*
Farrar, Jill
  See Morris, Jill
Farrar, Susan Clement 1917- *33*
Farrell, Ben
  See Cebulash, Mel
Farrell, John 1951- *204*
Farrell, Patrick
  See Odgers, Sally Farrell
Farrell, Sally
  See Odgers, Sally Farrell
Farrer, Vashti *167*
Farrington, Benjamin 1891-1974
  Obituary *20*
Farrington, S(elwyn) Kip, Jr. 1904-1983 ...... *20*
Farris, Christine King 1927- *206*
Farshtey, Greg(ory T.) 1965- *148*
Farthing, Alison 1936- *45*
  Brief entry *36*
Farthing-Knight, Catherine 1933- *92*
Fassler, Joan (Grace) 1931- *11*
Fast, Howard 1914-2003 .... *7*
  Autobiography Feature *107*
Fast, Howard Melvin
  See Fast, Howard
Fasulo, Michael 1963- *83*
Fatchen, Max 1920- *84*
  Earlier sketch in SATA *20*
  See also SAAS *20*

Fate, Marilyn
  See Collins, Paul
Father Goose
  See Ghigna, Charles
Fatigati, (Frances) Evelyn 1948- *24*
Fatio, Louise 1904-1993 .... *6*
Fatus, Sophie 1957- *182*
Faulhaber, Martha 1926- *7*
Faulkner, Anne Irvin 1906- *23*
Faulkner, Frank
  See Ellis, Edward S.
Faulkner, Nancy
  See Faulkner, Anne Irvin
Faulknor, Cliff(ord Vernon) 1913- *86*
Favole, Robert J(ames) 1950- *125*
Fax, Elton Clay 1909-1993 .... *25*
Faxon, Lavinia
  See Russ, Lavinia (Faxon)
Feagles, Anita M(acRae) 1927- *9*
Feagles, Elizabeth
  See Day, Beth (Feagles)
Feague, Mildred H. 1915- *14*
Fearnley, Jan 1965- *205*
  Earlier sketch in SATA *153*
Fearrington, Ann (Peyton) 1945- *146*
Fecher, Constance
  See Heaven, Constance (Christina)
Feder, Chris Welles 1938- *81*
Feder, Harriet K. 1928- *73*
Feder, Paula (Kurzband) 1935- *26*
Federici, Debbie 1965- *175*
Federici, Debbie Tanner
  See Federici, Debbie
Feelings, Muriel 1938- *16*
  See also CLR *5*
  See also SAAS *8*
Feelings, Muriel Lavita Grey
  See Feelings, Muriel
Feelings, Thomas 1933-2003 .... *69*
  Obituary *148*
  Earlier sketch in SATA *8*
  See also CLR *58*
  See also SAAS *19*
Feelings, Tom
  See Feelings, Thomas
Fehler, Gene 1940- *201*
  Earlier sketch in SATA *74*
Fehrenbach, T(heodore) R(eed, Jr.) 1925- *33*
Feiffer, Jules 1929- *201*
  Earlier sketches in SATA *8, 61, 111, 157*
Feiffer, Jules Ralph
  See Feiffer, Jules
Feiffer, Kate 1964- *206*
  Earlier sketch in SATA *170*
Feig, Barbara Krane 1937- *34*
Feikema, Feike
  See Manfred, Frederick (Feikema)
Feil, Hila 1942- *12*
Feilen, John
  See May, Julian
Feinberg, Barbara Jane 1938- *123*
  Earlier sketch in SATA *58*
Feinberg, Barbara Silberdick
  See Feinberg, Barbara Jane
Feinstein, John 1956- *195*
  Earlier sketch in SATA *163*
Feldman, Anne (Rodgers) 1939- *19*
Feldman, Elane *79*
Feldman, Jody *200*
Felin, M. Sindy *194*
Felix
  See Vincent, Felix
Fell, Derek 1939- *167*
Fell, Derek John
  See Fell, Derek
Fellowes, Julian 1950- *198*
Fellows, Muriel H. *10*
Fellows, Stan 1957- *177*
Fellows, Stanley
  See Fellows, Stan

Felsen, Henry Gregor 1916-1995 .... *1*
  See also SAAS *2*
Felstead, Cathie 1954- *192*
Feltenstein, Arlene (H.) 1934- *119*
Felton, Harold William 1902-1991 .... *1*
Felton, Ronald Oliver 1909- *3*
Felts, Shirley 1934- *33*
Fenderson, Lewis H., Jr. 1907-1983 .... *47*
  Obituary *37*
Fenner, Carol (Elizabeth) 1929-2002 .... *89*
  Obituary *132*
  Earlier sketch in SATA *7*
  See also SAAS *24*
Fenner, Phyllis R(eid) 1899-1982 .... *1*
  Obituary *29*
Fensham, Elizabeth *169*
Fenten, Barbara D(oris) 1935- *26*
Fenten, D(onald) X. 1932- *4*
Fenton, Carroll Lane 1900-1969 .... *5*
Fenton, Edward 1917-1995 .... *7*
  Obituary *89*
Fenton, Mildred Adams 1899-1995 .... *21*
Fenwick, Patti
  See Grider, Dorothy
Feravolo, Rocco Vincent 1922- *10*
Ferber, Brenda A. 1967- *184*
Ferber, Edna 1887-1968 .... *7*
Fergus, Charles *114*
Ferguson, Alane 1957- *182*
  Earlier sketch in SATA *85*
Ferguson, Bob
  See Ferguson, Robert Bruce
Ferguson, Cecil 1931- *45*
Ferguson, Peter 1968- *199*
Ferguson, Robert Bruce 1927-2001 .... *13*
Ferguson, Sarah 1959- *180*
  Earlier sketches in SATA *66, 110*
Ferguson, Sarah Margaret
  See Ferguson, Sarah
Ferguson, Walter (W.) 1930- *34*
Fergusson, Erna 1888-1964 .... *5*
Fermi, Laura 1907-1977 .... *6*
  Obituary *28*
Fern, Eugene A. 1919-1987 .... *10*
  Obituary *54*
Fern, Tracey E. *202*
Fernandes, Eugenie 1943- *205*
  Earlier sketches in SATA *77, 139*
Fernandez, Laura 1960- *171*
Ferrari, Maria *123*
Ferreiro, Carmen 1958- *158*
Ferrell, Nancy Warren 1932- *70*
Ferri, Giuliano 1965- *197*
Ferrier, Lucy
  See Penzler, Otto
Ferris, Helen Josephine 1890-1969 .... *21*
Ferris, James Cody
  See McFarlane, Leslie
Ferris, Jean 1939- *202*
  Brief entry *50*
  Earlier sketches in SATA *56, 105, 149*
Ferris, Jeri Chase 1937- *84*
Ferry, Charles 1927- *92*
  Earlier sketch in SATA *43*
  See also CLR *34*
  See also SAAS *20*
Fetz, Ingrid 1915- *30*
Feydy, Anne Lindbergh
  See Sapieyevski, Anne Lindbergh
Fiammenghi, Gioia 1929- *66*
  Earlier sketch in SATA *9*
Fiarotta, Noel
  See Ficarotta, Noel
Fiarotta, Phyllis
  See Ficarotta, Phyllis
Ficarotta, Noel 1944- *15*
Ficarotta, Phyllis 1942- *15*
Fichter, George S. 1922-1993 .... *7*
Ficocelli, Elizabeth *189*

Fidler, Kathleen (Annie) 1899-1980 87
 Obituary 45
 Earlier sketch in SATA 3
Fiedler, Jean(nette Feldman) 4
Fiedler, Joseph Daniel 159
Fiedler, Lisa 185
Field, Dorothy 1944- 97
Field, Edward 1924- 109
 Earlier sketch in SATA 8
Field, Elinor Whitney 1889-1980
 Obituary 28
Field, Eugene 1850-1895 16
Field, Gans T.
 See Wellman, Manly Wade
Field, James 1959- 113
Field, Peter
 See Drago, Harry Sinclair
 and Dresser, Davis
 and Mann, E(dward) B(everly)
Field, Rachel (Lyman) 1894-1942 15
 See also CLR 21
Fielding, Kate
 See Oldfield, Jenny
Fields, Bryan W. 1958(?)- 188
Fields, Terri 1948- 191
Fields, T.S.
 See Fields, Terri
Fienberg, Anna 1956- 183
 Earlier sketch in SATA 112
Fiery, Ann
 See Barrows, Annie
Fife, Dale (Odile Hollerbach) 1901- 18
Fighter Pilot, A
 See Johnston, H(ugh) A(nthony) S(tephen)
Figler, Jeanie 1949- 123
Figley, Marty Rhodes 1948- 158
 Earlier sketch in SATA 88
Figueredo, D(anilo) H. 1951- 155
Figueroa, Pablo 1938- 9
Fijan, Carol 1918- 12
Filderman, Diane E(lizabeth) 1959- 87
Files, Meg 1946- 107
Fillmore, Parker H(oysted) 1878-1944
 See YABC 1
Filstrup, Chris
 See Filstrup, E(dward) Christian
Filstrup, E(dward) Christian 1942- 43
Filstrup, Janie
 See Merrill, Jane
Finchler, Judy 1943- 93
Finder, Martin
 See Salzmann, Siegmund
Findlay, Jamieson 1958- 169
Findon, Joanne 1957- 161
Fine, Anne 1947- 197
 Earlier sketches in SATA 29, 72, 111, 160
 See also CLR 25
 See also SAAS 15
Fine, Edith Hope 169
Fine, Howard 1961- 181
Fine, Jane
 See Ziefert, Harriet
Finger, Charles J(oseph) 1869(?)-1941 42
Fink, William B(ertrand) 1916- 22
Finke, Blythe Foote 1922- 26
Finkel, George (Irvine) 1909-1975 8
Finkelstein, Norman H. 1941- 137
 Earlier sketch in SATA 73
Finkelstein, Norman Henry
 See Finkelstein, Norman H.
Finlay, Alice Sullivan 1946- 82
Finlay, Winifred Lindsay Crawford
 (McKissack) 1910-1989 23
Finlayson, Ann 1925- 8
Finley, Martha 1828-1909 43
Finley, Mary Peace 1942- 83
Finney, Jack 1911-1995 109
Finney, Patricia 1958- 163
Finney, Shan 1944- 65
Finney, Walter Braden
 See Finney, Jack

Firer, Ben Zion
 See Firer, Benzion
Firer, Benzion 1914- 64
Fireside, Bryna J. 1932- 73
Firmin, Charlotte 1954- 29
Firmin, Peter 1928- 58
 Earlier sketch in SATA 15
Firth, Barbara 179
Fischbach, Julius 1894-1988 10
Fischer, John
 See Fluke, Joanne
Fischer, R.J.
 See Fluke, Joanne
Fischer, Scott M. 1971- 195
Fischer-Nagel, Andreas 1951- 56
Fischer-Nagel, Heiderose 1956- 56
Fischler, Shirley (Walton) 66
Fischler, Stan(ley I.) 66
 Brief entry 36
Fischtrom, Harvey 1933-1974 3
Fishback, Margaret
 See Antolini, Margaret Fishback
Fishbone, Greg R. 195
Fisher, Aileen (Lucia) 1906-2002 73
 Obituary 143
 Earlier sketches in SATA 1, 25
 See also CLR 49
Fisher, Barbara 1940- 44
 Brief entry 34
Fisher, Carolyn 1968- 154
Fisher, Catherine 1957- 155
Fisher, Chris 1958- 80
Fisher, Clavin C(argill) 1912- 24
Fisher, Cynthia 195
Fisher, Dorothy (Frances) Canfield 1879-1958
 See YABC 1
 See also CLR 71
Fisher, Gary L. 1949- 86
Fisher, John 1909-1996 15
Fisher, John Oswald Hamilton
 See Fisher, John
Fisher, Laura Harrison 1934- 5
Fisher, Leonard Everett 1924- 176
 Autobiography Feature 122
 Earlier sketches in SATA 4, 34, 73, 120
 See also CLR 18
 See also SAAS 1
Fisher, Lois I. 1948- 38
 Brief entry 35
Fisher, Margery (Turner) 1913-1992 20
 Obituary 74
Fisher, Marshall Jon 1963- 113
Fisher, Nikki
 See Strachan, Ian
Fisher, Robert (Tempest) 1943- 47
Fisher, Suzanne
 See Staples, Suzanne Fisher
Fisher, Valorie 177
Fishman, Cathy Goldberg 1951- 106
Fisk, Nicholas
 See Higginbottom, David
Fisk, Pauline 1948- 160
 Earlier sketch in SATA 66
Fiske, Tarleton
 See Bloch, Robert (Albert)
Fisscher, Catharina G. M. 1958- 142
Fisscher, Tiny
 See Fisscher, Catharina G. M.
Fitch, Clarke
 See Sinclair, Upton
Fitch, John IV
 See Cormier, Robert
Fitch, Sheree 1956- 178
 Earlier sketch in SATA 108
Fitschen, Dale 1937- 20
Fitzalan, Roger
 See Trevor, Elleston
Fitzgerald, Captain Hugh
 See Baum, L. Frank
FitzGerald, Cathleen 1932-1987
 Obituary 50

Fitzgerald, Dawn 175
Fitzgerald, Edward Earl 1919-2001 20
Fitzgerald, F(rancis) A(nthony) 1940- 15
Fitzgerald, Joanne 1956- 198
Fitzgerald, John D(ennis) 1907(?)-1988 20
 Obituary 56
 See also CLR 1
Fitzgerald, Merni Ingrassia 1955- 53
Fitzgibbon, Terry 1948- 121
Fitzhardinge, Joan Margaret 1912- 73
 Earlier sketch in SATA 2
 See also CLR 5
 See also SAAS 3
Fitzhugh, Louise (Perkins) 1928-1974 45
 Obituary 24
 Earlier sketch in SATA 1
 See also CLR 72
Fitzhugh, Percy Keese 1876-1950 65
Fitzpatrick, Marie-Louise 1962- 189
 Earlier sketch in SATA 125
FitzRalph, Matthew
 See McInerny, Ralph
Fitz-Randolph, Jane (Currens) 1915- 51
Fitzsimons, Cecilia 1952- 97
Fitzsimons, Cecilia A.L.
 See Fitzsimons, Cecilia
Flack, Marjorie 1897-1958 100
 See also YABC 2
 See also CLR 28
Flack, Naomi John White -1999 40
 Brief entry 35
Flake, Sharon G. 166
Flanagan, John 1944- 180
Flanagan, John Anthony
 See Flanagan, John
Flannery, Kate
 See De Goldi, Kathleen Domenica
Flatt, Lizann 1966- 88
Fleagle, Gail S(hatto) 1940- 117
Fleetwood, Jenni 1947- 80
Fleischer, Jane
 See Oppenheim, Joanne
Fleischhauer-Hardt, Helga 1936- 30
Fleischman, Albert Sidney
 See Fleischman, Sid
Fleischman, John 1948- 145
Fleischman, Paul 1952- 156
 Brief entry 32
 Earlier sketches in SATA 39, 72, 110
 See also CLR 66
 See also SAAS 20
Fleischman, Sid 1920- 185
 Earlier sketches in SATA 8, 59, 96, 148
 See also CLR 15
Fleischner, Jennifer 1956- 188
 Earlier sketch in SATA 93
Fleisher, Paul 1948- 132
 Earlier sketch in SATA 81
Fleisher, Robbin 1951-1977 52
 Brief entry 49
Fleishman, Seymour 1918- 66
 Brief entry 32
Fleming, A. A.
 See Arthur, Robert, (Jr.)
Fleming, Alice Mulcahey 1928- 9
Fleming, Candace 1962- 190
 Earlier sketches in SATA 94, 143
Fleming, Denise 1950- 173
 Earlier sketches in SATA 81, 126
Fleming, Elizabeth P. 1888-1985
 Obituary 48
Fleming, Ian 1908-1964 9
Fleming, Ian Lancaster
 See Fleming, Ian
Fleming, Ronald Lee 1941- 56
Fleming, Sally
 See Walker, Sally M(acArt)
Fleming, Stuart
 See Knight, Damon (Francis)
Fleming, Susan 1932- 32
Fleming, Thomas 1927- 8

Fleming, Thomas James
  See Fleming, Thomas
Fleming, Virginia (Edwards) 1923- 84
Flesch, Y.
  See Flesch, Yolande (Catarina)
Flesch, Yolande (Catarina) 1950- 55
Fletcher, Charlie May Hogue 1897-1977 3
Fletcher, Colin 1922-2007 28
Fletcher, Dirk
  See Cunningham, Chet
Fletcher, George U.
  See Pratt, (Murray) Fletcher
Fletcher, Helen Jill 1910- 13
Fletcher, Ralph 1953- 195
  Earlier sketches in SATA *105, 149*
  See also CLR *104*
Fletcher, Ralph J.
  See Fletcher, Ralph
Fletcher, Richard E. 1917(?)-1983
  Obituary 34
Fletcher, Rick
  See Fletcher, Richard E.
Fletcher, Susan 1951- 181
  Earlier sketches in SATA *70, 110*
Fletcher, Susan Clemens
  See Fletcher, Susan
Fleur, Paul
  See Pohl, Frederik
Flexner, James Thomas 1908-2003 9
Flinn, Alex 1966- 198
  Earlier sketch in SATA *159*
Flint, Helen 1952- 102
Flint, Russ 1944- 74
Flitner, David P(erkins), Jr. 1949- 7
Floca, Brian 190
  Earlier sketch in SATA *155*
Floethe, Louise Lee 1913-1988 4
Floethe, Richard 1901-1998 4
Floherty, John Joseph 1882-1964 25
Flood, Bo
  See Flood, Nancy Bo
Flood, Nancy Bo 1945- 130
Flood, Pansie Hart 1964- 140
Flood, William 1942- 129
Flooglebuckle, Al
  See Spiegelman, Art
Flora, James (Royer) 1914-1998 30
  Obituary 103
  Earlier sketch in SATA *1*
  See also SAAS *6*
Flores-Galbis, Enrique 1952- 186
Florian, Douglas 1950- 177
  Earlier sketches in SATA *19, 83, 125*
Flory, Jane Trescott 1917- 22
Flournoy, Valerie 1952- 95
Flournoy, Valerie Rose
  See Flournoy, Valerie
Flowerdew, Phyllis -1994 33
Flowers, Pam 1946- 136
Flowers, Sarah 1952- 98
Floyd, Gareth 1940- 62
  Brief entry 31
Fluchere, Henri 1914-1991 40
Fluke, Joanne 1943- 88
Flutsztejn-Gruda, Ilona 1930- 170
Flynn, Barbara 1928- 9
Flynn, Jackson
  See Bensen, Donald R.
  and Shirreffs, Gordon D(onald)
Flynn, Nicholas
  See Odgers, Sally Farrell
Flynn, Rachel 1953- 171
  Earlier sketch in SATA *109*
Flynn, Warren (G.) 1950- 154
Fodor, R(onald) V(ictor) 1944- 25
Fogelin, Adrian 1951- 175
  Earlier sketch in SATA *129*
Foley, (Anna) Bernice Williams 1902-1987 . 28
Foley, Greg E. 1969- 190
Foley, June 1944- 44

Foley, (Mary) Louise Munro 1933- 106
  Brief entry 40
  Earlier sketch in SATA *54*
Foley, Rae
  See Denniston, Elinore
Folke, Will
  See Bloch, Robert (Albert)
Follett, Helen Thomas 1884(?)-1970
  Obituary 27
Folsom, Franklin (Brewster) 1907-1995 5
  Obituary 88
Folsom, Michael (Brewster) 1938-1990 40
  Obituary 88
Fontenot, Mary Alice 1910- 91
  Earlier sketch in SATA *34*
Fontes, Justine 172
Fontes, Ron 1952- 183
Foon, Dennis 1951- 119
Fooner, Michael 22
Foote, Timothy (Gilson) 1926- 52
Forberg, Ati
  See Forberg, Beate Gropius
Forberg, Beate Gropius 1925- 22
Forbes, Anna 1954- 101
Forbes, Bryan 1926- 37
Forbes, Cabot L.
  See Hoyt, Edwin P(almer), Jr.
Forbes, Esther 1891-1967 100
  Earlier sketch in SATA *2*
  See also CLR *147*
Forbes, Graham B. 1
Forbes, Kathryn
  See McLean, Kathryn (Anderson)
Forbes, Robert
  See Arthur, Robert, (Jr.)
Ford, Albert Lee
  See Stratemeyer, Edward L.
Ford, Barbara 56
  Brief entry 34
Ford, Brian J(ohn) 1939- 49
Ford, Carolyn (Mott) 1938- 98
Ford, Christine 1953- 176
Ford, David
  See Baldacci, David
  and Baldacci, David
Ford, David B.
  See Baldacci, David
Ford, David Baldacci
  See Baldacci, David
Ford, Elbur
  See Hibbert, Eleanor Alice Burford
Ford, Ellen 1949- 89
Ford, George (Jr.) 31
Ford, Hilary
  See Youd, Samuel
Ford, Hildegarde
  See Morrison, Velma Ford
Ford, Jerome W. 1949- 78
Ford, Jerry
  See Ford, Jerome W.
Ford, Juwanda G(ertrude) 1967- 102
Ford, Marcia
  See Radford, Ruby L(orraine)
Ford, Nancy K(effer) 1906-1961
  Obituary 29
Ford, Peter 1936- 59
Ford, S. M.
  See Uhlig, Susan
Forde, Catherine 1961- 170
Foreman, Mark 199
Foreman, Michael 1938- 184
  Earlier sketches in SATA *2, 73, 129, 135*
  See also CLR *32*
  See also SAAS *21*
Foreman, Wilmoth 1939- 153
Forest, Antonia 1915-2003 29
  Obituary 149
Forest, Dial
  See Gault, William Campbell
Forest, Heather 1948- 185
  Earlier sketch in SATA *120*

Forester, C(ecil) S(cott) 1899-1966 13
Forman, Brenda 1936- 4
Forman, James
  See Forman, James D.
Forman, James D. 1932- 70
  Earlier sketch in SATA *8*
Forman, James Douglas
  See Forman, James D.
Forman, Ruth 1970- 186
Forrest, Elizabeth
  See Salsitz, Rhondi Vilott
Forrest, Mary
  See Pausacker, Jenny
Forrest, Sybil
  See Markun, Patricia Maloney
Forrestal, Elaine 1941- 165
  Earlier sketch in SATA *117*
Forrester, Frank H. 1919(?)-1986
  Obituary 52
Forrester, Helen
  See Bhatia, Jamunadevi
Forrester, Jade
  See Pausacker, Jenny
Forrester, Marian
  See Schachtel, Roger
Forrester, Sandra 1949- 166
  Earlier sketch in SATA *90*
Forrester, Victoria 1940- 40
  Brief entry 35
Forsee, (Frances) Aylesa -1986 1
Forsey, Chris 1950- 59
Forshay-Lunsford, Cin 1965- 60
Forster, E(dward) M(organ) 1879-1970 57
Forsyth, Kate 1966- 154
Fort, Paul
  See Stockton, Francis Richard
Forte, Maurizio 1961- 110
Fortey, Richard 1946- 109
Fortey, Richard A.
  See Fortey, Richard
Fortey, Richard Alan
  See Fortey, Richard
Forth, Melissa D(eal) 96
Fortnum, Peggy
  See Nuttall-Smith, Margaret Emily Noel
Fortune, Eric 182
Forward, Robert L(ull) 1932-2002 82
Foster, Alan Dean 1946- 70
Foster, Brad W. 1955- 34
Foster, Doris Van Liew 1899-1993 10
Foster, E(lizabeth) C(onnell) 1902- 9
Foster, Elizabeth 1902- 12
Foster, Elizabeth 1905-1963 10
Foster, F. Blanche 1919- 11
Foster, G(eorge) Allen 1907-1969 26
Foster, Genevieve (Stump) 1893-1979 2
  Obituary 23
  See also CLR *7*
Foster, Gerald L. 198
Foster, Hal
  See Foster, Harold
Foster, Harold 1892-1982 31
Foster, Jeanne
  See Williams, Jeanne
Foster, John
  See Foster, John L(ouis)
  and Furcolo, Foster
Foster, John (Thomas) 1925- 8
Foster, John L(ouis) 1941- 102
Foster, Juliana 1961- 196
Foster, Laura Louise (James) 1918- 6
Foster, Leila Merrell 1929- 73
Foster, Lynne 1937- 74
Foster, Margaret Lesser 1899(?)-1979
  Obituary 21
Foster, Marian Curtis 1909-1978 23
Foster, Mark 1961- 197
Foster, Sally 58
Fotheringham, Edwin 201
Foulds, E. V.
  See Foulds, Elfrida Vipont

Foulds, Elfrida Vipont 1902-1992 .... *52*
Fountas, Angela Jane *180*
Fourie, Corlia 1944- *91*
Fourth Brother, The
   See Aung, (Maung) Htin
Fowke, Edith (Margaret) 1913-1996 .... *14*
Fowles, John 1926-2005 .... *22*
   Obituary *171*
Fowles, John Robert
   See Fowles, John
Fowles, Shelley 1956- *205*
Fox, Aileen 1907-2005 .... *58*
   Obituary *170*
Fox, Aileen Mary
   See Fox, Aileen
Fox, Annie 1950- *175*
Fox, Charles Philip 1913-2003 .... *12*
   Obituary *150*
Fox, Christyan *188*
Fox, Diane *188*
Fox, Eleanor
   See St. John, Wylly Folk
Fox, Fontaine Talbot, Jr. 1884-1964
   Obituary *23*
Fox, Fred 1903(?)-1981
   Obituary *27*
Fox, Freeman
   See Hamilton, Charles (Harold St. John)
Fox, Geoffrey 1941- *73*
Fox, Grace
   See Anderson, Grace Fox
Fox, Helen 1962- *181*
Fox, Larry *30*
Fox, Lorraine 1922-1976 .... *27*
   Earlier sketch in SATA *11*
Fox, Louisa
   See Kroll, Virginia L.
Fox, Mary Virginia 1919- *152*
   Brief entry *39*
   Earlier sketches in SATA *44, 88*
Fox, Mem
   See Fox, Merrion Frances
Fox, Merrion Frances 1946- *155*
   Earlier sketches in SATA *51, 103*
   See also CLR *80*
Fox, Michael W(ilson) 1937- *15*
Fox, Paula 1923- *167*
   Earlier sketches in SATA *17, 60, 120*
   See also CLR *96*
Fox, Robert J. 1927- *33*
Fox-Davies, Sarah 1956- *199*
Foyt, Victoria *187*
Fradin, Dennis
   See Fradin, Dennis Brindell
Fradin, Dennis Brindell 1945- *185*
   Earlier sketches in SATA *29, 90, 135*
Fradin, Judith Bloom 1945- *185*
   Earlier sketches in SATA *90, 152*
Frailey, Paige (Menefee) 1965- *82*
Frame, Janet 1924-2004 .... *119*
Frame, Paul 1913-1994 .... *60*
   Brief entry *33*
   Obituary *83*
Frances, Miss
   See Horwich, Frances R(appaport)
Franchere, Ruth *18*
Francis, Charles
   See Holme, Bryan
Francis, Dee
   See Haas, Dorothy F.
Francis, Dorothy 1926- *127*
   Earlier sketch in SATA *10*
Francis, Dorothy B.
   See Francis, Dorothy
Francis, Dorothy Brenner
   See Francis, Dorothy
Francis, Jaye
   See Pausacker, Jenny
Francis, Pamela (Mary) 1926- *11*
Franck, Eddie
   See Cooke, Frank E.

Franco, Betsy *188*
   Earlier sketch in SATA *150*
Franco, Eloise (Bauder) 1910- *62*
Franco, Johan (Henri Gustave) 1908-1988 ... *62*
Franco, Marjorie *38*
Francois, Andre 1915-2005 .... *25*
Francoise
   See Seignobosc, Francoise
Frank, Anne(lies Marie) 1929-1945 .... *87*
   Brief entry *42*
   See also CLR *101*
Frank, Daniel B. 1956- *55*
Frank, Emily R.
   See Frank, E.R.
Frank, E.R. 1967- *157*
Frank, Helene
   See Vautier, Ghislaine
Frank, Hillary 1976- *148*
Frank, John *199*
Frank, Josette 1893-1989 .... *10*
   Obituary *63*
Frank, Lucy 1947- *166*
   Earlier sketch in SATA *94*
Frank, Mary 1933- *34*
Frank, R., Jr.
   See Ross, Frank (Xavier), Jr.
Frankau, Mary Evelyn Atkinson 1899-1974 .. *4*
Frankel, Alona 1937- *66*
Frankel, Bernice *9*
Frankel, Edward 1910- *44*
Frankel, Ellen 1951- *78*
Frankel, Julie 1947- *40*
   Brief entry *34*
Frankenberg, Robert 1911- *22*
Franklin, Cheryl J. 1955- *70*
Franklin, Harold 1926- *13*
Franklin, Kristine L. 1958- *124*
   Earlier sketch in SATA *80*
Franklin, Lance
   See Lantz, Francess L(in)
Franklin, Madeleine
   See L'Engle, Madeleine
Franklin, Madeleine L'Engle
   See L'Engle, Madeleine
Franklin, Madeleine L'Engle Camp
   See L'Engle, Madeleine
Franklin, Max
   See Deming, Richard
Franklin, Steve
   See Stevens, Franklin
Franson, Leanne R. 1963- *111*
Franson, Scott E. 1966- *192*
Franzen, Nils-Olof 1916- *10*
Frascino, Edward *48*
   Brief entry *33*
   See also SAAS *9*
Frasconi, Antonio 1919- *131*
   Earlier sketches in SATA *6, 53*
   See also SAAS *11*
Fraser, Betty
   See Fraser, Elizabeth Marr
Fraser, Elizabeth Marr 1928- *31*
Fraser, Eric (George) 1902-1983 .... *38*
Fraser, Mary Ann 1959- *137*
   Earlier sketch in SATA *76*
   See also SAAS *23*
Fraser, Wynnette (McFaddin) 1925- *90*
Frasier, Debra 1953- *182*
   Earlier sketches in SATA *69, 112*
Fraustino, Lisa Rowe 1961- *146*
   Autobiography Feature *146*
   Earlier sketch in SATA *84*
Frazee, Marla 1958- *187*
   Earlier sketches in SATA *105, 151*
Frazetta, Frank 1928- *58*
Frazier, Craig 1955- *177*
Frazier, Neta (Osborn) Lohnes 1890-1990 ..... *7*
Frazier, Sundee T. 1968- *198*
Frazier, Sundee Tucker
   See Frazier, Sundee T.

Frederic, Mike
   See Cox, William R(obert)
Fredericks, Anthony D. 1947- *113*
Freed, Alvyn M. 1913-1993 .... *22*
Freedman, Benedict 1919- *27*
Freedman, Claire *185*
Freedman, Deborah 1960- *191*
Freedman, Jeff 1953- *90*
Freedman, Nancy 1920- *27*
Freedman, Russell 1929- *175*
   Earlier sketches in SATA *16, 71, 123*
   See also CLR *71*
Freedman, Russell Bruce
   See Freedman, Russell
Freeman, Barbara C. 1906-1999 .... *28*
Freeman, Barbara Constance
   See Freeman, Barbara C.
Freeman, Bill
   See Freeman, William Bradford
Freeman, Don 1908-1978 .... *17*
   See also CLR *90*
Freeman, Ira Maximilian 1905-1987 .... *21*
Freeman, Kimberley
   See Wilkins, Kim
Freeman, Laura *200*
Freeman, Lucy (Greenbaum) 1916-2004 ...... *24*
Freeman, Mae 1907-1985 .... *25*
Freeman, Mae Blacker
   See Freeman, Mae
Freeman, Marcia S. 1937- *102*
Freeman, Martha 1956- *201*
   Earlier sketches in SATA *101, 152*
Freeman, Nancy 1932- *61*
Freeman, Peter J.
   See Calvert, Patricia
Freeman, Sarah (Caroline) 1940- *66*
Freeman, Tor 1977- *164*
Freeman, VicToria
   See Freeman, Tor
Freeman, William Bradford 1938- *58*
   Brief entry *48*
Fregosi, Claudia (Anne Marie) 1946- *24*
Freitas, Donna 1972- *205*
French, Allen 1870-1946
   See YABC *1*
French, Dorothy Kayser 1926- *5*
French, Fiona 1944- *132*
   Earlier sketches in SATA *6, 75*
   See also CLR *37*
   See also SAAS *21*
French, Jackie *186*
   Autobiography Feature *139*
   Earlier sketches in SATA *108, 139*
   See French, Jackie Anne
   and French, Jacqueline Anne
French, Kathryn
   See Mosesson, Gloria R(ubin)
French, Martin *176*
French, Michael 1944- *49*
   Brief entry *38*
French, Paul
   See Asimov, Isaac
French, Simon 1957- *147*
   Earlier sketch in SATA *86*
French, Vivian *165*
Frenette, Liza *126*
Freschet, Gina 1960- *175*
   Earlier sketch in SATA *139*
Frewer, Glyn (M.) 1931- *11*
Frey, Darcy *98*
Freymann, Saxton 1958(?)- *178*
Freymann-Weyr, (Rhoda) Garret (Michaela)
   1965- *145*
Frick, C. H.
   See Irwin, Constance (H.) Frick
Frick, Constance
   See Irwin, Constance (H.) Frick
Fricke, Aaron 1962- *89*
Fridell, Ron 1943- *124*
Fried, Janice *197*
Friedlander, Joanne K(ohn) 1930- *9*

Friedman, Aimee 1979- *189*
Friedman, D. Dina 1957- *180*
Friedman, Debra 1955- *150*
Friedman, Estelle (Ehrenwald) 1920- *7*
Friedman, Frieda 1905- *43*
Friedman, Ina R(osen) 1926- *136*
  Brief entry *41*
  Earlier sketch in SATA *49*
Friedman, Jerrold David
  See Gerrold, David
Friedman, Judi 1935- *59*
Friedman, Laurie 1964- *179*
  Earlier sketch in SATA *138*
Friedman, Marvin 1930- *42*
  Brief entry *33*
Friedman, Robin 1968- *162*
Friedmann, Stan 1953- *80*
Friedrich, Otto (Alva) 1929-1995 .... *33*
Friedrich, Priscilla 1927- *39*
Friend, Catherine 1957(?)- *194*
Friend, David Michael 1975- *195*
Friend, Natasha 1972- *184*
Friendlich, Dick
  See Friendlich, Richard J.
Friendlich, Richard J. 1909- *11*
Friermood, Elisabeth Hamilton 1903-1992 .... *5*
Friesen, Bernice (Sarah Anne) 1966- *105*
Friesen, Gayle 1960- *200*
  Earlier sketch in SATA *109*
Friesen, Jonathan 1967(?)- *206*
Friesner, Esther M. 1951- *168*
  Earlier sketch in SATA *71*
Friis-Baastad, Babbis Ellinor 1921-1970 .... *7*
Frimmer, Steven 1928- *31*
Frischmuth, Barbara 1941- *114*
Friskey, Margaret (Richards) 1901-1995 .... *5*
Fritts, Mary Bahr
  See Bahr, Mary (Madelyn)
Fritz, Jean (Guttery) 1915- *163*
  Autobiography Feature *122*
  Earlier sketches in SATA *1, 29, 72, 119*
  See also CLR *96*
  See also SAAS *2*
Froehlich, Margaret W(alden) 1930- *56*
Frois, Jeanne 1953- *73*
Froissart, Jean 1338(?)-1410(?) *28*
Froman, Elizabeth Hull 1920-1975 .... *10*
Froman, Robert (Winslow) 1917- *8*
Fromm, Lilo 1928- *29*
Frommer, Harvey 1937- *41*
Frost, A(rthur) B(urdett) 1851-1928 .... *19*
Frost, Elizabeth
  See Frost-Knappman, Elizabeth
Frost, Erica
  See Supraner, Robyn
Frost, Helen 1949- *194*
  Autobiography Feature *194*
  Earlier sketches in SATA *157, 183*
Frost, Helen Marie
  See Frost, Helen
Frost, Lesley 1899-1983 .... *14*
  Obituary *34*
Frost, Robert 1874-1963 .... *14*
  See also CLR *67*
Frost, Robert Lee
  See Frost, Robert
Frost, Shelley 1960- *138*
Frost-Knappman, Elizabeth 1943- *179*
Froud, Brian 1947- *150*
Fry, Annette R(iley) *89*
Fry, Christopher 1907-2005 .... *66*
Fry, Edward Bernard 1925- *35*
Fry, Rosalie Kingsmill 1911-1992 .... *3*
  See also SAAS *11*
Fry, Virginia Lynn 1952- *95*
Frye, Sally
  See Moore, Elaine
Fuchs, Bernie 1932- *162*
  Earlier sketch in SATA *95*
Fuchs, Erich 1916- *6*
Fuchsshuber, Annegert 1940- *43*

Fuerst, Jeffrey B. 1956- *143*
Fuertes, Gloria 1918-1998 .... *115*
Fuge, Charles 1966- *144*
  Earlier sketch in SATA *74*
Fujikawa, Gyo 1908-1998 .... *76*
  Brief entry *30*
  Obituary *110*
  Earlier sketch in SATA *39*
  See also CLR *25*
  See also SAAS *16*
Fujita, Tamao 1905-1999 .... *7*
Fujiwara, Kim 1957- *81*
Fujiwara, Michiko 1946- *15*
Fuka, Vladimir 1926-1977
  Obituary *27*
Fulcher, Jennifer
  See Westwood, Jennifer
Fuller, Catherine Leuthold 1916- *9*
Fuller, Edmund (Maybank) 1914- *21*
Fuller, Iola
  See McCoy, Iola Fuller
Fuller, John G(rant, Jr.) 1913-1990 .... *65*
Fuller, Kathleen
  See Gottfried, Theodore Mark
Fuller, Lois Hamilton 1915- *11*
Fuller, Margaret 1810-1850 .... *25*
Fuller, Maud
  See Petersham, Maud
Fuller, Roy (Broadbent) 1912-1991 .... *87*
Fuller, Sarah Margaret
  See Fuller, Margaret
Fults, John Lee 1932- *33*
Funk, Thompson 1911- *7*
Funk, Tom
  See Funk, Thompson
Funke, Cornelia 1958- *174*
  Earlier sketch in SATA *154*
  See also CLR *145*
Funke, Cornelia Caroline
  See Funke, Cornelia
Funke, Lewis 1912-1992 .... *11*
Fuqua, Jonathon Scott 1966- *141*
Furbee, Mary R.
  See Furbee, Mary Rodd
Furbee, Mary Rodd 1954- *138*
Furchgott, Terry 1948- *29*
Furlong, Monica (Mavis) 1930-2003 .... *86*
  Obituary *142*
Furman, Gertrude Lerner Kerman 1909- *21*
Furniss, Tim 1948- *49*
Furrow, Robert 1985- *172*
Furukawa, Toshi 1924- *24*
Fusillo, Archimede 1962- *137*
Futcher, Jane P. 1947- *76*
Futehali, Zahida
  See Whitaker, Zai
Fyleman, Rose (Amy) 1877-1957 .... *21*
Fyson, Jenny Grace
  See Fyson, J.G.
Fyson, J.G. 1904-1998 .... *42*

G

Gaan, Margaret 1914- *65*
Gaber, Susan 1956- *169*
  Earlier sketch in SATA *115*
Gaberman, Judie Angell
  See Angell, Judie
Gabhart, Ann
  See Gabhart, Ann H.
Gabhart, Ann H. 1947- *75*
Gable, Brian 1949- *195*
Gabler, Mirko 1951- *77*
Gabriel, Adriana
  See Rojany, Lisa
Gabrys, Ingrid Schubert
  See Schubert-Gabrys, Ingrid

Gackenbach, Dick 1927- *79*
  Brief entry *30*
  Earlier sketch in SATA *48*
Gadd, Jeremy 1949- *116*
Gaddis, Vincent H. 1913-1997 .... *35*
Gadler, Steve J. 1905-1985 .... *36*
Gaeddert, Lou Ann (Bigge) 1931- *103*
  Earlier sketch in SATA *20*
Gaeddert, Louann
  See Gaeddert, Lou Ann (Bigge)
Gaer, Joseph 1897-1969 .... *118*
Gaer, Yossef
  See Gaer, Joseph
Gaetz, Dayle Campbell 1947- *138*
Gaffney, Timothy R. 1951- *170*
  Earlier sketch in SATA *69*
Gaffron, Norma (Bondeson) 1931- *97*
Gag, Flavia 1907-1979
  Obituary *24*
Gag, Wanda (Hazel) 1893-1946 .... *100*
  See also YABC *1*
  See also CLR *4*
Gage, Brian *162*
Gage, Wilson
  See Steele, Mary Q(uintard Govan)
Gagliano, Eugene M. 1946- *150*
Gagliardo, Ruth Garver 1895(?)-1980
  Obituary *22*
Gagnon, Cecile 1936- *58*
Gaillard, Jason 1965- *200*
Gaiman, Neil 1960- *197*
  Earlier sketches in SATA *85, 146*
  See also CLR *109*
Gaiman, Neil Richard
  See Gaiman, Neil
Gainer, Cindy 1962- *74*
Gaines, Ernest J. 1933- *86*
  See also CLR *62*
Gaines, Ernest James
  See Gaines, Ernest J.
Gaither, Gloria 1942- *127*
Gal, Laszlo 1933- *96*
  Brief entry *32*
  Earlier sketch in SATA *52*
  See also CLR *61*
Galbraith, Ben 1980- *200*
Galbraith, Kathryn O(sebold) 1945- *85*
Galdone, Paul 1907(?)-1986 .... *66*
  Obituary *49*
  Earlier sketch in SATA *17*
  See also CLR *16*
Galindo, Claudia 1979- *203*
Galinsky, Ellen 1942- *23*
Gall, Chris 1961- *176*
Gallagher, Diana G. 1946- *153*
Gallagher, Lurlene Nora
  See McDaniel, Lurlene
Gallagher-Cole, Mernie 1958- *206*
Gallant, Roy A(rthur) 1924- *110*
  Earlier sketches in SATA *4, 68*
  See also CLR *30*
Gallardo, Evelyn 1948- *78*
Gallaz, Christophe 1948- *162*
  See also CLR *126*
Gallego Garcia, Laura 1977- *173*
Gallico, Paul (William) 1897-1976 .... *13*
Gallo, Donald R. 1938- *112*
  Autobiography Feature *104*
Gallo, Donald Robert
  See Gallo, Donald R.
Galloway, Owateka (S.) 1981- *121*
Galloway, Priscilla 1930- *112*
  Earlier sketch in SATA *66*
Gallup, Joan 1957- *128*
Galouchko, Annouchka Gravel 1960- *95*
Galt, Thomas Franklin, Jr. 1908-1989 .... *5*
Galt, Tom
  See Galt, Thomas Franklin, Jr.
Galvin, Matthew R. 1950- *93*
Galvin, Matthew Reppert
  See Galvin, Matthew R.

Gamble, Kim 1952- *183*
  Earlier sketches in SATA *81, 124*
Gambrell, Jamey *82*
Gamerman, Martha 1941- *15*
Gammell, Stephen 1943- *128*
  Earlier sketches in SATA *53, 81*
  See also CLR *83*
Ganly, Helen (Mary) 1940- *56*
Gannett, Ruth Chrisman (Arens)
  1896-1979 .... *33*
Gannett, Ruth Stiles 1923- *3*
Gannon, Ned 1974- *205*
Gannon, Robert Haines 1931- *8*
Gano, Lila 1949- *76*
Gans, Roma 1894-1996 .... *45*
  Obituary *93*
Gant, Matthew
  See Hano, Arnold
Gantner, Susan (Verble) 1939- *63*
Gantos, Jack 1951- *169*
  Earlier sketches in SATA *20, 81, 119*
  See also CLR *85*
Gantos, John Bryan, Jr.
  See Gantos, Jack
Ganz, Yaffa 1938- *61*
  Brief entry *52*
Garafano, Marie 1942- *84*
Garant, Andre J. 1968- *123*
Garbe, Ruth Moore
  See Moore, Ruth (Ellen)
Garber, Esther
  See Lee, Tanith
Garcia, Emma 1969- *198*
Garcia, Yolanda P. 1952- *113*
Garcia, Yolanda Pacheco
  See Garcia, Yolanda P.
Gard, Janice
  See Latham, Jean Lee
Gard, Joyce
  See Reeves, Joyce
Gard, Robert Edward 1910-1992 .... *18*
  Obituary *74*
Gard, (Sanford) Wayne 1899-1986
  Obituary *49*
Gardam, Jane 1928- *130*
  Brief entry *28*
  Earlier sketches in SATA *39, 76*
  See also CLR *12*
  See also SAAS *9*
Gardam, Jane Mary
  See Gardam, Jane
Gardella, Tricia 1944- *96*
Garden, Nancy 1938- *147*
  Autobiography Feature *147*
  Earlier sketches in SATA *12, 77, 114*
  See also CLR *51*
  See also SAAS *8*
Gardiner, John Reynolds 1944-2006 .... *64*
  Obituary *174*
Gardiner, Lindsey 1971- *144*
Gardner, Craig Shaw 1949- *99*
Gardner, Dic
  See Gardner, Richard (M.)
Gardner, Graham *159*
Gardner, Hugh 1910-1986
  Obituary *49*
Gardner, Jane Mylum 1946- *83*
Gardner, Jeanne LeMonnier 1925- *5*
Gardner, John, Jr. 1933-1982 .... *40*
  Obituary *31*
Gardner, John Champlin, Jr.
  See Gardner, John, Jr.
Gardner, John E(dward) 1917- *192*
Gardner, Lyn *192*
Gardner, Martin 1914- *142*
  Earlier sketch in SATA *16*
Gardner, Miriam
  See Bradley, Marion Zimmer
Gardner, Richard (M.) 1931- *24*
Gardner, Richard A(lan) 1931-2003 .... *13*
  Obituary *144*

Gardner, Sally *177*
Gardner, Sandra 1940- *70*
Gardner, Scot 1968- *143*
Gardner, Sheldon 1934- *33*
Gardner, Ted
  See Gardner, Theodore Roosevelt II
Gardner, Theodore Roosevelt
  See Gardner, Theodore Roosevelt II
Gardner, Theodore Roosevelt II 1934- *84*
Garelick, May 1910-1989 .... *19*
Garfield, James B. 1881-1984 .... *6*
  Obituary *38*
Garfield, Leon 1921-1996 .... *76*
  Obituary *90*
  Earlier sketches in SATA *1, 32*
  See also CLR *21*
Garfinkle, Debra L.
  See Garfinkle, D.L.
Garfinkle, D.L. *187*
Garis, Howard R. 1873-1962 .... *13*
Garis, Howard Roger
  See Garis, Howard R.
Garland, Mark 1953- *79*
Garland, Mark A.
  See Garland, Mark
Garland, Michael 1952- *168*
Garland, Sarah 1944- *135*
  Earlier sketch in SATA *62*
Garland, Sherry 1948- *145*
  Autobiography Feature *145*
  Earlier sketches in SATA *73, 114*
Garner, Alan 1934- *69*
  Autobiography Feature *108*
  Earlier sketch in SATA *18*
  See also CLR *130*
Garner, David 1958- *78*
Garner, Eleanor Ramrath 1930- *122*
Garner, James Finn 1960(?)- *92*
Garnet, A. H.
  See Slote, Alfred
Garnett, Eve C. R. 1900-1991 .... *3*
  Obituary *70*
Garofoli, Viviana 1970- *186*
Garou, Louis P.
  See Bowkett, Stephen
Garraty, John A. 1920-2007 .... *23*
  Obituary *189*
Garraty, John Arthur
  See Garraty, John A.
Garren, Devorah-Leah
  See Devorah-Leah
Garret, Maxwell R. 1917- *39*
Garretson, Victoria Diane 1945- *44*
Garrett, Helen 1895- *21*
Garrett, Randall 1927-1987 .... *180*
Garrett, Richard 1920- *82*
Garrigue, Sheila 1931- *21*
Garrison, Barbara 1931- *163*
  Earlier sketch in SATA *19*
Garrison, Frederick
  See Sinclair, Upton
Garrison, Mary 1952- *146*
Garrison, Peter
  See Gardner, Craig Shaw
Garrison, Webb B(lack) 1919-2000 .... *25*
Garrity, Jennifer Johnson 1961- *124*
Garrity, Linda K. 1947- *128*
Garsee, Jeannine *199*
Garst, Doris Shannon 1894-1981 .... *1*
Garst, Shannon
  See Garst, Doris Shannon
Garth, Will
  See Hamilton, Edmond
  and Kuttner, Henry
Garthwaite, Marion H(ook) 1893-1981 .... *7*
Garton, Malinda D(ean) (?)-1976
  Obituary *26*
Garvie, Maureen 1944- *175*
Garvie, Maureen McCallum
  See Garvie, Maureen
Garza, Carmen Lomas 1948- *182*

Garza, Xavier *184*
Gascoigne, Bamber 1935- *62*
Gaskins, Pearl Fuyo 1957- *134*
Gasperini, Jim 1952- *54*
  Brief entry *49*
Gater, Dilys 1944- *41*
Gates, Doris 1901-1987 .... *34*
  Obituary *54*
  Earlier sketch in SATA *1*
  See also SAAS *1*
Gates, Frieda 1933- *26*
Gates, Susan 1950- *153*
Gates, Viola R. 1931- *101*
Gathorne-Hardy, Jonathan G. 1933- *124*
  Earlier sketch in SATA *26*
Gatti, Anne 1952- *103*
Gatty, Juliana Horatia
  See Ewing, Juliana (Horatia Gatty)
Gauch, Patricia Lee 1934- *80*
  Earlier sketch in SATA *26*
  See also CLR *56*
  See also SAAS *21*
Gaudasinska, Elzbieta 1943- *190*
Gaul, Randy 1959- *63*
Gault, Clare 1925- *36*
Gault, Frank 1926-1982 .... *36*
  Brief entry *30*
Gault, William Campbell 1910-1995 .... *8*
Gauthier, Gail 1953- *203*
  Earlier sketches in SATA *118, 160*
Gaver, Becky
  See Gaver, Rebecca
Gaver, Rebecca 1952- *20*
Gavin, Jamila 1941- *125*
  Earlier sketch in SATA *96*
Gay, Amelia
  See Hogarth, Grace (Weston Allen)
Gay, Francis
  See Gee, H(erbert) L(eslie)
Gay, Kathlyn 1930- *144*
  Earlier sketch in SATA *9*
Gay, Marie-Louise 1952- *179*
  Earlier sketches in SATA *68, 126*
  See also CLR *27*
  See also SAAS *21*
Gay, Michel 1947- *162*
Gay, Zhenya 1906-1978 .... *19*
Gaze, Gillian
  See Barklem, Jill
Gear, Kathleen M. O'Neal
  See Gear, Kathleen O'Neal
Gear, Kathleen O'Neal 1954- *166*
  Earlier sketch in SATA *71*
Gear, W. Michael 1955- *166*
  Earlier sketch in SATA *71*
Geary, Rick 1946- *142*
Geason, Susan 1946- *122*
Gedalof, Robin
  See McGrath, Robin
Gedge, Pauline (Alice) 1945- *101*
Gee, H(erbert) L(eslie) 1901-1977
  Obituary *26*
Gee, Maurice 1931- *101*
  Earlier sketch in SATA *46*
  See also CLR *56*
Gee, Maurice Gough
  See Gee, Maurice
Geehan, Wayne (E.) 1947- *107*
Geer, Charles 1922- *42*
  Brief entry *32*
Geeslin, Campbell 1925- *163*
  Earlier sketch in SATA *107*
Gehman, Mary W. 1923- *86*
Gehr, Mary 1910(?)-1997 .... *32*
  Obituary *99*
Geipel, Eileen 1932- *30*
Geis, Alissa Imre 1976- *189*
Geis, Darlene Stern 1918(?)-1999 .... *7*
  Obituary *111*
Geisel, Helen 1898-1967 .... *26*

Geisel, Theodor Seuss
    See Dr. Seuss
Geisert, Arthur 1941- *171*
    Brief entry *52*
    Earlier sketches in SATA *56, 92, 133*
    See also CLR *87*
    See also SAAS *23*
Geisert, Arthur Frederick
    See Geisert, Arthur
Geisert, Bonnie 1942- *165*
    Earlier sketch in SATA *92*
Geist, Ken *191*
Geldart, William 1936- *15*
Gelinas, Paul J. 1904-1996 .... *10*
Gellis, Roberta 1927- *128*
Gellis, Roberta Leah Jacobs
    See Gellis, Roberta
Gellman, Marc *112*
Gelman, Amy 1961- *72*
Gelman, Jan 1963- *58*
Gelman, Rita Golden 1937- *131*
    Brief entry *51*
    Earlier sketch in SATA *84*
Gelman, Steve 1934- *3*
Gemming, Elizabeth 1932- *11*
Gendel, Evelyn W. 1916(?)-1977
    Obituary *27*
Gennaro, Joseph F(rancis), Jr. 1924- *53*
Gentieu, Penny *204*
Gentile, Petrina 1969- *91*
Gentle, Mary 1956- *48*
Gentleman, David (William) 1930- *7*
Geoghegan, Adrienne 1962- *143*
George, Barbara
    See Katz, Bobbi
George, Emily
    See Katz, Bobbi
George, Gail
    See Katz, Bobbi
George, Jean
    See George, Jean Craighead
George, Jean C.
    See George, Jean Craighead
George, Jean Craighead 1919- *170*
    Earlier sketches in SATA *2, 68, 124*
    See also CLR *136*
George, John L(othar) 1916- *2*
George, Kristine O'Connell 1954- *156*
    Earlier sketch in SATA *110*
George, Lindsay Barrett 1952- *206*
    Earlier sketches in SATA *95, 155*
George, S(idney) C(harles) 1898- *11*
George, Sally
    See Orr, Wendy
George, Twig C. 1950- *114*
George, W(illiam) Lloyd 1900(?)-1975
    Obituary *30*
Georgiou, Constantine 1927- *7*
Georgiou, Theo
    See Odgers, Sally Farrell
Geraghty, Paul 1959- *130*
Gerard, Jean Ignace Isidore 1803-1847 .... *45*
Geras, Adele 1944- *180*
    Autobiography Feature *180*
    Earlier sketches in SATA *23, 87, 129, 173*
    See also SAAS *21*
Geras, Adele Daphne Weston
    See Geras, Adele
Gerber, Merrill Joan 1938- *170*
    Autobiography Feature *170*
    Earlier sketches in SATA *64, 127*
Gerber, Perren 1933- *104*
Gerberg, Mort 1931- *64*
Gergely, Tibor 1900-1978 .... *54*
    Obituary *20*
Geringer, Laura 1948- *164*
    Earlier sketches in SATA *29, 94*
Gerler, William R(obert) 1917-1996 .... *47*
Gerrard, Jean 1933- *51*

Gerrard, Roy 1935-1997 .... *90*
    Brief entry *45*
    Obituary *99*
    Earlier sketch in SATA *47*
    See also CLR *23*
Gerritsen, Paula 1956- *177*
Gerrold, David 1944- *144*
    Earlier sketch in SATA *66*
Gershator, David 1937- *180*
Gershator, Phillis 1942- *188*
    Earlier sketches in SATA *90, 158*
Gershon, Dann 1955- *187*
Gershon, Gina 1962- *187*
Gerson, Corinne 1927- *37*
Gerson, Mary-Joan *136*
    Earlier sketch in SATA *79*
Gerson, Noel Bertram 1914-1988 .... *22*
    Obituary *60*
Gerstein, Mordicai 1935- *178*
    Brief entry *36*
    Earlier sketches in SATA *47, 81, 142*
    See also CLR *102*
Gertridge, Allison 1967- *132*
Gervais, Bernadette 1959- *80*
Gervay, Susanne *183*
Gesner, Clark 1938-2002 .... *40*
    Obituary *143*
Gessner, Lynne 1919- *16*
Geter, Tyrone *150*
Getz, David 1957- *91*
Getzinger, Donna 1968- *128*
Gevirtz, Eliezer 1950- *49*
Gevry, Claudine *188*
Gewe, Raddory
    See Gorey, Edward (St. John)
Ghan, Linda (R.) 1947- *77*
Ghent, Natale 1962- *148*
Gherman, Beverly 1934- *123*
    Earlier sketch in SATA *68*
Ghigna, Charles 1946- *153*
    Earlier sketch in SATA *108*
Giacobbe, Beppe 1953- *174*
Giambastiani, Kurt R. A. 1958- *141*
Giannini, Enzo 1946- *68*
Gibala-Broxholm, Scott 1959(?)- *205*
Gibbons, Alan 1953- *198*
    Earlier sketch in SATA *124*
Gibbons, Faye 1938- *103*
    Earlier sketch in SATA *65*
Gibbons, Gail 1944- *201*
    Earlier sketches in SATA *23, 72, 104, 160*
    See also CLR *8*
    See also SAAS *12*
Gibbons, Gail Gretchen
    See Gibbons, Gail
Gibbons, Kaye 1960- *117*
Gibbs, Adrea 1960- *126*
Gibbs, Alonzo (Lawrence) 1915-1992 .... *5*
Gibbs, (Cecilia) May 1877-1969
    Obituary *27*
Gibbs, Tony
    See Gibbs, Wolcott, Jr.
Gibbs, Wolcott, Jr. 1935- *40*
Giblin, James Cross 1933- *197*
    Earlier sketches in SATA *33, 75, 122*
    See also CLR *29*
    See also SAAS *12*
Gibson, Andrew (William) 1949- *72*
Gibson, Barbara L. *205*
Gibson, Barbara Leonard
    See Gibson, Barbara L.
Gibson, Betty 1911- *75*
Gibson, Jo
    See Fluke, Joanne
Gibson, Josephine
    See Hine, Sesyle Joslin
    and Hine, Al(fred Blakelee)
Gibson, William 1914-2008 .... *66*
    Obituary *199*
Gibson, William Ford
    See Gibson, William

Gidal, Nachum
    See Gidal, Tim Nachum
Gidal, Sonia (Epstein) 1922- *2*
Gidal, Tim Nachum 1909-1996 .... *2*
Gidalewitsch, Nachum
    See Gidal, Tim Nachum
Gideon, Melanie 1963- *175*
Giegling, John A(llan) 1935- *17*
Gifaldi, David 1950- *76*
Giff, Patricia Reilly 1935- *203*
    Earlier sketches in SATA *33, 70, 121, 160*
Giffard, Hannah 1962- *83*
Gifford, Clive 1966- *198*
Gifford, Griselda 1931- *171*
    Earlier sketch in SATA *42*
Gifford, Kerri 1961- *91*
Gifford, Peggy 1952- *191*
Gilbert, Ann
    See Taylor, Ann
Gilbert, Anne Yvonne 1951- *185*
Gilbert, Barbara Snow 1954- *97*
Gilbert, Catherine
    See Murdock, Catherine Gilbert
Gilbert, Frances
    See Collings, Gillian
Gilbert, Harriett 1948- *30*
Gilbert, (Agnes) Joan (Sewell) 1931- *10*
Gilbert, John (Raphael) 1926- *36*
Gilbert, Nan
    See Gilbertson, Mildred Geiger
Gilbert, Roby Goodale 1966- *90*
Gilbert, Ruth Gallard Ainsworth
    See Ainsworth, Ruth (Gallard)
Gilbert, Sara (Dulaney) 1943- *82*
    Earlier sketch in SATA *11*
Gilbert, Sheri L. *157*
Gilbert, Suzie 1956- *97*
Gilbert, W(illiam) S(chwenck) 1836-1911 ... *36*
Gilbert, Yvonne
    See Gilbert, Anne Yvonne
Gilbertson, Mildred Geiger 1908-1988 .... *2*
Gilbreath, Alice 1921- *12*
Gilbreth, Frank B., Jr. 1911-2001 .... *2*
Gilbreth, Frank Bunker
    See Gilbreth, Frank B., Jr.
Gilchrist, Jan Spivey 1949- *130*
    Earlier sketch in SATA *72*
Gilden, Mel 1947- *97*
Giles, Gail *196*
    Earlier sketch in SATA *152*
Gilfond, Henry *2*
Gilge, Jeanette 1924- *22*
Gili, Phillida 1944- *70*
Gill, Derek (Lewis Theodore) 1919-1997 ...... *9*
Gill, Margery Jean 1925- *22*
Gill, Shelley *176*
Gill, Stephen 1932- *63*
Gillespie, Carol Ann 1951- *158*
Gillett, Mary (Bledsoe) *7*
Gillette, Henry Sampson 1915- *14*
Gillette, J(an) Lynett 1946- *103*
Gilley, Jeremy 1969- *174*
Gillham, Bill
    See Gillham, W(illiam) E(dwin) C(harles)
Gillham, W(illiam) E(dwin) C(harles)
    1936- *42*
Gilliam, Stan 1946- *39*
    Brief entry *35*
Gilliland, Alexis A(rnaldus) 1931- *72*
Gilliland, (Cleburne) Hap 1918- *92*
Gilliland, Judith Heide *180*
Gillmor, Don 1954- *127*
Gilman, Dorothy 1923- *5*
Gilman, Esther 1925- *15*
Gilman, Laura Anne *178*
Gilman, Phoebe 1940-2002 .... *104*
    Obituary *141*
    Earlier sketch in SATA *58*
Gilmore, Iris 1900-1982 .... *22*
Gilmore, Kate 1931- *87*
Gilmore, Mary (Jean Cameron) 1865-1962 . *49*

Gilmore, Susan 1954- *59*
Gilpin, Stephen *177*
Gilroy, Beryl (Agatha) 1924- *80*
Gilson, Barbara
  See Gilson, Charles James Louis
Gilson, Charles James Louis 1878-1943
  See YABC *2*
Gilson, Jamie 1933- *176*
  Brief entry *34*
  Earlier sketches in SATA *37, 91*
Ginsburg, Mirra 1909-2000 .... *92*
  Earlier sketch in SATA *6*
  See also CLR *45*
Giovanni, Nikki 1943- *107*
  Earlier sketch in SATA *24*
  See also CLR *73*
Giovanni, Yolanda Cornelia
  See Giovanni, Nikki
Giovanni, Yolande Cornelia
  See Giovanni, Nikki
Giovanni, Yolande Cornelia, Jr.
  See Giovanni, Nikki
Giovanopoulos, Paul (Arthur) 1939- *7*
Gipson, Billie
  See Letts, Billie
Gipson, Fred(erick Benjamin) 1908-1973 ...... *2*
  Obituary *24*
Girard, Linda (Walvoord) 1942- *41*
Girion, Barbara 1937- *78*
  Earlier sketch in SATA *26*
  See also SAAS *14*
Girouard, Patrick 1957- *155*
Girzone, Joseph F. 1930- *76*
Girzone, Joseph Francis
  See Girzone, Joseph F.
Gise, Joanne
  See Mattern, Joanne
Gist, E.M. *206*
Gittings, Jo (Grenville) Manton 1919- *3*
Gittings, Robert (William Victor) 1911-1992 . *6*
  Obituary *70*
Givens, Janet E(aton) 1932- *60*
Givner, Joan 1936- *171*
Givner, Joan Mary
  See Givner, Joan
Gladstone, Eve
  See Werner, Herma
Gladstone, Gary 1935- *12*
Gladstone, M(yron) J. 1923- *37*
Glanville, Brian (Lester) 1931- *42*
Glanzman, Louis S. 1922- *36*
Glaser, Byron 1954- *154*
Glaser, Dianne E(lizabeth) 1937- *50*
  Brief entry *31*
Glaser, Isabel Joshlin 1929- *94*
Glaser, Milton 1929- *151*
  Earlier sketch in SATA *11*
Glaser, Shirley *151*
Glaspell, Susan 1882(?)-1948
  See YABC *2*
Glass, Andrew 1949- *150*
  Brief entry *46*
  Earlier sketch in SATA *90*
Glass, Linzi *175*
Glass, Linzi Alex
  See Glass, Linzi
Glasscock, Amnesia
  See Steinbeck, John (Ernst)
Glassman, Bruce 1961- *76*
Glauber, Uta (Heil) 1936- *17*
Glazer, Thomas (Zachariah) 1914-2003 ...... *9*
Glazer, Tom
  See Glazer, Thomas (Zachariah)
Gleasner, Diana (Cottle) 1936- *29*
Gleason, Judith 1929- *24*
Gleason, Katherine (A.) 1960- *104*
Gleeson, Libby 1950- *142*
  Autobiography Feature *142*
  Earlier sketches in SATA *82, 118*
Gleiter, Jan 1947- *111*

Gleitzman, Morris 1953- *156*
  Earlier sketch in SATA *88*
  See also CLR *88*
Glen, Maggie 1944- *88*
Glendinning, Richard 1917-1988 .... *24*
Glendinning, Sally
  See Glendinning, Sara W(ilson)
Glendinning, Sara W(ilson) 1913-1993 .... *24*
Glenn, John W. *195*
Glenn, Mel 1943- *93*
  Brief entry *45*
  Earlier sketch in SATA *51*
  See also CLR *51*
Glenn, Patricia Brown 1953- *86*
Glenn, Sharlee *159*
Glenn, Sharlee Mullins
  See Glenn, Sharlee
Glennon, Karen M. 1946- *85*
Gles, Margaret Breitmaier 1940- *22*
Glick, Carl (Cannon) 1890-1971 .... *14*
Glick, Ruth (Burtnick) 1942- *125*
Glick, Virginia Kirkus 1893-1980
  Obituary *23*
Gliewe, Unada (Grace) 1927- *3*
Glimmerveen, Ulco 1958- *85*
Glines, Carroll V(ane), Jr. 1920- *19*
Gliori, Debi 1959- *189*
  Earlier sketches in SATA *72, 138*
Globe, Leah Ain 1900- *41*
Glori Ann
  See Blakely, Gloria
Glovach, Linda 1947- *105*
  Earlier sketch in SATA *7*
Glover, Denis (James Matthews) 1912-1980 . *7*
Glubok, Shirley (Astor) *146*
  Autobiography Feature *146*
  Earlier sketches in SATA *6, 68*
  See also CLR *1*
  See also SAAS *7*
Gluck, Felix 1923-1981
  Obituary *25*
Glyman, Caroline A. 1967- *103*
Glynne-Jones, William 1907-1977 .... *11*
Gobbato, Imero 1923- *39*
Gobbletree, Richard
  See Quackenbush, Robert M(ead)
Goble, Dorothy *26*
Goble, Paul 1933- *131*
  Earlier sketches in SATA *25, 69*
  See also CLR *21*
Goble, Warwick (?)-1943 .... *46*
Godden, (Margaret) Rumer 1907-1998 .... *36*
  Obituary *109*
  Earlier sketch in SATA *3*
  See also CLR *20*
  See also SAAS *12*
Gode, Alexander
  See Gode von Aesch, Alexander (Gottfried
  Friedrich)
Gode von Aesch, Alexander (Gottfried
  Friedrich) 1906-1970 .... *14*
Godfrey, Jane
  See Bowden, Joan Chase
Godfrey, Martyn
  See Godfrey, Martyn N.
  and Godfrey, Martyn N.
Godfrey, Martyn N. 1949-2000 .... *95*
  See also CLR *57*
Godfrey, William
  See Youd, Samuel
Godkin, Celia (Marilyn) 1948- *145*
  Earlier sketch in SATA *66*
Godon, Ingrid 1958- *186*
Godwin, Laura 1956- *179*
Godwin, Sam
  See Pirotta, Saviour
Goedecke, Christopher (John) 1951- *81*
Goekler, Susan
  See Wooley, Susan Frelick
Goembel, Ponder *204*
Goertzen, Glenda *172*

Goettel, Elinor 1930- *12*
Goetz, Delia 1898-1996 .... *22*
  Obituary *91*
Goffe, Toni 1936- *61*
Goffstein, Brooke
  See Goffstein, M(arilyn) B(rooke)
Goffstein, M(arilyn) B(rooke) 1940- *70*
  Earlier sketch in SATA *8*
  See also CLR *3*
Goforth, Ellen
  See Francis, Dorothy
Gogol, Sara 1948-2004 .... *80*
Goh, Chan Hon 1969- *145*
Going, Kelly L.
  See Going, K.L.
Going, Kelly Louise
  See Going, K.L.
Going, K.L. *199*
  Earlier sketch in SATA *156*
Golann, Cecil Paige 1921-1995 .... *11*
Golbin, Andree 1923- *15*
Gold, Alison Leslie 1945- *104*
Gold, Bernice *150*
Gold, Phyllis
  See Goldberg, Phyllis
Gold, Robert S(tanley) 1924- *63*
Gold, Sharlya *9*
Gold, Susan
  See Gold, Susan Dudley
Gold, Susan Dudley 1949- *147*
Goldberg, Grace 1956- *78*
Goldberg, Herbert S. 1926- *25*
Goldberg, Jacob 1943- *94*
Goldberg, Jake
  See Goldberg, Jacob
Goldberg, Phyllis 1941- *21*
Goldberg, Stan J. 1939- *26*
Goldberg, Susan 1948- *71*
Goldberg, Whoopi 1955- *119*
Goldberger, Judith M. 1948- *80*
Goldblatt, Stacey 1969(?)- *191*
Golden, Christie 1963- *167*
  Earlier sketch in SATA *116*
Goldentyer, Debra 1960- *84*
Goldfeder, Cheryl
  See Pahz, Cheryl Suzanne
Goldfeder, James
  See Pahz, James Alon
Goldfeder, Jim
  See Pahz, James Alon
Goldfinger, Jennifer P. 1963- *185*
Goldfrank, Helen Colodny 1912- *6*
Goldin, Augusta 1906-1999 .... *13*
Goldin, Barbara Diamond 1946- *129*
  Autobiography Feature *129*
  Earlier sketch in SATA *92*
  See also SAAS *26*
Goldin, David 1963- *101*
Golding, Julia 1969- *188*
Golding, Theresa Martin 1960- *150*
Golding, William 1911-1993
  See CLR *130*
Golding, William Gerald
  See Golding, William
Goldman, Alex J. 1917- *65*
Goldman, E(leanor) M(aureen) 1943- *103*
Goldman, Elizabeth 1949- *90*
Goldring, Ann 1937- *149*
Goldsborough, June 1923- *19*
Goldschmidt, Judy *202*
Goldsmith, Connie 1945- *147*
Goldsmith, Howard 1943- *108*
  Earlier sketch in SATA *24*
Goldsmith, John Herman Thorburn 1903-1987
  Obituary *52*
Goldsmith, Oliver 1730(?)-1774 .... *26*
Goldsmith, Ruth M. 1919- *62*
Goldstein, Nathan 1927- *47*
Goldstein, Philip 1910-1997 .... *23*
Goldston, Robert (Conroy) 1927- *6*
Goldstone, Bruce *183*

Goldstone, Lawrence A.
  See Treat, Lawrence
Goldszmit, Henryk 1878-1942 65
Golembe, Carla 1951- 79
Golenbock, Peter 1946- 99
Goll, Reinhold W(eimar) 1897-1993 26
Gollub, Matthew 1960- 134
  Earlier sketch in SATA 83
Gomes, Filomena 1965- 183
Gomez, Elena 191
Gomez, Elizabeth 133
Gomez-Freer, Elizabeth
  See Gomez, Elizabeth
Gomi, Taro 1945- 103
  Earlier sketch in SATA 64
  See also CLR 57
Gondosch, Linda 1944- 58
Gonyea, Mark 194
Gonzalez, Catherine Troxell 1917-2000 87
Gonzalez, Christina
  See Gonzalez, Maya Christina
Gonzalez, Gloria 1940- 23
Gonzalez, Julie 1958- 174
Gonzalez, Lucia M. 1957- 202
Gonzalez, Maya
  See Gonzalez, Maya Christina
Gonzalez, Maya Christina 1964- 175
  Earlier sketch in SATA 115
Gonzalez, Rigoberto 1970- 147
Goobie, Beth 1959- 128
Good, Alice 1950- 73
Good, Clare
  See Romano, Clare
Goodall, Daphne Machin
  See Machin Goodall, Daphne (Edith)
Goodall, Jane 1934- 111
Goodall, John S(trickland) 1908-1996 66
  Obituary 91
  Earlier sketch in SATA 4
  See also CLR 25
Goodbody, Slim
  See Burstein, John
Goode, Diane 1949- 170
  Earlier sketches in SATA 15, 84, 114
Goode, Diane Capuozzo
  See Goode, Diane
Goode, Stephen Ray 1943- 55
  Brief entry 40
Goodenow, Earle 1913- 40
Goodhart, Pippa 1958- 196
  Earlier sketch in SATA 153
Goodhue, Thomas W. 1949- 143
Goodin, Sallie (Brown) 1953- 74
Goodman, Alison 1966- 111
Goodman, Deborah Lerme 1956- 50
  Brief entry 49
Goodman, Elaine 1930- 9
Goodman, Joan Elizabeth 1950- 162
  Earlier sketches in SATA 50, 94
Goodman, Susan E. 1952- 181
Goodman, Walter 1927-2002 9
Goodrich, Samuel Griswold 1793-1860 23
Goodsell, Jane Neuberger 1921(?)-1988
  Obituary 56
GoodWeather, Hartley
  See King, Thomas
Goodweather, Hartley
  See King, Thomas
Goodwin, Hal
  See Goodwin, Harold L(eland)
Goodwin, Harold L(eland) 1914-1990 51
  Obituary 65
  Earlier sketch in SATA 13
Goodwin, William 1943- 117
Goor, Nancy (Ruth Miller) 1944- 39
  Brief entry 34
Goor, Ron(ald Stephen) 1940- 39
  Brief entry 34
Goossen, Agnes
  See Epp, Margaret A(gnes)
Goossens, Philippe 1963- 195

Gootman, Marilyn E. 1944- 179
Gopnik, Adam 1956- 171
Gorbachev, Valeri 1944- 184
  Autobiography Feature 143
  Earlier sketches in SATA 98, 143
Gordion, Mark
  See Turtledove, Harry
Gordon, Ad
  See Hano, Arnold
Gordon, Amy 1949- 197
  Earlier sketches in SATA 115, 156
Gordon, Bernard Ludwig 1931- 27
Gordon, Colonel H. R.
  See Ellis, Edward S.
Gordon, David
  See Garrett, Randall
Gordon, Donald
  See Payne, Donald Gordon
Gordon, Dorothy 1893-1970 20
Gordon, Esther S(aranga) 1935- 10
Gordon, Frederick 1
Gordon, Gaelyn 1939-1997
  See CLR 75
Gordon, Garrett
  See Garrett, Randall
Gordon, Gary
  See Edmonds, I(vy) G(ordon)
Gordon, Hal
  See Goodwin, Harold L(eland)
Gordon, Jeffie Ross
  See Enderle, Judith (Ann) Ross
  and Gordon, Stephanie Jacob
Gordon, John
  See Gesner, Clark
Gordon, John (William) 1925- 84
Gordon, Lew
  See Baldwin, Gordon C(ortis)
Gordon, Margaret (Anna) 1939- 9
Gordon, Mike 1948- 101
Gordon, Mildred 1912-1979
  Obituary 24
Gordon, Selma
  See Lanes, Selma Gordon
Gordon, Sheila 1927- 88
  See also CLR 27
Gordon, Shirley 1921- 48
  Brief entry 41
Gordon, Sol 1923- 11
Gordon, Stephanie Jacob 1940- 89
  Autobiography Feature 114
  Earlier sketch in SATA 64
  See also SAAS 26
Gordon, Stewart
  See Shirreffs, Gordon D(onald)
Gordons, The
  See Gordon, Mildred
  and Gordon, Gordon
Gore, Leonid 185
Gorelick, Molly C(hernow) 1920-2003 9
  Obituary 153
Gorey, Edward (St. John) 1925-2000 70
  Brief entry 27
  Obituary 118
  Earlier sketch in SATA 29
  See also CLR 36
Gorham, Charles Orson 1868-1936 36
Gorham, Michael
  See Folsom, Franklin (Brewster)
Gorman, Carol 187
  Earlier sketch in SATA 150
Gorman, Jacqueline Laks 1955- 148
Gorman, Mike 206
Gormley, Beatrice 1942- 202
  Brief entry 35
  Earlier sketches in SATA 39, 127
Gorog, Judith (Katharine Allen) 1938- 75
  Earlier sketch in SATA 39
Gorrell, Gena K. 1946- 170
Gorsline, Douglas (Warner) 1913-1985 11
  Obituary 43
Gorsline, (Sally) Marie 1928- 28

Gorsline, S. M.
  See Gorsline, (Sally) Marie
Gorton, Kaitlyn
  See Emerson, Kathy Lynn
Gorton, Kathy Lynn
  See Emerson, Kathy Lynn
Goryan, Sirak
  See Saroyan, William
Goscinny, Rene 1926-1977 47
  Brief entry 39
  See also CLR 37
Goss, Clay(ton E.) 1946- 82
Goss, Gary 1947- 124
Goss, Mini 1963- 186
Goto, Scott 203
Gott, Barry 197
Gottesman, S. D.
  See Kornbluth, C(yril) M.
  and Lowndes, Robert A(ugustine) W(ard)
  and Pohl, Frederik
Gottfried, Ted
  See Gottfried, Theodore Mark
Gottfried, Theodore Mark 1928- 150
  Earlier sketch in SATA 85
Gottlieb, Gerald 1923- 7
Gottlieb, William P. 1917-2006 24
Gottlieb, William Paul
  See Gottlieb, William P.
Goudey, Alice E(dwards) 1898-1993 20
Goudge, Eileen 1950- 88
Goudge, Elizabeth (de Beauchamp)
  1900-1984 2
  Obituary 38
  See also CLR 94
Gough, Catherine
  See Mulgan, Catherine
Gough, Philip 1908-1986 45
Gough, Sue 1940- 106
Goulart, Ron 1933- 67
  Earlier sketch in SATA 1
Goulart, Ronald Joseph
  See Goulart, Ron
Gould, Alberta 1945- 96
Gould, Chester 1900-1985 49
  Obituary 43
Gould, Jean R(osalind) 1909-1993 11
  Obituary 77
Gould, Lilian 6
Gould, Marilyn 1928- 76
  Earlier sketch in SATA 15
Gould, Robert 154
Gould, Steven 1955- 95
Gould, Steven Charles
  See Gould, Steven
Gourley, Catherine 1950- 190
  Earlier sketch in SATA 95
Gourse, Leslie 1939-2004 89
Govan, (Mary) Christine Noble 1898-1985 ... 9
Gove, Doris 1944- 72
Govenar, Alan 1952- 189
Govenar, Alan Bruce
  See Govenar, Alan
Govern, Elaine 1939- 26
Gowen, L. Kris 1968- 156
Graaf, Peter
  See Youd, Samuel
Graber, Alexander 1914-1997 98
  Earlier sketch in SATA 7
Graber, (George) Alexander 1914-1997 98
Graber, Janet 1942- 170
Graber, Richard (Fredrick) 1927- 26
Grabianski, Janusz 1928-1976 39
  Obituary 30
Graboff, Abner 1919-1986 35
Grace, Fran(ces Jane) 45
Grace, N.B.
  See Harper, Suzanne
Grace, Theresa
  See Mattern, Joanne
Gracza, Margaret Young 1928- 56

Graduate of Oxford, A
  See Ruskin, John
Grady, Denise 1952- 189
Graeber, Charlotte Towner 106
  Brief entry 44
  Earlier sketch in SATA 56
Graef, Renee 1956- 204
Graeme, Roderic
  See Jeffries, Roderic
Graf, Michael
  See Graf, Mike
Graf, Mike 1960- 164
Grafe, Max 198
Graff, Lisa 1981- 188
Graff, Polly Anne Colver
  See Colver, Anne
Graff, (S.) Stewart 1908- 9
Graham, Ada 1931- 11
Graham, Alastair 1945- 74
Graham, Arthur Kennon
  See Harrison, David L.
Graham, Bob 1942- 187
  Earlier sketches in SATA 63, 101, 151
  See also CLR 31
Graham, Brenda Knight 1942- 32
Graham, Charlotte
  See Bowden, Joan Chase
Graham, Eleanor 1896-1984 18
  Obituary 38
Graham, Ennis
  See Molesworth, Mary Louisa
Graham, Frank, Jr. 1925- 11
Graham, Georgia 1959- 190
Graham, Ian 1953- 112
Graham, John 1926-2007 11
Graham, Kennon
  See Harrison, David L.
Graham, Larry
  See Graham, Lawrence
Graham, Lawrence 1962- 63
Graham, Lawrence Otis
  See Graham, Lawrence
Graham, Linda
  See Graham-Barber, Lynda
Graham, Lorenz (Bell) 1902-1989 74
  Obituary 63
  Earlier sketch in SATA 2
  See also CLR 10
  See also SAAS 5
Graham, Margaret Bloy 1920- 11
Graham, Robin Lee 1949- 7
Graham, Shirley 1896(?)-1977
  See Du Bois, Shirley Graham
Graham-Barber, Lynda 1944- 159
  Earlier sketch in SATA 42
Graham-Cameron, M.
  See Graham-Cameron, M(alcolm) G(ordon)
Graham-Cameron, M(alcolm) G(ordon)
  1931- 53
  Brief entry 45
Graham-Cameron, Mike
  See Graham-Cameron, M(alcolm) G(ordon)
Grahame, Kenneth 1859-1932 100
  See also YABC 1
  See also CLR 135
Gralley, Jean 166
Gramatky, Hardie 1907-1979 30
  Obituary 23
  Earlier sketch in SATA 1
  See also CLR 22
Grambling, Lois G. 1927- 206
  Earlier sketches in SATA 71, 148
Grambo, Rebecca L(ynn) 1963- 109
Grammer, June Amos 1927- 58
Grand, Samuel 1912-1988 42
Grandits, John 1949- 192
GrandPre, Mary 1954- 184
Grandville, J. J.
  See Gerard, Jean Ignace Isidore
Grandville, Jean Ignace Isidore Gerard
  See Gerard, Jean Ignace Isidore

Granfield, Linda 1950- 160
  Earlier sketch in SATA 96
Grange, Peter
  See Nicole, Christopher (Robin)
Granger, Margaret Jane 1925(?)-1977
  Obituary 27
Granger, Michele 1949- 88
Granger, Peggy
  See Granger, Margaret Jane
Granowsky, Alvin 1936- 101
Granstaff, Bill 1925- 10
Granstrom, Brita 1969- 167
  Earlier sketch in SATA 111
Grant, Bruce 1893-1977 5
  Obituary 25
Grant, Cynthia D. 1950- 147
  Earlier sketches in SATA 33, 77
Grant, Eva 1907-1996 7
Grant, Evva H. 1913-1977
  Obituary 27
Grant, Gordon 1875-1962 25
Grant, Gwen(doline Ellen) 1940- 47
Grant, Katie M.
  See Grant, K.M.
Grant, K.M. 175
Grant, (Alice) Leigh 1947- 10
Grant, Matthew G.
  See May, Julian
Grant, Maxwell
  See Gibson, Walter B(rown)
  and Lynds, Dennis
Grant, Melvyn 183
Grant, Myrna (Lois) 1934- 21
Grant, Neil 1938- 154
  Earlier sketch in SATA 14
Grant, Nicholas
  See Nicole, Christopher (Robin)
Grant, Richard 1948- 80
Grant, Skeeter
  See Spiegelman, Art
Grater, Michael 1923- 57
Gravel, Fern
  See Hall, James Norman
Gravelle, Karen 1942- 166
  Earlier sketch in SATA 78
Graves, Charles Parlin 1911-1972 4
Graves, Keith 191
  Earlier sketch in SATA 156
Graves, Robert 1895-1985 45
Graves, Robert von Ranke
  See Graves, Robert
Graves, Valerie
  See Bradley, Marion Zimmer
Gravett, Emily 1972(?)- 189
Gray, Betsy
  See Poole, Gray Johnson
Gray, Caroline
  See Nicole, Christopher (Robin)
Gray, Dianne E. 183
Gray, Elizabeth Janet
  See Vining, Elizabeth Gray
Gray, Genevieve S(tuck) 1920-1995 4
Gray, Harold (Lincoln) 1894-1968 33
  Brief entry 32
Gray, Jenny
  See Gray, Genevieve S(tuck)
Gray, John Lee
  See Jakes, John
Gray, Judith A. 1949- 93
Gray, Judith Anne
  See Gray, Judith A.
Gray, Keith 151
Gray, Kes 1960- 153
Gray, Les 1929- 82
Gray, Libba Moore 1937- 83
Gray, Luli 1945- 149
  Earlier sketch in SATA 90
Gray, Marian
  See Pierce, Edith Gray
Gray, Nicholas Stuart 1922-1981 4
  Obituary 27

Gray, Nigel 1941- 104
  Earlier sketch in SATA 33
Gray, (Lucy) Noel (Clervaux) 1898-1983 47
Gray, Patricia (Clark) 7
Gray, Patsey
  See Gray, Patricia (Clark)
Gray, Rita 184
Graydon, Shari 1958- 158
Grayland, V. Merle
  See Grayland, Valerie (Merle Spanner)
Grayland, Valerie (Merle Spanner) 7
Grayson, Devin (Kalile) 1970- 119
Grayson, Kristine
  See Rusch, Kristine Kathryn
Grayson, Paul 1946- 79
Graystone, Lynn
  See Brennan, Joseph Lomas
Great Comte, The
  See Hawkesworth, Eric
Greaves, Margaret 1914-1995 87
  Earlier sketch in SATA 7
Greaves, Nick 1955- 77
Gree, Alain 1936- 28
Green, Adam
  See Weisgard, Leonard (Joseph)
Green, Anne Canevari 1943- 62
Green, Brian
  See Card, Orson Scott
Green, Cliff(ord) 1934- 126
Green, Connie Jordan 1938- 80
Green, D.
  See Casewit, Curtis W(erner)
Green, Elizabeth Shippen 1871-1954 139
Green, Hannah
  See Greenberg, Joanne (Goldenberg)
Green, Jane 1937- 9
Green, John 1977(?)- 170
Green, Mary Moore 1906- 11
Green, Morton 1937- 8
Green, Norma B(erger) 1925- 11
Green, Phyllis 1932- 20
Green, Roger (Gilbert) Lancelyn 1918-1987 . 2
  Obituary 53
Green, (James Le)Roy 1948- 89
Green, Sheila Ellen 1934- 148
  Earlier sketches in SATA 8, 87
Green, Timothy 1953- 91
Greenaway, Kate 1846-1901 100
  See also YABC 2
  See also CLR 111
Greenbank, Anthony Hunt 1933- 39
Greenberg, David 1954- 171
Greenberg, David T.
  See Greenberg, David
Greenberg, Harvey R. 1935- 5
Greenberg, Jan 1942- 125
  Earlier sketch in SATA 61
Greenberg, Joanne (Goldenberg) 1932- 25
Greenberg, Melanie Hope 1954- 72
Greenberg, Polly 1932- 52
  Brief entry 43
Greenblat, Rodney Alan 1960- 106
Greenburg, Dan 1936- 175
  Earlier sketch in SATA 102
Greene, Bette 1934- 161
  Earlier sketches in SATA 8, 102
  See also CLR 140
  See also SAAS 16
Greene, Carla 1916- 67
  Earlier sketch in SATA 1
Greene, Carol 102
  Brief entry 44
  Earlier sketch in SATA 66
Greene, Constance C(larke) 1924- 72
  Earlier sketch in SATA 11
  See also CLR 62
  See also SAAS 11
Greene, Edgar
  See Papademetriou, Lisa
Greene, Ellin 1927- 23
Greene, Graham 1904-1991 20

Greene, Graham Henry
 See Greene, Graham
Greene, Jacqueline Dembar 1946- *131*
 Earlier sketch in SATA *76*
Greene, Laura Offenhartz 1935- *38*
Greene, Meg
 See Malvasi, Meg Greene
Greene, Michele 1962- *178*
Greene, Michele Dominguez
 See Greene, Michele
Greene, Rhonda Gowler 1955- *160*
 Earlier sketch in SATA *101*
Greene, Stephanie 1953- *173*
 Earlier sketch in SATA *127*
Greene, Wade 1933- *11*
Greene, Yvonne
 See Flesch, Yolande (Catarina)
Greenfeld, Howard (Scheinman) 1928- *140*
 Earlier sketch in SATA *19*
Greenfeld, Josh(ua Joseph) 1928- *62*
Greenfield, Eloise 1929- *155*
 Earlier sketches in SATA *19, 61, 105*
 See also CLR *38*
 See also SAAS *16*
Greenhaus, Thelma Nurenberg 1903-1984
 Obituary *45*
Greenhut, Josh
 See Mercer, Sienna
Greenhut, Josh
 See Mercer, Sienna
Greening, Hamilton
 See Hamilton, Charles (Harold St. John)
Greenlaw, M. Jean 1941- *107*
Greenleaf, Barbara Kaye 1942- *6*
Greenleaf, Peter 1910-1997 .... *33*
Greenlee, Sharon 1935- *77*
Greeno, Gayle 1949- *81*
Greenseid, Diane 1948- *178*
 Earlier sketch in SATA *93*
Greenspun, Adele Aron 1938- *142*
 Earlier sketch in SATA *76*
Greenstein, Elaine 1959- *150*
 Earlier sketch in SATA *82*
Greenwald, Sheila
 See Green, Sheila Ellen
Greenwood, Barbara 1940- *129*
 Earlier sketch in SATA *90*
Greenwood, Mark 1958- *202*
Greenwood, Pamela D. 1944- *115*
Greer, Richard
 See Garrett, Randall
 and Silverberg, Robert
Gregg, Andrew K. 1929- *81*
Gregg, Charles T(hornton) 1927- *65*
Gregg, Walter H(arold) 1919- *20*
Gregor, Arthur 1923- *36*
Gregor, Lee
 See Pohl, Frederik
Gregori, Leon 1919- *15*
Gregorian, Joyce Ballou 1946-1991 .... *30*
 Obituary *83*
Gregorich, Barbara 1943- *184*
 Earlier sketch in SATA *66*
Gregorowski, Christopher 1940- *30*
Gregory, Diana (Jean) 1933- *49*
 Brief entry *42*
Gregory, Harry
 See Gottfried, Theodore Mark
Gregory, Jean
 See Ure, Jean
Gregory, Kristiana 1951- *136*
 Earlier sketch in SATA *74*
Gregory, Nan 1944- *192*
 Earlier sketch in SATA *148*
Gregory, Philippa 1954- *122*
Gregory, Stephen
 See Penzler, Otto
Gregory, Valiska 1940- *82*
Greif, Jean-Jacques 1944- *195*
Greisman, Joan Ruth 1937- *31*

Grendon, Stephen
 See Derleth, August (William)
Grenville, Pelham
 See Wodehouse, P(elham) G(renville)
Gretz, Susanna 1937- *7*
Gretzer, John *18*
Grewdead, Roy
 See Gorey, Edward (St. John)
Grey, Carol
 See Lowndes, Robert A(ugustine) W(ard)
Grey, Christopher *191*
Grey, Christopher Peter
 See Grey, Christopher
Grey, Jerry 1926- *11*
Grey, Mini *205*
 Earlier sketch in SATA *166*
Greybeard the Pirate
 See Macintosh, Brownie
Grey Owl
 See Belaney, Archibald Stansfeld
Gri
 See Denney, Diana
Gribbin, John 1946- *159*
Gribbin, John R.
 See Gribbin, John
Grice, Frederick 1910-1983 .... *6*
Grider, Dorothy 1915- *31*
Gridley, Marion E(leanor) 1906-1974 .... *35*
 Obituary *26*
Grieco-Tiso, Pina 1954- *108*
Grieder, Walter 1924- *9*
Griego, Tony A. 1955- *77*
Griese, Arnold A(lfred) 1921- *9*
Griessman, Annette 1962- *170*
 Earlier sketch in SATA *116*
Grieve, James 1934- *146*
Grifalconi, Ann 1929- *133*
 Earlier sketches in SATA *2, 66*
 See also CLR *35*
 See also SAAS *16*
Griffin, Adele 1970- *195*
 Earlier sketches in SATA *105, 153*
Griffin, Elizabeth May 1985- *89*
Griffin, Gillett Good 1928- *26*
Griffin, Judith Berry *34*
Griffin, Kitty 1951- *137*
Griffin, Peni R. 1961- *193*
 Earlier sketches in SATA *67, 99*
Griffin, Steven A. 1953- *89*
Griffin, Steven Arthur
 See Griffin, Steven A.
Griffin, W.E.B. 1929- *5*
Griffith, Connie 1946- *89*
Griffith, Gershom 1960- *85*
Griffith, Helen V(irginia) 1934- *87*
 Autobiography Feature *107*
 Earlier sketch in SATA *39*
Griffith, Jeannette
 See Eyerly, Jeannette
Griffith, Saul 1974- *200*
Griffiths, Andy 1961- *196*
 Earlier sketch in SATA *152*
Griffiths, G(ordon) D(ouglas) 1910-1973
 Obituary *20*
Griffiths, Helen 1939- *86*
 Earlier sketch in SATA *5*
 See also CLR *75*
 See also SAAS *5*
Grigson, Jane (McIntire) 1928-1990 .... *63*
Grimes, Lee 1920- *68*
Grimes, Nikki 1950- *174*
 Earlier sketches in SATA *93, 136*
 See also CLR *42*
Grimly, Gris *186*
Grimm, Jacob Ludwig Karl 1785-1863 .... *22*
 See also CLR *112*
Grimm, Wilhelm Karl 1786-1859 .... *22*
 See also CLR *112*
Grimm, William C(arey) 1907-1992 .... *14*

Grimm and Grim
 See Grimm, Jacob Ludwig Karl
 and Grimm, Wilhelm Karl
Grimm Brothers
 See Grimm, Jacob Ludwig Karl
 and Grimm, Wilhelm Karl
Grimsdell, Jeremy 1942- *83*
Grimshaw, Nigel (Gilroy) 1925- *23*
Grimsley, Gordon
 See Groom, Arthur William
Grindley, Jane Sally
 See Grindley, Sally
Grindley, Sally 1953- *148*
Gringhuis, Dirk
 See Gringhuis, Richard H.
Gringhuis, Richard H. 1918-1974 .... *6*
 Obituary *25*
Grinnell, David
 See Wollheim, Donald A(llen)
Grinnell, George Bird 1849-1938 .... *16*
Grinspoon, David
 See Grinspoon, David H.
Grinspoon, David H. 1959- *156*
Grinspoon, David Harry
 See Grinspoon, David H.
Gripe, Maria 1923- *74*
 Earlier sketch in SATA *2*
 See also CLR *5*
Gripe, Maria Kristina
 See Gripe, Maria
Grobler, Piet 1959- *201*
Groch, Judith (Goldstein) 1929- *25*
Grode, Redway
 See Gorey, Edward (St. John)
Groener, Carl
 See Lowndes, Robert A(ugustine) W(ard)
Groening, Matt 1954- *116*
 Earlier sketch in SATA *81*
Grohmann, Susan 1948- *84*
Grohskopf, Bernice *7*
Grol, Lini R(icharda) 1913- *9*
Grollman, Earl A. 1925- *22*
Groom, Arthur William 1898-1964 .... *10*
Grooms, Duffy 1964- *169*
Gross, Alan 1947- *54*
 Brief entry *43*
Gross, Ernie 1913- *67*
Gross, Philip 1952- *164*
 Earlier sketch in SATA *84*
Gross, Philip John
 See Gross, Philip
Gross, Ruth Belov 1929- *33*
Gross, Sarah Chokla 1906-1976 .... *9*
 Obituary *26*
Grosser, Morton 1931- *74*
Grosser, Vicky 1958- *83*
Grossman, Bill 1948- *126*
 Earlier sketch in SATA *72*
Grossman, Nancy 1940- *29*
Grossman, Patricia 1951- *73*
Grossman, Robert 1940- *11*
Grote, JoAnn A. 1951- *113*
Groten, Dallas 1951- *64*
Groth, John (August) 1908-1988 .... *21*
 Obituary *56*
Groth-Fleming, Candace
 See Fleming, Candace
Grove, Vicki 1948- *151*
 Autobiography Feature *151*
 Earlier sketch in SATA *122*
Grover, Lorie Ann 1964- *168*
Grover, Wayne 1934- *69*
Groves, Georgina
 See Symons, (Dorothy) Geraldine
Groves, Maketa 1950- *107*
Groves, Seli *77*
Grubb, Lisa *160*
Gruber, Michael 1940- *173*
Gruber, Terry (deRoy) 1953- *66*

Gruelle, John 1880-1938 35
  Brief entry 32
  See also CLR 34
Gruelle, Johnny
  See Gruelle, John
Gruenberg, Sidonie Matsner 1881-1974 2
  Obituary 27
Gruhzit-Hoyt, Olga (Margaret) 1922- 127
  Earlier sketch in SATA *16*
Grummer, Arnold E(dward) 1923- 49
Grunewalt, Pine
  See Kunhardt, Edith
Grunwell, Jeanne Marie 1971- 147
Grupper, Jonathan 137
Gryski, Camilla 1948- 72
Guarino, Dagmar
  See Guarino, Deborah
Guarino, Deborah 1954- 68
Guay, Georgette (Marie Jeanne) 1952- 54
Guback, Georgia 88
Guccione, Leslie Davis 1946- 111
  Earlier sketch in SATA *72*
Guck, Dorothy 1913-2002 27
Guerny, Gene
  See Gurney, Gene
Guest, Elissa Haden 1953- 125
Guest, Jacqueline 1952- 135
Guevara, Susan 167
  Earlier sketch in SATA *97*
Gugler, Laurel Dee 95
Gugliotta, Bobette 1918-1994 7
Guianan, Eve 1965- 102
Guiberson, Brenda Z. 1946- 124
  Earlier sketch in SATA *71*
Guibert, Emmanuel 1964- 181
Guile, Melanie 1949- 152
  Earlier sketch in SATA *104*
Guillaume, Jeanette G. Flierl 1899-1990 8
Guillot, Rene 1900-1969 7
  See also CLR 22
Guisewite, Cathy (Lee) 1950- 57
Gulbis, Stephen 1959- 142
Gulley, Judie 1942- 58
Gump, P. Q.
  See Card, Orson Scott
Gump, P.Q.
  See Card, Orson Scott
Gundrey, Elizabeth 1924- 23
Gunn, James E. 1923- 35
Gunn, James Edwin
  See Gunn, James E.
Gunn, Robin Jones 1955- 84
Gunnella 1956- 197
Gunning, Monica Olwen 1930- 161
Gunston, Bill
  See Gunston, William Tudor
Gunston, William Tudor 1927- 9
Gunterman, Bertha Lisette 1886(?)-1975
  Obituary 27
Gunther, John 1901-1970
Guravich, Dan 1918- 74
Gurko, Leo 1914- 9
Gurko, Miriam 1910(?)-1988 9
  Obituary 58
Gurney, Gene 1924- 65
Gurney, James 1958- 120
  Earlier sketch in SATA *76*
Gurney, John Steven 1962- 143
  Earlier sketch in SATA *75*
Gustafson, Sarah R.
  See Riedman, Sarah R(egal)
Gustafson, Scott 1956- 34
Gustavson, Adam 176
Guthrie, A(lfred) B(ertram), Jr. 1901-1991 .. 62
  Obituary 67
Guthrie, Anne 1890-1979 28
Guthrie, Donna W. 1946- 105
  Earlier sketch in SATA *63*
Gutierrez, Akemi 172
Gutierrez, Rudy 203

Gutman, Bill 128
  Brief entry 43
  Earlier sketch in SATA *67*
Gutman, Dan 1955- 188
  Earlier sketches in SATA *77, 139*
Gutman, Naham 1899(?)-1981
  Obituary 25
Gutmann, Bessie Pease 1876-1960 73
Guy, Geoffrey 1942- 153
Guy, Ginger Foglesong 1954- 171
Guy, Rosa (Cuthbert) 1925- 122
  Earlier sketches in SATA *14, 62*
  See also CLR 137
Guy, Susan 1948- 149
Guymer, (Wilhelmina) Mary 1909- 50
Guzman, Lila 1952- 168
Guzman, Rick 1957- 168
Gwaltney, Doris 1932- 181
Gwynne, Fred(erick Hubbard) 1926-1993 41
  Brief entry 27
  Obituary 75
Gwynne, Oscar A.
  See Ellis, Edward S.
Gwynne, Oswald A.
  See Ellis, Edward S.

H

Haab, Sherri 1964- 169
  Earlier sketch in SATA *91*
Haar, Jaap ter
  See ter Haar, Jaap
Haarsma, P.J. 183
Haas, Carolyn Buhai 1926- 43
Haas, Dan 1957- 105
Haas, Dorothy F. 46
  Brief entry 43
  See also SAAS 17
Haas, Irene 1929- 96
  Earlier sketch in SATA *17*
Haas, James E(dward) 1943- 40
Haas, (Katherine) Jessie 1959- 135
  Autobiography Feature 135
  Earlier sketch in SATA *98*
Haas, Merle S. 1896(?)-1985
  Obituary 41
Habenstreit, Barbara 1937- 5
Haber, Karen 1955- 78
Haber, Louis 1910-1988 12
Hacker, Randi 1951- 185
Hacker, Randi Dawn
  See Hacker, Randi
Hackett, John Winthrop 1910-1997 65
Hacks, Peter 1928-2003
  Obituary 151
Haddix, Margaret Peterson 1964- 187
  Earlier sketches in SATA *94, 125*
Haddon, Mark 1962- 155
Hader, Berta (Hoerner) 1891(?)-1976 16
Hader, Elmer (Stanley) 1889-1973 16
Hadithi, Mwenye
  See Hobson, Bruce
Hadley, Franklin
  See Winterbotham, R(ussell) R(obert)
Hadley, Lee 1934-1995 89
  Brief entry 38
  Obituary 86
  Earlier sketch in SATA *47*
  See also CLR 40
  See also SAAS 14
Haeffele, Deborah 1954- 76
Haenel, Wolfram 1956- 89
  See also CLR 64
Hafner, Marylin 1925- 179
  Earlier sketches in SATA *7, 121*
Haft, Erin
  See Ehrenhaft, Daniel
Hager, Alan 1940- 176

Hager, Alice Rogers 1894-1969
  Obituary 26
Hager, Betty 1923- 89
Hager, Sarah 171
Hager, Thomas 1953- 119
Hager, Tom
  See Hager, Thomas
Hagerup, Klaus 1946- 186
Haggard, H(enry) Rider 1856-1925 16
Haggerty, James J(oseph) 1920- 5
Hagon, Priscilla
  See Allan, Mabel Esther
Hague, (Susan) Kathleen 1949- 49
  Brief entry 45
Hague, Michael 1948- 185
  Brief entry 32
  Earlier sketches in SATA *48, 80, 129*
Hague, Michael R.
  See Hague, Michael
Hahn, Emily 1905-1997 3
  Obituary 96
Hahn, Hannelore 8
Hahn, James (Sage) 1947- 9
Hahn, (Mona) Lynn 1949- 9
Hahn, Mary Downing 1937- 157
  Autobiography Feature 157
  Brief entry 44
  Earlier sketches in SATA *50, 81, 138*
  See also SAAS 12
Hahn, Michael T. 1953- 92
Haig-Brown, Roderick (Langmere)
  1908-1976 12
  See also CLR 31
Haight, Anne Lyon 1895-1977
  Obituary 30
Haight, Rip
  See Carpenter, John
Haight, Sandy 1949- 79
Haij, Vera
  See Jansson, Tove (Marika)
Haines, Gail Kay 1943- 11
Haines, Margaret Ann Beck
  See Beck, Peggy
Haining, Peter 1940-2007 14
  Obituary 188
Haining, Peter Alexander
  See Haining, Peter
Hains, Harriet
  See Watson, Carol
Hajdusiewicz, Babs Bell 163
Hakim, Joy 1931- 173
  Earlier sketch in SATA *83*
Halacy, D. S., Jr. 1919-2002 36
  See also SAAS 8
Halacy, Dan
  See Halacy, D. S., Jr.
Halam, Ann
  See Jones, Gwyneth A(nn)
Haldane, Roger John 1945- 13
Hale, Arlene 1924-1982 49
Hale, Bruce 1957- 203
  Earlier sketch in SATA *123*
Hale, Christy
  See Apostolou, Christine Hale
Hale, Edward Everett 1822-1909 16
Hale, Glenn
  See Walker, Robert W.
Hale, Helen
  See Mulcahy, Lucille Burnett
Hale, Irina 1932- 26
Hale, Kathleen 1898-2000 66
  Obituary 121
  Earlier sketch in SATA *17*
Hale, Linda (Howe) 1929- 6
Hale, Lucretia P.
  See Hale, Lucretia Peabody
Hale, Lucretia Peabody 1820-1900 26
  See also CLR 105
Hale, Marian 194
Hale, Nancy 1908-1988 31
  Obituary 57

Hale, Shannon 200
  Earlier sketch in SATA 158
Haley, Amanda 205
Haley, Gail E(inhart) 1939- 161
  Autobiography Feature 161
  Brief entry 28
  Earlier sketches in SATA 43, 78, 136
  See also CLR 21
  See also SAAS 13
Haley, Neale 52
Hall, Adam
  See Trevor, Elleston
Hall, Adele 1910- 7
Hall, Anna Gertrude 1882-1967 8
Hall, Barbara 1960- 68
Hall, Becky 1950- 186
Hall, Beverly B. 1918- 95
Hall, Borden
  See Yates, Raymond F(rancis)
Hall, Brian P(atrick) 1935- 31
Hall, Cameron
  See del Rey, Lester
Hall, Caryl
  See Hansen, Caryl (Hall)
Hall, Donald 1928- 97
  Earlier sketch in SATA 23
Hall, Donald Andrew, Jr.
  See Hall, Donald
Hall, Douglas 1931- 43
Hall, Elizabeth 1929- 77
Hall, Elvajean 1910-1984 6
Hall, Francie 1940- 166
Hall, James Norman 1887-1951 21
Hall, Jesse
  See Boesen, Victor
Hall, Katy
  See McMullan, Kate
Hall, Kirsten Marie 1974- 67
Hall, Lynn 1937- 79
  Earlier sketches in SATA 2, 47
  See also SAAS 4
Hall, Malcolm 1945- 7
Hall, Marcellus 203
Hall, Marjory
  See Yeakley, Marjory Hall
Hall, Melanie W. 1949- 169
  Earlier sketches in SATA 78, 116
Hall, Patricia 1940- 136
Hall, Rosalys Haskell 1914- 7
Hall, Willis 1929-2005 66
Hallard, Peter
  See Catherall, Arthur
Hallas, Richard
  See Knight, Eric
Hall-Clarke, James
  See Rowland-Entwistle, (Arthur) Theodore
    (Henry)
Hallensleben, Georg 1958- 173
Haller, Dorcas Woodbury 1946- 46
Hallett, Mark 1947- 83
Halliburton, Richard 1900-1939(?) 81
Halliburton, Warren J. 1924- 19
Halliday, Brett
  See Dresser, Davis
  and Johnson, (Walter) Ryerson
  and Terrall, Robert
Halliday, William R(oss) 1926- 52
Hallin, Emily Watson 1916-1995 6
Hallinan, P(atrick) K(enneth) 1944- 39
  Brief entry 37
Hallman, Ruth 1929- 43
  Brief entry 28
Hallowell, Tommy
  See Hill, Thomas
Hall-Quest, (Edna) Olga W(ilbourne)
  1899-1986 11
  Obituary 47
Halls, Kelly Milner 1957- 131
Hallstead, William F(inn III) 1924- 11
Hallward, Michael 1889-1982 12
Halperin, Michael 156

Halperin, Wendy Anderson 1952- 200
  Earlier sketches in SATA 80, 125
Halpern, Julie 1975- 198
Halpin, Brendan 1968- 193
Halpin, Marlene 1927- 88
Halsell, Grace (Eleanor) 1923-2000 13
Halsey, Megan 185
Halsted, Anna Roosevelt 1906-1975
  Obituary 30
Halter, Jon C(harles) 1941- 22
Halverson, Deborah 202
Halvorson, Marilyn 1948- 123
Hamalian, Leo 1920- 41
Hamberger, John 1934- 14
Hamblin, Dora Jane 1920- 36
Hambly, Barbara 1951- 108
Hambly, Barbara Joan
  See Hambly, Barbara
Hamer, Martyn
  See Eldin, Peter
Hamerstrom, Frances 1907-1998 24
Hamil, Thomas Arthur 1928- 14
Hamill, Ethel
  See Webb, Jean Francis (III)
Hamilton, (John) Alan 1943- 66
Hamilton, Alice
  See Cromie, Alice Hamilton
Hamilton, Anita 1919- 92
Hamilton, Buzz
  See Hemming, Roy G.
Hamilton, Carol (Jean Barber) 1935- 94
Hamilton, Charles (Harold St. John)
  1876-1961 13
Hamilton, Charles 1913-1996 65
  Obituary 93
Hamilton, Clive
  See Lewis, C.S.
Hamilton, Dorothy (Drumm) 1906-1983 12
  Obituary 35
Hamilton, Edith 1867-1963 20
Hamilton, Edmond 1904-1977 118
Hamilton, (Muriel) Elizabeth (Mollie)
  1906- 23
Hamilton, Emma Walton 1962- 177
Hamilton, Franklin
  See Silverberg, Robert
Hamilton, Gail
  See Corcoran, Barbara (Asenath)
  and Dodge, Mary Abigail
Hamilton, Kersten 1958- 204
  Earlier sketch in SATA 134
Hamilton, K.R.
  See Hamilton, Kersten
Hamilton, Martha 1953- 183
  Earlier sketch in SATA 123
Hamilton, Mary (E.) 1927- 55
Hamilton, Mollie
  See Kaye, M.M.
Hamilton, Morse 1943-1998 101
  Earlier sketch in SATA 35
Hamilton, Peter F. 1960- 109
Hamilton, Priscilla
  See Gellis, Roberta
Hamilton, Ralph
  See Stratemeyer, Edward L.
Hamilton, Virginia 1936-2002 123
  Obituary 132
  Earlier sketches in SATA 4, 56, 79
  See also CLR 127
Hamilton, Virginia Esther
  See Hamilton, Virginia
Hamilton-Paterson, James 1941- 82
Hamlet, Ova
  See Lupoff, Richard A(llen)
Hamley, D. C.
  See Hamley, Dennis
Hamley, Dennis 1935- 69
  Earlier sketch in SATA 39
  See also CLR 47
  See also SAAS 22

Hamley, Dennis C.
  See Hamley, Dennis
Hamlin, Peter J. 1970- 84
Hamm, Diane Johnston 1949- 78
Hammer, Charles 1934- 58
Hammer, Richard 1928- 6
Hammerman, Gay M(orenus) 1926- 9
Hammill, Matt 1982- 206
Hammond, Andrew 1970- 181
Hammond, Ralph
  See Hammond Innes, Ralph
Hammond, Winifred G(raham) 1899-1992 ... 29
  Obituary 107
Hammond Innes, Ralph 1913-1998 116
Hammontree, Marie (Gertrude) 1913- 13
Hample, Zack 1977- 161
Hampshire, Joyce Gregorian
  See Gregorian, Joyce Ballou
Hampshire, Susan 1942- 98
Hampson, (Richard) Denman 1929- 15
Hampson, Frank 1918(?)-1985
  Obituary 46
Hampton, Wilborn 1940- 196
  Earlier sketch in SATA 156
Hamre, Leif 1914- 5
Hamsa, Bobbie 1944- 52
  Brief entry 38
Han, Jenny 1981- 175
Han, Lu
  See Stickler, Soma Han
Han, Soma
  See Stickler, Soma Han
Han, Suzanne Crowder 1953- 89
Hancock, Mary A. 1923- 31
Hancock, Sibyl 1940- 9
Hand, Elizabeth 1957- 167
  Earlier sketch in SATA 118
Handford, Martin (John) 1956- 64
  See also CLR 22
Handforth, Thomas (Schofield) 1897-1948 .. 42
Handler, Daniel
  See Snicket, Lemony
Handville, Robert (Tompkins) 1924- 45
Hane, Roger 1940-1974
  Obituary 20
Hanel, Wolfram
  See Haenel, Wolfram
Haney, Lynn 1941- 23
Hanff, Helene 1916-1997 97
  Earlier sketch in SATA 11
Hanft, Josh 1956- 197
Hanft, Joshua E.
  See Hanft, Josh
Hanley, Boniface Francis 1924- 65
Hanlon, Emily 1945- 15
Hann, Jacquie 1951- 19
Hann, Judith 1942- 77
Hanna, Bill
  See Hanna, William (Denby)
Hanna, Cheryl 1951- 84
Hanna, Dan 200
Hanna, Jack (Bushnell) 1947- 74
Hanna, Nell(ie L.) 1908- 55
Hanna, Paul R(obert) 1902-1988 9
Hanna, William (Denby) 1910-2001 51
  Obituary 126
Hannam, Charles 1925- 50
Hannan, Peter 1954- 187
Hannigan, Katherine 170
Hannon, Ezra
  See Hunter, Evan
Hann-Syme, Marguerite 127
Hano, Arnold 1922- 12
Hano, Renee Roth
  See Roth-Hano, Renee
Hanover, Terri
  See Huff, Tanya
Hansen, Ann Larkin 1958- 96
Hansen, Brooks 1965- 104
Hansen, Caryl (Hall) 1929- 39
Hansen, Ian V. 1929- 113

Hansen, Jennifer 1972- *156*
Hansen, Joyce 1942- *172*
  Autobiography Feature *172*
  Brief entry *39*
  Earlier sketches in SATA *46, 101*
  See also CLR *21*
  See also SAAS *15*
Hansen, Joyce Viola
  See Hansen, Joyce
Hansen, Mark Victor *112*
Hansen, Ron 1947- *56*
Hansen, Ronald Thomas
  See Hansen, Ron
Hanser, Richard (Frederick) 1909-1981 .... *13*
Hanson, Joan 1938- *8*
Hanson, Joseph E. 1894(?)-1971
  Obituary *27*
Hanson, Mary Elizabeth *188*
Hanson, Warren 1949- *155*
Hansson, Gunilla 1939- *64*
Hantman, Clea *200*
Harald, Eric
  See Boesen, Victor
Harcourt, Ellen Knowles 1890(?)-1984
  Obituary *36*
Hard, Charlotte (Ann) 1969- *98*
Hardcastle, Michael 1933- *47*
  Brief entry *38*
Harding, Lee 1937- *32*
  Brief entry *31*
Hardt, Helga Fleischhauer
  See Fleischhauer-Hardt, Helga
Hardwick, Richard Holmes, Jr. 1923- *12*
Hardy, Alice Dale *67*
  Earlier sketch in SATA *1*
Hardy, David A(ndrews) 1936- *9*
Hardy, Jon 1958- *53*
Hardy, LeAnne 1951- *154*
Hardy, Stuart
  See Schisgall, Oscar
Hare, Norma Q(uarles) 1924- *46*
  Brief entry *41*
Harel, Nira 1936- *154*
Harford, Henry
  See Hudson, W(illiam) H(enry)
Hargrave, Leonie
  See Disch, Thomas M.
Hargreaves, (Charles) Roger 1935-1988
  Obituary *56*
Hargrove, James 1947- *57*
  Brief entry *50*
Hargrove, Jim
  See Hargrove, James
Harik, Elsa
  See Marston, Elsa
Harik, Elsa M.
  See Marston, Elsa
Harik, Elsa Marston
  See Marston, Elsa
Hariton, Anca I. 1955- *79*
Hark, Mildred
  See McQueen, Mildred Hark
Harkaway, Hal
  See Stratemeyer, Edward L.
Harkins, Philip 1912-1997 .... *6*
  Obituary *129*
Harlan, Elizabeth 1945- *41*
  Brief entry *35*
Harlan, Glen
  See Cebulash, Mel
Harlan, Judith 1949- *135*
  Earlier sketch in SATA *74*
  See also CLR *81*
Harland, Richard 1947- *152*
Harlee, J. V.
  See Leese, Jennifer L.B.
Harler, Ann
  See Van Steenwyk, Elizabeth (Ann)
Harley, Avis *183*
Harley, Bill 1954- *87*
Harlow, Joan Hiatt 1932- *157*

Harman, Fred 1902(?)-1982
  Obituary *30*
Harman, Hugh 1903-1982
  Obituary *33*
Harmelink, Barbara (Mary) *9*
Harmer, Mabel 1894-1992 .... *45*
Harmon, Dan
  See Harmon, Daniel E(lton)
Harmon, Daniel E(lton) 1949- *157*
Harmon, Margaret 1906- *20*
Harmon, Michael 1969- *189*
Harmon, Michael B.
  See Harmon, Michael
Harmon, William (Ruth) 1938- *65*
Harnan, Terry 1920- *12*
Harness, Cheryl 1951- *178*
  Earlier sketch in SATA *131*
Harnett, Cynthia (Mary) 1893-1981 .... *5*
  Obituary *32*
Harper, Anita 1943- *41*
Harper, Betty 1946- *126*
Harper, Charise
  See Harper, Charise Mericle
Harper, Charise Mericle *179*
Harper, Elaine
  See Hallin, Emily Watson
Harper, Ellen
  See Noble, Marty
Harper, Jamie *174*
Harper, Jessica 1949- *148*
Harper, Jo 1932- *169*
  Earlier sketch in SATA *97*
Harper, Lee *201*
Harper, Mary Wood
  See Dixon, Jeanne
Harper, Piers 1966- *161*
  Earlier sketch in SATA *105*
Harper, Suzanne *194*
Harper, Wilhelmina 1884-1973 .... *4*
  Obituary *26*
Harrah, Madge 1931- *154*
Harrah, Michael 1940- *41*
Harrah, Monique
  See Harrah, Madge
Harrar, George E. 1949- *124*
Harrell, Beatrice Orcutt 1943- *93*
Harrell, Janice 1945- *70*
Harries, Joan 1922- *39*
Harrill, Ronald 1950- *90*
Harrington, Denis J(ames) 1932- *88*
Harrington, Evelyn Davis 1911- *5*
Harrington, Janice N. 1956- *187*
Harrington, Lyn
  See Harrington, Evelyn Davis
Harris, Alan 1944- *71*
Harris, Aurand 1915-1996 .... *37*
  Obituary *91*
Harris, Bob
  See Harris, Robert J.
Harris, Carol Flynn 1933- *135*
Harris, Catherine
  See Ainsworth, Catherine Harris
Harris, Christie
  See Harris, Christie (Lucy) Irwin
Harris, Christie (Lucy) Irwin 1907-2002 ...... *74*
  Autobiography Feature *116*
  Earlier sketch in SATA *6*
  See also CLR *47*
  See also SAAS *10*
Harris, Christine 1955- *105*
Harris, Colver
  See Colver, Anne
Harris, David 1942- *118*
Harris, David William
  See Harris, David
Harris, Dorothy Joan 1931- *153*
  Earlier sketch in SATA *13*
Harris, Geraldine (Rachel) 1951- *54*
Harris, Jacqueline L. 1929- *62*
Harris, Janet 1932-1979 .... *4*
  Obituary *23*

Harris, Jesse
  See Standiford, Natalie
Harris, Joan 1946- *146*
Harris, Joe 1928- *201*
Harris, Joel Chandler 1848-1908 .... *100*
  See also YABC *1*
  See also CLR *128*
Harris, John (Wyndham Parkes Lucas) Beynon
  1903-1969 .... *118*
Harris, Johnson
  See Harris, John (Wyndham Parkes Lucas)
  Beynon
Harris, Jonathan 1921-1997 .... *52*
Harris, Larry Vincent 1939- *59*
Harris, Lavinia
  See St. John, Nicole
Harris, Leon A., Jr. 1926-2000 .... *4*
Harris, Lois V. *199*
Harris, Lorle K(empe) 1912-2001 .... *22*
Harris, Marilyn
  See Springer, Marilyn Harris
Harris, Mark Jonathan 1941- *84*
  Earlier sketch in SATA *32*
Harris, Mary K(athleen) 1905-1966 .... *119*
Harris, Robert J. 1955- *195*
Harris, Robie H. 1940- *203*
  Brief entry *53*
  Earlier sketches in SATA *90, 147*
Harris, Robin
  See Shine, Deborah
Harris, Rosemary (Jeanne) *82*
  Earlier sketch in SATA *4*
  See also CLR *30*
  See also SAAS *7*
Harris, Ruth Elwin 1935- *164*
Harris, Sherwood 1932-2009 .... *25*
Harris, Steven Michael 1957- *55*
Harris, Trudy 1949- *191*
  Earlier sketch in SATA *128*
Harris-Filderman, Diane
  See Filderman, Diane E(lizabeth)
Harrison, C(hester) William 1913-1994 .... *35*
Harrison, Carol
  See Harrison, Carol Thompson
Harrison, Carol Thompson *113*
Harrison, David L. 1937- *186*
  Earlier sketches in SATA *26, 92, 150*
Harrison, Deloris 1938- *9*
Harrison, Edward Hardy 1926- *56*
Harrison, Elizabeth (Allen) Cavanna
  1909-2001 .... *30*
  Earlier sketch in SATA *1*
  See also SAAS *4*
Harrison, Harry 1925- *4*
Harrison, Harry Max
  See Harrison, Harry
Harrison, Mette Ivie 1970- *202*
  Earlier sketch in SATA *149*
Harrison, Michael 1939- *106*
Harrison, Molly (Hodgett) 1909-2002 .... *41*
Harrison, Sarah 1946- *63*
Harrison, Ted
  See Harrison, Edward Hardy
Harsh, Fred (T.) 1925- *72*
Harshaw, Ruth H(etzel) 1890-1968 .... *27*
Harshman, Marc 1950- *109*
  Earlier sketch in SATA *71*
Hart, Alexandra 1939- *14*
Hart, Alison
  See Leonhardt, Alice
Hart, Bruce 1938-2006 .... *57*
  Brief entry *39*
Hart, Carole 1943- *57*
  Brief entry *39*
Hart, Carolyn 1936- *74*
Hart, Carolyn G.
  See Hart, Carolyn
Hart, Carolyn Gimpel
  See Hart, Carolyn
Hart, Jan Siegel 1940- *79*
Hart, Joyce 1954- *148*

Hart, Karen *185*
Hart, Lenore *171*
Hart, Philip S. 1944- *180*
Hart, Virginia 1949- *83*
Harte, (Francis) Bret(t) 1836(?)-1902 .... *26*
Harter, Debbie 1963- *107*
Hartfield, Claire 1957- *147*
Hartinger, Brent 1964- *174*
   Earlier sketch in SATA *145*
Hartland, Jessie *171*
Hartley, Ellen (Raphael) 1915-1980 .... *23*
Hartley, Fred Allan III 1953- *41*
Hartley, William B(rown) 1913-1980 .... *23*
Hartling, Peter
   See Hartling, Peter
Hartling, Peter 1933- *66*
   See also CLR *29*
Hartman, Cassie *202*
Hartman, Dan 1955- *202*
Hartman, Evert 1937- *38*
   Brief entry *35*
Hartman, Jane E(vangeline) 1928- *47*
Hartman, Louis F(rancis) 1901-1970 .... *22*
Hartman, Rachel *174*
Hartman, Victoria 1942- *91*
Hartnett, Sonya 1968- *176*
   Earlier sketches in SATA *93, 130*
Hartshorn, Ruth M. 1928- *11*
Hartung, Susan Kathleen *192*
   Earlier sketch in SATA *150*
Hartwig, Manfred 1950- *81*
Harvey, Brett 1936- *61*
Harvey, Edith 1908(?)-1972
   Obituary *27*
Harvey, Gill *189*
Harvey, Karen D. 1935- *88*
Harvey, Roland 1945- *179*
   Earlier sketches in SATA *71, 123*
Harvey-Fitzhenry, Alyxandra 1974- *189*
Harwick, B. L.
   See Keller, Beverly L(ou)
Harwin, Brian
   See Henderson, LeGrand
Harwood, Pearl Augusta (Bragdon)
   1903-1998 .... *9*
Haseley, Dennis 1950- *157*
   Brief entry *44*
   Earlier sketches in SATA *57, 105*
Hashmi, Kerri 1955- *108*
Haskell, Arnold L(ionel) 1903-1981(?) *6*
Haskins, James
   See Haskins, James S.
Haskins, James S. 1941-2005 .... *132*
   Autobiography Feature *132*
   Earlier sketches in SATA *9, 69, 105*
   See also CLR *39*
   See also SAAS *4*
Haskins, Jim
   See Haskins, James S.
Hasler, Eveline 1933- *181*
Hasler, Joan 1931- *28*
Hass, Robert 1941- *94*
Hassall, Joan 1906-1988 .... *43*
   Obituary *56*
Hassett, Ann 1958- *162*
Hassett, John *162*
Hassler, Jon 1933-2008 .... *19*
   Obituary *191*
Hassler, Jon Francis
   See Hassler, Jon
Hastings, Beverly
   See Barkin, Carol
   and James, Elizabeth
Hastings, Graham
   See Jeffries, Roderic
Hastings, Ian 1912- *62*
Hastings, Victor
   See Disch, Thomas M.
Haszard, Patricia Moyes 1923-2000 .... *63*
Hatch, Lynda S. 1950- *90*
Hathaway, Barbara *164*

Hathorn, Elizabeth
   See Hathorn, Elizabeth Helen
Hathorn, Elizabeth Helen 1943- *156*
   Autobiography Feature *156*
   Earlier sketches in SATA *74, 120*
Hathorn, Libby 1943-
   See Hathorn, Elizabeth Helen
Hatkoff, Craig 1954- *192*
Hatlo, Jimmy 1898-1963
   Obituary *23*
Hatton, Caroline 1957- *205*
Haugaard, Erik Christian 1923- *68*
   Earlier sketch in SATA *4*
   See also CLR *11*
   See also SAAS *12*
Haugaard, Kay *117*
Haugen, Hayley Mitchell 1968- *172*
Haugen, Tormod 1945- *66*
Hauman, Doris 1898-1984 .... *32*
Hauman, George 1890-1961 .... *32*
Hauptly, Denis J(ames) 1945- *57*
Hauser, Jill Frankel 1950- *127*
Hauser, Margaret L(ouise) 1909- *10*
Hausherr, Rosmarie 1943- *86*
Hausman, Gerald 1945- *180*
   Earlier sketches in SATA *13, 90, 132*
   See also CLR *89*
Hausman, Gerry
   See Hausman, Gerald
Hauth, Katherine B. 1940- *99*
Hautman, Pete 1952- *173*
   Earlier sketches in SATA *82, 128*
Hautman, Peter Murray
   See Hautman, Pete
Hautzig, Deborah 1956- *106*
   Earlier sketch in SATA *31*
Hautzig, Esther Rudomin 1930-2009 .... *148*
   Earlier sketches in SATA *4, 68*
   See also CLR *22*
   See also SAAS *15*
Havel, Geoff 1955- *152*
Havel, Jennifer
   See Havill, Juanita
Havelin, Kate 1961- *143*
Havighurst, Walter (Edwin) 1901-1994 .... *1*
   Obituary *79*
Haviland, Virginia 1911-1988 .... *6*
   Obituary *54*
Havill, Juanita 1949- *155*
   Earlier sketch in SATA *74*
Hawes, Judy 1913- *4*
Hawes, Louise 1943- *180*
   Earlier sketch in SATA *60*
Hawke, Rosanne 1953- *165*
   Earlier sketch in SATA *124*
Hawke, Rosanne Joy
   See Hawke, Rosanne
Hawkes, Kevin 1959- *201*
   Earlier sketches in SATA *78, 150*
Hawkes, Nigel 1943- *119*
Hawkesworth, Eric 1921- *13*
Hawking, Lucy 1969- *197*
Hawkins, Arthur 1903-1985 .... *19*
Hawkins, Colin 1945- *162*
   Earlier sketch in SATA *112*
Hawkins, Jacqui *162*
   Earlier sketch in SATA *112*
Hawkins, Jimmy 1941- *188*
Hawkins, Laura 1951- *74*
Hawkins, (Helena Ann) Quail 1905-2002 ...... *6*
   Obituary *141*
Hawkinson, John (Samuel) 1912-1994 .... *4*
Hawkinson, Lucy (Ozone) 1924-1971 .... *21*
Hawks, Robert 1961- *85*
Hawley, Mabel C. *67*
   Earlier sketch in SATA *1*
Hawthorne, Captain R. M.
   See Ellis, Edward S.
Hawthorne, Nathaniel 1804-1864
   See YABC *2*
   See also CLR *103*

Hay, Jeff T. *154*
Hay, John 1915- *13*
Hay, Timothy
   See Brown, Margaret Wise
Hayashi, Leslie Ann 1954- *115*
Hayashi, Nancy 1939- *186*
   Earlier sketch in SATA *80*
Haycak, Cara 1961- *180*
Haycock, Kate 1962- *77*
Haycraft, Howard 1905-1991 .... *6*
   Obituary *70*
Haycraft, Molly Costain 1911- *6*
Hayden, Gwendolen Lampshire 1904- *35*
Hayden, Robert C(arter), Jr. 1937- *47*
   Brief entry *28*
Hayden, Robert E(arl) 1913-1980 .... *19*
   Obituary *26*
Hayden, Torey L. 1951- *163*
   Earlier sketch in SATA *65*
Hayden, Torey Lynn
   See Hayden, Torey L.
Hayes, Carlton J(oseph) H(untley)
   1882-1964 .... *11*
Hayes, Daniel 1952- *109*
   Earlier sketch in SATA *73*
Hayes, Geoffrey 1947- *91*
   Earlier sketch in SATA *26*
Hayes, Joe 1945- *131*
   Earlier sketch in SATA *88*
Hayes, John F. 1904-1980 .... *11*
Hayes, Rosemary *158*
Hayes, Sheila 1937- *51*
   Brief entry *50*
Hayes, Will *7*
Hayes, William D(imitt) 1913-1976 .... *8*
Haynes, Betsy 1937- *94*
   Brief entry *37*
   Earlier sketch in SATA *48*
   See also CLR *90*
Haynes, David 1955- *97*
Haynes, Linda
   See Swinford, Betty (June Wells)
Haynes, Mary 1938- *65*
Haynes, Max 1956- *72*
Hays, H(offmann) R(eynolds) 1904-1980 .... *26*
Hays, Thomas Anthony 1957- *84*
Hays, Tony
   See Hays, Thomas Anthony
Hays, Wilma Pitchford 1909- *28*
   Earlier sketch in SATA *1*
   See also CLR *59*
   See also SAAS *3*
Hayward, Linda 1943- *185*
   Brief entry *39*
   Earlier sketch in SATA *101*
Haywood, Carolyn 1898-1990 .... *75*
   Obituary *64*
   Earlier sketches in SATA *1, 29*
   See also CLR *22*
Hazell, Rebecca (Eileen) 1947- *141*
Hazen, Barbara Shook 1930- *178*
   Earlier sketches in SATA *27, 90*
Hazen, Lynn E. *202*
Head, Gay
   See Hauser, Margaret L(ouise)
Head, Tom 1978- *167*
Headley, Elizabeth
   See Harrison, Elizabeth (Allen) Cavanna
Headley, Justina Chen 1968- *176*
Headstrom, (Birger) Richard 1902-1985 .... *8*
Heady, Eleanor B(utler) 1917-1979 .... *8*
Heagy, William D. 1964- *76*
Heal, Edith 1903-1995 .... *7*
Heal, Gillian 1934- *89*
Heale, Jay (Jeremy Peter Wingfield) 1937- .. *84*
Healey, Brooks
   See Albert, Burton
Healey, Larry 1927- *44*
   Brief entry *42*
Heap, Sue 1954- *187*
   Earlier sketch in SATA *150*

Heaps, Willard A(llison) 1908-1987 26
Hearn, Diane Dawson 1952- 79
Hearn, Emily
    See Valleau, Emily
Hearn, Julie 1958- 152
Hearn, Lian
    See Rubinstein, Gillian
Hearn, Sneed
    See Gregg, Andrew K.
Hearne, Betsy 1942- 146
    Earlier sketches in SATA 38, 95
Heath, Charles D(ickinson) 1941- 46
Heath, Veronica
    See Blackett, Veronica Heath
Heaven, Constance (Christina) 1911- 7
Hebert-Collins, Sheila 1948- 111
Hecht, George J(oseph) 1895-1980
    Obituary 22
Hecht, Henri Joseph 1922- 9
Hechtkopf, Henryk 1910- 17
Heck, Bessie (Mildred) Holland 1911-1995 . 26
Heck, Ed 1963- 173
Heckert, Connie K(aye Delp) 1948- 82
Hector, Julian 205
Hedderwick, Mairi 1939- 145
    Earlier sketches in SATA 30, 77
Hedges, Sid(ney) G(eorge) 1897-1974 28
Hedrick, Irene Hope 1920- 175
Heelan, Jamee Riggio 1965- 146
Heerboth, Sharon
    See Leon, Sharon
Heffernan, John 1949- 168
    Earlier sketch in SATA 121
Heffron, Dorris 1944- 68
Hefter, Richard 1942- 31
Hegarty, Reginald Beaton 1906-1973 10
Hehenberger, Shelly 1968- 126
Heidbreder, Robert 1947- 196
    Earlier sketch in SATA 130
Heidbreder, Robert K.
    See Heidbreder, Robert
Heide, Florence Parry 1919- 192
    Earlier sketches in SATA 32, 69, 118
    See also CLR 60
    See also SAAS 6
Heiderstadt, Dorothy 1907-2001 6
Heidi Louise
    See Erdrich, Louise
Heidler, David S(tephen) 1955- 132
Heidler, Jeanne T. 1956- 132
Heilbroner, Joan Knapp 1922- 63
Heilbrun, Lois Hussey 1922(?)-1987
    Obituary 54
Heiligman, Deborah 1958- 193
    Earlier sketches in SATA 90, 144
Heilman, Joan Rattner 50
Heimann, Rolf 1940- 164
    Earlier sketch in SATA 120
Hein, Lucille Eleanor 1915-1994 20
Heine, Helme 1941- 135
    Earlier sketch in SATA 67
    See also CLR 18
Heinlein, Robert A. 1907-1988 69
    Obituary 56
    Earlier sketch in SATA 9
    See also CLR 75
Heinlein, Robert Anson
    See Heinlein, Robert A.
Heins, Ethel L(eah) 1918-1997 101
Heins, Paul 1909- 13
Heintze, Carl 1922- 26
Heinz, Bill
    See Heinz, W.C.
Heinz, Brian J. 1946- 181
    Earlier sketch in SATA 95
Heinz, Brian James
    See Heinz, Brian J.
Heinz, W.C. 1915-2008 26
Heinz, Wilfred Charles
    See Heinz, W.C.

Heinzen, Mildred
    See Masters, Mildred
Heisel, Sharon E(laine) 1941- 125
    Earlier sketch in SATA 84
Heitzmann, William Ray 1948- 73
Heitzmann, Wm. Ray
    See Heitzmann, William Ray
Helakoski, Leslie 178
Helberg, Shirley Adelaide Holden 1919- ... 138
Helfer, Andrew 187
Helfer, Ralph 1937- 177
Helfman, Elizabeth S(eaver) 1911-2001 3
Helfman, Harry Carmozin 1910-1995 3
Helgerson, Joseph 1950- 181
Hellard, Susan 182
Hellberg, Hans-Eric 1927- 38
Heller, Linda 1944- 46
    Brief entry 40
Heller, Mike
    See Hano, Arnold
Heller, Ruth M. 1924- 112
    Earlier sketch in SATA 66
Hellman, Hal
    See Hellman, Harold
Hellman, Harold 1927- 4
Helman, Andrea (Jean) 1946- 160
    Earlier sketch in SATA 107
Helmer, Diana Star 1962- 86
Helmer, Marilyn 160
    Earlier sketch in SATA 112
Helps, Racey 1913-1971 2
    Obituary 25
Helquist, Brett 187
    Earlier sketch in SATA 146
Helweg, Hans H. 1917- 50
    Brief entry 33
Helyar, Jane Penelope Josephine 1933- 5
    Autobiography Feature 138
    See also SAAS 2
Hemmant, Lynette 1938- 69
Hemming, Roy G. 1928-1995 11
    Obituary 86
Hemphill, Helen 1955- 179
Hemphill, Kris (Harrison) 1963- 118
Hemphill, Martha Locke 1904-1973 37
Hemphill, Stephanie 190
Hemstock, Gillian 1956- 173
Henba, Bobbie 1926- 87
Henbest, Nigel 1951- 55
    Brief entry 52
Henderley, Brooks 1
Henderson, Aileen Kilgore 1921- 178
Henderson, Aileen Mary
    See Fox, Aileen
Henderson, Gordon 1950- 53
Henderson, Kathy 1949- 155
    Brief entry 53
    Earlier sketches in SATA 55, 95
Henderson, Lauren 1966- 201
Henderson, LeGrand 1901-1965 9
Henderson, Nancy Wallace 1916- 22
Henderson, Zenna (Chlarson) 1917-1983 5
Hendrickson, Walter Brookfield, Jr. 1936- 9
Hendry, Diana 1941- 106
    Earlier sketch in SATA 68
Hendry, Frances Mary 1941- 171
    Earlier sketch in SATA 110
Hendry, Linda (Gail) 1961- 83
Heneghan, James 1930- 160
    Earlier sketches in SATA 53, 97
Henkes, Kevin 1960- 154
    Earlier sketches in SATA 43, 76, 108
    See also CLR 108
Hennessy, Barbara G.
    See Hennessy, B.G.
Hennessy, Barbara Gulbrandsen
    See Hennessy, B.G.
Hennessy, B.G. 1951- 175
Henney, Carolee Wells 1928- 102
Henriod, Lorraine 1925- 26

Henriquez, Emile F. 1937- 170
    Earlier sketch in SATA 89
Henry, April 1959- 174
Henry, Ernest 1948- 107
Henry, Joanne Landers 1927- 6
Henry, Maeve 1960- 75
Henry, Marguerite 1902-1997 100
    Obituary 99
    See also CLR 4
    See also SAAS 7
Henry, Marie H. 1935- 65
Henry, Marilyn 1939- 117
Henry, Marion
    See del Rey, Lester
Henry, O. 1862-1910
    See YABC 2
Henry, Oliver
    See Henry, O.
Henry, T. E.
    See Rowland-Entwistle, (Arthur) Theodore
        (Henry)
Henschel, Elizabeth Georgie 56
Henson, Heather 206
Henson, James Maury
    See Henson, Jim
Henson, Jim 1936-1990 43
    Obituary 65
Henstra, Friso 1928- 73
    Earlier sketch in SATA 8
    See also SAAS 14
Hentoff, Nat(han Irving) 1925- 133
    Brief entry 27
    Earlier sketches in SATA 42, 69
    See also CLR 52
Henty, G(eorge) A(lfred) 1832-1902 64
    See also CLR 76
Heo, Yumi 1964- 206
    Earlier sketches in SATA 94, 146
Hepler, Heather 177
Herald, Kathleen
    See Peyton, Kathleen Wendy
Herb, Angela M. 1970- 92
Herbert, Cecil
    See Hamilton, Charles (Harold St. John)
Herbert, Don 1917-2007 2
    Obituary 184
Herbert, Donald Jeffrey
    See Herbert, Don
Herbert, Frank 1920-1986 37
    Obituary 47
    Earlier sketch in SATA 9
Herbert, Frank Patrick
    See Herbert, Frank
Herbert, Helen (Jean) 1947- 57
Herbert, Janis 1956- 139
Herbert, Wally 1934-2007 23
Herbert, Walter William
    See Herbert, Wally
Herbst, Judith 1947- 74
Herda, D.J. 1948- 80
Herge
    See Remi, Georges
Heritage, Martin
    See Horler, Sydney
Herkimer, L(awrence) R(ussell) 1925(?)- 42
Herlihy, Dirlie Anne 1935- 73
Herman, Charlotte 1937- 203
    Earlier sketches in SATA 20, 99
Hermanson, Dennis (Everett) 1947- 10
Hermes, Jules 1962- 92
Hermes, Patricia 1936- 191
    Earlier sketches in SATA 31, 78, 141
Hermes, Patricia Mary
    See Hermes, Patricia
Hernandez, Natalie Nelson 1929- 123
Herndon, Ernest 91
Herold, Ann Bixby 1937- 72
Herrera, Juan Felipe 1948- 127
Herrick, Steven 1958- 156
    Earlier sketch in SATA 103
Herriman, George (Joseph) 1880-1944 140

Herriot, James 1916-1995
  See Wight, James Alfred
Herrmanns, Ralph 1933- 11
Herrold, Tracey
  See Dils, Tracey E.
Herron, Carolivia 1947- 203
Herron, Edward A(lbert) 1912- 4
Herschler, Mildred Barger 130
Hersey, John 1914-1993 25
  Obituary 76
Hersey, John Richard
  See Hersey, John
  and Hersey, John
Hershberger, Priscilla (Gorman) 1951- 81
Hershenhorn, Esther 1945- 151
Hershey, Kathleen M. 1934- 80
Hershey, Mary 173
Hersom, Kathleen 1911- 73
Hertz, Grete Janus 1915- 23
Herzig, Alison Cragin 1935- 87
Herzog, Brad 1968- 131
Heslewood, Juliet 1951- 82
Hess, Lilo 1916- 4
Hess, Paul 1961- 134
Hesse, Hermann 1877-1962 50
Hesse, Karen 1952- 158
  Autobiography Feature 113
  Earlier sketches in SATA *74, 103*
  See also CLR *141*
  See also SAAS *25*
Hest, Amy 1950- 193
  Earlier sketches in SATA *55, 82, 129*
Heuer, Karsten 1968(?)- 202
Heuer, Kenneth John 1927- 44
Heuman, William 1912-1971 21
Heuston, Kimberley 1960- 167
Heuston, Kimberley Burton
  See Heuston, Kimberley
Hewes, Agnes Danforth 1874-1963 35
Hewett, Anita 1918-1989 13
Hewett, Joan 1930- 140
  Earlier sketch in SATA *81*
Hewett, Richard 1929- 81
Hewitson, Jennifer 1961- 97
Hewitt, Margaret 1961- 84
Hewitt, Sally 1949- 127
Hext, Harrington
  See Phillpotts, Eden
Hey, Nigel S(tewart) 1936- 20
Heyduck-Huth, Hilde 1929- 8
Heyer, Carol 1950- 130
  Earlier sketch in SATA *74*
Heyer, Marilee 1942- 102
  Earlier sketch in SATA *64*
Heyerdahl, Thor 1914-2002 52
  Earlier sketch in SATA *2*
Heyes, (Nancy) Eileen 1956- 150
  Earlier sketch in SATA *80*
Heyliger, William 1884-1955
  See YABC *1*
Heyman, Ken(neth Louis) 1930- 114
  Earlier sketch in SATA *34*
Heyward, (Edwin) DuBose 1885-1940 21
Heywood, Karen 1946- 48
Hezlep, William (Earl) 1936- 88
Hibbert, Arthur Raymond
  See Hibbert, Christopher
Hibbert, Christopher 1924-2008 4
  Obituary 201
Hibbert, Eleanor Alice Burford 1906-1993 2
  Obituary 74
Hickman, Estella (Lee) 1942- 111
Hickman, Janet 1940- 127
  Earlier sketch in SATA *12*
Hickman, Martha Whitmore 1925- 26
Hickman, Pamela 1958- 186
  Earlier sketch in SATA *128*
Hickock, Will
  See Harrison, C(hester) William
Hickok, Lorena A. 1893-1968 20
Hickox, Rebecca (Ayres) 116

Hicks, Barbara Jean 1953- 165
Hicks, Betty 191
Hicks, Clifford B. 1920- 50
Hicks, Eleanor B.
  See Coerr, Eleanor (Beatrice)
Hicks, Harvey
  See Stratemeyer, Edward L.
Hicks, Peter 1952- 111
Hicyilmaz, Gaye 1947- 157
  Earlier sketch in SATA *77*
Hieatt, Constance B(artlett) 1928- 4
Hiebert, Ray Eldon 1932- 13
Higdon, Hal 1931- 4
Higginbottom, David 1923- 87
  Earlier sketch in SATA *25*
Higginbottom, J(effrey) Winslow 1945- 29
Higgins, Joanna 1945- 125
Higgins, Simon (Richard) 1958- 105
Higginsen, Vy 79
High, Linda Oatman 1958- 188
  Autobiography Feature 188
  Earlier sketches in SATA *94, 145*
High, Philip E. 1914- 119
High, Philip Empson
  See High, Philip E.
Higham, David (Michael) 1949- 50
Higham, Jon Atlas
  See Higham, Jonathan Huw
Higham, Jonathan Huw 1960- 59
Highet, Helen
  See MacInnes, Helen (Clark)
Hightman, Jason 1971(?)- 189
Hightman, J.P.
  See Hightman, Jason
Hightower, Florence Cole 1916-1981 4
  Obituary 27
Highwater, Jamake (Mamake)
  1942(?)-2001 69
  Brief entry 30
  Earlier sketch in SATA *32*
  See also CLR *17*
Hilb, Nora 1953- 178
Hildebrandt, Greg 1939- 172
  Brief entry 33
  Earlier sketch in SATA *55*
Hildebrandt, Tim 1939-2006 55
  Brief entry 33
Hildebrandt, Timothy
  See Hildebrandt, Tim
Hildebrandts, The
  See Hildebrandt, Greg
  and Hildebrandt, Tim
Hilder, Rowland 1905-1993 36
  Obituary 77
Hildick, E. W.
  See Hildick, Wallace
Hildick, Wallace 1925-2001 68
  Earlier sketch in SATA *2*
  See also SAAS *6*
Hilgartner, Beth 1957- 58
Hill, Alexis
  See Craig, Mary (Francis) Shura
  and Glick, Ruth (Burtnick)
Hill, Anthony R. 1942- 164
  Earlier sketch in SATA *91*
Hill, Anthony Robert
  See Hill, Anthony R.
Hill, David 1942- 152
  Earlier sketch in SATA *103*
Hill, Donna (Marie) 1921- 124
  Earlier sketch in SATA *24*
Hill, Douglas 1935-2007 78
  Earlier sketch in SATA *39*
Hill, Douglas Arthur
  See Hill, Douglas
Hill, Elizabeth Starr 1925- 143
  Earlier sketch in SATA *24*
Hill, Eric 1927- 133
  Brief entry 53
  Earlier sketch in SATA *66*
  See also CLR *13*

Hill, Gordon
  See Eldin, Peter
Hill, Grace Brooks 67
  Earlier sketch in SATA *1*
Hill, Grace Livingston 1865-1947
  See YABC *2*
Hill, Helen M(orey) 1915- 27
Hill, John
  See Koontz, Dean R.
Hill, Johnson
  See Kunhardt, Edith
Hill, Judy I. R.
  See Roberts, Judy I.
Hill, Kathleen Louise 1917- 4
Hill, Kay
  See Hill, Kathleen Louise
Hill, Kirkpatrick 1938- 188
  Earlier sketches in SATA *72, 126*
Hill, Laban
  See Hill, Laban Carrick
Hill, Laban Carrick 170
Hill, Lee Sullivan 1958- 96
Hill, Lorna 1902-1991 12
Hill, Margaret (Ohler) 1915- 36
Hill, Meg
  See Hill, Margaret (Ohler)
Hill, Meredith
  See Craig, Mary (Francis) Shura
Hill, Monica
  See Watson, Jane Werner
Hill, Pamela Smith 1954- 112
Hill, Ralph Nading 1917-1987 65
Hill, Robert W(hite) 1919-1982 12
  Obituary 31
Hill, Ruth A.
  See Viguers, Ruth Hill
Hill, Ruth Livingston
  See Munce, Ruth Hill
Hill, Stuart 1958- 186
Hill, Susan 1942- 183
Hill, Susan Elizabeth
  See Hill, Susan
Hill, Susanna Leonard 1965- 193
Hill, Thomas 1960- 82
Hillcourt, William 1900-1992 27
Hillenbrand, Will 1960- 147
  Earlier sketch in SATA *84*
Hiller, Ilo (Ann) 1938- 59
Hillerman, Anthony Grove
  See Hillerman, Tony
Hillerman, Tony 1925-2008 6
  Obituary 198
Hillert, Margaret 1920- 91
  Earlier sketch in SATA *8*
Hilliard, Richard 183
Hillman, Ben 1957- 202
Hillman, Elizabeth 1942- 75
Hillman, John 1952- 120
Hillman, Martin
  See Hill, Douglas
Hillman, Priscilla 1940- 48
  Brief entry 39
Hillman, Shane 200
Hills, C.A.R. 1955- 39
Hills, Charles Albert Reis
  See Hills, C.A.R.
Hills, Tad 173
Hilton, Irene Pothus -1979 7
Hilton, James 1900-1954 34
Hilton, Margaret Lynette 1946- 105
  Earlier sketch in SATA *68*
  See also CLR *25*
  See also SAAS *21*
Hilton, Nette
  See Hilton, Margaret Lynette
Hilton, Ralph 1907-1982 8
Hilton, Suzanne 1922- 4
Hilton-Bruce, Anne
  See Hilton, Margaret Lynette
Him, George 1937-1982
  Obituary 30

Himelblau, Linda -2005 .... *179*
Himelstein, Shmuel 1940- 83
Himler, Ann 1946- 8
Himler, Ronald 1937- *183*
  Earlier sketches in SATA *6, 92, 137*
Himler, Ronald Norbert
  See Himler, Ronald
Himmelman, John C(arl) 1959- *159*
  Earlier sketches in SATA *47, 94*
Hinckley, Helen
  See Jones, Helen Hinckley
Hind, Dolores (Ellen) 1931- 53
  Brief entry 49
Hindin, Nathan
  See Bloch, Robert (Albert)
Hindley, Judy 1940- *179*
  Earlier sketch in SATA *120*
Hinds, P(atricia) Mignon 98
Hine, Sesyle Joslin 1929- 2
Hines, Anna Grossnickle 1946- *141*
  Brief entry 45
  Earlier sketches in SATA *51, 95*
  See also SAAS *16*
Hines, Gary (Roger) 1944- *136*
  Earlier sketch in SATA *74*
Hinojosa, Maria (de Lourdes) 1961- 88
Hinton, Nigel 1941- *166*
Hinton, Sam 1917-2009 43
Hinton, S.E. 1950- *160*
  Earlier sketches in SATA *19, 58, 115*
  See also CLR *23*
Hinton, Susan Eloise
  See Hinton, S.E.
Hintz, Martin 1945- *128*
  Brief entry 39
  Earlier sketch in SATA *47*
Hintz, Stephen V. 1975- *129*
Hippopotamus, Eugene H.
  See Kraus, (Herman) Robert
Hirano, Cathy 1957- 68
Hirao, Amiko *203*
Hirsch, Karen 1941- 61
Hirsch, Odo *157*
  Earlier sketch in SATA *111*
Hirsch, Phil 1926- 35
Hirsch, S. Carl 1913-1990 2
  See also SAAS *7*
Hirschfelder, Arlene B. 1943- *138*
  Earlier sketch in SATA *80*
Hirschi, Ron 1948- *192*
  Earlier sketches in SATA *56, 95*
Hirschmann, Linda (Ann) 1941- 40
Hirsh, Marilyn 1944-1988 7
  Obituary 58
Hirshberg, Al(bert Simon) 1909-1973 38
Hiscock, Bruce 1940- *204*
  Earlier sketches in SATA *57, 137*
Hiser, Constance 1950- 71
Hiser, Iona Seibert -1998 4
Hislop, Julia Rose Catherine 1962- 74
Hissey, Jane 1952- *130*
  Autobiography Feature *130*
  Earlier sketches in SATA *58, 103*
Hissey, Jane Elizabeth
  See Hissey, Jane
Hitchcock, Alfred (Joseph) 1899-1980 27
  Obituary 24
Hite, Sid 1954- *175*
  Earlier sketches in SATA *75, 136*
Hitte, Kathryn 1919- 16
Hitz, Demi 1942- *152*
  Earlier sketches in SATA *11, 66, 102*
  See also CLR *58*
Hitzeroth, Deborah L. 1961- 78
Hnizdovsky, Jacques 1915- 32
Ho, Louise *185*
Ho, Minfong 1951- *151*
  Earlier sketches in SATA *15, 94*
  See also CLR *28*
Hoagland, Edward (Morley) 1932- 51
Hoare, Robert J(ohn) 1921-1975 38

Hoban, Lillian 1925-1998 69
  Obituary *104*
  Earlier sketch in SATA *22*
  See also CLR *67*
Hoban, Russell 1925- *136*
  Earlier sketches in SATA *1, 40, 78*
  See also CLR *139*
Hoban, Russell Conwell
  See Hoban, Russell
Hoban, Tana 1917(?)-2006 .... *104*
  Obituary *173*
  Earlier sketches in SATA *22, 70*
  See also CLR *76*
  See also SAAS *12*
Hobart, Lois (Elaine) 7
Hobbie, Holly 1944- *178*
  See also CLR *88*
Hobbie, Jocelyn *190*
Hobbie, Nathaniel *196*
Hobbs, Leigh 1953- *166*
Hobbs, Valerie 1941- *193*
  Autobiography Feature *145*
  Earlier sketches in SATA *93, 145*
Hobbs, Will 1947- *177*
  Autobiography Feature *127*
  Earlier sketches in SATA *72, 110*
  See also CLR *59*
Hobbs, William Carl
  See Hobbs, Will
Hoberman, Mary Ann 1930- *158*
  Earlier sketches in SATA *5, 72, 111*
  See also CLR *22*
  See also SAAS *18*
Hobson, Bruce 1950- 62
Hobson, Burton (Harold) 1933- 28
Hobson, Laura Z(ametkin) 1900-1986 52
Hobson, Sally 1967- *172*
  Earlier sketch in SATA *84*
Hoce, Charley E. *174*
Hochman, David *202*
Hochschild, Arlie Russell 1940- 11
Hockaby, Stephen
  See Mitchell, Gladys (Maude Winifred)
Hockenberry, Hope
  See Newell, Hope Hockenberry
Hodge, Deborah 1954- *163*
  Earlier sketch in SATA *122*
Hodge, P. W.
  See Hodge, Paul W(illiam)
Hodge, Paul W(illiam) 1934- 12
Hodgell, P(atricia) C(hristine) 1951- 42
Hodges, C. Walter 1909-2004 2
  Obituary *158*
Hodges, Carl G. 1902-1964 10
Hodges, Cyril Walter
  See Hodges, C. Walter
Hodges, Elizabeth Jamison *1*
Hodges, Margaret 1911-2005 .... *167*
  Obituary *172*
  Earlier sketches in SATA *1, 33, 75, 117*
  See also SAAS *9*
Hodges, Margaret Moore
  See Hodges, Margaret
Hodgetts, Blake Christopher 1967- 43
Hodgkins, Fran 1964- *199*
Hodgkinson, Leigh 1975- *202*
Hodgman, Ann 1956- *198*
Hodgson, Harriet (W.) 1935- 84
Hoehne, Marcia 1951- 89
Hoellwarth, Cathryn Clinton
  See Clinton, Cathryn
Hoestlandt, Jo 1948- 94
Hoestlandt, Jocelyne
  See Hoestlandt, Jo
Hoexter, Corinne K. 1927- 6
Hoeye, Michael 1947- *136*
Hoff, Carol 1900-1979 11
Hoff, Mary (King) 1956- *157*
  Earlier sketch in SATA *74*

Hoff, Syd(ney) 1912-2004 .... *138*
  Obituary *154*
  Earlier sketches in SATA *9, 72*
  See also CLR *83*
  See also SAAS *4*
Hoffman, Edwin D. 49
Hoffman, Elizabeth P(arkinson) 1921-2003
  Obituary *153*
Hoffman, Mary 1945- *144*
  Earlier sketches in SATA *59, 97*
  See also SAAS *24*
Hoffman, Mat 1972- *150*
Hoffman, Nina Kiriki 1955- *160*
Hoffman, Phyllis M(iriam) 1944- 4
Hoffman, Rosekrans 1926- 15
Hoffmann, E(rnst) T(heodor) A(madeus)
  1776-1822 27
  See also CLR *133*
Hoffmann, Felix 1911-1975 9
Hoffmann, Heinrich 1809-1894
  See CLR *122*
Hoffmann, Margaret Jones 1910- 48
Hoffmann, Peggy
  See Hoffmann, Margaret Jones
Hofher, Catherine Baxley 1954- *130*
Hofher, Cathy
  See Hofher, Catherine Baxley
Hofmeyr, Dianne (Louise) *138*
Hofsepian, Sylvia A. 1932- 74
Hofsinde, Robert 1902-1973 21
Hogan, Bernice Harris 1929- 12
Hogan, Inez 1895-1973 2
Hogan, James P(atrick) 1941- 81
Hogan, Jamie *192*
Hogan, Linda 1947- *132*
Hogarth, Burne 1911-1996 89
  Earlier sketch in SATA *63*
Hogarth, Grace (Weston Allen) 1905-1995 .. *91*
Hogarth, Jr.
  See Kent, Rockwell
Hogarth, (Arthur) Paul 1917-2001 41
Hogg, Garry 1902-1976 2
Hogg, Gary 1957- *172*
  Earlier sketch in SATA *105*
Hogner, Dorothy Childs 4
Hogner, Nils 1893-1970 25
Hogrogian, Nonny 1932- 74
  Autobiography Feature *127*
  Earlier sketch in SATA *7*
  See also CLR *95*
  See also SAAS *1*
Hoh, Diane 1937- *102*
  Brief entry 48
  Earlier sketch in SATA *52*
Hoke, Helen
  See Watts, Helen L. Hoke
Hoke, Helen L.
  See Watts, Helen L. Hoke
Hoke, John (Lindsay) 1925- 7
Hokenson, Terry 1948- *193*
Hol, Coby 1943- *126*
Holabird, Katharine 1948- *135*
  Earlier sketch in SATA *62*
Holaday, Bobbie 1922- *153*
Holbeach, Henry
  See Rands, William Brighty
Holberg, Ruth L(angland) 1889-1984 .... *1*
Holbrook, Kathy 1963- *107*
Holbrook, Peter
  See Glick, Carl (Cannon)
Holbrook, Sabra
  See Erickson, Sabra Rollins
Holbrook, Sara *131*
Holbrook, Stewart Hall 1893-1964 2
Holcomb, Jerry (Leona) Kimble 1927- *113*
Holcomb, Nan
  See McPhee, Norma H.
Holden, Elizabeth Rhoda
  See Lawrence, Louise
Holding, James (Clark Carlisle, Jr.)
  1907-1997 .... *3*

Hole, Stian 1969- 204
Holeman, Linda 1949- 136
  Autobiography Feature 136
  Earlier sketch in SATA *102*
Holinger, William (Jacques) 1944- 90
Holisher, Desider 1901-1972 6
Holl, Adelaide Hinkle 1910- 8
Holl, Kristi D(iane) 1951- 51
Holland, Gay W. 1941- 128
Holland, Isabelle (Christian) 1920-2002 70
  Autobiography Feature 103
  Obituary 132
  Earlier sketch in SATA *8*
  See also CLR *57*
Holland, Janice 1913-1962 18
Holland, John L(ewis) 1919- 20
Holland, Joyce
  See Morice, Dave
Holland, Julia 1954- 106
Holland, Lynda (H.) 1959- 77
Holland, Lys
  See Gater, Dilys
Holland, Marion 1908-1989 6
  Obituary 61
Hollander, John 1929- 13
Hollander, Nicole 1940(?)- 101
Hollander, Paul
  See Silverberg, Robert
Hollander, Phyllis 1928- 39
Hollander, Zander 1923- 63
Holldobler, Turid 1939- 26
Holliday, Joe
  See Holliday, Joseph
Holliday, Joseph 1910- 11
Holling, Holling C(lancy) 1900-1973 15
  Obituary 26
  See also CLR *50*
Hollingsworth, Alvin C(arl) 1930- 39
Hollingsworth, Mary 1947- 166
  Earlier sketch in SATA *91*
Holloway, Teresa (Bragunier) 1906- 26
Hollyer, Belinda 204
Holm, (Else) Anne (Lise) 1922-1998 1
  See also CLR *75*
  See also SAAS *7*
Holm, Jennifer L. 1968(?)- 183
  Earlier sketches in SATA *120, 163*
Holm, Matthew 1974- 174
Holm, Sharon Lane 1955- 114
  Earlier sketch in SATA *78*
Holman, Felice 1919- 82
  Earlier sketch in SATA *7*
  See also SAAS *17*
Holm and Hamel
  See Holm, Jennifer L.
Holmberg, Bo R. 1945- 203
Holme, Bryan 1913-1990 26
  Obituary 66
Holmes, Barbara Ware 1945- 127
  Earlier sketch in SATA *65*
Holmes, Elizabeth 1957- 191
Holmes, Elizabeth Ann
  See Holmes, Elizabeth
Holmes, John
  See Souster, (Holmes) Raymond
Holmes, Marjorie (Rose) 1910-2002 43
Holmes, Martha 1961- 72
Holmes, Mary Tavener 1954- 199
Holmes, Mary Z(astrow) 1943- 80
Holmes, Oliver Wendell 1809-1894 34
Holmes, Peggy 1898- 60
Holmes, Raymond
  See Souster, (Holmes) Raymond
Holmes, Rick
  See Hardwick, Richard Holmes, Jr.
Holmes, Sara Lewis 186
Holmgren, Helen Jean 1930- 45
Holmgren, Sister George Ellen
  See Holmgren, Helen Jean
Holmgren, Virginia C(unningham) 1909- 26
Holmquist, Eve 1921- 11

Holt, Kimberly Willis 1960- 179
  Earlier sketch in SATA *122*
Holt, Margaret 1937- 4
Holt, Margaret Van Vechten (Saunders)
  1899-1963 32
Holt, Michael (Paul) 1929- 13
Holt, Rackham
  See Holt, Margaret Van Vechten (Saunders)
Holt, Rochelle L.
  See DuBois, Rochelle Holt
Holt, Stephen
  See Thompson, Harlan
Holt, Victoria
  See Hibbert, Eleanor Alice Burford
Holton, Leonard
  See Wibberley, Leonard
Holtz, Thomas R., Jr. 1965- 203
Holtze, Sally Holmes 1952- 64
Holtzman, Jerome 1926-2008 57
  Obituary 194
Holub, Joan 1956- 149
  Earlier sketch in SATA *99*
Holub, Josef 1926- 175
Holubitsky, Katherine 1955- 165
  Earlier sketch in SATA *121*
Holyer, Erna Maria 1925- 22
Holyer, Ernie
  See Holyer, Erna Maria
Holz, Loretta (Marie) 1943- 17
Homel, David 1952- 97
Homze, Alma C. 1932- 17
Honey, Elizabeth 1947- 137
  Autobiography Feature 137
  Earlier sketch in SATA *112*
Honeycutt, Natalie 1945- 97
Hong, Lily Toy 1958- 76
Hong, Maxine Ting Ting
  See Kingston, Maxine Hong
Honig, Donald 1931- 18
Honness, Elizabeth H. 1904- 2
Hoobler, Dorothy 1941- 161
  Earlier sketches in SATA *28, 109*
Hoobler, Thomas 161
  Earlier sketches in SATA *28, 109*
Hood, Joseph F. 1925- 4
Hood, Robert E. 1926- 21
Hood, Sarah
  See Killough, (Karen) Lee
Hook, Brendan 1963- 105
Hook, Frances 1912-1983 27
Hook, Geoffrey R(aynor) 1928- 103
Hook, Jeff
  See Hook, Geoffrey R(aynor)
Hook, Martha 1936- 27
Hooker, Richard
  See Heinz, W.C.
Hooker, Ruth 1920-1998 21
hooks, bell 1952(?)- 170
  Earlier sketch in SATA *115*
Hooks, William H(arris) 1921- 94
  Earlier sketch in SATA *16*
Hoon, Patricia Easterly 1954- 90
Hooper, Byrd
  See St. Clair, Byrd Hooper
Hooper, Mary 1948- 205
  Earlier sketch in SATA *160*
Hooper, Maureen Brett 1927- 76
Hooper, Meredith 1939- 159
  Earlier sketches in SATA *28, 101*
Hooper, Meredith Jean
  See Hooper, Meredith
Hooper, Patricia 1941- 95
Hoopes, Lyn Littlefield 1953- 49
  Brief entry 44
Hoopes, Ned E(dward) 1932- 21
Hoopes, Roy 1922- 11
Hoose, Phillip M. 1947- 137
Hoover, H(elen) M(ary) 1935- 132
  Brief entry 33
  Earlier sketches in SATA *44, 83*
  See also SAAS *8*

Hoover, Helen (Drusilla Blackburn)
  1910-1984 12
  Obituary 39
Hope, Christopher 1944- 62
Hope, Christopher David Tully
  See Hope, Christopher
Hope, Laura Lee
  See Goulart, Ron
  and Stanley, George Edward
Hope Simpson, Jacynth 1930- 12
Hopf, Alice (Martha) L(ightner) 1904-1988 ... 5
  Obituary 55
Hopkins, A. T.
  See Turngren, Annette
Hopkins, C. M.
  See Hopkins, Cathy
Hopkins, Cathy 1953- 165
Hopkins, Cathy M.
  See Hopkins, Cathy
Hopkins, Clark 1895-1976
  Obituary 34
Hopkins, Ellen 1955- 128
  See Hopkins, Ellen L.
Hopkins, Ellen L.
  See Hopkins, Ellen
Hopkins, Jackie
  See Hopkins, Jackie Mims
Hopkins, Jackie Mims 1952- 178
  Earlier sketch in SATA *92*
Hopkins, Joseph G(erard) E(dward) 1909- ... 11
Hopkins, (Hector) Kenneth 1914-1988
  Obituary 58
Hopkins, Lee Bennett 1938- 168
  Earlier sketches in SATA *3, 68, 125*
  See also CLR *44*
  See also SAAS *4*
Hopkins, Lyman
  See Folsom, Franklin (Brewster)
Hopkins, Marjorie 1911-1999 9
Hopkins, Mary R(ice) 1956- 97
Hopkinson, Amanda 1948- 84
Hopkinson, Deborah 1952- 180
  Autobiography Feature 180
  Earlier sketches in SATA *76, 108, 159*
  See also CLR *118*
Hopman, Philip 1961- 177
Hoppe, Joanne 1932- 42
Hoppe, Matthias 1952- 76
Hopper, Nancy J. 1937- 38
  Brief entry 35
Hopping, Lorraine Jean
  See Egan, Lorraine Hopping
Horacek, Petr 163
Horenstein, Henry 1947- 108
Horgan, Paul (George Vincent O'Shaughnessy)
  1903-1995 13
  Obituary 84
Horlak, E.E.
  See Tepper, Sheri S.
Horler, Sydney 1888-1954 102
Horn, Sandra Ann 1944- 154
Hornblow, Arthur, Jr. 1893-1976 15
Hornblow, Leonora 1920-2005 18
  Obituary 171
Hornblow, Leonora Schinasi
  See Hornblow, Leonora
Horne, Constance 1927- 149
Horne, Richard 1960-2007 169
  Obituary 180
  Earlier sketch in SATA *111*
Horne, Richard Henry Hengist
  1802(?)-1884 29
Horner, Althea (Jane) 1926- 36
Horner, Dave 1934- 12
Horner, Jack
  See Horner, John R(obert)
Horner, John R(obert) 1946- 106
Hornik, Laurie Miller 159
Horniman, Joanne 1951- 167
  Earlier sketch in SATA *98*
Hornos, Axel 1907-1994 20

Hornstein, Reuben Aaron 1912- 64
Horowitz, Anthony 1955- 195
    Earlier sketch in SATA 137
Horowitz, Dave 1970- 204
    Earlier sketch in SATA 172
Horowitz, Ruth 1957- 136
Horrocks, Anita 1958- 169
Horse, Harry
    See Horne, Richard
Horsfield, Alan 1939- 153
Hort, Lenny 179
Horton, James O. 1943- 173
Horton, James Oliver
    See Horton, James O.
Horton, Madelyn (Stacey) 1962- 77
Horvath, Betty 1927- 4
Horvath, David 1972(?)- 192
Horvath, Polly 1957- 194
    Earlier sketches in SATA 85, 140
    See also CLR 90
Horwich, Frances R(appaport) 1908-2001 11
    Obituary 130
Horwitz, Elinor Lander 45
    Brief entry 33
Horwood, William 1944- 85
Hosford, Dorothy (Grant) 1900-1952 22
Hosford, Jessie 1892-1990 5
Hoshi, Shin'ichi 1926- 101
Hoshino, Felicia 1968- 189
Hoskyns-Abrahall, Clare (Constance
    Drury) 13
Hosler, Danamarie 1978- 184
Hossack, Sylvia 1939- 83
Hossack, Sylvie Adams
    See Hossack, Sylvia
Hosseini, Khaled 1965- 156
Hossell, Karen Price
    See Price, Karen
Hosta, Dar 192
Hostetler, Marian 1932- 91
Houck, Carter 1924- 22
Hough, Charlotte 1924-2008 9
    Obituary 202
Hough, Helen Charlotte
    See Hough, Charlotte
Hough, Judy Taylor 1932- 63
    Brief entry 51
    Earlier sketch in SATA 56
Hough, Richard (Alexander) 1922-1999 17
Houghton, Eric 1930- 7
Houk, Randy 1944- 97
Houlehen, Robert J. 1918- 18
Houlton, Peggy Mann 1925(?)-1990 6
Household, Geoffrey (Edward West)
    1900-1988 14
    Obituary 59
Housman, Laurence 1865-1959 25
Houston, Dick 1943- 74
Houston, Gloria 138
    Autobiography Feature 138
    Earlier sketch in SATA 81
Houston, James A(rchibald) 1921-2005 74
    Obituary 163
    Earlier sketch in SATA 13
    See also CLR 3
    See also SAAS 17
Houston, James D. 1933-2009 78
    Obituary 203
Houston, James Dudley
    See Houston, James D.
Houston, James Dudley
    See Houston, James D.
Houston, Jeanne Toyo Wakatsuki
    See Houston, Jeanne Wakatsuki
Houston, Jeanne Wakatsuki 1934- 168
    Autobiography Feature 168
    Earlier sketch in SATA 78
Houston, Juanita C. 1921- 129
Houton, Kathleen
    See Kilgore, Kathleen
Houts, Amy E. 164

Hovey, Kate 158
Howard, Alan 1922- 45
Howard, Alyssa
    See Buckholtz, Eileen (Garber)
    and Glick, Ruth (Burtnick)
    and Titchener, Louise
Howard, Arthur 1948- 165
Howard, Arthur Charles
    See Howard, Arthur
Howard, Elizabeth Fitzgerald 1927- 119
    Earlier sketch in SATA 74
Howard, Ellen 1943- 184
    Earlier sketches in SATA 67, 99
Howard, Jane R(uble) 1924- 87
Howard, Norman Barry 1949- 90
Howard, P. M.
    See Howard, Pauline Rodriguez
Howard, Paul 1967- 190
    Earlier sketch in SATA 118
Howard, Pauline Rodriguez 1951- 124
Howard, Prosper
    See Hamilton, Charles (Harold St. John)
Howard, Robert West 1908-1988 5
Howard, Todd 1964- 135
Howard, Tristan
    See Currie, Stephen
Howard, Vernon (Linwood) 1918-1992 40
    Obituary 73
Howard, Warren F.
    See Pohl, Frederik
Howarth, Daniel 188
Howarth, David (Armine) 1912-1991 6
    Obituary 68
Howarth, Lesley 1952- 94
Howe, Deborah 1946-1978 29
Howe, James 1946- 161
    Earlier sketches in SATA 29, 71, 111
    See also CLR 9
Howe, John F. 1957- 79
Howe, Norma 1930- 126
Howell, Pat 1947- 15
Howell, S.
    See Styles, (Frank) Showell
Howell, Virginia
    See Ellison, Virginia H(owell)
Howes, Barbara 1914-1996 5
Howie, Diana 1945- 122
Howie, Diana Melson
    See Howie, Diana
Howker, Janni 1957- 72
    Brief entry 46
    See also CLR 14
    See also SAAS 13
Howland, Ethan 1963- 131
Hoy, Linda 1946- 65
Hoy, Nina
    See Roth, Arthur J(oseph)
Hoyle, Geoffrey 1942- 18
Hoyt, Ard 190
Hoyt, Edwin P(almer), Jr. 1923- 28
Hoyt, Erich 1950- 140
    Earlier sketch in SATA 65
Hoyt, Olga
    See Gruhzit-Hoyt, Olga (Margaret)
Hrdlitschka, Shelley 1956- 167
    Earlier sketch in SATA 111
Hrdlitschka, Shelley Joanne
    See Hrdlitschka, Shelley
Htin Aung, U.
    See Aung, (Maung) Htin
Hu, Ying-Hwa 173
Huang, Benrei 1959- 86
Hubalek, Linda K. 1954- 111
Hubbard, Margaret Ann
    See Priley, Margaret (Ann) Hubbard
Hubbard, Michelle Calabro 1953- 122
Hubbard, Patricia 1945- 124
Hubbard, Woodleigh Marx 160
    Earlier sketch in SATA 98
Hubbell, Patricia 1928- 186
    Earlier sketches in SATA 8, 132

Hubery, Julia 195
Hubley, Faith Elliot 1924-2001 48
    Obituary 133
Hubley, John 1914-1977 48
    Obituary 24
Huck, Charlotte S. 1922- 136
    Earlier sketch in SATA 82
Hudak, Michal 1956- 143
Hudson, Cheryl Willis 1948- 160
    Earlier sketch in SATA 81
Hudson, Jan 1954-1990 77
    See also CLR 40
Hudson, Jeffery
    See Crichton, Michael
Hudson, Jeffrey
    See Crichton, Michael
Hudson, (Margaret) Kirsty 1947- 32
Hudson, Margaret
    See Shuter, Jane (Margaret)
Hudson, W(illiam) H(enry) 1841-1922 35
Hudson, Wade 1946- 162
    Earlier sketch in SATA 74
Huelsmann, Eva 1928- 16
Huerlimann, Bettina 1909-1983 39
    Obituary 34
Huerlimann, Ruth 1939- 32
    Brief entry 31
Huff, Barbara A. 1929- 67
Huff, Tanya 1957- 171
    Earlier sketch in SATA 85
Huff, Tanya Sue
    See Huff, Tanya
Huff, T.S.
    See Huff, Tanya
Huff, Vivian 1948- 59
Huffaker, Sandy 1943- 10
Huffman, Tom 24
Huggins, Nathan Irvin 1927-1989 63
Huggins, Peter 1951- 178
Hughes, Carol 1955- 108
Hughes, Dean 1943- 139
    Earlier sketches in SATA 33, 77
    See also CLR 76
Hughes, Eden
    See Griffin, W.E.B.
Hughes, Edward James
    See Hughes, Ted
Hughes, James Langston
    See Hughes, Langston
Hughes, Langston 1902-1967 33
    Earlier sketch in SATA 4
    See also CLR 17
Hughes, Libby 71
Hughes, Matilda
    See MacLeod, Charlotte (Matilda)
Hughes, Monica 1925-2003 162
    Earlier sketches in SATA 15, 70, 119
    See also CLR 60
    See also SAAS 11
Hughes, Monica Ince
    See Hughes, Monica
Hughes, Pat 197
Hughes, Richard (Arthur Warren)
    1900-1976 8
    Obituary 25
Hughes, Sara
    See Saunders, Susan
Hughes, Shirley 1927- 159
    Earlier sketches in SATA 16, 70, 110
    See also CLR 15
Hughes, Ted 1930-1998 49
    Brief entry 27
    Obituary 107
    See also CLR 131
Hughes, Thomas 1822-1896 31
Hughes, Virginia
    See Campbell, Hope
Hughes, Walter (Llewellyn) 1910-1993 26
Hughey, Roberta 1942- 61
Hugo, Pierre Brackers de
    See Brackers de Hugo, Pierre

Hugo, Victor 1802-1885 47
Hugo, Victor Marie
    See Hugo, Victor
Huline-Dickens, Frank William 1931- 34
Huling, Jan 172
Huliska-Beith, Laura 175
Hull, Eleanor (Means) 1913- 21
Hull, Eric Traviss
    See Harnan, Terry
Hull, H. Braxton
    See Jacobs, Helen Hull
Hull, Jesse Redding
    See Hull, Jessie Redding
Hull, Jessie Redding 1932- 51
Hull, Katharine 1921-1977 23
Hull, Lise (E.) 1954- 148
Hull, Maureen 1949- 142
Hulme, Joy N. 1922- 161
    Earlier sketches in SATA *74, 112*
Hults, Dorothy Niebrugge 1898-2000 6
Humble, Richard 1945- 60
Hume, Lachie 189
Hume, Lotta Carswell 7
Hume, Ruth Fox 1922-1980 26
    Obituary 22
Hume, Stephen Eaton 1947- 136
Hummel, Berta 1909-1946 43
Hummel, Sister Maria Innocentia
    See Hummel, Berta
Humphrey, Carol Sue 1956- 167
Humphrey, Henry (III) 1930- 16
Humphrey, Kate
    See Forsyth, Kate
Humphrey, Sandra McLeod 1936- 95
Humphreys, Martha 1943- 71
Humphreys, Susan L.
    See Lowell, Susan
Hundal, Nancy 1957- 128
Huneck, Stephen 1949- 183
    Earlier sketch in SATA *129*
Hungerford, Hesba Fay
    See Brinsmead, H(esba) F(ay)
Hungerford, Pixie
    See Brinsmead, H(esba) F(ay)
Hunkin, Timothy Mark Trelawney 1950- 53
Hunt, Angela Elwell 1957- 159
    Earlier sketch in SATA *75*
Hunt, Bernice 1920- 4
Hunt, Francesca
    See Holland, Isabelle (Christian)
Hunt, Irene 1907-2001 91
    Earlier sketch in SATA *2*
    See also CLR *1*
Hunt, Janie Louise 1963- 102
Hunt, Jonathan 1966- 84
Hunt, Joyce 1927- 31
Hunt, Linda 1940- 39
Hunt, Lisa B(ehnke) 1967- 84
Hunt, Mabel Leigh 1892-1971 1
    Obituary 26
Hunt, Morton M(agill) 1920- 22
Hunt, Nigel
    See Greenbank, Anthony Hunt
Hunt, Peter (Leonard) 1945- 76
Hunter, Anne B. 1966- 118
Hunter, Bernice Thurman 1922-2002 85
    Brief entry 45
Hunter, Bobbi Dooley 1945- 89
Hunter, Captain Marcy
    See Ellis, Edward S.
Hunter, Chris
    See Fluke, Joanne
Hunter, Clingham M.D.
    See Adams, William Taylor
Hunter, Edith Fisher 1919- 31
Hunter, Erin
    See Cary, Kate
Hunter, Evan 1926-2005 25
    Obituary 167
Hunter, George E.
    See Ellis, Edward S.

Hunter, Hilda 1921- 7
Hunter, Jana
    See Hunter, Jana Novotny
Hunter, Jana Novotny 190
Hunter, Jim 1939- 65
Hunter, Kristin
    See Lattany, Kristin Hunter
Hunter, Leigh
    See Etchison, Birdie L(ee)
Hunter, Lieutenant Ned
    See Ellis, Edward S.
Hunter, Mel 1927-2004 39
Hunter, Mollie 1922- 139
    Autobiography Feature 139
    Earlier sketches in SATA *2, 54, 106*
    See also CLR *25*
    See also SAAS *7*
Hunter, Ned
    See Ellis, Edward S.
Hunter, Norman (George Lorimer)
    1899-1995 84
    Earlier sketch in SATA *26*
Hunter, Ryan Ann
    See Greenwood, Pamela D.
    and Macalaster, Elizabeth G.
Hunter, Sara Hoagland 1954- 98
Hunter Blair, Pauline
    See Clarke, Pauline
Huntington, Amy 1956- 180
    Earlier sketch in SATA *138*
Huntington, Geoffrey 145
Huntington, Harriet E(lizabeth) 1909- 1
Huntsberry, William E(mery) 1916- 5
Hurd, Clement (G.) 1908-1988 64
    Obituary 54
    Earlier sketch in SATA *2*
    See also CLR *49*
Hurd, Edith Thacher 1910-1997 64
    Obituary 95
    Earlier sketch in SATA *2*
    See also CLR *49*
    See also SAAS *13*
Hurd, (John) Thacher 1949- 94
    Autobiography Feature 123
    Brief entry 45
    Earlier sketch in SATA *46*
Hurley, Jo
    See Dower, Laura
Hurlimann, Bettina
    See Huerlimann, Bettina
Hurlimann, Ruth
    See Huerlimann, Ruth
Hurmence, Belinda 1921- 77
    See also CLR *25*
    See also SAAS *20*
Hurst, Carol Otis 1933-2007 185
    Earlier sketch in SATA *130*
Hurt-Newton, Tania 1968- 84
Hurwin, Davida Wills 1950- 180
Hurwitz, Johanna 1937- 175
    Earlier sketches in SATA *20, 71, 113*
    See also SAAS *18*
Hurwood, Bernhardt J. 1926-1987 12
    Obituary 50
Husain, Shahrukh 1950- 108
Huser, Glen 1943- 151
Hutchens, Paul 1902-1977 31
Hutchins, Carleen M.
    See Hutchins, Carleen Maley
Hutchins, Carleen Maley 1911-2009 9
    Obituary 206
Hutchins, Hazel J. 1952- 175
    Brief entry 51
    Earlier sketches in SATA *81, 135*
    See also SAAS *24*
Hutchins, Pat 1942- 178
    Earlier sketches in SATA *15, 70, 111*
    See also CLR *20*
    See also SAAS *16*
Hutchins, Ross Elliott 1906- 4
Hutchison, Linda 1942- 152

Huthmacher, J. Joseph 1929- 5
Hutto, Nelson (Allen) 1904-1985 20
Hutton, Kathryn 1915- 89
Hutton, Sam
    See Jones, Allan Frewin
Hutton, Warwick 1939-1994 20
    Obituary 83
    See also SAAS *17*
Huxley, Aldous (Leonard) 1894-1963 63
Huxley, Elspeth (Josceline Grant)
    1907-1997 62
    Obituary 95
Hyde, Catherine R.
    See Hyde, Catherine Ryan
Hyde, Catherine Ryan 1955- 141
Hyde, Dayton O(gden) 9
Hyde, Hawk
    See Hyde, Dayton O(gden)
Hyde, Jeannette
    See Eyerly, Jeannette
Hyde, Margaret O. 1917- 139
    Earlier sketches in SATA *1, 42, 76*
    See also CLR *23*
    See also SAAS *8*
Hyde, Margaret Oldroyd
    See Hyde, Margaret O.
Hyde, Shelley
    See Reed, Kit
Hyde, Wayne Frederick 1922- 7
Hylander, Clarence J(ohn) 1897-1964 7
Hyman, Robin P(hilip) 1931- 12
Hyman, Trina Schart 1939-2004 95
    Obituary 158
    Earlier sketches in SATA *7, 46*
    See also CLR *50*
Hymes, Lucia M(anley) 1907-1998 7
Hyndman, Jane Andrews Lee 1912-1978 46
    Obituary 23
    Earlier sketch in SATA *1*
Hyndman, Robert Utley 1906-1973 18
Hynes, Pat 98

I

Iannone, Jeanne
    See Balzano, Jeanne (Koppel)
Ibatoulline, Bagram 1965(?)- 174
Ibbitson, John Perrie 1955- 102
Ibbotson, Eva 1925- 156
    Earlier sketches in SATA *13, 103*
Ibbotson, M. C(hristine) 1930- 5
Icenoggle, Jodi 1967- 168
Icenoggle, Jodi O.
    See Icenoggle, Jodi
Ichikawa, Satomi 1949- 146
    Brief entry 36
    Earlier sketches in SATA *47, 78*
    See also CLR *62*
Iggulden, Hal 1972- 196
Ignoffo, Matthew 1945- 92
Igus, Toyomi 1953- 112
    Earlier sketch in SATA *76*
Ihimaera, Witi (Tame) 1944- 148
Ikeda, Daisaku 1928- 77
Ilowite, Sheldon A. 1931- 27
Ilsey, Dent
    See Chapman, John Stanton Higham
Ilsley, Dent
    See Chapman, John Stanton Higham
Ilsley, Velma (Elizabeth) 1918- 12
Imai, Ayano 1980- 190
Imai, Miko 1963- 90
Imershein, Betsy 1953- 62
Immel, Mary Blair 1930- 28
Immell, Myra H. 1941- 92
Impey, Rose 1947- 152
    Earlier sketch in SATA *69*
Ingelow, Jean 1820-1897 33
Ingermanson, Randall 1958- 134

Ingermanson, Randy
    See Ingermanson, Randall
Ingersoll, Norman 1928- 79
Ingham, Colonel Frederic
    See Hale, Edward Everett
Ingman, Bruce 1963- 182
    Earlier sketch in SATA 134
Ingman, Nicholas 1948- 52
Ingold, Jeanette 128
Ingpen, Robert 1936- 166
    Earlier sketch in SATA 109
Ingpen, Robert Roger
    See Ingpen, Robert
Ingraham, Erick 1950- 145
Ingraham, Leonard W(illiam) 1913-2003 4
Ingram, Scott 1948- 167
    Earlier sketch in SATA 92
Ingram, W. Scott
    See Ingram, Scott
Ingrams, Doreen 1906-1997 97
    Earlier sketch in SATA 20
Ingrid, Charles
    See Salsitz, Rhondi Vilott
Ingves, Gunilla (Anna Maria Folkesdotter)
    1939- 101
Inkpen, Mick 1952- 154
    Earlier sketch in SATA 99
Innes, (Ralph) Hammond
    See Hammond Innes, Ralph
Innes, Ralph Hammond
    See Hammond Innes, Ralph
Innocenti, Roberto 1940- 159
    Earlier sketch in SATA 96
    See also CLR 126
Innocenti and Gallaz
    See Gallaz, Christophe
    and Innocenti, Roberto
Inyart, Gene
    See Namovicz, Gene Inyart
Ionesco, Eugene 1912-1994 7
    Obituary 79
Ipcar, Dahlov (Zorach) 1917- 147
    Autobiography Feature 147
    Earlier sketches in SATA 1, 49
    See also SAAS 8
Ireland, Karin 151
    Earlier sketch in SATA 101
Ironside, Jetske 1940- 60
Irvin, Fred 1914- 15
Irvine, Georgeanne 1955- 72
Irvine, Joan 1951- 80
Irving, Alexander
    See Hume, Ruth Fox
Irving, Robert
    See Adler, Irving
Irving, Washington 1783-1859
    See YABC 2
    See also CLR 97
Irwin, Ann(abelle Bowen) 1915-1998 89
    Brief entry 38
    Obituary 106
    Earlier sketch in SATA 44
    See also CLR 40
    See also SAAS 14
Irwin, Constance (H.) Frick 1913-1995 6
Irwin, Hadley
    See Hadley, Lee
    and Irwin, Ann(abelle Bowen)
Irwin, Keith Gordon 1885-1964 11
Isaac, Joanne 1934- 21
Isaacs, Anne 1949- 185
    Earlier sketch in SATA 90
Isaacs, Jacob
    See Kranzler, George G(ershon)
Isaacson, Philip M(arshal) 1924- 87
Isadora, Rachel 1953(?)- 204
    Brief entry 32
    Earlier sketches in SATA 54, 79, 121, 165
    See also CLR 7
Isbell, Rebecca T(emple) 1942- 125
Isham, Charlotte H(ickock) 1912- 21

Ishida, Jui 176
Ish-Kishor, Judith 1892-1972 11
Ish-Kishor, Sulamith 1896-1977 17
Ishmael, Woodi 1914-1995 31
    Obituary 109
Isle, Sue 1963- 105
Israel, Elaine 1945- 12
Israel, Marion Louise 1882-1973
    Obituary 26
Iterson, S(iny) R(ose) Van
    See Van Iterson, S(iny) R(ose)
Ivanko, John D. 1966- 111
Ivanko, John Duane
    See Ivanko, John D.
Iversen, Jeremy 1980(?)- 174
Iversen, Jeremy Watt
    See Iversen, Jeremy
Iverson, Carol (L.) 1941- 145
Iverson, Diane 1950- 122
Iverson, Eric G.
    See Turtledove, Harry
Ivery, Martha M. 1948- 124
Ives, David 1951- 173
Ives, Morgan
    See Bradley, Marion Zimmer
Iwai, Melissa 183
Iwamatsu, Jun Atsushi 1908-1994 81
    Earlier sketch in SATA 14
    See also CLR 4
Iwasaki (Matsumoto), Chihiro 1918-1974
    See CLR 18

                        J

Jablonski, Carla 184
Jac, Lee
    See Morton, Lee Jack, Jr.
Jacka, Martin 1943- 72
Jackson, Alison 1953- 160
    Earlier sketches in SATA 73, 108
Jackson, Anne 1896(?)-1984
    Obituary 37
Jackson, Barry
    See Jackson, Barry E.
Jackson, Barry E. 200
Jackson, C(aary) Paul 1902-1991 6
Jackson, Caary
    See Jackson, C(aary) Paul
Jackson, Charlotte E. (Cobden) 1903(?)-1989
    Obituary 62
Jackson, Dave
    See Jackson, J. David
Jackson, Donna M. 1959- 206
Jackson, Ellen B. 1943- 167
    Earlier sketches in SATA 75, 115
Jackson, Garnet Nelson 1944- 87
Jackson, Geoffrey (Holt Seymour) 1915-1987
    Obituary 53
Jackson, Gina
    See Fluke, Joanne
Jackson, Guida M. 1930- 71
Jackson, J. David 1944- 91
Jackson, Jacqueline 1928- 65
Jackson, Jacqueline Dougan
    See Jackson, Jacqueline
Jackson, Jesse 1908-1983 29
    Obituary 48
    Earlier sketch in SATA 2
    See also CLR 28
Jackson, Marjorie 1928- 127
Jackson, Melanie 1956- 141
Jackson, Mike 1946- 91
Jackson, Neta J. 1944- 91
Jackson, O. B.
    See Jackson, C(aary) Paul
Jackson, Rob 1961- 176
Jackson, Robert B(lake) 1926- 8
Jackson, Robert Bradley
    See Jackson, Rob

Jackson, Sally
    See Kellogg, Jean (Defrees)
Jackson, Shirley 1919-1965 2
Jackson, Woody 1948- 92
Jackson Issa, Kai 205
Jacob, Helen Pierce 1927- 21
Jacobin
    See Bisson, Terry
Jacobs, Deborah Lynn 187
Jacobs, Flora Gill 1918-2006 5
    Obituary 178
Jacobs, Francine 1935- 150
    Brief entry 42
    Earlier sketch in SATA 43
Jacobs, Frank 1929- 30
Jacobs, Helen Hull 1908-1997 12
Jacobs, Joseph 1854-1916 25
Jacobs, Judy 1952- 69
Jacobs, Laurie A. 1956- 89
Jacobs, Leah
    See Gellis, Roberta
Jacobs, Leland Blair 1907-1992 20
    Obituary 71
Jacobs, Linda
    See Altman, Linda Jacobs
Jacobs, Lou(is), Jr. 1921- 2
Jacobs, Shannon K. 1947- 77
Jacobs, Susan
    See Quinn, Susan
Jacobs, William Jay 1933- 89
    Earlier sketch in SATA 28
Jacobsen, Laura 177
Jacobson, Daniel 1923- 12
Jacobson, Jennifer
    See Jacobson, Jennifer Richard
Jacobson, Jennifer Richard 1958- 170
Jacobson, Morris K(arl) 1906- 21
Jacobson, Rick 170
Jacopetti, Alexandra
    See Hart, Alexandra
Jacques, Brian 1939- 176
    Earlier sketches in SATA 62, 95, 138
    See also CLR 21
Jacques, Robin 1920-1995 32
    Brief entry 30
    Obituary 86
    See also SAAS 5
Jaekel, Susan M. 1948- 89
Jaffe, Michele 179
Jaffe, Michele Sharon
    See Jaffe, Michele
Jaffee, Al(lan) 1921- 66
    Earlier sketch in SATA 37
Jagendorf, Moritz (Adolf) 1888-1981 2
    Obituary 24
Jahn, Joseph Michael
    See Jahn, Michael
Jahn, Michael 1943- 28
Jahn, Mike
    See Jahn, Michael
Jahn-Clough, Lisa 1967- 193
    Earlier sketches in SATA 88, 152
Jahsmann, Allan Hart 1916- 28
Jakes, John 1932- 62
Jakes, John William
    See Jakes, John
James, Andrew
    See Kirkup, James
James, Ann 1952- 168
    Earlier sketches in SATA 82, 117
James, Betsy 183
James, Brian 1976- 140
James, Bronte
    See Nash, Renea Denise
James, Captain Lew
    See Stratemeyer, Edward L.
James, Charlie 1961- 185
James, Curtis E. 182
James, Dynely
    See Mayne, William (James Carter)

James, Edwin
  See Gunn, James E.
James, Elizabeth 1942- 97
  Earlier sketches in SATA *39, 45, 52*
James, Emily
  See Standiford, Natalie
James, Gordon C. 1973- 195
James, Harry Clebourne 1896-1978 .... *11*
James, J. Alison 1962- *146*
  Earlier sketch in SATA *83*
James, Josephine
  See Sterne, Emma Gelders
James, Mary
  See Meaker, Marijane
James, Matt 201
James, Philip
  See del Rey, Lester
  and Moorcock, Michael
James, Robin 1953- 50
James, Robin Irene
  See James, Robin
James, Simon 202
  See Kunen, James Simon
James, T. F.
  See Fleming, Thomas
James, Tegan
  See Odgers, Sally Farrell
James, Will(iam Roderick) 1892-1942 .... *19*
Jameson, W. C. 1942- 93
Jamieson, Ian R.
  See Goulart, Ron
Jamiolkowski, Raymond M. 1953- 81
Jane, Mary Childs 1909- *6*
Jane, Pamela 158
Janeczko, Paul B(ryan) 1945- 155
  Earlier sketches in SATA *53, 98*
  See also CLR *47*
  See also SAAS *18*
Janes, Edward C. 1908-1984 25
Janes, J(oseph) Robert 1935- 148
  Brief entry 50
  Earlier sketch in SATA *101*
Janeway, Elizabeth (Hall) 1913-2005 .... *19*
Janger, Kathleen N. 1940- 66
Janice
  See Brustlein, Janice Tworkov
Janisch, Heinz 1960- 181
Janosch
  See Eckert, Horst
Janover, Caroline (Davis) 1943- 141
  Earlier sketch in SATA *89*
Janovitz, Marilyn 194
Jansen, Jared
  See Cebulash, Mel
Janson, Dora Jane (Heineberg) 1916- 31
Janson, H(orst) W(oldemar) 1913-1982 .... *9*
Jansson, Tove (Marika) 1914-2001 41
  Earlier sketch in SATA *3*
  See also CLR *125*
Janus, Grete
  See Hertz, Grete Janus
Jaques, Faith 1923-1997 97
  Earlier sketches in SATA *21, 69*
Jaquith, Priscilla 1908- 51
Jaramillo, Mari-Luci 1928- *139*
Jarman, Julia 1946- 198
  Earlier sketch in SATA *133*
Jarman, Rosemary Hawley 1935- 7
Jarrell, Mary Von Schrader 1914- 35
Jarrell, Randall 1914-1965 7
  See also CLR *111*
Jarrett, Clare 1952- 201
Jarrett, Roxanne
  See Werner, Herma
Jarrow, Gail 1952- 185
  Earlier sketch in SATA *84*
Jarvis, E.K.
  See Ellison, Harlan
  and Silverberg, Robert
Jarvis, Robin 1963- 181
Jaskol, Julie 1958- 127

Jasner, W. K.
  See Watson, Jane Werner
Jassem, Kate
  See Oppenheim, Joanne
Jauss, Anne Marie 1902(?)-1991 .... *10*
  Obituary 69
Javernick, Ellen 1938- 89
Jay, Alison 196
Jayne, Lieutenant R. H.
  See Ellis, Edward S.
Jaynes, Clare
  See Mayer, Jane Rothschild
Jeake, Samuel, Jr.
  See Aiken, Conrad
Jean-Bart, Leslie 1954- *121*
Jeapes, Ben 1965- *174*
Jecan, Gavriel 1962- *200*
Jefferds, Vincent H(arris) 1916- *59*
  Brief entry 49
Jefferies, (John) Richard 1848-1887 .... *16*
Jeffers, Dawn 189
Jeffers, Oliver 1977- 175
Jeffers, Susan 1942- 202
  Earlier sketches in SATA *17, 70, 129, 137*
  See also CLR *30*
Jefferson, Sarah
  See Farjeon, (Eve) Annabel
Jeffries, Roderic 1926- *4*
Jeffries, Roderic Graeme
  See Jeffries, Roderic
Jenkin-Pearce, Susie 1943- 80
Jenkins, A.M. 174
Jenkins, Amanda McRaney
  See Jenkins, A.M.
Jenkins, Debra Reid
  See Reid Jenkins, Debra
Jenkins, Emily 1967- 174
  Earlier sketch in SATA *144*
Jenkins, Jean 98
Jenkins, Jerry B. 1949- 149
Jenkins, Jerry Bruce
  See Jenkins, Jerry B.
Jenkins, Leonard 189
Jenkins, Marie M(agdalen) 1909- 7
Jenkins, Patrick 1955- 72
Jenkins, Steve 1952- 188
  Earlier sketch in SATA *154*
Jenkins, William A(twell) 1922-1998 9
Jenkyns, Chris 1924- 51
Jennings, Christopher S. 1971(?)- 201
Jennings, Coleman A(lonzo) 1933- 64
Jennings, C.S.
  See Jennings, Christopher S.
Jennings, Dana Andrew 1957- 93
Jennings, Elizabeth (Joan) 1926-2001 66
Jennings, Gary 1928-1999 9
  Obituary 117
Jennings, Gary Gayne
  See Jennings, Gary
Jennings, Patrick 1962- 205
  Earlier sketches in SATA *96, 160*
Jennings, Paul 1943- 165
  Earlier sketch in SATA *88*
  See also CLR *40*
Jennings, Richard W. 1945- 185
  Earlier sketch in SATA *136*
Jennings, Robert
  See Hamilton, Charles (Harold St. John)
Jennings, S. M.
  See Meyer, Jerome Sydney
Jennings, Sharon 1954- 95
Jennings, Sharon Elizabeth
  See Jennings, Sharon
Jennison, C. S.
  See Starbird, Kaye
Jennison, Keith Warren 1911-1995 .... *14*
Jensen, Kathryn 1949- 81
Jensen, Kristine Mary 1961- 78
Jensen, Niels 1927- 25
Jensen, Vickie (Dee) 1946- 81
Jensen, Virginia Allen 1927- 8

Jenson-Elliott, Cynthia L(ouise) 1962- *143*
Jeram, Anita 1965- *154*
  Earlier sketches in SATA *71, 102*
Jerman, Jerry 1949- 89
Jernigan, E. Wesley 1940- 85
Jernigan, Gisela (Evelyn) 1948- 85
Jeschke, Susan 1942- 42
  Brief entry 27
Jessel, Camilla (Ruth) 1937- *143*
  Earlier sketch in SATA *29*
Jessell, Tim 177
Jessey, Cornelia
  See Sussman, Cornelia Silver
Jewel
  See Kilcher, Jewel
Jewell, Nancy 1940- 109
  Brief entry 41
Jewett, Eleanore Myers 1890-1967 5
Jewett, (Theodora) Sarah Orne 1849-1909 ... *15*
Jezard, Alison 1919- 57
  Brief entry 34
Jiang, Cheng An 1943- 109
Jiang, Ji-li 1954- *101*
Jiang, Zheng An
  See Jiang, Cheng An
Jiler, John 1946- 42
  Brief entry 35
Jimenez, Francisco 1943- 108
Jinks, Catherine 1963- 155
  Earlier sketch in SATA *94*
Jobb, Jamie 1945- 29
Jobling, Curtis 131
Jocelyn, Ann Henning 1948- 92
Jocelyn, Marthe 1956- 198
  Earlier sketches in SATA *118, 163*
Joerns, Consuelo 44
  Brief entry 33
Joey D
  See Macaulay, Teresa (E.)
Johansen, Krista V.
  See Johansen, K.V.
Johansen, K.V 1968- 186
Johansen, K.V. 1968- 186
  Earlier sketch in SATA *129*
Johansson, Philip 163
John, Antony 1972- 206
John, Joyce 59
Johns, Avery
  See Cousins, Margaret
Johns, Elizabeth 1943- 88
Johns, Janetta
  See Quin-Harkin, Janet
Johns, Linda 1945- 173
Johns, W(illiam) E(arle) 1893-1968 55
Johns, Captain W. E.
  See Johns, W(illiam) E(arle)
Johnson, A.
  See Johnson, Annabell
Johnson, A. E.
  See Johnson, Annabell
  and Johnson, Edgar (Raymond)
Johnson, Angela 1961- 188
  Earlier sketches in SATA *69, 102, 150*
  See also CLR *33*
Johnson, Annabel
  See Johnson, Annabell
Johnson, Annabell 1921- 72
  Earlier sketch in SATA *2*
Johnson, Art 1946- 123
Johnson, B. F. 1920- 1
Johnson, Benjamin F., of Boone
  See Riley, James Whitcomb
Johnson, Bettye 1858-1919
  See Rogers, Bettye
Johnson, Caryn
  See Goldberg, Whoopi
Johnson, Caryn E.
  See Goldberg, Whoopi
Johnson, Caryn Elaine
  See Goldberg, Whoopi
Johnson, Charles R. 1925- *11*

Johnson, Charlotte Buel
   See von Wodtke, Charlotte Buel Johnson
Johnson, Chuck
   See Johnson, Charles R.
Johnson, Crockett
   See Leisk, David (Johnson)
Johnson, D(ana) William 1945- 23
Johnson, Daniel Shahid 1954- 73
Johnson, David
   See Johnson, David A.
Johnson, David A. 1951- 191
Johnson, D.B. 1944- 183
   Earlier sketch in SATA 146
Johnson, Dianne 1960- 130
Johnson, Dinah
   See Johnson, Dianne
Johnson, Dolores 1949- 69
Johnson, Donald B.
   See Johnson, D.B.
Johnson, Dorothy M(arie) 1905-1984 6
   Obituary 40
Johnson, E(ugene) Harper 44
Johnson, Edgar (Raymond) 1912-1990 72
   Earlier sketch in SATA 2
Johnson, Eleanor Murdock 1892-1987
   Obituary 54
Johnson, Elizabeth 1911-1984 7
   Obituary 39
Johnson, Eric W(arner) 1918-1994 ....
   Obituary 82
   Earlier sketch in SATA 8
Johnson, Evelyne 1922- 20
Johnson, Fred 19(?)-1982 63
Johnson, Gaylord 1884-1972 7
Johnson, Gerald White 1890-1980 19
   Obituary 28
Johnson, Harper
   See Johnson, E(ugene) Harper
Johnson, Harriett 1908-1987
   Obituary 53
Johnson, James Ralph 1922- 1
Johnson, James Weldon 1871-1938 31
   See also CLR 32
Johnson, Jane 1951- 48
Johnson, Joan J. 1942- 59
Johnson, John E(mil) 1929- 34
Johnson, Johnny 1901-1995
   See Johnson, (Walter) Ryerson
Johnson, Kathleen Jeffrie 1950- 186
Johnson, La Verne B(ravo) 1925- 13
Johnson, Layne 187
Johnson, Lee Kaiser 1962- 78
Johnson, Lissa H(alls) 1955- 65
Johnson, Lois Smith 1894-1993 6
Johnson, Lois Walfrid 1936- 130
   Earlier sketches in SATA 22, 91
Johnson, Margaret S(weet) 1893-1964 35
Johnson, Marguerite Annie
   See Angelou, Maya
Johnson, Mary Frances K. 1929(?)-1979
   Obituary 27
Johnson, Maud Battle 1918(?)-1985
   Obituary 46
Johnson, Maureen 1973- 200
Johnson, Meredith Merrell 1952- 104
Johnson, Milton 1932- 31
Johnson, Neil 1954- 135
   Earlier sketch in SATA 73
Johnson, Pamela 1949- 71
Johnson, Patricia Polin 1956- 84
Johnson, Paul Brett 1947- 132
   Earlier sketch in SATA 83
Johnson, Rebecca L. 1956- 147
   Earlier sketch in SATA 67
Johnson, Rick L. 1954- 79
Johnson, (Walter) Ryerson 1901-1995 10
   Obituary 106
Johnson, Scott 1952- 119
   Earlier sketch in SATA 76
Johnson, Sherrie 1948- 87
Johnson, Shirley K(ing) 1927- 10

Johnson, Siddie Joe 1905-1977
   Obituary 20
Johnson, Spencer 1938- 145
   Brief entry 38
Johnson, Stacie
   See Myers, Walter Dean
Johnson, Stephen T. 1964- 189
   Earlier sketches in SATA 84, 141
Johnson, Steve 1960- 177
Johnson, Sue Kaiser 1963- 78
Johnson, Sylvia A. 166
   Brief entry 52
   Earlier sketch in SATA 104
Johnson, William R. 38
Johnson, William Weber 1909-1992 7
Johnson-Feelings, Dianne
   See Johnson, Dianne
Johnston, Agnes Christine
   See Dazey, Agnes J(ohnston)
Johnston, Annie Fellows 1863-1931 37
Johnston, Dorothy Grunbock 1915-1979 54
Johnston, Ginny 1946- 60
Johnston, H(ugh) A(nthony) S(tephen)
   1913-1967 14
Johnston, Janet 1944- 71
Johnston, Jeffry W. 188
Johnston, Johanna 1914(?)-1982 12
   Obituary 33
Johnston, Julie 1941- 110
   Autobiography Feature 128
   Earlier sketch in SATA 78
   See also CLR 41
   See also SAAS 24
Johnston, Lynn 1947- 118
Johnston, Lynn Beverley
   See Johnston, Lynn
Johnston, Mark 194
Johnston, Norma
   See St. John, Nicole
Johnston, Portia
   See Takakjian, Portia
Johnston, Susan Taylor 1942- 180
   Earlier sketches in SATA 8, 83, 128
Johnston, Tim(othy Patrick) 1962- 146
Johnston, Tony
   See Johnston, Susan Taylor
Joinson, Carla 160
Jolin, Paula 186
Jonas, Ann 1932- 135
   Brief entry 42
   Earlier sketch in SATA 50
   See also CLR 74
Jonell, Lynne 1956- 196
   Earlier sketch in SATA 109
Jones, Adrienne 1915-2000 82
   Earlier sketch in SATA 7
   See also SAAS 10
Jones, Allan Frewin 1954- 204
Jones, Annabel
   See Lewis, Mary
Jones, Betty Millsaps 1940- 54
Jones, Carol 1942- 153
   Earlier sketch in SATA 79
Jones, Carrie 1971- 191
Jones, Charles M. 1912-2002 53
   Obituary 133
Jones, Charlotte Foltz 1945- 122
   Earlier sketch in SATA 77
Jones, Chuck
   See Jones, Charles M.
Jones, Constance 112
Jones, Constance A.
   See Jones, Constance
Jones, David 1956- 202
Jones, Diana Wynne 1934- 160
   Earlier sketches in SATA 9, 70, 108
   See also CLR 120
   See also SAAS 7
Jones, Douglas B. 202
Jones, Douglas C(lyde) 1924-1998 52
Jones, Elizabeth McDavid 155

Jones, Elizabeth Orton 1910-2005 18
   Obituary 164
Jones, Evan 1915-1996 3
Jones, Frewin
   See Jones, Allan Frewin
Jones, Geraldine
   See McCaughrean, Geraldine
Jones, Gillingham
   See Hamilton, Charles (Harold St. John)
Jones, Gwyneth A(nn) 1952- 159
Jones, Harold 1904-1992 14
   Obituary 72
Jones, Helen Hinckley 1903-1991 26
Jones, Helen L(ouise) 1903-1973
   Obituary 22
Jones, Hettie 1934- 42
   Brief entry 27
Jones, Hortense P. 1918- 9
Jones, J. Sydney 1948- 101
Jones, Jasmine
   See Papademetriou, Lisa
Jones, Jennifer (Berry) 1947- 90
Jones, Jessie Mae Orton 1887(?)-1983
   Obituary 37
Jones, John R(obert) 1926- 76
Jones, Jon Sydney
   See Jones, J. Sydney
Jones, Kimberly K. 1957- 187
Jones, Marcia Thornton 1958- 115
   Earlier sketch in SATA 73
Jones, Martha T(annery) 1931- 130
Jones, Mary Alice 1898(?)-1980 6
Jones, McClure 34
Jones, Noah Z. 182
Jones, Patrick 1961- 136
Jones, Penelope 1938- 31
Jones, Rebecca C(astaldi) 1947- 99
   Earlier sketch in SATA 33
Jones, Robin D(orothy) 1959- 80
Jones, Sanford W.
   See Thorn, John
Jones, Sylvie 185
Jones, Sylvie Michelle
   See Jones, Sylvie
Jones, Terence Graham Parry 1942- 127
   Brief entry 51
   Earlier sketch in SATA 67
Jones, Terry
   See Jones, Terence Graham Parry
Jones, Tim Wynne
   See Wynne-Jones, Tim
Jones, Traci L. 186
Jones, V(ictoria) M(ary) 1958- 147
Jones, Veda Boyd 1948- 119
Jones, Volcano
   See Mitchell, Adrian
Jones, Weyman (B.) 1928- 4
   See also SAAS 11
Jones, William Glynne
   See Glynne-Jones, William
Jonk, Clarence 1906-1987 10
Jonsberg, Barry 1951- 168
Joos, Francoise 1956- 78
Joos, Frederic 1953- 78
Joosse, Barbara M. 1949- 164
   Earlier sketches in SATA 52, 96
Joosse, Barbara Monnot
   See Joosse, Barbara M.
Jordan, Alexis Hill
   See Glick, Ruth (Burtnick)
   and Titchener, Louise
Jordan, Anne Devereaux 1943- 80
Jordan, Chris
   See Philbrick, Rodman
Jordan, Deloris 191
Jordan, Don
   See Howard, Vernon (Linwood)
Jordan, Hope Dahle 1905-1995 15
Jordan, Jael (Michal) 1949- 30

Jordan, June 1936-2002 .... *136*
  Earlier sketch in SATA *4*
  See also CLR *10*
Jordan, June Meyer
  See Jordan, June
Jordan, Lee
  See Scholefield, Alan
Jordan, Martin George 1944- *84*
Jordan, Robert 1948-2007 .... *95*
Jordan, Robert K.
  See Jordan, Robert
Jordan, Rosa 1939- *191*
Jordan, Roslyn M. *189*
Jordan, Sherryl 1949- *122*
  Earlier sketch in SATA *71*
  See also SAAS *23*
Jordan, Shirley 1930- *154*
Jordan, Tanis 1946- *84*
Jorgensen, Ivar
  See Ellison, Harlan
  and Garrett, Randall
Jorgensen, Mary Venn -1995 .... *36*
Jorgensen, Norman 1954- *157*
Jorgenson, Ivar
  See Silverberg, Robert
Jorisch, Stephane *178*
Joseph, Anne
  See Coates, Anna
Joseph, James (Herz) 1924- *53*
Joseph, Joan 1939- *34*
Joseph, Joseph M(aron) 1903-1979 .... *22*
Joseph, Patrick
  See O'Malley, Kevin
Josephs, Rebecca
  See Talbot, Toby
Josephson, Judith Pinkerton 1943- *198*
Josh
  See Twain, Mark
Joshua, Peter
  See Stone, Peter
Joslin, Mary 1953- *176*
Joslin, Sesyle
  See Hine, Sesyle Joslin
Joubert, Beverly 1957- *204*
Joubert, Dereck *204*
Journet, Mireille
  See Marokvia, Mireille
Joyce, Bill
  See Joyce, William
Joyce, J(ames) Avery 1902-1987 .... *11*
  Obituary *50*
Joyce, Peter 1937- *127*
Joyce, William 1957- *118*
  Brief entry *46*
  Earlier sketch in SATA *72*
  See also CLR *26*
Joyner, Jerry 1938- *34*
Juan, Ana 1961- *179*
Jubert, Herve *185*
Juby, Susan 1969- *202*
  Earlier sketch in SATA *156*
Jucker, Sita 1921- *5*
Judah, Aaron 1923- *118*
Judd, Cyril
  See Kornbluth, C(yril) M.
  and Merril, Judith
  and Pohl, Frederik
Judd, Denis (O'Nan) 1938- *33*
Judd, Frances K.
  See Benson, Mildred
Jude, Conny *81*
Judge, Lita *192*
Judson, Clara Ingram 1879-1960 .... *38*
  Brief entry *27*
Judy, Stephen
  See Tchudi, Stephen N.
Judy, Stephen N.
  See Tchudi, Stephen N.
Juhasz, Victor 1954- *177*

Jukes, Mavis 1947- *111*
  Brief entry *43*
  Earlier sketch in SATA *72*
  See also SAAS *12*
Jules, Jacqueline 1956- *183*
  Earlier sketch in SATA *148*
Julesberg, Elizabeth Rider Montgomery
  1902-1985 .... *34*
  Obituary *41*
  Earlier sketch in SATA *3*
Julian, Jane
  See Wiseman, David
Jumpp, Hugo
  See MacPeek, Walter G.
Jungman, Ann *165*
Jupo, Frank J. 1904-1981 .... *7*
Jurmain, Suzanne 1945- *169*
  Earlier sketch in SATA *72*
Jurmain, Suzanne Tripp
  See Jurmain, Suzanne
Juster, Norton 1929- *132*
  Earlier sketch in SATA *3*
  See also CLR *112*
Justus, May 1898-1989 .... *1*
  Obituary *106*
Juvenilia
  See Taylor, Ann

K

Kaaberbol, Lene
  See Kaaberbol, Lene
Kaaberbol, Lene 1960- *159*
Kabdebo, Tamas
  See Kabdebo, Thomas
Kabdebo, Thomas 1934- *10*
Kabibble, Osh
  See Jobb, Jamie
Kacer, Kathy 1954- *184*
  Earlier sketch in SATA *142*
Kaczman, James *156*
Kadair, Deborah Ousley *184*
Kadesch, Robert R(udstone) 1922- *31*
Kadohata, Cynthia 1956(?)- *180*
  Earlier sketch in SATA *155*
  See also CLR *121*
Kaempfert, Wade
  See del Rey, Lester
Kaestner, Erich 1899-1974 .... *14*
  See also CLR *4*
Kahl, Jonathan (D.) 1959- *77*
Kahl, M(arvin) P(hilip) 1934- *37*
Kahl, Virginia (Caroline) 1919-2004 .... *48*
  Brief entry *38*
  Obituary *158*
Kahn, Joan 1914-1994 .... *48*
  Obituary *82*
Kahn, Katherine Janus 1942- *167*
  Earlier sketch in SATA *90*
Kahn, Peggy
  See Katz, Bobbi
Kahn, Roger 1927- *37*
Kahukiwa, Robyn 1940- *134*
Kains, Josephine
  See Goulart, Ron
Kaizuki, Kiyonori 1950- *72*
Kakimoto, Kozo 1915- *11*
Kalashnikoff, Nicholas 1888-1961 .... *16*
Kalb, Jonah 1926- *23*
Kalbacken, Joan 1925- *96*
Kalechofsky, Roberta 1931- *92*
Kaler, James Otis 1848-1912 .... *15*
Kalish, Claire M. 1947- *92*
Kallen, Stuart A(rnold) 1955- *126*
  Earlier sketch in SATA *86*
Kallevig, Christine Petrell 1955- *164*
Kalman, Bobbie 1947- *63*

Kalman, Maira 1949- *137*
  Earlier sketch in SATA *96*
  See also CLR *32*
Kalnay, Francis 1899-1992 .... *7*
Kaloustian, Rosanne 1955- *93*
Kalow, Gisela 1946- *32*
Kalstein, Dave *175*
Kamen, Gloria 1923- *98*
  Earlier sketch in SATA *9*
Kamerman, Sylvia E.
  See Burack, Sylvia K.
Kamm, Josephine (Hart) 1905-1989 .... *24*
Kammerman, Sylvia K.
  See Burack, Sylvia K.
Kandel, Michael 1941- *93*
Kandell, Alice S. 1938- *35*
Kane, Bob 1916-1998 .... *120*
Kane, Henry Bugbee 1902-1971 .... *14*
Kane, L. A.
  See Mannetti, Lisa
Kane, Robert W. 1910- *18*
Kane, Wilson
  See Bloch, Robert (Albert)
Kanefield, Teri 1960- *135*
Kaner, Etta 1947- *198*
  Earlier sketch in SATA *126*
Kanetzke, Howard W(illiam) 1932- *38*
Kangas, Juli 1958- *200*
Kann, Elizabeth *180*
Kann, Victoria *180*
Kanninen, Barbara *196*
Kanninen, Barbara J.
  See Kanninen, Barbara
Kanoza, Muriel Canfield
  See Canfield, Muriel
Kantner, Seth 1965- *179*
Kanzawa, Toshiko
  See Furukawa, Toshi
Kanzler, John 1963- *188*
Kaplan, Andrew 1960- *78*
Kaplan, Anne Bernays
  See Bernays, Anne
Kaplan, Bess 1927- *22*
Kaplan, Boche 1926- *24*
Kaplan, Elizabeth 1956- *83*
Kaplan, Elizabeth A.
  See Kaplan, Elizabeth
Kaplan, Irma 1900- *10*
Kaplan, Jean Caryl Korn 1926- *10*
Kaplow, Robert 1954- *70*
Karageorge, Michael
  See Anderson, Poul
Karas, G. Brian 1957- *178*
Karas, George Brian
  See Karas, G. Brian
Karasz, Ilonka 1896-1981
  Obituary *29*
Karen, Ruth 1922-1987 .... *9*
  Obituary *54*
Kark, Nina Mary
  See Bawden, Nina
Karl, Herb 1938- *73*
Karl, Jean E(dna) 1927-2000 .... *122*
  Earlier sketch in SATA *34*
  See also SAAS *10*
Karlin, Bernie 1927- *68*
Karlin, Eugene 1918- *10*
Karlin, Nurit *103*
  Earlier sketch in SATA *63*
Karnes, Frances A. 1937- *110*
Karp, Naomi J. 1926- *16*
Karpinski, J. Rick
  See Karpinski, John Eric
Karpinski, John Eric 1952- *81*
Karpinski, Rick
  See Karpinski, John Eric
Karr, Kathleen 1946- *127*
  Earlier sketch in SATA *82*
Karr, Phyllis Ann 1944- *119*
Karwoski, Gail 1949- *127*

Karwoski, Gail Langer
See Karwoski, Gail
Kashiwagi, Isami 1925- 10
Kaslik, Ibi
See Kaslik, Ibolya Emma
Kaslik, Ibolya Emma 1973- 185
Kassem, Lou 1931- 62
Brief entry 51
Kastel, Warren
See Silverberg, Robert
Kastner, Erich
See Kaestner, Erich
Kastner, Jill (Marie) 1964- 117
Earlier sketch in SATA 70
Kasuya, Masahiro 1937- 51
Kasza, Keiko 1951- 191
Earlier sketch in SATA 124
Kataphusin
See Ruskin, John
Katchen, Carole 1944- 9
Katcher, Brian 1975- 203
Kathryn
See Searle, Kathryn Adrienne
Kato, Aya 1982- 202
Katona, Robert 1949- 21
Katsarakis, Joan Harries
See Harries, Joan
Katz, Alan 185
Katz, Avi 1949- 199
Katz, Avner 1939- 103
Katz, Bobbi 1933- 179
Earlier sketch in SATA 12
Katz, Fred(eric Phillip) 1938- 6
Katz, Jane B(resler) 1934- 33
Katz, Karen 1947- 195
Earlier sketch in SATA 158
Katz, Marjorie P.
See Weiser, Marjorie P(hillis) K(atz)
Katz, Susan 1945- 156
Katz, Welwyn Wilton 1948- 96
Autobiography Feature 118
Earlier sketch in SATA 62
See also CLR 45
Katz, William 1940- 98
Katz, William Loren 1927- 13
Kaufman, Bel 57
Kaufman, Jeff 1955- 84
Kaufman, Joe 1911-2001 33
Kaufman, Joseph
See Kaufman, Joe
Kaufman, Mervyn D. 1932- 4
Kaufmann, Angelika 1935- 15
Kaufmann, John 1931- 18
Kaula, Edna Mason 1906-1987 13
Kaur Khalsa, Dayal
See Khalsa, Dayal Kaur
Kavaler, Lucy 1930- 23
Kavanagh, Jack 1920- 85
Kavanagh, P(atrick) J(oseph Gregory)
1931- 122
Kavanaugh, Ian
See Webb, Jean Francis (III)
Kay, Alan N. 1965- 144
Kay, Elizabeth 1949- 165
Kay, Guy Gavriel 1954- 167
Earlier sketch in SATA 121
Kay, Helen
See Goldfrank, Helen Colodny
Kay, Jackie 1961- 165
Earlier sketch in SATA 97
Kay, Jacqueline Margaret
See Kay, Jackie
Kay, Julia 205
Kay, Mara 13
Kay, Verla 1946- 120
Kaye, Danny 1913-1987
Obituary 50
Kaye, Geraldine (Hughesdon) 1925- 85
Earlier sketch in SATA 10
Kaye, Judy
See Baer, Judy

Kaye, Marilyn 1949- 110
Earlier sketch in SATA 56
Kaye, Mary Margaret
See Kaye, M.M.
Kaye, M.M. 1908-2004 62
Obituary 152
Kaye, Mollie
See Kaye, M.M.
Kaye, Peggy 1948- 143
Keach, James P. 1950- 125
Keams, Geri 1951- 117
Keane, Bil 1922- 4
Keaney, Brian 1954- 188
Earlier sketch in SATA 106
Kearney, Meg 1964- 178
Kearny, Jillian
See Goulart, Ron
Keating, Bern
See Keating, Leo Bernard
Keating, Frank 1944- 143
Keating, Lawrence A. 1903-1966 23
Keating, Leo Bernard 1915- 10
Keats, Emma 1899(?)-1979(?) 68
Keats, Ezra Jack 1916-1983 57
Obituary 34
Earlier sketch in SATA 14
See also CLR 35
Keefer, Catherine
See Ogan, George F.
and Ogan, Margaret E. (Nettles)
Keefer, Janice Kulyk
See Kulyk Keefer, Janice
Keegan, Marcia 1943- 104
Earlier sketch in SATA 9
Keehn, Sally M. 1947- 165
Earlier sketch in SATA 87
Keel, Frank
See Keeler, Ronald F(ranklin)
Keeler, Patricia 183
Keeler, Patricia A.
See Keeler, Patricia
Keeler, Ronald F(ranklin) 1913-1983 47
Keely, Jack 1951- 119
Keen, Martin L. 1913-1992 4
Keenan, Sheila 1953- 95
Keene, Ann T(odd) 1940- 86
Keene, Carolyn
See Benson, Mildred
and Goulart, Ron
and Lerangis, Peter
and McFarlane, Leslie
and Stanley, George Edward
and Stratemeyer, Edward L.
Keens-Douglas, Richardo 1953- 154
Earlier sketch in SATA 95
Keep, Linda Lowery
See Lowery, Linda
Keep, Richard 1949- 170
Keep, Richard Cleminson
See Keep, Richard
Keeping, Charles (William James)
1924-1988 69
Obituary 56
Earlier sketch in SATA 9
See also CLR 34
Keeshan, Robert J. 1927-2004 32
Obituary 151
Kehlenbeck, Angela 1959- 186
Kehret, Peg 1936- 149
Autobiography Feature 149
Earlier sketches in SATA 73, 108
Keillor, Garrison 1942- 58
Keillor, Gary Edward
See Keillor, Garrison
Keir, Christine
See Pullein-Thompson, Christine
Keister, Douglas 1948- 88
Keith, Doug 1952- 81
Keith, Eros 1942- 52
Keith, Hal 1934- 36

Keith, Harold (Verne) 1903-1998 74
Earlier sketch in SATA 2
Keith, Robert
See Applebaum, Stan
Keleinikov, Andrei 1924- 65
Kelemen, Julie 1959- 78
Kelen, Emery 1896-1978 13
Obituary 26
Kelleam, Joseph E(veridge) 1913-1975 31
Kelleher, Anne 1959- 97
Kelleher, Annette 1950- 122
Kelleher, Daria Valerian 1955- 79
Kelleher, Victor (Michael Kitchener)
1939- 129
Brief entry 52
Earlier sketch in SATA 75
See also CLR 36
Keller, Beverly L(ou) 91
Earlier sketch in SATA 13
Keller, Charles 1942- 82
Earlier sketch in SATA 8
Keller, Debra 1958- 94
Keller, Dick 1923- 36
Keller, Emily 96
Keller, Gail Faithfull
See Faithfull, Gail
Keller, Holly 1942- 157
Brief entry 42
Earlier sketches in SATA 76, 108
See also CLR 45
Keller, Irene (Barron) 1927-2002 36
Obituary 139
Keller, Laurie 1961(?)- 196
Keller, Ellen A. 185
Kelley, Ellen A. 185
Kelley, Ellen Chavez
See Kelley, Ellen A.
Kelley, Gary 1945- 183
Kelley, Leo P(atrick) 1928- 32
Brief entry 31
Kelley, Patrick (G.) 1963- 129
Kelley, Patte 1947- 93
Kelley, True 1946- 179
Kelley, True (Adelaide) 1946- 130
Brief entry 39
Earlier sketches in SATA 41, 92
Kelley, True Adelaide
See Kelley, True
Kellin, Sally Moffet 1932- 9
Kelling, Furn L. 1914-2000 37
Kellogg, Gene
See Kellogg, Jean (Defrees)
Kellogg, Jean (Defrees) 1916-1978 10
Kellogg, Steven 1941- 177
Earlier sketches in SATA 8, 57, 130
See also CLR 6
Kellogg, Steven Castle
See Kellogg, Steven
Kellow, Kathleen
See Hibbert, Eleanor Alice Burford
Kelly, C. M. O.
See Gibbs, (Cecilia) May
Kelly, Clint 1950- 140
Kelly, Eric P(hilbrook) 1884-1960
See YABC 1
Kelly, Fiona
See Coleman, Michael
and Hendry, Frances Mary
and Oldfield, Jenny
and Welford, Sue
Kelly, Fiona
See Jones, Allan Frewin
Kelly, Irene 1957- 147
Kelly, Jeff
See Kelly, Jeffrey
Kelly, Jeffrey 1946- 65
Kelly, Joanne (W.) 1934- 87
Kelly, Kate 1958- 91
Kelly, Kathleen M. 1964- 71
Kelly, Katy 1955- 169
Kelly, Lauren
See Oates, Joyce Carol

Kelly, Laurene 1954- 123
Kelly, Martha Rose 1914-1983 37
Kelly, Marty
  See Kelly, Martha Rose
Kelly, Mij 166
Kelly, Ralph
  See Geis, Darlene Stern
Kelly, Regina Z(immerman) 1898-1986 5
Kelly, Rosalie (Ruth) 43
Kelly, Tom 1961- 191
Kelly, Walt(er Crawford) 1913-1973 18
Kelsey, Alice Geer 1896-1982 1
Kelsey, Elin 1961- 159
Kemly, Kathleen 1958- 197
Kemnitz, Thomas Milton, Jr. 1984- 152
Kemnitz, Tom, Jr.
  See Kemnitz, Thomas Milton, Jr.
Kemp, Gene 1926- 75
  Earlier sketch in SATA 25
  See also CLR 29
Kempner, Mary Jean 1913-1969 10
Kempter, Christa 1945- 187
Kempton, Jean Welch 1914- 10
Kenah, Katharine 1949- 182
Kenda, Margaret 1942- 71
Kendall, Carol (Seeger) 1917- 74
  Earlier sketch in SATA 11
  See also SAAS 7
Kendall, Katherine
  See Applegate, Katherine
Kendall, Lace
  See Stoutenburg, Adrien (Pearl)
Kendall, Martha E. 87
Kendall, Russ 1957- 83
Kenealy, James P. 1927- 52
  Brief entry 29
Kenealy, Jim
  See Kenealy, James P.
Kennaway, Adrienne 1945- 171
  Earlier sketch in SATA 60
Kennedy, Anne 1955- 198
Kennedy, Anne Vittur
  See Kennedy, Anne
Kennedy, Brendan 1970- 57
Kennedy, Dana Forrest 1917- 74
Kennedy, Dorothy M(intzlaff) 1931- 53
Kennedy, Doug 1963- 189
  Earlier sketch in SATA 122
Kennedy, Frances 1937- 192
Kennedy, John Fitzgerald 1917-1963 11
Kennedy, Joseph Charles 1929- 130
  Autobiography Feature 130
  Earlier sketches in SATA 14, 86
  See also CLR 27
  See also SAAS 22
  See Kennedy, X. J.
Kennedy, Kim 189
Kennedy, Pamela (J.) 1946- 87
Kennedy, Paul E(dward) 1929- 113
  Earlier sketch in SATA 33
Kennedy, Richard (Pitt) 1910-1989
  Obituary 60
Kennedy, (Jerome) Richard 1932- 22
Kennedy, Robert 1938- 63
Kennedy, T.A. 1953- 42
  Brief entry 35
Kennedy, Teresa
  See Kennedy, T.A.
Kennedy, Teresa A.
  See Kennedy, T.A.
Kennedy, William 1928- 57
Kennedy, William Joseph
  See Kennedy, William
Kennedy, X. J.
  See CLR 27
  See also SAAS 22
  See Kennedy, Joseph Charles
Kennell, Ruth Epperson 1893-1977 6
  Obituary 25
Kennemore, Tim 1957- 133
Kennen, Ally 190

Kennett, David 1959- 206
  Earlier sketch in SATA 121
Kennison, Ruth 202
Kenny, Ellsworth Newcomb 1909-1971
  Obituary 26
Kenny, Herbert Andrew 1912-2002 13
Kenny, Jude
  See Daly, Jude
Kenny, Kathryn
  See Bowden, Joan Chase
  and Krull, Kathleen
  and Sanderlin, Owenita (Harrah)
  and Stack, Nicolete Meredith
Kenny, Kevin
  See Krull, Kathleen
Kensinger, George
  See Fichter, George S.
Kensington, Kathryn Wesley
  See Rusch, Kristine Kathryn
Kent, Alexander
  See Reeman, Douglas Edward
Kent, David
  See Lambert, David
Kent, Deborah Ann 1948- 155
  Brief entry 41
  Earlier sketches in SATA 47, 104
Kent, Jack
  See Kent, John Wellington
Kent, John Wellington 1920-1985 24
  Obituary 45
Kent, Lisa 1942- 90
Kent, Mallory
  See Lowndes, Robert A(ugustine) W(ard)
Kent, Margaret 1894- 2
Kent, Rockwell 1882-1971 6
Kent, Rose 188
Kent, Sherman 1903-1986 20
  Obituary 47
Kenward, Jean 1920- 42
Kenworthy, Leonard S. 1912-1991 6
Kenyon, Karen (Smith) 1938- 145
Kenyon, Kate
  See Adorjan, Carol (Madden)
  and Ransom, Candice F.
Kenyon, Ley 1913-1990 6
Keown, Elizabeth 78
Kepes, Juliet A(ppleby) 1919-1999 13
Kephart, Beth 1960- 196
Kerby, Mona 1951- 202
  Earlier sketch in SATA 75
Kerigan, Florence 1896-1984 12
Kerley, Barbara 1960- 191
  Earlier sketch in SATA 138
Kerman, Gertrude
  See Furman, Gertrude Lerner Kerman
Kerns, Thelma 1929- 116
Kerr, Anne Louise
  See Mackey, Weezie Kerr
Kerr, Bob 1951- 120
Kerr, Jessica 1901-1991 13
Kerr, (Anne-)Judith 1923-1970 24
Kerr, M. E.
  See Meaker, Marijane
Kerr, P.B.
  See Kerr, Philip
Kerr, Philip 1956- 168
Kerr, Phyllis Forbes 1942- 72
Kerr, Tom 1950- 77
Kerrin, Jessica Scott 174
Kerry, Frances
  See Kerigan, Florence
Kerry, Lois
  See Duncan, Lois
Kershen, (L.) Michael 1982- 82
Kerven, Rosalind 1954- 83
Ker Wilson, Barbara 1929- 121
  Earlier sketches in SATA 20, 70
  See also SAAS 18
Keselman, Gabriela 1953- 128
Kesey, Ken 1935-2001 66
  Obituary 131

Kesey, Ken Elton
  See Kesey, Ken
Kesler, Jay 1935- 65
Kessel, Joyce Karen 1937- 41
Kessler, Cristina 190
Kessler, Ethel 1922- 44
  Brief entry 37
Kessler, Leonard P. 1921- 14
Kessler, Liz 1966- 206
Kest, Kristin 1967- 168
  Earlier sketch in SATA 118
Kesteven, G. R.
  See Crosher, G. R.
Ketcham, Hank
  See Ketcham, Henry King
Ketcham, Henry King 1920-2001 28
  Brief entry 27
  Obituary 128
Ketcham, Sallie 1963- 124
Ketchum, Liza 1946-
  See Murrow, Liza Ketchum
Ketner, Mary Grace 1946- 75
Kettelkamp, Larry (Dale) 1933- 2
  See also SAAS 3
Ketteman, Helen 1945- 167
  Earlier sketches in SATA 73, 115
Kettle, Peter
  See Glover, Denis (James Matthews)
Kevles, Bettyann Holtzmann 1938- 23
Key, Alexander (Hill) 1904-1979 8
  Obituary 23
Key, Samuel M.
  See de Lint, Charles
Key, Watt 1970- 189
Keyes, Daniel 1927- 37
Keyes, Fenton 1915-1999 34
Keyes, Greg 1963- 116
Keyes, J. Gregory
  See Keyes, Greg
Keyser, Marcia 1933- 42
Keyser, Sarah
  See McGuire, Leslie (Sarah)
Khalid, Mohamed Nor
  See Lat
Khalsa, Dayal Kaur 1943-1989 62
  See also CLR 30
Khan, Rukhsana 1962- 165
  Earlier sketch in SATA 118
Khanshendel, Chiron
  See Rose, Wendy
Kheirabadi, Masoud 1951- 158
Khemir, Sabiha 87
Kherdian, David 1931- 74
  Autobiography Feature 125
  Earlier sketch in SATA 16
  See also CLR 24
Khing, T.T. 1933- 192
Kibbe, Pat (Hosley) 60
Kidd, Diana 1933-2000 150
Kidd, Richard 1952-2008 152
  Obituary 194
Kidd, Ronald 1948- 173
  Earlier sketches in SATA 42, 92
Kiddell, John 1922- 3
Kiddell-Monroe, Joan 1908-1972 55
Kidwell, Carl 1910- 43
Kiefer, Irene 1926- 21
Kiefer, Kathleen Balmes 1957- 142
Kiepper, Shirley Morgan 1933- 10
Kierstead, Vera M.
  See Kierstead-Farber, Vera M.
Kierstead-Farber, Vera M. 1913- 121
Kierstead-Farber, Vera May
  See Kierstead-Farber, Vera M.
Kiesel, Stanley 1925- 35
Kiesler, Kate (A.) 1971- 152
  Earlier sketch in SATA 90
Kihn, Greg 1952- 110
Kikukawa, Cecily H(arder) 1919- 44
  Brief entry 35
Kilcher, Jewel 1974- 109

Kile, Joan 1940- 78
Kilgore, Kathleen 1946- 42
Kilian, Crawford 1941- 35
Killdeer, John
  See Mayhar, Ardath
Killien, Christi 1956- 73
Killilea, Marie (Lyons) 1913-1991 2
Killingback, Julia 1944- 63
Killough, (Karen) Lee 1942- 64
Kilpatrick, Don 206
Kilreon, Beth
  See Walker, Barbara (Jeanne) K(erlin)
Kilworth, Garry 1941- 94
Kilworth, Garry D.
  See Kilworth, Garry
Kilworth, Garry Douglas
  See Kilworth, Garry
Kim, David 1977- 201
Kim, Helen 1899-1970 98
Kim, Joung Un 1970- 205
Kimball, Gayle 1943- 90
Kimball, Violet T(ew) 1932- 126
Kimball, Yeffe 1914-1978 37
Kimber, Murray 1964- 171
Kimble, Warren 176
Kimbrough, Emily 1899-1989 2
  Obituary 59
Kimeldorf, Martin 1948- 121
Kimeldorf, Martin R.
  See Kimeldorf, Martin
Kimenye, Barbara 1940(?)- 121
Kimmel, Elizabeth Cody 170
Kimmel, Eric A. 1946- 176
  Earlier sketches in SATA 13, 80, 125
Kimmel, Margaret Mary 1938- 43
  Brief entry 33
Kimmelman, Burt 1947- 180
Kimmelman, Leslie (Grodinsky) 1958- 156
  Earlier sketch in SATA 85
Kincaid, Jamaica 1949-
  See CLR 63
Kincher, Jonni 1949- 79
Kindl, Patrice 1951- 128
  Earlier sketch in SATA 82
  See also CLR 132
Kindred, Wendy (Good) 1937- 7
Kinerk, Robert 199
Kines, Pat Decker 1937- 12
King, Adam
  See Hoare, Robert J(ohn)
King, Alison
  See Martini, Teri
King, (Maria) Anna 1964- 72
King, Billie Jean 1943- 12
King, Christopher (L.) 1945- 84
King, (David) Clive 1924- 144
  Earlier sketch in SATA 28
King, Colin 1943- 76
King, Cynthia 1925- 7
King, Daniel (John) 1963- 130
King, Daren 1972- 197
King, Elizabeth 1953- 83
King, Frank O. 1883-1969
  Obituary 22
King, Frank R. 1904-1999 127
King, Jane
  See Currie, Stephen
King, Jeanette (Margaret) 1959- 105
King, Larry L. 1929- 66
King, Laurie R. 1952- 88
King, Marian 1900(?)-1986 23
  Obituary 47
King, Martin Luther, Jr. 1929-1968 14
King, Mary Ellen 1958- 93
King, Paul
  See Drackett, Phil(ip Arthur)
King, Paula
  See Downing, Paula E.
King, Stephen 1947- 161
  Earlier sketches in SATA 9, 55
  See also CLR 124

King, Stephen Edwin
  See King, Stephen
King, Stephen Michael 157
King, Steve
  See King, Stephen
King, Thomas 1943- 96
King, Thomas Hunt
  See King, Thomas
King, Tony 1947- 39
King, Willie Christine
  See Farris, Christine King
Kingman, Dong (Moy Shu) 1911-2000 44
Kingman, Lee
  See Natti, Lee
Kingsland, Leslie William 1912- 13
Kingsley, Charles 1819-1875
  See YABC 2
  See also CLR 77
Kingsley, Emily Perl 1940- 33
Kingsley, Kaza 193
King-Smith, Dick 1922- 192
  Brief entry 38
  Earlier sketches in SATA 47, 80, 135
  See also CLR 40
Kingston, Maxine Hong 1940- 53
Kingston, Maxine Ting Ting Hong
  See Kingston, Maxine Hong
Kinney, C. Cle(land) 1915- 6
Kinney, Harrison 1921- 13
Kinney, Jean Stout 1912- 12
Kinney, Jeff 1971- 187
Kinsey, Elizabeth
  See Clymer, Eleanor
Kinsey, Helen 1948- 82
Kinsey-Warnock, Natalie 1956- 167
  Earlier sketches in SATA 71, 116
Kinzel, Dorothy 1950- 57
Kinzel, Dottie
  See Kinzel, Dorothy
Kipling, (Joseph) Rudyard 1865-1936 100
  See also YABC 2
  See also CLR 65
Kippax, Frank
  See Needle, Jan
Kirby, David K. 1944- 78
Kirby, David Kirk
  See Kirby, David K.
Kirby, Margaret
  See Bingley, Margaret (Jane Kirby)
Kirby, Susan E. 1949- 62
Kirk, Connie Ann 1957- 167
Kirk, Daniel 1952- 196
  Earlier sketches in SATA 107, 153
Kirk, David 1955- 161
  Earlier sketch in SATA 117
Kirk, Heather 1949- 166
Kirk, Ruth (Kratz) 1925- 5
Kirkham, Dinah
  See Card, Orson Scott
Kirkland, Will
  See Hale, Arlene
Kirkpatrick, Katherine (Anne) 1964- 113
Kirkup, James 1918-2009 12
Kirkus, Virginia
  See Glick, Virginia Kirkus
Kirkwood, Kathryn
  See Fluke, Joanne
Kirshenbaum, Binnie 79
Kirshner, David S. 1958- 123
Kirtland, G. B.
  See Hine, Sesyle Joslin
  and Hine, Al(fred Blakelee)
Kirwan, Wednesday 198
Kish, Eleanor M(ary) 1924- 73
Kish, Ely
  See Kish, Eleanor M(ary)
Kishida, Eriko 1929- 12
Kisinger, Grace Gelvin (Maze) 1913-1965 .. 10
Kissin, Eva H. 1923- 10
Kissinger, Rosemary K.
  See Updyke, Rosemary K.

Kistler, John M. 1967- 160
Kitamura, Satoshi 1956- 201
  Earlier sketches in SATA 62, 98, 143
  See also CLR 60
Kitchen, Bert
  See Kitchen, Herbert Thomas
Kitchen, Herbert Thomas 1940- 70
Kite, L. Patricia
  See Kite, Pat
Kite, Pat 1940- 78
Kitt, Tamara
  See de Regniers, Beatrice Schenk (Freedman)
Kittinger, Jo S(usenbach) 1955- 148
  Earlier sketch in SATA 96
Kituomba
  See Odaga, Asenath (Bole)
Kitzinger, Sheila 1929- 57
Kiwak, Barbara 1966- 103
Kjelgaard, James Arthur 1910-1959 17
  See also CLR 81
  See Kjelgaard, Jim
Kjelgaard, Jim
  See Kjelgaard, James Arthur
Kjelle, Marylou Morano 1954- 146
Klages, Ellen 1954- 196
Klagsbrun, Francine (Lifton) 36
Klaits, Barrie 1944- 52
Klam, Cheryl 191
Klaperman, Gilbert 1921- 33
Klaperman, Libby Mindlin 1921-1982 33
  Obituary 31
Klass, David 1960- 142
  Earlier sketch in SATA 88
Klass, Morton 1927-2001 11
Klass, Sheila Solomon 1927- 99
  Autobiography Feature 126
  Earlier sketch in SATA 45
  See also SAAS 26
Klause, Annette Curtis 1953- 175
  Earlier sketch in SATA 79
  See also CLR 104
Klaveness, Jan O'Donnell 1939- 86
Kleberger, Ilse 1921- 5
Kleeberg, Irene (Flitner) Cumming 1932- 65
Klein, Aaron E. 1930-1998 45
  Brief entry 28
Klein, Bill 1945- 89
Klein, David 1919-2001 59
Klein, Frederick C. 1938- 154
Klein, Gerda Weissmann 1924- 44
Klein, H(erbert) Arthur 8
Klein, James 1932- 115
Klein, Leonore (Glotzer) 1916- 6
Klein, Mina C(ooper) 1906-1979 8
Klein, Norma 1938-1989 57
  Earlier sketch in SATA 7
  See also CLR 19
  See also SAAS 1
Klein, Rachel S. 1953- 105
Klein, Robin 1936- 164
  Brief entry 45
  Earlier sketches in SATA 55, 80
  See also CLR 21
Klemin, Diana 65
Klemm, Barry 1945- 104
Klemm, Edward G., Jr. 1910-2001 30
Klemm, Roberta K(ohnhorst) 1884-1975 30
Kleven, Elisa 1958- 173
  Earlier sketch in SATA 76
  See also CLR 85
Klevin, Jill Ross 1935- 39
  Brief entry 38
Kliban, B(ernard) 1935-1990 35
  Obituary 66
Klimowicz, Barbara 1927- 10
Kline, Christina Baker 1964- 101
Kline, James
  See Klein, James
Kline, Jim
  See Kline, Jim
Kline, Lisa Williams 1954- 143

Kline, Suzy 1943- *193*
   Autobiography Feature *193*
   Brief entry *48*
   Earlier sketches in SATA *67, 99, 152*
Kliros, Thea 1935- *106*
Klise, Kate *181*
Klise, M. Sarah 1961- *180*
   Earlier sketch in SATA *128*
Klots, Alexander Barrett 1903-1989
   Obituary *62*
Klug, Ron(ald) 1939- *31*
Knaak, Richard A. 1961- *166*
   Earlier sketch in SATA *86*
Knaak, Richard Allen
   See Knaak, Richard A.
Knapman, Timothy *200*
Knapp, Edward
   See Kunhardt, Edith
Knapp, Ron 1952- *34*
Knebel, Fletcher 1911-1993 .... *36*
   Obituary *75*
Kneeland, Linda Clarke 1947- *94*
Knickerbocker, Diedrich
   See Irving, Washington
Knifesmith
   See Cutler, Ivor
Knigge, Robert (R.) 1921(?)-1987 .... *50*
Knight, Anne (Katherine) 1946- *34*
Knight, Brenda *112*
Knight, Christopher G. 1943- *96*
Knight, Damon (Francis) 1922-2002 .... *9*
   Obituary *139*
Knight, David C(arpenter) 1925-1984 .... *14*
   See also CLR *38*
Knight, Eric 1897-1943 .... *18*
Knight, Eric Mowbray
   See Knight, Eric
Knight, Francis Edgar 1905- *14*
Knight, Frank
   See Knight, Francis Edgar
Knight, Hilary 1926- *132*
   Earlier sketches in SATA *15, 69*
Knight, Joan (MacPhail) *159*
   Earlier sketch in SATA *82*
Knight, Joan
   See Knight, Joan (MacPhail)
Knight, Kathryn Lasky
   See Lasky, Kathryn
Knight, Mallory T.
   See Hurwood, Bernhardt J.
Knight, Ruth Adams 1898-1974
   Obituary *20*
Knight, Theodore O. 1946- *77*
Knobloch, Dorothea 1951- *88*
Knoepfle, John (Ignatius) 1923- *66*
Knorr, Laura 1971- *200*
Knott, Bill
   See Knott, William C(ecil, Jr.)
Knott, William C(ecil, Jr.) 1927- *3*
Knotts, Howard (Clayton, Jr.) 1922- *25*
Knowles, Anne 1933- *37*
Knowles, Jo 1970- *197*
Knowles, Johanna Beth
   See Knowles, Jo
Knowles, John 1926-2001 .... *89*
   Obituary *134*
   Earlier sketch in SATA *8*
   See also CLR *98*
Knox, Calvin M.
   See Silverberg, Robert
Knox, (Mary) Eleanor Jessie 1909-2000 ...... *59*
   Earlier sketch in SATA *30*
Knox, Elizabeth 1959- *176*
Knox, Elizabeth Fiona
   See Knox, Elizabeth
Knox, James
   See Brittain, William
Knox, Jolyne 1937- *76*
Knudsen, James 1950- *42*
Knudsen, Michelle *171*

Knudson, R. R.
   See Knudson, Rozanne
Knudson, Richard L(ewis) 1930- *34*
Knudson, Rozanne 1932-2008 .... *79*
   Earlier sketch in SATA *7*
   See also SAAS *18*
Knutson, Barbara 1959-2005 .... *166*
Knutson, Kimberley *115*
Knye, Cassandra
   See Disch, Thomas M.
Kobayashi, Masako Matsuno 1935- *6*
Koch, Dorothy Clarke 1924- *6*
Koch, Kenneth 1925-2002 .... *65*
Koch, Kenneth Jay
   See Koch, Kenneth
Koch, Phyllis (Mae) McCallum 1911- *10*
Kochalka, James 1967- *196*
Kocsis, J. C.
   See Paul, James
Koda-Callan, Elizabeth 1944- *140*
   Earlier sketch in SATA *67*
Kodman, Stanislawa *201*
Koehler, Phoebe 1955- *85*
Koehler-Pentacoff, Elizabeth 1957- *160*
   Earlier sketch in SATA *96*
Koehn, Ilse
   See Van Zwienen, Ilse Charlotte Koehn
Koeller, Carol *192*
Koenig, Viviane 1950- *80*
Koering, Ursula 1921-1976 .... *64*
Koerner, W(illiam) H(enry) D(avid)
   1878-1938 .... *21*
Koertge, Ronald 1940- *131*
   Earlier sketches in SATA *53, 92*
Koestler-Grack, Rachel A. 1973- *156*
Koff, Richard Myram 1926- *62*
Koffinke, Carol 1949- *82*
Kogan, Deborah
   See Kogan Ray, Deborah
Kogan Ray, Deborah 1940- *203*
   Earlier sketches in SATA *8, 50, 161*
Kogawa, Joy Nozomi 1935- *99*
Kogler, Jennifer Anne 1982(?)- *174*
Kohl, Herbert 1937- *47*
Kohl, Herbert R.
   See Kohl, Herbert
Kohl, MaryAnn F(aubion) 1947- *144*
   Earlier sketch in SATA *74*
Kohler, Julilly H(ouse) 1908-1976
   Obituary *20*
Kohn, Bernice
   See Hunt, Bernice
Kohn, Rita (T.) 1933- *89*
Kohner, Frederick 1905-1986 .... *10*
   Obituary *48*
Koide, Tan 1938-1986 .... *50*
Koike, Kay 1940- *72*
Koja, Kathe 1960- *199*
   Earlier sketch in SATA *155*
Koja, Stephan *198*
Kolar, Bob 1960(?)- *206*
Kolb, Larry J. 1953- *175*
Kolba, St. Tamara *22*
Kolibalova, Marketa
   See Kolibalova, Marketa
Kolibalova, Marketa 1953- *126*
Koller, Jackie French 1948- *157*
   Earlier sketches in SATA *72, 109*
   See also CLR *68*
Kolodny, Nancy J. 1946- *76*
Kolosov, Jacqueline 1967- *199*
Komaiko, Leah 1954- *164*
   Earlier sketch in SATA *97*
Komisar, Lucy 1942- *9*
Komoda, Beverly 1939- *25*
Komoda, Kiyo 1937- *9*
Kompaneyets, Marc 1974- *169*
Komroff, Manuel 1890-1974 .... *2*
   Obituary *20*

Konigsburg, E.L. 1930- *194*
   Earlier sketches in SATA *4, 48, 94, 126*
   See also CLR *81*
Konigsburg, Elaine Lobl
   See Konigsburg, E.L.
Koning, Hans 1921-2007 .... *5*
   Obituary *182*
Koningsberger, Hans
   See Koning, Hans
Konkle, Janet Everest 1917- *12*
Kono, Erin Eitter 1973- *177*
Konzak, Burt 1946- *151*
Koob, Theodora (J. Foth) 1918- *23*
Kooiker, Leonie
   See Kooyker-Romijn, Johanna Maria
Koons, James
   See Pernu, Dennis
Koontz, Dean
   See Koontz, Dean R.
Koontz, Dean R. 1945- *165*
   Earlier sketch in SATA *92*
Koontz, Dean Ray
   See Koontz, Dean R.
Koontz, Robin Michal 1954- *136*
   Earlier sketch in SATA *70*
Kooyker, Leonie
   See Kooyker-Romijn, Johanna Maria
Kooyker-Romijn, Johanna Maria 1927- *48*
Kooyker-Romyn, Johanna Maria
   See Kooyker-Romijn, Johanna Maria
Kopelke, Lisa 1963- *154*
Kopper, Lisa (Esther) 1950- *105*
   Brief entry *51*
Koppes, Steven N. 1957- *169*
Koppes, Steven Nelson
   See Koppes, Steven N.
Korach, Mimi 1922- *9*
Koralek, Jenny 1934- *140*
   Earlier sketch in SATA *71*
Korczak, Janusz
   See Goldszmit, Henryk
Koren, Edward (Benjamin) 1935- *148*
   Earlier sketch in SATA *5*
Koren, Edward 1935- *206*
Korinets, Iurii Iosifovich
   See Korinetz, Yuri (Iosifovich)
Korinetz, Yuri (Iosifovich) 1923- *9*
   See also CLR *4*
Korman, Bernice 1937- *78*
Korman, Gordon 1963- *167*
   Brief entry *41*
   Earlier sketches in SATA *49, 81, 119*
   See also CLR *25*
Korman, Gordon Richard
   See Korman, Gordon
Korman, Justine 1958- *70*
Kornblatt, Marc 1954- *147*
   Earlier sketch in SATA *84*
Kornprobst, Jacques 1937- *177*
Korte, Gene J. 1950- *74*
Korthues, Barbara 1971- *203*
Korty, Carol 1937- *15*
Koscielniak, Bruce 1947- *153*
   Earlier sketches in SATA *67, 99*
Koshin, Alexander (A.) 1952- *86*
Kositsky, Lynne 1947- *158*
Koskenmaki, Rosalie
   See Maggio, Rosalie
Koss, Amy Goldman 1954- *158*
   Earlier sketch in SATA *115*
Kossin, Sandy (Sanford) 1926- *10*
Kossman, Nina 1959- *84*
Kostecki-Shaw, Jenny Sue *203*
Kostick, Conor 1964- *186*
Kotzwinkle, William 1938- *146*
   Earlier sketches in SATA *24, 70*
   See also CLR *6*
Kouhi, Elizabeth 1917- *54*
   Brief entry *49*
Kouts, Anne 1945- *8*
Koutsky, Jan Dale 1955- *146*

Kovacs, Deborah 1954- 132
  Earlier sketch in SATA 79
Kovalski, Maryann 1951- 175
  Earlier sketches in SATA 58, 97
  See also CLR 34
  See also SAAS 21
Kowalski, Kathiann M. 1955- 151
  Earlier sketch in SATA 96
Kraft, Betsy Harvey 1937- 157
Kraft, Erik P. 193
Krahn, Fernando 1935- 49
  Brief entry 31
  See also CLR 3
Krakauer, Hoong Yee Lee 1955- 86
Krakauer, Jon 1954- 108
Kramer, George
  See Heuman, William
Kramer, Nora 1896(?)-1984 26
  Obituary 39
Kramer, Remi (Thomas) 1935- 90
Krantz, Hazel (Newman) 12
Kranzler, George G(ershon) 1916- 28
Kranzler, Gershon
  See Kranzler, George G(ershon)
Krasilovsky, Phyllis 1926- 38
  Earlier sketch in SATA 1
  See also CLR 83
  See also SAAS 5
Krasne, Betty
  See Levine, Betty K(rasne)
Krasner, Steven 1953- 154
Krasno, Rena 1923- 104
Kratman, Tom 175
Kraus, Joanna Halpert 1937- 87
Kraus, (Herman) Robert 1925-2001 93
  Obituary 130
  Earlier sketches in SATA 4, 65
  See also SAAS 11
Krauss, Ruth (Ida) 1911-1993 30
  Obituary 75
  Earlier sketch in SATA 1
  See also CLR 42
Krautter, Elisa (Bialk) 1912(?)-1990 1
  Obituary 65
Krautwurst, Terry 1946- 79
Kray, Robert Clement 1930- 82
Krech, Bob 1956- 185
Krech, Robert
  See Krech, Bob
Kredel, Fritz 1900-1973 17
Kreikemeier, Gregory Scott 1965- 85
Kreloff, Elliot 189
Krementz, Jill 1940- 134
  Earlier sketches in SATA 17, 71
  See also CLR 5
  See also SAAS 8
Kremer, Marcie
  See Sorenson, Margo
Krenina, Katya 1968- 101
Krensky, Stephen 1953- 188
  Brief entry 41
  Earlier sketches in SATA 47, 93, 136
Krensky, Stephen Alan
  See Krensky, Stephen
Kresh, Paul 1919-1997 61
  Obituary 94
Kress, Nancy 1948- 147
  Autobiography Feature 147
  Earlier sketch in SATA 85
Kricher, John C. 1944- 113
Krieger, Melanie 96
Krinitz, Esther Nisenthal 1927-2001 194
Kripke, Dorothy Karp 30
Krisher, Trudy 1946- 160
  Earlier sketch in SATA 86
Krisher, Trudy B.
  See Krisher, Trudy
Krishnaswami, Uma 1956- 182
  Earlier sketch in SATA 144
Kristof, Jane 1932- 8
Kroeber, Theodora (Kracaw) 1897-1979 1

Kroeger, Mary Kay 1950- 92
Krohn, Katherine E(lizabeth) 1961- 125
  Earlier sketch in SATA 84
Kroll, Francis Lynde 1904-1973 10
Kroll, Steven 1941- 135
  Autobiography Feature 135
  Earlier sketches in SATA 19, 66, 125
  See also SAAS 7
Kroll, Virginia L. 1948- 168
  Earlier sketches in SATA 76, 114
Kroll, Virginia Louisa
  See Kroll, Virginia L.
Kromhout, Rindert 1958- 189
Krommes, Beth 1956- 181
  Earlier sketch in SATA 128
Kronenwetter, Michael 1943- 62
Kroniuk, Lisa
  See Berton, Pierre (Francis de Marigny)
Kropp, Paul 1948- 38
  Brief entry 34
  See also CLR 96
Kropp, Paul Stephan
  See Kropp, Paul
Krosoczka, Jarrett J. 1977- 200
  Earlier sketch in SATA 155
Krovatin, Christopher 1985- 171
Kruess, James
  See Kruss, James
Kruglik, Gerald 187
Krull, Kathleen 1952- 184
  Autobiography Feature 106
  Brief entry 39
  Earlier sketches in SATA 52, 80, 149
  See also CLR 44
Krumgold, Joseph (Quincy) 1908-1980 48
  Obituary 23
  Earlier sketch in SATA 1
Krupinski, Loretta 1940- 161
  Earlier sketches in SATA 67, 102
Krupnick, Karen 1947- 89
Krupp, E(dwin) C(harles) 1944- 123
  Earlier sketch in SATA 53
Krupp, Robin Rector 1946- 53
Krush, Beth 1918- 18
Krush, Joe 1918-
  See Krush, Joseph P.
Krush, Joseph P. 1918- 18
Kruss, James 1926-1997 8
  See also CLR 9
Kruusval, Catarina 1951- 201
Krykorka, Vladyana 1945- 96
Krystoforski, Andrej 1943- 196
Kubie, Eleanor Gottheil
  See Kubie, Nora Gottheil Benjamin
Kubie, Nora Benjamin
  See Kubie, Nora Gottheil Benjamin
Kubie, Nora Gottheil Benjamin 1899-1988 . 39
  Obituary 59
Kubinyi, Laszlo 1937- 94
  Earlier sketch in SATA 17
Kudlinski, Kathleen V. 1950- 150
Kuehnert, Stephanie 1979- 205
Kuenstler, Morton 1927- 10
Kuh, Charlotte 1892(?)-1985
  Obituary 43
Kuharski, Janice 1947- 128
Kuhn, Dwight 199
Kuijer, Guus 1942- 179
Kujoth, Jean Spealman 1935-1975
  Obituary 30
Kuklin, Susan 1941- 163
  Earlier sketches in SATA 63, 95
  See also CLR 51
Kulikov, Boris 1966- 205
  Earlier sketch in SATA 170
Kulka, Joe 188
Kulling, Monica 1952- 89
Kullman, Harry 1919-1982 35
Kulyk Keefer, Janice 1952- 132
Kumin, Maxine 1925- 12

Kumin, Maxine Winokur
  See Kumin, Maxine
Kunhardt, Dorothy (Meserve) 1901-1979 53
  Obituary 22
Kunhardt, Edith 1937- 67
Kunjufu, Jawanza 1953- 73
Kunstler, Morton
  See Kuenstler, Morton
Kuntz, J(ohn) L. 1947- 91
Kuntz, Jerry 1956- 133
Kupferberg, Herbert 1918-2001 19
Kuratomi, Chizuko 1939- 12
  See also CLR 32
Kurczok, Belinda 1978- 121
Kurelek, William 1927-1977 8
  Obituary 27
  See also CLR 2
Kurian, George 1928- 65
Kurjian, Judi(th M.) 1944- 127
Kurland, Gerald 1942- 13
Kurland, Michael 1938- 118
  Earlier sketch in SATA 48
Kurland, Michael Joseph
  See Kurland, Michael
Kuroi, Ken 1947- 120
Kurokawa, Mitsuhiro 1954- 88
Kurten, Bjorn (Olof) 1924-1988 64
Kurtz, Jane 1952- 139
  Earlier sketch in SATA 91
  See also CLR 123
Kurtz, Katherine 1944- 182
  Earlier sketches in SATA 76, 126
Kurtz, Katherine Irene
  See Kurtz, Katherine
Kurz, Rudolf 1952- 95
Kushner, Donn (J.) 1927- 52
  See also CLR 55
Kushner, Ellen 1955- 202
  Earlier sketch in SATA 98
Kushner, Ellen Ruth
  See Kushner, Ellen
Kushner, Jill Menkes 1951- 62
Kushner, Lawrence 1943- 169
  Earlier sketch in SATA 83
Kushner, Tony 1956- 160
Kuskin, Karla 1932-2009 164
  Obituary 206
  Earlier sketches in SATA 2, 68, 111
  See also CLR 4
  See also SAAS 3
Kuskin, Karla Seidman
  See Kuskin, Karla
Kusugak, Michael 1948- 143
Kusugak, Michael Arvaarluk
  See Kusugak, Michael
Kutner, Merrily 1948- 196
Kuttner, Paul 1922- 18
Kuyper, Sjoerd 1952- 177
Kuzma, Kay 1941- 39
Kvale, Velma R(uth) 1898-1979 8
Kvasnosky, Laura McGee 1951- 182
  Earlier sketches in SATA 93, 142
Kwasney, Michelle D. 1960- 162
Kyle, Benjamin
  See Gottfried, Theodore Mark
Kyle, Elisabeth
  See Dunlop, Agnes M. R.
Kyte, Kathy S. 1946- 50
  Brief entry 44

L

L., Barry
  See Longyear, Barry B(rookes)
L., Tommy
  See Lorkowski, Thomas V(incent)
Labouisse, Eve Curie
  See Curie, Eve

Labouisse, Eve Denise
  See Curie, Eve
Lace, William W. 1942- *126*
Lacey, Joshua
  See Doder, Josh
Lachner, Dorothea
  See Knobloch, Dorothea
Lachtman, Ofelia Dumas 1919- *179*
Lackey, Mercedes R. 1950- *127*
  Earlier sketch in SATA *81*
Lackey, Mercedes Ritchie
  See Lackey, Mercedes R.
Lacoe, Addie *78*
Lacombe, Benjamin 1982- *198*
Lacome, Julie 1961- *174*
  Earlier sketch in SATA *80*
Lacy, Leslie Alexander 1937- *6*
Ladd, Cheryl (Jean) 1951- *113*
Ladd, London 1972(?)- *206*
Ladd, Louise 1943- *97*
Ladd, Veronica
  See Miner, Jane Claypool
Laden, Nina 1962- *148*
  Earlier sketch in SATA *85*
Lader, Lawrence 1919-2006 .... *6*
  Obituary *178*
LaDoux, Rita C. 1951- *74*
Lady, A
  See Taylor, Ann
Lady Mears
  See Tempest, Margaret Mary
Lady of Quality, A
  See Bagnold, Enid
La Farge, Oliver 1901-1963 .... *19*
La Farge, Oliver Hazard Perry
  See La Farge, Oliver
La Farge, Phyllis *14*
LaFave, Kim *196*
LaFaye, A. 1970- *156*
  Earlier sketch in SATA *105*
LaFaye, Alexandria R.T.
  See LaFaye, A.
LaFevers, R.L. *191*
LaFevers, Robin L.
  See LaFevers, R.L.
Laffin, John (Alfred Charles) 1922- *31*
LaFontaine, Bruce 1948- *176*
  Earlier sketch in SATA *114*
La Fontaine, Jean de 1621-1695 .... *18*
Lafrance, Marie 1955- *197*
Lager, Claude
  See Lapp, Christiane (Germain)
Lager, Marilyn 1939- *52*
Lagercrantz, Rose (Elsa) 1947- *39*
Lagerloef, Selma
  See Lagerlof, Selma
Lagerlof, Selma 1858-1940 .... *15*
  See also CLR *7*
Laguna, Sofie 1968- *158*
LaHaye, Tim F. 1926- *149*
LaHaye, Timothy F.
  See LaHaye, Tim F.
Laidlaw, Rob *205*
Laiken, Deirdre S(usan) 1948- *48*
  Brief entry *40*
Laimgruber, Monika 1946- *11*
Lain, Anna
  See Lamb, Nancy
Laing, Alexander (Kinnan) 1903-1976 .... *117*
Laing, Martha 1951- *39*
Laird, Christa 1944- *108*
  Autobiography Feature *120*
  See also SAAS *26*
Laird, Elizabeth (Mary Risk) 1943- *159*
  Earlier sketches in SATA *77, 114*
  See also CLR *65*
Laird, Jean E(louise) 1930- *38*
Laite, Gordon 1925- *31*
Lake, Harriet
  See Taylor, Paula (Wright)
Lakin, Patricia 1944- *190*

Laklan, Carli 1907-1988 .... *5*
Laliberte, Louise-Andree 1958- *169*
Lalicki, Barbara *61*
Lalicki, Tom 1949- *186*
Lally, Soinbhe 1945- *119*
LaMarche, Jim *162*
Lamb, Albert *187*
Lamb, Beatrice Pitney 1904-1997 .... *21*
Lamb, Charles 1775-1834 .... *17*
Lamb, Elizabeth Searle 1917- *31*
Lamb, G(eoffrey) F(rederick) *10*
Lamb, Harold (Albert) 1892-1962 .... *53*
Lamb, Lynton (Harold) 1907-1977 .... *10*
Lamb, Mary Ann 1764-1847 .... *17*
Lamb, Nancy 1939- *80*
Lamb, Robert (Boyden) 1941- *13*
Lamba, Marie *195*
Lambert, David 1932- *84*
  Brief entry *49*
Lambert, David Compton
  See Lambert, David
Lambert, Janet 1895(?)-1973 .... *25*
Lambert, Martha L. *113*
Lambert, Saul 1928- *23*
Lambert, Stephen *174*
Lamburn, Richmal Crompton 1890-1969 .... *5*
Lamensdorf, Len 1930- *120*
Lamensdorf, Leonard
  See Lamensdorf, Len
Laminack, Lester L. 1956- *163*
  Earlier sketch in SATA *120*
Lamont, Priscilla *200*
Lamorisse, Albert (Emmanuel) 1922-1970 ... *23*
Lampert, Emily 1951- *52*
  Brief entry *49*
Lamplugh, Lois 1921- *17*
Lampman, Evelyn Sibley 1907-1980 .... *87*
  Obituary *23*
  Earlier sketch in SATA *4*
Lamprey, Louise 1869-1951
  See YABC *2*
Lampton, Chris
  See Lampton, Christopher F.
Lampton, Christopher
  See Lampton, Christopher F.
Lampton, Christopher F. *67*
  Brief entry *47*
Lamstein, Sarah 1943- *174*
  Earlier sketch in SATA *126*
Lamstein, Sarah Marwil
  See Lamstein, Sarah
Lanagan, Margo 1960- *201*
  Earlier sketch in SATA *163*
Lancaster, Bruce 1896-1963 .... *9*
Lancaster, Matthew 1973(?)-1983
  Obituary *45*
Lance, Kathryn 1943- *76*
Land, Barbara (Neblett) 1923- *16*
Land, Jane
  See Borland, Kathryn Kilby
  and Speicher, Helen Ross S(mith)
Land, Myrick (Ebben) 1922-1998 .... *15*
Land, Ross
  See Borland, Kathryn Kilby
  and Speicher, Helen Ross S(mith)
Landau, Elaine 1948- *141*
  Earlier sketches in SATA *10, 94*
Landau, Jacob 1917- *38*
Landeck, Beatrice 1904-1978 .... *15*
Landin, Les 1923- *2*
Landis, J(ames) D(avid) 1942- *60*
  Brief entry *52*
Landis, James D.
  See Landis, J(ames) D(avid)
Landis, Jill Marie 1948- *101*
Landmann, Bimba 1968- *176*
Landon, Dena 1978(?)- *168*
Landon, Lucinda 1950- *56*
  Brief entry *51*
Landon, Margaret (Dorothea Mortenson)
  1903-1993 .... *50*

Landry, Leo *202*
Landshoff, Ursula 1908-1989 .... *13*
Landstrom, Lena 1943- *206*
  Earlier sketch in SATA *146*
Landstrom, Olof 1943- *146*
Lane, Carolyn 1926-1993 .... *10*
Lane, Connie
  See Laux, Constance
Lane, Dakota 1959- *166*
  Earlier sketch in SATA *105*
Lane, Jerry
  See Martin, Patricia Miles
Lane, John (Richard) 1932- *15*
Lane, Leena *199*
Lane, Margaret 1907-1994 .... *65*
  Brief entry *38*
  Obituary *79*
Lane, Rose Wilder 1887-1968 .... *29*
  Brief entry *28*
Lanes, Selma Gordon 1929- *3*
Lanfredi, Judy 1964- *83*
Lang, Andrew 1844-1912 .... *16*
  See also CLR *101*
Lang, Aubrey *169*
Lang, Paul 1948- *83*
Lang, Susan S. 1950- *68*
Lang, T.T.
  See Taylor, Theodore
Langart, Darrell T.
  See Garrett, Randall
Langdo, Bryan 1973- *191*
  Earlier sketch in SATA *138*
Lange, John
  See Crichton, Michael
Lange, Karen E. *190*
Lange, Suzanne 1945- *5*
Langley, Andrew 1949- *166*
  Earlier sketch in SATA *104*
Langley, Charles P(itman) III 1949- *103*
Langley, Jonathan 1952- *122*
Langley, Noel 1911-1980
  Obituary *25*
Langley, Wanda *173*
Langner, Nola
  See Malone, Nola Langner
Langone, John (Michael) 1929- *46*
  Brief entry *38*
Langreuter, Jutta 1944- *122*
Langrish, Katherine *177*
Langsen, Richard C. 1953- *95*
Langstaff, John 1920-2005 .... *68*
  Obituary *172*
  Earlier sketch in SATA *6*
  See also CLR *3*
Langstaff, John Meredith
  See Langstaff, John
Langstaff, Launcelot
  See Irving, Washington
Langston, Laura 1958- *186*
Langton, Jane 1922- *200*
  Autobiography Feature *140*
  Earlier sketches in SATA *3, 68, 129, 140*
  See also CLR *33*
  See also SAAS *5*
Lanier, Sidney 1842-1881 .... *18*
Lanier, Sterling E. 1927-2007 .... *109*
Lanier, Sterling Edmund
  See Lanier, Sterling E.
Lanino, Deborah 1964- *123*
Lankford, Mary D. 1932- *112*
  Earlier sketch in SATA *77*
Lannin, Joanne 1951- *121*
Lannin, Joanne A.
  See Lannin, Joanne
Lansdale, Joe R. 1951- *116*
Lansdale, Joe Richard
  See Lansdale, Joe R.
Lansing, Alfred 1921-1975 .... *35*
Lansing, Karen E. 1954- *71*
Lansky, Vicki 1942- *177*
Lanthier, Jennifer 1964- *204*

Lantier-Sampon, Patricia 1952- 92
Lantz, Fran
   See Lantz, Francess L(in)
Lantz, Francess L(in) 1952-2004 153
   Autobiography Feature 153
   Obituary 159
   Earlier sketches in SATA 63, 109
Lantz, Paul 1908- 45
Lantz, Walter 1900-1994 37
   Obituary 79
Lanza, Barbara 1945- 101
Lapp, Christiane (Germain) 1948- 74
Lappin, Peter 1911-1999 32
Larbalestier, Justine 178
Lardy, Philippe 1963- 168
LaReau, Jenna 181
LaReau, Kara 181
Larios, Julie 1949- 178
Larios, Julie Hofstrand
   See Larios, Julie
Larkin, Amy
   See Burns, Olive Ann
Larkin, Maia
   See Wojciechowska, Maia (Teresa)
Laroche, Giles 1956- 126
   Earlier sketch in SATA 71
LaRochelle, David 1960- 171
   Earlier sketch in SATA 115
Larom, Henry V. 1903(?)-1975
   Obituary 30
LaRose, Linda 125
Larrabee, Lisa 1947- 84
Larrecq, John M(aurice) 1926-1980 44
   Obituary 25
Larrick (Crosby), Nancy 1910-2004 4
Larsen, Anita 1942- 78
Larsen, Egon 1904- 14
Larsen, Rebecca 1944- 54
Larson, Eve
   See St. John, Wylly Folk
Larson, Gary 1950- 57
Larson, Hope 1982- 205
Larson, Ingrid D(ana) 1965- 92
Larson, Jean Russell 1930- 121
Larson, Kirby 1954- 181
   Earlier sketch in SATA 96
Larson, Norita D(ittberner) 1944- 29
Larson, William H. 1938- 10
Larsson, Carl (Olof) 1853-1919 35
LaSalle, Charles A.
   See Ellis, Edward S.
LaSalle, Charles E.
   See Ellis, Edward S.
Lasell, Elinor H. 1929- 19
Lasell, Fen H.
   See Lasell, Elinor H.
Lasenby, Jack 1931- 172
   Earlier sketches in SATA 65, 103
Laser, Michael 1954- 117
Lash, Joseph P. 1909-1987 43
Lasher, Faith B. 1921- 12
Lasker, David 1950- 38
Lasker, Joe
   See Lasker, Joseph Leon
Lasker, Joseph Leon 1919- 83
   Earlier sketch in SATA 9
   See also SAAS 17
Laski, Marghanita 1915-1988 55
Laskin, Pamela L. 1954- 75
Lasky, Kathryn 1944- 157
   Earlier sketches in SATA 13, 69, 112
   See also CLR 140
Lasky Knight, Kathryn
   See Lasky, Kathryn
Lass, Bonnie 131
Lassalle, C. E.
   See Ellis, Edward S.
Lassiter, Mary
   See Hoffman, Mary
Lassiter, Rhiannon 1977- 157
Lat 1951- 196

Latham, Barbara 1896- 16
Latham, Frank B(rown) 1910-2000 6
Latham, Jean Lee 1902-1995 68
   Earlier sketch in SATA 2
   See also CLR 50
Latham, Mavis
   See Clark, Mavis Thorpe
Latham, Philip
   See Richardson, Robert S(hirley)
Lathrop, Dorothy P(ulis) 1891-1980 14
   Obituary 24
Lathrop, Francis
   See Leiber, Fritz (Reuter, Jr.)
Latimer, Jim 1943- 80
Latta, Rich
   See Latta, Richard
Latta, Richard 1946- 113
Latta, Sara L. 1960- 174
Lattany, Kristin
   See Lattany, Kristin Hunter
Lattany, Kristin (Eggleston) Hunter 1931- . 154
   Autobiography Feature 154
   Earlier sketch in SATA 132
Lattany, Kristin Hunter 1931- 132
   Earlier sketch in SATA 12
   See also CLR 3
   See also SAAS 10
Lattimore, Eleanor Frances 1904-1986 7
   Obituary 48
Lattin, Ann
   See Cole, Lois Dwight
Lauber, Patricia (Grace) 1924- 138
   Earlier sketches in SATA 1, 33, 75
   See also CLR 16
Laugesen, Mary E(akin) 1906-1995 5
Laughbaum, Steve 1945- 12
Laughlin, Florence Young 1910-2001 3
Laughlin, Rosemary 1941- 123
Launder, Sally 206
Laure, Ettagale
   See Blauer, Ettagale
Laure, Jason 1940- 50
   Brief entry 44
Laurence, Ester Hauser 1935- 7
Laurence, Jean Margaret Wemyss
   See Laurence, Margaret
Laurence, Margaret 1926-1987
   Obituary 50
Laurie, Rona 1916- 55
Laurin, Anne
   See McLaurin, Anne
Lauritzen, Jonreed 1902-1979 13
Lauscher, Hermann
   See Hesse, Hermann
Lauture, Denize 1946- 86
Laux, Connie
   See Laux, Constance
Laux, Constance 1952- 97
Laux, Dorothy 1920- 49
Lavallee, Barbara 1941- 166
   Earlier sketch in SATA 74
Lavender, David (Sievert) 1910-2003 97
   Obituary 145
   Earlier sketch in SATA 64
Lavender, William D. 1921- 143
Laverne, Christine 175
Lavert, Gwendolyn Battle 1951-
   See Battle-Lavert, Gwendolyn
Laverty, Donald
   See Blish, James
   and Knight, Damon (Francis)
Lavigne, Louis-Dominique 107
Lavine, David 1928- 31
Lavine, Sigmund Arnold 1908-1986 82
   Earlier sketch in SATA 3
   See also CLR 35
Lavond, Paul Dennis
   See Kornbluth, C(yril) M.
   and Lowndes, Robert A(ugustine) W(ard)
   and Pohl, Frederik

Lawford, Paula Jane 1960- 57
   Brief entry 53
Lawhead, Stephen R. 1950- 109
Lawhead, Steve
   See Lawhead, Stephen R.
Lawlor, Laurie 1953- 137
   Earlier sketch in SATA 80
Lawlor, William
   See Lawlor, William T.
Lawlor, William T. 1951- 183
Lawrence, Ann (Margaret) 1942-1987 41
   Obituary 54
Lawrence, Caroline 1954- 203
Lawrence, Iain 1955- 183
   Earlier sketch in SATA 135
Lawrence, J. T.
   See Rowland-Entwistle, (Arthur) Theodore
   (Henry)
Lawrence, Jerome 1915-2004 65
Lawrence, John 1933- 30
Lawrence, Josephine 1890(?)-1978
   Obituary 24
Lawrence, Louise 1943- 119
   Earlier sketches in SATA 38, 78
Lawrence, Louise de Kiriline 1894-1992 13
Lawrence, Lynn
   See Garland, Sherry
Lawrence, Margery H. 1889-1969 120
Lawrence, Michael 1943- 132
Lawrence, Mildred Elwood 1907-1997 3
Lawrence, R(onald) D(ouglas) 1921- 55
Lawrinson, Julia 1969- 141
Lawson, Amy
   See Gordon, Amy
Lawson, Carol (Antell) 1946- 42
Lawson, Don(ald Elmer) 1917-1990 9
Lawson, Joan 1906- 55
Lawson, Julie 1947- 126
   Earlier sketch in SATA 79
   See also CLR 89
Lawson, Marion Tubbs 1896-1994 22
Lawson, Robert 1892-1957 100
   See also YABC 2
   See also CLR 73
Lawton, Clive A. 1951- 145
Laxdal, Vivienne 1962- 112
Laybourn, Emma 193
Laycock, George (Edwin) 1921- 5
Layne, Laura
   See Knott, William C(ecil, Jr.)
Layne, Steven L. 171
Layton, Neal 1971- 187
   Earlier sketch in SATA 152
Layton, Neal Andrew
   See Layton, Neal
Lazare, Gerald John 1927- 44
Lazare, Jerry
   See Lazare, Gerald John
Lazarevich, Mila 1942- 17
Lazarus, Keo Felker 1913-1993 21
   Obituary 129
Lea, Alec 1907- 19
Lea, Bob 1952- 203
Lea, Joan
   See Neufeld, John (Arthur)
Leach, Maria 1892-1977 39
   Brief entry 28
Leacock, Elspeth 1946- 131
Leacroft, Helen (Mabel Beal) 1919- 6
Leacroft, Richard (Vallance Becher) 1914- 6
Leaf, Margaret P. 1909(?)-1988
   Obituary 55
Leaf, (Wilbur) Munro 1905-1976 20
   See also CLR 25
Leaf, VaDonna Jean 1929- 26
Leah, Devorah
   See Devorah-Leah
Leakey, Richard E(rskine Frere) 1944- 42
Leander, Ed
   See Richelson, Geraldine

Lear, Edward 1812-1888 .... *100*
  Earlier sketch in SATA *18*
  See also CLR *75*
Lears, Laurie 1955- *127*
Leasor, James 1923-2007 .... *54*
Leasor, Thomas James
  See Leasor, James
Leavitt, Jerome E(dward) 1916- *23*
Leavitt, Martine 1953- *170*
LeBar, Mary E(velyn) 1910-1982 .... *35*
LeBlanc, Annette M. 1965- *68*
LeBlanc, L(ee) 1913- *54*
LeBox, Annette 1943- *145*
Lebrun, Claude 1929- *66*
Le Cain, Errol (John) 1941-1989 .... *68*
  Obituary *60*
  Earlier sketch in SATA *6*
Lechner, Jack *201*
Lechner, John 1966- *200*
Lecourt, Nancy (Hoyt) 1951- *73*
Ledbetter, Suzann 1953- *119*
Leder, Jane Mersky 1945- *61*
  Brief entry *51*
Lederer, Muriel 1929- *48*
Lederer, William J(ulius) 1912- *62*
Lee, Amanda
  See Baggett, Nancy
  and Buckholtz, Eileen (Garber)
  and Glick, Ruth (Burtnick)
Lee, Benjamin 1921- *27*
Lee, Betsy 1949- *37*
Lee, Carol
  See Fletcher, Helen Jill
Lee, Carol Ann 1969- *185*
Lee, Chinlun *182*
Lee, Cora
  See Anderson, Catherine Corley
Lee, Dennis (Beynon) 1939- *102*
  Earlier sketch in SATA *14*
  See also CLR *3*
Lee, Dom 1959- *146*
  Autobiography Feature *121*
  Earlier sketch in SATA *83*
  See also SAAS *26*
Lee, Doris Emrick 1905-1983 .... *44*
  Obituary *35*
Lee, Edward
  See Lee, J. Edward
Lee, Elizabeth Rogers 1940- *90*
Lee, Harper 1926- *11*
Lee, Hector Viveros 1962- *115*
Lee, Howard N.
  See Goulart, Ron
Lee, Huy Voun 1969- *129*
Lee, J. Edward 1953- *130*
Lee, Jeanne M. 1943- *138*
Lee, John R(obert) 1923-1976 .... *27*
Lee, Jordan
  See Scholefield, Alan
Lee, Joseph Edward
  See Lee, J. Edward
Lee, Julian
  See Latham, Jean Lee
Lee, Linda
  See Eyerly, Jeannette
Lee, Liz
  See Lee, Elizabeth Rogers
Lee, Lucy
  See Talbot, Charlene Joy
Lee, Lyn 1953- *128*
Lee, Manning de Villeneuve 1894-1980 ...... *37*
  Obituary *22*
Lee, Marian
  See Clish, (Lee) Marian
Lee, Marie G. 1964- *178*
  Earlier sketches in SATA *81, 130*
Lee, Marie Myung-Ok
  See Lee, Marie G.
Lee, Mary Price 1934- *82*
  Earlier sketch in SATA *8*

Lee, Mildred
  See Scudder, Mildred Lee
Lee, Nelle Harper
  See Lee, Harper
Lee, Richard S. 1927- *82*
Lee, Robert C. 1931- *20*
Lee, Robert E(dwin) 1918-1994 .... *65*
  Obituary *82*
Lee, Robert J. 1921- *10*
Lee, Roy
  See Hopkins, Clark
Lee, Sally 1943- *67*
Lee, Suzy *193*
Lee, Tammie
  See Townsend, Thomas L.
Lee, Tanith 1947- *185*
  Earlier sketches in SATA *8, 88, 134*
Leech, Ben
  See Bowkett, Stephen
Leeds, Contance *188*
Leedy, Loreen 1959- *175*
  Brief entry *50*
  Earlier sketches in SATA *54, 84, 128*
Leedy, Loreen Janelle
  See Leedy, Loreen
Lee-Hostetler, Jeri 1940- *63*
Leekley, Thomas B(riggs) 1910-2001 .... *23*
Leeming, Jo Ann
  See Leeming, Joseph
Leeming, Joseph 1897-1968 .... *26*
Leemis, Ralph B. 1954- *72*
Leese, Jennifer L.B. 1970- *163*
Leeson, Muriel 1920- *54*
Leeson, R. A.
  See Leeson, Robert (Arthur)
Leeson, Robert (Arthur) 1928- *76*
  Earlier sketch in SATA *42*
Lee Tae-Jun 1904-1956(?) *194*
Lee-Tai, Amy 1964- *189*
Leffland, Ella 1931- *65*
Leffler, Silke *197*
Lefler, Irene (Whitney) 1917- *12*
LeFrak, Karen *182*
Le Gallienne, Eva 1899-1991 .... *9*
  Obituary *68*
Legg, Gerald 1947- *143*
Legg, Sarah Martha Ross Bruggeman (?)-1982
  Obituary *40*
LeGrand
  See Henderson, LeGrand
Le Guin, Ursula K. 1929- *194*
  Earlier sketches in SATA *4, 52, 99, 149*
  See also CLR *91*
Le Guin, Ursula Kroeber
  See Le Guin, Ursula K.
Legum, Colin 1919-2003 .... *10*
Lehman, Barbara 1963- *170*
  Earlier sketch in SATA *115*
Lehman, Bob *91*
Lehman, Elaine *91*
Lehmann, Debra Lynn
  See Vanasse, Deb
Lehn, Cornelia 1920- *46*
Lehne, Judith Logan 1947- *93*
Lehr, Delores 1920- *10*
Lehr, Norma 1930- *71*
Leiber, Fritz (Reuter, Jr.) 1910-1992 .... *45*
  Obituary *73*
Leibold, Jay 1957- *57*
  Brief entry *52*
Leichman, Seymour 1933- *5*
Leick, Bonnie *205*
Leigh, Nila K. 1981- *81*
Leigh, Tom 1947- *46*
Leigh-Pemberton, John 1911-1997 .... *35*
Leighton, Clare (Veronica Hope)
  1899-1989 .... *37*
Leighton, Margaret (Carver) 1896-1987 .... *1*
  Obituary *52*
Leiner, Al(an) 1938- *83*
Leiner, Katherine 1949- *93*

Leipold, L. Edmond 1902-1983 .... *16*
Leisk, David (Johnson) 1906-1975 .... *30*
  Obituary *26*
  Earlier sketch in SATA *1*
  See also CLR *98*
Leister, Mary 1917- *29*
Leitch, Patricia 1933- *98*
  Earlier sketch in SATA *11*
Leitner, Isabella 1924- *86*
Lekich, John *202*
Leland, Bob 1956- *92*
Leland, Robert E.
  See Leland, Bob
Lematre, Pascal 1967- *176*
Lember, Barbara Hirsch 1941- *92*
LeMieux, A.C. 1954- *125*
  Earlier sketch in SATA *90*
LeMieux, Anne
  See LeMieux, A.C.
LeMieux, Anne Connelly
  See LeMieux, A.C.
Lemieux, Michele 1955- *139*
Lemke, Horst 1922- *38*
Lenain, Thierry 1959- *201*
Lenanton, Carola Mary Anima Oman
  See Oman, Carola (Mary Anima)
Lenard, Alexander 1910-1972
  Obituary *21*
L'Engle, Madeleine 1918-2007 .... *128*
  Obituary *186*
  Earlier sketches in SATA *1, 27, 75*
  See also CLR *57*
  See also SAAS *15*
L'Engle, Madeleine Camp Franklin
  See L'Engle, Madeleine
Lengyel, Cornel Adam 1915- *27*
Lengyel, Emil 1895-1985 .... *3*
  Obituary *42*
Lennon, John 1940-1980 .... *114*
Lennon, John Ono
  See Lennon, John
Leno, Jay 1950- *154*
LeNoir, Janice 1941- *89*
Lens, Sidney 1912-1986 .... *13*
  Obituary *48*
Lenski, Lois 1893-1974 .... *100*
  Earlier sketches in SATA *1, 26*
  See also CLR *26*
Lent, Blair 1930-2009 .... *133*
  Obituary *200*
  Earlier sketch in SATA *2*
Lent, Henry Bolles 1901-1973 .... *17*
Lent, John 1948- *108*
Leodhas, Sorche Nic
  See Alger, Leclaire (Gowans)
Leokum, Arkady 1916(?)- *45*
Leon, Sharon 1959- *79*
Leonard, Alison 1944- *70*
Leonard, Constance (Brink) 1923- *42*
  Brief entry *40*
Leonard, Dutch
  See Leonard, Elmore
Leonard, Elmore 1925- *163*
Leonard, Elmore John, Jr.
  See Leonard, Elmore
Leonard, Jonathan N(orton) 1903-1975 .... *36*
Leonard, Laura 1923- *75*
Leonetti, Mike 1958- *202*
Leong, Gor Yun
  See Ellison, Virginia H(owell)
Leonhardt, Alice 1950- *152*
Lerangis, Peter 1955- *171*
  Earlier sketch in SATA *72*
Lerner, Aaron 1920-2007 .... *35*
  Obituary *179*
Lerner, Aaron Bunsen
  See Lerner, Aaron
Lerner, Carol 1927- *86*
  Earlier sketch in SATA *33*
  See also CLR *34*
  See also SAAS *12*

Lerner, Gerda 1920- 65
Lerner, Harriet 1944- 101
Lerner, Marguerite Rush 1924-1987 11
    Obituary 51
Lerner, Sharon (Ruth) 1938-1982 11
    Obituary 29
Leroe, Ellen W(hitney) 1949- 99
    Brief entry 51
    Earlier sketch in SATA 61
Leroux, Gaston 1868-1927 65
Leroux-Hugon, Helene 1955- 132
LeRoy, Gen 52
    Brief entry 36
Lerrigo, Marion Olive 1898-1968
    Obituary 29
LeShan, Eda J(oan) 1922-2002 21
    See also CLR 6
LeSieg, Theo.
    See Dr. Seuss
Lesinski, Jeanne M. 1960- 120
Leslie, Robert Franklin 1911-1990 7
Leslie, Roger 1961- 168
Leslie, Roger James
    See Leslie, Roger
Leslie, Sarah
    See McGuire, Leslie (Sarah)
LeSourd, Catherine
    See Marshall, (Sarah) Catherine (Wood)
Lessac, Frane
    See Lessac, Frane
Lessac, Frane 1954- 148
    Earlier sketch in SATA 61
Lessem, Dino Don
    See Lessem, Don
Lessem, Don 1951- 182
    Earlier sketches in SATA 97, 155
Lesser, Margaret 1899(?)-1979
    Obituary 22
Lesser, Rika 1953- 53
Lester, Alison 1952- 129
    Earlier sketches in SATA 50, 90
Lester, Helen 1936- 189
    Earlier sketches in SATA 46, 92, 145
Lester, Julius 1939- 157
    Earlier sketches in SATA 12, 74, 112
    See also CLR 143
Lester, Julius Bernard
    See Lester, Julius
Lester, Mike 1955- 206
    Earlier sketch in SATA 131
Le Sueur, Meridel 1900-1996 6
Lethcoe, Jason 191
Le Tord, Bijou 1945- 95
    Earlier sketch in SATA 49
Letts, Billie 1938- 121
Letts, Elizabeth
    See Alalou, Elizabeth
Leuck, Laura 1962- 192
    Earlier sketches in SATA 85, 146
Leutscher, Alfred (George) 1913- 23
Levai, Blaise 1919- 39
Levenkron, Steven 1941- 86
Leverich, Kathleen 1948- 103
LeVert, (William) John 1946- 55
Levete, Sarah 1961- 153
Levin, Betty 1927- 201
    Earlier sketches in SATA 19, 84, 137
    See also SAAS 11
Levin, Ira 1929-2007 66
    Obituary 187
Levin, Ira Marvin
    See Levin, Ira
Levin, Ira Marvin
    See Levin, Ira
Levin, Marcia Obrasky 1918- 13
Levin, Meyer 1905-1981 21
    Obituary 27
Levin, Miriam (Ramsfelder) 1962- 97
Levine, Abby 1943- 54
    Brief entry 52
Levine, Betty K(rasne) 1933- 66

Levine, David 1926- 43
    Brief entry 35
Levine, Edna S(imon) 35
Levine, Ellen 1939- 190
Levine, Evan 1962- 77
    Earlier sketch in SATA 74
Levine, Gail Carson 1947- 195
    Earlier sketches in SATA 98, 161
    See also CLR 85
Levine, I(srael) E. 1923-2003 12
    Obituary 146
Levine, Joan Goldman 11
Levine, Joseph 1910- 33
Levine, Marge 1934- 81
Levine, Rhoda 14
Levine, Sarah 1970- 57
Levine, Shar 1953- 131
Levine-Freidus, Gail
    See Provost, Gail Levine
Levinson, Nancy Smiler 1938- 140
    Earlier sketches in SATA 33, 80
Levinson, Riki 99
    Brief entry 49
    Earlier sketch in SATA 52
Levithan, David 1972- 166
Levitin, Sonia 1934- 192
    Autobiography Feature 131
    Earlier sketches in SATA 4, 68, 119, 131
    See also CLR 53
    See also SAAS 2
Levitt, Sidney (Mark) 1947- 68
Levon, O. U.
    See Kesey, Ken
Levoy, Myron 49
    Brief entry 37
Levy, Barrie 112
Levy, Constance 1931- 140
    Earlier sketch in SATA 73
    See also SAAS 22
Levy, Elizabeth 1942- 169
    Earlier sketches in SATA 31, 69, 107
    See also SAAS 18
Levy, Janice 172
Levy, Marilyn 1937- 67
Levy, Nathan 1945- 63
Levy, Robert 1945- 82
Lewees, John
    See Stockton, Francis Richard
Lewin, Betsy 1937- 169
    Autobiography Feature 115
    Earlier sketches in SATA 32, 90
Lewin, Hugh 1939- 72
    Brief entry 40
    See also CLR 9
Lewin, Ted 1935- 195
    Autobiography Feature 115
    Earlier sketches in SATA 21, 76, 119, 165
Lewis, Alice C. 1936- 46
Lewis, Alice Hudson 1895(?)-1971
    Obituary 29
Lewis, Amanda 1955- 80
Lewis, Anthony 1927- 27
Lewis, Anthony 1966- 120
Lewis, Barbara A. 1943- 73
Lewis, Beverly 1949- 80
Lewis, Brenda Ralph 1932- 72
Lewis, Brian 1963- 128
Lewis, Claudia (Louise) 1907-2001 5
Lewis, Clive Staples
    See Lewis, C.S.
Lewis, C.S. 1898-1963 100
    Earlier sketch in SATA 13
    See also CLR 109
Lewis, Cynthia Copeland 1960- 111
Lewis, E. M. 123
    Earlier sketch in SATA 20
Lewis, Earl Bradley
    See Lewis, E.B.
Lewis, E.B. 1956- 168
    Earlier sketches in SATA 93, 124

Lewis, Elizabeth Foreman 1892-1958 121
    See also YABC 2
Lewis, Francine
    See Wells, Helen
Lewis, Hilda (Winifred) 1896-1974
    Obituary 20
Lewis, J. Patrick 1942- 205
    Earlier sketches in SATA 69, 104, 162
Lewis, Jack P(earl) 1919- 65
Lewis, Jean 1924- 61
Lewis, Jon Samuel
    See Lewis, J.S.
Lewis, Joseph Anthony
    See Lewis, Anthony
Lewis, J.S. 1972- 203
Lewis, Julinda
    See Lewis-Ferguson, Julinda
Lewis, Kevin 173
Lewis, Kim 1951- 136
    Earlier sketch in SATA 84
Lewis, Linda (Joy) 1946- 67
Lewis, Lucia Z.
    See Anderson, Lucia (Lewis)
Lewis, Marjorie 1929- 40
    Brief entry 35
Lewis, Mary 1907(?)-1988 64
    Obituary 56
Lewis, Mervyn
    See Frewer, Glyn (M.)
Lewis, Michael
    See Untermeyer, Louis
Lewis, Naomi 1911-2009 144
    Earlier sketch in SATA 76
Lewis, Paeony 1960- 173
Lewis, Paul
    See Gerson, Noel Bertram
Lewis, Richard 1935- 3
Lewis, Rob 1962- 72
Lewis, Roger
    See Zarchy, Harry
Lewis, Shannon
    See Llywelyn, Morgan
Lewis, Shari 1934-1998 35
    Brief entry 30
    Obituary 104
Lewis, Sylvan R.
    See Aronson, Virginia
Lewis, Thomas P(arker) 1936- 27
Lewis, Wendy A. 1966- 150
Lewis-Ferguson, Julinda 1955- 85
Lewison, Wendy Cheyette 177
Lewiton, Mina 1904-1970 2
Lew-Vriethoff, Joanne 186
Lexau, Joan M. 130
    Earlier sketches in SATA 1, 36
Ley, Willy 1906-1969 2
Leydon, Rita (Floden) 1949- 21
Leyland, Eric (Arthur) 1911- 37
L'Hommedieu, Dorothy Keasley 1885-1961
    Obituary 29
Li, Xiao Jun 1952- 86
Liao, Jimmy 1958- 202
Liatsos, Sandra Olson 1942- 103
Libby, Alisa M. 189
Libby, Barbara M. 153
Libby, Bill
    See Libby, William M.
Libby, William M. 1927-1984 5
    Obituary 39
Liberty, Gene 1924- 3
Lichtenheld, Tom 152
Lichtman, Wendy 1946- 193
Liddell, Kenneth 1912-1975 63
Lidz, Jane 120
Lieberman, E(dwin) James 1934- 62
Liebers, Arthur 1913-1984 12
Lieblich, Irene 1923- 22
Liers, Emil E(rnest) 1890-1975 37
Lies, Brian 1963- 190
    Earlier sketch in SATA 131
Liestman, Vicki 1961- 72

Lietz, Gerald S. 1918- *11*
Life, Kay (Guinn) 1930- *83*
Lifton, Betty Jean *118*
  Earlier sketch in SATA *6*
Lifton, Robert Jay 1926- *66*
Lightburn, Ron 1954- *91*
Lightburn, Sandra 1955- *91*
Lightner, A. M.
  See Hopf, Alice (Martha) L(ightner)
Lightner, Alice
  See Hopf, Alice (Martha) L(ightner)
Lignell, Lois 1911- *37*
Liles, Maurine Walpole 1935- *81*
Lillegard, Dee *184*
Lilley, Stephen R. 1950- *97*
Lilley, Stephen Ray
  See Lilley, Stephen R.
Lillington, Kenneth (James) 1916-1998 .... *39*
Lilly, Nate *182*
Lilly, Ray
  See Curtis, Richard
Lim, John 1932- *43*
Liman, Ellen (Fogelson) 1936- *22*
Limb, Sue 1946- *203*
  Earlier sketch in SATA *158*
Limburg, Peter R(ichard) 1929- *13*
Lin, Grace 1974- *198*
  Earlier sketches in SATA *111, 162*
Lincoln, C(harles) Eric 1924-2000 .... *5*
Lincoln, Hazel *187*
Lincoln, James
  See Bates, Katharine Lee
Lindbergh, Anne
  See Sapieyevski, Anne Lindbergh
Lindbergh, Anne Morrow 1906-2001 .... *33*
  Obituary *125*
Lindbergh, Anne Spencer Morrow
  See Lindbergh, Anne Morrow
Lindbergh, Charles A(ugustus, Jr.)
  1902-1974 .... *33*
Lindbergh, Reeve 1945- *163*
  Earlier sketch in SATA *116*
Lindblom, Steven (Winther) 1946- *94*
  Brief entry *39*
  Earlier sketch in SATA *42*
Linde, Gunnel 1924- *5*
Lindenbaum, Pija 1955- *183*
  Earlier sketches in SATA *77, 144*
Lindgren, Astrid (Anna Emilia Ericsson)
  1907-2002 .... *38*
  Obituary *128*
  Earlier sketch in SATA *2*
  See also CLR *119*
Lindgren, Barbro 1937- *120*
  Brief entry *46*
  Earlier sketch in SATA *63*
  See also CLR *86*
Lindman, Maj (Jan) 1886-1972 .... *43*
Lindop, Edmund 1925- *5*
Lindquist, Jennie Dorothea 1899-1977 .... *13*
Lindquist, Rowena Cory 1958- *98*
Lindquist, Willis 1908-1988 .... *20*
Lindsay, Norman Alfred William
  1879-1969 .... *67*
  See also CLR *8*
Lindsay, (Nicholas) Vachel 1879-1931 .... *40*
Lindsey, Kathleen D(orothy) 1949- *153*
Line, David
  See Davidson, Lionel
Line, Les 1935- *27*
Lines, Kathleen Mary 1902-1988
  Obituary *61*
Linfield, Esther *40*
Lingard, Joan (Amelia) 1932- *130*
  Autobiography Feature *130*
  Earlier sketches in SATA *8, 74, 114*
  See also CLR *89*
  See also SAAS *5*
Link, Martin 1934- *28*
Linn, Margot
  See Ziefert, Harriet

Linnea, Sharon 1956- *82*
Lion, Melissa 1976- *176*
Lionni, Leo(nard) 1910-1999 .... *72*
  Obituary *118*
  Earlier sketch in SATA *8*
  See also CLR *71*
Lipinsky de Orlov, Lino S. 1908- *22*
Lipkind, William 1904-1974 .... *15*
Lipman, David 1931-2008 .... *21*
Lipman, Matthew 1923- *14*
Lipp, Frederick *204*
Lippincott, Bertram 1898(?)-1985
  Obituary *42*
Lippincott, Gary A. 1953- *119*
  Earlier sketch in SATA *73*
Lippincott, Joseph W(harton) 1887-1976 ..... *17*
Lippincott, Sarah Lee 1920- *22*
Lippman, Peter J. 1936- *31*
Lipsyte, Robert 1938- *198*
  Earlier sketches in SATA *5, 68, 113, 161*
  See also CLR *76*
Lipsyte, Robert Michael
  See Lipsyte, Robert
Lisandrelli, Elaine Slivinski 1951- *94*
Lisker, Sonia O. 1933- *44*
Lisle, Holly 1960- *98*
Lisle, Janet Taylor 1947- *150*
  Brief entry *47*
  Earlier sketches in SATA *59, 96*
  See also SAAS *14*
Lisle, Rebecca *162*
Lisle, Seward D.
  See Ellis, Edward S.
Lisowski, Gabriel 1946- *47*
  Brief entry *31*
Liss, Howard 1922-1995 .... *4*
  Obituary *84*
Lissiat, Amy
  See Thompson, Colin
Lisson, Deborah 1941- *110*
  Earlier sketch in SATA *71*
List, Ilka Katherine 1935- *6*
Liston, Robert A. 1927- *5*
Litchfield, Ada B(assett) 1916-1999 .... *5*
Litchfield, Jo 1973- *116*
Lithgow, John (Arthur) 1945- *145*
Litowinsky, Olga (Jean) 1936- *26*
Littke, Lael J. 1929- *140*
  Earlier sketches in SATA *51, 83*
Little, A. Edward
  See Klein, Aaron E.
Little, Douglas 1942- *96*
Little, (Flora) Jean 1932- *149*
  Earlier sketches in SATA *2, 68, 106*
  See also CLR *4*
  See also SAAS *17*
Little, Lessie Jones 1906-1986 .... *60*
  Obituary *50*
Little, Mary E. 1912-1999 .... *28*
Littlechild, George 1958- *85*
Littledale, Freya (Lota) 1929-1992 .... *74*
  Earlier sketch in SATA *2*
Littlefield, Bill 1948- *83*
Littlefield, Holly 1963- *97*
Littlesugar, Amy 1953- *176*
  Earlier sketch in SATA *122*
Littleton, Mark R. 1950- *142*
  Earlier sketch in SATA *89*
Littman, Sarah Darer *175*
Litty, Julie 1971- *181*
Litzinger, Rosanne 1948- *196*
Lively, Penelope 1933- *164*
  Earlier sketches in SATA *7, 60, 101*
  See also CLR *7*
Lively, Penelope Margaret
  See Lively, Penelope
Liverakos, L.A.
  See Gilman, Laura Anne
Liversidge, (Henry) Douglas 1913- *8*
Livesey, Claire (Warner) 1927- *127*
Livingston, Carole 1941- *42*

Livingston, (M.) Irene 1932- *150*
Livingston, Myra Cohn 1926-1996 .... *68*
  Obituary *92*
  Earlier sketch in SATA *5*
  See also CLR *7*
  See also SAAS *1*
Livingston, Richard R(oland) 1922- *8*
Livo, Norma J. 1929- *76*
Liwska, Renata *199*
Ljungkvist, Laura *180*
Llerena Aguirre, Carlos 1952- *19*
Llerena Aguirre, Carlos Antonio
  See Llerena Aguirre, Carlos
Llewellyn, Claire 1954- *196*
  Earlier sketches in SATA *77, 143*
Llewellyn, Grace 1964- *110*
Llewellyn, Richard
  See Llewellyn Lloyd, Richard Dafydd Vivian
Llewellyn, Sam 1948- *185*
  Earlier sketch in SATA *95*
Llewellyn Lloyd, Richard Dafydd Vivian
  1906-1983 .... *11*
  Obituary *37*
Llewelyn, T. Harcourt
  See Hamilton, Charles (Harold St. John)
Lloyd, Alan
  See Lloyd, A.R.
Lloyd, Alan Richard
  See Lloyd, A.R.
Lloyd, A.R. 1927- *168*
  Earlier sketch in SATA *97*
Lloyd, David
  See Lloyd, David T.
Lloyd, David T. 1954- *167*
Lloyd, E. James
  See James, Elizabeth
Lloyd, Errol 1943- *22*
Lloyd, Hugh
  See Fitzhugh, Percy Keese
Lloyd, James
  See James, Elizabeth
Lloyd, Megan 1958- *189*
  Earlier sketches in SATA *77, 117*
Lloyd, Norman 1909-1980
  Obituary *23*
Lloyd, (Mary) Norris 1908-1993 .... *10*
  Obituary *75*
Lloyd, Sam *183*
Lloyd-Jones, Sally 1960- *179*
Lloyd Webber, Andrew 1948- *56*
Llywelyn, Morgan 1937- *109*
Lo, Ginnie *165*
Lo, Virginia M.
  See Lo, Ginnie
Lobato, Jose Bento Monteiro 1882-1948 ... *114*
Lobel, Anita (Kempler) 1934- *162*
  Earlier sketches in SATA *6, 55, 96*
Lobel, Arnold (Stark) 1933-1987 .... *55*
  Obituary *54*
  Earlier sketch in SATA *6*
  See also CLR *5*
Lobel, Gillian *181*
Lobsenz, Amelia *12*
Lobsenz, Norman M(itchell) 1919- *6*
Lochak, Michele 1936- *39*
Lochlons, Colin
  See Jackson, C(aary) Paul
Locke, Clinton W. *1*
Locke, Elsie (Violet) 1912-2001 .... *87*
Locke, Gary 1963- *197*
Locke, Lucie 1904-1989 .... *10*
Locke, Robert 1944- *63*
  See also CLR *39*
Locker, Thomas 1937- *109*
  Earlier sketch in SATA *59*
  See also CLR *14*
Lockhart, E.
  See Jenkins, Emily
Lockridge, Hildegarde (Dolson)
  1908-1981 .... *121*
  Earlier sketch in SATA *5*

Lockwood, Mary
  See Spelman, Mary
Lodge, Bernard 1933- 107
  Earlier sketch in SATA 33
Lodge, Jo 1966- 173
  Earlier sketch in SATA 112
Loeb, Jeffrey 1946- 57
Loeb, Robert H., Jr. 1917- 21
Loefgren, Ulf 1931- 3
Loehfelm, Bill 1969- 153
Loehr, Mallory 184
Loehr, Patrick 1968(?)- 194
Loeper, John J(oseph) 1929- 118
  Earlier sketch in SATA 10
Loescher, Ann Dull 1942- 20
Loescher, Gil(burt Damian) 1945- 20
Loewer, Jean Jenkins
  See Jenkins, Jean
Loewer, (Henry) Peter 1934- 98
LoFaro, Jerry 1959- 77
Lofo
  See Heimann, Rolf
Lofthouse, Liz 199
Lofting, Hugh (John) 1886-1947 100
  Earlier sketch in SATA 15
  See also CLR 143
Lofts, Norah (Robinson) 1904-1983 8
  Obituary 36
Logan, Jake
  See Knott, William C(ecil, Jr.)
  and Krepps, Robert W(ilson)
  and Pearl, Jacques Bain
  and Riefe, Alan
  and Rifkin, Shepard
  and Smith, Martin Cruz
Logan, Mark
  See Nicole, Christopher (Robin)
Logan, Rochelle 1954- 169
Logston, Anne 1962- 112
Logue, Christopher 1926- 23
Logue, Mary 1952- 161
  Earlier sketch in SATA 112
Logue, Mary Louise
  See Logue, Mary
Loh, Morag 1935- 73
Lohans, Alison 1949- 101
Loizeaux, William 185
Loken, Newton Clayton 1919- 26
Lomas, Steve
  See Brennan, Joseph Lomas
Lomask, Milton (Nachman) 1909-1991 20
Lombard, Jenny 178
Lombino, Salvatore
  See Hunter, Evan
LoMonaco, Palmyra 1932- 102
London, Jack 1876-1916 18
  See also CLR 108
London, Jane
  See Geis, Darlene Stern
London, John Griffith
  See London, Jack
London, Jonathan (Paul) 1947- 157
  Earlier sketches in SATA 74, 113
Lonergan, (Pauline) Joy (MacLean) 1909- ... 10
Lonette, Reisie (Dominee) 1924- 43
Long, Cathryn J. 1946- 89
Long, Earlene (Roberta) 1938- 50
Long, Emmett
  See Leonard, Elmore
Long, Ethan 1968(?)- 182
Long, Helen Beecher 1
Long, Judith Elaine 1953- 20
Long, Judy
  See Long, Judith Elaine
Long, Kim 1949- 69
Long, Laura Mooney 1892-1967
  Obituary 29
Long, Laurel 203
Long, Loren 1966(?)- 188
  Earlier sketch in SATA 151
Long, Melinda 1960- 152

Long, Sylvia 1948- 179
  Earlier sketch in SATA 120
Longbeard, Frederick
  See Longyear, Barry B(rookes)
Longfellow, Henry Wadsworth 1807-1882 ... 19
  See also CLR 99
Longfellow, Layne (A.) 1937- 102
Longman, Harold S. 1919- 5
Longsworth, Polly 1933- 28
Longtemps, Kenneth 1933- 17
Longway, A. Hugh
  See Lang, Andrew
Longyear, Barry B(rookes) 1942- 117
Look, Lenore 180
Loomans, Diane 1955- 90
Loomis, Christine 160
  Earlier sketch in SATA 113
Loomis, Jennifer A. 1942- 101
Loomis, Robert D. 5
Lopez, Angelo (Cayas) 1967- 83
Lopez, Barry (Holstun) 1945- 67
Lopez, Jack 1950- 178
Lopez, Loretta 1963- 190
Lopez, Lorraine M. 1956- 181
Lopez, Rafael 1961(?)- 198
Lopshire, Robert M(artin) 1927- 6
Loraine, Connie
  See Reece, Colleen L.
Lorbiecki, Marybeth 1959- 172
  Earlier sketch in SATA 121
Lord, Athena V. 1932- 39
Lord, Beman 1924-1991 5
  Obituary 69
Lord, Bette Bao 1938- 58
Lord, Cynthia 182
Lord, Doreen Mildred Douglas
  See Lord, Douglas
Lord, Douglas 1904-1992 12
Lord, Janet 204
Lord, John Vernon 1939- 21
Lord, Michele 201
Lord, Nancy
  See Titus, Eve
Lord, Patricia C. 1927-1988
  Obituary 58
Lord, Walter 1917-2002 3
Lorde, Diana
  See Reno, Dawn E(laine)
Lorenz, Albert 1941- 115
Lorenzini, Carlo 1826-1890 100
  Earlier sketch in SATA 29
  See also CLR 120
Lorey, Dean 1967- 193
Lorimer, Janet 1941- 60
Loring, Emilie (Baker) 1864(?)-1951 51
Lorkowski, Thomas V(incent) 1950- 92
Lorkowski, Tom
  See Lorkowski, Thomas V(incent)
Lorraine, Walter (Henry) 1929- 16
Lorrimer, Claire
  See Clark, Patricia Denise
Loss, Joan 1933- 11
Lothrop, Harriet Mulford Stone 1844-1924 . 20
Lottridge, Celia Barker 1936- 157
  Earlier sketch in SATA 112
LoTurco, Laura 1963- 84
Lotz, Wolfgang 1912-1981 65
Louie, Ai-Ling 1949- 40
  Brief entry 34
Louis, Catherine 1963- 186
Louis, Pat
  See Francis, Dorothy
Louisburgh, Sheila Burnford
  See Burnford, Sheila (Philip Cochrane Every)
Louise, Anita
  See Riggio, Anita
Louise, Tina 1934- 191
Lourie, Helen
  See Storr, Catherine (Cole)
Lourie, Peter 1952- 183
  Earlier sketches in SATA 82, 142

Lourie, Peter King
  See Lourie, Peter
Love, Ann 1947- 168
  Earlier sketch in SATA 79
Love, D. Anne 1949- 180
  Earlier sketches in SATA 96, 145
Love, Douglas 1967- 92
Love, Judith Dufour
  See Love, Judy
Love, Judy 188
Love, Katherine (Isabel) 1907- 3
Love, Kathleen Ann
  See Love, Ann
Love, Sandra (Weller) 1940- 26
Lovejoy, Jack 1937- 116
Lovelace, Delos Wheeler 1894-1967 7
Lovelace, Maud Hart 1892-1980 2
  Obituary 23
Lovell, Ingraham
  See Bacon, Josephine Dodge (Daskam)
Loverseed, Amanda (Jane) 1965- 75
Lovett, Margaret (Rose) 1915- 22
Low, Alice 1926- 156
  Earlier sketches in SATA 11, 76
Low, Elizabeth Hammond 1898-1991 5
Low, Joseph 1911-2007 14
Low, Penelope Margaret
  See Lively, Penelope
Low, William 177
Lowe, Helen 1961- 206
Lowe, Jay, Jr.
  See Loeper, John J(oseph)
Lowell, Pamela 187
Lowell, Susan 1950- 206
  Earlier sketches in SATA 81, 127
Lowenstein, Dyno 1914-1996 6
Lowenstein, Sallie 1949- 116
Lowery, Linda 1949- 151
  Earlier sketch in SATA 74
Lowitz, Anson C. 1901(?)-1978 18
Lowitz, Sadyebeth Heath 1901-1969 17
Lowndes, Robert A(ugustine) W(ard)
  1916-1998 117
Lowrey, Janette Sebring 1892-1986 43
Lowry, Lois 1937- 177
  Autobiography Feature 127
  Earlier sketches in SATA 23, 70, 111
  See also CLR 72
  See also SAAS 3
Lowry, Lois Hammersberg
  See Lowry, Lois
Lowry, Peter 1953- 7
Lowther, George F. 1913-1975
  Obituary 30
Loyie, Larry 1933- 150
Lozansky, Edward D. 1941- 62
Lozier, Herbert 1915- 26
Lubar, David 1954- 190
  Earlier sketch in SATA 133
Lubell, Cecil 1912-2000 6
Lubell, Winifred (A. Milius) 1914- 6
Lubin, Leonard
  See Lubin, Leonard B.
Lubin, Leonard B. 1943-1994 45
  Brief entry 37
Lubka, S. Ruth 1948- 154
Lubner, Susan 185
Luby, Thia 1954- 124
Lucado, Max (Lee) 1955- 104
Lucas, Cedric 1962- 101
Lucas, E(dward) V(errall) 1868-1938 20
Lucas, Eileen 1956- 113
  Earlier sketch in SATA 76
Lucas, George 1944- 56
Lucas, Jerry 1940- 33
Lucas, Margeaux 186
Lucas, Victoria
  See Plath, Sylvia
Lucashenko, Melissa 1967- 104
Luccarelli, Vincent 1923- 90
Luce, Celia (Geneva Larsen) 1914- 38

Luce, Willard (Ray) 1914-1990 38
Lucht, Irmgard 1937- 82
Lucke, Deb 202
Luckett, Dave 1951- 167
  Earlier sketch in SATA *106*
Luckhardt, Mildred Corell 1898-1990 5
Ludden, Allen (Ellsworth) 1918(?)-1981
  Obituary 27
Ludel, Jacqueline 1945- 64
Ludlow, Geoffrey
  See Meynell, Laurence Walter
Ludlum, Mabel Cleland
  See Widdemer, Mabel Cleland
Ludwig, Helen 33
Ludwig, Lyndell 1923- 63
Ludwig, Trudy 1959- 166
Lueders, Edward (George) 1923- 14
Luenn, Nancy 1954- 79
  Earlier sketch in SATA *51*
Lufkin, Raymond H. 1897- 38
Lugard, Flora Louisa Shaw 1852-1929 21
Luger, Harriett Mandelay 1914- 23
Luhrmann, Winifred B(ruce) 1934- 11
Luis, Earlene W. 1929- 11
Lujan, Jorge 201
Luke, Pauline 178
Luke, Pauline R.
  See Luke, Pauline
Lum, Peter
  See Crowe, (Bettina) Peter Lum
Lumry, Amanda (R.) 159
Lund, Deb 157
Lund, Doris Herold 1919- 12
Lunde, Darrin 202
Lung, Chang
  See Jordan, Robert
Lunge-Larsen, Lise 1955- 184
  Earlier sketch in SATA *138*
Lunn, Carolyn (Kowalczyk) 1960- 67
Lunn, Janet (Louise Swoboda) 1928- 110
  Earlier sketches in SATA *4, 68*
  See also CLR *18*
  See also SAAS *12*
Lunsford, Cin Forshay
  See Forshay-Lunsford, Cin
Lupica, Michael
  See Lupica, Mike
Lupica, Michael Thomas
  See Lupica, Mike
Lupica, Mike 1952- 177
Lupoff, Dick
  See Lupoff, Richard A(llen)
Lupoff, Richard A(llen) 1935- 60
Lurie, Alison 1926- 112
  Earlier sketch in SATA *46*
Lurie, Morris 1938- 72
Lussert, Anneliese 1929- 101
Lusted, Marcia Amidon 1962- 143
Lustig, Arnost 1926- 56
Lustig, Loretta 1944- 46
Luthardt, Kevin 1973- 172
Luther, Frank 1905-1980
  Obituary 25
Luther, Rebekah (Lyn) S(tiles) 1960- 90
Luttmann, Gail
  See Damerow, Gail
Luttrell, Guy L. 1938- 22
Luttrell, Ida (Alleene) 1934- 91
  Brief entry 35
  Earlier sketch in SATA *40*
Luttrell, William (J. III) 1954- 149
Lutz, John 1939- 180
Lutz, John Thomas
  See Lutz, John
Lutz, Norma Jean 1943- 122
Lutzeier, Elizabeth 1952- 72
Lutzker, Edythe 1904-1991 5
Luxbacher, Irene M. 1970- 153
Luzadder, Patrick 1954- 89
Luzzati, Emanuele 1921-2007 7
Luzzatto, Paola Caboara 1938- 38

Lybbert, Tyler 1970- 88
Lydon, Michael 1942- 11
Lyfick, Warren
  See Reeves, Lawrence F.
Lyle, Katie Letcher 1938- 8
Lynch, Chris 1962- 171
  Earlier sketches in SATA *95, 131*
  See also CLR *58*
Lynch, Jay 1945- 204
Lynch, Lorenzo 1932- 7
Lynch, Marietta 1947- 29
Lynch, P(atrick) J(ames) 1962- 122
  Earlier sketch in SATA *79*
Lynch, Patricia (Nora) 1898-1972 9
Lynds, Dennis 1924-2005 47
  Brief entry 37
Lyne, Alison Davis 188
Lyngseth, Joan
  See Davies, Joan
Lynn, Elizabeth A(nne) 1946- 99
Lynn, Mary
  See Brokamp, Marilyn
Lynn, Patricia
  See Watts, Mabel Pizzey
Lynn, Tracy 175
Lyon, Elinor 1921-2008 6
  Obituary 192
Lyon, Elinor Bruce
  See Lyon, Elinor
Lyon, George Ella 1949- 148
  Autobiography Feature 148
  Earlier sketches in SATA *68, 119*
Lyon, Lyman R.
  See de Camp, L. Sprague
Lyons, Dorothy M(arawee) 1907-1997 3
Lyons, Grant 1941- 30
Lyons, Marcus
  See Blish, James
Lyons, Mary E. 1947- 195
  Autobiography Feature 195
  Earlier sketches in SATA *93, 142*
Lyons, Mary Evelyn
  See Lyons, Mary E.
Lystad, Mary (Hanemann) 1928- 11
Lytle, Elizabeth Stewart 1949- 79
Lytle, Robert A. 1944- 119
Lyttle, Richard B(ard) 1927- 23
Lytton, Edward G(eorge) E(arle) L(ytton)
  Bulwer-Lytton Baron 1803-1873 23

M

Ma, Wenhai 1954- 84
Maar, Leonard (Frank, Jr.) 1927- 30
Maartens, Maretha 1945- 73
Maas, Selve -1997 14
Maass, Robert 195
Mabie, Grace
  See Mattern, Joanne
Mac
  See MacManus, Seumas
  and Maccari, Ruggero
Macalaster, Elizabeth G. 1951- 115
MacAlister, Katie 159
MacAllan, Andrew
  See Leasor, James
MacAodhagain, Eamon
  See Egan, E(dward) W(elstead)
MacArthur-Onslow, Annette Rosemary
  1933- 26
Macaulay, David (Alexander) 1946- 137
  Brief entry 27
  Earlier sketches in SATA *46, 72*
  See also CLR *14*
Macaulay, Teresa (E.) 1947- 95
Macavinta, Courtney 176
MacBeth, George (Mann) 1932-1992 4
  Obituary 70
MacBride, Roger Lea 1929-1995 85

MacCarter, Don 1944- 91
MacClintock, Dorcas 1932- 8
MacCready, Robin Merrow 1959(?)- 190
MacCullough, Carolyn 174
MacDonald, Alan 1958- 192
MacDonald, Amy 1951- 156
  Autobiography Feature 156
  Earlier sketches in SATA *76, 136*
MacDonald, Anne Elizabeth Campbell Bard
  -1958
  See MacDonald, Betty
MacDonald, Anson
  See Heinlein, Robert A.
MacDonald, Betty 1908-1958
  See YABC *1*
Macdonald, Blackie
  See Emrich, Duncan (Black Macdonald)
Macdonald, Caroline 1948- 86
  Obituary 111
  See also CLR *60*
MacDonald, Dwight 1906-1982 29
  Obituary 33
MacDonald, George 1824-1905 100
  Earlier sketch in SATA *33*
  See also CLR *67*
MacDonald, Golden
  See Brown, Margaret Wise
Macdonald, Guy 195
Macdonald, James D. 1954- 67
  Earlier sketches in SATA *81, 114, 165, 1*
Macdonald, Marcia
  See Hill, Grace Livingston
MacDonald, Margaret Read 1940- 194
  Earlier sketches in SATA *94, 164*
Macdonald, Marianne 1934- 113
Macdonald, Mary
  See Gifford, Griselda
Macdonald, Maryann 1947- 189
  Earlier sketch in SATA *72*
MacDonald, Ross 1957- 201
Macdonald, Shelagh 1937- 25
MacDonald, Suse 1940- 193
  Brief entry 52
  Earlier sketches in SATA *54, 109*
Macdonald, Zillah K(atherine) 1885-1979 ... 11
MacDonnell, Megan
  See Stevens, Serita
MacDougal, John
  See Blish, James
Mace, Elisabeth 1933- 27
Mace, Varian 1938- 49
MacEachern, Stephen 206
MacEwen, Gwendolyn (Margaret)
  1941-1987 50
  Obituary 55
Macfarlan, Allan A. 1892-1982 35
MacFarlane, Iris 1922- 11
MacGill-Callahan, Sheila 1926-2000 78
MacGregor, Carol Lynn 153
MacGregor, Ellen 1906-1954 39
  Brief entry 27
MacGregor-Hastie, Roy (Alasdhair Niall)
  1929- 3
MacGrory, Yvonne 1948- 142
Machado, Ana Maria 1941- 150
MacHale, D.J. 1956- 175
MacHale, Donald James
  See MacHale, D.J.
Machetanz, Frederick 1908- 34
Machin Goodall, Daphne (Edith) 37
Macht, Norm
  See Macht, Norman L.
Macht, Norman L. 1929- 122
Macht, Norman Lee
  See Macht, Norman L.
MacInnes, Helen (Clark) 1907-1985 22
  Obituary 44
Macintosh, Brownie 1950- 98
MacIntyre, Elisabeth 1916- 17
MacIntyre, Rod
  See MacIntyre, R.P.

MacIntyre, R.P. 1947- 203
MacIntyre, R.P. 1947- 203
MacIntyre, Wendy 1947- 196
Mack, Jeff 194
Mack, L.V.
    See Kimmelman, Burt
Mack, Stan(ley) 17
Mack, Todd 168
Mack, Tracy 1968- 183
    Earlier sketch in SATA *128*
Mackall, Dandi D.
    See Mackall, Dandi Daley
Mackall, Dandi Daley 1949- 182
    Earlier sketches in SATA *118, 177*
Mackay, Claire 1930- 97
    Autobiography Feature 124
    Earlier sketch in SATA *40*
    See also CLR *43*
Mackay, Constance D'Arcy (?)-1966 125
Mackay, Donald 1914-2005 81
    Obituary 173
Mackay, Donald Alexander
    See Mackay, Donald
MacKaye, Percy (Wallace) 1875-1956 32
Mackel, Kathryn 1950- 162
Mackel, Kathy
    See Mackel, Kathryn
MacKellar, William 1914- 4
Macken, JoAnn Early 1953- 201
Macken, Walter 1915-1967 36
MacKenzie, Jill (Kelly) 1947- 75
Mackenzie, Robert 1974- 204
Mackey, Ernan
    See McInerny, Ralph
Mackey, Weezie Kerr 188
Mackie, Maron
    See McNeely, Jeannette
Mackin, Edward
    See McInerny, Ralph
MacKinnon, Bernie 1957- 69
MacKinnon Groomer, Vera 1915- 57
MacKinstry, Elizabeth 1879-1956 42
Mackler, Carolyn 1973- 156
MacLachlan, Emily
    See Charest, Emily MacLachlan
MacLachlan, Patricia 1938- 168
    Brief entry 42
    Earlier sketches in SATA *62, 107*
    See also CLR *14*
MacLane, Jack
    See Crider, Bill
MacLean, Alistair (Stuart) 1922(?)-1987 23
    Obituary 50
Maclean, Art
    See Shirreffs, Gordon D(onald)
MacLean, Christine Kole 1962- 177
MacLean, Glynne 1964- 150
MacLeod, Beatrice 1910- 162
    Earlier sketch in SATA *10*
MacLeod, Beatrice Beach
    See MacLeod, Beatrice
MacLeod, Charlotte (Matilda) 1922-2005 28
    Obituary 160
MacLeod, Doug 1959- 201
    Earlier sketch in SATA *60*
MacLeod, Elizabeth 184
    Earlier sketch in SATA *158*
MacLeod, Ellen Jane (Anderson) 1916- 14
MacManus, James
    See MacManus, Seumas
MacManus, Seumas 1869-1960 25
MacMaster, Eve (Ruth) B(owers) 1942- 46
MacMillan, Annabelle
    See Quick, Annabelle
MacMillan, Dianne M(arie) 1943- 125
    Earlier sketch in SATA *84*
Macnaughton, Tina 182
Macneill, Janet
    See McNeely, Jeannette
MacPeek, Walter G. 1902-1973 4
    Obituary 25

MacPhail, Catherine 1946- 197
    Earlier sketch in SATA *130*
MacPherson, Margaret 1908-2001 9
    See also SAAS *4*
MacPherson, Thomas George 1915-1976
    Obituary 30
MacPherson, Winnie 1930- 107
MacRae, Tom 1980- 181
Macrae, Travis
    See Feagles, Anita M(acRae)
MacRaois, Cormac 1944- 72
Macumber, Mari
    See Sandoz, Mari(e Susette)
Macy, Sue 1954- 134
    Earlier sketch in SATA *88*
Madaras, Lynda 1947- 151
Madden, Don 1927- 3
Madden, Kerry 1961- 168
Madden-Lunsford, Kerry
    See Madden, Kerry
Maddern, Eric 1950- 166
Maddigan, Beth 1967- 174
Maddison, Angela Mary 1923- 10
    See also CLR *24*
Maddock, Reginald (Bertram) 1912-1994 15
Madenski, Melissa (Ann) 1949- 77
Madian, Jon 1941- 9
Madison, Alan 182
Madison, Arnold 1937- 6
Madison, Winifred 5
Madonna 1958- 149
Madsen, Gunnar 171
Madsen, Jim 1964- 202
Madsen, Ross Martin 1946- 82
Madsen, Susan A. 1954- 90
Madsen, Susan Arrington
    See Madsen, Susan A.
Maehlqvist, Stefan 1943- 30
Maestro, Betsy (Crippen) 1944- 106
    Brief entry 30
    Earlier sketch in SATA *59*
    See also CLR *45*
Maestro, Giulio 1942- 106
    Earlier sketches in SATA *8, 59*
    See also CLR *45*
Maeterlinck, Maurice 1862-1949 66
Magee, Doug 1947- 78
Magee, Wes 1939- 64
Maggio, Rosalie 1943- 69
Magid, Ken(neth Marshall) 65
Magnus, Erica 1946- 77
Magoon, Scott 182
Magorian, James 1942- 92
    Earlier sketch in SATA *32*
Magorian, Michelle 1947- 128
    Earlier sketch in SATA *67*
Magorian, Michelle Jane
    See Magorian, Michelle
Magovern, Peg 103
Maguire, Anne
    See Nearing, Penny
Maguire, Gregory 1954- 200
    Autobiography Feature 200
    Earlier sketches in SATA *28, 84, 129*
    See also SAAS *22*
Maguire, Gregory Peter
    See Maguire, Gregory
Maguire, Jack 1920-2000 74
Maguire, Jesse
    See Smith, Sherwood
Maguire, Jessie
    See Smith, Sherwood
Maher, Ramona 1934- 13
Mahlqvist, Stefan
    See Maehlqvist, Stefan
Mahon, Julia C(unha) 1916- 11
Mahony, Elizabeth Winthrop
    See Winthrop, Elizabeth
Mahood, Kenneth 1930- 24

Mahy, Margaret 1936- 171
    Earlier sketches in SATA *14, 69, 119*
    See also CLR *78*
Mahy, Margaret May
    See Mahy, Margaret
Maiden, Cecil (Edward) 1902-1981 52
Maidoff, Ilka
    See List, Ilka Katherine
Maifair, Linda Lee 1947- 83
Maik, Henri
    See Hecht, Henri Joseph
Maillu, David G(ian) 1939- 111
Maine, Trevor
    See Catherall, Arthur
Mains, Randolph P. 1946- 80
Maione, Heather 189
Maiorano, Robert 1946- 43
Maisner, Heather 1947- 89
Maison, Della
    See Katz, Bobbi
Maitland, Antony Jasper 1935- 25
Maitland, Barbara 102
Mai-Wyss, Tatjana 1972- 187
Major, Kevin (Gerald) 1949- 134
    Earlier sketches in SATA *32, 82*
    See also CLR *11*
Majure, Janet 1954- 96
Makhijani, Pooja 188
Makie, Pam 1943- 37
Makowski, Silk
    See Makowski, Silvia Ann
Makowski, Silvia Ann 1940- 101
Malam, John 1957- 152
    Earlier sketch in SATA *89*
Maland, Nick 195
Malcolm, Dan
    See Silverberg, Robert
Malcolm, Jahnna N.
    See Beecham, Jahnna
Malcolmson, Anne
    See von Storch, Anne B.
Malcolmson, David 1899-1978 6
Maletta, Dr. Arlene
    See Feltenstein, Arlene (H.)
Maley, Carleen
    See Hutchins, Carleen Maley
Mali, Jane Lawrence 1937-1995 51
    Brief entry 44
    Obituary 86
Malkin, Nina 1959(?)- 179
Mallett, Jerry J. 1939- 76
Malley, Gemma 198
Malley, G.R.
    See Malley, Gemma
Mallory, Kenneth 1945- 185
    Earlier sketch in SATA *128*
Mallowan, Agatha Christie
    See Christie, Agatha (Mary Clarissa)
Malmberg, Carl 1904-1979 9
Malmgren, Dallin 1949- 65
Malo, John W. 1911-2000 4
Malone, James Hiram 1930- 84
Malone, Nola Langner 1930-2003 8
    Obituary 151
Malone, Patricia 1932- 155
Malone, Peter 1953- 191
Maloney, Pat
    See Markun, Patricia Maloney
Malory, Sir Thomas 1410(?)-1471(?) 59
    Brief entry 33
Maltese, Michael 1909(?)-1981
    Obituary 24
Malvasi, Meg Greene 143
Malvern, Corinne 1905-1956 34
Malvern, Gladys (?)-1962 23
Mama G.
    See Davis, Grania
Mammano, Julie 1962- 202
    Earlier sketch in SATA *107*
Mamonova, Tatyana 1943- 93
Manchel, Frank 1935- 10

Manchess, Gregory 1955- 203
Manchester, William (Raymond)
  1922-2004 65
Mandabach, Brian 1962(?)- 197
Mandel, Brett H. 1969- 108
Mandel, Peter 1957- 87
Mandel, Sally (Elizabeth) 1944- 64
Mandell, Muriel (Hortense Levin) 1921- 63
Manders, John 1957- 175
Manes, Stephen 1949- 99
  Brief entry 40
  Earlier sketch in SATA 42
Manfred, Frederick (Feikema) 1912-1994 30
Mangin, Marie France 1940- 59
Mangione, Gerlando 1909-1998 6
  Obituary 104
Mangione, Jerre
  See Mangione, Gerlando
Mango, Karin N. 1936- 52
Mangurian, David 1938- 14
Mania, Cathy 1950- 102
Mania, Robert 1952- 102
Mania, Robert C., Jr.
  See Mania, Robert
Maniatty, Taramesha 1978- 92
Maniscalco, Joseph 1926- 10
Manley, Deborah 1932- 28
Manley, Seon 1921- 15
  See also CLR 3
  See also SAAS 2
Mann, Elizabeth 1948- 153
Mann, Josephine
  See Pullein-Thompson, Josephine (Mary
    Wedderburn)
Mann, Kenny 1946- 91
Mann, Pamela 1946- 91
Mann, Patrick
  See Waller, Leslie
Mann, Peggy
  See Houlton, Peggy Mann
Mannetti, Lisa 1953- 57
  Brief entry 51
Mannheim, Grete (Salomon) 1909-1986 10
Manniche, Lise 1943- 31
Manning, Jane K. 185
Manning, Mick 1959- 176
Manning, Rosemary 1911-1988 10
Manning, Sarra 162
Manning-Sanders, Ruth (Vernon)
  1895(?)-1988 73
  Obituary 57
  Earlier sketch in SATA 15
Mannion, Diane
  See Paterson, Diane
Mannis, Celeste Davidson 173
Mannon, Warwick
  See Hopkins, (Hector) Kenneth
Manos, Helen 199
Mansir, A. Richard 1932- 170
Manson, Ainslie Kertland 1938- 115
Manson, Beverlie 1945- 57
  Brief entry 44
Manthorpe, Helen 1958- 122
Mantinband, Gerda (B.) 1917- 74
Manton, Jo
  See Gittings, Jo (Grenville) Manton
Manuel, Lynn 1948- 179
  Earlier sketch in SATA 99
Manushkin, Fran 1942- 205
  Earlier sketches in SATA 7, 54, 93, 166
Manushkin, Frances
  See Manushkin, Fran
Man Without a Spleen, A
  See Chekhov, Anton (Pavlovich)
Manzano, Sonia 1950- 167
Mapes, Mary A.
  See Ellison, Virginia H(owell)
Maple, Marilyn 1931- 80
Mappin, Strephyn 1956- 109
Mara, Barney
  See Roth, Arthur J(oseph)

Mara, Jeanette
  See Cebulash, Mel
Marais, Josef 1905-1978
  Obituary 24
Marasmus, Seymour
  See Rivoli, Mario
Marbach, Ethel
  See Pochocki, Ethel (Frances)
Marcal, Annette B.
  See Callaway, Bernice (Anne)
Marcelino
  See Agnew, Edith J(osephine)
Marcellino, Fred 1939-2001 118
  Obituary 127
  Earlier sketch in SATA 68
March, Carl
  See Fleischman, Sid
Marchant, Bessie 1862-1941
  See YABC 2
Marchant, Catherine
  See Cookson, Catherine (McMullen)
Marcher, Marion Walden 1890-1987 10
Marchesi, Stephen 1951- 114
Marchesi, Steve
  See Marchesi, Stephen
  and Older, Effin
  and Older, Jules
Marchetta, Melina 1965- 170
Marciano, John Bemelmans 1970- 167
  Earlier sketch in SATA 118
  See also CLR 93
Marco, Lou
  See Gottfried, Theodore Mark
Marcus, Leonard S. 1950- 187
  Earlier sketch in SATA 133
Marcus, Paul 1953- 82
Marcus, Rebecca B(rian) 1907- 9
Marcuse, Aida E. 1934- 89
Marek, Margot L. 1934(?)-1987
  Obituary 54
Maren, Julie 1970- 199
Margaret, Karla
  See Andersdatter, Karla M(argaret)
Margolin, Harriet
  See Ziefert, Harriet
Margolis, Jeffrey A. 1948- 108
Margolis, Leslie 187
Margolis, Richard J(ules) 1929-1991 86
  Obituary 67
  Earlier sketch in SATA 4
Margolis, Vivienne 1922- 46
Mariana
  See Foster, Marian Curtis
Marie, Geraldine 1949- 61
Mariner, Scott
  See Pohl, Frederik
Marino, Dorothy Bronson 1912- 14
Marino, Jan 1936- 114
Marino, Nick
  See Deming, Richard
Marino, Peter 1960- 179
Mario, Anna
  See Odgers, Sally Farrell
Marion, Henry
  See del Rey, Lester
Maris, Ron 71
  Brief entry 45
Mark, Jan 1943-2006 164
  Obituary 173
  Earlier sketches in SATA 22, 69, 114
  See also CLR 11
Mark, Janet Marjorie
  See Mark, Jan
Mark, Joan T. 1937- 122
Mark, Pauline (Dahlin) 1913-1997 14
Mark, Polly
  See Mark, Pauline (Dahlin)
Mark, Ted
  See Gottfried, Theodore Mark
Markel, Michelle 169
Marker, Sherry 1941- 76

Markert, Jennifer 1965- 83
Markert, Jenny
  See Markert, Jennifer
Markham, Lynne 1947- 102
Markham, Marion M. 1929- 60
Markham, Wendy
  See Staub, Wendy Corsi
Markins, W. S.
  See Jenkins, Marie M(agdalen)
Markle, Sandra L. 1946- 185
  Brief entry 41
  Earlier sketches in SATA 57, 92, 148
Markle, Sandra Lee
  See Markle, Sandra L.
Marko, Katherine D(olores) 28
Markoosie
  See Patsauq, Markoosie
Marks, Alan 1957- 187
  Earlier sketches in SATA 77, 151
Marks, Burton 1930- 47
  Brief entry 43
Marks, Graham 158
Marks, Hannah K.
  See Trivelpiece, Laurel
Marks, J.
  See Highwater, Jamake (Mamake)
Marks, J(ames) M(acdonald) 1921- 13
Marks, Laurie J. 1957- 68
Marks, Margaret L. 1911(?)-1980
  Obituary 23
Marks, Mickey Klar -1986 12
Marks, Peter
  See Smith, Robert Kimmel
Marks, Rita 1938- 47
Marks, Stan(ley) 14
Marks-Highwater, J.
  See Highwater, Jamake (Mamake)
Markun, Patricia Maloney 1924- 15
Markusen, Bruce (Stanley Rodriguez)
  1965- 141
Marley, Louise 1952- 173
  Earlier sketch in SATA 120
Marlin, Hilda
  See Van Stockum, Hilda
Marlow, Layne 204
Marlow, Max
  See Nicole, Christopher (Robin)
Marlow, Susan K. 1953- 178
Marlowe, Amy Bell 67
  Earlier sketch in SATA 1
Marlowe, Jack
  See Deary, Terry
Marney, Dean 1952- 90
Marokvia, Artur 1909- 31
Marokvia, Mireille 1908-2008 5
  Obituary 197
Marokvia, Mireille Journet
  See Marokvia, Mireille
Marol, Jean-Claude 1946- 125
Marr, John S(tuart) 1940- 48
Marr, Melissa 1972- 189
Marric, J. J.
  See Butler, William Vivian
  and Creasey, John
Marrin, Albert 1936- 193
  Brief entry 43
  Earlier sketches in SATA 53, 90, 126
  See also CLR 53
Marriott, Alice Lee 1910-1992 31
  Obituary 71
Marriott, Janice 1946- 134
Marriott, Pat(ricia) 1920- 35
Marroquin, Patricio
  See Markun, Patricia Maloney
Mars, W. T.
  See Mars, Witold Tadeusz J.
Mars, Witold Tadeusz J. 1912-1985 3
Marsden, Carolyn 1950- 175
  Earlier sketch in SATA 140

Marsden, John 1950- 146
　Earlier sketches in SATA *66, 97*
　See also CLR *34*
　See also SAAS *22*
Marsh, Carole 1946- 127
Marsh, Dave 1950- 66
Marsh, J. E.
　See Marshall, Evelyn
Marsh, James 1946- 73
Marsh, Jean
　See Marshall, Evelyn
Marsh, Joan F. 1923- 83
Marsh, Paul
　See Hopkins, (Hector) Kenneth
Marsh, Valerie 1954- 89
Marshall, Anthony D(ryden) 1924- 18
Marshall, Bonnie C. 1941- 141
　Earlier sketch in SATA *18*
Marshall, Bridget M(ary) 1974- 103
Marshall, (Sarah) Catherine (Wood)
　1914-1983 2
　Obituary 34
Marshall, Douglas
　See McClintock, Marshall
Marshall, Edmund
　See Hopkins, (Hector) Kenneth
Marshall, Edward
　See Marshall, James
Marshall, Evelyn 1897-1991 11
Marshall, Felicity 1950- 116
Marshall, Garry 1934- 60
Marshall, H. H.
　See Jahn, Michael
Marshall, James 1942-1992 75
　Earlier sketches in SATA *6, 51*
　See also CLR *21*
Marshall, James Edward
　See Marshall, James
Marshall, James Vance
　See Payne, Donald Gordon
Marshall, Janet (Perry) 1938- 97
Marshall, Jeff
　See Laycock, George (Edwin)
Marshall, Kim
　See Marshall, Michael (Kimbrough)
Marshall, Michael (Kimbrough) 1948- 37
Marshall, Percy
　See Young, Percy M(arshall)
Marshall, S(amuel) L(yman) A(twood)
　1900-1977 21
Marsoli, Lisa Ann 1958- 101
　Brief entry 53
Marsten, Richard
　See Hunter, Evan
Marston, Elsa 1933- 156
Marston, Hope Irvin 1935- 127
　Earlier sketch in SATA *31*
Marszalek, John F. 1939- 167
Marszalek, John Francis, Jr.
　See Marszalek, John F.
Marszalek, John Francis 1939-
　See Marszalek, John F.
Martchenko, Michael 1942- 154
　Earlier sketches in SATA *50, 95*
Martel, Aimee
　See Thurlo, Aimee
　and Thurlo, David
Martel, Suzanne 1924- 99
Martignoni, Margaret E. 1908(?)-1974
　Obituary 27
Martin, Ann M. 1955- 192
　Brief entry 41
　Earlier sketches in SATA *44, 70, 126*
　See also CLR *32*
Martin, Bill, Jr. 1916-2004 145
　Brief entry 40
　Earlier sketches in SATA *40, 67*
　See also CLR *97*
Martin, Charles E(lmer)
　See Mastrangelo, Charles E(lmer)

Martin, Christopher
　See Hoyt, Edwin P(almer), Jr.
Martin, Claire 1933- 76
Martin, Courtney Autumn 1984- 205
Martin, David Stone 1913-1992 39
Martin, Del 1921-2008 47
Martin, Donald
　See Honig, Donald
Martin, Dorothy
　See Martin, Del
Martin, Dorothy L.
　See Martin, Del
Martin, Eugene 1
Martin, Eva M. 1939- 65
Martin, Frances M(cEntee) 1906-1998 36
Martin, Francesca 1947- 101
Martin, Fred 1948- 119
Martin, Fredric
　See Christopher, Matt(hew Frederick)
Martin, George Raymond Richard
　See Martin, George R.R.
Martin, George R.R. 1948- 118
Martin, J(ohn) P(ercival) 1880(?)-1966 15
Martin, Jacqueline Briggs 1945- 188
　Earlier sketches in SATA *98, 149*
Martin, Jane Read 1957- 84
Martin, Jeremy
　See Levin, Marcia Obrasky
Martin, Les
　See Schulman, L(ester) M(artin)
Martin, Linda 1961- 82
Martin, Lynne 1923- 21
Martin, Marcia
　See Levin, Marcia Obrasky
Martin, Marvin 1926- 126
Martin, Melanie
　See Pellowski, Michael (Joseph)
Martin, Nancy
　See Salmon, Annie Elizabeth
Martin, Patricia 200
Martin, Patricia A.
　See Martin, Patricia
Martin, Patricia Miles 1899-1986 43
　Obituary 48
　Earlier sketch in SATA *1*
Martin, Peter
　See Chaundler, Christine
Martin, Rafe 1946- 175
Martin, Rene 1891-1977 42
　Obituary 20
Martin, Rupert (Claude) 1905- 31
Martin, S. R.
　See Mappin, Strephyn
Martin, Stefan 1936- 32
Martin, Vicky
　See Storey, Victoria Carolyn
Martin, Webber
　See Silverberg, Robert
Martin, Wendy
　See Martini, Teri
Martin, William Ivan, Jr.
　See Martin, Bill, Jr.
Martineau, Diane 1940- 178
Martineau, Harriet 1802-1876
　See YABC *2*
Martinet, Jeanne 1958- 80
Martinez, Agnes 167
Martinez, Arturo O. 1933- 192
Martinez, Ed(ward) 1954- 98
Martinez, Elizabeth Coonrod 1954- 85
Martinez, Victor 1954- 95
Martini, Teri 1930- 3
Martini, Therese
　See Martini, Teri
Martino, Alfred C. 1964- 174
Martinson, Janis
　See Herbert, Janis
Marton, Jirina 1946- 144
　Earlier sketch in SATA *95*
Marton, Pierre
　See Stone, Peter

Martson, Del
　See Lupoff, Richard A(llen)
Martyr, Paula (Jane)
　See Lawford, Paula Jane
Maruki, Toshi 1912-2000 112
　See also CLR *19*
Marvin, Isabel R(idout) 1924- 84
Marx, Patricia Windschill
　See Marx, Trish
Marx, Robert F(rank) 1936- 24
Marx, Trish 1948- 202
　Earlier sketches in SATA *112, 160*
Marzani, Carl (Aldo) 1912-1994 12
Marzollo, Jean 1942- 190
　Autobiography Feature 190
　Earlier sketches in SATA *29, 77, 130*
　See also SAAS *15*
Masefield, John (Edward) 1878-1967 19
Masoff, Joy 1951- 118
Mason, Adrienne 1962- 163
Mason, Cherie 170
Mason, Edwin A. 1905-1979
　Obituary 32
Mason, Ernst
　See Pohl, Frederik
Mason, F(rancis) van Wyck 1901-1978 3
　Obituary 26
Mason, Frank W.
　See Mason, F(rancis) van Wyck
Mason, George Frederick 1904-2000 14
Mason, Miriam E(vangeline) 1900-1973 2
　Obituary 26
Mason, Prue 195
Mason, Simon 1962- 178
Mason, Tally
　See Derleth, August (William)
Mason, Van Wyck
　See Mason, F(rancis) van Wyck
Mass, Wendy 1967- 196
　Earlier sketch in SATA *158*
Mass, William
　See Gibson, William
Masselman, George 1897-1971 19
Massie, Dianne Redfield 1938- 125
　Earlier sketch in SATA *16*
Massie, Elizabeth 108
Masson, Sophie 1959- 179
　Earlier sketch in SATA *133*
Masters, Anthony (Richard) 1940-2003 112
　Obituary 145
Masters, Kelly R(ay) 1897-1987 3
Masters, Mildred 1932- 42
Masters, William
　See Cousins, Margaret
Masters, Zeke
　See Bensen, Donald R.
　and Goulart, Ron
Mastrangelo, Charles E(lmer) 1910-1995 70
　Earlier sketch in SATA *69*
Masuda, Takeshi 1944- 56
Matas, Carol 1949- 194
　Autobiography Feature 112
　Earlier sketch in SATA *93*
　See also CLR *52*
Matchette, Katharine E. 1941- 38
Math, Irwin 1940- 42
Mathabane, Mark 1960- 123
Mather, Kirtley F(letcher) 1888-1978 65
Mathers, Petra 1945- 176
　Earlier sketch in SATA *119*
　See also CLR *76*
Matheson, Richard (Christian) 1953- 119
Matheson, Shirlee Smith 1942- 155
Mathews, Eleanor
　See Mathews, Ellie
Mathews, Ellie 1946(?)- 193
Mathews, Janet 1914-1992 41
Mathews, Judith
　See Goldberger, Judith M.
Mathews, Louise
　See Tooke, Louise Mathews

Mathiesen, Egon 1907-1976
Obituary 28
Mathieu, Joe 1949- 185
Brief entry 36
Earlier sketches in SATA 43, 94
Mathieu, Joseph P.
See Mathieu, Joe
Mathis, Sharon Bell 1937- 58
Earlier sketch in SATA 7
See also CLR 147
See also SAAS 3
Matlin, Marlee 1965- 181
Matlin, Marlee Beth
See Matlin, Marlee
Matloff, Gregory 1945- 73
Matott, Justin 1961- 109
Matranga, Frances Carfi 1922- 78
Matray, James I. 1948- 161
Matray, James Irving
See Matray, James I.
Matson, Emerson N(els) 1926- 12
Matsui, Tadashi 1926- 8
Matsuno, Masako
See Kobayashi, Masako Matsuno
Matsuoka, Mei 1981- 192
Matte, (Encarnacion) L'Enc 1936- 22
Mattern, Joanne 1963- 122
Mattheson, Jenny 180
Matthew, James
See Barrie, J(ames) M(atthew)
Matthews, Aline
See De Wire, Elinor
Matthews, Andrew 1948- 138
Matthews, Caitlin 1952- 122
Matthews, Downs 1925- 71
Matthews, Elizabeth 1978- 194
Matthews, Ellen
See Bache, Ellyn
Matthews, Ellen 1950- 28
Matthews, Harold Downs
See Matthews, Downs
Matthews, Jacklyn Meek
See Meek, Jacklyn O'Hanlon
Matthews, John (Kentigern) 1948- 116
Matthews, Laura S.
See Matthews, L.S.
Matthews, Liz
See Pellowski, Michael (Joseph)
Matthews, L.S. 183
Matthews, Morgan
See Pellowski, Michael (Joseph)
Matthews, Nicola
See Browne, N.M.
Matthews, Patricia 1927-2006 28
Matthews, Patricia Anne
See Matthews, Patricia
Matthews, Tina 1961- 190
Matthews, Tom L.
See Lalicki, Tom
Matthews, William Henry III 1919- 45
Brief entry 28
Matthiessen, Peter 1927- 27
Mattingley, Christobel (Rosemary) 1931- 85
Earlier sketch in SATA 37
See also CLR 24
See also SAAS 18
Matulay, Laszlo 1912- 43
Matus, Greta 1938- 12
Maugham, W. S.
See Maugham, W(illiam) Somerset
Maugham, W(illiam) Somerset 1874-1965 .. 54
Maugham, William Somerset
See Maugham, W(illiam) Somerset
Maurer, Diane Philippoff
See Maurer-Mathison, Diane V(ogel)
Maurer, Diane Vogel
See Maurer-Mathison, Diane V(ogel)
Maurer-Mathison, Diane V(ogel) 1944- 89
Mauser, Pat Rhoads
See McCord, Patricia

Mauser, Patricia Rhoads
See McCord, Patricia
Maves, Mary Carolyn 1916- 10
Maves, Paul B(enjamin) 1913-1994 10
Mavor, Salley 1955- 125
Mawicke, Tran 1911- 15
Max 1906-1989
See Diop, Birago (Ismael)
Max, Peter 1939- 45
Maxon, Anne
See Best, (Evangel) Allena Champlin
Maxwell, Arthur S. 1896-1970 11
Maxwell, Edith 1923- 7
Maxwell, Gavin 1914-1969 65
Maxwell, Katie
See MacAlister, Katie
Maxwell, William (Keepers, Jr.) 1908-2000
Obituary 128
Maxwell-Hyslop, Miranda 1968- 154
May, Charles Paul 1920- 4
May, Elaine Tyler 1947- 120
May, J. C.
See May, Julian
May, Julian 1931- 11
May, Robert Lewis 1905-1976
Obituary 27
May, Robert Stephen 1929-1996 46
May, Robin
See May, Robert Stephen
Mayall, Beth 171
Mayberry, Florence V(irginia) Wilson 10
Maybury, Richard J. 1946- 72
Maybury, Rick
See Maybury, Richard J.
Mayer, Agatha
See Maher, Ramona
Mayer, Albert Ignatius, Jr. 1906-1994
Obituary 29
Mayer, Ann M(argaret) 1938- 14
Mayer, Bill 200
Mayer, Danuta 1958- 117
Mayer, Hannelore Valencak 1929- 42
Mayer, Jane Rothschild 1903-2001 38
Mayer, Marianna 1945- 132
Earlier sketches in SATA 32, 83
Mayer, Mercer 1943- 137
Earlier sketches in SATA 16, 32, 73, 129
See also CLR 11
Mayerson, Charlotte Leon 36
Mayerson, Evelyn Wilde 1935- 55
Mayfield, Katherine 1958- 118
Mayfield, Sue 1963- 146
Earlier sketch in SATA 72
Mayhar, Ardath 1930- 38
Mayhew, James 1964- 204
Earlier sketches in SATA 85, 149
Maynard, Olga 1920- 40
Mayne, William (James Carter) 1928- 122
Earlier sketches in SATA 6, 68
See also CLR 123
See also SAAS 11
Maynes, J. O. Rocky, Jr.
See Maynes, J. Oscar, Jr.
Maynes, J. Oscar, Jr. 1929- 38
Mayo, Gretchen Will 1936- 163
Earlier sketch in SATA 84
Mayo, Margaret 1935- 165
Earlier sketches in SATA 38, 96
Mayo, Margaret Mary
See Mayo, Margaret
Mayr, Diane 1949- 197
Mays, Lucinda L(a Bella) 1924- 49
Mays, (Lewis) Victor (Jr.) 1927- 5
Mazer, Anne 1953- 192
Earlier sketches in SATA 67, 105
Mazer, Harry 1925- 167
Earlier sketches in SATA 31, 67, 105
See also CLR 16
See also SAAS 11

Mazer, Norma Fox 1931-2009 198
Earlier sketches in SATA 24, 67, 105, 168
See also CLR 23
See also SAAS 1
Mazille, Capucine 1953- 96
Mazza, Adriana 1928- 19
Mazzio, Joann 1926- 74
Mbugua, Kioi Wa 1962- 83
McAfee, Carol 1955- 81
McAllister, Amanda
See Dowdell, Dorothy (Florence) Karns
and Hager, Jean
and Meaker, Eloise
McAllister, Angela 182
McAllister, Margaret I. 1956- 169
Earlier sketch in SATA 117
McAllister, M.I.
See McAllister, Margaret I.
McArdle, Paula 1971- 198
McArthur, Nancy 96
McAvoy, Jim 1972- 142
McBain, Ed
See Hunter, Evan
McBain, Georgina 189
McBratney, Sam 1943- 203
Earlier sketches in SATA 89, 164
See also CLR 44
McBrier, Michael
See Older, Effin
and Older, Jules
McCafferty, Jim 1954- 84
McCaffery, Janet 1936- 38
McCaffrey, Anne 1926- 152
Autobiography Feature 152
Earlier sketches in SATA 8, 70, 116
See also CLR 130
See also SAAS 11
McCaffrey, Anne Inez
See McCaffrey, Anne
McCaffrey, Mary
See Szudek, Agnes S(usan) P(hilomena)
McCain, Becky Ray 1954- 138
McCain, Murray (David, Jr.) 1926-1981 7
Obituary 29
McCall, Edith (Sansom) 1911- 6
McCall, Virginia Nielsen 1909-2000 13
McCall, Wendell
See Pearson, Ridley
McCallum, Phyllis
See Koch, Phyllis (Mae) McCallum
McCallum, Stephen 1960- 91
McCampbell, Darlene Z. 1942- 83
McCann, Edson
See del Rey, Lester
and Pohl, Frederik
McCann, Gerald 1916- 41
McCann, Helen 1948- 75
McCannon, Dindga 41
McCants, William D. 1961- 82
McCarter, Neely Dixon 1929- 47
McCarthy, Agnes 1933- 4
McCarthy, Colin (John) 1951- 77
McCarthy, Mary 1951- 203
McCarthy, Meghan 199
Earlier sketch in SATA 168
McCarthy, Ralph F. 1950- 139
McCarthy-Tucker, Sherri N. 1958- 83
McCarty, Peter 1966- 182
McCarty, Rega Kramer 1904-1986 10
McCaslin, Nellie 1914-2005 12
McCaughrean, Geraldine 1951- 173
Earlier sketches in SATA 87, 139
See also CLR 38
McCaughren, Tom 1936- 75
McCauley, Adam 1965- 128
McCay, (Zenas) Winsor 1869-1934 134
Earlier sketch in SATA 41
McClafferty, Carla Killough 1958- 137
McClary, Jane Stevenson 1919-1990
Obituary 64

McCleery, Patsy R. 1925- 133
 Earlier sketch in SATA 88
McClements, George 196
McClintock, Barbara 1955- 146
 Earlier sketches in SATA 57, 95
McClintock, Marshall 1906-1967 3
McClintock, May Garelick
 See Garelick, May
McClintock, Mike
 See McClintock, Marshall
McClintock, Norah 178
McClintock, Theodore 1902-1971 14
McClinton, Leon 1933- 11
McCloskey, Kevin 1951- 79
McCloskey, (John) Robert 1914-2003 100
 Obituary 146
 Earlier sketches in SATA 2, 39
 See also CLR 7
McCloy, James F(loyd) 1941- 59
McClung, Robert M(arshall) 1916- 135
 Earlier sketches in SATA 2, 68
 See also CLR 11
 See also SAAS 15
McClure, Gillian Mary 1948- 31
McColley, Kevin 1961- 80
 See also SAAS 23
McConduit, Denise Walter 1950- 89
McConnell, James Douglas Rutherford
 1915-1988 40
 Obituary 56
McCord, Anne 1942- 41
McCord, David (Thompson Watson)
 1897-1997 18
 Obituary 96
 See also CLR 9
McCord, Jean 1924- 34
McCord, Pat Mauser
 See McCord, Patricia
McCord, Patricia 1943- 159
 Earlier sketch in SATA 37
McCord, Patricia Sue Rhoads Mauser
 See McCord, Patricia
McCormick, Brooks
 See Adams, William Taylor
McCormick, Dell J. 1892-1949 19
McCormick, (George) Donald (King)
 1911-1998 14
McCormick, Edith (Joan) 1934- 30
McCormick, Kimberly A. 1960- 153
McCormick, Patricia 1956- 181
 Earlier sketch in SATA 128
McCourt, Edward (Alexander) 1907-1972
 Obituary 28
McCourt, Lisa 1964- 159
 Earlier sketch in SATA 117
McCourt, Malachy 1931- 126
McCoy, Iola Fuller 3
McCoy, J(oseph) J(erome) 1917- 8
McCoy, Karen Kawamoto 1953- 82
McCoy, Lois (Rich) 1941- 38
McCrady, Lady 1951- 16
McCrea, James (Craig, Jr.) 1920- 3
McCrea, Ruth (Pirman) 1921- 3
McCreigh, James
 See Pohl, Frederik
McCrumb, Sharyn 1948- 109
McCue, Lisa 1959- 177
 Earlier sketch in SATA 65
McCue, Lisa Emiline
 See McCue, Lisa
McCullen, Andrew
 See Arthur, Robert, (Jr.)
McCullers, (Lula) Carson (Smith)
 1917-1967 27
McCulloch, Derek (Ivor Breashur) 1897-1967
 Obituary 29
McCulloch, John Tyler
 See Burroughs, Edgar Rice
McCulloch, Sarah
 See Ure, Jean
McCullough, David 1933- 62

McCullough, David Gaub
 See McCullough, David
McCullough, Frances Monson 1938- 8
McCullough, Sharon Pierce 1943- 131
McCully, Emily Arnold
 See Arnold, Emily
McCune, Dan
 See Haas, Dorothy F.
McCunn, Ruthanne Lum 1946- 63
McCurdy, Michael (Charles) 1942- 147
 Earlier sketches in SATA 13, 82
McCutcheon, Elsie (Mary Jackson) 1937- ... 60
McCutcheon, John 1952- 97
McDaniel, Becky Bring 1953- 61
McDaniel, Lurlene 1944- 146
 Earlier sketch in SATA 71
McDaniels, Pellom III 1968- 121
McDaniels, Preston 1952- 192
McDearmon, Kay 20
McDermott, Beverly Brodsky 1941- 11
McDermott, Eleni 156
McDermott, Gerald (Edward) 1941- 163
 Earlier sketches in SATA 16, 74
 See also CLR 9
McDermott, Michael 1962- 76
McDevitt, Jack 1935- 155
 Earlier sketch in SATA 94
McDevitt, John Charles
 See McDevitt, Jack
McDole, Carol
 See Farley, Carol (J.)
McDonald, Collin 1943- 79
McDonald, Gerald D(oan) 1905-1970 3
McDonald, Jamie
 See Heide, Florence Parry
McDonald, Janet 1953-2007 204
 Earlier sketch in SATA 148
McDonald, Jill (Masefield) 1927-1982 13
 Obituary 29
McDonald, Joyce 1946- 164
 Earlier sketch in SATA 101
McDonald, Lucile Saunders 1898-1992 10
McDonald, Mary Ann 1956- 84
McDonald, Megan 1958- 202
 Autobiography Feature 151
 Earlier sketches in SATA 67, 99, 148, 151
 See also CLR 94
McDonald, Meme 1954- 112
McDonald, Mercedes 1956- 169
 Earlier sketch in SATA 97
McDonald, Rae A. 1952- 201
McDonell, Chris 1960- 138
McDonnell, Christine 1949- 115
 Earlier sketch in SATA 34
McDonnell, Flora (Mary) 1963- 146
 Earlier sketch in SATA 90
McDonnell, Kathleen 1947- 186
McDonnell, Lois Eddy 1914-2001 10
McDonnell, Patrick 1956- 179
McDonough, Yona Zeldis 1957- 73
McElligott, Matt 1968- 196
 Earlier sketch in SATA 135
McElligott, Matthew
 See McElligott, Matt
McElmeel, Sharron L. 1942- 128
McElmurry, Jill 198
 Earlier sketch in SATA 159
McElrath, William N. 1932- 65
McElrath-Eslick, Lori 1960- 204
 Earlier sketch in SATA 96
McEntee, Dorothy (Layng) 1902- 37
McEwen, Katherine 183
McEwen, Robert (Lindley) 1926-1980
 Obituary 23
McFadden, Kevin Christopher
 See Pike, Christopher
McFall, Christie 1918- 12
McFall, Gardner 1952- 183
McFarlan, Donald M(aitland) 1915- 59
McFarland, Henry "Hammer"
 See McFarland, Henry O.

McFarland, Henry O. 1934- 143
McFarland, Kenton D(ean) 1920- 11
McFarland, Martha
 See Smith-Ankrom, M. E.
McFarlane, Leslie 1902-1977 100
 Earlier sketches in SATA 31, 1, 65, 67
 See also CLR 118
McFarlane, Leslie Charles
 See McFarlane, Leslie
McFarlane, Peter (William) 1940- 95
McFarlane, Sheryl P. 1954- 86
McFarlane, Todd 1961- 117
McGaw, Jessie Brewer 1913-1997 10
McGee, Barbara 1943- 6
McGee, Marni 163
McGhee, Alison 1960- 196
McGiffin, (Lewis) Lee (Shaffer) 1908-1978 ... 1
McGill, Alice 159
McGill, Ormond 1913- 92
McGinley, Jerry 1948- 116
McGinley, Phyllis 1905-1978 44
 Obituary 24
 Earlier sketch in SATA 2
McGinnis, Lila S(prague) 1924- 44
McGinty, Alice B. 1963- 202
 Earlier sketch in SATA 134
McGivern, Justin 1985- 129
McGivern, Maureen Daly
 See Daly, Maureen
McGivern, Maureen Patricia Daly
 See Daly, Maureen
McGough, Elizabeth (Hemmes) 1934- 33
McGovern, Ann 1930- 132
 Earlier sketches in SATA 8, 69, 70
 See also CLR 50
 See also SAAS 17
McGowen, Thomas E. 1927- 109
 Earlier sketch in SATA 2
McGowen, Tom
 See McGowen, Thomas E.
McGrady, Mike 1933- 6
McGrath, Barbara Barbieri 1953- 169
 Earlier sketch in SATA 108
McGrath, Robin 1949- 121
McGrath, Thomas (Matthew) 1916-1990 41
 Obituary 66
McGraw, Eloise Jarvis 1915-2000 67
 Obituary 123
 Earlier sketch in SATA 1
 See also SAAS 6
McGraw, William Corbin 1916-1999 3
McGreal, Elizabeth
 See Yates, Elizabeth
McGregor, Barbara 1959- 82
McGregor, Craig 1933- 8
McGregor, Iona 1929- 25
McGrory, Anik 193
McGuffey, Alexander Hamilton 1816-1896 . 60
McGuigan, Mary Ann 1949- 106
McGuire, Edna 1899- 13
McGuire, Leslie (Sarah) 1945- 94
 Brief entry 45
 Earlier sketch in SATA 52
McGuire, Robert 187
McGuirk, Leslie (A.) 1960- 152
McGurk, Slater
 See Roth, Arthur J(oseph)
McHargue, Georgess 1941- 77
 Earlier sketch in SATA 4
 See also CLR 2
 See also SAAS 5
McHenry, E.B. 1963(?)- 193
McHugh, (Berit) Elisabet 1941- 55
 Brief entry 44
McIlvaine, Jane
 See McClary, Jane Stevenson
McIlwraith, Maureen Mollie Hunter
 See Hunter, Mollie
McInerney, Judith W(hitelock) 1945- 49
 Brief entry 46
McInerny, Ralph 1929- 93

McInerny, Ralph Matthew
See McInerny, Ralph
McKaughan, Larry (Scott) 1941- 75
McKay, Donald 1895- 45
McKay, Hilary (Jane) 1959- 145
Earlier sketch in SATA 92
See also SAAS 23
McKay, Lawrence, Jr. 1948- 114
McKay, Robert W. 1921- 15
McKay, Sharon E. 1954- 165
McKay, Simon
See Nicole, Christopher (Robin)
McKean, Dave 1963- 197
McKean, David Jeff
See McKean, Dave
McKeating, Eileen 1957- 81
McKee, David (John) 1935- 158
Earlier sketches in SATA 70, 107
See also CLR 38
McKee, Tim 1970- 111
McKeever, Marcia
See Laird, Jean E(louise)
McKelvey, Carole A. 1942- 78
McKelvy, Charles 1950- 124
McKendrick, Melveena (Christine) 1941- 55
McKendry, Joe 1972- 170
McKenna, Colleen O'Shaughnessy 1948- .. 136
Earlier sketch in SATA 76
McKenzie, Dorothy Clayton 1910-1981
Obituary 28
McKenzie, Ellen Kindt 1928- 80
McKernan, Victoria 1957- 171
McKie, Robin 112
McKillip, Patricia A. 1948- 174
Earlier sketches in SATA 30, 80, 126
McKillip, Patricia Anne
See McKillip, Patricia A.
McKim, Audrey Margaret 1909-1999 47
McKimmie, Chris 194
McKinley, Jennifer Carolyn Robin
See McKinley, Robin
McKinley, Robin 1952- 195
Brief entry 32
Earlier sketches in SATA 50, 89, 130
See also CLR 127
McKinney, Barbara Shaw 1951- 116
McKinney, Nadine 1938- 91
McKinty, Adrian 186
McKissack, Fredrick L. 1939- 162
Brief entry 53
Earlier sketches in SATA 73, 117
See also CLR 55
McKissack, Fredrick Lemuel
See McKissack, Fredrick L.
McKissack, Patricia C. 1944- 195
Earlier sketches in SATA 51, 73, 117, 162
See also CLR 129
McKissack, Patricia L'Ann Carwell
See McKissack, Patricia C.
McKissack and McKissack
See McKissack, Fredrick L.
and McKissack, Patricia C.
McKown, Robin (?)-1976 6
McKy, Katie 1956- 184
McLaren, Clemence 1938- 158
Earlier sketch in SATA 105
McLaughlin, Frank 1934- 73
McLaurin, Anne 1953- 27
McLean, Andrew 1946- 172
Earlier sketch in SATA 113
McLean, J. Sloan
See Gillette, Virginia M(ary)
and Wunsch, Josephine (McLean)
McLean, Jacqueline
See Kolosov, Jacqueline
McLean, Janet 1946- 113
McLean, Kathryn (Anderson) 1909-1966 9
McLean, Virginia Overton 1946- 90
McLean-Carr, Carol 1948- 122
McLeish, Kenneth 1940-1997 35

McLenighan, Valjean 1947- 46
Brief entry 40
McLennan, Connie 171
McLennan, Will
See Wisler, G(ary) Clifton
McLeod, Bob 1951- 173
McLeod, Chum 1955- 95
McLeod, Emilie Warren 1926-1982 23
Obituary 31
McLeod, Kirsty
See Hudson, (Margaret) Kirsty
McLeod, Margaret Vail
See Holloway, Teresa (Bragunier)
McLerran, Alice 1933- 137
Earlier sketch in SATA 68
McLimans, David 1949- 182
McLoughlin, John C. 1949- 47
McManus, Patrick F. 1933- 46
McManus, Patrick Francis
See McManus, Patrick F.
McMeekin, Clark
See McMeekin, Isabel McLennan
McMeekin, Isabel McLennan 1895-1973 3
McMenemy, Sarah 1965- 156
McMillan, Bruce 1947- 192
Earlier sketches in SATA 22, 70, 129
See also CLR 47
McMillan, Naomi
See Grimes, Nikki
McMorey, James L.
See Moyer, Terry J.
McMorrow, Annalisa 1969- 104
McMullan, Jim 1934- 150
Earlier sketch in SATA 87
McMullan, K. H.
See McMullan, Kate
McMullan, Kate 1947- 189
Brief entry 48
Earlier sketches in SATA 52, 87, 132
McMullan, Kate Hall
See McMullan, Kate
McMullan, Margaret 1960- 203
McMurtrey, Martin A(loysias) 1921- 21
McNabb, Linda 1963- 147
McNair, Kate 3
McNair, Sylvia 1924-2002 74
McNamara, Margaret C(raig) 1915-1981
Obituary 24
McNaught, Harry 32
McNaughton, Colin 1951- 134
Earlier sketches in SATA 39, 92
See also CLR 54
McNaughton, Janet 1953- 162
Earlier sketch in SATA 110
McNeal, Laura 194
McNeal, Tom 194
McNeely, Jeannette 1918- 25
McNeer, May (Yonge) 1902-1994 81
Earlier sketch in SATA 1
McNeese, Tim 1953- 139
McNeill, Janet
See Alexander, Janet
McNicholas, Shelagh 191
McNickle, (William) D'Arcy 1904-1977
Obituary 22
McNicoll, Sylvia (Marilyn) 1954- 113
See also CLR 99
McNulty, Faith 1918-2005 168
Earlier sketches in SATA 12, 84, 139
McPhail, David 1940- 183
Brief entry 32
Earlier sketches in SATA 47, 81, 140
McPhail, David M.
See McPhail, David
McPhail, David Michael
See McPhail, David
McPhee, Norma H. 1928- 95
McPhee, Richard B(yron) 1934- 41
McPherson, James M. 1936- 141
Earlier sketch in SATA 16

McPherson, James Munro
See McPherson, James M.
McQueen, Lucinda 1950- 58
Brief entry 48
McQueen, Mildred Hark 1908-1978 12
McQuillan, Mary 200
McRae, Russell (William) 1934- 63
McShean, Gordon 1936- 41
Mc Swigan, Marie 1907-1962 24
McTavish, Sandy
See Eyerly, Jeannette
McVeity, Jen 148
McVey, Vicki 1946- 80
McVicker, Charles (Taggart) 1930- 39
McVicker, Chuck
See McVicker, Charles (Taggart)
McWhirter, A(lan) Ross 1925-1975 37
Obituary 31
McWhirter, Norris (Dewar) 1925-2004 37
McWilliams, Karen 1943- 65
Mdurvwa, Hajara E. 1962- 92
Meacham, Margaret 1952- 203
Earlier sketch in SATA 95
Meachum, Virginia 1918- 133
Earlier sketch in SATA 87
Mead, Alice 1952- 146
Earlier sketch in SATA 94
Mead, Margaret 1901-1978
Obituary 20
Mead, Russell (M., Jr.) 1935- 10
Mead, Stella (?)-1981
Obituary 27
Meade, Ellen
See Roddick, Ellen
Meade, Marion 1934- 127
Earlier sketch in SATA 23
Meader, Stephen W(arren) 1892-1977 1
Meadmore, Susan
See Sallis, Susan (Diana)
Meadow, Charles T(roub) 1929- 23
Meadowcroft, Enid LaMonte
See Wright, Enid Meadowcroft (LaMonte)
Meadows, Graham (W.) 1934- 161
Meadows, Michelle 202
Meaker, M. J.
See Meaker, Marijane
Meaker, Marijane 1927- 160
Autobiography Feature 111
Earlier sketches in SATA 20, 61, 99
See also CLR 29
See also SAAS 1
Meaker, Marijane Agnes
See Meaker, Marijane
Means, Florence Crannell 1891-1980 1
Obituary 25
See also CLR 56
Mearian, Judy Frank 1936- 49
Mecca, Judy Truesdell 1955- 127
Mechling, Lauren 1978(?)- 194
Mechner, Jordan 1964- 205
Medary, Marjorie 1890-1980 14
Meddaugh, Susan 1944- 176
Earlier sketches in SATA 29, 84, 125
Medearis, Angela Shelf 1956- 123
Earlier sketch in SATA 72
Medearis, Mary 1915- 5
Medina, Jane 1953- 167
Earlier sketch in SATA 122
Medina, Nico 1982- 193
Medlicott, Mary 1946- 88
Mee, Charles L., Jr. 1938- 72
Earlier sketch in SATA 8
Meehl, Brian 204
Meek, Jacklyn O'Hanlon 1933- 51
Brief entry 34
Meek, S(terner St.) P(aul) 1894-1972
Obituary 28
Meeker, Clare Hodgson 1952- 96
Meeker, Oden 1919(?)-1976 14
Meeker, Richard
See Brown, Fornan

Meeks, Esther MacBain 1
Meggs, Libby Phillips 1943- 130
Mehdevi, Alexander (Sinclair) 1947- 7
Mehdevi, Anne (Marie) Sinclair 1947- 8
Meidell, Sherry 1951- 73
Meier, Minta 1906- 55
Meighan, Donald Charles 1929- 30
Meigs, Cornelia Lynde 1884-1973 6
   See also CLR 55
Meilach, Dona Z(weigoron) 1926- 34
Meilman, Philip W(arren) 1951- 79
Meinstereifel, Ronald L. 1960- 134
Meisel, Paul 184
Meister, Cari 204
Melanson, Luc 198
Melcher, Daniel 1912-1985
   Obituary 43
Melcher, Frederic Gershom 1879-1963
   Obituary 22
Melcher, Marguerite Fellows 1879-1969 10
Meldrum, Christina 206
Melendez, Francisco 1964- 72
Melhuish, Eva 199
Melin, Grace Hathaway 1892-1973 10
Mellersh, H(arold) E(dward) L(eslie)
   1897- 10
Melling, David 186
Melmoth, Sebastian
   See Wilde, Oscar
Melnikoff, Pamela (Rita) 97
Meltzer, Amy 1968- 202
Meltzer, Milton 1915-2009 201
   Autobiography Feature 124
   Earlier sketches in SATA *1, 50, 80, 128*
   See also CLR 13
   See also SAAS 1
Melville, Anne
   See Potter, Margaret
Melville, Herman 1819-1891 59
Melwood, Mary
   See Lewis, E. M.
Melzack, Ronald 1929- 5
Memling, Carl 1918-1969 6
Menchin, Scott 188
Mendel, Jo
   See Bond, Gladys Baker
   and Gilbertson, Mildred Geiger
Mendelson, Steven T. 1958-1995 86
Mendelson-Stevens, Serita Deborah
   See Stevens, Serita
Mendes, Valerie 1939- 157
Mendez, Raymond A. 1947- 66
Mendonca, Susan
   See Smith, Susan Vernon
Mendoza, George 1934- 41
   Brief entry 39
   See also SAAS 7
Menendez, Shirley (C.) 1937- 146
Meng, Cece 194
Meng, Heinz (Karl) 1924- 13
Mennen, Ingrid 1954- 85
Menotti, Gian Carlo 1911-2007 29
   Obituary 180
Menuhin, Sir Yehudi 1916-1999 40
   Obituary 113
Menville, Douglas 1935- 64
Menzel, Barbara Jean 1946- 63
Mercati, Cynthia 164
Mercati, Cynthia J.
   See Mercati, Cynthia
Mercer, Charles (Edward) 1917-1988 16
   Obituary 61
Mercer, Jessie 21
Mercer, Sienna 192
Meredith, Arnold
   See Hopkins, (Hector) Kenneth
Meredith, David William
   See Miers, Earl Schenck
Meringoff, Laurene Krasny
   See Brown, Laurene Krasny

Meriwether, Louise 1923- 52
   Brief entry 31
Merlin, Arthur
   See Blish, James
Merlin, Christina
   See Heaven, Constance (Christina)
Merriam, Eve 1916-1992 73
   Earlier sketches in SATA *3, 40*
   See also CLR *14*
Merrill, Jane 1946- 42
Merrill, Jane Merrill
   See Merrill, Jane
Merrill, Jean (Fairbanks) 1923- 82
   Earlier sketch in SATA *1*
   See also CLR 52
Merrill, Phil
   See Merrill, Jane
Merriman, Alex
   See Silverberg, Robert
Merriman, Rachel 1971- 149
   Earlier sketch in SATA *98*
Merrit, Elizabeth
   See Goudge, Eileen
Merski, Patricia K.
   See Merski, P.K.
Merski, P.K. 172
Mertz, Barbara
   See Peters, Elizabeth
Mertz, Barbara Gross
   See Peters, Elizabeth
Merveille, David 200
Merz, Jennifer J. 196
Meschel, Susan V. 1936- 83
Messenger, Charles (Rynd Milles) 1942- 59
Messick, Dale 1906-2005 64
   Brief entry 48
Messier, Claire 1956- 103
Messieres, Nicole de
   See de Messieres, Nicole
Messinger, Carla 198
Messmer, Otto 1892(?)-1983 37
Mesta, Gabriel
   See Moesta, Rebecca
Metcalf, Doris H(unter) 91
Metcalf, Suzanne
   See Baum, L. Frank
Metos, Thomas H(arry) 1932- 37
Metter, Bert(ram Milton) 1927- 56
Metzenthen, David 1958- 167
   Earlier sketch in SATA *106*
Meunier, Brian 1954- 195
Meyer, Barbara 1939- 77
Meyer, Carolyn 1935- 142
   Autobiography Feature 142
   Earlier sketches in SATA *9, 70, 118*
   See also SAAS 9
Meyer, Carolyn Mae
   See Meyer, Carolyn
Meyer, Edith Patterson 1895-1993 5
Meyer, F(ranklyn) E(dward) 1932- 9
Meyer, Jean Shepherd 11
Meyer, Jerome Sydney 1895-1975 3
   Obituary 25
Meyer, June
   See Jordan, June
Meyer, Kerstin 1966- 190
Meyer, L. A.
   See Meyer, Louis A(lbert), Jr.
Meyer, Louis A(lbert), Jr. 1942- 144
   Earlier sketch in SATA *12*
Meyer, Renate 1930- 6
Meyer, Stephenie 1973- 193
   See also CLR 142
Meyer, Susan E. 1940- 64
Meyers, Susan 1942- 164
   Earlier sketches in SATA *19, 108*
Meynell, Laurence Walter 1899-1989
   Obituary 61
Meynier, Yvonne (Pollet) 1908- 14
Mezey, Robert 1935- 33
Micale, Albert 1913- 22

Michael, James
   See Scagnetti, Jack
Michael, Livi 1960- 172
Michael, Manfred
   See Winterfeld, Henry
Michael, Olivia
   See Michael, Livi
Michaels, Barbara
   See Peters, Elizabeth
Michaels, Jamie 195
Michaels, Joanne Louise
   See Teitelbaum, Michael
Michaels, Kristin
   See Williams, Jeanne
Michaels, Molly
   See Untermeyer, Louis
Michaels, Neal
   See Teitelbaum, Michael
Michaels, Rune 194
Michaels, Ski
   See Pellowski, Michael (Joseph)
Michaels, Steve 1955- 71
Michaels, William M. 1917- 77
Michel, Anna 1943- 49
   Brief entry 40
Michel, Francois 1948- 82
Michelin, Linda 183
Michelson, Richard 198
   Earlier sketch in SATA *173*
Micich, Paul 74
Micklish, Rita 1931- 12
Micklos, John, Jr. 1956- 173
   Earlier sketch in SATA *129*
Micklos J., John, Jr. 1956-
   See Micklos, John, Jr.
Micucci, Charles (Patrick, Jr.) 1959- 144
   Earlier sketch in SATA *82*
Middleton, Haydn 1955- 152
   Earlier sketch in SATA *85*
Miers, Earl Schenck 1910-1972 1
   Obituary 26
Migdale, Lawrence 1951- 89
Miglio, Paige 1966- 201
Mikaelsen, Ben 1952- 173
   Earlier sketches in SATA *73, 107*
Mikaelsen, Benjamin John
   See Mikaelsen, Ben
Miklowitz, Gloria D. 1927- 129
   Earlier sketches in SATA *4, 68*
   See also SAAS 17
Mikolaycak, Charles 1937-1993 78
   Obituary 75
   Earlier sketch in SATA *9*
   See also SAAS 4
Mild, Warren (Paul) 1922- 41
Milelli, Pascal 1965- 135
Miles, Betty 1928- 78
   Earlier sketch in SATA *8*
   See also SAAS 9
Miles, Miska
   See Martin, Patricia Miles
Miles, (Mary) Patricia 1930- 29
Miles, Patricia A.
   See Martin, Patricia Miles
Miles, Victoria 1966- 188
Milgrim, David 187
   Earlier sketch in SATA *158*
Milgrom, Harry 1912-1978 25
Milhous, Katherine 1894-1977 15
Milich, Zoran 174
Milios, Rita 1949- 79
Militant
   See Sandburg, Carl (August)
Millais, Raoul 1901- 77
Millar, Barbara F. 1924- 12
Millar, Margaret (Ellis Sturm) 1915-1994 61
   Obituary 79
Millard, Glenda 203
Millard, Kerry 204
Millbank, Captain H. R.
   See Ellis, Edward S.

Millen, C(ynthia) M. 1955- *114*
Miller, Albert G(riffith) 1905-1982 .... *12*
  Obituary *31*
Miller, Alice Ann 1958- *150*
Miller, Alice P(atricia McCarthy) *22*
Miller, Debbie 1951- *160*
  Earlier sketch in SATA *103*
Miller, Debbie S.
  See Miller, Debbie
Miller, Deborah Uchill 1944- *61*
Miller, Don 1923- *15*
Miller, Doris R.
  See Mosesson, Gloria R(ubin)
Miller, Eddie
  See Miller, Edward
Miller, Edna Anita 1920- *29*
Miller, Edward 1905-1974 .... *8*
Miller, Edward 1964- *183*
Miller, Elizabeth 1933- *41*
Miller, Ellanita 1957- *87*
Miller, Eugene 1925- *33*
Miller, Frances A. 1937- *52*
  Brief entry *46*
Miller, Helen M(arkley) -1984 .... *5*
Miller, Helen Topping 1884-1960
  Obituary *29*
Miller, Jane (Judith) 1925-1989 .... *15*
Miller, Jewel 1956- *73*
Miller, John
  See Samachson, Joseph
Miller, Judi *117*
Miller, Kate 1948- *193*
Miller, Kirsten 1973- *185*
Miller, Louise (Rolfe) 1940- *76*
Miller, M. L. *85*
Miller, Madge 1918- *63*
Miller, Margaret J.
  See Dale, Margaret J(essy) Miller
Miller, Marilyn (Jean) 1925- *33*
Miller, Marvin *65*
Miller, Mary
  See Northcott, (William) Cecil
Miller, Mary Beth 1942- *9*
Miller, Mary Beth 1964- *185*
Miller, Maryann 1943- *73*
Miller, Natalie 1917-1976 .... *35*
Miller, Robert H. 1944- *91*
Miller, Ron 1947- *185*
Miller, Ruth White
  See White, Ruth C.
Miller, Sandra
  See Miller, Sandy
Miller, Sandra Peden
  See Miller, Sandy
Miller, Sandy 1948- *41*
  Brief entry *35*
Miller, Sarah 1969- *175*
Miller, Virginia
  See Austin, Virginia
Miller, William R. 1959- *116*
Milligan, Bryce 1953- *170*
Milligan, Spike
  See Milligan, Terence Alan
Milligan, Terence Alan 1918-2002 .... *29*
  Obituary *134*
  See also CLR *92*
Millington, Ada
  See Deyneka, Anita
Millman, Isaac 1933- *140*
Mills, Adam
  See Stanley, George Edward
Mills, Claudia 1954- *191*
  Brief entry *41*
  Earlier sketches in SATA *44, 89, 145*
Mills, Elaine (Rosemary) 1941- *72*
Mills, G. Riley *196*
Mills, Joyce C. 1944- *102*
Mills, Judith Christine 1956- *130*
Mills, Yaroslava Surmach 1925- *35*
Millspaugh, Ben P. 1936- *77*
Millstead, Thomas E. *30*

Millward, Gwen *202*
Milne, A. A. 1882-1956 .... *100*
  See also YABC *1*
  See also CLR *108*
Milne, Alan Alexander
  See Milne, A. A.
Milne, Lorus J. *5*
  See also CLR *22*
  See also SAAS *18*
Milne, Margery *5*
  See also CLR *22*
  See also SAAS *18*
Milne, Terry
  See Milne, Theresa Ann
Milne, Theresa Ann 1964- *84*
Milnes, Irma McDonough 1924- *101*
Milonas, Rolf
  See Myller, Rolf
Milone, Karen
  See Dugan, Karen
Milone-Dugan, Karen
  See Dugan, Karen
Milord, Susan 1954- *200*
  Earlier sketches in SATA *74, 147*
Milotte, Alfred G(eorge) 1904-1989 .... *11*
  Obituary *62*
Milstein, Linda 1954- *80*
Milton, Ann *134*
Milton, Hilary (Herbert) 1920- *23*
Milton, John R(onald) 1924- *24*
Milton, Joyce 1946- *101*
  Brief entry *41*
  Earlier sketch in SATA *52*
Milverton, Charles A.
  See Penzler, Otto
Milway, Katie Smith 1960- *203*
Minahan, John A. 1956- *92*
Minar, Barbra (Goodyear) 1940- *79*
Minard, Rosemary 1939- *63*
Minarik, Else Holmelund 1920- *127*
  Earlier sketch in SATA *15*
  See also CLR *33*
Miner, Jane Claypool 1933- *103*
  Brief entry *37*
  Earlier sketch in SATA *38*
Miner, Lewis S. 1909-1971 .... *11*
Mines, Jeanette 1948- *61*
Mines, Jeanette Marie
  See Mines, Jeanette
Minier, Nelson
  See Stoutenburg, Adrien (Pearl)
Minnitt, Ronda Jacqueline
  See Armitage, David
Minor, Wendell 1944- *199*
  Earlier sketches in SATA *78, 109, 164*
Minter, Daniel 1961- *176*
Mintonye, Grace *4*
Miranda, Anne 1954- *109*
  Earlier sketch in SATA *71*
Mirocha, Paul *192*
Mirsky, Jeannette 1903-1987 .... *8*
  Obituary *51*
Mirsky, Reba Paeff 1902-1966 .... *1*
Misako Rocks! *192*
Mishica, Clare 1960- *91*
Miskovits, Christine 1939- *10*
Miss Frances
  See Horwich, Frances R(appaport)
Miss Read
  See Saint, Dora Jessie
Mister Rogers
  See Rogers, Fred McFeely
Mitchard, Jacquelyn 1956- *168*
  Earlier sketch in SATA *98*
Mitchell, Adrian 1932-2008 .... *166*
  Obituary *200*
  Earlier sketch in SATA *104*
Mitchell, Allison
  See Griffin, W.E.B.
Mitchell, Betty Jo
  See Mitchell, B.J.

Mitchell, B.J. 1931- *120*
Mitchell, Clyde
  See Ellison, Harlan
  and Silverberg, Robert
Mitchell, Cynthia 1922- *29*
Mitchell, (Sibyl) Elyne (Keith) 1913- *10*
Mitchell, Gladys (Maude Winifred)
  1901-1983 .... *46*
  Obituary *35*
Mitchell, Jay
  See Roberson, Jennifer
Mitchell, Joyce Slayton 1933- *142*
  Brief entry *43*
  Earlier sketch in SATA *46*
Mitchell, K. L.
  See Lamb, Elizabeth Searle
Mitchell, Kathy 1948- *59*
Mitchell, Lori 1961- *128*
Mitchell, Margaree King 1953- *84*
Mitchell, Marianne 1947- *145*
Mitchell, Rhonda *89*
Mitchell, Stephen 1943- *199*
Mitchell, Todd 1974- *191*
Mitchell, Yvonne 1925-1979
  Obituary *24*
Mitchelson, Mitch
  See Mitchelson, Peter Richard
Mitchelson, Peter Richard 1950- *104*
Mitchison, Naomi (Margaret Haldane)
  1897-1999 .... *24*
  Obituary *112*
Mitchnik, Helen 1901-1982 .... *41*
  Brief entry *35*
Mitchum, Hank
  See Knott, William C(ecil, Jr.)
  and Murray, Stuart A. P.
  and Newton, D(wight) B(ennett)
  and Sherman, Jory (Tecumseh)
Mitgutsch, Ali 1935- *76*
Mitsuhashi, Yoko *45*
  Brief entry *33*
Mitton, Jacqueline 1948- *162*
  Earlier sketches in SATA *66, 115*
Mitton, Simon 1946- *66*
Mitton, Tony 1951- *203*
  Earlier sketches in SATA *104, 149*
Miura, Taro 1968- *181*
Mizner, Elizabeth Howard 1907- *27*
Mizumura, Kazue *18*
Mlynowski, Sarah 1977(?)- *180*
Mobin-Uddin, Asma *172*
Mobley, Joe A. 1945- *91*
Moche, Dinah (Rachel) L(evine) 1936- *44*
  Brief entry *40*
Mochi, Ugo (A.) 1889-1977 .... *38*
Mochizuki, Ken 1954- *146*
  Earlier sketch in SATA *81*
  See also SAAS *22*
Modarressi, Mitra 1967- *200*
  Earlier sketch in SATA *126*
Modell, Frank B. 1917- *39*
  Brief entry *36*
Modesitt, Jeanne 1953- *143*
  Earlier sketch in SATA *92*
Modesitt, L.E., Jr. 1943- *164*
  Earlier sketch in SATA *91*
Modesitt, Leland Exton, Jr.
  See Modesitt, L.E., Jr.
Modrell, Dolores 1933- *72*
Moe, Barbara 1937- *20*
Moe, Jorgen (Ingebretsen) 1813-1882
  See CLR *104*
Moed-Kass, Pnina *169*
Moerbeek, Kees 1955- *98*
Moeri, Louise 1924- *93*
  Earlier sketch in SATA *24*
  See also SAAS *10*
Moesta, Rebecca 1956- *182*
Moffett, Jami 1952- *84*
Moffett, Mark W. 1957(?)- *203*
Moffett, Martha (Leatherwood) 1934- *8*

Mogensen, Suzanne A(ncher) 1946- *129*
Mohammed, Khadra *197*
Mohn, Peter B(urnet) 1934- *28*
Mohn, Viola Kohl 1914- *8*
Mohr, Nicholasa 1938- *97*
   Autobiography Feature *113*
   Earlier sketch in SATA *8*
   See also CLR *22*
   See also SAAS *8*
Mok, Esther 1953- *93*
Molan, Christine 1943- *84*
Molarsky, Osmond 1909- *16*
Moldon, Peter L(eonard) 1937- *49*
Mole, John 1941- *103*
   Earlier sketch in SATA *36*
   See also CLR *61*
Molesworth, Mary Louisa 1839-1921 .... *98*
Molin, Charles
   See Mayne, William (James Carter)
Molina, Silvia 1946- *97*
Molk, Laurel 1957- *162*
   Earlier sketch in SATA *92*
Mollel, Tololwa M. 1952- *88*
Molloy, Anne Baker 1907-1999 .... *32*
Molloy, Michael (John) 1940- *162*
Molloy, Paul (George) 1924- *5*
Moloney, James 1954- *202*
   Autobiography Feature *144*
   Earlier sketches in SATA *94, 144*
Momaday, N. Scott 1934- *48*
   Brief entry *30*
Momaday, Navarre Scott
   See Momaday, N. Scott
Monaco, Octavia 1963- *169*
Monagle, Bernie 1957- *121*
Moncure, Jane Belk 1926- *23*
Monjo, F(erdinand) N(icholas III)
   1924-1978 .... *16*
   See also CLR *2*
Monk, Isabell 1952- *136*
Monks, Lydia *189*
Monroe, Lyle
   See Heinlein, Robert A.
Monroe, Marion
   See Cox, Marion Monroe
Monroy, Manuel 1970- *196*
Monsell, Helen Albee 1895-1971 .... *24*
Monson-Burton, Marianne 1975- *139*
Montana, Bob 1920-1975
   Obituary *21*
Montecalvo, Janet *177*
Montenegro, Laura Nyman 1953- *95*
Montero, Gloria 1933- *109*
Montes, Marisa 1951- *144*
Montgomerie, Norah (Mary) 1913- *26*
Montgomery, Constance
   See Cappel, Constance
Montgomery, Elizabeth
   See Julesberg, Elizabeth Rider Montgomery
Montgomery, Elizabeth Rider
   See Julesberg, Elizabeth Rider Montgomery
Montgomery, Hugh (Edward) 1962- *146*
Montgomery, L(ucy) M(aud) 1874-1942 .... *100*
   See also YABC *1*
   See also CLR *145*
Montgomery, Raymond A. (Jr.) 1936- *39*
Montgomery, Rutherford George 1894-1985 . *3*
Montgomery, Sy 1958- *184*
   Autobiography Feature *132*
   Earlier sketches in SATA *114, 132*
Montgomery, Vivian *36*
Monthei, Betty *179*
Montijo, Rhode *179*
Montileaux, Donald F. 1948- *183*
Montpetit, Charles 1958- *101*
Montresor, Beni 1926-2001 .... *38*
   Earlier sketch in SATA *3*
   See also SAAS *4*
Montserrat, Pep *181*

Monty Python
   See Chapman, Graham
   and Cleese, John (Marwood)
   and Gilliam, Terry
   and Idle, Eric
   and Jones, Terence Graham Parry
   and Palin, Michael
Moodie, Craig 1956- *172*
Moodie, Fiona 1952- *133*
Moody, Minerva
   See Alcott, Louisa May
Moody, Ralph Owen 1898-1982 .... *1*
Moon, Carl 1879(?)-1948 .... *25*
Moon, Grace (Purdie) 1877(?)-1947 .... *25*
Moon, Lily
   See Warnes, Tim
Moon, Nicola 1952- *147*
   Earlier sketch in SATA *96*
Moon, Pat 1946- *113*
Moon, Sheila 1910-1991 .... *5*
   Obituary *114*
Moon, Sheila Elizabeth
   See Moon, Sheila
Mooney, Bel 1946- *95*
Mooney, Bill 1936- *122*
Mooney, Elizabeth C(omstock) 1918-1986
   Obituary *48*
Mooney, William
   See Mooney, Bill
Moor, Emily
   See Deming, Richard
Moorcock, Michael 1939- *166*
   Earlier sketch in SATA *93*
Moorcock, Michael John
   See Moorcock, Michael
Moore, Anne Carroll 1871-1961 .... *13*
Moore, Cheri
   See Ladd, Cheryl (Jean)
Moore, Clement Clarke 1779-1863 .... *18*
Moore, Cyd 1957- *186*
   Earlier sketches in SATA *83, 133*
Moore, Don W. 1905(?)-1986
   Obituary *48*
Moore, Elaine 1944- *86*
Moore, Eva 1942- *103*
   Earlier sketch in SATA *20*
Moore, Ishbel (Lindsay) 1954- *140*
Moore, Jack (William) 1941- *46*
   Brief entry *32*
Moore, Janet Gaylord 1905-1992 .... *18*
Moore, Jim 1946- *42*
Moore, John Travers 1908- *12*
Moore, Lilian 1909-2004 .... *137*
   Obituary *155*
   Earlier sketch in SATA *52*
   See also CLR *15*
Moore, Liz
   See Moore, M. Elizabeth
Moore, M. Elizabeth 1959- *156*
Moore, Margaret R(umberger) 1903- *12*
Moore, Margie *176*
Moore, Marianne (Craig) 1887-1972 .... *20*
Moore, Patrick (Alfred Caldwell) 1923- *49*
   Brief entry *39*
   See also SAAS *8*
Moore, Patrick 1959- *184*
Moore, Perry *193*
Moore, Peter 1963- *175*
Moore, Peter G.
   See Moore, Peter
Moore, Ray (S.) 1905(?)-1984
   Obituary *37*
Moore, Regina
   See Dunne, Mary Collins
Moore, Rosalie (Gertrude) 1910-2001 .... *9*
Moore, Ruth (Ellen) 1908-1989 .... *23*
Moore, Ruth Nulton 1923- *38*
Moore, S(arah) E. *23*
Moore, Sarah Margaret
   See Hodges, Margaret
Moore, Tara 1950- *61*

Moore, Yvette 1958- *154*
   Earlier sketches in SATA *69, 70*
Moores, Dick
   See Moores, Richard (Arnold)
Moores, Richard (Arnold) 1909-1986
   Obituary *48*
Mooser, Stephen 1941- *75*
   Earlier sketch in SATA *28*
Mora, Francisco X(avier) 1952- *90*
Mora, Pat 1942- *186*
   Earlier sketches in SATA *92, 134*
   See also CLR *58*
Mora, Patricia
   See Mora, Pat
Morales, Yuyi *180*
   Earlier sketch in SATA *154*
Moran, Tom 1943- *60*
Moranville, Sharelle Byars *196*
   Earlier sketch in SATA *152*
Moray Williams, Ursula 1911-2006 .... *3*
   Obituary *177*
   See also SAAS *9*
Mordvinoff, Nicolas 1911-1973 .... *17*
More, Caroline
   See Cone, Molly (Lamken)
   and Strachan, Margaret Pitcairn
Moreno, Rene King *190*
Moreton, Andrew Esq.
   See Defoe, Daniel
Morey, Charles
   See Fletcher, Helen Jill
Morey, Walt(er Nelson) 1907-1992 .... *51*
   Obituary *70*
   Earlier sketch in SATA *3*
   See also SAAS *9*
Morgan, Alfred P(owell) 1889-1972 .... *33*
Morgan, Alison (Mary) 1930- *85*
   Earlier sketch in SATA *30*
Morgan, Anne 1954- *121*
Morgan, Christopher 1956- *199*
Morgan, Clay 1950- *198*
Morgan, Douglas
   See Macdonald, James D.
Morgan, Ellen
   See Bumstead, Kathleen Mary
Morgan, Geoffrey 1916- *46*
Morgan, Helen (Gertrude Louise)
   1921-1990 .... *29*
Morgan, Jane
   See Cooper, James Fenimore
   and Franklin, Jane (Morgan)
   and Moren, Sally M(oore)
Morgan, Lenore H. 1908-1976 .... *8*
Morgan, Mary 1957- *114*
   Earlier sketch in SATA *81*
Morgan, McKayla
   See Basile, Gloria Vitanza
Morgan, Michaela
   See Basile, Gloria Vitanza
Morgan, Nicola 1961- *161*
Morgan, Nina 1953- *110*
Morgan, Pierr 1952- *122*
   Earlier sketch in SATA *77*
Morgan, Robin (Evonne) 1941- *80*
Morgan, Roxanne
   See Gentle, Mary
Morgan, Sarah (Nicola) 1959- *68*
Morgan, Shirley
   See Kiepper, Shirley Morgan
Morgan, Stacy T(owle) 1959- *104*
Morgan, Stevie
   See Davies, Nicola
Morgan, Tom 1942- *42*
Morgan, Wendy
   See Staub, Wendy Corsi
Morgan-Vanroyen, Mary
   See Morgan, Mary
Morgenstern, Susie Hoch 1945- *133*
Mori, Hana 1909-1990(?) *88*

Mori, Kyoko 1957- *122*
  Autobiography Feature *126*
  See also CLR *64*
  See also SAAS *26*
Moriarty, Jaclyn *162*
Moriarty, William J. 1930- *127*
Morice, Dave 1946- *93*
Morin, Isobel V. 1928- *110*
Morine, Hoder
  See Conroy, John Wesley
Morley, Taia *199*
Morley, Wilfred Owen
  See Lowndes, Robert A(ugustine) W(ard)
Morningstar, Mildred (Whaley) 1912-1997 .. *61*
  Obituary *114*
Morozumi, Atsuko *110*
Morpurgo, Michael 1943- *184*
  Earlier sketches in SATA *93, 143*
  See also CLR *51*
Morrah, Dave
  See Morrah, David Wardlaw, Jr.
Morrah, David Wardlaw, Jr. 1914-1991 .... *10*
Morreale-de la Garza, Phyllis
  See De la Garza, Phyllis
Morressy, John 1930-2006 .... *23*
Morrill, Leslie H(olt) 1934-2003 .... *48*
  Brief entry *33*
  Obituary *148*
  See also SAAS *22*
Morris, Chris(topher Crosby) 1946- *66*
Morris, Deborah 1956- *91*
Morris, Desmond 1928- *14*
Morris, Desmond John
  See Morris, Desmond
Morris, Don 1954- *83*
Morris, Gerald 1963- *150*
  Earlier sketch in SATA *107*
Morris, Gerald Paul
  See Morris, Gerald
Morris, Gilbert (Leslie) 1929- *104*
Morris, Jackie *202*
  Earlier sketch in SATA *151*
Morris, Janet (Ellen) 1946- *66*
Morris, Jay
  See Tatham, Julie Campbell
Morris, (Margaret) Jean 1924- *98*
Morris, Jeffrey B(randon) 1941- *92*
Morris, Jennifer E. 1969- *179*
Morris, Jill 1936- *165*
  Earlier sketch in SATA *119*
Morris, Juddi *85*
Morris, Judy K. 1936- *61*
Morris, Oradel Nolen *128*
Morris, Robert A(da) 1933- *7*
Morris, William 1913-1994 .... *29*
Morrison, Bill 1935- *66*
  Brief entry *37*
Morrison, Chloe Anthony Wofford
  See Morrison, Toni
Morrison, Dorothy Nafus *29*
Morrison, Frank 1971- *185*
Morrison, Gordon 1944- *183*
  Earlier sketches in SATA *87, 128*
Morrison, Joan 1922- *65*
Morrison, Lillian 1917- *108*
  Earlier sketch in SATA *3*
Morrison, Lucile Phillips 1896- *17*
Morrison, Martha A. 1948- *77*
Morrison, Meighan 1966- *90*
Morrison, P.R. *196*
Morrison, Richard
  See Lowndes, Robert A(ugustine) W(ard)
Morrison, Robert
  See Lowndes, Robert A(ugustine) W(ard)
Morrison, Roberta
  See Webb, Jean Francis (III)
Morrison, Susan Dudley
  See Gold, Susan Dudley
Morrison, Taylor 1971- *187*
  Earlier sketches in SATA *95, 159*

Morrison, Toni 1931- *144*
  Earlier sketch in SATA *57*
  See also CLR *99*
Morrison, Velma Ford 1909- *21*
Morrison, Wilbur Howard 1915- *64*
Morrison, William
  See Samachson, Joseph
Morriss, James E(dward) 1932- *8*
Morrissey, Dean *183*
Morrow, Barbara Olenyik 1952- *167*
Morrow, Betty
  See Bacon, Elizabeth
Morse, C. Scott
  See Morse, Scott
Morse, Carol
  See Yeakley, Marjory Hall
Morse, C.S.
  See Morse, Scott
Morse, Dorothy B(ayley) 1906-1979
  Obituary *24*
Morse, Flo 1921- *30*
Morse, Scott 1973- *200*
Morse, Tony 1953- *129*
Mort, Vivian
  See Cromie, Alice Hamilton
Mortensen, Denise Dowling *179*
Mortimer, Anne 1958- *206*
  Earlier sketch in SATA *116*
Mortimer, Mary H.
  See Coury, Louise Andree
Morton, Alexandra (Hubbard) 1957- *144*
Morton, Anthony
  See Arthur, Robert, (Jr.)
Morton, Jane 1931- *50*
Morton, Joseph C. 1932- *156*
Morton, Lee Jack, Jr. 1928- *32*
Morton, Miriam 1918(?)-1985 .... *9*
  Obituary *46*
Mosatche, Harriet
  See Mosatche, Harriet
Mosatche, Harriet 1949- *122*
Moscow, Alvin 1925- *3*
Mosel, Arlene (Tichy) 1921-1996 .... *7*
Moseley, James W(illett) 1931- *139*
Moseng, Elisabeth 1967- *90*
Moser, Barry 1940- *185*
  Earlier sketches in SATA *56, 79, 138*
  See also CLR *49*
  See also SAAS *15*
Moser, Don(ald Bruce) 1932- *31*
Moser, Laura *194*
Moser, Lisa *192*
Moses, Sheila P. 1961- *168*
Moses, Will 1956- *178*
  Earlier sketch in SATA *120*
Mosesson, Gloria R(ubin) *24*
Mosher, Richard 1949- *120*
Moskin, Marietta D(unston) 1928- *23*
Moskof, Martin Stephen 1930- *27*
Mosley, Francis 1957- *57*
Moss, Don(ald) 1920- *11*
Moss, Elaine (Dora) 1924- *57*
  Brief entry *31*
Moss, Jeff(rey) 1942-1998 .... *73*
  Obituary *106*
Moss, Marissa 1959- *163*
  Earlier sketches in SATA *71, 104*
  See also CLR *134*
Moss, Miriam 1955- *202*
  Earlier sketches in SATA *76, 140*
Moss, Thylias 1954- *108*
Moss, Thylias Rebecca Brasier
  See Moss, Thylias
Most, Bernard 1937- *134*
  Brief entry *40*
  Earlier sketches in SATA *48, 91*
Mosz, Gosia 1972- *194*
Mott, Evelyn Clarke 1962- *133*
  Earlier sketch in SATA *75*
Motz, Lloyd 1909-2004 .... *20*
Mould, Chris *205*

Mould, Edwin
  See Whitlock, Ralph
Mouly, Francoise *155*
Mountain, Robert
  See Montgomery, Raymond A. (Jr.)
Mountfield, David
  See Grant, Neil
Mourlevat, Jean-Claude 1952- *187*
Mourning, Tuesday *206*
Moussard, Jacqueline 1924- *24*
Mowat, Claire 1933- *123*
Mowat, Claire Angel Wheeler
  See Mowat, Claire
Mowat, Farley 1921- *55*
  Earlier sketch in SATA *3*
  See also CLR *20*
Mowat, Farley McGill
  See Mowat, Farley
Mowll, Joshua 1970(?)- *188*
Mowry, Jess 1960- *131*
  Autobiography Feature *131*
  Earlier sketch in SATA *109*
  See also CLR *65*
Moxley, Sheila 1966- *96*
Moyer, Terry J. 1937- *94*
Moyes, Patricia
  See Haszard, Patricia Moyes
Moyler, Alan (Frank Powell) 1926- *36*
Mozelle, Shirley *179*
Mozley, Charles 1915- *43*
  Brief entry *32*
Mphahlele, Es'kia 1919-2008 .... *119*
  Obituary *198*
Mphahlele, Ezekiel
  See Mphahlele, Es'kia
Mphahlele, Zeke
  See Mphahlele, Es'kia
Mr. McGillicuddy
  See Abisch, Roslyn Kroop
Mr. Sniff
  See Abisch, Roslyn Kroop
Mr. Tivil
  See Lorkowski, Thomas V(incent)
Mr. Wizard
  See Herbert, Don
Mrs. Fairstar
  See Horne, Richard Henry Hengist
Muchamore, Robert 1972- *175*
Muchmore, Jo Ann 1937- *103*
Mude, O.
  See Gorey, Edward (St. John)
Mudgeon, Apeman
  See Mitchell, Adrian
Mueller, Jorg 1942- *67*
  See also CLR *43*
Mueller, Miranda R. *201*
Mueller, Virginia 1924- *28*
Muggs
  See Watkins, Lois
Muir, Diana
  See Appelbaum, Diana Muir Karter
Muir, Frank (Herbert) 1920-1998 .... *30*
Muir, Helen 1937- *65*
Mukerji, Dhan Gopal 1890-1936 .... *40*
  See also CLR *10*
Mulcahy, Lucille Burnett *12*
Mulford, Philippa G. 1948- *112*
  Earlier sketch in SATA *43*
Mulford, Philippa Greene
  See Mulford, Philippa G.
Mulgan, Catherine 1931- *24*
Mulila, Vigad G.
  See Maillu, David G(ian)
Mull, Brandon 1974- *190*
Mullen, Michael 1937- *122*
Muller, Billex
  See Ellis, Edward S.
Muller, Jorg
  See Mueller, Jorg
Muller, (Lester) Robin 1953- *86*
Mullin, Caryl Cude 1969- *130*

Mullins, Edward S(wift) 1922- *10*
Mullins, Hilary 1962- *84*
Mulock, Dinah Maria
  See Craik, Dinah Maria (Mulock)
Mulvihill, William Patrick 1923- *8*
Mumford, Ruth
  See Dallas, Ruth
Mumy, Bill 1954- *112*
Mun
  See Leaf, (Wilbur) Munro
Munari, Bruno 1907-1998 .... *15*
  See also CLR 9
Munce, Ruth Hill 1898- *12*
Mundy, Simon 1954- *64*
Mundy, Simon Andrew James Hainault
  See Mundy, Simon
Munger, Nancy *170*
Munowitz, Ken 1935-1977 .... *14*
Munoz, William 1949- *92*
  Earlier sketch in SATA 42
Munro, Alice 1931- *29*
Munro, Alice Anne
  See Munro, Alice
Munro, Eleanor 1928- *37*
Munro, Roxie 1945- *184*
  Earlier sketches in SATA 58, 136
Munsch, Bob
  See Munsch, Robert (Norman)
Munsch, Robert (Norman) 1945- *120*
  Brief entry *48*
  Earlier sketches in SATA 50, 83
  See also CLR 19
Munsinger, Lynn 1951- *177*
  Earlier sketches in SATA 33, 94
Munson, Derek 1970- *139*
Munson, R. W.
  See Karl, Jean E(dna)
Munson-Benson, Tunie 1946- *15*
Munsterberg, Peggy 1921- *102*
Muntean, Michaela *182*
Munthe, Nelly 1947- *53*
Munves, James (Albert) 1922- *30*
Munzer, Martha E. 1899-1999 .... *4*
Murawski, Darlyne A. *193*
Murch, Mel
  See Manes, Stephen
Murdoch, David H(amilton) 1937- *96*
Murdoch, Patricia 1957- *192*
Murdock, Catherine Gilbert *185*
Murhall, J(acqueline) J(ane) 1964- *143*
Murphy, Barbara Beasley 1933- *130*
  Earlier sketch in SATA 5
Murphy, Claire Rudolf 1951- *137*
  Earlier sketch in SATA 76
Murphy, E(mmett) Jefferson 1926- *4*
Murphy, Jill (Frances) 1949- *142*
  Earlier sketches in SATA 37, 70
  See also CLR 39
Murphy, Jim 1947- *185*
  Brief entry *32*
  Earlier sketches in SATA 37, 77, 124
  See also CLR 53
Murphy, Joseph E., Jr. 1930- *65*
Murphy, Kelly 1977- *190*
  Earlier sketch in SATA 143
Murphy, Louise 1943- *155*
Murphy, Mary 1961- *196*
Murphy, Pat
  See Murphy, E(mmett) Jefferson
Murphy, Patricia J. 1963- *132*
Murphy, Rita *180*
Murphy, Robert (William) 1902-1971 .... *10*
Murphy, Shirley Rousseau 1928- *126*
  Earlier sketches in SATA 36, 71
  See also SAAS 18
Murphy, Stuart J. 1942- *157*
  Earlier sketch in SATA 115
Murphy, Thomas Basil, Jr. 1935- *191*
Murphy, Tim
  See Murphy, Jim

Murphy, Tom
  See Murphy, Thomas Basil, Jr.
Murray, John 1923- *39*
Murray, Kirsty 1960- *165*
  Earlier sketch in SATA 108
Murray, Marguerite 1917- *63*
Murray, Marian *5*
Murray, Martine 1965- *125*
Murray, (Judith) Michele (Freedman)
  1933-1974 .... *7*
Murray, Ossie 1938- *43*
Murray, Peter
  See Hautman, Pete
Murrow, Liza Ketchum 1946- *132*
  Earlier sketch in SATA 78
Musgrave, Florence 1902-1999 .... *3*
Musgrove, Margaret W(ynkoop) 1943- *124*
  Earlier sketch in SATA 26
Mussey, Virginia Howell
  See Ellison, Virginia H(owell)
Mussey, Virginia T.H.
  See Ellison, Virginia H(owell)
Mussi, Sarah *206*
Mutel, Cornelia F. 1947- *74*
Muth, Jon J. *206*
  Earlier sketch in SATA 165
Mutz
  See Kuenstler, Morton
Mwangi, Meja 1948- *174*
My Brother's Brother
  See Chekhov, Anton (Pavlovich)
Myers, Anna *160*
Myers, Arthur 1917- *91*
  Earlier sketch in SATA 35
Myers, Bernice *81*
  Earlier sketch in SATA 9
Myers, Caroline Elizabeth Clark
  1887-1980 .... *28*
Myers, Christopher 1975- *183*
  See also CLR 97
Myers, Edward 1950- *172*
  Earlier sketch in SATA 96
Myers, Elisabeth P(erkins) 1918- *36*
Myers, (Mary) Hortense (Powner)
  1913-1987 .... *10*
Myers, Jack 1913-2006 .... *83*
  Obituary *178*
Myers, Jack Edgar
  See Myers, Jack
Myers, Lou 1915-2005 .... *81*
  Obituary *171*
Myers, Louis
  See Myers, Lou
Myers, R.E. 1924- *119*
Myers, Robert Eugene
  See Myers, R.E.
Myers, Tim 1953- *176*
  Earlier sketch in SATA 147
Myers, Timothy Joseph
  See Myers, Tim
Myers, Walter Dean 1937- *193*
  Brief entry *27*
  Earlier sketches in SATA 41, 71, 109, 157
  See also CLR 110
  See also SAAS 2
Myers, Walter M.
  See Myers, Walter Dean
Myller, Rolf 1926-2006 .... *27*
  Obituary *175*
Myra, Harold L(awrence) 1939- *46*
  Brief entry *42*
Myracle, Lauren 1969- *204*
  Earlier sketch in SATA 162
Myrus, Donald (Richard) 1927- *23*
Mysterious Traveler, The
  See Arthur, Robert, (Jr.)

N

Na, An *149*
Naaslund, Goorel Kristina 1940- *170*
Nadel, Laurie 1948- *74*
Naden, Corinne J. 1930- *166*
  Earlier sketch in SATA 79
Nadimi, Suzan *188*
Nagda, Ann Whitehead *199*
Nagel, Andreas Fischer
  See Fischer-Nagel, Andreas
Nagel, Heiderose Fischer
  See Fischer-Nagel, Heiderose
Nagle, Shane *176*
Naidoo, Beverley 1943- *180*
  Earlier sketches in SATA 63, 135
  See also CLR 29
Nakae, Noriko 1940- *59*
Nakata, Hiroe *205*
Nakatani, Chiyoko 1930-1981 .... *55*
  Brief entry *40*
  See also CLR 30
Nally, Susan W. 1947- *90*
Namioka, Lensey 1929- *157*
  Autobiography Feature *116*
  Earlier sketches in SATA 27, 89
  See also CLR 48
  See also SAAS 24
Namovicz, Gene Inyart 1927- *6*
Nanji, Shenaaz 1954- *204*
  Earlier sketch in SATA 131
Nanogak Agnes 1925- *61*
Napier, Mark
  See Laffin, John (Alfred Charles)
Napoli, Donna Jo 1948- *190*
  Earlier sketches in SATA 92, 137
  See also CLR 51
  See also SAAS 23
Napp, Daniel 1974- *204*
Narahashi, Keiko 1959- *115*
  Earlier sketch in SATA 79
Narayan, Rasipuram Krishnaswami
  See Narayan, R.K.
Narayan, R.K. 1906-2001 .... *62*
Nascimbene, Yan 1949- *173*
  Earlier sketch in SATA 133
Nash, Bruce M(itchell) 1947- *34*
Nash, Frediric Ogden
  See Nash, Ogden
Nash, Linell
  See Smith, Linell Nash
Nash, Mary (Hughes) 1925- *41*
Nash, Ogden 1902-1971 .... *46*
  Earlier sketch in SATA 2
Nash, Renea Denise 1963- *81*
Nast, Elsa Ruth
  See Watson, Jane Werner
Nast, Thomas 1840-1902 .... *51*
  Brief entry *33*
Nastick, Sharon 1954- *41*
Natale, Vince *196*
Natarajan, Srividya *187*
Nathan, Adele (Gutman) 1900(?)-1986
  Obituary *48*
Nathan, Amy *155*
  Earlier sketch in SATA 104
Nathan, Dorothy (Goldeen) (?)-1966 .... *15*
Nathan, Robert (Gruntal) 1894-1985 .... *6*
  Obituary *43*
Nathanson, Laura Walther 1941- *57*
Natti, Lee 1919- *67*
  Earlier sketch in SATA 1
  See also SAAS 3
Natti, Susanna 1948- *125*
  Earlier sketch in SATA 32
Nau, Thomas *186*
Naughtie, Eleanor
  See Updale, Eleanor
Naughton, Bill
  See Naughton, William John (Francis)
Naughton, James Franklin 1957- *85*

Naughton, Jim
  See Naughton, James Franklin
Naughton, William John (Francis)
  1910-1992 86
Navarra, John Gabriel 1927- 8
Naylor, Penelope 1941- 10
Naylor, Phyllis 1933- 152
  Autobiography Feature 152
  Earlier sketches in SATA *12, 66, 102*
  See also CLR *135*
  See also SAAS *10*
Naylor, Phyllis Reynolds 1933-
  See Naylor, Phyllis
Nazarian, Nikki
  See Nichols, Cecilia Fawn
Nazaroff, Alexander I(vanovich) 1898-1981 .. 4
Nazoa, Aquiles 1920-1976 198
Neal, Harry Edward 1906-1993 5
  Obituary 76
Neal, Michael
  See Teitelbaum, Michael
Nearing, Penny 1916- 47
  Brief entry 42
Nebel, Gustave E. 45
  Brief entry 33
Nebel, Mimouca
  See Nebel, Gustave E.
Nee, Kay Bonner 10
Needham, Kate 1962- 95
Needle, Jan 1943- 98
  Earlier sketch in SATA *30*
  See also CLR *43*
  See also SAAS *23*
Needleman, Jacob 1934- 6
Neel, David 1960- 82
Neel, Preston 1959- 93
Negri, Rocco 1932- 12
Negrin, Fabian 1963- 189
Neidigh, Sherry 1956- 204
Neier, Aryeh 1937- 59
Neigoff, Anne 13
Neigoff, Mike 1920- 13
Neilan, Eujin Kim 1969- 200
Neilson, Frances Fullerton (Jones)
  1910-2001 14
Neimark, Anne E. 1935- 145
  Earlier sketch in SATA *4*
Neimark, Paul G. 1934- 80
  Brief entry 37
Neitzel, Shirley 1941- 134
  Earlier sketch in SATA *77*
Nell
  See Hanna, Nell(ie L.)
Nelscott, Kris
  See Rusch, Kristine Kathryn
Nelson, Blake 1960- 177
Nelson, Catherine Chadwick 1926- 87
Nelson, Cordner 1918-2009 54
  Brief entry 29
Nelson, Drew 1952- 77
Nelson, Esther L. 1928- 13
Nelson, Jim A.
  See Stotter, Mike
Nelson, Julie L. 1970- 117
Nelson, Kadir 181
  Earlier sketch in SATA *154*
Nelson, Kris
  See Rusch, Kristine Kathryn
Nelson, Lawrence E(rnest) 1928-1977
  Obituary 28
Nelson, Marilyn 1946- 60
  Autobiography Feature 180
Nelson, Mary Carroll 1929- 23
Nelson, O. Terry 1941- 62
Nelson, Peter N. 1953- 73
Nelson, R.A. 197
Nelson, Richard K(ing) 1941- 65
Nelson, Robin Laura 1971- 141
Nelson, Roy Paul 1923- 59
Nelson, S.D. 181
Nelson, Sharlene (P.) 1933- 96

Nelson, Suzanne 1976- 184
Nelson, Ted (W.) 1931- 96
Nelson, Theresa 1948- 143
  Autobiography Feature 143
  Earlier sketch in SATA *79*
Nemeth, Sally 187
Neri, G. 197
Neri, Greg
  See Neri, G.
Neri, Gregory
  See Neri, G.
Nerlove, Miriam 1959- 53
  Brief entry 49
Nesbit, E. 1858-1924 100
  See also YABC *1*
  See also CLR *70*
Nesbit, Edith
  See Nesbit, E.
Nesbit, Troy
  See Folsom, Franklin (Brewster)
Nespojohn, Katherine V(eronica) 1912-1975 . 7
Ness, Evaline (Michelow) 1911-1986 26
  Obituary 49
  Earlier sketch in SATA *1*
  See also CLR *6*
  See also SAAS *1*
Nestor, Larry 1940- 149
Nestor, William P(rodromos) 1947- 49
Nethery, Mary 93
Neubecker, Robert 170
Neuberger, Julia (Babette Sarah) 1950- 142
  Earlier sketch in SATA *78*
Neufeld, John (Arthur) 1938- 131
  Autobiography Feature 131
  Earlier sketches in SATA *6, 81*
  See also CLR *52*
  See also SAAS *3*
Neuhaus, David 1958- 83
Neumeyer, Peter F(lorian) 1929- 13
Neurath, Marie (Reidemeister) 1898-1986 1
Neuschwander, Cindy 1953- 157
  Earlier sketch in SATA *107*
Neusner, Jacob 1932- 38
Neville, Charles
  See Bodsworth, (Charles) Fred(erick)
Neville, Emily Cheney 1919- 1
  See also SAAS *2*
Neville, Mary
  See Woodrich, Mary Neville
Nevins, Albert (Francis) J(erome)
  1915-1997 20
Nevius, Carol 1955- 186
Newberger, Devra
  See Speregen, Devra Newberger
Newberry, Clare Turlay 1903-1970 1
  Obituary 26
Newbery, John 1713-1767 20
  See also CLR *147*
Newbery, Linda 1952- 184
  Earlier sketch in SATA *142*
Newbigging, Martha 198
Newbold, Greg 199
Newcomb, Ellsworth
  See Kenny, Ellsworth Newcomb
Newcombe, Eugene A. 1923-1990 45
  Brief entry 33
Newcombe, Jack
  See Newcombe, Eugene A.
Newcome, Robert 1955- 91
Newcome, Zita 1959- 88
Newell, Crosby
  See Bonsall, Crosby Barbara (Newell)
Newell, Edythe W(eatherford) 1910-1989 11
Newell, Hope Hockenberry 1896-1965 24
Newfeld, Frank 1928- 26
Newgarden, Mark 1959- 194
Newlon, (Frank) Clarke 1905(?)-1982 6
  Obituary 33
Newman, Barbara Johansen 191
Newman, C.J.
  See Newman, Coleman J.

Newman, Coleman J. 1935- 82
Newman, Daisy 1904-1994 27
  Obituary 78
Newman, Gerald 1939- 46
  Brief entry 42
Newman, Jerry
  See Newman, Coleman J.
Newman, Leslea 1955- 134
  Earlier sketches in SATA *71, 128*
Newman, Margaret
  See Potter, Margaret
Newman, Marjorie 146
Newman, Matthew (Harrison) 1955- 56
Newman, Nanette 1934- 162
Newman, Robert (Howard) 1909-1988 87
  Obituary 60
  Earlier sketch in SATA *4*
Newman, Shirlee P(etkin) 144
  Earlier sketches in SATA *10, 90*
Newsom, Carol 1948- 92
  Earlier sketch in SATA *40*
Newsom, Tom 1944- 80
Newth, Mette 1942- 140
Newton, David E(dward) 1933- 67
Newton, James R(obert) 1935- 23
Newton, Jill 1964- 200
Newton, Robert 1965- 191
Newton, Suzanne 1936- 77
  Earlier sketch in SATA *5*
Newton, Vanessa
  See Newton, Vanessa Brantley
Newton, Vanessa Brantley 1962(?)- 206
Ney, John 1923- 43
  Brief entry 33
Nez, John 155
Ng, Franklin 82
Nguyen, Vincent 187
Nichol, B(arrie) P(hillip) 1944-1988 66
Nicholas, Louise D.
  See Watkins, Dawn L.
Nicholls, Judith (Ann) 1941- 61
Nichols, Cecilia Fawn 1906-1987 12
Nichols, Grace 1950- 164
  Earlier sketch in SATA *98*
Nichols, Janet (Louise) 1952- 67
Nichols, Judy 1947- 124
Nichols, Leigh
  See Koontz, Dean R.
Nichols, Paul
  See Hawks, Robert
Nichols, Peter
  See Youd, Samuel
Nichols, (Joanna) Ruth 1948- 15
Nichols, Travis 206
Nicholson, C. R.
  See Nicole, Christopher (Robin)
Nicholson, Christina
  See Nicole, Christopher (Robin)
Nicholson, Joyce Thorpe 1919- 35
Nicholson, Lois P. 1949- 88
Nicholson, Robin
  See Nicole, Christopher (Robin)
Nicholson, William 180
Nicholson, William 1872-1949
  See CLR *76*
Nickel, Barbara 1966- 188
Nickell, Joe 1944- 167
  Earlier sketch in SATA *73*
Nickelsburg, Janet 1893-1983 11
Nickerson, Betty 1922- 14
Nickerson, Elizabeth
  See Nickerson, Betty
Nickl, Barbara (Elisabeth) 1939- 56
Nicklaus, Carol 62
  Brief entry 33
Nickle, John 181
Nickless, Will 1902-1979(?) 66
Nic Leodhas, Sorche
  See Alger, Leclaire (Gowans)
Nicol, Ann
  See Turnbull, Ann

Nicolas
  See Mordvinoff, Nicolas
Nicolay, Helen 1866-1954
  See YABC *1*
Nicole, Christopher (Robin) 1930- *5*
Nicoll, Helen 1937- *87*
Nicolson, Cynthia Pratt 1949- *141*
Ni Dhuibhne, Eilis 1954- *91*
Niehaus, Paddy Bouma
  See Bouma, Paddy
Nields, Nerissa 1967- *166*
Nielsen, Kay (Rasmus) 1886-1957 .... *16*
  See also CLR *16*
Nielsen, Laura F. 1960- *93*
Nielsen, Laura Farnsworth
  See Nielsen, Laura F.
Nielsen, Nancy J. 1951- *77*
Nielsen, Susin 1964- *195*
Nielsen, Virginia
  See McCall, Virginia Nielsen
Nielsen-Fernlund, Susin
  See Nielsen, Susin
Niemann, Christoph 1970- *191*
Nieuwsma, Milton J(ohn) 1941- *142*
Nightingale, Sandy 1953- *76*
Nikolajeva, Maria 1952- *127*
Nikola-Lisa, W. 1951- *180*
  Earlier sketch in SATA *71*
Niland, Deborah 1951- *172*
  Earlier sketch in SATA *27*
Niland, Kilmeny *75*
Nilsen, Anna 1948- *174*
  Earlier sketch in SATA *96*
Nilsson, Eleanor 1939- *117*
  Earlier sketch in SATA *81*
  See also SAAS *23*
Nilsson, Per 1954- *159*
Nimmo, Jenny 1944- *144*
  Earlier sketch in SATA *87*
  See also CLR *44*
Nishimura, Kae *196*
Niven, Larry 1938- *171*
  Earlier sketch in SATA *95*
Niven, Laurence VanCott
  See Niven, Larry
Nivola, Claire A. 1947- *140*
  Earlier sketch in SATA *84*
Nix, Garth 1963- *143*
  Earlier sketch in SATA *97*
  See also CLR *68*
Nixon, Hershell Howard 1923- *42*
Nixon, Joan Lowery 1927-2003 .... *115*
  Obituary *146*
  Earlier sketches in SATA *8, 44, 78*
  See also CLR *24*
  See also SAAS *9*
Nixon, K.
  See Nixon, Kathleen Irene (Blundell)
Nixon, Kathleen Irene (Blundell)
  1894-1988(?) *14*
  Obituary *59*
Nobati, Eugenia 1968- *201*
Nobisso, Josephine 1953- *121*
  Earlier sketch in SATA *78*
Noble, Iris (Davis) 1922-1986 .... *5*
  Obituary *49*
Noble, Marty 1947- *125*
  Earlier sketch in SATA *97*
Noble, Trinka Hakes 1944- *197*
  Brief entry *37*
  Earlier sketch in SATA *123*
Nobleman, Marc Tyler 1972- *203*
Noda, Takayo 1961- *168*
Nodelman, Perry 1942- *101*
Nodset, Joan L.
  See Lexau, Joan M.
Noel Hume, Ivor 1927- *65*
Noestlinger, Christine
  See Nostlinger, Christine
Noguere, Suzanne 1947- *34*

Nolan, Dennis 1945- *166*
  Brief entry *34*
  Earlier sketches in SATA *42, 92*
Nolan, Han 1956- *157*
  Earlier sketch in SATA *109*
Nolan, Janet 1956- *191*
  Earlier sketch in SATA *145*
Nolan, Jeannette Covert 1897-1974 .... *2*
  Obituary *27*
Nolan, Paul T(homas) 1919- *48*
Nolan, William F(rancis) 1928- *88*
  Brief entry *28*
Nolen, Jerdine 1953- *157*
  Earlier sketch in SATA *105*
Noll, Sally 1946- *82*
Noonan, Brandon 1979- *184*
Noonan, Diana 1960- *146*
Noonan, Julia 1946- *148*
  Earlier sketches in SATA *4, 95*
Norac, Carl 1960- *166*
Norcross, John
  See Conroy, John Wesley
Nordan, Robert W(arren) 1934-2004 .... *133*
Nordhoff, Charles Bernard 1887-1947 .... *23*
Nordlicht, Lillian *29*
Nordstrom, Ursula 1910-1988 .... *3*
  Obituary *57*
Nordtvedt, Matilda 1926- *67*
Norling, Beth 1969- *149*
Norman, Charles 1904-1996 .... *38*
  Obituary *92*
Norman, Howard
  See Norman, Howard A.
Norman, Howard A. 1949- *81*
Norman, James
  See Schmidt, James Norman
Norman, Jay
  See Arthur, Robert, (Jr.)
Norman, Lilith 1927- *120*
  Earlier sketch in SATA *86*
Norman, Mary 1931- *36*
Norman, Steve
  See Pashko, Stanley
Norment, Lisa 1966- *91*
Norris, Gunilla Brodde 1939- *20*
North, Andrew
  See Norton, Andre
North, Anthony
  See Koontz, Dean R.
North, Captain George
  See Stevenson, Robert Louis (Balfour)
North, Captain George
  See Stevenson, Robert Louis (Balfour)
North, Howard
  See Trevor, Elleston
North, Joan 1920- *16*
North, Milou
  See Erdrich, Louise
North, Robert
  See Withers, Carl A.
North, Sara
  See Bonham, Barbara Thomas
  and Hager, Jean
North, Sherry *201*
North, Sterling 1906-1974 .... *45*
  Obituary *26*
  Earlier sketch in SATA *1*
Northcott, (William) Cecil 1902-1987
  Obituary *55*
Northeast, Brenda V(ictoria) 1948- *106*
Northmore, Elizabeth Florence 1906-1974 . *122*
Norton, Alice Mary
  See Norton, Andre
Norton, Andre 1912-2005 .... *91*
  Earlier sketches in SATA *1, 43*
  See also CLR *50*
Norton, Browning
  See Norton, Frank R. B(rowning)
Norton, Frank R. B(rowning) 1909-1989 ..... *10*

Norton, Mary 1903-1992 .... *60*
  Obituary *72*
  Earlier sketch in SATA *18*
  See also CLR *140*
Nosredna, Trebor
  See Anderson, Bob
Nostlinger, Christine 1936- *162*
  Brief entry *37*
  Earlier sketch in SATA *64*
  See also CLR *12*
Nourse, Alan E(dward) 1928-1992 .... *48*
  See also CLR *33*
Novak, Matt 1962- *204*
  Brief entry *52*
  Earlier sketches in SATA *60, 104, 165*
Novelli, Luca 1947- *61*
Nowell, Elizabeth Cameron *12*
Noyes, Deborah 1965- *194*
  Earlier sketch in SATA *145*
Nugent, Cynthia 1954- *205*
Nugent, Nicholas 1949- *73*
Numeroff, Laura 1953- *206*
  Earlier sketches in SATA *28, 90, 142*
  See also CLR *85*
Numeroff Joffe, Laura
  See Numeroff, Laura
Nunes, Lygia Bojunga 1932- *154*
  Earlier sketch in SATA *75*
Nunn, Laura (Donna) Silverstein 1968- *124*
Nurenberg, Thelma
  See Greenhaus, Thelma Nurenberg
Nurnberg, Maxwell 1897-1984 .... *27*
  Obituary *41*
Nussbaumer, Paul (Edmund) 1934- *16*
Nutt, Ken 1951- *163*
  Earlier sketch in SATA *97*
Nuttall-Smith, Margaret Emily Noel 1919- .. *26*
Nuygen, Mathieu 1967- *80*
Nuzum, K.A. *195*
Nyberg, (Everett Wayne) Morgan 1944- *87*
Nyce, (Nellie) Helene von Strecker
  1885-1969 .... *19*
Nyce, Vera 1862-1925 .... *19*
Nye, Naomi Shihab 1952- *198*
  Earlier sketches in SATA *86, 147*
  See also CLR *59*
Nye, Robert 1939- *6*
Nyeu, Tao *206*
Nyikos, Stacy A. 1969- *164*
Nystrom, Carolyn 1940- *130*
  Earlier sketch in SATA *67*

O

Oakes, Elizabeth H. 1964- *132*
Oakes, Vanya 1909-1983 .... *6*
  Obituary *37*
Oakley, Don(ald G.) 1927- *8*
Oakley, Graham 1929- *84*
  Earlier sketch in SATA *30*
  See also CLR *7*
Oakley, Helen (McKelvey) 1906- *10*
Oana, Katherine 1929- *53*
  Brief entry *37*
Oates, Eddie H. 1943- *88*
Oates, Joyce Carol 1938- *159*
Oates, Stephen B(aery) 1936- *59*
Obed, Ellen Bryan 1944- *74*
Oberle, Joseph 1958- *69*
Oberman, Sheldon 1949-2004 .... *85*
  Autobiography Feature *114*
  Obituary *153*
  See also CLR *54*
  See also SAAS *26*
Obligado, Lilian (Isabel) 1931- *61*
  Brief entry *45*
Obrant, Susan 1946- *11*
O'Brian, E.G.
  See Clarke, Arthur C.

O'Brien, Anne Sibley 1952- 80
  Brief entry 48
  Earlier sketch in SATA 53
O'Brien, E.G.
  See Clarke, Arthur C.
O'Brien, Esse Forrester 1895(?)-1975
  Obituary 30
O'Brien, Patrick 1960- 193
O'Brien, Robert C.
  See Conly, Robert Leslie
O'Brien, Thomas C(lement) 1938- 29
O'Callaghan, Julie 1954- 113
O'Callahan, Jay 1938- 88
O'Carroll, Ryan
  See Markun, Patricia Maloney
Ochiltree, Dianne 1953- 117
Ockham, Joan Price
  See Price, Joan
O'Connell, Margaret F(orster) 1935-1977 30
  Obituary 30
O'Connell, Peg
  See Ahern, Margaret McCrohan
O'Connell, Rebecca 1968- 130
O'Connor, Barbara 1950- 193
  Earlier sketch in SATA 154
O'Connor, Francine M(arie) 1930- 90
O'Connor, Genevieve A. 1914- 75
O'Connor, George 183
O'Connor, Ian 1965- 188
O'Connor, Jane 1947- 186
  Brief entry 47
  Earlier sketches in SATA 59, 103, 150
O'Connor, Karen 1938- 89
  Earlier sketch in SATA 34
O'Connor, Patrick
  See Wibberley, Leonard
O'Connor, Richard 1915-1975
  Obituary 21
O'Conor, Jane 1958- 78
Odaga, Asenath (Bole) 1937- 130
  Earlier sketch in SATA 67
  See also SAAS 19
O Danachair, Caoimhin
  See Danaher, Kevin
Odanaka, Barbara 159
O'Daniel, Janet 1921- 24
O'Day, Cathy
  See Crane, Barbara (Joyce)
O'Dell, Scott 1898-1989 134
  Earlier sketches in SATA 12, 60
  See also CLR 126
Odenwald, Robert P(aul) 1899-1965 11
Odgers, Sally
  See Odgers, Sally Farrell
Odgers, Sally Farrell 1957- 139
  Earlier sketch in SATA 72
O'Donnell, Dick
  See Lupoff, Richard A(llen)
  and Thompson, Don(ald Arthur)
Odriozola, Elena 186
Oechsli, Kelly 1918-1999 5
Oesterle, Virginia Rorby
  See Rorby, Ginny
Ofek, Uriel 1926- 36
  See also CLR 28
Offenbacher, Ami 1958- 91
Offit, Sidney 1928- 10
Ofosu-Appiah, L(awrence) H(enry) 1920- ... 13
Ogan, George F. 1912-1983 13
Ogan, M. G.
  See Ogan, George F.
  and Ogan, Margaret E. (Nettles)
Ogan, Margaret E. (Nettles) 1923-1979 13
Ogburn, Charlton (Jr.) 1911-1998 3
  Obituary 109
Ogburn, Jacqueline K. 162
Ogilvie, Elisabeth May 1917-2006 40
  Brief entry 29
  Obituary 176
Ogilvy, Gavin
  See Barrie, J(ames) M(atthew)

Ogilvy, Ian 1943- 177
Ogilvy, Ian Raymond
  See Ogilvy, Ian
Ogle, Lucille Edith 1904-1988
  Obituary 59
Ogletree, Charles J. 1952- 175
O'Green, Jennifer
  See Roberson, Jennifer
O'Green, Jennifer Roberson
  See Roberson, Jennifer
O'Hagan, Caroline 1946- 38
O'Hanlon, Jacklyn
  See Meek, Jacklyn O'Hanlon
O'Hara, Elizabeth
  See Ni Dhuibhne, Eilis
O'Hara, Kenneth
  See Morris, (Margaret) Jean
O'Hara, Mary
  See Alsop, Mary O'Hara
O'Hara (Alsop), Mary
  See Alsop, Mary O'Hara
O'Hare, Jeff(rey A.) 1958- 105
Ohi, Ruth 1964- 95
Ohiyesa
  See Eastman, Charles A(lexander)
Ohlsson, Ib 1935- 7
Ohmi, Ayano 1959- 115
Ohtomo, Yasuo 1946- 37
o huigin, sean 1942- 138
  See also CLR 75
Oiseau
  See Moseley, James W(illett)
Oke, Janette 1935- 97
O'Keefe, Susan Heyboer 176
  Earlier sketch in SATA 133
O'Keeffe, Frank 1938- 99
O'Kelley, Mattie Lou 1908-1997 97
  Earlier sketch in SATA 36
Okimoto, Jean Davies 1942- 103
  Earlier sketch in SATA 34
Okomfo, Amasewa
  See Cousins, Linda
olafsdottir, Gudrun Elin
  See Gunnella
Olaleye, Isaac O. 1941- 96
  See also SAAS 23
Olcott, Frances Jenkins 1872(?)-1963 19
Old, Wendie C(orbin) 1943- 154
Old Boy
  See Hughes, Thomas
Oldenburg, E(gbert) William 1936-1974 35
Older, Effin 1942- 114
Older, Jules 1940- 156
  Earlier sketch in SATA 114
Oldfield, Jenny 1949- 140
Oldfield, Margaret J(ean) 1932- 56
Oldfield, Pamela 1931- 86
Oldham, June 70
Oldham, Mary 1944- 65
Olds, Elizabeth 1896-1991 3
  Obituary 66
Olds, Helen Diehl 1895-1981 9
  Obituary 25
Oldstyle, Jonathan
  See Irving, Washington
O'Leary, Brian (Todd) 1940- 6
O'Leary, Patsy B(aker) 1937- 97
Oleynikov, Igor 1953- 202
Oliphant, B.J.
  See Tepper, Sheri S.
Oliver, Burton
  See Burt, Olive Woolley
Oliver, Chad
  See Oliver, Symmes C.
Oliver, John Edward 1933- 21
Oliver, Lin 202
Oliver, Marilyn Tower 1935- 89
Oliver, Narelle 1960- 197
  Earlier sketch in SATA 152
Oliver, Shirley (Louise Dawkins) 1958- 74
Oliver, Symmes C. 1928-1993 101

Oliviero, Jamie 1950- 84
Olmsted, Lorena Ann 1890-1989 13
Olney, Ross R. 1929- 13
Olschewski, Alfred (Erich) 1920- 7
Olsen, Barbara 148
Olsen, Carol 1945- 89
Olsen, Ib Spang 1921- 81
  Earlier sketch in SATA 6
Olsen, Violet (Mae) 1922-1991 58
Olson, Arielle North 1932- 67
Olson, David J. 1974- 198
Olson, Gene 1922- 32
Olson, Gretchen 187
Olson, Helen Kronberg 48
Olson, Kay Melchisedech 1948- 175
Olson, Marianne
  See Mitchell, Marianne
Olson-Brown, Ellen 1967- 183
Olten, Manuela 1970- 197
Olugebefola, Ademole 1941- 15
Oluonye, Mary N(kechi) 1955- 111
Om
  See Gorey, Edward (St. John)
O'Malley, Kevin 1961- 191
  Earlier sketch in SATA 157
Oman, Carola (Mary Anima) 1897-1978 35
O'Mara, Carmel 1965- 166
O'Mara-Horwitz, Carmel
  See O'Mara, Carmel
O'Meara, Walter (Andrew) 1897-1989 65
Ommanney, F(rancis) D(ownes) 1903-1980 . 23
O Mude
  See Gorey, Edward (St. John)
Oneal, Elizabeth 1934- 82
  Earlier sketch in SATA 30
  See also CLR 13
O'Neal, Katherine Pebley 1957- 204
O'Neal, Reagan
  See Jordan, Robert
O'Neal, Regan
  See Jordan, Robert
Oneal, Zibby
  See Oneal, Elizabeth
O'Neill, Amanda 1951- 111
O'Neill, Catharine 203
O'Neill, Gerard K(itchen) 1927-1992 65
O'Neill, Judith (Beatrice) 1930- 34
O'Neill, Mary L(e Duc) 1908(?)-1990 2
  Obituary 64
O'Neill, Reagan
  See Jordan, Robert
Onslow, Annette Rosemary MacArthur
  See MacArthur-Onslow, Annette Rosemary
Onslow, John 1906-1985
  Obituary 47
Onyefulu, Ifeoma 1959- 157
  Earlier sketches in SATA 81, 115
Opie, Iona (Margaret Balfour) 1923- 118
  Earlier sketches in SATA 3, 63
  See also SAAS 6
Opie, Peter (Mason) 1918-1982 118
  Obituary 28
  Earlier sketches in SATA 3, 63
Oppel, Kenneth 1967- 199
  Earlier sketches in SATA 99, 153
Oppel, Kenneth Kerry
  See Oppel, Kenneth
Oppenheim, Joanne 1934- 174
  Earlier sketches in SATA 5, 82, 136
Oppenheim, Shulamith Levey 1928- 177
Oppenheimer, Joan L(etson) 1925- 28
Oppong, Joseph Ransford 1953- 160
Optic, Oliver
  See Adams, William Taylor
  and Stratemeyer, Edward L.
Oram, Hiawyn 1946- 101
  Earlier sketch in SATA 56
Orbach, Ruth Gary 1941- 21
Orback, Craig 197
Orczy, Emma
  See Orczy, Baroness Emmuska

Orczy, Emma Magdalena Rosalia Maria Josefa
  See Orczy, Baroness Emmuska
Orczy, Emmuska
  See Orczy, Baroness Emmuska
Orczy, Baroness Emmuska 1865-1947 40
Orde, A.J.
  See Tepper, Sheri S.
O'Reilly, Jackson
  See Jordan, Robert
Orenstein, Denise Gosliner 1950- 157
Orgad, Dorit 1936- 199
Orgel, Doris 1929- 148
  Earlier sketches in SATA *7, 85*
  See also CLR 48
  See also SAAS 19
Orgill, Roxane 198
Oriolo, Joe
  See Oriolo, Joseph D.
Oriolo, Joseph D. 1913-1985
  Obituary 46
Orleans, Ilo 1897-1962 10
Orlev, Uri 1931- 135
  Earlier sketch in SATA *58*
  See also CLR 30
  See also SAAS 19
Ormai, Stella 57
  Brief entry 48
Ormerod, Jan 1946- 132
  Brief entry 44
  Earlier sketches in SATA *55, 70*
  See also CLR 20
Ormes, Jackie
  See Ormes, Zelda J.
Ormes, Zelda J. 1914-1986
  Obituary 47
Ormondroyd, Edward 1925- 14
Ormsby, Virginia H(aire) 1906-1990 11
Orona-Ramirez, Kristy 1964- 189
Orozco, Jose-Luis 1948- 179
Orr, Katherine S(helley) 1950- 72
Orr, Wendy 1953- 206
  Earlier sketches in SATA *90, 141*
Orris
  See Ingelow, Jean
Orth, Richard
  See Gardner, Richard (M.)
Ortiz Cofer, Judith
  See Cofer, Judith Ortiz
Orwell, George
  See Blair, Eric
Orwin, Joanna 1944- 141
Osborn, Elinor 1939- 145
Osborn, Kathy 1955(?)- 199
Osborn, Lois D(orothy) 1915- 61
Osborne, Charles 1927- 59
Osborne, Chester G(orham) 1915-1987 11
Osborne, David
  See Silverberg, Robert
Osborne, George
  See Silverberg, Robert
Osborne, Leone Neal 1914-1996 2
Osborne, Mary Pope 1949- 144
  Earlier sketches in SATA *41, 55, 98*
  See also CLR 88
Osceola
  See Blixen, Karen
Osgood, William E(dward) 1926- 37
O'Shaughnessy, Darren
  See Shan, Darren
O'Shaughnessy, Ellen Cassels 1937- 78
O'Shea, Catherine Patricia Shiels
  See O'Shea, Pat
O'Shea, Pat 1931-2007 87
  See also CLR 18
Osmond, Edward 1900- 10
Ossoli, Sarah Margaret
  See Fuller, Margaret
Ostendorf, (Arthur) Lloyd, (Jr.) 1921-2000 .. 65
  Obituary 125
Ostow, Micol 1976- 170

Otfinoski, Steven 1949- 116
  Earlier sketch in SATA *56*
Otis, James
  See Kaler, James Otis
O'Toole, Thomas 1941- 71
O'Trigger, Sir Lucius
  See Horne, Richard Henry Hengist
Otten, Charlotte
  See Otten, Charlotte F.
Otten, Charlotte F. 1926- 98
Otten, Charlotte Fennema
  See Otten, Charlotte F.
Ottley, Matt 1962- 171
  Earlier sketch in SATA *102*
Ottley, Reginald Leslie 1909-1985 26
  See also CLR 16
Otto, Margaret Glover 1909-1976
  Obituary 30
Otto, Svend
  See Soerensen, Svend Otto
Oughton, Jerrie (Preston) 1937- 131
  Earlier sketch in SATA *76*
Oughton, (William) Taylor 1925- 104
Ouida
  See De La Ramee, Marie Louise
Ousley, Odille 1896-1976 10
Outcalt, Todd 1960- 123
Overmyer, James E. 1946- 88
Overton, Jenny (Margaret Mary) 1942- 52
  Brief entry 36
Owen, Ann
  See Qualey, Marsha
Owen, Annie 1949- 75
Owen, Caroline Dale
  See Snedeker, Caroline Dale (Parke)
Owen, Clifford
  See Hamilton, Charles (Harold St. John)
Owen, Dilys
  See Gater, Dilys
Owen, (Benjamin) Evan 1918-1984 38
Owen, (John) Gareth 1936-2002 162
  Earlier sketch in SATA *83*
  See also CLR 31
  See also SAAS 14
Owen, James A. 185
Owens, Bryant 1968- 116
Owens, Dana Elaine
  See Queen Latifah
Owens, Gail 1939- 54
Owens, Mary Beth 191
Owens, Thomas S(heldon) 1960- 86
Owens, Tom
  See Owens, Thomas S(heldon)
Oxenbury, Helen 1938- 149
  Earlier sketches in SATA *3, 68*
  See also CLR 70
Oxendine, Bess Holland 1933- 90
Oz, Frank (Richard) 1944- 60
Ozer, Jerome S. 1927- 59

P

Paananen, Eloise (Katherine) 1923-1993 9
Pace, Lorenzo 1943- 131
Pace, Mildred Mastin 1907- 46
  Brief entry 29
Pachter, Hedwig (?)-1988 63
Pack, Janet 1952- 77
Pack, Robert 1929- 118
Packard, Edward 1931- 148
  Earlier sketches in SATA *47, 90*
Packer, Kenneth L. 1946- 116
Packer, Vin
  See Meaker, Marijane
Pad, Peter
  See Stratemeyer, Edward L.
Page, Eileen
  See Heal, Edith

Page, Eleanor
  See Coerr, Eleanor (Beatrice)
Page, Gail 1950- 205
Page, Jake 1936- 81
Page, James Keena, Jr.
  See Page, Jake
Page, Lou Williams 1912-1997 38
Page, Mary
  See Heal, Edith
Page, Robin 1943- 154
Pagnucci, Susan 1944- 90
Pahlen, Kurt 1907-2003
  Obituary 147
Pahz, Cheryl
  See Pahz, Cheryl Suzanne
Pahz, Cheryl Suzanne 1949- 11
Pahz, James Alon 1943- 11
Paice, Margaret 1920- 10
Paige, Harry W(orthington) 1922- 41
  Brief entry 35
Paige, Richard
  See Koontz, Dean R.
Paige, Robin
  See Albert, Susan Wittig
Paine, Penelope Colville 1946- 87
Paine, Roberta M. 1925- 13
Paisley, Tom 1932- 11
  See also CLR 3
Palatini, Margie 174
  Earlier sketch in SATA *134*
Palazzo, Anthony D.
  See Palazzo, Tony
Palazzo, Tony 1905-1970 3
Palder, Edward L. 1922- 5
Palecek, Josef 1932- 56
Palecek, Libuse 1937- 89
Palen, Debbie 195
Palin, Michael 1943- 67
Palin, Michael Edward
  See Palin, Michael
Palladini, David (Mario) 1946- 40
  Brief entry 32
Pallas, Norvin 1918-1983 23
Pallister, John C(lare) 1891-1980
  Obituary 26
Pallotta, Gerard Larry
  See Pallotta, Jerry
Pallotta, Jerry 1953- 186
Pallotta-Chiarolli, Maria 1960- 117
Palmer, Bernard (Alvin) 1914-1998 26
Palmer, C. Everard 1930- 14
Palmer, (Ruth) Candida 1926- 11
Palmer, Cyril Everard
  See Palmer, C. Everard
Palmer, Don
  See Benson, Mildred
Palmer, Hap 1942- 68
Palmer, Heidi 1948- 15
Palmer, Helen Marion
  See Geisel, Helen
Palmer, Jessica 1953- 120
Palmer, Judd 1972- 153
Palmer, Juliette 1930- 15
Palmer, Kate Salley 1946- 97
Palmer, Maria
  See Strachan, Ian
Palmer, Maria
  See Brennan, Herbie
Palmer, Robin 1909-2000 43
Palmero Caceres, Ana 198
Palmisciano, Diane 202
Paltrowitz, Donna 1950- 61
  Brief entry 50
Paltrowitz, Donna Milman
  See Paltrowitz, Donna
Paltrowitz, Stuart 1946- 61
  Brief entry 50
Pamela, Todd 1950- 124
Pamintuan, Macky 178
Panagopoulos, Janie Lynn 149
Panati, Charles 1943- 65

Panchyk, Richard 1970- 138
Panetta, George 1915-1969 15
Panetta, Joseph N. 1953- 96
Pang, YaWen Ariel 206
Panik, Sharon 1952- 82
Panowski, Eileen Thompson 1920- 49
Pansy
  See Alden, Isabella (Macdonald)
Pantell, Dora (Fuchs) 39
Panter, Carol 1936- 9
Paolini, Christopher 1983- 157
  See also CLR 102
Papademetriou, Lisa 175
Paparone, Pam 185
Paparone, Pamela
  See Paparone, Pam
Papas, Bill
  See Papas, William
Papas, William 1927-2000 50
Papashvily, George 1898-1978 17
Papashvily, Helen (Waite) 1906-1996 17
Pape, D. L.
  See Pape, Donna (Lugg)
Pape, Donna (Lugg) 1930- 82
  Earlier sketch in SATA 2
Paperny, Myra (Green) 1932- 51
  Brief entry 33
Papp, Robert 1967- 205
Paradis, Adrian A(lexis) 1912- 67
  Earlier sketch in SATA 1
  See also SAAS 8
Paradis, Marjorie Bartholomew
  1886(?)-1970 17
Paradiz, Valerie 1963- 176
Paratore, Coleen
  See Paratore, Coleen Murtagh
Paratore, Coleen Murtagh 1958- 200
Parenteau, Shirley 1935- 199
  Brief entry 40
  Earlier sketch in SATA 47
Parish, Margaret 1927-1988 73
  Obituary 59
  Earlier sketch in SATA 17
  See also CLR 22
Parish, Margaret Holt
  See Holt, Margaret
Parish, Peggy
  See Parish, Margaret
Park, Barbara 1947- 123
  Brief entry 35
  Earlier sketches in SATA 40, 78
  See also CLR 34
Park, Bill
  See Park, W(illiam) B(ryan)
Park, Frances 1955- 171
Park, Ginger 173
Park, Janie Jaehyun 150
Park, Jordan
  See Kornbluth, C(yril) M.
  and Pohl, Frederik
Park, Linda Sue 1960- 200
  Earlier sketches in SATA 127, 173
  See also CLR 84
Park, Nick 1958- 113
Park, (Rosina) Ruth (Lucia) 1923(?)- 93
  Earlier sketch in SATA 25
  See also CLR 51
Park, W(illiam) B(ryan) 1936- 22
Parke, Marilyn 1928- 82
Parker, Barbara Keevil 1938- 157
Parker, Daniel
  See Ehrenhaft, Daniel
Parker, Elinor Milnor 1906- 3
Parker, Julie F. 1961- 92
Parker, Kim 1963- 174
Parker, Kristy 1957- 59
Parker, Lois M(ay) 1912-1996 30
Parker, Margot M. 1937- 52
Parker, Marjorie Blain 1960- 205
  Earlier sketch in SATA 145
Parker, Mary Jessie 1948- 71

Parker, Nancy Winslow 1930- 132
  Earlier sketches in SATA 10, 69
  See also SAAS 20
Parker, Richard 1915-1990 14
Parker, Robert
  See Boyd, Waldo T.
  and Parker, Robert Andrew
Parker, Robert Andrew 1927- 200
Parker, Toni Trent 1947-2005 142
  Obituary 169
Parker-Rees, Guy 193
Parkes, Lucas
  See Harris, John (Wyndham Parkes Lucas)
  Beynon
Parkhill, John
  See Cox, William R(obert)
Parkins, David 1955- 176
Parkinson, Ethelyn M(inerva) 1906-1999 11
Parkinson, Kathryn N. 1954- 71
Parkinson, Kathy
  See Parkinson, Kathryn N.
Parkinson, Siobhan
  See Parkinson, Siobhán
Parkinson, Siobhán 1954- 178
Parks, Deborah A. 1948- 133
  Earlier sketch in SATA 91
Parks, Edd Winfield 1906-1968 10
Parks, Gordon 1912-2006 108
  Obituary 175
  Earlier sketch in SATA 8
Parks, Gordon Roger Alexander
  See Parks, Gordon
Parks, Peggy J. 1951- 143
Parks, PJ
  See Parks, Peggy J.
Parks, Rosa 1913-2005 83
  Obituary 169
Parks, Rosa Louise Lee
  See Parks, Rosa
Parks, Van Dyke 1943- 62
Parley, Peter
  See Goodrich, Samuel Griswold
Parlin, John
  See Graves, Charles Parlin
Parme, Fabrice 1966- 191
Parnall, Peter 1936- 69
  Earlier sketch in SATA 16
  See also SAAS 11
Parotti, Phillip (Elliott) 1941- 109
Parr, Ann 1943- 144
Parr, Danny
  See Parr, Ann
Parr, Letitia (Evelyn) 1906-1985(?) 37
Parr, Lucy 1924- 10
Parr, Todd 179
  Earlier sketch in SATA 134
Parrish, Anne 1888-1957 27
Parrish, Mary
  See Cousins, Margaret
Parrish, Maxfield
  See Parrish, (Frederick) Maxfield
Parrish, (Frederick) Maxfield 1870-1966 14
Parry, Marian 1924- 13
Parson Lot
  See Kingsley, Charles
Parsons, Alexandra 1947- 92
Parsons, Ellen
  See Dragonwagon, Crescent
Parsons, Garry 197
Parsons, Martin 1951- 116
Parsons, Martin Leslie
  See Parsons, Martin
Parsons, Tom
  See MacPherson, Thomas George
Parsons-Yazzi, Evangeline 172
Partch, Virgil Franklin II 1916-1984 39
  Obituary 39
Parton, Dolly 1946- 94
Parton, Dolly Rebecca
  See Parton, Dolly

Partridge, Benjamin W., Jr. 1915-2005 28
  Obituary 163
Partridge, Benjamin Waring, Jr.
  See Partridge, Benjamin W., Jr.
Partridge, Cora Cheney
  See Cheney, Cora
Partridge, Elizabeth 134
Partridge, Jenny (Lilian) 1947- 52
  Brief entry 37
Pasachoff, Naomi 1947- 147
Pascal, David 1918- 14
Pascal, Francine 1938- 143
  Brief entry 37
  Earlier sketches in SATA 51, 80
  See also CLR 25
Paschal, Nancy
  See Trotter, Grace V(iolet)
Paschkis, Julie 1957- 177
Pascudniak, Pascal
  See Lupoff, Richard A(llen)
Pashko, Stanley 1913-1982 29
Passailaigue, Thomas E.
  See Paisley, Tom
Pastel, Elyse 201
Pateman, Robert 1954- 84
Patent, Dorothy Hinshaw 1940- 162
  Autobiography Feature 162
  Earlier sketches in SATA 22, 69, 120
  See also CLR 19
  See also SAAS 13
Paterson, A(ndrew) B(arton) 1864-1941 97
Paterson, Banjo
  See Paterson, A(ndrew) B(arton)
Paterson, Diane 1946- 177
  Brief entry 33
  Earlier sketch in SATA 59
Paterson, John (Barstow) 1932- 114
Paterson, Katherine 1932- 204
  Earlier sketches in SATA 13, 53, 92, 133
  See also CLR 127
Paterson, Katherine Womeldorf
  See Paterson, Katherine
Patience, John 1949- 90
Patneaude, David 1944- 159
  Earlier sketch in SATA 85
Paton, Alan 1903-1988 11
  Obituary 56
Paton, Alan Stewart
  See Paton, Alan
Paton, Jane (Elizabeth) 1934- 35
Paton, Priscilla 1952- 98
Paton Walsh, Gillian
  See Paton Walsh, Jill
Paton Walsh, Jill 1937- 190
  Autobiography Feature 190
  Earlier sketches in SATA 4, 72, 109
  See also CLR 128
  See also SAAS 3
Patrick, Susan
  See Clark, Patricia Denise
Patron, Susan 1948- 182
  Earlier sketch in SATA 76
Patsauq, Markoosie 1942-
  See CLR 23
Patschke, Steve 1955- 125
Patten, Brian 1946- 152
  Earlier sketch in SATA 29
Patterson, Charles 1935- 59
Patterson, Geoffrey 1943- 54
  Brief entry 44
Patterson, James 1947- 197
  Earlier sketch in SATA 164
Patterson, James B.
  See Patterson, James
Patterson, Lillie G. -1999 88
  Earlier sketch in SATA 14
Patterson, Nancy Ruth 1944- 148
  Earlier sketch in SATA 72
Pattison, Darcy (S.) 1954- 126
  Earlier sketch in SATA 72
Pattou, Edith 164

Patz (Blaustein), Nancy 154
Paul, Aileen 1917- 12
Paul, Alison 196
Paul, Ann Whitford 1941- 168
    Earlier sketches in SATA 76, 110
Paul, David (Tyler) 1934-1988
    Obituary 56
Paul, Dominique 1973- 184
Paul, Elizabeth
    See Crow, Donna Fletcher
Paul, Hamish Vigne Christie 1951- 151
    See also CLR 87
Paul, James 1936- 23
Paul, Korky
    See Paul, Hamish Vigne Christie
Paul, Robert
    See Roberts, John G(aither)
Paul, Tessa 1944- 103
Pauli, Hertha (Ernestine) 1909-1973 3
    Obituary 26
Paull, Grace A. 1898- 24
Paulsen, Gary 1939- 189
    Earlier sketches in SATA 22, 50, 54, 79, 111,
    158
    See also CLR 82
Paulson, Jack
    See Jackson, C(aary) Paul
Pauquet, Gina Ruck
    See Ruck-Pauquet, Gina
Pausacker, Jenny 1948- 72
    See also SAAS 23
Pausewang, Gudrun 1928- 165
    Earlier sketch in SATA 104
Pavel, Frances 1907- 10
Paver, Michelle 170
Paxton, Thomas R. 1937- 70
Paxton, Tom
    See Paxton, Thomas R.
Paye, Won-Ldy 185
Payne, Alan
    See Jakes, John
Payne, Bernal C., Jr. 1941- 60
Payne, C. Douglas
    See Payne, C.D.
Payne, C.D. 1949- 133
Payne, C.F. 1956- 179
Payne, Chris Fox
    See Payne, C.F.
Payne, Donald Gordon 1924- 37
Payne, Emmy
    See West, Emily Govan
Payne, Nina 135
Payne, Rachel Ann
    See Jakes, John
Payson, Dale 1943- 9
Payzant, Charles 18
Paz, A.
    See Pahz, James Alon
Paz, Natalia Toledo
    See Toledo, Natalia
Paz, Zan
    See Pahz, Cheryl Suzanne
Peace, Mary
    See Finley, Mary Peace
Peacock, Shane 1957- 192
Peake, Mervyn 1911-1968 23
Peale, Norman Vincent 1898-1993 20
    Obituary 78
Pearce, Ann Philippa
    See Pearce, Philippa
Pearce, Emily Smith 1975- 199
Pearce, Jacqueline 1962- 146
Pearce, Margaret 104
Pearce, Philippa 1920-2006 129
    Obituary 179
    Earlier sketches in SATA 1, 67
    See also CLR 9
Peare, Catherine Owens 1911- 9
Pearsall, Shelley 1966- 190
Pearson, Gayle 1947- 119
    Earlier sketch in SATA 53

Pearson, Jean Mary
    See Gardam, Jane
Pearson, Kit 1947- 77
    Autobiography Feature 117
    See also CLR 26
Pearson, Mary E. 1955- 134
Pearson, Ridley 1953- 182
Pearson, Susan 1946- 166
    Brief entry 27
    Earlier sketches in SATA 39, 91
Pearson, Tracey Campbell 1956- 155
    Earlier sketch in SATA 64
Pease, (Clarence) Howard 1894-1974 2
    Obituary 25
Peavy, Linda 1943- 54
Peck, Anne Merriman 1884-1976 18
Peck, Beth 1957- 190
    Earlier sketch in SATA 79
Peck, Jan 159
Peck, Jeanie J. 1967- 147
Peck, Marshall III 1951- 92
Peck, Richard 1934- 190
    Autobiography Feature 110
    Earlier sketches in SATA 18, 55, 97, 110, 158
    See also CLR 142
    See also SAAS 2
Peck, Richard Wayne
    See Peck, Richard
Peck, Robert Newton 1928- 156
    Autobiography Feature 108
    Earlier sketches in SATA 21, 62, 111
    See also CLR 45
    See also SAAS 1
Peck, Sylvia 1953- 133
Peck-Whiting, Jeanie J.
    See Peck, Jeanie J.
Peddicord, Jane Ann 199
Pedersen, Janet 193
Pederson, Sharleen
    See Collicott, Sharleen
Pedler, Caroline 197
Peebles, Anne
    See Galloway, Priscilla
Peek, Merle 1938- 39
Peel, John 1954- 79
Peel, Norman Lemon
    See Hirsch, Phil
Peeples, Edwin A(ugustus, Jr.) 1915-1994 6
Peers, Judi 1956- 119
Peers, Judith May West
    See Peers, Judi
Peet, Bill
    See Peet, William Bartlett
Peet, Creighton B. 1899-1977 30
Peet, Mal 171
Peet, Malcolm
    See Peet, Mal
Peet, William Bartlett 1915-2002 78
    Obituary 137
    Earlier sketches in SATA 2, 41
    See also CLR 12
Peguero, Leone 116
Pelaez, Jill 1924- 12
Pelham, David 1938- 70
Pell, Ed(ward) 1950- 157
Pelletier, Andrew T. 195
Pelletier, Andrew Thomas
    See Pelletier, Andrew T.
Pellowski, Anne 1933- 20
Pellowski, Michael (Joseph) 1949- 151
    Brief entry 48
    Earlier sketch in SATA 88
Pellowski, Michael Morgan
    See Pellowski, Michael (Joseph)
Pelta, Kathy 1928- 18
Peltier, Leslie C(opus) 1900-1980 13
Pemberton, Bonnie 191
Pemberton, John Leigh
    See Leigh-Pemberton, John
Pembury, Bill
    See Groom, Arthur William

Pemsteen, Hans
    See Manes, Stephen
Pendennis, Arthur Esquir
    See Thackeray, William Makepeace
Pender, Lydia Podger 1907- 61
Pendery, Rosemary (Schmitz) 7
Pendle, Alexy 1943- 29
Pendle, George 1906-1977
    Obituary 28
Pendleton, Don
    See Cunningham, Chet
    and Garside, Jack
    and Jagninski, Tom
    and Krauzer, Steven M(ark)
    and Obstfeld, Raymond
Pendleton, Thomas 1965- 206
Pendziwol, Jean E. 1965- 177
Pene du Bois, William (Sherman)
    1916-1993 68
    Obituary 74
    Earlier sketch in SATA 4
    See also CLR 1
Penn, Audrey 1950- 22
Penn, Ruth Bonn
    See Rosenberg, Eth Clifford
Pennac, Daniel 1944- 155
Pennage, E. M.
    See Finkel, George (Irvine)
Penner, Fred 1946- 169
    Earlier sketch in SATA 67
Penner, Frederick Ralph Cornelius
    See Penner, Fred
Penney, Grace Jackson 1904-2000 35
Penney, Ian 1960- 76
Penney, Sue 1957- 152
    Earlier sketch in SATA 102
Pennington, Eunice 1923- 27
Pennington, Lillian Boyer 1904-2003 45
Pennypacker, Sara 1951- 187
Penrose, Gordon 1925- 66
Penson, Mary E. 1917- 78
Penzler, Otto 1942- 38
Pepe, Phil 1935- 20
Pepe, Philip
    See Pepe, Phil
Peppe, Rodney (Darrell) 1934- 74
    Earlier sketch in SATA 4
    See also SAAS 10
Pepper, Frank S. 1910-1988
    Obituary 61
Percy, Charles Henry
    See Smith, Dorothy Gladys
Percy, Rachel 1930- 63
Perdrizet, Marie-Pierre 1952- 79
Perenyi, Constance 1954- 93
Perenyi, Constance Marie
    See Perenyi, Constance
Perera, Hilda 1926- 105
Perera, Thomas Biddle 1938- 13
Peretti, Frank E. 1951- 141
    Earlier sketch in SATA 80
Perez, L. King 1940- 199
Perez, Lana
    See Perez, Marlene
Perez, Lucia Angela 1973- 182
Perez, Marlene 170
Pericoli, Matteo 1968- 178
Perkins, Al(bert Rogers) 1904-1975 30
Perkins, Lucy Fitch 1865-1937 72
Perkins, Lynne Rae 1956- 172
    Earlier sketch in SATA 131
Perkins, (Richard) Marlin 1905-1986 21
    Obituary 48
Perkins, Mitali 1963- 188
    Earlier sketch in SATA 88
Perks, Anne-Marie 1955- 122
Perl, Erica S. 188
Perl, Lila 72
    Earlier sketch in SATA 6
Perl, Susan 1922-1983 22
    Obituary 34

Perlman, Rhea 1948- *183*
Perlmutter, O(scar) William 1920-1975 .... *8*
Pernu, Dennis 1970- *87*
Perrault, Charles 1628-1703 .... *25*
   See also CLR *134*
Perret, Delphine 1980- *190*
Perret, Gene (Richard) 1937- *76*
Perrine, Mary 1913-1976 .... *2*
Perrins, Lesley 1953- *56*
Perrow, Angeli 1954- *121*
Perry, Andrea 1956- *190*
   Earlier sketch in SATA *148*
Perry, Barbara Fisher
   See Fisher, Barbara
Perry, Elizabeth 1959- *174*
Perry, Elizabeth Goodwin
   See Perry, Elizabeth
Perry, Marie Fritz *165*
Perry, Patricia 1949- *30*
Perry, Phyllis J(ean) 1933- *152*
   Earlier sketches in SATA *60, 101*
Perry, Ritchie (John Allen) 1942- *105*
Perry, Roger 1933- *27*
Perry, Steve(n Carl) 1947- *76*
Pershall, Mary K. 1951- *172*
   Earlier sketch in SATA *70*
Pershing, Marie
   See Schultz, Pearle Henriksen
Perske, Robert 1927- *57*
Persun, Morgan Reed
   See Watkins, Dawn L.
Petach, Heidi *149*
Peter
   See Stratemeyer, Edward L.
Peters, Alexander
   See Hollander, Zander
Peters, Andrew Fusek 1965- *169*
   Earlier sketch in SATA *107*
Peters, Caroline
   See Betz, Eva Kelly
Peters, David
   See David, Peter
Peters, Elizabeth 1927- *49*
Peters, Emma
   See Price, Karen
Peters, Gabriel
   See Matott, Justin
Peters, Julie Anne 1952- *197*
   Earlier sketches in SATA *82, 128*
Peters, Linda
   See Catherall, Arthur
Peters, Lisa Westberg 1951- *161*
   Earlier sketches in SATA *74, 115*
Peters, Patricia 1953- *84*
Peters, Russell M. 1929- *78*
Peters, S. H.
   See Henry, O.
   and Proffitt, Nicholas
Petersen, David 1946- *109*
   Earlier sketch in SATA *62*
Petersen, Gwenn Boardman 1924- *12*
Petersen, P(eter) J(ames) 1941- *118*
   Brief entry *43*
   Earlier sketches in SATA *48, 83*
Petersen, Palle 1943- *85*
Petersham, Maud 1890-1971 .... *17*
   See also CLR *24*
Petersham, Maud Sylvia Fuller
   See Petersham, Maud
Petersham, Miska 1888-1960 .... *17*
   See also CLR *24*
Peterson, Cris 1952- *174*
   Earlier sketches in SATA *84, 145*
Peterson, Dawn 1934- *86*
Peterson, Esther (Allen) 1934- *35*
Peterson, Hans 1922- *8*
Peterson, Harold L(eslie) 1922-1978 .... *8*
Peterson, Helen Stone 1910- *8*
Peterson, Jean Sunde 1941- *108*
Peterson, Jeanne Whitehouse 1939- *159*
   Earlier sketch in SATA *29*

Peterson, Kathleen B. 1951- *119*
Peterson, Lorraine 1940- *56*
   Brief entry *44*
Peterson, Shelley 1952- *146*
Peterson, Will
   See Cocks, Peter
Petie, Haris
   See Petty, Roberta
Petricic, Dusan 1946- *176*
Petrides, Heidrun 1944- *19*
Petrie, Catherine 1947- *52*
   Brief entry *41*
Petrone, Valeria *186*
Petrosino, Tamara *193*
Petroski, Catherine (Ann Groom) 1939- *48*
Petrovich, Michael B(oro) 1922- *40*
Petrovskaya, Kyra
   See Wayne, Kyra Petrovskaya
Petruccio, Steven James 1961- *67*
Petry, Ann (Lane) 1908-1997 .... *5*
   Obituary *94*
   See also CLR *12*
Pettit, Jayne 1932- *108*
Petty, J.T. 1977- *189*
Petty, Kate 1951-2007 .... *204*
Petty, Roberta 1915- *10*
Pevsner, Stella *131*
   Earlier sketches in SATA *8, 77*
   See also SAAS *14*
Peyo
   See Culliford, Pierre
Peyton, K. M.
   See Peyton, Kathleen Wendy
Peyton, Kathleen Wendy 1929- *157*
   Earlier sketches in SATA *15, 62*
   See also CLR *3*
   See also SAAS *17*
Pfanner, (Anne) Louise 1955- *68*
Pfeffer, Susan Beth 1948- *180*
   Earlier sketches in SATA *4, 83*
   See also CLR *11*
   See also SAAS *17*
Pfeffer, Wendy 1929- *204*
   Earlier sketches in SATA *78, 142*
Pfeiffer, Janet (B.) 1949- *96*
Pfister, Marcus *150*
   Earlier sketch in SATA *83*
   See also CLR *42*
Pfitsch, Patricia Curtis 1948- *148*
Pflieger, Pat 1955- *84*
Pham, LeUyen 1973- *201*
   Earlier sketch in SATA *175*
Phelan, Mary Kay 1914- *3*
Phelan, Matt 1970- *172*
Phelan, Terry Wolfe 1941- *56*
Phelps, Ethel Johnston 1914-1984 .... *35*
Philbrick, Rodman 1951- *163*
Philbrick, W. R.
   See Philbrick, Rodman
Philbrick, W. Rodman
   See Philbrick, Rodman
Philbrook, Clem(ent E.) 1917- *24*
Phillips, Aileen Paul
   See Paul, Aileen
Phillips, Betty Lou
   See Phillips, Elizabeth Louise
Phillips, Bob 1940- *95*
Phillips, Douglas A. 1949- *161*
Phillips, Elizabeth Louise *58*
   Brief entry *48*
Phillips, Irv(ing W.) 1905-2000 .... *11*
   Obituary *125*
Phillips, Jack
   See Sandburg, Carl (August)
Phillips, Leon
   See Gerson, Noel Bertram
Phillips, Loretta (Hosey) 1893-1987 .... *10*
Phillips, Louis 1942- *102*
   Earlier sketch in SATA *8*

Phillips, Mark
   See Garrett, Randall
   and Janifer, Laurence M(ark)
Phillips, Mary Geisler 1881-1964 .... *10*
Phillips, Michael
   See Nolan, William F(rancis)
Phillips, (Woodward) Prentice 1894-1981 .... *10*
Phillpotts, Eden 1862-1960 .... *24*
Phin
   See Thayer, Ernest Lawrence
Phipson, Joan
   See Fitzhardinge, Joan Margaret
Phiz
   See Browne, Hablot Knight
Phleger, Fred B. 1909-1993 .... *34*
Phleger, Marjorie Temple 1908(?)-1986 .... *1*
   Obituary *47*
Piaget, Jean 1896-1980
   Obituary *23*
Piatti, Celestino 1922- *16*
Picard, Barbara Leonie 1917- *89*
   Earlier sketch in SATA *2*
   See also SAAS *10*
Pichon, Liz *174*
Pickard, Charles 1932- *36*
Pickering, James Sayre 1897-1969 .... *36*
   Obituary *28*
Pickering, Jimmy *195*
Pickering, Robert B. 1950- *93*
Pielichaty, Helena 1955- *142*
Pienkowski, Jan (Michal) 1936- *131*
   Earlier sketches in SATA *6, 58*
   See also CLR *6*
Pierce, Edith Gray 1893-1977 .... *45*
Pierce, Katherine
   See St. John, Wylly Folk
Pierce, Meredith Ann 1958- *127*
   Brief entry *48*
   Earlier sketch in SATA *67*
   See also CLR *20*
Pierce, Ruth (Ireland) 1936- *5*
Pierce, Sharon
   See McCullough, Sharon Pierce
Pierce, Tamora 1954- *187*
   Brief entry *49*
   Earlier sketches in SATA *51, 96, 153*
Pierce, Terry *178*
Pierik, Robert 1921- *13*
Piernas-Davenport, Gail *199*
Piers, Robert
   See Anthony, Piers
Pig, Edward
   See Gorey, Edward (St. John)
Pike, Bob
   See Pike, Robert W(ilson)
Pike, Christopher 1954(?)- *156*
   Earlier sketch in SATA *68*
   See also CLR *29*
Pike, Deborah 1951- *89*
Pike, E(dgar) Royston 1896-1980 .... *22*
   Obituary *56*
Pike, R. William 1956- *92*
Pike, Robert W(ilson) 1931- *102*
Pilarski, Laura 1926- *13*
Pilgrim, Anne
   See Allan, Mabel Esther
Pilkey, Dav 1966- *166*
   Earlier sketches in SATA *68, 115*
   See also CLR *48*
Pilkey, David Murray, Jr.
   See Pilkey, Dav
Pilkington, Francis Meredyth 1907-1993 .... *4*
Pilkington, Roger (Windle) 1915-2003 .... *10*
   Obituary *144*
Pin, Isabel 1975- *183*
Pinchot, David 1914(?)-1983
   Obituary *34*
Pincus, Harriet 1938- *27*
Pinczes, Elinor J(ane) 1940- *81*
Pine, Nicholas 1951- *91*
Pine, Tillie S(chloss) 1896-1999 .... *13*

Pini, Richard (Alan) 1950- 89
Pini, Wendy 1951- 89
Pinkerton, Kathrene Sutherland (Gedney)
   1887-1967
   Obituary 26
Pinkett, Jada
   See Smith, Jada Pinkett
Pinkney, Andrea Davis 1963- 160
   Earlier sketch in SATA *113*
Pinkney, Brian 1961- 206
   Earlier sketches in SATA *74, 148*
   See also CLR *54*
Pinkney, Gloria Jean 1941- 85
Pinkney, J. Brian
   See Pinkney, Brian
Pinkney, Jerry 1939- 198
   Autobiography Feature 198
   Brief entry 32
   Earlier sketches in SATA *41, 71, 107, 151*
   See also CLR *43*
   See also SAAS *12*
Pinkney, John 97
Pinkney, Sandra L. 193
   Earlier sketch in SATA *128*
Pinkwater, D. Manus
   See Pinkwater, Daniel
Pinkwater, Daniel 1941- 158
   Earlier sketches in SATA *8, 46, 76, 114*
   See also CLR *4*
   See also SAAS *3*
Pinkwater, Daniel M.
   See Pinkwater, Daniel
Pinkwater, Daniel Manus
   See Pinkwater, Daniel
Pinkwater, Jill 188
Pinkwater, Manus
   See Pinkwater, Daniel
Pinner, Joma
   See Werner, Herma
Pinto, Sara 200
Pioneer
   See Yates, Raymond F(rancis)
Piowaty, Kim Kennelly 1957- 49
Piper, Roger
   See Fisher, John
Pirner, Connie White 1955- 72
Piro, Richard 1934- 7
Pirot, Alison Lohans
   See Lohans, Alison
Pirotta, Saviour 184
Pirsig, Robert M(aynard) 1928- 39
Pita
   See Rendon, Maria
Pitcher, C.
   See Pitcher, Caroline
Pitcher, Caroline 1948- 128
Pitcher, Caroline Nell
   See Pitcher, Caroline
Pitman, (Isaac) James 1901-1985
   Obituary 46
Pitre, Felix 1949- 84
Pitrone, Jean Maddern 1920- 4
Pittman, Helena Clare 1945- 71
Pitz, Henry C(larence) 1895-1976 4
   Obituary 24
Pitzer, Susanna 1958- 181
Piven, Hanoch 1963- 173
Pixley, Marcella 194
Pizer, Vernon 1918- 21
Place, Marian T(empleton) 1910- 3
Place, Robin (Mary) 1926- 71
Plaidy, Jean
   See Hibbert, Eleanor Alice Burford
Plain, Belva 1919- 62
Plaine, Alfred R. 1898(?)-1981
   Obituary 29
Plath, Sylvia 1932-1963 96
Platt, Chris 1959- 185
Platt, Kin 1911- 86
   Earlier sketch in SATA *21*
   See also SAAS *17*

Platt, Randall 1948- 95
Platt, Randall Beth
   See Platt, Randall
Platt, Richard 1953- 166
   Earlier sketch in SATA *120*
Playfellow, Robin
   See Ellis, Edward S.
Playsted, James
   See Wood, James Playsted
Plecas, Jennifer 1966- 149
   Earlier sketch in SATA *84*
Plimpton, George 1927-2003 10
   Obituary 150
Plimpton, George Ames
   See Plimpton, George
Plomer, William Charles Franklin
   1903-1973 24
Plotz, Helen Ratnoff 1913-2000 38
Plourde, Lynn 1955- 168
   Earlier sketch in SATA *122*
Plowden, David 1932- 52
Plowden, Martha Ward 1948- 98
Plowhead, Ruth Gipson 1877-1967 43
Plowman, Stephanie 1922- 6
Pluckrose, Henry (Arthur) 1931- 141
   Earlier sketch in SATA *13*
Plum, J.
   See Wodehouse, P(elham) G(renville)
Plum, Jennifer
   See Kurland, Michael
Plumb, Charles P. 1900(?)-1982
   Obituary 29
Plume, Ilse 170
   Brief entry 43
Plumme, Don E.
   See Katz, Bobbi
Plummer, Margaret 1911- 2
Plum-Ucci, Carol 184
Pochocki, Ethel (Frances) 1925- 76
Podendorf, Illa (E.) 1903(?)-1983 18
   Obituary 35
Podwal, Mark 1945- 160
   Earlier sketch in SATA *101*
Podwal, Mark H.
   See Podwal, Mark
Poe, Edgar Allan 1809-1849 23
Poe, Ty (Christopher) 1975- 94
Pogany, William Andrew 1882-1955 44
   Brief entry 30
Pogany, Willy
   See Pogany, William Andrew
Pohl, Frederik 1919- 24
Pohlmann, Lillian (Grenfell) 1902-1997 11
Pohrt, Tom 1953- 195
   Earlier sketches in SATA *67, 152*
Pointon, Robert
   See Rooke, Daphne
Points, Larry G. 1945- 177
   Earlier sketch in SATA *133*
Points, Larry Gene
   See Points, Larry G.
Pokeberry, P.J.
   See Mitchell, B.J.
POLA
   See Watson, Pauline
Polacco, Patricia 1944- 180
   Earlier sketches in SATA *74, 123*
   See also CLR *40*
Polacco, Patricia Ann
   See Polacco, Patricia
Polak, Monique 1960- 178
Polatnick, Florence T. 1923- 5
Polder, Markus
   See Kruss, James
Polese, Carolyn 1947- 58
Polese, James 1914- 87
Polette, Nancy (Jane) 1930- 42
Polhamus, Jean Burt 1928- 21
Policoff, Stephen Phillip 1948- 77
Polikoff, Barbara G. 1929- 162
   Earlier sketch in SATA *77*

Polikoff, Barbara Garland
   See Polikoff, Barbara G.
Polisar, Barry Louis 1954- 134
   Earlier sketch in SATA *77*
Politi, Leo 1908-1996 47
   Obituary 88
   Earlier sketch in SATA *1*
   See also CLR *29*
Polking, Kirk 1925- 5
Pollack, Jill S. 1963- 88
Pollack, Merrill S. 1924-1988
   Obituary 55
Polland, Barbara K(ay) 1939- 44
Polland, Madeleine A(ngela Cahill) 1918- ... 68
   Earlier sketch in SATA *6*
   See also SAAS *8*
Pollema-Cahill, Phyllis 1958- 123
Pollock, Bruce 1945- 46
Pollock, Mary
   See Blyton, Enid
Pollock, Penny 1935- 137
   Brief entry 42
   Earlier sketch in SATA *44*
Pollowitz, Melinda Kilborn 1944- 26
Polner, Murray 1928- 64
Polonsky, Arthur 1925- 34
Polseno, Jo 17
Pomaska, Anna 1946- 117
Pomerantz, Charlotte 1930- 177
   Earlier sketches in SATA *20, 80*
Pomeroy, Pete
   See Roth, Arthur J(oseph)
Pond, Alonzo W(illiam) 1894-1986 5
Pontiflet, Ted 1932- 32
Poole, Gray Johnson 1906- 1
Poole, Josephine
   See Helyar, Jane Penelope Josephine
Poole, (Jane Penelope) Josephine
   See Helyar, Jane Penelope Josephine
Poole, Lynn 1910-1969 1
Poole, Peggy 1925- 39
Poortvliet, Rien 1932- 65
   Brief entry 37
Pope, Elizabeth Marie 1917-1992 38
   Brief entry 36
Pope, Kevin 1958- 183
Popescu, Christine
   See Pullein-Thompson, Christine
Poploff, Michelle 1956- 67
Popp, K. Wendy 91
Poppel, Hans 1942- 71
Porfirio, Guy 1958- 197
Portal, Colette 1936- 6
Porte, Barbara Ann 1943- 152
   Brief entry 45
   Earlier sketches in SATA *57, 93*
Porter, A(nthony) P(eyton) 1945- 68
Porter, Connie (Rose) 1959(?)- 129
   Earlier sketch in SATA *81*
Porter, Donald Clayton
   See Gerson, Noel Bertram
Porter, Eleanor H(odgman) 1868-1920
   See CLR *110*
Porter, Gene Stratton
   See Stratton-Porter, Gene
Porter, Janice Lee 1953- 108
   Earlier sketch in SATA *68*
Porter, Katherine Anne 1890-1980 39
   Obituary 23
Porter, Kathryn
   See Swinford, Betty (June Wells)
Porter, Pamela 1956- 193
Porter, Sheena 1935- 24
   See also SAAS *10*
Porter, Sue
   See Limb, Sue
Porter, Sue 1951- 76
Porter, Tracey 191
Porter, William Sydney
   See Henry, O.
Portis, Antoinette 189

Porto, Tony 1960- 153
Portteus, Eleanora Marie Manthei (?)-1983
  Obituary 36
Posada, Mia 187
Posell, Elsa Z(eigerman) -1995 3
Posten, Margaret L(ois) 1915- 10
Posthuma, Sieb 1960- 150
Postier, Jim 1965- 202
Potok, Chaim 1929-2002 106
  Obituary 134
  Earlier sketch in SATA 33
  See also CLR 92
Potok, Herbert Harold -2002
  See Potok, Chaim
Potok, Herman Harold
  See Potok, Chaim
Potter, Beatrix 1866-1943 132
  Earlier sketch in SATA 100
  See also YABC 1
  See also CLR 73
Potter, Giselle 187
  Earlier sketch in SATA 150
Potter, Helen Beatrix
  See Potter, Beatrix
Potter, Margaret 1926-1998 21
  Obituary 104
Potter, Marian 1915- 9
Potter, Miriam Clark 1886-1965 3
Poulin, Stephane 1961- 98
  See also CLR 28
Poulton, Kimberly 1957(?)- 136
Pournelle, Jerry (Eugene) 1933- 161
  Earlier sketches in SATA 26, 91
Povelite, Kay 1955- 102
Pow, Tom 1950- 163
Powe-Allred, Alexandra
  See Allred, Alexandra Powe
Powell, A. M.
  See Morgan, Alfred P(owell)
Powell, Consie 174
Powell, E. Sandy 1947- 72
Powell, E.S.
  See Powell, E. Sandy
Powell, Pamela 1960- 78
Powell, Patricia Hruby 1951- 136
Powell, Randy 1956- 118
Powell, Richard Stillman
  See Barbour, Ralph Henry
Powell, Robert (Stephenson Smyth) Baden
  See Baden-Powell, Robert (Stephenson
  Smyth)
Powell, Stephanie 1953- 93
Power, Margaret (M.) 1945- 125
  Earlier sketch in SATA 75
Powers, Anne
  See Schwartz, Anne Powers
Powers, Bill 1931- 52
  Brief entry 31
Powers, Daniel 1959- 164
Powers, Jessica Lynn
  See Powers, J.L.
Powers, J.L. 1974- 195
Powers, Margaret
  See Heal, Edith
Powers, Tim 1952- 107
Powers, Timothy Thomas
  See Powers, Tim
Powledge, Fred 1935- 37
Poydar, Nancy 190
Poynter, Margaret 1927- 27
Prachaticka, Marketa
  See Kolibalova, Marketa
Prachatika, Marketa
  See Kolibalova, Marketa
Prager, Arthur 44
Prager, Ellen J. 1962- 136
Prange, Beckie 172
Prap, Lila 1955- 177
Praprotnik-Zupancic, Lilijana
  See Prap, Lila

Pratchett, Terence David John
  See Pratchett, Terry
Pratchett, Terry 1948- 185
  Earlier sketches in SATA 82, 139
  See also CLR 64
Prater, John 1947- 149
  Earlier sketches in SATA 72, 103
Prato, Rodica 184
Pratt, (Murray) Fletcher 1897-1956 102
Pratt, Kristin Joy 1976- 87
Pratt, Pierre 1962- 166
  Earlier sketch in SATA 95
Preiss, Byron 1953-2005 166
  Brief entry 42
  Earlier sketch in SATA 47
Preiss, Byron Cary
  See Preiss, Byron
Preller, James 1961- 88
Prelutsky, Jack 1940- 171
  Earlier sketches in SATA 22, 66, 118
  See also CLR 115
Prentice, Amy
  See Kaler, James Otis
Prescott, Casey
  See Morris, Chris(topher Crosby)
Presnall, Judith (Ann) Janda 1943- 96
Pressler, Mirjam 1940- 155
Preston, Douglas 1956- 113
Preston, Edna Mitchell 40
Preston, Lillian Elvira 1918- 47
Preussler, Otfried 1923- 24
Prevert, Jacques (Henri Marie) 1900-1977
  Obituary 30
Prevost, Guillaume 1964- 192
Prevost, Mikela 203
Price, Beverley Joan 1931- 98
Price, Charlie 187
Price, Christine (Hilda) 1928-1980 3
  Obituary 23
Price, Garrett 1896-1979
  Obituary 22
Price, Jennifer
  See Hoover, Helen (Drusilla Blackburn)
Price, Joan 1931- 124
Price, Jonathan (Reeve) 1941- 46
Price, Karen 1957- 125
Price, Kathy Z. 1957- 172
Price, Lucie Locke
  See Locke, Lucie
Price, Olive 1903-1991 8
Price, Susan 1955- 128
  Earlier sketches in SATA 25, 85
Price, Willard 1887-1983 48
  Brief entry 38
Price-Groff, Claire 127
Priceman, Marjorie 1958- 168
  Earlier sketches in SATA 81, 120
Prichard, Katharine Susannah 1883-1969 66
Prideaux, Tom 1908-1993 37
  Obituary 76
Priestley, Alice 1962- 95
Priestley, Chris 1958- 198
Priestley, Lee (Shore) 1904-1999 27
Priestly, Doug 1954- 122
Priestly, Douglas Michael
  See Priestly, Doug
Prieto, Mariana Beeching 1912-1999 8
Priley, Margaret (Ann) Hubbard 1909-1992
  Obituary 130
Primavera, Elise 1954- 185
  Brief entry 48
  Earlier sketches in SATA 58, 109
Prime, Derek (James) 1931- 34
Prince, Alison (Mary) 1931- 86
  Earlier sketch in SATA 28
Prince, April Jones 1975- 180
Prince, J(ack) H(arvey) 1908- 17
Prince, Joshua 188
Prince, Maggie 102
Prineas, Sarah 204
Pringle, Eric 138

Pringle, Laurence 1935- 201
  Autobiography Feature 201
  Earlier sketches in SATA 4, 68, 104, 154
  See also CLR 57
  See also SAAS 6
Pringle, Laurence Patrick
  See Pringle, Laurence
Prinz, Yvonne 1960- 175
Prior, Natalie Jane 1963- 106
Pritchett, Elaine H(illyer) 1920- 36
Pritchett, Laura 1971- 178
Pritchett, Laura Rose
  See Pritchett, Laura
Pritts, Kim Derek 1953- 83
Prochazkova, Iva 1953- 68
Proctor, Everitt
  See Montgomery, Rutherford George
Proeysen, Alf 1914-1970 67
  See also CLR 24
Professor Scribbler
  See Hollingsworth, Mary
Proimos, James 1955- 173
Prose, Francine 1947- 198
  Earlier sketches in SATA 101, 149
Protopopescu, Orel 186
Protopopescu, Orel Odinov
  See Protopopescu, Orel
Provensen, Alice 1918- 147
  Earlier sketches in SATA 9, 70
  See also CLR 11
Provensen, Martin 1916-1987 70
  Obituary 51
  Earlier sketch in SATA 9
  See also CLR 11
Provensen, Martin Elias
  See Provensen, Martin
Provenzo, Eugene (F., Jr.) 1949- 142
  Earlier sketch in SATA 78
Provist, d'Alain 1906-1989
  See Diop, Birago (Ismael)
Provost, Gail Levine 1944- 65
Provost, Gary (Richard) 1944-1995 66
Proysen, Alf
  See Proeysen, Alf
Pruett, Candace (J.) 1968- 157
Pryor, Bonnie H. 1942- 69
Pryor, Boori (Monty) 1950- 112
Pryor, Helen Brenton 1897-1972 4
Pryor, Michael 1957- 153
Pucci, Albert John 1920- 44
Pudney, John (Sleigh) 1909-1977 24
Pugh, Ellen (Tiffany) 1920- 7
Pullein-Thompson, Christine 1925-2005 82
  Obituary 172
  Earlier sketch in SATA 3
Pullein-Thompson, Diana
  See Farr, Diana
Pullein-Thompson, Joanna Maxwell
  1898-1961 82
Pullein-Thompson, Josephine (Mary
  Wedderburn) 82
  Earlier sketch in SATA 3
Pullen, Zachary 189
Pullman, Philip 1946- 198
  Earlier sketches in SATA 65, 103, 150
  See also CLR 84
  See also SAAS 17
Pullman, Philip Nicholas
  See Pullman, Philip
Pulver, Harry, Jr. 1960- 129
Pulver, Robin 1945- 133
  Earlier sketch in SATA 76
Puner, Helen W(alker) 1915-1989 37
  Obituary 63
Purdy, Carol 1943- 120
  Earlier sketch in SATA 66
Purdy, Susan G(old) 1939- 8
Purkiss, Diane 1961- 194
Purmell, Ann 1953- 206
  Earlier sketch in SATA 147
Purnell, Idella 1901-1982 120

Purscell, Phyllis 1934- 7
Purtill, Richard L. 1931- 53
Pushker, Gloria 1927- 162
   Earlier sketch in SATA 75
Pushker, Gloria Teles
   See Pushker, Gloria
Pushkin, Aleksandr Sergeevich
   See Pushkin, Alexander
Pushkin, Alexander 1799-1837 61
Putnam, Alice 1916- 61
Putnam, Arthur Lee
   See Alger, Horatio, Jr.
Putnam, Peter B(rock) 1920-1998 30
   Obituary 106
Puttapipat, Niroot 199
Puttock, Simon 178
Puvilland, Alex 205
Puvilland, Alexandre
   See Puvilland, Alex
Puybaret, Eric 1976- 195
Pyle, Howard 1853-1911 100
   Earlier sketch in SATA 16
   See also CLR 117
Pyle, Katharine 1863-1938 66
Pyne, Mable Mandeville 1903-1969 9
Pyrnelle, Louise-Clarke 1850-1907 114

Q

Quackenbush, Robert M(ead) 1929- 133
   Autobiography Feature 133
   Earlier sketches in SATA 7, 70
   See also CLR 122
   See also SAAS 7
Qualey, Marsha 1953- 124
   Earlier sketch in SATA 79
Qualls, Sean 177
Quammen, David 1948- 7
Quark, Jason
   See Eldin, Peter
Quarles, Benjamin 1904-1996 12
Quarles, Benjamin Arthur
   See Quarles, Benjamin
Quatermass, Martin
   See Carpenter, John
Quattlebaum, Mary 1958- 185
   Earlier sketches in SATA 88, 134
Quay, Emma 173
   Earlier sketch in SATA 119
Queen, Ellery
   See Deming, Richard
   and Dannay, Frederic
   and Davidson, Avram (James)
   and Fairman, Paul W.
   and Flora, Fletcher
   and Holding, James (Clark Carlisle, Jr.)
   and Hoch, Edward D.
   and Kane, Henry
   and Lee, Manfred B.
   and Marlowe, Stephen
   and Powell, (Oval) Talmage
   and Sheldon, Walter J(ames)
   and Sturgeon, Theodore (Hamilton)
   and Tracy, Don(ald Fiske)
   and Vance, Jack
Queen Latifah 1970- 185
Quennell, Marjorie Courtney 1884-1972 29
Quentin
   See Sheldon, David
Quentin, Brad
   See Bisson, Terry
Quest, (Edna) Olga W(ilbourne) Hall
   See Hall-Quest, (Edna) Olga W(ilbourne)
Quick, Annabelle 1922-1986 2
Quigg, Jane (Hulda) (?)-1986
   Obituary 49
Quill, Monica
   See McInerny, Ralph

Quin-Harkin, Janet 1941- 165
   Earlier sketches in SATA 18, 90, 119
Quin-Harkin, Janet Elizabeth
   See Quin-Harkin, Janet
Quinlan, Susan E. 1954- 88
Quinlan, Susan Elizabeth
   See Quinlan, Susan E.
Quinn, Elisabeth 1881-1962 22
Quinn, Pat 1947- 130
Quinn, Patrick 1950- 73
Quinn, Rob 1972- 138
Quinn, Susan 1940- 30
Quinn, Susan Taft
   See Quinn, Susan
Quinn, Theodora K.
   See Kroeber, Theodora (Kracaw)
Quinn, Vernon
   See Quinn, Elisabeth
Quintano, D.M.
   See Sheldon, Dyan
Quirk, Anne (E.) 1956- 99
Quixley, Jim 1931- 56
Quyth, Gabriel
   See Jennings, Gary

R

Ra, Carol F. 1939- 76
Raab, Evelyn 1951- 129
Rabb, Margo 1972- 188
Rabb, M.E.
   See Rabb, Margo
Rabe, Berniece (Louise) 1928- 148
   Autobiography Feature 148
   Earlier sketches in SATA 7, 77
   See also SAAS 10
Rabe, Olive H(anson) (?)-1968 13
Rabin, Staton 1958- 162
   Earlier sketch in SATA 84
Rabinowich, Ellen 1946- 29
Rabinowitz, Sandy 1954- 52
   Brief entry 39
Rachlin, Carol K(ing) 1919- 64
Rachlin, Harvey 1951- 47
Rachlin, Harvey Brant
   See Rachlin, Harvey
Rachlin, Nahid 64
Rachlis, Eugene (Jacob) 1920-1986
   Obituary 50
Rackham, Arthur 1867-1939 100
   Earlier sketch in SATA 15
   See also CLR 57
Raczka, Bob 1963- 191
   Earlier sketch in SATA 163
Radencich, Marguerite C. 1952-1998 79
Rader, Laura 197
Radford, Ruby L(orraine) 1891-1971 6
Radin, Ruth Yaffe 1938- 107
   Brief entry 52
   Earlier sketch in SATA 56
Radlauer, David 1952- 28
Radlauer, Edward 1921- 15
Radlauer, Ruth Shaw 1926- 98
   Earlier sketch in SATA 15
Radley, Gail 1951- 112
   Earlier sketch in SATA 25
Radunsky, Vladimir 177
Rae, Gwynedd 1892-1977 37
Raebeck, Lois 1921- 5
Rael, Elsa Okon 1927-
   See CLR 84
Raffi
   See Cavoukian, Raffi
Raftery, Gerald (Bransfield) 1905-1986 11
Ragan-Reid, Gale 1956- 90
Rahaman, Vashanti 1953- 98
Rahn, Joan Elma 1929- 27
Rai, Bali 1971- 152
Raible, Alton (Robert) 1918- 35

Raiff, Stan 1930- 11
Raines, Shirley C(arol) 1945- 128
Rainey, W. B.
   See Blassingame, Wyatt Rainey
Rake, Jody 1961- 157
Rallison, Janette 1966- 183
Ralston, Jan
   See Dunlop, Agnes M. R.
Rama, Sue 190
Ramal, Walter
   See de la Mare, Walter (John)
Ramanujan, A(ttipat) K(rishnaswami)
   1929-1993 86
Rame, David
   See Divine, Arthur Durham
Ramirez, Jose 1967- 198
Ramirez, Orlando L. 1972- 194
Ramos, Jorge 1958- 205
Ramstad, Ralph L. 1919- 115
Rana, Indi
   See Rana, Indira Higham
Rana, Indira Higham 1944- 82
Rana, J.
   See Bhatia, Jamunadevi
Ranadive, Gail 1944- 10
Rand, Ann (Binkley) 30
Rand, Gloria 1925- 156
   Earlier sketch in SATA 101
Rand, Paul 1914-1996 6
Randall, Carrie
   See Ransom, Candice F.
Randall, David 1972- 167
Randall, Florence Engel 1917-1997 5
Randall, Janet
   See Young, Janet Randall
   and Young, Robert W(illiam)
Randall, Robert
   See Garrett, Randall
   and Silverberg, Robert
Randall, Ruth (Elaine) Painter 1892-1971 3
Randell, Beverley
   See Price, Beverley Joan
Randle, Kristen D. 1952- 92
   Autobiography Feature 119
   See also SAAS 24
Randle, Kristen Downey
   See Randle, Kristen D.
Randolph, Boynton M.D.
   See Ellis, Edward S.
Randolph, Ellen
   See Rawn, Melanie
Randolph, Geoffrey
   See Ellis, Edward S.
Randolph, J. H.
   See Ellis, Edward S.
Randolph, Lieutenant J. H.
   See Ellis, Edward S.
Rands, William Brighty 1823-1882 17
Raney, Ken 1953- 74
Rankin, Joan 1940- 148
   Earlier sketch in SATA 88
Rankin, Laura 1953(?)- 176
Ranney, Agnes V. 1916-1985 6
Ransom, Candice F. 1952- 183
   Brief entry 49
   Earlier sketches in SATA 52, 89, 135
Ransom, Jeanie Franz 1957- 187
Ransome, Arthur (Michell) 1884-1967 22
   See also CLR 8
Ransome, James E. 1961- 178
   Earlier sketches in SATA 76, 123
   See also CLR 86
Rant, Tol E.
   See Longyear, Barry B(rookes)
Raphael, Elaine
   See Bolognese, Elaine
Raposo, Joseph Guilherme 1938-1989
   Obituary 61
Rapp, Adam 1968- 148
Rappaport, Doreen 151
Rappaport, Eva 1924- 6

Rappoport, Ken 1935- *167*
  Earlier sketch in SATA *89*
Rarick, Carrie 1911-2002 .... *41*
Raschka, Chris 1959- *166*
  Earlier sketches in SATA *80, 117*
Raschka, Christopher
  See Raschka, Chris
Rascol, Sabina I. *159*
Rash, Andy *162*
Raskin, Edith Lefkowitz 1908-1987 .... *9*
Raskin, Ellen 1928-1984 .... *139*
  Earlier sketches in SATA *2, 38*
  See also CLR *12*
Raskin, Joseph 1897-1982 .... *12*
  Obituary *29*
Rathjen, Carl Henry 1909-1984 .... *11*
Rathmann, Peggy 1953- *157*
  Earlier sketch in SATA *94*
  See also CLR *77*
Ratliff, Thomas M. 1948- *118*
Ratner, Sue Lynn
  See Alexander, Sue
Rattigan, Jama Kim 1951- *99*
Ratto, Linda Lee 1952- *79*
Rattray, Simon
  See Trevor, Elleston
Ratz de Tagyos, Paul 1958- *198*
  Earlier sketch in SATA *76*
Rau, Dana Meachen 1971- *167*
  Earlier sketch in SATA *94*
Rau, Margaret 1913- *168*
  Earlier sketch in SATA *9*
  See also CLR *8*
Rauch, Mabel Thompson 1888-1972
  Obituary *26*
Raucher, Herman 1928- *8*
Raude, Karina *199*
Rauh, Sherry
  See North, Sherry
Raum, Elizabeth 1949- *155*
Raven, Margot Theis *184*
RavenWolf, Silver 1956- *155*
Ravielli, Anthony 1916-1997 .... *3*
  Obituary *95*
Ravilious, Robin 1944- *77*
Ravishankar, Anushka 1961- *200*
Rawding, F(rederick) W(illiam) 1930- *55*
Rawlings, Marjorie Kinnan 1896-1953 .... *100*
  See also YABC *1*
  See also CLR *63*
Rawlins, Donna 1956- *206*
Rawlinson, Julia *175*
Rawls, (Woodrow) Wilson 1913-1984 .... *22*
  See also CLR *81*
Rawlyk, George Alexander 1935- *64*
Rawn, Melanie 1954- *98*
Rawn, Melanie Robin
  See Rawn, Melanie
Rawson, Katherine 1955- *190*
Ray, Carl 1943-1978 .... *63*
Ray, Deborah
  See Kogan Ray, Deborah
Ray, Delia 1963- *179*
  Earlier sketch in SATA *70*
Ray, Irene
  See Sutton, Margaret Beebe
Ray, Jane 1960- *196*
  Earlier sketches in SATA *72, 152*
Ray, JoAnne 1935- *9*
Ray, Mary (Eva Pedder) 1932- *127*
  Earlier sketch in SATA *2*
Ray, Mary Lyn 1946- *154*
  Earlier sketch in SATA *90*
Rayban, Chloe 1944- *167*
Rayevsky, Robert 1955- *190*
  Earlier sketch in SATA *81*
Raymond, James Crossley 1917-1981
  Obituary *29*
Raymond, Robert
  See Alter, Robert Edmond
Rayner, Catherine *204*

Rayner, Hugh *151*
Rayner, Mary 1933- *87*
  Earlier sketch in SATA *22*
  See also CLR *41*
Rayner, Shoo
  See Rayner, Hugh
Rayner, William 1929- *55*
  Brief entry *36*
Raynor, Dorka *28*
Rayson, Steven 1932- *30*
Razzell, Arthur (George) 1925- *11*
Razzell, Mary (Catherine) 1930- *102*
Razzi, James 1931- *10*
Read, Elfreida 1920- *2*
Read, Nicholas 1956- *146*
Read, Piers Paul 1941- *21*
Reade, Deborah 1949- *69*
Reader, Dennis 1929- *71*
Reading, Richard P(atrick) 1962- *161*
Readman, Jo 1958- *89*
Ready, Kirk L(ewis) 1943- *39*
Reaney, James 1926-2008 .... *43*
Reaney, James Crerar
  See Reaney, James
Reardon, Joyce
  See Pearson, Ridley
Reaver, Chap 1935-1993 .... *69*
  Obituary *77*
Reaver, Herbert R.
  See Reaver, Chap
Reaves, J. Michael
  See Reaves, (James) Michael
Reaves, (James) Michael 1950- *99*
Reber, Deborah *189*
Recorvits, Helen *191*
Redding, Robert Hull 1919- *2*
Redekopp, Elsa *61*
Redlich, Ben 1977- *181*
Redsand, Anna 1948- *184*
Redway, Ralph
  See Hamilton, Charles (Harold St. John)
Redway, Ridley
  See Hamilton, Charles (Harold St. John)
Reece, Colleen L. 1935- *116*
Reece, Gabrielle 1970- *108*
Reed, Betty Jane 1921- *4*
Reed, Dallas
  See Pendleton, Thomas
Reed, E.
  See Evans, Mari
Reed, Gwendolyn E(lizabeth) 1932- *21*
Reed, Kit 1932- *184*
  Autobiography Feature *184*
  Earlier sketches in SATA *34, 116*
Reed, Lynn Rowe *171*
Reed, Neil 1961- *99*
Reed, Talbot Baines 1852-1893
  See CLR *76*
Reed, Thomas (James) 1947- *34*
Reed, William Maxwell 1871-1962 .... *15*
Reeder, Carolyn 1937- *97*
  Earlier sketch in SATA *66*
  See also CLR *69*
Reeder, Colin (Dawson) 1938- *74*
Reeder, Colonel Red
  See Reeder, Russell P(otter), Jr.
Reeder, Russell P(otter), Jr. 1902-1998 .... *4*
  Obituary *101*
Reeder, Stephanie Owen 1951- *102*
Reed-Jones, Carol 1955- *112*
Reef, Catherine 1951- *189*
  Earlier sketches in SATA *73, 128*
Reekie, Jocelyn (Margaret) 1947- *145*
Reeman, Douglas Edward 1924- *63*
  Brief entry *28*
Rees, Celia 1949- *124*
Rees, David (Bartlett) 1936-1993 .... *69*
  Obituary *76*
  Earlier sketch in SATA *36*
  See also SAAS *5*
Rees, Douglas 1947- *169*

Rees, Ennis (Samuel, Jr.) 1925- *3*
Rees, (George) Leslie (Clarence)
  1905-2000 .... *105*
  Obituary *135*
Reese, Bob
  See Reese, Robert A.
Reese, Carolyn Johnson 1938- *64*
Reese, Della 1931(?)- *114*
Reese, Lyn
  See Reese, Carolyn Johnson
Reese, Robert A. 1938- *60*
  Brief entry *53*
Reese, (John) Terence 1913-1996 .... *59*
Reeve, Joel
  See Cox, William R(obert)
Reeve, Kirk 1934- *117*
Reeve, Philip *201*
  Earlier sketch in SATA *170*
Reeve, Rosie *186*
Reeve, Rosie *188*
Reeves, Faye Couch 1953- *76*
Reeves, James
  See Reeves, John Morris
Reeves, Jeni 1947- *111*
Reeves, John Morris 1909-1978 .... *87*
  Earlier sketch in SATA *15*
Reeves, Joyce 1911- *17*
Reeves, Lawrence F. 1926- *29*
Reeves, Ruth Ellen
  See Ranney, Agnes V.
Regan, Dian Curtis 1950- *149*
  Autobiography Feature *149*
  Earlier sketches in SATA *75, 133*
Regehr, Lydia 1903-1991 .... *37*
Reger, James P. 1952- *106*
Reggiani, Renee 1925- *18*
Rehm, Karl M. 1935- *72*
Reich, Ali
  See Katz, Bobbi
Reich, Susanna 1954- *113*
Reiche, Dietlof 1941- *159*
Reichert, Edwin C(lark) 1909-1988
  Obituary *57*
Reichert, Mickey Zucker
  See Reichert, Miriam Zucker
Reichert, Miriam Zucker 1962- *85*
Reichert, Renee *172*
Reichhold, Jane(t E.) 1937- *147*
Reid, Alastair 1926- *46*
Reid, Barbara 1922- *21*
Reid, Barbara (Jane) 1957- *93*
  See also CLR *64*
Reid, Desmond
  See Moorcock, Michael
  and McNeilly, Wilfred (Glassford)
Reid, Eugenie Chazal 1924- *12*
Reid, John Calvin *21*
Reid, (Thomas) Mayne 1818-1883 .... *24*
Reid, Meta Mayne 1905-1991 .... *58*
  Brief entry *36*
Reid, Robin (Nicole) 1969- *145*
Reid Banks, Lynne 1929- *165*
  Earlier sketches in SATA *22, 75, 111*
  See also CLR *86*
Reider, Katja 1960- *126*
Reid Jenkins, Debra 1955- *87*
Reiff, Stephanie Ann 1948- *47*
  Brief entry *28*
Reig, June 1933- *30*
Reigot, Betty Polisar 1924- *55*
  Brief entry *41*
Reilly, Joan *195*
Reim, Melanie (K.) 1956- *104*
Reinach, Jacquelyn (Krasne) 1930-2000 .... *28*
Reiner, Carl 1922- *151*
Reiner, William B(uck) 1910-1976 .... *46*
  Obituary *30*
Reinfeld, Fred 1910-1964 .... *3*
Reinhardt, Dana 1971- *175*
Reinhart, Matthew 1971- *197*
  Earlier sketch in SATA *161*

Reiniger, Lotte 1899-1981 .... *40*
  Obituary *33*
Reinsma, Carol 1949- *91*
Reinstedt, Randall A. 1935- *101*
Reinstedt, Randy
  See Reinstedt, Randall A.
Reisberg, Mira 1955- *82*
Reisberg, Veg
  See Reisberg, Mira
Reiser, Lynn 1944- *180*
  Earlier sketches in SATA *81, 138*
Reiser, Lynn Whisnant
  See Reiser, Lynn
Reisgies, Teresa (Maria) 1966- *74*
Reiss, Johanna (de Leeuw) 1929(?)- *18*
  See also CLR *19*
Reiss, John J. *23*
Reiss, Kathryn 1957- *144*
  Earlier sketch in SATA *76*
Reit, Seymour Victory 1918-2001 .... *21*
  Obituary *133*
Reit, Sy
  See Reit, Seymour Victory
Relf, Patricia 1954- *134*
  Earlier sketch in SATA *71*
Remi, Georges 1907-1983 .... *13*
  Obituary *32*
  See also CLR *114*
Remington, Frederic S(ackrider)
  1861-1909 .... *41*
Remkiewicz, Frank 1939- *152*
  Earlier sketch in SATA *77*
Rempt, Fiona 1973- *198*
Remy, Georges
  See Remi, Georges
Renaud, Bernadette 1945- *66*
Renault, Mary
  See Challans, Mary
Rendell, Joan *28*
Rendina, Laura (Jones) Cooper 1902- *10*
Rendon, Marcie R. 1952- *97*
Rendon, Maria 1965- *116*
Renee, Janina 1956- *140*
Renfro, Ed 1924- *79*
Renick, Marion (Lewis) 1905-1983 .... *1*
Renier, Aaron 1977- *202*
Renken, Aleda 1907- *27*
Renlie, Frank H. 1936- *11*
Rennert, Richard Scott 1956- *67*
Rennison, Louise 1951- *149*
Reno, Dawn E(laine) 1953- *130*
Rensie, Willis
  See Eisner, Will
Renton, Cam
  See Armstrong, Richard
Renvoize, Jean *5*
Resau, Laura 1973- *190*
Resciniti, Angelo G. 1952- *75*
Resnick, Michael David
  See Resnick, Mike
Resnick, Mike 1942- *159*
  Earlier sketches in SATA *38, 106*
Resnick, Seymour 1920- *23*
Retla, Robert
  See Alter, Robert Edmond
Rettig, Liz *199*
Reuter, Bjarne (B.) 1950- *142*
  Earlier sketch in SATA *68*
Reuter, Carol (Joan) 1931- *2*
Revena
  See Wright, Betty Ren
Revsbech, Vicki
  See Liestman, Vicki
Rex, Adam *186*
Rex, Michael *191*
Rey, H. A. 1898-1977 .... *100*
  Earlier sketches in SATA *1, 26, 69*
  See also CLR *93*
Rey, Hans Augusto
  See Rey, H. A.
Rey, Luis V. 1955- *201*

Rey, Margret 1906-1996 .... *86*
  Obituary *93*
  Earlier sketch in SATA *26*
  See also CLR *93*
Rey, Margret Elisabeth
  See Rey, Margret
Reyher, Becky
  See Reyher, Rebecca Hourwich
Reyher, Rebecca Hourwich 1897-1987 .... *18*
  Obituary *50*
Reynold, Ann
  See Bernardo, Anilu
Reynolds, Aaron 1970- *197*
Reynolds, Adrian 1963- *192*
Reynolds, C. Buck 1957- *107*
Reynolds, Dickson
  See Reynolds, Helen Mary Greenwood Campbell
Reynolds, Helen Mary Greenwood Campbell
  1884-1969
  Obituary *26*
Reynolds, Jan 1956- *180*
Reynolds, John
  See Whitlock, Ralph
Reynolds, Madge
  See Whitlock, Ralph
Reynolds, Malvina 1900-1978 .... *44*
  Obituary *24*
Reynolds, Marilyn 1935- *121*
  See also SAAS *23*
Reynolds, Marilyn M.
  See Reynolds, Marilyn
Reynolds, Marilynn 1940- *141*
  Earlier sketch in SATA *80*
Reynolds, Pamela 1923- *34*
Reynolds, Peter H. 1961- *128*
Reynolds, Peter J. 1961- *179*
Reynolds, Susan *179*
Rhine, Richard
  See Silverstein, Alvin
  and Silverstein, Virginia B.
Rhoades, Diane 1952- *90*
Rhodes, Bennie (Loran) 1927- *35*
Rhodes, Donna McKee 1962- *87*
Rhodes, Frank Harold Trevor 1926- *37*
Rhue, Morton
  See Strasser, Todd
Rhyne, Nancy 1926- *66*
Rhynes, Martha E. 1939- *141*
Ribbons, Ian 1924- *37*
  Brief entry *30*
  See also SAAS *3*
Ricciuti, Edward R(aphael) 1938- *10*
Rice, Alice (Caldwell) Hegan 1870-1942 ..... *63*
Rice, Bebe Faas 1932- *89*
Rice, Charles D(uane) 1910-1971
  Obituary *27*
Rice, Dale R. 1948- *42*
Rice, Dale Richard
  See Rice, Dale R.
Rice, Dick
  See Rice, R. Hugh
Rice, Earle (Wilmont), Jr. 1928- *151*
  Earlier sketch in SATA *92*
Rice, Edward 1918-2001 .... *47*
  Brief entry *42*
Rice, Elizabeth 1913-1976 .... *2*
Rice, Eve 1951- *91*
  Earlier sketch in SATA *34*
Rice, Eve Hart
  See Rice, Eve
Rice, Inez 1907- *13*
Rice, James 1934- *93*
  Earlier sketch in SATA *22*
Rice, John F. 1958- *82*
Rice, R. Hugh 1929- *115*
Rice, Richard H.
  See Rice, R. Hugh
Rich, Barbara
  See Graves, Robert
Rich, Elaine Sommers 1926- *6*

Rich, Josephine Bouchard 1912- *10*
Rich, Louise Dickinson 1903-1991 .... *54*
  Obituary *67*
Richard, Adrienne 1921- *5*
  See also SAAS *9*
Richard, James Robert
  See Bowen, Robert Sydney
Richards, Chuck 1957- *170*
Richards, Frank
  See Hamilton, Charles (Harold St. John)
Richards, Hilda
  See Hamilton, Charles (Harold St. John)
Richards, Jackie 1925- *102*
Richards, Jean 1940- *135*
Richards, Justin *169*
Richards, Kay
  See Baker, Susan (Catherine)
Richards, Laura E(lizabeth Howe) 1850-1943
  See YABC *1*
  See also CLR *54*
Richards, Leigh
  See King, Laurie R.
Richards, Marlee
  See Brill, Marlene Targ
Richards, Norman 1932- *48*
Richards, R(onald) C(harles) W(illiam)
  1923- *59*
  Brief entry *43*
Richards, Walter Alden (Jr.) 1907-1988
  Obituary *56*
Richardson, Andrew (William) 1986- *120*
Richardson, Carol 1932- *58*
Richardson, Frank Howard 1882-1970
  Obituary *27*
Richardson, Grace Lee
  See Dickson, Naida
Richardson, Jean (Mary) *59*
Richardson, Judith Benet 1941- *77*
Richardson, Nigel 1957- *187*
Richardson, Robert S(hirley) 1902-1981 .... *8*
Richardson, Sandy 1949- *116*
Richardson, V.A. *189*
Richardson, Willis 1889-1977 .... *60*
Richelson, Geraldine 1922- *29*
Richemont, Enid 1940- *82*
Richler, Mordecai 1931-2001 .... *98*
  Brief entry *27*
  Earlier sketch in SATA *44*
  See also CLR *17*
Richman, Sophia 1941- *142*
Rich-McCoy, Lois
  See McCoy, Lois (Rich)
Richmond, Robin 1951- *75*
Richoux, Pat(ricia) 1927- *7*
Richter, Alice 1941- *30*
Richter, Conrad (Michael) 1890-1968 .... *3*
Richter, Hans Peter 1925-1993 .... *6*
  See also CLR *21*
  See also SAAS *11*
Richter, Jutta 1955- *184*
Rickard, Graham 1949- *71*
Rico, Don(ato) 1917-1985
  Obituary *43*
Riddell, Chris 1962- *166*
  Earlier sketch in SATA *114*
Riddell, Christopher Barry
  See Riddell, Chris
Riddell, Edwina 1955- *82*
Ridden, Brian (John) 1934- *123*
Riddle, Tohby 1965- *151*
  Earlier sketch in SATA *74*
Riddleburger, Sam *202*
Riddles, Libby 1956- *140*
Rideout, Sandy *194*
Ridge, Antonia (Florence) (?)-1981 .... *7*
  Obituary *27*
Ridge, Martin 1923-2003 .... *43*
Ridley, Philip *171*
  Earlier sketch in SATA *88*
Ridlon, Marci
  See Balterman, Marcia Ridlon

Riedman, Sarah R(egal) 1902-1995 .... *1*
Riehecky, Janet 1953- *164*
Ries, Lori *185*
Riesenberg, Felix, Jr. 1913-1962 .... *23*
Rieu, E(mile) V(ictor) 1887-1972 .... *46*
  Obituary *26*
Riffenburgh, Beau 1955- *175*
Rigg, Sharon
  See Creech, Sharon
Riggio, Anita 1952- *148*
  Earlier sketch in SATA *73*
Riggs, Shannon *190*
Riggs, Sidney Noyes 1892-1975
  Obituary *28*
Riggs, Stephanie 1964- *138*
Riglietti, Serena 1969- *189*
Rigney, James Oliver, Jr.
  See Jordan, Robert
Rikhoff, Jean 1928- *9*
Rikki
  See Ducornet, Erica
Riley, James A. 1939- *97*
Riley, James Whitcomb 1849-1916 .... *17*
Riley, Jocelyn 1949- *60*
  Brief entry *50*
Riley, Jocelyn Carol
  See Riley, Jocelyn
Riley, Linda Capus 1950- *85*
Riley, Martin 1948- *81*
Rimbauer, Steven
  See Pearson, Ridley
Rimes, (Margaret) LeAnn 1982- *154*
Rinaldi, Ann 1934- *202*
  Brief entry *50*
  Earlier sketches in SATA *51, 78, 117, 161*
  See also CLR *46*
Rinard, Judith E(llen) 1947- *140*
  Earlier sketch in SATA *44*
Rinder, Lenore 1949- *92*
Ring, Elizabeth 1920- *79*
Ringdahl, Mark
  See Longyear, Barry B(rookes)
Ringgold, Faith 1930- *187*
  Earlier sketches in SATA *71, 114*
  See also CLR *30*
Ringi, Kjell (Arne Soerensen) 1939- *12*
Rinkoff, Barbara Jean (Rich) 1923-1975 .... *4*
  Obituary *27*
Rinn, Miriam 1946- *127*
Riordan, James 1936- *95*
Riordan, Rick *174*
Rios, Tere
  See Versace, Marie Teresa Rios
Ripken, Cal, Jr. 1960- *114*
Ripken, Calvin Edward, Jr.
  See Ripken, Cal, Jr.
Ripley, Catherine 1957- *82*
Ripley, Elizabeth Blake 1906-1969 .... *5*
Ripper, Charles L(ewis) 1929- *3*
Ripper, Chuck
  See Ripper, Charles L(ewis)
Riq
  See Atwater, Richard (Tupper)
Rish, David 1955- *110*
Riskind, Mary 1944- *60*
Rissinger, Matt 1956- *93*
Rissman, Art
  See Sussman, Susan
Rissman, Susan
  See Sussman, Susan
Ritchie, Barbara Gibbons *14*
Ritter, Felix
  See Kruss, James
Ritter, John H. 1951- *137*
  Earlier sketch in SATA *129*
Ritter, Lawrence S(tanley) 1922-2004 .... *58*
  Obituary *152*
Ritthaler, Shelly 1955- *91*
Ritts, Paul 1920(?)-1980
  Obituary *25*

Ritz, Karen 1957- *202*
  Earlier sketch in SATA *80*
Rivera, Geraldo (Miguel) 1943- *54*
  Brief entry *28*
Rivers, Elfrida
  See Bradley, Marion Zimmer
Rivers, Karen 1970- *131*
Riverside, John
  See Heinlein, Robert A.
Rivkin, Ann 1920- *41*
Rivoli, Mario 1943- *10*
Roach, Marilynne K. 1946- *9*
Roach, Marilynne Kathleen
  See Roach, Marilynne K.
Roach, Portia
  See Takakjian, Portia
Robb, Don 1937- *194*
Robb, Laura 1937- *95*
Robberecht, Thierry 1960- *182*
Robbins, Frank 1917-1994(?) *42*
  Brief entry *32*
Robbins, Ken 1945- *147*
  Brief entry *53*
  Earlier sketch in SATA *94*
Robbins, Raleigh
  See Hamilton, Charles (Harold St. John)
Robbins, Ruth 1917(?)- *14*
Robbins, Tony
  See Pashko, Stanley
Robbins, Wayne
  See Cox, William R(obert)
Robel, S. L.
  See Fraustino, Lisa Rowe
Roberson, Jennifer 1953- *72*
Roberson, John R(oyster) 1930- *53*
Robert, Adrian
  See St. John, Nicole
Roberts, Bethany *202*
  Earlier sketch in SATA *133*
Roberts, Bruce (Stuart) 1930- *47*
  Brief entry *39*
Roberts, Charles G(eorge) D(ouglas)
  1860-1943 .... *88*
  Brief entry *29*
  See also CLR *33*
Roberts, David
  See Cox, John Roberts
Roberts, David 1970- *191*
Roberts, Diane 1937- *184*
Roberts, Elizabeth 1944- *80*
Roberts, Elizabeth Madox 1886-1941 .... *33*
  Brief entry *27*
  See also CLR *100*
Roberts, Jim
  See Bates, Barbara S(nedeker)
Roberts, John G(aither) 1913-1993 .... *27*
Roberts, Judy I. 1957- *93*
Roberts, Katherine 1962- *152*
Roberts, M. L.
  See Mattern, Joanne
Roberts, Nancy Correll 1924- *52*
  Brief entry *28*
Roberts, Priscilla 1955- *184*
Roberts, Terence
  See Sanderson, Ivan T(erence)
Roberts, Willo Davis 1928-2004 .... *150*
  Autobiography Feature *150*
  Obituary *160*
  Earlier sketches in SATA *21, 70, 133*
  See also CLR *95*
  See also SAAS *8*
Robertson, Barbara (Anne) 1931- *12*
Robertson, Don 1929-1999 .... *8*
  Obituary *113*
Robertson, Dorothy Lewis 1912- *12*
Robertson, Ellis
  See Ellison, Harlan
  and Silverberg, Robert
Robertson, James I., Jr. 1930- *182*
Robertson, James Irvin
  See Robertson, James I., Jr.

Robertson, Janet (E.) 1935- *68*
Robertson, Jennifer Sinclair 1942-1998 .... *12*
Robertson, Jenny
  See Robertson, Jennifer Sinclair
Robertson, Keith (Carlton) 1914-1991 .... *85*
  Obituary *69*
  Earlier sketch in SATA *1*
  See also SAAS *15*
Robertson, Mark
  See Robertson, M.P.
Robertson, M.P. 1965- *197*
Robertson, Stephen
  See Walker, Robert W.
Robertus, Polly M. 1948- *73*
Robeson, Kenneth
  See Dent, Lester
  and Goulart, Ron
Robeson, Kenneth
  See Johnson, (Walter) Ryerson
Robinet, Harriette Gillem 1931- *104*
  Earlier sketch in SATA *27*
  See also CLR *64*
Robins, Deri 1958- *166*
  Earlier sketch in SATA *117*
Robins, Patricia
  See Clark, Patricia Denise
Robins, Rollo, Jr.
  See Ellis, Edward S.
Robins, Seelin
  See Ellis, Edward S.
Robinson, Adjai 1932- *8*
Robinson, Aminah Brenda Lynn 1940- *159*
  Earlier sketch in SATA *77*
Robinson, Barbara (Webb) 1927- *84*
  Earlier sketch in SATA *8*
Robinson, C(harles) A(lexander), Jr.
  1900-1965 .... *36*
Robinson, Charles 1870-1937 .... *17*
Robinson, Charles 1931- *6*
Robinson, Dorothy W. 1929- *54*
Robinson, Elizabeth Keeler 1959- *204*
Robinson, Eve
  See Tanselle, Eve
Robinson, Glen 1953- *92*
Robinson, Glendal P.
  See Robinson, Glen
Robinson, Jan M. 1933- *6*
Robinson, Jean O. 1934- *7*
Robinson, Joan (Mary) G(ale Thomas)
  1910-1988 .... *7*
Robinson, Kim Stanley 1952- *109*
Robinson, Lee 1948- *110*
Robinson, Lloyd
  See Silverberg, Robert
Robinson, Lynda S(uzanne) 1951- *107*
Robinson, Marileta 1942- *32*
Robinson, Maudie Millian Oller 1914- *11*
Robinson, Maurice R(ichard) 1895-1982
  Obituary *29*
Robinson, Nancy K(onheim) 1942-1994 ...... *91*
  Brief entry *31*
  Obituary *79*
  Earlier sketch in SATA *32*
Robinson, Ray 1920- *23*
Robinson, Raymond Kenneth
  See Robinson, Ray
Robinson, Shari
  See McGuire, Leslie (Sarah)
Robinson, Sharon 1950- *197*
  Earlier sketch in SATA *162*
Robinson, Spider 1948- *118*
Robinson, Sue
  See Robinson, Susan Maria
Robinson, Susan Maria 1955- *105*
Robinson, Susan Patricia
  See Gates, Susan
Robinson, Suzanne
  See Robinson, Lynda S(uzanne)
Robinson, T(homas) H(eath) 1869-1950 ...... *17*
Robinson, Tim 1963- *205*
Robinson, (Wanda) Veronica 1926- *30*

Robinson, W(illiam) Heath 1872-1944 .... *17*
Robison, Bonnie 1924- *12*
Robison, Nancy L(ouise) 1934- *32*
Robles, Harold E. 1948- *87*
Robottom, John 1934- *7*
Robson, Eric 1939- *82*
Roca, Francois 1971- *200*
Rocco, John 1967- *188*
Roche, A. K.
    See Abisch, Roslyn Kroop
    and Kaplan, Boche
Roche, Denis 1967- *196*
    Earlier sketch in SATA *99*
Roche, Denis Mary
    See Roche, Denis
Roche, Luane 1937- *170*
Roche, P(atricia) K. 1935- *57*
    Brief entry *34*
Roche, Terry
    See Poole, Peggy
Rochman, Hazel 1938- *105*
Rock, Lois
    See Joslin, Mary
Rock, Maxine 1940- *108*
Rocker, Fermin 1907- *40*
Rocklin, Joanne 1946- *134*
    Earlier sketch in SATA *86*
Rockwell, Anne F. 1934- *194*
    Earlier sketches in SATA *33, 71, 114, 162*
    See also SAAS *19*
Rockwell, Anne Foote
    See Rockwell, Anne F.
Rockwell, Bart
    See Pellowski, Michael (Joseph)
Rockwell, Harlow 1910-1988 .... *33*
    Obituary *56*
Rockwell, Lizzy 1961- *185*
Rockwell, Norman (Percevel) 1894-1978 .... *23*
Rockwell, Thomas 1933- *70*
    Earlier sketch in SATA *7*
    See also CLR *6*
Rockwood, Joyce 1947- *39*
Rockwood, Roy
    See McFarlane, Leslie
    and Stratemeyer, Edward L.
Rodanas, Kristina 1952- *155*
Rodari, Gianni 1920-1980
    See CLR *24*
Rodd, Kathleen Tennant
    See Rodd, Kylie Tennant
Rodd, Kylie Tennant 1912-1988 .... *57*
    Obituary *55*
    Earlier sketch in SATA *6*
Rodda, Emily 1948- *146*
    Earlier sketch in SATA *97*
    See also CLR *32*
Roddenberry, Eugene Wesley 1921-1991 ..... *45*
    Obituary *69*
Roddenberry, Gene
    See Roddenberry, Eugene Wesley
Roddick, Ellen 1936- *5*
Roddie, Shen *153*
Roddy, Lee 1921- *57*
Rodenas, Paula *73*
Rodgers, Frank 1944- *69*
Rodgers, Mary 1931- *130*
    Earlier sketch in SATA *8*
    See also CLR *20*
Rodman, Emerson
    See Ellis, Edward S.
Rodman, Eric
    See Silverberg, Robert
Rodman, Maia
    See Wojciechowska, Maia (Teresa)
Rodman, Mary Ann *185*
Rodman, (Cary) Selden 1909-2002 .... *9*
Rodowsky, Colby 1932- *164*
    Earlier sketches in SATA *21, 77, 120*
    See also SAAS *22*
Rodowsky, Colby F.
    See Rodowsky, Colby

Rodriguez, Alejo 1941- *83*
Rodriguez, Alex 1975- *189*
Rodriguez, Christina 1981- *177*
Rodriguez, Edel 1971- *196*
Rodriguez, Luis J. 1954- *125*
Rodriguez, Rachel *180*
Rodriguez, Rachel Victoria
    See Rodriguez, Rachel
Roeder, Virginia Marsh 1926- *98*
Roehrig, Catharine H. 1949- *67*
Roennfeldt, Robert 1953- *78*
Roessel-Waugh, C. C.
    See Waugh, Carol-Lynn Rossel
    and Waugh, Charles G(ordon)
Roets, Lois F. 1937- *91*
Roever, J(oan) M(arilyn) 1935- *26*
Rofes, Eric 1954-2006 .... *52*
Rofes, Eric Edward 1954-2006
    See Rofes, Eric
Roffey, Maureen 1936- *33*
Rogak, Lisa 1962- *80*
Rogak, Lisa Angowski
    See Rogak, Lisa
Rogan, S. Jones *199*
Rogan, Sally Jones
    See Rogan, S. Jones
Rogasky, Barbara 1933- *144*
    Earlier sketch in SATA *86*
Rogers, (Thomas) Alan (Stinchcombe)
    1937- *81*
    Earlier sketch in SATA *2*
Rogers, Bettye 1858-1919 .... *103*
Rogers, Cindy 1950- *89*
Rogers, Emma 1951- *74*
Rogers, Frances 1888-1974 .... *10*
Rogers, Fred McFeely 1928-2003 .... *33*
    Obituary *138*
Rogers, Hal
    See Sirimarco, Elizabeth
Rogers, Jean 1919- *55*
    Brief entry *47*
Rogers, Matilda 1894-1976 .... *5*
    Obituary *34*
Rogers, Pamela 1927- *9*
Rogers, Paul 1950- *98*
    Earlier sketch in SATA *54*
Rogers, Robert
    See Hamilton, Charles (Harold St. John)
Rogers, Sherry *193*
Rogers, W(illiam) G(arland) 1896-1978 .... *23*
Rohan, M. S.
    See Rohan, Michael Scott
Rohan, Michael Scott 1951- *98*
Rohan, Mike Scott
    See Rohan, Michael Scott
Rohmann, Eric 1957- *171*
    See also CLR *100*
Rohmer, Harriet 1938- *56*
Rohrer, Doug 1962- *89*
Rojan
    See Rojankovsky, Feodor (Stepanovich)
Rojankovsky, Feodor (Stepanovich)
    1891-1970 .... *21*
Rojany, Lisa *94*
Rokeby-Thomas, Anna E(lma) 1911- *15*
Roland, Albert 1925-2002 .... *11*
Roland, Mary
    See Lewis, Mary
Roleff, Tamara L. 1959- *143*
Rolerson, Darrell A(llen) 1946- *8*
Roll, Winifred 1909-1998 .... *6*
Rollins, Charlemae Hill 1897-1979 .... *3*
    Obituary *26*
Rollock, Barbara T(herese) 1924- *64*
Romack, Janice Reed
    See LeNoir, Janice
Romain, Trevor *134*
Romanenko, Vitaliy 1962- *101*
Romano, Clare 1922- *111*
    Earlier sketch in SATA *48*
Romano, Louis G. 1921- *35*

Romano, Melora A. 1966- *118*
Romano, Ray 1957- *170*
Romano, Raymond
    See Romano, Ray
Romijn, Johanna Maria Kooyker
    See Kooyker-Romijn, Johanna Maria
Romyn, Johanna Maria Kooyker
    See Kooyker-Romijn, Johanna Maria
Rong, Yu 1970- *174*
Rongen, Bjoern 1906- *10*
Rongen, Bjorn
    See Rongen, Bjoern
Ronson, Mark
    See Alexander, Marc
Rood, Ronald (N.) 1920- *12*
Rook, Sebastian
    See Jeapes, Ben
Rooke, Daphne 1914-2009 .... *12*
Rooke, Daphne Marie
    See Rooke, Daphne
Roop, Connie 1951- *167*
    Brief entry *49*
    Earlier sketches in SATA *54, 116*
Roop, Constance Betzer
    See Roop, Connie
Roop, Peter 1951- *167*
    Brief entry *49*
    Earlier sketches in SATA *54, 116*
Roop, Peter G.
    See Roop, Peter
Roop, Peter Geiger
    See Roop, Peter
Roos, Stephen 1945- *128*
    Brief entry *41*
    Earlier sketches in SATA *47, 77*
Roose-Evans, James 1927- *65*
Roosevelt, (Anna) Eleanor 1884-1962 .... *50*
Root, Barry *182*
Root, Betty *84*
Root, Kimberly Bulcken *192*
Root, Phyllis 1949- *184*
    Brief entry *48*
    Earlier sketches in SATA *55, 94, 145*
Root, Shelton L., Jr. 1923-1986
    Obituary *51*
Roper, Laura (Newbold) Wood 1911-2003 .. *34*
    Obituary *150*
Roper, Robert 1946- *142*
    Earlier sketch in SATA *78*
Roraback, Robin (Ellan) 1964- *111*
Rorby, Ginny 1944- *94*
Rorer, Abigail 1949- *85*
Rosamel, Godeleine de 1968- *151*
Roscoe, D(onald) T(homas) 1934- *42*
Rose, Anne *8*
Rose, Deborah Lee 1955- *185*
    Earlier sketches in SATA *71, 124*
Rose, Elizabeth (Jane Pretty) 1933- *68*
    Brief entry *28*
Rose, Florella
    See Carlson, Vada F.
Rose, Gerald (Hembdon Seymour) 1935- *68*
    Brief entry *30*
Rose, Malcolm 1953- *168*
    Earlier sketch in SATA *107*
Rose, Nancy A.
    See Sweetland, Nancy A(nn)
Rose, Ted 1940- *93*
Rose, Wendy 1948- *12*
Rosen, Elizabeth 1961- *205*
Rosen, Lillian (Diamond) 1928- *63*
Rosen, Marvin 1933- *161*
Rosen, Michael 1946- *181*
    Brief entry *40*
    Earlier sketches in SATA *48, 84, 137*
    See also CLR *45*
Rosen, Michael J. 1954- *199*
    Earlier sketch in SATA *86*
Rosen, Michael Wayne
    See Rosen, Michael
Rosen, Sidney 1916- *1*

Rosen, Winifred 1943- 8
Rosenbaum, Maurice 1907-1987 6
Rosenberg, Amye 1950- 74
Rosenberg, Dorothy 1906- 40
Rosenberg, Eth Clifford 1915- 92
  See also SAAS 22
Rosenberg, Jane 1949- 58
Rosenberg, Liz 1958- 129
  Earlier sketch in SATA 75
Rosenberg, Maxine B(erta) 1939- 93
  Brief entry 47
  Earlier sketch in SATA 55
Rosenberg, Nancy (Sherman) 1931- 4
Rosenberg, Sharon 1942- 8
Rosenberry, Vera 1948- 144
  Earlier sketch in SATA 83
Rosenblatt, Arthur
  See Rosenblatt, Arthur S.
Rosenblatt, Arthur S. 1938- 68
  Brief entry 45
Rosenblatt, Lily 1956- 90
Rosenbloom, Joseph 1928- 21
Rosenblum, Richard 1928- 11
Rosenburg, John M. 1918- 6
Rosenfeld, Dina 1962- 99
Rosenstiehl, Agnes 1941- 203
Rosenthal, Amy Krouse 1965- 177
Rosenthal, Betsy R. 1957- 178
Rosenthal, Harold 1914-1999 35
Rosenthal, M(acha) L(ouis) 1917-1996 59
Rosenthal, Marc 1949- 193
Rosenthal, Mark A(lan) 1946- 64
Rosing, Norbert 1953- 196
Rosman, Steven M 1956- 81
Rosman, Steven Michael
  See Rosman, Steven M
Rosoff, Meg 1956- 160
Ross, Alan
  See Warwick, Alan R(oss)
Ross, Christine 1950- 172
  Earlier sketch in SATA 83
Ross, Clare
  See Romano, Clare
Ross, Dana Fuller
  See Cockrell, Amanda
  and Gerson, Noel Bertram
Ross, Dave
  See Ross, David
Ross, David 1896-1975 49
  Obituary 20
Ross, David 1949- 133
  Earlier sketch in SATA 32
Ross, Deborah J.
  See Wheeler, Deborah
Ross, Diana
  See Denney, Diana
Ross, Edward S(hearman) 1915- 85
Ross, Eileen 1950- 115
Ross, Frank (Xavier), Jr. 1914- 28
Ross, Jane 1961- 79
Ross, John 1921- 45
Ross, Judy 1942- 54
Ross, Katharine Reynolds
  See Ross, Kathy
Ross, Kathy 1948- 169
  Earlier sketch in SATA 89
Ross, Kent 1956- 91
Ross, Lillian Hammer 1925- 72
Ross, Michael Elsohn 1952- 170
  Earlier sketches in SATA 80, 127
Ross, Pat(ricia Kienzle) 1943- 53
  Brief entry 48
Ross, Ramon R(oyal) 1930- 62
Ross, Stewart 1947- 134
  Earlier sketch in SATA 92
  See also SAAS 23
Ross, Tom 1958- 84
Ross, Tony 1938- 176
  Earlier sketches in SATA 17, 65, 130
Ross, Wilda 1915- 51
  Brief entry 39

Rossel, Seymour 1945- 28
Rossell, Judith 1953- 187
Rossel-Waugh, C. C.
  See Waugh, Carol-Lynn Rossel
Rossetti, Christina 1830-1894 20
  See also CLR 115
Rossetti, Christina Georgina
  See Rossetti, Christina
Rossi, Joyce 1943- 116
Rossotti, Hazel Swaine 1930- 95
Rostkowski, Margaret I. 1945- 59
Roth, Arnold 1929- 21
Roth, Arthur J(oseph) 1925-1993 43
  Brief entry 28
  Obituary 75
  See also SAAS 11
Roth, David 1940- 36
Roth, Julie Jersild 180
Roth, Matthue 1978(?)- 174
Roth, Roger 190
Roth, Stephanie 202
Roth, Susan L. 181
  Earlier sketch in SATA 134
Rothberg, Abraham 1922- 59
Roth-Hano, Renee 1931- 85
Rothkopf, Carol Z. 1929- 4
Rothman, Joel 1938- 7
Rotner, Shelley 1951- 169
  Earlier sketch in SATA 76
Rottman, S.L. 1970- 157
  Earlier sketch in SATA 106
Rottman, Susan Lynn
  See Rottman, S.L.
Roueche, Berton 1911-1994 28
Roughsey, Dick 1921(?)-1985 35
  See also CLR 41
Roughsey, Goobalathaldin
  See Roughsey, Dick
Rounds, Glen (Harold) 1906-2002 112
  Obituary 141
  Earlier sketches in SATA 8, 70
Rourke, Constance Mayfield 1885-1941
  See YABC 1
Rovetch, Gerda 1925(?)- 202
Rovetch, L. Bob
  See Rovetch, Lissa
Rovetch, Lissa 201
Rowan, Deirdre
  See Williams, Jeanne
Rowe, Jennifer
  See Rodda, Emily
Rowe, John A. 1949- 198
  Earlier sketch in SATA 146
Rowe, Viola Carson 1903-1969
  Obituary 26
Rowh, Mark 1952- 90
Rowland, Florence Wightman 1900-1997 8
  Obituary 108
Rowland-Entwistle, (Arthur) Theodore (Henry)
  1925- 94
  Earlier sketch in SATA 31
Rowling, J.K. 1965- 174
  Earlier sketch in SATA 109
  See also CLR 112
Rowling, Joanne Kathleen
  See Rowling, J.K.
Rowsome, Frank (Howard), Jr. 1914-1983 .. 36
Roy, Gabrielle 1909-1983 104
Roy, Jacqueline 1954- 74
Roy, Jennifer
  See Roy, Jennifer Rozines
Roy, Jennifer Rozines 1967- 178
Roy, Jessie Hailstalk 1895-1986
  Obituary 51
Roy, Liam
  See Scarry, Patricia (Murphy)
Roy, Ron(ald) 1940- 110
  Brief entry 35
  Earlier sketch in SATA 40
Roybal, Laura 1956- 85

Roybal, Laura Husby
  See Roybal, Laura
Royds, Caroline 1953- 55
Royston, Angela 1945- 169
  Earlier sketch in SATA 120
Rozakis, Laurie E. 1952- 84
Rozen, Anna 1960- 206
Rubel, Nicole 1953- 181
  Earlier sketches in SATA 18, 95, 135
Rubin, Eva Johanna 1925- 38
Rubin, Susan Goldman 1939- 182
  Earlier sketches in SATA 84, 132
Rubin, Vicky 1964- 193
Rubinetti, Donald 1947- 92
Rubinstein, Gillian 1942- 158
  Autobiography Feature 116
  Earlier sketches in SATA 68, 105
  See also CLR 35
  See also SAAS 25
Rubinstein, Gillian Margaret
  See Rubinstein, Gillian
Rubinstein, Patricia -2003
  See Forest, Antonia
Rubinstein, Robert E(dward) 1943- 49
Rublowsky, John M(artin) 1928- 62
Rubright, Lynn 1936- 171
Ruby, Laura 181
  Earlier sketch in SATA 155
Ruby, Lois 1942- 184
  Autobiography Feature 105
  Brief entry 34
  Earlier sketches in SATA 35, 95
Ruby, Lois F.
  See Ruby, Lois
Ruchlis, Hy(man) 1913-1992 3
  Obituary 72
Rucker, Mike 1940- 91
Ruckman, Ivy 1931- 93
  Earlier sketch in SATA 37
Ruck-Pauquet, Gina 1931- 40
  Brief entry 37
Ruditis, Paul 190
Rudley, Stephen 1946- 30
Rudolph, Marguerita 1908- 21
Rudomin, Esther
  See Hautzig, Esther Rudomin
Rue, Leonard Lee III 1926- 142
  Earlier sketch in SATA 37
Rueda, Claudia 183
Ruedi, Norma Paul
  See Ainsworth, Norma
Ruelle, Karen Gray 1957- 126
  Earlier sketch in SATA 84
Ruemmler, John D(avid) 1948- 78
Ruepp, Krista 1947- 143
Ruffell, Ann 1941- 30
Ruffins, Reynold 1930- 125
  Earlier sketch in SATA 41
Rugg, Jim 206
Rugoff, Milton 1913- 30
Ruhen, Olaf 1911-1989 17
Rukeyser, Muriel 1913-1980
  Obituary 22
Rumbaut, Hendle 1949- 84
Rumford, James 1948- 193
  Earlier sketch in SATA 116
Rumsey, Marian (Barritt) 1928- 16
Rumstuckle, Cornelius
  See Brennan, Herbie
Runnerstroem, Bengt Arne 1944- 75
Runyan, John
  See Palmer, Bernard (Alvin)
Runyon, Catherine 1947- 62
Ruoff, A. LaVonne Brown 1930- 76
Rupp, Rebecca 185
Rusch, Elizabeth 1966- 198
Rusch, Kris
  See Rusch, Kristine Kathryn
Rusch, Kristine Kathryn 1960- 113
Rush, Alison 1951- 41
Rush, Peter 1937- 32

Rushdie, Ahmed Salman
  See Rushdie, Salman
Rushdie, Salman 1947-
  See CLR *125*
Rushford, Patricia H(elen) 1943- *134*
Rushmore, Helen 1898-1994 .... *3*
Rushmore, Robert (William) 1926-1986 ...... *8*
  Obituary *49*
Ruskin, Ariane
  See Batterberry, Ariane Ruskin
Ruskin, John 1819-1900 .... *24*
Russ, Lavinia (Faxon) 1904-1992 .... *74*
Russell, Charlotte
  See Rathjen, Carl Henry
Russell, Ching Yeung 1946- *107*
Russell, Don(ald Bert) 1899-1986
  Obituary *47*
Russell, Franklin (Alexander) 1926- *11*
Russell, Gertrude Barrer
  See Barrer-Russell, Gertrude
Russell, Helen Ross 1915- *8*
Russell, James 1933- *53*
Russell, Jim
  See Russell, James
Russell, Joan Plummer 1930- *139*
Russell, P(hilip) Craig 1951- *162*
  Earlier sketch in SATA *80*
Russell, Patrick
  See Sammis, John
Russell, Paul (Gary) 1942- *57*
Russell, Sarah
  See Laski, Marghanita
Russell, Sharman Apt 1954- *123*
Russell, Solveig Paulson 1904-1985 .... *3*
Russo, Marisabina 1950- *188*
  Earlier sketches in SATA *106, 151*
Russo, Monica J. 1950- *83*
Russo, Susan 1947- *30*
Russon, Penni 1974- *179*
Rutgers van der Loeff, An
  See Rutgers van der Loeff-Basenau, An(na)
  Maria Margaretha
Rutgers van der Loeff-Basenau, An(na) Maria
  Margaretha 1910- *22*
Ruth, Rod 1912-1987 .... *9*
Rutherford, Douglas
  See McConnell, James Douglas Rutherford
Rutherford, Meg 1932- *34*
Ruthin, Margaret
  See Catherall, Arthur
Rutledge, Jill Zimmerman 1951- *155*
Rutz, Viola Larkin 1932- *12*
Ruurs, Margriet 1952- *147*
  Earlier sketch in SATA *97*
Ruzicka, Rudolph 1883-1978
  Obituary *24*
Ruzzier, Sergio 1966- *159*
, Ryan
  See Ryan, John
Ryan, Betsy
  See Ryan, Elizabeth (Anne)
Ryan, Cheli Duran *20*
Ryan, Darlene 1958- *176*
Ryan, Elizabeth (Anne) 1943- *30*
Ryan, Jeanette
  See Mines, Jeanette
Ryan, John 1921-2009 .... *22*
Ryan, Margaret 1950- *166*
  Earlier sketch in SATA *78*
Ryan, Mary E. 1953- *61*
Ryan, Mary Elizabeth
  See Ryan, Mary E.
Ryan, Pam Munoz 1951- *197*
  Earlier sketch in SATA *134*
Ryan, Patrick 1957- *138*
Ryan, Peter (Charles) 1939- *15*
Ryan-Lush, Geraldine 1949- *89*
Rybakov, Anatoli (Naumovich) 1911-1998 .. *79*
  Obituary *108*
Rybakov, Anatolii (Naumovich)
  See Rybakov, Anatoli (Naumovich)

Rybolt, Thomas R. 1954- *62*
Rybolt, Thomas Roy
  See Rybolt, Thomas R.
Rybolt, Tom
  See Rybolt, Thomas R.
Rydberg, Ernest E(mil) 1901-1993 .... *21*
Rydberg, Lou(isa Hampton) 1908- *27*
Rydell, Katy 1942- *91*
Rydell, Wendell
  See Rydell, Wendy
Rydell, Wendy *4*
Ryden, Hope *91*
  Earlier sketch in SATA *8*
Ryder, Joanne (Rose) 1946- *163*
  Brief entry *34*
  Earlier sketches in SATA *65, 122*
  See also CLR *37*
Ryder, Pamela
  See Lamb, Nancy
Rye, Anthony
  See Youd, Samuel
Rylant, Cynthia 1954- *195*
  Brief entry *44*
  Earlier sketches in SATA *50, 76, 112, 160*
  See also CLR *86*
  See also SAAS *13*
Rymer, Alta May 1925- *34*
Rymond, Lynda Gene *199*

S

S. L. C.
  See Twain, Mark
S., Svend Otto
  See Soerensen, Svend Otto
Saaf, Donald W(illiam) 1961- *124*
Saal, Jocelyn
  See Sachs, Judith
Sabbeth, Carol (Landstrom) 1957- *125*
Saberhagen, Fred 1930-2007 .... *89*
  Obituary *184*
  Earlier sketch in SATA *37*
Saberhagen, Fred T.
  See Saberhagen, Fred
Saberhagen, Fred Thomas
  See Saberhagen, Fred
Saberhagen, Frederick Thomas
  See Saberhagen, Fred
Sabin, Edwin L(egrand) 1870-1952
  See YABC *2*
Sabin, Francene *27*
Sabin, Lou
  See Sabin, Louis
Sabin, Louis 1930- *27*
Sabre, Dirk
  See Laffin, John (Alfred Charles)
Sabuda, Robert (James) 1965- *120*
  Earlier sketch in SATA *81*
Sabuda, Robert 1965- *170*
Sabuda, Robert James
  See Sabuda, Robert
Sachar, Louis 1954- *154*
  Brief entry *50*
  Earlier sketches in SATA *63, 104*
  See also CLR *79*
Sachs, Elizabeth-Ann 1946- *48*
Sachs, Judith 1947- *52*
  Brief entry *51*
Sachs, Marilyn 1927- *164*
  Autobiography Feature *110*
  Earlier sketches in SATA *3, 68*
  See also CLR *2*
  See also SAAS *2*
Sachs, Marilyn Stickle
  See Sachs, Marilyn
Sackett, S(amuel) J(ohn) 1928- *12*
Sackson, Sid 1920- *16*
Sacre, Antonio 1968- *152*

Saddler, Allen
  See Richards, R(onald) C(harles) W(illiam)
Saddler, K. Allen
  See Richards, R(onald) C(harles) W(illiam)
Sadie, Stanley 1930-2005 .... *14*
Sadie, Stanley John
  See Sadie, Stanley
Sadiq, Nazneen 1944- *101*
Sadler, Catherine Edwards 1952- *60*
  Brief entry *45*
Sadler, Marilyn (June) 1950- *79*
Sadler, Mark
  See Lynds, Dennis
Saffer, Barbara *144*
Sagan, Carl 1934-1996 .... *58*
  Obituary *94*
Sagan, Carl Edward
  See Sagan, Carl
Sage, Angie 1952- *197*
Sage, Juniper
  See Brown, Margaret Wise
  and Hurd, Edith Thacher
Sagsoorian, Paul 1923- *12*
Said, S.F. 1967- *174*
Saidman, Anne 1952- *75*
Saint, Dora Jessie 1913- *10*
St. Anthony, Jane *175*
St. Antoine, Sara L. 1966- *84*
St. Clair, Byrd Hooper 1905-1976
  Obituary *28*
Saint-Exupery, Antoine de 1900-1944 .... *20*
  See also CLR *142*
Saint-Exupery, Antoine Jean Baptiste Marie
  Roger de
  See Saint-Exupery, Antoine de
St. George, Judith 1931- *161*
  Earlier sketches in SATA *13, 99*
  See also CLR *57*
  See also SAAS *12*
St. George, Judith Alexander
  See St. George, Judith
St. James, Blakely
  See Gottfried, Theodore Mark
  and Platt, Charles
St. James, Blakely
  See Griffin, W.E.B.
St. James, Sierra
  See Rallison, Janette
Saint James, Synthia 1949- *152*
  Earlier sketch in SATA *84*
St. John, Nicole *143*
  Autobiography Feature *143*
  Earlier sketches in SATA *29, 89*
  See also CLR *46*
  See also SAAS *7*
St. John, Patricia Mary 1919-1993
  Obituary *79*
St. John, Philip
  See del Rey, Lester
St. John, Wylly Folk 1908-1985 .... *10*
  Obituary *45*
St. Max, E. S.
  See Ellis, Edward S.
St. Meyer, Ned
  See Stratemeyer, Edward L.
St. Mox, E. A.
  See Ellis, Edward S.
St. Myer, Ned
  See Stratemeyer, Edward L.
St. Tamara
  See Kolba, St. Tamara
Saito, Michiko
  See Fujiwara, Michiko
Sakaki, Ichiro 1969- *192*
Sakamoto, Miki *198*
Sakers, Don 1958- *72*
Sakharnov, S.
  See Sakharnov, Svyatoslav
Sakharnov, Svyatoslav 1923- *65*
Sakharnov, Svyatoslav Vladimirovich
  See Sakharnov, Svyatoslav

Saksena, Kate *148*
Sakurai, Gail 1952- *153*
  Earlier sketch in SATA 87
Salamanca, Lucy
  See del Barco, Lucy Salamanca
Salassi, Otto R(ussell) 1939-1993 .... *38*
  Obituary *77*
Salat, Cristina *82*
Saldana, Rene, Jr. *186*
Saldutti, Denise 1953- *39*
Sale, Tim 1956- *153*
Salem, Kay 1952- *92*
Salerno, Steven *176*
Salinger, J.D. 1919- *67*
  See also CLR 18
Salinger, Jerome David
  See Salinger, J.D.
Salisbury, Graham 1944- *195*
  Earlier sketches in SATA 76, 108, 161
Salisbury, Joyce E(llen) 1944- *138*
Salkey, (Felix) Andrew (Alexander)
  1928-1995 .... *118*
  Earlier sketch in SATA 35
Salley, Coleen *166*
Sallis, Susan (Diana) 1929- *55*
Salmon, Annie Elizabeth 1899- *13*
Salonen, Roxane Beauclair 1968- *184*
Salsi, Lynn 1947- *130*
Salsitz, R. A. V.
  See Salsitz, Rhondi Vilott
Salsitz, Rhondi Vilott *115*
Salten, Felix
  See Salzmann, Siegmund
Salter, Cedric
  See Knight, Francis Edgar
Saltman, Judith 1947- *64*
Saltzberg, Barney 1955- *194*
  Earlier sketch in SATA 135
Saltzman, David (Charles Laertes)
  1967-1990 .... *86*
Salvadori, Mario (George) 1907-1997 .... *97*
  Earlier sketch in SATA 40
Salwood, F.K.
  See Kilworth, Garry
Salzer, L. E.
  See Wilson, Lionel
Salzman, Marian 1959- *77*
Salzmann, Siegmund 1869-1945 .... *25*
Samachson, Dorothy (Mirkin) 1914-1997 ...... *3*
Samachson, Joseph 1906-1980 .... *3*
  Obituary *52*
Sammis, John 1942- *4*
Sampson, Emma (Keats) Speed 1868-1947 . *68*
Sampson, Fay (Elizabeth) 1935- *151*
  Brief entry *40*
  Earlier sketch in SATA 42
Sampson, Michael 1952- *143*
  Earlier sketch in SATA 95
Samson, Anne S(tringer) 1933- *2*
Samson, Joan 1937-1976 .... *13*
Samson, Suzanne M. 1959- *91*
Samuels, Barbara *199*
Samuels, Charles 1902-1982 .... *12*
Samuels, Cynthia K(alish) 1946- *79*
Samuels, Gertrude 1910(?)-2003 .... *17*
  Obituary *147*
Sanborn, Duane 1914-1996 .... *38*
Sancha, Sheila 1924- *38*
Sanchez, Alex 1957- *151*
Sanchez, Sonia 1934- *136*
  Earlier sketch in SATA 22
  See also CLR 18
Sanchez-Silva, Jose Maria 1911- *132*
  Earlier sketch in SATA 16
  See also CLR 12
Sand, George X. *45*
Sandak, Cass R(obert) 1950-2001 .... *51*
  Brief entry *37*
Sandberg, (Karin) Inger 1930- *15*
Sandberg, Karl C. 1931- *35*
Sandberg, Lasse (E. M.) 1924- *15*

Sandburg, Carl (August) 1878-1967 .... *8*
  See also CLR 67
Sandburg, Charles
  See Sandburg, Carl (August)
Sandburg, Charles A.
  See Sandburg, Carl (August)
Sandburg, Helga 1918- *3*
  See also SAAS 10
Sandell, Lisa Ann 1977- *175*
Sander, Heather L. 1947- *157*
Sanderlin, George 1915- *4*
Sanderlin, Owenita (Harrah) 1916- *11*
Sanders, Betty Jane
  See Monthei, Betty
Sanders, Nancy I. 1960- *141*
  Earlier sketch in SATA 90
Sanders, Scott Russell 1945- *109*
  Earlier sketch in SATA 56
Sanders, Winston P.
  See Anderson, Poul
Sanderson, Irma 1912- *66*
Sanderson, Ivan T(erence) 1911-1973 .... *6*
Sanderson, Margaret Love
  See Keats, Emma
  and Sampson, Emma (Keats) Speed
Sanderson, Ruth 1951- *172*
  Earlier sketches in SATA 41, 109
Sanderson, Ruth L.
  See Sanderson, Ruth
Sandin, Joan 1942- *197*
  Earlier sketches in SATA 12, 94, 153
Sandison, Janet
  See Cameron, Elizabeth Jane
Sandler, Martin W. *160*
Sandom, J. Gregory
  See Welsh, T.K.
Sandom, J.G.
  See Welsh, T.K.
Sandoz, Mari(e Susette) 1900-1966 .... *5*
Sanford, Agnes (White) 1897-1976 .... *61*
Sanford, Doris 1937- *69*
Sanford, Rose
  See Simmonds, Posy
Sanger, Amy Wilson 1967- *205*
Sanger, Marjory Bartlett 1920- *8*
San Jose, Christine 1929- *167*
Sankey, Alice (Ann-Susan) 1910- *27*
San Souci, Daniel *192*
  Earlier sketch in SATA 96
San Souci, Robert D. 1946- *158*
  Earlier sketches in SATA 40, 81, 117
  See also CLR 43
Santamaria, Benjamin 1955- *184*
Santat, Dan *188*
Santesson, Hans Stefan 1914(?)-1975
  Obituary *30*
Santiago, Esmeralda 1948- *129*
Santore, Charles 1935- *200*
Santos, Helen
  See Griffiths, Helen
Santrey, Louis
  See Sabin, Louis
Santucci, Barbara 1948- *130*
Sapergia, Barbara 1943- *181*
Sapieyevski, Anne Lindbergh 1940-1993 ..... *81*
  Brief entry *32*
  Earlier sketches in SATA 35, 78
Saport, Linda 1954- *123*
Sapp, Allen 1929- *151*
Sarac, Roger
  See Caras, Roger A(ndrew)
Sarah, Duchess of York
  See Ferguson, Sarah
Sarasin, Jennifer
  See Sachs, Judith
Sardinha, Rick *192*
Sarg, Anthony Frederick
  See Sarg, Tony
Sarg, Tony 1882-1942
  See YABC 1

Sargent, Pamela 1948- *78*
  Earlier sketch in SATA 29
Sargent, Robert 1933- *2*
Sargent, Sarah 1937- *44*
  Brief entry *41*
Sargent, Shirley 1927-2004 .... *11*
Sarnoff, Jane 1937- *10*
Saroff, Phyllis V. *202*
Saroyan, William 1908-1981 .... *23*
  Obituary *24*
Sarton, Eleanor May
  See Sarton, May
Sarton, May 1912-1995 .... *36*
  Obituary *86*
Sasaki, Chris *182*
Sasaki, Ellen Joy *206*
Saseen, Sharon (Dillon) 1949- *59*
Sasek, Miroslav 1916-1980 .... *16*
  Obituary *23*
  See also CLR 4
Sasso, Sandy Eisenberg 1947- *162*
  Earlier sketches in SATA 86, 116
Sathre, Vivian 1952- *133*
  Earlier sketch in SATA 79
Satterfield, Charles
  See del Rey, Lester
  and Pohl, Frederik
Sattgast, L. J.
  See Sattgast, Linda J.
Sattgast, Linda J. 1953- *91*
Sattler, Helen Roney 1921-1992 .... *74*
  Earlier sketch in SATA 4
  See also CLR 24
Sauer, Julia Lina 1891-1983 .... *32*
  Obituary *36*
Sauerwein, Leigh 1944- *155*
Saul, Carol P. 1947- *117*
  Earlier sketch in SATA 78
Saul, John III
  See Saul, John
Saul, John 1942- *98*
Saul, John W.
  See Saul, John
Saul, John W. III
  See Saul, John
Saul, John Woodruff III
  See Saul, John
Saul, (Ellen) Wendy 1946- *42*
Saulnier, Karen Luczak 1940- *80*
Saunders, Caleb
  See Heinlein, Robert A.
Saunders, Dave 1939- *85*
Saunders, Julie 1939- *85*
Saunders, (William) Keith 1910-1994 .... *12*
Saunders, Rubie (Agnes) 1929- *21*
Saunders, Steven
  See Jones, Allan Frewin
Saunders, Susan 1945- *96*
  Brief entry *41*
  Earlier sketch in SATA 46
Saunders-Smith, Gail 1952- *169*
Sauvain, Philip Arthur 1933- *111*
Savadier, Elivia 1950- *164*
  Earlier sketch in SATA 79
Savage, Alan
  See Nicole, Christopher (Robin)
Savage, Blake
  See Goodwin, Harold L(eland)
Savage, Candace 1949- *142*
Savage, Deborah 1955- *76*
Savage, Jeff 1961- *97*
Savage, Katharine James 1905-1989
  Obituary *61*
Savage, Stephen 1965- *194*
Savage, Thomas 1915-2003
  Obituary *147*
Savageau, Cheryl 1950- *96*
Savery, Constance (Winifred) 1897-1999 .... *1*
Saville, Andrew
  See Taylor, Andrew

Saville, (Leonard) Malcolm 1901-1982 23
  Obituary 31
Saviozzi, Adriana
  See Mazza, Adriana
Savitt, Sam 1917-2000 8
  Obituary 126
Savitz, Harriet May 1933- 72
  Earlier sketch in SATA 5
  See also SAAS 26
Sawicki, Mary 1950- 90
Sawyer, (Frederick) Don(ald) 1947- 72
Sawyer, Kem Knapp 1953- 84
Sawyer, Robert J. 1960- 149
  Earlier sketch in SATA 81
Sawyer, Robert James
  See Sawyer, Robert J.
Sawyer, Ruth 1880-1970 17
  See also CLR 36
Saxby, H.M.
  See Saxby, (Henry) Maurice
Saxby, (Henry) Maurice 1924- 71
Saxon, Andrew
  See Arthur, Robert, (Jr.)
Saxon, Antonia
  See Sachs, Judith
Say, Allen 1937- 161
  Earlier sketches in SATA 28, 69, 110
  See also CLR 135
Sayers, Frances Clarke 1897-1989 3
  Obituary 62
Sayles, Elizabeth 1956- 163
  Earlier sketch in SATA 108
Saylor-Marchant, Linda 1963- 82
Sayre, April Pulley 1966- 191
  Earlier sketches in SATA 88, 131
Sazer, Nina 1949- 13
Scabrini, Janet 1953- 13
Scagell, Robin 1946- 107
Scagnetti, Jack 1924- 7
Scamander, Newt
  See Rowling, J.K.
Scamell, Ragnhild 1940- 180
  Earlier sketch in SATA 77
Scanlon, Marion Stephany 11
Scannel, John Vernon
  See Scannell, Vernon
Scannell, Vernon 1922-2007 59
  Obituary 188
Scarborough, Elizabeth
  See Scarborough, Elizabeth Ann
Scarborough, Elizabeth Ann 1947- 171
  Earlier sketch in SATA 98
Scarf, Maggi
  See Scarf, Maggie
Scarf, Maggie 1932- 5
Scariano, Margaret M. 1924- 86
Scarlett, Susan
  See Streatfeild, Noel
Scarry, Huck
  See Scarry, Richard McClure, Jr.
Scarry, Patricia (Murphy) 1924- 2
Scarry, Patsy
  See Scarry, Patricia (Murphy)
Scarry, Richard (McClure) 1919-1994 75
  Obituary 90
  Earlier sketches in SATA 2, 35
  See also CLR 41
Scarry, Richard McClure, Jr. 1953- 35
Schachner, Judith Byron 1951- 178
  Earlier sketch in SATA 88
Schachner, Judy
  See Schachner, Judith Byron
Schachtel, Roger 1949- 38
Schachtel, Roger Bernard
  See Schachtel, Roger
Schade, Susan 189
Schaedler, Sally 116
Schaefer, Carole Lexa 173
Schaefer, Jack (Warner) 1907-1991 66
  Obituary 65
  Earlier sketch in SATA 3

Schaefer, Lola M. 1950- 183
  Earlier sketches in SATA 91, 144
Schaeffer, Mead 1898- 21
Schaeffer, Susan Fromberg 1941- 22
Schaer, Brigitte 1958- 112
Schaller, George
  See Schaller, George B.
Schaller, George B. 1933- 30
Schaller, George Beals
  See Schaller, George B.
Schanzer, Rosalyn (Good) 1942- 138
  Earlier sketch in SATA 77
Schatell, Brian 66
  Brief entry 47
Schechter, Betty (Goodstein) 1921- 5
Schechter, Simone
  See Elkeles, Simone
Schecter, Ellen 1944- 85
Scheeder, Louis 1946- 141
Scheer, Julian (Weisel) 1926-2001 8
Scheffer, Victor B(lanchard) 1906- 6
Scheffler, Axel 1957- 180
Scheffler, Ursel 1938- 81
Scheffrin-Falk, Gladys 1928- 76
Scheidl, Gerda Marie 1913- 85
Scheier, Michael 1943- 40
  Brief entry 36
Schell, Mildred 1922- 41
Schell, Orville (Hickok) 1940- 10
Scheller, Melanie 1953- 77
Schellie, Don 1932- 29
Schembri, Jim 1962- 124
Schembri, Pamela 1969- 195
Schemm, Mildred Walker 1905-1998 21
  Obituary 103
Schenker, Dona 1947- 133
  Earlier sketch in SATA 68
Scher, Paula 1948- 47
Scherer, Jeffrey 194
Scherf, Margaret 1908-1979 10
Schermer, Judith (Denise) 1941- 30
Schertle, Alice 1941- 192
  Earlier sketches in SATA 36, 90, 145
Schick, Alice 1946- 27
Schick, Eleanor 1942- 144
  Earlier sketches in SATA 9, 82
Schick, Joel 1945- 31
  Brief entry 30
Schields, Gretchen 1948- 75
Schiff, Ken(neth Roy) 1942- 7
Schiller, Andrew 1919- 21
Schiller, Barbara (Heyman) 1928- 21
Schiller, Pamela (Byrne) 127
Schindel, John 1955- 115
  Earlier sketch in SATA 77
Schindelman, Joseph 1923- 67
  Brief entry 32
Schindler, S.D. 1952- 198
  Brief entry 50
  Earlier sketches in SATA 75, 118, 171
Schindler, Steven D.
  See Schindler, S.D.
Schinto, Jeanne 1951- 93
Schisgall, Oscar 1901-1984 12
  Obituary 38
Schlaepfer, Gloria G. 1931- 154
Schlee, Ann 1934- 44
  Brief entry 36
Schleichert, Elizabeth 1945- 77
Schlein, Miriam 1926-2004 130
  Obituary 159
  Earlier sketches in SATA 2, 87
  See also CLR 41
Schlesinger, Arthur M., Jr. 1917-2007 61
  Obituary 181
  See Schlesinger, Arthur Meier
Schlesinger, Arthur Meier 1888-1965
Schlessinger, Laura (Catherine) 1947- 160
  Earlier sketch in SATA 110
Schlitz, Laura Amy 184
Schloat, G. Warren, Jr. 1914-2000 4

Schmatz, Pat 197
Schmid, Eleonore 1939- 126
  Earlier sketches in SATA 12, 84
Schmiderer, Dorothy 1940- 19
Schmidt, Annie M. G. 1911-1995 67
  Obituary 91
  See also CLR 22
Schmidt, C.A. 196
Schmidt, Diane 1953- 70
Schmidt, Elizabeth 1915- 15
Schmidt, Gary D. 1957- 193
  Earlier sketches in SATA 93, 135
Schmidt, James Norman 1912-1983 21
Schmidt, Karen Lee 1953- 185
  Earlier sketch in SATA 94
Schmidt, Lynette 1952- 76
Schneider, Antonie 1954- 167
  Earlier sketch in SATA 89
Schneider, Christine M. 1972(?)- 171
  Earlier sketch in SATA 120
Schneider, Dick
  See Schneider, Richard H.
Schneider, Elisa
  See Kleven, Elisa
Schneider, Herman 1905-2003 7
  Obituary 148
Schneider, Howie -2007 181
Schneider, Josh 1980- 196
Schneider, Laurie
  See Adams, Laurie
Schneider, Nina 1913-2007 2
  Obituary 186
Schneider, Nina Zimet
  See Schneider, Nina
Schneider, Rex 1937- 44
Schneider, Richard H. 1922- 171
Schneider, Richard Henry
  See Schneider, Richard H.
Schneider, Robyn 1986- 187
Schnirel, James R. 1931- 14
Schnitter, Jane T. 1958- 88
Schnitzlein, Danny 134
Schnur, Steven 1952- 144
  Earlier sketch in SATA 95
Schnurre, Wolfdietrich 1920-1989
  Obituary 63
Schoberle, Cecile 1949- 80
Schock, Pauline 1928- 45
Schoell, William 1951- 160
Schoen, Barbara (Taylor) 1924-1993 13
Schoenherr, Ian 177
Schoenherr, John (Carl) 1935- 66
  Earlier sketch in SATA 37
  See also SAAS 13
Schofield, Sandy
  See Rusch, Kristine Kathryn
Scholastica, Sister Mary
  See Jenkins, Marie M(agdalen)
Scholefield, A. T.
  See Scholefield, Alan
Scholefield, Alan 1931- 66
Scholefield, Edmund O.
  See Griffin, W.E.B.
Scholey, Arthur 1932- 28
Scholz, Jackson Volney 1897-1986
  Obituary 49
Schone, Virginia 22
Schongut, Emanuel 1936- 184
  Brief entry 36
  Earlier sketch in SATA 52
Schoonover, Frank (Earle) 1877-1972 24
Schoor, Gene 1921- 3
Schories, Pat 1952- 164
  Earlier sketch in SATA 116
Schorr, Melissa 1972- 194
Schorr, Melissa Robin
  See Schorr, Melissa
Schott, Jane A. 1946- 172
Schotter, Roni 190
  Earlier sketches in SATA 105, 149

Schraff, Anne E(laine) 1939- 92
  Earlier sketch in SATA 27
Schram, Peninnah 1934- 119
Schrank, Joseph 1900-1984
  Obituary 38
Schrecengost, Maity 1938- 118
Schrecengost, S. Maitland
  See Schrecengost, Maity
Schreck, Karen
  See Schreck, Karen Halvorsen
Schreck, Karen Halvorsen 1962- 185
Schrecker, Judie 1954- 90
Schreiber, Elizabeth Anne (Ferguson)
  1947- 13
Schreiber, Ralph W(alter) 1942- 13
Schreiner, Samuel A(gnew), Jr. 1921- 70
Schroeder, Alan 1961- 98
  Earlier sketch in SATA 66
Schroeder, Binette
  See Nickl, Barbara (Elisabeth)
Schroeder, Russell (K.) 1943- 146
Schroeder, Ted 1931(?)-1973
  Obituary 20
Schubert, Dieter 1947- 101
  Earlier sketch in SATA 62
Schubert, Leda 1950(?)- 181
Schubert-Gabrys, Ingrid 1953- 101
  Earlier sketch in SATA 62
Schuelein-Steel, Danielle
  See Steel, Danielle
Schuelein-Steel, Danielle Fernande
  See Steel, Danielle
Schuerger, Michele R. 110
Schuett, Stacey 1960- 168
  Earlier sketch in SATA 75
Schulke, Flip Phelps Graeme 1930- 57
Schulman, Arlene 1961- 105
Schulman, Janet 1933- 137
  Earlier sketch in SATA 22
Schulman, L(ester) M(artin) 1934- 13
Schulte, Elaine L(ouise) 1934- 36
Schultz, Betty K(epka) 1932- 125
Schultz, Gwendolyn 21
Schultz, James Willard 1859-1947
  See YABC 1
Schultz, Pearle Henriksen 1918- 21
Schulz, Charles M. 1922-2000 10
  Obituary 118
Schulz, Charles Monroe
  See Schulz, Charles M.
Schumacher, Julie 1958- 191
Schumaker, Ward 1943- 96
Schuman, Michael A. 1953- 134
  Earlier sketch in SATA 85
Schur, Maxine
  See Schur, Maxine Rose
Schur, Maxine Rose 1948- 135
  Autobiography Feature 135
  Brief entry 49
  Earlier sketches in SATA 53, 98
Schurfranz, Vivian 1925- 13
Schutzer, A. I. 1922- 13
Schuyler, Pamela R. 1948- 30
Schwabach, Karen 185
Schwager, Tina 1964- 110
Schwandt, Stephen (William) 1947- 61
Schwark, Mary Beth 1954- 51
Schwartz, Alvin 1927-1992 56
  Obituary 71
  Earlier sketch in SATA 4
  See also CLR 89
Schwartz, Amy 1954- 189
  Brief entry 41
  Earlier sketches in SATA 47, 83, 131
  See also CLR 25
  See also SAAS 18
Schwartz, Anne Powers 1913-1987 10
Schwartz, Carol 1954- 77
Schwartz, Charles W(alsh) 1914- 8
Schwartz, David M. 1951- 110
  Earlier sketch in SATA 59

Schwartz, David Martin
  See Schwartz, David M.
Schwartz, Elizabeth Reeder 1912- 8
Schwartz, Ellen 1949- 117
Schwartz, Jerome L.
  See Lawrence, Jerome
Schwartz, Joel L. 1940- 54
  Brief entry 51
Schwartz, Joyce R. 1950- 93
Schwartz, Julius 1907-2004 45
Schwartz, Perry 1942- 75
Schwartz, Sheila (Ruth) 1929- 27
Schwartz, Stephen (Lawrence) 1948- 19
Schwartz, Virginia Frances 1950- 184
  Earlier sketch in SATA 131
Schwarz, Silvia Tessa Viviane
  See Schwarz, Viviane
Schwarz, Viviane 1977- 204
Schwarz, (Silvia Tessa) Viviane 1977- 141
Schweitzer, Byrd Baylor
  See Baylor, Byrd
Schweitzer, Iris 59
  Brief entry 36
Schweninger, Ann 1951- 168
  Earlier sketches in SATA 29, 98
Schwerin, Doris H(alpern) 1922- 64
Schy, Yael 197
Scieszka, Jon 1954- 199
  Earlier sketches in SATA 68, 105, 160
  See also CLR 107
Scillian, Devin 199
  Earlier sketch in SATA 128
Scioscia, Mary (Hershey) 1926- 63
Sciurba, Katie 1957- 196
Scofield, Penrod 1933- 62
  Obituary 78
Scoggin, Margaret C(lara) 1905-1968 47
  Brief entry 28
Scoltock, Jack 1942- 141
  Earlier sketch in SATA 72
Scoppettone, Sandra 1936- 92
  Earlier sketch in SATA 9
Scot, Michael
  See Rohan, Michael Scott
Scot-Bernard, P.
  See Bernard, Patricia
Scotland, Jay
  See Jakes, John
Scott, Alastair
  See Allen, Kenneth S.
Scott, Ann Herbert 1926- 140
  Autobiography Feature 140
  Brief entry 29
  Earlier sketches in SATA 56, 94
Scott, Bill
  See Scott, William N(eville)
Scott, Bill 1920(?)-1985
  Obituary 46
Scott, Cora Annett (Pipitone) 1931- 11
Scott, Dan
  See Barker, S. Omar
Scott, Elaine 1940- 198
  Earlier sketches in SATA 36, 90, 164
Scott, Elizabeth 194
Scott, Jack Denton 1915-1995 83
  Earlier sketch in SATA 31
  See also CLR 20
  See also SAAS 14
Scott, Jane (Harrington) 1931- 55
Scott, Jessica
  See De Wire, Elinor
Scott, John 1912-1976 14
Scott, John Anthony 1916- 23
Scott, John M(artin) 1913- 12
Scott, Mary
  See Mattern, Joanne
Scott, Melissa 1960- 109
Scott, Richard
  See Rennert, Richard Scott
Scott, Roney
  See Gault, William Campbell

Scott, Sally 1909-1978 43
Scott, Sally 1948- 44
Scott, Sally Elisabeth
  See Scott, Sally
Scott, W. N.
  See Scott, William N(eville)
Scott, Sir Walter 1771-1832
  See YABC 2
Scott, Warwick
  See Trevor, Elleston
Scott, William N(eville) 1923- 87
Scotti, Anna
  See Coates, Anna
Scotton, Rob 1960- 177
Scribner, Charles, Jr. 1921-1995 13
  Obituary 87
Scribner, Joanne L. 1949- 33
Scribner, Kimball 1917- 63
Scrimger, Richard 1957- 164
  Earlier sketch in SATA 119
Scrimsher, Lila Gravatt 1897-1974
  Obituary 28
Scroder, Walter K. 1928- 82
Scroggs, Kirk 187
Scruggs, Sandy 1961- 89
Scudder, Brooke 1959- 154
Scudder, Mildred Lee 1908- 6
  See also SAAS 12
Scull, Marie-Louise 1943-1993 77
Scuro, Vincent 1951- 21
Seabrooke, Brenda 1941- 148
  Earlier sketches in SATA 30, 88
Seaman, Augusta Huiell 1879-1950 31
Seamands, Ruth 1916- 9
Searcy, Margaret Zehmer 1926- 54
  Brief entry 39
Searight, Mary W(illiams) 1918- 17
Searle, Kathryn Adrienne 1942- 10
Searle, Ronald (William Fordham) 1920- 70
  Earlier sketch in SATA 42
Sears, Stephen W. 1932- 4
Sebastian, Lee
  See Silverberg, Robert
Sebestyen, Igen
  See Sebestyen, Ouida
Sebestyen, Ouida 1924- 140
  Earlier sketch in SATA 39
  See also CLR 17
  See also SAAS 10
Sebrey, Mary Ann 1951- 62
Sechrist, Elizabeth Hough 1903-1991 2
Sedges, John
  See Buck, Pearl S.
Sedgwick, Marcus 1968- 197
  Earlier sketch in SATA 160
Seed, Cecile Eugenie 1930- 86
  Earlier sketch in SATA 8
  See also CLR 76
Seed, Jenny
  See Seed, Cecile Eugenie
Seed, Sheila Turner 1937(?)-1979
  Obituary 23
Seeger, Elizabeth 1889-1973
  Obituary 20
Seeger, Laura Vaccaro 200
  Earlier sketch in SATA 172
Seeger, Pete 1919- 139
  Earlier sketch in SATA 13
Seeger, Peter R.
  See Seeger, Pete
Seeley, Laura L. 1958- 71
Seever, R.
  See Reeves, Lawrence F.
Sefozo, Mary 1925- 82
Sefton, Catherine
  See Waddell, Martin
Segal, John 178
Segal, Joyce 1940- 35
Segal, Lore 1928- 163
  Earlier sketches in SATA 4, 66
  See also SAAS 11

Segal, Lore Groszmann
  See Segal, Lore
Segar, E(lzie) C(risler) 1894-1938 .... *61*
Segovia, Andres 1893(?)-1987
  Obituary *52*
Seguin, Marilyn W(eymouth) 1951- *91*
Seguin-Fontes, Marthe 1924- *109*
Seibold, J. Otto 1960- *196*
  Earlier sketches in SATA *83, 149*
  See also SAAS *22*
Seidel, Ross *95*
Seidelman, James Edward 1926- *6*
Seiden, Art(hur) *107*
  Brief entry *42*
Seidensticker, John 1944- *200*
Seidler, Ann (G.) 1925- *131*
Seidler, Tor 1952- *149*
  Brief entry *46*
  Earlier sketches in SATA *52, 98*
Seidman, Karla
  See Kuskin, Karla
Seidman, Laurence Ivan 1925- *15*
Seigel, Kalman 1917-1998 .... *12*
  Obituary *103*
Seignobosc, Françoise 1897-1961 .... *21*
Seinfeld, Jerry 1954- *146*
Seitz, Jacqueline 1931- *50*
Seixas, Judith S. 1922- *17*
Sejima, Yoshimasa 1913- *8*
Selberg, Ingrid (Maria) 1950- *68*
Selden, George
  See Thompson, George Selden
Selden, Neil R(oy) 1931- *61*
Self, Margaret Cabell 1902-1996 .... *24*
Selfors, Suzanne 1963- *193*
Selick, Henry 1952- *183*
Selig, Sylvie 1942- *13*
Selkirk, Jane
  See Chapman, John Stanton Higham
Sellers, Naomi
  See Flack, Naomi John White
Selman, LaRue W. 1927- *55*
Selsam, Millicent E(llis) 1912-1996 .... *29*
  Obituary *92*
  Earlier sketch in SATA *1*
  See also CLR *1*
Seltzer, Meyer 1932- *17*
Seltzer, Richard 1946- *41*
Seltzer, Richard Warren, Jr.
  See Seltzer, Richard
Selvadurai, Shyam 1965(?)- *171*
Selway, Martina 1940- *169*
  Earlier sketch in SATA *74*
Selzer, Adam 1980- *192*
Selznick, Brian 1966- *171*
  Earlier sketches in SATA *79, 117*
Semel, Nava 1954- *107*
Semloh
  See Holmes, Peggy
Sendak, Jack 1924(?)-1995 .... *28*
Sendak, Maurice 1928- *165*
  Earlier sketches in SATA *1, 27, 113*
  See also CLR *131*
Sendak, Maurice Bernard
  See Sendak, Maurice
Sender, Ruth M(insky) 1926- *62*
Sengler, Johanna 1924- *18*
Senisi, Ellen B. 1951- *116*
Senisi, Ellen Babinec
  See Senisi, Ellen B.
Senn, J(oyce) A(nn) 1941- *115*
Senn, Steve 1950- *60*
  Brief entry *48*
Sensel, Joni 1962- *204*
Serafini, Frank *201*
Serage, Nancy 1924- *10*
Seredy, Kate 1899-1975 .... *1*
  Obituary *24*
  See also CLR *10*
Serfozo, Mary 1925- *194*

Seroff, Victor I(lyitch) 1902-1979 .... *12*
  Obituary *26*
Serra, Sebastia 1966- *202*
Serraillier, Ian (Lucien) 1912-1994 .... *73*
  Obituary *83*
  Earlier sketch in SATA *1*
  See also CLR *2*
  See also SAAS *3*
Serros, Michele *175*
Serros, Michele M.
  See Serros, Michele
Servello, Joe 1932- *10*
Service, Pamela F. 1945- *64*
Service, Robert
  See Service, Robert W.
Service, Robert W. 1874(?)-1958 .... *20*
Serwadda, W(illiam) Moses 1931- *27*
Serwer-Bernstein, Blanche L(uria)
  1910-1997 .... *10*
Sescoe, Vincent E. 1938- *123*
Seth, Mary
  See Lexau, Joan M.
Seton, Anya 1904(?)-1990 .... *3*
  Obituary *66*
Seton, Ernest (Evan) Thompson 1860-1946 . *18*
  See also CLR *59*
Seton-Thompson, Ernest
  See Seton, Ernest (Evan) Thompson
Seuling, Barbara 1937- *193*
  Earlier sketches in SATA *10, 98, 145*
  See also SAAS *24*
Severn, Bill
  See Severn, William Irving
Severn, David
  See Unwin, David S(torr)
Severn, William Irving 1914- *1*
Sewall, Marcia 1935- *119*
  Earlier sketches in SATA *37, 69*
Seward, Prudence 1926- *16*
Sewell, Anna 1820-1878 .... *100*
  Earlier sketch in SATA *24*
  See also CLR *17*
Sewell, Helen (Moore) 1896-1957 .... *38*
Sexton, Anne (Harvey) 1928-1974 .... *10*
Seymour, Alta Halverson *10*
Seymour, Jane 1951- *139*
Seymour, Tres 1966- *164*
  Earlier sketch in SATA *82*
Sfar, Joann 1971- *182*
Shachtman, Tom 1942- *49*
Shackleton, C.C.
  See Aldiss, Brian W.
Shader, Rachel
  See Sofer, Barbara
Shadow, Jak
  See Sutherland, Jon
Shadyland, Sal
  See Cooper, Louise
Shafer, Audrey *183*
Shafer, Robert E(ugene) 1925- *9*
Shaffer, Terea 1968- *79*
Shahan, Sherry 1949- *134*
  Earlier sketch in SATA *92*
Shahn, Ben(jamin) 1898-1969
  Obituary *21*
Shahn, Bernarda Bryson
  See Bryson, Bernarda
Shaik, Fatima *114*
Shalant, Phyllis 1949- *150*
Shan, Darren 1972- *199*
  Earlier sketches in SATA *129, 168*
Shan, D.B.
  See Shan, Darren
Shanahan, Lisa *199*
Shanberg, Karen
  See Shragg, Karen (I.)
Shane, Harold Gray 1914-1993 .... *36*
  Obituary *76*
Shange, Ntozake 1948- *157*
Shanks, Ann Zane (Kushner) *10*

Shannon, David 1959- *152*
  Earlier sketch in SATA *107*
  See also CLR *87*
Shannon, George 1952- *202*
  Earlier sketches in SATA *35, 94, 143*
Shannon, George William Bones
  See Shannon, George
Shannon, Jacqueline *63*
Shannon, Margaret
  See Silverwood, Margaret Shannon
Shannon, Monica 1905(?)-1965 .... *28*
Shannon, Terry
  See Mercer, Jessie
Shannon, Terry Miller 1951- *148*
Shapiro, Irwin 1911-1981 .... *32*
Shapiro, Jody Fickes 1940- *193*
Shapiro, Karen Jo 1964- *186*
Shapiro, Michelle 1961- *196*
Shapiro, Milton J. 1926- *32*
Shapiro, Tricia
  See Andryszewski, Tricia
Shapp, Charles M(orris) 1906-1989
  Obituary *61*
Shapp, Martha Glauber 1910- *3*
Sharenow, Robert *193*
Sharfman, Amalie *14*
Sharma, Partap 1939- *15*
Sharma, Rashmi
  See Singh, Rashmi Sharma
Sharman, Alison
  See Leonard, Alison
Sharmat, Marjorie Weinman 1928- *133*
  Earlier sketches in SATA *4, 33, 74*
Sharmat, Mitchell 1927- *127*
  Earlier sketch in SATA *33*
Sharp, Anne Wallace 1947- *144*
Sharp, Luke
  See Alkiviades, Alkis
Sharp, Margery 1905-1991 .... *29*
  Obituary *67*
  Earlier sketch in SATA *1*
  See also CLR *27*
Sharp, Zerna A. 1889-1981 ....
  Obituary *27*
Sharpe, Jon
  See Duncan, Alice
  and Knott, William C(ecil, Jr.)
  and Messman, Jon
Sharpe, Mitchell R(aymond) 1924- *12*
Sharpe, Susan 1946- *71*
Sharratt, Nick 1962- *199*
  Earlier sketches in SATA *104, 153*
Shasha, Mark 1961- *80*
Shattuck, Roger 1923-2005 .... *64*
  Obituary *174*
Shattuck, Roger Whitney
  See Shattuck, Roger
Shaw, Arnold 1909-1989 .... *4*
  Obituary *63*
Shaw, Carolyn V. 1934- *91*
Shaw, Charles (Green) 1892-1974 .... *13*
Shaw, Evelyn S. 1927- *28*
Shaw, Flora Louisa
  See Lugard, Flora Louisa Shaw
Shaw, Janet 1937- *146*
  Earlier sketch in SATA *61*
  See also CLR *96*
Shaw, Janet Beeler
  See Shaw, Janet
Shaw, Lisa
  See Rogak, Lisa
Shaw, Margret 1940- *68*
Shaw, Mary 1965- *180*
Shaw, Nancy 1946- *162*
  Earlier sketch in SATA *71*
Shaw, Ray *7*
Shaw, Richard 1923- *12*
Shawn, Frank S.
  See Goulart, Ron
Shay, Art
  See Shay, Arthur

Shay, Arthur 1922- 4
Shay, Lacey
    See Shebar, Sharon Sigmond
Shea, Bob 188
Shea, George 1940- 54
    Brief entry 42
Shea, Pegi Deitz 1960- 172
    Earlier sketches in SATA 77, 137
Shearer, Alex 1949- 204
Shearer, John 1947- 43
    Brief entry 27
    See also CLR 34
Shearer, Ted 1919- 43
Shearing, Leonie 1972- 184
Sheban, Chris 182
Shebar, Sharon Sigmond 1945- 36
Shecter, Ben 1935- 16
Shedd, Warner 1934- 147
    Earlier sketch in SATA 87
Sheedy, Alexandra Elizabeth 1962- 39
    Earlier sketch in SATA 19
Sheehan, Ethna 1908-2000 9
Sheehan, Patty 1945- 77
Sheehan, Sean 1951- 154
    Earlier sketch in SATA 86
Sheen, Barbara 1949- 143
Shefelman, Janice 1930- 205
    Earlier sketches in SATA 58, 129
Shefelman, Janice Jordan
    See Shefelman, Janice
Shefelman, Tom 1927- 204
    Earlier sketch in SATA 58
Sheffer, H. R.
    See Abels, Harriette S(heffer)
Sheffield, Charles 1935-2002 109
Sheffield, Janet N. 1926- 26
Sheikh, Nazneen
    See Sadiq, Nazneen
Sheinkin, Steve 1968- 204
Shekerjian, Regina Tor 16
Shelby, Anne 1948- 85
    Autobiography Feature 121
    See also SAAS 26
Sheldon, Ann
    See Antle, Nancy
Sheldon, Ann 67
    Earlier sketch in SATA 1
Sheldon, Aure 1917-1976 12
Sheldon, David 185
Sheldon, Dyan 181
Sheldon, John
    See Bloch, Robert (Albert)
Sheldon, Muriel 1926- 45
    Brief entry 39
Shell, Barry 1951- 176
Shelley, Frances
    See Wees, Frances Shelley
Shelley, John 1959- 202
Shelley, Mary Wollstonecraft (Godwin)
    1797-1851 29
    See also CLR 133
Shelton, William Roy 1919-1995 5
    Obituary 129
Shemie, Bonnie (Jean Brenner) 1949- 96
Shemin, Margaretha (Hoeneveld) 1928- 4
Shen, Michele 1953- 173
Shenker, Michele
    See Shen, Michele
Shenton, Edward 1895-1977 45
Shepard, Aaron 1950- 187
    Earlier sketches in SATA 75, 113
Shepard, Ernest Howard 1879-1976 100
    Obituary 24
    Earlier sketches in SATA 3, 33
    See also CLR 27
Shepard, James R.
    See Shepard, Jim
Shepard, Jim 1956- 164
    Earlier sketch in SATA 90
Shepard, Mary
    See Knox, (Mary) Eleanor Jessie

Shephard, Esther 1891-1975 5
    Obituary 26
Shepherd, Amanda 201
Shepherd, Donna Walsh
    See Walsh Shepherd, Donna
Shepherd, Elizabeth 4
Shepherd, Irana 173
Shepherd, Roni
    See Shepherd, Irana
Sheppard, Kate 195
Shepperson, Rob 178
Sherburne, Zoa (Lillian Morin) 1912-1995 3
    See also SAAS 18
Sherk-Savage, Candace
    See Savage, Candace
Sherlock, Patti 71
Sherman, D(enis) R(onald) 1934- 48
    Brief entry 29
Sherman, Diane (Finn) 1928- 12
Sherman, Elizabeth
    See Friskey, Margaret (Richards)
Sherman, Harold (Morrow) 1898-1987 37
    Obituary 137
Sherman, Josepha 163
    Earlier sketch in SATA 75
Sherman, Michael
    See Lowndes, Robert A(ugustine) W(ard)
Sherman, Nancy
    See Rosenberg, Nancy (Sherman)
Sherman, Pat 174
Sherman, Peter Michael
    See Lowndes, Robert A(ugustine) W(ard)
Sherrard, Valerie (Anne) 1957- 141
Sherrod, Jane
    See Singer, Jane Sherrod
Sherry, Clifford J. 1943- 84
Sherry, (Dulcie) Sylvia 1932- 122
    Earlier sketch in SATA 8
Sherwan, Earl 1917- 3
Sherwood, Jonathan
    See London, Jonathan (Paul)
Sheth, Kashmira 186
Shetterly, Will 1955- 78
    Autobiography Feature 106
Shetterly, William Howard
    See Shetterly, Will
Shiefman, Vicky 1942- 22
Shields, Brenda Desmond (Armstrong)
    1914- 37
Shields, Carol Diggory 174
Shields, Charles 1944- 10
Shields, Gillian 203
Shiels, Barbara
    See Adams, Barbara Johnston
Shiffman, Lena 1957- 101
Shiina, Makoto 1944- 83
Shimin, Symeon 1902-1984 13
Shimko, Bonnie 1941- 191
Shine, Andrea 1955- 104
Shine, Deborah 1932- 71
Shinn, Everett 1876-1953 21
Shinn, Sharon 1957- 164
    Earlier sketch in SATA 110
Shippen, Katherine B(inney) 1892-1980 1
    Obituary 23
    See also CLR 36
Shippey, T. A. 1943- 143
Shippey, Thomas Alan
    See Shippey, T. A.
Shipton, Eric Earle 1907-1977 10
Shipton, Paul 1963- 196
Shiraz, Yasmin 173
Shirer, William L(awrence) 1904-1993 45
    Obituary 78
Shirley, Debra 203
Shirley, Gayle C 1955- 96
Shirley, Gayle Corbett
    See Shirley, Gayle C
Shirley, Jean 1919- 70
Shirreffs, Gordon D(onald) 1914-1996 11
Shirts, Morris A(lpine) 1922- 63

Shlichta, Joe 1968- 84
Shmurak, Carole B. 1944- 118
Sholokhov, Mikhail (Aleksandrovich)
    1905-1984
    Obituary 36
Shore, Diane Z. 179
Shore, Diane ZuHone
    See Shore, Diane Z.
Shore, June Lewis 30
Shore, Nancy 1960- 124
Shore, Robert 1924- 39
Short, Michael 1937- 65
Short, Roger
    See Arkin, Alan
Shortall, Leonard W. 19
Shortt, Tim(othy Donald) 1961- 96
Shotwell, Louisa Rossiter 1902-1993 3
Shoup, Barbara 1947- 156
    Earlier sketch in SATA 86
    See also SAAS 24
Shoveller, Herb 184
Showalter, Jean B(reckinridge) 12
Showell, Ellen Harvey 1934- 33
Showers, Paul C. 1910-1999 92
    Obituary 114
    Earlier sketch in SATA 21
    See also CLR 6
    See also SAAS 7
Shpakow, Tanya 1959(?)- 94
Shpitalnik, Vladimir 1964- 83
Shragg, Karen (I.) 1954- 142
Shreeve, Elizabeth 1956- 156
Shreve, Susan
    See Shreve, Susan Richards
Shreve, Susan Richards 1939- 152
    Brief entry 41
    Earlier sketches in SATA 46, 95
Shriver, Jean Adair 1932- 75
Shriver, Maria 1955- 134
Shriver, Maria Owings
    See Shriver, Maria
Shrode, Mary
    See Hollingsworth, Mary
Shtainmets, Leon 32
Shub, Elizabeth 1915(?)-2004 5
Shuken, Julia 1948- 84
Shulevitz, Uri 1935- 165
    Earlier sketches in SATA 3, 50, 106
    See also CLR 61
Shulman, Alix Kates 1932- 7
Shulman, Dee 1957- 146
Shulman, Irving 1913-1995 13
Shulman, Lisa 202
Shulman, Mark 1962- 184
Shulman, Max 1919-1988
    Obituary 59
Shulman, Milton 1913-2004
    Obituary 154
Shulman, Neil B(arnett) 1945- 89
Shumsky, Zena
    See Collier, Zena
Shura, Mary Francis
    See Craig, Mary (Francis) Shura
Shusterman, Neal 1962- 201
    Autobiography Feature 140
    Earlier sketches in SATA 85, 121, 140
Shuter, Jane (Margaret) 1955- 151
    Earlier sketch in SATA 90
Shuttlesworth, Dorothy Edwards 3
Shwartz, Susan (Martha) 1949- 94
Shyer, Christopher 1961- 98
Shyer, Marlene Fanta 13
Siberell, Anne 29
Sibley, Don 1922- 12
Siburt, Ruth 1951- 121
Siculan, Daniel 1922- 12
Siddon, Barbara
    See Bradford, Barbara Taylor
Sidgwick, Ethel 1877-1970 116
Sidjakov, Nicolas 1924- 18

Sidman, Joyce 1956- *181*
　Earlier sketch in SATA *145*
Sidney, Frank
　See Warwick, Alan R(oss)
Sidney, Margaret
　See Lothrop, Harriet Mulford Stone
Siebert, Diane 1948- *189*
Siegal, Aranka 1930- *88*
　Brief entry *37*
Siegel, Beatrice *36*
Siegel, Helen
　See Siegl, Helen
Siegel, Robert 1939- *39*
Siegel, Robert Harold
　See Siegel, Robert
Siegel, Siena Cherson 1967(?)- *185*
Siegelson, Kim L. 1962- *114*
Sieger, Ted 1958- *189*
Siegl, Helen 1924- *34*
Siepmann, Mary Aline
　See Wesley, Mary (Aline)
Sierra, Judy 1945- *195*
　Earlier sketches in SATA *104, 162*
Sieswerda, Paul L. 1942- *147*
Sievert, Terri
　See Dougherty, Terri (L.)
Silas
　See McCay, (Zenas) Winsor
Silcock, Sara Lesley 1947- *12*
Silin-Palmer, Pamela *184*
Sill, Cathryn 1953- *141*
　Earlier sketch in SATA *74*
Sill, John 1947- *140*
　Earlier sketch in SATA *74*
Sillitoe, Alan 1928- *61*
Sills, Leslie (Elka) 1948- *129*
Silly, E. S.
　See Kraus, (Herman) Robert
Silsbe, Brenda 1953- *73*
Silva, Joseph
　See Goulart, Ron
Silver, Ruth
　See Chew, Ruth
Silverberg, Robert 1935- *91*
　Autobiography Feature *104*
　Earlier sketch in SATA *13*
　See also CLR *59*
Silverman, Erica 1955- *165*
　Earlier sketches in SATA *78, 112*
Silverman, Janis L. 1946- *127*
Silverman, Mel(vin Frank) 1931-1966 .... *9*
Silverman, Robin L. 1954- *96*
Silverman, Robin Landew
　See Silverman, Robin L.
Silverstein, Alvin 1933- *124*
　Earlier sketches in SATA *8, 69*
　See also CLR *25*
Silverstein, Herma 1945- *106*
Silverstein, Robert Alan 1959- *124*
　Earlier sketch in SATA *77*
Silverstein, Shel 1932-1999 .... *92*
　Brief entry *27*
　Obituary *116*
　Earlier sketch in SATA *33*
　See also CLR *96*
Silverstein, Sheldon Allan
　See Silverstein, Shel
Silverstein, Virginia B. 1937- *124*
　Earlier sketches in SATA *8, 69*
　See also CLR *25*
Silverstein, Virginia Barbara Opshelor
　See Silverstein, Virginia B.
Silverthorne, Elizabeth 1930- *35*
Silverwood, Margaret Shannon 1966- *137*
　Earlier sketch in SATA *83*
Silvey, Diane F. 1946- *135*
Sim, David 1953- *162*
Sim, Dorrith M. 1931- *96*
Simak, Clifford D(onald) 1904-1988
　Obituary *56*
Simard, Remy 1959- *168*

Simmie, Lois (Ann) 1932- *106*
Simmonds, Posy 1945- *130*
　See also CLR *23*
Simmonds, Rosemary Elizabeth
　See Simmonds, Posy
Simmons, Andra 1939- *141*
Simmons, Elly 1955- *134*
Simmons, Michael 1970- *185*
Simms, Laura 1947- *117*
Simner, Janni Lee *113*
Simon, Charlie May
　See Fletcher, Charlie May Hogue
Simon, Francesca 1955- *111*
Simon, Gabriel 1972- *118*
Simon, Hilda Rita 1921- *28*
　See also CLR *39*
Simon, Howard 1903-1979 .... *32*
　Obituary *21*
Simon, Joe
　See Simon, Joseph H.
Simon, Joseph H. 1913- *7*
Simon, Martin P(aul William) 1903-1969 .... *12*
Simon, Mina Lewiton
　See Lewiton, Mina
Simon, Norma (Feldstein) 1927- *129*
　Earlier sketches in SATA *3, 68*
Simon, Seymour 1931- *202*
　Earlier sketches in SATA *4, 73, 138*
　See also CLR *63*
Simon, Shirley (Schwartz) 1921- *11*
Simon, Solomon 1895-1970 .... *40*
Simonetta, Linda 1948- *14*
Simonetta, Sam 1936- *14*
Simons, Barbara B(rooks) 1934- *41*
Simont, Marc 1915- *126*
　Earlier sketches in SATA *9, 73*
Simpson, Colin 1908-1983 .... *14*
Simpson, Harriette
　See Arnow, Harriette (Louisa) Simpson
Simpson, Jacynth Hope
　See Hope Simpson, Jacynth
Simpson, Lesley 1963- *150*
Simpson, Margaret 1943- *128*
Simpson, Myrtle L(illias) 1931- *14*
Sims, Blanche *168*
　Earlier sketch in SATA *75*
Sims, Blanche L.
　See Sims, Blanche
Simundsson, Elva 1950- *63*
Sinclair, Clover
　See Gater, Dilys
Sinclair, Emil
　See Hesse, Hermann
Sinclair, Jeff 1958- *77*
Sinclair, Olga 1923- *121*
Sinclair, Rose
　See Smith, Susan Vernon
Sinclair, Upton 1878-1968 .... *9*
Sinclair, Upton Beall
　See Sinclair, Upton
Singer, A.L.
　See Lerangis, Peter
Singer, Arthur 1917-1990 .... *64*
Singer, Isaac
　See Singer, Isaac Bashevis
Singer, Isaac Bashevis 1904-1991 .... *27*
　Obituary *68*
　Earlier sketch in SATA *3*
　See also CLR *1*
Singer, Jane Sherrod 1917-1985 .... *4*
　Obituary *42*
Singer, Julia 1917- *28*
Singer, Kurt D. 1911-2005 .... *38*
　Obituary *172*
Singer, Marilyn 1948- *201*
　Autobiography Feature *158*
　Brief entry *38*
　Earlier sketches in SATA *48, 80, 125, 158*
　See also CLR *48*
　See also SAAS *13*

Singer, Muff 1942-2005 .... *104*
　Obituary *160*
Singer, Nicky 1956- *194*
Singer, Susan (Mahler) 1941- *9*
Singh, Rashmi Sharma 1952- *90*
Singleton, Linda Joy 1957- *166*
　Earlier sketch in SATA *88*
Singleton, L.J.
　See Singleton, Linda Joy
Sinykin, Sheri
　See Sinykin, Sheri Cooper
Sinykin, Sheri Cooper 1950- *142*
　Autobiography Feature *142*
　Earlier sketches in SATA *72, 133*
Sinykin, Sheril Terri Cooper
　See Sinykin, Sheri Cooper
Sipiera, Paul P., (Jr.) 1948- *144*
　Earlier sketch in SATA *89*
Siracusa, Catherine (Jane) 1947- *82*
Sirett, Dawn (Karen) 1966- *88*
Sirimarco, Elizabeth 1966- *158*
Sirof, Harriet 1930- *94*
　Earlier sketch in SATA *37*
Sirois, Allen L. 1950- *76*
Sirvaitis (Chernyaev), Karen (Ann) 1961- ... *79*
Sis, Peter 1949- *192*
　Earlier sketch in SATA *149*
　See also CLR *110*
Sisson, Rosemary Anne 1923- *11*
Sister Mary Terese
　See Donze, Mary Terese
Sita, Lisa 1962- *87*
Sitarski, Anita *200*
Sitomer, Alan Lawrence *174*
Sitomer, Harry 1903-1985 .... *31*
Sitomer, Mindel 1903-1987 .... *31*
Sittenfeld, Curtis 1975(?)- *164*
Sive, Helen R(obinson) 1951- *30*
Sivulich, Sandra (Jeanne) Stroner 1941- *9*
Siy, Alexandra *193*
Skarmeta, Antonio 1940- *57*
Skelly, James R(ichard) 1927- *17*
Skelton, Matthew 1971- *185*
Skinner, Constance Lindsay 1877-1939
　See YABC *1*
Skinner, Cornelia Otis 1901-1979 .... *2*
Skipper, G. C. 1939- *46*
　Brief entry *38*
Sklansky, Amy E. 1971- *204*
Sklansky, Amy E(dgar) 1971- *145*
Skofield, James *95*
　Brief entry *44*
Skold, Betty Westrom 1923- *41*
Skorpen, Liesel Moak 1935- *3*
Skott, Maria
　See Nikolajeva, Maria
Skrypuch, Marsha Forchuk 1954- *134*
Skultety, Nancy Laney 1960- *175*
Skurzynski, Gloria 1930- *145*
　Autobiography Feature *145*
　Earlier sketches in SATA *8, 74, 122*
　See also SAAS *9*
Skurzynski, Gloria Joan
　See Skurzynski, Gloria
Skutch, Robert 1925- *89*
Skye, Maggie
　See Werner, Herma
Skye, Obert *200*
　Earlier sketch in SATA *170*
Slack, Michael 1969- *189*
Slackman, Charles B. 1934- *12*
Slade, Arthur G. 1967- *149*
　Earlier sketch in SATA *106*
Slade, Arthur Gregory
　See Slade, Arthur G.
Slade, Christian 1974- *193*
Slade, Richard 1910-1971 .... *9*
Slangerup, Erik Jon 1969- *130*
Slate, Joseph 1928- *174*
　Earlier sketches in SATA *38, 122*

Slate, Joseph Frank
  See Slate, Joseph
Slater, Dashka 1963- 179
Slater, Ray
  See Lansdale, Joe R.
Slaughter, Hope 1940- 84
Slaughter, Jean
  See Doty, Jean Slaughter
Slaughter, Tom 1955- 152
Slavicek, Louise Chipley 1956- 144
Slavin, Bill 1959- 199
  Earlier sketches in SATA 76, 148
Slaymaker, Melissa Eskridge 1958- 158
Sleator, William 1945- 161
  Earlier sketches in SATA 3, 68, 118
  See also CLR 128
Sleator, William Warner III
  See Sleator, William
Slegers, Liesbet 1975- 154
Sleigh, Barbara 1906-1982 86
  Obituary 30
  Earlier sketch in SATA 3
Slepian, Jan 1921- 85
  Brief entry 45
  Earlier sketch in SATA 51
  See also SAAS 8
Slepian, Janice B.
  See Slepian, Jan
Slicer, Margaret O. 1920- 4
Slier, Debby
  See Shine, Deborah
Sloan, Brian 1966- 172
Sloan, Carolyn 1937- 116
  Earlier sketch in SATA 58
Sloan, Glenna (Davis) 1930- 120
Sloane, Eric 1910(?)-1985 52
  Obituary 42
Sloane, Todd 1955- 88
Sloat, Teri 1948- 164
  Earlier sketches in SATA 70, 106
Slobodkin, Florence Gersh 1905-1994 5
  Obituary 107
Slobodkin, Louis 1903-1975 26
  Earlier sketch in SATA 1
Slobodkina, Esphyr 1908-2002 1
  Obituary 135
  See also SAAS 8
Sloggett, Nellie 1851-1923 44
Sloss, Lesley Lord 1965- 72
Slote, Alfred 1926- 72
  Earlier sketch in SATA 8
  See also CLR 4
  See also SAAS 21
Slote, Elizabeth 1956- 80
Small, Charlie
  See Ward, Nick
Small, David 1945- 183
  Brief entry 46
  Earlier sketches in SATA 50, 95, 126
  See also CLR 53
Small, Ernest
  See Lent, Blair
Small, Mary 1932- 165
Small, Terry 1942- 75
Smallcomb, Pam 1954- 159
Smallman, Steve 197
Smalls, Irene
  See Smalls-Hector, Irene
Smalls-Hector, Irene 1950- 146
  Earlier sketch in SATA 73
  See also CLR 103
Smallwood, Norah (Evelyn) 1910(?)-1984
  Obituary 41
Smaridge, Norah (Antoinette) 1903-1994 6
Smath, Jerry 1933- 198
Smee, Nicola 1948- 167
  Earlier sketch in SATA 76
Smiley, Virginia Kester 1923- 2
Smit, Noelle 1972- 199
Smith, Alexander McCall 1948- 179
  Earlier sketch in SATA 73

Smith, Anne Warren 1938- 41
  Brief entry 34
Smith, Barry (Edward Jervis) 1943- 75
Smith, Beatrice S(chillinger) 12
Smith, Betsy Covington 1937- 55
  Earlier sketch in SATA 43
Smith, Betty (Wehner) 1904-1972 6
Smith, Bradford 1909-1964 5
Smith, Brenda 1946- 82
Smith, C. Pritchard
  See Hoyt, Edwin P(almer), Jr.
Smith, Caesar
  See Trevor, Elleston
Smith, Cat Bowman 1939- 201
Smith, Charles R., Jr. 1969- 203
  Earlier sketch in SATA 159
Smith, Craig 1955- 172
  Earlier sketches in SATA 81, 117
Smith, Cynthia Leitich 1967- 152
Smith, Datus C(lifford), Jr. 1907-1999 13
  Obituary 116
Smith, Debra 1955- 89
Smith, Derek 1943- 141
Smith, Dick King
  See King-Smith, Dick
Smith, Dodie
  See Smith, Dorothy Gladys
Smith, Doris Buchanan 1934-2002 75
  Obituary 140
  Earlier sketch in SATA 28
  See also SAAS 10
Smith, Dorothy Gladys 1896-1990 82
  Obituary 65
Smith, Dorothy Stafford 1905- 6
Smith, Duane 1974- 202
Smith, E(lmer) Boyd 1860-1943
  See YABC 1
Smith, E(dric) Brooks 1917- 40
Smith, Elwood H. 1941- 203
Smith, Emma 1923- 52
  Brief entry 36
Smith, (Katherine) Eunice (Young)
  1902-1993 5
Smith, Frances C(hristine) 1904-1986 3
Smith, Gary R. 1932- 14
Smith, Geof 1969- 102
Smith, George Harmon 1920- 5
Smith, Gordon 1951- 184
Smith, Greg Leitich 152
Smith, H(arry) Allen 1907-1976
  Obituary 20
Smith, Helene 1937- 142
Smith, Hope Anita 202
Smith, Howard E(verett), Jr. 1927- 12
Smith, Hugh L(etcher) 1921-1968 5
Smith, Imogene Henderson 1922- 12
Smith, Jacqueline B. 1937- 39
Smith, Jada Pinkett 1971- 161
Smith, James D. 1955- 176
Smith, James Noel 1950- 193
Smith, Janet (Buchanan) Adam
  See Adam Smith, Janet (Buchanan)
Smith, Janice Lee 1949- 155
  Earlier sketch in SATA 54
Smith, Jean
  See Smith, Frances C(hristine)
Smith, Jean Pajot 1945- 10
Smith, Jeff 1958- 161
  Earlier sketch in SATA 93
Smith, Jeff Allen
  See Smith, Jeff
Smith, Jenny 1963- 90
Smith, Jessie
  See Kunhardt, Edith
Smith, Jessie Willcox 1863-1935 21
  See also CLR 59
Smith, Joan (Mary) 1933- 54
  Brief entry 46
Smith, Johnston
  See Crane, Stephen

Smith, Jos A. 1936- 181
  Earlier sketches in SATA 73, 120
Smith, Joseph Arthur
  See Smith, Jos A.
Smith, Judie R. 1936- 80
Smith, Lafayette
  See Higdon, Hal
Smith, Lane 1959- 179
  Earlier sketches in SATA 76, 131
  See also CLR 47
Smith, Lee
  See Albion, Lee Smith
Smith, Lendon H(oward) 1921- 64
Smith, Lillian H(elena) 1887-1983
  Obituary 32
Smith, Linda 1949- 177
Smith, Linell Nash 1932- 2
Smith, Lucia B. 1943- 30
Smith, Maggie 1965- 190
Smith, Margaret Emily Noel Nuttall
  See Nuttall-Smith, Margaret Emily Noel
Smith, Marion Hagens 1913- 12
Smith, Marion Jaques 1899-1987 13
Smith, Mary Ellen 10
Smith, Marya 1945- 78
Smith, Mike
  See Smith, Mary Ellen
Smith, Nancy Covert 1935- 12
Smith, Norman F. 1920- 70
  Earlier sketch in SATA 5
Smith, Patricia Clark 1943- 96
Smith, Pauline C.
  See Arthur, Robert, (Jr.)
Smith, Pauline C(oggeshall) 1908-1994 27
Smith, Philip Warren 1936- 46
Smith, R. Alexander McCall
  See Smith, Alexander McCall
Smith, Rebecca 1946- 123
Smith, Robert Kimmel 1930- 77
  Earlier sketch in SATA 12
Smith, Robert Paul 1915-1977 52
  Obituary 30
Smith, Roland 1951- 193
  Earlier sketches in SATA 115, 161
Smith, Rosamond
  See Oates, Joyce Carol
Smith, Ruth Leslie 1902- 2
Smith, Samantha 1972-1985
  Obituary 45
Smith, Sandra Lee 1945- 75
Smith, Sarah Stafford
  See Smith, Dorothy Stafford
Smith, Sharon 1947- 82
Smith, Sherri L. 1971- 156
Smith, Sherwood 1951- 206
  Autobiography Feature 206
  Earlier sketches in SATA 82, 140
Smith, Shirley Raines
  See Raines, Shirley C(arol)
Smith, Susan Carlton 1923- 12
Smith, Susan Mathias 1950- 43
  Brief entry 35
Smith, Susan Vernon 1950- 48
  Brief entry 45
Smith, Tim(othy R.) 1945- 151
Smith, Ursula 1934- 54
Smith, Vian (Crocker) 1920-1969 11
Smith, Wanda VanHoy 1926- 65
Smith, Ward
  See Goldsmith, Howard
Smith, William A. 1918- 10
Smith, William Jay 1918- 154
  Autobiography Feature 154
  Earlier sketches in SATA 2, 68
  See also SAAS 22
Smith, Winsome 1935- 45
Smith, Z.Z.
  See Westheimer, David
Smith-Ankrom, M. E. 1942- 130
Smith-Griswold, Wendy 1955- 88
Smith-Rex, Susan J. 1950- 94

Smithsen, Richard
  See Pellowski, Michael (Joseph)
Smits, Teo
  See Smits, Theodore R(ichard)
Smits, Theodore R(ichard) 1905-1996 45
  Brief entry 28
Smolinski, Dick 1932- 86
Smothers, Ethel Footman 1944- 149
  Earlier sketch in SATA 76
Smucker, Barbara 1915-2003 130
  Earlier sketches in SATA 29, 76
  See also CLR 10
  See also SAAS 11
Smucker, Barbara Claassen
  See Smucker, Barbara
Smyth, Iain 1959- 105
Snedeker, Caroline Dale (Parke) 1871-1956
  See YABC 2
Sneed, Brad 191
Sneider, Marian 1932-2005 197
Snell, Nigel (Edward Creagh) 1936- 57
  Brief entry 40
Snellgrove, L(aurence) E(rnest) 1928- 53
Snelling, Dennis (Wayne) 1958- 84
Sneve, Virginia Driving Hawk 1933- 95
  Earlier sketch in SATA 8
  See also CLR 2
Snicket, Lemony 1970- 187
  Earlier sketch in SATA 126
  See also CLR 79
Sniegoski, Thomas E. 195
Sniegoski, Tom
  See Sniegoski, Thomas E.
Snodgrass, Mary Ellen 1944- 75
Snodgrass, Quentin Curtius
  See Twain, Mark
Snodgrass, Thomas Jefferson
  See Twain, Mark
Snook, Barbara (Lillian) 1913-1976 34
Snow, Alan 1959- 190
Snow, Donald Clifford 1917-1979 16
Snow, Dorothea J(ohnston) 1909- 9
Snow, Richard F(olger) 1947- 52
  Brief entry 37
Snyder, Anne 1922-2001 4
  Obituary 125
Snyder, Bernadette McCarver 1930- 97
Snyder, Carol 1941- 35
Snyder, Gerald S(eymour) 1933- 48
  Brief entry 34
Snyder, Jerome 1916-1976
  Obituary 20
Snyder, Midori 1954- 106
Snyder, Paul A. 1946- 125
Snyder, Zilpha Keatley 1927- 163
  Autobiography Feature 163
  Earlier sketches in SATA 1, 28, 75, 110
  See also CLR 121
  See also SAAS 2
Snyderman, Reuven K. 1922- 5
So, Meilo 162
Sobel, June 1950- 149
Soble, Jennie
  See Cavin, Ruth (Brodie)
Sobol, Donald J. 1924- 132
  Earlier sketches in SATA 1, 31, 73
  See also CLR 4
Sobol, Harriet Langsam 1936- 47
  Brief entry 34
Sobol, Rose 1931- 76
Sobott-Mogwe, Gaele 1956- 97
Soderlind, Arthur E(dwin) 1920- 14
Soentpiet, Chris K. 1970- 159
  Earlier sketch in SATA 97
Soerensen, Svend Otto 1916- 67
Sofer, Barbara 1949- 109
Sofer, Rachel
  See Sofer, Barbara
Softly, Barbara Frewin 1924- 12
Soglow, Otto 1900-1975
  Obituary 30

Sohl, Frederic J(ohn) 1916- 10
Sohr, Daniel 1973- 190
Sokol, Bill
  See Sokol, William
Sokol, William 1923- 37
Sokolov, Kirill 1930- 34
Solbert, Romaine G. 1925- 2
Solbert, Ronni
  See Solbert, Romaine G.
Solheim, James 133
Solomon, Heather M. 188
Solomon, Joan 1930- 51
  Brief entry 40
Solomons, Ikey Esquir
  See Thackeray, William Makepeace
Solonevich, George 1915-2003 15
Solot, Mary Lynn 1939- 12
Soman, David 1965- 200
Somerlott, Robert 1928-2001 62
Somers, Kevin 205
Somervill, Barbara A(nn) 1948- 140
Sommer, Angela
  See Sommer-Bodenburg, Angela
Sommer, Carl 1930- 175
  Earlier sketch in SATA 126
Sommer, Elyse 1929- 7
Sommer, Robert 1929- 12
Sommer-Bodenburg, Angela 1948- 113
  Earlier sketch in SATA 63
Sommerdorf, Norma 1926- 131
Sommerdorf, Norma Jean
  See Sommerdorf, Norma
Sommerfelt, Aimee 1892-1975 5
Son, John 160
Sones, Sonya 131
Sonneborn, Ruth (Cantor) 1899-1974 4
  Obituary 27
Sonnenblick, Jordan 1969- 185
  See also CLR 144
Sonnenmark, Laura A. 1958- 73
Soo, Kean 201
Sopko, Eugen 1949- 58
Sorel, Edward 1929- 126
  Brief entry 37
  Earlier sketch in SATA 65
Sorensen, Henri 1950- 115
  Earlier sketch in SATA 77
Sorensen, Svend Otto
  See Soerensen, Svend Otto
Sorensen, Virginia 1912-1991 2
  Obituary 72
  See also SAAS 15
Sorenson, Jane 1926- 63
Sorenson, Margo 1946- 96
Sorley Walker, Kathrine 41
Sorra, Kristin 185
Sorrells, Walter 177
Sorrentino, Joseph N. 1937- 6
Sortor, June Elizabeth 1939- 12
Sortor, Toni
  See Sortor, June Elizabeth
Sosa, Hernan 1977- 203
Soskin, V. H.
  See Ellison, Virginia H(owell)
Soto, Gary 1952- 174
  Earlier sketches in SATA 80, 120
  See also CLR 38
Sotomayor, Antonio 1902-1985 11
Souci, Robert D. San
  See San Souci, Robert D.
Soudley, Henry
  See Wood, James Playsted
Souhami, Jessica 176
Soule, Gardner (Bosworth) 1913-2000 14
Soule, Jean Conder 1919- 10
Souster, (Holmes) Raymond 1921- 63
South, Sheri Cobb 1959- 82

Southall, Ivan 1921-2008 134
  Autobiography Feature 134
  Earlier sketches in SATA 3, 68
  See also CLR 2
  See also SAAS 3
Southall, Ivan Francis
  See Southall, Ivan
Southey, Robert 1774-1843 54
Southgate, Vera 54
Sovak, Jan 1953- 115
Sowden, Celeste
  See Walters, Celeste
Sowter, Nita 69
Spafford, Suzy 1945- 160
Spagnoli, Cathy 1950- 134
  Earlier sketch in SATA 79
Spain, Sahara Sunday 1991- 133
Spain, Susan Rosson 185
Spalding, Andrea 1944- 150
  Earlier sketch in SATA 101
Spalenka, Greg 1958- 198
Spanfeller, James J. 1930- 19
  See also SAAS 8
Spanfeller, Jim
  See Spanfeller, James J.
Spangenberg, Judith Dunn 1942- 5
Spanyol, Jessica 1965- 206
  Earlier sketch in SATA 137
Spar, Jerome 1918- 10
Sparks, Barbara 1942- 78
Sparks, Beatrice (Mathews) 1918- 44
  Brief entry 28
  See also CLR 139
Sparks, Mary W. 1920- 15
Spaulding, Douglas
  See Bradbury, Ray
Spaulding, Leonard
  See Bradbury, Ray
Spaulding, Norma 107
Speare, Elizabeth George 1908-1994 62
  Obituary 83
  Earlier sketch in SATA 5
  See also CLR 8
Spearing, Judith (Mary Harlow) 1922- 9
Spears, Rick 182
Speck, Katie 196
Speck, Nancy 1959- 104
Specking, Inez 1890-1960(?) 11
Speed, Nell
  See Keats, Emma
  and Sampson, Emma (Keats) Speed
Speed, Nell (Ewing) 1878-1913 68
Speer, Bonnie Stahlman 1929- 113
Speer-Lyon, Tammie L. 1965- 89
Speicher, Helen Ross S(mith) 1915- 8
Speir, Nancy 1958- 81
Spellman, John W(illard) 1934- 14
Spellman, Roger G.
  See Cox, William R(obert)
Spelman, Cornelia Maude 1946- 144
  Earlier sketch in SATA 96
Spelman, Mary 1934- 28
Spelvin, George
  See Lerangis, Peter
  and Phillips, David Atlee
Spence, Cynthia
  See Eble, Diane
Spence, Eleanor (Rachel) 1928- 21
  See also CLR 26
Spence, Geraldine 1931- 47
Spencer, Ann 1918- 10
Spencer, Britt 206
Spencer, Cornelia
  See Yaukey, Grace S(ydenstricker)
Spencer, Donald D(ean) 1931- 41
Spencer, Elizabeth 1921- 14
Spencer, Leonard G.
  See Garrett, Randall
  and Silverberg, Robert
Spencer, William 1922- 9
Spencer, Zane A(nn) 1935- 35

Sper, Emily 1957- *142*
Speregen, Devra Newberger 1964- *84*
Sperling, Dan(iel Lee) 1949- *65*
Sperry, Armstrong W. 1897-1976 .... *1*
   Obituary *27*
Sperry, Raymond
   See Garis, Howard R.
Sperry, Raymond, Jr. *1*
Spetter, Jung-Hee 1969- *134*
Spicer, Dorothy Gladys -1975 .... *32*
Spiegel, Beth *184*
Spiegelman, Art 1948- *158*
   Earlier sketch in SATA *109*
Spiegelman, Judith M. *5*
Spielberg, Steven 1947- *32*
Spier, Peter (Edward) 1927- *54*
   Earlier sketch in SATA *4*
   See also CLR 5
Spilhaus, Athelstan (Frederick) 1911-1998 .. *13*
   Obituary *102*
Spilka, Arnold 1917- *6*
Spillane, Frank Morrison
   See Spillane, Mickey
Spillane, Mickey 1918-2006 .... *66*
   Obituary *176*
Spinelli, Eileen 1942- *186*
   Earlier sketches in SATA *38, 101, 150*
Spinelli, Jerry 1941- *195*
   Earlier sketches in SATA *39, 71, 110, 158*
   See also CLR 82
Spink, Reginald (William) 1905-1994 .... *11*
Spinka, Penina Keen 1945- *72*
Spinner, Stephanie 1943- *132*
   Earlier sketches in SATA *38, 91*
Spinossimus
   See White, William, Jr.
Spiotta-DiMare, Loren *173*
Spires, Ashley 1978- *183*
Spires, Elizabeth 1952- *111*
   Earlier sketch in SATA *71*
Spiridellis, Gregg 1971(?)- *199*
Spirin, Gennadii
   See Spirin, Gennady
Spirin, Gennadij
   See Spirin, Gennady
Spirin, Gennady 1948- *204*
   Earlier sketches in SATA *95, 134*
   See also CLR 88
Spivak, Dawnine *101*
Spizman, Robyn Freedman *194*
Spohn, David 1948- *72*
Spohn, Kate 1962- *147*
   Earlier sketch in SATA *87*
Spollen, Christopher 1952- *12*
Spooner, Michael (Tim) 1954- *92*
Spowart, Robin 1947- *177*
   Earlier sketch in SATA *82*
Spradlin, Michael P. *204*
Sprague, Gretchen 1926-2003 .... *27*
Spranger, Nina 1969- *203*
Sprengel, Artie
   See Lerangis, Peter
Sprigge, Elizabeth (Miriam Squire)
   1900-1974 .... *10*
Spring, (Robert) Howard 1889-1965 .... *28*
Springer, Margaret 1941- *78*
Springer, Marilyn Harris 1931- *47*
Springer, Nancy 1948- *172*
   Earlier sketches in SATA *65, 110*
Springstubb, Tricia 1950- *78*
   Brief entry *40*
   Earlier sketch in SATA *46*
Spudvilas, Anne 1951- *199*
   Earlier sketch in SATA *94*
Spurll, Barbara 1952- *78*
Spurr, Elizabeth *172*
Spykman, E(lizabeth) C(hoate) 1896-1965 .. *10*
   See also CLR 35
Spyri, Johanna (Heusser) 1827-1901 .... *100*
   Earlier sketch in SATA *19*
   See also CLR 115

Squires, Phil
   See Barker, S. Omar
Srba, Lynne *98*
Sreenivasan, Jyotsna 1964- *101*
S-Ringi, Kjell
   See Ringi, Kjell (Arne Soerensen)
Stacey, Cherylyn 1945- *96*
Stacy, Donald
   See Pohl, Frederik
Stadler, John *204*
Stadtler, Bea 1921- *17*
Stafford, Jean 1915-1979
   Obituary *22*
Stafford, Liliana 1950- *141*
Stafford, Paul 1966- *116*
Stahl, Ben(jamin) 1910-1987 .... *5*
   Obituary *54*
Stahl, Hilda 1938-1993 .... *48*
   Obituary *77*
Stahler, David, Jr. *162*
Stainton, Sue *187*
Stair, Gobin (John) 1912- *35*
Stalder, Valerie *27*
Stamaty, Mark Alan 1947- *12*
Stambler, Irwin 1924- *5*
Standiford, Natalie 1961- *169*
   Earlier sketch in SATA *81*
Stanek, Lou Willett 1931- *63*
Stang, Judit 1921-1977 .... *29*
Stang, Judy
   See Stang, Judit
Stangl, (Mary) Jean 1928- *67*
Stanhope, Eric
   See Hamilton, Charles (Harold St. John)
Stankevich, Boris 1928- *2*
Stanley, Diane 1943- *164*
   Brief entry *32*
   Earlier sketches in SATA *37, 80, 115*
   See also CLR 46
   See also SAAS 15
Stanley, Elizabeth 1947- *206*
Stanley, George Edward 1942- *67*
   Earlier sketches in SATA *53, 111, 157, 1*
Stanley, Jerry 1941- *127*
   Earlier sketch in SATA *79*
Stanley, Mandy *165*
Stanley, Robert
   See Hamilton, Charles (Harold St. John)
Stanley, Sanna 1962- *145*
Stanli, Sue
   See Meilach, Dona Z(weigoron)
Stanstead, John
   See Groom, Arthur William
Stanton, Karen 1960- *190*
Stanton, Schuyler
   See Baum, L. Frank
Staples, Suzanne Fisher 1945- *151*
   Earlier sketches in SATA *70, 105*
   See also CLR 137
Stapleton, Marjorie (Winifred) 1932- *28*
Stapp, Arthur D(onald) 1906-1972 .... *4*
Starbird, Kaye 1916- *6*
   See also CLR 60
Stark, Evan 1942- *78*
Stark, James
   See Goldston, Robert (Conroy)
Stark, Ken 1943- *199*
Stark, Ulf 1944- *124*
Starke, Ruth (Elaine) 1946- *129*
Starkey, Marion L(ena) 1901-1991 .... *13*
Starr, Ward
   See Manes, Stephen
Starret, William
   See McClintock, Marshall
Starr Taylor, Bridget 1959- *99*
Stasiak, Krystyna *49*
Staub, Frank 1949- *116*
Staub, Frank Jacob
   See Staub, Frank
Staub, Wendy Corsi 1964- *114*

Stauffacher, Sue 1961- *199*
   Earlier sketch in SATA *155*
Stauffer, Don
   See Berkebile, Fred D(onovan)
Staunton, Schuyler
   See Baum, L. Frank
Staunton, Ted 1956- *167*
   Earlier sketch in SATA *112*
Stead, Rebecca 1968(?)- *188*
Steadman, Ralph 1936- *123*
   Earlier sketch in SATA *32*
Steadman, Ralph Idris
   See Steadman, Ralph
Stearman, Kaye 1951- *118*
Stearns, Monroe (Mather) 1913-1987 .... *5*
   Obituary *55*
Steckler, Arthur 1921-1985 .... *65*
Steding, Laurie 1953- *119*
Steel, Danielle 1947- *66*
Steel, Danielle Fernande
   See Steel, Danielle
Steele, Addison II
   See Lupoff, Richard A(llen)
Steele, Alexander 1958- *116*
Steele, Henry Maxwell
   See Steele, Max
Steele, Mary 1930- *94*
Steele, Mary Q(uintard Govan) 1922-1992 .. *51*
   Obituary *72*
   Earlier sketch in SATA *3*
Steele, Max 1922-2005 .... *168*
   Earlier sketch in SATA *10*
Steele, Philip 1948- *140*
   Earlier sketch in SATA *81*
Steele, William O(wen) 1917-1979 .... *51*
   Obituary *27*
   Earlier sketch in SATA *1*
Steelhammer, Ilona 1952- *98*
Steelsmith, Shari 1962- *72*
Stefanik, Alfred T. 1939- *55*
Steffanson, Con
   See Cassiday, Bruce (Bingham)
   and Goulart, Ron
Steffens, Bradley 1955- *166*
   Earlier sketch in SATA *77*
Steffensmeier, Alexander 1977- *195*
Stegeman, Janet Allais 1923- *49*
   Brief entry *49*
Steggall, Susan 1967- *182*
Steig, William 1907-2003 .... *111*
   Obituary *149*
   Earlier sketches in SATA *18, 70*
   See also CLR 103
Steig, William H.
   See Steig, William
Stein, David Ezra *180*
Stein, M(eyer) L(ewis) 1920- *6*
Stein, Mathilde 1969- *195*
Stein, Mini *2*
Stein, R(ichard) Conrad 1937- *154*
   Earlier sketches in SATA *31, 82*
Stein, Wendy 1951- *77*
Steinbeck, John (Ernst) 1902-1968 .... *9*
Steinberg, Alfred 1917-1995 .... *9*
Steinberg, David 1962- *200*
Steinberg, D.J.
   See Steinberg, David
Steinberg, Fannie 1899-1990 .... *43*
Steinberg, Fred J. 1933- *4*
Steinberg, Phillip Orso 1921- *34*
Steinberg, Rafael (Mark) 1927- *45*
Steinberg, Saul 1914-1999 .... *67*
Steincrohn, Maggie
   See Davis, Maggie S.
Steiner, Barbara A(nnette) 1934- *83*
   Earlier sketch in SATA *13*
   See also SAAS 13
Steiner, Charlotte 1900-1981 .... *45*
Steiner, George 1929- *62*
Steiner, Joan *199*
   Earlier sketch in SATA *110*

Steiner, Jorg
 See Steiner, Jorg
Steiner, Jorg 1930- 35
Steiner, K. Leslie
 See Delany, Samuel R., Jr.
Steiner, Stan(ley) 1925-1987 14
 Obituary 50
Steins, Richard 1942- 79
Stem, Jacqueline 1931- 110
Stemple, Jason 179
Steneman, Shep 1945- 132
Stengel, Joyce A. 1938- 158
Stephanie, Gordon
 See Gordon, Stephanie Jacob
Stephens, Alice Barber 1858-1932 66
Stephens, Casey
 See Wagner, Sharon B.
Stephens, Henrietta Henkle 1909-1993 6
Stephens, J.B.
 See Lynn, Tracy
Stephens, Mary Jo 1935- 8
Stephens, Rebecca 1961- 141
Stephens, Reed
 See Donaldson, Stephen R.
Stephens, Suzanne
 See Kirby, Susan E.
Stephens, William M(cLain) 1925- 21
Stephensen, A. M.
 See Manes, Stephen
Stephenson, Lynda 1941- 179
Stephenson, Lynda A.
 See Stephenson, Lynda
Stepp, Ann 1935- 29
Stepto, Michele 1946- 61
Steptoe, Javaka 1971- 151
Steptoe, John (Lewis) 1950-1989 63
 Earlier sketch in SATA 8
 See also CLR 12
Sterling, Brett
 See Bradbury, Ray
 and Hamilton, Edmond
 and Samachson, Joseph
Sterling, Dorothy 1913-2008 83
 Autobiography Feature 127
 Obituary 200
 Earlier sketch in SATA 1
 See also CLR 1
 See also SAAS 2
Sterling, Helen
 See Watts, Helen L. Hoke
Sterling, Philip 1907-1989 8
 Obituary 63
Sterling, Shirley (Anne) 1948- 101
Stern, Ellen Norman 1927- 26
Stern, Judith M. 1951- 75
Stern, Madeleine
 See Stern, Madeleine B.
Stern, Madeleine B. 1912-2007 14
Stern, Madeleine Bettina
 See Stern, Madeleine B.
Stern, Maggie 1953- 156
Stern, Philip Van Doren 1900-1984 13
 Obituary 39
Stern, Simon 1943- 15
Sterne, Emma Gelders 1894- 6
Steurt, Marjorie Rankin 1888-1978 10
Stevens, Bryna 1924- 65
Stevens, Carla M(cBride) 1928- 13
Stevens, Chambers 1968- 128
Stevens, Diane 1939- 94
Stevens, Franklin 1933- 6
Stevens, Greg
 See Cook, Glen
Stevens, Gwendolyn 1944- 33
Stevens, Jan Romero 1953- 95
Stevens, Janet 1953- 193
 Earlier sketches in SATA 90, 148
Stevens, Kathleen 1936- 49
Stevens, Leonard A. 1920- 67
Stevens, Lucile Vernon 1899-1994 59

Stevens, Margaret Dean
 See Aldrich, Bess Streeter
Stevens, Patricia Bunning 1931- 27
Stevens, Peter
 See Geis, Darlene Stern
Stevens, Serita 1949- 70
Stevens, Serita Deborah
 See Stevens, Serita
Stevens, Serita Mendelson
 See Stevens, Serita
Stevens, Shira
 See Stevens, Serita
Stevenson, Anna (M.) 1905- 12
Stevenson, Augusta 1869(?)-1976 2
 Obituary 26
Stevenson, Burton Egbert 1872-1962 25
Stevenson, Drew 1947- 60
Stevenson, Harvey 1960- 148
 Earlier sketch in SATA 80
Stevenson, James 1929- 195
 Brief entry 34
 Earlier sketches in SATA 42, 71, 113, 161
 See also CLR 17
Stevenson, Janet 1913- 8
Stevenson, Robert Louis (Balfour)
 1850-1894 100
 See also YABC 2
 See also CLR 107
Stevenson, Sucie
 See Stevenson, Sucie
Stevenson, Sucie 1956- 194
 Earlier sketch in SATA 104
Stewart, A(gnes) C(harlotte) 15
Stewart, Amber 181
Stewart, Chantal 1945- 173
 Earlier sketch in SATA 121
Stewart, Charles
 See Zurhorst, Charles (Stewart, Jr.)
Stewart, Eleanor
 See Porter, Eleanor H(odgman)
Stewart, Elisabeth J(ane) 1927- 93
Stewart, Elizabeth Laing 1907- 6
Stewart, Gail B. 1949- 141
Stewart, George Rippey 1895-1980 3
 Obituary 23
Stewart, Jennifer J(enkins) 1960- 128
Stewart, Joel 151
Stewart, John 1920- 14
Stewart, Mary (Florence Elinor) 1916- 12
Stewart, Mary Rainbow
 See Stewart, Mary (Florence Elinor)
Stewart, Melissa 1968- 167
 Earlier sketch in SATA 111
Stewart, Paul 1955- 199
 Earlier sketches in SATA 114, 163
Stewart, Robert Neil 1891-1972 7
Stewart, Sarah 143
Stewart, Scott
 See Zaffo, George J.
Stewart, W(alter) P. 1924- 53
Stewart, Whitney 1959- 167
 Earlier sketch in SATA 92
Stewig, John Warren 1937- 162
 Earlier sketches in SATA 26, 110
Stickler, Soma Han 1942- 128
Stidworthy, John 1943- 63
Stiegemeyer, Julie 180
Stier, Catherine 198
Stiles, Martha Bennett 108
 Earlier sketch in SATA 6
Still, James 1906-2001 29
 Obituary 127
Stille, Darlene R. 1942- 170
 Earlier sketch in SATA 126
Stille, Darlene Ruth
 See Stille, Darlene R.
Stillerman, Marci 104
Stillerman, Robbie 1947- 12
Stilley, Frank 1918- 29
Stilton, Geronimo 158

Stimpson, Gerald
 See Mitchell, Adrian
Stine, Catherine 165
Stine, G(eorge) Harry 1928-1997 136
 Earlier sketch in SATA 10
Stine, Jovial Bob
 See Stine, R.L.
Stine, R.L. 1943- 194
 Earlier sketches in SATA 31, 76, 129
 See also CLR 111
Stine, Robert Lawrence
 See Stine, R.L.
Stinetorf, Louise (Allender) 1900-1992 10
Stinson, Kathy 1952- 98
Stirling, Arthur
 See Sinclair, Upton
Stirling, Ian 1941- 77
Stirling, Nora B(romley) 1900-1997 3
Stirnweis, Shannon 1931- 10
Stobbs, William 1914-2000 17
 Obituary 120
Stock, Carolmarie 1951- 75
Stock, Catherine 1952- 158
 Earlier sketches in SATA 65, 114
Stockdale, Susan 1954- 206
 Earlier sketch in SATA 98
Stockham, Peter (Alan) 1928- 57
Stockton, Francis Richard 1834-1902 44
 Brief entry 32
Stockton, Frank R.
 See Stockton, Francis Richard
Stockwell-Moniz, Marc J. 1954- 164
Stoddard, Edward G. 1923- 10
Stoddard, Hope 1900-1987 6
Stoddard, Sandol 1927- 98
 Earlier sketch in SATA 14
Stoehr, Shelley 1969- 107
Stoeke, Janet Morgan 1957- 202
 Earlier sketches in SATA 90, 136
Stohner, Anu 1952- 179
Stoiko, Michael 1919- 14
Stojic, Manya 1967- 156
Stoker, Abraham 1847-1912 29
Stoker, Bram
 See Stoker, Abraham
Stokes, Cedric
 See Beardmore, George
Stokes, Jack (Tilden) 1923- 13
Stokes, Olivia Pearl 1916- 32
Stolarz, Laurie Faria 203
Stolz, Mary 1920-2006 133
 Obituary 180
 Earlier sketches in SATA 10, 71
 See also SAAS 3
Stolz, Mary Slattery
 See Stolz, Mary
Stone, Alan
 See Svenson, Andrew E(dward)
Stone, David K(arl) 1922- 9
Stone, David Lee 1978- 166
Stone, Eugenia 1879-1971 7
Stone, Gene
 See Stone, Eugenia
Stone, Helen V(irginia) 6
Stone, Idella Purnell
 See Purnell, Idella
Stone, Ikey
 See Purnell, Idella
Stone, Irving 1903-1989 3
 Obituary 64
Stone, Jeff 178
Stone, Jon 1931-1997 39
 Obituary 95
Stone, Josephine Rector
 See Dixon, Jeanne
Stone, Kyle M. 1972- 202
Stone, Lesley
 See Trevor, Elleston
Stone, Peter 1930-2003 65
 Obituary 143

Stone, Phoebe 205
Earlier sketch in SATA *134*
Stone, Raymond *1*
Stone, Rosetta
See Dr. Seuss
Stone, Tanya Lee 1965- *182*
Stonehouse, Bernard 1926- 140
Earlier sketches in SATA *13, 80*
Stones, (Cyril) Anthony 1934- 72
Stong, Phil(ip Duffield) 1899-1957 .... *32*
Stoops, Erik D(aniel) 1966- *142*
Earlier sketch in SATA *78*
Stoppelmoore, Cheryl Jean
See Ladd, Cheryl (Jean)
Stops, Sue 1936- 86
Storace, Patricia *193*
Storad, Conrad J. 1957- *119*
Storey, Margaret 1926- *9*
Storey, Victoria Carolyn 1945- *16*
Storme, Peter
See Stern, Philip Van Doren
Storr, Catherine (Cole) 1913-2001 87
Obituary *122*
Earlier sketch in SATA *9*
Story, Josephine
See Loring, Emilie (Baker)
Stotko, Mary-Ann 1960- *154*
Stott, Dorothy (M.) 1958- 99
Earlier sketch in SATA *67*
Stott, Dot
See Stott, Dorothy (M.)
Stotter, Mike 1957- *108*
Stout, William 1949- *132*
Stoutenburg, Adrien (Pearl) 1916-1982 .... *3*
Stoutland, Allison 1963- *130*
Stover, Allan C(arl) 1938- *14*
Stover, Jill (Griffin) 1958- 82
Stover, Marjorie Filley 1914- *9*
Stowe, Harriet (Elizabeth) Beecher 1811-1896
See YABC *1*
See also CLR *131*
Stowe, Leland 1899-1994 60
Obituary 78
Stowe, Rosetta
See Ogan, George F.
and Ogan, Margaret E. (Nettles)
Stower, Adam *195*
Strachan, Bruce 1959- *205*
Strachan, Ian 1938- 85
Strachan, Linda *167*
Strachan, Margaret Pitcairn 1908-1998 .... *14*
Strahinich, H. C.
See Strahinich, Helen C.
Strahinich, Helen C. 1949- 78
Strait, Treva Adams 1909-2002 35
Strand, Mark 1934- *41*
Strange, Philippa
See Coury, Louise Andree
Stranger, Joyce
See Wilson, Joyce M.
Strangis, Joel 1948- *124*
Strannigan, Shawn 1956- 93
Strannigan, Shawn Alyne
See Strannigan, Shawn
Strasser, Todd 1950- *153*
Earlier sketches in SATA *41, 45, 71, 107*
See also CLR *11*
Stratemeyer, Edward L. 1862-1930 .... *100*
Earlier sketches in SATA *1, 67*
See Adams, Harrison
Stratford, Philip 1927- *47*
Stratton, Allan 1951- *178*
Stratton, J. M.
See Whitlock, Ralph
Stratton, Thomas
See Coulson, Robert S(tratton)
and DeWeese, Thomas Eugene
Stratton-Porter, Gene 1863-1924 .... *15*
See also CLR *87*
Strauss, Gwen 1963- 77
Strauss, Joyce 1936- *53*

Strauss, Linda Leopold 1942- *127*
Strauss, Susan (Elizabeth) 1954- 75
Strayer, E. Ward
See Stratemeyer, Edward L.
Streano, Vince(nt Catello) 1945- 20
Streatfeild, Mary Noel
See Streatfeild, Noel
Streatfeild, Noel 1897(?)-1986 20
Obituary 48
See also CLR *83*
Street, Janet Travell 1959- 84
Street, Julia Montgomery 1898-1993 .... *11*
Streissguth, Thomas 1958- *116*
Strelkoff, Tatiana 1957- 89
Stren, Patti 1949- 88
Brief entry *41*
See also CLR *5*
Strete, Craig Kee 1950- 96
Earlier sketch in SATA *44*
Stretton, Barbara (Humphrey) 1936- *43*
Brief entry 35
Strickland, Brad 1947- *200*
Earlier sketches in SATA *83, 137, 142*
Strickland, Craig (A.) 1956- *102*
Strickland, Dorothy S(alley) 1933- 89
Strickland, Michael R. 1965- *144*
Earlier sketch in SATA *83*
Strickland, Tessa *173*
Strickland, William Bradley
See Strickland, Brad
Striegel, Jana 1955- *140*
Striegel-Wilson, Jana
See Striegel, Jana
Striker, Lee
See Clark, Margaret (D.)
Striker, Susan 1942- 63
Stringer, Lauren 1957- *183*
Earlier sketch in SATA *129*
Stroeyer, Poul 1923- *13*
Stromoski, Rick 1958- *111*
Strong, Charles
See Epstein, Beryl
and Epstein, Samuel
Strong, David
See McGuire, Leslie (Sarah)
Strong, Jeremy 1949- *175*
Earlier sketches in SATA *36, 105*
Strong, J.J.
See Strong, Jeremy
Strong, Pat
See Hough, Richard (Alexander)
Strong, Stacie 1965- 74
Stroud, Bettye 1939- *165*
Earlier sketch in SATA *96*
Stroud, Jonathan 1970- *159*
Earlier sketch in SATA *102*
See also CLR *134*
Stroyer, Poul
See Stroeyer, Poul
Strug, Kerri 1977- *108*
Stryer, Andrea Stenn 1938- *192*
Stryker, Daniel
See Morris, Chris(topher Crosby)
and Stump, Jane Barr
Stuart, David
See Hoyt, Edwin P(almer), Jr.
Stuart, Derek
See Foster, John L(ouis)
Stuart, Forbes 1924- *13*
Stuart, Ian
See MacLean, Alistair (Stuart)
Stuart, Jesse (Hilton) 1906-1984 .... *2*
Obituary 36
Stuart, Ruth McEnery 1849(?)-1917 .... *116*
Stuart, Sheila
See Baker, Mary Gladys Steel
Stuart-Clark, Christopher (Anthony) 1940- .. *32*
Stubis, Talivaldis 1926- *5*
Stubley, Trevor (Hugh) 1932- 22
Stucky, Naomi R. 1922- 72

Stucley, Elizabeth
See Northmore, Elizabeth Florence
Stultifer, Morton
See Curtis, Richard
Sture-Vasa, Mary
See Alsop, Mary O'Hara
Sturges, Philemon *174*
Sturtevant, Katherine 1950- *180*
Earlier sketch in SATA *130*
Sturton, Hugh
See Johnston, H(ugh) A(nthony) S(tephen)
Sturtzel, Howard A(llison) 1894-1985 .... *1*
Sturtzel, Jane Levington 1903-1996 .... *1*
Stutley, D(oris) J(ean) 1959- *142*
Stutson, Caroline 1940- *104*
Stuve-Bodeen, Stephanie 1965- *158*
Earlier sketch in SATA *114*
Stux, Erica 1929- *140*
Styles, (Frank) Showell 1908- *10*
Stynes, Barbara White *133*
Suarez, Maribel 1952- *201*
Suba, Susanne *4*
Subond, Valerie
See Grayland, Valerie (Merle Spanner)
Sudbery, Rodie 1943- 42
Suen, Anastasia 1956(?)- *157*
Sufrin, Mark 1925- 76
Sugarman, Joan G. 1917- 64
Sugarman, Tracy 1921- 37
Sugita, Yutaka 1930- 36
Suhl, Yuri (Menachem) 1908-1986 .... *8*
Obituary 50
See also CLR *2*
See also SAAS *1*
Suhr, Joanne *129*
Suid, Murray 1942- 27
Sullivan, Edward T. *206*
Sullivan, George (Edward) 1927- *147*
Earlier sketches in SATA *4, 89*
Sullivan, Jacqueline Levering *203*
Sullivan, Jody
See Rake, Jody
Sullivan, Kathryn A. 1954- *141*
Sullivan, Mary Ann 1954- 63
Sullivan, Mary W(ilson) 1907- *13*
Sullivan, Pat
See Messmer, Otto
Sullivan, Paul 1939- *106*
Sullivan, Sarah G. 1953- *179*
Sullivan, Silky
See Makowski, Silvia Ann
Sullivan, Sue
See Sullivan, Susan E.
Sullivan, Susan E. 1962- *123*
Sullivan, Thomas Joseph, Jr. 1947- *16*
Sullivan, Tom
See Sullivan, Thomas Joseph, Jr.
Sully, Tom 1959- *104*
Sumichrast, Jozef 1948- 29
Sumiko
See Davies, Sumiko
Summerforest, Ivy B.
See Kirkup, James
Summers, Barbara 1944- *182*
Summers, James L(evingston) 1910-1973 57
Brief entry 28
Summertree, Katonah
See Windsor, Patricia
Sun, Chyng Feng 1959- 90
Sunderlin, Sylvia (S.) 1911-1997 28
Obituary 99
Sung, Betty Lee 26
Supeene, Shelagh Lynne 1952- *153*
Supplee, Suzanne *204*
Supraner, Robyn 1930- *101*
Earlier sketch in SATA *20*
Supree, Burt(on) 1941-1992 73
Surface, Mary Hall 1958- *126*
Surge, Frank 1931- *13*
Susac, Andrew 1929- 5
Susi, Geraldine Lee 1942- 98

Sussman, Cornelia Silver 1914-1999 59
Sussman, Irving 1908-1996 59
Sussman, Susan 1942- 48
Sutcliff, Rosemary 1920-1992 78
  Obituary 73
  Earlier sketches in SATA 6, 44
  See also CLR 138
Sutcliffe, Jane 1957- 138
Sutherland, Colleen 1944- 79
Sutherland, Efua (Theodora Morgue)
  1924-1996 25
Sutherland, Jon 1958- 167
Sutherland, Jonathan D.
  See Sutherland, Jon
Sutherland, Jonathan David
  See Sutherland, Jon
Sutherland, Margaret 1941- 15
Sutherland, Zena Bailey 1915-2002 37
  Obituary 137
Suttles, Shirley (Smith) 1922- 21
Sutton, Ann (Livesay) 1923- 31
Sutton, Eve(lyn Mary) 1906-1992 26
Sutton, Felix 1910(?)-1973 31
Sutton, Jane 1950- 52
  Brief entry 43
Sutton, Larry M(atthew) 1931- 29
Sutton, Margaret Beebe 1903-2001 1
  Obituary 131
Sutton, Myron Daniel 1925- 31
Sutton, Roger 1956- 93
Suzanne, Jamie
  See Hawes, Louise
  and Lantz, Francess L(in)
  and Singleton, Linda Joy
  and Zach, Cheryl (Byrd)
Suzuki, David 1936- 138
Suzuki, David Takayoshi
  See Suzuki, David
Svendsen, Mark 1962- 181
  Earlier sketch in SATA 120
Svendsen, Mark Nestor
  See Svendsen, Mark
Svenson, Andrew E(dward) 1910-1975 2
  Obituary 26
Swaab, Neil 1978- 191
Swaim, Jessica 1950- 202
Swain, Carol 1962- 172
Swain, Gwenyth 1961- 134
  Earlier sketch in SATA 84
Swain, Ruth
  See Swain, Ruth Freeman
Swain, Ruth Freeman 1951- 161
  Earlier sketch in SATA 119
Swain, Su Zan (Noguchi) 1916- 21
Swallow, Pamela Curtis 178
Swamp, Jake 1941- 98
Swan, Susan 1944- 108
  Earlier sketch in SATA 22
Swann, Brian (Stanley Frank) 1940- 116
Swann, E. L.
  See Lasky, Kathryn
Swann, Ruth Rice 1920- 84
Swanson, Diane 1944- 203
Swanson, Helen M(cKendry) 1919- 94
Swanson, June 1931- 76
Swanson, Wayne 1942- 167
Swarthout, Glendon (Fred) 1918-1992 26
Swarthout, Kathryn 1919- 7
Swayne, Sam(uel F.) 1907- 53
Swayne, Zoa (Lourana) 1905- 53
Sweat, Lynn 1934- 168
  Earlier sketch in SATA 57
Swede, George 1940- 67
Sweeney, James B(artholomew) 1910-1999 . 21
Sweeney, Joyce 1955- 167
  Earlier sketches in SATA 65, 68, 108
Sweeney, Joyce Kay
  See Sweeney, Joyce
Sweeney, Karen O'Connor
  See O'Connor, Karen
Sweeney, Matthew (Gerard) 1952- 156

Sweet, Melissa 1956- 172
Sweet, Sarah C.
  See Jewett, (Theodora) Sarah Orne
Sweetland, Nancy A(nn) 1934- 48
Swenson, Allan A(rmstrong) 1933- 21
Swenson, May 1919-1989 15
Swentzell, Rina 1939- 79
Swiatkowska, Gabi 1971(?)- 180
Swift, Bryan
  See Knott, William C(ecil, Jr.)
Swift, David
  See Kaufmann, John
Swift, Hildegarde Hoyt 1890(?)-1977
  Obituary 20
Swift, Jonathan 1667-1745 19
  See also CLR 53
Swift, Merlin
  See Leeming, Joseph
Swiger, Elinor Porter 1927- 8
Swinburne, Laurence (Joseph) 1924- 9
Swinburne, Stephen R. 1952- 188
  Earlier sketch in SATA 150
Swinburne, Steve
  See Swinburne, Stephen R.
Swindells, Robert (Edward) 1939- 150
  Brief entry 34
  Earlier sketches in SATA 50, 80
  See also SAAS 14
Swinford, Betty (June Wells) 1927- 58
Swinford, Bob
  See Swinford, Betty (June Wells)
Swithen, John
  See King, Stephen
Switzer, Ellen 1923- 48
Swope, Sam 156
Swope, Samuel
  See Swope, Sam
Sybesma, Jetske
  See Ironside, Jetske
Sydney, Frank
  See Warwick, Alan R(oss)
Sykes, Julie 1963- 202
Sylvada, Peter 1964- 202
Sylvester, Natalie G(abry) 1922- 22
Syme, (Neville) Ronald 1913-1992 87
  Earlier sketch in SATA 2
Symes, R. F. 77
Symes, Ruth Louise 1962- 179
Symons, (Dorothy) Geraldine 1909- 33
Symons, Stuart
  See Stanley, George Edward
Symynkywicz, Jeffrey B. 1954- 87
Symynkywicz, Jeffrey Bruce
  See Symynkywicz, Jeffrey B.
Synge, (Phyllis) Ursula 1930- 9
Sypher, Lucy Johnston 1907- 7
Szasz, Suzanne (Shorr) 1915-1997 13
  Obituary 99
Szekeres, Cyndy 1933- 157
  Autobiography Feature 157
  Earlier sketches in SATA 5, 60, 131
  See also SAAS 13
Szekessy, Tanja 98
Szpura, Beata 1961- 93
Szudek, Agnes S(usan) P(hilomena) 57
  Brief entry 49
Szulc, Tad 1926-2001 26
Szydlow, Jarl
  See Szydlowski, Mary Vigliante
Szydlowski, Mary Vigliante 1946- 94
Szymanski, Lois 1957- 91

                         T

Taback, Simms 1932- 170
  Brief entry 36
  Earlier sketches in SATA 40, 104
  See also CLR 100

Taber, Gladys (Bagg) 1899-1980
  Obituary 22
Tabor, Nancy Maria Grande 1949- 161
  Earlier sketch in SATA 89
Tabrah, Ruth Milander 1921- 14
Tackach, James 1953- 123
Tackach, James M.
  See Tackach, James
Tadgell, Nicole 1969- 177
Tafuri, Nancy 1946- 192
  Autobiography Feature 192
  Earlier sketches in SATA 39, 75, 130
  See also CLR 74
  See also SAAS 14
Tagg, Christine Elizabeth 1962- 138
Tagliaferro, Linda 173
Taha, Karen T(erry) 1942- 156
  Earlier sketch in SATA 71
Tai, Sharon O. 1963- 153
Tait, Douglas 1944- 12
Takabayashi, Mari 1960- 156
  Earlier sketch in SATA 115
Takahashi, Rumiko 1957- 163
Takakjian, Portia 1930- 15
Takashima, Misako
  See Misako Rocks!
Takashima, Shizuye 1928- 13
Takayama, Sandi 1962- 106
Takeda, Pete(r M.) 1964- 148
Tal, Eve 1947- 176
Talbert, Marc (Alan) 1953- 154
  Autobiography Feature 154
  Earlier sketches in SATA 68, 99
Talbot, Charlene Joy 1928- 10
Talbot, Toby 1928- 14
Talbott, Hudson 1949- 131
  Earlier sketch in SATA 84
Taliaferro, Dorothy L.
  See Martin, Del
Talifero, Gerald 1950- 75
Talker, T.
  See Rands, William Brighty
Tallarico, Tony 1933- 116
Tallcott, Emogene 10
Tallec, Olivier 1970- 197
Tallis, Robyn
  See Smith, Sherwood
Tallon, Robert 1939- 43
  Brief entry 28
Talmadge, Marian 14
Tamaki, Jillian 1980- 201
Tamar, Erika 1934- 150
  Earlier sketches in SATA 62, 101
Tamarin, Alfred H. 1913-1980 13
Tamburine, Jean 1930- 12
Tames, Richard (Lawrence) 1946- 102
  Earlier sketch in SATA 67
Tamminga, Frederick W(illiam) 1934- 66
Tammuz, Benjamin 1919-1989
  Obituary 63
Tan, Amy 1952- 75
Tan, Amy Ruth
  See Tan, Amy
Tan, Shaun 1974- 198
Tanaka, Beatrice 1932- 76
Tanaka, Shelley 136
Tang, Charles 1948- 81
Tang, Greg 172
Tang, You-Shan 1946- 53
Tania B.
  See Blixen, Karen
Tankard, Jeremy 1973- 191
Tannen, Mary 1943- 37
Tannenbaum, Beulah Goldstein 1916- 3
Tannenbaum, D(onald) Leb 1948- 42
Tanner, Jane 1946- 74
Tanner, Louise S(tickney) 1922-2000 9
Tanobe, Miyuki 1937- 23
Tanselle, Eve 1933- 125
Tapio, Pat Decker
  See Kines, Pat Decker

Tapp, Kathy Kennedy 1949- 88
  Brief entry 50
Tarbescu, Edith 1939- 107
Tarkington, (Newton) Booth 1869-1946 17
Tarpley, Natasha A(nastasia) 1971- 147
Tarr, Judith 1955- 149
  Earlier sketch in SATA 64
Tarry, Ellen 1906- 16
  See also CLR 26
  See also SAAS 16
Tarshis, Jerome 1936- 9
Tarshis, Lauren 187
Tarsky, Sue 1946- 41
Taschek, Karen 1956- 185
Tashjian, Janet 1956- 151
  Earlier sketch in SATA 102
Tashjian, Virginia A. 1921-2008 3
Tasker, James 1908- 9
Tate, Don(ald E.) 159
Tate, Eleanora E. 1948- 191
  Earlier sketches in SATA 38, 94
  See also CLR 37
Tate, Eleanora Elaine
  See Tate, Eleanora E.
Tate, Ellalice
  See Hibbert, Eleanor Alice Burford
Tate, Joan 1922- 86
  Earlier sketch in SATA 9
  See also SAAS 20
Tate, Mary Anne
  See Hale, Arlene
Tate, Nikki 134
Tate, Richard
  See Masters, Anthony (Richard)
Tate, Suzanne 1930- 91
Tatham, Betty 142
Tatham, Campbell
  See Elting, Mary
Tatham, Julie
  See Tatham, Julie Campbell
Tatham, Julie Campbell 1908-1999 80
Tavares, Matt 198
  Earlier sketch in SATA 159
Tavares, Victor 1971- 176
Taves, Isabella 1915- 27
Taylor, Alastair 1959- 130
Taylor, Andrew 1951- 70
Taylor, Andrew John Robert
  See Taylor, Andrew
Taylor, Ann 1782-1866 41
  Brief entry 35
Taylor, Audilee Boyd 1931- 59
Taylor, Barbara J. 1927- 10
Taylor, Ben
  See Strachan, Ian
Taylor, Brooke 205
Taylor, Carl 1937- 14
Taylor, Cheryl Munro 1957- 96
Taylor, Cora (Lorraine) 1936- 103
  Earlier sketch in SATA 64
  See also CLR 63
Taylor, Dave 1948- 78
Taylor, David
  See Taylor, Dave
Taylor, David 1900-1965 10
Taylor, Debbie A. 1955- 169
Taylor, Eleanor 1969- 206
Taylor, Elizabeth 1912-1975 13
Taylor, Florance Walton 9
Taylor, Florence M(arian Tompkins)
  1892-1983 9
Taylor, Gage 1942-2000 87
Taylor, Geoff 1946- 204
Taylor, G.P. 1958(?)- 156
Taylor, Graham Peter
  See Taylor, G.P.
Taylor, Herb(ert Norman, Jr.) 1942-1987 22
  Obituary 54
Taylor, J. David
  See Taylor, Dave

Taylor, Jane 1783-1824 41
  Brief entry 35
Taylor, Jerry D(uncan) 1938- 47
Taylor, John Robert
  See Taylor, Andrew
Taylor, Judy
  See Hough, Judy Taylor
Taylor, Kenneth N. 1917-2005 26
Taylor, Kenneth Nathaniel
  See Taylor, Kenneth N.
Taylor, Kim 180
Taylor, L(ester) B(arbour), Jr. 1932- 27
Taylor, Lois Dwight Cole
  See Cole, Lois Dwight
Taylor, Louise Todd 1939- 47
Taylor, Margaret 1950- 106
Taylor, Mark 1927- 32
  Brief entry 28
Taylor, Mildred D. 1943- 135
  See also CLR 144
  See also SAAS 5
Taylor, Mildred Delois
  See Taylor, Mildred D.
Taylor, Paula (Wright) 1942- 48
  Brief entry 33
Taylor, Robert Lewis 1912-1998 10
Taylor, Sean 1965- 192
Taylor, Sydney (Brenner) 1904(?)-1978 28
  Obituary 26
  Earlier sketch in SATA 1
Taylor, Theodore 1921-2006 128
  Obituary 177
  Earlier sketches in SATA 5, 54, 83
  See also CLR 30
  See also SAAS 4
Taylor, William 1938- 164
  Earlier sketches in SATA 78, 113
  See also CLR 63
Tazewell, Charles 1900-1972 74
Tchana, Katrin
  See Tchana, Katrin Hyman
Tchana, Katrin H.
  See Tchana, Katrin Hyman
Tchana, Katrin Hyman 1963- 177
  Earlier sketch in SATA 125
Tchekhov, Anton
  See Chekhov, Anton (Pavlovich)
Tchen, Richard 120
Tchudi, Stephen N. 1942- 55
Teague, Bob
  See Teague, Robert
Teague, Mark 1963- 205
  Earlier sketches in SATA 68, 99, 170
Teague, Mark Christopher
  See Teague, Mark
Teague, Robert 1929- 32
  Brief entry 31
Teal, Val 1902-1997 10
  Obituary 114
Teal, Valentine M.
  See Teal, Val
Teale, Edwin Way 1899-1980 7
  Obituary 25
Teasdale, Sara 1884-1933 32
Tebbel, John (William) 1912-2004 26
Teckentrup, Britta 1969- 200
Teensma, Lynne Bertrand
  See Bertrand, Lynne
Tee-Van, Helen Damrosch 1893-1976 10
  Obituary 27
Tegner, Bruce 1928- 62
Teitelbaum, Michael 1953- 116
  Earlier sketch in SATA 59
Tejima
  See Tejima, Keizaburo
Tejima, Keizaburo 1931- 139
  See also CLR 20
Telander, Todd (G.) 1967- 88
Teleki, Geza 1943- 45
Telemaque, Eleanor Wong 1934- 43

Telescope, Tom
  See Newbery, John
Tellis, Annabel 1967- 191
Temkin, Sara Anne Schlossberg 1913-1996 . 26
Temko, Florence 13
Tempest, Margaret Mary 1892-1982
  Obituary 33
Templar, Maurice
  See Groom, Arthur William
Temple, Arthur
  See Northcott, (William) Cecil
Temple, Charles 1947- 79
Temple, Frances (Nolting) 1945-1995 85
Temple, Herbert 1919- 45
Temple, Paul
  See McConnell, James Douglas Rutherford
Temple, William F(rederick) 1914-1989 107
Tenggren, Gustaf 1896-1970 18
  Obituary 26
Tennant, Kylie
  See Rodd, Kylie Tennant
Tennant, Veronica 1947- 36
Tenneshaw, S.M.
  See Beaumont, Charles
  and Garrett, Randall
  and Silverberg, Robert
Tenniel, John 1820-1914 74
  Brief entry 27
  See also CLR 146
Tepper, Sheri S. 1929- 113
Terada, Alice M. 1928- 90
Terban, Marvin 1940- 54
  Brief entry 45
Teresi, Judith M.
  See Goldberger, Judith M.
ter Haar, Jaap 1922- 6
  See also CLR 15
Terhune, Albert Payson 1872-1942 15
Terkel, Susan N(eiburg) 1948- 103
  Earlier sketch in SATA 59
Terlouw, Jan (Cornelis) 1931- 30
Terrell, John Upton 1900-1988
  Obituary 60
Terrill, Beth 198
Terrill, Elizabeth
  See Terrill, Beth
Terris, Susan 1937- 77
  Earlier sketch in SATA 3
Terry, Luther L(eonidas) 1911-1985 11
  Obituary 42
Terry, Margaret
  See Dunnahoo, Terry Janson
Terry, Walter 1913-1982 14
Terry, Will 1966- 205
Terzian, James P. 1915- 14
Tessendorf, K(enneth) C(harles) 1925-2003 . 75
  Obituary 142
Tessler, Manya 200
Tessler, Stephanie Gordon
  See Gordon, Stephanie Jacob
Tester, Sylvia Root 1939- 64
  Brief entry 37
Tether, (Cynthia) Graham 1950- 46
  Brief entry 36
Tetzner, Lisa 1894-1963 169
Thach, James Otis 1969- 195
Thacher, Mary McGrath 1933- 9
Thackeray, William Makepeace 1811-1863 .. 23
Thaler, Michael C.
  See Thaler, Mike
Thaler, Mike 1936- 93
  Brief entry 47
  Earlier sketch in SATA 56
Thaler, Shmuel 1958- 126
  Earlier sketch in SATA 72
Thamer, Katie 1955- 42
Thane, Elswyth 1900-1984(?) 32
Tharp, Louise (Marshall) Hall 1898-1992 3
  Obituary 129
Tharp, Tim 1957- 189
Thayer, Ernest Lawrence 1863-1940 60

Thayer, Jane
　See Woolley, Catherine
Thayer, Marjorie 1908-1992 74
　Brief entry 37
Thayer, Peter
　See Wyler, Rose
Thelwell, Norman 1923-2004 14
Themerson, Stefan 1910-1988 65
Thermes, Jennifer 1966- 155
Theroux, Paul 1941- 109
　Earlier sketch in SATA 44
Theroux, Paul Edward
　See Theroux, Paul
Thesman, Jean 124
　Earlier sketch in SATA 74
The Tjong-Khing
　See Khing, T.T.
Thieda, Shirley Ann 1943- 13
Thiele, Colin 1920-2006 125
　Earlier sketches in SATA 14, 72
　See also CLR 27
　See also SAAS 2
Thiele, Colin Milton
　See Thiele, Colin
Thiesing, Lisa 1958- 159
　Earlier sketch in SATA 95
Thimmesh, Catherine 189
Thiry, Joan (Marie) 1926- 45
Thistlethwaite, Miles 1945- 12
Thollander, Earl 1922- 22
Thomas, Abigail 1941- 112
Thomas, Andrea
　See Hill, Margaret (Ohler)
Thomas, Art(hur Lawrence) 1952- 48
　Brief entry 38
Thomas, Carroll
　See Ratliff, Thomas M.
　and Shmurak, Carole B.
Thomas, Dylan (Marlais) 1914-1953 60
Thomas, Egbert S.
　See Ellis, Edward S.
Thomas, Estelle Webb 1899-1982 26
Thomas, Frances 1943- 171
　Earlier sketch in SATA 92
Thomas, H. C.
　See Keating, Lawrence A.
Thomas, Ianthe 1951- 139
　Brief entry 42
　See also CLR 8
Thomas, J. F.
　See Fleming, Thomas
Thomas, Jan 1958- 197
Thomas, Jane Resh 1936- 171
　Earlier sketches in SATA 38, 90
Thomas, Jerry D. 1959- 91
Thomas, Joan Gale
　See Robinson, Joan (Mary) G(ale Thomas)
Thomas, Joyce Carol 1938- 137
　Autobiography Feature 137
　Earlier sketches in SATA 40, 78, 123
　See also CLR 19
　See also SAAS 7
Thomas, Lee
　See Floren, Lee
　and Pendleton, Thomas
Thomas, Lowell Jackson, Jr. 1923- 15
Thomas, Margaret
　See Thomas, Peggy
Thomas, Meredith 1963- 119
Thomas, Michael
　See Wilks, Michael Thomas
Thomas, Middy 1931- 191
Thomas, Patricia 1934- 199
　Earlier sketch in SATA 51
Thomas, Peggy 174
Thomas, Rob 1965- 97
Thomas, Scott 1959- 147
Thomas, Velma Maia 1955- 171
Thomas, Vernon (Arthur) 1934- 56

Thomas, Victoria
　See DeWeese, Thomas Eugene
　and Kugi, Constance Todd
Thomasma, Kenneth R. 1930- 90
Thomassie, Tynia 1959- 92
Thompson, Brenda 1935- 34
Thompson, Carol 1951- 189
　Earlier sketch in SATA 85
Thompson, China
　See Lewis, Mary
Thompson, Colin 1942- 198
　Earlier sketches in SATA 95, 163
Thompson, David H(ugh) 1941- 17
Thompson, Eileen
　See Panowski, Eileen Thompson
Thompson, George Selden 1929-1989 73
　Obituary 63
　Earlier sketch in SATA 4
　See also CLR 8
Thompson, Harlan 1894-1987 10
　Obituary 53
Thompson, Hilary 1943- 56
　Brief entry 49
Thompson, Joanna Maxwell Pullein
　See Pullein-Thompson, Joanna Maxwell
Thompson, Julian F(rancis) 1927- 155
　Brief entry 40
　Earlier sketches in SATA 55, 99
　See also CLR 24
　See also SAAS 13
Thompson, K(athryn Carolyn) Dyble
　1952- 82
Thompson, Kate 1956- 204
Thompson, Kay 1912(?)-1998 16
　See also CLR 22
Thompson, Lauren 1962- 200
　Earlier sketches in SATA 132, 174
Thompson, Lauren Stevens
　See Thompson, Lauren
Thompson, Megan Lloyd
　See Lloyd, Megan
Thompson, Richard 1951- 184
Thompson, Ruth Plumly 1891-1976 66
Thompson, Sharon 1952- 119
Thompson, Sharon Elaine
　See Thompson, Sharon
Thompson, Stith 1885-1976 57
　Obituary 20
Thompson, Vivian L(aubach) 1911- 3
Thomson, Bill 1963- 187
Thomson, Celia
　See Lynn, Tracy
Thomson, David (Robert Alexander)
　1914-1988 40
　Obituary 55
Thomson, Melissa 1979- 205
Thomson, Pat 1939- 122
　Earlier sketch in SATA 77
Thomson, Peggy 1922- 31
Thomson, Sarah L. 178
Thon, Melanie Rae 1957- 132
Thong, Roseanne 174
Thorburn, John
　See Goldsmith, John Herman Thorburn
Thorn, John 1947- 59
Thorndyke, Helen Louise
　See Benson, Mildred
Thorne, Ian
　See May, Julian
Thorne, Jean Wright
　See May, Julian
Thornhill, Jan 1955- 148
　Earlier sketch in SATA 77
Thornton, Hall
　See Silverberg, Robert
Thornton, W. B.
　See Burgess, Thornton Waldo
Thornton, Yvonne S(hirley) 1947- 96
Thorpe, E(ustace) G(eorge) 1916- 21
Thorpe, J. K.
　See Nathanson, Laura Walther

Thorvall, Kerstin 1925- 13
Thorvall-Falk, Kerstin
　See Thorvall, Kerstin
Thrasher, Crystal (Faye) 1921- 27
Threadgall, Colin 1941- 77
Three Little Pigs
　See Lantz, Francess L(in)
Thum, Gladys 1920- 26
Thum, Marcella 28
　Earlier sketch in SATA 3
Thundercloud, Katherine
　See Witt, Shirley Hill
Thurber, James (Grover) 1894-1961 13
Thurlo, Aimee 161
Thurlo, David 161
Thurman, Judith 1946- 33
Thurman, Mark (Gordon Ian) 1948- 63
Thwaite, Ann (Barbara Harrop) 1932- 14
Tibbetts, Peggy 127
Tibbles, Jean-Paul 1958- 115
Tibo, Gilles 1951- 107
　Earlier sketch in SATA 67
Tiburzi, Bonnie 1948- 65
Ticheburn, Cheviot
　See Ainsworth, William Harrison
Tichenor, Tom 1923-1992 14
Tichnor, Richard 1959- 90
Tichy, William 1924- 31
Tickle, Jack
　See Chapman, Jane
Tiegreen, Alan F. 1935- 94
　Brief entry 36
Tierney, Frank M. 1930- 54
Tierney, Tom 1928- 113
Tiffault, Benette W. 1955- 77
Tiller, Ruth L. 1949- 83
Tilley, Debbie 190
Tilly, Nancy 1935- 62
Tilton, Madonna Elaine 1929- 41
Tilton, Rafael
　See Tilton, Madonna Elaine
Timberlake, Amy 156
Timberlake, Carolyn
　See Dresang, Eliza (Carolyn Timberlake)
Timmers, Leo 1970- 190
Timmins, William F(rederick) 10
Tinbergen, Niko(laas) 1907-1988
　Obituary 60
Tincknell, Cathy 194
Tiner, John Hudson 1944- 32
Tingle, Dolli (?)-
　See Brackett, Dolli Tingle
Tingle, Rebecca 174
Tingum, Janice 1958- 91
Tinkelman, Murray 1933- 12
Tinkham, Kelly A. 188
Tinkle, (Julien) Lon 1906-1980 36
Tinling, Marion (Rose) 1904- 140
Tipene, Tim 1972- 141
Tippett, James S(terling) 1885-1958 66
Tirone Smith, Mary-Ann 1944- 143
Titlebaum, Ellen 195
Titler, Dale M(ilton) 1926- 35
　Brief entry 28
Titmarsh, Michael Angelo
　See Thackeray, William Makepeace
Titus, Eve 1922- 2
Tjia, Sherwin 1975- 204
Tjong Khing, The 1933- 76
Tobias, Katherine
　See Gottfried, Theodore Mark
Tobias, Tobi 1938- 82
　Earlier sketch in SATA 5
　See also CLR 4
Todd, Anne Ophelia
　See Dowden, Anne Ophelia Todd
Todd, Barbara 1961- 173
Todd, Barbara K(eith) 1917- 10
Todd, Chuck 195
Todd, H(erbert) E(atton) 1908-1988 84
　Earlier sketch in SATA 11

Todd, Loreto 1942- 30
Todd, Peter
    See Hamilton, Charles (Harold St. John)
Toews, Miriam 1964- 165
Tofel, Richard J. 1957- 140
Toft, Kim Michelle 1960- 170
Tokunbo, Dimitrea 187
Tolan, Stephanie S. 1942- 142
    Earlier sketches in SATA 38, 78
Toland, John (Willard) 1912-2004 38
Tolbert, Steve 1944- 143
Toledo, Francisco 1940- 198
Toledo, Natalia 1967- 197
Tolkien, John Ronald Reuel
    See Tolkien, J.R.R
Tolkien, J.R.R 1892-1973 100
    Obituary 24
    Earlier sketches in SATA 2, 32
    See also CLR 56
Toll, Emily
    See Cannon, Eileen E(mily)
Toll, Nelly S. 1935- 78
Tolland, W. R.
    See Heitzmann, William Ray
Tolles, Martha 1921- 76
    Earlier sketch in SATA 8
Tolliver, Ruby C(hangos) 1922- 110
    Brief entry 41
    Earlier sketch in SATA 55
Tolmie, Kenneth Donald 1941- 15
Tolstoi, Lev
    See Tolstoy, Leo (Nikolaevich)
Tolstoy, Leo (Nikolaevich) 1828-1910 26
Tolstoy, Count Leo
    See Tolstoy, Leo (Nikolaevich)
Tomalin, Ruth 29
Tomaselli, Rosa
    See Pausacker, Jenny
Tomecek, Steve 172
Tomes, Margot (Ladd) 1917-1991 70
    Brief entry 27
    Obituary 69
    Earlier sketch in SATA 36
Tomey, Ingrid 1943- 77
Tomfool
    See Farjeon, Eleanor
Tomic, Tomislav 1977- 202
Tomkins, Jasper
    See Batey, Tom
Tomline, F. Latour
    See Gilbert, W(illiam) S(chwenck)
Tomlinson, Heather 192
Tomlinson, Jill 1931-1976 3
    Obituary 24
Tomlinson, Reginald R(obert) 1885-1979(?)
    Obituary 27
Tomlinson, Theresa 1946- 165
    Earlier sketch in SATA 103
    See also CLR 60
Tommaso, Rich 1970(?)- 200
Tompert, Ann 1918- 139
    Earlier sketches in SATA 14, 89
Tompkins, Troy
    See Cle, Troy
Toner, Raymond John 1908-1986 10
Tong, Gary S. 1942- 66
Tong, Paul 188
Took, Belladonna
    See Chapman, Vera (Ivy May)
Tooke, Louise Mathews 1950- 38
Tooke, Susan 173
Toonder, Martin
    See Groom, Arthur William
Toothaker, Roy Eugene 1928- 18
Tooze, Ruth (Anderson) 1892-1972 4
Topek, Susan Remick 1955- 78
Topping, Audrey R(onning) 1928- 14
Tor, Regina
    See Shekerjian, Regina Tor
Torbert, Floyd James 1922- 22

Torgersen, Don Arthur 1934- 55
    Brief entry 41
Torley, Luke
    See Blish, James
Torrecilla, Pablo 1967- 206
Torres, Andres Segovia
    See Segovia, Andres
Torres, Daniel 1958- 102
Torres, John A. 1965- 163
    Earlier sketch in SATA 94
Torres, John Albert
    See Torres, John A.
Torres, Laura 1967- 146
    Earlier sketch in SATA 87
Torres, Leyla 1960- 155
Torrey, Rich
    See Torrey, Richard
Torrey, Richard 189
Torrie, Malcolm
    See Mitchell, Gladys (Maude Winifred)
Toten, Teresa 1955- 99
Totham, Mary
    See Breinburg, Petronella
Touponce, William F. 1948- 114
Tournier, Michel 1924- 23
Tournier, Michel Edouard
    See Tournier, Michel
Towle, Wendy 1963- 79
Towne, Mary
    See Spelman, Mary
Townley, Rod
    See Townley, Roderick
Townley, Roderick 1942- 177
Townsend, Brad W. 1962- 91
Townsend, John Rowe 1922- 132
    Autobiography Feature 132
    Earlier sketches in SATA 4, 68
    See also CLR 2
    See also SAAS 2
Townsend, Michael 1981- 194
Townsend, Sue
    See Townsend, Susan Lilian
Townsend, Susan Lilian 1946- 93
    Brief entry 48
    Earlier sketch in SATA 55
Townsend, Thomas L. 1944- 59
Townsend, Tom
    See Townsend, Thomas L.
Townsend, Wendy 1962- 201
Townson, Hazel 134
Toye, William Eldred 1926- 8
Traherne, Michael
    See Watkins-Pitchford, Denys James
Trahey, Jane 1923-2000 36
    Obituary 120
Trapani, Iza 1954- 116
    Earlier sketch in SATA 80
Trapp, Maria Augusta von
    See von Trapp, Maria Augusta
Travers, P(amela) L(yndon) 1899-1996 100
    Obituary 90
    Earlier sketches in SATA 4, 54
    See also CLR 93
    See also SAAS 2
Travis, Lucille 133
    Earlier sketch in SATA 88
Treadgold, Mary 1910- 49
Trease, (Robert) Geoffrey 1909-1998 60
    Obituary 101
    Earlier sketch in SATA 2
    See also CLR 42
    See also SAAS 6
Treat, Lawrence 1903-1998 59
Tredez, Alain 1926- 17
Tredez, Denise 1930- 50
Treece, Henry 1912-1966 2
    See also CLR 2
Tregarthen, Enys
    See Sloggett, Nellie
Tregaskis, Richard 1916-1973 3
    Obituary 26

Treherne, Katie Thamer 1955- 76
Trell, Max 1900-1996 14
    Obituary 108
Tremain, Ruthven 1922- 17
Trembath, Don 1963- 168
    Earlier sketch in SATA 96
Tremens, Del
    See MacDonald, Amy
Trent, Robbie 1894-1988 26
Trent, Timothy
    See Malmberg, Carl
Treseder, Terry Walton 1956- 68
Tresilian, (Cecil) Stuart 1891-(?) 40
Tresselt, Alvin 1916-2000 7
    See also CLR 30
Trevino, Elizabeth B(orton) de 1904- 29
    Earlier sketch in SATA 1
    See also SAAS 5
Trevor, Elleston 1920-1995 28
Trevor, Frances
    See Teasdale, Sara
Trevor, Glen
    See Hilton, James
Trevor, (Lucy) Meriol 1919-2000 113
    Obituary 122
    Earlier sketch in SATA 10
Trewellard, J.M. 195
Trewellard, Juliet
    See Trewellard, J.M.
Trez, Alain
    See Tredez, Alain
Trez, Denise
    See Tredez, Denise
Trezise, Percy 1923-
    See CLR 41
Trezise, Percy James
    See Trezise, Percy
Triggs, Tony D. 1946- 70
Trimble, Marshall I(ra) 1939- 93
Trimby, Elisa 1948- 47
    Brief entry 40
Tring, A. Stephen
    See Meynell, Laurence Walter
Tripp, Eleanor B(aldwin) 1936- 4
Tripp, Janet 1942- 108
Tripp, Jenny 188
Tripp, John
    See Moore, John Travers
Tripp, Nathaniel 1944- 101
Tripp, Paul 1916-2002 8
    Obituary 139
Tripp, Valerie 1951- 168
    Earlier sketch in SATA 78
Tripp, Wallace (Whitney) 1940- 31
Trivelpiece, Laurel 1926- 56
    Brief entry 46
Trivett, Daphne Harwood 1940- 22
Trivizas, Eugene 1946- 84
Trnka, Jiri 1912-1969 43
    Brief entry 32
Trollope, Anthony 1815-1882 22
Trost, Lucille W(ood) 1938- 149
    Earlier sketch in SATA 12
Trott, Betty 1933- 91
Trotter, Deborah W. 184
Trotter, Grace V(iolet) 1900-1991 10
Trottier, Maxine 1950- 175
    Earlier sketch in SATA 131
Troughton, Joanna (Margaret) 1947- 37
Trout, Kilgore
    See Farmer, Philip Jose
Trout, Richard E. 123
Trudeau, Garretson Beekman
    See Trudeau, G.B.
Trudeau, Garry
    See Trudeau, G.B.
Trudeau, Garry B.
    See Trudeau, G.B.
Trudeau, G.B. 1948- 168
    Earlier sketch in SATA 35

Trueit, Trudi
   See Trueit, Trudi Strain
Trueit, Trudi Strain 1963- *179*
Trueman, Matthew *183*
Trueman, Terry 1947- *178*
   Earlier sketch in SATA *132*
Truesdell, Judy
   See Mecca, Judy Truesdell
Truesdell, Sue
   See Truesdell, Susan G.
Truesdell, Susan G. *108*
   Brief entry *45*
Trumbauer, Lisa (Trutkoff) 1963- *149*
Truss, Jan 1925- *35*
Truss, Lynne 1955(?)- *194*
Tryon, Leslie *194*
   Earlier sketch in SATA *139*
Tubb, Jonathan N. 1951- *78*
Tubby, I. M.
   See Kraus, (Herman) Robert
Tucker, Caroline
   See Nolan, Jeannette Covert
Tudor, Edward
   See Browne, Anthony
Tudor, Tasha 1915-2008 .... *160*
   Obituary *205*
   Earlier sketches in SATA *20, 69*
   See also CLR *13*
Tuerk, Hanne 1951- *71*
Tugeau, Jeremy *199*
Tulloch, Richard 1949- *180*
   Earlier sketch in SATA *76*
Tulloch, Richard George
   See Tulloch, Richard
Tulloch, Shirley *169*
Tully, John (Kimberley) 1923- *14*
Tumanov, Vladimir A. 1961- *138*
Tung, Angela 1972- *109*
Tunis, Edwin (Burdett) 1897-1973 .... *28*
   Obituary *24*
   Earlier sketch in SATA *1*
   See also CLR *2*
Tunis, John R(oberts) 1889-1975 .... *37*
   Brief entry *30*
Tunnell, Michael
   See Tunnell, Michael O.
Tunnell, Michael O. 1950- *157*
   Earlier sketch in SATA *103*
Tunnell, Michael O'Grady
   See Tunnell, Michael O.
Tunnicliffe, C(harles) F(rederick)
   1901-1979 .... *62*
Turck, Mary C. 1950- *144*
Turk, Hanne
   See Tuerk, Hanne
Turk, Ruth 1917- *82*
Turkle, Brinton 1915- *79*
   Earlier sketch in SATA *2*
Turlington, Bayly 1919-1977 .... *5*
   Obituary *52*
Turnbull, Agnes Sligh 1888-1982 .... *14*
Turnbull, Ann 1943- *160*
   Earlier sketch in SATA *18*
Turnbull, Ann Christine
   See Turnbull, Ann
Turner, Alice K. 1940- *10*
Turner, Ann 1945- *188*
   Autobiography Feature *188*
   Earlier sketches in SATA *14, 77, 113, 178*
Turner, Ann Warren
   See Turner, Ann
Turner, Bonnie 1932- *75*
Turner, Elizabeth 1774-1846
   See YABC *2*
Turner, Glennette Tilley 1933- *183*
   Earlier sketch in SATA *71*
Turner, Josie
   See Crawford, Phyllis
Turner, Megan Whalen 1965- *174*
   Earlier sketch in SATA *94*

Turner, Philip (William) 1925- *83*
   Earlier sketch in SATA *11*
   See also CLR *89*
   See also SAAS *6*
Turner, Robyn 1947- *77*
Turner, Sheila R.
   See Seed, Sheila Turner
Turngren, Annette 1902(?)-1980
   Obituary *23*
Turngren, Ellen (?)-1964 .... *3*
Turska, Krystyna (Zofia) 1933- *31*
   Brief entry *27*
Turteltaub, H.N.
   See Turtledove, Harry
Turtledove, Harry 1949- *166*
   Earlier sketch in SATA *116*
Turtledove, Harry Norman
   See Turtledove, Harry
Tusa, Tricia 1960- *111*
   Earlier sketch in SATA *72*
Tusiani, Joseph 1924- *45*
Twain, Mark 1835-1910 .... *100*
   See also YABC *2*
   See also CLR *66*
Tweit, Susan J 1956- *94*
Tweit, Susan Joan
   See Tweit, Susan J
Tweton, D. Jerome 1933- *48*
Twinem, Neecy 1958- *92*
Twohill, Maggie
   See Angell, Judie
Tworkov, Jack 1900-1982 .... *47*
   Obituary *31*
Tyche
   See Papademetriou, Lisa
Tyers, Jenny 1969- *89*
Tyers, Kathy 1952- *82*
Tyler, Anne 1941- *173*
   Earlier sketches in SATA *7, 90*
Tyler, Linda
   See Tyler, Linda W(agner)
Tyler, Linda W(agner) 1952- *65*
Tyler, Vicki 1952- *64*
Tyne, Joel
   See Schembri, Jim
Tyrrell, Frances 1959- *107*

U

Ubell, Earl 1926-2007 .... *4*
   Obituary *182*
Uchida, Yoshiko 1921-1992 .... *53*
   Obituary *72*
   Earlier sketch in SATA *1*
   See also CLR *56*
   See also SAAS *1*
Udall, Jan Beaney 1938- *10*
Uden, (Bernard Gilbert) Grant 1910- *26*
Uderzo, Albert 1927-
   See CLR *37*
Udovic, David 1950- *189*
Udry, Janice May 1928- *152*
   Earlier sketch in SATA *4*
Uegaki, Chieri 1969- *153*
Ueno, Noriko
   See Nakae, Noriko
Ugliano, Natascia *196*
Uhlberg, Myron *174*
Uhlig, Richard 1970- *195*
Uhlig, Susan 1955- *129*
Ulam, S(tanislaw) M(arcin) 1909-1984 .... *51*
Ullman, James Ramsey 1907-1971 .... *7*
Ulm, Robert 1934-1977 .... *17*
Ulmer, Louise 1943- *53*
Ulmer, Wendy K. 1950- *201*
Ulrich, Maureen 1958- *206*
Ulyatt, Kenneth 1920- *14*
Umansky, Kaye 1946- *188*
   Earlier sketch in SATA *158*

Unada
   See Gliewe, Unada (Grace)
Uncle Carter
   See Boucher, (Clarence) Carter
Uncle Eric
   See Maybury, Richard J.
Uncle Gus
   See Rey, H. A.
Uncle Mac
   See McCulloch, Derek (Ivor Breashur)
Uncle Ray
   See Coffman, Ramon Peyton
Uncle Shelby
   See Silverstein, Shel
Underhill, Alice Mertie (Waterman)
   1900-1971 .... *10*
Underhill, Liz 1948- *53*
   Brief entry *49*
Underwood, Deborah 1962- *206*
Unger, Harlow G. 1931- *75*
Unger, Jim 1937- *67*
Ungerer, (Jean) Thomas 1931- *106*
   Earlier sketches in SATA *5, 33*
   See also CLR *77*
Ungerer, Tomi 1931-
   See Ungerer, (Jean) Thomas
Unkelbach, Kurt 1913-1992 .... *4*
Unnerstad, Edith (Totterman) 1900-1982 .... *3*
   See also CLR *36*
Unobagha, Uzo *139*
Unrau, Ruth 1922- *9*
Unstead, R(obert) J(ohn) 1915-1988 .... *12*
   Obituary *56*
Unsworth, Walt(er) 1928- *4*
Untermeyer, Bryna Ivens 1909-1985 .... *61*
Untermeyer, Louis 1885-1977 .... *37*
   Obituary *26*
   Earlier sketch in SATA *2*
Unwin, David S(torr) 1918- *14*
Unwin, Nora S(picer) 1907-1982 .... *3*
   Obituary *49*
Unzner, Christa 1958- *141*
   Earlier sketch in SATA *80*
Unzner-Fischer, Christa
   See Unzner, Christa
Updale, Eleanor 1953- *175*
Updyke, Rosemary K. 1924- *103*
Upitis, Alvis *109*
Urban, Helle (Denise) 1957- *149*
Urban, Linda *199*
Urbanovic, Jackie *189*
Urbigkit, Cat 1965- *196*
Ure, Jean 1943- *192*
   Autobiography Feature *192*
   Earlier sketches in SATA *48, 78, 129*
   See also CLR *34*
   See also SAAS *14*
U'Ren, Andrea 1968- *142*
Uris, Leon 1924-2003 .... *49*
   Obituary *146*
Uris, Leon Marcus
   See Uris, Leon
Ursu, Anne *177*
Ury, Allen B. 1954- *98*
Uschan, Michael V. 1948- *129*
Usher, Margo Scegge
   See McHargue, Georgess
Uslan, Michael E. 1951- *169*
Uston, Ken(neth Senzo) 1935-1987 .... *65*
Uttley, Alice Jane 1884-1976 .... *88*
   Obituary *26*
   Earlier sketch in SATA *3*
Uttley, Alison
   See Uttley, Alice Jane
Utz, Lois (Marie) 1932-1986 .... *5*
   Obituary *50*

V

Vaeth, J. Gordon 1921- 17
Vaeth, Joseph Gordon
    See Vaeth, J. Gordon
Vagin, Vladimir (Vasilevich) 1937- 142
Vail, Rachel 1966- 201
    Earlier sketches in SATA *94, 163*
Vainio, Pirkko 1957- 123
    Earlier sketch in SATA *76*
Valen, Nanine 1950- 21
Valencak, Hannelore
    See Mayer, Hannelore Valencak
Valens, Amy 1946- 70
Valens, E(vans) G(ladstone), Jr. 1920-1992 ... *1*
Valentine, Johnny 72
Valerio, Geraldo 1970- 180
Valgardson, W(illiam) D(empsey) 1939- 151
    Earlier sketch in SATA *101*
Valleau, Emily 1925- 51
Van Abbe, Salaman 1883-1955 18
Van Allsburg, Chris 1949- 156
    Earlier sketches in SATA *37, 53, 105*
    See also CLR *113*
Van Anrooy, Francine 1924- 2
Van Anrooy, Frans
    See Van Anrooy, Francine
Vanasse, Deb 1957- 170
Van Buren, David 203
Vance, Eleanor Graham 1908-1985 11
Vance, Gerald
    See Garrett, Randall
    and Silverberg, Robert
Vance, Marguerite 1889-1965 29
VanCleave, Janice 1942- 116
    Autobiography Feature 123
    Earlier sketch in SATA *75*
Vandenburg, Mary Lou 1943- 17
Vander Boom, Mae M. 14
Vander-Els, Betty 1936- 63
van der Heide, Iris 1970- 183
van der Linde, Laurel 1952- 78
van der Meer, Ron 1945- 98
van de Ruit, John 1975- 199
Van der Veer, Judy 1912-1982 4
    Obituary 33
Vanderwerff, Corrine 1939- 117
Vander Zee, Ruth 199
    Earlier sketch in SATA *159*
Vande Velde, Vivian 1951- 141
    Earlier sketches in SATA *62, 95*
    See also CLR *145*
Vandivert, Rita (Andre) 1905-1986 21
Van Draanen, Wendelin 122
Van Dusen, Chris 173
Van Duyn, Janet 1910- 18
Van Dyne, Edith
    See Baum, L. Frank
    and Sampson, Emma (Keats) Speed
    and van Zantwijk, Rudolf (Alexander
    Marinus)
Vane, Mitch
    See Vane, Mitchelle
Vane, Mitchelle 176
van Frankenhuyzen, Gijsbert 1951- 132
Van Genechten, Guido 1957- 165
van Haeringen, Annemarie 193
Van Hook, Beverly H. 1941- 99
Van Horn, William 1939- 43
van Hout, Mies 1962- 178
Van Iterson, S(iny) R(ose) 26
Van Kampen, Vlasta 1943- 163
    Earlier sketch in SATA *54*
Van Laan, Nancy 1939- 105
van Lawick-Goodall, Jane
    See Goodall, Jane
Van Leeuwen, Jean 1937- 141
    Autobiography Feature 141
    Earlier sketches in SATA *6, 82, 132*
    See also SAAS *8*

van Lhin, Erik
    See del Rey, Lester
van Lieshout, Maria 201
Van Loon, Hendrik Willem 1882-1944 18
van Ommen, Sylvia 1978- 186
VanOosting, James 1951- 170
Van Orden, M(erton) D(ick) 1921- 4
Van Patter, Bruce 183
Van Reek, Wouter 204
Van Rensselaer, Alexander (Taylor Mason)
    1892-1962 14
Van Riper, Guernsey, Jr. 1909-1995 3
van Rossum, Heleen 1962- 174
Van Rynbach, Iris 1952- 102
Vansant, Rhonda Joy Edwards 1950- 92
Van Steenwyk, Elizabeth (Ann) 1928- 89
    Earlier sketch in SATA *34*
Van Stockum, Hilda 1908-2006 5
    Obituary 179
van Straaten, Harmen 1961- 195
Van Tuyl, Barbara 1940- 11
van Vogt, A(lfred) E(lton) 1912-2000 14
    Obituary 124
Van Wassenhove, Sue 1951- 202
Van Woerkom, Dorothy (O'Brien)
    1924-1996 21
Van Wormer, Joe
    See Van Wormer, Joseph Edward
Van Wormer, Joseph Edward 1913-1998 35
Van Wright, Cornelius 173
Van Zwienen, Ilse Charlotte Koehn
    1929-1991 34
    Brief entry 28
    Obituary 67
Van Zyle, Jon 1942- 176
    Earlier sketch in SATA *84*
Varela, Barry 180
Varga, Judy
    See Stang, Judit
Varley, Dimitry V. 1906-1984 10
Varley, Susan 1961- 134
    Earlier sketch in SATA *63*
Varon, Sara 195
Vasileva, Tatiana
    See Wassiljewa, Tatjana
Vasiliev, Valery 1949- 80
Vasilieva, Tatiana
    See Wassiljewa, Tatjana
Vasiliu, Mircea 1920- 2
Vass, George 1927- 57
    Brief entry 31
Vaughan, Carter A.
    See Gerson, Noel Bertram
Vaughan, Harold Cecil 1923- 14
Vaughan, Marcia (K.) 1951- 159
    Earlier sketches in SATA *60, 95*
Vaughan, Richard 1947- 87
Vaughan, Sam(uel) 1928- 14
Vaughn, Ruth 1935- 14
Vaught, Susan 1965- 195
Vaupel, Robin 198
Vautier, Ghislaine 1932- 53
Vavra, Robert James 1935- 8
Vecsey, George Spencer 1939- 9
Vedral, Joyce L(auretta) 1943- 65
Vega, Denise 174
Vega, Denise B.
    See Vega, Denise
Veglahn, Nancy (Crary) 1937- 5
Vejjajiva, Jane 1963- 189
Velasquez, Eric 192
Velasquez, Gloria 1949- 113
Velasquez, Gloria 1949-
    See Velasquez, Gloria
Velthuijs, Max 1923-2005 110
    Obituary 160
    Earlier sketch in SATA *53*
Venable, Alan (Hudson) 1944- 8
Venezia, Mike 1945- 150
Ventura, Anthony
    See Pellowski, Michael (Joseph)

Ventura, Piero (Luigi) 1937- 61
    Brief entry 43
    See also CLR *16*
Vequin, Capini
    See Quinn, Elisabeth
Verba, Joan Marie 1953- 78
Verboven, Agnes 1951- 103
verDorn, Bethea (Stewart) 1952- 76
Vere, Ed 197
Verissimo, Erico (Lopes) 1905-1975 113
Verne, Jules (Gabriel) 1828-1905 21
    See also CLR *88*
Verner, Gerald 1897(?)-1980
    Obituary 25
Verney, John 1913-1993 14
    Obituary 75
Verniero, Joan C. 1949- 181
Vernon, (Elda) Louise A(nderson) 1914- 14
Vernon, Rosemary
    See Smith, Susan Vernon
Vernon, Ursula 204
Vernor, D.
    See Casewit, Curtis W(erner)
Verr, Harry Coe
    See Kunhardt, Edith
Verral, Charles Spain 1904-1990 11
    Obituary 65
Verrillo, Erica 1953- 199
Verrillo, Erica F.
    See Verrillo, Erica
Verrone, Robert J. 1935(?)-1984
    Obituary 39
Versace, Marie Teresa Rios 1917- 2
Vertreace, Martha M(odena) 1945- 78
Vesey, A(manda) 1939- 62
Vesey, Mark (David) 1958- 123
Vesey, Paul
    See Allen, Samuel W(ashington)
Vestergaard, Hope 178
Vestly, Anne-Cath(arina) 1920- 14
    See also CLR *99*
Vevers, (Henry) Gwynne 1916-1988 45
    Obituary 57
Viator, Vacuus
    See Hughes, Thomas
Vicar, Henry
    See Felsen, Henry Gregor
Vick, Helen Hughes 1950- 88
Vicker, Angus
    See Felsen, Henry Gregor
Vickers, Sheena 1960- 94
Vickery, Kate
    See Kennedy, T.A.
Victor, Edward 1914- 3
Victor, Joan Berg 1942- 30
Vidrine, Beverly Barras 1938- 188
    Earlier sketch in SATA *103*
Viereck, Ellen K. 1928- 14
Viereck, Phillip 1925- 3
Viertel, Janet 1915- 10
Vigliante, Mary
    See Szydlowski, Mary Vigliante
Vigna, Judith 1936- 102
    Earlier sketch in SATA *15*
Viguers, Ruth Hill 1903-1971 6
Villareal, Ray 187
Villasenor, Edmund
    See Villasenor, Victor E.
Villasenor, Edmundo
    See Villasenor, Victor E.
Villasenor, Victor
    See Villasenor, Victor E.
Villasenor, Victor E. 1940- 171
Villasenor, Victor Edmundo
    See Villasenor, Victor E.
Villiard, Paul 1910-1974 51
    Obituary 20
Villiers, Alan (John) 1903-1982 10
Vilott, Rhondi
    See Salsitz, Rhondi Vilott
Vincent, Eric Douglas 1953- 40

Vincent, Erin 1969- *188*
Vincent, Felix 1946- *41*
Vincent, Gabrielle 1928-2000 .... *121*
  Earlier sketch in SATA *61*
  See also CLR *13*
Vincent, Mary Keith
  See St. John, Wylly Folk
Vincent, William R.
  See Heitzmann, William Ray
Vinegar, Tom
  See Gregg, Andrew K.
Vinest, Shaw
  See Longyear, Barry B(rookes)
Vinge, Joan (Carol) D(ennison) 1948- *113*
  Earlier sketch in SATA *36*
Vining, Elizabeth Gray 1902-1999 .... *6*
  Obituary *117*
Vinson, Kathryn 1911-1995 .... *21*
Vinton, Iris 1906(?)-1988 .... *24*
  Obituary *55*
Viola, Herman J(oseph) 1938- *126*
Viorst, Judith 1931- *172*
  Earlier sketches in SATA *7, 70, 123*
  See also CLR *90*
Vip
  See Partch, Virgil Franklin II
Vipont, Charles
  See Foulds, Elfrida Vipont
Vipont, Elfrida
  See Foulds, Elfrida Vipont
Viscott, David S(teven) 1938-1996 .... *65*
Visser, W(illem) F(rederik) H(endrik)
  1900-1968 .... *10*
Vitale, Stefano 1958- *180*
  Earlier sketch in SATA *114*
Vivas, Julie 1947- *96*
Vivelo, Jackie 1943- *63*
Vivelo, Jacqueline J.
  See Vivelo, Jackie
Vivelo, Jacqueline Jean
  See Vivelo, Jackie
Vizzini, Ned 1981- *179*
  Earlier sketch in SATA *125*
Vlahos, Olivia 1924- *31*
Vlasic, Bob
  See Hirsch, Phil
Voake, Charlotte *180*
  Earlier sketch in SATA *114*
Voake, Steve 1961- *178*
Vo-Dinh, Mai 1933- *16*
Vogel, Carole Garbuny 1951- *105*
  Earlier sketch in SATA *70*
Vogel, Ilse-Margret 1918- *14*
Vogel, John H., Jr. 1950- *18*
Vogt, Esther Loewen 1915-1999 .... *14*
Vogt, Gregory L. *94*
Vogt, Marie Bollinger 1921- *45*
Voight, Virginia Frances 1909-1989 .... *8*
Voigt, Cynthia 1942- *160*
  Brief entry *33*
  Earlier sketches in SATA *48, 79, 116*
  See also CLR *141*
Voigt, Erna 1925- *35*
Voigt-Rother, Erna
  See Voigt, Erna
Vojtech, Anna 1946- *108*
  Earlier sketch in SATA *42*
Vollstadt, Elizabeth Weiss 1942- *121*
Volponi, Paul *175*
Volting, Dr. R.E.
  See Lerangis, Peter
Von Ahnen, Katherine 1922- *93*
von Buhler, Cynthia *185*
Vondra, J. Gert
  See Vondra, Josef
Vondra, Josef 1941- *121*
Vondra, Josef Gert
  See Vondra, Josef
Von Gunden, Kenneth 1946- *113*
Von Hagen, Victor Wolfgang 1908-1985 ...... *29*

von Klopp, Vahrah
  See Malvern, Gladys
von Schmidt, Eric 1931-2007 .... *50*
  Brief entry *36*
  Obituary *181*
von Storch, Anne B. 1910- *1*
von Trapp, Maria Augusta 1905-1987 .... *16*
von Wodtke, Charlotte Buel Johnson
  1918-1982 .... *46*
von Ziegesar, Cecily 1970- *161*
Vos, Ida 1931-2006 .... *121*
  Earlier sketch in SATA *69*
  See also CLR *85*
Vosburgh, Leonard (W.) 1912- *15*
Votaw, Carol 1961- *201*
Voyle, Mary
  See Manning, Rosemary
Vrettos, Adrienne Maria *187*
Vriens, Jacques 1946- *151*
Vugteveen, Verna Aardema
  See Aardema, Verna
Vulture, Elizabeth T.
  See Gilbert, Suzie
Vuong, Lynette Dyer 1938- *110*
  Earlier sketch in SATA *60*

W

Waas, Uli
  See Waas-Pommer, Ulrike
Waas-Pommer, Ulrike 1949- *85*
Waber, Bernard 1924- *155*
  Brief entry *40*
  Earlier sketches in SATA *47, 95*
  See also CLR *55*
Wachtel, Shirley Russak 1951- *88*
Wachter, Oralee (Roberts) 1935- *61*
  Brief entry *51*
Waddell, Evelyn Margaret 1918- *10*
Waddell, Martin 1941- *129*
  Autobiography Feature *129*
  Earlier sketches in SATA *43, 81, 127*
  See also CLR *31*
  See also SAAS *15*
Waddy, Lawrence (Heber) 1914- *91*
Wade, Mary Dodson 1930- *151*
  Earlier sketch in SATA *79*
Wade, Suzanne
  See Kirby, Susan E.
Wade, Theodore E., Jr. 1936- *37*
Wademan, Peter John 1946- *122*
Wademan, Spike
  See Wademan, Peter John
Wadsworth, Ginger 1945- *157*
  Earlier sketch in SATA *103*
Wagenheim, Kal 1935- *21*
Wagner, Michele R. 1975- *157*
Wagner, Sharon B. 1936- *4*
Wagoner, David (Russell) 1926- *14*
Wahl, Jan (Boyer) 1933- *132*
  Earlier sketches in SATA *2, 34, 73*
  See also SAAS *3*
Wahl, Mats 1945- *186*
Waide, Jan 1952- *29*
Wainscott, John Milton 1910-1981 .... *53*
Wainwright, Richard M. 1935- *91*
Wainwright, Ruth
  See Symes, Ruth Louise
Wait, Lea 1946- *137*
Waite, Judy *174*
Waite, Judy Bernard
  See Bernard, Patricia
Waite, Michael
  See Waite, Michael P.
Waite, Michael P. 1960- *101*
Waite, P(eter) B(usby) 1922- *64*
Waites, Joan C. *187*
Waitley, Douglas 1927- *30*

Wakefield, Jean L.
  See Laird, Jean E(louise)
Wakin, Daniel (Joseph) 1961- *84*
Wakin, Edward 1927- *37*
Wakiyama, Hanako 1966- *192*
Walck, Henry Z. 1908(?)-1984
  Obituary *40*
Walden, Amelia Elizabeth *3*
Walden, Mark *188*
Waldherr, Kris 1963- *76*
Waldman, Bruce 1949- *15*
Waldman, Neil 1947- *203*
  Earlier sketches in SATA *51, 94, 142*
Waldrep, Richard *198*
Waldron, Ann Wood 1924- *16*
Waldron, Kathleen Cook *176*
Wales, Dirk 1931- *205*
Walgren, Judy 1963- *118*
Walker, Addison
  See Walker, (Addison) Mort
Walker, Alice 1944- *31*
Walker, Alice Malsenior
  See Walker, Alice
Walker, Barbara (Jeanne) K(erlin) 1921- *80*
  Earlier sketch in SATA *4*
Walker, Barbara M(uhs) 1928- *57*
Walker, (James) Braz(elton) 1934-1983 .... *45*
Walker, David 1965- *197*
Walker, David G(ordon) 1926- *60*
Walker, David Harry 1911-1992 .... *8*
  Obituary *71*
Walker, Diana 1925- *9*
Walker, Diane Marie Catherine
  See Walker, Kate
Walker, Dick
  See Pellowski, Michael (Joseph)
Walker, Frank 1931-2000 .... *36*
Walker, Holly Beth
  See Bond, Gladys Baker
Walker, Kate 1950- *165*
  Earlier sketch in SATA *82*
Walker, Kathrine Sorley
  See Sorley Walker, Kathrine
Walker, Lou Ann 1952- *66*
  Brief entry *53*
Walker, Louise Jean 1891-1976
  Obituary *35*
Walker, Mary Alexander 1927- *61*
Walker, Mildred
  See Schemm, Mildred Walker
Walker, (Addison) Mort 1923- *8*
Walker, Pamela 1948- *142*
  Earlier sketch in SATA *24*
Walker, Paul Robert 1953- *154*
Walker, Robert W. 1948- *66*
Walker, Sally M(acArt) 1954- *135*
Walker, Stephen J. 1951- *12*
Walker-Blondell, Becky 1951- *89*
Wallace, Barbara Brooks 1922- *136*
  Earlier sketches in SATA *4, 78*
  See also SAAS *17*
Wallace, Beverly Dobrin 1921- *19*
Wallace, Bill 1947- *169*
  Brief entry *47*
  Earlier sketches in SATA *53, 101*
Wallace, Daisy
  See Cuyler, Margery
Wallace, Ian 1950- *141*
  Earlier sketches in SATA *53, 56*
  See also CLR *37*
Wallace, John 1966- *155*
  Earlier sketch in SATA *105*
Wallace, John A(dam) 1915-2004 .... *3*
  Obituary *155*
Wallace, Karen 1951- *188*
  Earlier sketches in SATA *83, 139*
Wallace, Nancy Elizabeth 1948- *186*
  Earlier sketch in SATA *141*
Wallace, Nigel
  See Hamilton, Charles (Harold St. John)
Wallace, Paula S. *153*

Wallace, Rich 1957- *196*
Earlier sketches in SATA *117, 158*
Wallace, Robert 1932-1999 47
Brief entry 37
Wallace, Ruby Ann 1923(?)- 77
Wallace, William Keith
See Wallace, Bill
Wallace-Brodeur, Ruth 1941- *169*
Brief entry 41
Earlier sketches in SATA *51, 88*
Wallenta, Adam 1974- *123*
Waller, Leslie 1923-2007 20
Walley, Byron
See Card, Orson Scott
Wallis, Diz 1949- 77
Wallis, G. McDonald
See Campbell, Hope
Wallner, Alexandra 1946- *156*
Brief entry 41
Earlier sketches in SATA *51, 98*
Wallner, John C. 1945- *133*
Earlier sketches in SATA *10, 51*
Wallower, Lucille *11*
Walrod, Amy 1973(?)- *182*
Walsh, Ann 1942- *176*
Earlier sketch in SATA *62*
Walsh, Ellen Stoll 1942- *194*
Earlier sketches in SATA *49, 99, 147*
Walsh, George Johnston 1889-1981 53
Walsh, Gillian Paton
See Paton Walsh, Jill
Walsh, Jill Paton
See Paton Walsh, Jill
Walsh, Joanna 1970- *182*
Walsh, Lawrence 1942- *170*
Walsh, Marissa 1972- *195*
Walsh, Mary Caswell 1949- *118*
Walsh, Mitzy
See Walsh, Marissa
Walsh, Suella *170*
Walsh, V. L.
See Walsh, Vivian
Walsh, Vivian 1960- *120*
Walsh Shepherd, Donna 1948- 78
Walter, Frances V. 1923- *71*
Walter, Mildred Pitts 1922- *133*
Brief entry 45
Earlier sketch in SATA *69*
See also CLR *61*
See also SAAS *12*
Walter, Villiam Christian
See Andersen, Hans Christian
Walter, Virginia
See Walter, Virginia A.
Walter, Virginia A. *134*
Walters, Audrey 1929- *18*
Walters, Celeste 1938- *126*
Walters, Eric 1957- *205*
Earlier sketches in SATA *99, 155*
Walters, Eric Robert
See Walters, Eric
Walters, Helen B. (?)-1987
Obituary 50
Walters, Hugh
See Hughes, Walter (Llewellyn)
Walther, Thomas A. 1950- *31*
Walther, Tom
See Walther, Thomas A.
Waltner, Elma 1912-1987 40
Waltner, Willard H. 1909- 40
Walton, Darwin McBeth 1926- *119*
Walton, Fiona L. M. 1959- *89*
Walton, Richard J. 1928- *4*
Walton, Rick 1957- *204*
Earlier sketches in SATA *101, 151*
Waltrip, Lela (Kingston) 1904-1995 .... *9*
Waltrip, Mildred 1911- *37*
Waltrip, Rufus (Charles) 1898-1988 .... *9*
Walworth, Nancy Zinsser 1917- *14*

Wangerin, Walter, Jr. 1944- 98
Brief entry 37
Earlier sketch in SATA *45*
Waniek, Marilyn Nelson 1946-
See Nelson, Marilyn
Wannamaker, Bruce
See Moncure, Jane Belk
Warbler, J. M.
See Cocagnac, Augustin Maurice(-Jean)
Warburg, Sandol Stoddard
See Stoddard, Sandol
Ward, E. D.
See Gorey, Edward (St. John)
and Lucas, E(dward) V(errall)
Ward, Ed
See Stratemeyer, Edward L.
Ward, Helen 1962- *206*
Earlier sketches in SATA *72, 144*
Ward, Jay 1920-1989
Obituary 63
Ward, Jennifer 1963- *146*
Ward, John (Stanton) 1917- 42
Ward, Jonas
See Ard, William
and Cox, William R(obert)
and Garfield, Brian (Francis Wynne)
Ward, Lynd (Kendall) 1905-1985 .... *36*
Obituary 42
Earlier sketch in SATA *2*
Ward, Martha (Eads) *5*
Ward, Melanie
See Curtis, Richard
and Lynch, Marilyn
Ward, Nicholas John
See Ward, Nick
Ward, Nick 1955- *190*
Ward, Tom
See Stratemeyer, Edward L.
Wardell, Dean
See Prince, J(ack) H(arvey)
Wardlaw, Lee 1955- *115*
Earlier sketch in SATA *79*
Ware, Cheryl 1963- *101*
Ware, Chris 1967- *140*
Ware, Leon (Vernon) 1909-1976 .... *4*
Wargin, Kathy-jo 1964- *145*
Warhola, James 1955- *187*
Warner, Frank A. 67
Earlier sketch in SATA *1*
Warner, Gertrude Chandler 1890-1979 .... *9*
Obituary 73
Warner, J(ohn) F. 1929- 75
Warner, Lucille Schulberg 30
Warner, Matt
See Fichter, George S.
Warner, Oliver (Martin Wilson) 1903-1976 . 29
Warner, Sally 1946- *131*
Warner, Sunny (B.) 1931- *108*
Warnes, Tim 1971- *166*
Earlier sketch in SATA *116*
Warnes, Timothy
See Warnes, Tim
Warnick, Elsa 1942- *113*
Warren, Andrea 1946- 98
Warren, Betsy
See Warren, Elizabeth Avery
Warren, Billy
See Warren, William Stephen
Warren, Cathy 1951- *62*
Brief entry 46
Warren, Elizabeth
See Supraner, Robyn
Warren, Elizabeth Avery 1916- *46*
Brief entry 38
Warren, Jackie M. 1953- *135*
Warren, Joshua P(aul) 1976- *107*
Warren, Joyce W(illiams) 1935- *18*
Warren, Mary Phraner 1929- *10*
Warren, Robert Penn 1905-1989 .... *46*
Obituary 63
Warren, Scott S. 1957- *79*

Warren, William Stephen 1882-1968 .... *9*
Warrick, Patricia Scott 1925- 35
Warriner, John 1907(?)-1987
Obituary 53
Warsh
See Warshaw, Jerry
Warshaw, Jerry 1929- 30
Warshaw, Mary 1931- *89*
Warshofsky, Fred 1931- 24
Warshofsky, Isaac
See Singer, Isaac Bashevis
Wartski, Maureen (Ann Crane) 1940- 50
Brief entry 37
Warwick, Alan R(oss) 1900-1973 42
Wa-Sha-Quon-Asin
See Belaney, Archibald Stansfeld
Wa-sha-quon-asin
See Belaney, Archibald Stansfeld
Washburn, Bradford 1910-2007 38
Obituary *181*
Washburn, Henry Bradford, Jr.
See Washburn, Bradford
Washburn, Jan(ice) 1926- 63
Washburn, Lucia *193*
Washburne, Carolyn Kott 1944- 86
Washburne, Heluiz Chandler 1892-1970 ...... *10*
Obituary 26
Washington, Booker T(aliaferro)
1856-1915 28
Washington, Donna L. 1967- *159*
Earlier sketch in SATA *98*
Wasserstein, Wendy 1950-2006 94
Obituary *174*
Wassiljewa, Tatjana 1928- *106*
Watanabe, Shigeo 1928- *131*
Brief entry 32
Earlier sketch in SATA *39*
See also CLR *8*
Waters, John F(rederick) 1930- *4*
Waters, Summer
See Sykes, Julie
Waters, Tony 1958- 75
Waterton, Betty 1923- 99
Brief entry 34
Earlier sketch in SATA *37*
Waterton, Betty Marie
See Waterton, Betty
Watkins, Dawn L. *126*
Watkins, Gloria Jean
See hooks, bell
Watkins, Lois 1930- 88
Watkins, Peter 1934- 66
Watkins, Yoko Kawashima 1933- 93
Watkins-Pitchford, Denys James
1905-1990 87
Obituary 66
Earlier sketch in SATA *6*
See also SAAS *4*
Watling, James 1933- *117*
Earlier sketch in SATA *67*
Watson, Aldren A(uld) 1917- 42
Brief entry 36
Watson, Amy Zakrzewski 1965- 76
Watson, B. S.
See Teitelbaum, Michael
Watson, Carol 1949- 78
Watson, C.G. *193*
Watson, Clyde 1947- 68
Earlier sketch in SATA *5*
See also CLR *3*
Watson, Helen Orr 1892-1978
Obituary 24
Watson, James 1936- *106*
Earlier sketch in SATA *10*
Watson, Jane Werner 1915- 54
Earlier sketch in SATA *3*
Watson, Jesse Joshua *199*
Watson, John H.
See Farmer, Philip Jose
Watson, Mary 1953- *117*
Watson, N. Cameron 1955- *81*

Watson, Nancy Dingman 32
Watson, Pauline 1925- 14
Watson, Richard F.
    See Silverberg, Robert
Watson, Richard Jesse 1951- 62
Watson, Sally (Lou) 1924- 3
Watson, Wendy (McLeod) 1942- 142
    Earlier sketches in SATA *5, 74*
Watson Taylor, Elizabeth 1915- 41
Watt, Melanie 1975- 193
    Earlier sketch in SATA *136*
Watt, Thomas 1935- 4
Wattenberg, Jane 174
Watterson, Bill 1958- 66
Watt-Evans, Lawrence 1954- 121
Watts, (Anna) Bernadette 1942- 103
    Earlier sketch in SATA *4*
Watts, Ephraim
    See Horne, Richard Henry Hengist
Watts, Franklin (Mowry) 1904-1978 46
    Obituary 21
Watts, Helen L. Hoke 1903-1990
    Obituary 65
Watts, Irene N(aemi) 1931- 111
    Earlier sketch in SATA *56*
Watts, Isaac 1674-1748 52
Watts, James K(ennedy) M(offitt) 1955- 59
Watts, Jeri Hanel 1957- 170
Watts, Julia 1969- 103
Watts, Leander 1956- 146
Watts, Leslie Elizabeth 1961- 168
Watts, Mabel Pizzey 1906-1994 11
Watts, Nigel 1957-1999 121
Waugh, C. C. Roessel
    See Waugh, Carol-Lynn Rossel
    and Waugh, Charles G(ordon)
Waugh, Carol-Lynn Rossel 1947- 41
Waugh, Dorothy -1996 11
Waugh, Sylvia 1935- 169
Waugh, Virginia
    See Sorensen, Virginia
Wax, Wendy A. 1963- 163
    Earlier sketch in SATA *73*
Wayland, April Halprin 1954- 143
    Earlier sketch in SATA *78*
    See also SAAS *26*
Wayland, Patrick
    See O'Connor, Richard
Wayne, (Anne) Jenifer 1917-1982 32
Wayne, Kyra Petrovskaya 1918- 8
Wayne, Richard
    See Decker, Duane
Wayshak, Deborah Noyes
    See Noyes, Deborah
Waystaff, Simon
    See Swift, Jonathan
Weales, Gerald (Clifford) 1925- 11
Weary, Ogdred
    See Gorey, Edward (St. John)
Weatherford, Carole Boston 1956- 181
    Earlier sketch in SATA *138*
Weatherill, Cat 203
Weatherly, Lee 1967- 192
Weatherly, Myra 1926- 130
Weatherly, Myra S.
    See Weatherly, Myra
Weaver, Harriett E. 1908-1993 65
Weaver, John L. 1949- 42
Weaver, Robyn
    See Conley, Robyn
Weaver, Robyn M.
    See Conley, Robyn
Weaver, Tess 197
Weaver, Ward
    See Mason, F(rancis) van Wyck
Weaver, Will 1950- 161
    Earlier sketches in SATA *88, 109*
Weaver, William Weller
    See Weaver, Will
Weaver-Gelzer, Charlotte 1950- 79

Webb, Christopher
    See Wibberley, Leonard
Webb, Jacqueline
    See Pearce, Margaret
Webb, Jacquelyn
    See Pearce, Margaret
    and Pearce, Margaret
Webb, Jean Francis (III) 1910-1991 35
Webb, Kaye 1914- 60
Webb, Lois Sinaiko 1922- 82
Webb, Margot 1934- 67
Webb, Sharon 1936- 41
Webb, Sophie 1958- 135
Webber, Andrew Lloyd
    See Lloyd Webber, Andrew
Webber, Desiree Morrison 1956- 170
Webber, Irma E(leanor Schmidt)
    1904-1995 14
Weber, Alfons 1921- 8
Weber, Bruce 1942- 120
    Earlier sketch in SATA *73*
Weber, Debora 1955- 58
Weber, EdNah New Rider 1919(?)- 168
Weber, Jill 1950- 127
Weber, Judith E(ichler) 1938- 64
Weber, Ken(neth J.) 1940- 90
Weber, Lenora Mattingly 1895-1971 2
    Obituary 26
Weber, Michael 1945- 87
Weber, Sandra 1961- 158
Weber, William J(ohn) 1927- 14
Webster, Alice Jane Chandler 1876-1916 17
Webster, David 1930- 11
Webster, Frank V. 67
    Earlier sketch in SATA *1*
Webster, Gary
    See Garrison, Webb B(lack)
Webster, James 1925-1981 17
    Obituary 27
Webster, Jean
    See Webster, Alice Jane Chandler
Wechsler, Doug 189
Wechsler, Herman J. 1904-1976
    Obituary 20
Wechter, Nell (Carolyn) Wise 1913-1989 .. 127
    Earlier sketch in SATA *60*
Weck, Thomas L. 1942- 62
Wedd, Kate
    See Gregory, Philippa
Weddle, Ethel Harshbarger 1897-1996 11
Wedekind, Annie 204
Weeks, Sarah 194
    Earlier sketch in SATA *158*
Weems, David B(urnola) 1922- 80
Wees, Frances Shelley 1902-1982 58
Weevers, Peter 1944- 59
Wegen, Ronald 1946-1985 99
Wegman, William (George) 1943- 135
    Earlier sketches in SATA *78, 129*
Wegner, Fritz 1924- 20
Weidhorn, Manfred 1931- 60
Weidt, Maryann N. 1944- 85
Weigel, Jeff 1958- 170
Weigelt, Udo 1960- 201
    Earlier sketch in SATA *168*
Weihs, Erika 1917- 107
    Earlier sketch in SATA *15*
Weik, Mary Hays 1898(?)-1979 3
    Obituary 23
Weil, Ann Yezner 1908-1969 9
Weil, Lisl 1910- 7
Weilerstein, Sadie Rose 1894-1993 3
    Obituary 75
Weill, Cynthia 1959- 167
Wein, Elizabeth E(ve) 1964- 151
    Earlier sketch in SATA *82*
Weinberg, Larry
    See Weinberg, Lawrence (E.)
Weinberg, Lawrence (E.) 92
    Brief entry 48
Weinberger, Tanya 1939- 84

Weiner, Sandra 1922- 14
Weingarten, Violet (Brown) 1915-1976 3
    Obituary 27
Weingartner, Charles 1922- 5
Weinheimer, Beckie 1958- 186
Weinstein, Ellen Slusky 1959- 200
Weinstein, Nina 1951- 73
Weinstock, Robert 1967- 204
Weir, Bob 1947- 76
Weir, Diana (R.) Loiewski 1958- 111
Weir, Joan S(herman) 1928- 99
Weir, LaVada 2
Weir, Rosemary (Green) 1905-1994 21
Weir, Wendy 1949- 76
Weis, Margaret 1948- 164
    Earlier sketch in SATA *38, 92*
Weisberger, Bernard A(llen) 1922- 21
Weisburd, Stefi 1957- 202
Weiser, Marjorie P(hillis) K(atz) 1934- 33
Weisgard, Leonard (Joseph) 1916-2000 85
    Obituary 122
    Earlier sketches in SATA *2, 30*
    See also SAAS *19*
Weiss, Adelle 1920- 18
Weiss, Ann E(dwards) 1943- 69
    Earlier sketch in SATA *30*
    See also SAAS *13*
Weiss, Edna
    See Barth, Edna
Weiss, Ellen 1953- 44
Weiss, Harvey 1922- 76
    Earlier sketches in SATA *1, 27*
    See also CLR *4*
    See also SAAS *19*
Weiss, Jaqueline Shachter 1926- 65
Weiss, Malcolm E. 1928- 3
Weiss, Margaret Edith
    See Weis, Margaret
Weiss, Miriam
    See Schlein, Miriam
Weiss, Mitch 1951- 183
    Earlier sketch in SATA *123*
Weiss, Nicki 1954- 86
    Earlier sketch in SATA *33*
Weiss, Renee Karol 1923- 5
Weissberger, Ela 1930- 181
Weissberger, Ela Stein
    See Weissberger, Ela
Weissenborn, Hellmuth 1898-1982
    Obituary 31
Weitzman, David L. 1936- 172
    Earlier sketch in SATA *122*
Wekesser, Carol A. 1963- 76
Welber, Robert 26
Welch, Amanda (Jane) 1945- 75
Welch, D'Alte Aldridge 1907-1970
    Obituary 27
Welch, Holly 206
Welch, Jean-Louise
    See Kempton, Jean Welch
Welch, Pauline
    See Bodenham, Hilda Morris
Welch, Ronald
    See Felton, Ronald Oliver
Welch, Sheila Kelly 1945- 130
Welch, Willy 1952- 93
Weldin, Frauke 1969- 188
Welford, Sue 1942- 75
Weller, George 1907-2002 31
    Obituary 140
Weller, George Anthony
    See Weller, George
Welling, Peter J. 1947- 135
Wellington, Monica 1957- 157
    Earlier sketches in SATA *67, 99*
Wellman, Alice 1900-1984 51
    Brief entry 36
Wellman, Manly Wade 1903-1986 6
    Obituary 47
Wellman, Paul I. 1898-1966 3

Wellman, Paul Iselin
  See Wellman, Paul I.
Wellman, Sam(uel) 1939- *122*
Wells, H(erbert) G(eorge) 1866-1946 .... *20*
  See also CLR *133*
Wells, Helen
  See Campbell, Hope
Wells, Helen 1910-1986 .... *49*
  Earlier sketch in SATA *2*
Wells, J. Wellington
  See de Camp, L. Sprague
Wells, June
  See Swinford, Betty (June Wells)
Wells, Robert
  See Welsch, Roger L(ee)
Wells, Robert E. *184*
Wells, Rosemary 1943- *156*
  Earlier sketches in SATA *18, 69, 114*
  See also CLR *69*
  See also SAAS *1*
Wells, Susan (Mary) 1951- *78*
Wels, Byron G(erald) 1924-1993 .... *9*
Welsbacher, Anne 1955- *89*
Welsch, Roger L(ee) 1936- *82*
Welsh, David
  See Hills, C.A.R.
Welsh, Mary Flynn 1910(?)-1984
  Obituary *38*
Welsh, T.K. 1956- *184*
Weltner, Linda R(iverly) 1938- *38*
Welton, Jude 1955- *143*
  Earlier sketch in SATA *79*
Welty, S. F.
  See Welty, Susan F.
Welty, Susan F. 1905- *9*
Wemmlinger, Raymond *190*
Wendelin, Rudolph 1910-2000 .... *23*
Weninger, Brigitte 1960- *189*
Wentworth, Robert
  See Hamilton, Edmond
Werlin, Nancy 1961- *161*
  Earlier sketches in SATA *87, 119*
Werner, Elsa Jane
  See Watson, Jane Werner
Werner, Herma 1926- *47*
  Brief entry *41*
Werner, Jane
  See Watson, Jane Werner
Werner, K.
  See Casewit, Curtis W(erner)
Wersba, Barbara 1932- *58*
  Autobiography Feature *103*
  Earlier sketch in SATA *1*
  See also CLR *78*
  See also SAAS *2*
Werstein, Irving 1914(?)-1971 .... *14*
Werth, Kurt 1896-1983 .... *20*
Wesley, Alison
  See Barnes, Michael
Wesley, Kathryn
  See Rusch, Kristine Kathryn
Wesley, Mary (Aline) 1912-2002 .... *66*
Wesley, Valerie Wilson 1947- *168*
  Earlier sketch in SATA *106*
West, Andrew
  See Arthur, Robert, (Jr.)
West, Anna 1938- *40*
West, Barbara
  See Price, Olive
West, Betty 1921- *11*
West, Bruce 1951- *63*
West, C. P.
  See Wodehouse, P(elham) G(renville)
West, Dorothy
  See Benson, Mildred
West, Emily Govan 1919- *38*
West, Emmy
  See West, Emily Govan
West, James
  See Withers, Carl A.

West, Jerry
  See Svenson, Andrew E(dward)
West, (Mary) Jessamyn 1902-1984
  Obituary *37*
West, John
  See Arthur, Robert, (Jr.)
West, Owen
  See Koontz, Dean R.
West, Ward
  See Borland, Harold Glen
Westall, Robert (Atkinson) 1929-1993 .... *69*
  Obituary *75*
  Earlier sketch in SATA *23*
  See also CLR *13*
  See also SAAS *2*
Westaway, Jane 1948- *121*
Westcott, Nadine Bernard 1949- *130*
Westera, Marleen 1962- *187*
Westerberg, Christine 1950- *29*
Westerduin, Anne 1945- *105*
Westerfeld, Scott 1963- *161*
Westervelt, Virginia Veeder 1914-2005 .... *10*
Westheimer, David 1917-2005 .... *14*
  Obituary *170*
Westheimer, David Kaplan
  See Westheimer, David
Westmacott, Mary
  See Christie, Agatha (Mary Clarissa)
Westman, Barbara *70*
Westman, Paul (Wendell) 1956- *39*
Westmoreland, William C. 1914-2005 .... *63*
Westmoreland, William Childs
  See Westmoreland, William C.
Weston, Allen
  See Hogarth, Grace (Weston Allen)
  and Norton, Andre
Weston, Carol 1956- *135*
Weston, Carrie *190*
Weston, John (Harrison) 1932- *21*
Weston, Martha 1947- *119*
  Earlier sketch in SATA *53*
Westphal, Arnold Carl 1897- *57*
Westrup, Hugh *102*
Westwood, Jennifer 1940-2008 .... *10*
  Obituary *192*
Wexler, Jerome (LeRoy) 1923- *14*
Weyland, Jack 1940- *81*
Weyn, Suzanne 1955- *164*
  Earlier sketches in SATA *63, 101*
Weyr, Garret
  See Freymann-Weyr, (Rhoda) Garret
  (Michaela)
Wezyk, Joanna 1966- *82*
Whaley, Joyce Irene 1923- *61*
Whalin, W. Terry 1953- *93*
Wharf, Michael
  See Weller, George
Wharmby, Margot *63*
Wharton, Edith (Newbold Jones) 1862-1937
  See CLR *136*
Whatley, Bruce 1954- *177*
Wheatley, Arabelle 1921- *16*
Wheatley, Nadia 1949- *147*
Wheeler, Cindy 1955- *49*
  Brief entry *40*
Wheeler, Deborah 1947- *83*
Wheeler, Janet D. *1*
Wheeler, Jill C. 1964- *136*
  Earlier sketch in SATA *86*
Wheeler, Jody 1952- *148*
  Earlier sketch in SATA *84*
Wheeler, Lisa 1963- *200*
  Earlier sketch in SATA *162*
Wheeler, Opal 1898- *23*
Whelan, Elizabeth M(urphy) 1943- *14*
Whelan, Gloria 1923- *178*
  Earlier sketches in SATA *85, 128*
  See also CLR *90*
Whelan, Gloria Ann
  See Whelan, Gloria

Whipple, A(ddison) B(eecher) C(olvin)
  1918- *64*
Whipple, Cal
  See Whipple, A(ddison) B(eecher) C(olvin)
Whisp, Kennilworthy
  See Rowling, J.K.
Whistler, Reginald John 1905-1944 .... *30*
Whistler, Rex
  See Whistler, Reginald John
Whitaker, Zai *183*
Whitcher, Susan (Godsil) 1952- *96*
Whitcomb, Jon 1906-1988 .... *10*
  Obituary *56*
Whitcomb, Laura 1958- *171*
White, Anne Terry 1896-1980 .... *2*
White, Bessie (Felstiner) 1892(?)-1986
  Obituary *50*
White, Carolyn 1948- *130*
White, Dale
  See Place, Marian T(empleton)
White, Dori 1919- *10*
White, E. B. 1899-1985 .... *100*
  Obituary *44*
  Earlier sketches in SATA *2, 29*
  See also CLR *107*
White, Eliza Orne 1856-1947
  See YABC *2*
White, Elwyn Brooks
  See White, E. B.
White, Florence M(eiman) 1910- *14*
White, Laurence B(arton), Jr. 1935- *10*
White, Lee *176*
White, Martin 1943- *51*
White, Nancy 1942- *126*
White, Ramy Allison *67*
  Earlier sketch in SATA *1*
White, Robb 1909-1990 .... *83*
  Earlier sketch in SATA *1*
  See also CLR *3*
  See also SAAS *1*
White, Ruth C. 1942- *186*
  Autobiography Feature *186*
  Earlier sketches in SATA *39, 117, 165*
White, T(erence) H(anbury) 1906-1964 .... *12*
  See also CLR *139*
White, Tekla N. 1934- *115*
White, Timothy (Thomas Anthony)
  1952-2002 .... *60*
White, Tom 1923- *148*
White, William, Jr. 1934- *16*
Whitehead, Don(ald) F. 1908-1981 .... *4*
Whitehead, Jenny 1964- *191*
Whitehead, Kathy 1957- *176*
Whitehouse, Arch
  See Whitehouse, Arthur George Joseph
Whitehouse, Arthur George Joseph
  1895-1979 .... *14*
  Obituary *23*
Whitehouse, Elizabeth S(cott) 1893-1968 .... *35*
Whitehouse, Jeanne
  See Peterson, Jeanne Whitehouse
Whitelaw, Nancy 1933- *166*
  Earlier sketch in SATA *76*
Whitesel, Cheryl Aylward *162*
Whiting, Sue 1960- *205*
Whiting, Susan Allana
  See Whiting, Sue
Whitinger, R. D.
  See Place, Marian T(empleton)
Whitley, Mary Ann
  See Sebrey, Mary Ann
Whitley, Peggy 1938- *140*
Whitlock, Pamela 1921(?)-1982
  Obituary *31*
Whitlock, Ralph 1914-1995 .... *35*
Whitman, Alice
  See Marker, Sherry
Whitman, Sylvia (Choate) 1961- *135*
  Earlier sketch in SATA *85*
Whitman, Walt(er) 1819-1892 .... *20*
Whitmore, Arvella 1922- *125*

Whitmore, Benette 1955- 203
Whitney, Alex(andra) 1922- 14
Whitney, David C(harles) 1921- 48
   Brief entry 29
Whitney, Kim Ablon 162
Whitney, Phyllis A. 1903-2008 30
   Obituary 189
   Earlier sketch in SATA 1
   See also CLR 59
Whitney, Phyllis Ayame
   See Whitney, Phyllis A.
Whitney, Phyllis Ayame
   See Whitney, Phyllis A.
Whitney, Sharon 1937- 63
Whitney, Thomas P. 1917-2007 25
   Obituary 189
Whitney, Thomas Porter
   See Whitney, Thomas P.
Whittington, Mary K(athrine) 1941- 75
Whitworth, John 1945- 123
Whybrow, Ian 202
   Earlier sketch in SATA 132
Whyte, Mal(colm Kenneth, Jr.) 1933- 62
Whyte, Mary 1953- 148
   Earlier sketch in SATA 94
Whyte, Ron 1942(?)-1989
   Obituary 63
Whytock, Cherry 177
Wiater, Stanley 1953- 84
Wibbelsman, Charles J(oseph) 1945- 59
Wibberley, Leonard 1915-1983 45
   Obituary 36
   Earlier sketch in SATA 2
   See also CLR 3
Wibberley, Leonard Patrick O'Connor
   See Wibberley, Leonard
Wiberg, Harald (Albin) 1908- 93
   Brief entry 40
Wick, Walter 1953- 148
Wickberg, Susan
   See Rottman, S.L.
Wickens, Elaine 86
Wicker, Ireene 1905(?)-1987
   Obituary 55
Wickstrom, Sylvie 1960- 169
Wickstrom, Thor 1960- 200
Widdemer, Mabel Cleland 1902-1964 5
Widener, Terry 1950- 105
Widerberg, Siv 1931- 10
Wiebe, Rudy 1934- 156
Wiebe, Rudy Henry
   See Wiebe, Rudy
Wieler, Diana (Jean) 1961- 109
Wiener, Lori 1956- 84
Wier, Ester (Alberti) 1910-2000 3
Wiese, Kurt 1887-1974 36
   Obituary 24
   Earlier sketch in SATA 3
   See also CLR 86
Wiesel, Elie 1928- 56
Wiesel, Eliezer
   See Wiesel, Elie
Wiesner, David 1956- 181
   Earlier sketches in SATA 72, 117, 139
   See also CLR 84
Wiesner, Portia
   See Takakjian, Portia
Wiesner, William 1899-1984 5
Wiggers, Raymond 1952- 82
Wiggin, Eric E. 1939- 167
   Earlier sketch in SATA 88
Wiggin, Eric Ellsworth 1939-
   See Wiggin, Eric E.
Wiggin (Riggs), Kate Douglas (Smith)
   1856-1923
   See YABC 1
   See also CLR 52
Wiggins, VeraLee (Chesnut) 1928-1995 89

Wight, James Alfred 1916-1995 135
   Brief entry 44
   Earlier sketch in SATA 86
   See also CLR 80
Wignell, Edel 1936- 69
Wijnberg, Ellen 85
Wikland, Ilon 1930- 93
   Brief entry 32
Wikler, Madeline 1943- 114
Wilber, Donald N(ewton) 1907-1997 35
Wilbur, C. Keith 1923- 27
Wilbur, Frances 1921- 107
Wilbur, Helen L. 1948- 204
Wilbur, Richard 1921- 108
   Earlier sketch in SATA 9
Wilbur, Richard Purdy
   See Wilbur, Richard
Wilburn, Kathy 1948- 68
Wilcox, Charlotte 1948- 72
Wilcox, R(uth) Turner 1888-1970 36
Wilcox, Roger
   See Collins, Paul
Wild, Jocelyn 1941- 46
Wild, Kate 1954- 192
Wild, Margaret 1948- 197
   Earlier sketch in SATA 151
Wild, Robin (Evans) 1936- 46
Wild, Robyn 1947- 117
Wilde, D. Gunther
   See Hurwood, Bernhardt J.
Wilde, Oscar 1854(?)-1900 24
   See also CLR 114
Wilde, Oscar Fingal O'Flahertie Willis
   See Wilde, Oscar
Wilder, Buck
   See Smith, Tim(othy R.)
Wilder, Laura (Elizabeth) Ingalls
   1867-1957 100
   Earlier sketches in SATA 15, 29
   See also CLR 111
Wildsmith, Brian 1930- 124
   Earlier sketches in SATA 16, 69
   See also CLR 52
   See also SAAS 5
Wiles, Deborah 171
Wilhelm, Doug 1952- 190
Wilhelm, Hans 1945- 196
   Autobiography Feature 196
   Earlier sketches in SATA 58, 135
   See also CLR 46
   See also SAAS 21
Wilkie, Katharine E(lliott) 1904-1980 31
Wilkin, Eloise 1904-1987 49
   Obituary 54
Wilkins, Frances 1923- 14
Wilkins, Kim 147
Wilkins, Marilyn (Ruth) 1926- 30
Wilkins, Marne
   See Wilkins, Marilyn (Ruth)
Wilkins, Mary Huiskamp 1926- 2
   See also CLR 42
Wilkins, Mary Huiskamp Calhoun
   See Wilkins, Mary Huiskamp
Wilkins, Rose 180
Wilkinson, (Thomas) Barry 1923- 50
   Brief entry 32
Wilkinson, Beth 1925- 80
Wilkinson, Brenda 1946- 91
   Earlier sketch in SATA 14
   See also CLR 20
Wilkinson, (John) Burke 1913-2000 4
Wilkinson, Sylvia 1940- 56
   Brief entry 39
Wilkon, Jozef 1930- 133
   Earlier sketches in SATA 31, 71
Wilkowski, Sue 193
Wilks, Michael Thomas 1947- 44
Wilks, Mike
   See Wilks, Michael Thomas
Will
   See Lipkind, William

Willard, Barbara (Mary) 1909-1994 74
   Earlier sketch in SATA 17
   See also CLR 2
   See also SAAS 5
Willard, Mildred Wilds 1911-1978 14
Willard, Nancy 1936- 191
   Brief entry 30
   Earlier sketches in SATA 37, 71, 127
   See also CLR 5
Willcox, Isobel 1907-1996 42
Willems, Mo 180
   Earlier sketch in SATA 154
   See also CLR 114
Willett, Edward 1959- 115
Willett, Edward C.
   See Willett, Edward
Willey, Bee 184
Willey, Margaret 1950- 86
Willey, Robert
   See Ley, Willy
Willhoite, Michael A. 1946- 71
William, Kate
   See Armstrong, Jennifer
Williams, Arlene 171
Williams, Barbara 1925- 107
   Earlier sketch in SATA 11
   See also CLR 48
   See also SAAS 16
Williams, Barbara 1937- 62
Williams, Beryl
   See Epstein, Beryl
Williams, Brian (Peter) 1943- 54
Williams, Carol Lynch 1959- 110
Williams, Charles
   See Collier, James Lincoln
Williams, Clyde C. 1881-1974 8
   Obituary 27
Williams, Coe
   See Harrison, C(hester) William
Williams, Colleen Madonna Flood 1963- .. 156
Williams, Cynthia G. 1958- 123
Williams, Dar 1967- 168
Williams, Donna Reilly 1945- 83
Williams, Dorothy
   See Williams, Marcia
Williams, Dorothy Snowden
   See Williams, Dar
Williams, Eric (Ernest) 1911-1983 14
   Obituary 38
Williams, Ferelith Eccles
   See Eccles Williams, Ferelith
Williams, Frances B.
   See Browin, Frances Williams
Williams, Garth (Montgomery) 1912-1996 .. 66
   Obituary 90
   Earlier sketch in SATA 18
   See also CLR 57
   See also SAAS 7
Williams, Guy R(ichard) 1920- 11
Williams, Hawley
   See Heyliger, William
Williams, Helen 1948- 77
Williams, J. R.
   See Williams, Jeanne
Williams, J. Walker
   See Wodehouse, P(elham) G(renville)
Williams, Jay 1914-1978 41
   Obituary 24
   Earlier sketch in SATA 3
   See also CLR 8
Williams, Jeanne 1930- 5
Williams, Jenny 1939- 60
Williams, Karen Lynn 1952- 99
   Earlier sketch in SATA 66
Williams, Kit 1946(?)- 44
   See also CLR 4
Williams, Laura E. 180
Williams, Laura Ellen
   See Williams, Laura E.
Williams, L.E.
   See Williams, Laura Ellen

Williams, Leslie 1941- *42*
Williams, Linda 1948- *59*
Williams, Louise Bonino 1904(?)-1984
  Obituary *39*
Williams, Lynn
  See Hale, Arlene
Williams, Marcia 1945- *159*
  Earlier sketches in SATA *71, 97*
Williams, Marcia Dorothy
  See Williams, Marcia
Williams, Margery
  See Bianco, Margery Williams
Williams, Mark
  See Arthur, Robert, (Jr.)
Williams, Mark London 1959- *140*
Williams, Maureen 1951- *12*
Williams, Michael
  See St. John, Wylly Folk
Williams, Patrick J.
  See Griffin, W.E.B.
Williams, Pete
  See Faulknor, Cliff(ord Vernon)
Williams, S. P.
  See Hart, Virginia
Williams, Sam *177*
  Earlier sketch in SATA *124*
Williams, Selma R(uth) 1925- *14*
Williams, Sherley Anne 1944-1999 .... *78*
  Obituary *116*
Williams, Sheron 1955- *77*
Williams, Shirley
  See Williams, Sherley Anne
Williams, Slim
  See Williams, Clyde C.
Williams, Sophy 1965- *135*
Williams, Susan
  See Beckhorn, Susan Williams
Williams, Suzanne 1953- *202*
  Earlier sketch in SATA *71*
Williams, Ursula Moray
  See Moray Williams, Ursula
Williams, Vera B(aker) 1927- *102*
  Brief entry *33*
  Earlier sketch in SATA *53*
  See also CLR *9*
Williams-Andriani, Renee 1963- *98*
Williams-Ellis, (Mary) Amabel (Nassau
  Strachey) 1894-1984 .... *29*
  Obituary *41*
Williams-Garcia, Rita 1957- *160*
  Earlier sketch in SATA *98*
  See also CLR *36*
Williamson, Gwyneth 1965- *109*
Williamson, Henry (William) 1895-1977 ..... *37*
  Obituary *30*
Williamson, Joanne S(mall) 1926- *122*
  Earlier sketch in SATA *3*
Williamson, Melanie *196*
Willis, Charles
  See Clarke, Arthur C.
Willis, Connie 1945- *110*
  See also CLR *66*
Willis, Jeanne 1959- *195*
  Earlier sketches in SATA *61, 123*
Willis, Jeanne Mary
  See Willis, Jeanne
Willis, Meredith Sue 1946- *101*
Willis, Nancy Carol 1952- *139*
  Earlier sketch in SATA *93*
Willis, Paul J. 1955- *113*
Willms, Russ *95*
Willoughby, Lee Davis
  See Avallone, Michael (Angelo, Jr.)
  and Brandner, Gary (Phil)
  and Deming, Richard
  and DeAndrea, William L(ouis)
  and Laymon, Richard (Carl)
  and Streib, Dan(iel Thomas)
  and Toombs, John
  and Webb, Jean Francis (III)

Willson, Robina Beckles
  See Beckles Willson, Robina
Wilma, Dana
  See Faralla, Dana
Wilsdorf, Anne 1954- *191*
Wilson, April *80*
Wilson, Barbara Ker
  See Ker Wilson, Barbara
Wilson, Beth P(ierre) *8*
Wilson, Budge 1927- *55*
  Brief entry *51*
Wilson, Carletta 1951- *81*
Wilson, Carter 1941- *6*
Wilson, Charles Morrow 1905-1977 .... *30*
Wilson, Christopher B. 1910(?)-1985
  Obituary *46*
Wilson, Darryl B(abe) 1939- *90*
Wilson, Diane Lee *172*
Wilson, Dirk
  See Pohl, Frederik
Wilson, Dorothy Clarke 1904-2003 .... *16*
Wilson, Edward A(rthur) 1886-1970 .... *38*
Wilson, Ellen (Janet Cameron) (?)-1976 .... *9*
  Obituary *26*
Wilson, Eric (H.) 1940- *34*
  Brief entry *32*
Wilson, Erica *51*
Wilson, Forrest 1918- *27*
Wilson, Gahan 1930- *35*
  Brief entry *27*
Wilson, Gina 1943- *85*
  Brief entry *34*
  Earlier sketch in SATA *36*
Wilson, (Leslie) Granville 1912- *14*
Wilson, Hazel (Hutchins) 1898-1992 .... *3*
  Obituary *73*
Wilson, J(erry) M. 1964- *121*
Wilson, Jacqueline 1945- *199*
  Brief entry *52*
  Earlier sketches in SATA *61, 102, 153*
Wilson, John 1922- *22*
Wilson, John 1951- *182*
Wilson, John Alexander
  See Wilson, John
Wilson, Johnniece Marshall 1944- *75*
Wilson, Jonathan 1950- *181*
Wilson, Joyce M. *84*
  Earlier sketch in SATA *21*
  See also SAAS *24*
Wilson, Karma *174*
Wilson, Leslie 1952- *166*
Wilson, Linda Miller 1936- *116*
Wilson, Lionel 1924-2003 .... *33*
  Brief entry *31*
  Obituary *144*
Wilson, Marjorie
  See Wilson, Budge
Wilson, Martin 1973- *205*
Wilson, Maurice (Charles John) 1914- *46*
Wilson, Nancy Hope 1947- *138*
  Earlier sketch in SATA *81*
Wilson, Nathan D.
  See Wilson, N.D.
Wilson, N.D. 1978- *194*
Wilson, Nick
  See Ellis, Edward S.
Wilson, Phil 1948- *181*
Wilson, Ron(ald William) 1941- *38*
Wilson, Sarah 1934- *142*
  Earlier sketch in SATA *50*
Wilson, Tom 1931- *33*
  Brief entry *30*
Wilson, Troy 1970- *169*
Wilson, Walt(er N.) 1939- *14*
Wilson-Max, Ken 1965- *170*
  Earlier sketch in SATA *93*
Wilton, Elizabeth 1937- *14*
Wilton, Hal
  See Pepper, Frank S.
Wilwerding, Walter Joseph 1891-1966 .... *9*

Wimmer, Mike 1961- *194*
  Earlier sketch in SATA *70*
Winborn, Marsha (Lynn) 1947- *75*
Winch, John 1944- *165*
  Earlier sketch in SATA *117*
Winchester, James H(ugh) 1917-1985 .... *30*
  Obituary *45*
Winchester, Stanley
  See Youd, Samuel
Windawi, Thura al- 1983(?)- *165*
Winders, Gertrude Hecker -1987 .... *3*
Windham, Basil
  See Wodehouse, P(elham) G(renville)
Windham, Kathryn T(ucker) 1918- *14*
Windham, Sophie *184*
Windling, Terri 1958- *151*
Windrow, Martin
  See Windrow, Martin Clive
Windrow, Martin C.
  See Windrow, Martin Clive
Windrow, Martin Clive 1944- *68*
Windsor, Claire
  See Hamerstrom, Frances
Windsor, Linda 1950- *124*
Windsor, Patricia 1938- *78*
  Earlier sketch in SATA *30*
  See also SAAS *19*
Wineman-Marcus, Irene 1952- *81*
Winer, Yvonne 1934- *120*
Winerip, Michael *175*
Winfield, Arthur M.
  See Stratemeyer, Edward L.
Winfield, Edna
  See Stratemeyer, Edward L.
Winfield, Julia
  See Armstrong, Jennifer
Wing, Natasha 1960- *200*
  Earlier sketch in SATA *82*
Winick, Judd 1970- *124*
Winks, Robin William 1930-2003 .... *61*
Winn, Alison
  See Wharmby, Margot
Winn, Chris 1952- *42*
Winn, Janet Bruce 1928- *43*
Winn, Marie 1936(?)- *38*
Winnick, Karen B(eth) B(inkoff) 1946- *51*
Winn-Lederer, Ilene *198*
Winslow, Barbara 1947- *91*
Winstead, Rosie *180*
Winston, Clara 1921-1983 .... *54*
  Obituary *39*
Winston, Richard 1917-1979 .... *54*
Winston, Sherri 1964(?)- *201*
Winter, Janet 1926- *126*
Winter, Jeanette 1939- *184*
  Earlier sketch in SATA *151*
Winter, Jonah 1962- *179*
Winter, Milo (Kendall) 1888-1956 .... *21*
Winter, Paula Cecelia 1929- *48*
Winter, R. R.
  See Winterbotham, R(ussell) R(obert)
Winter, Susan *182*
Winterbotham, R(ussell) R(obert)
  1904-1971 .... *10*
Winterbotham, Russ
  See Winterbotham, R(ussell) R(obert)
Winterfeld, Henry 1901-1990 .... *55*
Winters, J. C.
  See Cross, Gilbert B.
Winters, Jon
  See Cross, Gilbert B.
Winters, Katherine 1936- *153*
  Earlier sketch in SATA *103*
Winters, Kay
  See Winters, Katherine
Winters, Nina 1944- *62*
Winters, Paul A. 1965- *106*
Winterson, Jeanette 1959- *190*
Winterton, Gayle
  See Adams, William Taylor

Winthrop, Elizabeth 1948- *164*
　Autobiography Feature *116*
　Earlier sketch in SATA *8, 76*
　See also CLR *89*
Winton, Ian (Kenneth) 1960- *76*
Winton, Tim 1960- *98*
Wintz-Litty, Julie
　See Litty, Julie
Wirt, Ann
　See Benson, Mildred
Wirt, Mildred A.
　See Benson, Mildred
Wirtenberg, Patricia Z. 1932-2007 .... *10*
Wirtenberg, Patricia Zarrella
　See Wirtenberg, Patricia Z.
Wirth, Beverly 1938- *63*
Wirths, Claudine (Turner) G(ibson)
　1926-2000 .... *104*
　Earlier sketch in SATA *64*
Wise, Bill 1958- *191*
Wise, Lenny
　See Wise, Leonard
Wise, Leonard 1940- *167*
Wise, Leonard A.
　See Wise, Leonard
Wise, Leonard Allan
　See Wise, Leonard
Wise, William 1923- *163*
　Earlier sketch in SATA *4*
Wise, Winifred E. *2*
Wiseman, Ann (Sayre) 1926- *31*
Wiseman, B(ernard) 1922-1995 .... *4*
Wiseman, David 1916- *43*
　Brief entry *40*
Wishinsky, Frieda 1948- *166*
　Earlier sketches in SATA *70, 112*
Wisler, G(ary) Clifton 1950- *103*
　Brief entry *46*
　Earlier sketch in SATA *58*
Wismer, Donald (Richard) 1946- *59*
Wisner, Bill
　See Wisner, William L.
Wisner, William L. 1914(?)-1983 .... *42*
Wisnewski, David 1953-2002
　See Wisniewski, David
Wisniewski, David 1953-2002 .... *95*
　Obituary *139*
　See also CLR *51*
Wister, Owen 1860-1938 .... *62*
Witham, (Phillip) Ross 1917- *37*
Withers, Carl A. 1900-1970 .... *14*
Withers, Pam 1956- *182*
Withrow, Sarah 1966- *199*
　Earlier sketch in SATA *124*
Witt, Dick 1948- *80*
Witt, Shirley Hill 1934- *17*
Wittanen, Etolin 1907- *55*
Wittels, Harriet Joan 1938- *31*
Wittig, Susan
　See Albert, Susan Wittig
Wittlinger, Ellen 1948- *189*
　Autobiography Feature *128*
　Earlier sketches in SATA *83, 122*
Wittman, Sally (Anne Christensen) 1941- *30*
Witty, Paul 1898-1976 .... *50*
　Obituary *30*
Wodehouse, P(elham) G(renville)
　1881-1975 .... *22*
Wodge, Dreary
　See Gorey, Edward (St. John)
Woelfle, Gretchen 1945- *145*
Wohlberg, Meg 1905-1990 .... *41*
　Obituary *66*
Wohlrabe, Raymond A. 1900-1977 .... *4*
Wohnoutka, Mike *195*
Wojciechowska, Maia (Teresa) 1927-2002 ... *83*
　Autobiography Feature *104*
　Obituary *134*
　Earlier sketches in SATA *1, 28*
　See also CLR *1*
　See also SAAS *1*

Wojciechowski, Susan *126*
　Earlier sketch in SATA *78*
Wojnarowski, Adrian 1970- *190*
Wolcott, Patty 1929- *14*
Wold, Allen L. 1943- *64*
Wold, Jo Anne 1938- *30*
Woldin, Beth Weiner 1955- *34*
Wolf, Allan 1963- *192*
Wolf, Bernard 1930- *102*
　Brief entry *37*
Wolf, Erica (Van Varick) 1978- *156*
Wolf, Gita 1956- *101*
Wolf, Janet 1957- *78*
Wolf, J.M.
　See Wolf, Joan M.
Wolf, Joan M. 1966- *193*
Wolf, Sallie 1950- *205*
　Earlier sketch in SATA *80*
Wolfe, Art 1952- *76*
Wolfe, Burton H. 1932- *5*
Wolfe, Gene 1931- *165*
　Earlier sketch in SATA *118*
Wolfe, Gene Rodman
　See Wolfe, Gene
Wolfe, Gillian *199*
Wolfe, Louis 1905-1985 .... *8*
　Obituary *133*
Wolfe, Rinna (Evelyn) 1925- *38*
Wolfenden, George
　See Beardmore, George
Wolfer, Dianne 1961- *167*
　Autobiography Feature *117*
　Earlier sketch in SATA *104*
Wolff, Alexander (Nikolaus) 1957- *137*
　Earlier sketch in SATA *63*
Wolff, Ashley 1956- *203*
　Earlier sketches in SATA *50, 81, 155*
Wolff, Diane 1945- *27*
Wolff, Ferida 1946- *164*
　Earlier sketch in SATA *79*
Wolff, Jennifer Ashley
　See Wolff, Ashley
Wolff, Nancy *202*
Wolff, Robert Jay 1905-1977 .... *10*
Wolff, Sonia
　See Levitin, Sonia
Wolff, Virginia Euwer 1937- *137*
　Earlier sketch in SATA *78*
　See also CLR *62*
Wolfman, Judy 1933- *138*
Wolfson, Evelyn 1937- *62*
Wolitzer, Hilma 1930- *31*
Wolkoff, Judie (Edwards) *93*
　Brief entry *37*
Wolkstein, Diane 1942- *138*
　Earlier sketches in SATA *7, 82*
Wollheim, Donald A(llen) 1914-1990
　Obituary *69*
Wolny, P.
　See Janeczko, Paul B(ryan)
Wolters, Richard A. 1920-1993 .... *35*
Wondriska, William 1931- *6*
Wong, Jade Snow 1922-2006 .... *112*
　Obituary *175*
Wong, Janet S. 1962- *148*
　Earlier sketch in SATA *98*
　See also CLR *94*
Wood, Anne (Savage) 1937- *64*
Wood, Audrey *198*
　Brief entry *44*
　Earlier sketches in SATA *50, 81, 139*
　See also CLR *26*
Wood, Catherine
　See Etchison, Birdie L(ee)
Wood, David 1944- *87*
Wood, Don 1945- *50*
　Brief entry *44*
　See also CLR *26*
Wood, Douglas 1951- *180*
　Earlier sketches in SATA *81, 132*

Wood, Douglas Eric
　See Wood, Douglas
Wood, Edgar A(llardyce) 1907-1998 .... *14*
Wood, Esther
　See Brady, Esther Wood
Wood, Frances Elizabeth *34*
Wood, Frances M. 1951- *97*
Wood, James Playsted 1905- *1*
Wood, Jenny 1955- *88*
Wood, John Norris 1930- *85*
Wood, June Rae 1946- *120*
　Earlier sketch in SATA *79*
　See also CLR *82*
Wood, Kerry
　See Wood, Edgar A(llardyce)
Wood, Kim Marie *134*
Wood, Laura N.
　See Roper, Laura (Newbold) Wood
Wood, Linda C(arol) 1945- *59*
Wood, Marcia 1956- *80*
Wood, Marcia Mae
　See Wood, Marcia
Wood, Nancy
　See Wood, Nancy C.
Wood, Nancy C. 1936- *178*
　Earlier sketch in SATA *6*
Wood, Nuria
　See Nobisso, Josephine
Wood, Owen 1929- *64*
Wood, Phyllis Anderson 1923- *33*
　Brief entry *30*
Wood, Richard 1949- *110*
Wood, Tim(othy William Russell) 1946- *88*
Wood, Wallace 1927-1981
　Obituary *33*
Woodard, Carol 1929- *14*
Woodburn, John Henry 1914- *11*
Woodbury, David Oakes 1896-1981 .... *62*
Woodford, Peggy 1937- *25*
Woodhouse, Barbara (Blackburn)
　1910-1988 .... *63*
Woodhull, Ann Love *194*
Wooding, Chris 1977- *166*
Wooding, Sharon
　See Wooding, Sharon L(ouise)
Wooding, Sharon L(ouise) 1943- *66*
Woodman, Allen 1954- *76*
Woodrich, Mary Neville 1915- *2*
Woodruff, Elvira 1951- *162*
　Earlier sketches in SATA *70, 106*
Woodruff, Joan Leslie 1953- *104*
Woodruff, Liza 1971(?)- *182*
Woodruff, Marian
　See Goudge, Eileen
Woodruff, Noah 1977- *86*
Woods, George A(llan) 1926-1988 .... *30*
　Obituary *57*
Woods, Geraldine 1948- *111*
　Brief entry *42*
　Earlier sketch in SATA *56*
Woods, Harold 1945- *56*
　Brief entry *42*
Woods, Lawrence
　See Lowndes, Robert A(ugustine) W(ard)
Woods, Margaret 1921- *2*
Woods, Nat
　See Stratemeyer, Edward L.
Woods, Titania
　See Weatherly, Lee
Woodson, Jack
　See Woodson, John Waddie Jr.
Woodson, Jacqueline 1964- *189*
　Earlier sketches in SATA *94, 139*
　See also CLR *49*
Woodson, Jacqueline Amanda
　See Woodson, Jacqueline
Woodson, John Waddie Jr. 1913- *10*
Woodtor, Dee
　See Woodtor, Delores Parmer
Woodtor, Dee Parmer 1945(?)-2002
　See Woodtor, Delores Parmer

Woodtor, Delores Parmer 1945-2002 .... *93*
Wood-Trost, Lucille
  See Trost, Lucille W(ood)
Woodward, (Landon) Cleveland 1900-1986 . *10*
  Obituary *48*
Woodworth, Chris 1957- *168*
Woodworth, Viki 1952- *127*
Woody, Regina Jones 1894-1983 .... *3*
Woodyadd, Charlotte
  See Hough, Charlotte
Woog, Adam 1953- *125*
  Earlier sketch in SATA *84*
Wooldridge, Connie Nordhielm 1950- *143*
  Earlier sketch in SATA *92*
Wooldridge, Frosty 1947- *140*
Wooldridge, Rhoda 1906-1988 .... *22*
Wooley, Susan Frelick 1945- *113*
Woolf, Paula 1950- *104*
Woolfe, Angela 1976- *169*
Woolley, Catherine 1904-2005 .... *3*
  Obituary *166*
Woolman, Steven 1969-2004 .... *163*
  Earlier sketch in SATA *90*
Woolsey, Janette 1904-1989 .... *3*
  Obituary *131*
Worcester, Donald E(mmet) 1915- *18*
Word, Reagan 1944- *103*
Work, Virginia 1946- *57*
  Brief entry *45*
Worline, Bonnie Bess 1914- *14*
Wormell, Christopher 1955- *154*
  Earlier sketch in SATA *103*
Wormell, Mary 1959- *96*
Wormser, Richard 1933- *106*
  Autobiography Feature *118*
  See also SAAS *26*
Wormser, Sophie 1897-1979 .... *22*
Worth, Richard 1945- *59*
  Brief entry *46*
Worth, Valerie 1933-1994 .... *81*
  Earlier sketches in SATA *8, 70*
  See also CLR *21*
Worthington, Leonie 1956- *200*
Wortis, Avi
  See Avi
Wortis, Edward Irving
  See Avi
Wosmek, Frances 1917- *29*
Woychuk, Denis 1953- *71*
Wrede, Patricia C(ollins) 1953- *146*
  Earlier sketch in SATA *67*
Wriggins, Sally Hovey 1922- *17*
Wright, Alexandra 1979- *103*
Wright, Betty Ren 1927- *109*
  Brief entry *48*
  Earlier sketch in SATA *63*
Wright, Cliff 1963- *168*
  Earlier sketch in SATA *76*
Wright, Courtni
  See Wright, Courtni C(rump)
Wright, Courtni C(rump) 1950- *84*
Wright, Courtni Crump
  See Wright, Courtni C(rump)
Wright, Dare 1914(?)-2001 .... *21*
  Obituary *124*
Wright, David K. 1943- *112*
  Earlier sketch in SATA *73*
Wright, Elinor
  See Lyon, Elinor
Wright, Enid Meadowcroft (LaMonte)
  1898-1966 .... *3*
Wright, Esmond 1915-2003 .... *10*
Wright, Frances Fitzpatrick 1897-1982 .... *10*
Wright, J. B.
  See Barkan, Joanne
Wright, Judith 1915-2000 .... *14*
  Obituary *121*
Wright, Judith Arundell
  See Wright, Judith
Wright, Katrina
  See Gater, Dilys

Wright, Kenneth
  See del Rey, Lester
Wright, Kit 1944- *87*
Wright, Leslie B(ailey) 1959- *91*
Wright, Michael 1954- *198*
Wright, Nancy Means *38*
Wright, R(obert) H(amilton) 1906- *6*
Wright, Rachel *134*
Wright, Susan Kimmel 1950- *97*
Wrightfrierson
  See Wright-Frierson, Virginia (Marguerite)
Wright-Frierson, Virginia (Marguerite)
  1949- *110*
  Earlier sketch in SATA *58*
Wrightson, (Alice) Patricia 1921- *112*
  Earlier sketches in SATA *8, 66*
  See also CLR *14*
  See also SAAS *4*
Wroble, Lisa A. 1963- *134*
Wrongo, I.B.
  See Katz, Alan
Wronker, Lili
  See Wronker, Lili Cassel
Wronker, Lili Cassel 1924- *10*
Wryde, Dogear
  See Gorey, Edward (St. John)
Wu, Elizabeth
  See Wu, Liz
Wu, Liz *184*
Wu, Norbert 1961- *155*
  Earlier sketch in SATA *101*
Wulf, Linda Press *205*
Wulffson, Don 1943- *155*
  Earlier sketches in SATA *32, 88*
Wulffson, Don L.
  See Wulffson, Don
Wummer, Amy 1955- *201*
Wunderli, Stephen 1958- *79*
Wunsch, Josephine (McLean) 1914- *64*
Wuorio, Eva-Lis 1918- *34*
  Brief entry *28*
Wurts, Janny 1953- *98*
Wyatt, B. D.
  See Robinson, Spider
Wyatt, David 1968- *185*
Wyatt, Jane
  See Bradbury, Bianca (Ryley)
Wyatt, Melissa 1963- *177*
Wyeth, Betsy James 1921- *41*
Wyeth, N(ewell) C(onvers) 1882-1945 .... *17*
  See also CLR *106*
Wyler, Rose 1909-2000 .... *18*
  Obituary *121*
Wylie, Betty Jane *48*
Wylie, Laura
  See Matthews, Patricia
Wylie, Laurie
  See Matthews, Patricia
Wyllie, Stephen *86*
Wyman, Andrea *75*
Wyman, Carolyn 1956- *83*
Wymer, Norman (George) 1911- *25*
Wynard, Talbot
  See Hamilton, Charles (Harold St. John)
Wyndham, John
  See Harris, John (Wyndham Parkes Lucas)
  Beynon
Wyndham, Lee
  See Hyndman, Jane Andrews Lee
Wyndham, Robert
  See Hyndman, Robert Utley
Wynne-Jones, Tim 1948- *186*
  Autobiography Feature *136*
  Earlier sketches in SATA *67, 96, 136*
  See also CLR *58*
Wynne-Jones, Timothy
  See Wynne-Jones, Tim
Wynter, Edward (John) 1914- *14*
Wynyard, Talbot
  See Hamilton, Charles (Harold St. John)

Wyss, Johann David Von 1743-1818 .... *29*
  Brief entry *27*
  See also CLR *92*
Wyss, Thelma Hatch 1934- *202*
  Earlier sketches in SATA *10, 140*

X

Xavier, Father
  See Hurwood, Bernhardt J.
Xuan, YongSheng 1952- *116*
  Autobiography Feature *119*

Y

Yaccarino, Dan *192*
  Earlier sketch in SATA *141*
Yadin, (Rav-Aloof) Yigael 1917-1984 .... *55*
Yaffe, Alan
  See Yorinks, Arthur
Yagher, Kevin 1962- *143*
Yakovetic, (Joseph Sandy) 1952- *59*
Yakovetic, Joe
  See Yakovetic, (Joseph Sandy)
Yamada, Utako 1963- *188*
Yamaguchi, Marianne (Illenberger) 1936- *7*
Yamaka, Sara 1978- *92*
Yamanaka, Lois-Ann 1961- *166*
Yamasaki, Katie *206*
Yancey, Diane 1951- *138*
  Earlier sketch in SATA *81*
Yancey, Richard *193*
Yancey, Rick
  See Yancey, Richard
Yang, Belle 1960- *170*
Yang, James 1960- *190*
Yang, Jay 1941- *12*
Yang, Mingyi 1943- *72*
Yarbrough, Camille 1938- *79*
  See also CLR *29*
Yarbrough, Ira 1910(?)-1983
  Obituary *35*
Yaroslava
  See Mills, Yaroslava Surmach
Yarrow, Peter 1938- *195*
Yashima, Taro
  See Iwamatsu, Jun Atsushi
Yates, Elizabeth 1905-2001 .... *68*
  Obituary *128*
  Earlier sketch in SATA *4*
  See also SAAS *6*
Yates, Janelle K(aye) 1957- *77*
Yates, John 1939- *74*
Yates, Philip 1958- *149*
  Earlier sketch in SATA *92*
Yates, Raymond F(rancis) 1895-1966 .... *31*
Yaukey, Grace S(ydenstricker) 1899-1994 ... *80*
  Earlier sketch in SATA *5*
Yazzie, Johnson 1946- *205*
Ye, Ting-xing 1952- *106*
Yeahpau, Thomas M. 1975- *187*
Yeakley, Marjory Hall 1908- *21*
Yeatman, Linda 1938- *42*
Yee, Brenda Shannon *133*
Yee, Lisa 1959- *160*
Yee, Paul (R.) 1956- *143*
  Earlier sketches in SATA *67, 96*
  See also CLR *44*
Yee, Tammy *206*
Yee, Wong Herbert 1953- *172*
  Earlier sketches in SATA *78, 115*
Yeh, Chun-Chan 1914- *79*
Ye Junjian
  See Yeh, Chun-Chan
Yelchin, Eugene 1956- *196*
Yenawine, Philip 1942- *85*
Yensid, Retlaw
  See Disney, Walt(er Elias)

Author Index

Yeo, Wilma (Lethem) 1918-1994 .... *81*
  Earlier sketch in SATA *24*
Yeoman, John 1934- *80*
  Earlier sketch in SATA *28*
  See also CLR *46*
Yep, Kathleen S. *203*
Yep, Laurence 1948- *176*
  Earlier sketches in SATA *7, 69, 123*
  See also CLR *132*
Yep, Laurence Michael
  See Yep, Laurence
Yepsen, Roger B(ennet), Jr. 1947- *59*
Yerian, Cameron John *21*
Yerian, Margaret A. *21*
Yerxa, Leo 1947- *181*
Yetska
  See Ironside, Jetske
Yezerski, Thomas F. 1969- *190*
Yin *194*
Ylvisaker, Anne 1965(?)- *172*
Yoder, Carolyn P. 1953- *149*
Yoder, Carolyn Patricia
  See Yoder, Carolyn P.
Yoder, Dorothy Meenen 1921- *96*
Yoder, Dot
  See Yoder, Dorothy Meenen
Yoder, Walter D. 1933- *88*
Yolen, Jane 1939- *194*
  Autobiography Feature *111*
  Earlier sketches in SATA *4, 40, 75, 112, 158*
  See also CLR *44*
  See also SAAS *1*
Yolen, Jane Hyatt
  See Yolen, Jane
Yonezu, Yusuke *196*
Yonge, Charlotte (Mary) 1823-1901 .... *17*
Yoo, Paula 1969(?)- *174*
Yoo, Taeeun *191*
Yoon, Salina 1972- *204*
Yorinks, Adrienne 1956- *171*
Yorinks, Arthur 1953- *200*
  Earlier sketches in SATA *33, 49, 85, 144*
  See also CLR *20*
York, Alison
  See Nicole, Christopher (Robin)
York, Andrew
  See Nicole, Christopher (Robin)
York, Carol Beach 1928- *77*
  Earlier sketch in SATA *6*
York, Rebecca
  See Buckholtz, Eileen (Garber)
  and Glick, Ruth (Burtnick)
York, Simon
  See Heinlein, Robert A.
Yoshida, Toshi 1911- *77*
Yoshikawa, Sachiko *181*
Yost, Edna 1889-1971
  Obituary *26*
Youd, C. S.
  See Youd, Samuel
Youd, Samuel 1922- *135*
  Brief entry *30*
  Earlier sketch in SATA *47*
  See also CLR *2*
  See also SAAS *6*
Young, Amy L. *185*
Young, Anne Mortimer
  See Mortimer, Anne
Young, Bob
  See Young, Robert W(illiam)
  and Young, James Robert
Young, Carol 1945- *102*
Young, Catherine
  See Olds, Helen Diehl
Young, Clarence
  See Stratemeyer, Edward L.
Young, Collier
  See Bloch, Robert (Albert)
Young, Dan 1952- *126*
Young, Dianne 1959- *88*
Young, Dorothea Bennett 1924- *31*

Young, Ed 1931- *173*
  Earlier sketches in SATA *10, 74, 122*
  See also CLR *27*
Young, Ed Tse-chun
  See Young, Ed
Young, Edward
  See Reinfeld, Fred
Young, Elaine L.
  See Schulte, Elaine L(ouise)
Young, James
  See Graham, Ian
Young, Jan
  See Young, Janet Randall
Young, Janet 1957- *188*
Young, Janet Randall 1919-1994 .... *3*
Young, Janet Ruth
  See Young, Janet
Young, Jeff C. 1948- *132*
Young, John
  See Macintosh, Brownie
Young, Judy 1956- *155*
Young, Judy (Elaine) Dockrey 1949- *72*
Young, Karen Romano 1959- *168*
  Earlier sketch in SATA *116*
Young, Ken 1956- *86*
Young, Lois Horton 1911-1981 .... *26*
Young, Louisa *161*
Young, Louise B. 1919- *64*
Young, Margaret B(uckner) 1922- *2*
Young, Mary 1940- *89*
Young, Miriam 1913-1974 .... *7*
Young, Noela 1930- *89*
Young, (Rodney Lee) Patrick (Jr.) 1937- *22*
Young, Percy M(arshall) 1912-2004 .... *31*
  Obituary *154*
Young, Richard Alan 1946- *72*
Young, Robert W(illiam) 1916-1969 .... *3*
Young, Ross B. 1955- *150*
Young, Ruth 1946- *67*
Young, Sara
  See Pennypacker, Sara
Young, Scott A. 1918-2005 .... *5*
Young, Scott Alexander
  See Young, Scott A.
Young, Selina 1971-2006 .... *201*
Young, Vivien
  See Gater, Dilys
Younger, Barbara 1954- *108*
Youngs, Betty 1934-1985 .... *53*
  Obituary *42*
Younkin, Paula 1942- *77*
Yount, Lisa (Ann) 1944- *124*
  Earlier sketch in SATA *74*
Yourgrau, Barry *179*
Yuditskaya, Tatyana 1964- *75*
Yumoto, Kazumi 1959- *153*

Z

Zach, Cheryl (Byrd) 1947- *98*
  Brief entry *51*
  Earlier sketch in SATA *58*
  See also SAAS *24*
Zacharias, Gary L. 1946- *153*
Zaffo, George J. (?)-1984 .... *42*
Zagarenski, Pamela 1969(?)- *183*
Zagwyn, Deborah Turney 1953- *138*
  Earlier sketch in SATA *78*
Zahares, Wade *193*
Zahn, Timothy 1951- *156*
  Earlier sketch in SATA *91*
Zaid, Barry 1938- *51*
Zaidenberg, Arthur 1908(?)-1990 .... *34*
  Obituary *66*
Zalben, Jane Breskin 1950- *170*
  Earlier sketches in SATA *7, 79, 120*
  See also CLR *84*
Zallinger, Jean (Day) 1918- *115*
  Earlier sketches in SATA *14, 80*

Zallinger, Peter Franz 1943- *49*
Zambreno, Mary Frances 1954- *140*
  Earlier sketch in SATA *75*
Zanderbergen, George
  See May, Julian
Zappa, Ahmet 1974- *180*
Zappa, Ahmet Emuukha Rodan
  See Zappa, Ahmet
Zappler, Lisbeth 1930- *10*
Zarchy, Harry 1912-1987 .... *34*
Zarin, Cynthia 1959- *192*
  Earlier sketch in SATA *108*
Zaring, Jane (Thomas) 1936- *40*
Zarins, Joyce Audy
  See dos Santos, Joyce Audy
Zaslavsky, Claudia 1917- *36*
Zaugg, Sandra L. 1938- *118*
Zaugg, Sandy
  See Zaugg, Sandra L.
Zaunders, Bo 1939- *137*
Zawadzki, Marek 1958- *97*
Zebra, A.
  See Scoltock, Jack
Zebrowski, George 1945- *67*
Zebrowski, George T.
  See Zebrowski, George
Zeck, Gerald Anthony 1939- *40*
Zeck, Gerry
  See Zeck, Gerald Anthony
Zed, Dr.
  See Penrose, Gordon
Zei, Alki 1925- *24*
  See also CLR *6*
Zeier, Joan T(heresa) 1931- *81*
Zeinert, Karen 1942-2002 .... *137*
  Earlier sketch in SATA *79*
Zeises, Lara M. 1976- *184*
  Earlier sketch in SATA *145*
Zelazny, Roger 1937-1995 .... *57*
  Brief entry *39*
Zelazny, Roger Joseph
  See Zelazny, Roger
Zeldis, Malcah 1931- *146*
  Earlier sketch in SATA *86*
Zelinsky, Paul O. 1953- *154*
  Brief entry *33*
  Earlier sketches in SATA *49, 102*
  See also CLR *55*
Zellan, Audrey Penn
  See Penn, Audrey
Zemach, Harve
  See Fischtrom, Harvey
Zemach, Kaethe 1958- *149*
  Brief entry *39*
  Earlier sketch in SATA *49*
Zemach, Margot 1931-1989 .... *70*
  Obituary *59*
  Earlier sketch in SATA *21*
Zemach-Bersin, Kaethe
  See Zemach, Kaethe
Zeman, Ludmila 1947- *153*
Zepeda, Gwendolyn 1971- *206*
Zephaniah, Benjamin 1958- *189*
  Earlier sketches in SATA *86, 140*
Zephaniah, Benjamin Obadiah Iqbal
  See Zephaniah, Benjamin
Zephaniah, Benjamin Pbadiah Iqubal
  See Zephaniah, Benjamin
Zephaniah, Benjamin Pbadiah Iqubal
  See Zephaniah, Benjamin
Zerman, Melvyn Bernard 1930- *46*
Zettner, Pat 1940- *70*
Zevin, Gabrielle *176*
Zhang, Christopher Zhong-Yuan 1954- *91*
Zhang, Song Nan 1942- *170*
  Earlier sketch in SATA *85*
Ziefert, Harriet 1941- *205*
  Earlier sketches in SATA *101, 154*
Ziegler, Jack (Denmore) 1942- *60*
Ziemienski, Dennis (Theodore) 1947- *10*

Ziliox, Marc
  See Fichter, George S.
Zillah
  See Macdonald, Zillah K(atherine)
Zim, Herbert S(pencer) 1909-1994 .... *30*
  Obituary *85*
  Earlier sketch in SATA *1*
  See also CLR *2*
  See also SAAS *2*
Zim, Sonia Bleeker 1909-1971 .... *2*
  Obituary *26*
Zima, Gordon 1920- *90*
Zimelman, Nathan 1921- *65*
  Brief entry *37*
Zimmer, Dirk 1943- *147*
  Earlier sketch in SATA *65*
Zimmer, Tracie Vaughn *169*
Zimmerman, Andrea 1950- *192*
  Earlier sketch in SATA *123*
Zimmerman, Andrea Griffing
  See Zimmerman, Andrea
Zimmerman, H. Werner 1951- *101*
Zimmerman, Heinz Werner
  See Zimmerman, H. Werner
Zimmerman, Naoma 1914-2004 .... *10*
Zimmermann, Arnold E. 1909- *58*
Zimmett, Debbie
  See Becker, Deborah Zimmett
Zimmy
  See Stratemeyer, Edward L.

Zimnik, Reiner 1930- *36*
  See also CLR *3*
Zindel, Bonnie 1943- *34*
Zindel, Lizabeth *187*
Zindel, Paul 1936-2003 .... *102*
  Obituary *142*
  Earlier sketches in SATA *16, 58*
  See also CLR *85*
Ziner, Feenie
  See Ziner, Florence
Ziner, Florence 1921- *5*
Zingara, Professor
  See Leeming, Joseph
Zinger, Yitskhok
  See Singer, Isaac Bashevis
Zion, Eugene 1913-1975 .... *18*
Zion, Gene
  See Zion, Eugene
Zoehfeld, Kathleen Weidner 1954- *193*
Zohorsky, Janet R. 1958- *148*
Zolkower, Edie Stoltz *171*
Zolkowski, Cathy (A.) 1969- *121*
Zollars, Jaime *191*
Zolotow, Charlotte 1915- *138*
  Earlier sketches in SATA *1, 35, 78*
  See also CLR *77*
Zolotow, Charlotte Gertrude Shapiro
  See Zolotow, Charlotte
Zolotow, Ellen
  See Dragonwagon, Crescent
Zonderman, Jon 1957- *92*

Zonia, Dhimitri 1921- *20*
Zonta, Pat 1951- *143*
Zubrowski, Bernard 1939- *90*
  Earlier sketch in SATA *35*
Zubrowski, Bernie
  See Zubrowski, Bernard
Zucker, Miriam S.
  See Reichert, Miriam Zucker
Zuckerman, Linda *190*
Zudeck, Darryl 1961- *61*
Zug, Mark *204*
Zupa, G. Anthony
  See Zeck, Gerald Anthony
Zupancic, Lilijana Praprotnik
  See Prap, Lila
Zurbo, Matt(hew) 1967- *98*
Zurhorst, Charles (Stewart, Jr.) 1913-1989 .. *12*
Zurlo, Tony 1941- *145*
Zuromskis, Diane
  See Stanley, Diane
Zuromskis, Diane Stanley
  See Stanley, Diane
Zusak, Markus 1975- *149*
Zwahlen, Diana 1947- *88*
Zweifel, Frances W. 1931- *14*
Zwerger, Lisbeth 1954- *194*
  Earlier sketches in SATA *66, 130*
  See also CLR *46*
  See also SAAS *13*
Zwinger, Ann (H.) 1925- *46*
Zymet, Cathy Alter 1965- *121*

DATE DUE
